ENCYCLOPEDIA OF THE RENAISSANCE

ENCYCLOPEDIA OF THE

RENAISSANCE

Paul F. Grendler

Editor in Chief

PUBLISHED IN ASSOCIATION WITH
THE RENAISSANCE SOCIETY OF AMERICA

VOLUME 2

Class – Furió Ceriol

CHARLES SCRIBNER'S SONS
An Imprint of The Gale Group
NEW YORK

Charles Scribner's Sons
1633 Broadway
New York, New York 10019

1 3 5 7 9 11 13 15 17 19   20 18 16 14 12 10 8 6 4 2

PRINTED IN THE UNITED STATES OF AMERICA

Library of Congress Cataloging-in-Publication Data
Encyclopedia of the Renaissance / Paul F. Grendler, editor in chief.
      p. cm.
    Includes bibliographical references and index.
    ISBN 0-684-80514-6 (set) — ISBN 0-684-80508-1 (v. 1) — ISBN 0-684-80509-X (v. 2)
  — ISBN 0-684-80510-3 (v. 3) — ISBN 0-684-80511-1 (v. 4) — ISBN 0-684-80512-X (v.
  5) — ISBN 0-684-80513-8 (v. 6)
    1. Renaissance—Encyclopedias.   I. Grendler, Paul F.   II. Renaissance Society of
America.
CB361.E52   1999
940.2'3'03—dc21   99-048290

The paper used in this publication meets the requirements of ANSI/NISO Z39.48-1992 (Permanence of Paper).

The typeface used in this book is ITC Garamond, a version of a typeface attributed to the French publisher and type founder Claude Garamond (c. 1480–1561).

CONTENTS OF OTHER VOLUMES

COMMON ABBREVIATIONS
USED IN THIS WORK

A.D.	*Anno Domini,* in the year of the Lord
A.H.	*Anno Hegirae,* in the year of the Hegira
b.	born
B.C.	before Christ
B.C.E.	before the common era (= B.C.)
c.	*circa,* about, approximately
C.E.	common era (= A.D.)
cf.	*confer,* compare
chap.	chapter
d.	died
D.	Dom, Portuguese honorific
diss.	dissertation
ed.	editor (pl., eds.), edition
e.g.	*exempli gratia,* for example
et al.	*et alii,* and others
etc.	*et cetera,* and so forth
f.	and following (pl., ff.)
fl.	*floruit,* flourished
HRE	Holy Roman Empire, Holy Roman Emperor
ibid.	*ibidem,* in the same place (as the one immediately preceding)
i.e.	*id est,* that is
MS.	manuscript (pl. MSS.)
n.	note
n.d.	no date
no.	number (pl., nos.)
n.p.	no place
n.s.	new series
N.S.	new style, according to the Gregorian calendar
O.F.M.	*Ordo Fratrum Minorum,* Order of Friars Minor; Franciscan
O.P.	*Ordo Predicatorum,* Order of Preachers; Dominican
O.S.	old style, according to the Julian calendar
p.	page (pl., pp.)
pt.	part
rev.	revised
S.	*san, sanctus, santo,* male saint
ser.	series

S.J.	*Societas Jesu,* Society of Jesus; Jesuit
SS.	*sancti, sanctae,* saints; *sanctissima, santissima,* most holy
Sta.	*sancta, santa,* female saint
supp.	supplement
vol.	volume
?	uncertain, possibly, perhaps

(CONTINUED)

CLASS, SOCIAL.   *See* **Social Status.**

CLASSICAL ANTIQUITY.   [This entry includes two subentries, the first on the discovery of classical antiquity, the second on the portrayal of classical antiquity in Renaissance art.]

Discovery of Classical Antiquity

Classical antiquity had long formed a conspicuous part of the entire Mediterranean landscape. Amphitheaters and temples, triumphal columns and arches, as well as the ruins of many other structures, had all been visible since the close of the Roman era. In Rome itself, antiquity was omnipresent not only in the topography but in the consciousness of its inhabitants, who lived amid these monumental remains. Yet as pilgrim guides and early maps attest, many of the ancient monuments had long since come to function more as mere landmarks in the cityscape of the new Christian Rome than as meaningful remnants of antique culture. While their classical forms had traversed the Middle Ages retaining at least something of their original significances, even some of Rome's grandest edifices had been much confused in medieval imaginations. In general, at the close of the fourteenth century, the topography of the city as a whole was scarcely understood and the relationship of its disparate ruins seldom pondered. At the dawn of the Renaissance, when the Colosseum alone might have held Rome's full population, the ancient city's scale and spread remained not only unknown but largely inconceivable.

Although popular memory had always retained the names, if not the functions and purposes, of the greatest of Rome's monuments—such as the Pantheon, the Arch of Constantine, and the Colosseum—many proved enigmatic. The Theater of Marcellus was known according to ancient topography as the Flaminian; by contrast, the Mausoleum of Hadrian was rechristened first the Domus Theodorici (c. 998), then the Castle of Crescentius (eleventh century), then finally the Castel Sant' Angelo (c. 1200). Similarly, while the bronze equestrian statue of Marcus Aurelius had been preserved largely because it had been wrongly identified as the great Christian emperor Constantine, the twin horsemen of Monte Cavallo had been regarded during the medieval period as two philosophers (strangely christened with the names of the famous Greek artists Praxiteles and Phidias) and thus their nudity was held to symbolize that all worldly knowledge was "naked and open to their minds."

The fate of the surviving writings of the ancient authors was little different. The historians' works had endured throughout the centuries, but so often little was known about the things of which they wrote. Much of the material fabric of life that had been described in Pliny's encyclopedic *Natural History,* or in a technical treatise like Vitruvius's book on architecture, remained a mystery. The poets had fared even worse. Virgil had become, according to legend, a medieval sorcerer or, by interpretation, a prophet of Christianity (*Eclogue* 4); Ovid's *Metamorphoses* had been allegorized as the vehicle of Christian doctrine; Homer, poorly latinized, or unreadable in Greek, was truly little more than a name. Thus, a blanket of debris, the deposit of many intervening centuries, covered not only all of the ancient cities, but nearly all that their culture had produced.

Of things not always visible or known, much was found wholly fortuitously. The history of Rome, as a material city, is the tale of the gradual revelation of the past and what lay buried beneath it. The stories are legion of how, whenever people dug in their suburban vineyards or excavated the foundations for a new urban building, they brought to light more marvels of the ancient past. As if to consciously contrast this continuing serendipity, Renaissance humanists and antiquarians constantly regaled one another with tales of their exertions as they deliberately set out to make new discoveries and record them. Poggio Bracciolini (1380–1459), the great Florentine humanist of the early fifteenth century, Pope Pius II Piccolomini (reigned 1458–1464), and Fra Giovanni Giocondo (c. 1435–1515), the famous architect and antiquarian of the following generation, all speak in their writings of the sweat and toil required for the recording of antiquities. Other scholars, however, refused to dirty their hands, preferring the study of manuscripts.

The profound endeavor in the discovery of antiquity was not the finding, unearthing, and collecting of these tantalizing vestiges of the distant past, but comprehending them—and, in so doing, rediscovering the society that produced them. Myriad inscriptions that had once declaimed to the public from the facades of great architectural monuments as well as the most humble tombs remained in large part a mystery until scholars could satisfactorily resolve the intricacies of their often highly specialized use of Latin and their many difficult abbreviations. Similarly, the material existence of that past, as it was described in the surviving ancient books, so often lacked reference to reality because many times these things were unknown to the Renaissance era. The spectacular architectural ruins provided the most striking exception, and consequently Renaissance artists assiduously studied their use, their structure, and their ancient architects' methods. Antonio Manetti (1423–1497), the biographer of the Florentine architect Filippo Brunelleschi (1377–1446), reports that when Brunelleschi was in Rome, he and the sculptor Donatello (c. 1386–1466) measured and drew whatever ancient remains they could find, so that by these means their structural principles might be divined. Leon Battista Alberti (1404–1472) describes what was to become a common procedure:

> [There was] no building of the ancients that had attracted praise, wherever it might be, but I immediately

examined it carefully, to see what I could learn from it. Therefore I never stopped exploring, considering, and measuring everything, and comparing the information through line drawings, until I had grasped and understood fully what each had to contribute in terms of ingenuity or skill. (*Ten Books on the Art of Building* 6.1)

Words and Things. What survived from the past was accessible to Renaissance understanding in various ways. The remnants can be classed broadly as either things or texts; in classical terms, *res* or *verba*. Not only did the interpretation of the monuments require the classical texts to explain them, but conversely, the texts themselves needed to be correlated with the things about which they spoke. A profound, new rapport with the classical world was constructed by the intense comparative study of this diverse and often fragmentary evidence. So, in 1489, Fra Giocondo would complain of the sorry state in which the ancient texts represented the thoughts of their authors, declaring in a letter to Lorenzo de' Medici that "even if [the ancient writers] were uncorrupted, they would still not be of much use to us, unless we ourselves were to see what they themselves saw." Thus, in 1511, when Giocondo turned his efforts to translating Vitruvius, he would write to Pope Julius II (reigned 1503–1513), "and do not think that my effort was slight, since everyone knows that to understand Vitruvius, I laboriously compared the meanings of his words again and again with the ruined remains and ancient buildings." As Raphael (1483–1520) would later say in his famous letter to Pope Leo X (reigned 1513–1521), Vitruvius's text might shed much light, but alone it was not sufficient for understanding. *Res* needed to be put in context to function as historical documents, and *verba* needed to be substantiated in vivid matter. Many examples illustrate fruits brought forth by such a marrying of the two orders of evidence, and one understands the drama of anecdotal histories that preserve the excited realization of those crucial, defining moments of Renaissance synthesis: Angelo Colocci's (1474–1544) reported excitement on discovering a realistic representation, at actual scale, of the measure of the Roman foot; Angelo Poliziano's (1454–1494) discovery of an ancient inscribed stone that might resolve the question of the spelling of Virgil's name as *Vergil,* with an *e;* or the recognition by Giuliano da Sangallo (c. 1445–1516) that the immense statue discovered on the Esquiline hill in 1506 was none other than that representation of Laocoön and his two sons mentioned by Pliny.

Such acts of intellectual synthesis depended on the systematic organization of all related evidence, no matter how slight or obscure. The fragmentary surviving writings of the late republican polymath and antiquarian Varro (116–27 B.C.) provided the pedigree for Renaissance antiquarian method. A summary of his attempt at a comprehensive survey of what were, for him, already ancient Roman institutions had been preserved in St. Augustine's treatise *The City of God*. Varro had collected and arranged his evidence and organized it by *genera,* or kinds, separating what pertained to men from what referred to the gods. Varro surely had his precursors. Origins had been among the Romans' great fascinations, and the history of their cities, their social institutions, and their leading families had been the objects of continued study, as well as many fraudulent claims to distinction. During the Renaissance this fascination was revived on a broad scale. Many cities traced their origins to Roman foundations, and the interpretation of their visible ruins played a role in the emergence of what amounted to a substantial literary genre. Observation confirmed the evidence provided in the ancient written sources, as each city attempted to anchor an account of its evolving social and political history within the grand framework of Rome's continuing myth. Early histories exist for cities such as Padua and Brescia, as well as others that could boast of their ancient heritage. Even the Florentines had long believed their Baptistery to be a Roman monument, and thus they too could lay claim, however mistakenly, to a classical foundation.

But it was in Rome, where the authenticity of the ancient past was most obviously confirmed by its monumental landscape, that such a historical consciousness had always been the strongest. There the idea of a civic history took on grand proportions, for it was the history of Rome—of its topography, society, and institutions—that the antiquarians sought continually to comprehend. Petrarch (1304–1374), Poggio Bracciolini, Flavio Biondo (1392–1463), Pomponio Leto (1428–1498), and Bernardo Ruccellai (1448–1514), among others, all made their attempts. The gradual evolution of the "Varronian" approach to these perennial historical questions was transformed during the course of the fifteenth century, as the systematic attempt at a comprehensive collection of testimonia gave way to questions concerning the relative value of each individual piece of evidence. The result was the emergence of a modern historical approach to the past marked by a profoundly new concern for the quality—as opposed to the quantity—of what had survived.

As Arnaldo Momigliano noted long ago, modern historical method began with the distinction between original and derivative authorities: between evidence contemporary with the events it attests, and the reports of later authorities whose sources can no longer be examined. The principles of this new discriminating approach were born from the study of the ancient texts. The surviving writings of the ancients were riddled with errors of the scribes who had continually copied them throughout the centuries. For any given literary work that survived in more than one manuscript, humanists faced the problem of which redaction, and which variant reading of the text, was to be preferred among those that the different manuscripts reported. Thus, Renaissance scholars collected multiple copies and collated them, discovering their differences, proposing which deviated from their original, and attempting to emend less satisfactory readings on the basis of others. Similarly, the work of one author who quoted another might verify or emend a difficult passage. More important still was that the relative merit of the surviving testimonia was evaluated, and so it was recognized that when historical accounts by two authors could be shown to have been derived one from the other, only one could be regarded as an independent authority. Even the physical character of the manuscripts themselves provided evidence, for study of their script forms could provide grounds for their relative dating, and those deemed older, and hence closer to the original, might be judged more reliable witnesses.

All these realizations were, to varying degrees, rooted in the profoundly new value placed on a revolutionary commitment to firsthand observation as opposed to the often blind adherence to received tradition. These new insights generated a series of interpretive principles with much broader historical application that pertained to a wide variety of the surviving remains of antiquity and subsequently transformed many fields of endeavor. The study of Roman topography provides a clear example. All early topographical texts followed the two known ancient models: Pliny's *Natural History* (book 2) and a late antique census, known as the Regionary Catalogs, that provided an account of the city's monuments region by region. Thus, almost all the early Renaissance discussions rehearse the same attested materials, in roughly the same order, to much the same effect. Only gradually did the humanists elaborate these sources, collating information drawn from other ancient authors, the discovery of inscriptions, and an interpretation of the monuments themselves. The result of such study fundamentally reconceived both the content and the form of later Renaissance topographical texts.

Early signs of such a change in approach are visible in the two great works of Flavio Biondo. In his *Roma instaurata* (c. 1445) the topographical order of the antique Regionary Catalogs that dominates the first and much of the second of his study's three books gives way in the final part to typological organization. The physical evidence of similar structures, the various imperial baths and "circuses" in particular, is arrayed with the literary sources that attest them, to allow comparative scrutiny of like with like. Mere accumulation gives way to methodical examination of the evidence, now weighed and ranked in value, as a means to interpretation. A little more than a decade later, Biondo's *Roma triumphans* (c. 1459) attempted to organize more thoroughly and methodically the evidence for Roman social practices and institutions, dividing the religious, military, and political spheres, and distinguishing the public from the private realm.

Interest in the ancient city and its remains propelled numerous antiquarians to attempt interpretations, and their differences of opinion gave rise to sometimes furious debate and criticism. Notable among these disputes was that concerning the site of the Forum Romanum, which was so overgrown and buried beneath a millennium's debris as to be wholly unrecognizable by the year 1500. Of the site's few visible monuments, not one was attested in the ancient sources as being in the Forum. A fierce argument emerged over the interpretation—and hence the authority—of the one passage from an ancient text that seemed specifically to suggest the Forum's location. Did it lie at the base of the Capitoline, stretching to the Arch of Titus, as the monumental topography suggested and as had long been (correctly) believed, or between the Capitol and the Palatine, as the writings of Dionysius of Halicarnassus suggested? In a striking triumph of the new scholarship and its principles, the evidence of an ancient text was proven wrong.

The emerging dominance of an essentially typological approach to the ancient world's remains, comparative rather than cumulative, can be seen in how the monuments were recorded in architects' sketchbooks. That the methods and principles established for textual criticism might be adapted for the study of the ancient monuments was advocated explicitly by Leon Battista Alberti:

> I would have [the architect] take the same approach as one might toward the study of letters, where no one would be satisfied until he had read and examined every author, good and bad, who had written anything on the subject in which he was interested. Likewise, wherever there is a work that has received general approval, he should inspect it with great care, record it in drawing, note its numbers, and construct models and examples of it; he should examine and study the order, position, type, and number of the individual parts, especially those employed by the architects of the biggest and most important buildings, who, it might be conjectured, were exceptional men, in that they were given control of so great an expenditure. (*Ten Books on Architecture*, 9.10)

The drawings of similar structures could be referred to each other, and eventually the individual studies systematically grouped for comparison. And with the addition of measurements, especially once the architects—Antonio da Sangallo (1455–1535), Baldassare Peruzzi (1481–1536), and also Sebastiano Serlio (1475–1554)—began to use the Roman foot as their unit of measure (to a great extent, the fruits of Angelo Colocci's researches), such comparative study became ever more explicit. With the use of the Roman foot it not only became more obvious what ancient modules for measurement had been employed in the design of any given building, but it was believed that this made more readily demonstrable any possible relationship of each structure to the principles described in Vitruvius's treatise.

Yet it was the philological principles employed by the humanists and antiquarians that bestowed the greatest historical value and authority on ancient inscriptions and coins. Both were contemporary with the events they described or depicted and were uncontaminated by the process of manuscript transmission. Thus they might serve as authentic models—for language usage, orthography, and ancient appearance. They were direct testimony—not interpretations—of ancient society and its various institutions. From the coinage, Guillaume Budé (*De asse;* Paris, 1515), Jacopo Questenberg (Vatican Library, Manuscript Vaticanus Latinus 3906, c. 1499), and Lorenzo da Porto (*De sestertio;* Venice, c. 1520) could attempt to recover the workings of the ancient monetary system, Andrea Fulvio (c. 1470–c. 1527) could establish a history of imperial iconography, and a multitude of scholars could employ coins as evidence in their interpretations of literary texts and Roman topography.

It was from the inscriptions that scholars could learn the most because their content was greater and more significant. With Poggio Bracciolini's discovery of the *Notae Juris,* a late antique manual of technical Latin abbreviations and administrative shorthand attributed to Valerius Probus, much of the mystifying content employed in the inscriptions could be deciphered. When found in situ, the epigraphic texts could explain a structure, as when Poggio recognized that it was Cestius, not Remus (as tradition had it), who was buried in the pyramid by the Porta Ostiense, just as the monument's inscription declared. Official imperial texts often established the dates of sites or monuments, not only for their construction but for their subsequent restorations. And the *Fasti,* the dated public lists of the successive consuls or triumphators, might allow other inscriptions, so often dated by reference to the current consuls, to be inserted precisely in historical chronology. What is more, it was all of these texts, collectively, that formed the basis and provided the standard for Latin orthography. In so many of the manuscript syllogai of inscriptions, unusual words or spellings were often signaled in the margins, and it was from a compilation of such annotations that Aldo Manuzio the Younger (1547–1597) would assemble the first comprehensive and authoritative treatise on ancient Latin usage, his *Orthographiae ratio* (Venice, 1566).

The great advance in the study of inscriptions, however, was made with the transformation of the manner in which they were organized. The early antiquarians had consistently listed them topographically, according to where the stones were then to be found—either in the field or mortared into a collector's cortile wall. What was required, if these texts were to be employed as historical evidence, was a system of classification according to the type of information each inscription preserved; thus materials on the same topic might be readily located and synthesizing interpretations produced. Such a scheme, devised on the great Varronian model, emerged in the mid-sixteenth century, the product of the collaborative and collective researches by an entire group of scholars at Rome: Antonio Agustin (1517–1586), Jean Matal (c. 1510–1600?), Onofrio Panvinio (1529–1568), and Martin de Smet (in Rome, 1545–1551). As a result, while around 1500 Fra Giocondo could annotate his collection of inscriptions with the realization that a text listing the street wardens of Rome offered evidence about the institutional organization of the city and its magistrates, by the 1550s Panvinio could attempt to assemble all the pertinent epigraphic sources in a comprehensive account of all such institutions, set within their historical context.

Commentary, Interpretation, Emulation. These new forms of scrutiny in turn produced innovative ways to present their results, visible in the

new organization and detailed publication of the inscriptions. They were not only arranged by type, but represented so as to include explicit evidence of their physical condition and appearance. A generation before, a new type of textual commentary had begun to be practiced by Angelo Poliziano, in his *Miscellanea* (1498), where short discussions of particular problems replaced the long-standardized form of a text accompanied by a running commentary. Not only the form changed: Poliziano gave new emphasis to the historical, as opposed to the grammatical, character of the surviving ancient literary works, so that their full value as evidence for the study of antiquity might begin to emerge. Thus was born the quintessentially modern form of the dissertation, as the antiquarians began to assemble and study the ancient remains, topic by topic, collating textual and physical evidence and offering an interpretation of the whole. The standards of ancient weights and measures, for example, posed numerous problems—for the study of architecture, numismatics, and various aspects of everyday life. Fra Giocondo and Angelo Colocci studied the problem assiduously, but it was Luca Peto (fl. 1550–1560) who eventually published a full account of the subject, *De mensuris et ponderibus* (On measures and weights) in 1573. Before the end of the sixteenth century many such treatises had begun to appear: both Lazare de Baïf (1496–1547) and Aldo Manuzio the Younger on ancient clothing; Baïf, as well, on ancient ships; and both Carlo Sigonio (c. 1524–1584) and Onofrio Panvinio on ancient Roman names. In all these works, the remains of the ancient monuments supplemented, indeed illustrated, the reports preserved in the surviving ancient texts.

Sixteenth-century topographical research and the ongoing study of the ancient monuments also reflect these developments. Although the historical topographical project initiated by Raphael for Pope Leo X was never completed it too clearly bore the signs of the new humanistic methods of scholarship in its emphasis on direct observation, comprehensiveness, and the organization of its materials by type. The same methodological approach can be seen in the great collections of drawings of antiquities known today as the Codex Coburgensis, the Codex Pighianus, and in the voluminous writings of Pirro Ligorio (c. 1513–1583). In all these essentially antiquarian productions, materials were comprehensively studied and systematically treated, not only by type but often alphabetically, thus demonstrating that scholars had made the capacity to retrieve information a goal.

A more profound knowledge of the past and its accomplishments gave birth to the systematic emulation, in form and content, of its surviving artifacts. The classical remains spawned a new architectural style. The ancient stone texts inspired a new style of lettering, in public inscriptions, in manuscripts, and eventually in the typefaces employed for print. The continuous discovery of manuscripts that brought to light new ancient texts fueled a revival of lost literary styles and genres, and played a role in the great Renaissance debate concerning whether one should imitate Cicero or try to develop an eclectic style based on many ancient authors, when writing in Latin. Yet the serendipitous survival of the remains engendered, inevitably, a belief that everything that endured throughout the ages had value. As a result, the antiquarian's immediate goal often became the mere assembly of all these ancient materials. They were often more concerned with the quantity than the quality—or authenticity—of what they collected. Indeed, one of the consequences of Renaissance scholarly enterprise was a belief that certain deficiencies in the surviving evidence might be rectified. Discoveries of whatever kind—texts or things—were, when possible, restored to what was believed to be their original state. Manuscripts were collated and editions published; architectural monuments reconstructed in drawings; statues were collected and their damage often repaired, fragmentary elements even combined so as to appear as if whole. At times, the fine line that distinguishes original from restoration, in any of these endeavors, seems to disappear. Paradoxically, the hard-won lessons of over a century's scholarly enterprise brought about a state of affairs that opened the way, not only to the overvaluation of any individual piece of material evidence about the past, but to an increasing demand for new discoveries—and a willingness to accept the new spate of imitations, and at times, outright forgeries (literary, sculptural, numismatic, and epigraphic) that came into being to satisfy that demand.

See also **Classical Scholarship; Manuscripts;** *and biographies of figures mentioned in this entry.*

BIBLIOGRAPHY

Alberti, Leon Battista. *De re aedificatoria: On the Art of Building in Ten Books.* Translated by Joseph Rykwert, Neil Leach, and Robert Tavernor. Cambridge, Mass., 1988.

Barkan, Leonard. *Unearthing the Past.* New Haven, Conn., 2000.

Bober, Phyllis Pray, and Ruth Rubinstein. *Renaissance Artists and Antique Sculpture: A Handbook of Sources.* Oxford and New York, 1986.

Bolgar, R. R. *The Classical Heritage and Its Beneficiaries.* Cambridge, U.K., 1954.

Buddensieg, T. "Criticism and Praise of the Pantheon in the Middle Ages and the Renaissance." In *Classical Influences on European Culture, A.D. 500–1500.* Edited by R. R. Bolgar. Cambridge, U.K., 1971. Pages 259–267.

Burns, Howard. "Pirro Ligorio's Reconstruction of Ancient Rome: The *Anteiquae Urbis Imago* of 1561." In *Pirro Ligorio: Artist and Antiquarian.* Edited by Robert W. Gaston. Florence, 1988. Pages 19–92.

Ciapponi, L. "Fra Giocondo da Verona and His Edition of Vitruvius." *Journal of the Warburg and Courtauld Institutes* 47 (1984): 72–90. *Convegno di studi su Angelo Colocci, 1969.* Iesi, Italy, 1972.

Crawford, M. H., ed. *Antonio Agustín: From Renaissance to Counter-Reform.* London, 1993.

Daly Davis, Margaret. "Zum Codex Coburgensis: Frühe Archäologie und Humanismus im Kreis des Marcello Cervini." In *Antikenzeichnung und Antikenstudium in Renaissance und Frühbarock.* Edited by Henning Wrede and Richard Harprath. Mainz, Germany, 1989. Pages 185–199.

Fanelli, Vittorio. *Ricerche su Angelo Colocci e sulla Roma cinquecentesca.* Vatican City, 1979.

Ferrary, Jean-Louis. *Onofrio Panvinio et les antiquités romaines.* Rome, 1996.

Gordon, Phyllis W. G., ed. *Two Renaissance Bookhunters: The Letters of Poggius Bracciolini to Nicolaus de Niccolis.* New York, 1974.

Graevius, Joannes Georgius. *Thesaurus antiquitatum romanarum.* 12 vols. Venice, 1732–1737.

Grafton, Anthony. *Commerce with the Classics: Ancient Books and Renaissance Readers.* Ann Arbor, Mich., 1997.

Grafton, Anthony. *Joseph Scaliger: A Study in the History of Classical Scholarship.* Vol. 1. Oxford, 1983.

Günther, Hubertus. "L'idea di Roma antica nella Roma Instaurata di Flavio Biondo." *Le due Rome del Quattrocento: Melozzo, Antoniazzo e la cultura artistica del '400 romano.* Edited by Sergio Rossi and Stefano Valeri. Rome, 1997. Pages 380–393.

Günther, Hubertus. *Das Studium der antiken Architektur in den Zeichnungen der Hochrenaissance.* Tübingen, Germany, 1988.

Harprath, Richard, and Henning Wrede, eds. *Antikenzeichnung und Antikenstudium in Renaissance und Frühbarock.* Mainz, Germany, 1989.

Jacks, Philip. *The Antiquarian and the Myth of Antiquity: The Origins of Rome in Renaissance Thought.* Cambridge, U.K., 1993.

Momigliano, Arnaldo. "Ancient History and the Antiquarian." *Journal of the Warburg and Courtauld Institutes* 13 (1950): 285–315.

Rizzo, Silvia. *Il lessico filologico degli umanisti.* 1973. Reprint, Rome, 1984.

Rowland, Ingrid D. *The Culture of the High Renaissance. Ancients and Moderns in Sixteenth-Century Rome.* Cambridge, U.K., 1998.

Rowland, Ingrid D. "Raphael, Angelo Colocci, and the Genesis of the Architectural Orders." *Art Bulletin* (1994): 81–104.

Vagenheim, Ginette. "La falsification chez Pirro Ligorio: A la lumière des Fasti Capitolini et des inscriptions de Préneste." *Eutopia* 3 (1994): 67–113.

Vagenheim, Ginette. "Les inscriptions ligoriennes: Notes sur la tradition manuscrite." *Italia medioevale e umanistica* 30 (1987): 199–309.

Valentini, R., and G. Zucchetti. *Codice topografico della città di Roma.* 4 vols. Rome, 1940–1953.

Weiss, Roberto. *The Renaissance Discovery of Classical Antiquity.* Oxford, 1965; rev. ed., Oxford, 1988.

MICHAEL KOORTBOJIAN

Classical Antiquity in Renaissance Art

Representation of the classical world in Renaissance art reflects all the complexity of the humanist movement's sense of the past: irrevocably remote at one moment, immediately present at the next, and always bound up with Christianity, whose development coincided closely, after all, with the growth of the Roman Empire. One of the most evocative examples of these complex attitudes is a drawing from the 1530s by Maerten van Heemskerck (Berlin Sketchbook, I, fol. 72) that portrays the antiquities collection of the Florentine merchant Jacopo Galli. Amid crumbling remains of ancient Roman sarcophagi, Greek statues, and an Egyptian sphinx stands Michelangelo's *Bacchus* (Florence, Bargello), missing a hand as if it, too, is another battered monument from the "shipwreck" of antiquity.

Models. Artists gathered their ideas of the ancient world from their Bibles and from the literary works of ancient Greek and Roman authors. Italian artists in particular could also observe their own physical surroundings, from imposing Roman ruins, immemorial landscapes, smaller artifacts like coins, cameos, and statues, and the occasional remains of ancient Roman and Etruscan painting. However, the sense of chronology that they applied to these relics was no more reliable than that of the humanists who took ninth-century Carolingian minuscule script as the true writing of the ancients rather than the much older rustic capitals of manuscripts like the fourth-century Vatican Virgil. Fifteenth-century Florentines believed that their Romanesque Baptistery was an ancient building, so that an architect like Filippo Brunelleschi designed ostensibly ancient-looking arcades that rested on columns (as in his Ospedale degli Innocenti of 1419) rather than piers, as in genuinely ancient Roman buildings like the Colosseum.

Still, the impulse toward some kind of chronological accuracy often governed Renaissance artists' decisions in portraying the ancient world. To indicate Christ's precise chronological moment, as well as to foreshadow the eventual triumph of Christianity, painters often set their Nativity scenes within crumbling Roman ruins, with Joseph clad in a toga and the Madonna in a Roman matron's stola (a long draped robe). Togas and stolas were also appropriate garb for many saints. The Magi, those visitors to the Christ child from ancient Persia, presented an-

other problem entirely; for lack of ancient models, artists might clothe them in the flowing robes and elaborate turbans of contemporary Ottoman Turks. The look of the Holy Land itself posed yet another challenge: from the fertile flatlands of the Low Countries to the rugged mountains of southern Italy, Europe contained a rich variety of landscapes, but none that bore the slightest resemblance to the deserts of Egypt or Palestine. Sienese artists came as close as any of their peers by setting works like the Osservanza Master's *Temptation of Saint Anthony* (c. 1435; New York, Metropolitan Museum of Art) in the rugged, eroded chalk formations called the *Crete Senesi* in the hills outside of Siena. Botticelli's *Scenes from the Life of Moses* (1481–1482) on the Sistine Chapel walls are more typical with their lush Tuscan landscape pressed into service to represent the land of the pharaohs.

Egypt. Egypt, indeed, posed a particular challenge for Renaissance art; the country itself, under Turkish domination, had become inaccessible for all but the most intrepid merchants. Thus the ancient Egyptian sage Hermes Trismegistus appears in Turkish turban and robes on the inlaid marble floor of Siena Cathedral. In Rome itself, Egyptian obelisks and artifacts provided firsthand knowledge of ancient Egyptian art; sphinxes and crouching lions appear in sketchbooks of antiquities like that of Maarten van Heemskerck done in the 1530s, in grotesque decorations and, with exquisite refinement, in the decorative arts. Ironically, however, some of the best-known examples of Egyptian art for Renaissance artists were actually Roman pastiches: the funeral pyramid of the Roman official Gaius Cestius, known as the "Tomb of Remus," and the pyramidal "Tomb of Romulus" demolished in the 1490s by Pope Alexander VI, were both elongated Roman monuments, quite unlike the broadly massive pyramids of Gizeh: both appear in vivid detail on Filarete's bronze doors for Pope Eugenius IV at St. Peter's (1434).

Another Egyptian artifact, a bronze offering table inlaid with silver scenes of Isis and engraved with hieroglyphs, came to light in about 1525 and entered the collection of the humanist Pietro Bembo; this "Tabula Bembina" or "Mensa Isiaca" was thought for centuries to reveal profound secrets of Egyptian religion, but in fact its hieroglyphs are nonsense, created by an ancient Roman artist for a devout but uninformed Roman client. The first evidence of explicit sensitivity to the stylistic peculiarities of Egyptian art comes from a spectacular illuminated manuscript,

Classical Antiquity in Renaissance Art. *The Triumph of Julius Caesar* by Andrea Mantegna. One of a series of nine paintings made for the ruler of Mantua in the late fifteenth century purchased by Charles I in 1629. Tempera on canvas; c. 1474–1490s. HAMPTON COURT PALACE, LONDON/ALINARI/ART RESOURCE

the *Missal* created circa 1530 for Cardinal Pompeo Colonna (Manchester, John Rylands Library), in which the column of the Colonna coat of arms is likened to an Egyptian obelisk, carrying this venerable family's ancestry back to the most ancient of civilizations. Many evocations of ancient Egypt, on the other hand, like Pinturicchio's frescoes of Isis and Osiris for the Vatican apartment of Pope Alexander VI (reigned 1492–1503), or the lavish woodcut illustrations for the *Hypnerotomachia Poliphili* (Dream of Poliphilo), printed in Venice in 1499, are almost entirely fanciful.

Greece. Greece loomed large in the Renaissance imagination, especially in the wake of the Ottoman conquest of Constantinople in 1453. Thereafter, Greek scholars came to Italy, and humanists began to see the learning of Greek as an indispensable part of their education. Greek art, however, meant Byzantine art; when the fifteenth-century traveler Cyriac of Ancona sketched the Parthenon in Athens, he

paid so little attention to the task that he made the Doric building Ionic. The imposing Greek ruins of Sicily and southern Italy seem to have made almost no impression on Renaissance artists. Greek vases, largely found in Etruscan tombs, were regarded as Etruscan. Many Roman statues either bore Greek inscriptions or were signed by Greek artists; the cosmopolitan mix of ancient Roman culture made distinction between Greek and Roman style nearly impossible more than a millennium later. Raphael, according to Giorgio Vasari, was one of the first artists to solicit drawings of the monuments of Greece itself in order to garner a sense of their distinctive qualities. Raphael's *Letter to Pope Leo X* (1519) shows that he trained the same sensitivity to style on late antique art and architecture.

Etruria. For Tuscan artists, the ancient world importantly included their Etruscan ancestors, who formed an important part of their civic identity and hence of their identity as artists. If awareness of the difference between Greek and Roman art is hard to discern in the work of Renaissance artists, their feel for the art of Etruria is easily identified. For his Medici patrons, who established the first museum of Etruscan antiquities, Botticelli evoked Etruscan art in paintings like his *Mars and Venus,* where Venus's dress and her contorted pose are both directly drawn from Etruscan sarcophagi, or the *Primavera,* whose hook-nosed, winged blue Zephyr recreates an Etruscan underworld demon with rare accuracy. The columnar facade of the Villa Medici at Poggio a Caiano, designed by another Tuscan artist, Giuliano da Sangallo, recreates the widely spaced columns and deep porch of an Etruscan temple.

Ancient history. The most ambitious of Renaissance artists also tried to re-create famous ancient works of art from the descriptions (*ekphraseis*) left by ancient authors. Botticelli tried his hand at re-creating the busy *Calumny* painted by Apelles, Alexander the Great's favorite artist, and described in detail by Pliny the Elder (*Natural History,* 35.36). For the bedroom of the wealthy Roman banker Agostino Chigi, Sodoma (Giovanni Antonio Bazzi) frescoed a *Marriage of Alexander and Roxane* (1518) inspired by the Greek author Lucian's description of a painting by Aëtion. Titian chose to recreate Apelles's masterpiece, *Venus Rising from the Sea,* a painting reportedly purchased by the emperor Augustus for the staggering price of one hundred talents.

Ancient history furnished the subject matter for what was regarded as one of the most exalted genres of painting, history painting. Andrea Mantegna's colorful rendering of the *Triumph of Caesar* (Hampton Court) combines the Mantuan artist's stately style with his close observation of ancient Roman historical reliefs, especially those on Trajan's Column. Baldassare Peruzzi's frescoes for the bishop's palace at Ostia re-create both the themes and the grisaille coloring of Roman relief. Giorgio Vasari's biography of this most talented artist reports that he executed many similar decorative schemes, most of which have not survived; for example, his "Loves of the Gods" from the exterior of Agostino Chigi's Roman villa (1511; now known as the Villa Farnesina) survive only in exiguous fragments.

Many Roman palaces boasted grisaille facade paintings based on Roman historical relief; those of the Palazzo Ricci and the Palazzo Massimo are still fairly well preserved. In the case of the Palazzo Massimo, the historical incidents detailed on the facade were intended to remind viewers that the family traced its ancestry, implausibly, back to the Roman hero Fabius Maximus. The Raphael workshop's Sala di Costantino in the Vatican (1520s) not only incorporates individual motifs from Trajan's Column and other Roman reliefs, but also experiments with the representation of space, again drawing from careful observation of Roman art; here the transformation of the Roman Empire into a Christian empire provides the underlying motive for such close scrutiny and such exact evocation of ancient Roman art.

BIBLIOGRAPHY

Panofsky, Erwin. *Renaissance and Renascences in Western Art.* Stockholm, 1960.

Curran, Brian A. "Ancient Egypt and Egyptian Antiquities in the Italian Renaissance Art and Culture." Ph.D. dissertation, Princeton University, 1997.

Bober, Phyllis Pray, and Ruth O. Rubinstein. *Renaissance Artists and Antique Sculpture: A Handbook of Sources.* Rev. ed. London, 1987.

Bonfante, Larissa, ed. *Etruscan Life and Afterlife: A Handbook of Etruscan Studies.* Detroit, Mich., 1986.

INGRID D. ROWLAND

CLASSICAL MYTHOLOGY. *See* **Myth.**

CLASSICAL SCHOLARSHIP. The attempt to recover, restore, and revive the culture of antiquity was one of the most characteristic features of the Renaissance. The mainspring of this revival was classical scholarship: the intensive study of the remains, primarily literary but also material, of Greek and Roman civilization. Classical scholarship in this period was closely associated with the movement known as humanism. Drawing on their expert knowledge of the language, literature, thought, and history of Rome and, to a lesser extent, Greece, Renaissance humanists sought to regain and preserve the legacy of the classical past. In addition, they helped to make this heritage accessible to the wider society through their activities as teachers, editors, and translators.

The Beginnings of Classical Scholarship in Italy. In the late thirteenth and the early fourteenth century, a small group of lawyers and notaries in northern Italy began to take an enthusiastic interest in Roman literature and history. These so-called prehumanists wrote Latin poetry echoing Roman poets virtually unknown to the Middle Ages: the symbolic return of Catullus, unread for centuries, to his hometown of Verona, in the shape of a single corrupt manuscript, was celebrated by a local poet in the early decades of the fourteenth century. Members of this circle studied the meter and prosody of

Seneca's tragedies, with a view to writing Senecan tragedies of their own, and imitated Livy, Sallust, and Julius Caesar in their historical works. In the field of literary history, the works of Pliny, thought in the Middle Ages to belong to one author, were correctly assigned to two: the Elder, who composed *Historia naturalis* (Natural history), and the Younger, who wrote nine books of letters.

Petrarch (1304–1374) transformed these early glimmerings of classical scholarship into a comprehensive program, one that would set the agenda for several generations of Italian humanists. First, he discovered lost works of Latin literature, including Cicero's speeches and letters to Atticus. Second, he tried to improve the transmitted text of classical authors by comparing different manuscripts and by using his knowledge of Latin to detect and emend errors; in the case of Livy's history of Rome, he reconstructed the first three decades from different manuscripts. Third, he attempted to learn Greek—although to no avail—in order to gain access to the literature of ancient Greece. Fourth, Petrarch made extensive use of his classical studies in his own works of poetry, history, and moral philosophy. These four elements would remain at the center of classical scholarship throughout the Renaissance.

Recovery and Dissemination of Classical Literature.

Many of the great discoveries of Latin literature in the early fifteenth century were made by Poggio Bracciolini (1380–1459). For most of his life Poggio worked in the papal Curia, which enabled him to travel widely in northern Europe, where he made a number of important manuscript finds. Among his discoveries were the complete text of Quintilian's rhetorical treatise, known before only in a mutilated form; new speeches of Cicero; Lucretius's Epicurean poem on the universe, *De rerum natura;* and three other monuments of Roman poetry: Statius's *Silvae,* Silius Italicus's *Punica,* and Marcus Manilius's *Astronomica.*

In this great age of discovery new works continually came to light, sometimes by unexpected avenues. The desire of Coluccio Salutati (1331–1406), the humanist chancellor of Florence, to locate a manuscript of Cicero's letters to Atticus, originally discovered by Petrarch, led to the unearthing in Vercelli of a collection of Cicero's letters to his friends. Other manuscripts also turned up in Italy: a codex containing some rhetorical works of Cicero, previously either unknown or incomplete, was found near Milan in 1421. Many others were transported to Italy, the home of classical studies, by foreign visitors: twelve new plays by Plautus were brought from Germany in 1429 by the amateur manuscript hunter and future cardinal Nicholas of Cusa. The minor works of the Roman historian Tacitus ended up in Rome in 1455, as a result of an expedition to northern libraries in search of new classical texts sponsored by the first humanist pope, Nicholas V (reigned 1447–1455). Books 1 to 6 of Tacitus's *Annales,* preserved for centuries in a single manuscript in the Benedictine abbey of Corvey, came into the possession of the future pope Leo X (reigned 1513–1521) in 1508.

More Roman historical writing was recovered when a German scholar found the surviving books of Livy's fifth decade in the monastery of Lorsch, thus completing the work of reconstruction begun by Petrarch. This discovery, one of the last major Latin finds of the Renaissance, was made in 1527, the year Rome was sacked by the imperial troops. Preeminence in classical studies, like the balance of political power, was now shifting to northern Europe. The new Livy manuscript did not travel to Italy in the way that past discoveries had done but instead went to Basel, where four years later it appeared in print.

Printing. Since its invention in the mid-fifteenth century, the printing press had provided an unparalleled opportunity for the dissemination of classical literature. In the past newly discovered texts had been diffused through the laborious and time-consuming process of copying out the manuscript by hand, either oneself or by hiring professional scribes—whose standards of accuracy often left much to be desired. Even the most popular classical texts could achieve only limited circulation in manuscript. The printing press changed matters dramatically, making it possible to produce hundreds, and sometimes thousands, of copies of individual works. At the end of the fifteenth century most of classical Latin literature—writers such as Cicero and Virgil who had been read throughout the Middle Ages, along with Lucretius and other recently recovered authors—was available in a variety of printed editions at prices, moreover, that any scholar could afford.

Classical Greek literature. In the 1490s the humanist publisher Aldo Manuzio began an ambitious program of printing the ancient Greek classics. Despite the efforts of his publishing house and a few other scholarly presses, the printing of Greek books remained a trickle compared with the steady stream of classical Latin works coming out each year. Ancient Greek literature, unlike Latin, did not have a continuous tradition of study in western Europe: those Greek authors, such as Aristotle and Galen, who were read in the Middle Ages were invariably encountered in Latin translation. By the fourteenth century, however, Greek manuscripts began to appear in Italy: Petrarch owned works by both Homer and Plato, though he never attained sufficient knowledge of Greek to read them.

Over the course of the fifteenth century an increasing number of Greek manuscripts came into circulation. Many of these contained works unknown in the West: Ptolemy's *Outline of Geography,* for instance, and the historians Herodotus and Thucydides, not to mention the poets and dramatists who for centuries had been little more than names, if that, to Western readers. Some texts were brought to Italy by humanists like Francesco Filelfo (1398–1481) and Giovanni Aurispa (1369?–1459) who traveled to Byzantium in the first half of the fifteenth century; Aurispa established a profitable trade in Greek manuscripts. Others codices came in the train of Byzantine scholars who fled to Italy to escape the Turks: Cardinal Bessarion (1403–1472) not only brought Greek books with him when he settled in Italy in 1440 but also sought out other works to be copied for his collection, attempting to preserve as much of the Greek heritage as possible in the face of the collapse of the Byzantine empire. In 1468 Bessarion bequeathed his books, including almost five hundred Greek manuscripts, to Venice, where they eventually became the core of the Marciana Library. Another Greek émigré, Janus Lascaris (c. 1445–c. 1535), was sent to the East in the early 1490s by Lorenzo de' Medici (1449–1492) and returned with more than two hundred manuscripts. By the end of the fifteenth century, virtually all Greek literature that survives today had reached Italy.

The dissemination of Greek works required, however, more than just circulation in manuscript or, later, in print. Since relatively few Renaissance scholars acquired a comfortable reading knowledge of Greek, it was necessary for these texts to be translated into Latin in order to reach a wide audience. Latin versions of Greek works new to the West, such as the speeches of Demosthenes and Isocrates, started to be made early in the fifteenth century; in addition, works well known in the Middle Ages, above all the treatises of Aristotle, were retranslated in a less literal and more classical style. The number of Platonic dialogues in Latin slowly expanded throughout the century, until the complete corpus finally became accessible to Western scholars for the first time in the Latin version made for Cosimo the Elder (1389–1464) and Lorenzo de' Medici by Marsilio Ficino (1433–1499) and printed in 1484.

Like the Medici, other patrons sponsored the translation of Greek works into Latin. Cardinal Nicholas of Cusa, an enthusiastic reader of Platonic philosophy, commissioned a Byzantine émigré to translate Plato's dialogue *Parmenides* and had an Italian scholar do the same for Proclus's *Platonic Theology,* a manuscript of which Nicholas himself had brought back from Constantinople in 1438. The ambitions of Pope Nicholas V to found a library that would rival that of Alexandria included a plan to have the major Greek prose works translated into Latin, for which he engaged the services both of Byzantine scholars and of Italian humanists who had mastered Greek such as Lorenzo Valla (1407–1457).

Libraries. Nicholas V's projected papal library became a reality in the 1470s under Sixtus IV (reigned 1471–1484). He appointed the humanist Bartolommeo Platina (1421–1481) as Vatican librarian in 1475 and set aside four specially designed rooms to hold the growing collection of manuscripts—numbering thirty-six hundred at Sixtus's death—a large proportion of which contained classical texts. Renaissance scholars were given access to these works, provided they observed minimum standards of decorum (putting books back in their place and not quarreling with other readers), and could even borrow manuscripts for private study.

Another important contribution to the dissemination of classical texts came from the Florentine humanist and book collector Niccolò de' Niccoli (c. 1364–1437). He made provision in his will that his large collection of manuscripts be freely available to scholars; and his friend Cosimo de' Medici carried out this wish by establishing a public library in the Dominican monastery of San Marco in Florence in 1444. It was from this library, a century later, that the Florentine classical scholar Pietro Vettori (1499–1585) borrowed two important Greek manuscripts of Aeschylus, which he used in his 1557 edition: the most ancient witness to the text, dating from the tenth century; and a fourteenth-century codex containing several hundred previously unknown lines of *Agamemnon.*

From the Renaissance to the present. Discoveries like Vettori's became increasingly rare as the sixteenth century wore on. The amount of Greek and Latin literature known in the West had radically expanded since the Middle Ages, so that by the end of the Renaissance it closely resembled our own canon of ancient texts. A few manuscript discoveries remained to be made: a codex of Petronius's *Cena Trimalchionis* (Trimalchio's dinner party), first discovered by Poggio in the 1420s but completely lost for more than two centuries, turned up in Dalmatia around 1650; and in 1743 a French scholar found a Greek manuscript in the Vatican Library that contained two new chapters of Theophrastus's *Charaktēres* (Characters). The most important post-Renaissance additions to the repertoire of classical literature, however, were made in the nineteenth and twentieth centuries: Latin works, most notably Cicero's *De republica,* erased and written over in palimpsests, have been restored; and Greek works, such as Aristotle's *Athenaion politeia* (Athenian constitution), have been discovered among the Egyptian papyri.

Textual Criticism and Exegesis. In the process of transmission from antiquity to the Renaissance, classical works suffered varying degrees of textual corruption due to errors induced by medieval scribes. Humanists attempted to solve this problem by two methods: collation, that is, comparing the readings found in different manuscripts; and conjectural emendation, that is, using one's ingenuity and knowledge to divine what the original text must have been. The margins of manuscripts owned by Petrarch are filled with annotations revealing his use of both procedures. He did not, however, distinguish between his conjectural emendations and the variants he found in different manuscripts; nor did he ever discuss textual problems. Following in Petrarch's footsteps, most fifteenth-century humanists used collation and conjectural emendation to purge classical texts of errors; but they, too, for the most part failed to explain how they came to their interventions, many of which later proved mistaken.

Valla, who had acquired Petrarch's annotated copy of Livy, not only added new corrections of his own but also indicated the reasons for his alterations of the text. In a polemical work of 1447, directed against two humanists who had incompetently emended a manuscript of Livy, he adduced arguments based on his careful observation of the letter forms found in medieval manuscripts and the ways in which they were commonly misread by copyists, on his unrivaled command of classical Latin, and on his knowledge of Roman history to demonstrate the inaccuracy of his opponents' emendations and the soundness of his own.

Angelo Poliziano. These advances in textual criticism were carried much further by the greatest classical scholar of the second half of the fifteenth century—and arguably of the entire Renaissance—Angelo Poliziano (1454–1494). Following in the tradition of Petrarch, Poliziano was a poet who put his knowledge of classical literature to good use in his own writings. Unlike his predecessor, however, he succeeded in attaining an almost native command of Greek and was familiar with all aspects of the Greek literary heritage, which he drew on extensively in his Italian, Latin, and Greek poetry, as well as in his Latin letters and prose compositions.

In the field of textual criticism Poliziano was in a league of his own, devising methods that anticipated the revolutionary achievements of nineteenth-century classical philology. He distinguished clearly between conjectural emendation and variant readings based on collation. In recording his collations, he indicated which readings came from which manuscripts and identified each manuscript by its owner or present location, appearance, and history. By analyzing the errors found in all copies of a given text, he was sometimes able to determine the archetype, or original manuscript, from which the others had descended. He showed, for instance, that the manuscript of Cicero's letters to his friends sent to Salutati from Vercelli was the source of all other known copies of the text, since they reproduced the mistaken order caused by its misbound leaves; this meant that an editor need only consult the archetype and could eliminate the copies from consideration. Finally, when collating a particularly ancient manuscript, such as the Codex Bembinus of Terence, he recorded not only the variants that appeared better than the received text, as humanists normally did, but even obvious mistakes, on the grounds that these might contain traces of the correct reading, which could provide the basis for later emendation.

Poliziano also went further than previous humanists in the area of textual exegesis. Because of his exceptionally wide and deep knowledge of Greek literature, he was able to identify many of the Greek models behind Latin poetry. He recognized, for example, that a phrase in Cicero's letters was a quotation from the early Latin poet Ennius, who had translated the verse from Euripides's *Medea;* and he explained the meaning of an obscure line in the Roman elegist Propertius with reference to a myth found in a hymn by Callimachus, a Hellenistic poet, and in Nonnus's *Dionysiaca,* a recondite poem from the early Byzantine era. In 1493 Poliziano's friend, the Venetian humanist Ermolao Barbaro (1454–1493), demonstrated the potential of this comparative method for textual criticism, using Greek scientific sources to correct the highly corrupt Latin text of Pliny the Elder's *Historia naturalis.*

While Barbaro adopted the traditional style of commentary, presenting a continuous exposition of a single text, Poliziano used a new format, based on *Noctes Atticae* (Attic nights) of Aulus Gellius and consisting of brief chapters that dealt with specific textual or exegetical problems arising in a variety of Greek and Latin works. His *Miscellanea* (Miscellaneous notes) provided an ideal showcase for the sort of insights produced by his masterly brand of philology. It developed into a popular genre among sixteenth-century classical scholars under the title *variae lectiones* (variant readings).

The sixteenth century. By the opening years of the sixteenth century, the vast majority of Latin classical texts had appeared in printed editions. This had both advantages and disadvantages for textual criticism. The main advantage was that printing quickly led to the formation of a *textus receptus,* a standard or received text, which provided a common point of reference for the entire scholarly community, making it much easier for corrections to be communicated and shared. The main disadvantage was that the received text tended to be based not on the oldest and most reliable manuscripts but on whatever ones the early editors had to hand, which were often recent and corrupt. Moreover, as scholars soon began to realize, printing permitted the widespread circulation of ill-founded conjectural emendations.

It was one of Vettori's aims to eliminate such distortions from classical texts by exploiting the methods of manuscript collation devised by Poliziano. Vettori performed a systematic recension, or critical evaluation of the text of each manuscript, so that he could identify the archetype, or at any rate the oldest witness to the text, and use that as the basis of his edition. In his annotations he set out the reasons for any corrections he made to the received text, which usually depended on an improved reading found in what he had determined to be the best manuscript. When this procedure did not produce a solution to an obviously corrupt word or phrase, he would reluctantly emend the text, preferably altering only one letter so that he could conserve, as far as possible, the manuscript reading. In his 1558 edition of Cicero's letters to his friends, Vettori went so far as to produce what was essentially a transcription of the Vercelli manuscript that Poliziano had shown to be the archetype. In 1553 the father-and-son team of Lelio and Francesco Torelli, who shared Vettori's views on editing, published a critical edition of the late sixth-century Florentine codex of the *Digest,* or *Pandects,* the largest part of the compilation of Roman law promulgated in the sixth century. They attempted to reproduce the unusual spelling found in this manuscript, which Poliziano, after intensive study, had concluded was the very codex first written by the officials of Emperor Justinian.

This conservative style of textual criticism did not, in general, find favor in France, which in the sixteenth century replaced Italy as the leading center of classical scholarship. French editors were inclined to shun the drudgery of systematic manuscript collation, so highly valued by their Italian counterparts, and preferred to indulge in conjectural emendation, which allowed them to show off their philological acumen. It was Poliziano's interest in the Greek sources of Latin literature, rather than his methods for evaluating the age and independence of manuscripts, that exerted the greatest influence among French scholars. Although the Parisian professor Denys Lambin (c. 1520–1572) improved the texts of Horace, Lucretius, and Cicero by using readings from a number of different manuscripts, he did so somewhat randomly, without attempting to work out the relationship between them. What made his editions of these authors stand out were the lengthy—in truth, rather long-winded—annotations, which revealed Lambin's remarkable ability to detect the Greek models behind Latin texts.

Joseph Justus Scaliger (1540–1609), the son of an Italian scholar who had immigrated to France, achieved mastery of both the Italian and the French style of textual criticism. In his 1577 edition of Catullus he made a thorough study of the manuscript tradition and, outdoing the Italians in their own area of specialization, used the shared errors in the extant manuscripts to reconstruct a hypothetical lost archetype—a methodological leap forward that, like the innovations of Poliziano, would not become part of the accepted practice of textual critics until the nineteenth century. Two years later, however, in his 1579 edition of Manilius's *Astronomica,* Scaliger returned to the French editorial methods in which he had been schooled: refusing to examine the manuscript evidence, he relied entirely on conjectural emendation. The challenges presented by this extremely difficult didactic poem presented him with an opportunity to earn a reputation for brilliance by producing a bravura display of critical ingenuity, linguistic flair, and arcane astronomical knowledge.

The Netherlands and Germany. In 1593 Scaliger became a professor at the University of Leiden.

He was hired to replace the Flemish scholar Justus Lipsius (1547–1606), who had decided to return to Louvain (in the southern Netherlands) and to the Catholic faith, after a twelve-year sojourn in Protestant Leiden. Lipsius specialized in the works of the Latin prose authors Tacitus and Seneca. His most significant achievement as a textual critic was his 1574 edition of the works of Tacitus, in which the *Historiae* and the *Annales,* previously regarded as one work, were distinguished for the first time. His 1605 edition of Seneca, though less innovative and impressive than the Tacitus, contained masterly annotations that elucidated the Roman philosopher's concise, elliptical, and epigrammatic style, and presented a detailed exposition of Seneca's Stoic doctrines. Lipsius wanted not only to expound and edit the writings of both authors but also to apply their ideas to contemporary needs. His *Politica* of 1589 turned the prudence described by Tacitus and other Roman writers into practical lessons for Renaissance rulers and subjects, while his *De constantia* of 1584 drew on the wisdom of Seneca to provide ethical guidance for individuals caught up in the turmoil of the wars of religion.

The application of classical learning to the needs of the present was also a hallmark of much German scholarship, especially among humanists such as Beatus Rhenanus (1485–1547) who were inspired by the ideals of Desiderius Erasmus (c. 1466–1536). Beatus, the most distinguished editor of Tacitus before Lipsius, devoted particular attention to the *Germania,* taking patriotic pride in this account of the moral virtues of the ancient German tribes but also using it to highlight the sorry state into which his country had fallen. Another Erasmian, Ulrich Zasius (1461–1535), discovered important Roman legal manuscripts and made use of his extensive knowledge of ancient Roman civil law as a practicing lawyer in Freiburg.

German classical scholarship made advances in the study of Greek as well as Latin authors. The Augsburg humanist Wilhelm Holtzmann (1532–1576), known by the Greek version of his name, Xylander, in 1559 produced the first edition and Latin translation of the *Meditations* of Emperor Marcus Aurelius, which would eventually become a key philosophical text in the Neostoic revival. Hieronymus Wolf (1516–1580), also of Augsburg, made a name for himself with his definitive editions of the Athenian orators Demosthenes and Aristides and of the Stoic philosopher Epictetus; in 1557 he produced the first corpus of Byzantine historians. His student David Hoeschel (1556–1617) continued along these lines, with his 1601 edition of the *Bibliotheca* (Library) of the ninth-century patriarch of Constantinople, Photius, which preserved excerpts from 280 lost Greek works.

Although Janus Gruter (1560–1627) spent most of his career as a librarian in Heidelberg, he was born in Antwerp, educated in England and in Leiden under Scaliger, with whose assistance he compiled a collection of ancient Latin inscriptions. Gruter's modest achievements as an editor of classical texts—he worked out the generally accepted chapter division of the books of Livy's Roman history—were overshadowed by other scholars also trained at Leiden, most notably Scaliger's favorite pupil, Daniel Heinsius (1580–1655), whose 1611 edition of Aristotle's *Poetics* and essay on the Aristotelian theory of tragedy made an enormous impact on neoclassical drama, especially in France. His editorial work on Roman poets, especially Ovid, was carried on, with greater success, by his son Nicholas Heinsius (1620–1681), the seventeenth century's finest editor and interpreter of Latin poetry.

The Classical Languages. Latin had been taught and studied since the Middle Ages, and the early Renaissance humanists did little more than modify traditional methods and textbooks, placing greater emphasis on classical forms and models. A real break with the past occurred in the middle of the fifteenth century with the appearance of Valla's *Elegantiae linguae latinae libri sex* (Six books of the elegances of the Latin language; 1471), a guide to Latin usage and syntax based on a careful empirical study of Roman literature. Valla believed that the return to the classical style of writing Latin, which had begun with Petrarch, was bringing with it a gradual renewal of all disciplines, from law and medicine to philosophy, and had even contributed to the revival of the visual arts. Much had been achieved, but there was more still to do. Valla saw his book as propelling forward the broad cultural transformation now referred to as the Renaissance.

Valla's *Elegantiae* may not have fulfilled his grandiose ambitions, but it did give an important impetus to the reform of Latin, teaching contemporaries to imitate the great Roman authors in their prose and poetry. Other reference works also played a role in the humanist movement to classicize Latin and remove every vestige of medieval vocabulary and usage. *Cornucopiae linguae Latinae* (Horn of plenty of the Latin language) of Niccolò Perotti (1430–1480), first printed in 1489, was often consulted as a Latin dictionary; but it was in reality a lexicographical commentary on the first book of Martial's epigrams and consequently had the advantage, from a humanist point of view, of containing only words that were current in first-century Rome. Another work of humanist lexicography, *De orthographia,* by Giovanni Tortelli (1400–1466), which was in print by 1471, focused on the Greek roots of Latin terms, explaining, for instance, that its title derived from the Greek words for "correct" and "writing."

Until the end of the fifteenth century the teaching of the Greek language remained largely the preserve of émigré scholars, who adapted and simplified Byzantine methods for Western use. Manuel Chrysoloras (c. 1353–1415), who taught Greek in Florence at the end of the fourteenth century to a generation of young Italian humanists, wrote a textbook called *Erotemata sive quaestiones* (Questions), which circulated widely, especially in the Greek-Latin redaction by Guarino Guarini (1374–1460) of Verona. In 1476 a similarly titled work by another Byzantine, Constantine Lascaris (1434–1501), became the first wholly Greek book to reach print. Byzantine dictionaries, too, dominated the scene at first; but in the sixteenth century Westerners began to compile their own lexicons. The massive dictionary, entirely in Greek, by Varino Favorino (1450–1537), the bishop of Nocera, was printed in 1523; while the French humanist Guillaume Budé (1467–1540) produced a Greek counterpart to Valla's *Elegantiae* in his *Commentarii linguae Graece* (Commentaries on the Greek language) of 1529. Much of Budé's work was later incorporated into the greatest monument of Greek scholarship in the Renaissance, the 1572 *Thesaurus linguae Graecae* (Treasure-house of the Greek language), by the scholarly printers Robert (1503–1559) and Henri Estienne (d. 1598).

History and Antiquarianism. Renaissance classical scholars took a keen interest in ancient history, which provided the essential background to their literary and linguistic studies. Italian humanists, seeing themselves as descendants of the Romans, naturally enough focused on the history of Rome and quickly learned to combine information gleaned from the material remains of Roman civilization, in which Italy was so rich, with literary sources such as Livy and Sallust. Flavio Biondo (1392–1463), in his *De Roma instaurata* (Rome restored) of 1444–1446, reconstructed the architecture and topography of ancient Rome using inscriptions and surviving monuments together with the works of classical historians.

Inscriptions were highly valued not only for the historical data they yielded but also because they provided an authentic record of the Latin language as it was written in antiquity, free from the errors inherent in manuscript transmission. Many humanists collected inscriptions, searching them out wherever they went. Cyriacus of Ancona (1391–1452) on his travels to the East in the 1430s and 1440s, took great care to record all the Greek inscriptions he encountered and drew surviving monuments. Fra Giocondo (c. 1433–1515), a practicing architect and editor of Vitruvius, produced beautiful and meticulous drawings of Latin inscriptions, which he put together in topographically arranged notebooks. Material from his notebooks found its way into a large illustrated collection of inscriptions from ancient Rome, published in 1521 by Jacopo Mazzocchi, a book that immediately became a valuable resource for historians.

Humanists since the time of Petrarch had used ancient coins as historical evidence. In the fifteenth century collecting coins, along with other antiquities, became a popular pursuit among wealthy and cultivated patrons like Pope Paul II (reigned 1464–1471) and Lorenzo de' Medici. Numismatics as a serious discipline was inaugurated by Budé, whose 1514 treatise on Roman coinage and measures, *De asse* (On the Roman penny), established the scholarly credentials of antiquarian studies in general. The Spanish lawyer and humanist Antonio Agustín (1517–1586), the author of an important work on numismatics and epigraphy published in 1587, in his old age came to believe that coins and inscriptions were far more reliable witnesses to Roman history than written documents. Usually, however, historians availed themselves of both types of evidence: thus Carlo Sigonio (1524–1584), a distinguished sixteenth-century editor of Livy, wrote a commentary on *Fasti consulares,* a list of consuls inscribed on an arch in the Roman forum, in which he compared this epigraphical material with information in literary sources.

Impact of Renaissance Classical Scholarship. The advances made in classical scholarship during the Renaissance had important repercussions for theology, law, medicine, and philosophy. These disciplines were all based on ancient texts and therefore presented problems similar to those involved in the study of Greek and Latin literature. The authoritative text for theologians was, of course, the Bible. Medieval scholars had grappled with its many textual difficulties; but in the Renaissance techniques devised to deal with classical works began to be applied systematically to the Bible. Valla approached the Vulgate New Testament in much the same spirit as he approached Livy's history of Rome, regarding both as texts that had suffered corruption over the centuries due to scribal errors and consequently needed emendation. In addition, the Vulgate, as a Latin version of a Greek work, was marred by mistranslations that could only be corrected by reference to the original.

Valla's annotations on the New Testament, which were published in 1505, were edited by the Dutch humanist Erasmus, who was inspired by this new philological approach to the most sacred of texts. In 1516 Erasmus published a Greek and Latin edition of the New Testament, using the methods of textual criticism developed by generations of classical scholars. The Bible was, however, a special case, as Erasmus quickly realized when he caused a theological uproar by deleting a Trinitarian passage (1 John 5:7–8) from the Vulgate on the grounds that it could not be found in any manuscripts of the Greek and had presumably been added at a late stage for dogmatic purposes. Although he reinserted the verses in later editions—a Greek manuscript containing them, no doubt written for the occasion, turned up—the overall effect of his editorial work, which included making a revised Latin translation of the New Testament, was to undermine the authority of the Vulgate.

When Poliziano began to lecture on Aristotle's *Prior Analytics* in 1492, the philosophers at the University of Florence complained that he had invaded their territory. Poliziano replied that as a classical scholar he had the right and the ability to interpret any ancient text, whether its content was philosophical, legal, or medical. Throughout the fifteenth and sixteenth centuries, humanists like Poliziano took an interest in the Aristotelian corpus, which remained the basis of the philosophy curriculum. They produced more accurate and readable translations, studied and edited the Greek text of Aristotle's works, and made the large body of ancient Greek commentaries on Aristotle available to professional philosophers. Classical scholars also enlarged the range of philosophical material known in the Renaissance by editing and translating Greek works from the Platonic, Stoic, and Epicurean traditions, as well as discovering important new Latin philosophical works such as the Epicurean poem of Lucretius.

When Poliziano collated the Florentine codex of the *Digest,* or *Pandects,* and the Torelli produced a critical edition of it, they were treating a foundational work of Roman law just like any other ancient text. Since the Middle Ages legal scholars had attempted to adapt ancient Roman law to present political circumstances; but in the sixteenth century a group of French humanists, including Budé, started to study the texts of Roman law as historical documents. Moreover, they recognized that these texts had gone through the same damaging process of manuscript transmission as other works from antiquity—the Greek passages in particular had become garbled beyond recognition—and required emendation by experts in classical languages.

In the final years of his life Poliziano embarked on a study of Greek medical texts and became interested in the problem of translating the technical terms in such works into Latin. His contemporary Niccolò Leoniceno (1428–1524), both a physician and a humanist, brought together these two areas of expertise by writing a treatise (1492) on the medical errors in Pliny's *Historia naturalis,* demonstrating that the Roman author had misunderstood various Greek terms for medicinal plants and herbs. In the sixteenth century doctors with humanistic training edited and made new translations of the works of Galen and Hippocrates, with the aim (only partially achieved) of placing these ancient Greek texts at the center of medical education and practice.

All in all, few aspects of Renaissance intellectual and cultural life escaped the pervasive influence of classical scholarship.

Conclusion.   From Petrarch in the fourteenth century to Daniel Heinsius in the early seventeenth, classical scholars dramatically increased and radically transformed the knowledge of antiquity available to Renaissance readers. Scholars gradually came to understand the process by which written documents—whether literary, historical, philosophical, legal, or medical—had been transmitted and to devise ways to counter the inevitable corruption the documents had suffered. They also invented techniques for studying material artifacts such as coins, inscriptions, and architectural remains. This newly recovered information was not only studied for its intrinsic and historical value, but was also exploited for the benefits it might bring to the present. From the mid-fifteenth century onward, the printing press made it easier to communicate scholarly advances and discoveries, which were now rapidly disseminated throughout Europe. Italy, which had been at the forefront of classical studies in the early Renaissance, was overtaken in the course of the sixteenth century by France, which itself yielded supremacy to the Netherlands after 1600.

BIBLIOGRAPHY

Bentley, Jerry H. *Humanists and Holy Writ: New Testament Scholarship in the Renaissance.* Princeton, N.J., 1983.

Billanovich, Giuseppe. "Petrarch and the Textual Tradition of Livy." *Journal of the Warburg and Courtauld Institutes* 14 (1951):137–208.

D'Amico, John F. *Theory and Practice in Renaissance Textual Criticism: Beatus Rhenanus between Conjecture and History*. Berkeley, Calif., 1988. Study of a sixteenth-century northern classical scholar.

Dionisotti, A. C., Anthony Grafton, and Jill Kraye, eds. *The Uses of Greek and Latin: Historical Essays*. London, 1988. Articles on the role of classical scholarship in biblical, patristic, philosophical, medical, and legal studies.

Gaisser, Julia Haig. *Catullus and His Renaissance Readers*. Oxford, U.K., 1993. Study of fifteenth- and sixteenth-century editions of and commentaries on the Roman poet.

Grafton, Anthony. *Commerce with the Classics: Ancient Books and Renaissance Readers*. Ann Arbor, Mich., 1997. Includes chapters on Leon Battista Alberti, Giovanni Pico della Mirandola, Guillaume Budé, and Johannes Kepler.

Grafton, Anthony. *Joseph Scaliger: A Study in the History of Classical Scholarship*. 2 vols. Oxford, U.K., 1983–1993. Vol. 1 discusses Poliziano's philological method and its influence in Italy, France, and the Low Countries.

Grafton, Anthony. "Quattrocento Humanism and Classical Scholarship." In *Renaissance Humanism: Foundations, Forms, and Legacy*. Vol. 3. Edited by Albert Rabil. Philadelphia, 1988. Pages 23–66.

Grafton, Anthony, ed. *Rome Reborn: The Vatican Library and Renaissance Culture*. Washington, D.C., 1993. Essays on the history of one of the most important Renaissance collections of Greek and Latin manuscripts.

Kenney, E. J. *The Classical Text: Aspects of Editing in the Age of the Printed Book*. Berkeley, Calif., 1974.

Kraye, Jill, ed. *The Cambridge Companion to Renaissance Humanism*. Cambridge, U.K., 1996. Includes chapters on classical and biblical scholarship, on Latin grammar and teaching, and on the transition from manuscripts to printing.

McCuaig, William. *Carlo Sigonio: The Changing World of the Late Renaissance*. Princeton, N.J., 1989. Study of a sixteenth-century Italian humanist and historian of ancient Rome.

Percival, W. Keith. "Renaissance Grammar." In *Renaissance Humanism: Foundations, Forms, and Legacy*. Vol. 3. Edited by Albert Rabil. Philadelphia, 1988. Pages 67–83.

Pfeiffer, Rudolf. *History of Classical Scholarship from 1300 to 1850*. Oxford, U.K., 1976.

Reynolds, L. D., and Nigel Guy Wilson. *Scribes and Scholars: A Guide to the Transmission of Greek and Latin Literature*. 3d ed. Oxford, U.K., 1991. Contains chapters on classical scholarship in the Renaissance and after and on textual criticism.

Reynolds, L. D., and Peter K. Marshall, eds. *Texts and Transmission: A Survey of the Latin Classics*. Oxford, U.K., 1983. Contains information about the role played by Renaissance scholars in the textual transmission of Latin authors.

Ullman, Berthold L., and Philip A. Stadter. *The Public Library of Renaissance Florence: Niccolò Niccoli, Cosimo de' Medici, and the Library of San Marco*. Padua, Italy, 1972. History of the library and its collection of Greek and Latin manuscripts.

Weiss, Roberto. *The Renaissance Discovery of Classical Antiquity*. 2d ed. Oxford, U.K., 1988. Survey of the study of the material remains of antiquity (coins, inscriptions, monuments, and so on).

Wilson, Nigel Guy. *From Byzantium to Italy: Greek Studies in the Italian Renaissance*. London, 1992. Discusses the Greek scholarship of Byzantine émigrés and Italian scholars.

JILL KRAYE

CLAVIUS, CHRISTOPHER (1538–1612), Jesuit mathematician and astronomer, important for his relationship with Galileo Galilei. Christopher Clavius (possibly a latinization of Clau or Schlüssel) was born in Bamberg, Germany, or its vicinity. Nothing is known of his family or his life before 1 February 1555, when he was admitted to the Jesuit novitiate in Rome by Ignatius Loyola. In the autumn of that year he was sent to Portugal, and from 1556 he studied in the College of Arts at Coimbra: Latin and rhetoric with Pedro Juan Perpiñá (Petrus Perpinianus) and Cipriano Soares, philosophy with Pedro da Fonseca.

There was no professor of mathematics at the college, though that subject was taught in the University of Coimbra by Pedro Nuñes, often said to be his teacher. However, Nuñes was hostile to the Jesuits; Clavius indicated acquaintance with his works and said that he was self-taught in mathematics, beginning with Euclid's *Elements*. The authors providing his foundation were the classical Greeks, Nuñes, Francesco Maurolico, mathematician-philologists like Federico Commandino and Guidobaldo dal Monte, and German algebraists like Michael Stiefel and Johann Scheubel. He also knew all the significant works of ancient and Renaissance mathematicians.

In 1560 Clavius was recalled to Rome, probably to allow him to gain expertise with specialists. Before departing, on 21 August, he observed a total solar eclipse. His description of this in his *In Sphaeram Ioannis de Sacro Bosco commentarius* (Commentary on the Sphere of John of Sacrobosco; Rome, 1570, with sixteen editions to 1612), the first of its kind in Western astronomical literature, was much discussed (Tycho Brahe rejected it, but Johannes Kepler firmly accepted it). Up to 1566 he followed the course in theology at the Collegio Romano, the Jesuit school of higher learning in Rome, and from November 1563 he taught mathematics there, but usually with other assignments.

Clavius ceased teaching public courses around 1590; thereafter his students substituted for him while he devoted himself to courses for specialists— Jesuits, but also laity. From 1594 these courses had the official title of Academy of Mathematics. Up to around 1640 they formed practically all the professors of mathematics in the European colleges of the Jesuits and the missionaries who carried European science to India, China, and Japan. Among Clavius's direct or indirect students were Matteo Ricci, Christopher Grienberger, Paul Guldin, Odo van Maelcote, Gregory of Saint Vincent, Luca Valerio, Johann Schreck, and Marino Ghetaldi. Clavius's books were widely used up to about 1650, even in non-Jesuit schools and universities, and played a major role in the spread of mathematics in America and Asia.

Clavius showed no deep interest in subjects other than mathematics, but he composed sacred music, probably performed only among Jesuits. About fifteen compositions are extant, mainly motets. A notable part of the mathematical work he took on concerned applications, and this perhaps prevented him from making more original contributions to the field. This work consisted predominantly of commentaries, textbooks, and treatises originating from his teaching or from his work on ecclesiastical commissions. He was the central figure of the commission for the reform of the calendar and devoted some works to explain and defend it. His *Explicatio* of the new Gregorian calendar (Rome, 1603), written at the request of Pope Clement VIII, still is the fullest treatment of the subject.

Clavius's most well-known works were his *Commentarius* on Sacrobosco, probably the most used elementary textbook on astronomy after the Middle Ages, and his *Euclidis Elementorum libri XV* (The fifteen books of Euclid's *Elements;* Rome, 1574, with nine editions to 1612), which enjoyed the same popularity for basic mathematics. In these and in other smaller works, Clavius's technique was to take a classic of a mathematical science, or a portion of it, commenting on it and adding the contributions of other authors from Greek times to his contemporaries. For that reason, though these works are philological in form, their content approaches that of original treatises. Other works, like *Astrolabium* (Astrolabes; Rome, 1593), *Gnomonices libri VIII* (Theory of sundials; Rome, 1591), and *Algebra* (Rome, 1608), were written directly as mathematical treatises. Clavius is regarded more as a learned expositor and teacher than as a researcher, but he did contribute some original results.

His historical importance notwithstanding, Clavius is known mostly for his relationship with Galileo, who showed him his own first paper on mathematics and in 1611 obtained, through Clavius, the approval of the Jesuits for his telescopic observations. Clavius first knew of Copernicus's *De revolutionibus* (On the revolutions) before 1580 and the work of Tycho Brahe around 1590; he was well aware of the crisis these presented for geocentrism. Nonetheless, the limits imposed by Aristotelian physics and fidelity to scripture prevented him from considering heliocentrism as a real possibility. They put him in a theoretical bind, which he recognized in the last edition of the *Commentarius* he personally edited. This situation, both doctrinal and psychological, explains the behavior of his students in the crisis of 1615–1616, when Cardinal Robert Bellarmine—once Clavius's fellow student—used them as consultants to the Congregations of the Holy Office and the Index when deciding the final form of the prohibition of Copernicus's doctrine because of their favorable views of Galileo and heliocentrism.

BIBLIOGRAPHY

Primary Works

Backer, Augustin de. *Bibliothèque de la Compagnie de Jésus.* New edition by Carlos Sommervogel. 12 vols. 1890–1932. Reprint, Louvain, Belgium, 1960. Vol. 2, cols. 1212–1224 lists all of Clavius's writings.

Baldini, Ugo, and Pier Daniele Napolitani, eds. *Christoph Clavius: Corrispondenza.* 7 vols. in 14 fascicles. Pisa, Italy, 1992. A critical edition of Clavius's correspondence.

Secondary Works

Baldini, Ugo, ed. *Christoph Clavius e l'attività dei Gesuiti nell'età di Galileo.* Rome, 1995.

Coyne, George V., Michael A. Hoskin, and Olaf Pedersen, eds. *Gregorian Reform of the Calendar: Proceedings of the Vatican Conference to Commemorate Its Four Hundredth Anniversary.* Rome, 1983.

Knobloch, Eberhard. "Sur la vie et l'oeuvre de Christophore Clavius." *Revue d'histoire des sciences* 42 (1988): 331–356.

Lattis, James M. *Between Copernicus and Galileo: Christoph Clavius and the Collapse of Ptolemaic Astronomy.* Chicago, 1994.

UGO BALDINI

Translated from Italian by William A. Wallace

CLEMENT VII (Giulio de' Medici; 1478–1534), pope (1523–1534). Born illegitimately a month after the murder of his father, Giuliano, in the Pazzi Conspiracy, Giulio de' Medici probably spent seven years in the care of the architect Antonio da Sangallo before joining the family of his uncle, Lorenzo "the Magnificent," in the Medici Palace in Florence. Alongside his cousins Giuliano and Giovanni, he studied under the direction of the humanist bishop of Arezzo, Gentile Becchi. When Giovanni was inducted into the college of cardinals (1492), Giulio entered his service. After Giovanni became Pope Leo X (1513), he named Giulio archbishop of Florence and elevated him to the cardinalate. In 1517 Giulio succeeded Cardinal Bernardo Dovizi (Bibbiena) as vice-chancellor of the church. Renowned for diplomatic skill, he helped forge an alliance with Charles V (1500–1558), the Spanish king and Holy Roman Emperor–designate, to counterbalance French designs on Italy. Beginning in 1519, he also served as de facto ruler of Florence.

Succeeding Adrian VI as pope, Clement initially maintained a pro-imperial policy but, fearing that Spain threatened papal political autonomy, he soon adopted a pose of neutrality. In late 1524, when incursions of French and Spanish troops into Italy rendered that strategy untenable, Clement allied with France, a choice that issued in disaster with the Spanish victory at the Battle of Pavia (24 February 1525) in which Francis I of France was captured. Clement soon reached terms with Charles V, but once Francis had returned to power, Clement joined France, Milan, and Venice in the League of Cognac (22 May 1526) against Charles.

Clement alternately prosecuted war and sought peace in accordance with the league's fortunes. In March 1527, as Charles de Bourbon (1490–1527) led an imperial army toward Rome, the pope concluded an armistice with the viceroy of Naples, Charles de Lannoy (c. 1487–1527), but Bourbon and his men ignored it, and on 6 May they sacked Rome. Pope Clement watched helplessly from the Castel Sant' Angelo as the occupying troops committed atrocities in the city below. That December he escaped to Orvieto, returning to Rome only the following autumn. By May 1529, Clement again concluded peace with Charles V, whose grip on the Italian Peninsula had become decisive, and in February 1530 he crowned Charles Holy Roman Emperor. That summer an imperial army restored the Medici to power in Florence, from which they had been expelled three years earlier. Thus family advancement compensated somewhat for papal political losses.

Clement perforce subordinated ecclesiastical goals to those of political survival and economic solvency. Early on he sought to establish standards for the training and moral reform of the secular clergy and supported the founding of the Theatine order. Not until 1527 did he resort to creating cardinals to augment revenues. Yet he resisted calls for a general council of the church, partly because such a council might use his illegitimate birth as a pretext for deposing him. In response to Henry VIII's petitions for the annulment of his marriage to Catherine of Aragon, Clement temporized, finally affirming the marriage's validity in March 1534. The papacy's intermittent anti-imperial policy also complicated Charles V's attempts to resolve the Lutheran schism in Germany. Ultimately Clement bequeathed Paul III a church severely fragmented and little prepared for reform.

His efforts to further family interests intensified over time. When he was gravely ill in January 1529, he elevated his nephew Ippolito de' Medici (1510–-1535) to the cardinalate. In 1532 he had Alessandro de' Medici (1510–1537)—who some historians believe was actually Clement's son—installed as duke of Florence. Clement also sought politically beneficial marriage alliances, orchestrating (1529) the betrothal of Alessandro to the emperor's natural daughter, Margaret (1522–1586), and the marriage (1533) of Catherine de' Medici (1519–1589) to Henri of Orléans (1519–1559).

Clement's initial promise as artistic patron gave way to disappointment as political and fiscal crises diminished or stalled his designs. A discerning Maecenas whose commissions included Raphael's *Transfiguration,* Sebastiano del Piombo's *Raising of Lazarus,* and Michelangelo's *Last Judgment,* he began ambitious architectural projects including the facade and new sacristy for the Church of San Lorenzo in Florence, but the former was never realized, and the latter did not reach completion within his lifetime.

Historians have traditionally concurred with the Florentine historian Francesco Vettori (1474–1539), who famously remarked that Clement "endured a great hardship to become, from a great and much-admired cardinal, a small and little-esteemed pope." Scholars today tend to attribute his failures less to character flaws (timidity and indecisiveness) than to the well-nigh insurmountable political, fiscal, and ecclesiastical crises that confronted him—challenges that would require transformation of the imagery as well as the policies that had most distinguished the Renaissance papacy.

[For images of Clement VII, see the entry on **Historical Themes in Renaissance Art** and the biographies of the emperor Charles V and Pope Leo X.]

See also **Papacy**; **Wars of Italy**.

BIBLIOGRAPHY

Primary Works

Guicciardini, Francesco. *The History of Italy.* Translated by Sidney Alexander. New York, 1969. Abridged. A thorough account of the years after 1492 by the foremost historian of his generation.

Guicciardini, Luigi. *The Sack of Rome.* Translated and edited by James H. McGregor. New York, 1993. A near-contemporary account of the disaster and Clement's role in it. A competent translation marred by a severely flawed critical apparatus.

Secondary Works

Pastor, Ludwig von. *The History of the Popes from the Close of the Middle Ages Drawn from the Secret Archives of the Vatican and Other Original Sources.* 40 vols. 3d ed. Edited and translated from the German by Frederick I. Antrobus et al. London, 1891–1953. Vols. 9 and 10 detail Clement VII and his pontificate.

Prosperi, Adriano. "Clement VII, papa." *Dizionario biografico degli Italiani.* Rome, 1960–. Vol. 26, pp. 237–259. Reliable, concise biography with extensive bibliography.

Reiss, Sheryl E. "Cardinal Giulio de' Medici as a Patron of Art, 1513–1523." 3 vols. Ph.D. diss., Princeton University, 1992. A richly documented study.

Zimmermann, T. C. Price. *Paolo Giovio: The Historian and the Crisis of Sixteenth-Century Italy.* Princeton, N.J., 1995. An outstanding and eloquent biography of Clement VII's official historian, set in political and cultural context.

KENNETH GOUWENS

CLEMENT VIII (Ippolito Aldobrandini; 1536–1605), pope (1592–1605). Born at Fano in the Papal States, the son of a Florentine exile and papal governmental official, young Ippolito studied law at Padua, Perugia, and Bologna. With the favor of Pius V (pontificate 1566–1572) he rose to judge of the Rota, the papal tribunal, in 1569. His fortunes diminished under the reign of Gregory XIII (1572–1585). In 1580 the genuinely pious Ippolito was ordained priest, probably under the influence of Philip Neri (1515–1595), to whom he always remained devoted. In 1585 Sixtus V (reigned 1585–1590) both appointed him to the important office of datary and raised the relatively obscure Ippolito to the cardinalate. A highly successful mission as papal legate in 1588 to mediate the conflict over the Polish succession further raised his profile. His position in the Curia made him a natural candidate to succeed Sixtus. Spanish reservations hindered this in the conclaves that elected the next three, short-lived popes; once the reservations dissolved, he was elected unanimously on 30 January 1592.

Clement combined promotion of church reform with political realism and the nepotism typical of the time. His greatest achievement was the restoration of France as a Catholic balance to Spain and so the liberation of the papacy from undue Spanish influence, and this without alienating Spain. Clement absolved Henry IV on 17 September 1595, thus preparing the way for Henry's coronation, and he accepted the Edict of Nantes in 1598 with its limited toleration of the Huguenots. As *padre commune* (common father) of Christendom, Clement played a major role in mediating the Peace of Vervins between France and Spain in 1598. This conclusion of the religious wars in France greatly facilitated Catholic renewal there. The pope wisely did not press Henry to fulfill his promise to secure the formal acceptance of the Tridentine decrees, but he did obtain the readmission of the Jesuits in 1603 to the areas of the kingdom from which they had been expelled. Henry IV, for his part, gave decisive support for the

Pope Clement VIII. Bronze bust on the facade of Ferrara Cathedral by Giorgio Albenga (fl. 1586–1605), early seventeenth century. The papacy became the ruler of Ferrara in 1597 after the death of the last duke; Clement entered the city in 1598. ALINARI/ART RESOURCE

papal recovery of the duchy of Ferrara in 1598. More of a threat for Clement than the heretics were the Turks, who were at war with the empire from 1593 to 1606, but his constant efforts to organize and finance a league against them failed for the most part. Expenditures on Turkish campaigns and gifts to his family depleted the papal treasury. In 1593 Clement created as cardinals his two nephews, the cousins Cinzio Passeri-Aldobrandini (d. 1610) and Pietro Aldobrandini (d. 1621), but the rivalry between the two proved to be an annoyance to the pope until Pietro emerged as the more influential by 1598.

Shortly after his election, the pope called his former fellow student, the Neoplatonist philosopher Francesco Patrizi (1529–1597), to Rome to teach, a move that some at the papal court as well as some modern scholars have interpreted as a tentative first step toward an intellectual opening, but Patrizi's vigorous anti-Aristotelianism was unpopular and his principal work was subsequently condemned. In 1592 Clement authorized the publication of a revision of the Vulgate Bible published by Sixtus V in 1590. This new edition became known as the Sixto-Clementine Vulgate. Clement fostered the publication of Caesar Baronius's *Annales ecclesiastici* (Annals of the church; 12 vols., 1598–1607) and Robert Bellarmine's *Disputationes de controversiis christianae fidei huius temporis haereticos* (Lectures on the controversies of the Christian faith against the heretics of this time; 3 vols., 1586–1596), and he completed work on the Vatican Palace, including the magnificent Clementine Hall for audiences. Cardinal Pietro undertook the construction of the Villa Aldobrandini at Frascati. The controversy over grace and free will between the Dominicans and the Jesuits was summoned to Rome in 1595, and in 1602 Clement himself presided over sixty-eight sessions, but he was unable to resolve the thorny issue, which he left to his successor.

BIBLIOGRAPHY

Primary Work

Clement VIII. *Die Hauptinstruktionen Clemens' VIII. für die Nuntien und Legaten an den europäischen Fürstenhöfen, 1592–1605.* Edited by Klaus Jaitner. 2 vols. Tübingen, Germany, 1984. Richly annotated, with a 273-page introduction.

Secondary Works

Borromeo, Agostino. "Clemente VIII." In *Dizionario biogràfico degli Italiani.* Vol. 26. Rome, 1982. Pages 259–282.

Lutz, Georg, ed. *Das Papsttum, die Christenheit und die Staaten Europas 1592–1605. Forschungen zu den Hauptinstruktionen Clemens' VIII.* Tübingen, Germany, 1994. Eight solid contributions by distinguished scholars.

von Pastor, Ludwig. *History of the Popes, from the Close of the Middle Ages.* Vols. 23–24, *Clement VIII (1592–1605).* Edited by Ralph Francis Kerr. London, 1933.

ROBERT BIRELEY

CLERGY.

[This entry includes two subentries, one on the Catholic clergy, the other on the Protestant clergy.]

Catholic Clergy

In the Western Church the canonical concept of a *kleros* (meaning "lot" or "hereditary portion") designates that group of baptized, celibate men chosen to be part of the church hierarchy or to carry out ecclesiastical duties. In Catholic theology, the "chosen" ("elected") are called by the Holy Spirit. During the Renaissance a man or boy entered the clerical state with the rite of "first tonsure" when a bishop cut his hair; with this he became dedicated to the divine ministry. Theologically, clergy were distinguished from the laity (*laos,* people) by divine origin and alone received both the power of orders for the sanctification of the church's membership through the sacraments, and the power of jurisdiction to direct members toward their eternal goal.

The lowest clerical ranks, the minor orders, consisted of acolyte, porter, lector, and exorcist. These were not directly instituted by Christ and the primitive church, and one could depart from these orders and reenter the lay state. From minor orders and from the subdiaconate (considered a major order during the Renaissance) one could be called to the other major orders of deacon, priest, and bishop, which were conferred by an ordination ritual administered by a bishop who confirmed the calling of the Holy Spirit. These last three ranks constituted the sacrament of holy orders. (In the early church, an acolyte assisted priests and deacons in the celebration of the liturgy; a porter, or doorkeeper, kept unauthorized persons from attending the liturgy; a lector read the scripture [except the Gospel] at the liturgy; an exorcist was empowered to expel evil spirits, though in the Middle Ages and the Renaissance the office was a formality, a step in the progression to the priesthood. A deacon and subdeacon in the early church assisted the bishop in temporal ministries, such as distribution of alms; they later assisted in the celebration of the liturgy; by the Renaissance both offices were more formal steps to the priesthood than practical ministries.)

At the top of the jurisdictional hierarchy was the pope, or supreme pontiff, who when elected in conclave by the college of cardinals (a select group of bishops, priests, and deacons from the churches of Rome and its environs who advise the pope), and freely accepting the election, became bishop of Rome. By divine law the pope received in his person the primacy of jurisdiction, or supreme jurisdiction, over the universal church in matters of faith, morals, correction, and direction; he also made or confirmed appointments for the administrative territories of the church: archbishops for archdioceses (provinces), bishops for dioceses. Bishops enjoyed full jurisdiction within their dioceses; beneath them were priests (presbyters) who assisted the bishops in the administration of their dioceses. Priests were granted permission by their bishops to preach and to exercise their power to celebrate mass and administer the sacraments of baptism, confession, Holy Communion, and the last anointing, and to officiate at marriages. On local levels various ranks of clergy exercised jurisdiction derivatively according to their competence, such as pastors in parishes, chaplains in lay religious communities, confraternities, and ecclesiastical associations. In the jurisdictional hierarchy were many ranks of function and honor, such as patriarch, primate, vicar apostolic, cardinal, nuncio, and so forth, but only the episcopacy and the primacy of the papacy were considered of divine institution.

The entire clergy was divided into the secular clergy ("living in the world"), for example, parish priests and bishops; and the regular clergy or "regulars" ("living according to a religious rule"), such as Benedictines, Franciscans, and Dominicans, who took perpetual vows of poverty, chastity, and obedience. In the Middle Ages and Renaissance many clergy lived in chapter houses as canons secular, or in communities as canons regular. A canon generally served on the staff of a cathedral or collegiate church. Clergy could hold an ecclesiastical benefice (office or estate) and receive ecclesiastical revenues and pensions. The laity were to pay reverence to the clergy, and at the risk of ecclesiastical sanctions refrained from injuring their physical person. Completely exempt before civil courts, clergy could be tried only in ecclesiastical courts, and were exempt from taxation and military service.

In the Middle Ages and Renaissance, the growing complexity of the Roman church's administrative functions created a need for good "clerical" skills for composing documents and carrying out other bureaucratic duties; clerical status often allowed for rapid career advancement. In the Roman Curia clerical titles and offices proliferated, such as protonotary apostolic, referendary, abbreviator. Bishops, too, had their own diocesan offices or chanceries whose clerics received titles reflective of the administrative and jurisdictional offices and dignities, such as archpresbyter or dean for a cathedral, collegiate chapter, or deanery (a territorial subdivision of a diocese). On local levels, pastors ruled parishes; chantry priests (that is, priests with stipends to say or sing masses for the deceased, and who used these revenues to support their work of teaching or visiting the sick) were hired by the laity; and chaplains conducted liturgical and paraliturgical functions for lay or religious associations outside regular parish liturgical life.

Among the regular clergy, titles of rank also proliferated: principals of religious orders received titles as superior general, vicar general, procurator general, and provincial; monastic orders designated their superiors as abbots over monasteries, priors over convents, and rectors over lesser religious houses. Titles differentiated degrees of status within religious houses; a friar (brother) was a member of a mendicant order (that is, begging, meaning forbidden to acquire property); lay brothers, or nonclerical religious, were ignorant of Latin and attended to the material needs of monastic living. The Renaissance saw the introduction of a new category of male religious, that of clerics regular, with the foundation of the Theatines in 1524. The most famous of the clerics regular were the Jesuits, founded in 1540. Unlike monks, they were not bound to stability in a monastery; unlike mendicant friars they did not live off begging or recite the Divine Office in choir. Although not clerics, women religious, or nuns, also differentiated themselves into ranks such as canonesses, nuns, sisters, lay sisters, and so on, ruled over by abbesses and prioresses; they dwelt in communities similar to those of their male counterparts and enjoyed clerical privileges. Secular clergy, regular clergy, and women religious had canonically prescribed times for administrative meetings. As the universal church met in a general council, bishops met in regional synods and religious met in chapters and congregations.

In the Renaissance the orderly ranks of the ecclesiastical hierarchy were celebrated as the earthly reflections of the angelic choirs of angels and of cosmic order; the concept was widely popularized in the Middle Ages and Renaissance through the early sixth-century works of Pseudo-Dionysius (*The Celestial Hierarchy* and *The Ecclesiastical Hierarchy*).

See also **Papacy**; **Religious Orders**, *subentries on* **Orders of Men** *and* **Orders and Congregations of Women**; **Seminaries**.

BIBLIOGRAPHY

Claeys-Bouuaert, F. "Clerc." In *Dictionnaire de droit canonique*. Paris, 1942. Vol. 3, pp. 827–872.

Dolhagaray, B. "Clercs." In *Dictionnaire de théologie catholique*. Paris, 1923. Vol. 3, pp. 225–235.

Faivre, Alexandre. "Klerus, Kleriker." In *Lexikon für Theologie und Kirche*. Freiburg, Germany, 1997. Vol. 6, pp. 131–133.

Hay, Denys. *The Church in Italy in the Fifteenth Century*. Cambridge, U.K., 1977.

Skeeters, Martha C. *Community and Clergy: Bristol and the Reformation, c. 1530– c. 1570*. Oxford, 1993. Pages 11–33.

FREDERICK J. MCGINNESS

Protestant Clergy

With the Reformation there evolved a fundamentally new understanding of the ministry, with far-reaching social consequences: the legitimate family of the pastor was a starting point of a new civil class within European Protestantism of the sixteenth century. The novelty of this understanding lay in the rejection of the sacral character of the ministry.

The Lutheran Movement. In opposition to the old faith, the German Reformer Martin Luther (1483–1546) began formulating a new interpretation of the traditional doctrine of the "priesthood of all believers" in 1520, thereby eliminating the distinction between clergy and laity. This view challenged the legitimacy of the hierarchy of the Roman church, because in Luther's opinion the power to forgive sins rested with the church as the communion of all believers and not with the pope or officeholders. Luther continued to propose a theory of the "special office of the church," but the definition of this special office remained ambiguous. He characterized it as "service to the Word" or "service to the Gospel." An officeholder should not have any authority over his fellow believers; a minister received his special authority only because he was serving the Word. This characterization of ministry as a "mediation of the Holy Scripture" in opposition to the priesthood as "mediation of salvation" was meant as a functional understanding of ministry: wherever the Word is being proclaimed, there is the ministry. Luther did see the necessity of having only specially appointed people perform official clerical functions. This interpretation became even clearer after 1525, as a consequence of his disputes with Spiritualist forces of the Radical Reformation.

An appointment to the ministry should result from election by the congregation or by secular authority (as part of the believing community); the legitimacy of this appointment was subject to strict injunctions. Luther did not make any differentiation within the ministry according to different tasks nor did he define a resulting hierarchy of the ministry. Only in his preface to Philipp Melanchthon's *Unterricht der Visitatoren* (Instructions for visitors; 1528) did Luther emphasize the necessity of a superior clerical authority. In Luther's lifetime Melanchthon (1497–1560) further defined the ministry in the official confessional documents of the emerging Lutheran church (for example, in article 5 of the Augsburg Confession of 1530). He regarded the ministry as founded by God; it is a special service to be performed by people especially appointed for it. The priesthood of all believers was reduced to the right of electing the pastor and the ministry of the bishop as a superior clerical authority was explicitly confirmed.

The church ordinances formulated in the late sixteenth century, including that of Johannes Bugenhagen (1485–1558) in Pomerania, formalized the first steps toward a hierarchy. Bugenhagen also found himself in dispute with the radical wing of the Reformation. All constitutions regarded the ministry as a special service, with regional differences in the regulations of the appointment by election. From the beginning a leading position was assigned to a superintendent (with substitute), who had to exercised supervisory duties. Since the end of the sixteenth century all pastors and superintendents of the Lutheran churches (also in the countries of northern Europe) were subordinate to a clerical administrative authority, the *consistorium* (consistory). The Lutheran movement was characterized by the opposition of the ministry to the parish, which underlined the special value of the ministry and also gave it a special social status within the parish.

Zwinglians and Calvinists. All magisterial Reformers opposed both the sacramental interpretation of ministry promoted by the Roman church and the elimination of the spiritual office as sought by the Radical Reformation. The Zurich Reformer Huldrych Zwingli (1484–1531) agreed with Luther and Melanchthon that the ministry as well as the priesthood of all believers was based on the New Testament. But the two offices are not to be mingled; no one should be allowed to claim to be a teacher or preacher without a legitimate mission. This, according to Zwingli, was the fundamental mistake of the Spiritual wing of the Reformation. Zwingli emphasized, even more than Luther, that this constitution of the office was biblically based; he asserted that its existence derived from the apostolic age. The most important function of a preacher, therefore, is the explanation of Holy Scripture and pastoral care. Zwingli did not differentiate between these functions nor did he define any hierarchy within the ministry.

This view was quite different from that of John Calvin (1509–1564), the French Reformer of Geneva. In his church *institutio* (ordinances) of 1559, he established a system of church offices based on the New Testament. The pastor as clerical counselor has the same status as the teacher, who expounds Holy Scripture. The presbyter—the elder of the parish who shares disciplinary authority with the pastor—is put beside the deacon, who is responsible for poor relief. Like Melanchthon and Zwingli, Calvin emphasized that ministry has a divine foundation. Christ the King leads the church through people who do his will, whence comes the strong authority of every officeholder. The minister's appointment by election (by the congregation) was considered a confirmation of the divine will.

Luther's understanding of the priesthood of all believers had no significance in this doctrine of offices within the ministry. But Calvin also did not put any hierarchic order into the various offices of the ministry. He rejected a graduation within the different functions, like the German Reformers. Calvin's doctrine of offices within the ministry remained the principle of order in all Reformed church constitutions of the late sixteenth century. These constitutions became effective in the Netherlands, Switzerland, and in the states of the Holy Roman Empire that adopted a Reformed church order. In these places, appointment to the ministry required election by the congregation.

The Church of England. The course of the English Reformation resulted in a different development of the understanding of ministry. It remained close to the Roman understanding of clergy because the ministry of the bishop was considered of divine foundation (*iure divino*). Moreover, terminology and designation and hierarchic graduation (deacon, priest, bishop) continued. The major difference was that the superior authority of the pope was replaced by that of the king of England in 1534. Also, the priests of the Anglican church had no sacral obligation associated with the ministry. The Anglican church constitutions considered the administration of sacraments and the exercising of ecclesiastical discipline to be the major duties of the clergy, because these constitutions were influenced by the Reformer Martin Bucer (1491–1551) of Strasbourg and therefore by the continental Reformed tradition. Appointment to a ministry was carried out by ordination by a bishop involving blessing and prayer. The Lutheran notion of the priesthood of all believers had as little significance in England as the election of the preacher by the parish.

The legitimacy of marriage for the clergy of the Lutheran, Reformed, and Anglican churches resulted in the incorporation of the clergy in non-noble society.

Anabaptists and Spiritualist Movements. The Radical Reformation differed from the magisterial Reform movements with regard to institutional organization because of their radical criticism of the clergy. Despite the differences between the various trends of the Radical Reformation (antitrinitarians, various Anabaptist movements, the followers of Thomas Müntzer, and others), they all rejected a special clerical ministry. Not priest nor monk but the pious laity were the real clergy. The biblical priesthood of all believers, as postulated by Luther, was also fundamental for Anabaptist and Spiritualist ecclesiology. They insisted that every Christian has the right to proclaim the Gospel; there is no necessity for special appointment. A similar criticism of the ministry could be found later in Pietism in the seventeenth century.

BIBLIOGRAPHY

Eastwood, Cyril. *The Royal Priesthood of the Faithful: An Investigation of the Doctrine from Biblical Times to the Reformation.* Minneapolis, 1963.

Karant-Nunn, Susan. *Luther's Pastors: The Reformation in Ernestine Saxony.* Philadelphia, 1979.

O'Day, Rosemary. *The English Clergy: The Emergence and Consolidation of a Profession, 1558–1642.* Leicester, U.K., 1979.

Schorn-Schütte, Luise. *Evangelische Geistlichkeit in der Frühneuzeit.* Guterslöh, Germany, 1996.

LUISE SCHORN-SCHÜTTE
Translated from German by Christin Merkel

CLEVE, JOOS VAN (Joos van Cleef; c. 1485/90–1540/41), Netherlandish painter. The exact date and place of Joos van Cleve's birth are unknown, but he probably came from the province or city of Kleve in the Lower Rhine. From sometime between 1505/06 until their completion in 1508/09, Joos assisted Jan Joest in painting the wings of the high altar in the church of Saint Nicolai in Kalkar, not far from Kleve. The wings joined the carved center portion that was finished in 1500/01. Joest is sometimes considered to have been Joos's teacher. There is, however, a self-portrait of Joos in the *Raising of Lazarus* panel, and this possibly unique occurrence suggests that Joos enjoyed a special status beyond that of the usual apprentice or journeyman. The earliest paintings attributed to Joos van Cleve are the wings of an altarpiece depicting Adam and Eve (Paris, Musée du Louvre), each dated 1507. The panels show the influence not only of Jan Joest but also of the Bruges painters Hans Memling (c. 1430/40–1494) and Gerard David (c. 1460–1523). It has been suggested that Joos could have spent several years in Bruges, from 1507 on, before emigrating to Antwerp.

Joos van Cleve is first documented in Antwerp in 1511, the year that he became a master in the Guild of Saint Luke. In the centuries following his death Joos's artistic identity was lost and his paintings attributed to a variety of Netherlandish or Lower Rhenish artists. One of his finest early works, the *Death of the Virgin* altarpiece (Cologne, Wallraf-Richartz-Museum) was a key to his rediscovery. In 1894 Eduard Firmenich-Richartz interpreted a monogram in a window in the center panel as referring to the initials of Joos van der Beke, thus identifying the author with the artist known from documents in Antwerp. The altarpiece can be dated to 1515 and was originally installed in the chapel of the Hackeney family house in Cologne.

One of the most salient features of Joos van Cleve's art was his ability to combine and reconcile traditional and progressive features. Joos was one of the first to assimilate the innovative landscape style of Joachim Patinir (c. 1485–1524), who was active in Antwerp from 1515 until his death. Patinir's influence

Joos van Cleve. Self-Portrait. Oil on panel; c. 1519; 38 × 27 cm (15 × 10.6 in.). MUSEO THYSSEN-BORNEMISZA, MADRID

can be seen, for example, in Joos's *Crucifixion* riptych (Naples, Museo Nazionale di Capodimonte; c. 1516/18). Similarly, Joos's depictions of the *Adoration of the Magi* (examples in Dresden, Berlin, Prague, and Naples) are allied in their extravagant costumes and ornament to the work of the largely anonymous group known as the Antwerp mannerists.

Of particular interest is Joos van Cleve's awareness of Italian art as well as the fact that several of his paintings were exported to Italy. The *Lamentation* altarpiece (Paris, Musée du Louvre; c. 1525/27) was originally in the church of Santa Maria della Pace in Genoa. The pose of the dead Christ can be associated with a composition by Andrea del Sarto (1486–1530), while the *Last Supper* in the predella is derived from Leonardo da Vinci's (1452–1519) famous fresco of the same subject (Milan, Santa Maria delle Grazie). The *Virgin and Child* (Cambridge, Fitzwilliam Museum; c. 1525/28) demonstrates an understanding of Leonardo's subtle, sfumato shading, while the pose of the Christ Child in Joos's *Holy Family* (Manchester, N.H., Currier Gallery of Art; c. 1525) recalls Raphael's (1483–1520)

Bridgewater *Madonna* (Edinburgh, National Galleries of Scotland).

Joos van Cleve and his workshop produced numerous pictures of the Madonna and Child and the Holy Family that were elegant and potent devotional images most likely destined for the homes of middle- and upper-class citizens. His paintings of Saint Jerome, such as the panel dated 1528 (Princeton, N.J., Princeton University Art Museum), have been analyzed in the context of the humanism of Erasmus and the unsettled climate in Antwerp at the time of the Reformation.

Joos was an excellent portraitist, as can be seen in such works as the pendant pair *Joris Vezeleer* and *Margaretha Boghe* (Washington, D.C., National Gallery of Art), probably done on the occasion of their marriage in 1518. A *Self-portrait* (Madrid, Fundación Colección Thyssen-Bornemisza) may date to the time of his engagement and marriage to Anna Vijds (Vijdts), and the artist included self-portraits in several of his altarpieces. Lodovico Guicciardini's *Descrittione* (Description of the Low Countries; 1567) states that Joos was called to France to depict the king and queen and court nobility. The fact that Joos is not documented in Antwerp between 1529 and 1535 and the existence of portraits of *Francis I* (Philadelphia Museum of Art) and of his wife, *Eleonore of Austria* (London, Hampton Court; Vienna, Kunsthistorisches Museum), argue for Joos's presence in France from 1529/30 on.

BIBLIOGRAPHY

Friedländer, Max J. *Early Netherlandish Painting.* Vol. 9, parts 1–2. Leiden, Netherlands, and Brussels, Belgium, 1972–1973.

Hand, John Oliver. "Joos van Cleve (van der Beke)." *Dictionary of Art.* Vol. 7. New York, 1996. Pages 423–426.

JOHN OLIVER HAND

CLIENTAGE. *See* **Patronage.**

CLOCKS. The simplest definition of a clock is: a device that maintains a regular mechanical movement to indicate the passage of time. At minimum a clock requires a driving mechanism as a source of power and a controlling mechanism to regulate the motion. The earliest form, known from antiquity, was the water clock or *clepsyra,* a simplified version of which was used by Galileo Galilei for his inclined-plane experiments of 1638. The development of clocks in the Renaissance saw a gradual shift from weight-driven clocks, already in use in the Middle Ages, to spring-driven clocks, and a steady improvement in controlling mechanisms or escapements,

German Clock. Weight-driven German wrought-iron clock, c. 1570. COURTESY OF THE TIME MUSEUM, ROCKFORD, ILLINOIS

culminating in the pendulum clock. The last was pioneered by Galileo but brought to perfection by Christiaan Huygens in 1656.

Weight-driven Clocks. The prototype of the weight-driven clock was an astronomical clock built between 1348 and 1362 by Giovanni de' Dondi (1318–1389), physician to Emperor Charles IV and professor of astronomy at Padua. A geared equatorium driven by clockwork, this clock provided a graphic display of Ptolemaic astronomy. Its hexagonal frame housed dials for the sun, moon, and the five planets, below which was a twenty-four-hour dial and displays showing the times of sunrise and sunset, fixed feasts, movable feasts, and the nodes of the moon's orbit. It was seen in 1463 by Johannes Regiomontanus, who reported in 1474 that he had a similar mechanism under construction in his workshop at Nürnberg. A modern replica is now stored at the National Museum of American History in Washington, D.C.

Clocks of this type that still survive are the Strasbourg Clock (1354), the Salisbury Clock (1386), the Rouen Clock (1389), the Wells Clock (1392/3), and the Nürnberg Striking Clock (between 1400 and

1450), which struck one blow at each hour. Their escapements were generally of the verge and foliot balance type, whose time of swing on later models was regulated by small adjustable weights. All were poor timekeepers, requiring continuous care and adjustment.

Spring-driven Clocks. An early spring-driven portable clock is portrayed in a painting dated about 1440 at the Antwerp Fine Arts Museum. The first surviving models date from around 1500 and are the work of a locksmith of Nürnberg, Peter Henlein (c. 1480–1542). The use of a mainspring posed serious difficulties because its pull varies greatly as the spring winds down. Two devices were used to equalize the pull, the stackfreed and the fusee. The stackfreed consisted of a strong curved spring and a cam, whose mutual action offset the unequal pulls. The fusee was a cone-shaped pulley that, when connected to the spring by a catgut cord, supplied a differential radius for the application of the spring's force. The cord was replaced around 1560 by a flexible chain.

The advantage of the spring drive was its portability and small size, making it suitable for domestic clocks, clock watches, and the pocket watch, the last invented by Henlein in 1502. An outstanding astronomical clock was that of Eberhart Baldewin (1525–1593), built in 1561 for Landgrave William IV of Hesse, which employed clock trains to portray the celestial motions of Ptolemaic astronomy. Baldewin was the teacher of Jost Bürgi (1552–1632), an instrument maker first for William IV and then for Emperor Rudolf II at Prague, where he was an assistant to Johannes Kepler. Bürgi invented the cross-beat or double-verge escapement and built several experimental clocks using combined weight and spring drives. His masterpiece was a spring-driven clock for Rudolf II, built shortly after 1604, which had separate dials for hours, minutes, and seconds.

The Pendulum Clock. Galileo had been interested in pendulums from his youth, when in 1582 he observed their isochronism in the swing of the sanctuary lamp in the cathedral at Pisa. He later experimented with them extensively, and in 1617 worked on a time regulator based on a pendulum's oscillation alone, without clockwork. It was not until 1637, when he was already going blind, that he began work on a pendulum to regulate a mechanical clock. In 1641 he discussed plans for building such a clock with his son Vincenzio, but Galileo's death in 1642 effectively put an end to the project.

The most important feature of Vincenzio's model, a drawing of which still survives, is its novel escapement. This was a form of dead-beat escapement acting by means of pins on a band instead of teeth cut in the periphery of a wheel, as in later types. The first use of Galileo's escapement was in the repair of the great public clock of the Palazzo Vecchio in Florence. This was carried out in 1667 by the Augsburg clockmaker Georg Lederle, who was hired for the task by Vincenzo Viviani (1622–1703), Galileo's favorite student and then court mathematician. The clock contains a pin-wheel escapement as sketched in Vincenzio's drawing and still ticks on to the present day.

BIBLIOGRAPHY

Baillie, G. H., C. Clutton, and C. A. Ilbert, eds. *Britten's Old Clocks and Watches and Their Makers: A Historical and Descriptive Account of the Different Styles of Clocks and Watches of the Past in England and Abroad, Containing a List of Nearly Fourteen Thousand Makers.* 7th ed. London, 1956. The first edition of this work by Frederick James Britten appeared in 1899; it was preceded by his *Former Clock and Watchmakers and Their Work* (1894).

Bedini, Sylvio A. "Galileo and Scientific Instrumentation." In *Reinterpreting Galileo.* Studies in Philosophy and the History of Philosophy, vol. 15. Edited by William A. Wallace. Washington, D.C., 1986. Pages 127–153.

Lloyd, H. Alan. *Some Outstanding Clocks over Seven Hundred Years 1250–1950.* London, 1958. Contains detailed descriptions and illustrations of the clocks discussed in this entry.

WILLIAM A. WALLACE

CLOTHING.   Clothing took on tremendous importance in the Renaissance, which experienced economic, political, and cultural changes that propelled dress into new directions of style and sartorial significance. The raising of hemlines for men (and the lengthening of them for women), the shift toward military uniforms, the impact of the Protestant Reformation on clerical dress, and the evolution of class distinctions through clothes all reflected larger historical developments. Clothing was also central in the shaping of identity, as color, cut, fold, and draping took on momentous importance in negotiating one's way through the times. As a result, changes in clothing reveal as much about national and class distinctions as they do about more abstract notions of masculinity and femininity, ideals of beauty, and the vicissitudes of self-creation in a new age.

Economic Developments.   Economic conditions toward the end of the fourteenth century became exceptionally favorable for the clothing trade. Political stability, greater disposable wealth, and expanding trade made it possible for industries to emerge in Italy and elsewhere based around the production, importation, and exportation of luxury goods and cloths. In Lucca, silk weaving—which had been introduced by Jews in the tenth century—expanded considerably after the mid-fourteenth century, while Venice benefited from its commercial network and large fleet to import precious silks and textiles from the east. Silk in general underwent an expansion in places such as Spain and later in France, but Italy remained central not only for the production of silks but of satins, velvets, taffetas, and eventually lace. Wool and linen would remain the predominant fabrics of the age, but the wearing of luxury cloth warranted enough attention as to produce a series of sumptuary laws across Europe, regulating the consumption and capricious wearing of clothing made from these fabrics.

The primary purpose of these laws was to limit luxury consumption, but their specificity in defining who could wear what—and what shape and style those clothes could be—reflect attempts by authorities to maintain control in a world that defined itself by dress.

With the economic transformations and the influx of precious metals that occurred after Columbus's journey to America, Italy was challenged by new manufacturing and trade centers in the north. These developments impelled it to step up its production and trading in luxury clothing and silks. For northern countries, new manufacturing equipment that had previously been prohibited by the old guild regulations began to appear, first the funding mill and later William Lee's knitting machine (invented in 1589). At the same time, technological innovations improved processes of weaving and dying. In England, landowners increased their own wool production by turning their arable land into pasture to produce more wool—an act that displaced populations and led to comments about the wastefulness of a court wearing "a whole flock on its shoulders."

Elite Men's and Women's Fashion.   Sartorial adornment preoccupied Renaissance men, for whom clothing was central to their projection of masculinity and power, especially at court. Every day the fashionable man undertook his dressing and toilette with the help of a servant, who was required to tie up the points (pieces of lace that held a garment together), lace the doublet, arrange the stomacher, and fasten the frilled shirt in an ordeal one Englishman called the "uprising in the morning." Costume varied across nations. In general, however, long garments—which still prevailed at church and

Elite Men's Fashion. Portrait of King James I of England (reigned 1603–1625) by Paul van Somer (c. 1576–c. 1622). THE ROYAL COLLECTION © HER MAJESTY QUEEN ELIZABETH II

university—went through a distinct shortening, much to the consternation of preachers and tailors. The latter were also threatened in their business when the surcoat (an outer coat or cloak) went out of fashion in favor of the exposed hose-enclosed leg. Attached to the hose was the pourpont, a chest- and waist-fitted doublet made of lined and quilted rich stuff that took many forms and cuts over the years and across regions. Regions, in turn, influenced one another in the wake of such events as Charles VIII's 1494 invasion of the Italian peninsula, which led to a mutual borrowing between French and Italian clothing cultures.

Toward the end of the sixteenth century, Spain began to set standards of fashion that would eventually dominate throughout Europe, resulting in a more austere, somber, and simplified line. Softness was replaced by a straight and stiff silhouette, the doublet would emphasize the slimness of the waist,

and black was to become the preferred color for Spaniards. In France, Henry II and his court (1547–1559) would be especially fond of dark hues overtraced with gold and stripped of ornamentation in the Italian style. In the succeeding reign of Henry III (1574–1589) in contrast, vulgarity and ostentation would signal a somewhat confused and brief return to the Italian style. It was during this time, especially in the Elizabethan age, that ruffs grew increasingly pronounced in size around the neck, until by 1579, according to one writer, the wearers could scarcely turn their heads, causing Henry III to declare that the result looked like "the head of John the Baptist in a charger."

Women and fashion had always provoked a vehement male response, especially from clerics such as Bernard of Clairvaux, who declared in the twelfth century, regarding women's trains, that "if women had needed a tail, God would have provided them with one." Sumptuary laws attempted to proscribe the measurements, the number of jewels, and the decolletage of women's wear, while writers such as Leon Battista Alberti described in works such as *Della famiglia* (1433–1434) an ideal of female beauty in clothing and body. Across Europe, by the end of the fifteenth century, the gown replaced all other garments for women except for the elegant surcoat, both of which fitted tightly to the upper part of the body while the skirt flowed and trailed on the ground, lengthening the line and accentuating the waist and hips. Necklines could vary—the square neckline was derived from Italian styles, whereas the Burgundians favored pointed neck openings— while sleeves tended to trail. In the sixteenth century, women, like men, were subject to Spanish fashions, most notably in the farthingale, a garment that circled the lower part of a woman's body with a series of hoops. The farthingale was a favorite garment of Marguerite de Valois (1553–1615), queen consort of Henry IV. It could take on many variations and required the building of special high chairs. The garment provoked Montaigne to ask, "Why do women cover themselves with so many barricades over the parts on which our admiration principally lingers?"

Accentuating women's adornment were cosmetic flourishes, jewels, headgear, and accessories. Elizabeth I, who made clothing a conscious part of her political strategies, wished to preserve the complexion appropriate to a virgin queen. She did so by applying half an inch of makeup to her already blanched face. Accessories became more important than ever before, for men as well as women: earrings, which had disappeared in the Middle Ages, reappeared with vigor, as did handkerchiefs; gloves were de rigeur, and could be made of cloth of gold encrusted with hundreds of pearls, or strategically perforated to offset ringed fingers. Fans, hand mirrors, and elaborately embroidered objects, especially in Elizabeth's age, completed the costumes that were in essence women's weapons in their social encounters. Away from court, prostitutes were given more leeway in dress and ornamentation than their more constricted, domesticated sisters, especially in such cities as Venice. Their dress influenced that of respectable women; prostitutes were often behind fads such as the towering wooden platform shoe—a shoe so tall that one commentator described the spectacle as watching a creature half wood and half woman totter down the streets.

Fashion and the Body. Clothing overlaid the body but it also changed, shaped, squeezed, and exaggerated the human form, pushing it up or in, elongating or suppressing portions of it, all according to ideals of beauty shaped by history and culture. For Renaissance men, puffy doublets gave the broad-shouldered appearance of a soldier in armor, while coats were padded with hay and straw at the shoulders. With hose male legs received a new emphasis, as did the waist, usually set off by a form-fitting doublet or tightened with a belt. In addition, increasingly prominent codpieces—which had originated in Germany—exaggerated male endowment to sometimes graphic effect, with the shell shape receiving particular favor. As for the female form, in sixteenth-century Italy women "full of flesh" were appreciated and compared favorably to wine barrels; to emphasize this full-figured ideal, women's clothes were thus overladen with brocades, velvets, precious stones, chains, gold, emerald, and pearl necklaces. Following Spanish influences, however, women's waists were gradually taken in, leading to increasingly rigid and torturous whalebone bodices that also tightly compressed the breasts. Montaigne noted that to achieve such a "fine Hispanized body, what Gehennas do women not suffer?"

Clothes of the Lesser Classes. Since clothing in essence announced the wearer's rank, class, and profession, it was important for authorities to issue sumptuary regulations. In the words of Philip Stubbes (1555–1610), a Puritan whose pamphlets denounced luxury, the laws ensured that "every man should be compelled to weare apparell according to his degree, estate, and condition." In England, with the rise of the gentry class, such distinctions became somewhat blurred, leading Stubbes to complain that "now there is such a confused mingle mangle of apparell . . . that it is verie hard to knowe who is noble, who is worshipfull, who is a gentleman, who is not." In response to this fluidity, students at Cambridge University were fined sixpence if found to be wearing hose of "unseemly greatness" and eightpence if they appeared in public without a suitable gown and hood. Servants or members of a City company were expected to clothe themselves in bright blue or gray livery—blue being the traditional color of servitude, while physicians, surgeons, teachers, and other professional men in England were to wear long gowns over their usual dress.

Clothing was simple and tended not to vary much among the lower orders, with women wearing skirts and aprons tucked up for work and topped with tight bodices and enveloping cloaks, while men wore buttoned jackets, short breeches, and wide-brimmed hats. Material consisted primarily of coarse woolen stuffs or unbleached linen, while colors were restricted primarily to black (in women's clothing) or to dull browns and grays. Those who worked in a luxury industry attempted to imitate the higher classes by wearing velvet on special occasions, but, in general, embellishments to these drab clothes consisted of silver buttons, taffeta scarves, or the occasional muff. Only at the end of the seventeenth century would developments in industrial production offer the lower orders a wider array of fabric and color, though the destitute continued to wear hand-me-down rags or coarse wool garments donated by tradesmen guilds or religious fraternities.

Clothing and the Military. Fashion in the Renaissance took many elements from the military, from breeches to the wearing of swords, which noblemen donned ceremoniously at court. Beginning in Germany, a mania for slashes and puffed sleeves moved across Europe and peaked in the sixteenth century. The style was said to have been derived from tattered Swiss mercenaries returning victorious from battling Charles the Bold, duke of Burgundy, in 1476. They seized the garments off the defeated dead, but the returning warriors found them too tight and thus slashed them or allowed the seams to rip, causing the garments underneath to puff out. Germans, who first noted this look, were responsible in turn for the military-derived "lattice" breeches made of wide strips of material and worn by the papal Swiss Guards today. The Thirty Years' War of the seventeenth century seems to have been especially influential, however, in disseminating among the larger population the soldier's soft, broad-brimmed hat (which later became the tricorn), the broad collar, and the rows of buttons that decorated the seams of the trousers.

Armor, though increasingly obsolete in the face of evolving realities in warfare, nevertheless reached new levels of decoration more appropriate to a ceremonial rather than functional level. In the sixteenth century the master armor maker was Filippo Negroli of Milan, whose intricately worked helmets, cuirasses, and shields for such clients as Charles V and Francis I evoked Roman emperors, classical themes, and mythological heroes such as Hercules. A fourth-generation member of an armor-making dynasty, the illustrious Filippo specialized in *all'antica*, a contemporary type of armor that evoked antiquity and called up images of lions, dragons, and Medusa heads. Among the more elaborate of his designs was a helmet created for Guidobaldo II della Rovere, a kind of monster mask consisting of flying batwing cheekpieces, fangs thrusting from the jaw, and a pair of ramlike horns protruding from the free-flowing hair.

After the sixteenth century the rise of infantry warfare involving masses of men would eventually generate a need for uniforms. A certain uniformity had always existed in the Renaissance era, and precursors to the more modern variety of uniform could be found, for example, in the fifteenth century, with Swiss wearing short and brightly colored slashed doublets and tight breeches, and in the sixteenth century, when Germans of the Imperial army in Nürnberg wore red coats in 1550 and English soldiers under the duke of Norfolk around the same time wore suits of blue piped with red. German *Landsknechten*, mercenaries recruited from the lower orders, pioneered the use of long breeches and cloaks in battle, as well as widened slashes and puffs. In general, however, uniforms of a more utilitarian variety would have to await modern developments in mass production and a greater degree of nation-state consolidation—changes that would emerge at the end of the seventeenth century.

Religious Clothing. Popes, cardinals, and other clergy were not immune from embracing sartorial resplendence, and as a result vestimentary laws, issued in 1464 by Pope Paul II, were directed to regulate the occasional outrages. Though not typical, Cardinal Francesco Gonzaga (1444–1483) threw himself into debt with his expenditures on Turkish style floor-length robes of crimson or green damask, various velvets and woven silks, and other garments, some lined with ermine. In another reaction to these

displays, the Dominican monk Girolamo Savonarola would inspire many "bonfires of vanities" directed toward clergy and laity alike in Florence in the 1490s, where precious veils and cosmetics, ornaments, and masses of false hair (especially fashionable blonde false hair) were thrown into the fire. Erasmus would also comment upon the increasingly labored refinement of the clerical orders in their obsession with girdles, cowls, gowns, and tonsures; "some," he continued, "are so strict in their observances that they will wear an outer garment which has to be made of Sicilian goat's hair and one of Milesian wool next to the skin, while others have linen on top and wool underneath."

The Protestant Reformation had an important effect on clothing, as white gowns, plain white surplices, and black scarves distinguished men of the new faith. In England, Cardinal Thomas Wolsey, with his scarlet satin robes and sable tippet, would give way to Archbishop Thomas Cranmer in his close dark cassock and leathern girdle. Luther himself had worn a cassocklike overcoat, fur-lined and sometimes sleeveless, which was worn by prosperous contemporaries and by some Lutheran clergymen today. More extreme were Calvinists—and later Puritans in England—who spurned any form of aestheticism in favor of black, which nevertheless failed to dislodge the Dutchman's continued attachment to the ruff.

Theatrical and Festive Costumes. Finally, festivals, processions, and special events proliferated in the Renaissance, generated by increased spending power, princely or civic displays, or a general desire for self-enhancing show. As a result clothing became subject to further creative innovations, especially in the seventeenth century, when the masque became a fully developed theatrical court genre. In England, so important was the masque that Francis Bacon would write a treatise on the subject, enjoining readers to "Let the suits of the masquers be graceful, and such as become the person when the vizars are off: not after examples of known attires: Turks, soldiers, mariners and the like." Since performances were always at night and usually illuminated by candlelight, the most flattering colors chosen in the design of these costumes were thought to be white, carnation, or a kind of "sea-water greene"; costumes could also be made of "tynsell," beads, and sequins, and further adorned with gold tassels, gilt bells, fringing, and silver and gold lace. Masks were usually made of velvet and built up to elaborate effect, which, combined with distorted shapes and intricately patterned

French Clothing. Series of figures showing dress of various social orders from a costume manual by Abraham de Bruyn, *Omnium paene gentium imagines,* Cologne, 1577.

surfaces in the clothes, caused foreign visitors to view the costumes as bordering on the outrageous and bizarre.

The French, however, were most noted for the dress displayed at glittering court events, gaining a reputation (in the words of one writer) for "a richness, a magnificence, and taste that outstrip anything one can see elsewhere." In seventeenth-century France, ballets became forums for performers to dress as Indians, Moors, Africans, and Asians, while court members indulged in their own kind of theater by dressing, at special events, as Persian shahs, Turks, rajahs, and native Americans. Louis XIV especially understood the importance of self-representation and spectacle through clothes, particularly as they offset his own sunny luster; indeed, it was under his guidance that France would finally cement its dominance in splendor, setting the sartorial stage for the new century, and all its excesses, to come.

See also **Arms and Armor; Sumptuary Laws.**

BIBLIOGRAPHY

Boucher, Francois. *20,000 Years of Fashion: The History of Costume and Personal Adornment.* Expanded ed. New York, 1987.
Davenport, Millia. *The Book of Costume.* Vol. 2. New York, 1948.
Laver, James. *Costume of the Western World.* Vol. 3: *The Tudors to Louis XIII.* New York, 1951.

SARAH COVINGTON

CLOUET, JEAN AND FRANÇOIS. *See* **France,** *subentry on* **Art in France.**

COBOS, FRANCISCO DE LOS (1477?–1547), chief secretary and adviser to Holy Roman Emperor Charles V. Born into impoverished low nobility, Cobos got his start serving his uncle, an accountant and secretary of Queen Isabella of Castile, rising in favor and recognition through a combination of secretarial talents and pleasing disposition. On Ferdinand of Aragon's death in 1516 he threw in his lot with Duke Charles of Burgundy in Flanders, thereby bringing to the future Holy Roman Emperor an already incomparable knowledge of the operation of the secretariat of both Aragon and Castile. Cobos served Charles V as chief secretary and financial adviser for his Spanish kingdoms. On 4 October 1529 he became a most trusted member of the Council of State. After Grand Chancellor Mercurino Gattinara's death in 1530, Cobos split with Nicholas Peronet (lord of Granvelle) the paperwork of Charles's diverse lands, taking the Spanish secretariat, and continuing in im-

perial favor and service down to his own death on 10 May 1547. Cobos left two achievements: the establishment of the first state archive, the depository for Habsburg papers at Simancas in 1544, and the development of a staff of public officials.

Described as one who never wasted his intelligence on subtleties and epigrams, Cobos combined bureaucratic ability with a relaxed, charming manner. In 1543 the emperor counselled his son Philip: "No one knows so much of my affairs as he, and you will always have reason to be glad of his service." Cobos was not alone in an age that liberally used office for personal enrichment. Among his many talents, self-advancement ranked high.

See also biographies of Charles V and Mercurino Gattinara.

BIBLIOGRAPHY

Keniston, Hayward. *Francisco de los Cobos: Secretary of the Emperor Charles V.* Pittsburgh, Pa., 1959. The basic study.

JOHN M. HEADLEY

COIMBRA, UNIVERSITY OF. The University of Lisbon-Coimbra was established in 1290 by King Dinis. In his bull confirming the founding of the university, Pope Nicholas IV authorized the licentiate to be granted to students of medicine, civil and canon law, and arts, but he forbade the university to teach theology. The pope did, however, delegate substantial authority to the clergy, whom he empowered to judge criminal cases involving students. This provision of the papal bull weakened Dinis's authority over his newly founded university.

In 1308 Dinis transferred the university to Coimbra (the first of five moves the university underwent). In 1338 Afonso IV transferred the university back to Lisbon, and in 1354 he moved it once again to Coimbra, where it remained until 1377, when King Ferdinand transferred it to Lisbon. Shortly thereafter the Vatican permitted theology to be taught at the university.

During the fifteenth and early sixteenth centuries, the university contributed to Portugal's expansion overseas. The university enjoyed the patronage of Prince Henry "the Navigator," who served as its official protector from 1418 until his death in 1460. Henry endowed a chair of theology in 1448, and he encouraged the teaching of arithmetic, geometry, and astronomy; these areas of learning were crucial to the Portuguese discoveries. King Manuel also established a chair of astronomy, one of several reforms that he instituted from 1500 to 1504.

Humanism made its appearance in Portugal during the fifteenth century and played a significant role in Portuguese intellectual life during the first half of the sixteenth century. Three of Portugal's most prominent Renaissance humanists, André de Gouveia (1497–1548), Garcia da Orta (c. 1500–1568), and Pedro Nunes (1502–1578), taught at the university. Although a medical doctor, Garcia da Orta lectured on natural philosophy. The area of research that most interested him, however, was tropical medicine. In 1534 he left Portugal for Goa, where he published studies on the medicinal uses of newly discovered plants and herbs; these studies became well known throughout Europe.

Pedro Nunes was Portugal's most distinguished Renaissance mathematician and astronomer. Under his Latinized name, Petrus Nonius, he published in Latin several treatises on navigation. He also invented a measuring device known as the "nonius," similar to the modern-day vernier. In addition to teaching mathematics, moral philosophy, and logic, he presided over the university as rector from 1536 to 1537. After John III (1502–1557) transferred the university to Coimbra in 1537, Nunes became the university's first chaired professor of mathematics.

In order to revitalize the university, John III invited professors from Spain, France, and Italy to teach there. Another reform that John III enacted concerned the administration: in an effort to assert its authority over the university, the crown would henceforth appoint the rector, who had hitherto been elected. A serious problem confronting John III involved the numerous Portuguese who were still studying abroad. In order to attract students to Coimbra, he established colleges affiliated with the university.

The most famous of these colleges was the Colégio das Artes (College of arts), which John III founded in 1547 to prepare young men for study at the university. The college was essentially a school of arts and humanities dedicated to teaching classical philosophy and languages. Earlier, in 1536, John had established the Portuguese Inquisition, which in 1550 imprisoned several faculty members for their heterodox ideas. Himself a devout Catholic, he directed the Jesuits to take jurisdiction of the college in 1555.

During the Spanish domination of Portugal from 1580 to 1640, several noted Spanish scholars taught at Coimbra. Foremost among them was the Jesuit Francisco Suárez (1548–1617), a philosopher, theologian, and jurist, the foremost metaphysician of the Renaissance. Suárez accepted a chair of theology at Coimbra in 1597 and there wrote his *De legibus* (On law), which he published in 1612.

Another Jesuit who gained an international reputation at Coimbra was Pedro da Fonseca (1528–1599). Under his direction, the college of arts published a series of commentaries on Aristotle titled the *Commentarii Collegii Conimbricensis Societatis Iesu* (Coimbra commentaries). Written between 1592 and 1606, these commentaries provide a summary of all branches of Aristotelian philosophy placed at the service of Catholic theology. Often reprinted for the next forty years, they were widely used throughout Europe and became the principal vehicle through which the founders of modern philosophy became acquainted with Scholasticism.

Among the Renaissance monuments of the University of Coimbra are the Chapel of Saint Michael; the Porta Férrea (Iron gate), which leads to the quadrangle of the university; and the Sala Grande dos Actos, also called the Sala dos Capelos (Great hall), where important academic ceremonies are still held. Some of these monuments date back to the sixteenth century, when the university was definitively established in Coimbra.

See also **Universities**.

BIBLIOGRAPHY

Primary Work
Chartularium Universitatis Portugalensis (1288–1537). Edited by A. Moreira de Sá. Vol. 5. Lisbon, Portugal, 1972.

Secondary Works
Ackerlind, Sheila R. *King Dinis of Portugal and the Alfonsine Heritage*. New York, 1990. See "The University of Lisbon-Coimbra," pp. 75–103.
Batllori, Miguel. *Humanismo y Renacimiento: Estudios hispano-europeos*. Barcelona, 1987. See "El Humanismo y el Renacimiento en Portugal," pp. 44–51.
Brandão, Mário. *O Colégio das Artes*. 2 vols. Coimbra, Portugal, 1924–1933.

SHEILA R. ACKERLIND

COINS, MEDALS, AND PLAQUETTES.

Portrait medals and coins are often discussed under the misleading heading of numismatics, while portrait medals and plaquettes are similarly lumped under the generic rubric of decorative arts. The three do share characteristics that encourage some such generalizations, but they are in fact fundamentally different enough that they should be described and understood separately.

Coins. The term "coins" refers to units of currency in gold, silver, and various copper alloys. Ancient coins became popular collectibles in fourteenth-

Florentine Coin. Reverse side of a gold *fiorino* (florin), c. 1400. The florin, first struck in 1252, was widely traded throughout western Europe during the Renaissance. ASHMOLEAN MUSEUM, OXFORD, U.K.

century Italy. Petrarch's collection of antiquities included a large selection of Roman coins and medallions, and his interest certainly influenced others in the intellectual community to begin collecting as well.

In 1252 Florence introduced the gold florin, with a lily on one side and Florence's patron saint, John the Baptist, on the other. The florin—along with the Venetian ducat of 1284 (the latter was stylistically based on Venice's silver *grosso*, introduced around 1202)—dominated traded currencies in western Europe throughout most of the fourteenth and fifteenth centuries. As a result, the florin influenced coinage design in much of the Continent. From the mid-1450s through the 1500s, much of Europe (following the examples of Milan and Naples) reintroduced realistic portraiture to coinage. In doing so, they were returning to precedents set by imperial Rome and probably following classicizing currents in the art world (such as portrait medals). Coins carrying a ruler's portrait—usually busts, but also half- and full-length figures, and equestrians—presented ideal vehicles of propaganda, and the Italian *testone* (from the Italian *testa*, head) was copied in southern Germany and Switzerland as the *Dicken*, in France as the *teston*, and in England as the *testoon* (also known as the shilling). Concurrently, a parallel development in numismatic design occurred when dynastic coats of arms began to replace portraits, as took place in Spain and Portugal, or obverse portraits were combined with heraldic motifs on their reverses.

Medals. Portrait medals arguably constitute the most focused visual embodiment of humanism in Renaissance Italy: they exalted the individual in indelible materials (thereby ensuring immortality) while harking back to classical Rome. Medals were not currency. They were double-sided, palm-sized, low-relief, roundel (disk-shaped) portraits that functioned as personal and political tools of propaganda. The obverse contained a profile portrait of a man or woman, surrounded by a Latin inscription of the sitter's name and position, while the reverse compositions, similarly surrounded by a Latin inscription, allegorized his or her personality. Medals served to court distant brides, were traded with friends and collected, or worn around the neck; they commemorated building projects and patrons, and were even buried in the foundations of buildings. Portrait medals were inspired by the medallions and coins of the Roman emperors, but unlike their classical predecessors, they were available to anyone with the financial resources to commission them. Much of the popularity of the medal was doubtless due to its tactile quality: medals were meant to be held, rubbed, turned over, and admired in an intimate context not extended to other media.

Most medals of the fifteenth century were cast from wax models, allowing a variety of sizes and relief depths. The "striking" process was applied to medals in the sixteenth century. Striking coins or medals required that a die be cut in a hard metal and then hammered against a softer (usually heated) metal to make its impression. The "pressing" process used a large screw-like machine to impress a die's design on the softer metal. The striking and pressing processes allowed extremely fine detail and large production runs, but restricted the depth of the medal's relief and its overall size.

It is generally agreed that the first modern portrait medal was the invention of Antonio di Puccio Pisano, called Pisanello (c. 1395–1455), though certain earlier objects anticipated aspects of Pisanello's landmark introduction. In the 1390s Francesco II da Carrara commemorated the recapture of Padua with a small struck "medal" based on Roman coins, and the Sesto family in Venice similarly imitated Roman numismatics in the early fifteenth century. Further, the 1413 inventory of the collection of Jean de France, duke of Berry, describes medal-like objects depicting the emperors Constantine and Heraclius (Bibliothèque Nationale, Paris), while the philosopher-architect-artist Leon Battista Alberti (1404–1472) may also have had a germinal influence on the first medal: his bronze relief self-portrait *all 'antica* (in the ancient style) of around 1435 (National Gallery, Washington; Louvre, Paris) displays many of the features inherent in portrait medals. These isolated efforts notwithstanding, it was not until Pisanello's initial roundel cast that the medal assumed what came to be its standard form in content, size, and general composition. Pisanello's first medal commemorated the visit of John VIII Palaeologus, emperor of Byzantium, and his retinue, to the council of Ferrara-Florence of around 1438–1439. Pisanello followed his inaugural work with a string of over twenty-six medals in twenty-two years, commissioned by many of the most esteemed patrons in Italy. His reverses display a creative facility with roundel compositions that has never been surpassed in the medium.

Matteo de' Pasti (active 1441–1467/68) was among the first artists to follow Pisanello's lead, executing medals for the Malatesta court at Rimini and elsewhere. Mantua became the locus of much of the fifteenth-century talent in medals by commissioning, training, or inspiring such artists as Cristoforo di Geremia (c. 1430–1476), Sperandio of Mantua (c. 1425–c. 1504), Pier Jacopo di Antonio Alari Bonacolsi, called Antico (c. 1460–1528), and Galeazza Mondella, called Moderno (1467–1528). Florence em-braced medallic production rather late in the fifteenth century. Bertoldo di Giovanni (c. 1440–1491), best known as a teacher of the young Michelangelo, cast several medals, including a commemoration of the Pazzi Conspiracy (1478). The most prolific of the Florentine medalists was Niccolò Fiorentino (1430–1514), who combined powerful portraits with uninspired reverses (often taken from classical prototypes) to dominate the Florentine school in the late fifteenth and early sixteenth centuries.

Most medals from the 1500s differ significantly from those of the preceding century due primarily to the innovation of the screw-press by Benvenuto Cellini (1500–1571). In Italy, Milan became a center of medallic style. Artists of distinction such as Leone Leoni (c. 1509–1590), Jacopo da Trezzo (c. 1514/19–1589), and Antonio Abondio (1538–1591) produced medals for many of the leading courts of Europe and profoundly influenced medallic style throughout the continent. Pastorino de' Pastorini (c. 1508–1592), the most prolific sixteenth-century Italian medalist, worked primarily in Ferrara, while two Florentine brothers, Gianpaolo (1518–c. 1582) and Domenico Poggini (1520–1590), found patronage in the Medici family and abroad. In Reggio d' Emilia, Bombarda (active 1540–1575) and Alfonso Ruspagiari (1521–1576) produced an intriguing and unprecedented group of extremely thin, whimsical, uniface portraits in lead.

The sixteenth century also witnessed talented artists working in medals in Germany, France, the Netherlands, and England. Medallic production in Germany was centered around the cities of Nürnberg and Augsburg. German medals were primarily cast from wood or stone models (as opposed to the Italian preference for wax as a modeling agent) and reveal a seemingly infinite capacity for detail and meticulous execution. In Nürnberg, artists such as the prolific Matthes Gebel (active 1523–1574), Joachim Deschler (1500–c. 1572), and Hans Bolsterer (d. 1573) composed medals that had a substantial influence on northern Europe throughout the century. Augsburg wood sculptors, goldsmiths, and medalists including Hans Schwartz (c. 1492–died after 1521), Christoph Weiditz (c. 1500–1559), and Friedrich Hagenauer (active 1525–1546) cast magnificently detailed portraits, sometimes eschewing the profile format for three-quarter likenesses. Hans Reinhart the Elder (c. 1510–1581), in Saxony, cast a series of adequate portraits, but is particularly remembered for the spectacular, high-relief silver *Trinity* medal, dated 1544 (Münzkabinet, Staatliche Museen, Berlin).

Portrait Medal. Portrait of the Genoese admiral Andrea Doria by Leone Leoni (1509–1590). CLICHÉ BIBLIOTHÈQUE NATIONALE DE FRANCE, PARIS. MED. ITALIENNE 65 A 13861.

France produced few medalists of distinction in the fifteenth and sixteenth centuries—with the notable exception of the sculptor Germain Pilon (c. 1525–1590)—but in the early years of the seventeenth century, Guillaume Dupré (c. 1579–c. 1642) produced medals displaying an unparalleled technical virtuosity. Jacques Jonghelinck (1530–1606) and Steven van Herwijck (c. 1530–1565/67), working in Antwerp and Utrecht, produced a large number of fine medals following the stylistic tendencies of the Milanese school.

Plaquettes. The replication in bronze of specific antique gems, from precise casts in wax or plaster taken directly from the stones themselves, provided one of the earliest classes of plaquettes. It was evidently through this medium, and, after the middle 1450s from Rome (under Pietro Barbo, later Pope Paul II), that glyptic imagery (imagery carved into gemstones, such as intaglios, or in relief, such as cameos) of the classical period was made available to the artist and the general public. Plaquettes—small, single-sided metal (usually bronze) reliefs of various shapes, usually without portraits or inscriptions, but featuring either mythological or religious imagery—were reproduced in large numbers and served any number of functions. They were sewn into hats and impressed onto leather book covers, attached to the hilts of swords and daggers, functioned as ornamental bases to candlesticks and inkwells, and adorned reliquary boxes, bells, and armor. Plaquettes were used as models for illuminated manuscripts, fresco and panel painting, majolica, monumental sculpture, and the reverse compositions to portrait medals.

Leon Battista Alberti's self-portrait relief of about 1435 might be classified as a plaquette, though it also shares unmistakable features with early portrait medals. The most accomplished of the artists working in plaquettes at the end of the 1400s was Galeazzo Mondella, called Moderno (1467–1528), noted for *The Flagellation of Christ* and for a series of smaller mythological reliefs. The identity of the Master IO.F.F. remains obscure, but his small plaquettes on mythological themes—often in round or shield shapes, and made for the pommels of swords and daggers—were among the best of the late fifteenth century. Andrea Briosco, called Riccio (c. 1470/75–1532), brought a new sense of drama to plaquettes with his large, heavy reliefs, such as the *Deposition,* in the early years of the sixteenth century, while Valerio Belli (1468–1546) and Giovanni Bernardi (1496–1553), engravers of crystal and gems, reproduced and disseminated many of their intaglio creations in small, low-relief bronzes.

As with medals, plaquettes in Germany became popular in the sixteenth century and were produced primarily in Nürnberg and Augsburg. Their influence extended to Scandinavia, England, and Russia. The early Nürnberg school was led by Peter Flötner (c. 1485–1546), and followed by Hans Peisser (b. 1500/ 1505–after 1571), and goldsmiths such as Elias Lencker the elder (active 1562–1583), and Nikolaus Schmidt (d. 1609). Toward the end of the century, the center for plaquette manufacture shifted to Augsburg, where plaquettes were often based on engraved prints. Goldsmiths including Paul Hübner (d. 1614) and Hans Jakob Bayr (1574–1628) produced several series of small reliefs that served as models for designs in several other media.

See also **Banking and Money**; **Heraldry**; **Sculpture**.

BIBLIOGRAPHY

Coins

Bernochhi, M. *Le monete della Republica Fiorentina.* 4 vols. Florence, 1975–1978.

Cairola, A. *Le monete del Rinascimento.* Rome, 1972.

Grierson, P., and M. Blackburn. *Medieval European Coinage.* Cambridge, U.K., 1986.

Medals

Hill, George Francis. *Medals of the Renaissance.* Oxford, 1920. Revised and enlarged by Graham Pollard. London, 1978.

Hill, George Francis. *A Corpus of Italian Medals of the Renaissance before Cellini.* 2 vols. London, 1930. Reprint. Florence, 1984.

Jones, Mark. *The Art of the Medal.* London, 1979.

Scher, Stephen, ed. *The Currency of Fame.* New York, 1994.

Trusted, Marjorie. *German Renaissance Medals: A Catalog of the Collection in the Victoria & Albert Museum.* London, 1990.

Plaquettes

Pope-Hennessy, John. *Renaissance Bronzes from the Samuel H. Kress Collection: Reliefs, Plaquettes, Statuettes, Utensils, and Mortars.* London, 1965.

Luchs, Alison, ed. *Studies in the History of Art.* Vol. 22: *Italian Plaquettes.* Washington, D.C., 1989.

Lewis, Douglas. *The Systematic Catalog of Renaissance and Baroque Plaquettes at the National Gallery of Art.* Washington, D.C., projected publication 1999–2000.

ARNE R. FLATEN

COLET, JOHN (1467–1519), English churchman and humanist. The oldest of twenty-two children, John Colet long survived all his siblings and inherited his father's large fortune at Sir Henry Colet's death in 1505. Thanks to John Colet's friendship with Erasmus, who published a long letter commemorating him two years after his death, Colet is one of very few early Tudors whom we can know with some intimacy. The fearful mortality among his brothers and sisters was bound to affect a reflective youngster. From his earliest days to his young manhood his home life was a continuous "procession of cradles and coffins" (Inge, *Lay Thoughts of a Dean,* p. 3).

Colet held an extremely low view of marriage. He saw "nothing good" to be said for it, as sexual relations "soiled" the bodies of both spouses (quoted in Gleason, *Jean Colet,* 1989). True marriage, he argued in his treatise *De Sacramentis* (On the sacraments), was not the union of man and woman on earth but the union of humankind with God in heaven. This is typical of the earnest spiritualizing of every human instinct that characterizes his writings.

He studied at Cambridge, then continued his studies during three years in Italy (1496–1499). His intellectual hero at this time was the Florentine humanist Marsilio Ficino (1433–1499), with whom he initiated a brief exchange of letters. Colet also studied and cited Giovanni Pico della Mirandola (1463–1494). His deep engagement with Neoplatonism remained a strong strain in his later thought and offered an idealistic framework for his theoretical renunciation of the goods of this world. Otherwise humanist culture left little mark on him. The Latin writers he preferred were not the classical authors but later Christian writers whose orthodox outlook, for Colet, more than made up for their literary inferiority. His own Latin style reflected his English education and was not free from errors in grammar and spelling. He never learned Greek. Apart from a single sermon, Colet published almost nothing in his lifetime; instead he devoted himself to preaching and education.

Upon his return from Italy in 1499 Colet resumed work toward the doctorate in divinity at Oxford. Thanks to his influential father he was made Dean of Saint Paul's immediately after he received his doctorate. Thus, at thirty-eight he became a leading figure in England's ecclesiastical establishment. He was widely respected for the fervor of his preaching, his stainless personal reputation, and his ardent protest against corruptions in the church.

His best-known work is a powerful sermon delivered before the convocation of the higher clergy of the province of Canterbury and therefore known as the Convocation Sermon (1510). The sermon divides neatly into two halves. The first details the ways in which the church is unworthily entangled in the worldliness of the age; the second points to ways of reform. The sermon is certainly vehement, especially in its first half, but it was not a bombshell. It does

John Colet. Drawing by Hans Holbein the Younger (c. 1497–1543). THE ROYAL COLLECTION © HER MAJESTY QUEEN ELIZABETH II

not mention the pope, the Mass, indulgences, or supposedly superstitious ceremonies—standard Protestant themes. Instead its proposals are couched in biblical terms and phrased with respect toward his eminent hearers.

Though Colet made enemies among some of the higher clergy, he made an ally of the greatest of them all, Cardinal Thomas Wolsey (c. 1472–1530), the leading figure of the government of Henry VIII. Wolsey made him a member of the Royal Council, which among other matters heard accusations of heresy. There Colet sat in judgment on Lollard heretics (followers of John Wycliffe) and joined with his colleagues in condemning them to their punishment. His career path makes it seem likely that if he had lived longer (he died of the sweating sickness at fifty-two), he would have risen to a major bishopric.

As dean, Colet was much occupied with writing commentaries on biblical books, especially the Epistles of St. Paul. Highly individual works, the commentaries followed the curve of Colet's own interests and show much of the vehemence and idealism to which he could not give full scope in preaching to a wider public. His method was not academic. Nor was he, as Victorian critics sought to make him, a historical critic. Instead, he believed that the first requirement for a successful exegete, or textual interpreter, was that he be "spiritual." Such an exegete began his work with prayer. Exegetes who relied on academic scholarship were doomed, he thought, to see only the superficial meanings of their text. The true exegete must "dig out" the meanings buried beneath the textual surface and accessible only to a seeker illumined by the Spirit. Unfamiliar, indeed strange, to the modern reader, this spiritual mode of interpretation enjoyed solid status in Colet's own time, when it was centered in the spirituality of the monastic life, not in the universities. He disdained the humanist approach to scripture, which increasingly required knowledge of the original languages. Colet read the Bible in Latin, confident that the man of faith would achieve insights hidden from the mere philologist, however learned.

But practical experience, especially as a preacher, had taught Colet that real reform had to begin with the as yet uncorrupted young. Probably the most important humanistic enterprise of his career was his endowment of a major new grammar school set in the heart of the capital, Saint Paul's School in London. It was to enroll 153 boys, the number of the miraculous draft of fishes in John 21:11. The school's aims were chiseled onto its facade: "School for the Instruction of Boys in the Faith," with "Good Literature" mentioned in second place. Colet's friend Erasmus wrote texts for use in the school. Erasmus also made the suggestion, which Colet eagerly adopted, of setting into the wall behind the master's chair an image of the Child Jesus and the Gospel quotation, "Ipsum audite"—"Hear ye him." This was the essential message of Colet's life and career.

BIBLIOGRAPHY

Primary Works
Colet, John. *Opera.* 5 vols., London, 1867–1876. Reprint, 5 vols. in 4, Ridgewood, N.J., 1965. Latin texts accompanied by facing English translations by Joseph H. Lupton. *De sacramentis,* the only Latin text not translated, is reedited and translated as an appendix to John Gleason's *John Colet* (below).

Secondary Works
Gleason, John B. *John Colet.* Berkeley, Calif., 1989. The standard treatment; extensive bibliography.
Inge, William Ralph. "Jean Colet." In *Lay Thoughts of a Dean.* New York and London, 1926.
Jayne, Sears. *John Colet and Marsilio Ficino.* Oxford, 1963.

JOHN B. GLEASON

COLIGNY, GASPARD II DE (1519–1572), admiral of France and Protestant leader, whose abortive assassination was the prelude to the Saint Bartholomew's Day massacre. The younger son of a French marshal, Gaspard I de Coligny, and Louise de Montmorency, Coligny had the best of court connections and introductions to military affairs. With his brothers, Odet de Châtillon (1517–1571) and François d'Andelot (1521–1569), he enjoyed the protection of the Constable Anne de Montmorency and King Henry II. In the first year of the latter's reign (1547), Coligny was made colonel-general of the infantry, and was subsequently nominated governor of the Île de France (1551) and admiral of France (1552). Among his most striking military contributions in the Habsburg-Valois conflict were in Picardy at the siege of Dinant (1552) and the battle of Renty (1554). It was for his contribution to the second battle that he was rewarded with the government of Picardy (1555) and his own company of lancers. After the disastrous defeat of the French army at Saint-Quentin (1557), he defended the town of Saint-Quentin for seventeen days, thus preventing an even more catastrophic advance of the Spanish Habsburg forces. Eventually captured by the Spanish, he spent two years at prison in Ghent.

Next to nothing is known for certain about Coligny's conversion to Protestantism. Not until January 1561 did he publicly attend a Protestant service, when his son was baptized into the Reformed faith. Thereafter, through the tense months of 1561, Coligny championed the new faith, while moderating Protestant ambitions. The new regent of France, Catherine de Médicis, invited him to take part at the colloquy of Poissy and in October made him the leading figure in the council of affairs. It was under his influence that the edict of January 1562 gave French Protestants limited legal rights of worship. Within two months, however, his delicately engineered compromise had collapsed, and he left court, joining the Huguenot army at Orléans and serving as lieutenant general under the prince of Condé. It was after Condé's death in battle at Jarnac in March 1569 that Coligny assumed the strategic and military high command of the Huguenot army, forcing the French crown to the peace of Saint-Germain in August 1570.

Coligny's reputation was controversial among his contemporaries and has remained so after his death. This was, in part, the result of his long-running feud with the house of Guise, which espoused the defense of Catholic France. The feud began during the military campaigns of the 1550s (notably the Battle

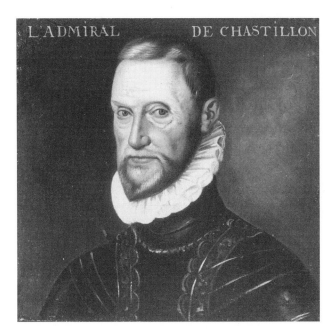

Gaspard de Coligny. Portrait by an anonymous artist in the Château de St.-Germain-Beaupré, Creuse, France. MUSÉE DE BLOIS, FRANCE/©COLLECTION VIOLLET

of Renty), but it became rancorous after the assassination of François, duc de Guise, in March 1563. Coligny was accused of complicity in that murder, and although he formally declared his innocence, the Guise never forgave him, and the dispute poisoned French politics for a decade. Controversy also surrounded his involvement in French politics in the last year of his life. Coligny returned to court in September 1571, determined to use the growing respect he enjoyed with the king to reinforce the pacification of Saint-Germain. In his mind, this would best be undertaken by a comprehensive reform of the French state and the channeling of the destructive energies of civil war into foreign expeditions in Flanders and the New World. Such initiatives created tensions with Catherine de Médicis and further inflamed the Guises' hatred of him. Coligny retired to his estates, returning to court only in the early summer of 1572.

Historians still debate the degree to which Coligny advocated these schemes and their role in the events that followed. But Coligny became a marked man to his numerous enemies, including Catherine de Médicis, the Guise, and Philip II of Spain. Each has been variously accredited with instigating the attempted assassination of Coligny in Paris on 22 August 1572. At that moment the Huguenot leadership was gathered in force in Paris for the marriage of Henry of Navarre (Henry IV) to Margaret of Valois. Apparently fearful that the Huguenots would seek vengeance for the attack on Coligny, Charles IX ordered the selective elimination of Huguenot leaders. Two days later, Coligny became the most prominent victim of what became known as the Saint Bartholomew's Day massacre. The king ordered his goods confiscated to the crown and his offspring dishonored. Protestant propaganda thereafter, both inside and outside France, made Coligny a hero of religious toleration and national identity and a martyr to Valois duplicity.

BIBLIOGRAPHY

Bourgeon, Jean-Louis. *L'assassinat de Coligny.* Geneva, 1994.

Crouzet, Denis. *La nuit de la Saint-Barthélemy: Un rêve perdu de la Renaissance.* Paris, 1994.

Delaborde, Jules. *Gaspard de Coligny.* 3 vols. Paris, 1879.

Kingdon, Robert M. *Myths about the Saint Bartholomew's Day Massacres, 1572–1576.* Cambridge, Mass., and London, 1988.

Shimizu, J. *Conflict of Loyalties: Politics, and Religion in the Career of Gaspard de Coligny: Admiral of France, 1519–1572.* Geneva, 1970.

Sutherland, N. M. *The Massacre of St. Bartholomew and the European Conflict, 1559–1572.* London and New York, 1973.

MARK GREENGRASS

COLLÈGE DE FRANCE. The Collège de France (also known as the Collège Royal), one of the most prestigious institutions of higher learning in France today, likes to trace its origin to 1530, when King Francis I—the so-called father of letters—set up four royal professorships, two in Greek and two in Hebrew, languages as yet unrepresented in the curriculum of the University of Paris. In time more professors were added to the original four, but they did not constitute a college, as such, until 18 March 1633, when a royal decree affirmed that the Regia Galliorum Schola was "a separate body free from all outside control." As late as 1568 the professors had no building of their own: they taught in various colleges of the University of Paris, notably those of Cambrai and Tréguier. Not until late in the reign of Henry IV were plans for a royal college building drawn up. The first stone was laid by the young Louis XIII in August 1610, but nothing more was done until 1774 when Jean-François-Thérèse Chalgrin built the college that exists today.

It was in February 1517 that Francis I responded to pressure from a group of court humanists, led by Guillaume Budé, by announcing his intention to found a college for the study of ancient languages. Although some Greek had been taught by Girolamo

Collège de France. Engraving by Claude Châtillon, 1612. GIRAUDON

Aleandro (Hieronymous Aleander) at the University of Paris in the fifteenth century, Latin was the only language taught and used by the university as a whole. In widening the scope of language teaching, the king could follow two foreign examples: the college of young Greeks founded in Rome by Pope Leo X in 1515 and the trilingual college being set up in Louvain under the will of Jerome Busleiden. Erasmus was invited to take charge of the new foundation, but he felt unable to accept despite the temptation of a rich prebend. Francis had to fall back on the services of Janus Lascaris, the principal of Leo X's college in Rome, who, as a first step, set up a college of young Greeks in Milan, which then belonged to France. However, Francis's interest in scholarship was easily supplanted by more pressing political concerns, and Budé constantly had to remind him of past promises. In January 1521 the king promised to set up a college for the study of Greek in Paris, but nothing was done. Meanwhile, Lascaris had to dissolve his college in Milan after his pleas for adequate funding had fallen on deaf ears.

No further action was taken with respect to the new college after war broke out between Francis I and the emperor Charles V in April 1521. Following the Treaty of Cambrai in 1529, Budé and his friends reminded the king of his undertaking to found a college. In 1530 Francis set up the four royal professorships. Pierre Danès and Jacques Toussaint were appointed to teach Greek, and François Vatable and Agazio Guidacerio to teach Hebrew. Oronce Fine

(Orontius Fineus) was then picked to teach mathematics, and in 1531 the third lecturer was appointed, also to teach Hebrew: Paul Canossa (Paradis), a converted Venetian Jew. As yet, no provision was made for the teaching of Latin, which was seen as the responsibility of the University of Paris, but many people thought its teaching could be updated. This end was served in 1534 when Barthélemy Le Masson (Latomus), a dedicated Ciceronian, was appointed to the college by the king. More disciplines were soon added to the list: medicine (Jacques Sylvius, c. 1535), oriental languages (Guillaume Postel, 1538), and Greek and Latin philosophy (Francesco Vimercato, 1542). Mathematics and medicine were each given a second chair. The long list of famous names who attended the courses of the *lecteurs royaux,* including Calvin, Rabelais, Ignatius Loyola, Jacques Amyot, Henri Estienne, and Pierre de Ronsard, may be taken as a measure of the success of those courses. Among the many eulogies in prose and verse addressed to them, the best known is Gargantua's letter in chapter 8 of Rabelais's *Pantagruel.*

Important as it was, the appointment of the *lecteurs royaux* represented a modest achievement compared to establishing the college originally envisaged by the king. No foundation charter has ever been found. The only archival documents relating to the royal initiative are a letter by Francis to Ludovico di Canossa, bishop of Bayeux, asking for the release of Toussaint so that he might take up the chair of Greek, and some entries in the accounts of the king's household concerning the professors' salaries. At the start, each was to receive 200 *écus*. It seems, however, that they were kept waiting for four or five years before being paid. This unhappy state of affairs lasted until the close of the century. The royal foundation only survived thanks to the generosity of humanist bishops like Jean du Bellay, Jacques Colin, and Pierre Du Chastel, who conferred ecclesiastical benefices on the professors.

Recent research has refuted the traditional assumption that the appointment of the *lecteurs royaux* was an enlightened gesture by Francis I in support of humanism and against the scholastic obscurantism of the University of Paris. The *lecteurs* never posed a threat to the university's privileges or interests. Moreover, they were often described as part of it. One should not read too much into the prosecution of four *lecteurs* by the Parlement of Paris in 1534 at the instance of Noël Béda, syndic of the Faculty of Theology. What he objected to was not their teaching of Greek and Hebrew but their right, as nontheologians, to teach Scripture without the faculty's permission. The fact that the case was referred to the king's council and that no verdict has come to light has been claimed by at least one historian (Lefranc) as a victory for the Renaissance spirit, yet the Faculty of Theology emerged from the affair without any loss of prestige.

See also **Humanism,** *subentry on* **France; Paris, University** of; *and biographies of figures mentioned in this entry.*

BIBLIOGRAPHY

Chastel, André. "François Ier et le Collège de France." In *Culture et demeures en France au XVI*ᵉ *siècle.* Edited by André Chastel. Paris, 1989.

Farge, James K. *Le parti conservateur au XVI*ᵉ *siècle: Université et Parlement de Paris à l'époque de la Renaissance et de la Réforme.* Paris, 1992.

Lefranc, Abel. *Histoire du Collège de France depuis ses origines jusqu'à la fin du premier empire.* Paris, 1893. Reprint, Geneva, 1970.

McNeil, David O. *Guillaume Budé and Humanism in the Reign of Francis I.* Geneva, 1975.

R. J. KNECHT

COLOGNE. Located on the lower Rhine, Cologne (Köln) was the largest and richest of the German towns during the late fifteenth and sixteenth centuries. Its population of around 40,000 included a high percentage of religious. Although under the authority of the archbishop of Cologne, the patrician and wealthy burgher classes dominated the political, social, cultural, and educational institutions of this imperial free city. The University of Cologne, with its enrollment of more than 2,000 students by the late fifteenth century, was second only to Louvain among the German universities. The reputation of the Cologne theologians as defenders of religious orthodoxy was well known across Europe. With the outbreak of the Reformation, however, its enrollments plummeted to only several hundred and its importance waned through the end of the century. The city's famous Gothic cathedral, only partially completed, held the relics of the three magi and was a popular destination for pilgrims. With eleven chapter churches, nineteen parishes, and numerous religious houses, Cologne remained "the faithful daughter of Rome," as proclaimed on the city seal. The strong clerical presence, along with imperial strategies to maintain Cologne as a Catholic city, stifled the Protestant presence as well as the moderate religious reform attempts of Archbishop Hermann von Wied (1477–1552) during the sixteenth century.

Cologne's reputation as a bastion of conservative Catholicism and a center of reactionary Scholasticism, while partly justified, has been overly emphasized in the historical literature. Scholars have pointed out that this characterization was largely the result of literary efforts by Ulrich von Hutten (1488–1523), Crotus Rubeanus (c. 1480–c. 1539), Hermann von dem Busche (1468–1534), and other radical humanists who circulated the most famous satire in pre-Reformation Germany, the *Epistolae obscurorum virorum* (Letters of obscure men), first published in 1515–1517 during the Reuchlin affair. These fictional letters depicted Jacob Hoogstraeten (c. 1460–1527), a Dominican theologian and inquisitor, and other conservative clerics in the city as obscurantist fools and moral degenerates.

A modest humanist presence continued in Cologne. There was, however, a modest humanist presence at the University of Cologne from the second half of the fifteenth century onward. This was a period of increasing enrollment, which reached a high in 1496, when 578 new students entered the university. Supported by influential families, such as the Rincks, wandering humanist poets and teachers visited the city during the fifteenth century. They included Jacobus Publicius, who arrived in 1468, Stephanus Surigonus, and Flavius Raimundus Mithridates, who taught arts and theology at the university during the 1480s. However, the traditional faculty organization and the scholastic curriculum at the late-medieval university stifled efforts to teach the new humanism. Some humanists, including Busche and Ortwin Gratius, provided instruction in poetry, rhetoric, and other humanistic subjects as elective courses in the university residences (*bursae*), while other humanists, such as the language scholars Johannes Caesarius and Johannes Potken, taught privately. Prompted by Count Hermann von Neuenahr and his circle, the attempts to introduce moderate humanist reforms at the university in 1523 and again in 1525 were only partially implemented. Perhaps more important for the spread of humanist ideas were the publishing activities of a number of scholar-printers in the city, who included Heinrich and Peter Quentell, Eucharius Cervicornus, Johann Gymnich, Johannes Soter, Konrad and Nikolaus Kaiser, and Gottfried Hittorp.

With the emergence of the Reformation the situation worsened for the humanists, since they were perceived by the theologians as being aligned with the Protestant cause. When Theodoricus Fabritius, returning from Wittenberg, tried to lecture on Greek and Hebrew in 1528, the city council banned all instruction in those ancient languages. During the Counter-Reformation, the Jesuits introduced a humanist program of study at their college, thereby providing new educational opportunities for the sons of important Cologne families into the modern period.

See also **Holy Roman Empire**; **Humanism**, *subentry on* **Germany and the Low Countries**; **Reuchlin Affair**.

BIBLIOGRAPHY

Mehl, James V., ed. *Humanismus in Köln/Humanism in Cologne.* Cologne, Germany, and Vienna, 1991. Contains five useful essays on the humanist presence in the city.

Meuthen, Erich. *Kölner Universitätsgeschichte.* Vol. 1, *Die alte Universität.* Cologne, Germany, and Vienna, 1988. Chapter 6 covers humanist activities at the university.

Nauert, Charles G. "Graf Hermann von Neuenahr and the Limits of Humanism in Cologne." *Historical Reflections/Réflexions Historiques* 15 (1988): 65–79.

JAMES V. MEHL

COLONNA, FRANCESCO (1433/34–1527), Italian monk and writer. Colonna is chiefly known as the author of the erudite prose work *Hypnerotomachia Poliphili* (The strife of love in a dream of Poliphilo). Little is known of his life. He was from the Veneto region and belonged to the Dominican order. Colonna is registered at the convent of Saints John and Paul in Venice beginning in 1472. The following year he obtained a baccalaureate degree in theology at the University of Padua. Some evidence suggests that Colonna may have encountered resistance to the more profane elements of his work on the part of his fellow clerics.

Although various scholars have attempted to attribute the anonymous *Hypnerotomachia* to other authors, the consensus now argues that the work was indeed written by Colonna, whose name is identified only in a cryptogram. *Hypnerotomachia* exercised a powerful influence on other humanist-hermetic writings of the later Renaissance, just as its numerous woodcuts, filled with antique decorative and architectural motifs, have never been attributed successfully to a particular artist. The illustrations, which often serve to veil meanings rather than to clarify the enigmatic text, exercised influence on many artists, including Titian, Giorgione, and Bernini. The first edition of the text was published by the renowned publisher Aldus Manutius in Venice in 1499. Aldus's heirs issued a second edition in 1545; numerous subsequent versions of the text appeared (Paris, 1546; London, 1592; and so on). Overall, the work enjoyed widespread attention in the Renaissance and was interpreted in four primary ways: as an allegorical romance, in the tradition of the *Romance of the Rose,* Boccaccio's romances, and courtly love; as the narrative of an alchemical-hermetic-mystical pilgrimage; as a humanist encyclopedia of erudition; and as an illustrated architectural compendium.

In *Hypnerotomachia,* Poliphilo dreams of a long journey through gardens, symbolic spaces, and ancient ruins. Eventually he is united with a nymph whom he recognizes as Polia, his beloved; she leads him to a temple of Venus. In the second half of the story, Polia is herself granted a voice. She rejects the physical love of Poliphilo and undergoes a kind of initiation rite. Finally, she dies and is assumed into the heavens.

Colonna wrote in a macaronic style based on the Venetian dialect and peppered with a Latin and (primarily in the case of certain adjectives) Greek lexicon. The linguistic structure is so tortured that "polyphilic language" became a colloquial term for undecipherable speech or writing in the Renaissance. Some scholars have convincingly argued that this odd language reflects an internal conflict between Colonna's religious vocation and his humanist literary tendencies. The name Poliphilo means, literally, the lover of Polia. Scholars have identified the female in the text as a real woman whom the monk Colonna himself may have loved. Or her name may contain a purely allegorical significance. Polia's name probably comes from the Greek word (*poliòs*) meaning "the gray or aged one." She may represent the moribund classical languages that are buried alive beneath the growing use of the vulgate in hu-

Colonna's *Hypnerotomachia Poliphili*. Poliphilo journeys through gardens, symbolic spaces, and ancient ruins. Illustration from the first edition (Venice: Aldus Manutius, 1499).

manist texts. One might say of *Hypnerotomachia* that it was truly valued as a beautiful object in its own time, above and beyond the difficult and arcane content.

BIBLIOGRAPHY

Primary Works

Colonna, Francesco. *Hypnerotomachia Poliphili.* Edited by Giovanni Pozzi and Lucia Ciapponi. Padua, Italy, 1964. Reprint, Padua, 1980. The best critical edition of the text, in its original macaronic language with commentary in Italian.

Colonna, Francesco. *Hypnerotomachia: The Strife of Love in a Dreame.* London, 1592. Reprint, Delmar, N.Y., 1973. The first English edition.

Secondary Works

Fierz-David, Linda. *The Dream of Poliphilo.* Translated by M. Hottinger. New York, 1950. Reprint, Dallas, Tex., 1987. An outline and interpretation of the work as an example of alchemy by a disciple of Jung.

Gombrich, Ernst. "Hypnerotomachiana." *Journal of the Warburg and Courtauld Institute* 14 (1951): 119–125.

Hunt, John Dixon, ed. *Word and Image* 14, nos. 1–2 (Jan.–June 1998). Dedicated to Colonna's text.

KAREN PINKUS

COLONNA, VITTORIA (1492–1547), Italian noblewoman, poet. Vittoria Colonna was born into the elite aristocracy of Rome, the daughter of military leader Fabrizio Colonna and Agnese da Montefeltro of Urbino. Wed in 1509 to Ferrante Francesco d'Avalos, the marquis of Pescara, she became one of the most important women of the sixteenth century, noted for her intellect, virtue, piety, and charm.

While her beloved husband spent years at war, Colonna held court for intellectuals and artists at home in Naples, befriending such luminaries as Jacopo Sannazaro, Bernardo Tasso, and Benedetto Gareth Cariteo. After her husband's death in 1525, the childless Colonna turned to intellectual pursuits and religious matters, opting to live in convents. As celebrated in widowhood as in youth, she embodied feminine nobility for her generation. She was consistently praised for her chaste existence, decorous behavior, piety, and honorable character.

Colonna's devotional inclinations drew her to the Roman Catholic reformists as well as to the intelligentsia who flocked to her gatherings in the Roman convent of San Silvestro. She associated with several religious figures usually called "Spirituali," notably

Juan de Valdés, Bernardino Ochino, Cardinal Reginald Pole, and Cardinal Gasparo Contarini. They emphasized interior Christianity and were attracted to justification by faith, but only Ochino became a Protestant. In the 1530s Colonna and the artist Michelangelo Buonarroti formed a friendship that grew into a profound love based on shared artistic and spiritual interests. The noblewoman's support of Roman Catholic reformation, her unconventional theological opinions, and her associations brought her to the attention of the Inquisition in the 1540s. Suspected of heresy, Colonna was demoralized during her final years. Suffering from a debilitating illness, she died on 25 February 1547, with Michelangelo at her side.

Colonna is considered one of Italy's foremost female poets. Although few of her compositions were issued with her consent, an unauthorized edition appeared in 1538 and was followed by twenty more editions in the sixteenth century alone, attesting to her popularity. Since 1547, editions generally divide her poetry into two sections: the love compositions for her deceased husband and the spiritual poems. Other works include epistolary sonnets and letters. Colonna's poetry, like her person, ideally suited Renaissance taste. Her works utilize Petrarchan motifs, form, rhetorical devices, and imagery. Philosophically, they are influenced by a markedly Christian version of Neoplatonic discourse. Stylistically mainstream, Colonna was nevertheless an excellent emulator, finding canonical models suitable instruments for expressing her feminine voice and individual themes.

Her lyric output is considerable: a 1982 edition of the *Rime* (Rhymes), edited by Alan Bullock, contains almost four hundred compositions. Colonna, penning her love poems in the years following the death of d'Avalos, modeled them after Petrarch's lyrics in praise of the dead Laura. Like the Petrarchan subject, Colonna's lost beloved is a spiritual guide who comes to embody all good. The love lyrics underscore the Christian aspect of Petrarchan love and serve to commemorate the departed. As Colonna grew older, the subject of her spiritual love shifted from man to God. Love poetry gave way to religious meditations on Christ and faith. The amorous verse and the devotional works are linked structurally and metaphorically by their common origin in sixteenth-century Petrarchism.

BIBLIOGRAPHY

Primary Work
Colonna, Vittoria. *Rime*. Edited by Alan Bullock. Rome and Bari, Italy, 1982.

Secondary Works
Bassanese, Fiora A. "Vittoria Colonna (1492–1547)." In *Italian Women Writers: A Bio-Bibliographical Sourcebook*. Edited by Rinaldina Russell. Westport, Conn., 1994. Pages 85–94.
Gibaldi, Joseph. "Vittoria Colonna: Child, Woman, and Poet." In *Women Writers of the Renaissance and Reformation*. Edited by Katharina M. Wilson. Athens, Ga., 1987. Pages 22–46. Includes translations of some poetry.
McAuliffe, Dennis J. "Neoplatonism in Vittoria Colonna's Poetry: From the Secular to the Divine." In *Ficino and Renaissance Neoplatonism*. Edited by Konrad Eisenbichler and Olga Zorzi Pugliese. Toronto, 1986. Pages 101–112.

FIORA A. BASSANESE

COLUMBINE LIBRARY. *See* **Libraries.**

COLUMBUS, CHRISTOPHER (1451–1506), explorer whose voyages to the Americas led to the European settlement of the Western Hemisphere. Columbus was born in the Italian republic of Genoa. His father worked as a wool weaver, wool merchant, tavern keeper, and political appointee. Christopher was the oldest of five children. After 1492, brothers Bartolomeo and Giacomo (Spanish Bartolomé and Diego) joined Columbus in Spain and the Caribbean.

Early Career. Columbus's early education was limited, but he read widely as an adult. He went to sea at an early age and sailed the Mediterranean as far east as the island of Chios, then under Genoese control. He acted as a merchant and possibly commanded a ship at least once. In the mid-1470s he joined the small colony of Italian merchants in Lisbon, a city at the center of Portuguese maritime activity in the Atlantic. On Portuguese vessels, he sailed north to England and Ireland, and possibly as far as Iceland. He also visited the Madeira and Canary Islands and sailed down the African coast as far as the Portuguese trading post at São Jorge da Mina. On these trips Columbus observed the winds and currents, the flora and fauna, and how the Portuguese made profits trading with African societies.

In Portugal, Columbus in 1478 or 1479 married Felipa Moniz, a member of an Italian-Portuguese family whose Italian progenitors had arrived sometime in the late fourteenth century and had attained noble status in Portugal. Her Portuguese forebears were noble and through them she was related to Queen Isabella of Castile. Felipa Moniz bore Columbus a son in 1480 named Diogo (Spanish Diego), who would later establish a bureaucratic career in the lands his father claimed for Spain. Presumably, Columbus had achieved a degree of wealth and distinction of his own even before his marriage, from which he secured connections to the Portuguese court and high nobility, ties to Madeira and Porto Santo, and at least some additional wealth.

For centuries, Asia and its spices and other lucrative commodities had attracted European attention, but in the fifteenth century it was almost impossible for European merchants to reach Asia overland. They could buy Asian goods from Muslim merchants in Alexandria and other ports but sought a sea route to Asia that would allow them to buy Asian goods directly at their source. In the 1480s the Portuguese were trying to find the southern tip of Africa and a passage into the Indian Ocean and from there a route to India itself. Taking a different approach, Columbus became convinced that Asia could be reached by sailing west from Europe. Columbus's geographical ideas probably evolved piecemeal, based on rumors of other islands yet to be found in the Atlantic; unusual objects drifting in from the western ocean; and wide reading of academic geography, including Pierre d'Ailly's *Imago mundi* (1410) and Ptolemy's second-century C.E. *Geographia* in the printed editions that became available with the invention of the printing press. Columbus, like other well-read Europeans, knew that the world was spherical, but he made a great error that inspired him to believe he could easily reach Asia by sailing west.

The foundations of his faulty theory were that the Asian continent stretched some thirty degrees farther to the east than it really does, and that Japan lay fifteen hundred miles east of the Asian mainland. Columbus also greatly underestimated the circumference of the earth. Although he used the conventional division of the globe into 360 degrees, he used too short an estimate of the length of a degree at the equator. On the basis of his calculations, Columbus thought the Canary Islands lay only 2,400 nautical miles from Japan. The actual distance is 10,600 nautical miles. Many experts in geography at the time held far more accurate ideas about the earth's size. Of course, neither Columbus nor anyone else in Europe even suspected that two vast continents lay in the way of a westward passage to Asia.

With miscalculations as the basis of his proposal, Columbus tried around 1483 to interest the Portuguese king John II in his scheme for a westward passage to Asia. The king turned him down for unrecorded reasons.

Columbus went to Spain around 1485 and through personal contacts met the king and queen for the first time early in 1486. Isabella and Ferdinand took an interest in his project and appointed a commission to investigate the feasibility of a westward voyage. Although the commission disputed Colum-

Christopher Columbus. Engraving by Tobias Stimmer.

bus's flawed geography, the spherical shape of the world was never in question; disagreement concerned the true magnitude of its circumference. The monarchs encouraged him to believe that they might support him once they finished their long war to conquer Muslim Granada, and provided him with subsidies from time to time.

During his years of waiting before 1492, Columbus established a liaison with a young woman in Córdoba named Beatriz Enríquez de Arana. Although they never married, they had a son named Fernando in 1488, whom Columbus later legitimized. Fernando accompanied Columbus on his fourth voyage to the Western Hemisphere and later wrote a biography of his father.

In January 1492 Isabella summoned Columbus back to court. The monarchs agreed that the potential benefit of supporting Columbus was worth a modest financial risk and were willing to discount the skepticism of their own experts. They helped to underwrite the voyage and promised to grant Columbus noble status and the titles of admiral, viceroy, and governor-general for any islands or mainlands he might discover.

The First Voyage. With royal backing and the support of the prominent mariner Martín Alonso Pinzón, Columbus outfitted three vessels for the voyage, two caravels named *Niña* and *Pinta,* and a larger ship named *Mariagalante,* often called *Santa María.* The fleet sailed first to the Canary Islands, where Columbus picked up winds that he assumed would take him directly to Japan. They left the Canaries on 6 September 1492, heading westward into the open ocean. Propelled by the prevailing winds blowing from northeast to southwest in those latitudes, Columbus and the other pilots in the fleet navigated by dead reckoning, a system using estimates of direction, time, and speed to plot their course and position. They determined direction by compass, time by a sand clock, and speed by eye and feel.

The voyage went smoothly, with fair winds and remarkably little grumbling among the crew. On 12 October at 2 o'clock in the morning, Juan Rodríguez Bermejo, the lookout on the *Pinta,* saw a light, and after dawn the fleet dropped anchor at an island in the Bahamas that local inhabitants (Taínos) called Guanahaní, and which Columbus renamed San Salvador. It was probably the island formerly named Watlings Island and renamed San Salvador in the twentieth century. Believing they were in Asia, they called the natives "Indians."

Aided by Taíno guides, Columbus's fleet continued sailing through the Bahamas and visited Cuba as he vainly sought the vast commerce and rich ports of Asia. Martín Alonso Pinzón took the *Pinta* without Columbus's permission and sailed off to explore and trade on his own. Columbus and the two remaining ships sailed to the island he named Hispaniola and explored its northern coast. Early Christmas morning, the *Mariagalante* ran aground and wrecked. With only the *Niña* still at his disposal, Columbus founded a settlement for the thirty-nine men he had to leave behind, naming it Villa de la Navidad, or Christmas Town. Columbus prepared to return to Spain in the *Niña* and sailed eastward along the coast of Hispaniola. Pinzón rejoined him, and on 16 January 1493, the *Niña* and *Pinta* set sail for home, bringing seven captured Indians with them, as proof of the exotic destinations Columbus and his crew had reached.

Through trial and error, Columbus eventually found winds blowing from the west that would take them home. Fierce storms separated the two ships as they approached the Azores. On 4 March, Columbus found himself just north of Lisbon, where they put in for rest and refitting. Columbus paid a courtesy call on King John II and departed for Spain on 13 March 1493, arriving in Palos two days later. Martín Alonso Pinzón brought the *Pinta* into Palos later that same day, and died shortly thereafter.

The Second Voyage. Isabella and Ferdinand received Columbus warmly in Barcelona. In addition to confirming all his promised privileges, they gave him permission for a second, larger voyage, and Columbus continued to assure them that the rich Asian mainland lay close to the islands he had found. They facilitated Columbus's colonizing effort with ships and men to send to Hispaniola, and the queen ordered that the native islanders be treated well and converted to Christianity. Columbus had no difficulty in finding 1,200 men to accompany him as settlers. Departing from Cádiz on 25 September 1493, the fleet of seventeen vessels reached the Canaries on 2 October and began their Atlantic crossing on 13 October. On 3 November they landed on an island in the Caribbean that Columbus named Dominica and then sailed to Hispaniola.

Much to their shock, they found in late November that all thirty-nine of the men left in La Navidad were dead, most of them killed in disputes with the islanders. Columbus founded a new settlement, located on a poor site with no fresh water, which later caused it to be abandoned. In addition to searching for gold and the location of the ports of the Grand Khan of China, Columbus began a slave trade. If the islanders peacefully accepted takeover by the Europeans, they were protected against enslavement as subjects of the Castilian crown, but if they made war they could be seized as slaves, according to European law. By the time Columbus's second expedition arrived, some islanders were certainly at war against the Europeans, and Columbus used their resistance as a justification for their outright conquest.

Leaving Hispaniola under the control of his brother Diego, Columbus on 24 April 1494 began an expedition to explore the southern shores of Cuba, which he believed was part of the Asian mainland; he even made his crew members sign a document to that effect so that he could claim to his royal backers that he had truly found Asia.

In command of a small fleet, Columbus's brother Bartolomé had arrived on Hispaniola during Columbus's absence, but the colony was in chaos. Disappointed colonists returned to Spain and spread stories about the ineptitude of Columbus and his brothers as administrators. The Spanish rulers sent out an investigator named Juan Aguado, who confirmed their worst fears: there were alarmingly high deaths among the Amerindians and the numbers of settlers were greatly reduced by disease and desertions. Columbus decided to defend his administration in person and sailed for Spain on 10 March 1496,

Columbus Departing. Columbus takes leave of Ferdinand and Isabella at Palos. Engraving by Théodor de Bry in *Americae* (Frankfurt, 1594). BY PERMISSION OF THE BRITISH LIBRARY

leaving his brother Bartolomé in charge on Hispaniola, and reached Cádiz on 11 June 1496.

By 1496 Ferdinand and Isabella had abandoned hope of short-term profits from Columbus's ventures. Despite reports about Columbus's failings as an administrator, the monarchs confirmed his previous grants and gave him permission for a third voyage, with 300 men and 30 women as additional colonists.

The Third and Fourth Voyages. Departing from Spain in May 1498, the fleet divided in the Canaries. Three vessels sailed directly for Hispaniola. Columbus took the other three to the Cape Verde Islands before heading westward on 4 July and reaching the island that Columbus named Trinidad on 31 July. He then sailed north and west to the mainland of South America, realizing from the vast flow of water of the Orinoco River that he had encountered an enormous land mass, which he speculated might be near the Garden of Eden described in the Bible. After briefly exploring the coast of Venezuela, Columbus sailed on to Hispaniola in mid-August.

There he found the situation in crisis. Some of the colonists had mutinied because they wanted greater freedom of action than Columbus's policies allowed. The Indians were increasingly hostile, and Columbus's brothers had not been able to maintain order. Columbus himself had little better luck. Forewarned by Columbus's own reports, Ferdinand and Isabella sent out Francisco de Bobadilla to investigate, empowering him to take extraordinary measures to restore authority if necessary. Quickly sizing up the situation, he arrested the three Columbus brothers for their failure to keep order in the colony, seized their money, and sent them home ignominiously in chains in October 1500.

The monarchs told him they had never ordered him to be chained, but they delayed granting his request for reinstatement to his official posts until September 1501. They allowed Columbus to keep some of his titles and all his property, but his titles would thereafter be empty of authority. They also delayed granting him permission for another voyage until March 1502. Instead, they began to build a bureaucratic structure outside Columbus's control, appointing Nicolás de Ovando as governor of Hispaniola.

Columbus's final fleet consisted of four small caravels in questionable repair, with second-rate crews. The fleet left Spain on 11 May 1502. Departing the Canaries on 25 May, they crossed the Atlantic and arrived at Hispaniola on 29 June, even though Ferdinand and Isabella had specifically forbidden Columbus to land there. He warned Governor Ovando of an approaching hurricane and asked to use the harbor at Hispaniola to ride it out. Ovando refused to believe him and ordered a scheduled fleet to depart. Just as Columbus had predicted, the hurricane struck, sinking twenty-five ships.

After Columbus left Hispaniola, he spent most of the remainder of the voyage along the coast of Central America. Local people fiercely resisted his efforts to found a settlement in Panama and forced him to leave, abandoning one ship. The three others were barely seaworthy, riddled by shipworm damage and leaking badly. Columbus abandoned yet another ship at sea and then was forced to put in at Jamaica. Grounding his two remaining worn-out vessels and shoring them up for use as strongholds, Columbus spent a miserable year before he was rescued. Broken in health, he arrived in Spain on 7 November 1504, never again to return to the Indies.

Columbus made every effort to have all his grants and titles restored. Even without them, he was a wealthy man, but he felt betrayed and slighted by his royal patrons. For their part, the Spanish sovereigns justified their withdrawal of support by Columbus's mismanagement and by his betrayal of their trust and of the agreements he had signed with them. Surrounded by his brother Diego, his sons Diego and Fernando, and friends from his voyages, Columbus died in Valladolid on 20 May 1506, rich but dissatisfied.

Myths and Realities. Although Columbus is one of the most familiar figures in history, myths about him abound, making it difficult to put his accomplishments into their proper context. There often has been little attempt to probe beyond the myths. Those who want to see Columbus as a hero often force his life into a heroic mold. They believe that he was the first to conceive of a spherical earth and that he had to fight traditional religious beliefs and prejudices before succeeding. They believe that he died poor and alone. They believe that he was a perfect hero, almost without human failings. None of this is true. Recently, politically motivated writers have begun to attempt to forge a countermyth, to depict Columbus as the first European despoiler of a supposedly pristine American continent, and to de-

pict him as the embodiment of evil. They offer a view as distorted as that produced by the Columbus hagiographers.

Columbus above all was a man of his time, strongly influenced by the powerful religious currents of his era as well as by the norms and laws surrounding mercantile enterprises. In pursuit of profits, he would urge the establishment of a slave trade in Caribbean natives, particularly those who practiced cannibalism, arguing that such slavery would also allow them to be converted and reformed. Far from opposing Christian beliefs, he considered that God had chosen him for his mission. He became obsessed with religion as he aged. He hoped that some of the profits from his ventures would be used to recapture Jerusalem from the Muslims, in fulfillment of Christian crusading prophesy and as a prelude to the conversion of the world to Christianity. Columbus was a complex human being who exemplified both the virtues and the flaws of his time and place in history.

In the mid-twentieth century, textbook writers tended to depict Columbus as a man who embodied the supposedly scientific spirit of the Renaissance. That view is no longer valid. It is true that Columbus made use of classical and more recent geographical and religious works in newly available printed editions, but in larger terms Columbus exemplified trends that had begun in the Middle Ages. His millenarianism, his enthusiasm for crusades, and his obsession with Asia were all centuries-old patterns.

Instead of finding a new route to Asia, Columbus made the lands and peoples of the Western Hemisphere known to Europeans and set in motion a chain of events that altered human history. The origin of many of the most characteristic features of the modern world, such as the interdependent global system of trade and the interconnections of all the world's societies, can be traced directly to the voyages of Columbus.

See also **Americas; Exploration.**

BIBLIOGRAPHY

Primary Works

Colón, Cristóbal. *Textos y documentos completos.* Edited by Consuelo Varela and Juan Gil. 2d ed. Madrid, 1992.

Columbus, Ferdinand. *The Life of the Admiral Christopher Columbus by His Son Ferdinand.* Translated by Benjamin Keen. New Brunswick, N.J., 1992.

Dunn, Oliver, and James E. Kelley, Jr., eds. and trans. *The Diario of Christopher Columbus' First Voyage to America, 1492–1493.* Norman, Okla., 1989.

Nader, Helen, ed. *The Book of Privileges Issued to Christopher Columbus by King Fernando and Queen Isabel, 1492–1502.* Berkeley, Calif., 1996.

West, Delno C., and August Kling. *The "Libro de las Profecías" of Christopher Columbus.* Gainesville, Fla., 1991.

Secondary Works

Deneven, William M. "The Pristine Myth: The Landscape of the Americas in 1492." *Annals of the Association of American Geographers* 82, no. 3 (1992): 369–385.

Henige, David. *In Search of Columbus: The Sources for the First Voyage.* Tucson, Ariz., 1991.

Lunenfeld, Marvin, ed. *1492—Discovery, Invasion, Encounter: Sources and Interpretations.* Lexington, Mass., 1991.

Morison, Samuel Eliot. *Admiral of the Open Sea: A Life of Christopher Columbus.* 2 vols. Boston, 1942.

Phillips, William D., Jr., and Carla Rahn Phillips. *The Worlds of Christopher Columbus.* Cambridge, 1992.

Sauer, Carl Ortwin. *The Early Spanish Main.* Berkeley, Calif., 1966.

WILLIAM D. PHILLIPS JR.

COMEDY. *See* **Drama.**

COMMANDINO, FEDERICO (1509–1575), Italian mathematician, physician, translator. From a noble family of Urbino, Italy, Commandino was educated first by his father, an architect, then trained in Latin and Greek by Giacopo Torelli and tutored in mathematics by Giovanni Pietro di Grassi. He served briefly in Rome as secretary to Pope Clement VII (1533–1534). On Clement's death he went to the University of Padua, where he studied philosophy and medicine for ten years, then to the University of Ferrara, where he took his medical degree around 1546. Thereupon he returned to Urbino, married, and had two daughters and a son; after this his wife died, and he never remarried.

About 1552 he entered the service of Duke Guidobaldo della Rovere and worked with him at Verona on military mapping and land surveying. When the duke fell ill Commandino treated him successfully, but he grew dissatisfied with medical practice "by reason of its uncertainty" and turned gradually to mathematics. He was physician, however, to Ranuccio Cardinal Farnese at Rome and Venice, and met Marcello Cardinal Cervini, the Vatican librarian, shortly before the latter was elected pope in 1555 as Marcellus II. Cervini asked him to reconstruct Ptolemy's *Analemma* (Sundials) from a codex containing the Latin translation of William of Moerbeke (c. 1220–1286), the Greek original being lost. The codex also contained Moerbeke's translation of Archimedes's *Floating Bodies,* and it was this encounter with Ptolemy and Archimedes that interested Commandino in reconstructions and translations of ancient texts. When the new pope died a few weeks after his election, Commandino reentered the service

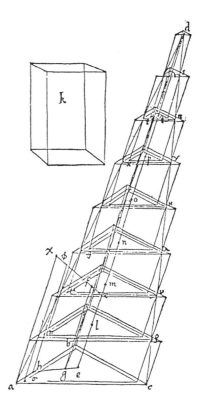

A Diagram by Commandino. Commandino's use of Archimedes's methods of approximation to determine the center of gravity of an inclined triangular pyramid. From Federico Commandino, *Liber de centro gravitatis solidorum* (Book on the center of gravity of solids; Bologna, 1565, fol. 19v).

of Cardinal Farnese, where he remained until Farnese's death in 1565. From then until he died Commandino lived in Urbino. There he was visited by John Dee (1527–1608), with whom he revised and published an Arabic work on the division of surfaces (Pesaro, 1570). He also taught mathematics to Guidobaldo del Monte (1545–1607) and Bernardino Baldi (1553–1617). The latter wrote a biography of Commandino in 1587, not published until 1714.

Commandino's original publications were a treatise on the calibrating of sundials (Rome, 1562) and a book on the center of gravity of solids (Bologna, 1565), in which he made skillful use of Archimedean methods of approximation; to these should be added a work on perspective edited by Rocco Sinisgalli (Florence, 1993). Commandino translated Archimedes's main Greek texts into Latin, which were published, along with his commentary, at Bologna in

1558. Seeking sources of these texts, he further investigated and translated parts of Apollonius's *Conics* and Pappus's *Collection,* as well as writings of Eutocius and Serenus (Bologna, 1566). Other works he translated into Latin include Ptolemy's *Planisphere,* to which he added his edition of Jordanus de Nemore's *Planisphere* (Venice, 1558); Euclid's *Elements,* for which he provided an extensive commentary (Pesaro, 1572); Aristarchus's *Sizes and Distances of the Sun and Moon,* along with Pappus's explanations (Pesaro, 1572); and Hero's *Pneumatics* (Urbino, 1575). His almost-finished translation of, and commentary on, Books 3–8 of Pappus's *Collections* was completed by his student Guidobaldo del Monte and published at Pesaro in 1588.

See also **Mathematics; Mechanics.**

BIBLIOGRAPHY

Primary Work
Commandino, Federico. *La prospettiva.* Edited by Rocco Sinisgalli. Florence, 1993.

Secondary Works
Bertoloni Meli, Domenico. "Guidobaldo dal Monte and the Archimedean Revival." *Nuncius* 7, no. 1 (1992): 3–34.
Drake, Stillman, and I. E. Drabkin, eds. *Mechanics in Sixteenth-Century Italy.* Madison, Wis., and London, 1969. Pages 41–51.
Neville, Pamela. "The Printer's Copy of Commandino's Translation of Archimedes, 1558." *Nuncius* 1, no. 2 (1986): 7–12.
Ramballi, Enrico I. "John Dee and Federico Commandino: An English and an Italian Interpretation of Euclid during the Renaissance." In *Italy and the English Renaissance.* Edited by Sergio Rossi and Dianella Savoia. Milan, 1989. Pages 123–153.
Rosen, Edward. "Commandino, Federico." In *Dictionary of Scientific Biography.* Vol. 3. New York, 1971. Pages 363–365.

WILLIAM A. WALLACE

COMMEDIA DELL'ARTE. A post-Renaissance term referring to a practice and organization of professional acting companies, commedia dell'arte has acquired a mythic identity and a place in theatrical vocabularies everywhere. But though the vision of spontaneously choreographed color and movement, acrobatic stage business, slapstick and sleight of hand, frisking Harlequins, pompous Pantaloons, and lyrical lovers that it conjures up is unmistakable (if inadequate), the name itself remains ambiguous. *Arte* has been taken to mean both professional category (or guild, though never organized as such) and skill in the craft, while *commedia* often indicates the whole establishment of commercial acting as well as one particular style and format: the improvisation on a three-act *soggetto,* or scenario, for which the *co-mici* were celebrated. Commedia dell'arte was theater for hire, known best for unscripted performance cobbled together out of whatever materials were procured by the talents and knowledge of actors.

The scenarios changed continually but demanded a nucleus of fixed types usually played by actors specializing in the roles. Every company required couples of fashionable young lovers accomplished in Tuscan flowers of rhetoric and poetry; these characters were played without masks, as were the essential roles of maidservants, including the middle-aged Franceschina, often performed by a man. Ordinarily masked or wearing some facial additions were the senior fixtures, the Bolognese *dottore* Graziano, the Venetian *magnifico* Pantalone, and the legion of *zanni* (clowns) who functioned as servants, clever or buffoonish, and varied their identities and dialects depending on the company's constitution and the actors' specialties. The basic Bergamask Zanni in time was joined by Neapolitan Pulcinella and a host of others with different regional as well as individual lexicons: Arlecchino, Pedrolino, Francatrippa, Scapino, Frittellino, Scaramuccia, and so on. Equally essential was the swaggering mustached captain with terrifying, often Hispanoid, names like Matamoros, Cardone, Spavento da Vall'Inferna, Coccodrillo, and Sbranaleoni. The many other parts called for in the scenarios—the gypsies, drunken Germans, Croatian mariners, Sicilian doctors, astrologers, policemen, Turks, hangmen, innkeepers, and peasants—could all be accommodated by doubling the roles. The troupe could also redispose itself as shepherds, nymphs, satyrs, magicians, kings, queens, warriors, spirits, and wild animals when pastorals and tragedies were to be improvised.

Beginnings. Ancient and romantic origins have been claimed for the commedia dell'arte, but as a phenomenon distinct from all other kinds of entertainment available in the Italian peninsula from antiquity through the Middle Ages, it comes into view only in the sixteenth century. Regarded as the earliest document of the commedia dell'arte is a contract signed at Padua in 1545 by eight men who agreed to travel about for the gainful purpose of acting comedies. Beginning in the 1560s, in addition to innumerable roaming troupes setting up trestle stages in piazzas and passing the hat, there grew up fairly prosperous companies like the Gelosi, the Accesi, the Desiosi, the Confidenti, and the Fideli, who could boast popular leading ladies and were invited to improvise before illustrious audiences and to participate in private theatricals, performing scripted

Stock Characters of the Commedia dell'Arte. Abraham Bosse's 1630 etching of the Hôtel de Bourgogne players of Paris depicts the characters Le Capitaine Fracasse, Turlupin, Gros Guillaume, and Gaultier Garguille. BIBLIOTHÈQUE NATIONALE DE FRANCE, PARIS, TB 34A FOL. 40R

regular comedies, tragedies, and pastorals. Such resources were routinely looted by the professional players. Typically, commedia dell'arte scenarios were skeletal reductions of the plots of regular or erudite comedy—urban domestic conflicts between generations, love affairs abetted by shrewd bawdy servants, involving tricks and high jinks, deceits and mistakes, disguises, transvestism, and disappearances, all ending happily in marriages and family reunions.

A description of wedding festivities at the imperial court of Munich in 1568 provides the earliest testimony to a specific "commedia all'italiana" performance, with the musician Orlando di Lasso improvising the role of Doctor Graziano from a scenario. Playing without a script required reading, practice, and teamwork. Like jazz musicians building on a melody, the actors brought to the plot and to their assigned roles in it personal repertories of memorized speeches, poems, patter, and cross talk, verbal and gestural *lazzi,* or gags, songs and dances, dialogues and skits, elastic, flexible, inexhaustibly variable in combination. A famous account of a Medici wedding in 1589 described Isabella Andreini of the Gelosi company in her celebrated mad scene, a star turn which she improvised variously, according to need. On this occasion she raved in snatches of Spanish, Greek, French, and several Italian dialects to mimic her fellow actors, in succession impersonating Graziano, Pantalone, Pedrolino, Francatrippa, Captain Cardone, and Franceschina. To please the bride, Christine of Lorraine, Isabella sang French songs. Music and dance were essential to the commedia dell'arte: lovers serenaded ladies with Petrarchan lyrics to lute and mandolin accompaniment, and early illustrations depict *zanni* and Pantalone in chorus. Various instruments were employed and both solo and group dances were expected from professional entertainers.

Cultural Contacts and Travels. Improvised comedies were not unjustly despised by many cultivated writers as being filched, shapeless, and obscene *zannate,* but if the players, on the margins of society and hungry for any material they could sell onstage, profited from contact with regular drama, many literary playwrights in turn learned from the *comici* how to enliven their compositions with theatrical rhythm and variety, physical action, and fuller female roles. Acting was not a respectable profession and was unstable at best, but successful troupes were often helped as well as burdened by ducal patrons like the Mantuan Gonzaga and the Florentine Medici and their royal French relations. In the last third of the century the *comici* began their foreign touring, to France and Spain, across the English Channel, and as far east as Poland. Ganassa's company was in Paris in 1571, the Gelosi followed in 1577, and the Accesi went for the marriage of Marie de Médicis and Henri IV in 1600 and stayed the year. The rapport established between Italian troupes and French audiences fixed an image of Italian comedy that later contributed to the character of Molière's art.

A number of *comici* printed the fruits of their experience. When he retired from the stage, Francesco Andreini copyrighted his role of Capitan Spavento by publishing the dialogues he had used (*Le bravure;* 1607) and did the same for his wife's witty love scenes, her "contrasti scenici." Other actors published entire plays, recasting the material improvised in three acts from scenarios into full-length five-act plays in the format of regular comedy. Bernardino Lombardi's *L'alchimista* (The alchemist; 1583) and Fabrizio Fornaris's *Angelica* (1585) were printed comedies incorporating and augmenting these actors' improvised successes. Although Isabella Andreini's pastoral *Mirtilla* (1588) is indistinguishable from literary pastoral plays, it too originated in her stage performances. Flaminio Scala printed two regular comedies and in 1611 an unprecedented collection of fifty detailed scenarios, *Teatro delle favole rappresentative* (Theater of stage plots), memorializing and condensing his long professional experience as actor and director for the use of dilettante improvisers, thereby producing a unique account of the commedia dell'arte in action. In 1634 Nicolò Barbieri, known onstage as Beltrame, published *La supplica* (The supplication), a serious defense of the acting profession, which by this time, though always an object of censorship and reform policy, was too deeply entrenched in the economy and the culture to be in danger of extinction. Suppressing the players would be like ridding Egypt of crocodiles, as Barbieri put it.

In the first half of the seventeenth century the commedia dell'arte flourished in conjunction and competition with the increasingly variegated forms of theater, as illustrated by the career of G. B. Andreini, who often took his Fedeli company to Paris and, while acting and directing, also published plays in genres ranging from comedies and pastorals featuring his own improvised role of Lelio *innamorato* to religious multimedia extravaganzas and a closet tragedy about Adam and Eve. Eventually the comedy of harlequins, pantaloons, and zanies was stylized into a mechanism; the companies purveying it became relatively bureaucratized and their function was downsized. In 1699 Andrea Perrucci's compilation and codification of the performing art, *Dell'arte rappresentativa,* classified the improvised style as humble and confined to city comedy, "la ridicolosità urbana." The masks were superseded in the eighteenth century by Carlo Goldoni's psychologically realistic comedy, leaving their legacy to all European theater and awaiting the scholarly attentions of the nineteenth century, as well as a twentieth-century reincarnation in the performances of Marcello Moretti and Dario Fo.

See also **Andreini, Isabella; Drama,** *subentry on* **Erudite Comedy.**

BIBLIOGRAPHY

Primary Works

Andreini, Isabella. *Selected Poems, Letters, Fragments, and Dramas.* Edited by Laura Stortoni. Translated by James Cook and Laura Stortoni. Chicago, forthcoming.

Ferrone, Siro, ed. *Commedie dell'arte.* 2 vols. Milan, 1985–1986. Five scripted plays published by actors.

Henke, Robert, and Siro Ferrone, eds. *Source Readings in the "Commedia dell'Arte."* New York and London, forthcoming. Primary readings on the commedia dell'arte.

Scala, Flaminio. *Scenarios of the Commedia dell'Arte.* Translated by Henry F. Salerno. New York and London, 1967. Approximate translation of *Il teatro delle favole rappresentative* (1611).

Secondary Works

Andrews, Richard. *Scripts and Scenarios: The Performance of Comedy in Renaissance Italy.* Cambridge, U.K., 1993.

Cairns, Christopher, ed. *The Commedia dell'Arte from the Renaissance to Dario Fo.* Lewiston, N.Y., 1989.

Heck, Thomas F. *Commedia dell'Arte: A Guide to the Primary and Secondary Literature.* New York, 1988.

Lea, Kathleen M. *Italian Popular Comedy: A Study in the Commedia dell'Arte 1560–1620, with Special Reference to the English Stage.* 2 vols. Oxford, 1934.

Nicoll, Allardyce. *The World of Harlequin: A Critical Study of the Commedia dell'Arte.* Cambridge, U.K., 1963.

Pietropaolo, Domenico, ed. *The Science of Buffoonery: Theory and History of the Commedia dell'Arte.* Toronto, 1989.

Richards, Kenneth, and Laura Richards. *The Commedia dell'Arte: A Documentary History.* Oxford, 1990.

Louise George Clubb

COMMONPLACE BOOKS. Commonplace books were collections of phrases widely used in speech and writing during the Renaissance. The basic format of the commonplace book and the manner in which it was generated remained remarkably stable from the second decade of the sixteenth century until the second half of the seventeenth. Pupils encountered the commonplace book early in their schooling, as soon as they could grasp continuous Latin. They were then instructed to assemble a large notebook of blank pages with headings and subheadings suggested by the teacher. These were normally topics of a general moral nature, like *pietas* (loving respect), which might be subdivided into respect for God, for country, for parents, for teachers, and so on. Under these headings, the pupil inserted quotations from the Latin works he was studying, including both prose and poetry, at first as directed by the teacher and later as he read them by himself.

Schoolboys would read pen in hand, attempting to extract the essence of the moral universe inhabited by the classical writers admired in the Renaissance, and copy it into their notebooks. Typically they chose short, quotable phrases exemplifying witty, pregnant aphorisms, apposite metaphors, similitudes, examples, and proverbial expressions. Reading adults continued to compile their commonplace books, often adding categories in other areas of enquiry; they normally cross-referenced between categories and back to the source texts. Commonplacing was ideally an exercise for the individual's intellectual initiative, but the demand for readymade repositories of quotations ensured a large market for printed commonplace books on the same model.

Ordering and Use. The headings in commonplace books were ordered in a variety of ways: they might be grouped alphabetically according to affinities and opposites; or based on well-known paradigms such as traditional virtues and vices, the Ten Commandments, and Aristotle's *Ethics*. Some were classed under the predicaments (categories of thought) found in Aristotelian logic; others replicated the order of the universe from God through humankind from all perspectives, down to stones. These various principles of ordering knowledge, so indelibly set in the imagination by systematic use, are a key to understanding the Renaissance mind.

The commonplace book was a tool for analyzing texts and resourcing composition. In the early stages of education it was used to assemble Latin vocabulary and phraseology. Later it supported the rhetorical analysis of texts into themes of discourse and figures of speech (pupils were encouraged to note how their chosen quotations exemplified tropes and figures). It could also be used to probe a text for its underlying procedures of rational development, named according to the "places" (*loci*) of dialectical argumentation, and related to the general theses represented by the notebook headings.

In the course of all these applications, the pupil was expected both to note down and to memorize. For generating discourse, both oral and written, the commonplace book provided a well-stocked, well-ordered, and searchable resource. The speaker or writer would go to his categories to find copious

supplies of material; he would use his quotations either as authoritative pronouncements supporting his case or as ideas to be adapted and expanded, and certainly as models of expression. In this way, the commonplace book was an integral part of the disciplines of grammar, rhetoric, and dialectic that made Renaissance writers so articulate. More advanced and discipline-specific commonplace books were produced for law, medicine, and particularly theology, where the accumulation of quotations under generally accepted heads provided the strategy and ammunition for controversy, and the subject matter of sermons, both Protestant and Catholic.

History. The commonplace book had many antecedents, beginning with the theory of "places" derived from Aristotle, Cicero, and Quintilian, for whom commonplaces were both general themes of discourse and model procedures for arguing, dialectically and rhetorically, for the plausibility of a case. Medieval *florilegia* or collections of quotations, usually random, preceded them, as did highly organized and largely alphabetical dictionaries of quotations from religious sources, used as a resource for sermon rhetoric in the late Middle Ages. Italian humanists assembled phrases exemplifying correct Latin usage in order to inculcate a classical style of writing.

The characteristic format of the commonplace book, systematically collecting quotations under headings, was developed by northern humanists following the *De formando studio* (The foundations of study; 1484) of Rudolf Agricola and the *De copia* (Foundations of the abundant style; 1512) of Erasmus. The advice offered by Erasmus for making such a notebook, together with Philipp Melanchthon's *De rhetorica* (On rhetoric; 1519), proved more or less definitive. For the next hundred years and more, printed commonplace books proliferated, becoming larger and larger, as did instructions for making private ones.

The commonplace book was the most important learning aid in all schools. Almost all serious books were annotated and indexed by commonplaces. For example, Erasmus's collections of sayings and similitudes, not originally organized as commonplace books, were rearranged to fit the format. Vernacular commonplace books were at first printed as translations, but by approximately 1600 contemporary English literature was also being commonplaced. Only in the middle of the seventeenth century did the commonplace book lose its prestige as a premier knowledge organizer and production mechanism. Its decline coincided with the search for scientific truth, which replaced forms of reasoning based on plausibility with a new concept of authorship and of social discourse that did not favor ostentatious displays of secondhand quotations.

The more wide ranging effects of the commonplace book include a verbal style combining aphorisms, virtuoso display of rhetorical argumentation and ornament, and allusions to a common stock of literary quotations. They produced a cultural elitism that tended to exclude those outside the Latin school, in particular most women. They demonstrated a shift to written repositories of knowledge, sidelining techniques for memorizing. Above all, the commonplace book maintained a common culture across Western Europe that was resistant to religious divisions, as well as an intellectual conservatism, because it assumed that any new book could be digested into preestablished categories. At the same time, commonplace books manifested an openness and a degree of scepticism, because no category was considered closed, and the quotations could always be augmented, made mutually contradictory, and moved across categories or cross-referenced to destabilize the apparently unmoveable headings meant to contain them. In many ways, commonplace books organized and reflected Renaissance thought.

See also **Classical Scholarship**; **Education**; **Rhetoric**.

BIBLIOGRAPHY

Primary Works
The most frequently reprinted commonplace books for school use were *Marci Tullii Ciceronis sententiae illustriores.* (Quotations from Cicero and others), edited by Petrus Lagnerius (Paris, 1546), and *Illustrium poetarum flores* (Quotations from poets), edited by Octavianus Mirandula (Strasbourg, 1538).

Secondary Works
Goyet, Francis. *Le Sublime du 'lieu commun': L'invention rhétorique dans l'Antiquité et à la Renaissance.* Paris, 1996. History of commonplaces and their use in rhetoric.
Moss, Ann. *Printed Commonplace Books and the Structuring of Renaissance Thought.* Oxford, 1996.

ANN MOSS

COMMUNICATION AND TRANSPORTATION.

During the Renaissance merchants, governments, and other corporate entities depended on the regular flow of information and goods, much as they had in earlier times.

Communication. The Hanseatic trading cities, located in northern Germany and other German settlements in northern Europe, had set up regular courier services among their members in the thirteenth century, and those services continued in the

A Mode of Transportation. A type of litter carried by horses in front and behind, in use during the fourteenth and fifteenth centuries. From Octave Uzanne, *La locomotion à travers l'histoire et les moeurs* (1900).

Renaissance. The trading network of Venice was sustained by couriers who formed a link between the Christian and Islamic worlds. By 1400 universities also ran their own services to carry letters for students and faculty. Edward IV of England (ruled 1471–1483) established stages to supply fresh horses to couriers along the road to Scotland. The first national postal system was supposedly established by Louis XI of France (ruled 1461–1483). Ferdinand of Aragon (ruled 1479–1516) and Isabel of Castile (ruled 1474–1504) also established a postal service for their combined realms.

Perhaps the most famous courier service in Renaissance times was established and run by the Habsburg dynasty to link their widespread possessions. Organized for Emperor Maximilian I (ruled 1493–1519) by Robert, first count of Thurn und Taxis, the imperial postal service became a source of state revenue and a model for other governments. Emperor Charles V (ruled 1519–1556) bestowed the title postmaster of the empire on the count of Thurn und Taxis. The imperial system connected the centers of Habsburg power in Spain, the Netherlands, the Germanies, and Italy with one another and with their allies and rivals. The Vatican postal service complemented the Habsburg network, especially during the reign of Philip II of Spain (1556–1598), when Rome arguably became the most important nexus of communications in Europe. The royal post in France was reorganized in 1560 but fell into disarray during the subsequent religious wars; it was reorganized again in the late 1590s to more lasting effect. Table 1 shows reported travel times between various European and Near Eastern cities. Despite the inevitable delays and often unreliable timetables, couriers provided a crucial network of communications for businesses, governments, corporate bodies, and private persons.

Travel. People traveled in the Renaissance for a variety of reasons besides the famous voyages of global exploration and trade. Business, politics, and diplomacy probably accounted for most travel. Ships, merchant caravans, and farmers' carts moved the goods that fueled the growing consumer economy of the Renaissance, and the itinerant peddlar was a frequent sight in the countryside, even in quite remote villages. Private business and the regular exchange of diplomatic missions added to the traffic by land and sea.

Religious pilgrimages. Apart from commercial and official travel, religious pilgrimages enjoyed great popularity, though their roots lay in much earlier traditions. Within the Christian community, the most revered pilgrimage sites included Jerusalem, Rome, Santiago de Compostela in Spain, and Canterbury in England. As the number of pilgrims grew, governments often tried to regulate their numbers by issuing passports, restricting travel to a limited number of ports, and controlling the movement of currency. With the advent of the printing press, guidebooks were written to advise pilgrims about every detail for a successful journey. A round-trip from central Germany to Jerusalem could be made in less than six months in the late fifteenth century, including numerous side trips and stopovers. Typical pilgrims were less concerned with speed, however, than with the spiritual benefits to be gained from the journey itself. Rome attracted a huge number of pilgrims in the Renaissance, thanks to the appeal of both Christian and ancient artifacts. After 1550, guidebooks to Rome were available not only in Latin, but also in Italian, German, French, Spanish, and Flemish, and the yearly total of visitors to the seat of western Christendom may have exceeded 500,000.

Recreational travel. Wealthy young men in the Renaissance traveled to complete their educational and cultural development, often with an eye to a career in government service back home. Visits to spas for health cures were also popular, and many obscure towns developed a lucrative tourist industry based on the supposedly curative powers of their local hot springs. Not surprisingly, the travel narrative became a popular literary genre in the Renaissance, similar to earlier pilgrimage reports but broader in the range and detail of information included.

Modes of Travel and Transport. During the Renaissance people relied on land and sea for transport and travel. Although the majority of men and women traveled by foot, class created some distinctions in terms of the way people traveled. Overland travel was hindered by poor road conditions in Europe throughout the Renaissance. Sea travel expanded significantly during the Renaissance, particularly in Europe, where shipbuilders created a wide variety of ships for the transport of goods and people.

Land. On land, people traveled mostly by foot or in the saddle before the seventeenth century, though the wealthy or infirm might use a sedan chair or a litter to ease the discomfort and strain of the journey. Horses were associated with elite transport, and mules or asses with the lower orders. Some elite travelers, though, preferred a fine-paced mule, and people of all sorts might hitch a ride on a cart or wagon carrying goods to market. Roads were notoriously bad throughout Europe, especially during the winter season, when many of them became impassable to wheeled traffic. Couriers could obtain fresh mounts at staged intervals on the official routes, but the most experienced couriers also knew how to improvise, especially if their pay depended on speed. Under most circumstances, a rider supplied with a change of horses around every twelve miles could travel approximately from thirty-five to fifty miles a day. Fast couriers could travel seventy-five miles or more a day in extraordinary circumstances. Private couriers were generally more flexible and sometimes faster than the official services and were used by governments as well as private parties. Overall, the speed of overland travel hardly changed from medieval times to the late eighteenth century.

Commercial goods might be carried by pack animals, carts, or wagons of various designs, depending on the terrain and the roads. Coaches designed especially for passenger travel were evidently first developed in Hungary in the early fifteenth century, and they slowly spread to wherever conditions made them feasible. Early passenger coaches were simply heavy wagons pulled by two or more pair of horses. A front-turning train became common on sixteenth-century coaches, which could carry eight or more persons and their luggage on established passenger routes. Lighter and smaller coaches suspended on

TABLE 1. Travel Times and Distances in Renaissance Europe and the Mediterranean World

From	To	Approximate Travel Time	Direct Distance miles (kilometers)
General Travel in Europe and the Mediterranean World			
	Europe	Per day by horse	25–35 (40–56)
	Europe	Per hour on foot	2.5–4 (4–7)
Dover (England)	Calais (France)	5 hours–2 days	50 (80)
Alexandria	Rosetta	1 day by donkey	35 (55)
Constantinople	Negropont	8 days by sea	330 (530)
Jerusalem	Jaffa	3 days	34 (55)
Trebizond	Tarsus	12–13 days by horse	425 (680)
Overland Horseback Courier Travel in Europe			
	Europe	Per day on horse	37–50 (60–80
Brussels	Granada	15 days	1,018 (1,642)
Brussels	Innsbruck	5–7 days	404 (651)
Brussels	Lyon	4 days	352 (567)
Brussels	Paris	44 hours	162 (262)
Brussels	Toledo (Spain)	12 days	856 (1,381)
	England	Per hour by law	5 (8)
London	Berwick	60 hours (by law)	300 (485)
London	Carlisle	5 days	261 (421)
London	Dover	12 hours	72 (116)
London	Strasbourg	11 days	403 (650)
London	Blois	5 days	295 (495)
London	Calais	8 days	92 (149)
London	Paris	7 days	211 (341)
France	Italy	Per day	75–125 (120–200)
Lyon	Rome	10–12 days	464 (748)
Paris	Naples	21 days	802 (1,295)
Paris	Rome	14 days or more	687 (1,108)
Rome	Bologna	3–4 days	187 (302)
Rome	Florence	3–4 days	143 (231)
Rome	Genoa	6–7 days	248 (401)
Rome	Milan	7–8 days	295 (476)
Rome	Naples	3–4 days	117 (189)
Rome	Venice	2–5 days	245 (395)
Rome	Cracow	25–30 days	666 (1,075)
Rome	Lisbon	33–37 days by sea	1,156 (1,866)
Rome	London	25–30 days	890 (1,434)
Rome	Madrid	26 days	846 (1,365)
Rome	Prague	16–19 days	572 (922)
Rome	Vienna	12–15 days	474 (764)
Toledo (Spain)	Chartres (France)	12 days	660 (1,065)
Land and Sea Route Courier Travel in Europe			
Antwerp	Medina del Campo (near Valladolid, Spain)	14–50 days	795 (1,280)
Rome	Constantinople	40 days	300 (485)
Rome	Messina	12 days	303 (489)

TABLE 1. *(continued)*

From	To	Approximate Travel Time	Direct Distance miles (kilometers)
European Trade Travel			
Amsterdam	Rotterdam	12 hours by boat	35 (56)
Delft	Leyden	4 hours by boat	14 (23)
Delft	Rotterdam	2 hours by boat	9 (15)
Harlem	Leyden	3.5 hours by boat	19 (30)
Poole (England)	St. Malo (France)	4–14 days	145 (235)
Lyon	Netherlands	15–20 days	435 (700)
Rhône River	(downriver)	Per day	up to 56 (90)
Roanne	Tours	4–5 days	180 (295)
Saône River	(upriver)	Per day	9–16 (14–25)
North coast of Spain	Burgos	Per day	11 (17)
Trebizond	Tarsus	30–32 days	425 (680)
Pilgrimage Travel in the Mediterranean World			
Candia	Modon (Peloponnese Peninsula)	5 days by sea	120 (190)
Corfu	Venice	16 days in storms by sea	485 (780)
Cyprus	Rhodes	1 day by sea	355 (570)
Jaffa	Rhodes	25 days by sea	479 (773)
Mainz	Venice	15 days overland	370 (590)
Modon	Corfu	7 days by sea	175 (280)
Modon	Venice	20 days by sea	765 (1,230)
Rhodes	Alexandria	4 days in storm by sea	373 (601)
Rhodes	Candia	2 days by sea	250 (400)
Rhodes	Modon	8 days by sea	350 (570)
Rosetta	Fohar	23 hours by Nile riverboat	60 (96)
Venice	Jaffa	24 days by sea	1,185 (1,910)
Venice	Modon	18 days with stops	735 (1,185)

straps were also developed to provide a more comfortable ride. By the late sixteenth century private carriages came into fashion among the upper classes, especially in the major cities. In the seventeenth century coaches increasingly gained in popularity, but in the countryside they might still move slower than a traveler on foot due to poor road conditions.

Sea. Transport by sea also increased during the Renaissance, employing a variety of ship types and sizes, each suitable for specific purposes and routes. European ships ranged in size from tiny fishing vessels that could hold one man and his gear to enormous carracks of nearly two thousand tons carrying capacity that could transport close to one thousand persons. It is as difficult to estimate the duration of an average voyage from one point to another as it is to estimate the size and characteristics of an average ship; everything depended on the season, the weather, the tides, the port, the cargo, the crew, the passengers, and myriad other factors. The only useful generalization is that during the Renaissance, Europeans had an arsenal of ships that suited the needs of trade and transportation.

See also **Grand Tour; Pilgrimage; Travel and Travel Literature.**

BIBLIOGRAPHY

Allen, E. John B. *Post and Courier Service in the Diplomacy of Early Modern Europe.* The Hague, Netherlands, 1972.

Gardiner, Robert, ed. *The Age of the Galley: Mediterranean Oared Vessels since Pre-Classical Times.* Annapolis, Md., 1995.

Gardiner, Robert, ed. *Cogs, Caravels, and Galleons: The Sailing Ship, 1000–1650.* London and Annapolis, Md., 1994.

Lay, M. G. *Ways of the World: A History of the World's Roads and of the Vehicles That Used Them.* New Brunswick, N.J., 1992.

Stagl, Justin. *A History of Curiosity: The Theory of Travel, 1550–1800.* Chur, Switzerland, 1995.

CARLA RAHN PHILLIPS *and* PATRICIA J. D. KULISHECK

COMMYNES, PHILIPPE DE (c. 1447–1511), French writer and diplomat. Commynes (also spelled Comines or Commines) is best known as the author of *Mémoires,* a work of history and political theory that remained popular and influential throughout the early modern period. He was also a statesman who served three successive French kings—Louis XI, Charles VIII, and Louis XII—in varying capacities, although primarily as a skillful negotiator of both internal and foreign disputes.

Born into a noble family in Flanders, Commynes was brought up at the Burgundian court, eventually becoming a squire to the duke of Burgundy's son, Charles, comte de Charolais, in 1464. After Charolais succeeded as duke of Burgundy, he gave Commynes a number of ambassadorial assignments, including a mission to England to aid the Anglo-Burgundian alliance against France. He continued to serve Charles the Bold until 1472, when, in the dead of night, he defected to Louis XI's camp (although there is evidence that he was already in pay of the king of France by 1471). His change in allegiance brought immediate financial gain: he was awarded the estate of Talmont in 1472 and the following year married Hélène de Chambes and became seigneur d'Argenton. He remained a trusted adviser and diplomat throughout Louis XI's reign.

After the king's death in 1483, Commynes was briefly on the regency council of Charles VIII, but his participation in Louis d'Orléans's machinations against the Beaujeu resulted in his ouster and brief imprisonment. After Charles VIII reached his majority, Commynes was once again put to work in an ambassadorial capacity and sent to Venice at the beginning of Charles VIII's ill-conceived expedition into Italy in 1494–1495. After Charles VIII's death in 1498, Commynes's familiarity with the tortuous politics of the Italian peninsula was once again brought to bear in an unofficial capacity as an adviser to Louis XII.

Commynes is primarily remembered as the author of his famous *Mémoires* (written between 1489 and 1498; published in 1524 and 1528, with a full edition in 1552), the lively and informative account of Louis XI's reign. The *Mémoires* go beyond other contemporary chronicles in providing not only a narrative account of events but also a deeper analysis of historical causation. Commynes understood and at-tempted to explain the complex interplay of human motivations and opportunity that together resulted in historical change. He preceded Machiavelli in his appreciation of a ruler who knew how to turn every opportunity to his advantage, a trait Commynes greatly admired in Louis XI. Indeed, Commynes's positive portrait of the Spider King is at odds with almost every other contemporary account of Louis XI, which has led later writers and modern historians to question the usefulness of Commynes's reportage. However, the clarity of his prose, his attention to the telling detail, and his desire to extrapolate from particular circumstances general rules about political behavior ensured that the *Mémoires* would exert tremendous influence on early modern historians and political theorists. By the end of the sixteenth century, the *Mémoires* had been translated into Latin, Dutch, English, German, and Italian, in addition to the publication of at least fifteen French editions; it has been republished with remarkable regularity ever since. His fusion of pageantry and pragmatism firmly establish Commynes as a significant transitional figure between the medieval and the modern.

See also **Historiography, Renaissance,** *subentry on* **French Historiography.**

BIBLIOGRAPHY

Primary Work

Commynes, Philippe de. *Memoires: The Reign of Louis XI, 1461–83.* Translated by Michael Jones. Harmondsworth, U.K., 1972.

Secondary Works

Bittman, Karl. *Ludwig XI und Karl der Kühne: Die Memoiren des Philippe de Commynes als historische Quelle.* Göttingen, Germany, 1964.

Dreyer, Kenneth. "Commynes and Machiavelli: A Study in Parallelism," *Symposium* 5 (1951): 38–61.

Dufournet, Jean. *Études sur Philippe de Commynes.* Paris, 1975.

Dufournet, Jean. *Philippe de Commynes: Un historien à l'aube des temps modernes.* Brussels, 1994.

ADRIANNA E. BAKOS

COMPLUTENSIAN POLYGLOT BIBLE. The Complutensian Polyglot Bible was a magnificent, six-volume edition of the Hebrew scriptures and the New Testament in their original languages, together with the most important translated versions, printed between 1513 and 1517. The first volume featured the Hebrew Pentateuch along with the Greek Septuagint and the Latin Vulgate versions, as well as an Aramaic paraphrase known as the Targum of Onkelos and a Latin translation. The next three volumes presented the remainder of the Hebrew scriptures,

Complutensian Polyglot Bible. A page from the book of Exodus with the Hebrew text *(upper left),* the Latin Vulgate version of Jerome *(center),* the Greek Septuagint version *(upper right),* the Aramaic paraphrase called the Targum of Onkelos *(lower right),* and the Latin translation of the Aramaic paraphrase *(lower left).* The Bible was printed at Alcalá de Henares between 1514 and 1517. THE PIERPONT MORGAN LIBRARY/ART RESOURCE, NY

with Septuagint and Vulgate versions. The fifth volume offered the earliest printed edition of the Greek New Testament: printers completed work on it, before any of the other volumes, on 10 January 1514. However, the project's sponsors did not obtain papal permission to bind and distribute their work until 1520, so Erasmus's edition of 1516 was the first actually published. The sixth Complutensian volume was a Hebrew-Aramaic-Latin lexicon.

The Complutensian Polyglot Bible was sponsored by Cardinal Francisco Jiménez de Cisneros, archbishop of Toledo and primate of Spain. He founded the University of Alcalá (Complutum in Latin) near Madrid in 1500 to promote instruction in Hebrew, Greek, and Latin. After several years of planning, the university opened in 1508. Meanwhile, the cardinal decided to prepare a printed edition of the scriptures in their original languages, in hopes of encouraging moral reform throughout Christendom. He recruited Hebrew and Greek scholars to teach at the University of Alcalá and work on the project. Editing of the Hebrew scriptures fell largely to three Spanish scholars who were of Jewish ancestry and had converted to Christianity: Pablo Coronel, Alfonso the physician, and the esteemed Hebrew scholar Alfonso de Zamora. The young humanist Juan de Vergara, the prominent Greek scholar Hernán Núñez, and students at Alcalá probably contributed to the Septuagint text. The Greek text of the New Testament was edited by the Byzantine refugee Demetrius Ducas and the conservative cleric Diego López Zúñiga, commonly known as Stunica. The humanist scholar Elio Antonio de Nebrija also contributed to the editing of the Vulgate New Testament and perhaps of the Greek text of the New Testament as well.

From a philological point of view, the Complutensian Polyglot Bible offered conservative texts of the scriptures. Jiménez instructed the editors to present the standard texts, introducing emendations only when ancient manuscripts supported them. This principle was especially distasteful to Nebrija, who wanted to replace the Vulgate with a revised Latin translation of the New Testament. When Jiménez and his coeditors objected, Nebrija resigned from the editorial team. The text of the Greek New Testament was especially conservative: the editors consistently chose variant readings that agreed with the Vulgate and supported medieval Roman Catholic theology. At one passage (1 John 5:7) they consciously altered the Greek text to bring it in line with the Vulgate. While they did not prepare critically edited texts like those of Erasmus, the Complutensian editors provided a valuable collection of scriptural texts and translations that stimulated further biblical scholarship.

See also **Alcalá de Henares, University of; Bible,** subentries on **Printed Bibles** and **Texts and Textual Criticism; Jiménez de Cisneros, Francisco.**

BIBLIOGRAPHY

Bentley, Jerry H. *Humanists and Holy Writ: New Testament Scholarship in the Renaissance.* Princeton, N.J., 1983.

Bentley, Jerry H. "New Light on the Editing of the Complutensian New Testament." *Bibliothèque d'humanisme et Renaissance* 42 (1980): 145–156.

Revilla Rico, Mariano. *La políglota de Alcalá.* Madrid, 1917.

JERRY H. BENTLEY

COMUNEROS, REVOLT OF THE. The rebellion of the comuneros (Castilian cities), occurring in 1520–1521, is often called the *comunidades.*

Causes. Three proximate causes of discontent triggered the rebellion. First, despite questions about the revolt's legal basis, Charles of Habsburg (1500–1558) had been brought from the Low Countries late in 1517 to serve as joint ruler with his incapacitated mother, Queen Joan I (born 1479; ruled 1504–1555), usually designated "the Mad." Her father, King Ferdinand of Aragon (1452–1516), had been serving as Castilian regent until his death. When Charles's grandfather, the Holy Roman Emperor Maximilian I (1459–1519), died, the young king's advisers thought it wise for him to go quickly to Germany to be crowned as the Emperor Charles V, and this decision was upsetting to many Castilian leaders who worried that the monarch's departure would only make worse the political crisis that had undermined effective royal government since the death of Queen Isabella in 1504. Throughout much of the fifteenth century, territorial aristocrats had used violence and personal favoritism to obtain huge grants of jurisdictions, royal revenues, and lands, usually at the expense of municipal corporations, and judicial administration had often been corrupted. Thus weakened, Castile had been the victim of frequent civil war and intervention by its Iberian neighbors.

Second, prominent Castilians were alarmed to see high royal offices and major ecclesiastical benefices granted by the king to foreigners under the perceived influence of Charles's Flemish advisers, especially Guillaume de Croy, lord of Chièvres (1458–1521). The most scandalous of these appointments were that of Chièvres's young nephew of the same name (1500–1521) as archbishop of Toledo, Castilian primate, and of Adrian of Utrecht (later Pope Adrian VI; 1459–1523) as Castilian regent during

Charles's absence. Third, there were riots in several major cities when Charles extracted in April 1520 from the Cortes (Castile's representative assembly), meeting in the unaccustomed northwestern port city of La Coruña, approval of an extraordinary tax just before he embarked for northern Europe.

Course of the Revolt. On 6 June 1520 the municipal council of Toledo sent a circular letter to the other seventeen cities with the right to be represented in the Cortes to propose a meeting at which Charles would be petitioned to cancel the new tax, reserve offices and benefices for Castilians, forbid the export of any royal revenues, and appoint a Castilian as regent. Response was tepid and only four other cities were represented when the Junta (often "Santa," to indicate a blessed or virtuous character), as the assembly was known, opened discussions in Ávila at the beginning of August. However, when the regent's forces later that month attacked and burned the great commercial center of Medina del Campo, the rebel assembly was promptly supported by fourteen Cortes cities, and many other municipal governments embraced the cause. Thus strengthened, the comunero forces in support of local rebels entered the town of Tordesillas where Queen Joan lived under the watchful eyes of aristocratic guardians, and the Junta reassembled there to govern in conjunction with the monarch. Rebel attempts to negotiate with Charles's administration were frustrated by the regent's lack of legitimacy and Charles's distance from Castile.

By September an increasing number of rural villages had taken advantage of the cities' rebellion to rise against their seigneurial lords, and this development would aid the royal government in two ways. First, many of these lords were major territorial aristocrats who were estranged from a crown government they felt was improperly dominated by foreigners. Frightened by rural rebellion and soothed when Charles brought two leading magnates into the regency, aristocratic houses began to use their resources to build a more effective royal army. Second, the major municipalities and important ecclesiastical institutions, as corporate entities, were also seigneurial lords, and their governing councils often split over continuing their own rebellion in the face of this new threat. Within many comunero cities, plebeians either overthrew existing municipal councils dominated by locally prominent families, as in the southeastern city of Murcia, or these leading families felt increasingly threatened by the development of popular parish assemblies and engineered a turn to-

ward support for the regency, as in the important northern commercial center of Burgos in November.

Thus strengthened, the royal army took Tordesillas and regained control of Queen Joan on 5 December, forcing the comunero representatives who escaped to reassemble in Valladolid. Leaders of the great southern cities of Córdoba and Seville, who had avoided joining the rebel Junta, convened other Andalusian towns in late January 1521 and in early February established their own league against the comuneros. Its military position deteriorating, the main comunero force, under the leadership of the Toledan Juan de Padilla (1490–1521), one of the rebellion's most prominent figures, was defeated at Villalar on 23 April 1521, and Padilla and others were executed the next day.

A French invasion the following 10 May of the neighboring kingdom of Navarre, which Ferdinand of Aragon had only conquered in 1512 and annexed to the crown of Castile in 1515, prevented the regency government from acting aggressively to overcome the remaining comunero resistance. However, Murcia had returned to the fold by fall, and after an abortive uprising in early February 1522, Toledo was completely secure. Charles returned to Castile in July 1522, and on 1 November issued a generous pardon.

The Comunero Revolt was significant because it conditioned subsequent political developments and ideas. The tiny Castilian elite of territorial aristocrats and locally notable municipal patricians, who enjoyed a highly disproportionate share of the kingdom's resources, recognized the degree to which they depended on a stable, respected royal administration organized according to a model of absolute monarchy elaborated during the preceding century, and the ruler and his close officials understood that they must seek the support of these wealthy groups by governing in conjunction with them. Because many of its leaders were executed, were exiled, or lived under the terms of a royal pardon, it is hard to trace the rebellion's direct influence on ideas, but it was considerable as the central problems of community and government then debated continued to appear in print, circulated manuscripts, and public discourse. This is evident in the humanist dialogue *De motu Hispaniae* (The movement of Spain), written by Juan Maldonado (c. 1485–c. 1554) just after the events discussed, but the rebellion also forms a necessary context for an understanding of the moral, political, and economic thought of Iberian Scholastics from Francisco de Vitoria (c. 1483–1546) to Francisco Suárez (1548–1617), of the more practical treatises like those of Juan de Mariana (1535/36–1624) and the Castilian *arbitristas,* of the writings and council debates of municipal and royal officials, and of the intense parliamentary struggles until the mid-seventeenth century over the proper course for the global Hispanic monarchy.

Interpretation. For several centuries after the revolt, Castilian writers tended to present the rebellion as the sort that often took place when royal authority was somehow weakened, and different moral and political arguments were developed on that basis, but the revolt of the comuneros has been much analyzed for its significance to modern Spanish history. The rebellion's historiographical prominence is due to the importance given it by leading Spanish intellectuals of the nineteenth-century liberal constitutionalist and nationalist movements who sought domestic roots for their political position in the comuneros. They explained their country's perceived weakness and backwardness as a legacy of the rebellion's defeat by the House of Habsburg (1516–1700) and the subsequent baleful effects of foreign domination, bigoted fanaticism, and arbitrary royal absolutism.

The liberal and nationalist appreciation for the comuneros provided support for the impressive six-volume documentary collection Manuel Danvila published (*Historia crítica y documentada de las comunidades de Castilla;* 1897–1899). The first volume (*Idearium español*) had not appeared, however, before Angel Ganivet's attempt to capture the essence of Spanishness (1896) painted the comuneros as representatives of the old Castilian tendency to resist innovation from northern Europe, thereby preserving the country's backward ways and leaving it vulnerable to decline and defeat. Ganivet's approach often found echoes among intellectuals of the Generation of '98 (that is, 1898) who sought a regeneration of Spain from its humiliating defeat at the hands of the United States. At times, both camps have shown interest in possible connections to the revolt of religious heterodoxy or Inquisition persecution of conversos (Christians of Jewish origin), but nothing that would help explain the Comunero Revolt has been discovered.

The rebellion is the focus of three major studies, none available in English, that first appeared within a decade of each other and continue to define our understanding of these events. In 1963 José Antonio Maravall published a book to demonstrate that the rebellion's goals were informed by a coherent political program to limit the exercise of the monarch's absolute authority. Seven years later Joseph Pérez's

massive French dissertation, based on an extensive review of archival sources, embodied the most complete account of the rebellion available. Among Pérez's important discoveries is the great role played by preaching friars in generating support for the rebellion. Then Juan Ignacio Gutiérrez Nieto discussed in detail the role of antiseigneurial revolts in the genesis and course of the comunero rebellion.

Besides the differences in purpose and scope, these works offer conflicting interpretations. Maravall and Pérez establish the significance of the comuneros and their ideas by comparing them to the programs of later revolutions and their theoretical significance, giving to Spain pride of place as the home of the "first modern revolution" (to translate Maravall's subtitle). As such, the Comunero Revolt often plays a prominent role in the work of those historians who want to establish a major watershed between periods labeled "medieval" and "modern." In contrast, in his book and later work Gutiérrez Nieto has been concerned to discover what their ideas meant to the rebels who formulated and used them based on perspectives developed since the fourteenth century. Most of the subsequent work on the rebellion has concentrated on its local context but has not closed the division over how the events should be understood.

BIBLIOGRAPHY

Gutiérrez Nieto, Juan Ignacio. *Las comunidades como movimiento antiseñorial: La formación del bando realista en la guerra civil castellana de 1520–1521.* Barcelona, Spain, 1973.

Haliczer, Stephen. *The Comuneros of Castile: The Forging of a Revolution, 1475–1521.* Madison, Wis., 1981. Chiefly valuable for bringing to light sources about the decades prior to the revolt and for making extensive use of the major earlier studies and of less-disseminated works like doctoral dissertations.

Maravall, José Antonio. *Las comunidades de Castilla: Una primera revolución moderna.* Madrid, 1963.

Owens, J. B. *Rebelión, monarquía y oligarquía murciana en la época de Carlos V.* Murcia, Spain, 1980.

Pérez, Joseph. *La révolution des "comunidades" de Castille (1520–1521).* Bordeaux, France, 1970.

Seaver, Henry Latimer. *The Great Revolt in Castile: A Study of the Comunero Movement of 1520–1521.* London, 1928. Reprint, New York, 1966. Still useful for English readers because it follows closely the major chronicles and uses the most important documents published in Danvila's collection.

J. B. OWENS

CONCILIARISM. Conciliarism is a theory that holds that a general council is the supreme authority in the Church. The roots of conciliarism are found in the writings of medieval canonists, as shown by

Brian Tierney. According to canonists the principle *prima sedes a nemine iudicatur* (the first see, Rome, is judged by no one) was to be set aside if the pope became a heretic. They extended the definition of heresy to include scandal, simony, and perseverance in schism. However, conciliarism was never a uniform system; conciliarists were divided into moderates—who would give the council superiority over the pope only in exceptional cases—and extremists—who would democratize the church's hierarchical structure.

During the western schism (1378–1417) conciliarism was advocated by Conrad of Gelnhausen (c. 1320–1390), Henry of Langenstein (1330–1397), Dietrich of Nieheim (c. 1340–1418), Pierre d'Ailly (1350–1420), and Jean Gerson (1363–1429), among others. They rejected extreme conciliarism, however, and did not deny the hierarchical structure of the Western Church. Still, the Western Schism provided conciliarism with a broad base, especially after the standard efforts to remove the rival popes brought no end to the schism.

With the convocation of the Council of Pisa (1409) a doctrine of the canonists was put into practice: in a state of emergency the convocation of a council devolves upon the cardinals (or the emperor, respectively). The Council of Pisa deposed the two rival popes, Gregory XII of Rome and Benedict XIII of Avignon, on the grounds of heresy and perseverance in schism. According to the council they were deposed because they opposed themselves to the doctrine of the one, holy, catholic Church. But Pisa did not bring about the unity of the Church. Instead, it complicated matters by electing a third pope, Alexander V, who was soon succeeded by John XXIII.

At the Council of Constance (1414–1418) conciliarist tendencies became powerful after the flight of John XXIII. On 6 April 1415 the decree *Haec sancta* was passed. It emphasized the superiority of the council on questions of faith, resolution of the schism, and reform of the Church. On 9 October 1417 the fathers of Constance tried to establish the council as a permanent institution of the Church. They decreed that the next council be convoked after five years, another after seven years, and then every ten years thereafter. At first the popes complied with the decree: Martin V (1417–1431) convoked the Council of Pavia-Siena (1423–1424), five years after the end of Constance. Seven years later he also convoked the Council of Basel (1431–1449).

However, the popes did not consider the decree *Haec sancta synodus* binding. That became obvious on 10 May 1418, when Martin V issued a prohibition against an appeal to a council. The fact that Martin V authorized an envoy to end the Council of Pavia-Siena confirms that he considered himself superior to the council. According to Martin V the pope's former position of primacy was reestablished once the schism ended.

At the Council of Basel conciliarism became more radical. On 16 May 1439 the council passed the so-called *Tres veritates* (three truths): that the council is superior to the pope; that the pope cannot dissolve, transfer, or adjourn the council; and that a violation of these truths is heresy. Also in 1439 the council deposed Pope Eugenius IV (1431–1447) and elected Felix V (1439–1449). The main representatives of conciliarism at Basel were Nicholas of Cusa (1401–1464), Nicholas de Tudeschis (1386–1445), John Stojkovich of Ragusa (c. 1390–1443), John Alfonsi Gonzalez of Segovia (1393–1458), and Thomas Ebendorfer (1388–1464). But with the deposition of Eugenius IV the fathers at Basel overestimated their power; the deposition was without effect, except in restricted areas. The faithful did not want a new schism. The efficacy of conciliarism was broken, and the schism begun by the Council of Basel ended in 1449.

In the course of the following decades conciliarism continued to lose influence but was still alive as proven by numerous appeals to the council (despite the bull *Execrabilis* [1460] of Pius II prohibiting such appeals), threats of calling councils, and attempts at holding a council. At the turn of the century conciliarist ideas were advocated by Filippo Decio (1454–1536), Giovanni Gozzadini (1477–1517), Jacques Almain (c. 1480–1515), John Major (1469–1550), and Matteo Ugonio (d. 1535). But the failure of the attempted council at Pisa in 1511 proved that conciliarism had only limited support within the church.

Conciliarism was strengthened by its connection to the concept of reform. The common opinion was that only a council had the power to bring about a reform of the church. These conceptions were revived during the Reformation. In 1518 the University of Paris appealed from the pope to a general council. Luther appealed to a council in 1518 and 1520. This was a tactical measure because according to him a council no longer had teaching authority. Pope Leo X (reigned 1513–1521) was dominated by fear of a council and therefore did not call one. The lingering effects of conciliarism were also obvious during the meeting of the imperial diet at Worms (1521). Only during the pontificate of Paul III (1534–1549) did the question of a council become a reality. Even in 1541 German bishops still referred to the decree *Frequens* from the Council of Constance. In 1545 the long awaited council took place. At the Council of Trent conciliarism became evident after the arrival of the French led by Cardinal Charles de Guise (1524–1574) and during the crisis of the council in 1562–1563. But it became obvious that conciliarism no longer had great influence. In fact, the Council of Trent led to a strengthening of papal authority since the popes themselves were charged with the implementation of reform decrees issued by the council.

After the Renaissance, conciliarism exercised some influence on Gallicanism and Jansenism in France and the theologians of the church in the Holy Roman Empire. Conciliarism was definitively rejected by the First Council of the Vatican (1870). There were echoes of conciliarism in the statement on the collegiality of bishops adopted at the Second Vatican Council (1962–1965).

See also **Basel, Council of; Constance, Council of; Florence, Council of; Lateran V, Council of; Trent, Council of.**

BIBLIOGRAPHY

Primary Works

Burns, James H., and Thomas M. Izbicki, eds. *Conciliarism and Papalism.* Cambridge, U.K., 1997. Contains translated selections from works of Tommaso de Vio (Cajetan), Jacques Almain, and John Major.

Crowder, Christopher M. D., ed. *Unity, Heresy, and Reform, 1378–1460: The Conciliar Response to the Great Schism.* London, 1977.

Spinka, Matthew, ed. *Advocates of Reform: From Wyclif to Erasmus.* Philadelphia, 1953. Contains translated selections from Henry of Langenstein, Jean Gerson, Dietrich of Nieheim, and John Major.

Secondary Works

Alberigo, Giuseppe. *Chiesa conciliare: Identità e significato del conciliarismo.* Brescia, Italy, 1981.

Bäumer, Remigius. *Nachwirkungen des konziliaren Gedankens in der Theologie und Kanonistik des frühen 16. Jahrhunderts.* Münster, Germany, 1971.

Landi, Aldo. *Concilio e papato nel Rinascimento (1449–1516): Un problema irrisolto.* Turin, Italy, 1997.

Sieben, Hermann J. *Traktate und Theorien zum Konzil: Von Beginn des grossen Schismas bis zum Vorabend der Reformation.* Frankfurt, 1984.

Tierney, Brian. *Foundations of the Conciliar Theory.* Cambridge, U.K., 1955. 3d ed., Cambridge, U.K., 1968.

REMIGIUS BÄUMER

Translated from German by Christin Merkel

CONCORDATS. Throughout the centuries, the church's supranational character has created day-to-day problems in its relations in individual states. Its claims to freedom have clashed with secular rulers' efforts to assert authority over both the persons and possessions of the clergy. To resolve these problems, compromises have been reached, sometimes tacit acknowledgments of the other party's rights, and at other times formal concordats, dealing with either general problems or particular issues. Between the Council of Constance (1414–1418) and the beginning of the Reformation various such settlements were reached, their form reflecting the balance of power (both ecclesiastical and political) between the papacy and the lay rulers of Christendom.

The Great Schism (1378–1417) had diminished papal power. Previously, powerful popes could lay down the law to kings; now weak popes had to salvage influence by negotiations with individual rulers. Between 1378 and 1414 the rivalries of contending papal claimants compelled them to seek assistance from lay rulers, whose price was the enhancement of their own power. Within the church, conciliar theory challenged the doctrines of papal supremacy. Four concordats after the Council of Constance between the papacy and Spain, France, Germany, and England reflected the need of the new universally accepted pope, Martin V (1417–1431), to define the relationship between the church's central government and national churches throughout Europe. The price of political acceptance was an acknowledgment of de facto limitations on his power. After the Council of Basel (1431–1449), the concordat with the German princes (1447) and the concordat of Vienna (1448) provided the political framework for restoring obedience to the pope.

Three of the 1418 concordats were seen as temporary (five-year) measures and were very similar. The fourth, with England, differed because many issues, such as appointments to benefices and appeals to Rome, were already regulated by English laws. Although Martin V waged a vigorous campaign to abrogate this legislation he had to accept its existence as the starting point in negotiations. In fact, kings were often more willing than their subjects to bargain with the papacy. In France, Gallican elements asserted greater claims to ecclesiastical freedom than did the king.

The Constance concordats with Spain, France, and Germany aimed, without success, to restrict the number of cardinals and lay down normal qualifications for appointment. Attempts were also made to prevent the appointment of close relatives of other cardinals. Most of the agreements dealt with ecclesiastical administration and the lay power in individual countries, papal taxation of the clergy, limitations on appeals to Rome, and appointments to major ecclesiastical offices. This last was crucial for church government, irrespective of theory, for if kings could appoint compliant men to high office, they could often disregard papal intervention in their lands. As kings, however, might be challenged from below by demands for free canonical election, they willingly cooperated with the papacy to set this aside, and the popes negotiated rights of appointment with them in return for support elsewhere. In the concordat of Gennazzano (1426), Pope Martin V conceded to the dauphin Charles three hundred nominations to benefices, although the latter had sought five hundred.

Political problems might destabilize the implementation of concordats. Nowhere was instability more marked than in France, which was involved in political as well as ecclesiastical disputes with the popes. Its adoption of the Council of Basel's reform decrees in the Pragmatic Sanction of Bourges (1438) as the law for the French church gave kings bargaining leverage in dealings with the papacy. Louis XI abolished the Pragmatic Sanction in 1461 and again in 1472, when a new concordat was agreed upon that clarified procedures for appointments. The Pragmatic Sanction was effectively resurrected in 1510 to try to rally Gallican support against the pope. Significantly, after the French victory at Marignano (1515), Francis I (1515–1547) could negotiate from strength, and by the concordat of Bologna (1516) the papacy effectively abandoned the French church to royal power. The king secured virtually free rights of nomination to major benefices, abrogating rights of free election, and by 1518 overcame the only real opposition to it, not from the pope but from the Parlement of Paris.

Particular circumstances affected the concessions to the lay power in individual countries. In 1452 Pope Nicholas V (1447–1455) granted generous rights on appointments to benefices to the duke of Savoy, confirmed by Leo X in 1515, probably in order to restore friendly relations between the papacy and Savoy, whose previous duke had been the Council of Basel's antipope. Innocent VIII's (1484–1492) indult to James III of Scotland (1460–1488) in 1487, by which he deferred provisions to major benefices for eight months to await royal recommendations, effectively left such appointments in royal hands. The motives for the papal concession are not clear, but at the time the pope was anxious for the goodwill of Scotland's ally France in Italian politics. Even without such formal grants other lay rulers, as in Spain, obtained concessions from the pope over appointments. This was the main issue in a concordat with Poland in 1519, which provided for an al-

ternation of months in presentations, although one with Portugal in 1516 dealt more with fiscal questions.

Only when the papacy possessed political power, as in Naples, did agreements operate in its favor. There the pope was both spiritual and temporal overlord, and where rival claimants to the throne were seeking papal goodwill, influence over the local church was a useful bargaining tool. An agreement between the clergy and their Aragonese king Alfonso I (1442–1458), ratified by Nicholas V in 1451, freed the church from various financial burdens and confirmed alienations of property to it, and a concordat between Innocent VIII and King Ferdinand I (1458–1494) in 1492 recognized rights of free election to benefices without royal assent, with the king accepting papal provisions. Such lay concessions to the church, and particularly to the papacy, were, however, exceptional. Generally the concordat system demonstrated decentralization of ecclesiastical power from the papacy to the lay rulers.

BIBLIOGRAPHY

Primary Works

Mercati, A., ed. *Raccolta di concordati su materie ecclesiastiche tra la Santa Sede e le autorità civili.* Vol. 1, *1098–1914.* Vatican City, 1954.

Theiner, Augustin. *Vetera monumenta hibernorum et scotorum historiam illustrantia.* Rome, 1864.

Secondary Works

Martin, Victor. *Les origines du gallicanisme.* Vol. 2. Paris, 1939.

Ourliac, Paul. "Le concordat de 1472: Étude sur les rapports de Louis XI et de Sixte IV." *Revue historique de droit français et étranger,* 4th ser., 21 (1942): 174–223 and 22 (1943): 117–154.

Thomson, John A. F. *Popes and Princes, 1417–1517.* London, 1980.

JOHN A. F. THOMSON

CONDOTTIERI. *See* **Mercenaries.**

CONFRATERNITIES. Known variously as *compagnie, confréries, guilds, Bruderschaften, scuole, casacce, cofradías, confrarias,* or *broederschappen,* confraternities were the primary organized expression of Catholic lay religious life from the thirteenth through the eighteenth centuries. They were strongest and most numerous in the Mediterranean area, where a common concern with social kinship ties transcended religious differences. There is evidence of Muslim confraternities active in Turkey, the Balkans, and the Levant; Jewish and Greek Orthodox confraternities in Venice; and Eastern Rite confraternities in the Ukraine.

The Work of a Confraternity. *The Works of Mercy: Visiting the Sick* by a follower of Domenico Ghirlandaio. Mural in the church of S. Martino dei Buonomini, Florence. SCALA/ART RESOURCE

At the heart of the confraternities' origins and periodic renewals in Catholic Europe was the desire of laypeople to live a regulated spiritual life, and the belief that salvation was secured collectively with a deliberately chosen group of spiritual kin. As with all corporate groups in the Renaissance, from this seed grew a multitude of activities connected by fluid notions of what it meant to be a Christian: regular communal worship, penitential exercises, civic shrines and processions, public instruction, moral policing, social charity, peacemaking, celebratory feasting, artistic, literary, and cultural patronage, and funerary rituals. These activities and the large memberships of confraternities brought political, economic, and social influence as well. Between 10 percent and 20 percent of urban adult males and females joined these groups, and a far higher percentage in rural areas and northern Europe where they often administered parish life. By their very ubiquity, confraternities defined the public face of the church for Christians of the Renaissance. Their

activities and character were shaped in turn by broader forces at work in Renaissance society that rendered the confraternities of 1600 quite different from those of 1400: the ennobling of old communal institutions, a politicization of piety, an approach to the Christianization of society that emphasized education, hierarchy, and obedience, and that subordinated those whose grasp of these was slight. In Protestant Europe, confraternities were suppressed on account of the thoroughly Catholic theology that animated their individual and collective activities. In Catholic Europe, the success of their cultic, charitable, and educational efforts made it inevitable that they would be drawn into the programs launched by reforming bishops and religious orders before and after the Council of Trent. It also ensured that they would play a fundamental part in lending religious legitimacy to, and organizing social charity for, the early modern state.

Origins and Corporate Life. Religious orders had long offered "letters of fraternity" that ex-

The Work of a Confraternity. *The Works of Mercy: Visiting Prisoners* by a follower of Domenico Ghirlandaio. Mural in the church of S. Martino dei Buonomini, Florence. SCALA/ART RESOURCE

tended auxiliary membership and spiritual benefits to far-flung supporters. Local fraternal groups emerged during the thirteenth century, sometimes in conjunction with devotional movements like the Flagellants of 1260 and the Bianchi of 1399, sometimes at the urging of a charismatic friar like Peter Martyr (c. 1205–1252), and sometimes promoted by mendicant orders generally. Their public vernacular worship, flagellant penitential exercises, and charitable and cultic activities were directed to civic peacemaking, but their heavy recruitment from the artisanal, mercantile, and professional classes meant that they identified most strongly with the popular commune in political struggles with noble and ecclesiastical overlords.

While the concept of kinship animated their corporate life and public activities, two models governed the size and scope of confraternities. The example of Christ's disciples inspired small and often secretive groups of a few dozen members oriented to penitential piety and mutual moral criticism. The

example of the holy community directed large groups of a few hundred members organized by neighborhood, quarter, occupation, or nationality. These met less often but more publicly and directed their piety to the needs of the community, writing vernacular songs for large worship services, leading public processions, and fulfilling the works of corporal and spiritual charity. Such charity was of two kinds: extensive aid schemes for members and their families when illness or death struck, and forms of public welfare such as burial of the poor, aid to prisoners or capital criminals, education of youth, or construction of hostels for pilgrims, abandoned children, the sick, and the dying.

Relations between confraternities and the clergy were mixed. Mendicant orders were particularly active as confraternal sponsors, and individual friars such as Peter Martyr, Vincent Ferrer (c. 1350–1419), and Bernardino of Siena (1380–1444) promoted them in their preaching campaigns. Some scholars have portrayed confraternities as "voluntary parishes" that challenged the local priest. Most of them certainly valued their autonomy as much as their Catholicism, but there are many examples of clergy and confraternities working cooperatively. On the whole, those in England and northern Europe were more often parochial in scope and function, being responsible for administration and maintenance of the parish church, charitable disbursements, mystery plays, and songs. Italian, Spanish, and French groups more often functioned apart from the parish, organizing themselves on the basis of sections of the city, occupations, nationality, social class, age, or devotions; these employed a spiritual director who was usually chosen from one of the mendicant orders.

Confraternal statutes established administrative structures, procedures for recruitment and discipline of members, mutual obligations, and spiritual exercises. These were written, or at least approved, by the lay membership. Administrative procedures followed contemporary guild conventions, with frequent turnover of officials, close auditing of elections and accounts, and restriction of office to male members. Recruitment and discipline followed the mendicant model. Nominees underwent a novitiate, a review of their character and social status, a vote before being accepted into the fraternity, and ongoing oversight of their moral and spiritual life. Violators of the strict behavioral codes set out in the statutes could be expelled. Members' mutual obligations covered the full range of temporal and spiritual needs for which one could expect the help of spiritual kin. By paying regular dues, members underwrote early forms of health and unemployment insurance, dowries, funerary processions and burial of members, and pensions for widows. Salvation was a collective concern, secured through indulgences, moral correction, requiem masses and anniversaries, and anticipated in annual feasts that celebrated the connections between living and dead members.

Piety, Patronage, and Charity. Confraternal piety adapted the regular devotional exercises of mendicant orders to the realities of lay life. Mental prayer and confession structured the individual's daily life, while weekly, monthly, and feast-day meetings brought members together for recitation of the Office of the Virgin, the Mass, mutual censure, sacramental confession and communion, and sermons presented by members or the confraternity's priest. Funerals and annual feasts commemorating the dead reminded members that their ultimate goal lay in securing the soul's passage to heaven. Although characteristically affective and imitative, con-

fraternal piety developed around two modes. Penitential groups oriented worship to the expiation of individual and collective sins through public and private flagellation, frequent confession and communion, private fasts, and public processions. Praising groups celebrated the mercies of Christ, the qualities of the Virgin Mary (to whom roughly one-third of European confraternities were dedicated), and the glories of the saints in works of music and drama that were performed publicly by members or professionals, often in conjunction with public religious services.

Since the arts were particularly appropriate vehicles for the public expression of affective piety, confraternities became significant cultural patrons. Italian *laude,* German *Geisslerlieder,* Spanish *cantigas,* and English carols were all examples of the vernacular monophonic and polyphonic hymns commissioned by confraternities. The simple rhyme schemes and affective lyrics of early hymns made them popular elements of confraternal worship and public processions, while later polyphonic versions provided models for the development of the oratorio and chorale. Similarly, English, German, and Italian confraternities were major patrons of the mystery plays that were the foundation of later secular dramatic traditions. Early confraternal commissions of music and drama were for works that could be performed by members of the brotherhood in corporate worship or public performance; as artwork became more technically complex, the confraternities employed professional musicians and actors.

Patronage of professional artists reached its highest point in confraternal shrines, oratories, and charitable institutions, particularly in Italy. Florence's Orsanmichele devoted considerable revenues to its lavish and richly decorated quarters in the city center, while competition between Venice's five leading confraternities, called *scuole grandi,* resulted in a series of elaborate structures built on the scale of urban palaces for the greater glory of the brotherhood and the state. The perpendicular Gothic parish churches built across England in the fifteenth century were underwritten by parish guilds. Altarpieces and frescoes adorned confraternal oratories, and when brothers issued from these spaces in procession, they bore a rich array of processional images and banners.

As these examples of charity, worship, artistic patronage, and processional activity demonstrate, Renaissance confraternities were seen by members and others alike as acting on behalf of the larger civic community. As new social challenges emerged in the fifteenth and sixteenth centuries, it was characteristically confraternities rather than civil governments, ecclesiastical structures, or guilds that first organized the lay charitable response. As the scale of these problems became clearer, these same authorities facilitated confraternal work with subsidies, tax exemptions, and legal privileges. The small loan pawnshops (*monti di pietà*) promoted by Italian Franciscan preachers were often put into operation by confraternities, as were the Dominican-inspired alms funds that secretly subsidized worthy families who had fallen on hard times but could not beg. After the emergence of venereal disease, the confraternal Company of Divine Love opened the first infirmaries for syphilitics in Genoa and Rome. Across Tuscany, Misericordia confraternities developed the ambulance service that still operates as a voluntary charitable activity; similarly named confraternities elsewhere in Europe undertook the burial of paupers. As demographic pressures increased across Europe, foundling homes and orphanages opened under confraternal administration to shelter abandoned infants and children. Similarly, in cities like Bologna, Turin, Rome, and Toledo, the new shelters that emerged during the mid-sixteenth century to house, educate, and discipline the poor employed confraternal administration and often incorporated existing confraternal institutions. With this aggressive charitable outreach, confraternities emerged as lay agents of the contemporary Catholic reform movement, acting with considerable autonomy and initiative. Both characteristics would be blunted by the Protestant Reformation and by the responses it set in motion at Rome and Trent.

Protestant Reformation. Wherever the Protestant cause was adopted, confraternities were part of the Catholic establishment marked for expropriation. English guilds were suppressed by Edward VI's government in 1547 and, despite some sporadic revivals under Mary Tudor, either disappeared entirely, metamorphosed into parish councils, or, in settlements once under an abbot's control, became the town government. Parallel suppressions in Ireland were less thorough, and some Dublin confraternities preserved Catholic worship, resources, and charitable activities into the seventeenth century. In German cities that embraced Lutheranism, confraternal resources were consigned to the Common Chest, and their ritual activities were suspended. Calvinist Emden allowed confraternities to continue providing some poor relief until the deacons of the Reformed Church took over charitable administra-

tion by the late sixteenth century. Apart from Dublin, the possible role of confraternities as a form of underground church in Protestant countries where substantial Catholic minorities continued worshiping secretly is yet to be studied systematically. The papacy certainly hoped for this subversive role of confraternities; in 1569, Pius V called on confraternities operating in Protestant territories to rent their properties to Catholics only, and to use the revenues in support of priests and missionaries.

The pretext for Protestant suppression was usually a charge of corruption directed against elaborate confraternal festive activities that, in England for example, could last two or three days. Erasmus derided them as "conventicles of Bacchus," and Luther criticized the twenty-one confraternities of Wittenberg for following a "swinish way of life." At the same time their fundamental purpose of helping Catholics secure salvation with indulgences, sacraments, requiems, and charitable works was hardly consonant with the Protestant creed of salvation by grace alone through faith. These theological differences have led many historians to ignore the confraternities when seeking the models for Protestant worship and congregational life. Yet there is hardly a single element of the "new" lay-oriented Protestant liturgies and Church Orders that does not have ample confraternal precedent: lay and/or vernacular preaching, vernacular hymnody, congregational autonomy, the power of discipline over members, the power to appoint and dismiss clergy. Historians of the Protestant Reformation have been curiously silent on this debt.

Catholic Reform. Ironically, these same elements were bled out of confraternities as the Catholic Reform found its clerical footing. Among the chief factors in this change were the development of uniform confraternities promoting particular devotions, the promotion of confraternities by new religious orders, the multiplication of parish confraternities and of archconfraternities, and the greater supervision of confraternities by bishops. Much of this was already under way by the late fifteenth century and became more pronounced after the Council of Trent.

The Brotherhood of the Rosary is an early example of uniform confraternities promoting particular devotions. Established around 1475 by Dominican Jacob Sprenger in Cologne to promote the devotion of the rosary, it recruited thousands of members throughout Germany, Italy, Portugal, and Spain. The main Brotherhood claimed an unsubstantiated membership of one million by the eve of the Reformation. The figure says as much about the undemanding na-

The Work of a Confraternity. Sixteenth-century votive tablet showing aid to plague victims at Sansepolcro. PINACOTECA COMUNALE, SANSEPOLCRO, ITALY/SCALA/ART RESOURCE, NY

ture of the confraternity as about the popularity of the devotion; by the late sixteenth century some local Rosary confraternities had a stronger corporate life, and more localized devotions. Eucharistic confraternities (Corpus Christi, Corpus Domini, SS. Sacramento) first emerged in the late fourteenth century but spread more deliberately across Europe in response to Protestant rejections of transubstantiation. They promoted eucharistic piety generally, sponsoring processions, advocating frequent communion, and assisting priests in the distribution of communion to the sick. Finally, Companies of Christian Doctrine developed during the mid-sixteenth century to undertake catechetical instruction of children and youths.

These confraternities functioned primarily as the lay agents of devotions or activities promoted by the regular or secular clergy. Some of the new orders of the sixteenth century had their origins in confraternities, as for instance the Theatines that arose out of the Company of Divine Love. Others, chiefly the Jesuits, used confraternities extensively both in their charitable and educational work, and as a means of recruitment into the order. In such cases, the orders themselves prescribed the statutes, establishing the group's devotional activities and removing its traditional independence from clerical authority. The same occurred at the level of the parish. Reforming bishops like Carlo Borromeo of Milan promoted networks of lay confraternities throughout their dioceses, but stipulated that these be under the authority of the parish priest, and that they promote the educational, charitable, and devotional aims of the bishop. The Council of Trent in session 22 (1562) established the supervisory authority of bishops over confraternal administration, worship, and charitable institutions, and empowered them to visit and require annual audits. So many confraternities resisted this that Clement VIII issued the bull *Quaecumque* (1604) confirming full episcopal control. Finally, from the 1530s, popes had encouraged centralization and uniformity through the creation of archconfraternities. These were primarily Roman confraternities endowed with special spiritual privileges and indulgences that could be shared through a process of affiliation. Confraternities affiliating with the arch-confraternity gained access to its spiritual treasury in return for fees and an agreement to follow the exercises and rules of the parent group. Rome's Holy Spirit in Sassia received 170 international affiliations through the sixteenth century, Holy Trinity 100, and others like Saint Roch and Holy Crucifix had more than 30.

Confraternities and the Catholic State.

Interference by the state also limited confraternal autonomy and reshaped charitable activities. Catholic rulers, like their Protestant counterparts, could redirect confraternal revenues for social purposes. Duke Cosimo I Medici suppressed one of Florence's wealthiest confraternities, the Company of the Bigallo, in 1542 and attached its name and revenues to a state magistracy charged with hospital administration. Acting with papal approval, Philip II of Spain (ruled 1556–1598) consolidated the eighty-nine charitable hospitals of Seville into two large institutions in 1587. More commonly, patricians moved into the charitable confraternities and effected similar consolidations and rationalizations from within. In Genoa, members of the Company of Divine Love designed a civic relief scheme in 1539 and established subordinate confraternities that ran shelters for syphilitics, orphaned boys, and abandoned girls. In Turin, the Company of St. Paul (1563) came to control the *monti di pietà,* conservatories for abandoned girls and reformed prostitutes, and to participate in administering the hostel for the poor; its function as a semiofficial almoner gave it such financial resources that it metamorphosed by the twentieth century into one of Italy's largest banks.

But beyond charity, piety itself was politicized through the sixteenth century. This is seen most overtly in the Wars of Religion in France. In the 1560s, local confraternities mobilized to defend the fabric and rituals of the church against the Huguenots in their midst, with arms if necessary. By the 1580s Catholics were turning on each other, as both Henry III and leaders of the Holy League competed by establishing networks of flagellant companies to demonstrate their personal piety and promote their policies. Finally, in the 1590s, confraternities of the Holy Name of Jesus were established to maintain order in Paris and Orléans, stirring reaction by League and church officials alike when they assumed more autonomy and authority than their sponsors had wished to grant them.

A more subtle politicization developed across Europe as patricians took a leading role in those confraternities with significant charitable or cultic functions. By sponsoring masses, dowries, infirmaries, pensions, ornamentation, rituals, and building campaigns for shrines, oratories, and hospitals, local patricians made their piety and their patronage public. Whether rooted in personal generosity, or in manipulation of existing confraternal resources, this patronage offered numerous benefits. Charitable patronage strengthened client relations, while religious or cultic patronage offered prestige and legitimacy. Both consolidated patrician group identity and offered leverage in negotiations with higher ecclesiastical and political authorities.

By 1600, confraternities had lost much of their earlier practical autonomy, were more socially stratified, and had become agencies for the implementation of goals established by state and church officials. In this new form, they multiplied rapidly across Europe as agents of the new Catholic social order. When that order was challenged in the late eighteenth century, confraternities were again expropriated and suppressed. Yet their ritual, social kinship, and mutual assistance influenced the newer fraternal lodges of the Enlightenment. As in the Protestant Reformation, the social forms of confraternal organization remained compelling even when the theological content was rejected.

See also **Hospitals and Asylums; Poverty and Charity; Religious Piety.**

BIBLIOGRAPHY

Bainbridge, Virginia R. *Gilds in the Medieval Countryside: Social and Religious Change in Cambridgeshire, c. 1350–1558.* Suffolk, U.K., and Rochester, N.Y., 1996.

Barnes, Andrew. *The Social Dimension of Piety: Associative Life and Devotional Change in the Penitent Confraternities of Marseilles (1499–1792).* New York, 1994.

Black, Christopher. *Italian Confraternities in the Sixteenth Century.* Cambridge, U.K., 1989.

Bowen, William, ed. *Confraternities in the Renaissance.* Special issue of *Renaissance and Reformation/Renaissance et Réform.* N.S. 13, no. 1 (1989).

Donnelly, John P., ed. *Confraternities and Catholic Reform in Italy, France, and Spain.* Kirksville, Mo., 1999.

Eisenbichler, Konrad, ed. *Crossing the Boundaries: Christian Piety and the Arts in Italian Medieval and Renaissance Confraternities.* Kalamazoo, Mich., 1991.

Flynn, Maureen. *Sacred Charity: Confraternities and Social Welfare in Spain 1400–1700.* Ithaca, N.Y., 1989.

Henderson, John. *Piety and Charity in Late Medieval Florence.* Oxford, 1994.

Pullan, Brian. *Rich and Poor in Renaissance Venice: The Social Institutions of a Catholic State, to 1620.* Oxford, 1971.

Terpstra, Nicholas. *Lay Confraternities and Civic Religion in Renaissance Bologna.* Cambridge, U.K., 1995.

Terpstra, Nicholas, ed. *The Politics of Ritual Kinship: Confraternities and Social Order in Early Modern Italy.* Cambridge, U.K., 2000.

Weissman, Ronald F. E. *Ritual Brotherhood in Renaissance Florence.* New York, 1982.

Wilson, Blake. *Music and Merchants: The Laudesi Companies of Republican Florence.* Oxford, 1992.

Wisch, Barbara, and Diane Cole Ahl, eds. *Ritual, Spectacle, Image: Confraternities and the Visual Arts in the Italian Renaissance.* Cambridge, 2000.

NICHOLAS TERPSTRA

CONSTANCE, COUNCIL OF

CONSTANCE, COUNCIL OF (1414–1418). Considered to be the last great assembly of Western Christendom, the Council of Constance met to end the schism caused by three rival popes (Rome, Avignon, and Pisa), to condemn heresies in England and Bohemia, and to reform the Church.

Origins. The schism of the Western Church, which began with the election of an antipope on 20 September 1378, could not be resolved by the Council of Pisa (1409), which instead actually exacerbated the schism by electing a third "pope," Alexander V (d. 1410). The convocation of another council seemed to offer the only possibility to reunite the Western Church. On 9 December 1413 the successor of Alexander V, John XXIII, called for a council to meet in Constance on 1 November 1414. Since the followers of popes Gregory XII (Rome) and Benedict XIII (Avignon) were expected not to comply with the convocation, they were invited by the Roman king Sigismund.

The council lasted from 5 November 1414 to 22 April 1418. In its course twenty-nine cardinals, about 250 bishops, numerous abbots and members of orders, envoys of sovereigns, laymen, and above all hundreds of doctors of theology and canon law, participated. The latter formed the most influential group. At first only the followers of John XXIII were present, but after his resignation on 4 July 1415, the followers of Gregory XII came. During the summer of 1417 the followers of Benedict XIII (from Spain and Scotland) gradually joined the council.

Union, Heresy, and Reform. The council, under the influence of the French cardinals Guillaume Fillastre and Pierre d'Ailly as well as the important jurist-cardinal Francesco Zabarella and the chancellor of the Sorbonne, Jean Gerson, adopted unusual procedures (including changing the customary conciliar voting procedures to give more power to delegates from outside Italy and to lower-level clerics and even laymen) to reunite the church under a commonly accepted, legitimate pope. John XXIII, fearing coercive measures by Sigismund, fled Constance on the night of 19–20 March 1415. Even though he resigned under the pressure of the circumstances, the council deposed him on 29 May 1415. In contrast, Gregory XII resigned voluntarily on 4 July 1415 through his envoy, Prince Carlo Malatesta of Rimini. Benedict XIII agreed to resign only on condition that afterward an undoubtedly legitimate election of a pope would be held. But Sigismund and the council did not want to accept this condition, even though they gave evidence of farsightedness and of a sense of responsibility and could have met Benedict's requirements. The council therefore deposed him (on 26 July 1417) on charges of of heresy and obstinate schism. The problem of unity was solved on 11 November 1417 by the election of Cardinal Oddo Colonna, who took the name Martin V. The election was unanimous and was greeted by everyone with great relief.

From the beginning the council had also kept in mind a reunification with the Eastern Orthodox Church, from which various delegations came to Constance. No concrete results were reached, but union with the Greek Orthodox remained a concern of the Western Church throughout the conciliar period.

The council also addressed the heresy of the Oxford theologian John Wyclif (c. 1330–1384) and of those spreading his teaching in Prague, Jan Hus and Jerome of Prague. The council condemned Wyclif's teachings on 4 May 1415, and on 6 July 1415 condemned the positions of Hus together with more statements of Wyclif. Despite the efforts of the council, Hus did not retract his teachings and was burned at the stake the same day. Jerome of Prague suffered the same fate on 30 May 1416 after retracting an abjuration he had made on 23 September 1415. The refusals of Hus and Jerome to abjure is most easily explained by the influence of their strong followers in Prague. The protest movement of Prague also considered the reception of the eucharistic chalice—for the laity—as necessary for salvation. This position was condemned by the council in the sessions of 15 June 1415 and 15 June 1417 because it was not only opposed to the eucharistic doctrine of the church but showed a strictly literal biblical interpretation, thereby ignoring the living tradition of the church. The council considered the legitimacy of tyrannicide in the decree *Quilibet tyrannus* (6 July 1415) and repudiated the ideas of the Prussian Dominican friar Johannes Falkenberg, who in his *Satira* called for an extermination of the Polish people for the benefit of the Teutonic Knights.

Finally, the council was supposed to bring about a reform of the church in head and members. Despite initial demands for religious and ethical reform, as in *Capita agendorum* by Cardinal d'Ailly, the council ordered only a more equitable distribution of church revenues and reforms in legal and administrative practice. On the other hand, impulses toward reform of a mainly religious character successfully moved the orders, especially the Benedictines and the Franciscans.

The Problem of Conciliarism. The council's decrees *Haec sancta* (6 April 1415) and *Frequens* (9 October 1417) are commonly considered to be the Magna Carta of conciliarism. The former established the superiority of a council over the pope; the latter established the council as a "democratic" organ for controlling the pope by ordering the periodic convocation of future councils (the first in five years, the next in seven years, and from then on one every ten years).

But this theory overlooks the fact that *Haec sancta* was not intended to deal with the normal situation of the church. It can be argued that the document refers to the doubtful and therefore not obviously legitimate status of the schismatic popes, particularly as *Haec sancta* was adopted only by the followers of John XXIII and not by a truly general council. Furthermore, *Frequens* may be seen as intended to prevent further schisms. A council that meets only every ten years would not be sufficient as a supervisory assembly. Instead, the conciliarism of Constance showed an obvious tendency to restore the papacy after the schism. Nevertheless there were also radical tendencies striving to achieve a fundamental superiority of the council over the pope. Both tendencies could be reconciled by a double-sided pragmatism. This pragmatism allowed for the conciliarist ideas to remain significant for overcoming a schism but excluded them in the normal situation of the church. It can be argued as well that there was no deposition of a single pope at Constance since there was no legitimate pope who could have been deposed.

The Achievement of Constance. The Council of Constance can be considered a truly general council once the followers of Benedict XIII joined. The pope elected by this council approved its decrees implicitly by his bulls *Inter cunctas* and *In eminentis* of 22 February 1418, which differentiated among the decrees. This approval was limited to the decrees against the Bohemian heresy and did not include *Haec sancta* and *Quilibet tyrannus. Fre-*

quens can be viewed as not having required papal approval since it was decreed by the council during a time when there was no legitimate pope. Other scholars insist that all the decrees of Constance are valid.

The question of whether this council was a success is to be answered positively: the greatest success was the resolution of the schism. The problem of Hussite Bohemia could not be solved. A revolutionary movement, including wide sections of the population, evolved there, erupted violently, and expanded far into the West. The struggles over the distribution of church revenue (through benefices and the like) could be mainly quieted, but the council's focus on this goal can be seen as a serious deficiency of theological-spiritual power. The councils of the fifteenth century should not be considered "reform councils"; in each case the main concern was the unity of the church.

Constance proved to have a great importance for the contemporary cultural movement of the Renaissance and humanism: it constituted a forum of communication that involved all of Europe and the Christian East, bringing together the intellectual elite of that time in a cramped space for three years. Extensive intellectual exchange was made possible by literary creations and production of books by council members, which still needs to be explored in its volume and intensity. The Council of Constance was not only the largest but also the longest-lasting meeting of the leading elite of the Western world. It was the last great self-representation of medieval Christianity before its eventual decay.

See also **Basel, Council of; Christianity,** *subentry on* **The Western Church; Conciliarism; Florence, Council of; Lateran V, Council of; Papacy.**

BIBLIOGRAPHY

Primary Works

Acta Concilii Constanciensis. 4 vols. Edited by Heinrich Finke, Johannes Hollnsteiner, and Hermann Heimpel. Münster, Germany, 1896–1928. Reprint, Münster, 1976–1982.

Magnum oecumenicum Constantiense concilium. 6 vols. Edited by Hermann von der Hardt. Frankfurt and Leipzig, Germany, 1697–1700.

Sacrorum conciliorum nova et amplissima Collectio. Edited by Johannes Dominicus Mansi. Venice, 1759–1798. Reprint, Graz, Austria, 1960. See vols. 27 and 28.

Tanner, Norman P., ed. *Decrees of the Ecumenical Councils.* Vol. 1: *Nicaea to Lateran V.* London and Washington, D.C., 1990. Pages 403–451. Original text established by Giuseppe Alberigo et al. Texts of the conciliar decisions in the original languages with English translation.

Secondary Works

Brandmüller, Walter. *Das Konzil von Konstanz 1414–1418.* 2 vols. Paderborn, Germany, 1991; 1997. Includes a bibliography for 1993–1997.

Brandmüller, Walter. *Papst und Konzil im Grossen Schisma. Studien und Quellen.* Paderborn, Munich, Vienna, and Zurich, 1990.

Crowder, Christopher. *Unity, Heresy, and Reform, 1378–1460: The Conciliar Response to the Great Schism.* London, 1977. Reprint, Kingston, Ontario, Canada, 1987.

Frenken, Ansgar. *Die Erforschung des Konstanzer Konzils (1414–1418) in den letzten 100 Jahren.* Paderborn, Germany, 1993. See pages 421–491 for an exhaustive bibliography.

Loomis, Louise R. *The Council of Constance: The Unification of the Church.* Edited by John H. Mundy and Kennerly M. Woody. New York and London, 1961.

Mladenovic, Petrz. *John Hus at the Council of Constance.* Translated by Matthew Spinka. New York and London, 1966.

Sieben, Hermann Josef. *Die katholische Konzilsidee von der Reformation bis zur Aufklärung.* Paderborn, Germany, 1988.

Stump, Phillip H. *The Reforms of the Council of Constance (1414–1418).* Leiden, Netherlands, and New York, 1994.

WALTER BRANDMÜLLER

Translated from German by Christin Merkel

CONSTANTINOPLE, FALL OF

(29 May 1453). The Fall of Constantinople was an epochal event, marking the end of the medieval Greek empire of Byzantium and the coming of age of the Ottoman Empire. More than a thousand years earlier Constantine the Great had recognized the exquisite defensive position and strategic location of ancient Byzantium on a neck of land jutting into the Bosporus between Europe and Asia. He gave the city his name and remade it into the magnificent new Christian capital of the Roman Empire. At its fall the Byzantine Empire was just a petty Balkan state, but its disappearance inaugurated a 250-year period when the Ottomans pressed hard on central Europe, including laying siege several times to Vienna.

The Ottoman Turks emerged as a Balkan power in the fourteenth century after the breakup of the Seljuk sultanate in Asia Minor. In 1394 the Ottoman sultan Bayezid I (ruled 1389–1403) began what amounted to an eight-year blockade of Constantinople, which ended only when he was defeated and captured by the Mongol khan Tamerlane in the battle of Ankara in 1402. In 1422 the Ottoman sultan Murād II (ruled 1421–1443) unsuccessfully besieged Constantinople. When his brilliant young son Mehmed II (ruled 1451–1481) acceded to the throne he quickly determined to take the city. He prepared an army of well over one hundred thousand men, eighty thousand of whom were regular soldiers, and

Siege of Constantinople, 1422. The sultan Murād II besieged the city in 1422. Miniature from Bertrandon de la Broquière's *Voyage d'outremer* (1432–1433). Murād's son, Mehmet, captured the city in 1453. CLICHÉ BIBLIOTHÈQUE NATIONALE DE FRANCE, PARIS. RES B 120 1

to this he added a substantial battery of cannons. His naval forces amounted to over a hundred ships.

The Byzantine emperor Constantine XI Palaeologus (ruled 1449–1453) had at his disposal fewer than seven thousand regular soldiers, predominantly Greek, but including the contingent of seven hundred men brought by the Genoese warrior Giovanni Giustiniani Longo as well as ships and volunteers of the Venetian colony in Constantinople. Pope Nicholas V (reigned 1447–1455) attempted to organize aid and the Venetians sent a relief flotilla, but it failed to arrive in time. The West's largest relief effort had in fact come a decade earlier. In the wake of the union of the Greek and Latin churches at the Council of Florence in 1439, a crusading army led by King Ladislas III of Poland and Hungary invaded the Balkans in 1444 but suffered a catastrophic defeat at Varna at the hands of Murād II.

Mehmed II began the siege with a bombardment on 6 April 1453. Yet after nearly two months against overwhelming odds, Constantinople still held out. Finally, Mehmed decided on one last all-out attack on 29 May. Constantine XI died in the ensuing melee and his body was never recovered. Mehmed allowed his troops to pillage for three days, but then regularized the rule of his new capital city, including the appointment as the new Greek patriarch Gennadius George Scholarius, the leader of Greek opposition to union with the Roman Catholic Church.

The Fall of Constantinople evoked calls for a crusade among Christians in the following decades. But the crusade orchestrated by Pope Pius II (reigned 1458–1464) never materialized as he died at the Adriatic port of Ancona in 1464 while vainly waiting for the crusade fleet to gather. Rather, the Ottomans under Mehmed II continued on the offensive, seizing the Greek principalities of Mistra and Trebizond and Venetian Negroponte.

See also **Greek Émigrés**; **Ottoman Empire**.

BIBLIOGRAPHY

Primary Works

Melville Jones, J. R., trans. *The Seige of Constantinople 1453: Seven Contemporary Accounts.* Amsterdam, 1972.

Pertusi, Agostino, trans. *La caduta di Costantinopoli.* 2 vols. Edited by Antonio Carile. Rome and Milan, 1976.

Pertusi, Agostino, trans. *Testi inediti e poco noti sulla caduta di Costantinopoli.* Edited by Antonio Carile. Bologna, Italy, 1983.

Secondary Works

Nicol, Donald M. *The Last Centuries of Byzantium, 1261–1453.* 2d ed. Cambridge, U.K., 1993.

Runciman, Steven. *The Fall of Constantinople 1453.* Cambridge, U.K., 1965.

Vacalopoulos, Apostolos E. *Origins of the Greek Nation: The Byzantine Period, 1204–1461.* Translated by Ian Moles. New Brunswick, N.J., 1970.

JOHN MONFASANI

CONSTITUTIONALISM. The term "constitution," in the political sense used here, dates especially from the eighteenth century in connection with the American and French Constitutions, but the ideas of "constitution" and of "constitutionalism" are as old as Aristotle's *Politics*.

Constitutionalism is a philosophy of government opposed to tyranny, where the tyrant is seen as governing arbitrarily. Constitutional government by contrast, whether monarchical, aristocratic, or democratic, must be in accordance with law and established procedures, and thus predictable. Such governments are seen as functioning in accordance with a "constitution," which may or may not have taken the form of one specific instrument. It is only when a government is overthrown by revolution that it becomes necessary to provide a *written* constitution for the new government.

The Italian Renaissance, according to Jakob Burckhardt, was characterized by the rise of the tyrant or despot, whose state was a "work of art," an artificial creation rather than a product of tradition. Of course, Burckhardt also recognized that constitutional regimes continued to exist in such cities as Florence and Venice.

The "constitution" of the Florentine commune rested in the Ordinances of Justice drawn up in the 1290s. They excluded the nobility from the executive councils of the city and established what was called a government of the people. Similar developments established popular governments in other cities and towns. "Popular" should be understood as meaning "bourgeois" rather than "democratic."

Italy and Spain. The history of Florence, after the establishment of the Ordinances of Justice, was marked by frequent changes of regime, but the changes were always defended as returns to the principles of the Ordinances. Florentines appealed to the Ordinances as Americans to their Constitution. Periodically amended, the Ordinances continued to serve as what we would call the constitution of Florence for three centuries, and justify our referring to Florence as a republic until, in the sixteenth century, members of the Medici family finally took the title of duke.

During the fourteenth century, Florentines praised their government for defending their liberties against outside enemies, but within the ideology of Guelfism, which assumed that liberty rested on an alignment of cities with the papacy and with the kingdom of France. When in the later years of the century it became evident that this alignment no longer corresponded with political reality, a new ideology made its appearance.

This ideology was in the first instance the work of Leonardo Bruni (1370–1444). In his *Laudatio florentinae urbis* (Eulogy of Florence; c. 1405) he praised the city not only for its buildings and culture, but specifically for the form (constitution) of its government. Using the language of Cicero, he described Florence as a republic. With the knowledge gained from his reading of Greek philosophers and historians he came to see Florence as a republican city-state, engaged like the cities of ancient Greece in a struggle to maintain their liberty and independence. Both in his rhetorical works and in his *Historiarum florentini populi* (History of the Florentine republic), completed in 1415, Bruni offered a justification of what had become a territorial state, which he saw at least in his early works as the heir to the ancient Roman republic and destined to play a comparable role in history.

The Medici who ruled Florence de facto from 1434 to 1494 did so while preserving the forms of the republic. They nevertheless came to be seen as tyrants, and when they were overthrown in 1494, Florentines spoke of the restoration of the republic. Based on a newly created Great Council of 1,500 citizens (a third of whom were convened at a time), it was more widely representative than any previous Florentine regime. The new republic (1494–1512), however, was not strong enough to resist Spanish conquest of the peninsula. Serving it from 1498 until its demise in 1512, Niccolò Machiavelli subsequently analyzed the weaknesses of the Florentine constitution in *The Prince,* completed in 1513, and other works. He considered that the establishment of a durable government would always require the creative and forceful act of a prince. Once established, it could become a constitutional regime, preferably (for Machiavelli) a government of the people.

The overthrow of existing regimes in Italy by the invading French and Spanish during the Wars of Italy (1494–1512) prompted numerous writers to devote thought to the ideal constitution. The republican ideas that emerged in seventeenth-century England and eighteenth-century France and America have been shown to have their roots in the ideas of Machiavelli and the following generation of Italian political theorists. The survival of the Venetian republic until 1797 also aroused the attention of political theorists and prompted the conclusion that this republic's longevity could be explained by the fact that its government was not popular but oligarchic.

Constitutional limitations on monarchy were expressed in their most extreme form in the so-called Aragonese Oath, according to which the prospective king was addressed by his electors in the Cortes (the Aragonese parliament) as follows: "We who are worth as much as you and can do more than you, elect you as king upon such and such conditions. . . ." (Giesey, *If Not, Not,* p. 20).

France. In France the troubles of the sixteenth century prompted both abstract and historical analysis of the French "constitution." An early example is that of Claude de Seyssel (*La grand monarchie de France,* 1519). John Calvin, after admonishing his readers to obey the king, added toward the end of his *Institutes of the Christian Religion* (*Institutio religionis Christianae,* 1536) the caveat that in countries where Estates existed, it was their duty to offer constitutional resistance to kings when they became tyrants. After the outbreak of the wars of religion (1562), Calvin's successor, Théodore Béza, composed a treatise on the *Right of Magistrates* (*Du droit des magistrats sur leurs subiets,* 1574). François Hotman asserted in his *Francogallia* (1573) that the French monarchy had been balanced by the Estates from early times, and that failure to convene the Estates General between 1484 and 1560 was an example of tyranny. The author of the *Vindiciae contra Tyrannos* (An indictment of tyrants, 1579) maintained on theoretical grounds that government should be representative. In Germany, Johannes Althisius systematized in his *Politica* (1603) the doctrine of popular sovereignty resting on a social contract. On the other hand, Jean Bodin had famously maintained that sovereignty could not be divided, and so he laid down a theoretical foundation for absolutism (*Six livres de la République* [Six books of the commonwealth; 1576]).

Theoretical justification of the Estates lost its appeal to the Calvinist party in France when in the later years of the civil war their Catholic opponents gained control of the Estates, both provincial and general, and when Henry of Navarre, the erstwhile Calvinist leader, became heir to the throne in 1584 and subsequently King Henry IV (ruled 1589–1610). The Catholic League convened an assembly of the Estates General in 1593 and pressed the antimonarchical arguments recently advanced by the Calvinists to the point of asserting that the monarchy should be elective. Their candidate, the granddaughter of Henry II, was the Infanta of Spain.

The readiness of the Catholic League to put the interest of party above the interest of France led to the formation of a third party, the Politiques. Jurists and members of the Parlement of Paris were prominent within the ranks of this group, which placed the interests of the country above either religious party. The Politiques found justification for Henry IV's kingship in what they called the Fundamental Laws, the unwritten constitution that had served to maintain national integrity during the Hundred Years' War. The precise content of the Fundamental Laws was a matter of dispute, but one of them was very widely accepted: the Salic Law requiring that succession to the throne must be through the male line.

The Netherlands. During the Revolt of the Netherlands from Spanish rule (1568–1648), administration of the country fell into the hands of the States General, but they did not at first embrace a republican form of government. Instead, Netherlanders sought a ruler who would recognize their traditional privileges. They drew up articles of a contract first with Matthias of the House of Habsburg in 1577. When his regime failed, they turned in 1581 to the duke of Anjou, brother of the king of France. Negotiations with him broke down over his demand that they recognize his "sovereignty." Next they turned in 1585 to Queen Elizabeth I of England, who sent the earl of Leicester to serve as military commander. He went further and accepted the title of governor-general. This led, however, to contention with the States General.

Thomas Wilkes, an English member of the Council of State, wrote *A Remonstrance to the States General and the States of Holland* on 16 October 1587, in which he argued that Leicester's authority rested on the sovereignty of the common people, and not with their servants in the States. The response of the States General was written by François Vranck of Gouda and dated 16 October of the same year. He argued that

> if people declare that sovereignty of the provinces resides with the States, they are not speaking about private persons or delegates, but about the constituents, that is, the nobles and towns of the country whom the members of the States represent by virtue of their commission. . . . It is, we declare, certain that sovereignty of the country resides with the States and that the States are now no less sovereign than under the rule of the former princes. (Kossmann and Mellink, eds., pp. 274–281)

It was only after the failure of the efforts to borrow an acceptable ruler from Germany, France, and England that the Netherlanders found themselves by default under a republican form of government. Even so, they accepted the leadership of the House of Orange, except for a more "republican" interval between 1640 and 1680.

See also **Machiavelli, Niccolò,** *subentry on* **The Political Theorist; Representative Institutions; Wars of Italy; Wars of Religion.**

BIBLIOGRAPHY

Primary Works

Althusius, Johannes. *Politica methodice digesta.* Edited by C. J. Friedrich. Cambridge, Mass., 1932.

Bodin, Jean. *The Six Books of a Commonweale.* Edited by Kenneth Douglas McRae. Translated by Richard Knolles. Cambridge, Mass., 1962.

Bruni, Leonardo. *Historiarum florentini populi libri XII.* Edited by Emilio Santini, et al. Città di Castello, Italy, 1914. Translation by Renée Neu Watkins of books 1 and 12 and part of book 4 and the preface appears in *Humanism and Liberty: Writings from Fifteenth-Century Florence.* Columbia, S.C., 1978.

Bruni, Leonardo. *Laudatio florentinae urbis.* In *From Petrarch to Leonardo Bruni.* Edited by Hans Baron. Chicago, 1968. Pages 232–263. Translation by Benjamin G. Kohl as "Panegyric to the City of Florence," in *The Earthly Republic.* Edited by Benjamin G. Kohl and Ronald G. Witt. Philadelphia, 1978.

Burd, L. Arthur, ed. *Il Principe, by Niccolò Machiavelli.* Oxford, U.K., 1891.

Calvin, John. *On God and Political Duty.* Translated by John T. McNeill. 2d (rev.) ed. Edited and with an introduction by J. T. McNeill. New York, 1956. Passages from Calvin, particularly the chapter "On Civil Government" from the fourth book of his *Institutes of the Christian Religion.*

Franklin, Julian H., ed. and trans. *Constitutionalism and Resistance in the Sixteenth Century: Three Treatises by Hotman, Beza, and Mornay.* New York, 1969. Contains *Francogallia* (Hotman), *Du droit des magistrats sur leurs subjets* (Beza), and *Vindiciae contra tyrannos* (attributed to Philippe de Mornay).

Hooker, Richard. *The Laws of Ecclesiastical Polity.* In *The Works of That Learned and Judicious Divine, Mr. Richard Hooker.* Edited by R. W. Church and F. Paget. Vol. 3. Oxford, U.K., 1888.

Kossmann, Ernst H., and Albert F. Mellink, eds. *Texts concerning the Revolt of the Netherlands.* London and New York, 1974.

Secondary Works

Allen, J. W. *A History of Political Theory in the Sixteenth Century.* London, 1928.

Carlyle, R. W., and A. J. Carlyle. *A History of Medieval Political Theory in the West.* Vol. 6, *Political Theory from 1300 to 1600.* New York, 1936.

Church, William Farr. *Constitutional Thought in Sixteenth-Century France: A Study in the Evolution of Ideas.* Cambridge, Mass., 1941.

Giesey, Ralph E. *If Not, Not: The Oath of the Aragonese and the Legendary Laws of Sobrarbe.* Princeton, N.J., 1968.

Mesnard, P. *L'essor de la philosophie politique au seizième siècle.* Paris, 1936.

Reynolds, Beatrice. *Proponents of Limited Monarchy in Sixteenth-Century France: Francis Hotman and Jean Bodin.* New York, 1931.

Skinner, Quentin. *The Foundations of Modern Political Thought.* Vol. 1, *The Renaissance.* Cambridge, U.K., 1978.

Weill, Georges. *Les theories sur le pouvoir royal en France pendant les guerres de religion.* Paris, 1892.

GORDON GRIFFITHS

CONTARINI, GASPARO (1483–1542), Venetian statesman, ambassador, cardinal; author of philosophical and technological works. Contarini was born into a patrician Venetian family that prided itself on belonging to the most ancient nobility. His branch of the family was called della Madonna dell'Orto, after the church near the Contarini palazzo. After attending schools in Venice, he studied philosophy and theology at the University of Padua from 1501 to 1509, when the war of the League of Cambrai interrupted his leisurely progress toward the doctorate he never completed.

The years from 1509 until his entrance into public life in 1518, spent in Venice, were of great importance for Contarini's intellectual and religious development, as shown by a series of letters to his close friends Tommaso Giustiniani and Vincenzo Querini. Contarini experienced inner turmoil and went through a crisis in his search for the right vocation. Despite the urging of his two friends, who had joined the strict Camaldolese order, he decided to remain in the world and follow a career in the service of Venice. Almost at the same time as the young Martin Luther, Contarini embraced the idea of justification by faith in the merits of Christ, which he repeatedly affirmed in later years. But unlike Luther, he did not break with the Catholic church; to the contrary, he firmly accepted ecclesiastical and papal authority. His conviction that people can err but that the institution of the church was of divine origin is characteristic of his thought.

Career. Contarini's rise to political prominence began with his appointment as ambassador to the emperor Charles V in 1521. For four years he resided at the imperial court, learning about the administration of the vast Habsburg empire, gathering information about its economic and political life, and transmitting reports to the Venetian senate, as ambassadors were required to do. Contarini's meticulous dispatches include information about the rise of the Lutheran movement in Germany and news about the conquest of Mexico. He returned to Venice in 1525 as a seasoned and respected diplomat. From 1528 to 1530 he was ambassador to Pope Clement VII, whom he tried in vain to persuade to cede some possessions of the Papal States to the Venetians. Empowered to negotiate with both emperor and pope at their meeting in Bologna in the winter of 1529–1530, Contarini was instrumental in the conclusion of a treaty that brought a period of peace to Venice and Italy. Between 1530 and 1535 he was elected to ever-more responsible offices of the Venetian government, including that of head of the Council of Ten.

In May 1535 Contarini was appointed cardinal by Pope Paul III, the former cardinal Alessandro Farnese, who had formed a favorable idea of him during his embassy to Pope Clement VII. Contarini received holy orders and soon moved to Rome with his small

familia, or entourage of secretaries and servants, which was all his modest income could support.

In 1536 he was appointed president of a commission of prelates who in March 1537 made recommendations about reform of the clergy and the church to Pope Paul III. This outspoken report, titled "Consilium de emendanda ecclesia," established Contarini as a leading figure among a group of reform-minded men and a few women who were called Spirituali by their contemporaries. During the next four years Contarini was a prominent member of several commissions entrusted with reforming curial offices, including the datary, which collected a fee for affixing the date to papal documents. His most important appointment was as papal legate to the colloquy between Catholic and Protestant theologians who met in the spring of 1541 in conjunction with an imperial diet at Regensburg, Germany. Contarini was instrumental in bringing about a short-lived accord on the contested issue of justification that was rejected by both the pope and Luther. His last mission was as legate to Bologna, then a key city of the Papal States. He died there in August 1542.

Works. Contarini was a prolific writer throughout his life, although his collected works were published only posthumously. In 1517 he wrote a lengthy reply to his famous philosophy teacher in Padua, Pietro Pomponazzi, whose *De immortalitate animae* (On the immortality of the soul) had appeared the previous year. Also in 1517 Contarini wrote a second and more original treatise concerning the duties of the bishop, *De officio viri probi ac boni episcopi* (On the duty of the upright man and the good bishop), which presented his vision of how an ideal shepherd of souls should govern his diocese. This work is clear evidence that reform of the church occupied Contarini even before he began his public career. The period between his embassy to Spain and 1535 was one of considerable literary activity during which his most famous work was written, *De magistratibus et republica Venetorum* (On the magistracies and republic of the Venetians). It not only accurately described the structure of Venetian government but fixed the "myth of Venice" as the perfectly organized state in the European imagination. Contarini's continuing interest in philosophy is evident in his *Primae philosophiae compendium* (Compendium of first philosophy), while a more significant treatise of these years shows his concern with Reformation thought: *Confutatio articulorum seu quaestionum Lutheranorum* (A confutation of the articles or questions of the Lutherans), an attempt to answer Philipp Melanchthon's Augsburg Confession of 1530. A short piece in defense of papal power, *De potestate pontificis* (On the power of the pontiff), may have influenced the decision of Paul III to appoint Contarini to the cardinalate.

Between 1535 and 1542 Contarini wrote numerous short but significant tracts, including *De potestate pontificis in compositionibus epistola* (A letter on the power of the pontiff in compositions) and *De usu potestatis clavium* (On the use of the power of the keys), both of which argue against the arbitrary use of papal power. Contarini's last longer work was a treatise on the sacraments of the Catholic church. His nephew Alvise Contarini guided the publication of his *Opera* (Works) in Paris in 1571.

Contarini was a thorough Venetian and an outspoken proponent of church reform whose sympathy with Protestant ideas did not change his firm adherence to the Catholic church. He exemplified irenic prelates who hoped that the break in Christian unity was not final and believed that the moral and civic life had to be based on order in both church and state. Contarini was one of the most attractive figures among sixteenth-century Catholic churchmen.

BIBLIOGRAPHY

Primary Works

Contarini, Gasparo. *Regesten und Briefe des Cardinals Gasparo Contarini*. Edited by Franz Dittrich. Braunsberg (Braniewo) Poland, 1881.

Secondary Works

Dittrich, Franz. *Gasparo Contarini, 1483–1542: Eine Monographie*. Braunsberg, Poland, 1885. Still indispensable.

Fragnito, Gigliola. *Gasparo Contarini: Un magistrato veneziano al servizio della cristianità*. Florence, Italy, 1988. Collection of important articles.

Gleason, Elisabeth G. *Gasparo Contarini: Venice, Rome, and Reform*. Berkeley and Los Angeles, 1993.

ELISABETH G. GLEASON

CONVERSOS. From the late Middle Ages the term "conversos," originally used to designate converts to Christianity in general, came to be used in Spain and Portugal for Jews baptized as Roman Catholics, whether forcibly or willingly. Along with the term "New Christians" (*cristianos nuevos* in Spanish and *cristãos novos* in Portuguese), it remained in use in Iberia and the countries under Spanish and Portuguese dominion throughout the Renaissance and early modern periods, referring to descendants of the original converts, even those born as Christians for several generations. It also referred, although to a lesser extent, to Moriscos, forced converts from Islam after 1500.

The Roots of the Converso Problem in Iberia. In 1391 riots broke out against the Jews of Castile and Aragon, perpetrated by the urban lower class, incited by the minor clergy. The rioters condemned the Jews for alleged hatred of Christianity, which was expressed, among other ways, in economic exploitation of Christians. Many Jewish communities dwindled or completely disappeared following the murder of thousands of Jews and the forced conversion of many more thousands, who sought to save their lives by means of baptism. Although the kings of Castile and Aragon strongly opposed the forced conversion and repressed the rebellion, they demanded that the conversos honor the sacrament of baptism and remain loyal to their new religion.

The conversions affected every stratum of Jewish society, but the conversion of well-known figures, courtiers closely associated with the crown, was very conspicuous. The anti-Jewish campaign (1411–1412) of the Dominican friar Vicente Ferrer, the economic and social restrictions imposed on the Jews of Castile in 1412, and the Tortosa Disputation (1413–1414), in which, under pressure and intimidation, representatives of the Jews were forced to contend with the attacks of the convert Jerónimo de Santa Fe against the Talmud, all created a climate of despair and prompted many Jews to convert to Christianity. Among wealthy Jews the temptation was greater, for conversion opened avenues of social and economic advancement which were closed to Jews, but many conversos were motivated by inner conviction. Such was Rabbi Solomon Halevi, the rabbi of Burgos, who converted in 1390, changed his name to Pablo de Santa María, and was appointed bishop of his city. Other Jewish scholars took that path, becoming indefatigable champions of their new faith. On the other hand, for some of the conversos, influenced by the radical philosophical rationalism of Averroes (Ibn Rushd; 1126–1198), which was current among the Jewish social elite, baptism appears to have been an expression of disappointment with all religious faith. Their religious nihilism led them to adopt Christianity for reasons of personal security and social advantage.

Despite the differences in the circumstances and motivations for conversion, both forced and willing converts belonged to the same ethnic group. Their common origin left its mark on their consciousness and identity, and their particular social and cultural character was not easily effaced. The large number of conversos, their concentration in certain regions and neighborhoods, which were often former Jewish quarters, and their continued engagement in professions that had been typical of the Jews (such as commerce, banking, finance, and also medicine, regarded as a Jewish profession) made the social identification of the conversos easy, although their acculturation within Hispanic Christian society was impressive. At the same time, their conflicting religious outlooks often gave rise to considerable friction among them, especially between sincere Christians and those suspected of Judaizing. The Jews maintained some solidarity with those conversos who wished to keep some Jewish traditions in secret. Although most rabbis condemned the conversos as apostates according to Jewish law, Jews and conversos maintained contact through family ties and old friendships. Jews often assisted conversos in the practice of Jewish customs and traditions, supplying information and certain religious services.

Persecution of the Conversos.

Toward the middle of the fifteenth century open aversion toward the conversos began to emerge, mainly in Castile. In Toledo riots broke out against converso tax farmers and their influence in the municipal council. They were accused of secret loyalty to Judaism and of denying the basic tenets of Christianity. After an inquisitorial trial, several of them were executed. The leaders of the rebellion passed an ordinance denying the conversos any official function or position of authority in the city. This was the first purity of blood statute instituted in Iberia, and although the Toledo ordinance was rescinded within a short time, after the suppression of the riots, similar ordinances became common in Spain, and later in Portugal as well, barring people of Jewish and Muslim origin from institutions such as city councils, religious and military orders, and universities. This discriminatory policy gained new impetus after 1555–1556, when the archbishop of Toledo, Juan Martínez Siliceo (1486–1557), obtained royal and papal permission to institute a statute of *limpieza de sangre* (purity of blood), preventing New Christians from obtaining positions in the cathedral chapter of the city, lest they exploit their office to exercise Judaizing influence. Such laws served the interests of those within Spanish society who feared competition from the conversos.

After the Toledo incident in 1449, a heated public dispute arose in Castile, with the participation of several highly prominent churchmen whose Jewish origins were particularly in evidence. These men, including Pablo de Santa María's son, Alonso de Cartagena, defended the conversos' loyalty to Christianity and argued that most of them had joined the church in sincere faith.

At that time satirical writing flourished in Castile, emphasizing the New Christians' peculiar customs and their retention of certain Jewish observances and customs under the cover of Christianity, including the consumption of Jewish foods, affinity for commerce and finance, and hostility to Christianity and its symbols. Some of the satirical poets were themselves conversos. Many of their poems, which exacerbated the stereotype of the Judaizing convert, were collected in *Cancionero de Juan Alfonso de Baena*. Hostility to the conversos was also manifest in pejorative epithets. They were called *marranos* (pigs), *tornadizos* (turncoats, because they changed their identity for the sake of convenience), or even *alboraycos* (after Muhammad's legendary horse, which could not be classed among ordinary animals).

The problem of the conversos took a special turn because of the policies of the Catholic monarchs, Isabella of Castile (ruled 1474–1504) and Ferdinand of Aragon (ruled 1479–1516), whose marriage brought about the unification of the kingdoms in 1479. The converso problem became a central political issue for them, the solution of which was necessary for the political and religious unity of Spain. They implemented some of the far-reaching proposals offered by the Franciscan Alfonso de Espina in his anticonverso work *Fortalitium fidei* (Fortress of faith; 1460), establishing the Spanish Inquisition, first in Castile and then in Aragon. Trials against conversos suspected of Judaizing strengthened the impression that a considerable portion of them had not abandoned their old faith, legitimizing the idea that they had to be segregated from the Jews, who were responsible for their infidelity. Under pressure from the Inquisition, the Jews were expelled first from Andalusia in 1483 and then in 1492 from all the kingdoms of Spain because of their alleged Judaizing influence on the conversos. The Edict of Expulsion led to a new wave of conversions, for thousands of Jews preferred to become Christians rather than leave Spain. The Catholic monarchs' policy toward the conversos remained ambivalent: they regarded them with suspicion, but at the same time they tried to attract more Jews to the Christian religion, including the expellees, who were offered attractive conditions to return and convert to Christianity.

An estimated 100,000 expelled Jews went to Portugal, increasing the general population there by 10 percent. Manuel I (ruled 1495–1521) of Portugal, who wished to marry the daughter of the Spanish monarchs, was constrained to accept their condition, so in late 1496 he proclaimed the expulsion of the Jews from his kingdom. Within a few months Manuel changed his mind and declared that all the Jews of Portugal, including the deportees from Spain, must accept the sacrament of baptism. In this manner all the Jews of Portugal became conversos, and after the expulsion of the Jews of Navarre in 1498, no Jews remained in Iberia except conversos. Those of Portugal were quite homogenous with respect to their identity and affinity with Judaism, and the fact that Christianity had been imposed upon them from above preserved their Jewish identity both for themselves and for those around them.

Since the Portuguese Inquisition was not founded until 1536, the conversos there were able to consolidate their own ways of observing Jewish traditions and customs in secret, almost without interference. When the Portuguese Inquisition began its activities, it acted more harshly to the conversos than did the Spanish Inquisition, which meanwhile had ceased to focus on the heresy of the Judaizers and was paying more attention to the Moriscos and to people suspected of Protestant inclinations. Persecution of conversos resumed in Spain after the annexation of Portugal in 1580, which led to a mass immigration of conversos hoping to escape the Portuguese Inquisition. The presence of conversos in the Spanish and Portuguese colonies was also one of the reasons for the establishment of inquisitional tribunals in Goa (1560), Lima (1570), Mexico (1571), and in Cartagena, Colombia (1610).

The Conversos' Beliefs and Thought. Although historians disagree about the extent of Judaizing among the New Christians, there is no disagreement that the phenomenon existed. Although crypto-Judaism decreased in Spain toward the middle of the sixteenth century, it survived among the conversos in Portugal, many of whom migrated to Spain in the seventeenth century. Generally speaking, the religion of the Judaizers diverged from its Jewish source over the generations, both because of separation from the Jewish world and also because of the scrutiny of the Inquisition, which denied them access to written Jewish sources. Central to their religious views was the conviction that the Law of Moses grants salvation, indicating their skepticism regarding the redemptive power of the Christian church. Nevertheless they internalized Christian symbols and attached them to Jewish beliefs, creating their own syncretistic theology. They retained certain ceremonies on Sabbaths, holidays, and Jewish fast days, which they observed without connec-

tion to their official date, for they were unable to consult the Jewish calendar. Some conversos remembered Jewish prayers by heart, in Spanish or Portuguese translation, and many refrained from eating pork and other foods prohibited by Jewish law. Converso women played a central role in educating the younger generation to observe their special rituals.

There was a continuous trickle of emigration of conversos to the Spanish and Portuguese communities in the Ottoman Empire, North Africa, Italy, and Palestine. Conversos even established communities of their own in Ferrara, Ancona, Venice, Pisa, Livorno, and elsewhere. During the seventeenth and eighteenth centuries, converso emigrants who returned openly to Judaism founded communities in western Europe, in Amsterdam, Hamburg, London, Bordeaux, Bayonne, and on the American continent.

However, the Iberian conversos were not all of a piece either with regard to their religious affinities or to their general views. Most of them were assimilated within Christianity, but even those faithful to the Christian religion displayed certain signs of marginality deriving from their delicate situation as individuals who aroused opposition and resistance within Christian society. Their yearning for a spiritual and antiritualistic Christianity attracted them to the humanism associated with Desiderius Erasmus. Such were the Augustinian friar and poet Luis de León (1527–1591) and the greatest Erasmian thinker in Spain, Juan Luis Vives (1492–1540). Conversos were also prominent among innovative Spanish mystics like Juan de Ávila and the Carmelite Teresa of Ávila (1515–1582), as well as among the *alumbrados* (Illuminati) who claimed direct divine illumination. Almost all the Hebraists at the universities of Salamanca and Alcalá de Henares during the sixteenth century were descendants of conversos, as were some leaders of the Jesuit order, such as Diego Lainez and Juan de Polanco.

The presence of conversos in Iberian literature was also considerable. Their writing was sometimes melancholic in tone, expressing reservations about the establishment and a subversive attitude toward some dominant values such as honor and pure Christian lineage. Prominent among them were Fernando de Rojas as well as the creators of the picaresque novel, Francisco Delicado and Mateo Alemán, and the fathers of the Spanish theater, Juan del Encina (1469–1529) and Bartolomé de Torres Naharro (c. 1485–c. 1520).

Although the tendency of crypto-Judaism among the conversos was stronger in Portugal than in Spain, this did not prevent their acculturation or their participation in Portuguese intellectual creativity. The converso Bernardim Ribeiro (1482–1552) was one of the harbingers of the Portuguese sentimental novel. Some conversos there stood out in cosmography and cartography, and there, too, the great concentration of converso physicians reinforced the Jewish image of that profession. Their critical approach was also epitomized by skeptical thinkers such as Francisco Sanches, who emigrated to Toulouse, and even Uriel d'Acosta (c. 1585–1640), who returned to Judaism in Hamburg but was excommunicated there and in Amsterdam because of his criticism of rabbinical Judaism and his Epicureanism.

Conversos who returned to Judaism and their descendants during the seventeenth century played a critical role in skeptical and critical tendencies within the Sephardic communities of western Europe. Benedict de Spinoza himself was the son of conversos who returned to Judaism in Amsterdam, and he was raised in a community of former conversos. The return of conversos to Judaism in western Europe did not separate them from Iberian culture. In their new homes they continued to write in Spanish and Portuguese and established literary academies in the Iberian style.

See also Inquisition, *subentries on* Spanish Inquisition *and* Portuguese Inquisition.

BIBLIOGRAPHY

Alcalá, Angel, ed. *The Spanish Inquisition and the Inquisitorial Mind.* Boulder, Colo., 1987. A collection of articles mainly concerned with the world of the conversos in Spain in the Renaissance and early modern periods, concentrating among other things on the religious and literary creativity of those who were assimilated into Christian society.

Beinart, Haim. *Conversos on Trial: The Inquisition in Ciudad Real.* Translated by Yael Guiladi. Jerusalem, 1981. By describing the trials against Judaizers before one of the first tribunals of the Inquisition in Castile, the author brings out the beliefs and opinions of a converso community which retained a strong affinity with Judaism.

Gitlitz, David M. *Secrecy and Deceit: The Religion of the Crypto-Jews.* Philadelphia and Jerusalem, 1996. A description and analysis of the religion, beliefs, and customs of the conversos in Iberia from 1391 on. Also includes a detailed treatment of the historiographical dispute surrounding the question of the religious identity of the conversos.

Kaplan, Yosef. *From Christianity to Judaism: The Story of Isaac Orobio de Castro.* Translated by Raphael Loewe. Oxford, 1989. A monograph about a seventeenth-century crypto-Jew who emigrated from Iberia to Holland. The book sheds light on the religious and cultural life of the conversos during the seventeenth century and concentrates on the reasons that brought them to return to Judaism.

Netanyahu, Benzion. *The Origins of the Inquisition in Fifteenth-Century Spain.* New York, 1995. This work treats the conversos in Spain between 1391 and the expulsion of the Jews in 1492. The author is a prominent exponent of the historiographical approach that maintains that the vast majority of the conversos in the fifteenth century regarded themselves as loyal Christians.

Novinsky, Anita. *Cristãos novos na Bahia.* São Paulo, Brazil, 1972. A case study of a colony of conversos on the American continent, emphasizing the anti-Catholic character of their views, while at the same time they assimilated into the Iberian cultural milieu.

Pullan, Brian. *The Jews of Europe and the Inquisition of Venice, 1550–1670.* Oxford, 1983. Contains a comprehensive analysis of the phenomenon of the Iberian conversos, their identity, and their religious affinities, with detailed treatment of those who settled in Venice and were active there.

Révah, Israel S. "Les Marranes." *Revue des Études Juives* 118 (1959–1960): 29–77. A general presentation of the phenomenon of the conversos in Iberia, emphasizing the Jewish potential latent in their religious life.

Saraiva, Antonio José. *Inquisicã e Cristãos-Novos.* 3d ed. Porto, Portugal, 1969. Presents the thesis that most of the conversos in Portugal had severed all ties with their original religion after their conversion, and that the Inquisition was established as an instrument in the class struggle waged against them.

Yerushalmi, Yosef Hayim. *From Spanish Court to Italian Ghetto: Isaac Cardoso: A Study in Seventeenth-Century Marranism and Jewish Apologetics.* New York and London, 1971. A comprehensive monograph on the transition of a fascinating intellectual figure in the world of the conversos from Christianity to Judaism. The introduction includes a comprehensive analysis of the converso phenomenon, including its religious, social, and cultural manifestations.

YOSEF KAPLAN

COOKING. *See* **Food and Drink.**

COPERNICUS, NICOLAUS (1473–1543), Polish astronomer, cathedral canon, founder of modern astronomy. Copernicus was born 19 February 1473 at Toruń, Poland. Nicolaus lost his parents before he was twelve. He was then supported by his maternal uncle, Lucas Watzelrode, a priest, who attended to Nicolaus's education and who was made bishop of Varmia (Ermland) in 1489. He went to the cathedral school at Włocławek and in 1491 matriculated at the University of Cracow, where he studied under Albert of Brudzewo. Through his uncle's influence, Nicolaus was elected to the cathedral chapter of Frauenburg (Frombork), whose members received a benefice for life.

In 1496 he was sent by the chapter to the University of Bologna to study canon law. He also pursued studies in astronomy there under Domenicos Maria Novara and made his first recorded observation on 9 March 1497, that of the occultation, or covering from sight, of the star Aldebaran by the moon. Through Novara's influence, Copernicus was invited in 1499 to give one or more lectures in Rome on his ideas on astronomy. While there lecturing on mathematics, on 6 November 1500 he observed a lunar eclipse. By late July 1501 he had returned to Frauenburg for his formal installation as a canon there. He thereupon was given permission to return to Italy to study medicine at Padua for two years. Copernicus completed the doctorate of canon law from the University of Ferrara on 31 May 1503. Already qualified as a physician, he returned to Frauenburg some time between 1504 and 1506. There he remained for the rest of his life, making important discoveries in astronomy and also serving the administrative and economic needs of the cathedral chapter. He died at Frauenburg on 24 May 1543.

Astronomical Works.   Records of the chapter show that on 31 March 1513 Copernicus bought materials from the cathedral's workshops to build a roofless astronomical tower on which he situated three instruments. These were a device for measuring the moon's parallax, that is, changes in its apparent position that enable one to calculate its distance from earth; a quadrant for tracking the sun; and an astrolabe, or armillary sphere, for observing the stars. Quickly thereafter, before 1 May 1514, he completed the first draft of a new astronomical system that was to revolutionize astronomy.

The reigning theory from antiquity was the geocentric or "earth centered" system of Ptolemy, which located the Earth at the center of the universe, around which rotated all of the heavenly bodies in larger and larger circles that were approximately homocentric. The order of the circles was, first, the moon, then Mercury, Venus, the sun, Mars, Jupiter, Saturn, and last the sphere of the fixed stars. Copernicus proposed a radical alternative, a heliocentric, or "sun centered," system in which the sun replaced the Earth at the center of the universe, and the Earth was moved to the fourth sphere to take the place vacated by the sun. The draft was entitled *Commentariolus* (Little commentary), and a few copies were circulated among discreet friends. In this work Copernicus explicitly stated that the center of the Earth is not the center of the universe and that the rotation of the heavens is only apparent, since it is attributable to the Earth's daily rotation on its axis. Similarly, the apparent passage of the sun along the ecliptic is caused by the Earth's annual revolution around the sun, and the alternate direct and retrograde motions of the planets are merely reflections of Earth's orbital travel. There can be no doubt that Copernicus thought of Earth's twofold motion as physically real

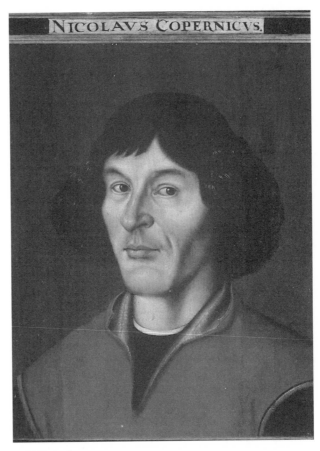

Nicolaus Copernicus. Anonymous portrait, 1575, in the museum at Toruń, Poland, Copernicus's birthplace. MUSEUM, TORUŃ, POLAND/ERICH LESSING/ART RESOURCE

and not merely a mathematical fiction useful for predicting the positions of the heavenly bodies as seen from Earth. In this, his position was clearly different from that expressed by Jean Buridan in the fourteenth century, who stated that for astronomers it was enough to assume a way of saving the appearances of the heavens, whether the motions assumed were real or not.

So profound were the implications of this new theory when taken realistically, and particularly its impact on scriptural teachings, that Copernicus pondered it for twenty-six years. A member of the Roman Curia, Cardinal Nikolaus von Schönberg, who apparently understood its import, suggested that Copernicus publish his discoveries. Tiedmann Giese, bishop of Kulm, urged their publication for many years as Copernicus's duty toward science and mankind. But the young Lutheran scholar Georg Rheticus finally prevailed on him, and Copernicus gave his manuscripts to Rheticus, allowing him to make a summary of their contents. Rheticus published the summary at Gdansk in 1540 as a "First Report" (*Narratio prima*) of their contents. In 1542 he then supervised at Nürnberg the publication of the trigonometric portion of the book, which was to appear the next year with the title *De revolutionibus orbium caelestium* (On the revolutions of the heavenly orbs; the "orbs" here refer not to the heavenly bodies themselves but to the spheres that carry them along or assist their motion).

Unable to complete the work when appointed professor at the University of Leipzig, Rheticus gave the remainder of *De revolutionibus* to an editor in Nürnberg who was favorable to a fictionalist view of scientific theories. The editor disregarded Copernicus's own commitment to realism, of which he had been informed in private correspondence. He suppressed the introduction Copernicus had planned and put in its place an unsigned preface written by Andreas Osiander (1498–1552), a Lutheran theologian. Osiander there disavowed any realist intention in the work, assuring the reader that it simply provided a means of calculating positions in the heavens that were consistent with observation but making no claim for their truth. The editor did include, however, Copernicus's dedication of the book to Pope Paul III in which he explained his reasons for making his discoveries public. The volume was finally published in 1543 and, according to one account, was presented to Copernicus on his deathbed.

The *De revolutionibus* is divided into six books. In many portions of these Copernicus's exposition parallels that of Ptolemy's *Almagest,* with appropriate adjustments made for the interchanged positions of the sun and the Earth. Book 1 is addressed to the general reader and gives a lucid and simplified account of the new world system, along with the philosophical grounds on which the account is based. The remaining books, 2 to 6, were written for professional astronomers. They give the rather complicated details of the system and are of the same grade of difficulty as the *Almagest* itself. They are not for the casual reader, but a brief summary of their contents may give some idea of the work as a whole.

In book 1 the fundamental principles are outlined, and these Copernicus reduces to seven axioms, which may be stated as follows: (1) there is no common center for all the heavenly circles or spheres; (2) the center of the Earth is not the center of the universe, but only a center of gravity and the lunar sphere; (3) all spheres rotate about the sun as their central point, and therefore the sun is the approximate center of the universe; (4) the distance of the Earth to the sun is negligible compared to that of the firmament, that is, the outermost sphere of stars that are "fixed" in constellations; (5) every movement observed in the firmament is caused by the motion of the Earth and not by that of the firmament; (6) what appears to us as movements of the sun are actually movements of the Earth, in diurnal rotation and yearly revolution; and (7) the apparent retrograde and direct motion of the planets is not due to their proper motions but to that of the Earth.

In chapter 10 of book 1 Copernicus then presents his revised sketch of the world system, numbering the spheres from one to seven. This begins with the outermost sphere of the fixed stars, which he presents as immovable, and it ends with the sun at the central point of the universe. The second sphere is that of Saturn, with a revolution around the sun of thirty years; the third is that of Jupiter, revolving in twelve years; the fourth is that of Mars, in two years; the fifth is that of Earth along with the moon, in a single year; the sixth that of Venus, in nine months; and the seventh that of Mercury, in eighty days.

Book 2 supplies the spherical trigonometry necessary to make calculations on the sphere of the heavens. Book 3 is the obverse of the third book of the *Almagest,* in which Ptolemy had given an account of Hipparchus's theory of the sun's motion; Copernicus here treats the motions of the Earth in a similar way. For him Earth is on an eccentric that itself moves on a very small epicycle around the sun, all moving at very slow angular velocities. Book 4 then gives Copernicus's account of the motions of the moon. This is geocentric, with the moon moving on a large epicycle around the Earth's center. Finally, books 5 and 6 provide the details of Copernicus's theory of the planets, which is much more complex, involving various combinations of eccentrics and epicycles of different sizes and varying angular velocities of rotation.

As can be seen from this account, eccentrics and epicycles were required in Copernicus's system just as they were in Ptolemy's. The difference is that Copernicus was able to reduce the total number of circles (eccentrics and epicycles) from fifty-five to thirty-four, mainly by eliminating the large epicycles that were used in the Ptolemaic system to explain the retrograde motions of the planets. It is often said that Copernicus greatly simplified the system of the world by making it heliocentric as opposed to geocentric. Some simplification was indeed achieved by doing this, but not as great as one might imagine, as can be seen by anyone who makes a comparative drawing of the two systems.

On its publication *De revolutionibus* was not a source of controversy, mainly because Osiander's unsigned preface was taken to have been written by Copernicus and thus as his disavowal of any realist intent. A Dominican at the Holy Office at Rome, Giovanni Tolosani, did express concern over the motion Copernicus was attributing to the Earth, and also over the sun's rest, but Tolosani died in 1549, and no censure was directed against the book. The problem did return, however, after Galileo's discoveries with the telescope, and in 1616 the Congregation of the Index forbade the reading of *De revolutionibus* "until corrected." Thereupon nine sentences in which Copernicus seemed to be offering demonstrations of the sun's rest or the Earth's motion were changed to have them read merely as hypothetical arguments. The complete removal of the work from the Index of Prohibited Books did not come, however, until 1758, when it disappeared from the revised Index issued in that year by Pope Benedict XIV.

Other Works. At Frauenburg Copernicus served as physician and personal secretary to his uncle; as a canon of the cathedral he took part in church services, and as a doctor he ministered to the needs of his clerical friends and to the poor. He was also chosen to be administrator of all church property in Ermland. In connection with the currency reform of Ermland and neighboring provinces in 1519, Copernicus wrote a treatise on coinage that antedates by forty years Sir Thomas Gresham's law of the behavior of debased currency. As administrator he compiled a sliding scale of ceiling prices for bread based on the varying local prices of grain. He also normalized the weights and measures throughout the area under his jurisdiction. His various writings about money survive in four versions, written at different times and on various occasions brought about by the changing political and military scene in Ermland and neighboring countries.

The *Commentariolus* and the *Letter against Werner* are Copernicus's minor astronomical works, the first of which has been discussed above. The second was a critical appraisal of an essay by a Catholic clergyman, Johann Werner (1468–1522), on the "Motion of the Eighth Sphere." In this Copernicus politely but firmly showed how Werner erred regarding the motion of the fixed stars and thus was maintaining an unsound position.

One of Copernicus's longer compositions was a Latin translation of eighty-five *Letters* of Theophylactus Simocatta, which had been published in Greek by Aldo Manuzio in 1499 and which fell into three categories: ethical, rustic, and erotic. Copernicus's translation was published in 1509. For him the work served a twofold purpose: it disseminated a code of conduct in the best tradition of Greek ethics, and, more importantly, it improved his knowledge of Greek so that he could work directly on Ptolemy's *Almagest,* which was not available at that time in Latin translation.

In addition, many administrative documents and seventeen letters came from Copernicus's pen. Extensive research was initiated on these materials on the fifth centenary of Copernicus's birth in 1973. In 1985 all the minor works became available in English translation, with full documentation, through the efforts of Edward Rosen and Erna Hilfstein.

Copernicus's accomplishments as a churchman, physician, economist, and administrator aside, his importance for the history of science can hardly be overestimated. The vastness of the mathematical problems he faced in formulating a workable heliocentric system required an unusual intellect. But in his case, that intellect was sustained by a moral heroism that, in humble pursuit of truth, dared to challenge a scientific tradition that had endured for two millennia. What is more, in his day this tradition was vigorously supported by the universal Church of which he was a loyal member. Copernicus's greatness did not consist in providing astronomers with new facts, for which he has been criticized by recent historians. Rather, in circumstances such as these, it consisted in his framing and elaborating a revolutionary theory in ways that were open to extensive development. That is why historians of science commonly date the Scientific Revolution as beginning in 1543, with the publication of *De revolutionibus,* and ending in 1687, with the publication of the *Principia* of Sir Isaac Newton. This places the Polish astronomer, and rightly so, in the company of Newton, along with Johannes Kepler and Galileo Galilei, as fathers of modern science.

See also **Astronomy**; **Ptolemy**.

BIBLIOGRAPHY

Primary Works
Rosen, Edward, trans. and ed. *Nicholas Copernicus on the Revolutions.* Baltimore and London, 1978.
Rosen, Edward, trans. and ed. *Three Copernican Treatises,* with an introduction by the editor. 3d ed. New York, 1971.
Rosen, Edward, and Erna Hilfstein, trans. and eds. *Nicholas Copernicus Minor Works.* Baltimore and London, 1985.

Secondary Works
Cohen, I. Bernard. *The Birth of a New Physics.* Revised and updated. New York and London, 1985.

Dijksterhuis, E. J. *The Mechanization of the World Picture: Pythagoras to Newton.* Translated by C. Dikshoorn. Foreword by D. J. Struik. Princeton, N. J., 1986.

Gingerich, Owen, ed. *The Nature of Scientific Discovery: A Symposium Commemorating the 500th Anniversary of the Birth of Nicholas Copernicus.* Washington, D.C., 1975.

Pedersen, Olaf. *Early Physics and Astronomy: A Historical Introduction.* Rev. ed. Cambridge, U.K., 1993. The best for technical details.

Westman, Robert S., ed. *The Copernican Achievement.* Berkeley, Los Angeles, and London, 1975.

WILLIAM A. WALLACE

COQUILLE, GUY

(1523–1603), French jurist and political thinker. Educated in Paris and Italy, Coquille settled in the Nivernais, where his family had originated. During the French Wars of Religion he was elected first magistrate of Nevers (1568) and then appointed attorney general of the duchy (1571). Having served as a delegate at the Estates General of Orléans (1560) and Blois (1576), he set about compiling a series of works on law and history, most notably *Institution au droit des François* (Elements of the law of the French; Paris, 1607), *Les coustomes du pays et duché de Nivernois* (Customs of the country and duchy of Nivernais; Paris, 1605), and his history of that same region, *Histoire du pays et duché de Nivernois* (Paris, 1612). In these discursive works, Coquille advocated two key propositions. First, he insisted that the rights and constitutional role of the feudal nobility were vital to the stability of France. Second, he distinguished between three categories of law and their origins: first, "perpetual laws," made at the Estates General and grounded upon the reciprocal relationship of king and people; second, customs, made by the people themselves, though authorized by the king; and third, general laws and ordinances, made by the king and published in sovereign courts, that had no specifically legislative power of their own. In Coquille's opinion, professional lawyers and royal officeholders in the France of his day were too numerous and too obtrusive, prompting kings to "command more absolutely" than was compatible with the principles he avowed. They were the principles of a constitutionalist, steeped in provincial traditions and out of sympathy with contemporary theorists of resistance and absolutism alike.

BIBLIOGRAPHY

Church, William Farr. *Constitutional Thought in Sixteenth-Century France: A Study in the Evolution of Ideas.* Cambridge, Mass., 1941.

Lloyd, Howell A. "Constitutionalism." In *The Cambridge History of Political Thought, 1450–1700.* Edited by J. H. Burns and Mark Goldie. Cambridge, U.K., 1991. Pages 254–297.

HOWELL A. LLOYD

CORNARO PISCOPIA, ELENA LUCREZIA

(1646–1684), Italian writer and scholar and the first female university graduate. Born into a prominent Venetian noble family, Cornaro Piscopia early manifested her learning and piety. She studied theology and philosophy privately and with tutors in Venice for many years. After performing brilliantly in a public disputation, a form of academic debate, in Venice on 30 May 1677, she asked, with her father's support, to be examined for the doctorate of theology from the University of Padua. Obtaining a degree by examination without attending university lectures was possible in the Italian university system. The archbishop of Padua, who served as chancellor of the university, objected but agreed that she might be examined for a doctorate of philosophy. Hence, the

Elena Lucrezia Cornaro Piscopia.

College of Doctors of Arts and Medicine examined her; she discussed issues based on Aristotle's *Posterior Analytics* and *Physics,* the required logical and philosophical texts. The college voted unanimously in her favor, and she received the doctorate of philosophy on 25 June 1678. But she did not establish a precedent. A Paduan professor immediately asked if his daughter might be examined for the doctorate of philosophy, but she was rebuffed.

A large statue of Cornaro Piscopia in the entrance of the main university building in Padua commemorates her accomplishment. She represents the highest educational achievement of a woman in the Renaissance, but also the limits imposed by society. The next female university graduate was Laura Bassi (1711–1778), a highborn Bolognese woman, who obtained a doctorate of philosophy from the University of Bologna on 12 May 1732 and taught at the university from 1732 to 1738. She was the first woman to teach at a university.

BIBLIOGRAPHY

Fusco, Nicola. *Elena Lucrezia Cornaro Piscopia 1646–1684.* Pittsburgh, Pa., 1975. Contains an English translation of the Latin diploma.

Maschietto, Francesco Ludovico. *Elena Lucrezia Cornaro Piscopia (1646–1684): Prima donna laureata nel mondo.* Padua, Italy, 1978. The basic source with documents.

PAUL F. GRENDLER

CORNER, CATERINA (Cornaro in Tuscan; c. 1454–1510), queen of Cyprus and proprietor of Asolo. Born into one of the oldest Venetian families, the Corner, Caterina descended on her mother's side from the Comnenos, emperors of Trebizond, on the Black Sea (1204–1461). In 1472 she married James II of Cyprus, natural son of the last Lusignan king. James had usurped the throne and was heavily indebted to the Corner family, who had large holdings on the island. A few days after the wedding James died and Caterina was left regent for a child yet unborn, who was to die one year later.

Throughout her reign, Caterina was enmeshed in a web of machinations and conspiracies spun by the local aristocrats, Italian princes, the pope, and the Genoese, as well as the Mamluks of Egypt, whose vassals the Lusignans had become. Venice intended to annex Cyprus and use it as an outpost against the expansion of the Ottoman Turks. The annexation occurred in 1489, when Caterina ceded the island to the republic in exchange for the sovereignty of Asolo, a hill town in Venetian-ruled northern Italy.

As the nominal lady of Asolo, Caterina instituted administrative and judicial reforms, establishing a

Caterina Corner. Anonymous portrait in the Museo Civico, Asolo, Italy. AKG LONDON/CAMERAPHOTO

new post of treasurer, a high court of appeal, and a pawnbroker institution. She commissioned a baptismal font for the cathedral and an altarpiece for the church of San Martino. For herself she built Villa Barca, and Villa dall'Aglio for Fiammetta, her favorite maid-in-waiting. Caterina was memorialized by Pietro Bembo's *Gli Asolani,* a work that depicted the conversations on love entertained by men and women of the Asolo court. She contributed significantly to the establishment of an aristocratic ideal of learning, worldly wisdom, and social elegance.

BIBLIOGRAPHY

Hunt, David, and Iro Hunt, eds. *Caterina Cornaro, Queen of Cyprus.* London, 1989. Includes contributions by Peters W. Edbury, Joachim G. Joachim, and Terence Mullaly.

Robbert, Louise Buenger. "Caterina Corner, Queen of Cyprus." In *Female Scholars: A Tradition of Learned Women before 1800.* Edited by J. R. Brink. Montreal, 1980. Pages 24–35.

RINALDINA RUSSELL

CORREGGIO (Antonio Allegri da Correggio; 1489/94–1534), Lombard painter. Correggio was one of the most influential artists of his generation, despite a relatively short career. Pervasive visual illusionism and psychological directness characterize his mature work, dating from 1518–1519 until his death in 1534. Correggio's figures are often powerful in physique, boldly foreshortened, and posed in dynamic *contrapposto* (counterposition, or "weight shift"), yet their eloquent gestures and sweetness of expression, rendered by a subtle use of value and sensual application of color, result in images of immense emotional appeal. Correggio is best known for frescoes that visually transcend their architectural settings as well as paintings that revivified the traditional formula of Renaissance altarpieces in Italy.

Biography. Apart from Giorgio Vasari's profile in his *Lives of the Artists* (1550; 2d ed. 1568), documentary evidence about the artist is scant, and precise information about Correggio's biography, artistic training, early work, and commissions is subject to debate. The artist died in his native town of Correggio on 5 March 1534; his birthdate has been variously calculated between 1489 and 1494. Modern scholarship favors the earlier birthdate and postulates that Correggio received his initial artistic training from his uncle, Lorenzo Allegri (d. 1527), believed to have been a local painter. Other aspects of his formal training remain unknown, although artists as diverse as Andrea Mantegna, the Modenese painter Francesco Bianchi de' Ferrari, and Francesco Raibolini of Bologna, better known as Francia, have been forwarded as possible teachers.

Whatever the specifics of his workshop experience and early career, it is clear that Correggio's style developed on a matrix of artistic principles nascent in fifteenth-century Lombard illusionism, particularly as practiced by Andrea Mantegna in Mantua, linked with a concern for compositional unity based on light and color found in Leonardo da Vinci's Milanese works. The influence of Raphael and Michelangelo is also evident in Correggio's artistic evolution and has led scholars since the eighteenth century to suggest that Correggio may have visited Rome, notwithstanding the absence of written documentation for such a trip and Vasari's assertion to the contrary. The presence of works by Raphael and Michelangelo in northern Italy as well as the increased availability and dissemination of drawings and engravings during this period may account for the influence of these Renaissance masters on Correggio's artistic thinking.

Early Career. Correggio's career is generally divided into two parts. Paintings created prior to the artist's arrival in Parma, c. 1518–1519, are considered early works, although few are signed or well documented. Two late-twentieth-century discoveries—

the appearance of Correggio's name in notarial records from 1512 concerning Andrea Mantegna's son, Francesco, and the attribution of two panels representing *David Before the Ark of the Covenant* (Turin, private collection), commissioned by the abbey of San Benedetto Po in 1514—confirm a long-standing tradition placing Correggio in Mantua within the circle of Mantegna and attest to Correggio's involvement with both Gonzaga and Benedictine patronage at an early point in his career. Correggio's name has also been connected with the decoration of Mantegna's funerary chapel in the Benedictine church of Sant' Andrea in Mantua, as well as two, much damaged, roundel frescoes (Museo Diocesano, Mantua), originally located in the atrium of the same church.

Only two securely documented works survive from this early period. Both are altarpieces painted for the artist's native town: the *Madonna of St. Francis* (Gemäldegalerie, Dresden) commissioned for the high altar of S. Francesco in August 1514, and the *Four Saints Altarpiece* (Metropolitan Museum, New York; c. 1514–1517), associated with the church of Santa Maria Verberator. Passages of subtle modeling in color and the delicacy of facial expression in these paintings anticipate qualities that characterize Correggio's later work. As manifestations of the artist's thinking, both altarpieces demonstrate Correggio's rapid assimilation and synthesis of significant pictorial trends in early-sixteenth-century Italy.

Parma. Correggio's arrival in Parma is perceived as coincident with the advent of his mature style, initiating a prolific decade during which he worked on a number of commissions simultaneously. A ceiling decoration painted c. 1518–1519, for Abbess Giovanna da Piacenza at the Benedictine monastery of San Paolo, is acknowledged as Correggio's first significant fresco commission in Parma. Within the private apartment of the abbess, Correggio's frescoes transform a small chamber into a fictive pergola, a verdant gazebo open to the sky, where the goddess Diana presides over a collection of classically inspired statues, accompanied by rambunctious putti, nude infants inspired by ancient Roman art, who playfully threaten to spill into the interior from the roof. The illusionistic structuring of space in this small chamber known as the "camera di San Paolo" became a hallmark of the artist's subsequent fresco work in Parma.

San Giovanni Evangelista. Documents dating from July 1520 through January 1524 detail Correggio's activity at the neighboring Benedictine monastery of San Giovanni Evangelista. This extensive

Correggio. *Madonna with St. Sebastian.* GEMÄLDEGALERIE, DRESDEN, GERMANY/ALINARI/ART RESOURCE, NY

commission included frescoes in the nave, cupola, choir, and apse, as well as a charming lunette depicting St. John above the door connecting church and cloister. Although the sequence of their execution is debated, Correggio's frescoes brought visual unity to the vast church interior, punctuating the visitor's experience of the building. Moreover, Correggio's iconographic and stylistic treatment of standard Christian narrative was inventive. Approaching the celebrated cupola frescoes, spectators are summoned by Christ, who descends earthward in a golden aura of light; only after shifting position does the viewer become privy to the *Vision of Saint John on Patmos,* as described in the Book of Revelation.

Beyond the cupola, Correggio's apse frescoes presented the *Coronation of the Virgin* as a timeless event, witnessed in the presence of several carefully selected saints: John the Baptist is paired with St. Benedict adjacent to Christ on the right while John the Evangelist appears on the left with St. John, first abbot of the church. Correggio's original work was destroyed in 1587 when the choir was extended but was soon replaced with a full-scale copy by Cesare Aretusi. A central fragment representing Christ and Mary (Galleria Nazionale) and its sinopia underdrawing (Biblioteca Palatina) are preserved in Parma; three smaller fragments exist in London (National Gallery). Correggio's innovative decorative scheme for the Del Bono chapel, with its paired lateral paintings of the unusual *Martyrdom of Four Saints* and dramatic *Lamentation* (both Galleria Nazionale, Parma), was widely adapted by the end of the century.

Cathedral of Parma and other works.

Instantaneous recognition of Correggio's achievement at San Giovanni Evangelista resulted in a prestigious commission to decorate the cathedral of Parma, dedicated to Santa Maria Assunta in honor of Parma's special veneration of the Virgin. As part of a comprehensive sixteenth-century renovation, Correggio was contracted to paint frescoes throughout the Romanesque church in November 1522. His cupola portrayal of the *Assumption of the Virgin* was a radical departure from prior representations of the scene. Yet despite its innovation and later influence, the extravagant foreshortening of Correggio's figures and the dizzying *di sotto in su,* the spectator's experience of looking up from underneath the images, in which Correggio presented the Virgin's ascent were not considered an unqualified success and may have prompted the artist's return to his native Correggio (c. 1530).

Correggio's unique ability to represent the nuanced iconography of the miraculous as a concrete reality is apparent in other religious work from this period. Three remarkable altarpieces, all in the Gemäldegalerie, Dresden, portray the Virgin and Child as the tranquil focus of emotions so powerful as to elicit a palpable physical response. The maidservant who recoils from the numinous brilliance of the infant Christ in the *Adoration of the Shepherds,* known since the seventeenth century as "La Notte," is contrasted by the donkey pressing eagerly toward the Child, despite St. Joseph's robust restraint. Similarly, altarpieces such as the *Madonna with St. Sebastian* (c. 1524) and the *Madonna with St. George* (before 1530), both painted for confraternities in Modena, render the spiritual joy felt in the presence of the Christ child and his mother as a profound corporeal experience.

Late Career. Physical pleasure in experiencing the divine also distinguishes Correggio's late masterpieces, the "Loves of Jupiter" series, painted for Federico II Gonzaga, duke of Mantua, after 1529. These four mythological canvases are the most erotic of Correggio's entire oeuvre and are more explicitly carnal than his earlier *Venus with Mercury and Cupid,* or "School of Love" (National Gallery, London), and *Venus and Cupid with Satyr* (Louvre, Paris), both painted c. 1523–1525 and known to have been in the collection of Nicola Maffei in Mantua before 1589. Undoubtedly aware of the tastes of his patron, the artist has consistently represented the literal and figurative climax of each narrative: *Io* (Kunsthistorisches Museum, Vienna) enraptured by the Jupiter cloud; *Ganymede* (Kunsthistorisches Museum, Vienna) submissively transported upward by means of an improbably levitating eagle; and *Danaë* (Borghese Gallery, Rome) in stunned acquiescence to Jupiter's golden shower from anatomically suggestive clouds. *Leda* (Gemäldegalerie, Berlin) differs from the others in that it was the only myth presented in episodic fashion and not based on Ovid's *Metamorphoses.*

Whether promising ecstatic union with God or the more terrestial pleasures afforded by visions of ancient goddesses or nude nymphs, Correggio's mature work appeals directly to the senses. Emotional directness anchors formal complexity; physical, psychological, and spatial relationships are intricate without appearing strained. Correggio's use of color, wedded to a structuring of pictorial space as a visual metaphor of spiritual transcendence, was essential to the development of baroque illusionism and a for-native influence on subsequent aesthetic principles and theory.

BIBLIOGRAPHY

Ekserdjian, David. *Correggio*. New Haven, Conn., and London, 1997.

Gould, Cecil. *The Paintings of Correggio*. Ithaca, N.Y., 1976.

Pungileoni, P. Luigi. *Memorie istoriche di Antonio Allegri detto il Correggio*. 3 vols. Parma, Italy, 1817; 1821.

Popham, Arthur E. *Correggio's Drawings*. London, 1957.

Ricci, Corrado. *Antonio Allegri da Correggio*. Translated by Florence Simmonds. London, 1896.

MAUREEN PELTA

CORTÉS, HERNÁN (1485–1547), Spanish explorer, conqueror of Mexico. Hernando (better known as Hernán) Cortés conquered the Aztec empire in Mexico from 1519 to 1521. He consequently became one of the wealthiest and most acclaimed personalities in Spain, was named a marquis, and married a woman from the nobility, Doña Juana de Zúñiga. Throughout his life, both before and after the conquest, Cortés behaved very much like a man of business, financing trading ventures to the Spice Islands and establishing a sugar plantation in Mexico maintained by slaves from Africa.

From a respectable gentry family in Medellín, Cortés was sent as a youth to study at the University of Salamanca. He remained but two years. In 1504 or 1506 he sailed to Santo Domingo, where he fought in Indian campaigns and was given an *encomienda* (a grant of Indian laborers). He joined Diego Velázquez's expedition to subdue Cuba in 1511 and was given even greater rewards.

When made aware of an advanced native civilization in Mexico, Governor Velázquez chose Cortés to lead a well-supplied expedition of around five hundred men, including twelve harquebusiers, some thirty crossbowmen, and sixteen horses, to negotiate and trade with it. Cortés, however, intended from the beginning to conquer the society on his own behalf, not that of Velázquez. As a person of stature, experience, and wealth in the Indies, Cortés fit the requirements for a successful *adelantado* (expedition leader). He and Velázquez financed the undertaking more or less equally.

Once in Mexico, Cortés found that some provinces within the Aztec empire were quite willing to ally themselves with the Spanish. In repeated military engagements against vast native armies over the next two years, the Spanish demonstrated their military superiority through their metal weapons, cavalry, and ruthlessness. When the Spaniards fought to kill, the Aztecs followed the ancient Mesoamerican military practice of attempting to capture their opponents. The natives also made poor use of their numerical superiority by emphasizing one-on-one combat rather than overrunning their greatly fewer opponents. They were also hurt by their tradition of capitulating when their commander was killed or captured. The Spanish soon learned to focus their attacks on the leader of the Aztec army.

Cortés's decision to capture the Aztec emperor Montezuma and to rule through him for as long as possible reflected long-established Spanish tactics in the Americas. More innovative was his construction of thirteen small ships to control the large lake that surrounded the Aztec island capital of Tenochtitlán. Cortés was dismayed that the only way he could defeat the besieged Aztecs was to level their city to prevent them from using its structures in defense. The capital fell to Cortés's force on 13 August 1521, and with it the Spanish controlled all of central Mexico.

The Spanish crown soon designated Cortés as governor and captain general of this colony of New Spain. Cortés distributed *encomiendas* to his men, reserving the largest for himself. He personally led an expedition against a rebellious subordinate in Central America from 1524 to 1526 and launched others throughout Mexico. He founded a dockyard on the Pacific coast that constructed vessels to trade with the Spice Islands (part of Indonesia) and later with newly conquered Peru.

Cortés's first wife died shortly after arriving in Mexico. His second wife bore him four children. He had five other children by several Indian women, including a sister of Montezuma. Shortly before his death near Seville, Spain, in 1547, Cortés composed a will recognizing these latter offspring and providing all his children with substantial bequests. His eldest legitimate son inherited his marquisate.

BIBLIOGRAPHY

Cortés, Hernán. *Letters from Mexico*. Edited and translated by Anthony Pagden. With an introduction by J. H. Elliott. New Haven, Conn., 1986.

Martínez, José Luis. *Hernán Cortés*. Mexico City, Mexico, 1990.

Thomas, Hugh. *Conquest: Montezuma, Cortés, and the Fall of Old Mexico*. New York, 1993.

JOHN E. KICZA

CORVINUS, MATTHIAS (Mátyás Hunyadi; 1440–1490), king of Hungary (1458–1490). Matthias Corvinus was the younger son of Johannes (János) Hunyadi (1387–1456). He contended for the throne with Emperor Frederick III (1415–1493) and was finally crowned on 29 March 1464. He was proclaimed king of Bohemia in 1469. In a war with Frederick, Matthias seized Vienna in 1485, which he held until his death.

Coming from a family of mercenary soldiers, and supported by the lesser nobility whose first major victory was his election, Matthias's self-fashioned persona was based on the Italian model. He received a humanist education supervised by Johannes Vitéz (1408–1472), then bishop of Várad, and by Gregor of Sanok (Gregorz za Sanoka, 1406–1477), the famous Polish humanist, later archbishop of Lwow (now L'viv, Ukraine; also spelled Lvov). Matthias showed a special gift for languages and frequently functioned as his father's interpreter. His education also included the martial arts.

Matthias became a true Renaissance ruler by successfully applying the contemporary western symbols of power; in addition, he enhanced his military and political fame with the image of a learned king, an enlightened patron of the arts. Matthias's court, in Buda, was a hub of prominent humanists from all over Europe. Many of them dedicated their work to the generous king. His diplomats were educated at European universities, and his chancery successfully handled the intricate issues involved in a complex state apparatus. The building boom and the beautification of the capital during his reign were noted enthusiastically by the foreign dignitaries visiting Matthias's court. His greatest pride was his library, the "Corviniana," a collection of over five hundred illuminated manuscripts. Matthias's book-collecting policies and copying workshops greatly contributed to the preservation, transcription, and translation (from Greek into Latin) of classical literature and science in central Europe.

Matthias's rule can be divided into three main periods. Until the 1460s, depending on the lesser nobles, he secured the country's geographical unity and independence. During the second period, Matthias proceeded with reforms in the army, in public affairs, and in the courts of law (modeled on the West). The third period, following his marriage to Beatrix of Naples and Aragon in 1476, was characterized by wars of expansion and dynastic ambition.

Matthias's expansionist policies, directed against the West, left the country's southern borders unprotected against the Turks. This led to an unsuccessful plot in 1472, designed to have him replaced on the throne by the young Casimir of Poland. The plot revealed a major flaw in Matthias's state-building. He had transformed his humanist prelates and nobles into feudal vassals, who then challenged him in order to protect their own interests.

Matthias Corvinus. Marble relief by Giancristoforo Romano, 1489. SZÉPMŰVÉSZETI MÚZEUM, BUDAPEST

Matthias's first wife, Catherine of Podiebrad, died childless, and Matthias's hopes to create a dynasty with Beatrix remained frustrated. Without a legitimate heir, Matthias tried to have the national party accept his natural son (Johannes Corvinus, 1473–1504), but Johannes lost to Władysław Jagiello (Uláiszló II, 1456–1516) and lost his life in a battle against the Turks as *banus* (the king's legal representative) of Croatia and Slavonia.

Since Matthias's reign coincided with the most glorious period of Hungarian history, his figure lives on in fiction and in folk tradition, often independent of factual records.

BIBLIOGRAPHY

Birnbaum, Marianna D. *The Orb and the Pen: Janus Pannonius, Matthias Corvinus, and the Buda Court.* Budapest, Hungary, 1996.

Csapodi, Csaba, and Klára Csapodi-Gárdonyi, eds. *Bibliotheca Corviniana, 1490–1990.* Budapest, Hungary, 1981.

Fraknói, Vilmos. *Matthias Corvinus, König von Ungarn, 1458–1490.* Freiburg, Germany, 1891.

Matthias Corvinus und die Renaissance in Ungarn, 1458–1541: Schallaburg '82 [Ausstellung], 8 Mai–1 November 1982. Vienna, 1982.

MARIANNA D. BIRNBAUM

COSMOLOGY. *See* **Astronomy.**

COSSA, FRANCESCO DEL. *See* **Ferrara,** *subentry on* **Art in Ferrara.**

COSTUME. *See* **Clothing.**

COUNTER-REFORMATION. *See* **Catholic Reformation and Counter-Reformation.**

COURT. The court brought together numerous individuals and elements of Renaissance society. Here the ruler, his family, associates, servants, artists, writers, and others advanced their own interests and, in so doing, created one of the most important and colorful centers of Renaissance life.

Structure. A Renaissance court was typically composed of two concentric circles: the councillors and officials whose work was directly supervised by the ruler—a king, pope, emperor, or duke, generically referred to as a prince—and the household officers who served the prince's personal needs. Together with the household of the consort, which was increasingly separate from the prince's, these circles created a structure loosely called the court, the functions of which were to regulate access to the ruler, to augment the ruler's splendor, and to integrate the rich and powerful of the realm with the government. Because the court was always the center of patronage, relations among its members were tense as ministers, favorites, aristocratic and middle-class councillors, ladies of the court, secretaries, artisans, and even jesters and dwarfs jostled for favor and patronage. The court was one sphere where women could convert social power into political power. Because Renaissance government was still somewhat informal, dividing lines between the court and the permanent bureaucracies are difficult to draw, as are those between the traditional noble officers and the middle-class officials and ministers upon whom Renaissance rulers increasingly relied. The household, usually presided over by a chamberlain, was organized to afford the prince protection and a degree of freedom from the incessant demands of petitioners; the extended court, usually presided over by a major domo or steward, provided the prince's contact with both the government and the ruled.

Growth. Political circumstances in the Renaissance favored the development of more elaborate courts. New dynasties such as the Sforza in Italy or the Tudors in England sought to obliterate in a blaze of splendor the recentness of their origins. Court festivals dazzled the populace and co-opted the nobility in ceremonies, important when mechanisms of authority were still weak. The rise of diplomacy likewise favored the growth of the court. Visiting princes or their emissaries were treated to spectacles calculated to impress them with the wealth and power of their host, and solemn entries, such as those greeting the arrival of a visiting sovereign or a bride for the prince, became occasions of spectacular display wherein artists, architects, artisans, actors, musicians, courtiers, and eventually (as spectators) the entire populace cooperated in a celebration, however ephemeral, of the dynasty and the state.

Protocol. As rulers sought to enhance their personal power, mechanisms of access were made more complex, and increasingly elaborate ceremony was devised to create distance and enhance the prince's aura. Among the courtiers, protocol and dress emphasized differences in rank and made the favors of the sovereign more significant. The ceremonies of the church provided a model for much court ceremonial. While in exile in Avignon (1309–1377), the papacy had perfected its own protocol, some of which—pontifical foot-kissing, for example—derived from the elaborate ceremonial of the Byzantine court. The papal master of ceremonies was a major official. At solemn banquets the pope was served with quasi-liturgical ceremony: butlers tasted his food and wine, which was then proffered him on bended knee while cardinals and curial officials either stood around or ate at lower tables. When the pope washed his hands or drank, laymen genuflected and clergy stood, mimicking the ritual of the mass. To varying degrees, secular monarchs followed suit. Formalization of court etiquette was also spurred by permanent embassies, as ambassadors of rival powers jealously watched each other's reception. When, at a public audience in 1570, the pope called for a stool to seat the grand duke of Tuscany, a privilege normally reserved for the Holy Roman Emperor, ambassadors of other powers stormed out in protest.

The many contemporary treatises on the organization and protocol of courts provide the basis for a growing literature of modern historical analysis and social theory, particularly when archival research in registers and account books can add quantification.

A sovereign was expected to have the most magnificent court and elaborate protocol, but territorial lords such as the dukes of Burgundy might vie with kings. Great nobles might expand their households into small courts. In his treatise on the cardinalate, the Roman humanist Paolo Cortesi (1465–1510) described a palace and court for a cardinal that could easily employ sixty gentlemen attendants and eighty servants. The desperate need for additional income for display increased the stakes in the hazardous game of winning and holding the favor of the prince. Secret misery was the lot of many a clerical or lay noble, forced by general expectation to live beyond his means; princes themselves were constantly endeavoring to curb the ever-increasing expenditures for their courts and to reduce the numbers of courtiers entitled to meals.

Space. Access to the prince was graded by space as well as protocol: the more intimate the setting, the greater the honor. The place of a guest's initial reception, the location and quality of assigned lodgings, the number and quality of the persons forming the reception party, the seating at the banquets to follow—all could be used to flatter, make distinctions, and send nuanced messages. The epicenter of the court was the bedroom of the prince. An ambassador would initially be formally received in the presence chamber or great hall and subsequently in a less public setting, a private interview in the bedroom being the greatest honor. A Renaissance variant on the medieval concept of the bedroom as the center of the palace was the eventual emergence of the prince's private study as the sanctum sanctorum.

As Renaissance rulers sought greater privacy, the household tended to retreat into itself. At Rome, for example, the "palatine family," or private household of the pope, was a separate division of the curia (the papal court). Not surprisingly, princes found the endless ceremony tedious and created refuges for themselves. Pope Innocent VIII (reigned 1484–1492) built the Villa Belvedere on the hill above the Vatican Palace; King Henry VII of England (ruled 1485–1509) instituted the privy chamber; kings and princes throughout Europe built hunting lodges and country villas. Life was wearying for courtiers as well. While he was a secretary at the court of the emperor Frederick III (ruled 1440–1493), the Italian humanist Enea Silvio Piccolomini (1405–1464), later Pope Pius II, wrote a treatise in letter form, "De curialium miseriis" (On the miseries of courtiers). Long waits in cold, drafty rooms, sleepless nights in un-comfortable—and generally shared—beds, bad food, tedium, snubs, and all manner of discomforts, rendered even worse when the court traveled, were the lot of the courtier. The rewards were festivities, feasts, and above all the chance for advancement. To advance, said the late-Renaissance theorist Giovanni Francesco Commendone (1524–1584), was the whole purpose of being a courtier.

Major Courts. In the mid-fifteenth century, Burgundy was the preeminent secular court, whose dukes maintained a truly royal state calculated to bind the nobility of their heterogeneous lands by a common tie. As described by Olivier de la Marche, master of the household and captain of the guard for Charles the Bold (ruled 1467–1477), elaborate ceremony ruled every aspect of court life. Court ideology centered on knighthood, and foreign visitors were particularly awed by the magnificent gatherings of the Order of the Golden Fleece, created to integrate the great nobles with the Burgundian court but an order in which even crowned heads were flattered to be enrolled. By 1474 over a thousand office-holders, most of whom had their own servants, lived at court at the duke's expense. The English diarist John Paston (1421–1466) could only think to compare it to King Arthur's court.

Italy had an abundance of princely courts that, as part of the Renaissance cult of magnificence, were centers of patronage and instrumental in the evolution of arts and letters. The sixteenth-century humanist Paolo Giovio (1486–1552) thought that the Renaissance had begun at the court of Galeazzo II Visconti of Milan (ruled 1354–1378), whose example had spurred the princes of Italy, including Pope Nicholas V (reigned 1447–1455), "to study magnificence." Petrarch (1304–1374) was Galeazzo's guest for several years, and although his fellow humanists complained of lack of leisure for their studies, they generally preferred appointments at court to university teaching. It was as schoolmasters and tutors to young princes and their noble companions, and subsequently as their secretaries, that humanists were able to promote their new educational program. To their increased status at courts, Renaissance artists owed much of their emancipation from mere artisan status under the urban guilds.

After the papacy, the leading Italian courts were those of Naples and Milan. At Asolo, however, the tiny court of Caterina Cornaro (1454–1510), the former queen of Cyprus, produced one of the most influential works of the Renaissance, Pietro Bembo's *Gli asolani* (Asolan dialogues; 1505). And thanks to the popularity of Baldassare Castiglione's *Il cortegiano* (*The Book of the Courtier;* 1528), the small court of Urbino, instituted by Duke Federico da Montefeltro (ruled 1444–1482) in an exquisite palace by the architect Francesco da Laurana (c. 1430–1502), holds a lasting place in the history of the court. From medieval chivalry and romance, which fascinated Italians no less than northerners, there evolved the arts of courtesy, heraldry, and emblems, as well as elaborate codes of honor.

Most of the small Italian courts were quasi-familial autocracies. The Ferrarese steward Cristoforo di Messisbugo listed the court personnel of Duke Ercole II (ruled 1534–1559): his family; court nobles, gentlemen, councillors, ambassadors, secretaries, chancellors; doctors, chaplains, and musicians; chamberlain and staff, including the master of the wardrobe and staff, valets, pages, and doorkeepers; master of the house, steward and staff, including butlers, purveyors, cooks, carvers, servers, porters, sweepers; master of the stables with grooms and muleteers; master of falcons and falconers, master of the hunt and huntsmen; castellan (governor of the castle), with architects, warders, and so forth. Equally brilliant was the Gonzaga court at Mantua, especially in the time of Marchioness Isabella d'Este (1474–1539). In Florence the great tradition of Medici patronage was continued when the city became the capital of a grand duchy under Cosimo I (ruled 1537–1574), whose paternalistic rule included systematic patronage as a means of enhancing the power and prestige of the dynasty.

After the parsimony of Louis XI (ruled 1461–1483) and the modest court of Louis XII (ruled 1498–1515), the glories of the French court revived under Francis I (ruled 1515–1547), thanks to the king's extensive patronage (inspired by his Italian visits) and to his magnificent palaces, particularly Fontainebleau. In England the household book of Edward IV (ruled 1461–1470, 1471–1483) distinguished the *Domus providencie,* or domestic household, under the lord steward, which focused on feeding and provisioning, from the *Domus regie magnificencie* under the lord chamberlain, which comprised the rest of the court functions, including the departments of the chapel, privy wardrobe, jewels, and signet, and the heralds, physicians, knights, esquires, carvers, servers, cupbearers, ushers, pages, minstrels, servants, and so on. Seeking greater freedom from the importunities of courtiers, the first Tudor king, Henry VII (ruled 1485–1509), instituted the privy chamber, served by mere gentlemen, not nobles, and presided over by an officer unique to the English court, the

groom of the stool. Relations between the Tudor court and government have been the subject of scholarly controversy; in the 1990s scholars tended to stress the importance of the household. Under Henry VIII (ruled 1509–1547), the privy chamber became the preserve of royal favorites, many of whom served as diplomats. Under Elizabeth I (ruled 1558–1603) it reverted to being private and was staffed by women who were allowed by the queen to meddle in patronage but not in politics.

In Spain the independence of the traditional nobility limited the role of the court, although Charles I (ruled Spain 1516–1556; as Charles V, Holy Roman Emperor, 1519–1556) attempted to introduce some Burgundian practices, as he later did in Germany. Philip II (ruled 1556–1598) was temperamentally unsuited to court life and during the latter part of his life buried himself in the combined monastery and palace of the Escorial. In Germany the Holy Roman emperor's court had always to compete with the rich and powerful princely courts; moreover, it suffered from the lack of a fixed capital and was overshadowed by the imperial diet (assembly). Since the quixotic emperor Maximilian I (ruled 1493–1519) spent most of his time in the relatively insignificant city of Innsbruck, his court, despite its apparent splendor, never fulfilled the function of integrating the German nobility.

Etiquette. In every country the court was the arbiter of manners. The nobility had long sent their sons to court as pages to learn manners. Manners gave the court identity and differentiated courtiers from other ranks of society. That courtliness could be a highly civilizing process is shown by Castiglione's ever-popular *Book of the Courtier,* with its emphasis on comeliness and grace of manners, morals, and intellect, and its cultivation of a humane outlook. Bishop Giovanni della Casa's *Galateo* (1558) provided a complementary guide to the particulars of good manners. Sociologists have stressed the special nature of a world where extreme competitiveness put its inhabitants constantly on guard because of their vulnerability to slander and intrigue, a world where they learned to read every nuance of a sovereign's looks and gestures and where, in consequence, they learned to control every nuance of their own.

If the court was a place where manners were perfected, it was also a place where morals were corrupted. Sexual license was a constant reproach to courts. The bitter description by Pietro Aretino (1492–1556) of the fate of a youth placed in a Roman court household may be an exaggeration, but the reality was often not very wholesome, especially as many Renaissance princes hardly provided models of chastity. Indeed, their mistresses were increasingly prominent at court. Francis I's second official mistress, Madame d'Étampes (1508–c. 1580), acquired so much influence that she was able to bring about the fall of the constable of France, Anne, duc de Montmorency. Federico Gonzaga of Mantua (ruled 1519–1540), who had spent some of his formative years at Francis's court, made his mother, Isabella d'Este, miserable by advancing his mistress over her. Vigilant queens and duchesses did their best to protect the young women committed to their charge, but with varying success. The walled garden was developed originally as a refuge for the women of the palace or castle to enjoy the outdoors in privacy, free from masculine intrusion.

As it advanced the centralization of political power, the Renaissance court increasingly fostered the adroit and self-seeking courtier, and the daily struggle to win the favor of the prince undermined many a character. "Say to the court," wrote a disillusioned Sir Walter Ralegh (1554–1618) in his poem "The Lie," "it glows and shines like rotten wood." With its ritual splendor the court dazzled and delighted; with its festivities it unified; but with its power it corrupted.

See also **Monarchy**; **Patronage**, *subentry on* **Patrons and Clients in Renaissance Society**; **Prince**.

BIBLIOGRAPHY

Anglo, Sydney. *Spectacle, Pageantry, and Early Tudor Policy.* 2d ed. Oxford, 1997.

Anglo, Sydney, ed. *Chivalry in the Renaissance.* Woodbridge, U.K., 1990.

Asch, Ronald G., and Adolf M. Birke, eds. *Princes, Patronage, and the Nobility: The Court at the Beginning of the Modern Age c. 1450–1650.* Oxford, 1991.

Bertelli, Sergio, et al., eds. *The Courts of the Italian Renaissance.* New York, 1986.

Chambers, David, and Jane Martineau. *Splendours of the Gonzaga: Catalogue.* London, 1981.

Dickens, A. G., ed. *The Courts of Europe: Politics, Patronage, and Royalty 1400–1800.* New York, 1977.

Elias, Norbert. *The Court Society.* Translated by Edmund Jephcott. New York, 1983.

Loades, David. *The Tudor Court.* Totowa, N.J., 1987.

Lubkin, Gregory. *A Renaissance Court: Milan under Galeazzo Maria Sforza.* Berkeley, Calif., 1994.

Potter, David. *A History of France, 1460–1560.* New York, 1995. See chapter 2, "The Court of France from Louis XI to Henri II," pp. 57–89.

Scaglione, Aldo. *Knights at Court: Courtliness, Chivalry, and Courtesy from Ottonian Germany to the Italian Renaissance.* Berkeley, Calif., 1991.

Starkey, David, et al., *The English Court: From the Wars of the Roses to the Civil War.* London, 1987.

T. C. Price Zimmerman

COURTS, LAW. *See* **Crime and Punishment.**

COVARRUBIAS Y LEIVA, DIEGO DE (1512–1577), Spanish jurist, bishop, president of the Council of Castile. Covarrubias was born in Toledo on 25 July 1512, to a nonnoble but highly distinguished Castilian family. His father, Alonso de Covarrubias, and his Flemish-born maternal uncles, Anton and Enrique de Egas, were leading architects in the service of the Holy Roman Emperor Charles V. In 1523 Covarrubias was sent to Salamanca, where he enjoyed a more broadly humanistic primary education than most of his fellow students; through the special efforts of his family, he studied Greek as well as Latin and read widely in ancient history and theology before matriculating, in 1527, in the faculty of canon and civil law. This humanistic foundation helped him to become one of the most erudite men in sixteenth-century Spain. In 1533 he earned the bachelor's degree in law. In 1538 he won a coveted fellowship in the Colegio Mayor de San Salvador de Oviedo, one of Salamanca's four elite residential colleges for graduate students in law and theology. He earned the licenciate degree in law in 1538, the doctorate in 1539, and his first university teaching chair in 1540. From then until 1548, when he left Salamanca, Covarrubias lectured on canon and civil law, becoming one of Spain's leading jurists. Beginning in 1545 he published a series of nine volumes of scholastic legal commentaries closely based on his academic lectures.

After leaving Salamanca in 1548, Covarrubias followed a career path typical of the more successful graduates of the *colegios mayores,* serving in both the royal bureaucracy and the church. He was a judge in the royal appeals court in Granada from 1548 until the late 1550s. In 1553 he was nominated as archbishop of Santo Domingo in the Indies, a post that for unknown reasons he never occupied. In 1560 he became bishop of Ciudad Rodrigo, and in this capacity he attended the third session of the Council of Trent in 1562–1563. In 1565 he was transferred to the bishopric of Segovia. In 1572, without renouncing this position, he became president of the Council of Castile, the highest administrative post in Philip II's government; he retained this post until his death. Named bishop of Cuenca in 1577, he died the same year before he could assume the office.

Not a particularly original thinker, Covarrubias was nonetheless widely admired for the learnedness and lucidity of his legal judgments; between 1568 and 1762 his *Opera omnia* were published in more than thirty editions in six countries, attesting to a broad and enduring readership. He practiced the traditional Bartolist method of legal interpretation (named for Bartolus of Sassoferrato, 1314–1357), also called the *mos italicus* (Italian method), an essentially practical, ahistorical approach. The bulk of his commentaries concern private-law matters like marriage, inheritance, and contracts, but he also dealt extensively with such topics as criminal law, ecclesiastical law, and the law of nations. In the latter field, his teachings were indebted to Salamanca theologian Francisco de Vitoria, whose lectures Covarrubias attended in the 1530s; Covarrubias is often identified as one of the "School of Salamanca," a label designating Vitoria's neo-Thomist disciples. Covarrubias's writings on natural law and the law of nations were cited respectfully not only by Catholic authors, but also by Protestant legal and political thinkers like Hugo Grotius and Johannes Althusius, whose own ideas went beyond the scholastic tradition.

Although best remembered as a jurist, Covarrubias also exercised his humanist learning as an amateur historian and antiquarian. In 1556 he published a treatise on numismatic history. He corresponded with scholars like Antonio Agustín and Pier Vettori about Roman and Spanish antiquities. In the 1570s, with his younger brother Antonio, he began to edit a version of the Visigothic Spanish law code, the *Fuero Juzgo,* which was never published.

BIBLIOGRAPHY

Primary Works
Covarrubias y Leiva, Diego de. *Opera omnia.* 2 vols. Geneva, 1762.
Covarrubias y Leiva, Diego de. *Textos jurídico-políticos.* Edited by Manuel Fraga Iribarne. Madrid, 1957.

Secondary Work
Gutiérrez, Constancio. *Españoles en Trento.* Valladolid, Spain, 1951.

KATHERINE ELLIOT VAN LIERE

CRACOW. The capital of Poland from 1038 until 1609, Cracow was the cultural center of the country during the Polish golden age (*Złoty Wiek*), which occurred during the reigns of the last two kings of the Jagiellonian dynasty, Sigismund I the Elder (Zygmunt Stary; 1506–1548) and Sigismund II Augustus (Zygmunt August; 1548–1572). During the four-teenth century Cracow, its government based on the Magdeburg Law (which provided a form of independent administration for towns), had become a major trading center situated on the crossroads of central Europe. By the end of the fifteenth century a patrician class of wealthy merchant families, most of whom were of German origin, took control of the urban administration and won the confidence of the king. The religious controversies of the age were not played out in the capital, but rather in the provinces, and in Prussia and Silesia, where the Reformation took hold.

Italian Renaissance humanism had first seeped into Poland through ecclesiastical contacts at the councils of Constance and Basel. Cardinal Zbigniew Oleśnicki (1389–1455), a correspondent of Enea Silvio Piccolomini (Pope Pius II), and his secretary Jan Długosz (1415–1480), the author of *Annales seu cronicae incliti regni Poloniae,* a monumental history of Poland, created an intellectual atmosphere receptive to the new learning. At the royal court, the refugee Filippo Buonaccorsi Callimachus (1437–1496) was made adviser to the kings Casimir IV Jagiellon (Kazimierz Jagiellończyk; ruled 1447–1492) and John I Albert (Jan Olbracht; ruled 1492–1501). Italian culture became intensified at the court with the marriage of Sigismund I to the princess Bona Sforza in 1518. Throughout the sixteenth century, the bishops of Cracow, such as Piotr Tomicki (1464–1535), who corresponded with Erasmus, and the chancellors of the crown, such as Jan Zamojski (1542–1605), who organized a humanist academy, promoted education and the arts.

The University of Cracow (founded in 1364) gained renown in the field of liberal arts, especially astronomy. Humanism was encouraged by Conrad Celtis, who matriculated at the university and stayed in Cracow from 1489 to 1491. Copernicus also studied at Cracow in the 1490s. Still, humanist learning was not integrated into the official university curriculum until the mid-sixteenth century.

Printing began at Cracow in the 1470s; the first book in Cyrillic appeared in 1491, and the first book in Polish was produced in 1513. The greatest literary figure of the period, Jan Kochanowski (1530–1584), studied at Cracow and Padua, and worked at the royal court in the 1560s. In 1566 a Cracow courtier, Łukasz Górnicki published *Dworzanin polski,* a Polish adaptation of Castiglioni's *Il cortegiano.* (*The Book of the Courtier*).

Although the Polish Renaissance produced no outstanding school of painting, the new style in music flourished from about 1520, with John of Lublin's

City of Cracow. From Hartmann Schedel and Anton Koberger, *Liber chronicarum* (The Nürnberg Chronicle; 1493).
STAPLETON COLLECTION, UK/THE BRIDGEMAN ART LIBRARY

(Jan z Lublina) *Tabulatura* (1537–1548) reflecting the popularity of dance at the court. In the 1520s and 1530s, Sigismund I employed Italian artisans for the renovation of the royal castle and cathedral, where the Florentine architect Bartolomeo Berrecci created his masterpiece, the Sigismund burial chapel (1519–1538). The architecture of Renaissance Cracow has been miraculously preserved; the royal castle and cathedral on Wawel hill, and the Italianate cloth hall (Sukiennice) and burghers' houses on the old town square may be visited today.

See also **Poland.**

BIBLIOGRAPHY

Białostocki, Jan. *The Art of the Renaissance in Eastern Europe: Hungary, Bohemia, Poland.* Ithaca, N.Y., 1976.

Bieniarzówna, Janina, and Jan M. Małecki. *Dzieje Krakowa.* Vol. 2, Kraków w wiekach XVI–XVIII. Cracow, 1984.

Fiszman, Samuel, ed. *The Polish Renaissance in Its European Context.* Bloomington, Ind., and Indianapolis, Ind., 1988.

Segel, Harold B. *Renaissance Culture in Poland: The Rise of Humanism, 1470–1543.* Ithaca, N.Y., and London, 1989.

JACQUELINE GLOMSKI

CRANACH, LUCAS (1472–1553), known as "the Elder," German painter, printmaker, and book illustrator in Wittenberg. Born in Kronach, near Bamberg, Cranach was trained by his father, Hans Maler. Almost nothing is known of his Kronach period, save that he absorbed the revolutionary style of Albrecht Dürer, either through trips to Nürnberg or through seeing Dürer's woodcuts. Taking the name of his birthplace as his own, he arrived in Vienna in 1502. There he entered a humanist circle centered on the university and led by the poet laureate Conrad Celtis (1459–1508). In Vienna Cranach made religious paintings of novel expressive power. Applying contrasting colors loosely, he gave figures a turbulence of arrangement and gesture that fit their pathos; and he set these in an agitated landscape that seems to respond sympathetically. These works, especially their rendering of nature, influenced other artists along the Danube, including Albrecht Altdorfer.

By 1505, Cranach moved to Wittenberg, where he became court painter of the Saxon elector, Frederick the Wise. Over the next half-century, he dominated the art of northern and eastern Germany through his output for the Saxon princes (he served three successive electors), and through work for the Protestant cause. His shop employed his sons Hans (1513?–1537) and Lucas, called the Younger (1515–1586), plus some ten apprentices and more assistants. Cranach adapted his Vienna style to collaboration by formalizing spontaneity: emphasizing linear outline and detail, he made a virtue of the quickness required by huge commissions.

Today Cranach's most prized later works are his secular allegories. In these gently erotic paintings, the outline of nudes plays against a dark, flat ground.

Other works, such as his hunting scenes, resemble patterned tapestry, reflecting their use as palace decoration. Cranach was Renaissance Germany's most prolific portraitist. Along with iconic likenesses of Saxon nobles, he portrayed Protestant reformers in paintings and prints that projected their cause well beyond Wittenberg.

Cranach's links to Martin Luther were both personal and professional. Godfather to each other's children, they collaborated on key projects, such as antipapal pamphlets, diagrams of reformed doctrine, and illustrations to Luther's Bible translations. In response to iconoclasm, Luther fostered through Cranach a legible style appropriate to a word-based faith. Cranach continued to work for Catholic patrons, notably Luther's foe, Albrecht of Brandenburg.

In 1550, after the 1547 defeat by Catholics of Prince Johann Frederick, Cranach accompanied his patron to Augsburg and then in 1552 to Weimar, where Cranach died in 1553. His shop still thrived under Lucas the Younger. Various and collaborative, Cranach's art coined a recognizable style that helped define visual culture for Lutheran Germany.

BIBLIOGRAPHY

Friedländer, Max J., and Jacob Rosenberg. *The Paintings of Lucas Cranach*. Ithaca, N.Y., 1978.

Grimm, Klaus, et al., eds. *Lucas Cranach: Ein Maler-Unternehmer aus Franken*. Munich, 1994. Exhibition catalog.

Jahn, Johannes. *1472–1553 Lucas Cranach der Ältere: Das gesamte graphische Werk*. Munich, 1972.

Koepplin, Dieter, and Tielman Falk. *Lukas Cranach*. 2 vols. Basel, 1974, 1976. Exhibition catalog.

Schade, Werner. *Cranach: A Family of Master Painters*. Translated by Helen Sebba. New York, 1980.

JOSEPH LEO KOERNER

CRANMER, THOMAS (1489–1556), archbishop of Canterbury (1533–1556). From a minor Nottinghamshire gentry family, Cranmer went to Jesus College, Cambridge, in 1503, and during his unspectacular academic career teaching theology, he displayed the mixture of traditionalist piety and humanist scholarship predictable from his devout background. By 1520, after his first wife died in childbirth, he was ordained a priest and was recruited, probably through his Cambridge friend Edward Lee, for royal diplomatic service, assisting on an embassy to Charles V in Spain in 1527 and meeting Henry VIII on his return. He left Cambridge in 1529 to join the theological team working on the annulment of Henry's marriage to Catherine of Aragon, benefiting from patronage by Henry's prospective wife, Anne Boleyn, and her family. In 1531 he produced the published English translation of Henry's annulment case, *The Determinations of the Universities (Censurae academiarum),* which reveals him experimenting with the limits of the vernacular for conveying academic argument. The collaborative research work he was undertaking is summarized in the manuscript compilation preserved in the British Library as *Collectanea satis copiosa* (Comprehensive enough collections; 1529–1532); this work, which radically questions papal jurisdiction and affirms royal supremacy over the church, may have stimulated Cranmer's move away from orthodoxy.

Also in 1531, through the English visit of the Basel reformer Simon Grynaeus, Cranmer made contact with the Strasbourg reform leader Martin Bucer, who became a lifelong friend. Cranmer's own increasingly reformist stance was revealed while he was on embassy to Germany in 1532: during his mission he deliberately flouted the traditional requirement that clerics be celibate by marrying Margarethe, niece of a Lutheran theologian from Nürnberg, Andreas Osiander. It proved necessary to conceal this marriage when royal esteem led to his unexpected appointment as archbishop of Canterbury in 1533. Confirmed in office with reluctant papal permission, he quickly presided over the annulment of Henry's marriage to Catherine of Aragon and Anne Boleyn's coronation. Through the 1530s he worked closely with the king's minister Thomas Cromwell to promote reformation: he gladly ceded power to Cromwell in a new office of royal vicegerent in spirituals, after his own visitation of the province of Canterbury in 1534–1535 revealed limitations in his traditional powers over his bishops. Already in February 1536 he openly preached that the pope was the Antichrist.

Cromwell rather than Cranmer forwarded legalization of an English Bible in 1537, but Cranmer was enthusiastic about this initiative and contributed a major statement on the importance of vernacular scripture in a preface added to the official Bible (the Great Bible) in 1540. He had begun drawing up drafts of a vernacular liturgy by 1539, although the first published fruit—an English litany still substantially preserved in the Book of Common Prayer—only appeared in 1544. After Cromwell's fall, Cranmer survived Henry's final unpredictable years to become the chief architect of the accelerated religious changes under Edward VI (1547–1553): he constructed two Prayer Books (1549, 1552) and the Ordinal, which dictated the rites for ordaining deacons, priests, and bishops (1550); drew up the Forty-Two Articles of faith for the new church (reconstructed in 1563 as Thirty-Nine Articles); and presided over an

Thomas Cranmer. Portrait by the English artist Gerlach Flicke. Oil on panel; 1546. NATIONAL PORTRAIT GALLERY, LONDON/THE BRIDGEMAN ART LIBRARY

abortive reform plan for canon law, later styled the *Reformatio legum.*

Cranmer's liturgical projects demonstrate a genius for drawing on very varied sources: he looked to the Sarum (Salisbury Cathedral) version of the traditional liturgy but also showed a lively awareness of both contemporary Lutheran experiment and the Roman church's liturgical reforms. He unhesitatingly cannibalized devotional publications in English. His theological program was increasingly radical, although it was only cautiously expressed in the 1549 Prayer Book, a consciously stopgap production. In general, his theology as archbishop through Henry's reign was close to Lutheranism, especially in relation to the Eucharist, where he continued to believe in the real presence (or "true presence") while rejecting transubstantiation. About 1546, like many English evangelical leaders, he reassessed his eucharistic beliefs and aligned himself with the view prevalent in south Germany and Switzerland that there was no bodily or real presence in the Eucharist, Christ being experienced only by the elect believer, in a spiritual sense. He spelled this belief out in two published treatises on the Eucharist (1550, 1551). He was concerned to make England a unifying force among religious reform movements in Europe and tried in vain to gather a general council of evangelicals to rival the Council of Trent. It is likely that he would have sponsored still more radical reform; with little sympathy for English cathedral life, he encouraged the dismantling of England's remaining sacred choral tradition in Edward's last year.

Although his relations with Edward's second minister, John Dudley, duke of Northumberland, became strained, he acquiesced in the unsuccessful attempt to make Jane Grey queen in place of Henry VIII's daughter Mary. Cranmer was convicted of treason by Mary's government in 1553 and of heresy in 1554, after theological disputations and a show trial; his morale collapsed in prison. He signed six recantations but was still condemned to burn at the stake at Oxford. At the ceremony preceding his burning he rejected his recantations and made an uncompromising statement of Protestant faith. Elizabeth I revived his work in her church settlement of 1559 but blocked all attempts at more radical reforms.

Surviving fragments of Cranmer's artistic patronage indicate an advanced classical taste, evidenced in seals commissioned for his official duties during the 1530s, in remains of building projects at his palaces, and in a celebrated portrait by Gerlach Flicke (1545), whose background utilizes exactly contemporary French decorative models. He also habitually used Arabic, not Latin, numeration in his private notes. Too fair-minded and cautious to be a readymade hero, he was an impressively learned if unoriginal scholar, gathering the largest library in mid-Tudor England apart from the Royal Library. He was keenly interested in the publishing trade, using evangelical printers like the Dutch Reyner Wolfe to liaise with European evangelicals. His widow married his own publisher, Edward Whitchurch (and subsequently was married yet again, to an associate of Whitchurch's). Cranmer's genius for formal prose, in particular his carefully restrained encouragement of humanist importations of Latin- and Greek-derived words into the vernacular, has left a lasting mark not merely on Anglican liturgy but on the shape of the English language.

BIBLIOGRAPHY

Primary Works

Cranmer, Thomas. *A Catechism Set Forth by Thomas Cranmer from the Nuremberg Catechism Translated into Latin by Justus Jonas.* Edited by David G. Selwyn. Appleford, U.K., 1978.

Cranmer, Thomas. *The Works of Thomas Cranmer.* 2 vols. Edited by John Edmund Cox. Cambridge, U.K., 1844–1846.

The Divorce Tracts of Henry VIII. Edited by Edward Surtz and Virginia Murphy. Angers, France, 1988. Gives the Latin text, with Cranmer's translation, helpfully annotated.

The Two Liturgies, A.D. 1549 and A.D. 1552: With Other Documents Set Forth by Authority in the Reign of King Edward VI. Edited by J. Ketley. Cambridge, U.K., 1844.

Secondary Works

Ayris, Paul, and David Selwyn, eds. *Thomas Cranmer: Churchman and Scholar.* Woodbridge, U.K., 1993. Valuable collection of essays on different aspects of Cranmer's career.

Brooks, Peter Newman. *Thomas Cranmer's Doctrine of the Eucharist: An Essay in Historical Development.* Rev. ed. Basingstoke, U.K., 1992. Useful analysis of Cranmer's changing views on the Eucharist, although it mislabels his last as a belief in "true presence."

MacCulloch, Diarmaid. *Thomas Cranmer: A Life.* New Haven, Conn., and London, 1996.

DIARMAID MacCULLOCH

CRIME AND PUNISHMENT.

This article deals with the definition of crimes in the Renaissance, how police and judicial systems dealt with the variety of offenses, whether courts treated commoners differently from aristocrats, the gender issues involved (were men participants in different sorts of criminal activity than women, and did the courts respond differently to the sex of the accused in judgment and punishment), how legal codes changed during the Renaissance, and whether there was a Renaissance system of laws and procedures.

Defining Crime.

Europeans shared a common legacy of colorful localism during the Middle Ages, which produced a variety of law codes. In each case laws were the embodiment of common will, of accepted social norms of behavior. The ecclesiastical courts were another source for defining crime. Whether in the monastic courts of rural England or the parish courts of urban Italy, crimes of morality, violations of the church conception of sin, were dealt with locally, at the parish level. A third source generating local definitions of crime were Europe's monarchies and principalities. With the introduction of Roman Law (the Codes of Justinian directed substantial power to the ruler) in the late Middle Ages, first in Italy, then in most of western Europe apart from England, the power to define crime shifted to the prince or king, eclipsing the older sources of definition. Thus, during the Renaissance, sin became almost completely secularized, and crime was defined from the top down.

The justice system divided criminal behavior into two general categories: crimes against persons and crimes against property; the former were more frequent. Clearly, some persons, particularly monarchs,

Punishment. Hanged men. *St. George and the Princess* (detail) by Antonio Pisanello (c. 1395–1455) in the church of S. Anastasia, Verona, Italy. SCALA/ART RESOURCE

were considered more important than others. With the growing acceptance of Roman Law, assassination, attempted assassination, and conspiracy against the monarch's government were pursued as especially serious crimes.

Other forms of violence against persons extended along a continuum from verbal insult (a speech act considered as a form of violence and recognized as such in statutes) to assault and murder. In Italy, some types of verbal insult were accompanied by the use of props of various kinds, which were delineated in communal statutes: animal horns placed over the target's doorway, excrement smeared over the door, signs posted in public places, and so on. A chance encounter between enemies on a public plaza could produce an exchange of stock verbal phrases intended to lead to the brink of violence. At this point the defense of honor became the paramount issue, and violence usually followed.

Not even the poorest Europeans engaged in violence without the use of some weapon. Every man who was not a cleric (and an unarmed man was assumed to be a cleric!) went about with a cudgel at the very least. If a confrontation occurred in a large city such as sixteenth-century Florence, where all weapons were banned within the city gates, then men and women fought with anything at hand—rocks, pots and pans—but never simply with fists. The Italian countryside of the sixteenth century had a true "arms race," as factions made or procured early types of firearms. The rape of women was also considered a violent crime. Then, as now, rape was a display of male power over women. The major difference was that, where family feuding still occurred, rape could be another dimension of the violence associated with a vendetta.

Criminal Justice. The system of criminal justice dealt with crimes of violence through imposition of various penalties, often in combination. Flexibility was the rule. Fines were imposed on those convicted of the least significant violations, but the level of punishment could escalate sharply if the crime was linked to a serious flare-up of a vendetta. Even a verbal insult, if it led to injury or a death in the context of a vendetta, could be punished according to a carefully calibrated scale of fines matched to the severity of injury, up to death.

Complicating matters everywhere in Europe was the ease with which an accused person could evade all punishment by fleeing the competent jurisdiction. There was a risk involved for those who fled, since they were automatically banned, deprived of the protection of law, and subject to being killed or captured by anyone without recourse. But this was a risk worth running, because the miscreant avoided the discomfort of a long prejudgment confinement. In effect, the justice system was forced to bargain with the accused for his return. At times the exilee could even negotiate down his punishment as a condition of return. The commutation might include a limited period of exile, payment of a fine in money or kind, or some combination of these penalties.

Nowhere in Europe were fines collected from the poor to any great extent. Northern Europe saw a growing reliance on afflictive penalties during the Renaissance. Afflictive penalties were supposed to make punishments equal for rich and poor alike, preventing the rich from getting off with lighter punishment because they could more easily pay fines. The Florentine system, after the first third of the sixteenth century, came increasingly to rely on commutation of all kinds of penalties to a period of *confino* (exile for a fixed period) within the state, such as in the town of Livorno. Execution was reserved for the rare career criminal, for the worst murderers, and for those bandits involved in brigandage. When caught, brigands were summarily hung in groups. The limited and declining use of capital penalties was a trend in northern Italy.

Crimes against Property. Crimes against property were less frequently committed than crimes against persons. It is worth noting that the balance did not change until the nineteenth century, when the Industrial Revolution and a consumer economy combined to produce a convergence of extensive poverty and many things that could be easily stolen. During the Renaissance crimes against property were many and various, but clearly on the increase through the sixteenth century, when more laws dealing with these crimes went on the books. Theft covered a broad range of violations, from stealing a fish or loaf of bread at market to the occasional fraudulent bankruptcy. The latter was considered theft akin to the failure to pay off a legitimate debt and was a jailable offense. In the countryside, highway robbery was a special problem since, unlike theft in the city, it was invariably done with the aid of a deadly weapon. Highway robbery differed from brigandage in scale and frequency. Brigandage was endemic in the sixteenth century. It had to be treated as a quasi-military problem, because of the number and size of the bands. Organizing an expensive temporary expeditionary force to hunt them down was the usual solution.

Beginning in sixteenth-century Florence, royal decrees established new types of property crimes. After 1537 fishing and hunting in large swathes of Tuscan forests and rivers, now established as aristocratic preserves, were declared off-limits to those without permits. These lands had formerly been open to all for gaming and fishing. The motivation for creating these reserves was twofold: to establish hunting as a defining characteristic of the aristocracy, and to create monopolies of fish and game, viewed as commodities to be supplied to a market, for Medici supporters. The Florentines initiated a practice increasingly adopted by the nobility of northern Eu-

Executions. Executions in Brussels, 1580s. From *De leone belgico* (1588).

rope. French nobles, for example, annexed open land for their private uses.

Other categories of crime against property were declared and elaborated as property owners sought to protect new uses of their land, such as conversion to sheep raising or silkworm cultivation in mulberry trees. Criminal courts, rather than civil courts, punished violators, thus resolving an earlier ambivalence concerning how disputes between the rich and poor over access to property should be resolved. Civil procedures were considered too long and drawn out, too expensive, and unsure of outcome.

Criminals. European systems of criminal justice dealt differently with commoners and aristocrats, largely as a matter of legal and sociopolitical principle. People were different according to their origins, and criminal courts recognized the differences. Another important part of the equation was the character of the crime, from less to more horrendous. When these elements were combined, the principle emerged that each crime was unique, because it comprised randomly combined factors, the relative

importance of which had to be evaluated in order to arrive at a just decision. Justice in criminal matters was not conceived as a general principle or set of principles to be applied to the common elements of general categories of cases. Justice was properly determined by identifying elements of difference in each individual crime and applying the appropriate type, level, or combination of penalties.

Distinctions among persons were constructed according to gender, socioeconomic status related to birth, family relationships when one family member committed a crime against another (patricide was considered very serious, sibling violence less so), whether the criminal was a native of the place where the crime occurred or a foreigner, and whether the victim was a native and the perpetrator a nonresident. Finally, political status, that is, whether the miscreant was a member of the royal family or one of its noble supporters, mattered. Vendetta was a separate category; any crime committed in connection with a vendetta was viewed within its context. Especially in Italy, the family vendetta was a complex phenomenon with a separate system of justice, whose rules and structure the state had to acknowledge.

The courts dealt with all classes and persons except for ecclesiastical personnel and members of the royal family. A member of a royal family seldom committed a crime. When he did, it was usually one of violence and was swept under the rug. Aristocrats, such as those linked to the Medici regime in Florence, committed crimes, but the Medici rulers dealt with them outside of the regular system or by manipulating the system. Sometimes aristocratic criminals were ignored. Women did not appear in court nearly as frequently as did men. They were accused of a very limited group of crimes, most often fights with other women, small thefts, and other nonviolent crimes. They were given the same kinds of punishment as men, usually fines or *confino*. The most serious crime of which women were accused was infanticide. However, prosecutions were rare because it was a difficult crime to prove in either secular or ecclesiastical courts.

Crimes against the regime, such as conspiracy, assassination, or attempted assassination, were the most serious crimes. Viewed as *laesa maesta,* that is, crimes against the royal person conceived as the state, they were punished by execution, imprisonment, or long periods of exile. Crimes of the poor against the wealthy, usually property crimes, were punished with fines, or exile within the state, or both. Crimes among persons of the same sociopolitical status, notably the poor, yielded the complete spectrum of penalties. The authorities found intrafamily crimes of violence particularly disturbing but punished them with fines or exile. They often suspected foreigners of thievery; indeed, most professional thieves were foreign, and were likely to be executed or banished. The occasional thrill-seeking noble might also become a thief.

Laws and Procedures. At the level of laws and procedures the Renaissance system of criminal justice comprised an eclectic mixture of old and new elements. By the sixteenth century, the legal codes of northern Europe and Spain followed the Italian codes by adopting Roman Law. They investigated alleged crime by means of inquisitorial (from the Latin *inquirere, inquisitum,* to inquire into or to search for evidence) procedure. Adopted first by the medieval church in order to deal with heretics, inquisitorial procedure was certainly a rational advance over the traditional system of ordeal and blood repudiated by the church at the fourth Lateran

Council in 1215. Inquisitional process was adopted by Italian communes (town governments) in the twelfth century, and throughout western continental Europe by the sixteenth century. It often existed alongside the older accusatorial procedures.

In accusatorial procedure, the aggrieved claimant brought a charge to court; he had to investigate and prove the case against the alleged culprit. If he failed to prove his case, the plaintiff was liable to pay court costs and to suffer the same penalty that the accused would have been assessed if convicted. This form of prosecution, which gave little power to judges, was common in medieval Europe and remained a lesser element of the Renaissance system.

In inquisitorial procedure governmental organs ex officio, that is, by virtue of office, conducted the entire investigation judicially in order to establish the substantive facts and the objective truth. This is a fair assessment of how officials tried to make the system work, and they did so with considerable success. Exceptions existed, especially if the ruler had a personal stake in the outcome. Occasionally a case might prove embarassing or inconvenient to the prince. Then the culprit might be murdered in his prison cell, or spirited into exile without benefit of a trial.

By the sixteenth century, in Florence for example, courts relied almost exclusively on a summary form of inquisitorial procedure, rather than the longer form typical of the fourteenth and fifteenth centuries. This saved time and moved the court toward the imposition of fines. For small monetary disputes between unimportant people, courts used an informal summary procedure, again saving time and money.

The difficulty in financing the justice system played a crucial role in determining its character and operation. Those accused of crimes were usually subject to lengthy pretrial incarceration in uncomfortable public jails, because they could not afford bail. The law required them to pay for their sustenance in jail, but most could not do so. Hence, the government had to support the prisoners. However, very little state funding went to this or any other public charge. Thus, those in jail, whether guilty or innocent, suffered hunger and other discomforts. The Florentines dealt with the problem by clearing the jails every six or nine months by releasing those unable to pay their fines.

Torture in order to obtain confession was a staple of a system incapable of producing other reliable evidence. But protracted torture was used only when professional theft was suspected. The use of torture was intended to shorten the time that individuals

Crime, Trial, Punishment, and Redemption. A painting attributed to Filippo di Lorenzo Dolciati, c. 1502, tells the story of the crime of Antonio Rinaldeschi. Influenced by a devil, Rinaldeschi, a Florentine who had been unlucky at dice, commits blasphemy by throwing a piece of horse dung at an image of the Virgin called S. Maria de' Ricci at the church of S. Maria degli Alberighi *(top row)*. He is arrested and imprisoned *(middle row)* and brought to trial *(bottom left)*. After confessing his sin to a priest *(bottom middle)*, he is hanged as angels and devils contend for his soul *(bottom right)*. Rinaldeschi's crime occurred on 12 July 1501; he was hanged on 22 July. MUSEO STIBBERT, FLORENCE/FMR/R. ORSI BATTAGLINI

spent in jail, which reduced costs. Indeed, very little of judicial procedure actually occurred in a courtroom, which was often only the setting for an exchange of written documents between lawyers, rather than examination of witnesses and oral arguments. The justice system clearly did not offer adequate procedural protections for the accused.

The overall quality of the judiciary was uneven in Renaissance Europe. Men without legal training served as judges in England and Florence. On the other hand, appointed jurists presided in some outlying regions of the Florentine state. Trained legal professionals presided in the French criminal justice system, but the opposite was the case in Germany, even though Germany, like France, had adopted inquisitorial procedure. Centralization of the justice system was the rule but was not uniformly applied. With tensions between old and new, between the theoretical and practical, crime and criminal justice in Renaissance Europe reflected the eclecticism and pragmatism typical of that marvelous, creative, but confused era.

See also **Law**; **Rape**; **Violence**.

BIBLIOGRAPHY

Bellamy, John G. *Criminal Law and Society in Late Medieval and Tudor England*. Gloucester, U.K., 1984.

Bowsky, William M. "The Medieval Commune and Internal Violence: Police Power and Public Safety in Siena, 1287–1355." *American Historical Review* 73 (1967): 1–17.

Brackett, John K. *Criminal Justice and Crime in Late-Renaissance Florence, 1537–1609*. Cambridge, U.K., 1992.

Cohn, Samuel, Jr. "Criminality and the State in Renaissance Florence, 1344–1466." *Journal of Social History* 14, no. 2 (1980): 211–239.

Dean, Trevor, and K. J. P. Lowe, eds. *Crime, Society and the Law in Renaissance Italy*. Cambridge, U.K., 1994.

Gatrell, V. A. C., Bruce Lenman, and Geoffrey Parker, eds. *Crime and the Law: The Social History of Crime in Western Europe since 1500*. London, 1980.

Langbein, John H. *Prosecuting Crime in the Renaissance: England, Germany, France*. Cambridge, Mass., 1974.

Padoa-Schioppa, Antonio, ed. *Legislation and Justice*. Oxford, 1997.

Peters, Edward. *Inquisition*. New York, 1988.

Ruggiero, Guido. *Violence in Early Renaissance Venice*. New Brunswick, N.J., 1980.

Soman, A. "Deviance and Criminal Justice in Western Europe, 1300–1800: An Essay in Structure." *Criminal Justice History* 16 (1980).

Stern, Laura Ikins. *The Criminal Law System of Medieval and Renaissance Florence*. Baltimore, Md., 1994.

Weisser, Michael. *Crime and Punishment in Early Modern Europe, 1350–1850*. Cambridge, U.K., 1979.

JOHN BRACKETT

CROATIA AND DALMATIA.

[This entry includes two subentries, one on the history of Croatia and Dalmatia in the Renaissance and the other on artists active in Croatia and Dalmatia.]

Croatia and Dalmatia in the Renaissance

The southern region of Croatia, known as Dalmatia, was under Venetian rule for nearly four hundred years, from 1409 to 1797. The Venetian influence on the formation of Croatian humanism in Dalmatia during the fifteenth and sixteenth centuries was enormous, especially in Split, Zadar, Šibenik, and Dubrovnik. Significant factors in the development of Dalmatian humanism were the cultural, political, and social influence of Venetian rule on the Dalmatian nobility, the literary connections between Venice and Dalmatia; and, most important, the education of Dalmatian humanists in Italy.

Italian Education. Croatian humanists who studied in Italy brought back to Croatia their knowledge and passion for humanism. After studying in Padua, Juraj Šižgorić (Georgius Sisgoreus; 1420–1504) from Šibenik wrote the first printed book of Croatian poems in 1477, entitled *Elegiarum et carminum libri tres* (Three books of elegies and lyric poems). Ivan Česmički (Janus Pannonius; 1434–1472), from northern Croatia, studied canon law in Italy and spent a major part of his life at the court of the Hungarian king Matthias Corvinus (ruled 1458–1490). Česmički is best known for his epigrams.

Another important poet, Marko Marulić (Marcus Marulus; 1450–1524), studied in his native city of Split in the school of the famous teacher Tideo Acciarini (who also taught Ludovik Crijević-Tuberon, Karlo Pucić, and Ilija Crijević, all important Croatian Latinists) before he went to Padua to continue his studies. Upon his return to Split, Marulić assembled around him a considerable group of Dalmatian humanists, educated by Italian teachers and in contact with Italy and its humanistic movement. Among them were Latinists such as Toma Niger, Petar Petracic, Jerolim Papalic, and Placid Grguric.

The Croatian humanist Ilija Crijević (Aelius Lampridus Cervinus; 1463–1520), who studied in Ferrara, acquired great fame after he was crowned *poeta laureatus* for his poetry at Rome. Another humanist, Franjo Petris (Francesco Patrizi; 1529–1597) of the island of Cres, taught as a professor of Platonic philosophy in Ferrara and Rome from 1577 until his death. Also, two students at Padua from Dubrovnik—Matija Ranjina and Dominko Zlatarić (c. 1556–c. 1610)—were elected student rectors of the university. Evidence of Zlatarić's role at the University of Padua exists to this day, with his coat of arms adorning one of the walls of the university.

Croatian Literature. Dalmatians were influenced both stylistically and thematically by important Italian writers such as Dante and Petrarch. The cult of Petrarch was first introduced to Dalmatia from 1384 to 1387 through Giovanni di Conversino da Ravenna, an admirer of Petrarch's. Some Petrarchists of Dalmatia, such as Sabo Bobaljevic Misetic and Lodovico Paskalic, wrote most of their poetry in Italian, while others translated Petrarch's works in Croatian. Dalmatian poets also found inspiration in Italian imitators of Petrarch, such as Serafino Ciminelli dell'Aquila (1466–1500). Serafino's odd similes are scattered throughout the Italian poems (*canzonieri*) of Dinko Ranjina (1536–1607).

Petrarch's influence is evident in the works of Marin Držić, an author of comedies who was born in Dubrovnik around 1508. Držić was a priest who had studied canon law and music in Siena and written several mediocre verses in an artificial Petrarchan style. After his return to Dubrovnik, Držić wrote several excellent pastoral plays and comedies in a similar style, pointing to Siena as a turning point in his development as a writer.

Dalmatian humanists preferred to utilize Latin in order to place themselves within a wider European sphere. They wrote historiographical works—based on sources they discovered—surveying Dalmatian history from earliest to Renaissance times in Latin. One example is Vinko Pribojevic's *De origine successibusque Slavorum,* published in Venice in 1532, which describes the history of the Slavs, Dalmatia, and Hvar in three parts. Another important Latinist was Marulić, who wrote the majority of his didactic moralistic books and lyric and epic poems in Latin. He was best known for his theological treatises, *Evangelistarium* (Evangelistary; 1516) and *De institutione bene beateque vivendi* (Instructions for a good and blessed life; 1506), which were later translated into many languages and reprinted many times.

Dalmatian humanists also utilized the Croatian vernacular. Marulić's epic poem *Judita* (Judith), for one, was published in Venice in 1521. Hanibal Lucić (1485–1553) published his Croatian love poems, entitled *Skladanja* (Compositions), in 1556, while Petar Hektorović (1487–1572) published *Ribanje i ribarsko prigovaranje* (Fishing and fisherman's talk) in 1568. Miksa Pelegrinović's *Jedupka* (Gypsy lady) was published in 1599 by Toma N. Budislovic in Venice. In 1595 Faust Vrančić published his five-language dictionary, including Croatian, in Venice. Venetians were therefore a vital element in discovering and publishing the works of Dalmatian humanists, both in Latin and the vernacular.

Croatian Patriotism. Even though the Italian influence on Dalmatian humanists was marked, Dalmatians were still able to develop a uniquely Croatian mode of expression. Dalmatian humanists showed their patriotic pride by adding the name of their birthplace, as in "Dalmata," to their humanist Latin names to identify their origin, and the literature they produced portrays the background and traditions of their native land. Marulić's epic poem *Judita* contains references to medieval Croatian literature and Dalmatian folk poetry and also intersperses its classical Latin forms with similes inspired by the breezes and storms at sea of his native Split. The Dalmatian landscape was depicted by other poets, such as Petar Zoranić (1508–1550), whose *Planine* (Mountains; 1569) was the first Croatian novel. Another local theme, that of concern over the Turkish threat to the Dalmatian hinterland, was treated with sensitivity in Juraj Šižgorić's *Elegia de Sibenicensis agri vastatione* (An elegy on the devastation of the Sibenik Plain), written in 1470.

Croatians remained conscious of belonging to a wider Slavic "nation" (in its pre-nationalistic sense) and thus felt a common bond with other Slavs such as the Czechs, Poles, and Russians. Vinko Pribojević's *De origine successibusque Slavorum* (On the origins of the Slavs and the events among them; 1532) was the first Pan-Slavic document to be written. At times, patriotism took the form of criticism directed at the Venetian Republic and its policies. Juraj Barakovic (1548–1628) was famous for his work *Vila Slovinka* (Slavic fairy), in which he laments the changes that occurred in Zadar after the Venetian takeover. Both Pribojević's and Barakovic's works were the earliest manifestations of Pan-Slavism, a philosophy that came to the forefront in Croatia during the Illyrian movement of the nineteenth century, effected by Ljudevit Gaj, which sought to unify the South Slavs against the then-dominant Hungarians.

See also **Dubrovnik.**

BIBLIOGRAPHY

Primary Works

Marulić, Marko. *Judith.* Edited by Henry R. Cooper. New York, 1991.

Vratovic, Vladimir, ed. *The Croatian Muses in Latin: A Trilingual Anthology, Latin-English-Croatian.* Zagreb, Croatia, 1998.

Vratovic, Vladimir, ed. *Latinism and Mediterraneanism.* Zagreb, Croatia, 1997. Both texts contain Latin and English versions of works from important Croatian humanists.

Secondary Works

Birnbaum, Marianna D. *Humanists in a Shattered World: Croatian and Hungarian Latinity in the Sixteenth Century.* Columbus, Ohio, 1986. An insightful look at the Croatian humanists in the Hungarian court, and their reactions to, among other things, the Ottoman threat to Croatia.

Franicevic, Marin. *Povijest hrvatske renesansne knjizevnosti.* (The history of Croatian renaissance literature). Zagreb, 1983. An authoritative text on Croatian Renaissance literature.

Kadić, Ante. *The Tradition of Freedom in Croatian Literature.* Bloomington, Ind., 1983. Interesting study of the political and philosophical significance of Croatian literature.

Kolumbic, Nikica. *Hrvatska knjizevnost od humanizma do manirizma.* (Croatian literature from humanism to mannerism). Zagreb, Croatia, 1980. A comprehensive study.

Petrovich, Michael Boro. "Croatian Humanism and the Italian Connection." *Journal of Croatian Studies* 27 (1986): 78–90. Well-documented essay dealing with Italy's influence in the formation of Croatian humanism.

Torbarina, Josip. *Italian Influence on the Poets of the Ragusan Republic.* London, 1931. A detailed account of Dubrovnik's humanists and their connections to Italy.

Usmiani, Mirko A. "Marko Marulić." *Harvard Slavic Studies* 3 (1957): 1–48. A concentrated study of Marulić's literature and its significance to Croatian humanism.

ANITA MIKULIĆ-KOVAČEVIĆ

Art in Croatia and Dalmatia

During the Renaissance, Croatian lands were divided between Venice, which governed Istria, Kvarner, and Dalmatia; and Hungary and Austria, which ruled over northern Istria, Croatia, and Slavonia. Only the Republic of Dubrovnik—reaching from Cavtat to Pelješac, and including the islands of Šipan, Lopud, and Koločep—was free and independent during that time. The historic division between northern and southern Croatia during the Renaissance is revealed in their contrasting cultural heritage: works of Renaissance style were being realized in Dalmatia, but the Turks occupied Slavonia, and constantly threatened to invade the remainder of northern Croatia.

The period of greatest intensity in architectural and artistic productivity for the eastern Adriatic coast and Croatian archipelago was the fifteenth and sixteenth centuries. This region freely chose between various artistic models and used them in a creative synthesis (combining Florentine and Venetian ideals with the ancient heritage of the Dalmatian region). In Croatia, the early Renaissance was evident before the middle of the fifteenth century. The cities of the Adriatic coast and islands were enlarged and embellished with Renaissance palaces and houses, churches, bell-towers, city halls, and lodges, and surrounded by new walls with cylindrical turrets and strongholds. The well-preserved walls and towers of Dubrovnik, Korčula, Hvar, the interesting small Renaissance town of Svetvinčenat in Istria, and the entire island of Šipan are especially notable.

Most of the monuments of the fifteenth and sixteenth centuries in Croatia are in the Renaissance style; yet three architectural works of that period—the Šibenik Cathedral, the Trogir Chapel, and the Sorkočevičev summer villa—make peculiar and original contributions to the advancement of the Renaissance in Europe. The Šibenik Cathedral, by Juraj Dalmatinac (Giorgio da Sebenico; Georgius Mathei Dalamticus; fl. 1441), marked the first appearance of the early Renaissance in Dalmatian architecture and sculpture. The illusionistic reliefs that appear in the niches of its polygonal apses employ a geometric perspective (1443), while a frieze of seventy-two sculpted heads is exceptional in the history of cathedral sculpture. Constructed entirely of stone, without the use of mortar, the cathedral incorporated large stone tiles, pilasters, and girdles, tied together by tongue and groove in the original use of that method of assembly construction. This use of precarved

Croatian Art. *The Annunciation* by N. Bozidarević (fl. 1430) in the Dominican Convent, Dubrovnik, Croatia. DOMINICAN CONVENT, DUBROVNIK/THE BRIDGEMAN ART LIBRARY

stone elements, an adaptation of the techniques of wood construction, is unique. The molding of the tripartite gable of the main facade—completed by Nikola Firentinac (Niccolò di Giovanni Fiorentino)—repeats the shape of the interior arches; thus the facade is not a false front (as in Italy), but rather a direct expression of the geometry of the interior stone arches, and hence the first and only functional version of a trefoil early Renaissance facade in Europe. Stone construction, the identity of interior and exterior expressed through architectural elements, and figural reliefs integrated as part of the architecture are fundamental characteristics of the central Dalmatian early Renaissance school. Juraj's student, Andrija Aleši, used giant monoliths, rather than pre-carved elements, to harmonize the exterior and interior in the Trogir Baptistery (1467).

The mortuary Chapel of the Blessed John of Trogir, in the Trogir Cathedral, by Nikola Firentinac (1468), uses the forms of early Renaissance Tuscan style, but its stone masonry and its unification of architecture and sculpture reflect Dalmatian practice. Drawing on ancient architectural niches (like those from tombs under St. Peter's in Rome and the Isola sacra next to Ostia) and those from Croatian Romanesque architecture, Firentinac adapted them to decorate the interior of the chapel with connecting niches of life-size sculptures placed above a relief slab with depictions of torch-bearers, and with a relief of "putti-telamoni" (unruly and chubby cherubs). This mausoleum, with the attentive faces of 150 children (those of the torch-bearers and putti) staring at us, is an example of the triumph of early Renaissance humanism.

Many residential structures in the territory of the Dubrovnik Republic exhibit a uniquely functional organization of their interior space within an asymmetrical L-shaped plan that balanced both architecture and garden design. Sorkočevičev's summer palace in Dubrovnik (1521) was an epoch-making achievement in the application of this functional asymmetry to project design.

Outstanding monuments of sixteenth-century Renaissance art in Croatia include the trefoiled facade of the Hvar Cathedral and St. Mary's Church in Zadar, works of distinctive Gothic-Renaissance style in Dubrovnik; the Ducal Palace (Michelozzo and local masters 1464) and Divon (P. Milićević, 1524), and city halls and lodges in Trogir, Šibenik, and Hvar. The thirty summer villas in the territory of Dubrovnik and the villas in Hvar belonging to the Renaissance poets Hanibal Lučić and Petar Hektorović are also notable. Many Croatian artists left for Italy and cre-ated masterpieces there (the Italians identified them as "Schiavoni"). In Ancona Juraj Dalmatinac built the portal of the "Loggia dei Mercanti" for Franciscan and Augustinian friars (c. 1450). The architect Luciano Laurana and the sculptor Francesco Laurana (from Vrana, Croatia, next to Zadar), the sculptor Giovanni Dalmata (Duknović, who was active in the court of the Hungarian king Matthias Corvinus), the painter Andrea Meldolla (Medulić), and the miniaturist Giulio Clovio (Juraj Klović), are only the most notable of these distinguished expatriates. Among painters in Croatia, the most significant was Nikola Božidarević (c. 1460–c. 1518) in Dubrovnik.

While in the south sacred and secular architecture flourished, in the northwestern regions of Croatia, Renaissance style in the sixteenth century only appeared in military architecture. The most outstanding of these fortifications are the monument of Veliki Tabor (an oval layout with semicircular towers), the fortifications surrounding the Zagreb Cathedral (six circular and two square towers) and the Karlovac (Karlstadt) Fortress in the shape of a true six-pointed star, symbol of an ideal Renaissance town plan (1579).

See also **Dubrovnik.**

BIBLIOGRAPHY

Ivančević, Radovan. *Art Treasures of Croatia*. Zagreb, Croatia, 1993.

Ivančević, Radovan. *Šibenik Cathedral*. Šibenik, Croatia, 1998.

RADOVAN IVANČEVIĆ

Translated from Croatian by Anita Mikulić-Kovačević

CROMBERGER PRESS. The Cromberger press (Seville, 1503–c. 1555) was one of the most important in the Iberian Peninsula during the first half of the sixteenth century. The German Jakob Cromberger settled in Seville in the 1490s and became associated with Meinardus Ungut and Stanislaus Polonus, the most prolific printers in fifteenth-century Spain. In 1500 he became a partner in their firm, taking control of it shortly afterward. At his death in 1528 he enjoyed a high reputation throughout Spain and Portugal as a printer, publisher, and bookseller. His son, Juan, was an equally energetic entrepreneur, establishing the first press in the Americas, which he sent to Mexico in 1539 as a branch office of his Seville firm. Although of historical significance, the importance to him of this Mexican press has been exaggerated; he probably agreed to found it only because he was granted in return a monopoly on book exports to New Spain and other commercial benefits associated with silver mining there. On

Juan's death in 1540, his widow appears to have taken charge of the Seville office until their son Jácome Cromberger was old enough, in the mid-1540s, to assume responsibility for the family business. While Jakob and Juan had been fine printers, Jácome's press was undercapitalized and had low production, and his work was shoddy; he was operating at a time when economic and ideological conditions in Spain were unfavorable to printing and when the domestic industry's center of gravity was shifting to northern Castile. The Cromberger press went into steep decline, its last surviving edition appearing in 1553. In 1559, Jácome emigrated to the New World in a bid to improve his fortunes, dying there in 1560 or 1561.

The three generations of Crombergers printed at least six hundred editions, which made their press prolific by Spanish standards. In the sixteenth century Spain provided a market for publishers in Italy, France, the Low Countries, and Germany. Consequently Spain tended to produce editions that could not be imported economically from abroad, such as service books for local dioceses and popular works in the vernacular. The Crombergers could not afford to specialize. Instead they alternated elaborate liturgical editions or Latin works by local humanists with cheap schoolbooks, ballads, and best-sellers printed in Castilian. While Seville was a center for vernacular printing and many of the Crombergers' staple products were medieval or of a medieval stamp (popular devotion, romances of chivalry), their output also reflected the impact of the Renaissance in Spain.

In the late 1520s the Crombergers commissioned a local humanist to prepare Latin editions of Lucan, Ovid, and Virgil, which they printed in a format imitating the famous octavo series issued at Venice by Aldus Manutius; these were the first books printed in Spain in the italic types so closely associated in the minds of contemporary readers with the new learning. The Crombergers printed important first editions concerning discoveries in the Americas (Cortés's second and third letters from Mexico, 1522 and 1523) and works that popularized classical learning (the first edition of Guevara's *Libro áureo de Marco Aurelio* [Golden book of Marcus Aurelius], 1528), and they were the earliest printers anywhere to issue a vernacular translation of Erasmus's *Tratado o sermón del niño Jesu "Concio de puero Jesu"* (Treatise or sermon on the infant Jesus; 1516). Their editions of translations of classical and Italian works epitomize the Spanish Renaissance. From their press issued Castilian versions of Roman history (Josephus's *Los siete libros de la guerra que tuvieron los judíos con los romanos* [*Bellum judaicum*], 1532 and 1536), of classical literature (Apuleius's *Asno de oro* [*The Golden Ass*], c. 1513), and of popular Italian Renaissance works (Boccaccio's *Libro llamado Fiameta* [*Fiammetta*], 1523, and *Libro de Juan Bocacio que trata de las ilustres mujeres* [*De claris mulieribus*], 1528; and Castiglione's *Libro llamado el cortesano* [*Book of the Courtier*], at least three editions in the 1540s).

BIBLIOGRAPHY

Griffin, Clive. *The Crombergers of Seville: The History of a Printing and Merchant Dynasty*. Oxford, 1988.

Griffin, Clive. "A Series of Classical Literary Texts Printed in Seville 1528–29." In *Letters and Society in Fifteenth-Century Spain: Studies Presented to P. E. Russell on His Eightieth Birthday*. Edited by Alan Deyermond and Jeremy Lawrance. Oxford and Llangrannog, U.K., 1993. Pages 39–57.

Norton, Frederick John. *A Descriptive Catalogue of Printing in Spain and Portugal, 1501–1520*. Cambridge, U.K., 1978.

Norton, Frederick John. *Printing in Spain, 1501–1520, with a Note on the Early Editions of the "Celestina."* Cambridge, U.K., 1966.

CLIVE GRIFFIN

CROMWELL, THOMAS (c. 1485–1540), chief minister of Henry VIII. Son of a cloth worker and brewer in south London, Cromwell left for the Continent at an early age and fought in Italy, where he may have been initiated into the money-lending career that he pursued on his return to England in 1512. He also practiced law and came in contact with Thomas More's circle. In 1517 he went for a second time to Rome, on behalf of a religious guild at Boston (Lincolnshire). During his trip he reportedly learned the New Testament by heart from Erasmus's new Latin edition.

By this time he had attracted Cardinal Wolsey's notice, entering his service in about 1514. He handled nearly all of Wolsey's legal business. Cromwell made his most important contribution to Wolsey's affairs in 1525, when he oversaw the suppression of several small monastic houses, the endowments of which were put to the founding of Wolsey's grammar school in Ipswich and a college (to become Christ Church) in Oxford. When Wolsey fell in 1529, Cromwell stood loyally by his master, perhaps not entirely out of disinterested motives.

Beginning with his entry into the parliament of 1529, Cromwell quickly transferred to royal service, becoming a privy councillor in early 1531. Over the next three years Cromwell largely engineered the king's breach with Rome, drafting most of the crucial legislation, especially the Act in Restraint of Appeals (1533), which declared England an empire, free to do as it wished in ecclesiastical as in secular matters. Throughout, Cromwell strove to establish uniform jurisdiction in England, continuing a policy that went back at least to Henry VII.

Little by little Cromwell acquired a large number of bureaucratic offices, which allowed him to centralize first the royal secretariat and then the crown's financial machinery, work largely accomplished from the office of lord privy seal that he received in 1536. He was a good judge of men and surrounded himself with efficient servants, especially Ralph Sadler and Thomas Audley. Cromwell oversaw the dissolution of the monasteries (1536–1540), which brought the crown a vast, if temporary, increase in revenues, and invented a new machinery, the Court of Augmentations, for handling them. He played a hand, if not the only one, in the creation of the Privy Council.

Cromwell displayed an interest in social and economic reforms and patronized thinkers, among them Thomas Starkey and Richard Morison, who could advise him about how best to undertake them. Cromwell proceeded with reforms systematically, drafting proposals (or having them drafted), boiling them down to specifics, and then executing them to the maximum degree possible. He was as good at mobilizing resources of propaganda, drawing on his stable of intellectuals, as he was at putting through practical reforms, including the establishment of parish registers (1538).

Cromwell's mark was perhaps clearest on the English church, which he refashioned beginning with the Act of Supremacy (1534). He was appointed vicegerent in spirituals in 1535, making him Henry's agent for religious affairs. He rigorously enforced the new royal supremacy, most notably in proceedings against Bishop John Fisher and Thomas More, in both of whose trials he took a personal role. Cromwell's religion is still unclear, but he undoubtedly fostered some kind of reformation, most notably through an English translation of the Bible published in 1539 and through frequently making common cause with Archbishop Thomas Cranmer, a Lutheran for much of Henry's reign. Among other Lutherans Cromwell patronized were Robert Barnes and Christopher Mont; the reformer Hugh Latimer enjoyed his support, as did John Bale, some of whose earliest plays may have been written for Cromwell. But it is at least clear that he stoutly supported an English via media (middle way) and wished to curtail the power of the clergy.

A humble commoner by origin, Cromwell worked very hard to achieve noble status, becoming a knight

Thomas Cromwell. Portrait after Hans Holbein the Younger. NATIONAL PORTRAIT GALLERY, LONDON

of the Garter in 1537, lord great chamberlain of England in 1539, and earl of Essex in April 1540. His grasping contributed to his fall, for it gave his numerous enemies among the nobility a lever with which to pry Cromwell away from the king. Cromwell played into their hands in 1538 and 1539 by following an increasingly ideologically determined foreign policy, which seriously annoyed Henry when Cromwell tried to force the king to accept Anne of Cleves as a wife in 1538. She was quite bad enough, as far as Henry was concerned, but the alliance with a German Protestant prince which threatened to isolate England in the face of the Catholic powers was worse. Although never himself inclined to Sacramentarian beliefs, Cromwell overlooked their dangerous inroads in Calais until it was almost too late; his success in bringing down the lord deputy, Lord Lisle, wound up contributing to the opposition to him.

In June 1540 Cromwell was arrested on charges of corruption, Sacramentarianism, and *scandalum magnatum* (which means, approximately, contempt of the great nobility). The duke of Norfolk, his inveterate enemy and one of the most exalted English

111

aristocrats, himself yanked Cromwell's insignias of office from his neck. Attainted by Parliament, Cromwell was executed on 28 July 1540. Henry quickly regretted his loss, mourning Cromwell as "the most faithful servant" the king had ever had.

Cromwell's role in the English Reformation and the development of the modern state has been widely discussed by historians since the 1950s because of the work of G. R. Elton, who put forward undoubtedly the most influential image of Cromwell. According to Elton, Cromwell was responsible for what Elton called the Tudor revolution in government, which brought into existence a modern, unitary state in England, grounded in the legislative omnicompetence of Parliament, whose orders were put into effect by a fully articulated, rationalized bureaucracy. Disputed by medievalists almost from the first, Elton's views came under heavy attack in the 1990s, and in his final summation he implicitly largely retracted his claims for Cromwell's uniqueness. Nevertheless, Elton never gave up his notion of Cromwell as an extraordinarily thoughtful and efficient administrator who left England a quite different place than he had found it.

BIBLIOGRAPHY

Primary Works

Brewer, J. S., et al., eds. *Letters and Papers, Foreign and Domestic, of the Reign of Henry VIII.* London, 1862–1932. Much of the material calendared between 1532 and 1540 stems from Cromwell's archive.

Secondary Works

Elton, G. R. *Policy and Police: The Enforcement of the Reformation in the Age of Thomas Cromwell.* Cambridge, U.K., 1972. This and the following two works offer the fullest study of Cromwell.

Elton, G. R. *Reform and Renewal: Thomas Cromwell and the Common Weal.* Cambridge, U.K., 1973.

Elton, G. R. *The Tudor Revolution in Government: Administrative Changes in the Reign of Henry VIII.* Cambridge, U.K., 1953.

Merriman, Roger B. *The Life and Letters of Thomas Cromwell.* Oxford, 1902. The only full-length (but not very sympathetic) biography.

THOMAS F. MAYER

CRUSADE. The crusade was deeply embedded in late-medieval Latin Christianity as both an ideological concept and an administrative and tax-raising structure. The movement began as a holy war against Islam with the Latin conquest of Jerusalem in 1099 and was extended, under papal direction, to attack fellow Christians, whether heretics, schismatics, or merely political opponents of the papacy. While copiously bolstered with Old Testament rhetoric, the crusade was not easily presented as a revival from antiquity, yet the noted humanist Pope Pius II was profoundly dedicated to the Turkish war and died while waiting to lead an abortive crusade in 1464. The movement's postmedieval history maintained its continuity in the Renaissance; the crusade was not destroyed by the disasters inflicted on Balkan expeditions by the Turks at Nicopolis in 1396 or Varna in 1444. The original intention of recovering Jerusalem for Western Christendom survived as a chivalric ideal; in 1513 it inspired Afonso de Albuquerque, the Portuguese ruler of India, to consider capturing Muhammed's body at Medina in order to exchange it for the Temple at Jerusalem. The crusade was a declared objective of chivalric orders such as the Golden Fleece and was celebrated in literature, most notably in Torquato Tasso's widely read poem *Gerusalemme liberata* (Jerusalem delivered; 1581).

The defense of eastern Europe throughout the intermittent Turkish war was a matter of survival for the Balkan Christians and of economic concern to the Latins in the Levant. For Venice in particular its eastern colonies had considerable value, but the economic balance shifted, however gradually, from the Mediterranean to the Atlantic and beyond. As Europe expanded overseas, it also shrank. The Turks were repulsed at Belgrade in 1456 and at Rhodes in 1480, but they won a great victory at Mohács in Hungary in 1526 and besieged Vienna in 1529 and 1683; Cyprus fell in 1571, and Crete in 1669; the Turks were halted, but only just, at Malta in 1565 and were defeated in a great galley battle at Lepanto in 1571. They conquered Mamluk Egypt in 1516–1517 and defeated the Portuguese at Alcazarquivir in Morocco in 1578.

Not all these conflicts were technically crusades and not all religious wars were fought against infidels. The completion of the Hispanic *reconquista* (reconquest) against the Muslims of Granada ended centuries of religious warfare sustained by papal taxation and indulgences, but the crusades against the Hussites of 1420 to 1431 in Bohemia were launched against heretical Catholics. Schismatic Greeks were eventually abandoned as a legitimate crusading target but the union of the Greek and Roman churches achieved at the Council of Florence in 1439 failed to prevent the fall of Constantinople in 1453. Some Catholics, such as Erasmus, and many Protestants, including Luther, objected on theological grounds to indulgences granted to finance the crusades, but they supported resistance to the Turks in defense of Germany. Elizabethan England rang its bells to celebrate the Ottoman failure at Malta in 1565 but itself

Crusader Pope. *Pius II at Ancona* by Pinturicchio (c. 1454–1513) in the Piccolomini Library, Siena Cathedral. ALINARI/ART RESOURCE

faced a Spanish armada financed by crusading taxes and indulgences in 1588. Outside Europe the Christian conquistadores turned, at times with extreme brutality, to the task of conversion. The military-religious orders were integrated into the crusade enterprise, their members being fully professed men and women involved for life in a perpetual holy war rather than in the limited obligation of the crusader who took the cross. The national orders in Spain and Portugal and the Teutonic Order, which fought harsh campaigns against Catholic Poles in Prussia and Orthodox Russians in Livonia, lost all military effectiveness during the sixteenth century, but the Hospitallers, at Rhodes until 1522 and from 1530 to 1798 on Malta, played a leading role in resisting the Turks and policing the Mediterranean against Muslim corsairs. The Order of Santo Stefano founded by the grand duke of Tuscany in 1562 was particularly efficient in its naval campaigns against the Turks.

Crusades had narrow national as well as universal objectives, but they served the papacy and the empire in particular. The crusade was a papal operation that functioned only when the pope issued a proclamation, licensed the necessary preaching and the issue and sale of indulgences, which derived their validity from the papal fund of spiritual grace, and sanctioned taxation of the clergy to finance the ever-more costly demands for mercenaries, guns, and galleys. The crusade permitted popes, and to a lesser extent emperors, to function as leaders of Catholic Christendom as they continually pressed crusading proposals in councils and congresses. However disrupting the effects of the northern Reformation, which virtually limited the crusade to the Catholic Mediterranean sphere, and however disillusioned individual Christians were with the often corrupt money-grubbing realities of the crusade, papal determination and leadership in securing peace in the West and papal grants of crusade taxation remained fundamental to the mechanics of any great campaign. The victories at Granada in 1492 and Lepanto in 1571 required years of diplomatic negotiation and haggling over ecclesiastical taxation before the necessary force could be mobilized. The crusade long remained a vital element in the defense of Catholic Europe.

BIBLIOGRAPHY

A History of the Crusades. Edited by Kenneth Mayer Setton. 2d ed. 6 vols. Madison, Wis., 1969–1989.

Housley, Norman. *The Later Crusades, 1274–1580: From Lyons to Alcazar.* Oxford, 1992.

The Oxford Illustrated History of the Crusades. Edited by Jonathan Riley-Smith. Oxford, 1995.

Setton, Kenneth Mayer. *The Papacy and the Levant: 1204–1571.* 4 vols. Philadelphia, 1976–1984.

ANTHONY LUTTRELL

CUISINE. *See* **Food and Drink.**

CURRENCY. *See* **Banking and Money.**

CUSA, NICHOLAS OF. *See* **Nicholas of Cusa.**

DADDI, BERNARDO. *See* **Giotto.**

DAILY LIFE. How does one define daily life in any period? Daily life does not solely involve politics, warfare, intellectual or artistic pursuits, economic activity and work, religion, or festivals, yet it contains elements of them all. Therefore, our picture of daily life will be a mosaic whose parts represent the shared activities of Renaissance Europeans.

The Mediterranean and the North: Different Patterns of Life. Renaissance Europe was not a homogeneous society, and distinct ecological, ethnic, linguistic, and demographic factors shaped everyday life in the various regions. Broadly, Mediterranean societies experienced hot, dry summers and cold, rainy winters, while the North experienced mild, temperate summers and long, rainy or snowy winters. The Mediterranean region had arid or semiarid mountain ranges, while the North was characterized by broad expanses of fertile plains and forest. The Mediterranean Sea connected the South with the more ancient cultures and peoples of northern Africa and Asia. Consequently, cities, long-distance shipping, and trade were features of life in the South much more so than in the North. The exceptions were the Hanseatic cities of northern Germany and the cosmopolitan industrial cities of the Low Countries. Everywhere else, Europe's population was thinly spread throughout rural areas, where peasants and nobles sometimes rubbed shoulders with sheepherders on the plains when they brought their flocks down from the high pastures in the fall and sought work for the winter.

Europeans were often on the move, going to market, to political centers to pay taxes, or on religious pilgrimages. Southerners traveled from one port city to another on ships or over land by foot or on the uncomfortable back of a donkey; northerners traveled by foot or, increasingly, by boat on canals and rivers. Hosting travelers were numberless inns, taverns, and religious establishments.

The Impact of Gender and Class. Gender and class also shaped daily life. Upper-class women were confined to the home or the court; when they went out, it was with accompaniment to the market, church, or special civic or religious events. Middle-class and poor women spent much time working—middle-class women perhaps in an artisanal trade or shop and poor women in the fields if they were peasants or in households if they were servants. Women of the elite classes supervised a domestic staff and oversaw the education of their children.

Noblemen spent their time at court, at war, or managing their country estates; in urbanized areas, especially in Italy, some of them engaged in business activity. Political life was open to some; but opportunities for nobles meaningfully to participate in politics declined during the Renaissance as princes and kings consolidated their authority. In smaller urban areas nobles of middling rank directed local politics under the authority of capitals of territorial states or on their own if they had not yet been integrated into the political structure of a regional state. Whatever the setting, political life was almost entirely the domain of upper-class men. Rural males participated in village affairs through parish or village councils, which were directed by priests or local lords.

Economic Trends and Standard of Living.

The performance of the economy is always a prime factor in the quality of life, since the relation between prices and wages determines purchasing power. The economic cycle that lasted from 1450 until 1550 began and ended in crisis. The earlier edge of the spectrum, around 1450, witnessed the beginnings of a recovery from the population losses and the consequent economic depression following the Black Death of 1347–1349. Population began to recover as did prosperity; workers' wages bought more and better food. Wages and prices entered into a harmonious relationship, remaining flat until about 1550. Then a rapid series of price increases ignited a severe inflation that by 1600 left prices 200 to 300 percent above what they had been fifty years earlier. To some extent, this inflation was due to the influx of gold from the Americas. The severity of inflation varied regionally, as did the ability of workers to subsist as wages lagged behind prices. In rural areas the expansion of a money economy produced a problem linking lord and peasant: how to convert wealth in land and goods into increasingly necessary cash. The seignorial class solved this problem by converting peasant obligations into cash payments; peasants then had to find some means of obtaining cash to pay the lord, through working for wages, producing surplus goods that they could sell, or engaging in such forms of criminal activity as smuggling.

Housing and Diet.

The quality of housing, urban and rural, followed a slow but steady course of improvement during the Renaissance. Europeans were the best housed and fed among civilizations and cultures on the major continents. Those of the seignorial class who had not fallen on hard times lived relatively comfortably in wooden or stone castles or manor houses. The movement toward building with stone increased from 1400 on, with an emphasis in France and elsewhere on remodeling medieval structures in stone according to architectural standards established in Renaissance Italy. The peasantry lived in houses made of wood or earth, with thatched roofs and earthen floors. The major improvements in these dwellings came with the incorporation of tile flooring, which was plentiful and inexpensive. There was little besides a screen to separate one room from another and the human occupants from the animal. Fleas and other insects probably kept constant company with the higher forms of life in these earthen dwellings. Bathrooms were unknown until the seventeenth century; narrow chimneys existed beginning in the high Middle Ages.

Furnishings differed according to status. In the homes of lords, beds, tables, and chairs were comfortable if not elaborate. Metal plates held food; in Italy in the fifteenth century, ceramic dinner services, a specialty of the Romagna, began to appear. For the poor, straw mattresses, chairs or a table fashioned from barrel halves, and some flowers and herbs to freshen up the place in the summer graced the living space. Cooking and eating might have centered on a metal stove, with a cooking pot and a common drinking cup.

Europeans were unique at this time in comparison with the rest of the world's peoples for the amount of meat and fish they ate, largely because the relatively sparse human population left ample space for raising herds of cattle, pigs, goats, and sheep. Flesh was eaten by all classes, though with more variety and in larger quantities by the rich. Workers in sixteenth-century Flanders ate rye bread, peas, beans, and cured herring. Those who were not rich generally ate more grains, including oats—in porridge, soup, and gruel—and more vegetables. When the poor ate meat, it was salted (for preservation); tuna fish was also available. The very poor might subsist on a diet of two or three pounds of bread a day and nothing else. The rich ate every variety of flesh available—meats roasted, grilled, or baked; fish prepared several different ways; birds roasted—sometimes with sauce. Meats would come heaped together on metal plates called *mets* in France, and the diners would help themselves. Dinner might consist of as many as eight courses, beginning with meats in broth and ending with sugared fruits and the like. Presentation of the meal was important only at the highest levels on special occasions. Otherwise, sheer abundance was sufficient.

Only the elites of cities enjoyed style, comfort, and beauty in housing, furnishings, and food. Italy was in the forefront of quality of life among the well-to-do. For example, while towns in northern Europe did not change their building materials from wood to stone until the sixteenth century, the Italians began this process in the Middle Ages and brought it to a high standard with the construction of Renaissance palaces in the fifteenth century. Elaborate and beautiful ceramic dinnerware, which was less expensive and improved the taste of food, replaced the metal plates of the earlier period. Table manners also emerged first among the Italians, along with relatively refined cookery, which then made its way to

France from about 1550 onward. The urban poor lived less well, evidence of the growing gap in cities between the rich and the poor.

The poor of Renaissance cities subsisted in deplorable conditions, as attested to by inventories made after their deaths. A typical poor person had only meager possessions: a few low-quality eating utensils, a blackened metal cooking pot, frying pans, dripping pans, a board for kneading bread, a few old clothes, a stool, a table, and a bench, the planks of which served as a bed, with perhaps a few sacks of straw as a mattress. Items such as these furnished life in crowded rented rooms, which were generally on the upper floors (reserved for the poor) of buildings; rooms were dark and dirty. The homeless poor lived in shantytowns—in 1560 in Pescara, for example, four hundred to five hundred people out of a population of two thousand lived in such conditions; in Genoa the poor sold themselves as galley slaves every winter; in Venice the miserable lived in small boats near quays or under the bridges of canals. In each circumstance the poor lived with fleas, lice, and other bugs. Poverty and destitution were highly visible everywhere.

Clothing and Fashion. Clothing and fashion were always changing and were indicators of social position. To some extent, the rich sought to use sumptuary legislation to prevent the poor and the middle classes from imitating their dress, but nothing could suppress the general desire to sacrifice everything for fashion. Whether it was peasants who went barefoot to market six days a week but wore ruffs to a parish feast or young men who wore gold-and-silver-trimmed hats to the taverns and girls with foot-high hairdos for trips to church on Sundays, some finery was necessary for making even an abbreviated social statement. A person's station was immediately apparent by his or her dress, as we can see from paintings of popular scenes, such as those by Brueghel of markets, where the fishermen, the peasants, and the bourgeoisie are all immediately distinguishable.

While the costumes of the bourgeoisie changed rapidly, changes in peasant clothing occurred less quickly. For peasants, underwear came into use in the thirteenth century in France. Men wore shirts of coarse cloth, and women wore dresses of similar material. Legs might be bare, feet shod with a sole held by a leather strap wound around the leg. Some peasants in Flanders wore wooden shoes, as did the urban cloth workers of Florence. Rich and poor alike slept naked in their beds. Bourgeois men and women wore Spanish-style high collars edged with simple fluting, which were later replaced by true ruffs worn by both sexes. Popular female costume was a turned-down open collar, bodice, and apron over a gathered skirt. Black, coming from Spain and reflecting that country's political and cultural dominance, was the color of choice in the sixteenth century. Noblemen at the court of Henry IV in France had to have as many as thirty suits and had to change them frequently in order to maintain respectability. Clothes began to be molded and fitted to the body, as paintings from the Renaissance confirm; these replaced bulky greatcoats, tall, fine hats, and long, pointed shoes, which previously had been the fashion. Silks and brocades of many different colors were worn in the seventeenth century, as the Spanish preference for black yielded to the French preference for color.

The Concept of Private Life. Not unconnected to matters of fashion and political dominance was the development in Western society of a concept of private life, which involved a general change in mental outlook (*mentalité*) related to the development of a sense of individualism. During the Middle Ages the public and private spheres were intermixed. People existed within various sodalities that de-emphasized individuality and submerged it in collective identities. Change began in the fifteenth century (and much earlier in Italy) with the development of commerce, cities, and wealth. Some individuals then had the means and the desire to distinguish themselves from others. In addition, monarchs and princes who were engaged in amassing political power effectively created a state organization that defined itself in contrast to persons. The practice of silent reading was a spur to the seeking of solitude. Finally, changes in religious life fostered inward reflection and communion with God. Also important was the changed role of the family, seen, from as early as the seventeenth century in some regions, as a place of refuge where one was spared public scrutiny.

To conclude, daily life in the Renaissance was full of contrasts of the most extreme types, reflective of a Europe assuming recognizably modern characteristics.

See also **Clothing**; **Food and Drink**.

BIBLIOGRAPHY

Ariès, Philippe, and Georges Duby. *A History of Private Life*. Vol. 3: *Passions of the Renaissance*. Edited by Roger Chartier. Translated by Arthur Goldhammer. Cambridge, Mass., 1989.

Brady, Thomas A., Jr., Heiko A. Oberman, and James D. Tracy. *Structures and Assertions*. Vol. 1 of *Handbook of European History, 1400–1600: Late Middle Ages, Renaissance, and Reformation*. New York, 1994.

Braudel, Fernand. *Capitalism and Material Life, 1400–1800*. New York, 1967.

Chabert, Alexandre R. E. "More about the Sixteenth-Century Price Revolution." In *Economy and Society in Early Modern Europe*. Edited by Peter Burke. New York, 1972. Pages 47–54.

Cipolla, Carlo. "The So-called 'Price Revolution': Reflections on 'The Italian Situation.'" In *Economy and Society in Early Modern Europe*. Edited by Peter Burke. New York, 1972. Pages 43–46.

Verlinden, C., J. Craeybeckx, and E. Scholliers. "Price and Wage Movements in Belgium in the Sixteenth Century." In *Economy and Society in Early Modern Europe*. Edited by Peter Burke. New York, 1972. Pages 55–84.

JOHN K. BRACKETT

DANCE. The first notated dance steps in Western culture appeared in dance master Domenico da Piacenza's *De arte saltandi et choreas ducendi* (The art of leaping and dancing; 1416). Dance, however, had a long history prior to this. In the Bible, the Israelites commonly dance as part of religious and secular celebrations. In medieval Europe, the existence of dance music and of numerous examples of dance in the visual arts show that dance occupied a similar role in society.

Dance in Renaissance Society.

By the beginning of the Renaissance, professional dance masters had appeared. A dance master's career could contain several varied roles, including that of performer, teacher (of not only dance but also music and martial arts), and choreographer. Not only were dance masters hired by aristocratic households, but also by members of the bourgeoisie. The advent of the printing press helped dance masters raise the profile of their profession by disseminating specific dances and the names of their creators throughout Europe. Dances appeared in carefully noted manuscripts and in hastily jotted notes as well. Since dance of the lower classes was undoubtedly passed on by rote, there are few written descriptions, though the visual arts show peasants doing circle dances outdoors, often accompanied by a small bagpipe or pipe and tabor.

The dances preserved in notated sources were primarily intended for indoor occasions by the nobility, though dancing also took place in courtyards or gardens. The most frequent occasion for dance in noble households was after dinner, when members of the family and invited guests would dance to the accompaniment of household musicians. Scenes from Giovanni Boccaccio's *Decameron* provide numerous examples of this setting.

> All the ladies and gentlemen could dance and many of them could play and sing, so when the tables were cleared . . . Dioneo took a lute and Fiametta a viol and began to play a dance tune . . . and then with slow steps [the queen] danced with the two young men and the other ladies. (First Day)

Dancing was the focal point at events called *festas* or balls, and weddings included dance as part of the festivities. Celebrations in honor of visiting royalty usually featured choreographed entries danced by courtiers and ladies, and dance masters performing their own specialities, such as solo virtuoso variations, mime routines, and mock combat with swords, shields, or other fighting apparatus.

Since dance was considered important for men as both a social grace and as martial arts training, the professional combination of dance master–fencing instructor was not unusual in Renaissance Europe. The place of the dance master in society was not always completely clear, though an interesting distinction is made in Baldassare Castiglione's *Il cortegiano* (1528; trans. *The Book of the Courtier*). Castiglione advises that gentlemen should dance with more reserve than professionals in public. In book two of his treatise he admonishes gentlemen to avoid public performance of raucous dances—such as the Morris dance, where bells are worn on dancers' legs—unless the gentlemen are masked. For women, dance provides exercise and a stage for displaying grace and stateliness.

Castiglione and other chroniclers of social mores demand a certain nonchalance or *sprezzatura* in the well-bred courtier or lady, clearly visible in the way they danced. Dance was a vital social attainment, considered a necessary part of education for those of aristocratic and bourgeois households alike, alongside music (both singing and playing instruments), riding, fencing, verbal banter, painting, and rhetoric.

Fifteenth Century.

In the fifteenth century, dances were designed for long lines of two or three dancers. In France the predominant dance was the Burgundian basse dance, a stately stylized processional with only five steps organized into patterns called *mesures*. The five steps—*reverence* (R), *branle* (b), *double* (d), *simple* (s), and *reprise* (r)—were arranged according to very specific rules. If all the rules were followed in the *mesures*, the dance was called *commune* (common). If there were irregularities, the dance was *incommune*.

Peasant Dance. From *Heures de Charles d'Angoulême,* fifteenth century. CLICHÉ BIBLIOTHÈQUE NATIONALE DE FRANCE, PARIS. MS. LATIN 1173, FOL. 20v

Dance sources such as *L'art et instruction de bien danser,* printed by Michel de Toulouze in the 1480s, contain detailed instructions for the steps and numerous choreographies with music in the form of "tenor" lines. These tenors supplied a base above which up to three improvised lines were placed. The tenors were generally performed by the slide trumpet or the sackbut, early versions of the trombone, while the improvisation was most often performed by shawms, members of the oboe family.

The instrumentation and music for the Italian *ballo* was much the same, but there was greater variety in the music and in the choreographies. The *ballo* was composed of four basic step patterns. Listed in order from slowest to fastest, they are the *bassadanza, quaternaria, saltarello,* and *piva.* The *saltarello* is the oldest, with surviving music examples from the fourteenth century. All but the *quaternaria* could also serve as independent dances that used the other three steps, in which case the step's basic tempo would change to fit its new context. The *bassadanza* step, for example, is normally slow. But

when placed in a *piva* context, the same movements are performed much faster. This level of formal complexity meant Italian dance treatises included more theoretical information about music and dance. Italian dance was often compared to other arts, especially architecture, because of similarities of proportion and order.

Sixteenth Century. Sixteenth-century dance masters took the glorification of dance to new heights, often referring to the ancient Greeks and Romans when describing the virtues of dance, and in one case using ancient poetic meters in the definitions of some step rhythms. Cesare Negri (c. 1535–c. 1604), one of the three best-known sixteenth-century dance masters because of his treatise *Le gratie d'amore* (Love's graces; 1602), compares dance and jousting by saying "jousting and riding are for Mars," while dancing is more appropriate for Venus, "the innkeeper of our gentle hearts." He even goes so far as to say "the whole world dances." Fabritio Caroso (c. 1527–c. 1605) who wrote *Il ballarino* (The dance master) and *Nobiltà di dame* (On the nobility of women) revised the steps of *Ballarino* (1581) to use poetic meters from *Nobiltà di dame* (1600). The *dactylic* step, with its one long step and two short steps, is only one example. In a rather transparent attempt to align dance with the more widely respected art of literature, Caroso specifically identifies the names of these steps as Latin, coming from the verses of Virgil and Ovid. The dances of the sixteenth century also became more elaborate, including dances for up to four couples, dances for single-sex groups of men or women, dances for as many as care to dance, and solo dances, all dedicated to noble patronesses and bearing fanciful titles.

The occasions for dance in the sixteenth century included the public and private events of the fifteenth century, plus theatrical events like the English masque, the Italian *mascherata* and the Italian *intermedio.* The masque originated as a series of poems, lute songs, choruses, and dances with a loose story line. Masques were frequently presented by ladies and gentlemen as part of wedding festivities. A good example is the masque by Thomas Campion created for the wedding of the earl of Somerset and Lady Frances Howard in 1614. Although the actual choreographies are not included in published masques, their placement in the production is clearly indicated and English manuscript sources provide examples of appropriate choreographies.

The *mascherata* was essentially a formal parade always in costume, sometimes in masks, that was performed as part of the gala amusements surrounding a state visit. One such *mascherata* was presented during the 1574 visit to Milan of Don Juan of Austria. In this event, characters played by members of the noble families of Milan represented human emotions. For example, "Love . . . had a bow in his left hand and two kinds of darts, lead and gold, in his right. Besides this he was, as usual, blindfolded." Each character was followed by a musician dressed as a shepherd. The entire event ended with a dance performed by eighty-two people.

The *intermedio* was one of the most stupendous entertainments of all time, rivaled only by late-nineteenth-century opera. The *intermedio* typically consisted of a prologue introducing a five-act pastoral play and interludes of music and dance between the acts, with a grandiose choreography concluding the performance. The most famous set of *intermedii* was created for a well-documented Florentine performance of *pellegrina*, a comedy by Girolamo Bargagli that was produced for the wedding of Christine of Lorraine and Ferdinand de' Medici in 1589.

The Geography of Dance.

During the sixteenth century, dances were recorded in France, Italy, Spain, and England and eventually became popular all over Europe.

France. In France, the *branles* were very popular and *branle* music is found throughout Europe in the sixteenth and early seventeenth centuries. There were two types of *branles*—the "single" included one basic step pattern, while the *couppé* incorporated more steps. The single *branles* were normally performed as a suite by a group of dancers organized in lines or, more commonly, in a circle. First came the *branle* double, a slow duple meter dance with two steps to the left and two steps to the right; then the *branle* simple with two steps to the left and one step to the right; then the *branle* gay, a lively triple meter kicking dance; and finally a regional *branle*, like the *Branle de Bourgogne* or the *Branle de Poictou*. The *branles couppé* included mime gestures like bowing the head as in prayer for the "hermit" *branle*, or pawing at the floor for the "horse" *branle*.

The French source with the most detail and with the largest variety of choreographies is *Orchésographie* (1588–1589) by Thoinot Arbeau (pseudonym of Jehan Tabourot, a provincial French cleric). *Orchésographie* presents a dialogue between Arbeau as teacher and the mythical Capriol (also the name of a dance step) as student. Probably addressing the controversy that surfaced during the Reformation concerning the place of dance in the life of Christians, Arbeau begins his treatise with references to the ancients and the Bible, justifying dancing as an innocent pastime that might be enjoyed by the virtuous with no damage to their moral fiber. He includes forty-six dances, each with its own tune. The harmonized versions of these tunes are found in numerous publications of music for lute or instrumental ensemble.

Italy. The most complex dances of the sixteenth century were recorded in Italy. These included several choreographical types such as *balletto, brando, cascarda,* and *entrata;* choreographical forms, like variations that could serve as part of a choreographical type or as independent choreographies; and individual dances that could serve, like the forms, as part of a larger structure or on their own. These included *alemana, canario, gagliarda, passamezzo, saltarello,* and *tordiglione.*

The choreographic types are general formats for choreographies. The *balletto,* danced by two to four dancers, usually includes at least two dance types, like the *pavana* and the *gagliarda,* requiring at least one change of meter and tempo. The *brando* is a much more complex structure meant to end major theatrical productions like the *intermedio.* It normally has at least four dance types and several changes of tempo and direction. The *entrata* is a simple choreographed entry. Forms like variations might present a couple dancing several sections together, followed by a few solo variations each, ending with a passage together. In other situations variations could be the sole form used for an entire choreography. Individual dances like the *canario* could have an entire choreography to themselves, or serve as a part of a larger choreography.

The music in the Italian sources, both printed and in manuscript form, is typically presented as a tune with chords written in lute tablature notation. A varied assortment of instruments were used including groups of lutes, harps, recorders, and viols (related to the violin family), among others.

Spain and England. There are more Spanish dances in the sources of other countries than there are in Spanish sources—Spain is represented in dance sources from every country. The few known Spanish sources are all in manuscript and are little more than a few notated choreographies without any music or any of the explanations of steps and manners that are typically found in sources from France and Italy. The dances found most frequently

Courtly Dance. An example of fifteenth-century Italian *bassadanza* accompanied by two shawms and slide trumpet. CLICHÉ BIBLIOTHÈQUE NATIONALE DE FRANCE, PARIS. MS. 5073, FOL. 117v

in Spanish sources are *entratas,* and the *pavana* arranged in variation form.

If the sources in Spain are sparse, those of England are even more so. The English sources—also all in manuscript—are greater in number, but sometimes include only one line of instruction that essentially advises the reader to find someone who knows how to do the dance and learn the dance from them. Dances popular in France, Italy, and Spain are all found in English sources, along with the two dances that were popular everywhere, the *pavane* and *gagliard*. Even the most English of the dances, the measures, was apparently taken from the Italian *passamezzo,* a stately processional dance in the tradition of the *bassedance*. England is, however, rich in literary references to dance. Shakespeare alone has copious references to specific dances in plays and poetry, and in *Orchestra, or a Poem of Dancing* (1594), Sir John Davies describes many dances and their affect as practiced in Renaissance England.

Italy produced the largest number of dance treatises, dance music, and detailed references to dance in volumes dedicated to etiquette, clearly trumpeting the importance of dance in everyday life as well as at stately court events. This was echoed in countries all over Europe. Ultimately, however, many Italian dance masters relocated to France and developed the movements that eventually became the classical ballet that we know today.

BIBLIOGRAPHY

Primary Works

Arbeau, Thoinot. *Orchesography*. Translated by Mary Stewart Evans. Edited with introduction and notes by Julia Sutton. New York, 1967. Translation of *Orchesographie*.

Arena, Anthonius. "Rules of Dancing." *Dance Research* 4, no. 2 (fall 1986): 3–53. Translated by John Guthrie and Marina Zorzi. Translation and document history of *Ad suos compagniones* (1529).

Caroso, Fabritio. *Courtly Dance of the Renaissance: A New Translation of the* Nobiltà di dame (1600). Edited by Julia Sutton: Music transcribed into modern notation by F. Marion Walker. New York, 1995.

Caroso, Marco Fabritio. *Il Ballarino* (The dance master). Venice, 1581. Facsimile ed., New York, 1967.

Cornazzano, Antonio. *The Book on the Art of Dancing*. Translated by Madeleine Inglehearn and Peggy Forsyth. London, 1981. Translation of *Il libro dell'arte del danzare* (1465). Contains table of basic dances and tempo relationships.

Ebreo, Guglielmo. *De pratica seu arte tripudii* (On the practice or art of dancing). Translated by Barbara Sparti. London, 1993.

Negri, Cesare. *The Graces of Love*. Translation and commentary by Gustavia Yvonne Kendall. DMA diss., Stanford University, 1985. Translation of *Le gratie d'amore* (1602).

Toulouze, Michel de. *L'art et instruction de bien dancer* (The art of dancing well). Paris, c. 1488. Facsimile edition, Geneva, 1985.

Secondary Works

Brainard, Ingrid. "Sir John Davies' *Orchestra* [London, 1594] as a Dance Historical Source." In *Songs of the Dove and the Nightingale: Sacred and Secular Music c. 900– c. 1600.* Edited by Greta Mary Hair and Robyn Smith. Basel, Switzerland, 1995. Pages 176–212.

Crane, Frederick. *Materials for the Study of the Fifteenth-Century Basse Danse.* New York, 1968. Discusses Tarragó, Brussels, and Toulouse.

Cunningham, James P. *Dancing in the Inns of Court.* London, 1965. Includes descriptions of events and publication of six dance manuscripts from 1560s–1670s.

Jones, Pamela Anne. "The Relation between Music and Dance in Cesare Negri's *Le gratie d'amore* (1602)." Ph.D. diss., King's College, University of London, 1989.

Saslow, James M. *The Medici Wedding of 1589: Florentine Festival as "Theatrum Mundi."* New Haven, Conn., 1996.

Walker, D. P. *Musique des intermèdes de "La Pellegrina": Les Fêtes de Florence—1589.* Paris, 1986. Music, text, choreography, and costume and set designs for this major event.

Ward, John. "The English Measure." *Early Music* 14, no. 1 (February 1986): 15–21.

G. YVONNE KENDALL

DANIEL, SAMUEL. *See* **Poetry, English,** *subentry on* **Elizabethan Poetry.**

DANTE IN THE RENAISSANCE. The Renaissance marks one of the most distinctive phases in Dante's critical fortune. During the fifteenth and sixteenth centuries Dante (1265–1321) shared with his Florentine compatriots Petrarch and Boccaccio the status of a contemporary classic. Dante's position, however, was not that of primus inter pares. During the Renaissance there appeared over 160 editions of Petrarch's works and even more of Boccaccio's. In contrast, by the end of the sixteenth century only 50 editions of *La divina commedia* (*The Divine Comedy*) had been printed. (Dante's minor works were also printed during the Renaissance: the first edition of the *Convivio* [The banquet] was published in 1490, *De vulgari eloquentia* [Concerning vernacular eloquence] in 1577, and *La vita nuova* [The new life] in 1576.)

The decline in Dante's critical fortune was largely owing to Pietro Bembo's comparison of Dante and Petrarch in *Prose della volgar lingua* (Prose of the vernacular language; 1525), a landmark dialogue on the status of the Italian vernacular. For Bembo, the most influential arbiter of literary matters of his time, Petrarch's refined lyricism represented the Italian language at its most illustrious. While Bembo acknowledged that Dante had contributed substantially to the elevation of the vernacular, he argued that Dante, in desiring to be more than a poet, was as a poet less than perfect, and noted that he was not consistent or orderly in his diction. Bembo condemned the *Comedy*'s many foreign and Latinate words as well as its many archaic and coarse expressions. Bembo claimed Dante had fashioned something on his own "without any sense of selection or rule," with the result that the *Comedy* "resembles a beautiful and spacious wheatfield, which mixes together wheat, rye, and sterile and dangerous grasses."

Notwithstanding the blow dealt to the *Comedy*'s fortunes by Bembo's pronouncements, Dante's works continued to command the critical attention of philosophers, poets, artists, scientists, and intellectuals, especially in his native Florence. Eminent intellectuals such as Francesco Filelfo and Cristoforo Landino gave lectures on the *Comedy;* politicians and merchants cited memorable verses from the *Comedy* during civic debates or recorded them as pithy dictums in their family account books or *ricordanze* (diaries); mathematicians and scientists such as Antonio Manetti and Galileo Galilei endeavored to calculate the dimensions of the *Inferno* and explored the poet's treatment of astronomical phenomena; and artists such as Domenico da Michelino, Botticelli, Bronzino, Giorgio Vasari, and Michelangelo illustrated scenes from the poem, depicted Dante himself, or, in the case of Michelangelo, portrayed figures such as Charon and Minos in his *Last Judgment* in ways that recalled Dante's descriptions of these characters. Studies of the libraries of Florentines show that most citizens, even those with fewer than five books or manuscripts, owned a copy of the *Comedy*. Florentines honored Dante as the consummate poet, political theoretician, philosopher, theologian, and champion of the vernacular. They sought repeatedly to retrieve the poet's remains, although the mysterious disappearance of the remains for several centuries thwarted their attempts.

While interest in Dante's masterpiece outside Florence did not permeate society to the same extent as in his native city, exposition of the poem continued through the course of the sixteenth century. Commentary on Dante assumed a wide range of forms: line-by-line exposition of the entire poem, marginal glosses culled from these larger commentaries, editions featuring two commentaries, and extended discussions of a particular passage. Among the commentaries written in Italy between 1400 and 1600 are those of Guiniforte Barzizza (whose exposition is limited to the *Inferno*, c. 1438). Martino Nidobeato (1477), Cristoforo Landino (1481), Trifone Gabriele (1526–1527), Alessandro Vellutello (1544), Bernardino Daniello (1568), and Lodovico Castelvetro (who commented on the first twenty-nine cantos of the *Inferno,* c. 1570).

Landino's commentary constitutes the most influential and widely diffused commentary of the Renaissance; it was printed sixteen times from 1481 to 1596, more often than any other commentary on the poem. Presented to the Florentine government on 30 August 1481 in a sumptuous folio edition with engravings attributed to Botticelli, Landino's commentary is a monument to Florentine patriotism, culture, the Florentine dialect, and Neoplatonism. The Neoplatonic tenor of the commentary is most evident in Landino's grandiloquent *proemio* (foreword), where he develops the philosopher Marsilio Ficino's conception of poetry as an earthly image of "divine harmony," which poets convey by relaying "the intimate senses of their minds." Whereas Landino emphasized philosophical concerns, Trifone Gabriele and Bernardino Daniello were more concerned with explicating Dante's language. While both of these commentaries provide learned discussions of scientific, philosophical, literary, and geographical matters, their most distinctive feature is thorough analysis of Dante's language and style. Both writers were greatly influenced by Bembo's treatment of the vernacular in *Prose della volgar lingua,* but they tend to be less critical of Dante's language. Vellutello's commentary represents a significant departure: he questioned the text of the poem printed by Aldus Manutius in 1502 as well as Bembo's views on literary matters. Vellutello did not share Bembo's emphasis on purity of diction, nor did he accept the elevation of Petrarch and the classics as models for imitation. Castelvetro's partial commentary constitutes yet another departure from earlier traditions. Informed largely by his admiration for Aristotle's philosophy and Petrarch's poetry, this exposition presents a lively and at times pugnacious treatment of the *Comedy.* It offers numerous comparisons of Dante's and Petrarch's poetry, often to the disadvantage of the former.

In addition to the aforementioned commentaries, a number of expositions on specific passages or cantos were published in the sixteenth century. The majority of these explications were based on public lectures given at the Accademia Fiorentina, a literary academy devoted to the elevation of vernacular literature that flourished from 1540 to 1589. Among the more famous academicians who gave lectures on Dante were Benedetto Varchi, Pier Francesco Giam-

bullari, and Giovanni Battista Gelli. Many of these critics sought to mitigate Bembo's harsh evaluation of Dante. While each commentator emphasized different issues—Giambullari sought to illustrate the richness of Dante's language, Varchi analyzed the poem's moral and philosophical dimension, and Gelli underscored the poet's scientific and ethical concerns—they shared a moral and philological approach to the poem.

Readers in the Renaissance adapted Dante's poem to their own concerns. If one of the most salient features of a masterpiece is its ability to assume a new life in different literary and social environments, one would be hard-pressed to find a period that offers a more complex interpretive history of the *Comedy* than the Renaissance.

See also **Italian Literature and Language.**

BIBLIOGRAPHY

Editions of Commentaries

Barzizza, Guiniforte. *Lo Inferno della* Commedia *di Dante Alighieri, col comento di Guiniforto delli Bargigi.* Edited by G. Zac[c]heroni. Marsilia, Italy, 1838.

Castelvetro, Lodovico. *Sposizione di Lodovico Castelvetro a venti-nove canti dell'Inferno dantesco.* Modena, Italy, 1886.

Daniello, Bernardino. *L'espositione di Bernardino Daniello da Lucca sopra la* Comedia *di Dante.* Edited by Robert Hollander et al. Hanover, N.H., and London, 1989. A reprint of the 1568 work.

Gabriele, Trifone. *Annotationi nel Dante fatte con M. Trifon Gabriele in Bassano.* Edited by Lino Pertile. Bologna, Italy, 1993.

Gelli, Giovan Battista. *Letture edite e inedite Giovan Battista Gelli sopra* La Divina Commedia. Edited by C. Negroni. Florence, 1887.

Landino, Cristoforo. *Comento di Christophoro Landino fiorentino sopra la* Comedia *di Danthe Alighieri poeta fiorentino.* Florence, 1481.

Nidobeato, Martino Paolo. *La Comedia di Dante Aldighieri, excelso poeta fiorentino.* Milan, 1477–1478.

Serravalle, Giovanni. *Fratris Johannis de Serravalle translatio et comentum totius libri Dantis Aldigherii.* Edited by Marcellino da Civezza and Teofilo Domenichelli. Prato, Italy, 1891.

Vellutello, Alessandro. La Comedia *di Dante Alighieri con la nova espositione di Alessandro Vellutello.* Venice, 1544.

Secondary Works

Barbi, Michele. *Dante nel Cinquecento.* Pisa, Italy, 1890. Reprint, Rome, 1975. Examines Dante's critical fortune in the Renaissance.

Dionisotti, Carlo. "Dante nel Quattrocento." In *Atti del congresso internazionale di studi Danteschi.* 2 vols. Florence, 1965. A look at fifteenth-century criticism of Dante.

Mazzacurati, Giancarlo. "Dante nell' Accademia Fiorentina (1540–1560) (Tra esegesi umanistica e razionalismo critico)." *Filologia e letteratura* 13 (1967): 258–308. Examines Renaissance commentators' different approaches to Dante in lectures given at the Accademia Fiorentina.

Parker, Deborah. *Commentary and Ideology: Dante in the Renaissance.* Durham, N.C., 1993. A sociohistorical treatment of Renaissance commentaries on *The Divine Comedy*.

Vallone, Aldo. *Storia della critica dantesca dal decimonono al ventesimo secolo.* 2 vols. Padua, Italy, 1981. Discusses criticism from the thirteenth century to the present.

DEBORAH PARKER

DANTISCUS, JOHANNES (1485–1548), Polish diplomat, bishop, poet. The son of the merchant Simon von Höfen (De Curiis) and grandson of a flax-worker, Johannes (or Joannes) called himself Dantiscus after his native city, Gdansk (Dantiscum in Latin). He studied at the University of Gryfia (Greifswald), where he met the poet Paulus Crosnensis (Paweł of Krosno, 1470–1517), and Cracow, where Krosno was appointed professor of rhetoric. From 1501 on, Dantiscus was in the service of the royal court. In 1502–1503 he participated in a campaign against the Tartars and Wallachians. In 1505 he took lower orders and in the following years undertook a number of diplomatic missions for King Sigismund I. In this capacity he traveled to Greece, Palestine, Italy, Spain, the Netherlands, and to the imperial court in Vienna. There he was crowned *poeta laureatus* by the emperor Maximilian I, awarded a doctorate in law, and made a member of the nobility (1516). Between 1519 and 1530 he repeatedly served as ambassador at the court of Charles V in Spain, and he was actively engaged in negotiations to have Queen Bona of Poland recognized as duchess of Bari. Between 1530 and 1532 he resided in the Netherlands. In 1532 he returned to Cracow and entered the see of Chełmno, of which he had been made bishop in 1530. In 1537 he became bishop of Warmia (Ermland). He died at the episcopal residence Lidbark (Heilsberg) and was buried at the cathedral of Frombork.

Dantiscus was in contact with the leading humanists and reformers of his day: Baldassare Castiglione, Desiderius Erasmus, Thomas More, Martin Luther, Philipp Melanchthon, and others. He made his literary debut with a collection of poems, *De virtutis et fortunae differentia somnium* (A dream of the difference between virtue and fortune; 1510). Other poems commemorated the wedding of King Sigismund I and Barbara Zapolya (1512), Sigismund's victory at Moscow (1514), and a diplomatic meeting at Vienna (1515). In 1530 he published an anti-Turkish poem, *De nostrorum temporum calamitatibus* (On the calamities of our times).

Dantiscus generously patronized Nicolaus Copernicus (1473–1543), a man of prodigious intellectual powers and a canon of the Warmia chapter. Dantis-cus's short epigram "In Copernici libellum" (On Copernicus's book) was published in Copernicus's treatise *De lateribus et angulis triangulorum* (On the sides and angles of the triangle; 1542). He was also the patron of Eustatius Cnobelsdorf (1519–1571), to whom he dedicated *Carmen paraeneticum* (A poem offering advice), his longest poem, about twelve hundred verses. Cnobelsdorf returned the compliment with his poem *De bello Turcico* (On the Turkish war; both poems were published in 1539), and he mentioned Dantiscus in his other poem, *Lutetiae Parisiorum descriptio* (Description of Paris; 1543), in which he referred to him as "the embellishment of poets and bishops." Dantiscus was also the author of *Hymni ecclesiastici* (1548), a collection of church hymns.

Dantiscus's poetry centers on the issues significant in his life: matters of court, politics, and religion. He often made references to the works of such Latin poets as Virgil and Ovid. His literary output comprises a great variety of genres, including threnodies, prayers, satires, elegies, epigrams, and political pamphlets; the majority of his works are of a parenetic (exhortatory) character.

Dantiscus was a master of free syntax of words; many of his works are written in elegiac couplets (most notably his autobiography), though other forms of versification are also found. Some critics maintain that there are small lapses in Dantiscus's Latin.

Dantiscus was one of the six Latin poets in Poland who achieved recognition in the first half of the sixteenth century. His poetry, as well as the poetry of his contemporaries, especially Klemens Janicius, paved the way for the poetic achievements of the eminent Polish poets, such as Johannes Cochanovius and Mathias Casimir Sarbievius, who gained prominence in the second half of the sixteenth and first part of the seventeenth century.

Though Dantiscus often stressed that his poetic creativity was the main objective of his life, it was his diplomatic activities that brought him fame, probably because his poetry was mainly occasional, written for specific circumstances while he was at the service of the king of Poland.

BIBLIOGRAPHY

Primary Work

Dantiscus, Johannes. *Carmina.* Edited by Stanislaus Skimina. Cracow, Poland, 1950.

Secondary Works

Backvis, Claude. "La poésie latine en Pologne pendant la première phase de l'humanisme." *Neohelicon* 3 (1975): 29–86. See pages 39–48 and 84.

IJsewijn, Jozef, and W. Brache, eds. *Studia Europaea II: Johannes Dantiscus (1485–1548) Polish Ambassador and Humanist. Proceedings of the International Colloquium, Brussels, May 22–23, 1995*. Brussels, 1996.

Moos, Ann. "Johannes Dantiscus: Hymn-Writer." In *Munera Philologica Georgio Starnawski . . . oblata*. Edited by Krzysztof A. Kuczyński et al. Lodz, Poland, 1992. Pages 155–162.

Müller-Blessing, Inge Brigitte. "Joannes Dantiscus von Hofen: Ein Diplomat und Bischof zwischen Humanismus und Reformation (1485–1548)." *Zeitschrift für die Geschichte und Altertumskunde Ermlands* 31–32 (1967–1968): 59–238.

Vocht, Henry de. *John Dantiscus and His Netherlandish Friends As Revealed by Their Correspondence, 1522–1546*. Louvain, Belgium, 1961.

JERZY STARNAWSKI

Translated from Polish by
Krystyna Kujawinska-Courtney

DATINI, FRANCESCO (c. 1335–1410), merchant and banker, founder of a substantial business empire. Francesco Datini was born in the town of Prato, near Florence, and was known to posterity as the Merchant of Prato. When he died in 1410, he left behind both an impressive fortune and an enormous collection of records and documents that provide a detailed view into the social and professional world of fourteenth-century Italy. Nearly 140,000 letters exist, as well as 500 or more commercial registers and account books and thousands of other documents. Datini's historical importance derives as much from these records as from his activities as a merchant.

Born of humble means, Datini lost both parents to the Black Death of 1348 and was entrusted to the care of relatives. In 1350 he went to Avignon, the home since 1305 of the papal court, and began working as an office boy in a Florentine business. He advanced in the company, from factor (traveling agent) to minor investor. Within eight years, by dint of hard work and shrewd investments, Datini had amassed sizable profits, sufficient to make him a man of ample means, though probably not yet wealthy. His early dealings in Avignon included commerce in the materials of war—armor, daggers, iron and tin—as well as in a wide range of nonmilitary commodities, including salt, saffron, dye, silks, precious stones, and works of art. There he married Margherita di Domenico Bandini, a much younger woman from the petty Florentine nobility.

In 1382, at age forty-seven, Datini returned to Prato. He remained there for the rest of his life. Datini maintained a particularly close friendship with the notary Lapo Mazzei and helped to pay for his university studies. Their voluminous surviving correspondence reveals Datini as a man of homespun

Francesco Datini. Anonymous fourteenth-century portrait of the Merchant of Prato in the Palazzo Municipale of Prato. ALINARI/ART RESOURCE, NY

wisdom, greatly burdened by the task of managing his business.

By 1395 Datini headed an impressive collection of trading and banking companies. From his headquarters in Prato, he maintained branches in Pisa, Avignon, Florence, Genoa, Barcelona, Valencia, and Palma de Mallorca, and correspondents in England and the Levant. In his native Prato, Datini set up a local bank as well as a wool cloth shop. He also invested heavily in real estate. By the time he died he possessed seventy-three properties, including twenty-five houses in Prato, two warehouses, and thirty-five plots of land in the countryside.

Datini's companies were notable as much for their internal structure as for the broad scope of their activities. Like the Medici, the Merchant of Prato arranged his empire like a modern holding company, with each branch a separate legal entity. Datini retained the controlling share of the capital.

Unlike many of his contemporaries, Datini eschewed involvement in politics, although he was elected *gonfaloniere* in Prato in 1386. His memory endures in the still extant charitable organization that came into being at his death, the Casa del Ceppo dei Poveri, which aids poor children. For students of Renaissance Italy, however, his greatest legacy remains the documents, a veritable gold mine of social and economic history.

See also **Accounting; Banking and Money.**

BIBLIOGRAPHY

Gavitt, Philip. *Charity and Children in Renaissance Florence.* Ann Arbor, Mich., 1990.

Melis, Federigo. *Aspetti della vita economica medievale.* Siena, Italy, 1962.

Origo, Iris. *The Merchant of Prato.* London, 1992.

Trexler, R. C. *Public Life in Renaissance Florence.* New York, 1980.

WILLIAM CAFERRO

DA VINCI, LEONARDO. *See* **Leonardo da Vinci.**

DEATH. Renaissance Europeans from the fourteenth through the sixteenth centuries displayed a marked fascination with death compared to their medieval predecessors. The men and women of this age showed a heightened awareness of death, perhaps because of recurring epidemics of bubonic plague that appeared unexpectedly and killed large segments of the population. This intensified awareness of the fragility of life was expressed in new forms of funeral rites, mourning practices, acts of remembrance, and the disposition of worldly goods. Accompanying these changes was a preoccupation with the "art of dying" (*ars moriendi*), which developed as a popular literary genre beginning in the fifteenth century. The themes of physical decay and the triumph of death over all persons figured prominently in contemporary visual depictions of death, especially in the tomb art of northern Europe. Although every society must confront the inevitable loss of its members through death, the ways in which Renaissance Europeans faced the facts of death reveal much about their social values, religious beliefs, and overall health status.

Causes and Patterns of Mortality. The single greatest killer in Renaissance Europe was bubonic plague, or the "Black Death." Bubonic plague arrived first in Sicily in December 1347 and spread up the Italian peninsula by the summer of 1348. It reached pandemic levels throughout continental Europe, especially in urban areas, by the end of 1349. This first wave of plague took an enormous but erratic toll on the European population, with estimates ranging from one-third to one-half of local populations succumbing to the disease in those two years. Beginning with the second appearance of plague in 1363, the disease became a standard feature of life in Renaissance Europe. The plague returned about every ten to twelve years until the last major outbreak in London in 1661, with some episodes being more virulent than others. Even though Europeans did not understand fully the causes of plague, they knew that certain practical measures such as quarantine and escape from infected areas were effective ways to cope. By the end of the fifteenth century, affluent urban dwellers, especially those in the Mediterranean basin, fled every summer into the countryside, where plague was spread less easily. These practices gradually concentrated plague victims among the poor and led to harsher municipal policies that quarantined laborers and artisans in plague hospitals (*lazzaretti*) by 1500. By the late sixteenth century, plague became a disease associated with poverty and poor hygiene.

Renaissance Europeans confronted other epidemic diseases as well. Most prominent among them was a virulent strain of syphilis that first appeared in 1494. This form of syphilis, or "the pox," was a painful venereal disease that killed its victims far more slowly than plague. The onset of a new debilitating and incurable disease gave rise to numerous charitable groups throughout Europe whose members tended to the horrible infirmities caused by syphilis. The "pox" regularly was blamed on those outside the immediate community. At some point the Italians, French, and Amerindians all bore the stigma of having caused and spread this disease. Unlike plague, which initially attacked all age groups and both sexes with equal virulence, syphilis was confined to sexually active adults. Moralizing treatises diffused the assumption that there was a connection between prostitution and venereal disease, a connection that played a partial role in the closure of state-run brothels in the later sixteenth century.

Europeans also commonly suffered from deadly respiratory illnesses such as tuberculosis. Men routinely fell victim to accidents on their business travels

Dance of Death. Death visits a printer's shop and a bookseller. From *Le grant danse macabre* (Lyon, 1499).

or in the course of agricultural work, while women frequently died in childbirth. Mortality was extremely high for children below the age of two, whether in urban or rural areas, primarily due to illness. In times of economic hardship, infanticide became a noticeable social problem, either because it actually increased as a way to limit family size or because it came to greater public attention as a criminal activity. Records from Italian courts indicate that infant girls were either killed or abandoned at roughly twice the frequency of baby boys. Part of the reason for this discrepancy lay in the fact that girls could not earn similarly high wages as boys; girls also needed a larger outlay of economic resources in the form of dowry in order to marry. Once children survived their critical early years, they had a reasonable chance of reaching adulthood.

Attitudes toward Death. Renaissance Europeans held a complex set of attitudes toward death, dying, and the afterlife that mixed traditional Christian beliefs with those of classical Greek and Roman authors. Perhaps the source that best reveals this cultural mix was the popular literary genre called the *ars moriendi,* or "art of dying." Beginning in the early fifteenth century, short tracts written in both Latin and vernacular languages started to teach a lay audience how a good Christian should approach im-

pending death. These tracts stressed that death should be welcomed rather than feared, since it was the death that gave meaning to a Christian's life. The whole of a Christian's life was seen as a preparation for the afterlife. Even an educated man like the Dutch humanist Desiderius Erasmus (1466?–1536) kept a human skull on his desk as a constant reminder of the brevity of life. Since anyone might fall ill suddenly, the *ars moriendi* treatises emphasized the importance of making a "good death." The ill person was advised to confess to a priest, forgive friends and family gathered around the deathbed, and dispose prudently of his or her effects, including making charitable donations or other financial compensation for past sins. These popular literary works stressed acceptance of death and planning for its inevitability as a way to control the unpredictable timing of one's demise. Making a good death helped the individual to gain entry into purgatory, where she or he could expiate remaining sins, rather than be condemned to hell.

Visual imagery in northern Europe emphasized a more macabre sense of death than did the artistic representations of Italy and Spain. In France and Holland, the "dance of death," with its grim reapers and skeletons, became a popular motif in the fifteenth century that mixed fascination and fear in equal parts. Northern European artists also developed a form of tomb sculpture that portrayed an effigy of the living person placed over a decaying corpse. This type of representation reinforced the notion that death triumphed over all persons regardless of wealth or status, and reminded viewers that the physical organism of the body was less enduring than the soul.

Attitudes and beliefs drawn from ancient philosophers became more familiar with the renewed interest in antiquity during the Renaissance. These attitudes generally were interpreted in ways that supported traditional Christian tenets. For example, Renaissance intellectuals like the Florentine chancellors Coluccio Salutati (c. 1331–1406) and Leonardo Bruni (1370–1444) integrated Roman Stoic ideals with standard Christian teachings. Stoic philosophy emphasized the importance of maintaining one's duty to the living and moderating public displays of grief in the interests of decorum. Renaissance thinkers proposed that the bereaved should contain their sorrow through self-discipline and should try to console themselves by combining work, duty, literary expression, and Christian resignation. Throughout the fifteenth century humanists in particular advocated more restrained forms of mourning for both women and men instead of traditional, open expressions of grief.

Wills and Bequests. The testament (or will) was a legal document witnessed by a notary that gave binding instructions about the testator's wishes. The will was both an instrument of personal expression and a way to encumber property and direct the activities of heirs from beyond the grave. The *ars moriendi* treatises suggested that drawing up a last will was an important step in planning for a good death. Despite this advice, the vast majority of Europeans died without leaving a testament. For the many who died intestate, local custom determined what happened to their mortal remains and worldly goods. Normally wives were buried in the tombs of their husbands, and close relatives inherited property according to time-honored practices. Burial in one's local parish church or cemetery was the norm in the absence of other instructions.

Still, many thousands of testaments survive from the Renaissance period. These legal documents provide rich sources for analyzing social values ranging from the strength of kinship ties to patterns of piety. Studies of French and Italian urban wills, which dominate historical scholarship, reveal that many more men than women left wills. In fourteenth- and fifteenth-century Italy, wills made by women (mostly widows) never exceeded thirty percent of extant documents. The transmission of property designated in wills followed very complex patterns that differed according to locale, class, gender, pious preferences, and time period. Over the course of the Renaissance era, many testators left greater sums of money and property to ensure their own remembrance in the form of tombs and commemorative masses. In some central Italian cities, men favored making substantial bequests to single institutions rather than fragmenting their charitable donations among many recipients. In these cities that followed focused patterns of giving, men of assorted classes tended to favor civic or clerical dowry funds that enabled poor young girls to marry. In other cities, however, an opposite pattern of giving prevailed, with men splitting up their donations among many different charitable groups. Women, especially widows, preferred to patronize nunneries to a greater extent than their male counterparts. They may have done so because they were related to nuns in particular convents or because they wanted to support these alternative institutions. Scholars have yet to evaluate all the information available in these documents.

Rituals of Death. Between 1300 and 1600 there were two main directions of change in the rituals surrounding death, mourning, and remembrance. The first trend was toward an increased flamboyance in funeral pomp and commemoration, especially in regions that remained Catholic after the religious reforms of the sixteenth century. This trend toward greater pomp began in the early fourteenth century and thus predated the first outbreak of plague in 1348. However, plague gave a marked push to new forms of conspicuous consumption in funeral rites, which became apparent throughout Europe by the 1360s, probably due to a combination of economic, social, and psychological motives. Wealthy merchants, landowners, and aspiring aristocrats spent ever larger sums on the trappings of the funeral procession, such as expensive cloth to drape the bier, a richer outfit in which to bury the deceased, a greater number of paid mourners and candles, and more elaborate mourning clothes for relatives. Funeral pomp declared one's social status and may have offered a kind of psychological barrier against the horrors of pandemic diseases. The funerals of even ordinary folk like artisans, petty merchants, and shopkeepers showed a spiraling interest in similar forms of conspicuous display. This new flamboyance also was expressed in larger numbers of commemorative masses said for the deceased, which hastened the soul's journey out of purgatory. The beautiful family funerary chapels decorated in the new Renaissance style formed part of this same pattern.

The second major trend in death rites during the Renaissance period ran exactly counter to the first. The desire to minimize funeral pomp formed part of an ascetic spiritual current that was closely associated with the mendicant orders, even before 1500. After the rise of Protestantism in the sixteenth century, however, a more subdued ceremonial style became commonplace in those regions of Europe that had rejected Catholicism. Adherents of Protestantism had to develop new liturgical and ceremonial practices that better fit their beliefs. English Protestants tried to balance an appropriate, dignified display of social status in their hierarchical society with the rejection of what was perceived as wasteful "popish" pomp. Protestant preachers advocated simple funeral ceremonies that focused attention on the hereafter. They also advised mourners to engage in only brief periods of grieving and rejected commemorative masses along with the notion of purgatory. By 1600 the ways in which Europeans buried and remembered their dead provided important clues about their deepest religious beliefs and helped to distinguish Catholics from Protestants in everyday life.

See also **Sickness and Disease.**

BIBLIOGRAPHY

Ariès, Philippe. *Western Attitudes toward Death: From the Middle Ages to the Present.* Translated by Patricia M. Ranum. Baltimore, 1974.

Cohn, Samuel K., Jr. *The Cult of Remembrance and the Black Death: Six Renaissance Cities in Central Italy.* Baltimore, 1992.

Cressy, David. *Birth, Marriage, and Death: Ritual, Religion, and the Life-Cycle in Tudor and Stuart England.* Oxford, 1997.

Gittings, Clare. *Death, Burial, and the Individual in Early Modern England.* Beckenham, U.K., 1984.

King, Margaret L. *The Death of the Child Valerio Marcello.* Chicago, 1994.

McClure, George W. *Sorrow and Consolation in Italian Humanism.* Princeton, N.J., 1991.

Strocchia, Sharon T. *Death and Ritual in Renaissance Florence.* Baltimore, 1992.

Tetel, Marcel, Ronald G. Witt, and Rona Goffen, eds. *Life and Death in Fifteenth-Century Florence.* Durham, N.C., 1989.

SHARON T. STROCCHIA

DECORATIVE ARTS. "Decorative arts" is a misleading term applied to objects that do not fall readily into the categories of painting, sculpture, and ar-

The Golden Pony. Isabella of Bavaria, queen of France, gave the Golden Pony altar to her husband, King Charles VI of France. He is portrayed kneeling in veneration of the Virgin and Child. Enamel, gold, and pearls; c. 1404. ALTÖTTING ABBEY, GERMANY/ERICH LESSING/ART RESOURCE

chitecture, but were in the Renaissance often more costly and prestigious on account of their raw materials and exquisite craftsmanship. Inventories, wills, descriptions of travelers and chroniclers, and contemporary depictions demonstrate the preeminence of goldwork, hardstone carvings, tapestries, embroideries, arms, armor, medals, and so forth. Isabella d'Este, marchioness of Mantua (1474–1539), bequeathed to her children ivories from her oratory, an emerald engraved with the head of Christ that had belonged to her father, antique marble and bronze sculptures, gems, coins of gold, silver, and bronze, cameos, and vases rendered in semi-precious stones mounted in gold. Her favorite ladies-in-waiting, in contrast, each received a painting of their choice. The sumptuous attire, accoutrements, and possessions of rulers, nobles, courtiers, and high-ranking ecclesiastics were affordable to very few. Gradations of quality distinguished the lofty from the lowly, the truly rich from the aspiring middle classes. The interconnectedness of the religious and the secular spheres of life in this period is reflected in the intersection between devotional and lay sumptuous arts: they were commissioned and used by the same patrons, created by the same craftsmen, and fashioned of the same materials.

Goldwork. Gem-embellished goldwork served as an eloquent symbol of status. Secular goldwork (including works in silver gilt and silver) took many forms: *joyaux* (decorative ensembles), *nefs* (elaborate table centerpieces), plate, crowns, chains, pendants, badges, and rings, all made even more exorbitantly expensive by inclusion of precious stones. Preserved examples, profuse lists in princely inventories, exaltation by chroniclers and travelers, and representations in paintings vividly convey the splendor of such objects and of their owners. Reliquaries, liturgical vessels and utensils, and sacred sculptural ensembles were likewise frequently rendered in precious metals and adorned with gems and pearls. Used in ecclesiastical settings they conveyed the wealth and prestige of the institution and its benefactors; employed in domestic worship by the elites they signaled wealth and piety of their princely and noble owners.

The *Golden Pony* (c. 1400; collegiate church of Altötting, Bavaria), a New Year's gift from Isabella of Bavaria to her husband, Charles VI, king of France, exemplifies both the splendor of royal goldwork and the frequent merging of religious and secular concerns in such objects: in this ensemble the king is depicted kneeling in adoration of the Virgin and Child. The figures are all cast gold forms covered with enamel, which provides color to flesh, garments, and other elements; gems and pearls enhance the aesthetic and monetary value of the piece. Such spectacular and enormously costly goldwork was a common type of New Year's Day offering in royal circles, for rulers were expected to possess and display such affluence and refinement, as well as to demonstrate piety both in their everyday actions and particularly in politically sensitive circumstances. They further proclaimed their worth through elaborate table centerpieces, such as Benvenuto Cellini's (1500–1571) enameled gold *Saltcellar* (1540–1543; Vienna, Kunsthistorisches Museum) created for Francis I, king of France (ruled 1515–1547), as well as through wrought gold and silver plate arranged on multi-shelf cupboards during feasts and diplomatic receptions. Princely goldwork was further exhibited to visiting dignitaries and exchanged as diplomatic gifts. Enameled gold badges bearing personal insignia were distributed to supporters and allies. Of course, goldwork also served as a literal depository of wealth: notwithstanding its artistic merits it was melted down in times of financial need.

Reliquaries, or receptacles for the physical remains of holy figures, were habitually fashioned of precious metals and adorned with gems to pay respect to, as well as to enhance the power of, their sacred contents. Reliquaries took many shapes, ranging from boxes to sculptural forms. The massive silver gilt and gem-embellished *Reliquary Bust of Saint Lambert*, created by Henri Soete for Bishop Erard de la Marck (5 feet, 3.75 inches high; 1505–1512; Liège, Cathedral of Saint Paul, Treasury), illustrates one common type of reliquary, as well as the tradition of high-ranking church officials both enriching their institutions and demonstrating their own refinement and authority through such commissions. The reliquary depicts the saint in a half-length, holding a book in one hand, and a crozier (bishop's staff) in the other, while the base below is decorated with scenes from his life, rendered in miniature sculpture. Liturgical vessels and crosses were also wrought in precious metals, the latter frequently elaborated with figures of Christ, the Virgin and Saint John, and the angels, cast in the round. The *Adelhauser Cross* fashioned from silver, silver gilt, enamel, and glass, exemplifies such objects (c. 1440; Freiburg im Breisgau, Augustinermusem).

Wealthy bourgeoisie also used gold work to express their status as well as piety, although on a less spectacular scale: they purchased drinking bowls, spoons, items of personal adornment, rosaries, devotional plaques and statuettes, and other such objects. Such pieces were mostly ready-made, rather than commissioned, and contained few, if any, gems. Petrus Christus's painting of *Saint Eligius,* the patron saint of goldsmiths (1449; New York, Metropolitan Museum), depicts a goldsmith's shop stocked with upper middle-class wares—rings with stones, brooches, a belt buckle, crystal container, pewter pitchers with gold terminals, and raw precious materials; a fashionably dressed couple select a ring.

Major centers of precious metalwork production included Bruges, Florence, London, Nürnberg, and Venice. A series of vessels and spoons from the Burgundian Netherlands, exemplified by the *Monkey Cup* (c. 1450s–1460s; New York, Metropolitan Museum, Cloisters), were fashioned in a technique of enamel painting over metal. Such objects appear in the Burgundian, Habsburg, and Medician inventories. Wenzel Jamnitzer of Nürnberg (1508–1585) catered to the Habsburg emperors—creating regalia, centerpieces, ceremonial cups, caskets, and ornamental fountains—and to Nürnberg patricians. Many artists trained as goldsmiths—Filippo Brunelleschi, Lorenzo Ghiberti, Albrecht Dürer—and also worked in other media, and painters furnished designs for goldwork: Hans Holbein the Younger (1497–1543), serving Henry VIII Tudor (ruled 1509–1547), executed patterns for clocks, fountains, and jewels to be rendered in precious material, and Raphael (1483–1520) designed plate for the papal banker Agostino Chigi.

Medals and Hardstones. Portrait medals, cast in gold, silver, bronze, or lead, and inspired by ancient coins, depicted persons of distinction, usually in profile and identified by inscription, while their reverses bore emblematic images or associated texts. Medals fulfilled the desire for glory and excellence, and were particularly popular among Italian upper classes. Produced in limited numbers, they circulated within select groups of friends or allies. Antonio Pisanello (c. 1395–1455), greatly admired for this art at courts across Italy, created such masterpieces as the *Medal of Leonello d'Este,* marchese of Ferrara (London, British Museum). From Italy the fashion spread elsewhere in Europe.

Princely inventories, moreover, shimmer with objects of great cost and refinement carved from semiprecious stones mounted in gold and silver. Medici of Florence inventories, for example, list numerous vessels of rock crystal, jasper, sardonyx, chalcedony, amethyst, and porphyry; intaglios and cameos of carnelian; and exorbitant gem-studded jewelry. Similar and richer collections were amassed by more exalted rulers: the Burgundian dukes, Habsburg emperors, English Tudor and French Valois kings. Church treasuries likewise preserve examples of such splendid containers. Many of these objects were remounted ancient, Byzantine, or Eastern carvings. Florence, Milan, and Venice were major centers of their manufacture.

Arms and Armor. The political and social importance of arms and armor, the high end of whose production also involved goldsmiths, was stimulated by constant warfare, numerous tournaments, and imperatives of military might and readiness for rulers and cities. The accumulation of armor beyond military need by princes and aristocracy indicates its significance as a marker of status; their equipment was distinguished by superior quantity and dazzling decoration in precious metals and gems. Among the booty captured from the duke of

Burgundy, Charles the Bold (ruled 1467–1477), by the Swiss at the battle of Granson (1476) was a sword set with seven large diamonds, as many rubies, and fifteen large pearls.

The finest armor was produced by Milanese, Augsburg, Nürnberg, and Innsbruck armorers. The *Parade Armor of Philip II of Spain* (1549–1550, 1552; Madrid, Real Armería)—embellished with minutely detailed decoration rendered in relief, engraved, and damascened with gold—was fashioned by the celebrated armorer Desiderius Helmschmid and goldsmith Jörg Sigman of Augsburg, cost approximately three thousand gold escudos, and took three years to complete. The great Milanese armorer Filippo Negroli and his goldsmith brother Francesco created the exquisite *Medusa Shield* for Emperor Charles V (1541; Madrid, Real Armería).

Textile Arts. Tapestries constituted one of the most splendid artforms in Renaissance Europe. Their expensive materials—gold, silver, silk, wool, and dyestuffs—extreme labor-intensiveness, vast scale, and programmatic subject matter rendered them valuable both materially and politically. Tapestries adorned the walls of princely palaces, tents during military operations, barges during maritime travel, church choirs and altars, creating sumptuous visual settings that distinguished secular and ecclesiastical elites as well as notable spaces. Akin to goldwork and armor, tapestries were given as gifts to rulers and displayed at strategically significant spatial and temporal junctures, creating carefully orchestrated environments to suit particular occasions. Rulers' vast accumulations of tapestries, alongside stores of goldwork and multiple suits of deluxe armor, conveyed wealth and power. Philip the Good, duke of Burgundy (ruled 1419–1467), owned between ninety and one hundred tapestry cycles, ranging from single pieces to sets of up to ten weavings; he stored them in a specially designed fireproof hall at Arras, staffed with guards, servants, and menders.

Netherlandish tapestries and their creators were preeminent across Europe; Arras, Tournai, and Brussels were the greatest production centers. The industry was nurtured by continuous demand from the Burgundian court and worthies of church and state throughout Europe, who not only purchased tapestries, but also recruited Netherlandish weavers to set up local workshops. Manufacture and sales were managed by merchants who provided capital, kept stocks of cartoons (preliminary drawings or designs), and employed weavers. The renowned Tournai merchant Pasquier Grenier supplied rulers

Benvenuto Cellini. Saltcellar. Cellini (1500–1571) made the saltcellar for King Francis I of France. Gold and enamel; c. 1539–1543. KUNSTHISTORISCHES MUSEUM, VIENNA/FOTO MARBURG/ART RESOURCE, NY

throughout Europe with such popular ensembles as the *Trojan War* series (1470–1490; New York, Metropolitan Museum). One of the most spectacular tapestries from this period, the *Three Coronations* altar hanging (c. 1480; Sens Cathedral, Treasury), depicts the Coronation of the Virgin flanked by two Old Testament scenes: Solomon crowning his mother Bathsheba on the left, and Ahasuerus touching the shoulder of Esther with his golden scepter on the right. This tapestry was apparently produced in Brussels and presented to the cathedral by Charles II of Bourbon, archbishop of Lyon in 1447, papal legate in 1465, and cardinal in 1476 (and nephew of Philip the Good, duke of Burgundy)—clearly an illustrious and powerful personage. Woven in wool, silk, gold, and silver, the *Three Coronations* tapestry preserves much of its original brilliant color and extraordinarily fine detail: the delicately modeled faces with slight blush on the cheeks and moist red lips, the glimmering jewels, soft furs, velvets, and brocades. The

spectacular aesthetic and technical achievement of this piece represents the high end of tapestry production accessible only to the most wealthy patrons. Like goldwork and armor, tapestries ranged widely in quality and price and could be custom-ordered, or purchased ready-made or secondhand. Many were probably produced on speculation. Their subjects spanned pastoral scenes and florals, depictions of heroes and heroines as well as courtiers, mythological and chivalric narratives, religious stories, and important historical events. Affluent burghers also purchased tapestries, but the fineness of weave and the inclusion of silk and metal threads was limited by their lesser finances.

Embroideries also carried great prestige. The ornamentation of garments with silk, gold, pearls, and gems was accessible only to the upper classes. The profusion of embroideries in princely inventories and church treasuries, their presentation to dignitaries, and their careful depiction in Renaissance paintings emphatically signal their importance to contemporary displays of status. Rich burghers and confraternities commissioned embroideries, but on a modest scale. Mid-fifteenth-century Flemish masters developed a particularly splendid embroidery technique of stitching polychrome silks over parallel gold threads, called *or nué*. The *Vestments of the Burgundian Order of the Golden Fleece* (c. 1425–1450; Vienna, Kunsthistorisches Museum) reveal the technical brilliance and extraordinary pictorial richness of such works, which remarkably convey the volumes and textures of depicted objects.

Embroidered panels were also applied to brocade and velvet liturgical garments. *The Mass of St. Giles* by the Master of Saint Giles (c. 1500; London, National Gallery) encapsulates the importance of luxury arts in the Renaissance royal and ecclesiastical settings: it depicts Saint Giles clad in a velvet chasuble adorned with embroidered panels, standing on an imported Oriental rug at the altar, whose front is decorated with a silk hanging dyed with an expensive red pigment, and elevating the host before a gem-studded gold altarpiece with relief figures of God the Father, saints, and angels (this altarpiece, so carefully reproduced in the painting, was, in fact, presented to the Abbey of Saint Denis, where the scene takes place, by King Charles the Bald [ruled 840–877]). The altarpiece is surmounted by a gem-encrusted gold cross in the foot of which is enclosed a small reliquary containing a fragment of the Cross of Our Lord. King Charles Martel, attired in a golden crown embellished with gems and an ermine-lined cloak thrown over a brocaded red dress, kneels at a *prie-dieu* covered with gold brocade as he witnesses the miracle of his sins, which he could not bring himself to confess, being delivered as a written note by the angel to Saint Giles.

Woodwork. Intarsia, or pictorial panels composed of colored wood inlays (using diverse species to achieve coloristic effects), arrived in Europe from the Islamic world. The first figurative intarsia appeared in Orvieto and Siena in the mid-fourteenth century. The rediscovery of linear perspective in the early fifteenth century engendered illusionistic depictions of three-dimensional objects and spaces rendered in flat wood mosaics. Intarsia benches and cabinets adorned Italian church choirs and vestries. The North Vestry of Florence Cathedral is decorated with a series of intarsia panels depicting saints in niches and liturgical objects and books in illusionistic cabinets, executed in two stages, one carried out by Antonio Manetti and Agnolo di Lazzaro in 1436–

1445, another by Giuliano da Maiano in 1460–1465. Masterpieces of this genre are the panels adorning the studies of the duke of Urbino, Federico da Montefeltro (1422–1482) at Urbino and Gubbio (1470s; New York, Metropolitan Museum; for the Urbino studiolo, see the color plates in volume 6), where illusionistic cabinets display books, armor, scientific and musical instruments; illusionistic benches underneath beckon the viewer to sit or behold other treasures they contain.

Ceramics. Italian majolica is best known. This technique also arrived in Europe from the Islamic East, where white tin-glazed pottery developed in imitation of Chinese porcelain. Hispano-Moresque ceramics were highly prized and actively imported into Italy during the fifteenth century, exerting great impact on local manufacture. Iznik ceramics, transported by the Venetians and Genoese, and Chinese Ming porcelain further influenced the forms, techniques, and decorations of Italian wares.

White tin-glaze offered a smooth, opaque, and stable surface on which ornamental designs could be applied and permanently preserved by firing. In later fifteenth-century Italy a broader palette of pigments was developed. Majolica techniques were elucidated by Cipriano Piccolpasso in *The Three Books of the Potter's Art* (1557): fired clay vessels were dipped into liquid glaze, painted with fine brushes preferably made from the whiskers of mice, coated with a clear glaze, and refired. Classical mythologies, histories, ancient Roman wall-paintings, religious narratives, portraits, and heraldic and ornamental motifs provided subject matter for majolica designs. Contemporary prints and paintings inspired historiated vessels. Alongside more elaborately decorated ceramics used and displayed by wealthy patrons, ceramic workshops also produced everyday domestic pottery. Castel Durante, Deruta, Faenza, Florence, Gubbio, Pesaro, Siena, Urbino, Venice, and Naples were major ceramic centers; leading masters included the Fontana of Urbino, Francesco Xanto Avelli da Rovigo, who created the *Hercules Service* (1532; Washington, Corcoran Gallery), and Giorgio Andreoli in Gubbio.

Enamels. Paintings in enamel on metal produced in Limoges in the late fifteenth and sixteenth centuries constituted an important branch of French Renaissance luxury arts. Enamel is a glass-like compound to which, when heated to a molten state, are added metallic oxides that produce a variety of colors. After cooling it is ground to powder and applied to a metal surface. Reheated to extremely high tem-

French Tapestry. *Battle of the Milvian Bridge* designed by Peter Paul Rubens and woven at the Comans-La Planche manu-factory of the firm of Hans Taye and Filippe Maëcht. At the Milvian Bridge near Rome, the emperor Constantine overcame his rival, Maxentius, in 312. One of seven tapestries in the series *The History of Constantine the Great* that King Louis XIII of France presented to the papal envoy Cardinal Francesco Barberini in 1625. Wool and silk with silver and gold threads; 1623–1625; 5 × 7.4 m (16 × 24.4 ft.). PHILADELPHIA MUSEUM OF ART, GIFT OF THE SAMUEL H. KRESS FOUNDATION

peratures it is fused to the base. The resultant objects possess jewel-like luster.

Enamel painting received particular stimulus in the 1530s from King Francis I (ruled 1515–1547), then striving to create a magnificent court at Fontainebleau. Around 1535 Léonard Limosin began to produce for the court fine enameled portraits of dignitaries, pictures based on Italian paintings, sumptuous vases, candlesticks, and saltcellars. Limosin and his contemporaries Pierre Reymond and Jean II Pénicaud—who also worked in white opaque enamel applied to black ground—manufactured vessels decorated with biblical, mythological, and secular scenes for local and foreign patrons. Pierre Reymond's *Pair of Saltcellars with the Story of Actaeon* (c. 1555; Baltimore, Walters Art Gallery) exemplifies this refined art.

Lesser Arts. Middle-class household implements and church furniture were often cast and hammered in brass or copper. The southern Netherlands mass-produced and exported great quantities of chandeliers, lecterns, bells, baptismal fonts, as well as handwashing sets, cooking and serving vessels, and other brassware collectively termed *dinanderie,* after the famous manufacturing city of Dinant. A particularly fine example of an eagle lectern, originally belonging to the collegiate church of Saint Peter at Louvain, is now at the Cloisters in New York. Churches of any importance usually acquired two lecterns, one for singing the Gospel and Epistle, another reserved for the choir books. The books rested on a stand placed on the outspread wings of the bird. The differentiation of textures and the fine polish contributes to the majestic appearance of this object.

See also Arms and Armor; Ceramics; Coins, Medals, and Plaquettes; Jewelry.

BIBLIOGRAPHY

Goldwork

Cellini, Benvenuto. *Autobiography.* Edited by John Pope-Hennessy. London, 1960.

Lightbown, Ronald. *Mediaeval European Jewellery.* London, 1992.

Lightbown, Ronald. *Secular Goldsmiths' Work in Medieval France: A History.* London, 1978.

Medals

The Currency of Fame: Portrait Medals of the Renaissance. Edited by Stephen K. Scher. New York, 1994.

Hardstones

Habsburg, Géza von. *Princely Treasures.* New York, 1997.

Massinelli, Anna Maria, and Filippo Tuena. *Treasures of the Medici.* New York, 1992.

Arms and Armor

Pfaffenbichler, Matthias. *Armourers.* London, 1992.

Pyhrr, Stuart W. et al., eds. *Heroic Armor of the Renaissance: Filippo Negroli and His Contemporaries.* New York, 1998.

Textiles

Cavallo, Adolph Salvatore. *Medieval Tapestries in the Metropolitan Museum of Art.* New York, 1993.

Eichberger, Dagmar. "Tapestry Production in the Burgundian Netherlands, Art for Export and Pleasure." *Australian Journal of Art* 10 (1992): 23–43.

Smith, Jeffrey Chipps. "Portable Propaganda—Tapestries as Princely Metaphors at the Courts of Philip the Good and Charles the Bold." *Art Journal* (1989): 123–129.

Souchal, Geneviève, ed. *Masterpieces of Tapestry from the Fourteenth to the Sixteenth Century.* New York, 1973. Exhibition catalog, Metropolitan Museum of Art.

Staniland, Kay. *Embroiderers.* London, 1991.

Woodwork

Raggio, Olga, and Antoine M. Wilmering. *The Liberal Arts Studiolo from the Ducal Palace at Gubbio.* New York, 1996. The Metropolitan Museum of Art.

Tormey, Alan. *Renaissance Intarsia: The Art of Geometry.* New York, 1982.

Ceramics

Caiger-Smith, Alan. *Tin-Glaze Pottery in Europe and the Islamic World.* London, 1973.

Piccolpasso, Cipriano, *The Three Books of the Potter's Art.* 2 vols. Translated by Ronald Lightbown and Alan Caiger-Smith. London, 1980. Translation of *I tre libri dell'arte del vasaio* (1557).

Rackham, Bernard. *Italian Maiolica.* London, 1963.

Enamels

Caroselli, Susan L., ed. *The Painted Enamels of Limoges: A Catalogue of the Collection of the Los Angeles County Museum of Art.* New York, 1993.

Charleston, Robert Jesse. *Glass and Stained Glass: Limoges and Other Painted Enamels.* Fribourg, Switzerland, 1977.

MARINA BELOZERSKAYA

DEDEKIND, FRIEDRICH

DEDEKIND, FRIEDRICH (1524–1598), German humanist and Lutheran pastor, author of the Latin satire *Grobianus.* Dedekind was born in Neustadt am Rübenberge, the son of a butcher. After studying at the universities of Marburg and Wittenberg, where he obtained a Magister of Arts degree in 1550, he settled in his hometown as a Lutheran pastor. In 1553 he married Juliana Cordus, the daughter of the famous humanist Euricius Cordus. In 1576 Dedekind became pastor in Lüneburg.

Although Dedekind wrote two little known Reformation plays, *Der christliche Ritter* (The Christian knight; 1576) and *Papista conversus* (The converted papist; 1596), his fame rests on his satire *Grobianus: De morum simplicitate libri duo* (Grobianus: Two books on the simplicity of manners; 1549). Inspired by and drawing on numerous Latin and German works from the literary genres of conduct literature and *Tischzuchten* (table disciplines), Dedekind fashioned a new work that, along with *Epistolae obscurorum virorum* (Letters of obscure men; 1515–1517) and Erasmus's *Moriae encomium* (1511; trans. *In Praise of Folly*), belongs to the great humanist satires of the sixteenth centuries. In two books and 2,600 Latin verses, Dedekind describes, and ironically endorses, the daily routine of a Grobianus, a coarse, boorish fellow who indulges in the most asocial, indecent behavior imaginable. At any stage, Grobianus asserts the primacy of the body and gratifies his desires: he belches, breaks wind, vomits, and defecates, constantly destroying or diminishing the pleasures and appetites of those around him.

The ironic, didactic technique of teaching good manners by demonstrating the worst possible behavior is based on the belief that negative examples will serve as a deterrent, just as the Spartans, the author claims, paraded drunken slaves in front of their children to discourage similar inclinations. Dedekind's ironic satire of negative precepts has been variously interpreted. While older critics saw in *Grobianus* a manifestation of the decline in manners in the sixteenth century, more recent critics have viewed the work as a satire on an age when members of the rising urban classes used their corporality as a weapon to assert their place "at the table of life," ruthlessly ousting rivals in an increasingly competitive environment. Others have placed *Grobianus* in the context of the civilizing process that marked emerging bourgeois society in early modern Europe.

Only two years after its publication, Dedekind's work was translated into German rhymed couplets by the Worms schoolmaster Caspar Scheidt (c. 1520–

1565) under the title *Von groben Sitten und unhöf-lichen Gebärden* (Of coarse manners and rude gestures). Dedekind himself published a second (1552) and third edition (1554), expanding the work to three books and introducing a female counterpart, the Grobiana. Both Latin and German versions experienced numerous editions in the sixteenth century.

Outside Germany, Dedekind's satire found translators and adaptors primarily in England. In 1605 a certain "R. F. Gent" rendered it rather faithfully into English. Four years later Thomas Dekker used large portions of Dedekind's work in *The Gul's Horne-book* (1609).

BIBLIOGRAPHY

Primary Works

Dedekind, Friedrich. *Grobianus. De Morum Simplicitate. Grobi-anus, von groben Sitten und unhöflichen Gebärden.* German version by Caspar Scheidt. With a preface by Barbara Könneker. Darmstadt, Germany, 1979.

R. F. Gent [pseudonym]. *The Schoole of Slovenrie, or Cato turnd Wrong Side Outward.* London, 1605. In Ernst Rühl. *Grobi-anus in England: Nebst Neudruck der ersten Übersetzung "The Schoole of Slovenrie" (1605) und erster Herausgabe des Schwankes "Grobiana's Nuptials" (c. 1640) aus Ms. 30 Bodl. Oxf. Plaestra, 38.* Berlin, 1904.

Secondary Works

Correll, Barbara. *The End of Conduct: Grobianus and the Renaissance Text of the Subject.* Ithaca, N.Y., and London, 1996. Only analysis that examines *Grobianus* under social-historical and cultural-historical aspects.

Könneker, Barbara. *Satire im 16. Jahrhundert: Epoche, Werke, Wirkung.* Munich, 1991. Pages 118–134.

ECKHARD BERNSTEIN

DEE, JOHN (1527–1608), English natural philosopher, alchemist, scholar. Described by Petrus Ramus as one of the few learned men in England, John Dee was born in London to Rowland Dee and Johanna Wild. His father, a member of the Merchant Tailors Guild, ensured that Dee had a fine education, first at Chelmsford Grammar School and then at Cambridge University, where he received his B.A. from St. John's College in 1546 and his M.A. from Trinity College in 1548. Although Dee's official course of study was humanistic, his book purchases reveal that he was also reading natural philosophy. Starting in 1547 Dee supplemented his formal education with visits to the European continent. He studied at the University of Louvain, traveled extensively, and consulted with prominent natural philosophers. Dee's most important published contributions to natural philosophy were his astronomical *Propaedeu-mata aphoristica* (London, 1558), the alchemical-cabalistic *Monas hieroglyphica* (Antwerp, 1564), his preface to the first English translation of Euclid's *Elements* (London, 1570), and *General and Rare Memorials Pertayning to the Perfect Arte of Navigation* (London, 1577). Dee's wide-ranging expertise also included geography, calendar reform, astrology, medicine, history, and magic. But Dee failed to gain sufficient patronage from four successive English monarchs (Edward VI, Mary I, Elizabeth I, and James I) and had to rely upon well-placed friends and clients, such as William Cecil and Robert Dudley, for financial support. By the late 1570s Dee had become dissatisfied not only with his position in England but also with the limits of his natural philosophical expertise. As the sixteenth century waned, Apocalypticism, with its insistence on the natural world's corruption, and the exploration of the New World, which revealed a confusing array of novel natural phenomena, challenged Dee's ability to practice natural philosophy. To resolve his difficulties Dee crafted a technique for communicating with angels about the natural world and its properties through a crystal stone with the assistance of a "scryer." Over two hundred transcripts of Dee's conversations with angels survive, most of which focus on linguistic, kabbalistic, alchemical, and apocalyptic topics. In 1583 Dee and his scryer Edward Kelly (with their families and much of Dee's library) journeyed to central Europe in search of a patron who would support their conversations. But potential patrons, including King Stephen Báthory of Poland, the Holy Roman Emperor Rudolf II, and Count Willem Rozmberk, were more interested in Dee's alchemical expertise than his angels. A disappointed Dee left central Europe in 1589; Kelly remained in Prague as one of Rudolf II's alchemists. For the next two decades Dee tried and largely failed to regain his position in England while continuing to seek angelic advice with the assistance of Bartholomew Hickman. Dee continued to pursue the financial support of Elizabeth I and James I successively, served for a time as warden of the University of Manchester, and entertained scholarly visitors from home and abroad. He died unappreciated and in poverty. Only in the twentieth century have his efforts to popularize mathematics, his serious study of alchemy, and his status as one of Elizabethan England's most illustrious "Renaissance men" been fully appreciated.

BIBLIOGRAPHY

French, Peter J. *John Dee: The World of an Elizabethan Magus.* London, 1972.

Harkness, Deborah E. *John Dee's Conversations with Angels: Cabala, Alchemy, and the End of Nature.* Cambridge, U.K., 1999.

Sherman, William H. *John Dee: The Politics of Reading and Writing in the English Renaissance.* Amherst, Mass., 1995.

DEBORAH E. HARKNESS

DELLA CASA, GIOVANNI (1503–1556), Italian writer. The author of *Galateo,* the famous Renaissance book of manners, Della Casa was the most important Italian poet in the years between Ludovico Ariosto and Torquato Tasso. He also played an important role in the implementation of the Counter-Reformation in Venice.

Born in Mugello, near Florence, to a distinguished Florentine family, he studied law at Bologna, spent some time in Padua, and moved to Rome in 1531. Like many well-to-do intellectuals of his generation, Casa spent an aimless and dissolute life in that city.

Casa's father directed him from early youth toward the Church, a normal career path of the upper levels of Italian society at the time. Casa's antifeminist treatise *An uxor sit ducenda* (On taking a wife), written probably in 1537, marks a transition from his reckless youth to a life dedicated to success within the Church. He became clerk of the Apostolic Chamber in 1538, dean of the same chamber in 1543, and was given the archbishopric of Benevento in 1544. The same year he was sent as nuncio, or papal legate, to Venice. This position was particularly delicate since the Republic, the most influential Italian state, maintained a forceful position of independence from the church in state affairs, including the enforcement of religious orthodoxy. Initially Casa's work met strong resistance from the Venetian government, but in 1547 the Republic relented its opposition because of a combination of factors, including the defeat of the Protestant princes at Mühlberg by Charles V, the doctrinal clarifications brought by the first phase of the Council of Trent, and the growing conviction that religious orthodoxy was essential to the internal security of the state. It is no surprise that Casa was finally able to establish the Roman Inquisition in 1547 in Venice and to make inroads toward the establishment of the Index of Prohibited Books. Eventually, however, the republic prevented the Index's implementation, mainly because it might damage the commercial success of the Venetian presses.

Casa's *Rime* (Lyric poems; 1558) are among the most beautiful poems of the century, and are notable for the introduction of broken rhythms and an often tragic sense of life. Around 1543 he wrote another short Latin treatise, *De officiis inter potentiores et ten-uoiores amicos* (On the duties between higher and lower friends), in which he dwelt on the nature of bureaucratic affairs and on the importance of money in human relationships. His *Galateo* (1558), which was eventually translated into Latin and into all the major European languages, is not only a clever treatise on table manners, but also a subtle restatement of the new philosophy of life, showing how people can overcome or at least survive the whims of fortune if they can combine education with riches and social standing. In this sense *Galateo* is a forceful statement supporting the aristocratization of Italian life. Finally, his two orations, one asking Venice to enter a league of Italian states, the other on the city of Piacenza, are evidence of the anti-Spanish sentiment in Italy and include the first usage of the term "reason of state."

BIBLIOGRAPHY

Primary Work

Della Casa, Giovanni. *Galateo.* Translated with introduction and note by Konrad Eisenbichler and Kenneth R. Bartlett. Toronto, 1994.

Secondary Works

Mutini, C. "Della Casa, Giovanni." In *Dizionario biografico degli italiani.* Rome, 1988. Vol. 36, pp. 699–719.

Santosuosso, Antonio. *Books, Readers, and Critics: The Bibliography of Giovanni della Casa, 1537–1975.* Florence, 1979.

Santosuosso, Antonio. *Vita di Giovanni della Casa.* Rome, 1979.

ANTONIO SANTOSUOSSO

DELLA PORTA, GIAMBATTISTA (c. 1535–1615), Neapolitan dramatist, investigator of nature, and writer of treatises. Della Porta's name has been linked with the development of modern optics, photography, cryptography, botany, and, discreditably, criminal anthropology. His belief in a tension between forces of sympathy and antipathy sustaining the universe distantly presages a modern astrophysical theory of the cosmological constant.

Magic and Science. Della Porta's encyclopedic writings on physiognomy, alchemy, agriculture, the art of memory, meteorology, mathematics, hydraulics, the doctrine of signatures, chiromancy, ciphers, the camera obscura, magnetism, astronomy, astrology, and illusionism belong to a time before the distinction between science and magic. With his brother Gian Vincenzo he maintained a famous collection, part *Wunderkammer* (miscellany of natural phenomena and remarkable artifacts), part scientific museum. He traveled within Italy and beyond and was consulted by visitors to Naples as a seer and "Mago." Sometime before 1580, the Inquisition investigated his practice of the occult arts. Although he insisted that his magic was natural or "white," rather than diabolic "black" magic, and eventually joined the Jesuit lay order to allay suspicion, his Accademia dei Segreti, formed between 1558 and 1579 to study the secrets of nature, was disbanded. For most of his life Della Porta was plagued by censors' bans and delays in publishing his treatises. He accused William Gilbert, the English discoverer of magnetism, of plagiarizing his revelations on magnetism and claimed to have invented the telescope before Galileo. From 1579 to 1586 he was financed by Cardinal Luigi d'Este in experiments with lens making at Murano and in his alchemical search for the philosophers' stone. Della Porta knew Paolo Sarpi, Galileo Galilei, Tommaso Campanella, and, probably, Giordano Bruno, although he avoided publicizing the dangerous acquaintance. In old age he flourished as a member of the Accademia dei Lincei and the Accademia degli Oziosi. His works, abundant in observation but lacking in system, were widely known and reprinted, especially *De humana physiognomonia* (Of human physiognomy; 1586) and *Magiae naturalis* (1558, augmented 1589), which was translated into Italian, French, German, and printed in England as *Natural Magick* in 1658.

Drama. In youth Della Porta attended plays in Naples sponsored by the Sanseverino family and translated Plautus's works, a formative influence on his comic dramaturgy. Perhaps to distract attention from his embattled scientific writings, he began publishing his *commedie erudite* with the appearance of *L'Olimpia* in 1589; it was followed by thirteen other regular comedies in prose and three verse plays: a tragicomedy, *La Penelope* (1591); a sacred drama, *Il Georgio* (1611), probably written in support of the Este dynasty's struggle to hold Ferrara; and in his last years a tragedy, *L'Ulisse* (1614). Laughter dominates some of the comedies, for example, *La fantesca* (The maidservant; 1592), *La trappolaria* (The trapper trapped; 1596), *La carbonaria* (The blackface play; 1601), and *Lo astrologo* (The astrologer; 1606). Others approach tragicomedy, such as *Gli duoi fratelli rivali* (The two rival brothers; 1601), *La sorella* (The sister, 1604), *Il Moro* (The Moor; 1607), and *La furiosa* (The play of madness; 1609). Observing the neo-Aristotelian unities of time, place, and action, and constructed of combinations of typical elements from the sixteenth-century theatrical repertory, all of them are vivaciously stageworthy models of stylized theatrical language and comic psychology reflecting the author's theories of physiognomy. Some contain Neapolitan dialect and comic turns characteristic of the commedia dell'arte, to which Della Porta gave many plots and rhetorical models. Although suspect because of his research into nature, Della Porta supported Catholic Reformation policies regarding the arts and the movement to preserve but improve on earlier humanistic achievements in rebuilding classical genres by perfecting dramatic structure and introducing new emotional content, fashionably modern and often didactically Christian. In print his plays were long circulated as examples of the best in Italian comedy. Among his immediate literary imitators were Francesco D' Isa, Fabrizio Marotta, Filippo Caetani, and Giulio Cesare Torelli. In the next century Carlo Goldoni kept Della Porta's comedies in his library. Jean de Rotrou derived *Célie* (performed 1645; published 1646) from *Gli duoi fratelli rivali* and *La soeur* (performed 1645; published 1647) from *La sorella;* Pierre de Larivey translated an adaptation of *Olimpia,* which Tristan l'Hermite adapted as *Le parasite* (1654); even Molière may indirectly have acquired debts to Della Porta. In England, Walter Hawkesworth cast *Cintia* into Latin as *Labyrinthus* (performed c. 1602/03; published 1636); Samuel Brooke made *Adelphe* (performed 1611/12) from *Sorella;* George Ruggle turned *Trappolaria* into the Cambridge hit *Ignoramus* (performed 1614/15; published 1630), later twice translated into English; Thomas Middleton used *Sorella* in *No Wit No Help Like a Woman's* (performed 1613; published 1657); and Thomas Tomkis adapted *Astrologo* as *Albumazar* (performed 1614/15; published 1615), a play with a long stage life.

See also **Commedia dell'Arte; Drama,** *subentry on* **Erudite Comedy; Magic and Astrology.**

BIBLIOGRAPHY

Primary Works

Della Porta, Giambattista. *Edizione Nazionale delle Opere di Giovan Battista della Porta.* Naples, 1996–. Two volumes have appeared as of 1999: vol. 3, *Ars reminiscendi,* edited by Raffaele Sirri, 1996, and vol. 8, *Coelestis physiognomonia,* edited by Alfonso Paolella, 1996.

Della Porta, Giambattista. *Natural magick.* Edited by Derek J. Price. New York, 1957. Reprint of anonymous translation (London, 1658) of *Magiae Naturalis libri XX* (1589).

Della Porta, Giambattista. *Gli duoi fratelli rivali/The Two Rival Brothers.* Edited and translated by Louise George Clubb. Berkeley, 1980.

Della Porta, Giambattista. *Teatro.* Edited by Raffaele Sirri, 4 vols. Naples, 1978–1980.

Secondary Works

Boas, Marie. *The Scientific Renaissance, 1450–1630.* New York, 1962. Reprint 1994.

Clubb, Louise George. *Giambattista Della Porta, Dramatist.* Princeton, N.J., 1965. See pp. 315–318 for a list of the first editions of all of Della Porta's scientific and literary works.

Muraro, Luisa. *Giambattista Della Porta mago e scienziato.* Milan, 1978.

Torrini, Maurizio, ed. *Giovan Battista Della Porta nell'Europa del suo tempo.* Naples, 1990.

LOUISE GEORGE CLUBB

DELLA ROBBIA FAMILY. *See* **Florence,** *subentry on* **Art of the Fifteenth Century.**

DELLA VALLE, FEDERICO (c. 1560–1628), poet, playwright, courtier. Della Valle was relatively ignored until Benedetto Croce fostered republication of his work in the twentieth century. At the court of Carlo Emanuele I of Savoy in Turin, Della Valle held the post of chief cavalry quartermaster to the duchess Caterina, daughter of Philip II of Spain, for whose marriage in 1585 he composed an epithalamium. Among Della Valle's literary and theatrical models were Torquato Tasso and Battista Guarini, whose celebrated tragicomedy *Il pastor fido* (1589; trans. *The Faithful Shepherd*) was first performed for the ducal wedding. In addition to four plays in unrhymed verse, Della Valle left *sonetti* on court subjects, forty-six octaves of an epic poem on the duke's proposed campaign against the Turks, a pair of funeral orations, and a political treatise, *Ragionamento fatto ne la raunanza degli stati de la Francia per l'elezione d'un re* (Discourse delivered at the gathering of the estates of France for an election of a king; 1593).

Adelonda di Frigia, a semipastoral blending of tragedy and comedy in the style of Guarini, was performed by court ladies, with Della Valle's own *intermedi* sung and danced, for the visit to Turin in 1595 of the cardinal archduke of Austria. The play is a Catholic reworking of *Iphigenia in Taurus,* with augmentations from the *romanzo* tradition of Ludovico Ariosto. Recast in sixteenth-century Petrarchistic verse, the plot becomes a representation of the instability of temporal life, and the action is conducted more lyrically than theatrically.

At about the same time Della Valle was working on the tragedy *La reina di Scozia* (The queen of Scots; 1628). Mary Stuart's ill-fated secretary Davide Rizzio belonged to the court of Savoy, where partisan Catholic support for the queen of Scots was intensified by personal acquaintance and anti-English court gossip. Compiled from contemporary Catholic accounts and dedicated to Pope Urban VIII, *Reina* was the first of several Italian tragedies about Mary Stuart. A neo-Senecan saint's play in five acts, it dramatizes Mary's last day and martyrdom. The action consists in Mary's transcendence of the world as she moves toward heaven, free from courts and power struggles. The tragedy is an example of Catholic dramaturgy, interiorizing and baptizing classical *sententiae* on the vanity of human wishes.

Perhaps moved by Mary Stuart's references to biblical heroines, likening herself at her trial to the advocate Esther rather than to the avenger Judith, Della Valle took them as subjects in *Iudit* and *Ester,* printed together in 1627 and dedicated to the Queen of Heaven, whose "shades" the devout author declared Judith and Esther to have been. Both works belong to the genre of sacred tragedy that was still flourishing later in the century when Jean Racine wrote his *Esther* and *Athalie.* Della Valle's *Ester* opens with a cloud figuring the insubstantiality of earthly life, depicts the tragic fall of Aman and his ambitious wife, scheming against Queen Esther's people, and closes with moving laments on human inconstancy and the futility of court life, as a chorus of Israelites urges reliance on God.

Iudit, sometimes considered Della Valle's finest work, is similar in its lyrical expression of tormented faith. It is the most dramatic of the tragedies, composed of contrasting atmospheres, including comic touches and a variety of characters. Holofernes is presented as a barbarian sensualist surrounded by courtiers and captains competing for his favor. The splendid figure of Judith, necessarily the most active of Della Valle's protagonists, achieves victory for God and Judaea, but a tragic ending focuses on the brave surviving enemy warrior Arimaspe and the vanquished chorus of Assyrian soldiers, terrified victims of their leaders' wars. A pessimistic thematics of power and a sense of death and suffering penetrate all the plays; earthly happiness is represented as evanescent, a mere foretaste of heavenly peace, ardently invoked by Della Valle's exquisitely modulated verse.

See also **Drama,** *subentry on* **Tragedy; Italian Literature and Language.**

BIBLIOGRAPHY

Primary Works

Della Valle, Federico. *Opere.* Edited by Maria Gabriella Stassi. Turin, Italy, 1995.

Della Valle, Federico. *Tragedie.* Edited by Andrea Gareffi. Milan, 1988.

Della Valle, Federico. *Tutte le opere.* Edited by Pietro Cazzani. Verona, Italy, 1955.

Secondary Works

Croce, Benedetto. "Le tragedie di Federigo della Valle di Asti." *La Critica* 27 (1929): 377–397.

Croce, Franco. *Federico Della Valle.* Florence, 1965.

White, Laura Sanguineti. *Dal detto alla figura: Le tragedie di Federico Della Valle.* Florence, 1992.

LOUISE GEORGE CLUBB

DELMEDIGO, ELIJAH (c. 1460–1497), Jewish philosopher. A native of Candia on the island of Crete, where he mastered the classics of rabbinic and philosophic literature, Delmedigo traveled to Italy in 1480. He spent the next ten years in Padua, Venice, Bassano, and Florence working as a freelance translator and commentator specializing in the philosophy of Aristotle as transmitted in the writings of the Muslim sage, Ibn Rushd (called Averroes). Among the patrons who commissioned Delmedigo to compose Latin treatises and translations based on the Hebrew texts of Ibn Rushd were Girolamo Donato, Domenico Grimani, Antonino Pizzamano, and Giovanni Pico della Mirandola. Delmedigo's work ranged from literal renditions of Ibn Rushd's summaries of Aristotle's *Metaphysics* and Plato's *Republic* to encyclopedic accounts of Ibn Rushd's various commentaries on Aristotle's *De anima*. In 1482 Delme-

Elijah Delmedigo. Portrait from *Sefer Elim* (Amsterdam, 1629).

digo translated into Hebrew the two treatises he originally wrote in Latin for Pico dealing with the definition of the intellective soul and the possibility of immortality. In 1485, again seeking to widen his audience within the Jewish community, Delmedigo translated into Hebrew the text he had earlier written in Latin for Pico dealing with Ibn Rushd's *De substantia orbis* (On the substance of the celestial sphere).

Returning to Crete at the end of 1490, Delmedigo composed a Hebrew treatise devoted to religious philosophy, *Behinat ha-dat* (The examination of religion). It is his last known work and the one most widely studied by modern scholars. It features Delmedigo's elaborate defense of the congenial relationship between prophetic revelation, rabbinic faith, and philosophic reason; his critique of Christian beliefs regarding salvation and the related doctrines of the Trinity, the Incarnation, and transubstantiation; his dissatisfaction with theology and mindless orthodoxy; and his attack against the exaggerated claims of Jewish mysticism, the Kabbalah.

Throughout his writings, Delmedigo consistently and unequivocally declared Aristotle to be the supreme philosopher and Ibn Rushd his only reliable exponent. Delmedigo defended such notions as the theoretical impossibility of a personal afterlife and the necessity that God is a self-contained mind whose transcendental thoughts guarantee the regularity of the natural world as well as its intelligibility to philosophically disciplined observers. A staunch Averroist, Delmedigo objected to the theologically inspired doctrines and interpretations of St. Thomas Aquinas and John of Jandun. Delmedigo's philosophic loyalties also aligned him against Giovanni Pico della Mirandola and other contemporaries, especially in Florence, who were steeped in kabbalistic lore and fascinated by Neoplatonic metaphysics. Despite his penchant for scholarly controversy, Delmedigo was also concerned with social order. He urged his community to avoid sectarian strife, to tolerate the beliefs of popular religion whenever possible, and to acknowledge the doctrines and practices cherished by rationalists, mystics, Talmudists, and simple folk alike. He cultivated secular philosophy, defending its freedom from the burden of serving traditional theological needs. He did so because he thought secular philosophy would help defend the Jewish community against its diverse opponents and because he assumed the obligations of a responsible interpreter of Aristotle and Ibn Rushd.

BIBLIOGRAPHY

Bland, Kalman. "Elijah Del Medigo's Averroist Response to the Kabbalahs of Fifteenth-Century Jewry and Pico Della Mirandola." *The Journal of Jewish Thought and Philosophy* 1 (1991): 23–53.

Geffen, David. "Insights into the Life and Thought of Elijah Del Medigo Based on His Published and Unpublished Works." *Proceedings of the American Academy for Jewish Research*. 41–42 (1973–1974): 69–86.

KALMAN P. BLAND

DEMOGRAPHY. For the late medieval and Renaissance periods, the European demographic system was characterized by modest overall growth.

General Population Development.

In the first three centuries of the new millennium, western Europe experienced a slow but continuous population growth. However, when the "Black Death" hit Europe in the mid-fourteenth century, it began a period in which phases of stagnation—or even of demographic regression—alternated with phases of rather intense population growth (see table 1).

The European population increased from 74 million in 1340 (only a few years before the huge epidemic of 1347–1350) to 95 million in 1700. In other words, the average annual rate of increase would have remained for a period of more than three and one-half centuries well below the threshold of 1 per 1,000. Although the growth phase, which ends in the first half of the fourteenth century, is not quantifiable with exactitude due to fragmentary and uncertain documentation, its magnitude is supported by concordant clues such as the cultivation of new fields, the expansion of city walls, an increase in population, and the foundation of new castles and villages. However, even before the coming of the plague in many parts of the Continent, there are clear signs of

TABLE 1. Population of Europe[a]

Year	Population (in millions)	Period	Annual population growth (per 1,000 people)
1200	49	1200–1250	3.0
1250	57	1250–1300	4.1
1300	70	1300–1340	1.4
1340	74	1340–1400	−5.9
1400	52	1400–1500	2.5
1500	67	1500–1600	2.8
1600	89	1600–1700	0.7
1700	95	—	
		1340–1700	0.7

Source: Biraben, "Essai sun l'evolution du nombre des hommes," p. 16.

[a]Not including territories of the former Soviet Union.

slowing population growth due to the mounting difficulty of increasing available resources to keep pace with the increase in population. Within these difficult circumstances, the spreading of the plague at the mid-fourteenth century—and the ensuing repeated epidemics, which die down only by the first half of the following century—made the continental population growth slow down dramatically. The population probably reached a minimum in the first decades of the fifteenth century, and only from the middle of that century does reasonable population growth occur. The rate of growth increases over the course of the sixteenth century, and toward the end of that century the population surpasses its former maximum for the first time.

However, this growth is not the start of the continuous growth that precedes demographic transition. The first signs of a true change in the demographic system take place only toward the middle of the eighteenth century, and these signs of change are restricted to a few limited areas of Europe. England is a prime example. Sixteenth-century growth led again, in a less dramatic way, to a situation of relative overpopulation, analogous to that recorded in the fourteenth century. The seventeenth century, devastated by war, prolonged famine, and fresh outbreaks of the plague, was a period of crises and of economic and especially demographic stagnation for Europe as a whole.

Differential Trends.

In addition to identifying these general tendencies for European populations, it is important to underline a differential trend: a consistent, longstanding tendency leading to a progressive shift in the demographic center of gravity between Mediterranean countries and those in northwestern Europe (see table 2).

At least in the beginning, the introduction of new agricultural techniques, which permitted annual cultivation of lands previously farmed only between long fallow intervals, probably allowed a substantial increase in the production of foodstuffs in northwestern Europe and thus a more rapid peopling of these lands than occurred in Mediterranean countries. Even within specific countries such as Italy, for which available sources allow fairly detailed estimates of the progression of regional populations (see table 3), important differences can be observed within similar phases of growth or recession. These differences were determined in part by the varying impact of the great mortality crises and in part by differing capacities of economic systems to produce the resources necessary to sustain a rising population.

TABLE 2. Differential Trends of the European Population

| Year | Population (in millions) | | |
	Southern Europe	Northern Europe	Europe
1000	24	8	32
1200	33	12	45
1500	39	23	62
1750	60	42	102

| Period | Average annual growth (per 1,000 people) | | |
	Southern Europe	Northern Europe	Europe
1000–1200	1.6	2.0	1.7
1200–1500	0.6	2.2	1.1
1500–1750	1.7	2.4	2.0

Source: Durand, "Historical Estimates of World Population," p. 256.

TABLE 3. Regional Italian Populations (according to present national boundaries of the nation), 1300–1650 (in millions)

Year	North	Central	South	Islands	Italy
1300	6.3	3.0	2.3	0.9	12.5
1450	3.9	1.4	1.6	0.6	7.5
1550	5.5	2.0	2.9	1.1	11.5
1600	6.5	2.2	3.3	1.5	13.5
1650	5.2	2.1	2.9	1.5	11.7

| Period | Average annual growth (per 1,000 people) | | | | |
	North	Central	South	Islands	Italy
1300–1450	−3.2	−5.1	−2.4	−2.7	−3.4
1450–1550	3.4	3.6	5.9	6.1	4.3
1550–1600	3.3	1.9	2.6	6.2	3.2
1600–1650	−4.5	−0.9	−2.6	0.0	−2.9

Source: Del Panta et al., *La popolazione italiana,* p. 277.

The Plague Cycle. In the long term, a clear link existed throughout Europe between the capacity of the economic system to increase its available resources (especially alimentary resources) and the possibility that populations could increase without heading for catastrophe or demographic stagnation. Nevertheless, European demographic history of the late medieval and Renaissance periods was especially affected by the plague cycle. It is important to underline that the cycle constituted an exogenous element with regard to the classic Malthusian mechanisms controlling demographic growth. The dead-liness of the plague was not strictly dependent on the population's level of nutrition. However, indirect relations between crises of subsistence and the diffusion and graveness of epidemics indirectly caused by the plague cannot be ignored.

The great crises of mortality linked to the spreading of plague epidemics affected the growth of European populations from the mid-fourteenth to the start of the eighteenth century. The frequency and intensity of the crises generated relatively long phases of stagnation, growth, and demographic decline. The plague can certainly be blamed for the demographic collapse in the second half of the fourteenth century. In England, for example, other epidemics of national scale hit the country (after the first in 1348) in 1361–1362, 1369, 1375, 1390, and 1400. A similar situation is recorded in Italian history, with epidemics in 1347–1350, 1360–1363, 1371–1374, 1381–1384, 1388–1390, and 1398–1400. The reduction of the frequency of the great pandemics made possible the weak resurgence that characterizes the fifteenth and sixteenth centuries. Ultimately the general crisis of the seventeenth century is confirmed by an almost nonexistent growth for the Continent as a whole throughout the century. This crisis, which was only partially attributable to the plague, was characterized by true catastrophes which caused sudden oscillations in demographic trends.

The Mechanics of Recuperation. Analysis of the developmental mechanisms of European populations of the past shows the capacity of these populations to react to damage caused by enormous population loss. Dissolved marriages, due to the death of a spouse, were re-formed when a widow or widower remarried. The death of one or more children was compensated by having more children. The rise in the birthrate after crises is not only a mechanical consequence of remarriage but also an index of a real increase in fertility, attributable in part to a changed attitude toward procreation. On the other hand, the repetition of large-scale, recurrent catastrophes interfered with the process of recuperation, especially in the second half of the fourteenth century. It generated such a lack of balance in the demographic structure that it prevented the population from reviving. Additionally, the population lacked a guaranteed flow of migrants from elsewhere into places where voids had occurred, which interfered with the process of recuperation.

The repercussions of the great pandemics were likewise linked to structural factors, including those related to family composition and settlement types.

These factors partly explain the different tendencies of populations hit by the huge disaster of the plague. For example, the size of nuclear families was inversely proportional to the probability that a family would be totally eliminated by a crisis: the large size of a family constituted a safeguard against its own extinction. Similar statements can be made about populations distributed in fairly large and fairly autonomous demographic aggregates; these include urban aggregates, towns of mixed economies, and small rural villages. Logically, a small population center was more likely to have been threatened or even completely exterminated by an epidemic. It would have surely been less capable to react, in demographic terms, to the consequences of crises, while cities often succeeded at putting into play the natural demographic mechanisms of recuperation as well as encouraging the immigration of qualified people. This immigration was able to reconstitute the productive fabric of the population, allowing the recuperation of economic activity.

The Auto-Regulatory System. European demography of the fourteenth to seventeenth centuries presents several interpretational difficulties—beyond the effects of the great epidemics. A system of auto-regulation of growth undoubtedly existed (in different contexts and with specific mechanisms) over relatively long periods of time and not only as a short-term response to the periods of destructiveness due to epidemics or large-scale famines. The latest techniques of demographic analysis permit us in many cases to highlight the distinct role of mortality (beyond that caused by exceptional crises) and fertility in the long-term evolution of European populations. Even the level of "normal" survival changed over time. Changes could have been the result of available foodstuffs but also could have been due to factors beyond the relation between population and resources. Demographic statistics also prove that populations in the past were capable of adaptation to economic and environmental constrictions by modifying their marriage regimes, if need be. Such changes could have had significant effects on reproductive capacities. The best example is that of the English population, which over the long run experienced relatively low mortality in comparison with the European average. The English population was extremely capable of maintaining its growth at a rate compatible with the availability of its resources. It was capable of maintaining an equilibrium by having adopted new marriage regimes and thus fertility levels.

Marriage Rates and Families. In general, fertility levels—the average number of surviving children—during the time of the Renaissance were modest. Fertility levels were also characterized by a marked geographic and temporal variability as well as a necessarily high infant mortality rate. According to the 1427 Florentine *catasto* (land register), which yields information about the Tuscan population of over 260,000 people, the average household was composed of only 4.42 people. This finding took place in an exceptional period for the history of Italian and European demographics, characterized by ravages of extremely grave and repeated returns of the plague. It is, however, still possible to assert that the average family size in Renaissance Europe was rarely larger than six people per household. Disasters caused by the late medieval catastrophes undoubtedly stimulated a series of recuperating mechanisms involving profound modifications in the formation of the family. The most obvious symptom of this devastation was the extremely low age at which girls married, evident throughout Europe in periods of great depopulation. In 1427 Tuscany, where this phenomenon is well documented, women married between the average ages of seventeen and twenty, in contrast with a significantly higher age of about twenty-two in 1481.

The modification of the marriage regime, as populations distanced themselves from the most disturbed times, occurs alongside an increase in the complexity of the family structure. These changes can be seen in several ways and in several parts of Europe from the fifteenth century onward. On one hand, the reformation of nuclear families represented a reactionary mechanism in the face of devastations caused by great plagues. But in many rural areas in Europe (and especially in Mediterranean rural areas), this process led to the establishment of complex familial forms, especially from the start of the early modern period. These complex forms were linked to the division of land into holdings of agricultural contracts requiring a stable presence of families proportionately sized in order to run the estates. The situation was completely different in the urban centers, where the nuclear family, in a reduced form, predominated within the artisanal as well as within the poorest classes. In the more well-off classes, including the nobility, the prevalence of divisible and patrilineal familial models, at least until the middle of the sixteenth century, often favored the formation of multiple families in both the horizontal sense (married siblings live together with their respective families) and the vertical sense (at least three generations of a family live together).

Urban Demographics. In the context of the history of European demographics, the differences between the city and the countryside must be underlined. The demographic regime of the cities presents characteristics fairly different from those of the countryside during the entire course of the late Middle Ages and Renaissance. The cities actually earned the nickname "man eaters," which indicates that their growth usually came about in spite of a more natural system characterized by an elevated mortality and a fairly modest fertility—a natural balance that over the long run remained basically negative. The demographic growth of cities was usually attributable to floods of migration, which was usually supported when it involved specialized workers and relatively qualified laborers. In periods of famine and economic difficulty, however, migration to cities was mainly composed of marginal and derelict people in search of food and assistance.

In general, the particularly unfavorable demographic regime of European cities in the past set fairly rigid limits for many centuries on the increase of the rate of urbanization. This unfavorable structure is evident if we consider the necessity to avoid crises—for example, to avoid straining the capacity of rural areas to produce foodstuffs for the urban populations. Even in Italy, where the process of urbanization came about earlier than in the rest of western Europe, it is estimated that at the start of the sixteenth century only slightly more than 10 percent of the population lived in towns with more than ten thousand people. After all, in the late Medieval and Renaissance periods, even the largest European cities rarely reached the size of modest towns by today's standards. Before 1348, some cities (Milan and Venice, for example) probably reached 100,000 in population. But at the start of the fifteenth century, the size of the most important urban centers was drastically reduced. The reduction is visible in the large empty spaces seen within city walls—walls constructed or planned before the arrival of the plague. Florence, whose population probably surpassed 100,000 before 1348, had a population of about 40,000 at the time of the 1427 land register and less than 60,000 at the time of the registered census of 1552.

On the whole, the sixteenth century in Europe was a period of rising urbanization that witnessed the success and development of the capitals of the new centralized states (see table 4). If at the start of

TABLE 4. Population of European Cities over 40,000

	c. 1500	c. 1600
Amsterdam		100–150,000
Antwerp	50,000	
Augsburg	50,000	50,000
Barcelona	50,000	50,000
Bologna	50,000	65,000
Bordeaux		50,000
Brescia	48,000	44,000
Bruges		50,000
Brussels		50,000
Cologne	50,000	50,000
Constantinople	150–200,000	200–400,000
Cordoba	60–100,000	50,000
Cremona	40,000	45,000
Danzig		50,000
Ferrara		41,000
Florence	50,000	60,000
Genoa	50,000	80,000
Ghent	50,000	50,000
Grenada	60–100,000	60–100,000
Haarlem		50,000
Hamburg		50,000
Leiden		50,000
Lisbon	50,000	100–150,000
London	50,000	150–200,000
Lyon	50,000	80,000
Madrid		60–100,000
Marseille		50,000
Messina		60,000
Milan	100,000	150,000
Moscow		60–100,000
Naples	200,000	250,000
Nürnberg		50,000
Palermo	50,000	100,000
Paris	150,000	250,000
Prague		50,000
Rome	50,000	100,000
Rouen	50,000	60–100,000
Seville	60–100,000	100–150,000
Toulouse	50,000	50,000
Valencia	50,000	60–100,000
Valladolid		50,000
Venice	150,000	175,000
Verona		46,000
Vienna		50,000

Sources: Ginatempo and Sandri, *L'Italia delle città*; Mols, "Population in Europe," pp. 42–43.

the century only four cities surpassed 100,000 inhabitants (Naples, Venice, Milan, and Paris), it is estimated that this threshold was surpassed by another eight cities (including London, Amsterdam, and Lisbon) by the start of the next century. Moreover, during the course of the seventeenth century, the progressive disruption of European economic balances, with the growth of some countries (such as Holland and England) and the decline of others (especially Italy and Spain), allowed the development of clearly differentiated trends in the demographic growth of cities. In particular, in countries like Italy, the crises of town economies led to a process of disinvestment in the manufacturing and service industries and a shifting of surplus manufacturing industries from large urban centers to small rural centers. On the whole, the rate of urbanization in these countries declined, while the development of some cities was mainly conditioned by the political and administrative roles they played in their regions.

See also **Census; Plague.**

BIBLIOGRAPHY

Barbagli, Marzio. *Sotto lo stesso tetto: Mutamenti della famiglia in Italia dal quindicesimo al ventesimo secolo.* Bologna, Italy, 1984.

Bardet, Jean-Pierre, and Jacques Dupâquier, eds. *Histoire des populations de l'Europe.* 3 vols. Paris, 1998.

Beloch, Julius. *Bevolkerungsgeschichte Italiens.* 3 vol. Berlin, 1937–1961.

Biraben, Jean-Noel. "Essai sur l'evolution du nombre des hommes." *Population* 34, no. 1 (1979): 13–25.

Cipolla, Carlo M. *Before the Industrial Revolution: European Society and Economy, 1000–1700.* New York, 1976.

Del Panta, Lorenzo, Massimo Livi Bacci, Giuliano Pinto, and Eugenio Sonnino. *La popolazione italiana dal medioevo a oggi.* Rome, 1996.

Durand, John D. "Historical Estimates of World Population: An Evaluation." *Population and Development Review* 3 (1977): 253–296.

Ginatempo, Maria, and Lucia Sandri. *L'Italia delle città: Il popolamento urbano tra Medioevo e Rinascimento (secoli XIII–XVI).* Florence, 1990.

Herlihy, David, and Christiane Klapisch-Zuber. *Tuscans and Their Families: A Study of the Florentine Catasto of 1427.* New Haven, Conn., and London, 1985.

Livi Bacci, Massimo. *Storia minima della popolazione del mondo.* Bologna, Italy, 1998.

McEvedy, Colin, and Richard Jones. *Atlas of World Population History.* New York, 1978.

Mols, Roger. *Introduction à la demographie historique des villes d'Europe du quatorzième au dix-huitième siecle.* 3 vols. Louvain, Belgium, 1954–1956.

Mols, Roger. "Population in Europe 1500–1700." In *The Fontana Economic History of Europe.* Vol. 2: *The Sixteenth and Seventeenth Centuries.* Edited by Carlo M. Cipolla. 2d ed. Glasgow, U.K., 1976.

Wrigley, E. A., and R. S. Schofield. *The Population History of England 1541–1871: A Reconstruction.* London, 1981.

Lorenzo Del Panta

Translated from Italian by Elizabeth Bernhardt

DENMARK. *See* **Scandinavian Kingdoms.**

DES PÉRIERS, BONAVENTURE (c. 1510–1544), French writer of short tales, poet, translator of Plato and Terence. Bonaventure Des Périers is remembered for two works: *Cymbalum mundi* (The cymbal of the world; 1537) and *Nouvelles récréations et joyeux devis* (New recreations and joyous discourses; 1558). Controversy surrounding Des Périers comes not from *Cymbalum,* the work he published anonymously, but from *Nouvelles récréations,* the book that has always borne his name. The untimely death of Des Périers in 1544 and the rather late first edition of the latter work by the printer Granjon lent support to the argument that a prominent figure such as Jacques Peletier or Denisot may have intervened to edit the work, but twentieth-century critics agree that Des Périers is the author. Anachronisms, both linguistic and historical, can be attributed to an editorial hand.

Des Périers's mastery of the short narrative tale—*la nouvelle*—helped define the genre in the Renaissance in ways rivaled only by Margaret of Navarre, whom he served as valet de chambre. As its name suggests, the *nouvelle* is a genre emerging from contemporary events—that which is new, newsworthy, innovative. While Margaret of Navarre's *Heptaméron* and the *Nouvelles récréations et joyeux devis* differ in many ways, they both combine ribald passages and moments of psychological insight that shed light on the vagaries of human behavior.

The *Cymbalum mundi,* an enigmatic and controversial work owing much to the paradoxical style of Lucian, presents a series of four dialogues poking fun at the contentious religious disputes that too vigorously try to probe divine secrets through human reason rather than preparing for illumination by faith and quiet meditation on God's love. The religious controversies of the period are represented through the thinly veiled anagrams of Luther, Martin Bucer, and Girard Roussel in Dialogue 2. The *Prognostications des prognostications,* published in the same year as the *Cymbalum mundi* (1537), echoes the author's views in the latter work that it is folly to try to foretell the future. Both works develop the evangelical concept that man should limit his intellectual probing to issues within his grasp, and that neither divine acts nor future events are fruitful or suitable objects of human inquiry. The noise of human speech, represented in the image of the title *Cymbalum mundi,* interferes with the faithful's quiet contemplation of God's word and God's love. Des Périers appropriates Saint Paul's view that speech without love is just a clanging cymbal (1 Corinthians 13:1). His insistence on indifference to things over which we have no control marks a link between his work and that of Rabelais and Margaret of Navarre.

BIBLIOGRAPHY

Primary Works

Des Périers, Bonaventure. *Cymbalum mundi.* Edited by Peter Hampshire Nurse. Geneva, 1983.

Des Périers, Bonaventure. *The Mirror of Mirth and Pleasant Conceits.* Edited by James Woodrow Hassell Jr. Columbia, S.C., 1959. Translation of *Nouvelles récréations et joyeux devis* (1558).

Des Périers, Bonaventure. *Nouvelles récréations et joyeux devis 1–110.* Edited by Krystyna Kasprzyk. Paris, 1980.

Des Périers, Bonaventure. *Oeuvres françoises de Bonaventure Des Périers.* 2 vols. Edited by Louis Lacour. Paris, 1856. Reprint, Nendeln, Liechtenstein, 1973.

Secondary Works

Cholakian, Rouben, and Patricia Cholakian, eds. and trans. *The Early French Novella: An Anthology of Fifteenth- and Sixteenth-Century Tales.* Albany, N.Y., 1972.

Hassel, J. W. *Sources and Analogues of the* Nouvelles récréations et joyeux devis *of Bonaventure Des Périers.* Vol. 1. Chapel Hill, N.C., 1957.

Winn, Colette H. "L'art de 'quémander' à la renaissance: L'exemple de Bonaventure Des Périers." *Neophilologus* 4 (1987): 505–512.

DEBORAH N. LOSSE

DESPORTES, PHILIPPE (1546–1606), French mannerist poet. Philippe Desportes, born in Chartres to a bourgeois family, traveled at a fairly young age to Italy in the entourage of the bishop of Le Puy. Italy introduced Desportes to neo-Petrarchism, the essential source for his poetic inspiration. Upon his return in 1567, Desportes wrote his *Stances,* closely modeled on the Italian *stanze* then much in vogue, which earned him instant renown at the court of Henry III. His reputation rests chiefly on his virtuoso renewal of such Petrarchan poetic forms, among them the stanza, the sonnet, the complaint, and the dialogue. Subsequently, Desportes formed a literary *cercle* with other poets, including Jean Bertaut and Jacques Davy Du Perron, although Desportes remained the most renowned among them. His work possessed a far-reaching and sometimes surprising impact. For example, Théodore-Agrippa d'Aubigné, the embattled Calvinist poet, slavishly imitated Desportes's *Meslanges* in his own *Odes.* After 1583, Desportes entered a profoundly religious period; he renounced his earlier, profane publications and embarked on a translation of the Psalms. This translation, intended to provide an alternative to the Calvinist Psalter as translated by the evangelical Clément Marot, initiated an important current of Catholic devotional poetry that reached its fullest development in the seventeenth century.

Other of Desportes's works include the *Imitations d'Arioste* (Imitations of Ariosto; 1572); the *Premières oeuvres* (First works; 1573), which came out in a new edition each year after its publication until his death; the *Derniers amours* (Last loves; 1583); and two books of *Elégies.* Prior to his religious period, Desportes preferred elegiac or love themes, drawing on his great predecessor, Pierre de Ronsard (whom his contemporaries esteemed Desportes to have eclipsed), equally with the poetry of Italian mannerists, for his content—often suggestive and erotic—and idiom. His poetic *oeuvre* constitutes the apogee of courtly, Italianate expression during the late sixteenth century. However, his style is less forceful than Ronsard's, as well as more precious in its application of imagery. Mathurin Régnier, his nephew and himself an accomplished court poet, referred to him as a "nonchalant," conveying Desportes's relaxed, worldly, epicurean attitude. Perhaps because most of his love poetry was commissioned by members of the nobility for their specific personal circumstances, Desportes's poems may not seem very profound, but in fact they embody considerable intellectual import, with their reliance on abstract concepts and their pre-Cartesian clarity of articulation and logic.

As one of the "second generation" following Ronsard, Desportes shows signs of the moral decadence of the Pléiade school of poets. At times, his poems display a disturbing coincidence of contrary sources of inspiration that do not always marry well: a conventional treatment coexists uneasily with hyperbole, extremism, and exaggeration. Nonetheless, the ingenuity as well as the clear, harmonious style of his poetry anticipate the limpid stylistics of classicism, while the purity of his literary language fosters his reputation as an artist of elegant, scintillating verse expression.

BIBLIOGRAPHY

Baïche, André. *La naisance du baroque français: Poésie et image de la Pléiade à Jean de La Ceppède.* Toulouse, France, 1976.

Clements, R. J. *The Peregrine Muse: Studies in Comparative Renaissance Literature.* Chapel Hill, N.C., 1969.

Lafay, Henri. *La poésie française du premier XVIIᵉ siècle: 1598–1630.* Paris, 1975.

Pineaux, Jacques. *La poésie de protestants de langue française.* Paris, 1971.

CATHARINE RANDALL

DESPOTISM. Once a standard feature in the literature on late medieval and early Renaissance Italy, the word "despot" and references to the "age of the despots" have vanished from the pages of most contemporary scholarship. This development corresponds to a fundamental shift in ways of interpreting the thirteenth- and fourteenth-century phenomenon of the *signoria* (lordship). Before examining this shift, one must consider the historical reality of the *signoria* itself.

During the late thirteenth century most of the previously self-governing communes of northern and central Italy granted extensive powers to the head of a prominent local family, who then became the effective ruler, or lord, of the city. The reasons for this development varied from place to place, but such grants were often motivated by the excessive factionalism that characterized late medieval communal politics. Concerns of this kind caused the commune of Verona, for example, to grant lordship to Alberto della Scala in 1277. Such grants increased power and efficiency at the center; towns headed by vigorous lords often saw their dominions expand to incorporate less fortunate territories. The threat posed by expansionist lords acted as a further stimulus to one-man rule, as when the Carrara were invested as lords of Padua in 1318, a move intended to counter the imminent takeover of the city by the Scala.

The original grants of lordship were made by the legally constituted communal organs acting voluntarily. The lords were not tyrants in the Aristotelian sense of ruling against the will of their subjects. The commune reserved certain powers to itself, among them the right to confirm or reject the nomination of successors. Lordship was not initially hereditary, nor was it despotic, given that the communal organs continued to exist and to exercise their functions. But over time the lords consolidated in their hands most of the powers that really counted: fiscal, political, and military. Considerable reinforcement of the lord's position also derived from securing recognition—often in the form of a title—from a higher authority, as in the pope or the emperor. A title conferred dynastic status and thus rendered the traditional communal sanction of the succession a mere formality.

Do such developments justify the use of the term "despotism" to describe the phenomenon of the *signoria?* Modern scholarly consensus is that they do not. Yet for more than a century—from Jakob Burckhardt's *Civilization of the Renaissance in Italy* (1860) to the 1960s and beyond—the terms "despot" and "despotism" were commonly adapted to this purpose, particularly in English-speaking countries. How and why this came about is a matter worth investigating. In order to do so, we need to consider the origins and history of the term "despotism" itself. Why, for example, was it not used by Renaissance legal and political theorists? How did it come to be applied at last to the Renaissance *signoria,* and what implications did such a label carry? On what grounds was the label finally rejected?

Vicissitudes of the Term "Despotism."

Like most modern political terminology, the word "despot" originates with the ancient Greeks. In the *Politics* (1252a) Aristotle used the word *despoteia* to designate the relationship of master to slave within a household. Properly speaking, the *despotes* is the master of slaves. In other passages, however, Aristotle moved beyond this original meaning and began to adopt the term in a more broadly political sense. *Despotikos,* for example, is the word used to describe the degenerate forms of all three of his fundamental types of government: tyranny (1279b), democracy (1292a), and oligarchy (1306b). Thus, while not one of Aristotle's fundamental types, despotic government has a connotation shared by all in their degenerate state: it signifies unlawful, arbitrary power wielded in the interests of the few rather than for the general good. This makes despotic rule akin to tyranny, yet the two are not quite one and the same. In other key passages (1285a, 1295a) Aristotle makes clear the distinction: tyranny is exercised against the will of the subjects and is based on fear; despotic rule is exercised over willing subjects and is based on consent.

Aristotle's terminology did not immediately enter the Roman world. What he called the *despotes* was expressed by the Latin word *dominus.* Not until medieval Scholasticism recovered the *Politics* were the terms *despoticus, despotice,* and *despotizare* again made familiar through the translation of Aristotle's work around 1260 by William of Moerbeke. By the fourteenth century, writers like Marsilius of Padua and William of Ockham were adopting both the language and the concept of despotic rule in their polemical battles against the temporal powers of the papacy. But just as the terms derived from Aristotle's notion of the *despotes* seemed destined to take their place in modern political vocabulary alongside *monarchia, aristokratia, demokratia,* and so on, humanist linguistic reform saw fit to reject them as impure borrowings from the Greek.

Coluccio Salutati (1331–1406), in *De tyranno* (1400), reduced the scope of *despoticus* to the household alone, thus depriving it of the wider political significance it was beginning to reacquire. Leonardo Bruni (c. 1370–1444), in his influential translation of the *Politics* (c. 1438), eliminated the incipient Latin neologism altogether; he translated "despot" as *dominus* and "despotic rule" as *dominatio*. Those who were later termed despots in English-language scholarship, that is, the lords of thirteenth- and fourteenth-century Italy, were known in good Latin as *domini* and in Italian as *signori*.

The question then is how English-language scholarship—but also German and French—came to use the terms "despot" and "despotism" to describe the phenomenon of the Italian Renaissance *signoria*.

If Bruni's ban on the word "despot" was effective in the short term, the concept of despotic rule nevertheless remained a part of political thought. In his *Six livres de la république* (Six books of the commonwealth; 1576), Jean Bodin (1529/30–1596) revisited Aristotle's tripartite typology of monarchy: monarchy could be *royale*, *seigneuriale* (lordly), or *tyrannique*. Here, the concept of despotic rule—halfway between legitimate, or royal, monarchy and tyranny—is designated by the word *seigneuriale*. Like Aristotle, Bodin associated despotic rule with the authority held by the head of a household over his slaves. Unlike Aristotle, however, he also saw it as the peculiar right of the conqueror over the conquered. This latter point was picked up by Thomas Hobbes (1588–1679) in the following century in *Leviathan* (1651). Hobbes not only used the concept of despotic rule, he also restored the word itself, both in English and in Latin. Meanwhile, in France the term *monarchie despotique* began in 1649 to circulate as an alternative to *tyrannique* in the pamphlet wars of the Frondeurs. Adherents of the parliamentarian cause used it to stigmatize the encroachments of royal government on traditional rights and privileges.

From this context it is but a short step to Montesquieu (1689–1755). In *L'Esprit des lois* (The spirit of laws; 1748), Montesquieu made despotism—by now this form of the word existed—one of the three fundamental types of government, along with republic and monarchy. As opposed to monarchy—where the rule of one is balanced by respect for law and the existence of corporate bodies whose powers act as a restraining force—despotism is rule by one with total and unlimited power. The evils of despotism—for example, that it is a system based on fear rather than honor—are meant to throw into high relief the benefits of the limited monarchy that Montesquieu believed should typify civilized European peoples like the French.

Despotism as a Concept in Renaissance Studies. In *Histoire des républiques italiennes du moyen âge* (History of the Italian republics in the Middle Ages; 1807–1818), J.-C.-L. Simonde de Sismondi celebrated the freedom of the medieval Italian city republics and deplored their subsequent degeneration into tyrannically governed *signorie* (lordships). Sismondi's work formed the backdrop for Jakob Burckhardt's *Civilization of the Renaissance in Italy* (1860), where the terms "despot" (*Herrscher* or *Gewaltherrscher*) and "despotism" (*Gewaltherrschaft*) were first used to designate the Italian *signori*. Burckhardt's use of these words was far from systematic: he made them virtually interchangeable with "tyrant" and "tyranny."

The translation of Burckhardt's book brought the terms "despot" and "despotism" into common use as descriptive of the late medieval Italian *signori*. The words conveyed the notions of unlimited power and freedom from constraint, which were presented as the necessary prelude to modernity. The English case is particularly instructive, since the S. G. C. Middlemore translation (1878) considerably augmented the use of the word "despot" and its derivatives with respect to the German original. In the meantime, moreover, the first volume of John Addington Symonds's *Renaissance in Italy, The Age of the Despots* (1875) had appeared. Under Burckhardt's influence, but with a late romantic literary sensitivity all his own, Symonds depicted the Italian despot in ever more vivid and heightened colors. His despot not only wields absolute power; he is also a sort of demiurge, an animating social principle.

The combination of Middlemore's Burckhardt and Symonds struck deeply. For nearly a century English scholarship on the late medieval Italian *signori* adopted "despotism" as its leitmotiv. Cecilia M. Ady, for example, used it in the subtitle of her book *The Bentivoglio of Bologna: A Study in Despotism* (1937). An interesting attempt to recover the more positive, Burckhardtian concept of the *signori* is Werner L. Gundersheimer's study of the Este in Ferrara (1973), subtitled *The Style of a Renaissance Despotism*.

In the mid-1960s a new generation of scholars challenged the applicability of the term "despotism" to the Italian *signori*. Their challenge was based on a distinction between the image of power and its practice. By relying too much on the former, traditional scholarship had greatly exaggerated the extent of seigneurial authority. The new studies revealed that the *signori* were not destroyers of the organs of traditional city government and their prerogatives as they had been labeled, and they were not bent on a policy of centralization at whatever cost; in short, they were not despots in the sense Burckhardt had suggested. Rather than erect their power by sheer force, the *signori* had followed a policy of compromise and mediation with the traditional organs of communal society. Far from disappearing altogether, these organs had continued to exist, and even flourish, under seigneurial rule.

While modern scholars agree that the Renaissance was marked by changing forms of governance, they focus not on any supposed consolidation of central power but on the survival of traditional institutions and on the way these were incorporated into a new superstructure in the age of the *signori*.

See also Bodin, Jean; Bruni, Leonardo; Political Thought; Prince; Renaissance, Interpretations of the, *subentries on* Jakob Burckhardt *and* John Addington Symonds.

BIBLIOGRAPHY

Bueno de Mesquita, D. M. "The Place of Despotism in Italian Politics." In *Europe in the Late Middle Ages.* Edited by J. R. Hale, J. R. L. Highfield, and B. Smalley. London, 1965. Pages 301–331.

Dean, Trevor. "Commune and Despot: The Commune of Ferrara under Este Rule, 1300–1450." In *City and Countryside in Late Medieval and Renaissance Italy: Essays Presented to Philip Jones.* Edited by Trevor Dean and Chris Wickham. London, 1990. Pages 183–197.

Hurstfield, Joel. "Was There a Tudor Despotism after All?" *Transactions of the Royal Historical Society,* 5th ser., 17 (1967): 83–108.

Jones, P. J. "Communes and Despots: The City State in Late-Medieval Italy." *Transactions of the Royal Historical Society,* 5th ser., 15 (1965): 71–96.

Koebner, R. "Despot and Despotism: Vicissitudes of a Political Term." *Journal of the Warburg and Courtauld Institutes* 14 (1951): 275–302.

Larner, John. *The Lords of Romagna: Romagnol Society and the Origins of the Signorie.* London and New York, 1965. Detailed study of the relationship between communes and *signori* in the Romagna area.

Law, John E. *The Lords of Renaissance Italy: The Signori, 1250–1500.* London, 1981. Brief but useful survey of the phenomenon of the *signori* in northern Italy.

GARY IANZITI

DES ROCHES, MADELEINE (1520–1587) and **CATHERINE** (1545–1587), French humanists, scholars, and poets known as the Dames des Roches. Madeleine des Roches and her daughter Catherine were celebrated members of the noted humanist circles of Poitiers. Madeleine was well-educated and was twice married to lawyers, to whose libraries she would have had access. She could have known the humanist poets who frequented the University of Poitiers from 1545 to 1551, such as Jacques Peletier, Jacques Tahureau, Jean-Antoine de Baïf, and Joachim Du Bellay. She encouraged female learning for its own sake and devoted herself to educating Catherine, her sole surviving child. Catherine never married, preferring to study, write, and publish with her mother.

The Dames des Roches began publishing their writings in the 1570s when they established a salon. The influential Parisian bookseller Abel L'Angelier published their first volume, *Les oeuvres,* in 1578. It sold out, and he published an enlarged edition in 1579. Their growing fame attracted to their salon Parisian lawyers present at the 1579 criminal assizes of the *grand jour* of Poitiers. Among them was Étienne Pasquier who, while conversing with Catherine des Roches, sighted a flea on her bosom and thereupon suggested a contest to see who could write the wittiest poem about it. This led to L'Angelier's unauthorized publication of *La puce de Madame des Roches* (The flea of Madame des Roches; 1582, 1583), a ninety-three folio collection of the *blasons* (blazons) written by the habitués of the salon. Before their death of the plague in 1587, the Dames des Roches published two more volumes of works: *Les secondes oeuvres* (New works; 1583) and *Les missives* (Letters; 1586), the first collection of private letters by women in France. Their published writings include a wide range of poetic genres, prose dialogues, salon responses, and letters, a pastoral play, a tragicomedy, and first translations of Latin works.

BIBLIOGRAPHY

Primary Works

Des Roches, Madeleine and Catherine. *Les oeuvres.* Edited by Anne R. Larsen. Geneva, 1993.

Des Roches, Madeleine and Catherine. *Les secondes oeuvres.* Edited by Anne R. Larsen. Geneva, 1998.

Des Roches, Catherine. *La puce de Madame des Roches.* Edited by D. Jouaust. Paris, 1868, 1872. Partial reprint of The flea of Madame des Roches (Paris, 1582, 1583).

Secondary Works

Diller, George E. *Les Dames des Roches: Étude sur la vie littéraire à Poitiers dans la deuxième moitié du seizième siècle.* Paris, 1936. Standard monograph on the Dames des Roches.

Jones, Ann Rosalind. *The Currency of Eros: Women's Love Lyric in Europe, 1540–1620.* Bloomington, Ind., 1990. Important chapter on Catherine des Roches's sonnet sequence.

Sankovitch, Tilde. *French Women Writers and the Book: Myths of Access and Desire.* Syracuse, N.Y., 1988. Important chapter on the Dames des Roches.

ANNE R. LARSEN

DEVIL IN RENAISSANCE ART. *See* **Supernatural World in Renaissance Art.**

DEVOTIO MODERNA. The name Devotio Moderna (modern devotion) was applied by Johannes

Busch (1399–1479/80) to a late medieval movement of spiritual renewal, originating in the Low Countries from the preaching of the deacon Geert (Gerard) Grote (1340–1384) of Deventer.

Geert Grote. Grote, whose father became burgomaster of Deventer in 1348, went to the University of Paris in 1355, receiving a master's degree in 1358. He continued studying canon law, natural philosophy, astrology, and probably theology in Paris and perhaps also in Cologne and Prague. In 1368 he obtained a canonry at Aachen, followed by a canonry in Utrecht in 1371. Seriously ill at Deventer in 1372, he renounced black magic at the instigation of the local parish priest and recovered. Under the influence of Henry Egher from Kalkar, prior of the Carthusian monastery in Monnikhuizen near Arnheim from 1368 to 1373, he decided to order his life according to the honor and service of God. He gave up his canonries. In September 1374 he set apart his parental house in Deventer for poor women who wanted to serve God, reserving one room for himself. From 1374 to 1377 he lived with the Carthusians in Monnikhuizen, who finally convinced him to work publicly for the salvation of souls, as a preacher. He was ordained a subdeacon and a deacon, which allowed him to undertake public preaching. From the end of 1379 to mid-1383 he wandered about, converting many people. Finally the bishop of Utrecht revoked his preaching license; Grote had gone too far in denouncing the way of life of many priests who lived with women. Grote withdrew first to Woudrichem, near the Augustinian monastery of Eemstein, then to Kampen, where a small community of "servants of God" had been formed, and finally to Deventer, in the meantime appealing to the pope.

In Deventer Grote's friend the priest Florens Radewijnsz (1350–1400) had given up his life as a canon at St. Lebuinus. In his house he assembled priests and students who were followers of Grote (c. 1381). They started a common life, contributing their earnings, especially as writing specialists, to the common treasury. Of their own free will they obeyed a chosen rector, but they did not take vows. They found the inspiring example of this way of life in the early church (Acts 2:42–47; 4:32). Florens established some rules for the Deventer priests and clerics, which were applied to other communities. The Deventer house (1383–1574) came to be considered the principal place of resort for these communities, such as the semireligious community in Zwolle, founded at the request of some of Grote's followers (1383/84). When members of the community wished to withdraw from the city, Grote allowed them to establish themselves at the Nemelerberg near Zwolle in 1384. This community transformed itself with episcopal consent into an Augustinian monastery (St. Agnietenberg; 1398–1561), where Thomas à Kempis (c. 1379–1471) acted as master of the novices. Some devouts, however, remained in Zwolle.

Brethren and Sisters of the Common Life. The Deventer and Zwolle Brethren of the Common Life were especially active in establishing communities elsewhere, including Germany (Münster) and Belgium. Nineteen houses were established in the Netherlands, twenty-five in Germany, and eight in Belgium and northern France. For the houses of the Sisters no complete survey is available. The houses of the Dutch Brethren were united in the Colloquium of Zwolle, those of northern Germany in the Colloquium of Münster, and those of southern Germany in the so-called Oberdeutsche Generalkapittel. All these communities were established according to the rules of secular law by transferring individual property to the community in the presence of a public notary. The devouts obliged themselves to live together, sustaining themselves by the work of their hands, especially by copying books. Episcopal approval of the establishment of such a community was granted afterward.

Congregation of Windesheim. Despite this approval, the Brethren were under constant pressure from ecclesiastical authorities to assume a canonically approved status within the church, especially by assuming a monastic rule. Grote advised his followers to establish a monastery of Augustinian canons, which came into being in 1387 at Windesheim, near Zwolle. Together with newly founded monasteries near Arnheim and Hoorn (1392) and the monastery of Eemstein (1382), Windesheim established a congregation under the direction of its prior superior and the guidance of the yearly convening general chapter. It was approved by Pope Boniface IX on 16 May 1395. One of the first acts of the general chapter was to give public testimony to the orthodoxy and canonical obedience of the Brethren at Deventer (19 March 1395). Other convents joined the congregation, among them St. Agnietenberg (1398). Convents for women, following the same rule, were founded in several places. They joined the chapter of Windesheim in due time. In 1413 the chapter of Groenendaal (Belgium) joined the congregation, as did the chapter of Neuss (Germany, 1430). Pope Eugenius IV prohibited the further incorporation of women's convents in the chapter of Windesheim in 1436. In 1511 the congregation numbered eighty-four convents for men and thirteen for women.

Some houses of the Brethren or Sisters went over to the Third Order of St. Francis or assumed the Windesheim rule. The communities in Münster, Cologne, and Wesel transformed themselves into secular chapters in 1439, retaining the community of possessions and their rules. The communities at Amersfoort and 's-Hertogenbosch followed their example in 1469.

By a decree from Pope Pius V (17 November 1568), the communities were ordered to assume a monastic rule or disband. This measure coincided with the Reformation, which put an end to the existence of monasteries and semireligious houses in Protestant countries. The priests were incorporated as parish vicars or given pensions. The secular authorities confiscated properties.

Education and Spirituality. The Brethren had their own schools in Deventer (c. 1469–1535; Erasmus was educated there), Utrecht (1475–1565), and Groningen (c. 1511–1566); in Butzbach, Königstein, Kulm, Magdeburg (Martin Luther was a student there), Marburg, Rostock, Trier, and Urach; and in Brussels, Cambrai, Geraardsbergen, Ghent, Louvain, and Liège. Famous convicts (dormitory houses) for boys were established in Zwolle, Doesburg, 's-Hertogenbosch (Erasmus studied there privately for three years), and elsewhere. Geert Grote was in close contact with Rector John Cele of the city school at Zwolle; the curriculum was revised in order to promote Christian education, a main goal of the Brethren. The restoration of the church and its culture was to start with children. The Zwolle school system was widely imitated, especially in the College of Montaigu in Paris. This Parisian model was influential in the organization of Jesuit schools.

The Devotio Moderna as a spiritual movement stressed simplicity of life, self-knowledge by repeated examination of conscience, inwardness, "walking with God," and imitation of Christ in poverty and humility. The famous *De imitatione Christi* (On the imitation of Christ), already in existence in 1427 as a compilation of four separate tracts, is nowadays firmly ascribed to Thomas à Kempis, the final composer of the autograph of 1441. It reflects the spiritual praxis of the Dutch-German communities and the Windesheim monasteries.

BIBLIOGRAPHY

Primary Work
Van Engen, John, trans. *Devotio Moderna: Basic Writings.* New York, 1988.

Secondary Works
Leesch, Wolfgang, Ernst Persoons, and Anton G. Weiler, eds. *Monasticon fratrum vitae communis.* 3 vols. Brussels, 1977–1999. History of every house of the Brethren in Belgium (vol. 1), Germany (vol. 2), and the Netherlands (vol. 3; in print); with extensive archival data and bibliography.
Kohl, Wilhelm, Ernst Persoons, and Anton G. Weiler, eds. *Monasticon Windeshemense.* 4 vols. Brussels, 1976–1984. History of every monastery of the Augustinian canons in Belgium (vol. 1), Germany (vol. 2), and the Netherlands (vol. 3); includes extensive archival data and bibliography. Vol. 4: Register.
Post, R. R. *The Modern Devotion. Confrontation with Reformation and Humanism.* Leiden, Netherlands, 1968.
Van Zijl, Theodore P. *Gerard Groote, Ascetic and Reformer (1340–1384).* Washington, D.C., 1963.
Weiler, Anton G. "The Dutch Brethren of the Common Life, Critical Theology, Northern Humanism, and Reformation." In *Northern Humanism in European Context, 1469–1625.* Edited by F. Akkerman, A. J. Vanderjagt, and A. H. van der Laon. Leiden, Netherlands, 1999. Pages 307–332.
Weiler, Anton G. *Volgens de norm van de vroege kerk: De geschiedenis van de huizen van de broeders van het Gemene leven in Nederland.* Nijmegen, Netherlands, 1997. With general bibliography on the Devotio Moderna and on each House separately.

ANTON G. WEILER

DIALECTIC. *See* **Logic.**

DIANE DE POITIERS (1499–1566), French noblewoman and mistress to King Henry II. In 1514 Diane married Louis de Brézé, the grand sénéchal of Normandy, and had two daughters with him. Her exceptional beauty, which she maintained until late in life, gained her entry to Francis I's court. In 1530 she met Henry when he and his brother returned from serving as hostages in Spain for their father's ransom. After her husband's death in 1531, she became the love of Henry's life, and he remained devoted to her to his death, although she was twenty years older. When Henry became king in 1547, Diane received the title of the duchess of Valentinois and the château of Chenonceau. At Henry's court she usually held the balance of power between Constable Anne de Montmorency and the family of Guise. Diane extended patronage to the group of poets known as the Pléiade and was the subject of many laudatory poems. Her beauty and position also made her the subject of numerous artworks, including the famed *Diana the Huntress* attributed to Jean Goujon. It was placed in her château of Anet, whose reconstruction was one of the highlights of mid-sixteenth-century French Renaissance culture. Philibert de L'Orme was the principal architect, and Rosso Fiorentino, Benvenuto Cellini, and Francesco Primatic-

Diane de Poitiers. *Diane de Poitiers as an Allegory of Peace* by Jean Capassin. MUSÉE GRANET, AIX-EN-PROVENCE, FRANCE/PHOTOGRAPH BY BERNARD TERLAY

cio produced works for decorating it. After Henry II was killed while jousting in 1559, his widow, Catherine de Médicis, took Chenonceau from Diane, who retired to Anet, where she died in 1566.

BIBLIOGRAPHY

Baumgartner, Frederic J. *Henry II, King of France, 1547–1559.* Durham, N.C., 1988.

Guiffrey, Georges, ed. *Les lettres inédites de Dianne de Poytiers.* Paris, 1866. The introduction to this collection of Diane's letters is the best scholarly treatment of her life.

Orliac, Jehanne d'. *The Moon Mistress: Diane de Poitiers, grant' sénéchalle de Normandy.* Translated by F. M. Atkinson. Philadelphia, 1930. Interesting popular biography.

FREDERIC J. BAUMGARTNER

DIARIES AND MEMOIRS. The literate of the Renaissance often kept personal records. This custom has increased historians' knowledge of personal and family life, urban life and trade, and patron-client relationships. Italian merchants, who benefited from urban public schools, recorded trade and family information in their account-book diaries; Italians called such secret books of records *ricordanze* or, to emphasize their miscellany, *zibaldoni.*

In the fourteenth century Petrarch's sonnets recorded the drama of his love for Laura; life writing took on poetic form in the works of the Florentine leader Lorenzo de' Medici (1449–1492), the French poet Louise Labé (c. 1524–1566), and the Englishman Thomas Tusser (1524–1580). While diaries and autobiographical poems were generally written in the vernacular—such as Dutch, Spanish, or English—memoirs were written either in the vernacular, such as those by Margaret of Valois (1553–1615), the French queen of Henry IV, or in Latin, such as those by Pope Pius II (1405–1464).

Imitating the formal third-person style of Julius Caesar's *Gallic Wars,* Pius II's *Commentaries* (first published in 1584) is a chronological memoir intended for posterity. The more intimate epistolary form of Margaret of Valois's memoirs, which were published in 1628, suggests that the genre of memoirs developed concomitantly with the genre of collected letters. In fact, a medieval precedent was Abelard's early twelfth-century account of his calamitous love for Héloïse, followed by her letters. Some people systematically corresponded and circulated their correspondence, following the ancient precedents of Cicero and Seneca. The Latin letters of Petrarch in the fourteenth century and of Erasmus in the sixteenth form in-depth personal accounts of their intellectual careers; likewise, the seventeenth-century publication of Latin letters by Cassandra Fedele (1465?–1558) and by Laura Cereta (1469–1499) attests to the ideas of these women humanists. Historians have found two sets of family letters particularly useful: those of the German Fuggers between 1568 and 1605, which in their international scope record the merchant family's relation to major events; and those of the English Pastons from 1422 to 1509, as well as those from Katherine to her son William between 1603 and 1627, which provide case studies of property transactions and marriage arrangements.

Of the more than one hundred Florentine diaries, those of Luca Landucci (1436?–1516), Buonaccorso Pitti (1354–c. 1431), and Gregorio Dati (1362–1436) are readily available in English. Merchants, doctors, lawyers, artists, and other professionals often kept memoranda books in which they recorded the contents of their home studies; among the published Italian memoranda detailing the purchasing of books and art objects for study are those of the Florentines Francesco di Matteo Castellani (1418–1494), Giovanni Chellini da San Miniato (1370–1461), and Giovanni Rucellai (1475–1525) and of the Venetian Alessandro Vittoria (1524–1608), as well as the letters of Isabella d'Este (1474–1539). While Venetian archives do not yield the wealth of local diaries the Florentine archives do, Venetian diary writing included the important medieval travel journal of Marco Polo (1254–1324), Niccolò da Canal's 1422 *zibaldone* recording thirteenth- and fourteenth-century events, and the autobiographical poetry of the sixteenth-century courtesans Gaspara Stampa (1524–1554) and Veronica Franco (1546–1591). In addition, French ambassadorial letters and the correspondence of Jewish traders yield observations on the life of other cultures in Renaissance Venice. In the tradition of merchant diaries is the seventeenth-century Yiddish diary of Glueckel of Hameln (1646–1724) in which she provided extensive advice, as well as details on her life as a trader and a mother.

Important developments occurred in the period between the lives of the poets Petrarch (1304–1374) and Giambattista Marino (1569–1625), when diaries and memoirs became more introspective. Petrarch's Latin *Secretum* (c. 1342), an internal dialogue influenced by St. Augustine's *Confessions,* opened up possibilities of in-depth psychological exploration. One sequel was the sixteenth-century dialogues between Madeleine des Roches (c. 1520–1587) and her daughter Catherine des Roches (1542–1587) con-

cerning woman's condition. Michel de Montaigne (1533–1592) recorded events of his life, dictated and wrote a private travel journal, and created the genre of collected essays. His *Essays* are filled with his personal encounters, state of health, psychological feelings and attitudes, relations with other people and with books, and thoughts. The self-exploration was so deep that Marie de Gournay (1565–1645) viewed Montaigne as a companion before she had met him personally (she later became the editor of his works, keeping his books in print throughout the early seventeenth century). By the early seventeenth century artificial exaggeration and more formal literary devices were bringing to a close the Renaissance style of life writing. Marino described his own life in poetic form. His poems, sometimes set to music, became valued in Italian, French, and English courts. While in the fifteenth century Leon Battista Alberti (1404–1472) measured himself in three-dimensional space and viewed his reflection as a model of the universal man, seventeenth-century baroque writers and artists, by focusing on the bizarre, marvelous, and distortions of the human image, brought new perspectives to the writing on the self.

See also **Biography and Autobiography**.

BIBLIOGRAPHY

Primary Works

Brucker, Gene, ed. *Two Memoirs of Renaissance Florence: The Diaries of Buonaccorso Pitti and Gregorio Dati.* Translated by Julia Martines. New York, 1967. Brucker's introduction, "Florentine Diaries and Diarists," is a useful overview.

Hughey, Ruth, ed. *The Correspondence of Lady Katherine Paston, 1603–1627.* Norfolk, U.K., 1941.

Wilson, Katharina M., ed. *Women Writers of the Renaissance and Reformation.* Athens, Ga., 1987.

Secondary Works

Mayer, Thomas F., and D. R. Woolf, eds. *The Rhetorics of Life-Writing in Early Modern Europe: Forms of Biography from Cassandra Fedele to Louis XIV.* Ann Arbor, Mich., 1995.

Thornton, Dora. *The Scholar in His Study: Ownership and Experience in Renaissance Italy.* New Haven, Conn., 1997. See the chapter "Concordance of Inventories and Memoranda."

MARYANNE CLINE HOROWITZ

Distortion of the Human Image. *Self-Portrait in a Convex Mirror* by Francesco Mazzola, called Parmigianino (1503–1540). Oil on panel; 1523–1524. KUNSTHISTORISCHES MUSEUM, VIENNA/ERICH LESSING/ART RESOURCE

DICTIONARIES AND ENCYCLOPEDIAS. The Renaissance produced an abundance of dictionaries and encyclopedias designed to gather and present to the reader the expanding universe of knowledge. Renaissance scholars organized these reference works according to humanistic approaches to language and philology.

The Medieval Legacy. The major reference works written between the thirteenth and fifteenth centuries were printed and used until 1500 and often later still. Late medieval encyclopedias and dictionaries were compiled primarily to support the production of theological books and sermons.

Well known to the early Renaissance were the *Speculum majus* (Greater mirror; c. 1220–1244) of Vincent de Beauvais (c. 1190–1264) and the *De proprietatibus rerum* (On the properties of things) of Bartholomaeus Anglicus (d. c. 1250). Vincent included a world history and covered all intellectual knowledge and moral philosophy. Bartholomaeus collected written information and a variety of lore about the natural world and arranged it alphabetically by subject in books that described the human mind and body, as well as the inhabitants of air, water, and earth. Moral and social encyclopedias, such as the *Summa* of John of Wales (dating from the third quarter of the thirteenth century), that provided material for sermons and reflected their rhetorical structure, retained their market until about 1520.

A slightly different encyclopedic tradition, going back to the fifth-century writer Martianus Capella, arranged information under the pedagogical disciplines and was exemplified most attractively for the early Renaissance by the *Margarita philosophica* (Philosophical pearl) of Gregor Reisch (d. 1525). The requirements of late-medieval preaching rhetoric had generated vast concordances of biblical words and phrases such as the *Summa praedicantium* (Summa for preachers) of John of Bromyard (d. 1352), as well as Latin dictionaries. The *Catholicon* of Joannes Balbus de Janua (or Genoa, d. 1298) was Europe's main lexicon until about the second decade of the sixteenth century. The *Catholicon* included a Latin grammar and frequently supplied extensive definitions of alphabetically listed words, with illustrations from the Latin Bible and other religious texts, to which early Renaissance editors added more classical references. The printed publication of these and other medieval dictionaries and encyclopedias ensured the continuation of medieval habits of thought into the early Renaissance and resulted in the appropriation of the sophisticated cataloging techniques of the late Middle Ages: alphabetical organization; cross-referencing systems; and diagrammatic division of material, using brackets to show how branches of knowledge were generated and interrelated.

Renaissance Innovations. The humanists' school program had demands different from medieval sermon rhetoric. For the humanists, words were defined by their use. New monolingual Latin dictionaries defined vocabulary by copious quotation from the approved classical writers. The *Elegantiae* (Elegances of the Latin language) of Lorenzo Valla (1405–1457) was a model of the new humanist resource, with entries arranged not alphabetically but grouped according to affinities and contraries. It was much reprinted, and its method was used by Guillaume Budé (1467–1540) in his *Commentarii linguae Graecae* (Commentaries on the Greek language; 1529) and by Étienne Dolet (1509–1546) in his *Commentarii linguae Latinae* (Commentaries on the Latin language; 1536–1538). These dictionary writers, like Erasmus, deplored alphabetization because it did not reproduce the interwoven fabric of language, but pragmatic needs quickly brought in alphabetical abbreviations of their works. Practicality and catholicity also ensured a market for the Latin dictionary of Ambrosius Calepinus (1435–1511), an alphabetically organized work that drew on previous humanist compendiums, listed examples of classical usage, and also included explanations of proper names and quotations from the Bible and other religious texts. Constantly revised, it remained the most comprehensively useful lexicon of the sixteenth century, although in the 1530s it had a temporary rival in the *Thesaurus* of Robert Estienne (1503–1559), which combined alphabetically arranged examples of Latin usage, more clearly displayed, with less use of religious texts, more use of legal material, and occasional recourse to the vernacular.

Humanist grammar was more than words. It also re-created the historical and cultural context of works studied, and it applied procedures to emend wrong and doubtful readings. These aspects of humanist grammar spawned encyclopedias of the ancient world built on the elucidation of text references. Annotation of just some of the epigrams of the Roman poet Martial alone produced the huge *Cornucopiae* of Niccolò Perotti (1429–1480), who followed the order of Martial's work, adding a multiplicity of cognate words and allusions. More utilitarian were alphabetical encyclopedias of proper names, from the little *Elucidarius carminum* (Explanation of poems) of Hermannus Torrentinus (c. 1450–1520) to the progressively amplified *Dictionarium historicum et poeticum* of Charles Estienne (1504–1564). In a conciliatory manner similar to Calepinus, Domitius Nanus Mirabellius produced a *Polyanthea* in 1503. It combined the virtues of humanist dictionary and encyclopedia with theological references and bracketed distinctions on words appropriate for sermon rhetoric, and was widely used in the first thirty years of the century.

Encyclopedias of knowledge growing to massive proportions from single words in classical texts substantiated the humanists' claim that philology was the key that unlocked all sciences. Even quite small keys opened up treasuries of information, as exemplified by works collecting more or less at random the solutions of expert critics to textual difficulties. The *Miscellanea* of Poliziano (1454–1494), the *Lectiónes antiquae* (Readings of ancient texts) of Ludovico Ricchieri (1469–1525), and the *Geniales dies* (Festive day) of Alexander ab Alexandro (1461–1523) reconstructed ancient culture around specific locutions, philosophical puzzles, and legal questions and these works were followed by countless *miscellanea, lectiones,* and *animadversiones.*

Miscellanies were related by title, if not by content, to vernacular collections of curiosities and marvels, most famously the much translated *Silva de varia lección* (Miscellany of diverse readings) of Pedro Mexía (1496–1552). Encyclopedic dictionaries also had their vernacular counterparts, notably the *Fabrica del mondo* (Fabric of the world) of Francesco Alunno (d. 1556), which provided Latin equivalents for Italian words and illustrations of their use from Dante, Petrarch, and Boccaccio.

The humanists promoted composition as systematically as comprehension. From the beginning, composition had its own supply of reference works: adages and similitudes collected by Erasmus, examples and epithets collected by Ravisius Textor (c. 1480–1524), and, most importantly, commonplace books, which toward the end of the sixteenth century grew into encyclopedias in size and content. Commonplace books were ordering mechanisms as well as collecting mechanisms. By the mid-sixteenth century, the professional disciplines of medicine, law, and especially theology were organized around their subject-specific topics or commonplaces, and this organization was reflected in the way their reference books were structured.

The combined influence of commonplace books and of the complex schemes for organization utilizing bracketed divisions that were associated with Petrus Ramus (Pierre de La Ramée, 1515–1572) can be detected in the *Theatrum vitae humanae* (Theater of human life) of Theodor Zwinger (1533–1588), a compilation of examples cataloged under heads; this combination was most rigorously applied in the enormous *Encyclopedia* of Johann Heinrich Alsted (1588–1638). Both encyclopedias collected information rather than methods of saying, and Alsted's

work encompasses a world of knowledge prodigiously expanded since Reisch. But the linguistic base is still visible: one of Alsted's rules of procedure states that philology precedes philosophy.

The Natural World. Renaissance encyclopedias of the natural sciences mirror a world viewed from the perspective of language and language use. In the late Middle Ages, the natural phenomena and animal behavior described by Bartholomaeus Anglicus were given moral interpretations suitable for sermons by Petrus Berchorius (1290–1362) in a *Reductorium morale* (Moral guide) printed for the same purpose early in the sixteenth century. Throughout the century, preaching rhetoric created a market for encyclopedic collections of similitudes derived from the natural world. But encyclopedias of natural history published without a particular rhetoric in view are more indicative of the fundamentally linguistic world that Renaissance readers inhabited.

The lavish *Historia animalium* produced between 1551 and 1558 by Conrad Gesner (1516–1565), and subsequently expanded, begins each entry with the name of the animal in various languages and proceeds through a description of physical characteristics, behavior, and habitat, based on prior written sources and collected lore. These sections are much more extensive than in Bartholomaeus, but not radically different. However, Gesner's entries conclude by assembling all possible traces of the animal in the figurative expressions of literary language (metaphors, similitudes, epithets, adages, emblems, and so on), with copious exemplification from classical sources. The animal thus becomes a commonplace head, generating discourse and signifying within the moral universe of human language use. Gesner's encyclopedias, which also include plants, minerals, and metals, were not superseded until the series of volumes on natural history compiled by Aldrovandi of Bologna (1522–1605) were published between 1599 and 1637. Aldrovandi included more information and more sources, but his parameters were the same as Gesner's and his verbal associations yet more florid.

Another feature that differentiates these encyclopedias from their medieval antecedents is their engravings, lifelike and generally very accurate. Other illustrated encyclopedias of animals, more limited in range, were produced by Pierre Belon (1517–1564) and Guillaume Rondelet (1507–1566), but their books, which did not contextualize their animals within the literary culture of the Renaissance, were only reprinted, if at all, in conjunction with Gesner.

One encyclopedia that had neither illustration nor literary context was the 1596 *Universae naturae theatrum* (Theater of universal nature) of Jean Bodin (1530–1596). This rather selective encyclopedia explicitly contains only features of the natural universe that its author claims to be incompletely or inaccurately described by ancient natural historians, such as Aristotle and Pliny. These details are written in continuous prose, interrupted by questions, and the leading question—"why?"—directs the whole work to a description of the causes of observed effects. The answers given are ascertained from observation (*experientia*) and from prior written sources corrected by observation. Bodin understands his material from the perspective of Aristotle, although at times he corrects Aristotle, and, although literary references are minimal and there is an attempt to impose a coherent structure, the work has close analogies with contemporary *miscellanea* productions.

Some encyclopedias made a more radical break with the linguistic universe of humanist culture by literally going outside it, in terms of scope and in terms of language. Sebastian Münster (1489–1552), who had already produced a trilingual dictionary of Latin, Greek, and Hebrew, published his *Cosmographia universalis* in German before its Latin version appeared. Marvelously illustrated and written in continuous prose, it covers in detail the topography, history, social organization, and natural environment of peoples and places beyond the perimeters of the ancient world and posterior to its history. The 1575 *Cosmographie universelle* of André Thevet (1502–1590) follows the same pattern, adding personal observation and exotic pictures to descriptions of recently explored lands.

There was also new territory for encyclopedias nearer home. Charles Estienne, in his Latin compilations of the 1530s on agriculture and horticulture, had had ancient Latin models at hand, but his French *Agriculture et maison rustique* (Agriculture and country household management), published in 1566, is a complete encyclopedia of farming and gardening relevant to the estate of a French country gentleman, written in continuous prose, as many vernacular encyclopedias were, but carefully indexed. This book and subsequent ones, like the *Théâtre d'agriculture* of Olivier de Serres (1539–1619), represented the definitive elevation of "mechanical arts" to the status of subjects fit for the printed encyclopedia; these arts had come to be seen as capable of methodical analysis, radically dependent on observation, and as instruments of a perspective on the natural world that had only the most marginal convergence with verbal culture.

Multilingual Dictionaries. The sixteenth century witnessed a language explosion as well as a printing explosion, and the two were closely connected. Bilingual and multilingual dictionaries ranged from simple word lists for children to dictionaries of the learned languages (Greek, Hebrew, Aramaic) fostered by philological Biblical scholarship. Latin remained the pivotal language into which works in other languages were translated. Modern languages were described in forms appropriate to Latin, and Latin was the standard against which they were measured.

From the late 1530s, Robert Estienne adapted his *Thesaurus* as a Latin-French dictionary by supplying French lexical equivalents for the Latin entries and excising the Latin quotations, thus leaving the cultural poverty of the French language exposed. The Latin dictionary of Calepinus acquired a new lease on life from the mid-1560s onward, as new languages were successively grafted into it until, by the mid-1580s, it had become a polyglot dictionary of eleven languages. However, its examples of language use were still drawn from exclusively Latin sources. By the end of the sixteenth century, bilingual dictionaries were bypassing Latin and discovering the fertile language territory displayed in Randle Cotgrave's *Dictionarie of the French and English Tongues* (1611).

See also **Commonplace Books.**

BIBLIOGRAPHY

Primary Works
Two bibliographical encyclopedias are indispensable for gaining access to the Renaissance world of knowledge: Conrad Gesner, *Pandectae sive partitiones universales* and the accompanying *Bibliotheca universalis* (Zurich, 1548–1549) and Antonio Possevino, *Bibliotheca selecta* (Rome, 1593).

Secondary Works
Blair, Ann. *The Theater of Nature: Jean Bodin and Renaissance Science.* Princeton, N.J., 1997.
Kelley, Donald R., and Richard H. Popkin, eds. *The Shapes of Knowledge from the Renaissance to the Enlightenment.* Dordrecht, Netherlands; Boston; and London; 1991.
Kenny, Neil. *The Palace of Secrets: Beroalde de Verville and Renaissance Conceptions of Knowledge.* Oxford, 1991.
Starnes, De Witt T. *Renaissance Dictionaries: English-Latin and Latin-English.* Austin, Tex., 1954.
Starnes, De Witt T., and E. W. Talbert. *Classical Myth and Legend in Renaissance Dictionaries.* Chapel Hill, N.C., 1955.
Tonelli, Giorgio. *A Short-Title List of Subject Dictionaries of the Sixteenth, Seventeenth, and Eighteenth Centuries.* London, 1971.

ANN MOSS

DIET. *See* **Food and Drink.**

DIFFUSION OF IDEAS.   During the Renaissance ideas were disseminated in a variety of ways, beginning with personal communication by letter, treatises, and word of mouth. As the Renaissance developed, new forms of education, libraries, translations from the classics, and even the bitter invectives that scholars hurled at one another helped spread the ideas of the humanists.

1350–1400.   The diffusion of Renaissance ideas began with Petrarch (1304–1374), who discovered Cicero's speech *Pro Archia* in 1333 and *Ad Atticum* (Letters to Atticus) in 1345. In these texts Petrarch discovered a rhetorical moral philosophy different from Scholasticism, a writer of personal letters who expressed his own feelings, and a model of elegant Latin. Petrarch wrote many personal letters (which he gathered in two collections), a practice followed by his immediate disciples, his successors—Coluccio Salutati (1331–1406), Leonardo Bruni (c. 1370–1444), and Poggio Bracciolini (1380–1459)—and Erasmus (c. 1466–1536). He also wrote letters to his favorite classical writers as if he were their contemporary.

Indeed, Petrarch regarded himself as closer to the ancients than to his contemporaries; he was, he said, a man born out of season. His notion that the fall of the Roman Empire was the great turning point in history, leading him to divide historical epochs into ancient, dark, and modern, contradicted the Christian view that the birth of Christ marked this point. Petrarch wrote lives of eminent men of the past (emulated by his disciple Boccaccio, who wrote lives of eminent women) and other works recalling the glory of ancient Rome, including an epic poem on Scipio Africanus (*Africa*). His coronation as poet laureate in 1341 was a high point of his life, in large part because of its association with the ancient glory of Rome.

Petrarch also aspired to knowledge of Greek antiquity; he possessed a manuscript of works by Plato unknown to the Middle Ages, but he could not read it, though he made one inadequate effort to learn Greek. Within one generation of Petrarch's death, his successors achieved an elegance in writing Latin much greater than his own; some of them also learned Greek. And they searched for classical manuscripts, making momentous discoveries of Cicero's and Quintilian's works on the training and practice of an orator. They also began to write (and copy manuscripts) in a new kind of script, the Roman script practiced in the Carolingian age (though the humanists believed it to be classical).

1400–1450.   Through education, what began with Petrarch spread through all of Italy during the fifteenth century and through the rest of western Europe during the sixteenth century. Pier Paolo Vergerio (1370–1444) wrote the earliest humanist treatise (1404) on the education of boys, *De ingenuis moribus* (Bruni penned one for girls in 1424). Vergerio modified the medieval trivium and quadrivium by giving special prominence to the *studia humanitatis,* those disciplines worthy of study by a free man: grammar, poetry, rhetoric, history, and moral philosophy. Taught in these subjects and using classical writers as examples of good usage, a new generation of teachers emerged, the most well known of whom were Gasparino Barzizza (c. 1360–c. 1431), Vittorino da Feltre (1378–1446), and Guarino da Verona (1370 or 1374–1460). Their famous schools, and less famous ones, throughout northern Italy created an environment for humanistic studies, which spread the ideas and principles of Petrarch and the other humanists. They generated the most significant educational revolution in more than one thousand years and one destined to hold its ground until well into the twentieth century.

The humanist revival of classical antiquity coincided with the artistic Renaissance in early fifteenth-century Florence. Consequently, the new enthusiasm for antiquity spread to artists. Donatello (1386?–1466) and Filippo Brunelleschi (1377–1446) studied the remains of classical architecture and sculpture in Rome. In his statue of St. Mark (completed 1413), Donatello revealed his knowledge of the classical sculptors' ability to create a freestanding human figure. Brunelleschi rediscovered Hellenistic illusionism, which he communicated by word of mouth to the humanist man of letters Leon Battista Alberti (1404–1472); Alberti described that discovery in an influential book, *Della pittura* (On painting), published in Latin in 1435 and in Italian in 1436. Masaccio (1401–1428), who learned Brunelleschi's rules from Brunelleschi himself, created the first painting based on one-point perspective (*The Holy Trinity with the Virgin and St. John;* 1425). Poggio Bracciolini, in his expeditions around Constance, also discovered and had copied Vitruvius's work on architecture, the only classical treatise on that subject. Although other copies were available, Vitruvius was not seriously studied until Alberti did so, using Vitruvian principles in his building designs after 1450 and writing his own *De re aedificatoria* (Treatise on architecture; completed 1452, printed 1485; editio princeps of Vitruvius 1486 at Rome).

Although most artists were not learned in the humanist sense, they were introduced to ideas by word of mouth. Communication between artisans and intellectuals is one of the most important ways in which ideas spread. So effective was this communication that during the fifteenth century artists ceased to be regarded as craftsmen and came to be viewed as practitioners of the liberal arts. Art gained greatly in prestige as artists achieved higher status. Pedigrees were even invented for them, notoriously so in the case of Michelangelo. Despite the fusion in theory of craft and the liberal arts, artists were still learning their classics from humanists by word of mouth at the end of the century. Botticelli (1445–1510) apparently was not learned in the mythical tradition so richly represented in his *Primavera* and *Birth of Venus,* but humanists were there to instruct him. By the following century, however, artists had become profound students of classical mythology, as reflected in painting and sculpture during the seventeenth and eighteenth centuries.

Research libraries were founded in Florence through the initiative of Niccolò de' Niccoli (1364–1437) and sustained through the money of Cosimo de' Medici, making it possible for humanist scholars to consult rare books. These early libraries became the basis for manuscript collections in the Laurenziana and Riccardiana libraries (Florence). Thus, even before the advent of printing, humanist scholarship had become a collective enterprise.

The manuscripts collected were not only in Latin but also in Greek. As early as 1397 the Byzantine scholar Manuel Chrysoloras (c. 1353–1415) had come to Florence through the initiative of Salutati, Petrarch's disciple and the chancellor of the city since 1375. Chrysoloras taught Greek there for three years, and by the time he left in 1400 to teach in other quarters, several Florentines had become proficient enough to translate Greek texts into Latin (Bruni translated several Aristotelian texts) and to incorporate ideas from those texts into their own writings (Bruni's *Laudatio Florentiane urbis* [Panegyric on the City of Florence], patterned after Athenaeus's oration on Athens, is one of the more famous examples). Before mid-century a number of Italian humanists had become proficient in Greek, some, like Francesco Filelfo (1398–1481) and Guarino da Verona, by studying in Greece. Thus, ideas from ancient Greece increasingly entered the discussions of scholars.

1450–1500. After 1450 several events coalesced to increase greatly the impact of all the tendencies thus far discussed. When Constantinople fell to the Turks in 1453 and Greek émigrés arrived in Italy, Greek studies and texts were augmented still further. The first humanist pope, Nicholas V (reigned 1447–1455), laid the foundation for the Vatican Library by making a concerted effort to collect Greek manuscripts and encouraging scholars through his patronage to copy them and render them into Latin.

Nothing conspired to magnify these tendencies so much as the invention of the printing press around 1450. Now texts could be disseminated in identical copies, facilitating emendation. Humanists published editions of ancient texts, beginning a process of standardization impossible in a manuscript tradition in which errors of the past were perpetuated and new ones created each time a text was copied. Two great philologists, Lorenzo Valla (1407–1457) and Angelo Poliziano (1454–1494), emerged during the latter half of the century, Poliziano establishing a method for the development of an accurate textual tradition. Although the French invasion of Italy, coinciding with the year of his death, delayed the immediate impact of Poliziano's work, the antiquarians of the seventeenth century and later greatly advanced what he had begun.

Translations were probably even more important for the diffusion of ideas. Perhaps the most important was the translation by Marsilio Ficino (1433–1499) of the complete works of Plato (as well as of Plotinus, Hermes Trismegistus, and other works associated with Platonism) in the 1460s, making Plato known in the West through his own voice for the first time in more than one thousand years. The resurgence of Platonism in late fifteenth-century Florence offered yet another countercurrent to Aristotelian Scholasticism. Platonic ideas played an important role in the development of love poetry in vernacular languages during the Renaissance and also may have affected the emergence of modern science. Editions and translations from Italy facilitated the development of humanism north of the Alps, making possible in one generation (1470–1500) what had taken three in Italy.

Humanists were above all rhetoricians and orators. Orations were delivered on all kinds of occasions, including visits from foreign dignitaries to one's city or court, the opening of an academic year, and sermons. Cassandra Fedele (1465?–1558) delivered an address welcoming the queen of Poland to Venice, as well as an address opening a university session she was forbidden to attend. Heinrich Agrippa of Nettesheim opened the 1509 academic year at the French University of Dôle with a declamation on the superiority of women over men. Sermons preached at the papal court and elsewhere increasingly reflected humanist themes through the fifteenth century. Imaginative speeches were equally common, and some have been enduringly important. Erasmus, for example, placed a declamation against war and military aggression in the mouth of Peace, a "complaint" that has been reprinted many times, most often when some European war is imminent. Even more famous is his *Moriae encomium* (trans. *Praise of Folly;* 1511), which was written as a speech by the goddess Folly in behalf of folly and became one of the great literary classics of the Renaissance. At least one aim of Folly's speech was to bring about religious reform.

After 1500. During the sixteenth century, even before the beginning of the Protestant Reformation, humanists added the Christian tradition to the classical traditions recovered by them. Lorenzo Valla wrote philological notes on the New Testament, which were discovered in 1504 by Erasmus, who had them printed. Thus inspired, Erasmus in 1516 published the first Greek New Testament with his own Latin translation; the work went through five editions in his lifetime and focused attention on the biblical text just as the Protestant Reformation began. At the same time, Erasmus and others published original-language editions (in Greek or Latin) of works by the fathers of the church. The philological work humanists undertook on nonscriptural texts was, by their successors, applied as well to the Bible.

Ideas spread through invective as much as through forms of persuasion intended to generate laughter and good feeling. Humanists regularly excoriated each other's ideas and character: Poggio and Valla are one famous example from the fifteenth century; Erasmus and critics of his biblical scholarship are an example from the sixteenth century. Invective reached a peak during the Protestant Reformation that the humanists could hardly have imagined; but without the humanists the Protestant and Catholic reformers could not have argued so well among themselves or against each other. Indeed, what had earlier been debates among the learned, commandeering only a small audience, became during the Reformation pamphlet warfare sometimes published in Latin but often in the European vernaculars. Undoubtedly, such warfare increased the need for literacy and helped turn the modern vernaculars into languages as supple and expressive as classical Greek and Latin. The printing press greatly facilitated the diffusion of opposing ideas, not only on religion but also on politics (the question of sovereignty, for example) and science (Copernicus's heliocentric theory).

See also **Classical Antiquity, Discovery of; Education; Greek Émigrés; Humanism; Libraries; Manuscripts; Printing and Publishing; Rhetoric; Vatican Library;** *and biographies of figures mentioned in this entry.*

BIBLIOGRAPHY

Primary Works

Agrippa, Heinrich Cornelius. *Declamation on the Nobility and Preeminence of the Female Sex.* Translated by Albert Rabil. Chicago, 1996.

Alberti, Leon Battista. *On Painting.* Translated by John R. Spencer. Rev. ed. New Haven, Conn., 1966.

Erasmus. *The Complaint of Peace.* In *The Essential Erasmus.* Edited by John P. Dolan. New York, 1964. Pages 174–204.

Fedele, Cassandra. "Oration on the Arrival of the Queen of Poland" and "Oration for Bertucio Lamberto, Receiving the Honors of the Liberal Arts." In *Her Immaculate Hand.* Edited by Margaret L. King and Albert Rabil Jr. Rev. ed. Binghamton, N.Y., 1992. Pages 48–50 and 69–73.

Gordan, Phyllis Walter Goodhart, ed., *Two Renaissance Book Hunters: The Letters of Poggius Bracciolini to Nicolaus de Niccolis.* New York, 1974.

Petrarch. *Letters of Old Age.* Translated by Aldo Bernardo, Saul Levin, and Reta Bernardo. 2 vols. Baltimore, 1992.

Petrarch. *Letters on Familiar Matters.* Translated by Aldo Bernardo. 3 vols. Vol. 1: Albany, N.Y., 1975. Vols. 2 and 3: Baltimore, 1982, 1985.

Valla, Lorenzo. *The Treatise of Lorenzo Valla on the Donation of Constantine.* Translated by Christopher Bush Coleman. Toronto, 1993.

Secondary Works

Edwards, Mark U., Jr. *Printing, Propaganda, and Martin Luther.* Berkeley, Calif., 1994.

Grafton, Anthony, and Ann Blair, eds. *The Transmission of Culture in Early Modern Europe.* Philadelphia, 1990.

Woodward, William Harrison, ed. *Vittorino da Feltre and Other Humanist Educators.* Toronto, 1996. Includes a foreword by Eugene F. Rice Jr.

ALBERT RABIL

DIGNITY OF MAN. Treatises on the dignity of the human species were an important genre of Renaissance moral thought and a major ingredient of the Renaissance philosophy of man. Although there are important classical and early Christian considerations of this theme, and some more limited discussion of it in the Middle Ages, the expression of a more affirmative attitude toward human existence is a significant aspect of Renaissance culture.

Origins. The first humanist treatment of this theme occurs in Petrarch's *De remedis utriusque fortunae* (Remedies for both kinds of fortune; 1366), the second book of which offers consolation for adverse fortune. In his *Epistolae rerum senilium* (Letter of his old age) to the grandprior of the Carthusians, Petrarch offers the *Remedies* in response to the prior's request that Petrarch should write the work that Pope Innocent III had promised to write at the end of his *De contemptu mundi* (On contempt for the world: The misery of the human condition; 1217), namely, *On the Dignity of the Human Condition*. In his *Remedies* Petrarch writes, "since the misery of human kind is palpably evident, while its happiness is small and hidden," this "must be explored in a deeper more sophisticated manner. . . . Now, considering essentials, is it a small joy to know that there is the likeness of God the Creator depicted within the human soul, your mind, your memory, foresight and speech . . ." (Rawski, vol. 3, p. 224). Petrarch follows with many details concerning the powers of the human soul, the beauty and gifts of the body, the glory that Christ's incarnation provides to man with its promise of resurrection—all themes that were developed in later humanist versions.

It was not until the mid-fifteenth century that the genre of the dignity of man reappeared. But important expressions of both the pessimistic theme of human misery and the optimistic vision of human majesty, joy, and power frequently appeared in humanist writings on other subjects. Coluccio Salutati (1331–1406) asserted in *De nobilitate legum et medicinae* (On the nobility of law and medicine; 1399): "By this excellence of goodness, which from the creation has been common to us and the angels, and will be common in the fatherland, human nature excels all corporeal creatures and any man transcends the dignity of his own body."

It should be noted that these anthropological writings included a theological element, with frequent allusions and references to the Biblical verses Genesis 1:26–27, in which men and women ("male and female he created them") are created in the image and likeness of God. Lorenzo Valla (1407–1457) also speaks of the greatness of God's gifts to mankind in *De voluptate* (On pleasure, or the true good; 1431) "That you might know how much more potent you are, for whom the whole world and all the heavens have been fabricated I say they are made for you alone. For although you also have others sharing with you, nevertheless all things are made for the sake of individuals."

The major development of humanist writing on the dignity of man occurred in the 1440s and 1450s. The Genoese humanist, Bartolomeo Facio (1400–1457), living under the patronage of King Alfonso of Naples, wrote a reply to Valla's *On Pleasure* called *De vitae felicitate* (The happiness of life). Although

he deprecates pleasure and praises virtue in the face of universal hardship, he also sees an element of dignity and fortitude in the struggle against the vices. However the true initiator of the reemergence of the dignity of man theme was an Olivetan monk, Antonio da Barga (c. 1390–1452) who later became Abbot of San Miniato in Florence. Barga was an admirer and friend of several prominent humanists, including Facio. In the 1440s Barga acknowledged receipt of a work on the dignity of man dedicated to him by Giannozzo Manetti. Although this work has not survived, Barga wrote an outline of such a work and gave it to Facio to fill out, a task that Facio undertook and completed by late 1447 or early 1448. This work is highly pious in tone, emphasizing man's creation in God's image and likeness, and the command God had given him to rule over the animals and the natural world.

Giannozzo Manetti. Barga's other protégé, Giannozzo Manetti (1396–1459), was a leading Florentine citizen-humanist, a man of wealth and political influence, governor of territories and ambassador to Venice and to the papal Curia, translator of the Greek New Testament and the Hebrew Psalms. As ambassador to King Alfonso of Naples he undertook to write *De dignitate et excellentia hominis* (The dignity and excellence of man) and completed it by 1453 (first published 1532).

The work is divided into four books; the first draws on Cicero's *De natura deorum* (On the Nature of the Gods; B.C. 45 or 44), Lactantius's *De opificio Dei* (The divine creation; A.D. 303 or 304), and on Aristotle, Galen, Avicenna, and Albert the Great to depict the wonders of human anatomy and physiology. According to Manetti, the beauty of the human body is so great that men imagined God in human likeness "in certain basilicas of the apostles and martyrs and other saints." Meanwhile, some men thought the body was made in the image of the universe so that man had been called a microcosm.

Manetti's second book deals with the soul, first on the basis of Cicero's *Tusculanae disputationes* and Lactantius's *On the Fabrication of Man,* and then on Aristotle and a long list of early Greek philosophers whom he knew mainly through Aristotle. On the authority of Cicero he disparaged Plato, who "spoke of the soul very obscurely, employing metaphors and figures of speech." Aristotle does not fare much better, since, Manetti says, "If he had wished to transgress and transcend the circumscribed limits of a natural philosopher, he would have added that man was created by Almighty God from nothing, marvel-

Dignity and Misery. The dignity of man places him above other creatures. Human nature comprehends mineral (exemplified by a rock, which *est,* exists), vegetable (exemplified by a tree, which *vivit,* lives), and animal (or sensible, exemplified by a horse, which *sentit,* feels) natures. But it is superior to them in that it possesses reason (which *intelligit,* knows). The powers appropriate to each nature are shown to the right. The *virtus* of the rational nature in man is to be studious. A human being given over to the powers of the lower natures, however, falls victim to vices appropriate to the nature: lust (*luxuria*) for the sensual or animal nature; gluttony (*gula*) for the vital or vegetable nature; and sloth (*acedia*) for the mineral nature. Woodcut; sixteenth century. BIBLIOTHÈQUE NATIONALE DE FRANCE, PARIS

lously as I think." Manetti's true authority was scripture, particularly the words of Moses, who saw God face to face, and who reports God's words in Genesis: "Let us make humankind in our image and likeness" (1:26). These words "according to a certain and unique explanation of all the theologians do not refer to the body but to the soul alone." Drawing on Augustine and Peter Lombard (c. 1095–1160), he argues over whether the words of Genesis refer to angels or men, or also refer to the Trinity. He quotes Hermes Trismegistus of the ancient world, who called the human form *theoides,* or godlike, and sees human powers as Promethean.

In his third book Manetti deals with man as a whole. Here he considers human beauty and ingenuity. The world, after its first creation, has been made over by humans:

> Everything seems to have been discovered, constructed and completed by us out of some singular and outstanding acuteness of the human mind. For those things are ours, that is they are human, which are seen to be produced by men: all homes, all towns, all cities . . . Ours are the paintings, ours the sculptures, ours the arts, ours the sciences, ours . . . are all discoveries, ours all the different kinds of languages and literatures.

He goes on to depict the human works of cultivation, irrigation, the "fashioning, as it were, of another nature within the bounds and precincts of the one we have." The office of man in the world, thus, is:

> to be such that he knows how and is able to govern and administer the world, made for his sake, and especially everything we see is established in this entire world, which he cannot entirely perfect and fully implement except by both knowing and doing. And so we say not unjustly that to know and to act is the proper function of man alone.

Manetti's work indicates how theology and practical achievement were combined during the Renaissance to bring about an activistic functional attitude that became a determining characteristic of modern humankind.

Dignity and Misery. Contrary to the theme of human dignity in Renaissance thought is that of human misery, and in the fourth book of his *Dignity* Manetti writes a confutation of many ancient and contemporary representatives of it, including that of Pope Innocent III, *On Contempt for the World.* By coincidence a fellow Florentine, Poggio Bracciolini (1380–1459) returned to Florence after long service in the papal Curia and wrote *De miseria humanae conditionis* (On the misery of the human condition) in 1455. Such pairings were frequent in the Renaissance.

An actual debate on this subject took place between two Bolognese humanists during the 1460s and 1470s. Giovanni Garzoni (1419–1505) had been a student of Lorenzo Valla and then became a physician. He wrote a series of short pessimistic pieces called *De miseria humana* (On human misery), *De miseria mundi* (On the misery of the world), *De varietate fortunae* (The variety of fortune), and *De contemptu mundi et felicitatis religione* (On contempt for the world and the happiness of religion). In reply to at least some of these, Benedetto Morandi (d. 1478) wrote *De felicitate humana* (Of human happiness) and *In calumniatorem naturae humanae secunda reluctatio* (Second refutation against a calumniator of human nature). Morandi said:

> Other living creatures are neither moved by the will nor have free choice, but are borne by the impulse of nature without election. Man alone chooses with reason, is led by it in his actions, uses his own will.... Wise indeed is the life of man who willing and loving by reason founds homes, cities, cultivates society, conserves it by laws, and whatever is common to him with animals he moderates by reason.

A similar view of man is expressed by Bartolomeo de' Sacchi (1421–1481), generally known as Platina, in his *De vero et falso bono* (On true and false good) of the early 1470s. Man through the development of his intellectual powers acquires the urge to improve himself in order to help others and better the conditions of human life. "Certainly an effort is made, as far as it can be done, that the same order, the same justice and constancy as he knows by contemplation and wisdom to be in heaven should be observed on earth."

A final example of this humanist stress on the excellence of the human condition may be drawn from Aurelio Brandolini (d. 1497 or 1498) in his *Dialogus*

de humanae vitae conditione et toleranda corporis aegritudine (On the condition of human life and on bearing bodily sickness), a work of consolation for King Matthias Corvinus of Hungary in his illness:

> Good God, how great and how admirable is that force of intellect conceded divinely to man alone by which he contemplates himself and all things which are located outside him? How great its speed? so that in a single moment of time it wanders far and wide through the entire world. . . . Finally, it is so great an image and similitude of the divine nature that it has been rendered capable and a participant of immortality and beatitude.

Ficino and Pico. The grand theme of the dignity and excellence of man achieved its most influential expression in the Renaissance, not among the humanists but in the writings of Marsilio Ficino (1433–1499) and Giovanni Pico della Mirandola (1463–1494). Ficino was a Neoplatonic philosopher, in fact the chief translator and transmitter of Platonic and Neoplatonic texts and thought to early modern Europe. Pico developed a synthesis of scholastic Aristotelianism, medieval Arabic and Judaic thought, and Platonism. But both men were closely associated and familiar with the humanist tradition, and continued and deepened the basic humanist theme of the dignity of man.

Marsilio Ficino dealt with this theme explicitly in books 13 and 14 of his *Theologia Platonica* of 1474. A few excerpts follow:

> The other animals either live without art, or have each one single art to the use of which they . . . are dragged by a law of fate. . . . On the contrary men are the inventors of innumerable arts which they practise according to their own decision. . . . Human arts make by themselves whatever nature itself makes, so that we seem not to be servants of nature, but competitors. . . . The force of man is almost similar to the divine nature since man by himself, that is through his intelligence and skill, governs himself without being in the least limited by his physical nature and imitates the individual works of the higher nature.
>
> Our soul is concerned not only with the necessities of the body like beasts subjected to the rule of nature, but with various delights of the senses as though a kind of food for the phantasy. And the soul not only flatters its phantasy with these various pleasures while daily seducing it with various games as if for jest, but meanwhile also the cogitative reason acts seriously . . . to show how strong its own inventive genius is through various silk and woolen textiles, paintings, sculptures and buildings. . . . In these industrial arts it may be observed how man everywhere utilizes all the materials of the universe as though they were subject to man. . . . Nor is he content with one element or a few, as animals,

but he uses all as though he was master of all. He tramps the earth, he sails the water, he ascends in the air by the highest towers, as I pass over the feathers of Daedalus or Icarus.

He goes on listing the powers of men over the elements, and over the animals, whom he nurtures, thus imitating "universal providence, proper to God who is the universal cause. Man is thus god of the animals, of all living things, of the elements." In these the dignity of man is that of *homo faber,* industrial man. But man also possesses the civil arts of government; he is also a builder; and he commands the liberal arts of language, music, and mathematics, as well as the creative arts of sculpture and painting. "Therefore he would be proven mad who would deny that the soul, which in the arts and in governing competes with God, is divine." Indeed, in commanding the elements, in transmuting the species of things and in other magical practices he shows his closeness to God.

Although Ficino puts forth this vision of human dignity in more extravagant terms than Manetti, the most thoroughgoing of his humanist predecessors, and places it in the setting of an effort to establish a Platonic theology, it is very close to the humanistic tradition that began with Petrarch and is also redolent of the industrial, civic, and artistic environment of fifteenth-century Florence.

Giovanni Pico della Mirandola's *De hominis dignitate* (Oration on the dignity of man) is the best-known Renaissance expression of this theme. Never delivered, but prepared in late 1486 to introduce his nine hundred theses on the concord of all philosophical schools and theologies, it was suspended when Pope Innocent VIII charged a commission with examining the theses. Pico's vision of human dignity has the entire universe created by God except for someone to behold and admire it. Hence God ordained that man should be a creature of indeterminate nature, free to "have and possess what abode, what form and what function thou thyself shalt desire." The words are highly admired by many interpreters of the Renaissance. The story of Pico's flight, eventual capture and arrest by papal forces, and eventual settlement in Florence under the protection of Lorenzo de' Medici are well known.

In 1488–1489 he wrote an interpretive commentary, called *Heptaplus,* on chapter 1 of Genesis, concerning God's six days of labor and seventh of rest. Here an elaborate vision of the centrality of man's position in the universe is set forth. Man is no longer free to choose his place in the cosmos but allegorically embodies the existence of every part of the universe as the image and likeness of God as set forth in Genesis 1:26–27.

> We are seeking something peculiar to man from which the dignity proper to him and the image of the divine substance may be found to be common to him and to no other creature. What else can this be except that the substance of man . . . comprehends in himself the substances of all natures and the plenitude of the entire universe through his very existence?

Man, as the image of God (not God, himself) "brings together and co-unites all natures of the entire world to the integrity of his own substance. This we can say of no other creature, whether angelic, celestial, or sensible." Pico's conception of human dignity in the *Oration* is frequently interpreted as refuting the notion of man as a microcosm, an idea frequently expressed in classical, medieval, and Renaissance thought, but in the *Heptaplus* he clearly portrays man as such.

> It is truly a divine possession of all these natures at the same time flowing into one, so that it pleases us to exclaim with Hermes, "A great miracle, Asclepius, is man." The human condition can especially be glorified for this reason, through which no created substances disdains to serve his. . . . No wonder that he is loved by all in whom all recognize something of their own, indeed their whole selves and all their possessions.

Pico's vision of man is theological and cosmological in contrast to the conception of Ficino in his *Theologia Platonica.* Ficino does become theological in book 14 where he characterizes the basic striving of man, not to be all natures as Pico, but to become God.

> But in what pertains to the desire for victory, the immense magnificence of our soul may be seen from this, that he will not be satisfied with the empire of the world, if, having conquered this one, he learns that there is another world which he has not yet subjugated. . . . Thus man wishes no superior and no equal and will not permit anything to be left out and excluded from his rule. This status belongs to God alone.

Therefore he seeks a divine condition. Yet this delineation of the extremity of human ambition is more compatible with the earlier humanist tradition of the dignity of man while Pico's version is highly theological and repentant.

These treatises and statements on the dignity of man continued to be repeated and echoed throughout the Renaissance. The theme of the dignity of man is one of the characteristic elements of Renaissance thought.

See also **Humanity, Concept of**; *and biographies of figures mentioned in this entry.*

BIBLIOGRAPHY

Primary Works

Ficino, Marsilio. *Théologie platonicienne de l'immortalité des âmes* (Platonic theology of the immortality of souls). Edited and translated by Raymond Marcel. Paris, 1964.

Manetti, Giannozzo. *De dignitate et excellentia hominis* (The dignity and excellence of man). Edited by Elizabeth R. Leonard. Padua, Italy, 1975.

Petrarch's Remedies for Fortune Fair and Foul. 5 vols. Translated by Conrad H. Rawski. Bloomington and Indianapolis, Ind., 1991.

Pico della Mirandola, Giovanni. On the Dignity of Man, *translated by Charles Glenn Wallis;* On Being and the One, *translated by Paul J. W. Miller;* Heptaplus (Sevenfold), *translated by Douglas Carmichael.* The Library of Liberal Arts. Indianapolis, Ind., 1965. Reprint, Indianapolis, Ind., 1998.

Salutati, Coluccio. *De fato et fortuna* (Fate and fortune). Edited by Concetta Bianca. Istituto nazionale di studi sul Rinascimento: Studi e testi, 10. Florence, 1985.

Valla, Lorenzo. *On Pleasure/De Voluptate.* Translated by A. Kent Hieatt and Maristella Lorch. New York, 1977.

Secondary Works

Cassirer, Ernst. *The Individual and the Cosmos in Renaissance Philosophy.* Translated with an introduction by Mario Domandi. New York, 1963.

Cassirer, Ernst, Paul Oskar Kristeller, and John Herman Randall Jr., eds. *The Renaissance Philosophy of Man.* Chicago, 1948.

Garin, Eugenio. *La cultura filosofica del Rinascimento italiano.* Florence, 1961.

Garin, Eugenio. *La Dignitas Hominis e la letturatura patristica.* Turin, Italy, 1972.

Garin, Eugenio. *Italian Humanism: Philosophy and Civic Life in the Renaissance.* Translated by Peter Munz. New York, 1965. Translation of *Umanesimo italiano.*

Kristeller, Paul Oskar. *Il pensiero filosofico di Marsilio Ficino.* Florence, 1988.

Kristeller, Paul Oskar. *The Philosophy of Marsilio Ficino.* Translated by Virginia Conant. New York, 1943. Reprint, Gloucester, Mass., 1964.

Kristeller, Paul Oskar. *Renaissance Concepts of Man and Other Essays.* New York, 1972.

Kristeller, Paul Oskar. *Renaissance Thought: The Classic, Scholastic, and Humanist Strains.* New York, 1961.

Kristeller, Paul Oskar. *Renaissance Thought II: Papers on Humanism and the Arts.* New York, 1961, 1965.

Sozzi, Lionello. *La "Dignitas Hominis" dans la littérature française de la renaissance.* Turin, Italy, 1972.

Trinkaus, Charles. *"In Our Image and Likeness," Humanity and Divinity in Italian Humanist Thought.* 2 vols. Notre Dame, Ind., 1995.

CHARLES TRINKAUS

DIPLOMACY. The accrediting by a sovereign power of a resident ambassador to another sovereign power developed in western Europe during the Renaissance. The use of resident ambassadors differed from the practice of medieval monarchs, who dispatched emissaries for a specified purpose and time; furthermore, resident ambassadors were sent not simply to negotiate, but to gather information useful to their governments.

The Emergence of Resident Ambassadors. There were medieval precedents for resident ambassadors, such as the *baiulo,* or commercial representative, employed at Constantinople by the Republic of Venice, and the procurators that western European rulers maintained at the papal curia. During the later Middle Ages, terms such as nuncio, legate, commissioner, and procurator were often used interchangeably for agents who were exchanged among popes, monarchs, feudal nobles, bishops, cities and towns, merchants, and even regional estates. But in the increasing status-conscious societies of Renaissance Europe, distinctions were made between ranks of diplomats and between those persons who had the right to send and receive them and those who did not. These distinctions, however, did not solidify into sharp definitions much before the eighteenth century.

In general, lower-ranking envoys were the nuncio *(nuncius),* a messenger who spoke the words of his principal, and the procurator *(procurator),* a legally empowered agent who negotiated on behalf of his principal. Ambassador *(ambaxator),* a term first used in the thirteenth century, and legate *(legatus)* were applied to envoys empowered by major rulers to speak and negotiate on their behalf in accordance to their written instructions. Humanists preferred the more classical term *orator* for ambassador and legate. The papacy restricted the title legate to its envoys of cardinal status, and the title of nuncio to all its other high-ranking diplomats. Kings in northern Europe, such as Louis XI of France (ruled 1461–1483), asserted against such semiautonomous nobles as the dukes of Orléans, Burgundy, and Brittany their exclusive right to send and receive ambassadors. In the sixteenth century it was generally accepted that only those who possessed the designation "majesty" could accredit ambassadors.

During a time of rising suspicions and increased tension, the need to continue embassies at foreign courts beyond some immediate purpose created the greatest impetus for the establishment of permanent embassies. As early as the mid-thirteenth century, Venice became the first to do this. Widespread employment of resident ambassadors developed first in Italy, where small city-states with well-organized governments were locked in bitter rivalries and repeated conflict over power and territory. For security, these states banded together in countervailing and ephemeral leagues, creating the need for continual communication between states and for the gathering of intelligence about an allied ruler and regime that might easily become an adversary.

The dukes of Milan appear to have pioneered the use of resident ambassadors. Duke Filippo Maria Visconti kept a resident agent at the court of Sigismund, king of Hungary and future Holy Roman Emperor, between 1425 and 1432; the emperor reciprocated with his own resident representative in Milan. Nicodemus of Pontremoli is often thought to have been the first true resident ambassador. Starting in 1446 he represented the duke of Milan in Florence for more than two decades, though not continuously. Following the Peace of Lodi (1454), during the effort to maintain the peace and political balance of Italy, this new diplomacy came into its own. In the 1450s Milan established resident embassies in Naples, Genoa, Rome, and Venice. The duke of Milan also appointed a resident ambassador at the French court in 1463. Other Italian states emulated Milan. The first Florentine resident ambassador to France was appointed in 1474, and the first Venetian resident ambassador followed in 1479.

This new diplomacy was adopted slowly by the northern European powers beginning in the late 1480s and the 1490s. As in Italy, the pace was quickened by increased conflict involving Spain, the Empire, France, and England from the Breton Wars (1487–1491) through the wars of Italy and Habsburg and Valois (1494–1559). Between 1487 and 1489 Ferdinand and Isabella of Spain established resident ambassadors in the Low Countries, Brittany, and England. Emperor-elect Maximilian I's secretary, Pierre Puissant, functioned as a resident envoy in England in 1491 and 1492. King Henry VII of England, while flattered to receive resident envoys, had at the end of his reign in 1509 only one resident ambassador outside the papal curia. The kings of France, surrounded by enemies, established by the end of the sixteenth century the most extensive diplomatic network. When he became king in 1515, Francis I employed one resident ambassador; at the end of his reign in 1547 he was supporting ten resident ambassadors throughout Europe.

In the 1560s, as a result of the religious antagonism spawned by the Reformation, Catholic and Protestant powers withdrew resident envoys from each other's courts, and regular diplomatic contacts between Catholic and Protestant Europe were not reestablished until the early seventeenth century. Poland-Lithuania, Russia, the Ottoman Empire, and the Scandinavian countries did not make use of resident diplomats. France and Protestant powers sent emissaries to Constantinople to enlist Turkish aid against the Habsburgs. The Habsburg ambassador Sigismund von Herberstein (1486–1566), made fifty-four missions to eastern European powers between 1515 and 1533, becoming a specialist on Muscovites and Slavonic languages. In the late sixteenth century England sent merchant envoys to Moscow seeking commercial ties with Russia. The sultan sent no ambassadors to the West, and until the time of Peter the Great (ruled 1682–1725), Russia had minimal contact with the western European courts.

The persistence of special ambassadors. The reliance on resident ambassadors did not end the sending of special ambassadors. Indeed, special embassies became part of the elaborate court ceremonial that proliferated during the Renaissance, and reflected the status consciousness of the princes who sent and received them. Special ambassadors were dispatched to congratulate a monarch upon his or her accession; to negotiate treaties of peace, alliance, and marriage; or to exchange articles of ratification and witness the swearing of oaths. In contrast to resident ambassadors, special ambassadors were men of rank, often nobles. Their rich clothing, gold chains, and number of horses in their train exhibited their status and the importance of the embassy. Special ambassadors were received amid elaborate entry ceremonies, which other diplomats observed carefully as indicators of the status, power, and relationships between states. Princes provided honorable hospitality to visiting envoys, including resident ambassadors. In the late fifteenth century, this hospitality included lodging, food, and drink, but a century later the government sending the embassy was expected to bear all of its costs. The giving of such gifts as cups, gold chains, money, and rich garments to visiting ambassadors remained an important part of diplomatic courtesy, and another occasion for the display of wealth and status.

Ambassadorial status. Precedence among ambassadors also involved issues of status and a sense of honor among monarchs and nations. Ambassadors at the papal curia squabbled over precedence, even coming to blows. Pope Julius II (reigned 1503–1513) issued an Order of Precedence, giving primacy of place among secular rulers to the emperor. Until the Reformation, and at Catholic courts afterwards, precedence was given to papal nuncios. Precedence was a point of rivalry between nations. Sir Thomas Egerton, Lord Ellesmere, minister to Elizabeth I (ruled 1558–1603) and James I (ruled 1603–1625), prepared legal arguments to show that England had precedence over Spain.

Qualifications of resident ambassadors. Despite the growing importance of diplomacy during the Renaissance, most governments lacked an organized diplomatic service. Nevertheless, those sent out as resident ambassadors had to have some basic skills, above all knowledge of Roman law and a humanistic education, with its emphasis on classical philosophy, history, and rhetoric. Latin was the common language of diplomacy, but use was also made of vernacular languages, especially in dispatches written by ambassadors to their governments. Rhetorical ability was particularly important in special embassies, which commenced with a solemn public oration given by one of the accredited ambassadors and a reply from a representative of the host government. Many of the great Renaissance humanists served as diplomats because of their linguistic and rhetorical abilities. Humanist diplomats preferred the title orator because it reflected their belief in the importance of rhetoric in the shaping of action.

The secretaries assigned to resident ambassadors needed to be educated as well. They kept all papers relating to the mission, including ciphers, and took down dictation for dispatches. In Italy these secretaries were state officials, but in northern Europe they were regarded as the ambassador's household servants. By the mid-sixteenth century, the increased number of resident envoys and the volume of diplomatic dispatches required the monarchies of Europe to appoint secretaries of state to prepare correspondence and instructions, oversee negotiations, and supervise the gathering of intelligence. The experience of foreign affairs gained as a resident ambassador became valuable in a minister of state. Diplomatic service was regarded not as a career in itself, but as a path to higher government service. Few were like Sigismund von Herberstein, who spent thirty-eight years as an envoy of the Habsburgs.

Paying the ambassadors. For the most part, payments to envoys were ad hoc, but some limited measures were taken to make maintenance of envoys more regular. Henry VII, recognizing the growing importance of diplomacy, established ambassadors as a recurrent category of state expenditure. Elizabeth I, despite her stinginess, made sure that her envoys were paid regularly. Pope Gregory XIII (reigned 1572–1585) assigned salaries for his nuncios, but was unable to insure that these salaries were paid regularly. Papal nuncios, because they were clergymen, had the revenues from their benefices and drew money from the collections of papal taxes and indulgences. Resident envoys of secular powers, unless they were already men of wealth, were often in financial difficulty. Their dispatches contained frequent complaints about the lack of money, the arrears of payment, the high costs of living in a foreign land, and the expense of couriers and messengers. The sending of money to ambassadors by bills of exchange often delayed delivery of money to envoys especially as they were traveling with a peripatetic court.

Speed and Security of Diplomatic Communication.

The dispatches sent and received by resident ambassadors were frequently intercepted and often took weeks to reach their destination. Couriers and messengers were commonly used in the Middle Ages, but the Gonzaga dukes of Mantua were the first to have special diplomatic couriers. Governments sent duplicates of diplomatic documents by various routes to insure that they reached the intended person. Merchants also conveyed diplomatic communications and documents, and were an alternate source of information. By the sixteenth century most governments of Europe were maintaining a postal service to aid diplomatic communication, but special couriers and post did not keep such communication secure from the prying eyes of foreign governments.

Ciphers. To maintain secrecy, the practice of cryptography was initiated during the Renaissance. Italy again led the way in the mid-thirteenth century. Early ciphers, which had associations with numerology and hermetic-kabbalistic mysticism, were simple and needed to be changed frequently. The Milanese, who had the most sophisticated diplomacy of the period, used two hundred different ciphers in the second half of the fifteenth century; most governments, however, especially in northern Europe, stuck to a single cipher for several years, making it easier for rivals to read their diplomatic letters. Methods of encryption became more sophisticated by the late sixteenth century. Johann von Trittenheim's *Polygraphiae libri sex* (Six books on the method of ciphering; 1518) was the first treatise on cryptography, followed by Giovanni Battista della Porta's *De furtivis litterarum notis* (On the secret knowledge of writing; 1563). Blaise de Vigenère's *Traité des chiffres* (A treatise on numbers; 1587) became the standard textbook for encryption for the next three centuries. As encryption became more sophisticated, governments employed specialists to decipher dip-

Diplomats. *The English Ambassadors Take Their Leave* by Vittore Carpaccio (c. 1460–1525/6) from a cycle illustrating the legend of St. Ursula. Clothing and setting are late-fifteenth-century Venetian. GALLERIE DELL'ACCADEMIA DI BELLE ARTI, VENICE/ANDERSON/ALINARI/ART RESOURCE

lomatic codes. The great mathematician François Viète (1540–1603) served Henry IV of France (ruled 1589–1610) in this capacity.

Diplomatic immunity. The security of diplomatic communication touched upon the issue of immunity enjoyed by resident ambassadors and their servants. The notion that envoys enjoyed some immunity from harassment and arrest was present in Roman law, but not widely established in Europe. The extensive use of resident ambassadors in the Renaissance led to more widespread recognition of certain types of immunity, which extended to the house

occupied by an ambassador. During the Reformation most governments allowed envoys of a different confession to practice their beliefs privately in their own house. This was not a universally recognized privilege, and Philip II of Spain (ruled 1556–1598) forbade the English ambassador to hold Protestant services in his house. It was also held throughout Europe that an ambassador who had committed a serious crime was subject to prosecution by the magistrates of the state or monarch to whom he was accredited. Angry and offended sovereigns had no compunction about imprisoning an ambassador. In

1516 Henry VIII arrested a papal envoy and threatened to put him on the rack. Francis I held Charles V's ambassador captive for six weeks in 1528. Governments had reason to be concerned about the activities of ambassadors. In the early 1560s Elizabeth I's resident ambassadors in France intrigued with the Huguenots, and in the 1570s Philip II's ambassador in London plotted with Catholics. Diplomats caught dabbling in treason were expelled.

Diplomacy and Morality. Despite the flowery humanistic rhetoric of peace, the milieu of Renaissance and Reformation politics was often one of mistrust and mutual antagonism, and ideas about diplomacy took on a hard-bitten reality, just as political theory seemed to do with Niccolò Machiavelli. In *Ambaxiator brevilogus* (A brief discourse on ambassadors; 1436), the first treatise about diplomacy, Bernard du Rosier argued that an ambassador, bound by the moral law, had to be concerned above all with the general welfare of the Christian commonwealth, which was peace. But in *De Officio Legati* (The duty of the legate; 1490), the first treatise to discuss the resident ambassador, Ermolao Barbaro asserted that while the resident diplomat should avoid dishonest behavior and deceitful practices, such as espionage and assassination, his primary responsibility was the preservation and aggrandizement of his state. A century later, the Elizabethan diplomat Sir Henry Wootton carried Barbaro's notion a step further into cynicism, saying that the resident ambassador was nothing more than "a man sent abroad to lie for his country's good."

See also Espionage; Field of Cloth of Gold.

BIBLIOGRAPHY

Primary Works

Dumont, Jean. *Corps universel diplomatique du droit des gens.* 8 vols. Amsterdam, 1726–1731. Texts of treaties and other diplomatic documents.

Hrabar, Vladimir E., ed. *De legatis et legationibus tractatus varii.* Dorpat, Estonia, 1905. Includes several treatises on diplomacy in the fifteenth and sixteenth centuries.

Secondary Works

Adair, Edward R. *The Exterritoriality of Ambassadors in the Sixteenth and Seventeenth Centuries.* New York, 1929.

Anderson, Matthew S. *The Rise of Modern Diplomacy, 1450–1919.* New York, 1993.

Krauske, Otto. *Die Entwicklung der ständigen Diplomatie vom 15. Jahrhundert bis zu den Beschlussen von 1815 und 1818.* Leipzig, Germany, 1885.

Maulde-La-Clavière, René. *La diplomatie au temps de Machiavel.* 3 vols. Paris, 1892–1893.

Mattingly, Garrett. *Renaissance Diplomacy.* Boston, 1955.

Queller, Donald E. *The Office of Ambassador in the Middle Ages.* Princeton, N.J., 1967.

Russell, Joycelyne G. *Diplomats at Work: Three Renaissance Studies.* Wolfboro Falls, N.H., 1992.

JOHN M. CURRIN

DISEASE. *See* **Sickness and Disease.**

DOLET, ÉTIENNE (1509–1546), French humanist printer. The brief but eventful career of Étienne Dolet exemplifies and exaggerates some of the most prominent tendencies of Renaissance humanism.

Born in Orléans, educated in Paris and Padua, briefly engaged in the service of the French ambassador to the Venetian Republic, Dolet first achieved notoriety as a law student at the University of Toulouse in 1533 when he delivered two Latin orations that earned him the applause of his fellow students and a brief imprisonment at the hands of the municipal authorities. Published under the title *Orationes Duae in Tholosam* (Two orations against Toulouse) in 1534, these speeches exemplify Dolet's ideal of civic humanism and reveal his deep engagement in the controversy over Ciceronianism that preoccupied so many European humanists of his era. As a rebuttal to Erasmus's earlier *Dialogus Ciceronianus* (The Ciceronian; 1528), Dolet published his own dialogue *De Imitatione Ciceroniana* (On the imitation of Cicero) in 1535, which established his reputation both as a preeminent Latinist and a vindictive polemicist. Drawing on the vast resources of his Ciceronian erudition, Dolet composed an innovative Latin dictionary entitled *Commentarii Linguae Latinae* (Commentaries on the Latin language), published in two volumes in 1536 and 1538, which constitutes his main contribution to Renaissance humanism and demonstrates the decisive intellectual influence of the greatest French humanist of his era, Guillaume Budé.

Unique among his contemporaries, Dolet distinguished himself not only as a renowned Latinist and advocate of pure Ciceronian style but also as an eloquent partisan of the vernacular, as can be seen in his treatise on translation, published together with two other French grammatical treatises in 1540 as part of a larger project entitled *l'Orateur Françoys* (The French orator). This project, although never completed, inspired an impressive tribute from Joachim Du Bellay in the *Deffence et illustration de la langue Francoyse* (Defense and enrichment of the French language; 1549).

Having set up his own printing business in Lyon in 1538, thus ensuring the diffusion of his own writings, Dolet began in 1542 to publish a series of controversial or prohibited texts associated with French evangelism, including Clément Marot's translation of the Psalms and Pierre-Robert Olivétan's translation of the Bible. This ambitious project, which may have represented a commercial strategy as well as an ideological commitment, earned the unpopular Dolet another imprisonment on charges of fomenting heresy. No sooner was he released from prison in the fall of 1543 than he again incurred the displeasure of the authorities, notably the Paris Parlement, on the same suspicion of publishing heretical works. Arrested in January 1544, he escaped from custody long enough to publish a compilation of French verse epistles entitled *Le Second Enfer* (The second hell), by which he sought unsuccessfully to win the intercession in his behalf of King Francis I and other powerful patrons. Rearrested at the end of the summer of 1544, Dolet spent two years in prison before being burnt at the stake in Paris on his thirty-seventh birthday, 3 August 1546, thus securing a posthumous reputation as a martyr of Renaissance idealism and intellectual courage.

BIBLIOGRAPHY

Primary Works

Dolet, Étienne. *De Imitatione Ciceroniana.* Edited by Emile Telle. Geneva, 1974.

Dolet, Étienne. *La maniere de bien traduire d'une langue en aultre* (The proper way to translate from one language to another). Reprint, Geneva, 1972.

Dolet, Étienne. *Orationes Duae in Tholosam.* Edited by Kenneth Lloyd-Jones and Marc Van Der Poel. Geneva, 1992.

Dolet, Étienne. *Le Second Enfer.* Edited by Claude Longeon. Geneva, 1978.

Secondary Works

Christie, Richard Copley. *Étienne Dolet: The Martyr of the Renaissance.* New York, 1899.

Pérouse, Gabriel-André, ed. *Etudes sur Étienne Dolet.* Geneva, 1993.

Scott, Izora. *Controversies over the Imitation of Cicero in the Renaissance.* New York, 1910. Reprint, Davis, Calif., 1991.

ERIC MACPHAIL

DONATELLO (Donato di Niccolò di Betto di Bardi; c. 1386/87–1466), Florentine sculptor, considered one of the founders of the Italian Renaissance style. Donatello extended the visual paradigms of every genre of sculpture, from freestanding figures, portraiture, and sacred narrative in relief to commemorative tomb monuments and chapel decoration, working across an impressive range of media, including marble, wood, bronze, terra-cotta, glass, brick, and stucco.

Life and Early Work. The earliest biography of Donatello is found in Giorgio Vasari's *Lives of the*

Donatello. *David with the Head of Goliath.* Made for the Medici between 1430 and 1440, this statue was first recorded in the courtyard of the Medici palace in 1469. Bronze; c. 1430–1440. MUSEO NAZIONALE DEL BARGELLO, FLORENCE/ALINARI/ART RESOURCE

169

Artists (1550). Yet Donatello is among the best-documented artists of the fifteenth century, with more than four hundred documentary references detailing his activities from 1401 until 1461 and frequent mentions in a variety of contemporary sources. Incidents recorded in contemporary biographies mentioning Donatello attest to his forceful personality and support the wealth of anecdote encountered in Vasari. Donatello was among the artists to whom Leon Battista Alberti dedicated his *Della pictura* (1436); he was praised for his talent and skill by Bartolomeo Fazio in *De viris illustribus* (Lives of illustrious men; 1456) and was celebrated posthumously in Cristoforo Landino's *Apologia* (1481). Significantly, these humanists note Donatello's artistic achievement in specific reference to antiquity. Donatello's acute interest and participation in the revival of classical culture were reflected in a number of activities, from restoring antiquities to advising collectors as distinguished as the humanist Poggio Bracciolini.

Donatello is first documented as an assistant in Lorenzo Ghiberti's Florence workshop (1403–1407), while Ghiberti was at work on models for the first set of bronze Baptistery doors. Although Donatello was described as a goldsmith and stonemason in the guild registry of St. Luke in 1412, earlier payment records from the cathedral workshops of Santa Maria del Fiore suggest that he was already autonomous; beginning in 1408 and continuing into the early 1420s, Donatello received a number of public and corporate commissions, mostly single figures in marble and terra-cotta. The earliest independent commissions that brought him to prominence were for Florence Cathedral and include the life-size marble *David* (1408–1409; Bargello), and a seated *St. John the Evangelist* (1408–1415; Museo dell Opera del Duomo), commissioned to flank the west doors of the cathedral facade. Too small for its intended location on a northern tribune buttress of the cathedral, the *David* was acquired by the Florentine city council for display in the Palazzo della Signoria in 1416. *David*'s decorative sway and original ornamentation—painted, gilded, and installed on an elaborate base inlaid with colored glass and mosaic—reflect contemporary taste for the International Gothic style. By contrast, the marble *St. John,* with its concentrated realism and optical corrections, carved to compensate for a viewer's angle of vision below, is often mentioned as a forerunner to Michelangelo's *Moses* (1513–1516; San Pietro in Vincoli, Rome).

The Period 1411–1420. During the second decade of the fifteenth century, Donatello received two commissions for Orsanmichele, a multipurpose structure that functioned as a center for the Florentine guilds: a marble *St. Mark* (1411–1414), commissioned by the Linen Drapers' Guild (noted for Donatello's realistic rendering of the Evangelist's robe and cushion), and a marble *St. George* (1414–1417; Bargello), patron saint of the Armorers' Guild, whose alert and tense expression was much admired for its realism. The exterior of the niche below marks the pioneering debut of Donatello's "rilievo schiacciato," or flattened relief technique, to illustrate the saint's rescue of the princess of Cappadoccia. Departing from earlier conventions, Donatello treated the surface of marble like wax, drawing with the corner of his chisel to create atmospheric effects and employing perspective to enhance the illusion of spatial depth.

At the same time, 1415–1418, he produced five marble sculptures for the bell tower of Florence Cathedral: the earliest were a *Bearded Prophet, Prophet with Scroll,* and *Abraham and Isaac* (Museo dell' Opera del Duomo). Execution of *Habakkuk* (the so-called Zuccone) and *Jeremiah* lasted into the 1430s; an early tradition claiming these as portraits testifies to their realism. The sandstone lion, the *Marzocco* (Bargello), was commissioned in 1418 and completed in 1420 for the entrance to the papal chambers at Santa Maria Novella, on the occasion of Pope Martin V's visit.

Works, 1420–1440. Donatello's growing engagement with bronze as well as an increase in private commissions can be observed throughout the 1420s. He produced his first gilded bronze, the *St. Louis of Toulouse* (1421–1425; now Museo di S. Croce), for the Guelph party at Orsanmichele in collaboration with Michelozzo, an experienced metallurgist in Ghiberti's workshop, resulting in an official workshop partnership from 1425 into the early 1430s. The vivid realism of the gilded bronze reliquary bust of *St. Rossore* (Museo di San Matteo, Pisa) has suggested to scholars that it was the earliest revival of classical portrait bust in the Renaissance.

The polychrome marble and bronze Tomb of Baldassare Coscia, Antipope John XXIII, in the Florentine Baptistery, was one of the most prestigious commissions of the 1420s. Its innovative composition features a vivid effigy in gilded bronze, lying "in state" under a marble baldachin. Three other tomb commissions date from this period: the Aragazzi Tomb in Montepulciano, the bronze Pecci Tomb relief with its unusual illusionism in the Siena cathedral, and the Brancacci Tomb ordered for Sant'An-

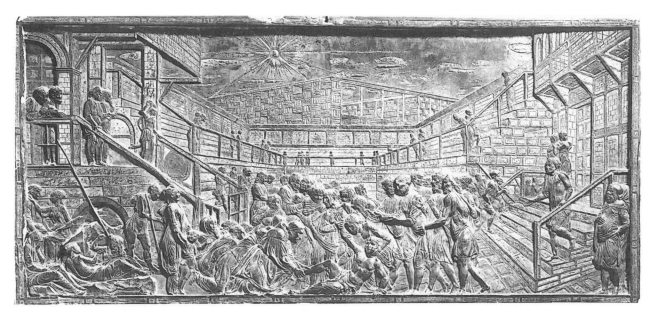

Donatello. *Miracle of the Wrathful Son.* Bronze relief showing St. Anthony healing a boy's foot, 1446–1453. Church of Sant' Antonio, Padua. 57 × 123 cm (22.5 × 48.5 in.). ANDERSON/ALINARI/ART RESOURCE

gelo a Nilo in Naples, where it was shipped from Pisa in 1428. In many respects a typical Neapolitan tomb updated with classicizing elements, Donatello's central marble relief of the *Assumption of the Virgin* reflects his increasing interest in narrative and his rapidly developing technique. Similar concerns were brilliantly explored in the gilded bronze panel of *Feast of Herod,* 1423–1427, for the Siena Baptistery font, assigned to Donatello after Jacopo della Quercia failed to fulfill the commission. Using multiple vanishing points, Donatello manipulated perspective as an expressive device linking pictorial space to narrative time; viewers watch the head of the Baptist move inexorably closer, from background to foreground, toward Herod, the banqueters, and us. In a series of small marble reliefs, which date from this period and include a number of Madonnas as well as the *Delivery of the Keys/Ascension of Christ* (Victoria and Albert Museum, London), Donatello's disregard for traditional finish and obvious chisel marks add to the works' expressiveness.

Donatello's exceptional experimentation with materials, techniques, and modes of expression continued in the 1430s, while his interest in ancient art intensified. Although tradition maintains that Donatello explored the ruins of Rome with Filippo Brunelleschi c. 1403, the artist's only documented trip occurred c. 1432, evidenced by the Crivelli Tomb in Santa Maria in Aracoeli and *Tabernacle with Burial of Christ,* now in the Beneficiati Sacristy of St. Peter's.

Upon his return to Florence, Donatello embarked on his first large-scale Medici commission, the decoration of a sacristy constructed by Brunelleschi to house the tomb of Giovanni de' Medici at the church of San Lorenzo. In addition to two sets of bronze doors, whose paired and actively gesticulating figures raised issues of decorum and finish, Donatello revived an ancient technique by modeling eight polychrome stucco roundels on site.

Difficulties in executing an exterior pulpit on the southwestern corner of Prato's cathedral, initially contracted to both Donatello and Michelozzo in July 1428, form a backdrop for Donatello's activities during this decade. In 1434, Donatello alone signed a second contract for the Prato Pulpit (Museo dell' Opera del Duomo, Prato), required for the semiannual outdoor display of a highly venerated relic, the girdle of the Virgin lowered to Thomas as a sign of her Assumption. Finally completed in 1438, individual marble panels on Prato's circular gallery present a continuum of joyously dancing angels.

Donatello's *Cantoria* (Museo dell'Opera del Duomo, Florence), a choir gallery commissioned for the cathedral of Florence in 1433 and completed in 1440, is related conceptually to the Prato pulpit but richer in ornamentation and expression. Its uninterrupted frieze of wildly cavorting angels is viewed through a screen of columns supporting a massive cornice. Other significant work from this period includes a stained-glass window of the coronation of the Virgin for the cathedral's dome; the deeply carved and tenderly expressive *Cavalcanti Annunciation Tabernacle* sandstone relief, Santa Croce; the polychrome and gilded wood *John the Baptist,* made in Florence for the Florentine merchants' chapel in Santa Maria Gloriosa dei Frari, Venice, 1438; and two iconographically mysterious bronzes now in the Bargello, the *Attis/Amor* and the controversial *David,* first recorded in the courtyard of the Medici palace in 1469.

Padua. Why Donatello left Florence for Padua around 1443 is uncertain; however, he was soon occupied with distinguished projects near and within the church of Sant'Antonio. Donatello's bronze equestrian portrait of the mercenary captain Erasmo da Narni (Gattamelata) was erected on its base outside Sant'Antonio in 1453. Inside the church, Donatello undertook an ambitious enterprise for a high altar complex entailing seven freestanding bronze figures and a series of reliefs in both marble and bronze that included four complex narratives recounting St. Anthony's miracles. The anatomically powerful bronze *Crucifix* (1444) was the earliest figure contracted for Sant'Antonio but probably not part of the original altar. The altar itself was left unfinished when Donatello left Padua in 1454, was dismantled in 1579, and reinstalled in 1895. Its intended appearance is subject to speculation.

Last Works. Documents indicate that Donatello resided in Florence from 1454 to 1457, when he moved to Siena to design a set of bronze doors for the Siena cathedral. He returned to Florence in 1459, where he remained until his death. Donatello's last works reveal a wide range of emotional tension, narrative invention, and drama. The penitent *Mary Magdalen* (Baptistery, Florence; c. 1455) in polychrome wood, and the bronze *John the Baptist* (c. 1457; Siena Cathedral) both appear as introspective aged ascetics empowered by their faith. The heroic and allegorical bronze *Judith Slaying Holofernes* (c. 1453–1457; Palazzo Vecchio, Florence) was probably commissioned as a fountain sculpture for the Medici palace. Donatello's final commission for the Medici, the so-called Resurrection and Passion Pulpits in San Lorenzo, remained unfinished at the time of his death and were not installed until 1515, yet their intricate perspectives and almost claustrophobic crowding of figures impart a new sense of urgency to their narratives. Donatello died in Florence on 13 December 1466 and was buried with obsequies in the crypt of San Lorenzo. Donatello's last works demonstrate the same profound intellect, restless imagination, expressive power, and confident handling of materials that marked the artist's work throughout his entire career.

BIBLIOGRAPHY

Avery, Charles. *Donatello: An Introduction.* New York, 1994.

Bennett, Bonnie, and David Wilkins. *Donatello.* Oxford, 1984.

Darr, A. P., ed. *Italian Renaissance Sculpture in the Time of Donatello: An Exhibition to Commemorate the Six Hundredth Anniversary of Donatello's Birth and the One Hundredth Anniversary of the Detroit Institute of Arts.* Detroit, Mich., 1985.

Janson, H. W. *The Sculpture of Donatello.* 2 vols. Princeton, N.J., 1957.

Wirtz, Rolf. *Donatello.* Cologne, Germany, 1998.

MAUREEN PELTA

DONI, ANTON FRANCESCO (1513–1574), Italian social critic, writer, journalist. Doni represents the antithesis of the typical Renaissance man of letters. His are the conflicting aspirations of the individual against the cultural and moral life of the century. Born into a family of artisans, he entered a monastic order to gain an education but was expelled in 1540. With a reputation for irreverence preceding him, Doni failed to secure a permanent position outside the traditional cultural centers of the Renaissance, the court and the church.

Instead, the success of Pietro Aretino (1492–1556) encouraged him to pursue a career as a freelance writer, from which pursuit there remain echoes of bizarre and vindictive behavior. Doni's life and career is of particular importance because it introduces the highs and lows of the new model of the intellectual tied to the fortunes of the commercial printing industry. Explanations for his behavior must be sought in the fluctuations of public taste and the necessity of generating a demand for his writings according to the suggestions of an editor burdened with probing the interests of a widening reading public.

Doni was a self-proclaimed "doctor in vernacular" who, without cultural pretenses, wrote popular light moral tales and humor, and covered cultural topics ranging from the classical age to his own times. Historical evidence indicates that he was one of the most popular authors of his time, but by the end of the sixteenth century he fell into oblivion as his elliptic style proved too difficult for the uninitiated to understand.

In his major original works he rejected the learning, politics, and social structure of contemporary Italy. The intense production in the years 1548–1553 in collaboration with the vernacular publishers Gabriele Giolito and Francesco Marcolini was marked by success but ended abruptly. In reaction to the Venetian censors' adaptation to the changed social, political, and religious climate of the Counter-Reformation, Doni went into voluntary exile in Monselice. Other authors who, like Doni, wrote in opposition to the political and religious institutions of their time suffered worse ends. Because of their free and unfettered writings they are known as "*poligrafi*" (polymaths, or writers on many subjects).

The most notable work of Doni's early career is *Le lettere* (The letters; 1544), known for the diversity of language used and for showing Doni's polemical spirit. His first real public success as a trendsetting author came when Marcolini published *La zucca* (The gourd; 1551–1552). Confidence in the novelty of this seminal work was such that it appeared at the same time in Spanish. *La zucca* contains a vast emporium of styles free from the traditional expectations of plot and replete with gossip, stories, and anecdotes. Here Doni anticipates all the thematic and structural novelties of his other works.

I marmi (The marble steps; 1553) is characterized by the structural breakdown of the typical printed book. Diverse themes are introduced in conversations held by the Florentine people congregating spontaneously on the steps of the cathedral of Santa Maria del Fiore. The author takes the role of observer in this *locus amoenus* (delightful place) that exists in critical opposition to more elevated cultural spaces, such as the court and the academy. *I mondi* (The worlds; 1552–1553) represents the maximum effort in the ethical and satirical itinerary of the author. It consists of a series of imaginary dialogues between abstract characters (fictitious academicians and mythological figures) and describes seven imaginary worlds and seven imaginary hells. Man is represented in the totality of his sins in opposition to an ideal world, such as that of Sir Thomas More's *Utopia* (1516).

BIBLIOGRAPHY

Primary Works

Doni, Anton Francesco. *I marmi*. Edited by Ezio Chiorboli. Bari, Italy, 1928.

Doni, Anton Francesco. *I mondi e gli inferni*. Edited by Patrizia Pellizzari. Turin, Italy, 1994.

Doni, Anton Francesco. *Opere di P. Aretino e A. F. Doni*. Edited by Carlo Cordiè. Milan, 1976.

Secondary Works

Candela, Giuseppe. *Manierismo e condizioni della scrittura in Anton Francesco Doni*. New York, 1993.

Grendler, Paul F. *Critics of the Italian World 1530–1560: Anton Francesco Doni, Nicolò Franco, and Ortensio Lando*. Madison, Wis., 1969.

Ricottini Marsili-Libelli, Cecilia. *Anton Francesco Doni: Scrittore e stampatore*. Florence, 1960.

GIUSEPPE CANDELA

DONNE, JOHN (1572–1631), English poet, courtier, preacher, writer of religious prose and sermons. Born into a recusant Catholic family in Elizabethan London, Donne was schooled first by Catholic tutors (including, perhaps, his Jesuit uncle, Jasper Heywood) before going with his younger brother to Oxford at the age of twelve. Little evidence of his life between 1584 and 1591 survives: R. C. Bald claims that Donne attended both Oxford and Cambridge, leaving the university before the age of sixteen, when he would have had to swear the Elizabethan oath of allegiance, which committed Catholics refused to do. Donne may subsequently have traveled on the Continent before reappearing in London in the early 1590s. Dennis Flynn has argued that Donne left Oxford early, was taken to France in the Catholic earl of Derby's retinue, and traveled for some years with fellow Catholics before returning for service in the Derby household. The portrait miniature of Donne at eighteen in military garb, with the Spanish motto *Antes muerto que mudado* (Sooner dead than changed), suggests he fought or was prepared to fight on the Catholic side in continental religious warfare.

Early Secular Career. Donne enrolled in Thavies Inn in 1591, an Inn of Chancery serving to prepare young men for entrance into one of the four Inns of Court, which trained common lawyers. In 1592 he entered Lincoln's Inn, using it as a route to possible advancement in courtly service. The Inns (which the poet and playwright Ben Jonson called "the noblest nourceries of humanity and liberty in the kingdom") were a center of intellectual and literary activity as well as a fashionable milieu for socially and politically ambitious young men desiring access to the court or aristocratic households. Like the majority of Inns students, Donne did not seriously study law but rather used his residence at an Inn of Court for intellectual broadening, fashionable recreation, and making social contacts with elite society and centers of power. He later wrote his friend Sir Henry Goodyer that he had been "diverted [from legal studies] by the worst voluptuousness, which is an Hydroptique immoderate desire of humane learning and languages." Sir Richard Baker described the young Donne as "very neat; a great visiter of Ladies, a great frequenter of Playes, a great writer of conceited Verses."

John Donne. Anonymous portrait at Newbattle Abbey; c. 1595. FROM THE COLLECTION OF THE MARQUESS OF LOTHIAN

With the possible exception of some Latin epigrams surviving only in English translation, Donne's first poetry and prose were written at Lincoln's Inn. Like other Inns authors such as John Marston and Sir John Davies, he composed both satiric and socially iconoclastic pieces (intellectually charged works distinguished from the genres and polite manner of courtly literature): epigrams, verse satires, love elegies, verse letters to friends, prose paradoxes, and some of his lyrics (for example, "Song: Go and Catch a Falling Star," "The Indifferent," "The Curse," "Loves Diet," and "Loves Usury"). Responding to the revival of interest in Roman erotic elegy, classical verse satire and epigram, and other courtly and anticourtly poetry, Donne was the first English writer to produce a vernacular collection of love elegies (though the dramatist and poet Christopher Marlowe had already done a translation of Ovid's *Amores*) and one of the first to compose a set of formal verse satires. In such love elegies as "The Bracelet" and "To His Mistress Going to Bed," he translated the social scene of Ovid's and Propertius's love elegies—and, in his first and second satires, of Horace's satires—to Elizabethan London.

These poems reflect the interests in philosophy, theology, science, and politics that made the Inns world one of intellectual and political ferment and the training ground for later active Parliamentarians. Donne designed these works and almost all his other secular prose and verse for manuscript circulation among select or "coterie" (usually educated male) readers, maintaining his status as a literary amateur in an age in which socially privileged and socially ambitious writers feared the social devaluation associated with the publishing literary author—what J. W. Saunders has called "the stigma of print." Such private circumstances also freed the poet to explore some topics that would expose him to censorship or political danger in the more public arena of print, or even in broad manuscript transmission.

Sometime, probably after the 1593 death of his younger brother Henry in prison (arrested for harboring a Catholic priest) and his entrance into government service in 1598, Donne probably backed away from the militant Catholicism of his family and moved toward Protestantism. Later, as a Protestant apologist, he referred to this as a slow process, in which he postponed his decision until he had "digested the whole body of Divinity, controverted between ours and the Romane Church." His religiously exploratory third satire, which is skeptical of the sectarian claims of both Catholicism and various forms of Protestantism, was probably composed in this transitional period—a time at which he lived in London, spending his small inheritance on maintaining the lifestyle of a young gentleman of fashion, probably composing some further elegies and lyric poems reflecting his involvement in courtly and polite amorousness.

Donne served as a "gentleman volunteer" in the late 1590s on two naval military expeditions against England's archenemy, Catholic Spain: the earl of Essex's raid on Cadiz in 1596 and the subsequent failed Azores expedition of 1597. His valedictory love elegy, "His Picture," was possibly connected with the former. His verse epistles to his closest friend from Lincoln's Inn, Christopher Brooke, "The Storme" and "The Calme," were associated with the latter: in them Donne announces his self-critical involvement in the larger political world. In between the two adventures, he may have written his dangerously anticourt and deeply pessimistic fourth satire. The friendship he formed on the second expedition with a fellow gentleman volunteer, the younger Thomas Egerton, led to employment as a secretary with the elder Thomas Egerton, Queen Elizabeth's lord keeper of the great seal (chief judicial officer), for whom he worked from 1598 to 1602, beginning a promising career in government service. His fifth satire, addressed to his employer and dealing with the abuses in the justice system Egerton was charged to reform, is the work of a political insider: Egerton, in fact, secured Donne a seat in the Parliament of 1601.

Donne continued to compose verse letters—for example, to his friend Sir Henry Wotton, with whom he shared much of his earlier verse and prose—but he also, no doubt, wrote love poems reflecting his involvement in the social life of the court and elite society: some in a polite, Petrarchan idiom, such as "Loves Deitie," "The Will," and "The Blossom," and others of a more cynical sort, such as "Loves Alchymie" and "Farewell to Love." Some lyrics associated with Donne's courtship of Ann More, who, like Donne, lived in Egerton's York House (under the care of Lady Egerton before the latter's death in January 1600) probably belong to this period: poems such as "The Broken Heart," "The Anniversarie," "The Good-Morrow," "Loves Growth," "Loves Infiniteness," "A Lecture upon the Shadow," and "A Valediction: Of My Name in the Window." These all utilize the sorts of intellectually adroit and emotionally sensitive dramatic speakers Donne developed in elegies like "On His Mistress" and "His Picture" and in the earlier lyrics that escape the sensibility of the Ovidian libertine lover. The dating of these and of most of Donne's lyrics later (posthumously) gathered as his *Songs and Sonnets* is uncertain, but we should keep in mind Ben Jonson's comment to the Scottish poet William Drummond that Donne wrote "all his best pieces err he was 25 years old" (that is, before 1598).

Secular Career from 1602 to 1615.

The crucial event in Donne's secular career was his unauthorized marriage to the seventeen-year-old Ann in 1601, an elopement that lost him his position with Egerton and, in effect, ruined his secular courtly career. Though he moved from near destitution back to social and political involvement, finally becoming a member of Parliament again in 1614, Donne repeatedly failed in the first fourteen years of his marriage to find secure employment.

Some of the love lyrics allude to Donne's marriage, his socially outcast state, and his lack of employment in the early years of the Jacobean era—especially "The Sun Rising" and "The Canonization." He may have written poems like "A Valediction: Of Weeping" and "A Valediction: Forbidding Mourning" on the occasion of the reentry into active social and political life signaled by his leaving home in

Donne the Preacher. Engraving by Matthäus Merian the Younger (1621–1687); frontispiece to *Eighty Sermons Preached by That Learned and Reverend Divine, John Donne* (1640). PRIVATE COLLECTION/THE BRIDGEMAN ART LIBRARY

1605 to travel on the Continent with Sir Walter Chute, a journey of over a year, after which he and his growing family moved to Mitcham, near London, so he could resume his search for preferment and patronage.

He was introduced to the powerful court lady Lucy, countess of Bedford, by his friend Henry Goodyer (to whom he tried to write weekly and with whom he shared his deepest thoughts and feelings), and Donne enjoyed her patronage from around 1607. For Lady Bedford he composed not only intellectually dense encomiastic verse epistles, but also some lyric poems in the manner of complimentary courtly amorousness: "Twicknam Garden" and perhaps "The Funeral," "The Feaver," and "Air and Angels." Although she was a literary patron of such writers as Ben Jonson, Samuel Daniel, and John Florio, Donne sought primarily political and social patronage from her, well aware of her role as a courtly power broker. She allowed herself to serve as godmother to Donne's daughter Lucy in 1608.

Donne also began a friendship with the devout Magdalen Herbert (later Lady Danvers) in this period. For her, Donne composed prose epistles and one verse letter ("Mad paper stay") as well as *La Corona,* a short set of holy sonnets. He was not only her close friend for the rest of her life, finally preaching her funeral sermon in 1627, but he also shared his friendship with her two poet-sons, Sir Edward and George—especially the former, with whom he engaged in competitive poetic exchanges with lyrics like "The Extasie" and "The Primrose," his 1610 verse epistle "To Sir Edward Herbert, at Julyers," his elegy on Prince Henry (written, Ben Jonson claims, "to match Sir Edward Herbert in obscureness"), and possibly the lyrics "The Undertaking" and "Negative Love."

During this same period, Donne composed most of his "Holy Sonnets," poems whose self-harrowing feelings mirror some of the depression and despair expressed in his contemporary letters to Goodyer, much of which is associated with his failure to find useful employment. Drawing on both Catholic and Protestant meditative disciplines, these powerful, theologically Calvinist poems are some of the best sacred poetry of the period, strongly influencing the religious verse of George Herbert.

Donne's "paradoxical" argument in favor of suicide, *Biathanatos,* was composed at this time but circulated only in manuscript to restricted readers. Donne also wrote prose "problems," "characters," and the comic *Catalogus librorum aulicorum* (The courtier's library)—works whose satire, skepticism, and personal bitterness bespeak deep social and political disillusionment. With his association with the religious polemicist Dean Thomas Morton, through whom he involved himself in the international controversy over the Jacobean oath of allegiance, Donne came to compose his first substantial religious prose, the polemical *Pseudo-Martyr* (1610), which argued, in opposition to Cardinal Robert Bellarmine and other Catholic writers, that English Catholics should not refuse to take the oath. He attempted to appeal to more moderate Catholics in criticizing the rigid position of the Jesuits, whom he subsequently attacked viciously in his Menippean satire, *Ignatius His Conclave* (published in both Latin and English in 1611). Beyond their immediate arguments, however, Donne's *Biathanatos, Pseudo-Martyr,* and *Ignatius His Conclave* (like the other prose from the first decade of James I's rule) contain implicit political criticism of Jacobean government and political ideology, demonstrating the kinds of critical and intellectual independence Donne valued throughout his writings.

In the years preceding his decision to abandon the pursuit of political preferment and to accept King James's suggestion that he find preferment by entering the ministry, Donne sought other patronage as he agonized over his spiritual life. He became a client of Sir Robert Drury, with whom he traveled to France in 1611 and 1612, and for whom he wrote and published two "Anniversaries" and a "Funeral Elegy," poems commemorating the death of his patron's fifteen-year-old daughter. These complex philosophical, theological, and moral meditations, however, proved so subject to misinterpretation that Donne regretted their printing. Jonson quipped to Drummond that "Done . . . for not being understood would perish." Donne also composed the intellectually convoluted elegy for Prince Henry and further verse letters to Lady Bedford and to other potential patronesses. To this period also belongs one of his best religious poems, "Goodfriday, 1613. Riding Westward," and his lay-theological *Essays in Divinity*—both of which works involve intense spiritual self-scrutiny.

Religious Career (1615–1631). At the end of 1614 Donne made his "valediction to the world" (as he put it in a letter to Goodyer), becoming ordained as an Anglican priest in January 1615. King James quickly made him a royal chaplain and pressured Cambridge University to grant him a doctor of divinity degree. The following year (in addition to two other appointments) Donne was made reader in divinity at Lincoln's Inn, a position that required him to preach fifty sermons per year.

From his ecclesiastical years 160 sermons survive, some having been published singly or in small groups during his lifetime, others published posthumously—in 1634 (*Six Sermons*), 1640 (*Eighty Sermons*), 1649 (*Fifty Sermons*), and 1661 (*Twenty-six Sermons*), the last three folio volumes edited by his son John, a minister. He usually preached from notes and only later wrote out texts of sermons for manuscript circulation or printing (most of them in two intense periods of composition in 1625 and 1630). Donne became one of the most highly esteemed preachers of his day, addressing congregations at Lincoln's Inn, at the Jacobean and Caroline courts, at parish churches, at Saint Paul's Cathedral, and in other public and private venues. As always, he was sensitive to the social and political contexts in which his words were received. His Lincoln's Inn sermons are highly charged intellectually, though no less fervent devotionally than his other sermons. Especially during the politically turbulent 1620s, he served as an apologist for royal foreign policy and the Anglican via media in his role as court preacher and as dean of Saint Paul's, criticizing both radical Protestantism and uncompromising Catholicism. Despite his Protestant English nationalism, however, he tried to promote religious reconciliation, emphasizing those fundamental theological issues on which he believed all Christians agreed.

Donne responded to the death of his wife in 1617 with an elegiac sonnet ("Since She Whom I Loved Hath Paid Her Last Debt"), a poem that has been seen as a conflicted expression of his love for her. R. C. Bald and others have argued that Donne's religious commitment deepened after this loss. In 1619 Donne left England for the Continent as chaplain on Viscount Doncaster's embassy to Germany, an occasion he marked with a "valedictory" sermon at Lincoln's Inn and one of his best religious poems, "A Hymn to Christ, at the Author's Last Going into Germany." At this time, he also left many of his poems and a manuscript copy of *Biathanatos* with his courtly friend Sir Robert Ker (the namesake and cousin of the earl of Somerset), explaining that the prose work was "written by *Jack Donne,* and not by D.[octor] *Donne*"—thus suggesting the contrast Sir Izaak Walton later highlighted in his biography between the fashionably iconoclastic secular intellectual and poet, on the one hand, and the serious divine and preacher, on the other.

Early in 1620, he returned to Lincoln's Inn, cultivating court connections like the powerful duke of Buckingham, through whom he obtained the prestigious deanship of Saint Paul's Cathedral, a post in which he preached as a self-conscious official ecclesiastical spokesperson. He was a strong defender of the king's policies—his first published sermon defended the "Directions for Preachers" James issued to silence criticism of his handling of domestic and international religiopolitical affairs.

In late 1623 Donne was seriously ill with relapsing fever and composed both "A Hymn to God My God, in My Sickness" and his prose *Devotions* (published 1624). He fell into his terminal illness late in 1630 and preached his last sermon at court on 25 February 1631 (posthumously published as *Death's Duel*), dying 31 March 1631 while his promotion to a bishopric was pending. He named as his literary executor

Donne's Effigy. Funeral monument in St. Paul's Cathedral, London, by Nicholas Stone; 1631. St. Paul's Cathedral, London/The Bridgeman Art Library

Henry King, who ushered the first collected edition of Donne's poems into print in 1633. Other editions followed in 1635, 1639, 1649, 1650, 1654, 1669, and 1719, and an edition of Donne's *Letters to Severall Persons of Honour* was brought out by his son in 1651.

Donne was arguably the most influential lyric poet in seventeenth-century England—his work was well known in manuscript circulation well before the appearance of the 1633 edition. His intellectualism, "conceited" and forceful style, urbanity, rhetorical complexity, and dramatic handling of the lyric form all had a strong impact on such successors as Thomas Carew, George Herbert, Abraham Cowley, and Andrew Marvell. Donne's reputation for the next two generations (reinforced by Walton's biography in 1640 and shaped by the published secular and religious writings) was both as a witty poet and as an eloquent preacher. Donne fell out of fashion in the eighteenth and nineteenth centuries, until, following Sir Edmund Gosse's biography (1899) and Sir Herbert Grierson's Oxford edition of the poetry (1921), he was rediscovered and appropriated by modernist poets and critics, including T. S. Eliot and the New Critics, the latter inaugurating a large body of formalist interpretations before more historically oriented scholars and critics of the last quarter of the twentieth century resituated Donne's poetry and prose in their original sociocultural matrix. His status in the canon of early modern English writing is now secure.

BIBLIOGRAPHY

Primary Works

Biathanatos. Edited by Ernest W. Sullivan II. Newark, N.J., and London, 1984.

The Courtier's Library; or, Catalogus Librorum Aulicorum. Edited by Evelyn M. Simpson, with a translation by Percy Simpson. London, 1930.

The Divine Poems of John Donne. 2d ed. Edited by Helen Gardner. Oxford, 1978.

The Elegies, and the Songs and Sonnets. Edited by Helen Gardner. Oxford, 1965.

The Epithalamions, Anniversaries, and Epicedes. Edited by W. Milgate. Oxford, 1978.

Essays in Divinity. Edited by Evelyn M. Simpson. Oxford, 1952.

Ignatius His Conclave. An edition of the Latin and English texts by T. S. Healy. Oxford, 1969.

Letters to Severall Persons of Honour (1651). A facsimile edition with an introduction by M. Thomas Hester. Delmar, N.Y., 1977.

Paradoxes and Problems. Edited by Helen Peters. Oxford, 1980.

Pseudo-Martyr. Edited by Anthony Raspa. Montreal and Buffalo, N.Y., 1993.

The Satires, Epigrams, and Verse Letters. Edited by W. Milgate. Oxford, 1967.

The Sermons of John Donne. Edited by George R. Potter and Evelyn M. Simpson. 10 vols. Berkeley and Los Angeles, 1953–1962.

The Variorum Edition of the Poetry of John Donne. General editor, Gary A. Stringer. Vol. 6, *The Anniversaries and the Epicedes and Obsequies*. Vol. 8, *The Epigrams, Epithalamions, Epitaphs, Inscriptions, and Miscellaneous Poems*. Blooming-

ton, Ind., 1995. When complete, this eight-volume edition will be the standard for Donne's poetry.

Secondary Works

Bald, R. C. *John Donne: A Life*. Oxford, 1970. Reprint, with corrections, Oxford, 1986. Still the basis for the study of Donne's life and his historical context.

Carey, John. *John Donne: Life, Mind and Art*. 2d ed. London, 1990. Lively discussion of all of Donne's writings, emphasizing the impact of Donne's apostasy on his life and work.

Flynn, Dennis. *John Donne and the Ancient Catholic Nobility*. Bloomington, Ind., 1995. Highly speculative, but useful for its information about Catholic recusant culture.

Gosse, Edmund. *The Life and Letters of John Donne*. 2 vols. London, 1899. Reprint, Gloucester, Mass., 1959. Useful for the letters it prints.

Jonson, Ben. "Conversations with William Drummond of Hawthornden." In *Ben Jonson*. Edited by C. H. Herford and Percy Simpson. Oxford, 1925. Vol. 1, pp. 128–178.

Marotti, Arthur F. *John Donne, Coterie Poet*. Madison, Wis., and London, 1986. Discusses Donne as a poet writing primarily for manuscript circulation to known, restricted audiences in various sociopolitical contexts.

Marotti, Arthur F., ed. *Critical Essays on John Donne*. New York, 1994. Recent historical analyses of Donne's writings.

Roberts, John R., ed. *Essential Articles for the Study of John Donne's Poetry*. Hamden, Conn., 1975. A large and rich selection of critical and scholarly essays on Donne.

Saunders, J. W. "The Stigma of Print: A Note on the Social Bases of Tudor Poetry." *Essays in Criticism* 1 (1951): 139–164.

Smith, A. J., ed. *John Donne: The Critical Heritage*. 2 vols. London and Boston, 1975–1996.

Webber, Joan. *Contrary Music: The Prose Style of John Donne*. Madison, Wis., 1963. Still the best general study of Donne's prose.

ARTHUR F. MAROTTI

DORIA, ANDREA (1466–1560), Genoese admiral and politician who played a key role in the political and military events in Italy during and after the Italian Wars (1494–1559). Doria was born into a minor branch of a Genoese noble family on 30 November 1466 at Oneglia, in western Liguria. Orphaned as a youth, he entered military service under Pope Innocent VIII at the age of eighteen, through the auspices of his cousin Nicolò Doria. After holding a series of commands under the papacy, the duchy of Urbino, and the kingdom of Naples, he entered Genoese service, again under Nicolò, this time commanding troops on behalf of the Casa San Giorgio. In 1507 the Casa gave him his own contract to put down a rebellion in Corsica.

By 1516 Doria was commanding a pair of galleys in a fleet led by Nicolò. Between 1513 and 1528 he held a variety of naval posts, usually as an ally of King Francis I of France, taking part in actions against the Turks and Barbary pirates led by the infamous Barbarossa. Rising to the rank of admiral,

Doria became the key figure in French and papal naval power in the Mediterranean.

By 1525 the emperor Charles V had begun to court Doria in an attempt to lure the Genoese into the imperial camp. Events in Genoa aided the emperor. For some time efforts had been under way to reform the Genoese constitution, and Doria was among those interested in political change and the survival of an independent Genoese republic. He was instrumental in getting the republic to switch its allegiance to the Habsburgs in 1528. That revolt overthrew French rule and installed a stable republican regime under the protection of Spain, whose king was Charles I (the emperor Charles V).

Doria profited both politically and personally under the new regime. His personal authority and prestige were instrumental in controlling the traditional factional rivalries that had so often torn the republic apart before 1528. His power was further augmented by the personal *asiento,* or contract, that he had negotiated directly with Charles V as part of his price for backing the Spanish. The contract paid money directly to Doria to supply galleys to the Spanish in the Mediterranean. This arrangement not only netted him handsome profits but also made him the official middleman between the fledgling Genoese republic and its Spanish protectors. As such he was indispensable for both the day-to-day operation of the government and its continued survival in Spain's shadow.

Doria ruled Genoa as a prince in fact, though wisely not in name, from 1528 until his death on 25 November 1560. He held the office of prior from 1528 for the rest of his life, and through a series of constitutional reforms he engineered a political compromise that channeled old factional rivalries into productive institutional venues, thereby preserving the state. In so doing he transformed the traditionally fractious Genoese nobility into a political class with common interests. Thus Doria followed a pattern typical of other Italian rulers who sought to quell traditionally quarrelsome civic elites. It is with some justification, therefore, that he is still considered by modern Genoese as the father of his country.

See also **Genoa.**

BIBLIOGRAPHY

Lingua, Paolo. *Andrea Doria*. Milan, 1984.

Perria, Antonio. *Andrea Doria il corsaro*. Milan, 1982.

There is no comprehensive English-language biography of Doria.

KARL APPUHN

DOSSI, DOSSO. *See* **Ferrara,** *subentry on* **Art in Ferrara.**

DOVIZI, BERNARDO (da Bibbiena; 1470–1520), Tuscan diplomat, cardinal, playwright. Best known as Il Bibbiena, after the Tuscan town of his birth, Bernardo Dovizi entered Medici service in Florence. When his patrons were expelled from Florence in 1494, he followed them to Rome, though he was often away on diplomatic missions and visits to northern Italian courts. A favorite of two duchesses of Urbino, Elisabetta and Eleonora Gonzaga, Bibbiena also enjoyed good relationships with Isabella d'Este Gonzaga, duchess of Mantua, and with the Venetian patrician Pietro Bembo, an important courtier, poet, and literary theorist. Widely praised for his sense of humor, Bibbiena appears as a character in Baldassare Castiglione's *Il cortegiano* (*The Book of the Courtier*),

Bernardo Dovizi. Portrait by Raphael. PITTI, FLORENCE/ALINARI/ART RESOURCE

discoursing at length on the nature and function of humor. His powers of observation and writerly talents are evident in his many dispatches and letters.

While in Rome the Medici increased their influence by achieving eminence in the Catholic Church, laying the groundwork for their return to Florence. Integral to their plans were the efforts of Bibbiena, whose negotiating skills made him indispensable to Pope Julius II, then embroiled in the Wars of Cambrai (1509–1517). With Julius's support, the Medici returned to Florence in 1512. The following year, after Julius's death, Cardinal Giovanni de' Medici became Pope Leo X, largely as a result of Bibbiena's efforts. Leo appointed Bibbiena papal treasurer, named him cardinal, and sent him on a variety of crucial diplomatic missions necessitated by the wars. Bibbiena died after a lingering illness; rumors of poisoning are now discounted. A patron of the arts, Bibbiena was the subject of a portrait by Raphael.

Shortly before Leo's election, Bibbiena's play *La calandria* (The follies of Calandro) was staged in Urbino as part of an elaborate theatrical spectacle. Combining influences from Roman theater, Boccaccio's *Decameron*, Neoplatonic theory, and the comedies of Ferrarese poet and playwright Ludovico Ariosto with elements of daily life in Rome pushed to absurd limits, *La calandria* marks the opening of the mature phase of Italian Renaissance theater. Critical reaction to it centers on two interpretations: the first as a commentary on the collapse of Italian political power and the decadence of contemporary society, and the second as a refined manipulation of theatrical conventions. Although often treated as mutually exclusive, both interpretations are supported by the play. The plot device of twins is borrowed from Plautus but changed from boy-boy to boy-girl, permitting an allusion to the Neoplatonic concept of the hermaphrodite, the cross-dressing of both characters, and a series of comic confusions. Love, one of the greatest preoccupations of Renaissance culture, is shown to exalt and strengthen women but to weaken and humiliate men, especially Calandro. It also makes the clever servant master of all. This damage to the image of the strong patriarchal male is compounded by references to contemporary military defeats of Italian states by foreign powers. Printed in 1521, *La calandria* was frequently staged and imitated in Italy and France.

BIBLIOGRAPHY

Primary Works

Dovizi, Bernardo. *La calandria*. In *La commedia del Cinquecento*. Edited by Guido Davico Bonino. Vol. 1. Turin, Italy, 1977. Pages 3–87.

Dovizi, Bernardo. *Epistolario di Bernardo Dovizi da Bibbiena*. Edited by Giuseppe Moncallero. 2 vols. Florence, 1955, 1965. Annotated correspondence of Bibbiena.

Dovizi, Bernardo. *The Follies of Calandro, 1513*. Translation by Oliver Evans of *La calandria*. In *The Genius of the Italian Theater*. Edited by Eric Bentley. New York, 1964. Pages 31–98.

Secondary Works

D'Amico, Jack. "Drama and the Court in *La calandria*." *Theatre Journal* 43 (1991): 93–106. Summarizes recent scholarship; situates *La calandria* in the context of contemporary theater and its equivocal relationship to power.

Fontes-Baratto, Anna. "Les fêtes à Urbin en 1513 et la *Calandria* de Bernardo Dovizi da Bibbiena." In *Les écrivains et le pouvoir en Italie à l'époque de la Renaissance*. Edited by André Rochon. Paris, 1974. Connects rise of vernacular theater and spread of Tuscan language with growth of Medici power. Pages 45–79.

Moncallero, Giuseppe. *Il cardinale Bernardo Dovizi da Bibbiena, umanista e diplomatico (1470–1520)*. Florence, 1953. Thorough and detailed biography; summarizes scholarship connecting *Calandria* to Roman and contemporary plays.

Ruffini, Franco. *Commedia e festa nel Rinascimento: La "Calandria" alla corte di Urbino*. Bologna, Italy, 1986. Sees Bibbiena as epitomizing complex, conflicting urges of the Renaissance, especially desire and reason.

LINDA L. CARROLL

DRAKE, FRANCIS (c. 1540–1596), seaman. The first Englishman to circumnavigate the globe, Francis Drake was raised at Chatham, where his father was chaplain to the dockyard. The family was of West Country stock and Drake was always associated with the port city of Plymouth, which he later served as mayor and member of Parliament. John Hawkins introduced him to the Caribbean; Drake accompanied Hawkins on his ill-fated third expedition of 1567 and, after much of Hawkins's fleet was destroyed by the Spanish at San Juan de Ulúa in the Gulf of Mexico, appears to have abandoned his commander and sailed home alone in his ship, the *Judith*. Hawkins, who lost all the other vessels except his own *Minion*, evidently understood and never reproached Drake.

Drake, eight years younger than Hawkins, now assumed the role of principal English navigator. He undertook three voyages to the West Indies between 1570 and 1572. His expedition of 1577 ultimately took him around the world, although circumnavigation was not part of his original plan. He passed the West Indies, sailed through the Strait of Magellan at the south tip of South America, and explored the coast of California, which he claimed for the English crown and named New Albion. Failing to find the northwest passage predicted by geographers, he then decided to sail west, through what became known as the East Indies, to Africa. Early in 1580

Francis Drake. Portrait by a follower of Marcus Gheeraerts. NATIONAL MARITIME MUSEUM, LONDON

Drake rounded the Cape of Good Hope, and after he reached Sierra Leone he rejoined an established trade route to England. His first words on reaching Plymouth in September, inquiring whether Queen Elizabeth was still alive, are famous. The *Golden Hind* thus became the first English ship to sail around the world, and Drake the second mariner of any nationality to accomplish the feat.

During Elizabeth's later years Drake was caught up in England's hostility to Spain. Because of the tragedy at San Juan de Ulúa, he had personal reasons for animosity to Philip II. In April 1587 he led a fleet of six of the queen's ships into the Spanish harbor at Cádiz. After several days' fighting the city surrendered, and Drake could claim that he had burned, sunk, or captured thirty-seven Spanish vessels. He had "singed the King of Spain's beard" and delayed the departure of the Spanish Armada for a year. On his way home he secured the surrender of Henry the Navigator's castle at Sagres and, at Cape St. Vincent, burned a large number of barrel staves which the Spanish had intended to make into casks to hold the Armada's provisions. Garrett Mattingly, the great historian of the Armada, believed that burning the staves was more important than burning the ships at Cádiz.

When the Spanish Armada did set sail in 1588 Drake played a leading role in the defense of England. His flagship, appropriately, was the *Revenge*. After the defeat of the Armada there were persistent rumors that Drake had been captured, wounded, or killed, but they were refuted by the English tract "A Pack of Spanish Lies." In a counter-Armada of 1589 Drake returned to Spain and destroyed much Spanish shipping.

Drake was also involved in the effort to colonize Virginia, but when his first attempt failed he brought the settlers back to England in 1586. He died off Portobello in a final unsuccessful expedition to the West Indies, which he commanded jointly with Hawkins in 1596.

See also **Exploration.**

BIBLIOGRAPHY

Andrews, Kenneth R. *Drake's Voyages*. London, 1967.
Cummins, John. *Francis Drake: The Lives of a Hero*. New York, 1995.
Mattingly, Garrett. *The Armada*. Boston, 1959.

STANFORD E. LEHMBERG

DRAMA. [This entry includes three subentries on drama in general:

Religious Drama
Tragedy
Erudite Comedy

For discussion of drama in England, in France, and in Spain, see the following three main entries.]

Religious Drama

Religious drama in the Renaissance encompassed a broad range of dramatic forms and subjects, some of which originated as early as the thirteenth century. Medieval forms of religious theater—Passion plays, miracle plays depicting the life and miracles of a favorite saint, and allegorical dramas portraying the constant struggle between virtue and vice—can be found in most of western and southern Europe from around 1350 until the early 1600s.

Passion or mystery plays (*mystères*) were the most expansive and costly works to perform. Lasting several days, if not weeks, they dominated the social, economic, and cultural life of the sponsoring city and, at their height around 1400 in England and 1500 in France and the Holy Roman Empire, engaged hundreds of townspeople at various outdoor locations in elaborate representations of biblical events from the Fall of Man through the Resurrection. In Italy, Passion and miracle plays were occasionally sponsored, acted, and written by nuns in convents but more frequently by members of confraternities, lay organizations whose brethren regularly participated in communal rituals of devotion. These *sacre rappresentazioni* (sacred representations), many of which focused on a single episode from Christ's life such as the Nativity or the Ascension, were generally performed, especially in Florence and Rome, as part of a grand religious pageant during Holy Week or in celebration of a patron saint. The repertoire ranged from plays with texts, biblical characters, allegorical figures in ornate costumes, and elaborate special effects to recitations of scriptural passages with musical accompaniment and *tableaux vivants* (posed biblical, allegorical, or hagiographical scenes with costumed players) on carts paraded throughout the city.

Allegorical morality plays were also performed by the Italian confraternities, but they were especially popular in the Low Countries and northern France, where the local chambers of rhetoric (*rederijkers*), amateur societies of poets, presented works such as *Elckerlijk* (Everyman; c. 1495) depicting man's spiritual journey from birth to death. In the early 1500s ecclesiastical authorities increasingly decried Passion and miracle plays as sacrilegious, and with the onset of the renewed piety of the Reformation and Counter-Reformation, such presentations were prohibited, albeit unsuccessfully, in France, England, Italy, and the Protestant lands of the Holy Roman Empire.

Many of the themes and characters of medieval theater found new life in the neoclassical dramas of humanist playwrights. Between 1450 and 1550 in England, France, the Low Countries, and the Holy Roman Empire, a large corpus of Latin drama arose, in which biblical subjects (Abraham, Joseph, the Prodigal Son, etc.) and hagiographical subjects (such as early Christian martyrs) were presented in the form and language of Roman comedy and tragedy (Plautus, Terence, and Seneca). These dramas were usually performed with modest decor in Latin grammar schools by youths desirous of combining Latin language skills with spiritual edification. After 1550, Jesuit and Benedictine school playwrights continued this humanist Latin tradition in Catholic lands until the late 1700s. Humanist religious drama also flourished in the vernacular on school, court, and civic stages in Italy, France, England, and the Holy Roman Empire throughout the 1500s, culminating in the religious tragedies of the Netherlander Joost van den Vondel (1587–1679) and John Milton (*Samson Agonistes;* 1671).

BIBLIOGRAPHY

Blackburn, Ruth H. *Biblical Drama under the Tudors.* The Hague, Netherlands; and Paris, 1971. Plot summaries of sixteenth-century religious plays with little regard for the sociohistorical context.

Parente, James A., Jr. *Religious Drama and the Humanist Tradition: Christian Theater in Germany and the Netherlands, 1500–1680.* Leiden, Netherlands; and New York, 1987. Humanist religious drama and its afterlife in seventeenth-century neoclassical theater.

Pieri, Marzia. *La nascita del teatro moderno: In Italia tra quindici e sedici secolo.* Turin, Italy, 1989. Contains chapter on Renaissance religious drama in Italy and its connection to other dramatic forms.

Street, J. S. *French Sacred Drama from Bèze to Corneille: Dramatic Forms and Their Purpose in Early Modern Theater.* Cambridge, U.K.; and New York, 1983. Best English-language survey of French religious drama.

JAMES A. PARENTE JR.

Tragedy

Ancient tragedy, as Lodovico Dolce claimed in his *Ifigenia* (1551), came from Athens to sixteenth-century Florence after a short stay in classical Rome. It was through Renaissance Italy that the noble genre, as it was called, made its way into modern Western culture. Indeed, Italian playwrights wishing to revive ancient theater paved the way for great tragedians like Jean Racine and William Shakespeare. Interest in the concept and function of tragedy was very much alive throughout the Middle Ages, as evinced by the writings of scholars such as Aelius Donatus, Isidore of Seville, and Dante, who thought of tragedy as a poem dealing mainly with the ghastly crimes of wicked kings. They placed little emphasis on tragedy as a theatrical representation other than making incidental references to its being recited or mimed in public. Clearly, they were working mostly in the dark, since the very few ancient dramatic texts that were known were mostly in excerpts or in anecdotal form.

Seneca and Aristotle. The idea of tragedy as a literary genre largely intended for a reading audience was further supported by the discovery of Seneca's plays in the early fourteenth century. The growing predilection for dramatic reading contributed to the production of a number of Latin tragedies that, adhering to medieval and Senecan poetics, emphasized the literary aspect of drama while neglecting its stage properties. It did not propose to revive the ancient art by depicting contemporary realities, although, in some instances, it dramatized recent historical events. Albertino Mussato's *Ecerinis* (c. 1315), one of the better-known early humanist tragedies, features relatively few modern elements and has virtually no theatrical qualities. The only modern aspect of the drama is its plot, which is based on the brutal deeds of Ezzelino III da Romano (1194–1259), ruler of Padua. While the play rivals Seneca in its atrocities and moral maxims, much in the text suggests that Mussato was more interested in imitating the classical art form than in reviving it. It is also clear that he, like other humanist playwrights, was never fully aware of the genre's theatrical qualities.

This one-dimensional view of tragedy prevailed well into the sixteenth century as the genre began to take hold in the literary consciousness of the Renaissance. Gian Giorgio Trissino's *Sofonisba* (1515), for instance, though reprinted six times and translated into French, was not performed until 1562. Giovanni Rucellai's *Rosmunda* (c. 1515) was reprinted at least five times in the course of the century, but there is no record of its being performed before the eighteenth century. While no tragedy had yet appeared on stage, there was a growing awareness of the genre's theatrical dimension. Playwrights and critics were beginning to identify the spectator rather than the reader as the intended audience of the genre. Trissino, reiterating a belief expressed earlier, wrote in the fifth section of his *Poetica* (1529), where he discusses tragic theory, that the scenery is the first thing that comes before the eyes of the spectator and is the principal source of pleasure.

Interest in the genre was intensified by the occasional discovery of ancient Greek texts. Eagerness to bring the content of newly found texts to a wide audience led to translations in the vernacular and reworkings appropriately called *vulgarizzamenti*. Alessandro de' Pazzi, for instance, translated Euripides's *Iphigenia in Tauris* (1524) and *Cyclops* (1525) and Sophocles's *Oedipus Rex* (1525), while Dolce translated Seneca's tragedies (1560). Enthusiasm for the classics was also felt in France, where Lazare de Baïf and Guillaume Bochetel translated Sophocles's *Electra* (1537) and Euripides's *Hecuba* (1544), respectively. In England, George Gascoigne and Francis Kinwelmersh translated Dolce's *Giocasta* (1566). The effort not only made ancient tragedy more accessible to audiences outside the learned community, it also provided firsthand knowledge of the genre's most basic features. Though fascinated by the classics and ancient culture, most Italian playwrights were not content merely to translate or imitate an art form whose aesthetic principles and cultural realities had long since vanished. Thus, with all

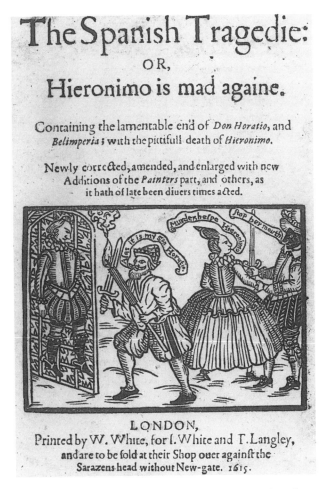

Thomas Kyd's *Spanish Tragedy.* Frontispiece to the 1615 edition.

due reverence to the genius of the past, they set out to give dramatic expression to their own culture and individual aspirations, inaugurating a revitalization process that would bring the ancient genre to life.

The process was facilitated by the diffusion in the second half of the sixteenth century of Aristotle's *Poetics,* which, together with Horace's *Ars poetica,* provided basic guidance and formal authority. However, ancient precepts, though of fundamental importance, were ultimately open to a wide range of interpretations. Debates spread through Europe, especially in France, England, and Spain where translations of Horace's *Ars poetica* and commentaries on Aristotle's *Poetics,* based in part on Ludovico Castelvetro's *Poetica di Aristotele vulgarizzata* (1570), provided arguments in support of or against one's dramatic notions or preferences. Playwrights would often appeal to the authority of Horace whenever their innovations departed from Aristotelian precepts, and vice versa. Differences of opinion led to lively disputes ranging from whether it was better to imitate the Greeks or the Romans and whether plots should be based on historical or fictional events.

Tragedy and Contemporary Society. If the debates over the aesthetics of tragedy failed to reach general consensus on several important issues, they succeeded in generating widespread interest in the genre, as questions of poetics, usually discussed by scholars in letters to their friends or influential patrons, reached an ever-widening audience. Appreciation went beyond pure literary gratification, as tragedy began to come out of the reading "closet" and slowly regained its rightful place on the stage. The honor of restoring tragedy to the stage was proudly claimed by Giambattista Cinzio Giraldi, one of the most prolific dramatists of the century and perhaps the most important. The 1541 performance of his *Orbecche,* the first regular Italian tragedy performed in Renaissance Italy, revived a long-lost theatrical tradition that was promptly received with great enthusiasm. Dramatic performances thus became ever more frequent as patrons commissioned plays and subsidized stage productions, which, in the absence of public theaters, were put on either at court or in private residences before large but select groups of spectators. The audience in Ferrara for Dolce's *Marianna* in 1565, for example, was so numerous that it actually hindered the performance.

Admittedly, tragedy never reached the level of popularity enjoyed by comedy. This was due in part to its high style and gravity, which appealed only to the educated few. However, a more pragmatic reason was undoubtedly the high cost associated with stage production. Unlike comedy, tragedy required the construction of majestic sets and the use of elaborate costumes for both the royal characters and their large retinues. The burden of such expenses made performances rare; on the other hand, the pageantry that they engendered made them appropriate for celebrating important events, state weddings and official state visits, in particular. Epistolary testimony, such as Filippo Pigafetta's description of the 1585 performance of Orsatto Giustiniani's *Edipo* at the Palladio in Vicenza, indicates that the occasion was normally characterized by carefully staged protocol and pageantry, reflecting the sponsors' wealth and political influence. Members of the nobility, in ostentatious display of family colors and prestige, participated in the festivities and sanctioned with their presence the sociopolitical system that legitimized their privileged status.

It is important to keep in mind that this overt political use of the genre did not extend to the dramatic text, but only to the pageantry occasioned by the performance. And, though the rhetoric of power spilled into the auditorium, where seating arrangements reflected status and influence, the performance remained largely an artistic presentation of a fictional world. The failure to distinguish between textual import and extratextual concerns has led critics to reduce Renaissance tragedy to the role of state propaganda and to view playwrights as noblemen typically servile to their own privileged class. Such a view is highly questionable because several important playwrights of the sixteenth century, such as Pietro Aretino, Dolce, and Luigi Groto, were not members of the nobility and had therefore little interest in promoting a political system that essentially excluded them. The suggestion is debatable also because it fails to take into account the irrepressible urge that normally inspires poetic creativity. Sponsors could commission the labor but not the genius, which alone determines a work's greatness or lack thereof.

Although the wish for patronage was undoubtedly a main motivation for the artists' work, the urge to rise above their rivals ultimately roused their poetic genius to greater achievements. They aimed to go beyond the mere imitation of the classics and to bring on stage a world that, while retaining its ancient allure, bore meaningful contrasts and similarities to their own. Building on the knowledge acquired through translations, playwrights composed their own plays, drawing plot material from historical legends of the near and distant past, classical mythology, collections of novelle, or simply adapting story lines already dramatized in antiquity. This last alternative was perhaps the most popular because it provided a rich source of tested material and a basic model of the genre's formal aims and limitations.

Excessive reliance on ancient dramas has caused modern scholars to dismiss the Italians as mere copyists lacking originality. This view is rather narrow, for it overlooks the advantages of recasting old plots. The most obvious advantage was that well-known plots allowed the spectators to concentrate less on the story line and more on the playwright's innovations. This view also assumes that good theater must be original. What, then, of Euripides, Sophocles, Aeschylus, and Seneca, all of whom rewrote popular stories?

Themes of Tragedy. Following the ancients, the Italians found guidance in the poetics of imitation, best exemplified by the classical simile of the bees that turn pollen from various flowers into a product that is ultimately unique. Their achievements were measured not in terms of the story line but of the innovations that characterized their work. Ultimately, what the audience came to appreciate was the playwright's dramaturgical skills that helped to narrow the gap between the fiction of the stage and the reality of the auditorium.

This bridging made it easier for theater to fulfill its basic function, "docere et diligere" (to teach and to entertain), the aim of all poetry. The didactic scope of a play was usually voiced by Prologue, an actor on the stage who often called attention to the forces of good and evil informing the dramatic action. It also exhorted the audience to learn from the tragic events they were about to see. Commenting on the moral role of theater, Prologue in Giraldi's *Selene* (1554?) asserts that theater was conceived for the purpose of teaching the way to a virtuous life to thousands of people. Through the dramatized events, Prologue continues, audiences would learn to follow virtue and eschew evil.

The notion of right and wrong, of good and evil, is not always absolute, for it is often shaped by changing cultural trends and is therefore peculiar to a specific moment in the history of a society. The humanists, for instance, considered honor, glory, and honesty intrinsic princely virtues. However, a generation later, with the proliferation of armed conflicts, fraud and violence became the basic qualities of an ideal prince. In turn, these Machiavellian qualities were eventually repudiated by reason-of-state writers, who found them incompatible with the prevailing Counter-Reformation ideology.

The didactic goal of theater, then, was not merely to teach the difference between right and wrong or to show the effects of good and evil in absolute terms. Rather, it was to encourage the audience to reflect on, define, or redefine the evolving values and ideological notions (moral, political, religious, social) underpinning their social institutions. A topic of great relevance to the times and dominant in many a Renaissance tragedy was the notion of kingship, which Machiavellian theory had brought to the forefront of political discourse. The ideology informing the role of most stage rulers clearly mirrors the ongoing debate on royal prerogatives and princely virtues. The king's usual dismissal of his counselor's advice to govern with justice, prudence, and other princely qualities dramatizes Machiavelli's rejection of humanist notions of kingship as too idealistic and incompatible with reality. However, in the violent

deaths of bloodthirsty stage tyrants, audiences recognized the rejection of Machiavellian amoralism and the emergence of a political philosophy that was more in keeping with moral and religious values of Counter-Reformation Italy.

Another topic with profound cultural implications that found a forum on the stage was the growing challenge to the traditional view of women. The issue was dramatized by conflicting perspectives articulating the role of the female tragic victim. On the one hand, she was characterized as subservient, of limited intellect, and given to the quick display of emotions and other frailties. On the other hand, she was portrayed as an intelligent and strong individual victimized by cultural prejudice. The contrast became dramatic as the heroine demanded the recognition of her intellectual ability and, inherently, the right to live with the human dignity that derives from freedom of action and expression. In most dramas, the debate ended with the heroine's tragic demise; however, the composed resolve with which victims, such as Sofonisba and Marianna, faced death earned them the admiration of both courtly stage and public theater audiences, elevating them to the status of their male counterparts.

A function of tragedy, then, was to provide a forum for expressing society's current views on its changing world, which prompted, as it evolved, the constant reassessment of existing beliefs and values. To be sure, Renaissance drama remained largely within the parameters of the classical Sophoclean conflict between the interests of the state and the rights of the individual. What set apart playwrights and their plays was the attention they called to specific aspects of the conflict, such as the tyrant's violence, claims of human dignity, ideals of liberty, or freedom of choice and expression. The specific nature of the conflict, then, made each tragedy unique and, at the same time, accounted for the ideological diversity that distinguished both the genre and the individual dramatist.

Performance and Audience. Whatever the issues informing the tragic conflict, the debate inevitably involved the audience, predisposing them in favor of one view or the other. Undoubtedly, vivid representations drew the attention of even the most indifferent spectators, forcing a social dialogue that could lead, depending on the issue and on the strength of its dramatization, to the questioning and perhaps the redefinition of existing beliefs and values. In this sense, tragedy was more than just the product and the mirror of profound ethical and political or religious crises, as has been suggested. It was also a vehicle that helped to generate constructive dialogue on issues of great social concern.

The extent to which theater succeeded as a significant cultural force largely hinged on its power to draw the audience into the dramatic action. To this end, playwrights followed the much debated notion of verisimilitude, which proposed that theatrical representations bear a strong resemblance to reality. Accordingly, the fictional world of the stage was to be represented in ways so realistic as to suspend the audience's instinctive reluctance to be drawn from their real world into the illusion of theater. To this purpose, dramatists, arguing against slavish imitation of long-dead traditions, insisted that plays be written in the vernacular and represent living customs. Dolce gave a simple but suggestive account of this principle of poetics when he proposed a new tragedy "con nuovi panni . . . vestita" (dressed in new clothes). A basic article of the new "clothes" was the language itself. Drawing heavily on literary tradition, playwrights took pride in their stylistic virtuosity, flaunting their familiarity with classics by such writers as Dante, Petrarch, and Ariosto. This emphasis on language contributed to a mostly verbal representation, earning Renaissance tragedy the reputation of being talky and static theater or simply more suitable for reading than for stage representation.

As with all generalizations, here too one finds exceptions, for many tragedies were better suited for the stage than for silent reading. The movements, the cries, the sounds, the blocking, and other audio and visual percepts articulating the theatricality of many a tragedy, such as Rucellai's *Oreste* (1515–1525?), make it difficult to sustain the critical contention that playwrights only rarely considered the relationship between the stage and the poetic text. Dramatists sensitive to the theatrical properties of the stage sought in earnest to enliven tragic representations. For instance, they opted, when possible, for a more visual representation either by actual showing or by spatial techniques. One such technique was the *hic et nunc,* or here and now, expedient, whereby the unrepresentable, such as the gathering of a crowd or a violent act, was described by an eyewitness as it was developing, there and then, out of sight but within earshot of the audience. Thus, the ghastly murder of King Sulmone at the hands of his daughter Orbecche, though perpetrated inside the palace, is brought, so to speak, into the open space of the stage by the chorus, who witnesses the killing and describes it to the spectators as it is taking place. In this way, the Italians avoided the gruesome scenes that

characterized the theater of Elizabethan dramatists, especially Thomas Kyd's *The Spanish Tragedie* (c. 1587) and Christopher Marlowe's *The Jew of Malta* (1588–1592).

Inherent in this technique was the notion that dramatic space expanded beyond the physical limits of the stage to include areas visually inaccessible to the audience. In several instances, this expansion led to the representation of events easily signified by sensorial signs, such as sounds and lighting. In Aretino's *Orazia* (1546), for instance, both the stage and the theater public are startled by the sounds of trumpets and cries of joy coming from afar. One of the most obvious and immediate effects of the noise is to expand the mimetic space of the dramatic action to the streets of Rome: the stage, as it were, of the events suggested by the uproar. Rome, then, visible only in scenic perspective, comes to life as the staging ground of events that through sensorial signs converge on the stage, where they acquire relevance to the main action.

Though language remained the most basic form of communication and indispensable for the full appreciation of theater, the increasing tendency to signify space and events through sensorial signs points to a growing awareness of the nature of theater as a mimesis of reality. The effect of these innovations was both entertaining and engaging, as spectators, always eager for entertainment, undoubtedly marveled at the ingenuity of the inventions. Most amusing was perhaps the realistic reproduction of certain natural phenomena, such as lightning and thunder, which in the past were often reported as having occurred somewhere offstage. In this way, the stage engaged the spectators both intellectually and sensorially, predisposing them to ignore the barrier between fiction and reality and accept more readily the illusion of theater. So totally involved in the representation, the audience could reflect on the contrasts and similarities that the fiction of the stage bore to the reality of their own world.

The genre that at the turn of the sixteenth century, when it first entered the literary consciousness of Renaissance Italy, represented a mere infatuation with the ancients had now become a theater in its own rights, grounded on living realities and on the aesthetic preferences of the times. Indeed, it spoke, as theater should, to the audience about their problems and preferences, in a manner that was both intelligible and entertaining. Its accomplishments and the lessons to be drawn from its failures constitute an important legacy to the art of theater both in Italy and abroad. Its most important legacy lies perhaps, as has been suggested, in having demonstrated that it was possible to create a modern tragic theater that might rival the ancient.

See also biographies of figures mentioned in this entry.

BIBLIOGRAPHY

Primary Works

Ariani, Marco, ed. *Il teatro italiano: La tragedia del Cinquecento.* 2 vols. Turin, Italy, 1977.

Cremante, Renzo, ed. *Teatro del Cinquecento. Vol. 1, La tragedia.* Milan, 1988.

Dolce, Lodovico. *La Medea: Tragedia de M. Lodovico Dolce.* Venice, 1560.

Giraldi, Giambattista. *Le tragedie di M. Gio. Battista Giraldi Cinthio, nobile ferrarese.* Venice, 1583.

Poggiali, Gaetano, ed. *Teatro italiano antico.* 10 vols. Milan, 1808–1812.

Secondary Works

Attolini, Giovanni. *Teatro e spettacolo nel Rinascimento.* Bari, Italy, 1988.

Barish, Jonas. "The Problem of Closet Drama in the Italian Renaissance." *Italica* 71, no. 1 (1994): 4–30.

Carlson, Marvin. *Theories of the Theatre: A Historical and Critical Survey from the Greeks to the Present.* Ithaca, N.Y., 1984.

Charlton, H. B. *The Senecan Tradition in Renaissance Tragedy.* Manchester, U.K., 1946.

Di Maria, Salvatore. "The Dramatic *hic et nunc* in the Tragedy of Renaissance Italy." *Italica* 72, no. 3 (1995): 275–297.

Herrick, Marvin. *Italian Tragedy in the Renaissance.* Urbana, Ill., 1965.

Marotti, Ferruccio. *Lo spettacolo dall'umanesimo al manierismo.* Milan, 1974.

Musumarra, Carmelo. *La poesia tragica italiana nel Rinascimento.* Florence, 1972.

Neri, Ferdinando. *La tragedia italiana del Cinquecento.* Florence, 1904.

Russo, Luigi. "La tragedia nel Cinque e Seicento." *Belfagor* 1 (1959): 14–22.

SALVATORE DI MARIA

Erudite Comedy

Commedia erudita (erudite comedy) was a defining theatrical phenomenon for modern European comedy, originating in fifteenth-century Italy and nourished both by the social demand for secular plays that produced various dramatizations of medieval narratives and by the purposeful neoclassicism that elicited translations, imitations, and variations on the comedies of Plautus and Terence. This neoclassicism fueled an avant-garde movement to assimilate, rival, and surpass the achievements of Roman theater and its Greek sources. The recovery in 1429 of a dozen "lost" comedies of Plautus heightened the spirit of emulation. Early results were Latin school plays and humanistic experiments like the *Chrysis* (1444) of Aenea Silvio Piccolomini. From the 1470s, among many kinds of theatrical spectacle, the Este court sponsored performances of Plautus, in Latin and in translation, as a demonstration of Ferrarese cultural superiority, and nurtured the first vernacular comedies of Ludovico Ariosto, *La cassaria* (The casket play) in 1508 and *I suppositi* (The pretenders) in 1509. Isabella d'Este endured the Latin plays for reasons of state but delighted in the Italian versions and imitations, importing them to her Gonzaga husband's court in Mantua, as her sister did to the Sforza court in Milan.

Similar experiments with the forms of ancient comedy were being conducted in courtly and academic circles elsewhere: In Florence, Terence's *Andria* had been edited by Angelo Poliziano and later translated by Niccolò Machiavelli, and Latin drama and Attic Old and New Comedy were studied and dissected by the intelligentsia who met in the Rucellai gardens; in Rome, Pomponio Leto's academy, an informal gathering of humanists, prepared the way for *commedia erudita* to flourish in the next century under the Medici pope Leo X. The acclaimed *La calandria* of Bernardo Dovizi, Cardinal Bibbiena, was introduced at Urbino in 1513, splendidly produced with *intermedi* and new sets in Rome the following year and often played thereafter, at Mantua in 1520, in Venice sometime before 1522. Medici patronage fanned the growing demand for regular comedy to which Machiavelli's *La mandragola* (The mandrake; c. 1518) and *La Clizia* (1525) responded in different ways.

The new comedy was referred to variously as *erudita,* because it was modeled on the comedy of the ancients, *osservata* or *regolare,* because its structure observed the "rules" derived from the classical genre, and *grave,* because it was conceived as serious art, written by the literati for private, courtly, or academic performance, principally by amateur male actors. Romantic nineteenth-century exaltation of individualistic originality above imitation of classical models long obscured the innovative character of *commedia erudita* and imparted a negative charge to the term; understood as a triumph of theatrical engineering, however, regular comedy offered playmakers of many kinds a revolutionary structure, simultaneously stable and expandable.

Characteristic Features. The genre is characterized by division into five acts and the use of vernacular prose (though a minority of playwrights preferred verse), essentially Tuscan or a "national" language based on Tuscan understandable throughout the peninsula, often with interpolations of dialect or of foreign or specialized vocabularies for particular characters. The setting is an Italian city street or piazza, populated by bourgeois characters, their servants and dependents, courtesans, procurers, innkeepers, travelers, peddlers, pedants, soldiers, charlatans, and friars. All but the friars and the humanistic pedants descend theatrically from Plautine and Terentian stock characters but, unlike their Latin ancestors, who were often given Greek names and settings, the characters of *commedia erudita* belong at all points to the urban society of early modern Italy. Whatever cityscape they inhabit becomes the locus of linguistic invention and display; the ubiquitous Italian fascination with the development of the vernacular language found in the genre a laboratory of usage and styles.

Typically, the dramatic conflicts are within and among families, pitting desire against interests, children against parents in plots drawn from Plautus and Terence, wives against husbands in those from Boccaccio's *Decameron.* This framework provided a controlled space hospitable to a range of topics: local satire, political allegory, psychological portraits, propaganda for patrons, vignettes of life on the streets, slapstick, love scenes, and debates on such subjects as education, food, marriage, literature, and the use of cosmetics. The plots, or *favole,* most admired at the time were those developed on the principle of Terentian *contaminatio* of two or more stories in the public domain, twisted in a complicated intrigue. The goddess Fortuna is the ruling spirit, always favoring wit and young love. Lustful, jealous, or tightfisted old men are routinely mocked and thwarted. Disguises or deceits are the weapons of the conflict, clever servants or parasites are the strategists or assistants to the young *innamorati,* and the *beffa,* or practical joke, is a favorite episode in the campaign of ridicule.

In Bibbiena's *Calandria,* a model *commedia erudita,* the story of male/female twin refugees, dressed alike and searching for each other throughout Rome, is entwined with a tale of adulterous love between the male twin and the unsatisfied wife of a womanizing dodderer named for Boccaccio's famous fool Calandrino. At the finale, the female twin makes a rich marriage with Calandro's son and her brother's affair is guaranteed secrecy and continuation. The action is an artful pattern of tricks, disguises, mistakes, and foolery, stage-managed by a clever servant. The dialogue is a lively literary patchwork of colloquial Tuscan patter, phrases from the *Decameron,* puns, and double-entendres. For years to come such figures would reappear in comedy, variously combined in similar encounters—lamenting love, gulling the fool, eavesdropping, advising and debating, commenting in asides, spinning tall tales, exchanging insults, conversing from windows. The choreographical and lexical registers would grow, ringing changes on basic actions—cross-dressing, misreading letters, switching bedmates in the dark. Such theatergrams—reshuffled units of plot, stage business, and speech—would be accumulated in a repertory that the regular comedy eventually transmitted to the European stage at large.

Structure. In their prologues writers of such comedies joked about Plautus and Terence, now boasting of kinship, now declaring independence, always eager to present themselves as the heirs and modern exponents of classical tradition. They routinely quoted the commentary on Terence of the fourth-century grammarian Aelius Donatus, "Cicero said that comedy is an imitation of life, a mirror of custom, an image of truth," and took as their charge the verisimilar portrayal of contemporary middle-class life, distancing themselves from the fairy tales, myths, miracles, and farces of medieval drama. With Horace's *Ars poetica* in mind, they maintained unity of time and place, limiting the fictional action to the events of a day transpiring on a single set representing a specific Italian city. The defining achievement of their common enterprise, as recognized by later practitioners of the genre, was the mastery of coherent structure, the dramatic logic of causal connection that gave beginning, middle, and end to a verisimilar action by exposition, complication, catastrophe, and denouement.

The sources were diverse and the ways of handling them still more so, but agreement on basic elements achieved by the new form would underlie the regular comedy for more than a century. Even the famous exceptions to the standard features prove the essential accord on structure. Machiavelli's *Mandragola* lacks a secondary plot; likewise *Il marescalco* (The stablemaster; 1533) of Pietro Aretino (1492–1556), whose episodic *La cortigiana* (The courtesan; 1525) might be said to have no plot at all. But both playwrights observe the rules regarding time and setting, divide the action into five acts, and focus on urban realism, and both would draw closer in their later comedies to the ideal intricacy of plot. The actor-playwright Angelo Beolco (c. 1502–1542), creator of the rustic clown Ruzante, whose choice of Paduan dialect for most of his work limited the size of his audience (indeed, it was only after his death that his works were published), in time moved away from monologues and loose eclogues toward the

Erudite Comedy. Woodcut illustration to a printed *commedia grave,* from Sforza degli Oddi's *Prigione d'amore* (Prisoner of love; 1591). THE BODLEIAN LIBRARY, UNIVERSITY OF OXFORD. DOUCE O17, FOL. 45 RECTO

shape of *commedia erudita* in *La moscheta* (The phony lingo; composed c. 1532), more so in *L'Anconitana* (The woman of Ancona; 1534–1535), and adapted Plautus directly in *La vaccaria* (The cow play; 1533). Even the exuberant multilingual plays of Gigio Artemio Giancarli hewed to the structures of regular comedy. Eventually the genre of regular comedy attracted writers of widely diverse regions and conditions, among them the quintessential Florentine satirist Antonfrancesco Grazzini, the versatile notary Giovanni Maria Cecchi, the political assassin Lorenzino de' Medici, the Venetian aristocrats Luigi Pasqualigo and Giovanni Francesco Loredano and the polymath Lodovico Dolce, the scholarly courtier Annibal Caro, and the heretical Calabrian priest and philosopher Giordano Bruno, who used the form for a closet drama of extravagant polemical and linguistic proportions, *Il candelaio* (The candle maker; 1582).

Romance Plots. A milestone in the history of the *commedia erudita* was the initiation on Epiphany, 6 January 1531/32, of the theatrical productions of the Intronati, a Sienese academy of university wits whose collaborative comedy *Gl'ingannati* (The deceived) engendered a large European progeny that eventually included Shakespeare's *Twelfth Night.* Into the new vessel of regular comedy the acade-

micians poured content from medieval romances, especially from the *Decameron* tales of heroic women that were the favorites of the Intronati's feminine audience. Alessandro Piccolomini (1508–1578) and his colleagues and successors in the academy subsequently produced a series of such plays featuring resourceful lovesick heroines, creating a lasting demand for romantic comedy. Regular comedy was by this time a fixture of high culture, played as a centerpiece of carnival or wedding festivities, with lyrical *intermedi,* on some occasions including ballets with spectacular scenery. News of theatrical events passed between cities and courts by diplomatic means along a major axis from Venice to Naples, traversing Padua, Florence, Siena, and Rome. Naples had long been hospitable to both popular and literary theater, and by the mid-sixteenth century the fashionable comedy was supported there by patrons like Ferrante Sanseverino as a display of culture and power.

Church and Stage. Catholic reform policy emerging from the sessions of the Council of Trent from 1545 to 1563 affected dramaturgy as well as the other arts, and writers of *commedia grave* increasingly introduced serious content into their works, often boasting of the gravity of both theme and structure achieved thereby. The results were seen everywhere, from Venice, Florence, and Rome—in comedies of Loredano, Girolamo Razzi, Raffaello Borghini, and Cristoforo Castelletti—to Naples in those of Giambattista Della Porta, Filippo Caetani, duke of Sermoneta, Francesco D'Isa, Fabrizio Marotta, and other luminaries of the southern literary establishment around the turn of the century. The abbot Bernardino Pino of Cagli, in the duchy of Pesaro, published a *Breve consideratione* on the high aims of comic structure and content, appended to Sforza Oddi's serious comedy *L'erofilomachia, ovoro, Il duello d'amore e d'amicitia* (The duel of love and friendship; 1572). One of Pino's own highly successful comedies, *I falsi sospetti* (False suspicions; 1579), appeared with a title-page advertisement of its moral value "for the instruction of prudent parents of families, obedient children and faithful servants." The gravity praised for bringing comedy closer to tragedy consisted in adding emotional as well as moral weight to the dramatic situations, loading them with dire consequences, threatened or apparent death or madness, promoting characters to courtly rank, mixing pathos and heroic examples with the usual intrigue and popular bawdry. In Oddi's *Prigione d'amore* (Prisoner of love; 1590) a self-sacrificing lady at the court of Ferrara dons her brother's clothes and assumes his place in the castle dungeon to await capital punishment. Borghini's *La donna costante* (The faithful woman; 1578) is a complicated version of the story of Romeo and Juliet with an athletic and enterprising heroine and a happy ending.

By augmenting the seriousness of the *commedia grave* such dramatists joined in the large-scale experimentation with dramatic genres aiming at creating a modern hybrid of comedy and tragedy unknown to the ancients but worthy of comparison with their dramatic forms and observant of the rules that Italian theorists were deriving from Aristotle's newly available *Poetics,* an aim that coincided with the Catholic mobilization of the stage to teach orthodoxy. The essentially Christian movement of tragicomedy toward redemption through suffering and its capacity for illustrating the superiority of Divine Providence to the capricious power of pagan Fortune that governed classical comedy pulled the theater toward a third genre. When tragicomedy was at last established, it took the form of pastoral drama, dominantly represented by Battista Guarini's *Il pastor fido* (1589; trans. *The Faithful Shepherd*), but the achievement depended on long practice with *commedia erudita*. So successful was the pastoral play

that it displaced regular comedy as the main attraction at theatrically festive occasions.

Relation to *Commedia dell'Arte*. The professional players of the *commedia dell'arte* were insatiable consumers of erudite comedies, memorizing them when hired to participate in private theatricals and then recycling the material in their popular three-act improvisations on sketchy scenarios. Some writers of regular comedy scorned these "clown plays" as being jerry-built, crowd pleasing and indecent, but others, including Della Porta and Castelletti, enhanced the theatricality of their own scripted plays by borrowing characters, gestures, and comic turns from the *commedia dell'arte,* enlarging the roles for women and giving greater physical scope to the clowns. Simultaneously, some professional actors began to print the results of their experience onstage, expanding the material into the five-act format of the *commedia erudita*. In the seventeenth century, comedy was published in various forms, including the fantastic *commedia ridicolosa* like Margarita Costa's *Li buffoni* (The clowns) and Spanish-influenced cape-and-sword plays and other three-acters, but the *commedia erudita* remained a model of high form, if no longer the one most imitated. As late as 1629, the actor Nicolò Barbieri published one of his starring vehicles, *L'inavertito* (Clueless) in five acts with modifications to make it conform to "good rules" and a dedication offering his devotion to his patron as a substitute for the excellence of Plautus and Terence.

See also **Aretino, Pietro; Commedia dell'Arte; Literary Theory, Renaissance; Music,** *subentry on* **Intermedi; Piccolomini, Alessandro; Plautus, Titus Maccius; Terence.**

BIBLIOGRAPHY

Primary Works

Beecher, Donald A., Douglas Campbell, and Massimo Ciavolella, eds. *Carleton Renaissance Plays in Translation: Translations from Dutch, Italian, French, Spanish, and German Plays 1380–1680.* Ottawa, 1980–. Continuing series includes Caro, Cecchi, Piccolomini, Bernini, Aretino, Bargagli, De'Sommi, Beolco, Ariosto, Della Porta, Bruno.

Borsellino, Nino, ed. *Commedie del cinquecento.* 2 vols. Milan, 1962–1967.

Davico Bonino, Guido, ed. *Il teatro italiano. II. La commedia del Cinquecento.* 3 vols. Turin, Italy, 1977–1978.

Penman, Bruce, ed. *Five Italian Renaissance Comedies.* Harmondsworth, U.K., 1978. Translation of Ariosto, Aretino, the Intronati Academy, Machiavelli, and Guarini.

Secondary Works

Clubb, Louise George. *Italian Drama in Shakespeare's Time.* New Haven, Conn., 1989.

Clubb, Louise George, and Robert Black. *Romance and Aretine Humanism in Sienese Comedy, 1516: Pollastra's* Parthenio *at the Studio di Siena.* Florence, 1993.

Cope, Jackson I. *Secret Sharers in Italian Comedy from Machiavelli to Goldoni.* Durham, N.C., and London, 1996.

Herrick, Marvin T. *Italian Comedy in the Renaissance.* Urbana, Ill., 1960.

Radcliff-Umstead, Douglas. *The Birth of Modern Comedy in Renaissance Italy.* Chicago, 1969.

LOUISE GEORGE CLUBB

DRAMA, ENGLISH. [This entry includes three subentries on English drama:

Elizabethan Drama
Jacobean Drama
Jacobean Court Masque

For discussion of drama in general, see the preceding entry, Drama. For discussion of drama in France and in Spain, see the following two main entries.]

Elizabethan Drama

The two phrases most commonly used to describe the English drama of the late sixteenth and early seventeenth centuries—Elizabethan drama and English Renaissance drama—are both unsatisfactory, for neither term fully represents the facts. Elizabeth's reign began in 1558, but not until the 1580s was there any system able to provide the public with a regular schedule of theatrical performances (interrupted only by Sundays, Lent, periods of court mourning, and the plague). And the drama continued to flourish until 1642—thirty-nine years after Elizabeth's death. Invocation of the Renaissance raises other, no less serious, problems. It is true that without the impulse to secular self-expression created by the recovery of Greco-Roman civilization the plays thus described could not have been written; but a parallel between English popular drama, as found in the drama of William Shakespeare, Christopher Marlowe, Robert Greene, Thomas Dekker, Ben Jonson, Thomas Heywood, John Webster, Thomas Middleton, and John Marston, and a Renaissance drama, represented centrally by such figures as Pietro Bembo, Niccolò Machiavelli, Leonardo da Vinci, and Ludovico Ariosto, can only be justified if we ignore the characteristics of both parties. The Italian efflorescence was sustained by an aristocratic ambition to re-create the culture of Greece and Rome. But the English drama was essentially a bourgeois and commercial enterprise, aiming to achieve success by attracting the plaudits and pennies of the semi-educated masses.

Taking these two insufficient descriptions together, in terms of their overlap and contradiction, does, however, allow us to arrive at a fair picture of the role of English performed drama in this period. The dialectic between homegrown tradition and continental innovation evident in the plays mirrors that in society at large in its mixture of parochialism and expansion, its obsession with local heritage coupled to the pleasure taken in novelty, its capacity to admire stasis and at the same time achieve radical change. The drama offered, of course, a sharpened version of the mixture. On the one hand, it endorsed the positive ethos of communitarian, anti-individualist values, piety, patriotism, and xenophobia. On the other hand, it depended for its popularity on its capacity to evoke an exciting counterculture that defied both the preachers who thundered against its immorality from their city pulpits and the civic authorities who thought the whole enterprise a seedbed of revolution and sought continuously to have it closed down. Indeed, the drama did offer a picture of life that looked socially dangerous, providing apprentices and men-about-town with a sense of the possibility of self-assertion (or of comic evasion) that was officially forbidden; yet it did so in terms that the culture in some of its aspects already endorsed.

Producing Plays. The structure of the theatrical profession was well suited to handle this paradox of contradiction inside compromise. The money required to set up commercial playhouses large enough to give a quick return on investment could only come from capitalist entrepreneurs in the city. The continually changing repertory of plays, designed to draw in a regular clientele, required, however, the collaboration of a different cohort. The humanist training provided by Renaissance schools and universities encouraged in the men they produced an intellectual expansiveness, a sense of innate capacity that was bound to be frustrated in the real world of Elizabethan social hierarchy. But university men like Marlowe, John Day, Greene, John Ford, Philip Massinger, Middleton, and perhaps also Heywood, as well as literate printers, scriveners, and journalists like Henry Chettle, Thomas Kyd, Anthony Munday, and Robert Yarrington, were able to find in playwriting not only an outlet but an income considerably beyond anything available in the standard graduate professions of schoolmaster or curate.

Writing plays for money was, however, rather shameful, and the professional playwrights were oppressed by the social disgrace of labor undertaken for wages and submitting it to the approval of an au-

Macbeth Meets the Witches. From the second edition of Raphael Holinshed's *Chronicle of Scotland* (1587), from which Shakespeare took the story of *Macbeth*. FOTOMAS INDEX, U.K.

dience of artisans. Yet, as it turned out, their humanist ideals were not entirely irrelevant. Eloquence is as much approved in the street as in the senate, and no doubt these reluctant playwrights relished the opportunity to display their linguistic powers and range of learning that looks labored and arcane today, but which they managed to communicate to the public as an exuberance of linguistic fancy, an almost physical projection of intellectual energy, and so a proper coordinate of continuous physical action.

In these characteristics the drama of the time fitted in beside other popular entertainments that used the same spaces and attracted the same audiences: fencing matches, bearbaiting, acrobatics (the "feats of activity" for which acting companies were often called to court). All of these were displays of energy that brought about immediate engagement between stage and audience—an engagement that can only be pallidly reproduced when the plays are understood through reading.

The account book of Philip Henslowe, the financier who owned the Rose and the Fortune playhouses (as well as bear pits and brothels), gives a marvelously detailed account of the intense activity that was necessary to keep the show running. What Henslowe and the actors were promoting was not, of course, the literary careers of authors (whose names were seldom known to the public). Speed of composition, a knowledge of the acting company's strengths and weaknesses, and a keen eye for the

taste of the moment seem to have been the qualities most in demand. The responsibility of the author for his creation had to be sacrificed to the need for a rapid turnover; collaboration and division of responsibilities were common. In these terms, the Elizabethan dramatist worked under conditions very like those of the modern newspaper reporter and with the modern reporter's instinct for the unstructured feelings of a popular audience.

A play written in 1624 but now known only through the lawsuit it occasioned gives us our most complete understanding of the methods used to rush out a topical work. Known by three titles, *The Late Murder in Whitechapel, The Late Murder of the Son upon the Mother,* and *Keep the Widow Waking,* it deals with two recent scandals, one a domestic tragedy and the other a cruel comedy of a rich widow who is kept drunk and sleepless in a local tavern until she agrees to marry a young fortune hunter. Thomas Dekker, who appears as a regular collaborator in Henslowe's account book, seems to have been in charge of the project. It was he, presumably, who sketched the outline of the plot. He wrote the first and last acts and entrusted the rest to Ford, William Rowley, and Webster, no doubt at the rate of one act apiece. A play of this kind demanded great speed because its commercial success depended on its topicality, on local interest due to fade as soon as the next scandal came along. To drum up support, the actors performed a ballad of the comic story in the street outside the widow's house and invited spectators to come to the playhouse (the Red Bull) and see their neighbors' lives in greater detail.

Plays and Audiences. Plays like *Keep the Widow Waking* offered theatergoers the excitement that later ages found in newspapers, radio, and television—stories of mishap and disaster disrupting lives very like their own. But the genre of "domestic" or "homiletic" tragedy offered not only spicy details of local lives but also an ethos that is not found in later redactions, an ethos that served to place the sinners inside the community that was watching their story. Plays such as the anonymous *Arden of Faversham* (1589–1592), *A Warning for Fair Women* (1598–1599), and *A Yorkshire Tragedy* (1605–1608), and Heywood's *A Woman Killed with Kindness* (1603) depict crime as a sudden slippage in the even tenor of local life (an actual possession by the devil in *A Yorkshire Tragedy*), as an aberration that suddenly cuts off the criminal from the fellowship of a Christian society. The tragic emotion thus emerges less in the violent deed itself than in the pain of this loss of a self that belongs to the community. Hence, a story's ending in legal punishment is not a sufficient closure of the case but demands the further meaning given by repentance. Confession of guilt and acceptance of punishment (seen as a representation of God's proper vengeance) allow the community to reabsorb the criminal into Christian charity.

It seems improbable that such plays of humble life were much appreciated in the higher strata of society, but it is clear that there was considerable overlap in the tastes of court and city. The court drama of Elizabeth and James never entirely separated itself from the popular drama of London. Elizabeth's parsimony prevented her from paying for players who would perform exclusively at court. The boys' companies of the early years came as close to such exclusivity as the system allowed, but even they showed their plays also in commercial playhouses. At court they were in competition with the adult companies of the great lords who, like their mistress, were willing to patronize acting companies if their wages could be subsidized by the public at large. When, in 1583, a group of twelve actors was "selected as the best out of the companies of divers great lords" to form Queen Elizabeth's Men, their status seems to have been as grooms of the chamber without pay. Their liveries, however, served them well when they toured the country and demanded

welcome from civic authorities and permission to charge the public for admission into civic spaces. There is no evidence that their repertory when they played at court differed from that of their commercial performances.

The best-liked plays of the period (as judged by the number of recorded performances or republications) seem to modern taste to be without much interest—they are rarely discussed or even reprinted—but their existence can hardly be ignored in a historical survey. The anonymous *A Most Pleasant Comedy of Mucedorus, the King's Son of Valentia and Amadine the King's Daughter of Aragon, with the Merry Conceits of Mouse* was probably written in the early 1590s. It was published first in 1598 ("*as it hath been sundry times played in the honourable City of London*"), with an epilogue that makes it clear it was performed before Elizabeth. In 1610 it was revised, given an augmented title page—"*Amplified with new additions, as it was acted before the King's Majesty at Whitehall on Shrove-Sunday night*"—and in this form republished fourteen times. In spite of this appeal to court-oriented tastes, the Grocer's wife in Francis Beaumont's *The Knight of the Burning Pestle* (1613) tells the "gentlemen" around her that Rafe, her apprentice, "hath played . . . *Mucedorus* before the wardens of our company" (induction, 27f.). Given the bombast and mock-heroics of Rafe's part in Beaumont's play, this is clearly meant to characterize *Mucedorus* as fodder suitable for tradesmen. Certainly it retained enough popular appeal to be selected for a sanction-busting tour through Oxfordshire villages in 1652. Yet the lord chamberlain and the master of the revels had clearly thought it appropriate entertainment for the sovereign.

What qualities in *Mucedorus* gave it this broad appeal? Clearly the variousness of the situations it offers must be part of the explanation. An induction introducing the revised version shows this variousness to be a self-conscious device. In it Comedy and Envy (alias Tragedy) argue for control of the stage, each claiming superior dramatic appeal. Comedy must win, for, with sovereigns as benign as Elizabeth or James, Envy cannot be expected to have success; but Comedy can only triumph after a great deal of terror and dismay.

If we are looking for characteristics like those of *Mucedorus*, we probably find them most easily in the romances written by Shakespeare at the end of his career. Of these plays, *The Late and Much Admired Play Called Pericles* (1606–1608) is certainly the least admired in modern times; yet once again the historical evidence contradicts modern judgment. The modern view is that the extant text of *Pericles* cannot represent Shakespeare's intention at all faithfully. Yet not only is this the only play in the canon that earned itself a novelistic retelling (*The Painful Adventures of Pericles, Prince of Tyre. Being the True History of the Play of Pericles* by George Wilkins), but it is the only one of these late plays to be printed in quarto (four times). The episodic structure of *Pericles,* the stop-and-start "adventures" it offers, and its intermingling of comic and tragic emotions seem once again to provide a formula that, up to the death of Shakespeare at any rate, had power to charm all classes.

A play that makes the same point but in quite different terms is *Greene's Tu Quoque, or, The Cittie Gallant* of 1611, the only known work of one Jo. Cooke, who is known only as the author of *Greene's Tu Quoque.* In this case the play is not a tissue of romantic adventures but a hardheaded examination of class conflicts in a mercantile London household. A prosperous London merchant is knighted and must give up trade. Frank Spendall, his journeyman, becomes master, lives up to his name, and is thrown into debtors prison. In a second plot another servant is ruined by unexpected wealth, which leads him this time through foolish social aspiration to general mockery. He hires his former master (now a fallen gentleman) to teach him manners, but he is hopelessly inept. He believes that the cant phrase "Tu quoque" (the same to you) will serve him in every social situation, and it is clear from the title that the comedic actor Thomas Greene used this phrase to create memorable comedy. A 1654 commentary tells us that this was one of the plays that could deter rioting apprentices from attacking the playhouse fabric, since it "could with ease insinuate [itself] into their capacities." But it was also played at court in 1611–1612 and 1624–1625. And its attractive power was sufficiently obvious as late as 1671 to lead a commentator, Edward Howard, to allow that the rude drama of the past was "not so rank but that it may in some degree tread with our present writers" (*The Six Days Adventure*). The ability to see *Greene's Tu Quoque* in this light is largely denied to modern readers, but the historical fact of its reputation must be registered as an important witness in the history of Elizabethan drama.

History Plays. The power of Elizabethan plays to overcome differences of audience is matched by their capacity to use old forms to say new things. Nowhere is this more obvious than in the English history play—a genre that retains even today the ability to entertain millions who know nothing of its local meanings. The old play *The Famous Victories of Henry V* (1583–1588) provides a clear picture of the simpleminded chauvinism that gave representations of English victories their original popular appeal. The young Henry V in this play is not only the victor over the French; he is also the enemy of all forms of social restriction on individual activities. The transformation of this figure into Shakespeare's Prince Hal marks the extent to which the history play can retain its jingoistic potential while adding an awareness of all the uncertainties that attach to the idea of manifest destiny. The moral ambiguity of Shakespeare's major historical figures, King John, Richard III, Richard II, Henry IV, Henry V, continues to intrigue by its refusal to separate contradictory moral and political judgments and by continually confronting us with central questions: Need a good king be a good man? Do national aims reflect national good or only the self-aggrandizement of leaders? The massively contradictory figure of Falstaff carries the moral anarchies of *The Famous Victories of Henry V* into a world that can neither accept them nor deny them, thereby allowing the audience both to enjoy and to speculate about what it is enjoying.

The careful work of such Tudor historians as Edward Hall, Raphael Holinshed, William Camden, and John Stow made it clear to the age how uncertain was the interpretation of the past and how obscure the relation between God's purposes and state policy. In the historical drama we see a parallel development as portrayals of the military deeds of kings in wars against foreigners and traitors give way to a sentimental concentration on their emotional lives. *Edward IV* (1592–1599), usually attributed to Heywood, centers on the martyr figure of the king's mistress, Jane Shore, whose personal virtue makes suspect the whole issue of dynastic legitimacy. In plays dealing with "the troubles of Queen Elizabeth," such as Dekker's *The Whore of Babylon* (1606–1607) and Heywood's two-part *If You Know Not Me, You Know Nobody* (1603–1605), the chief interest is in Elizabeth's miraculous capacity to survive persecution and murder plots. At the same time, though at a more theoretically sophisticated level, a new historiography brought the disenchanted views of Machiavelli and Francesco Guicciardini to bear on English statecraft, requiring the community to notice that political aims cannot be achieved on a basis of moral principles. What seems to be the last of the Elizabethan history plays to deal with a real political situation,

Ford's *The Chronicle History of Perkin Warbeck: A Strange Truth* (1629–1634), draws on Francis Bacon's Machiavellian *History of the Reign of King Henry VII* (1622) and adds to Bacon's skeptical view of kingship a contrast (perhaps derived from Shakespeare's *Richard II*) between the player king who dominates the stage and the efficient king who runs the country. The theater that celebrates royalty thus becomes a stage for suspicion of theatrical kingship, setting a sovereign who has none of the glamour of rule against a pretender whose rhetoric and bearing define him, in the theatrical vision, as the genuine article. Seeing it in these terms we can understand why Ford's play is often taken to mark the end of the history-play genre.

Problem Plays and City Comedies. In every genre, as the Elizabethan era gives way to the Jacobean and Caroline, the drama seems to find the strain of keeping contradiction inside compromise increasingly difficult. Late humanism, with its preference for Seneca over Cicero and for individual over public statement, as well as its taste for satire and the skeptical view of life found in Montaigne's essays, leads those playwrights attuned to intellectual fashion to shift the terms of their compromise with the popular audience.

In the early Tudor period, stories of the prodigal son had provided basic material for grammar-school study and performance of plays. The model provided classical structure and Christian morals since it used the basic plot of Terence but evaded his suspect morals by turning angry fathers into the Father in Heaven and construing his denouements as a discovery of Christian repentance and forgiveness. The pattern reappears in seventeenth-century plays of erring husbands and of naive country gentlemen caught in the nets spread by slick city merchants. In plays about husbands the pattern of rebellious sons and forgiving wives and fathers is given an extra twist, since the young man unwilling to submit to the restrictions of family and matrimony does so because he is the kind of macho male that the culture especially admired.

The anonymous play *Captain Thomas Stukeley* (1596) provides a good example of the moral ambiguity that results. Stukeley needs money for a military career. His dazzling prowess convinces his best friend that he should cancel his own betrothal to an alderman's daughter so that Stukeley can step into his place. Stukeley marries the daughter and immediately takes off with her dowry (as does Bertram in Shakespeare's *All's Well That Ends Well*). But even

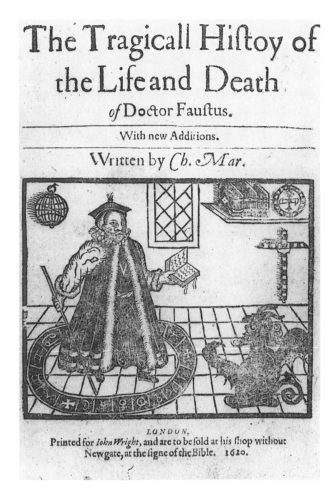

Christopher Marlowe's *Doctor Faustus*. Faustus conjures spirits as a devil rises from a trapdoor. BY PERMISSION OF THE BRITISH LIBRARY

on the battlefield, ambiguity cannot be evaded: Stukeley's desperate search for individual glory leads him into the service of the pope and Philip of Spain, and he dies in a contest between obscure Moorish factions in North Africa. Is he to be admired or condemned? The divided valuations that this play (and others like it) seems to require indicates that the "problem play" is not simply a Shakespearean genre but an aspect of the history of Elizabethan drama.

The city comedies of Middleton, Dekker and Webster, Jonson, Marston, and Richard Brome illustrate the same development of moral ambiguity, created this time by the changing economic and social structures of London society, which require that the battle between good and evil be replayed as a survival of the fittest. These plays show the traditional nobility of the fighting man and lover stranded in a world that refuses to accept traditional valuation.

Though they characteristically allow the hero (or gallant) to win at the end of the action, he can only do so by seeming to join his enemies, entering into the mind-sets of the usurers and con men who surround him. By playing their game more skillfully than they do, and gaining the advantage of surprise that he can play it at all, he finally gets the girl and recovers his estate. But the contradictions between social and economic value systems, gallantry and money, traditionalism and innovation, are not resolved. The hero finds it the better part of valor, for instance, at the end of Middleton's *Michaelmas Term* (1604–1606), to retreat from the city to the world of the manor house and the peasantry.

The Witch of Edmonton (c. 1621) by Dekker, Ford, and Rowley offers another interesting model of how popular subjects could persist and, at the same time, change. It has the same moral pattern as the domestic tragedies discussed above but ends with another ambiguous judgment. The domestic action is set this time not in the crowded streets of the city but in the village of Edmonton. Here, once again, the devil walks abroad seeking to seduce those caught in social desperation. He appears, characteristically enough, as a natural part of the village scene, in the apparently unthreatening guise of a black dog (in all these plays, ordinary life and the eternal verities are but a hairbreadth apart). Once again there is no possibility that those who succumb to the devil's suggestions for an easy option can evade punishment. But this time the social structure is also implicated. The "witch" (Mother Sawyer, whose history is taken from an actual witch trial of the time) has indeed accepted the devil-dog as her familiar. But the grandees of the village who preside over her trial are themselves revealed as guilty, and she seizes the opportunity not to repent but to convict her accusers. Their imposition of narrowly economic judgment and their intolerant self-righteousness have made the shield of a Christian community powerless to protect the weak.

Changes in the Playhouses.
The Witch of Edmonton, like Middleton's city comedies, operates on material very similar to the popular drama of earlier years, but the action is seen from a point of view more challenging to received morality. The small elite playhouse in Drury Lane called the Phoenix, where the play was performed, also has a role in this story of change. Small playhouses like the Phoenix and the Blackfriars were enclosed, expensive, and provided seating for all; they were places where, as we learn from Marston's *Jack Drum's Entertainment*

(1600), "a man shall not be choked with the smell of garlic, nor be pasted to the barmy jacket of a beer-brewer." In all aspects they were like the courtly playhouses of Elizabeth's reign, where choirboys presented plays (such as those by John Lyly) destined for the attention of the queen but open to a paying public on the pretext that they were only showing rehearsals.

These early boys' playhouses were closed down from 1590 to 1600 (presumably because of some political indiscretion). When they reopened, they had to operate in a different, more crassly commercial world and with an eye to young men-about-town, especially the young gentlemen of the Inns of Court, rather than the courtiers of Whitehall. This inevitably meant a change in repertory from Ovidian tales of gods and heroes, nymphs and shepherds (with delicate implications of court life), as in the plays of Lyly, to a satiric and ironic treatment of the cultural controversies of the City (in such plays as Jonson's *Poetaster* [1601] and Dekker and Marston's *Satiromastix* [1601]). It seems, however, that the artificial mode in which the behavior of adults was represented by choirboys aged twelve to sixteen was as appropriate to one repertory as the other. If what Rosencrantz tells Hamlet is true of current theatrical history, the success of this "aerie of children, little eyases that cry out on the top of question," was such that in 1601 or so the adult companies found it hard to survive. Perhaps they could only do so by co-opting some of the qualities of their rivals.

The 1608 transfer of the Blackfriars playhouse from the boys to the King's Men marks a convergence of the two theaters, boys and men, as does the 1604 "theft" of Martson's *The Malcontent* by the same King's Men, who were, it would seem, looking for a repertory that was both popular and elite (and perhaps found one in the works of Shakespeare). That convergence was itself a subject of tension is made clear in Beaumont's *The Knight of the Burning Pestle.* The action begins with an assumption that a play by the boys called "The London Merchant" is about to be performed. Gentlemen are sitting on the stage (as they did only in these "private" playhouses). But then the situation that has been set up is interrupted by the appearance of a grocer and his wife. They climb on to the stage, pay for stools, and take the gentlemanly privilege of criticizing the play. The grocer assumes that "The London Merchant" will be a satire on tradesmen like himself and proposes an alternative in which his apprentice, Rafe, can demonstrate the capacity of citizens to engage in chivalric adventures (as in Heywood's *The Four*

Prentices of London [1592–1600]). The resultant action, as scenes from both plays are performed alternately, enforces a parodic view of both plots, so that the tensions embodied in the actual playhouse are absorbed into the fictional structure of the play.

No such compromise was available to halt the on-going "gentrification" of the drama in real historical time. The big arena playhouses, built to cater to a mass audience—the Theatre, the Curtain, the Rose, the Globe, the Fortune, the Red Bull—were by their size and shape committed to broad effects suitable for a socially mixed audience (some sitting, some standing). To keep the thousands of spectators coming to the plays required not only a system that offered a different play every afternoon of the week and a new play once every two weeks but also a variety of tragic, comic, and historical effects inside each play.

By the first decade of the seventeenth century these playhouses seem no longer to have been the money spinners they once were. After the construction of the Red Bull in 1605 or 1606, no more large playhouses were built in London. The fashion in playgoing was now for smaller, "private" houses like the Blackfriars; the Whitefriars (occupied 1607–1613); the Phoenix and Cockpit in Drury Lane (in the newly fashionable West End), which opened in 1617; and the Salisbury Court, which opened in 1630. The old arena buildings, particularly the Red Bull, the Curtain, and the Fortune, came to be identified with violent lower-class audience behavior, noisy overacting, and sensationalist drama, so that when drama historians of the next generation looked back on the pre-1642 theatrical scene they saw it as divided along class lines, with private playhouses representing the defensible dramatic tradition and arena playhouses representing the taste of "citizens and the meaner sort of people."

Closing the Theaters.

The crisis that destroyed the drama in 1642 was related to this division in the theatrical scene. The ambiguities and obliquities that had long sustained the theater's compromises allowed it both to suggest and to deny relevance to contemporary political life, so that the battles with the censor (the Master of the Revels) appear as an almost necessary part of the process of playwriting. Gentrification meant a more direct relation to the political classes and so a narrowing and sharpening of the focus on politics.

The most talked-about theatrical event of the reign of James—the production of Middleton's *A Game at Chess* (1624)—was a nine days' wonder for just this reason. The play offered the kind of intervention in contemporary politics precisely forbidden in the first year of Elizabeth's reign, 1558, but perhaps in this case condoned or even encouraged by the authorities. It was the scandal of being apparently invited to participate in the mysteries of state that drew thousands to wait in line for admission to the Globe. The play did indeed contain scandalous lampoons of figures normally treated with deference but the real political issue between England and Spain in the matter of Prince Charles's "Spanish marriage" was in fact rendered in the play mainly as an old-fashioned allegory of good and evil. It was less what the play contained than the fact that people saw the actors as part of the political scene that marked the new and dangerous status the playhouses were acquiring.

A Game at Chess was a onetime event, though a portent of much more. A more common theatrical response to the dangerous proximity of players to politicians was a retreat from challenging formulations. The drama of John Fletcher and Massinger, Shakespeare's successors as playwrights-in-ordinary to the King's Men, shows a withdrawal from the general to the particular, solving political issues with individualistic answers. Massinger's *A New Way to Pay Old Debts* (1621–1625) rewrites Middleton's *A Trick to Catch the Old One* (1604–1607), another of the city comedies for boys discussed above, in which a landed gentleman finds himself bankrupted by city usury and can only recover his estate by out-tricking the tricksters. In Massinger's handling of the story for adult actors, the anarchic pleasure Middleton's hero takes in trickery has largely disappeared. The appeal of a noble nature in distress, the concomitant emotions of shame, despair, and gratitude, and a sharp distinction between the generous and predatory classes now control the action.

Fletcher is the more innovative of this pair and is often seen as the creator of prevailing standards in later drama. In *The Faithful Shepherdess* (1608–1609) he introduced to the English stage Giovanni Battista Guarini's concept of tragicomedy as a form that "wants death . . . yet brings some near it," so cutting the thread of inevitability that holds together the individual and the situation in the best drama of the preceding age. Where Fletcherian dramaturgy excels is in dramatizing situations of passionate indeterminacy, as when characters are faced with incompatible demands on their loyalty and are incapable of taking any action that would help. That eventual solutions are achieved by legerdemain did not weaken the age's admiration for the rhetorical power of these high moments, as when Philaster must both love and seek to kill Princess Arethusa or when, in *A King and No King* (1611), Arbaces must believe that the woman he passionately desires is his sister. *The Maid's Tragedy* (1608–1611) turns on a political point that demands political action, since the villain of the piece is the king; but political impropriety is avoided, in spite of noisy threats of regicide. Evadne, the king's mistress and the immediate source of all the misery and despair, is persuaded that she can cleanse her soul by killing her royal partner in crime, so leaving the courtiers (and the audience) able to retain the comforting standard belief that God forbids regicide but will himself stir up a scapegoat who can carry away the guilt of killing an anointed monarch.

Fletcher was the most admired playwright of his time, and after the puritan Parliament had closed the playhouses in 1642, he was remembered as a model of a vanished civilization in which refinement of feeling could resolve contradiction in personal rather than political terms. The folio volume of Beamount and Fletcher plays published in 1647 under the auspices of the former King's Men was designed as a ghostly memorial to the living playhouse and the Caroline courtly culture it had come to reflect. There is little in the thirty-eight prefatory verses by leading gentlemen-poets of the time, however, to indicate their awareness of how the theatrical tradition they praised had grown out of a ferment of real alternatives. That was a history they did not understand and could not have wished to understand.

See also **Theaters**; *and biographies of dramatists mentioned in this entry.*

BIBLIOGRAPHY

Primary Works

With the exception of the anonymous plays *A Warning for Fair Women,* edited by Charles D. Cannon (The Hague, Netherlands, 1975), and *The Famous Victories of Henry V,* edited by Geoffrey Bullough, in *Narrative and Dramatic Sources of Shakespeare,* vol. 4 (London, 1966), and Jo. Cooke's *Greene's Tu Quoque,* edited by Alan J. Berman (New York, 1984), all the plays mentioned here are accessible in one or another of the following anthologies.

Drama of English Renaissance. Edited by Russell Fraser and Norman Rabkin. 2 vols. New York, 1976.

Elizabethan and Stuart Plays. Edited by Charles Read Baskervill, Virgil B. Heltzel, and Arthur Hobart Nethercot. New York, 1962.

English Drama, 1580–1642. Edited by Tucker Brooke and Nathaniel Burton Paradise. Boston, 1933.

The Shakespeare Apocrypha. Edited by C. F. Tucker Brooke. Oxford, 1908.

Secondary Works

Bentley, Gerald E. *The Jacobean and Caroline Stage.* 7 vols. Oxford, 1941–1968.

Chambers, Edmund K. *The Elizabethan Stage.* 4 vols. Oxford, 1923.

Gurr, Andrew. *The Shakespearian Playing Companies.* Oxford, 1996.

Hunter, George K. *English Drama, 1586–1642.* Oxford, 1997.

G. K. HUNTER

Jacobean Drama

In older critical writing, the term "Jacobean drama" is frequently used to describe all Renaissance plays, regardless of who was on the throne when they were written. In the late twentieth century, however, critics have identified sharper divisions between Elizabethan, Jacobean, and Caroline plays (written during the reigns of Elizabeth I, James I, and Charles I, respectively), and have suggested and that English drama underwent a marked change in character after the death of Elizabeth I in March 1603, and the accession of James VI of Scotland as James I of England (ruled 1603–1625). The political dominance of the king's male favorites and James's willingness to sell honors led to a widespread sense that the new court was corrupt and unsavory.

The focus of Jacobean drama is primarily on the court and on London, which surrounded the court and took its cue from it. Plays in which characters seeking revenge have just causes give way to plays in which innocence is found only in pathetic victims. Women, behaving in ever more devious ways, are also more prominent. Although James banned any mention of living monarchs from the stage, there are oblique reflections of the political dissent that surfaced intermittently during his reign and climaxed in the reign of his son, Charles I (1625–1649): Jacobean drama puts many bad rulers on stage. English unease about James's attempt to engineer a union with Scotland and later fears about the marriage of Charles with a Catholic princess may also be reflected in the xenophobia of many of the plays.

The dominant dramatic modes of the period are city comedy, with its biting wit and dog-eat-dog world, and satiric tragedy, generally set in highly decadent foreign courts, which are often seen as transparent representations of James's England. Drama of the period was characterized by ever darker plots and themes and an abundance of horrors and violence. These plays are often termed "tragedies of state" because they deal with diseased societies, and their lack of explicit moral frameworks or guidance has led to accusations of decadence being leveled against them. The largely satirical and cynical tone of both genres is counterbalanced only by masques, which were written largely to offer favorable representations of the monarch and his court, and by the improbable romance-plots of the tragicomic mode favored by Francis Beaumont and John Fletcher and also adopted in the last plays of Shakespeare.

Middleton. One of the most interesting and prolific of all Jacobean dramatists is Thomas Middleton (c. 1580–1627). In the 1990s, critics using new techniques of computer-assisted authorship attribution credited Middleton with having written a considerable amount of material previously thought to be by other hands, including parts of Shakespeare's *Macbeth* (1606) and *Timon of Athens* (c. 1607), the little-known *Second Maiden's Tragedy* (which was rechristened variously in modern editions as *The Lady's Tragedy* and *The Maiden's Tragedy*), and, perhaps most important, *The Revenger's Tragedy* (1607). (Throughout this entry, dates for plays refer to dates of first performance.) The latter had been previously attributed to Cyril Tourneur (c. 1575–1626) on the grounds of apparent similarities to his only other known play, *The Atheist's Tragedy* (1611), a rather ludicrous affair in which the villain, suitably named D'Amville (French *âme vile,* vile soul), eventually falls victim to divine justice when, while attempting to execute his nephew, he accidentally strikes out his own brains with an axe.

The Revenger's Tragedy is often seen as the first work with a distinctively Jacobean stamp, and indeed as typifying many of the fundamental qualities of Jacobean drama. Set in Italy, it deals with the attempts of the hero, Vindice (whose name means "Revenger"), to achieve vengeance for the death of his fiancée, Gloriana, poisoned nine years before by the corrupt Duke. After adopting a series of elaborate and increasingly improbable disguises, Vindice brings about the downfall of the Duke's entire family, only to find himself and his brother and helper, Hippolito, arrested and condemned to death by the new ruler, Antonio. This conclusion is fully in line with the official view, of both church and state, that revenge was self-defeating and that the revenger would never prosper, but any suggestion that the play has so clear a message seems to be sharply undercut by the savagery of its black humor. This sacrifice of explicit morality to dark comedy is often taken to set the tone for Jacobean tragedy as a whole, but at the same time the play clearly looks backward not only to *Hamlet* (1600–1601), which it seems almost to parody in a scene with a man talking to a skull, but also to Elizabeth I herself, who seems clearly alluded to by the use of the name "Gloriana."

To see Middleton as the probable author of *The Revenger's Tragedy* is particularly interesting because it gives him a career spanning virtually the whole of James's reign. His output was divided among civic entertainments such as the Lord Mayor's Shows (in 1620 he was made city chronologer of London), city comedies, and tragedies. The comedies, often coauthored with writers such as Thomas Dekker (c. 1570–1632) and William Rowley (c. 1585–1626), include *A Trick to Catch the Old One* (1604–1606), *A Mad World, My Masters* (1608), *A Chaste Maid in Cheapside* (1611), *No Wit, No Help Like a Woman's* (1613), and *The Roaring Girl* (c. 1610), which because of its interest in cross-dressing and gender roles—it centers on the historical Mary Frith, who dressed and acted as a man—attracted the greatest amount of critical attention in the 1990s.

In Middleton's day, however, the play that seems to have had the greatest impact was *A Game at Chess* (1624), a biting satire on the Spanish ambassador written to protest the possibility of a Spanish marriage for the heir to the throne, Prince Charles. This work broke all previous records by being played on nine consecutive days, apparently with overnight rewritings to keep it fresh. The profusion of characters and complexity of interconnecting plots make it impossible to summarize the comedies, which create a powerful impression of the seething vitality and pace of city life; perhaps Middleton's most attractive feature is the apparently unfailing energy that animates his plotting and characterization. For the most part, the comedies are peopled by characters not unlike Ben Jonson's knaves and gulls, with a young and usually virtuous couple having to outwit their amoral elders, whose primary focus is money. Indeed, money and sex are the matters of crucial concern in Middleton's world, as evidenced by the names of characters such as Pecunius Lucre and Penitent Brothel.

The most famous of Middleton's tragedies is perhaps *The Changeling* (1622), which was cowritten with Rowley, primarily a comic actor but noted for his collaborations with a number of dramatists of the period. Here a tragic main plot of lust and deception, set in a fortress, is suggestively doubled and shadowed by a comic subplot set in an asylum (which is attributed to Rowley). Both *The Changeling* and *Women Beware Women* (1625), which deals with multiple murder at the court of Florence, have often been read as influenced by the career of Frances Howard, countess of Somerset, who had been in-

Jacobean Drama. Title page of Thomas Middleton's *A Game at Chess* (1625). BY PERMISSION OF THE BRITISH LIBRARY, C34D38

volved in a notorious divorce case and was found guilty of poisoning Sir Thomas Overbury, a friend of her second husband's who had advised him against marrying her. *Women Beware Women* is also notable for containing one of the most extravagant of all examples of that favored device of Jacobean drama, the banquet or play-within-a-play that turns into a bloodbath; this is all the more striking because the initial part of the play is set in the world of the bourgeoisie, which is observed in such detail that Middleton has sometimes been acclaimed as a forerunner of the Norwegian dramatist Henrik Ibsen (1828–1906). He has also been seen as a dramatist particularly sympathetic to women; and Beatrice-Joanna of *The Changeling* and Livia of *Women Beware Women* are certainly both colorful and intriguing roles that allow for strong performances.

Chapman and Marston. George Chapman (c. 1560–1634) and John Marston (1576–1634) both collaborated with Ben Jonson (1572–1637) on *Eastward Ho!* (1605), and share a tone that is frequently savagely cynical. Chapman, a serious scholar who seems to have attended both Oxford and Cambridge, read the Italian Neoplatonist Marsilio Ficino (1433–1499), and translated Homer, was listed among "the best Poets" in both comedy and tragedy by Francis Meres in *Palladis Tamia* in 1598. His comedy *The Widow's Tears* (before 1609) makes savage fun of the Scots who were swamping London in the wake of the accession of James I, satirizing them as Spartans; this parallel, which was thought appropriate because both Scotland and Sparta were poor, barren, and warlike nations, was often reused.

Chapman is also distinguished by his unusual interest in French history. To some extent, he seems to have positioned himself as the literary heir to Christopher Marlowe (1564–1593): he supplied a continuation of Marlowe's poem *Hero and Leander* (1598; he and Marlowe are both claimed as members of the "School of Night"—an alleged coterie of nobleman and intellectuals interested in esoteric philosophy and science—if such a school indeed existed), and he explores something of the same territory as Marlowe's *The Massacre at Paris* (c. 1593) in *Bussy d'Ambois* (1604), *The Conspiracy and Tragedy of Charles, Duke of Byron, Marshal of France* (1608), *The Revenge of Bussy D'Ambois* (c. 1610), and *Chabot, Admiral of France* (c. 1613). He is particularly interested in the character and attributes of the hero, and the nature of the heroic.

If Chapman's France was a dangerous place inhabited by unscrupulous politicians, so too was Marston's Italy, as we see most particularly in *The Malcontent* (1604), which contains probably the first version of the figure of the discontented courtier, lacking preferment, which recurred in so much of Jacobean drama, most notably in John Webster's *The White Devil* (1612) and *The Duchess of Malfi* (1613–1614). Marston's mother was Italian, and his plays not only contain long passages in the language but also show a clearer than usual sense of Italy's complex political groupings. Unusually, all his plays were written for presentation by children's companies, and are highly self-conscious: *Antonio and Mellida* (1602) has an induction in which the boys discuss their fitness for the roles they are to play; it is also distinguished by having its hero cross-dress as an Amazon and by the fact that though it is a comedy, its sequel, *Antonio's Revenge, or The Second Part of the History of Antonio and Mellida* (1602), is a tragedy. Marston also wrote single comedies, of which *The Dutch Courtesan* (1605) is the most famous. Initially strongly associated with the Inns of Court, and with the witty, cynical tone that they fostered, Marston gave up writing for the stage after he was ordained in 1609.

Dekker and Heywood. John Webster, in the preamble to *The White Devil,* praised "the right happy and copious industry of Mr. Shakespeare, Mr. Dekker and Mr. Heywood." Thomas Heywood (1573–1641) was copious indeed, since he claimed to have written or to have had "a main finger" in 220 plays, of which about 30 survive. He also acted in Philip Henslowe's company, the Lord Admiral's Men, and wrote some of the lord mayor's pageants, in succession to Thomas Dekker (c. 1570–1632). The best-remembered of his plays is his domestic tragedy *A Woman Killed with Kindness* (1603), which has excited interest primarily because of the self-starvation of its heroine and because it is the only one of the Elizabethan domestic tragedies not to be based on a true-crime story and is poised interestingly between naive and sophisticated art. *The Miseries of Enforced Marriage* (1607), whose title speaks for itself, struck a note heard increasingly in the light of new Protestant arguments in favor of the companionate marriage, while *The Fair Maid of the West* (1610) is interesting for its energetic heroine and its fanciful version of the English colonial enterprise. Heywood was also much interested in Marlowe, and it was under his auspices that *The Jew of Malta* was revised and finally published (1633).

Thomas Dekker was another prolific writer, who worked, singly or in collaboration, on fifty plays, and is remembered principally for committed Protestantism, the popularism of his perspective, and his penchant for including scraps of foreign languages in his plays. His greatest achievement is usually thought to be *The Shoemaker's Holiday* (1599), but the same feel for the problems and recreations of the lives of the lower and middle classes is also evident in *The Witch of Edmonton* (1621), which he coauthored with John Ford (1586–1640s) and William Rowley (1585–1626). This, along with Heywood's *The Late Lancashire Witches* (1634; coauthored with Richard Brome, 1590–1652), Middleton's *The Witch* (1610–1616), and Shakespeare's *Macbeth,* responds to the feverish increase in witch-hunting in the early seventeenth century.

Beaumont and Fletcher. Francis Beaumont (c. 1584–1616) was from a wealthy gentry family and the brother of the poet Sir John Beaumont, and John Fletcher (1579–1625) was the son of Richard, a bishop of London and brother of the Spenserian poets Phineas and Giles. Both playwrights experienced early individual failure: Beaumont with *The Knight*

of the Burning Pestle (1607), whose hilariously funny metatheatrical jokes may perhaps have been over the head of its original audience; and Fletcher with *The Faithful Shepherdess* (1608–1609), which may well have been too faithful for its audience, since it is a close adaptation of Italian pastoral. Together, however, they achieved instant and lasting success, particularly with *Philaster* (before 1610), *The Maid's Tragedy* (before 1611), and *A King and No King* (1611). These three plays, two of them written in the new genre of tragicomedy, which Beaumont and Fletcher marked as their own, focus on courts where, in that favorite Jacobean *topos,* the duties of kingship are not being properly discharged: in *Philaster* because the king is a usurper, in *The Maid's Tragedy* because he is a lecher, and in *A King and No King* because he lusts after his sister, though it is eventually revealed that, because of an exchange in the cradle, they are not actually related, and she, not he, is the rightful ruler.

Although Beaumont and Fletcher have sometimes been labeled servile apologists of the divine right of kings, these plays in fact suggest a fairly vigorous critique of royalty. There is even an anecdote that the two playwrights narrowly escaped arrest on charges of treason when they were overheard discussing which of them should take responsibility for the scene depicting the killing of the king. Their legal training seems to have led them to favor constructing plots on the general principle of the argument *in utramque partem,* on either side; the Inns of Court often encouraged their students to take a role and plead for justice in hypothetical cases where opposing interests were equally balanced, and the influence of this approach, where emotional considerations take second place to the interest in the nature of the problem and the skill with which the argument is presented, is clear in their preference for improbable situations and abrupt changes of direction and mood. Beaumont and Fletcher also wrote *The Woman's Prize; or, The Tamer Tamed* (after 1604), a sequel to Shakespeare's *The Taming of the Shrew* (1594) in which Petruchio, now a widower after the death of Katharina, is himself tamed by his second wife, Maria.

Many of the works customarily attributed to "Beaumont and Fletcher" are in fact by a variety of other combinations, usually Fletcher with Nathan Field (1587–c. 1619) or Philip Massinger (1583–1640) or both. It is said that Fletcher's preferred approach was to write the middle of the play, in which he would sketch out a situation where opposing imperatives are so evenly balanced that no solution seems possible, and leave both the untangling and the initial setting-out process to his collaborators. Massinger, who was the son of the earl of Pembroke's steward, and thus loosely connected to the famous literary circle at Wilton House in Wiltshire, where Sir Philip Sidney had written *The Countess of Pembroke's Arcadia* (1590, 1593), also collaborated independently with Field and Dekker, and produced a number of his plays on his own, including *A New Way to Pay Old Debts* (1621–1622), which, because of the great actability of the role of its villain, Sir Giles Overreach, stayed in the repertoire until the last century, and *The Roman Actor* (1626). Additionally, Fletcher also collaborated with Shakespeare on *The Two Noble Kinsmen* (1613), *Henry VIII* (1613), and the now lost *Cardenio*.

Ford. John Ford comes late in the period—indeed all his independent plays are technically Caroline rather than Jacobean—but is very close in spirit to his predecessors, with a particular interest in reworking plots and motifs of Shakespeare. A Devon man of good family, he was the great-nephew of the lord chief justice, Sir John Popham, and his numerous dedications to members of the aristocracy attest to a wide and well-connected social circle. He seems to have lived most if not all of his adult life at the Middle Temple, though little is known of what he did there and nothing at all of his later years.

His most famous play, *'Tis Pity She's a Whore* (1633), rewrites *Romeo and Juliet* (1594–1595), but with the shocking difference that this time the lovers are brother and sister; incest is often suggested or seems imminent in Jacobean drama, but, except in Middleton's *Women Beware Women,* had always before been averted at the last minute by a discovery of mistaken identity, as in Beaumont and Fletcher's *A King and No King.* The fact that the playwright never explicitly condemns the incestuous liaison has often led to accusations of decadence and sensationalism, but the society that he depicts in the play has little except each other to offer these two bright young people. *The Broken Heart* (1633) and *Perkin Warbeck* (1634) also look backward in time, imaginatively revisiting the beginning and the end of the Tudor dynasty. *Perkin Warbeck* also revives the almost forgotten genre of the chronicle history play. Another last gasp of the Jacobean era was James Shirley (1596–1666), whose play *The Cardinal* (1641) was the final flourish of the revenge tradition, and who provided one of the rare points of continuity between Renaissance and Restoration drama.

Women Dramatists. Although all the professional playwrights of the period were men, women produced closet drama (which was meant to be read rather than performed), to which considerable critical attention was paid in the late twentieth century. Mary Sidney Herbert, countess of Pembroke (1561–1621), the sister and muse of Sir Philip Sidney, translated *The Tragedy of Antonie* (1595) from the French of Robert Garnier, and her niece Mary Wroth (c. 1587–c. 1653) wrote a comedy, *Love's Victory* (1621). The most celebrated play by a woman is *The Tragedy of Mariam* (1613) by Elizabeth Cary (1585–1639), a bluestocking heiress who later displeased her husband by converting to Catholicism. The play, which centers on Mariam, the wife of Herod, deals with the question of women's position in marriage and their right to speak, and makes an interesting comparison with *Othello* (c. 1604) and with *Antony and Cleopatra* (c. 1606).

BIBLIOGRAPHY

Primary Works

Beaumont, Francis, and John Fletcher. *The Maid's Tragedy.* Edited by T. W. Craik. Manchester, U.K., 1988.

Cerasano, S. P., and Marion Wynne-Davies. *Renaissance Drama by Women: Texts and Documents.* London, 1996. Includes *The Tragedy of Antonie, The Tragedy of Mariam, Love's Victory,* and Lady Jane Cavendish and Lady Elizabeth Brackley's Civil War play *The Concealed Fancies.*

Chapman, George. *The Widow's Tears.* Edited by Ethel M. Smeak. Lincoln, Nebr., 1966.

Corbin, Peter, and Douglas Sedge, eds. *Three Jacobean Witchcraft Plays.* Manchester, U.K., 1986. Contains Marston's *Sophonisba,* Middleton's *The Witch,* and Dekker, Ford, and Rowley's *The Witch of Edmonton.*

Ford, John. *Three Plays.* Edited by Keith Sturgess. Harmondsworth, U.K., 1970. Contains *'Tis Pity She's a Whore, The Broken Heart,* and *Perkin Warbeck.*

Gibson, Colin, ed. *The Selected Plays of Philip Massinger.* Cambridge, U.K., 1978. Contains *A New Way to Pay Old Debts, The City Madam, The Duke of Milan,* and *The Roman Actor.*

Lindley, David, ed. *Court Masques.* Oxford, 1995. Contains numerous masques by Ben Jonson, Thomas Campion, Samuel Daniel, George Chapman, Aurelian Townshend, Thomas Carew, and William Davenant.

Marston, John. *The Malcontent.* Edited by George K. Hunter. Manchester, U.K., 1975.

Maus, Katharine Eisaman, ed. *Four Revenge Tragedies.* Oxford, 1995. Contains Kyd's *The Spanish Tragedy, The Revenger's Tragedy, The Revenge of Bussy D'Ambois,* and *The Atheist's Tragedy.*

Middleton, Thomas. *A Mad World, My Masters and Other Plays.* Edited by Michael Taylor. Oxford, 1995. In addition to the title play, also contains *Michaelmas Term, A Trick to Catch the Old One,* and *No Wit, No Help Like a Woman's.*

Sturgess, Keith, ed. *Three Elizabethan Domestic Tragedies.* Harmondsworth, U.K., 1985. Contains *Arden of Feversham, A Yorkshire Tragedy,* and *A Woman Killed with Kindness.*

Secondary Works

Bentley, G. E. *The Jacobean and Caroline Stage.* 7 vols. Oxford, 1941–1968.

Dollimore, Jonathan. *Radical Tragedy.* 2d ed. Durham, N.C., 1993. Includes discussions of Marston's Antonio plays, *The Revenger's Tragedy,* and *Bussy D'Ambois.*

Ellis-Fermor, Una. *The Jacobean Drama: An Interpretation.* 4th rev. ed. London, 1958.

Farley-Hills, David. *Jacobean Drama: A Critical Study of the Professional Drama, 1600–25.* New York, 1988.

Gibbons, Brian. *Jacobean City Comedy.* 2d ed. London and New York, 1980.

Greg, W. W. *A Bibliography of the English Printed Drama to the Restoration.* 4 vols. London, 1938. Reprint, London, 1970.

Holdsworth, R. V., ed. *Three Jacobean Revenge Tragedies: A Selection of Critical Essays.* Basingstoke, U.K., 1990. Contains essays on *The Revenger's Tragedy, Women Beware Women,* and *The Changeling.*

Hopkins, Lisa. *John Ford's Political Theatre.* Manchester, U.K., 1994.

Kirsch, Arthur. *Jacobean Dramatic Perspectives.* Charlottesville, Va., 1972.

McLuskie, Kathleen. *Renaissance Dramatists.* Atlantic Highlands, N.J., 1989. Wide-ranging and very useful feminist readings of a number of plays of the period.

McMullan, Gordon. *The Politics of Unease in the Plays of John Fletcher.* Amherst, Mass., 1994.

Ornstein, Robert. *The Moral Vision of Jacobean Tragedy.* Madison, Wis., 1960.

Salingar, Leo. *Dramatic Form in Shakespeare and the Jacobeans: Essays.* Cambridge, U.K., and New York, 1986.

Zimmerman, Susan, ed. *Erotic Politics: Desire on the Renaissance Stage.* New York and London, 1992. A variety of interesting essays on Shakespearean and non-Shakespearean drama, including two on *The Roaring Girl.*

LISA HOPKINS

Jacobean Court Masque

When Ben Jonson (1572–1637) and Inigo Jones (1573–1652) staged *The Masque of Blackness* in 1605, they initiated a partnership that dominated the production of court entertainments throughout King James's reign. In their hands the varied traditions of courtly pastime, reaching back to the "disguisings" of the early Tudor period, incorporating the panegyric of the elaborate progress entertainments offered to Queen Elizabeth, and influenced by Italian and French models, were integrated into a form flexible enough to fulfill the varied demands made upon these ephemeral but enormously significant events.

The masque, comprising music, dance, and scenic spectacle as well as the literary texts that are its primary record, was customarily performed as part of the Christmas festivities, or else staged to mark significant state events. For example, Jonson's *Oberon* marked the investiture of Henry as Prince of Wales in 1611, and a series of masques by, among others, Thomas Campion and George Chapman marked the marriage of Princess Elizabeth in 1613. The devisers of these entertainments faced a complex brief. Central to all masques was the entry of disguised courtiers, who performed a series of choreographed dances before taking out the members of the audience in the social dances (the "revels"), which occupied the bulk of the evening. The first task, then, was to construct a narrative that might explain the masquers' arrival—hence the frequency with which the "plot" spoke of visitors arriving to do homage to the monarch. At the same time, the device had to be appropriate to the particular occasion of its performance and might be called upon to meet the specific demands of its patrons (Jonson, for example, was fulfilling Queen Anne's request to appear as a "blackamoor" in *The Masque of Blackness*). Masques also had a public function in manifesting the magnificence of the court to an audience that frequently included foreign ambassadors. Most important of all, it was essential that the masque's fiction issue in praise of the monarch, who was its most important spectator.

Jonson addressed these competing demands in the preface to *Hymenaei* (1606), his key formulation of masque theory, but claimed also that by drawing upon "antiquity and solid learnings" the masque might reach through its particular occasion toward "more removed mysteries" that transcended the ephemeral splendor of the performance. For Jonson the masque was a learned, moral, and didactic genre. The seriousness with which he took his task is manifest in the elaborate footnotes he supplied for the manuscript of *The Masque of Queens* (1609), which he presented to Prince Henry. This masque has further significance in that Jonson's device responded to Queen Anne's suggestion that her entrance be preceded by "a foil or false masque" by providing an antimasque of witches to set against the embodiments of "good Fame," which the Queen and her ladies represented. After this date the antimasque—usually performed by professional actors—became a fixed feature of the genre. The dialectical opposition of figures of evil, deceit, or trickery in the antimasque and the heroic virtues of the masquers defined the moral debate enacted in the masque. In his later masques Jonson deployed the contrast with increasing subtlety. In masques such as *Love Restored* (1612) and *Pleasure Reconciled to Virtue* (1618) the main masque does not simply overturn and displace its antithesis, as it had done in *Queens,* but rather revises and redirects the impulses toward love and pleasure whose excesses are exhibited in the antimasque.

A Masque. Design for the set of Ben Jonson's *Masque of Oberon* by Inigo Jones; 1610. DEVONSHIRE COLLECTION, CHATSWORTH/REPRODUCED BY PERMISSION OF THE DUKE OF DEVONSHIRE AND THE CHATSWORTH SETTLEMENT TRUSTEES/PHOTOGRAPHIC SURVEY, COURTAULD INSTITUTE OF ART

Significant though the moral allegory of the masque is, much critical attention has focused on its responsiveness to particular political circumstance, its "sounding to present occasions," in Jonson's phrase. At times masques seem straightforwardly to articulate a royal agenda. For example, *The Golden Age Restored* (1616) reflected on the turmoil caused by the trial of Robert Carr for the murder of Sir Thomas Overbury. But not infrequently they could seek to educate the monarch through a circumspect and qualified praise. For example, Thomas Campion's *Lord Hay's Masque* (1607) staged contemporary hesitations about the union of England and Scotland so urgently desired by King James, and George Chapman's *Memorable Masque* (1613) encouraged a more active colonial policy within its praise of the Palatine marriage. Reading the politics of any particular masque requires careful attention to its context, to the interests of its sponsors, and to the factional politics of the court itself, where participation as a masquer could itself be a mark of royal favor or, as George Villiers found, a way of coming to the king's attention.

Not everyone consented to Jonson's high estimate of the genre. Although he was contemptuous of those who "cry out that all endeavour of learning, and sharpness in these transitory devices . . . is superfluous," there were many, both inside and outside the court, who would have assented to Francis Bacon's verdict, in his essay "Of Masques and Triumphs," that "these things are but toys." Samuel Daniel, in his preface to *Tethys' Festival* (1610), expressly challenged Jonson's proud assertiveness, characterizing masque writers as "the poor engineers for shadows" who "frame only images of no result." To many the masque seemed to symbolize the extravagance rather than the magnificence of James's court, and to others to typify its moral laxity. (It should be remembered, however, that masques, such as *The Coleorton Masque* [1618], might be performed in a domestic environment by those unsympathetic to the court itself.) The ambivalence of attitudes to the genre are clearly marked in the drama of the period, where Prospero's masque in *The Tempest* (1611) leads to reflections upon transitoriness and impermanence, and Middleton's *Women Be-*

ware Women (1625–1627) ends in a grotesque bloodbath in a perverted masque of Cupid.

It is precisely the tensions that permeate the masque which are the source of its fascination. Politically conservative, it was yet a genre that, in its adoption of the latest musical fashions, and in the ever-increasing ingenuity of Inigo Jones's stage machinery and elaborate perspectival settings, looked toward the theater of the Restoration. It aspired to the dramatization of transcendent truths, yet was profoundly enmeshed in the complexity of political realities.

BIBLIOGRAPHY

Primary Works

Herford, C. H., Percy Simpson, and Evelyn Simpson, eds. *Ben Jonson.* 11 vols. Oxford, 1925–1952. Vols. 7 and 10, text and commentary, are still the principal edition of Jonson's masques.

Lindley, David, ed. *Court Masques.* Oxford, 1995. A selection of eighteen masques.

Orgel, Stephen, and Roy Strong, eds. *Inigo Jones: The Theatre of the Stuart Court.* 2 vols. London, Berkeley, and Los Angeles, 1973. Texts of masques, together with all the surviving Inigo Jones drawings of sets and costumes, and an important introduction.

Sabol, Andrew J., ed. *Four Hundred Songs and Dances from the Stuart Masque.* Providence, R.I., 1978. The main source for the masque's music.

Spencer, T. J. B., and Stanley Wells, eds. *A Book of Masques.* Cambridge, U.K., 1967. Fourteen masques, with little overlap with Lindley's selection.

Secondary Works

Bevington, David, and Peter Holbrook, eds. *The Politics of the Stuart Court Masque.* Cambridge, U.K., 1998. Wide-ranging collection of essays on the genre.

Butler, Martin. "Private and Occasional Drama." In A. R. Braunmuller and Michael Hattaway, eds. *The Cambridge Companion to English Renaissance Drama.* Cambridge, U.K., 1990. Excellent brief introduction.

Gordon, D. J. *The Renaissance Imagination.* Edited by Stephen Orgel. Berkeley, Los Angeles, and London, 1975. Pp. 127–160. Includes key essays on the iconology of masque.

Lindley, David, ed. *The Court Masque.* Manchester, U.K., 1984. Collection of essays on a wide variety of topics.

Orgel, Stephen. *The Illusion of Power.* Berkeley, Los Angeles, and London, 1975. Powerful short essay on the politics of theater.

Orgel, Stephen. *The Jonsonian Masque.* Cambridge, Mass., 1965. Groundbreaking study of the dramatic form of the masque.

Peacock, John. *The Stage Designs of Inigo Jones: The European Context.* Cambridge, U.K., 1995. The most comprehensive study of Jones's contribution to the masque.

Walls, Peter. *Music in the English Courtly Masque, 1604–1640.* Oxford, 1996. Full account of perhaps the most neglected aspect of the genre.

DAVID LINDLEY

DRAMA, FRENCH. The period between 1450 and 1620 is still a neglected period in the literary history of France. The French are so proud of the seventeenth-century plays of Corneille, Molière, and Racine that they tend to regard earlier theater inferior by definition. This is unfortunate, especially given that theater was not as easily separable from daily life in the Renaissance as it is today. Church and municipality frequently organized dramatic ceremonies and spectacles, and while court life was not yet the stylized dramatic production it would become under Louis XIV, it also reveled in sumptuous weddings, jousts, and elaborately choreographed royal entries into important cities.

A further problem is the lack of agreement about dates: when, in France, did the Middle Ages end and the Renaissance begin? In fact, as historical criticism since 1960 has shown, there was no strongly marked break between the thought habits of the Middle Ages and the Renaissance. This article will treat plays of the late fifteenth century as well as those of the sixteenth century.

Popular Theater. A misleading term, "popular theater" could be better replaced with "plays written for a large and diverse audience." The sprawling mystery plays of the Middle Ages, which sometimes went on for days and mobilized much of the population of a town, continued to be performed until they were officially forbidden in 1548. Their content was almost exclusively religious, but they sometimes included a short farcical interlude. Other municipal performances are recorded in the sixteenth century, including a number of carnival plays and the 1512 *Jeu du prince des sots* (Play of the prince of fools) by the well-known poet Pierre Gringore, which comprised a *cry* (a long poem advertising the performance, read aloud by one of the company as they paraded through the streets), a *sottie* (fools' play), a morality play, and a farce. Gringore was an important member of a society called Enfans sans souci (Happy-go-lucky children) and played a stock character called Mère Sotte (Mother Folly).

Theater was obviously an important component of the life of some towns, and there are records related to a number of performances. It is sometimes difficult to decide what kind of plays we are dealing with, as the genres mentioned above can overlap. Morality plays are perhaps the easiest, since their characters are usually biblical figures or moral abstractions. They vary in length from two hundred to three thousand lines of verse and are usually heavily didactic (a badly taught child falls into Lust, and thence into Shame, Despair, and the scaffold; Charity triumphs over Cheating, Avarice, and Death), although *La condamnation de banquet* (The condemnation of feasting) has several hilarious interludes. None is as successful, to a modern reader's eye, as the English equivalent, *Everyman*.

Closely related, at least in content, to the morality plays are the *sotties* written either for the medieval *sociétés joyeuses* like the Enfans sans souci mentioned above or for the various associations of lawyers' clerks collectively known as the Basoche. *Sotties,* so called because their characters are most often labeled "First Fool," "Second Fool," and so on, are more likely than the morality plays to contain specific political satire, like Gringore's *Jeu du prince des sots.* But they do sometimes have very similar moral content, based on (often complicated) wordplay: the New People who eat the World and lead the fool from a bad lodging to a worse one ("le logent de mal en pire"), or the *rapporteurs* who are both talebearers and rat carriers. The best of these plays are still great fun to perform but almost impossible to translate.

More congenial to modern audiences are the farces, of which we possess several hundred, almost all written in octosyllabic verse, of widely varying length, subject, and poetic quality. In many cases, we have little or no information about their authors, intended public, or whether they were in fact performed. Some fall naturally into groups: husband and wife quarrel and come to blows; unfaithful wife manages to deceive suspicious husband; doting mother thinks idiot son will be priest or pope; trickster turns the tables on those trying to trick him. The characters are usually taken from ordinary life—family members, servants, priests, merchants, soldiers, shoemakers, butchers, fishwives—and thus are easily distinguishable from the allegorical characters of the morality and *sottie.* The amount of action varies, and action is sometimes replaced with verbal cut-and-thrust, whether poetically witty or largely obscene. A few entire farces are based on verbal play. In *L'arbalète* (The crossbow), a wife tries to remedy her husband's stupidity, but he takes each clichéd phrase she uses and literally acts it out, for instance apostrophizing the arrow on his crossbow when she says he needs to "parler à trait" (speak slowly/speak to an arrow). In several cases, the double meaning is an obscene one, as in the case of the women who want to have their cooking pots (*pots*) cleaned out, or their saddles (*bas*) stuffed.

The two best-known farces are quite often performed today. In *Le cuvier* (The tub; probably late fifteenth century), a downtrodden husband is bullied by his shrewish wife, abetted by her unpleasant mother, into compiling a list of all the household chores he must perform. The wife then falls into the washtub and cannot get out, so he sits calmly reading through his list to see if "helping wife out of washtub" figures on it. When he finds it does not, he agrees to help her on condition that from now on he will be master in the house—a happy ending, "if the bargain holds," as he rather pessimistically comments. To the Renaissance audience, plays like this undoubtedly had a moral: the husband's duty is to be master in his house, and when he fails in this duty he deserves nothing but ridicule.

The most famous farce, never forgotten from its day to modern times, is *Maistre Pierre Pathelin* (Master Peter Pathelin; c. 1460). It is at least twice the length of any other farce and has been claimed as France's first comedy, the equivalent of *Ralph Roister Doister* in England. Its "hero" is the epitome of the trickster, but his wife, Guillemette, is his accomplice, not his antagonist. The other characters are a deceitful merchant, a shepherd who is less of a fool than he looks, and an honest but hopelessly befuddled judge. Pathelin, a shady character with some legal qualifications but no money, first cheats the merchant out of a length of cloth by promising to pay him for it when he comes to his house and then pretending to have been confined to his bed, delirious, for weeks (a very funny scene in which Pathelin gabbles in a variety of languages and dialects, uncomprehensibly to the merchant but comprehensibly to the audience). Then the shepherd begs Pathelin to defend him against the merchant, his employer, who is taking him to court for eating the sheep he was supposed to be guarding. Pathelin tells him to say only "Baa" in reply to any questions or orders, and he follows these instructions faithfully (a hilarious scene before the judge, in which the merchant recognizes Pathelin and becomes hopelessly confused about the two crimes of which he is a victim). All goes well, until Pathelin demands his fee from the shepherd, who continues to reply "Baa" until Pathelin gives up in disgust.

One reason for calling *Pathelin* a comedy rather than a farce is the sophistication of its verbal play. The verb *pateliner* already meant to gabble or verbally deceive. Pathelin invites the merchant, whose name is Guillaume ("fool"), to his house to eat roast goose, and "to make someone eat goose" meant "to make a fool of someone." More important, after Pathelin has agreed to help him, the shepherd promises to pay "à vostre mot." Pathelin understands this as "at your word," meaning "whatever you ask," but the shepherd means "*with* your word," that is, the "Baa" Pathelin has suggested to him.

This play was clearly very popular. Rabelais quotes it a number of times, it was translated into Latin in the sixteenth century, and the Parisian humanist Étienne Pasquier discussed it at length in his *Recherches de la France* (Researches on France; 1560).

One more category of "popular theater" tends to be overlooked in general studies: dramatic monologue. While numerous nondramatic monologues have survived, especially of the genre known as *sermons joyeux* (facetious sermons), some surviving examples have authentic theatrical qualities. The best of these is the *Franc-archer de Bagnolet* (The bowman from Bagnolet; c. 1470), in which a mercenary soldier boasts of his cowardice and his pillaging exploits, then mistakes a scarecrow for an enemy soldier and talks to it at length before realizing his error. This little play should certainly be counted among the farces.

The whole farce genre was clearly as popular with intellectuals as with ordinary people and had some influence on later literature. John Heywood translated several farces (but not *Pathelin*) into English. Farces may well have influenced the Italian commedia dell'arte, which developed during the sixteenth century, and numerous echoes of them can be found in the plays of Molière in the next century.

Humanist Comedy. Again, literary historians have traditionally seen a dramatic break between the "popular" farces and mystery plays of the Middle Ages and the more "classical" and dignified five-act forms of the Renaissance. They have also tried to fit sixteenth-century comedy into a Molieresque mold. In reality, these plays are less regular, more farcelike, and much more interesting than has been thought, but they need to be evaluated on their own terms, and not according to the numerous statements on comedy in poetic treatises, commentaries on Terence, and play prefaces, which all follow the lead of Joachim Du Bellay, the theoretician of the Pléiade group of poets, in stressing imitation of classical models.

The traditional date assigned to the "dawn" of French Renaissance comedy is 1552, the date of performance of Étienne Jodelle's *Eugène*. Jodelle, too, was a member of the Pléiade group of poets surrounding Pierre de Ronsard, and *Eugène* has been hailed as a striking new form of comedy. This is a quite unjustified exaggeration. The play is indeed in five acts but written in octosyllables like a farce and with a plot combining farce with Roman comedy: struggle for power and sexual favors among Alix, her loutish husband Guillaume, her former lover Florimond, her current lover the priest Eugène, and Eugène's sister Hélène, who loves Florimond. All ends amorally well, with Florimond and Hélène together, and Guillaume and Eugène agreeing to share Alix. Characters, Paris setting, and language are all authentically French.

This kind of bourgeois setting will dominate "humanist" comedy for much of the rest of the century. If the five-act division is usually respected, at least nine later plays are in octosyllables, suggesting that authors and public were in no hurry to adopt Terentian prose. Plots derived from Terence (or Plautus), however, are in the majority, involving situations such as an adulterous wife juggling two lovers (Jacques Grévin, *La trésorière* [The treasurer's wife; 1559]), an adulterous husband trying to take advantage of an orphan girl who turns out to be an heiress (Rémy Belleau, *La reconnue* [The rediscovered daughter; composed c. 1563; published 1578]), a young woman apparently condemned to marry an older man (Grévin, *Les ébahis* [Taken by surprise; 1561]), or a much more complex imbroglio with two beleaguered heroines and two flighty young men (Jean de La Taille, *Les corrivaux* [The rivals; composed 1562; published 1573]; this is the first prose comedy).

The characters in all these plays are the expected family members, dissolute young men who prefer love to their studies, and helpful or treacherous servants, with a sprinkling of doctors, legal officials, military men, and one procuress. A few authors try to vary the scene with more exotic characters. Jean-Antoine de Baïf, another member of the Pléiade, produced an excellent adaptation of Plautus's *Miles gloriosus, Le brave* (The braggart) in 1567; his swaggering soldier is just about as comic as his source's and seems to have started a trend. There is another braggart, Rodomont, in what is generally agreed to be the best of these plays, Odet de Turnèbe's *Les contents* (Satisfaction all around; 1584); still another, this time a Spaniard, in François d'Amboise's *Les Néapolitaines* (The Neapolitan ladies; 1584); and no fewer than three in Pierre Troterel's *Les corrivaux* (The rivals; 1612). In François Perrin's *Les ecoliers* (The students; 1589), Sobrin disguises himself as a peasant and speaks in dialect; in Jean Godard's *Les déguisés* (The masqueraders; 1594), a passerby is persuaded to impersonate a young man's father. Jean de La Taille introduced a necromancer into *Le négromant,* which he adapted from Ludovico Ariosto in 1573; he also created Pierre Le Loyer, an astrologer, for his eccentric and sometimes Rabelaisian *Le muet insensé* (The crazy mute; 1576).

These plays are more dissimilar than this bald recital would suggest. They ring changes attractively on the age-old plots of bourgeois comedy, and there is after all no limit to the permutations of lovers' disguises and servant's ruses. Some of their hackneyed characters are genuinely appealing, and many of them would play quite well on stage.

Some of the best-constructed comedies of the period were adapted from Italian sources by Pierre de Larivey, a member of a well-known Italian printing family (Giunti) established in Troyes. He published six comedies in 1579 and a further three in 1611; the liveliest is probably *Les esprits* (The ghosts), in which the old miser Severin, finding his hidden purse stolen, bursts out in lamentations that Molière will remember when writing *L'avare* (The miser; 1668).

Toward the end of the century we find a group of unclassifiable, interesting plays to which insufficient attention has been paid. Pierre Le Loyer adapted Aristophanes in *La néphélococugie* (Cloud-cuckoo city; 1578), with an open-ended structure, varying verse forms, and a style oscillating between the "noble" and the crude. Gérard de Vivre's *De la fidelité nuptiale* (On marital fidelity; 1577) seems more interested in its detailed stage directions about scenery, costume, and delivery than in the plot. Claude Bonet's *La tasse* (The cup; 1595) is an extraordinary farrago with a farcelike plot in five acts, octosyllables, and four languages: French, Provençal, Italian, and Latin. The well-known poet Marc de Papillon's *La nouvelle tragicomique* (The tragicomic story; 1597) barely qualifies as theater, and Pierre Troterel's *Gillette* (1620), in octosyllables (whereas his *Corrivaux* is in alexandrines), is part melodrama and part pastoral.

It is impossible to tell how many comedies in this large and disparate collection were actually performed or even intended for performance. Some of them may simply have been entertaining intellectual exercises. But the majority of them are still worth reading and merit scholarly attention.

Humanist Tragedy. If the comic repertoire of the sixteenth century is large, the tragic one is enormous, both in Latin and French. There seem to have been a variety of reasons for humanists to write tragedies in imitation of Euripides and Seneca: religious propaganda, contemporary satire, a genuine desire to "re-create" classical literature in French, or a simple fondness for rhetorical exercise. This last looks much like the pretext for what is generally considered the first French Renaissance tragedy: Étienne Jodelle's *Cléopâtre captive* (Cleopatra in prison; 1552 or 1553). Critics point out that the prologue addresses Henry II directly, and that he no doubt saw himself in the character of Octavian, but the fact remains that the entire "action" of the play takes place after the death of Anthony, and that Jodelle clearly delights in varying verse forms (alexandrines, octosyllables, lines of six and four syllables) and in rhetorical set pieces, especially of lamentation, using all the resources of rhetorical tropes.

Cléopâtre is in fact not the first French tragedy; that distinction belongs to Théodore de Bèze's *Abraham sacrifiant* (Abraham's sacrifice; 1550), although it has no act-scene division and, obviously, ends happily. Its analysis of Abraham's mental anguish has a strong Protestant undertone. Several other authors chose biblical or Christian subjects, including Louis Des Masures (*Tragédies saintes* [Sacred tragedies; 1563]); Jean de La Taille (*Saül le furieux* [The madness of Saul; before 1563?]); André de Rivaudeau (*Aman;* 1566); and Pierre Troterel (*La tragédie de Sainte Agnès;* 1615). The most appealing is probably Robert Garnier's *Les juives* (The Israelite women; 1583), which adds touching female characters to the biblical account of the Sack of Jerusalem by Nebuchadnezzar, but one of the most influential was George Buchanan's *Jephthes* of about 1542, written in Latin for performance by his pupils and several times translated later in the century.

But the great majority of tragedies, whether imitations of Euripides, Seneca, Italian models, or the Latin plays of Buchanan or Marc-Antoine Muret, took classical subjects. These were sometimes Greek (Jean de La Péruse, *La Médée* [Medea; 1556]; Nicolas Filleul, *Achille,* 1563; Garnier, *Antigone,* 1580), but more often Roman. Julius Caesar inspired perhaps the first tragedy on a secular theme in France, written in Latin by Muret and performed in the 1540s, as well as Grévin's *La mort de César* (The death of Caesar; 1561) and a number of other plays. Mark Anthony and Lucretia were popular, while Jodelle produced a *Didon se sacrifiant* (The sacrifice of Dido), probably about 1560, and Nicolas de Montreux a *Cléopâtre* in 1595. There are even a few plays with more exotic subjects, like Gabriel Bonnin's *La sultane* (The sultan's wife) of 1561, or based on contemporary events, like the anonymous *Tragédie du sac de Cabrières* (The sack of Cabrières).

Critics generally agree that the most important writer of tragedies was Robert Garnier. Between 1568 and 1583 he published eight plays, seven of which were tragedies. All are based on classical sources and have five acts with a chorus and a high proportion of monologues, stichomythia (a classical form of argumentative dialogue), and long recitals of tragic or violent events—we are still in the domain of rhetoric. Nearly all portray the calamities resulting from internecine or fratricidal rivalry, which Garnier saw as very relevant to the horrors of the French Wars of Religion. Three Roman plays—*Porcie,* on the death of Brutus and his wife Portia's suicide; *Cornélie,* about the death of Pompey's wife, and *Marc Antoine*—are more talk than action but succeed in creating an atmosphere of tragic emotion.

Of his Greek plays, *Hippolyte, La Troade,* and *Antigone,* the most often discussed is *Hippolyte* (1573), which is interesting to compare with Jean Racine's *Phèdre.* Unlike most of Garnier's tragedies, it has a male protagonist and focuses on love rather than politics. Garnier plays down Seneca's violence and stresses inevitability and pathos, starting with the initial monologues by Hippolytus and the ghost of Aegeus. Phaedra is depicted as more remorseful, and thus less guilty, than in Racine's play.

These plays have usually been studied, if at all, as illustrations of the classically based theory of the period (increased interest in Aristotle's unities and other rules toward the end of the century), or as steps in the "evolution" from medieval mystery play to Racinian tragedy. In fact, as Donald Stone and Gillian Jondorf have shown, these plays owe more to the classical Latin theoreticians Aelius Donatus and Diomedes, and to the plays of Euripides and Seneca, than they do to Aristotle, and their main interest is not in stagecraft but in rhetoric and ethics. Most have five acts and a chorus (which was beginning to be abandoned around the turn of the century), and delight in variations of meter and rhetorical set pieces. And as many titles suggest, the focus of the play is likely to be moralizing about the evils of unbridled lust, tyranny, or ambition. Compared to the roughly contemporary drama of the Elizabethan stage, these tragedies might seem boring to a modern audience—but the same can be said of plays by Racine a century later.

Tragicomedy and Pastoral. As monologue tends to get left out of discussions of farce, so tragicomedy and pastoral are often omitted from surveys of French theater, although both were very popular in the late sixteenth and early seventeenth century.

The versatile Garnier chose an episode from Ariosto's *Orlando furioso* for his *Bradamante* (1582), and is credited with importing into France the Italian genre of tragicomedy, which would remain popular until the mid-seventeenth century and include Pierre Corneille's *Le Cid* in 1637 (although Corneille subsequently claimed that the play was a tragedy). However, a case can be made for calling Louis Le Jars's *Lucelle* (1576) the first French tragicomedy, even if the real heyday of the genre was 1620–1640.

The incredibly energetic Alexandre Hardy is reputed to have composed or adapted several hundred plays, including tragedies, tragicomedies, and pastorals; only thirty-four plays were published. The pastoral, imported from both Italy and Spain, was extremely popular in the early seventeenth century, in the theater as in fiction (Honoré d'Urfé, *L'Astrée;* 1607–1627). Mention should at least be made of the works of Jean Mairet, whose pastoral tragicomedies were performed in 1626 and 1630, even though most of these plays were produced outside the chronological limits of this article. It is curious that pastoral elements in fiction persist throughout the seventeenth century, whereas pastoral plays seem to have had a brief, if flourishing, life.

The theatrical output of this period is both prolific and extremely diverse. The French stage produced no towering genius to set beside Rabelais and Montaigne, and indeed the term "the French stage" already does the period a disservice. Farces, *sotties,* and morality plays were performed on makeshift platforms in the marketplace; some comedies, tragedies, tragicomedies, and pastorals were staged at court, others were intended only to be read in the classroom, and so on. Of the authors mentioned here, only Hardy wrote for a specific company of professional actors, and it is hard to imagine how some of the plays mentioned above can have been staged at all. The best way to enjoy this theater is to forget what we know both about the classical (seventeenth-century) theater that will shortly follow it, and about modern theater, and study each play on its own terms.

See also **Commedia dell'Arte; Drama,** *subentries on* **Tragedy** *and* **Erudite Comedy; Pléiade.**

BIBLIOGRAPHY

Primary Works

Aubailly, Jean-Claude, ed. *Deux jeux de carnaval de la fin du Moyen Age.* Geneva, 1977.

Balmas, Enea, ed. *Comédies du seizième siècle.* Paris, 1967.

Capitani, Patrizia de, et al., eds. *La tragédie à l'époque d'Henri II et de Charles IX.* Florence and Paris, 1986–.

Droz, Eugénie, ed. *Le recueil Trepperel: Les sotties.* Paris, 1935.

Helmich, Werner, ed. *Moralités françaises*. Geneva, 1980.

Tissier, André, ed. *Recueil de farces (1450–1550)*. 10 vols. Geneva, 1986–.

Turnèbe, Odet de. *Satisfaction All Around*. Ottawa, Canada, 1979. Translation of *Les contents*.

Secondary Works

Arden, Heather. *Fools' Plays: A Study of Satire in the Sottie*. Cambridge, U.K., 1980.

Jeffery, Brian. *French Renaissance Comedy 1552–1630*. Oxford, 1969.

Jondorf, Gillian. *French Renaissance Tragedy: The Dramatic Word*. Cambridge, U.K., 1990.

Knight, Alan E. *Aspects of Genre in Late Medieval French Drama*. Manchester, U.K., 1983.

Maddox, Donald. *Semiotics of Deceit: The Pathelin Era*. London, 1984. Includes English translation of *Maistre Pierre Pathelin*.

Perret, Donald. *Old Comedy in the French Renaissance 1576–1620*. Geneva, 1992.

Stone, Donald. *French Humanist Tragedy: A Reassessment*. Manchester, U.K., 1974.

BARBARA C. BOWEN

DRAMA, SPANISH.

Whatever controversy may exist about the origins of the Spanish theater and the prevalence of theater in Castile in the early Middle Ages, studies have confirmed the existence of a flourishing religious drama in fifteenth-century Castile. However, a departure in the history of the Spanish theater came late in the fifteenth century in the works of Juan del Encina, many of whose pastoral plays, even those with religious themes, are thinly disguised allegories of his relationship with his patrons. Slightly later, Bartolomé de Torres Naharro, working mostly in Italy, took the important step of creating theater that was illusionistic rather than ritualistic.

Sixteenth-century Spanish drama comprised several dramatic practices that served widely different audiences. These included popular religious plays performed on the major feasts of the ecclesiastical year; university and Jesuit collegiate plays composed in Latin, Castilian, or a mixture of both languages and aimed at a more learned audience; secular plays, often based on Italian or classical models and performed by itinerant professional companies; and courtly entertainments associated with royal or noble courts and ultimately derived from the medieval masque. Toward the end of the century, a group of playwrights working primarily in Valencia experimented with neoclassical tragedy.

Sacramental Plays and the *Comedia*.

The two most important dramatic genres in seventeenth-century Spain were the *auto sacramental* and the *comedia*. The Corpus Christi *autos sacramentales* (sacramental plays) were the culmination of the popular religious theater of the sixteenth century and a significant vehicle for the dissemination of Counter-Reformation theology. While all sacramental plays exalted the Eucharist, their allegorical plots could be based on Old Testament stories, biblical parables, classical mythology, or current events. By giving dramatic form to abstract religious concepts, the sacramental plays functioned as both theater and theology. In Madrid the town council financed the performance of four sacramental plays a year, staged in the open air on two to four pageant wagons, which contained elaborate scenery and hidden machines to create spectacular scenic effects.

The seventeenth-century *comedia*, while built on sixteenth-century dramatic practices, constituted another new departure. The *comedia*, literally "comedy," became the generic term for "play," and that shift in meaning underscored the comic pattern that underlay a high percentage of Spanish drama. This is not to say that tragic themes or undertones were lacking, although tragedy in the Aristotelian sense failed to prosper in Spain. *Comedia* was fundamentally escapist and provided audiences with a simplified view of life; although the characters sometimes faced serious dilemmas, they overcame all obstacles to arrive at a happy ending.

Theaters and Performance.

Largely the creation of Lope de Vega, the *comedia* was closely associated with the construction of the first public theaters. The public theaters brought together all social classes, from the gentry in their rented boxes to the groundlings who stood in the pit. Plays were performed during the day in *corrales*, that is, in interior courtyards (*patios*) surrounded by houses through whose windows the more affluent spectators could watch the performance. The *patio* proper consisted of lateral rows of benches and a central pit for the groundlings. At one end of the patio was a rectangular apron stage with most likely a curtained back with openings for entrances and exits. As required, the curtain could be drawn back to reveal an inner room, while the gallery above the stage could be used to represent a balcony, a mountain, and so forth. The stage was relatively bare, with the exception of a few significant stage properties. Since there was no scenery as such, poetry was used to "paint" the place of the action as well as to indicate—in the absence of lighting effects—the time of day. Stage machinery created spectacular scenic effects, which were extremely popular.

Since the *comedia* was written entirely in verse, the poetry itself constituted no mean part of the genre's popularity. The frequent wordplay and complicated imagery suggest that the spectators, whether literate or not, were sophisticated in their appreciation of verbal complexities. The plays are polymetric; the meter changes from one scene to another, resulting in subtle variations of tempo and rhythm. Versification is sometimes linked to characterization: peasants tend to speak in traditional Spanish meters, while the nobility often speak in Italian hendecasyllables.

In Spain, unlike other European countries, women were allowed to act in the public theaters, although their alleged—and sometimes real—immorality was censured by severe moralists. The conventional cast of characters included a pair of lovers and such blocking figures as rival suitors or an authoritarian father, husband, or brother. The *gracioso,* normally the protagonist's servant, provides comic relief through his witty repartee or by parodying the main plot. The plays normally end in marriage presided over by an authority figure like the king. In general, the audience preferred swiftly moving plots fraught with disguises, deceptions, and duels to plots involving the leisurely revelation of character. Characterization is accomplished largely through action and dialogic interaction among the characters.

The conventional three-act structure was framed by a *loa,* or prelude, before the main play and punctuated by an *entremés* (a short, comical skit) following act one, and another *entremés* or a *baile* (a danced dialogue) following act two. More singing and dancing followed the third act. Such breaks in tone could have quite different aesthetic effects, depending on whether the main play was comic or serious.

Almost anything could provide the basis for a *comedia:* proverbs, Italian short stories, episodes of national history, classical mythology, lives of the saints, and so forth. Lope de Vega himself was aware of the popularity of the honor theme, whose variations ran the gamut from the seduced maiden who dons masculine disguise to track down and marry her seducer to the murder of the wife merely suspected of infidelity.

The *comedia* was a highly conventionalized genre and often opted for conservative solutions to the characters' dilemmas. As such, the Spanish theater has been viewed as a highly efficient propaganda machine that promoted social conformity and exalted the shared values of seventeenth-century Spanish society. However, despite their generic similarities, the plays were also works of art whose ambiguity and subtlety allowed for questioning the very values they seemed to uphold.

See also Encina, Juan del; Spanish Literature and Language; Torres Naharro, Bartolomé de; Vega Carpio, Lope Félix de.

BIBLIOGRAPHY
McKendrick, Melveena. *Theatre in Spain 1490–1700.* Cambridge, U.K., 1989.
Shergold, N. D. *A History of the Spanish Stage from Medieval Times until the End of the Seventeenth Century.* Oxford, 1967.
Wilson, Margaret. *Spanish Drama of the Golden Age.* Oxford and New York, 1969.

RONALD E. SURTZ

DRAWING. During the Renaissance drawings became, for the first time, a significant and functional medium for creating artworks. The extraordinary growth in the number of preparatory sheets produced after 1450 attests to an increasing reliance on draftsmanship as the generative force of the creative process. Drawing revolutionized artistic practice because it helped meet the new demands for original solutions when reliance on formulas no longer sufficed.

Drawings were used in the workshop to train apprentices and facilitate production. Shop masters assembled model-books of drawings with accepted solutions to artistic problems. These drawings (*exempla*) could be copied by apprentices as a primary means of instruction and consulted or reused by the master for future paintings. Copying from the same model-book taught apprentices the workshop style and engendered a homogeneous workshop product. *Exempla* have a particular look due to their function. Since they were meant to be studied and copied, they had to be carefully executed with simple, strong and uninterrupted contours.

By 1450 workshops began to shift some resources away from rote copying of exempla to exploration of the natural world by means of observing and sketching it. The concept of experimental drawing emerged. At that point, drawing became a creative problem-solving tool. A thinking, or exploratory, sheet was made to work out ideas and search for original formal solutions. In its often rapidly executed, probing style and fragmentary character, it differs in look and purpose from carefully finished *exempla.* With this shift in the function of drawings, model-books were replaced by sketchbooks of drawings made from life.

The intensity of the analytical component in the drawing process was supported by a complex theoretical framework that evolved for *disegno* (drawing). This term signified not only the act of drawing, but also the intellectual process of translating an idea into a concrete form. Giorgio Vasari, who published the first biographies of artists in 1550, spoke for his era when he glorified *disegno* as the father of all the arts.

Techniques. The two components of a drawing are the marking medium and the surface. Renaissance artists used metalpoint, pen and ink, chalk, charcoal, and brush on parchment, paper, panel, canvas, and fresco.

Until the Renaissance, the absence of a suitable surface (paper) prohibited sketching freely. The increasing availability and decreasing cost of paper after the invention of the printing press revolutionized artistic practice because it allowed artists to work out ideas through innumerable drawings.

In the early Renaissance, when media choices were limited and conservatively employed, there was a persistent tension between technique and expression as artists tried to achieve pictorial goals for which traditional media (particularly silverpoint) became impediments rather than facilitators. By the late Renaissance, when a plethora of options was open to artists, there was a greater range, experimentation, and freedom in the use of media.

Silverpoint. In silverpoint a mark is made as the stylus passes over the calcium-coated surface of the paper, leaving behind minuscule particles of silver that tarnish, turning gray.

Because it is difficult to guide the stylus through the unyielding ground, the line tends to be thin, stiff, delicate, and uniform. Thicker lines can only be produced by a blunter instrument. Shading is achieved by hatching, or marking with fine, closely spaced lines. Texture and tonal effects are difficult to convey. To overcome these limitations, inherent in the medium, a three-tone sheet was devised by applying white highlighting with a brush on a tinted ground.

Silverpoint requires great skill, patience, concentration, and control. It demands accuracy and a sure hand because mistakes cannot be erased. Silverpoint sheets tend to be finished, linear, two-dimensional, and carefully thought out. Accordingly, this technique is not conducive to exploratory sketching and was gradually abandoned as this task became a necessity to the draftsman.

Pen and ink. The goose-quill pen, which came into use around 1100, is far more versatile than the metal stylus. It glides fluently over the paper and the line it produces is capable of spontaneity and variety.

By changing pressure applied to the quill, the contour of the line can swell, thicken, or taper to indicate tension of muscles under pressure. The quill also responds to speed of movement, producing an energetic and dynamic line. The flexibility and variation in the pen line renders it more expressive and calligraphic than the stylus line. The medium was prized for rapidly executed sketches as well as for carefully thought out, detailed studies.

By 1500 the range of effects of pen-and-ink drawings had greatly expanded as artists successfully sought ways to overcome the inherent linearity of the medium and increase their ability to express light-modeled form and atmosphere. Hatching proved unsatisfactory in achieving subtle tonal modulations. Another method was to use the paper as a middle ground and apply white highlighting and washes with a brush. Wash could define the fall of light on an object and indicate the structure of space and the placement of objects in space. However, wash had only limited ability to render subtle tonal transitions.

Chalk and charcoal. Only when artists became concerned with conveying smooth and imperceptible tonal modulation (c. 1475), particularly of light playing across the muscular structure of the nude, did they realize the possibilities of red and black chalk over pen and ink to achieve this goal. Chalk's advantages for rendering atmospheric effects of light and its broad pictorial qualities appealed to high-Renaissance artists in whose works these goals were paramount. It also permitted greater freedom of handling and spontaneity. Charcoal was used primarily for cartoons, but was increasingly favored for preliminary underdrawing as a guide because it erased so easily.

Types of Drawings. Types of drawing in the Renaissance include figure drawings, studies of heads, composition drawings, cartoons, and presentation drawings.

Figure drawings. A central goal of Renaissance art was to master the realistic representation of the nude in dramatic action. Anatomical structure, movement, proportional construction, and expression were analyzed and learned by drawing from the nude model. Studies range from stiff, two-dimensional figures (Pisanello) made in the early Renaissance, to scientific diagrams of proportions (Leonardo da Vinci), to freely manipulated and decoratively conceived figures appreciated by the mannerists (Pontormo) for their artifice and grace.

Drawing by Dürer. *Praying Hands* (study). Chalk on blue paper; 1508. GRAPHISCHE SAMMLUNG ALBERTINA, VIENNA/ERICH LESSING/ART RESOURCE

While ancient sculpture provided a visual catalyst, the theoretical impetus for the mastery of the figure was formulated by Leon Battista Alberti (*On Painting;* 1436), who encouraged artists to draw from the nude. Along with Leonardo, he admonished them to render "the movements of the mind" through pose and gesture.

Studies of heads. As with the nude, artists developed a scientific interest in rendering the head accurately and in perspective. Piero della Francesca and Leonardo methodically studied and diagramed the head, including mathematical ratios of facial features. The increased demand for portraits and for portrait heads inserted into paintings encouraged artists to abandon formulaic delineation and to observe and study the live model. Theoretical admonitions to use appropriate facial types and interest in facial expression encouraged subtle psychological portrayals. Independent portrait drawings proliferated.

Composition drawings. Two types of highly finished composition studies were common during the Renaissance: the contract sheet inserted in a legal document to be presented to a patron for his approval, and the *modello,* or small-scale version of the painting used to transfer to the cartoon. In contrast to these carefully prepared sheets, the exploratory composition sketch (*schizzo*), made early in the preparatory process, is often messy and filled with rejected ideas (*pentimenti*).

By 1500 a fairly standardized procedure for using drawings in the preparation of a painting developed. The artist began with a rudimentary idea of the composition (*primo pensiero*) to get the idea down on paper. He had little concern for correct form at this stage. Because he was still unsatisfied, he continued to explore alternative possibilities, finally working up a more fully developed composition study. When he achieved his desired concept he made studies from nature of individual parts to verify his forms and refine individual parts and their relationships. Then he carefully executed a *modello,* which he squared for transfer and enlargement to a cartoon.

Cartoons. In the early Renaissance, drawings for frescoes (*sinopia*) were sketched on the rough coating of plaster (*arriccio*) rather than on scarce paper. However, the *sinopia* was eventually covered by smooth fresh plaster (*intonaco*), on which the artist had to work from memory. The cartoon, a charcoal drawing in the exact dimensions of the painting, was delineated on paper and could be affixed to the wall on the *intonaco* and pricked along its outlines. Charcoal could then be "pounced" through the holes (*spolvero*) onto the *intonaco,* leaving dotted outlines of the objects. The artist used the cartoon, a drawing made in charcoal in the exact dimensions of the painting, to transfer his composition to the surface to be painted.

Presentation drawings. Independent, virtuoso works of art known as presentation drawings are highly finished and have the same aesthetic value as a painting. Their emergence at the end of the fifteenth century indicates the rising status and appreciation of drawings by this time.

Other major categories of Renaissance drawings are studies after the antique, landscape, and drapery studies.

See also **Human Body in Renaissance Art.**

BIBLIOGRAPHY

Ames-Lewis, Francis. *Drawing in Early Renaissance Italy.* New Haven, Conn., 1981.

Ames-Lewis, Francis, and Joanne Wright. *Drawing in the Italian Renaissance Workshop.* London, 1983. Exhibition catalog.

De Tolnay, Charles. *History and Technique of Old Master Drawings.* New York, 1943.

Grassi, Luigi. *Il disegno italiano dal trecento al seicento.* Rome, 1956.

Watrous, John. *The Craft of Old Master Drawings.* Madison, Wis., 1957.

JEAN GOLDMAN

DRAYTON, MICHAEL. *See* **Poetry, English,** *subentry on* **Elizabethan Poetry.**

DU BARTAS, GUILLAUME DE SALLUSTE

(1544–1590), French Calvinist poet and playwright. Guillaume Du Bartas was born in Montfort in Gascony to one of the oldest families among Huguenot nobility. He received a humanist education and exposure to both sacred and profane literature. A convinced Calvinist, he served Henry of Navarre, traveling to England and Scotland as well as to Germany (1586) to win support for the Huguenot cause. Du Bartas spoke many languages, and possessed an encyclopedic knowledge and interest in all things; a prolific writer, he also studied natural history and the sciences, musical composition, and was an accomplished artist. He married around 1572 and had four daughters. When his wife died, he lamented her passing in *La seconde sepmaine* (The second week; unfinished); they appear to have had a close and nurturing relationship. Appropriately, his grief and his art intertwined, as did all aspects of his life—a life dedicated always to a metaphysical purpose, his Calvinist understanding of the glory of God. Du Bartas befriended many poets and men of letters, among them Théodore-Agrippa d'Aubigné, his comrade-in-arms. He contributed enormously to literature in his day, influencing, most notably, John Milton, who—via Josuah Sylvester's masterful translation of Du Bartas's 1578 work *La sepmaine* (which conveys the agonizing climate of the Wars of Religion), as *The Divine Weekes and Workes* (London, 1605)—composed *Paradise Lost* as a sort of intertextual document weaving together the Bible and Du Bartas's vision of creation. Du Bartas's works were also

Guillaume de Salluste Du Bartas. BIBLIOTHÈQUE NATIONALE, PARIS/JEAN-LOUP CHARMET

Protestant poetic manifesto. Du Bartas's master-pieces—*La sepmaine* and *La seconde sepmaine*—put poetry to work at the service of both divine truth and moralizing science.

A disciple of the Pléiade poets when young, Du Bartas adopted their emphasis on epic poetry. Pierre de Ronsard, the author of the epic *La franciade,* recognized Du Bartas's mastery, and exclaimed upon reading *La sepmaine:* "O! Que n'ay-je fait ce poème!" (Oh! If only I had made thy poem!). However, Du Bartas was no secularist. Bitterly opposed to licentious court poetry and pagan sources for poetic inspiration, he joined his inspiration, the Bible, with his poetic flair and wide-sweeping knowledge to create a strong, new, Calvinist poetic voice. In his work, the Reformation powerfully uses poetry to articulate biblically based moral perspectives on mankind.

BIBLIOGRAPHY

Dauphiné, James. *Guillaume Salluste Du Bartas: Poète scientifique.* Paris, 1983.

Miernowski, Jan. *Dialectique et connaissance dans* La Sepmaine *de Du Bartas.* Geneva, 1992.

Pellissier, Georges. *La vie et les oeuvres de Du Bartas.* Geneva, 1969.

CATHARINE RANDALL

translated all over the Continent, going into many editions. In France, an entire generation of writers acknowledged their indebtedness to him. Simon Goulart, successor to John Calvin in Geneva, edited and commented on Du Bartas's works, claiming him not only as literary *confrère,* but as the crown of Calvinist literature.

Du Bartas's compendious *oeuvre* includes the play *La judit* (1574). Based on the biblical story of Judith and Holofernes, *La judit* conveys an acute, baroque consciousness of suffering and death, rendering its biblical model extremely dramatic. Du Bartas's *L'Uranie* develops his conception of "*la muse chrestienne*" (the Christian muse), or writing deriving its merit solely from the glory it gives to God, and expresses his desire to be the David, or psalmist, of his time. *L'Uranie*, like his other texts, attests to Du Bartas's deftness in reconciling classical models with Christian imperatives, much as Théodore de Bèze had counseled in the preface to his *Abraham sacrifiant.* Together, and joined with d'Aubigné's preface to *Les tragiques,* these documents elucidate a

DU BELLAY, JOACHIM (c. 1522–1560), French poet of the Pléiade. Du Bellay was the most important poet of the Pléiade after Pierre de Ronsard. He was born near Liré in Anjou into a family of diplomats, bishops, and soldiers. Because of his poor health and the loss of his parents when he was nine, his education was neglected. During most of his life Du Bellay was in poor health and had recurring deafness. He died of a stroke before the age of forty.

In 1545 he began law school in Poitiers, but he left his studies after he was introduced to poetry by Jacques Peletier du Mans. Peletier persuaded Du Bellay to choose the sonnet and the ode as poetic forms. In 1574 Du Bellay joined Ronsard and Jean-Antoine de Baïf at the Collège de Coqueret with Jean Dorat, an erudite professor of Greek, as principal. There Du Bellay learned to imitate the achievements of classical poets and eventually became a member of the Pléiade, a group of seven prominent French poets. In 1549 he published his manifesto, *Défense et illustration de la langue française* (Defense and illustration of the French language), which called for the renewal and enrichment of French through the imitation of Greco-Roman and Italian texts. His specific recommendations included adaptation of classical works and the use of neologisms, archaisms, and technical words.

Du Bellay's defense of vernacular French as a literary medium, the pagan and aesthetic implications of his theory of imitation, and his rejection of previous French poets in favor of the ancients all led to a lively debate in French letters and to the publication of other treatises on poetic theory. His sonnet sequence *L'Olive* (Olive; Paris, 1549–1550) was a landmark in literary history and a practical example of the precepts of the *Défense*. As the first French poetic love sequence, it was inspired by Du Bellay's admiration for Maurice Scève's *Délie* and for Ronsard's growing ascendancy in French letters.

A change in style occurred during his travels to Rome in 1553, where he resided at first with great expectations and ambitions for career advancement. But he soon became critical of Rome's mores. He found time, however, for friendships with cultivated writers in French diplomatic circles, and he wrote *Les antiquités de Rome* (Antiquities of Rome; 1558), *Les regrets* (Regrets), *Les divers jeux rustiques* (Diverse rustic games), and *Poemata* (Poems). *Les antiquités* forms a collection of thirty-two sonnets, followed by *Songe* (Dream), a further sequence of fifteen sonnets, all built around the motif of Rome's past glory and present decadence. *Les regrets,* which contains his most celebrated verse, describes in a poetic "journal" his life in Rome with its many disappointments and his return journey to France. Distancing himself from the elevated principles of *Défense* and from Ronsard's more erudite tendencies, Du Bellay turns the sonnet form into a medium for expressing more personal thoughts and feelings. The elegiac turn, recalling Ovid (*Tristia*), blends with the satirical strain that Du Bellay draws from Horace (*Satires*) and from contemporary Italian burlesque poetry.

Les divers jeux rustiques is a composite collection of recreational pieces reminiscent of Ronsard's *Folastries* (Frolickings) and Baïf's *Passetems* (Pastimes). The satirical strain is still present, as in the poem "Vieille courtisane" (The old courtesan) or the "Hymne de la surdité" (Hymn to deafness). The *Poemata* consist of four books of Latin verse. These collections differ from traditional Petrarchan poetry as Du Bellay uses the sonnet as a vehicle for themes other than love.

BIBLIOGRAPHY

Primary Works

Du Bellay, Joachim. *Oeuvres complètes.* Edited by Henri Chamard. 6 vols. Geneva, 1908–1913. Rev. ed., 1982–.

Secondary Works

Coleman, Dorothy G. *The Chaste Muse: A Study of Du Bellay's Poetry.* Leiden, Netherlands, 1980.

Dickinson, Gladys. *Du Bellay in Rome.* Leiden, Netherlands, 1960.

Gadoffre, Gilbert. *Du Bellay et le sacré.* Paris, 1978. A classic text on Du Bellay's life and works.

Katz, Richard A. *The Ordered Text: The Sonnet Sequences of Du Bellay.* New York, 1985.

Tucker, George Hugo. *The Poet's Odyssey: Joachim Du Bellay and the Antiquitez de Rome.* Oxford and New York, 1990.

ANNE R. LARSEN

DUBROVNIK. The Republic of Dubrovnik (called Ragusa in Italian), entered its "golden century" in the 1400s. Its merchant fleet ("argosy" in English) rivaled the fleets of Venice and Genoa and traded from the Levant to the English Channel. The value of its shipping reached 700,000 *ducats* in 1570, but by 1585 maritime trade had ceased to expand.

After 1358 the republic was autonomous, owing a nominal tribute to Hungary as its protector. It expanded greatly in these years, adding the island of Mljet over the course of the fourteenth century, the peninsula of Pelješac in 1333, the coast to the northwest (Primorje) in 1399, and the southeastern coastal region (Konavli) in the early fifteenth century. The city enjoyed remarkable political stability, achieving a peak population of possibly 7,000 within its walls and 25,000 more in the countryside. Dubrovnik's white flag bore the proud word *Libertas,* and its leaders generally succeeded in peaceable relations with Dubrovnik's former overlord, the Republic of Venice, and with its powerful new neighbors, the Ottoman Turks, who had won by conquest the neighboring Balkan lands. Internal political stability has, most likely, been overstated by the city-state's chroniclers, but it would be difficult to overestimate the republic's diplomatic achievements. Dubrovnik maintained amicable relations with most powers in an embattled Mediterranean world. It established a consular service that was the envy of its rivals and a boon to trade. The state generally avoided entangling political alliances, although a turn to Spain as protector in the sixteenth century meant that Dubrovnik sent a small contingent from its own fleet to join Philip II's ill-fated Armada in 1588.

The inhabitants were devout Catholics. One native son, Elias de Saraca, served as archbishop of the city. Despite his highly appreciated role in bringing Dubrovnik under Hungarian protection in the 1350s, after his tenure Dubrovnik requested that the pope never again appoint a native to the local see. Dubrovnik's constitutional concern with egalitarianism among the ruling patriciate may be seen at work here and also in the continuance of a weak executive office where an elected rector served only a single six-month term. Governing the republic fell to a Great Council composed of all men of aristocratic family over the age of twenty (repealed back to eighteen for some decades following the peak of the Black Death of 1348–1350). The Senate and the Small Council rounded out the civic offices. Although factionalism arose, the interrelated patriciate stifled it for the most part and displayed much skill in negotiating local disputes. In the Great Council the aristocracy still spoke an Adriatic dialect known locally as "Old Ragusan," although Slavic had become the language of preference and of high culture in this Balkan city-state by the Renaissance.

Nonetheless Dubrovnik-Ragusa remained bilingual through the Renaissance centuries. Philippus de Diversis's *Situs aedificiorum, politiae et laudabilium consuetudinum inclytae civitatis Ragusij* (The site of the buildings and praiseworthy customs of political life in the city of Ragusa; 1440) and Benedetto Cotrugli's *Della mercatura et del mercante perfetto* (On commerce and the perfect merchant; 1458), as well as Cotrugli's now-lost disquisition on the family, spread Dubrovnik's fame in the West. Both Lodovico Beccadelli, archbishop of Dubrovnik from 1555 to 1563, and the political theorist Jean Bodin promoted the Dubrovnik myth of a *republica perfetta* where proper deference was paid to one's social and moral superiors. These authors and various travelers' accounts may have prompted William Shakespeare to use the town as the setting for his comedy *Twelfth Night*.

Perhaps Dubrovnik's greatest cultural contribution lay in the emergence of a vernacular Slavic literature. The comedies of Marin Držić (d. 1567) and the tragedies of Ivan Gundulić (d. 1638) are among the greatest works in Slavic languages. In arts and letters Renaissance residents of Dubrovnik combined a unique local flavor with Italian humanist influences brought through their own travel and study abroad and spread through men like Beccadelli, who had belonged to the illustrious circle of Pietro Bembo and his friends. The sculptors and artists of Dubrovnik embellished their walled city, making it one of the most beautiful Mediterranean city-states.

BIBLIOGRAPHY

Primary Works
Cotrugli, Benedetto. *Il libro dell'arte di mercatura.* Edited by Ugo Tucci. Venice, 1990. A modern edition of *Della mercatura et del mercante perfetto* (Venice, 1583).

de Diversis de Quartigianis, Philippus. *Situs aedificiorum, politiae et laudabilium consuetudinum inclytae civitatis Ragusij.* Edited by V. Brunelli. Zara, 1882.
Držić, Marin. *Uncle Mario.* Translated by Sonia Bicanic. Dubrovnik, 1967. An enduring comedy still performed in Dubrovnik.
Gundulić, Ivan. *Osman.* Translated by E. D. Goy. Zagreb, 1991. Gundulić's most renowned work.
Luetić, Josip. *Mornarica dubrovačke republike.* Dubrovnik, 1962.
Tadić, Jorjo. *Dubrovnik portreti.* Belgrade, 1948.

Secondary Works
Krekic, Barisa. *Dubrovnik: A Mediterranean Urban Society, 1300–1600.* Aldershot, U.K., and Brookfield, Vt., 1997.
Krekic, Barisa. *Dubrovnik in the Fourteenth and Fifteenth Centuries: A City between East and West.* Norman, Okla., 1971.
Stuard, Susan Mosher. *A State of Deference: Ragusa/Dubrovnik in the Medieval Centuries.* Philadelphia, 1992. Contains material relevant to the Renaissance period.
Zlatar, Zdenko. *The Slavic Epic.* New York, 1995.

SUSAN MOSHER STUARD

DUCCIO DI BUONISEGNA. *See* **Siena,** *subentry on* **Art in Siena.**

DUDLEY, ROBERT (1533?–1588), earl of Leicester (1564). The fifth son of John Dudley, duke of Northumberland, and Jane Guildford Dudley, Robert Dudley served four monarchs: Edward VI, Mary I, Elizabeth I, and Mary, queen of Scots.

At the death of Edward VI in 1553, Dudley joined his father's efforts to make Lady Jane (Dudley) Grey queen. He was arrested, sent to the Tower in London (1553–1554), and his properties were confiscated. Military service during Mary I's reign partially restored his family's fortunes, but brought no offices. With Elizabeth I's accession, Leicester became an influential political figure, and the queen's great affection for Leicester permitted him to move in the highest circles at court. As a member of the Privy Council (1563–1588), Leicester joined with others of that group in advising the queen on matters of domestic and foreign policy and in executing a multitude of administrative duties throughout the realm. Although he failed in his efforts to become Elizabeth's chief adviser, Leicester used his political influence to good advantage in promoting religious and cultural issues. For example, Leicester was a leading sympathizer of the Puritans, and his position at court proved invaluable in his strong support and protection of this religious faction.

Leicester also utilized the authority granted by the queen to the Privy Council for the purpose of controlling dramatic performances by issuing licenses. In 1574 Leicester issued the first such license to a company of actors under his patronage. Other peers soon followed Leicester's example, and brought a sense of legitimacy to the stage, thus preparing the way for a golden age of theater in England.

As her beloved "Sweet Robin," Leicester hoped to marry Elizabeth. However, he was beset by scandal, accused of murdering his first wife, Amy Robsart (married 1550–1560), and abandoning his second, Lady Douglas Sheffield (married 1571–1573). Nevertheless, he remained the queen's favorite courtier, and was showered with gifts of estates and offices. In 1575, Leicester entertained Elizabeth at Kenilworth, one of those estates, for eighteen days of perhaps the most glittering pageantry of her reign. In 1578 he married Lettice Knollys, widow of the earl of Essex. This marriage lasted until his death in 1588.

Leicester was a patron to artists, playwrights, and actors (including William Kemp, Shakespeare's colleague). He maintained a company of players, Leicester's Men, and in 1574 obtained the first royal patent issued to a theatrical company. The poet Edmund Spenser modeled Prince Arthur in *The Faerie Queene* after him. Other protégés included chroniclers John Stow and Richard Grafton, surgeon Thomas Gale, physician William Clowes, and mathematicians Thomas Digges and John Dee. Leicester favored moderate Puritanism, but supported several radical theologians. He also cosponsored Italian philosopher Giordano Bruno's visit to Oxford in 1583. Hated by English Roman Catholics, he was reviled by a group of exiled papists as a sorcerer and murderer in the malicious *Leicester's Commonwealth* (1584).

Leicester led two major military expeditions: one to the United Provinces (1585–1587), following William of Orange's death, to prevent a Spanish takeover and the spread of Catholicism; and one to the south of England to command land forces in anticipation of a Spanish invasion (1588). Leicester died soon thereafter, on 4 September 1588, of malarial fever.

See also Elizabeth I.

BIBLIOGRAPHY

Haynes, Alan. *The White Bear: Robert Dudley, The Elizabethan Earl of Leicester.* London, 1987.

Strong, Roy C., and Jan A. Van Dorsten. *Leicester's Triumph.* London, 1964.

Wilson, Derek. *Sweet Robin: A Biography of Robert Dudley, Earl of Leicester, 1533–1588.* London, 1981.

LILLIAN HROMIKO

DUEL. The history of the duel extends beyond the Renaissance, but as an aspect of aristocratic culture, the practice belongs largely to the sixteenth and seventeenth centuries. It was then that the duel became ritualized and endowed with a code of conduct, and then too that it peaked in virulence within aristocratic circles. The importance of the duel lies not so much in the costs it inflicted, which were significant, as in its symbolic value as an expression of aristocratic self-consciousness at a particular moment.

The early history of the duel is bound up with the custom of trial by battle, which took various forms; early on, too, princes or monarchs often sanctioned duels as a means of publicly settling quarrels between gentlemen. Judicial combat or trial by duel, however, ended sometime in the mid-sixteenth century. The last such duel in France was probably the famous La Chastaigneraye–Jarnac duel in 1547 between two favorites of King Henry II, witnessed by an audience that included the Turkish ambassador, who registered his astonishment that such a practice should be permitted. Subsequently, official condemnation and even attempts to prosecute duelists became the order of the day. The Council of Trent (1545–1563) condemned the practice. In 1566 unauthorized dueling was declared a capital offense in France; in 1576 it was deemed a matter of *lèse majesté* (treason). And James I, who had ample exposure to intramural brawling during his reign in Scotland, made extirpation of the duel a personal mission, even writing a treatise against it.

Despite these prohibitions the duel reached epidemic proportions in the last part of the sixteenth and early seventeenth century. Several observers approximated the body count, but these figures may not be reliable. Writing in 1609, the Parisian diarist Pierre de l'Estoile estimated that in the previous twenty years the duel had claimed the lives of between seven and eight thousand noblemen. A contemporary put the figure at six thousand. These figures seem inflated, yet Venetian ambassadors, among others, confirmed them. For England the evidence suggests comparable numbers for about the same time. The English stage certainly saw an increase in dueling: theatrical depictions of the ritual combat more than doubled in the first half of the seventeenth century.

The duel does not seem to have been evenly distributed across Europe. It was concentrated in Italy, France, and England; Spain was largely untouched, while Holland and Germany adopted the practice only later in the seventeenth century. That it was a phenomenon with a limited chronological and geographical scope suggests that certain conditions were crucial to its development into a major form of

Training for the Duel. Fencing with long spears. From *Kunst des Fechtens* (Strasbourg, 1575). CULVER PICTURES

bloodletting. One was the emergence of a sophisticated code of honor, fashioned largely by Italian humanists in the fifteenth and sixteenth centuries, which dissected its meanings, encouraged a manly concern, even obsession, with personal honor, elaborated an entire etiquette of social interactions between gentlemen, and specified levels of insult when honor was aggrieved. The well-known legal scholar Andrea Alciato wrote an early code on the duel; Girolamo Muzio's *Il duello* (1550) was one of the most widely read treatises on the subject, and spawned many imitations. Even Baldassare Castiglione, who disapproved of the practice, acknowledged that a gentleman, once committed to a duel, must show "readiness and courage." In short, out of the Renaissance emerged an ideology for aristocrats that affirmed, as a defining feature of their class, their privilege to settle questions of personal honor with blood. Another factor in its rise was the development of the rapier, also an Italian invention, which began to appear throughout Europe in the mid-sixteenth century. Lightweight and deadly, this needle-sharp sword allowed gentlemen to walk about armed with a weapon at their side that could be drawn at the slightest imprecation or insult. Encounters that with cumbersome broadswords might have ended only in mutual exhaustion now turned fatal in an instant with the merest thrust.

These factors are not sufficient, however, to explain the duel's prominence in the late sixteenth and early seventeenth centuries. The heart of the matter relates to the anxieties and sensitivities that prompted aristocrats to cross swords at a moment's notice. It can be argued that a heightened concern for their status and privileges led many gentlemen to the duel. Two factors seem most salient in explaining their concern. One was the so-called military revolution, which generally challenged the aristocracy's traditional role in society as those who fought by replacing cavalry with infantry at the crux of battlefield tactics. Aristocrats continued to serve as officers in the military, but were forced to reconsider their role in an enterprise that increasingly valued esprit de corps over individualism, patient strategizing over brute impetuosity, leadership skills over heroism, and training over birthright. Another was the inflation of honors and the sale of offices, which greatly increased the pool of privileged elites. Under James I, England saw a dramatic inflation of honors, after the long depression of Elizabeth's reign, an upturn that indeed coincided with an outbreak of the dueling mania. In France, new titles were distributed throughout the sixteenth century, and especially during the religious wars. As with the military revolution, the competition from parvenus and outsiders could provoke anxiety and uncertainty among aristocrats, prompting them to seek relief in a ritual that, if nothing else, reaffirmed their self-image as great men whose sense of honor and sensitivity to injury set them far above others. "The greatest bond between them is that of the duel," observed the Venetian ambassador Pietro Proili in 1608, and his observation testifies to the importance of this custom as a feature of class solidarity, especially when the integrity of their class was called into question.

Such reasoning must remain speculative, for it is impossible to know for certain what motivated men to engage in a practice that seems so senseless and self-destructive. Indeed, the duel was not lacking in critics. The aristocracy itself was on record as opposing it: at the Estates General of 1588, it was the delegation from the second estate that called for the death penalty for duelists. Michel Montaigne bemoaned the propensity of Frenchmen to fall into quarrelling and condemned "these 'laws of honor' which are so often opposed in hostility to the laws of reason" ("On Cowardice, Mother of Cruelty"). But the duel had defenders, or at least apologists, as well. Jean Bodin thought the practice provided a safety-valve for aristocrats who otherwise might be prone to rebellion. The Jesuits tended to support the duel, arguing that because a gentleman's honor is as valuable as his property, he could defend it just as righteously. And the most famous depiction of a duelist, the playwright Pierre Corneille's *Le Cid,* presented theatergoers with a young aristocrat who, to be sure, defied a royal ban on dueling, but then gloriously led his king's troops into battle, saving his country. Kings, too, displayed a reluctance to prosecute warriors who violated the ban on dueling, especially when their services were so valued on the battlefield. In a society dominated by aristocrats and preoccupied with the demands of war, it is perhaps understandable that the prohibition on the duel should have been observed in the breach as much as in the observance.

See also **Aristocracy; Arms and Armor; Chivalry.**

BIBLIOGRAPHY

Billaçois, François. *Le duel dans la société française des XVIe–XVIIe siécles: essai de psychosociologie historique.* Paris, 1986.

Kiernan, V. G. *The Duel in European History: Honour and the Reign of Aristocracy.* Oxford, 1989.

Schneider, Robert A. "Statemaking and Swordplay: Aspects of the Campaign against the Duel in Early Modern France." In *Statemaking and Social Movements.* Edited by Charles Bright and Susan Harding. Ann Arbor, Mich., 1984. Pages 265–296.

Stone, Lawrence. *The Crisis of the Aristocracy, 1558–1641.* Oxford, 1965.

ROBERT A. SCHNEIDER

DU FAIL, NOËL (c. 1520–1591), French writer. Noël Du Fail, master of the short story, contributed to what literary historians have termed the golden age of French Renaissance narrative fiction, extending from 1540 to 1560. In this respect he is part of a trio including Margaret of Navarre and Bonaventure Des Périers. A country gentleman of Brittany born near Rennes, Du Fail belonged to both the well-entrenched minor nobility (provincial squires) and the legal profession (by virtue of his high judicial appointments). That he straddled two social backgrounds gives us an insight into the thematic tensions that characterize his work: past and present, city and country, decadence and utopia, Catholic and Protestant, conservatism and social criticism.

Writing under the anagrammatic pseudonym of Leon Ladulfi, Du Fail began his literary career in 1547 with his best-known work, the *Propos rustiques* (Country conversations), an ironic narrative that praises rural simplicity and contentment with a subtlety that belies its naive tone. Inspired by humanist learning and certain literary models (especially François Rabelais and Giovanni Boccaccio), Du Fail exhibits a shrewd grasp of village life, excelling in vivid montage, spontaneous dialogue, and a nonchalance that veils his facetious intent. If one views Du Fail's work as a whole, it is clear that he wanted to unshackle himself from the conventions of narrative fiction, especially the constraints of a sustained plot, in order more directly to criticize contemporary sociopolitical developments.

What he conserved from traditional narrative were dialogue and anecdote in order to deliver advice, praise, or blame. To accomplish these objectives, his last work, *Contes et discours d'Eutrapel* (Short stories and conversations of Eutrapel; 1585), combined the salmagundi of the earlier *Baliverneries* (Idle stories; 1548) and the essay style of *Mémoires . . . des arrests du Parlement de Bretagne* (Memoirs . . . of the decrees of the Parliament of Brittany; 1579). *Baliverneries* enabled him to mirror the disorders of his times with a jumble of conversations and episodes lacking cohesion, while the didactic, autobiographical quality of *Mémoires* used literary resources to comment and moralize on contemporary failings.

BIBLIOGRAPHY

Primary Works

Du Fail, Noël. *Propos rustiques* (Country conversations). Edited by Gabriel-André Pérouse, Roger Dubuis, and D. Bécache-Leval. Geneva, 1994. An excellent edition in French with painstakingly detailed notes, a glossary, and a bibliography that includes references to Du Fail's other works.

Krailsheimer, A. J., ed. *Three Sixteenth-Century Conteurs.* Oxford, 1966. Selected chapters in French from *Propos rustiques* and *Baliverneries* (Idle stories) with a useful introduction and notes in English. Also contains selected chapters from Margaret of Navarre's *Heptaméron* (The Heptameron; 1558–1559) and Bonaventure des Périers's *Nouvelles récréations* (New pastimes; 1558).

Secondary Work

Magnien-Simonin, Catherine. *Noël Du Fail écrivain: Actes et articles*. Paris, 1991. A collection of critical essays constituting the present state of studies on Du Fail.

MICHAEL J. GIORDANO

DUFAY, GUILLAUME (Du Fay; 1397?–1474), Flemish singer and preeminent composer of his generation. Dufay was likely born in Beersel les Bruxelles, then a Flemish-speaking town near Brussels; he was educated at Cambrai Cathedral from May 1409 to 1413–1414, when he gained his chaplaincy. His teachers would have been Nicolas Malin (until 1412) and the composer Richard Locqueville.

Details of Dufay's early career are gleaned from several of his compositions that can be dated precisely and associated with specific events. After a stay at the Council of Constance, he was employed in Italy by the Malatesta family in Pesaro and Rimini between 1420 and 1423. Evidence for his service with the Malatesta comes from his compositions *Vasilissa ergo gaude* and *Resvellieés vous* written for occasions in 1421 and 1423, respectively, and—less directly—from several Italian songs. Similarly, texts of two songs indicate that Dufay worked in Laon in the mid-1420s.

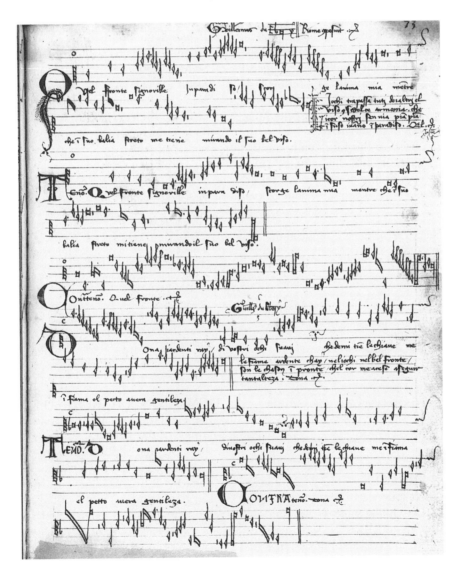

Guillaume Dufay. A page of Dufay's music. THE BODLEIAN LIBRARY, UNIVERSITY OF OXFORD, MS. CANON. MISC. 213, FOL. 73R

Dufay's peripatetic career path—common for northern musicians in the fifteenth century—continued through the 1430s. He served in Bologna with Cardinal Louis Alemán (1426–1428), in Rome in the papal choir (1428–1433), in Chambéry with Duke Louis of Savoy (1434–1435), and with Pope Eugenius IV (1435–1437) in Florence and Bologna. Dufay left the papal choir at the end of May 1437, just as the antipapal forces at the Council of Basel—led by his former patrons Louis Alemán and the duke of Savoy—intensified their attack on Eugenius. For the next two years Dufay again worked at the court of Savoy. His peregrinations briefly came to an end in December 1439 when he returned to Cambrai. Aside from his second residency at the court of Savoy (1452–1458), he remained based in Cambrai until his death.

From the lyricism of his songs and smaller motets, to the intellectual rigor of his isorhythmic motets, Dufay's compositions brought together the musical styles of France, England, and Italy. Among his lasting achievements was the regularization of the treatment of dissonance. Dufay's imposing isorhythmic motets (works based on separate melodic and rhythmic patterns) reach back to the fourteenth century in their formal schemes, just as his cantus firmus Mass settings helped to define cyclic masses based on a unifying tenor as a central genre for generations to come.

See also **Music in France; Music in Italy; Music in the Low Countries.**

BIBLIOGRAPHY

Fallows, David. *Dufay*. London, 1982. 2d rev. ed., London, 1987.

Planchart, Alejandro Enrique. "The Early Career of Guillaume Du Fay." *Journal of the American Musicological Society* 46 (1993): 341–368.

Planchart, Alejandro Enrique. "Guillaume Du Fay's Benefices and His Relationship to the Court of Burgundy." *Early Music History* 8 (1988): 117–171.

Wright, Craig. "Dufay's *Nuper rosarum flores,* King Solomon's Temple, and the Veneration of the Virgin." *Journal of the American Musicological Society* 47 (1994): 395–441.

CHRISTOPHER REYNOLDS

DU GUILLET, PERNETTE (c. 1520–1545), French poet. The chief source of the scant biographical knowledge of Du Guillet's life is Antoine Du Moulin, the learned chamberlain of Marguerite of Navarre. She was born in Lyon and married in 1536 or 1537; her maiden name is unknown. She was proficient in languages and spoke Latin, Castillian, and Tuscan, the literary language of Italy. Also talented musically, she performed on the lute, harpsichord, and other instruments.

Pernette actively participated in the intellectual life of Lyon. Her writings reveal a precocious mastery of her craft and show the influences of Clément Marot (c. 1496–1544) and the *rhétoriqueurs* and also Maurice Scève (c. 1501–c. 1560/64). Several of her epigrams were set to music by prominent composers of the day, including Pierre de Villiers. They appeared in various collections of *chansonniers* (witty songs) published in 1540 and 1541. A probable victim of the plague, Pernette died in July 1545.

At the request of her husband, Du Moulin collected her works, and Jean de Tournes published them in a single volume entitled *Rymes de gentile et vertueuse Dame, D. Pernette du Guillet, Lyonnoise* (Rhymes of a gentle and virtuous lady; 1545). The *Rymes* in several genres and meters consist of sixty epigrams, ten chansons, two letters, and five elegies. Many of Pernette's poems are closely connected with *Délie* (1544), Maurice Scève's most famous work. Scève, a poet of outstanding erudition, met Pernette in 1536. Their reciprocal love is clearly expressed in their poems, which alternate between chaste platonic principles and impassioned love.

BIBLIOGRAPHY

Primary Work

Du Guillet, Pernette. *Rymes*. Edited by Victor E. Graham. Geneva, 1968.

Secondary Works

Delaney, Susan. "Lyric Dialogue in the 'Ring' Poems of Pernette Du Guillet and Maurice Scève." *French Review* 68 (1995): 822–829.

Miller, Joyce. "In the Margins of Amatory Discourse, the *Responses* of Pernette Du Guillet." *Sixteenth Century Journal* 24 (1993): 351–368.

Mulhauser, Ruth. *Maurice Scève*. Boston, 1977.

CLEMENT A. MILLER

DUMOULIN, CHARLES (1500–1566), French jurist, legal theorist, and historian. The eldest son of a family of the Parisian *noblesse de robe* (nobility of the robe; that is, high magistrates), Charles Dumoulin studied law at the Universities of Orléans and Poitiers. Returning to Paris with his degree in 1522, he began his professional work as an *avocat* first in the municipal court (Châtelet) and then in the Parlement of Paris. His scholarly career began with the publication of his commentary on the *coutume* (custom) of Paris in 1539, which opened his campaign for the unification of French law, defined more specifically in his *Oratio de concordia et unione consuetudinum*

Franciae (Oration on the union and concord of the customs of France; 1546). From 1540 Dumoulin was also attracted to Protestantism, as is evident in his *Treatise contractum et usuarum redituumque pecunia constituorum* (Treatise on the law of contracts and of usury; 1545), which opposed the rigidity of canonist doctrines and justified lending at interest on the grounds of utility. His evangelical leanings were more apparent in his *Commentaruis ad edictum Henrici Secundi contra parvas datas* (Commentary on the edict of Henry II [1550] against the little dates [that is, the predating and sale of benefices in France by the pope]; 1552). This book was Dumoulin's contribution to the "Gallican crisis" of 1551, which almost led to a break between France and the papacy. Another work written in 1551 (though not published until 1561) was his *Treatise sur l'origine, progrès et excellence du royaume et monarchie des français et couronne de France* (Treatise on the origin, progress, and excellence of the French monarchy; 1561), which celebrated the antiquity and autonomy of France, its laws, and its institutions.

As these and other scholarly and polemical works indicate, Dumoulin's professional and religious agenda was threefold: the unity of French law, the autonomy of the Gallican church, and the grandeur of the French monarchy. As a jurist Dumoulin opposed the influence of Roman law (paternal power, arbitrary taxes, and associated inequities) and denied its relevance to France—the French king was an autonomous "emperor in his kingdom" and so exempt from imperial law. Against this Romanist thesis Dumoulin defended the Germanic legacy embodied in French customs, attacking, from a Gallican perspective, the canonist tradition for being ridden not only with superstition and "papist" error but also forgeries. As a national historian Dumoulin celebrated the French monarchy (in terms similar to those of the *Francogallia* of his younger friend François Hotman) as the most ancient and admirable government in all Europe.

Dumoulin's posthumous influence was extraordinary, especially on the sixteenth-century movement to reform the French customs and, in the longer term, to reduce French customs to a legal code; his influence extended down to the Revolution and beyond. Intellectually Dumoulin remained a nonconformist. His commentary on the "little dates," praised by radical Gallicans as well as Protestants, was censured by the Sorbonne, so he fled into exile in Switzerland and Germany, where he traveled, taught, and performed legal services. During the first of the Wars of Religion he published polemics against both Calvinism and Counter-Reformation Catholicism, especially the decrees of the Council of Trent and the agenda of the Jesuits. Besieged by private troubles as well as rival religious parties, Dumoulin died in a religious state somewhere between these extremes but politically still an unrepentant Gallican and royalist.

BIBLIOGRAPHY

Kelley, Donald R. "*Fides Historiae:* Charles Dumoulin and the Gallican View of History." *Traditio* 22 (1966): 347–402. Study of Dumoulin's work in civil, canon, and customary law, and his conception of French history.

Thireau, Jean-Louis. *Charles du Moulin, 1500–1566: Étude sur les sources, la méthode, les idées: Politiques et économique d'un juriste de la Renaissance.* Geneva, 1980. Scholarly biography and study of Dumoulin as a jurist, with particular attention to his economic ideas.

DONALD R. KELLEY

DUNSTAPLE, JOHN (Dunstable; c. 1390–1453), musician, mathematician, astronomer. Dunstaple was the foremost of an influential group of English composers active in the first half of the fifteenth century, internationally acclaimed during his lifetime and long after his death.

Evidently a gentleman of some property, probably a married layman, Dunstaple probably spent time at St. Albans. The abbot of St. Albans, John Wheathampstead, was close to Duke Humphrey of Gloucester and Queen Joan, both of whom Dunstaple served; all four were evidently interested in music, mathematics, astrology, and Italian humanism. Humphrey's connection with Leonello d'Este, duke of Ferrara (1441–1450), may explain why so much of Dunstaple's music (including two St. Albans–related motets) traveled to Ferrara.

Over seventy musical compositions, nearly all Mass music and motets, survive mainly in north Italian and Germanic manuscripts. The famous song *O rosa bella*—often attributed to Dunstaple—is probably by John Bedingham. Many English sources were destroyed before and during the Reformation, though new discoveries continue as fragments emerge. The surviving music is mostly in three parts, some in four, very few in five or six, and was originally intended for all-vocal performance. Some Mass movements constituted groups or cycles built on a shared tenor, a technique pioneered by Dunstaple and his English contemporaries. Twelve polytextual motets are all on sacred subjects; two were written by 1416 and another for St. Albans probably in 1426. His earliest datable motets (for Pentecost and John the Baptist) were allegedly performed at Canterbury in 1416 in the presence of Henry V and the emperor Sigismund. Most of his other works are settings of liturgical texts in a songlike style. Dunstaple's mellifluous music was hailed as the chief expression of a sweet new English style; indeed, the theorist Johannes Tinctoris (1470s) called him the founder of a new musical art.

BIBLIOGRAPHY

Primary Work
John Dunstable: Complete Works. 2d rev. ed. Edited by Margaret Bent, Ian Bent, and Brian Trowell. London, 1970.

Secondary Works
Bent, Margaret. *Dunstaple.* London, 1981.
Bent, Margaret. "A New Canonic Gloria and the Changing Profile of Dunstaple." *Plainsong and Medieval Music* 5 (1996)
Maclean, Charles. "The Dunstable Inscription in London." *Sammelbände der Internationalen Musikgesellschaft* 11 (1910): 232–249.
Wathey, Andrew. "Dunstable in France." *Music and Letters* 67 (1986): 1–36.
Trowell, Brian. "Proportion in the Music of Dunstable." *Proceedings of the Royal Musical Association* 105 (1978–1979): 100–141.

MARGARET BENT

DÜRER, ALBRECHT (1471–1528), German artist. A talented painter, printmaker, draftsman, designer, and theoretician, Albrecht Dürer spent most of his career in his native city of Nürnberg. He was the third of eighteen children of Albrecht the Elder (d. 1502), a noted goldsmith, and Barbara Holper (d. 1514). By the time of his death, Dürer was arguably Europe's best-known artist because of the broad dissemination of his prints. His works reveal a remarkable breadth of interests. Although many generations of scholars have overemphasized Dürer's significance, his influence was felt throughout Germany and beyond. For later audiences, he was the quintessential German artist.

Training and Early Years. Dürer initially trained to become a goldsmith with his father. He learned to work with a burin (a cutting tool) and to appreciate the characteristics of different metals. His fledgling talents as a draftsman were already evident in 1484 when he drew a delicate and slightly awkward silverpoint *Self-Portrait at Age Thirteen* (Vienna, Albertina). Produced at a time when artists rarely represented themselves, this proved to be the first of many self-portraits by Dürer. From November 1486 until 1489 Dürer apprenticed with Michael Wolgemut, a neighbor and Nürnberg's leading painter. Although Dürer later remarked on how difficult these years were, especially the inevitable torments that he suffered at the hands of the older apprentices in the studio, he learned the arts of drawing, painting, and printmaking. The young Dürer may have assisted Wolgemut in the design and execution of woodcuts for two ambitious book projects: Stephan Fridolin's *Schatzbehalter* (Treasure Chest; Nürnberg, 1491) and Hartmann Schedel's *Welt Kronik,* or *Liber chronicarum* (*Nürnberg Chronicle;* Nürnberg, 1493). The pupil's affection for his master is evident in his 1516 *Portrait of Michael Wolgemut at Age 82* (Nürnberg, Germanisches Nationalmuseum) with its laudatory inscription.

Upon completing his training in 1489, Dürer began his extended *Wanderjahr.* Although the precise itinerary of his travels as a journeyman is unknown, the documentary and artistic records indicate that he arrived in Colmar only to discover that Martin Schongauer, the famed engraver and painter, had died. Dürer worked in Basel and Strasbourg, both active publishing centers, where he made designs for book illustrations, including Terence's *Comedies* (unpublished) and, less certainly, Sebastian Brant's *Das Narrenschiff* (*Ship of Fools;* Basel, 1494).

The artist returned to Nürnberg in 1494, apparently at his father's bidding, where he married Agnes Frey, the daughter of Hans Frey, a talented coppersmith. Much has been written about their relationship and their lack of children. Even though Agnes did not always get along with Willibald Pirckheimer, the noted humanist and Dürer's best friend, she seems to have been a highly supportive spouse who helped manage the large workshop and often traveled to fairs to sell his prints. In the fall Dürer first journeyed across the Alps to Venice and other towns. Several exquisite watercolors record his route. While in northern Italy he first discovered the art of Andrea Mantegna, with its powerful evocation of classical antiquity, concern for the human body, and explorations of perspective, and that of Giovanni Bellini, Venice's leading painter, who taught Dürer new approaches to the use of color.

Woodcuts, Engravings, and Paintings: 1495–1505. Back in Nürnberg in 1495 Dürer established a workshop and entered one of the most productive periods of his career, in which he focused primarily on woodcuts and engravings. In his *Men's Bath* woodcut of 1496–1497 he explored complex spatial constructions, varied material surfaces, including the stunning use of the whiteness of the paper to suggest both solids and open passages, and complex poses. Here and especially in the woodcuts for his famed *Apocalypse* series of 1496–1498, pub-

Albrecht Dürer. *Adam and Eve.* Engraving; 1504. VICTORIA & ALBERT MUSEUM, LONDON

lished as a book in collaboration with Anton Koberger, his godfather, Dürer experimented with the expressive and descriptive potentials of line to communicate form, surface, texture, and light. Never had the terror of the *Four Horsemen* seemed so palpable as in Dürer's woodcut. Likewise, Dürer convincingly evoked the immateriality of an angel dissolving into a band of clouds in *St. John Eating the Book*. Through prints like these and the first edition of the *Large Passion* (1497–1499), Dürer's artistic ideas and fame reached a growing audience well beyond the walls of Nürnberg.

Dürer's early facility with a burin and his youthful admiration for the art of Martin Schongauer attracted him to engraving as early as 1494. The *Sea Monster* (c. 1498) offered the artist the opportunity to represent a voluptuous nude woman set against an exquisitely detailed landscape, one reminiscent of the watercolors from his first Italian trip. In several instances Dürer used his engravings as a means for communicating his growing fascination with antiquity and human proportions. *Nemesis* (1501–1503) is ostensibly an allegory of fortune and retribution, reward and punishment, based upon a humanistic text by Angelo Poliziano. His personification, a winged nude woman hovering above the Alpine town of Klausen, is actually an experiment in correct human proportions based upon the writings of the ancient Roman architect Vitruvius. Her head measures one-eighth the length of the body, the face is one-tenth, and her right foot is one-seventh. Although in later years he would abandon Vitruvius's scheme for one that better accommodated the variety of human bodies, the artist already was seeking a theoretical basis for his art. This quest is best observed in *Adam and Eve* (1504). The first couple is based loosely upon canonical examples of classical sculpture, the *Apollo Belvedere* and the *Medici Venus,* which he knew only indirectly. These are among the most complex and compelling nudes in German art. They inspired dozens of subsequent copies by other artists in a variety of media. His interest in the human body and the classical tradition are, however, couched in a northern artistic language, one stressing surfaces, varied lighting, and vivid contrasts between the figures and the dense forest behind.

Throughout this period Dürer also painted and created designs for stained glass, table fountains, and a host of other objects. In 1496 the artist executed a portrait of Frederick III the Wise, elector of Saxony (now in Berlin). This commission was the start of a long patronage by Frederick that resulted in such works as *Seven Sorrows of the Virgin* and the *Mater Dolorosa* (1496; Dresden and Munich), *Mary Altarpiece* (1496; Dresden), possibly the *Jabach Altarpiece* (1503–1504; Frankfurt, Cologne, and Munich), *Adoration of the Magi* (1504; Florence), and *Martyrdom of Ten Thousand* (1508; Vienna).

Dürer's theoretical ambitions are evident when comparing his self-portraits of 1498 in Madrid and 1500 in Munich. Adopting a compositional formula developed earlier in Netherlandish and Italian art, the twenty-six-year-old artist rests his arm on a ledge parallel to the picture plane. Behind, an Alpine vista appears through the open window. Dürer stresses his attractive appearance, notably his long flowing hair, and attentive gaze. This painting depicts a successful, if mildly narcissistic, sitter. By contrast, the 1500 portrait confronts the viewer. Dürer positions himself frontally. He gazes intensely outward, an effect heightened by the reflection of an unseen window off the surface of each eye. Intentionally iconic, indeed consciously Christlike, the likeness stresses the artist's creative capacities, especially his mathematical prowess in the generation of the picture's proportions and his phenomenal skill in rendering

material textures. The accompanying Latin inscription reads "Albrecht Dürer of Nürnberg has [depicted] myself in everlasting color at age twenty-eight," an allusion that the artist's likeness and his fame would be everlasting too.

Italy and Nürnberg: 1505–1520. When Dürer returned to Venice in the late summer of 1505 he was a far more renowned artist. As ten of his surviving letters written to Pirckheimer in Nürnberg attest, his fame prompted a certain jealousy in some of the Italian artists. Dürer wrote that "they copy my work in the churches and wherever they can find it; and then they revile it and say that the style is not antique and so not good" (Conway, *Writings,* p. 48). Dürer reported that he was awarded a much-coveted commission to paint the *Feast of the Rose Garlands Altarpiece* (1506; now in Prague) for the German merchants' Chapel of Saint Bartholomew. Stung by criticism of his painting talents, the artist labored on this picture. His colors and technique reflect the influence of the aged Giovanni Bellini, with whom he maintained friendly contacts. Dürer also had to contend with Marcantonio Raimondi's direct copying of his prints. In Venice and in his travels to Bologna, Rome, and likely Florence, Dürer continued his studies of perspective and the human body. He copied several of Leonardo's anatomical sketches and, indirectly, caricatures, as seen in his *Christ among the Doctors* (Madrid), executed in Rome in 1506.

Back home by January 1507 Dürer soon entered another highly productive period. As if to demonstrate the lessons of Italy, he painted life-size pendants of *Adam* and *Eve* (1507; Madrid). In contrast with the rigidity and rather academic quality of his 1504 engraved couple, the pair are far softer, more fluid, and more graceful. Perhaps his Venetian experience encouraged the artist to paint two large pictures: the *Heller Altarpiece* (1508), which exists only in drawings and in a copy (c. 1614; Frankfurt) made by Jobst Harrich; and the *All Saints' Altarpiece* (1508–1511; Nürnberg and Vienna), done for the Landauer Chapel in Twelve Brothers' House in Nürnberg. Both pictures show heavenly visions that occur just above deep, panoramic landscapes. Each includes a prominent portrait of Dürer holding an inscription tablet. The financial success of these and other projects permitted the artist to purchase a large stone and half-timber house near the Tiergärtner gate just beneath the castle.

Dürer's graphic activity also increased dramatically. In 1511 he published his *Mass of St. Gregory* and *Trinity* woodcuts, which with their elaborate

Albrecht Dürer. *Melencolia I.* There is little agreement on the significance of the two angelic figures and the dog or the many objects—among them carpenter's tools, scientific instruments, geometrical shapes, and a magic square that adds to 34—in Dürer's engraving or their multiple symbolism: The fireball (*upper left*) is an accurate picture of the widely witnessed fireball of the Ensisheim meteorite of 1492; it represents the mystery of stones and metal falling from the sky. The symmetry (harmony) and geometry of the truncated rhombohedron (*center left*) may represent the mystery of a "nature learned in geometry." The seven rungs of the ladder may refer to the seven liberal arts. Engraving; 1514. FOTO MARBURG/ART RESOURCE

shading systems are two of the most technically accomplished of his career; his *Life of the Virgin* series (c. 1504–1511); *Large Passion* series (1497–1499 and 1510–1511); and *Apocalypse* series, each now reissued with a new title page. His *Engraved Passion* series of 1508–1512 is perhaps Dürer's most complex narrative and emotional exposition. Next follow the three "master" engravings: *Knight, Death, and the Devil* (1513), *St. Jerome in His Study* (1514), and *Melencolia I* (1514). The precise perspectival design and the careful mimicry of textures in his *St. Jerome in His Study,* however brilliant, are secondary to the print's remarkable lighting effects. Warm sunlight bathes the saint's study. This symphony of light and shadow sets a tranquil mood conducive to Jerome's scholarly enterprise. Jerome's radiant halo conveys a convincing aura of sanctity. Dürer created the *Agony in the Garden* (1515) and the *Angel Holding the Sudarium* (1516), two of his most expressive etchings, a technique he used only rarely. The rough and energetic lines heighten the emotion of Christ's lonely burden and the angel's anguish.

Around 1512, if not a year or two earlier, Dürer started working for the emperor Maximilian I. The artist made now-lost drawings (c. 1512) for the bronze statues of King Arthur, King Theodoric, and Charlemagne for the emperor's tomb that later in the century was erected in the Hofkirche in Innsbruck. Soon after meeting Maximilian, who visited Nürnberg in 1512, Dürer and his workshop, following designs by imperial court artist Jörg Kölderer, began production of the 192 woodcuts for the *Triumphal Arch of Maximilian,* which was finished by 1515 but not published until 1517–1518. When assembled, the arch measures 134 in. by 115 in., making it the largest graphic project ever. Together with Albrecht Altdorfer, Hans Burgkmair, Lucas Cranach, and Hans Baldung, Dürer contributed pen drawings to the margins of the emperor's *Book of Hours* (1515; Munich). In 1515 Maximilian rewarded the artist with an annual stipend of one hundred guilders drawn from Nürnberg's imperial taxes. Three years later Dürer traveled with a city delegation to the imperial diet in Augsburg, where he sketched Maximilian's portrait, now in Vienna. The emperor died the following January before the artist had completed either the two painted portraits, today in Nürnberg and Vienna, or the large commemorative woodcut portrait (1519). He also was in the midst of designing the *Large Triumphal Chariot;* the drawing in Vienna was finished in 1518 but the subsequent woodcut was published only four years later. This composition was one of the models that Dürer provided for the redecoration of the great hall and exterior of Nürnberg's city hall that was painted by others in 1521–1522.

Final Years: 1520–1528. Dürer's fourth great journey occurred in 1520–1521 when, together with Agnes and a servant, he traveled to the Low Countries. Although prompted by his desire to have Charles V, the new emperor, reaffirm his annual stipend, the Nürnberg master used this occasion leisurely to explore the Netherlands from his primary base in Antwerp. As recounted in his remarkable diary—or, more accurately, annotated account book—Dürer was treated as a celebrity. He was feted by artists in most of the towns he visited. He befriended Joachim de Patinir, the noted landscapist, and exchanged works with Lucas van Leyden, Bernard van Orley, Jan Provost, and others. He supported his trip through the sale of prints, which apparently he brought in considerable quantities, through the execution of numerous portrait drawings and the occasional painting, and through the completion of a few other projects, such as *St. Jerome* (1521; Lisbon). The diary records Dürer's visits to view Jan van Eyck's *Ghent Altarpiece,* among other works of art, and his quest to view a beached whale. From the latter trip he developed a fever, perhaps malaria, that permanently damaged his health.

During the last years of his life, Dürer concentrated on portraiture and writing. He experimented with printed portraits that range from the huge woodcut of *Ulrich Varnbüler* of 1522 to the refined engraved likenesses of *Cardinal Albrecht von Brandenburg* (1519 and 1524), *Frederick III the Wise* (1524), and, from 1526, *Erasmus, Philipp Melanchthon,* and *Willibald Pirckheimer*. Most are arranged with a laudatory inscription tablet beneath the portrait. Melanchthon's reads, "Dürer was able to picture the features of the living Philipp, but his skilled hand was unable to picture his mind." Equally impressive are the three painted portraits of *Jacob Muffel* (Berlin), *Hieronymus Holzschuher* (Berlin), and *Johann Kleberger* (Vienna), all dating to 1526.

In 1512 or 1513 Dürer began drafting a manual entitled *Speis der Malerknaben* (Food for young painters), in which he argued that art is a combination of craft and knowledge. Although this project was never completed, he eventually wrote *Vnderweysung der Messung* (Art of measurement; Nürnberg, 1525), *Etliche Vnderricht, zu Befestigung der Stett, Schlosz vnd Flecken* (On fortification; Nürnberg, 1527), and *Hierinn sind begriffen vier Bücher von menschlicher Proportion* (Four books on human proportions; Nürnberg, 1528). The latter was published posthumously through the efforts of Agnes and Pirckheimer. In a land without a strong theoretical tradition and virtually no history of writing about art, Dürer's texts were pioneering. Indeed, he often had to invent his own artistic terms. While these texts were popular with later theoreticians, the practical impact on contemporary artists was limited.

Like others of his age, Dürer was keenly interested in the emerging religious debate. He belonged to the Sodalitas Staupitziana, a group of humanists and patricians who met in the local Augustinian church to discuss theological issues. Although Dürer avidly collected the writings of Martin Luther and in his 1520–1521 diary fretted over the rumor of the reformer's death, it is not clear whether he ever abandoned Catholicism; he probably assumed, like others at the time, that the different groups would ultimately reconcile. In 1526, the year after Nürnberg formally adopted Lutheranism, Dürer presented his *Four Apostles,* two life-sized panels (now in Munich), to the city council. The images of Saints John the Evangelist, Peter, Paul, and Mark, together with the accompanying inscription, stress the artist's faith in the word of God and the need to be steadfast in safeguarding it.

Dürer's Legacy. The course of German art would have been quite different without Dürer. Unlike most artists, Dürer's posthumous reputation continued to grow. Collectors avidly hunted for his drawings, prints, and paintings. The taste for his work or new works in his style between about 1570 and 1620 has been dubbed the Dürer Renaissance. By 1828 elaborate ceremonies honoring Germany's "greatest artist," the Teutonic counterpart to Italy's Raphael, were held in Nürnberg, Berlin, and other locales. For much of the nineteenth and early twentieth century, Dürer's fame tended to overshadow the very real contributions of his peers. Subsequently, a more nuanced understanding of both Dürer's art and the complexities of the Renaissance in Germany has emerged.

[Dürer's self portrait of 1500 appears in the color plates in this volume. Dürer's *Four Apostles* appears in the color plates in volume 5.]

See also **Germany, Art in.**

BIBLIOGRAPHY

Primary Works
Dürer, Albrecht. *The Writings of Albrecht Dürer.* Edited and translated by William Martin Conway. New York, 1958.
Rupprich, Hans, ed. *Schriftlicher Nachlass: Dürer.* 3 vols. Berlin, 1956–1969.

Secondary Works
Albrecht Dürer: Master Printmaker. Exhibition catalog. Boston Museum of Fine Arts. Boston, 1971.
Anzelewsky, Fedja. *Albrecht Dürer: Das malerische Werk.* 2 vols. Rev. ed. Berlin, 1991.
Anzelewsky, Fedja. *Dürer: His Art and Life.* Translated by Heide Grieve. Secaucus, N.J., 1980.
Bialostocki, Jan. *Dürer and His Critics.* Baden-Baden, Germany, 1986.
Gothic and Renaissance Art in Nuremberg, 1300–1550. Exhibition catalog. Nürnberg, Germanisches Nationalmuseum; New York, Metropolitan Museum of Art. New York and Munich, 1986.
Hutchison, Jane Campbell. *Albrecht Dürer: A Biography.* Princeton, N.J., 1990.
Koerner, Joseph Leo. *The Moment of Self-Portraiture in German Renaissance Art.* Chicago, 1993.
Landau, David, and Peter Parshall. *The Renaissance Print, 1470–1550.* New Haven, Conn., 1994.
Panofsky, Erwin. *The Life and Art of Albrecht Dürer.* 4th ed. Princeton, N.J., 1955.
Smith, Jeffrey Chipps. *Nuremberg, A Renaissance City: 1500–1618.* Austin, Tex., 1983.
Strauss, Walter. *Albrecht Dürer: Woodcuts and Wood Blocks.* New York, 1980.
Strauss, Walter. *The Complete Drawings of Albrecht Dürer.* 6 vols. New York, 1974.
Strauss, Walter, ed. *Intaglio Prints, Engravings, Etchings, and Drypoints: Albrecht Dürer.* New York, 1975.
Strieder, Peter. "Albrecht Dürer." In *Dictionary of Art.* Edited by Jane Turner. Vol. 9. New York, 1996. Pages 427–445.
Strieder, Peter. *The Hidden Dürer.* Oxford, 1978.
Talbot, Charles, ed. *Dürer in America: His Graphic Work.* Exhibition catalog. National Gallery of Art. Washington, D.C., 1971.
Thausing, Moritz. *Dürer: Geschichte seines Lebens und seiner Kunst.* 2 vols. Leipzig, 1884.
Wilckens, Leonie von, ed. *Albrecht Dürer, 1471–1971.* Exhibition catalog. Nürnberg, Germanisches Nationalmuseum. Munich, 1971.

JEFFREY CHIPPS SMITH

DU TILLET, JEAN (d. 1570), sieur de La Bussière, registrar of the Parlement of Paris, author of *Recueil des roys de France.* Between the 1530s and the 1560s, Du Tillet served as an archivist commissioned by French kings to inventory repositories and supply documents recording royal entries, funerals, visits to Parlement, coronations, estates meetings, and laws. He was an eminent historian who rejected unsubstantiated chronicles as fictions and grounded French history on facts drawn from reliable documents signed, dated, sealed.

His influential works, *Pour la majorité du roi treschrestien* (For the majority of the Christian king; Paris, 1560) and the *Recueil des roys de France* (Collection of the kings of France; Paris, 1577–1618), which demonstrated the legal humanists' belief in the indigenous nature of French law and institutions, spurred the search for an ancient constitution. Appropriating those sources to solve political crises during the religious wars, kings and queen-regents held that the royal majority (legal age to rule) was regulated by French law (an ordinance of 1375), not Roman law, and legitimated a new constitutional assembly, the *lit de justice,* convoked by kings in Parlement to treat constitutional issues. First convoked in 1527 and 1537, that assembly officially declared the royal majority (1563, 1614, 1651), then functioned as an inaugural ritual that displaced the coronation (1610, 1643).

With his brother of the same name, Jean Du Tillet (d. 1570), bishop of Saint-Brieux (1553) and of Meaux (1564–1570), whose discovery of a ninth-century Carolingian copy of Salic law exposed the current ordinance (forged in the fifteenth century to exclude women from rule in France) as fraudulent, Du Tillet (the registrar) helped to build the foundations for modern historical scholarship.

BIBLIOGRAPHY

Primary Work

Du Tillet, Jean (registrar). *Jean du Tillet and the French Wars of Religion: Five Tracts, 1562–1569.* Edited by Elizabeth A. R. Brown. Binghamton, N.Y., 1994. A modern edition of Du Tillet's previously unpublished works with useful introductory material about their author.

Secondary Works

Hanley, Sarah. *The Lit de Justice of the Kings of France: Constitutional Ideology in Legend, Ritual, and Discourse.* Princeton, N.J., 1983. Appearance of this innovative assembly in 1527 indebted to Du Tillet's sources; shows the articulation of several constitutional ideologies through the 1600s.

Hanley, Sarah. "Mapping Rulership in the French Body Politic: Political Identity, Public Law, and *The King's One Body.*" *Historical Reflections/Réflections Historiques* 23 (1997): 129–149. On the forgeries of Salic law in the 1400s meant to exclude women from rule in France.

Kelley, Donald R. *Foundations of Modern Historical Scholarship: Language, Law, and History in the French Renaissance.* New York, 1970. Classic exposition of the link between French law and history made by legal humanists in the 1500s, including the Du Tillet brothers.

SARAH HANLEY

DU VAIR, GUILLAUME (1556–1621), French moral philosopher and political figure. Trained as both a cleric and a jurist, Guillaume Du Vair was a member of the Parlement of Paris during the Catholic League uprising of 1588, when supporters of Henri, duc de Guise, seized the city in the name of the Catholic cause. Though at first a moderate Leaguer, Du Vair quickly aligned himself with the Politiques, who valued the political welfare of the kingdom more than its religious unity. He later became a trusted servant of Henry IV, acting as his agent on a mission to England (1596), as intendant of justice in Marseille (1596), and as first president of the Parlement of Provence (1598–1616). After the accession of Louis XIII, Du Vair became keeper of the seals (1616) and bishop of Lisieux (1617).

Best known today as a neo-Stoic philosopher, Du Vair wrote his most important works between 1584 and 1590 while serving in the Parlement of Paris. In contrast to most brands of Stoicism, which counsel detachment from worldly affairs, Du Vair articulated a more activist moral philosophy rooted in a sense of Christian charity. In *La philosophie morale des Stoiques* (The moral philosophy of the Stoics) he declares that love of country is second only to love of God. In *Exhortation à la vie civile* (Exhortation to civic life) he chides those who abandon public life during civil war for breaking the bonds of Christian charity that link them to their compatriots. And in his most famous treatise, *De la constance et consolation ès calamitez publiques* (Of constancy and consolation in public calamities), he defends the virtue of those loyalists like himself who remained in Leaguer Paris rather than abandon their public posts in the kingdom's greatest hour of need.

BIBLIOGRAPHY

Abel, Günter. *Stoizismus und frühe Neuzeit.* Berlin, 1978. See especially chapter 5.

Radouant, René. *Guillaume du Vair: L'homme et l'orateur jusqu'à la fin des troubles de la Lique (1556–1596).* Paris, 1908. Still the standard account.

Zanta, Léontine. *La renaissance du stoicisme au seizième siècle.* Paris, 1914. See in particular part 3, chapters 5–8.

ZACHARY S. SCHIFFMAN

DYNASTIC RIVALRY. Competition was the norm of European international relations from the fourteenth through the sixteenth centuries. Whether they were establishing colonial empires abroad or striving for economic advantage on the Continent, the kings and princes of the period viewed one another as rivals, either active or potential. While none among them sought to eliminate fellow rulers and their lines altogether, they were exceedingly alert to one another's ambitions and adjusted their own goals accordingly.

Territorial Claims and Disputes. Although the race for the fullest treasury was important to Europe's Renaissance rulers, it paled in comparison with the rivalry engendered by dynastic competition over successions and lands. Indeed, nothing did more to destabilize European state relations on a continuing basis throughout the entire Renaissance. Aside from the Ottoman-controlled areas of the Balkans, where indigenous ruling houses were eradicated altogether, no region of the Continent escaped the political and military effects of these rivalries. No territorial claim of a prince went unexamined for its dynastic implications. Assertions of rights over contested territories were often no more than a matter of official prerogative; the feudatory position held by the Holy Roman Empire in northern Italy is one example. Nevertheless, such statements were judged in the light of the dynastic interests of the emperors who enforced them. This was especially true in the fifteenth and sixteenth centuries, when the imperial office was filled by members of the House of Habsburg, who were arguably at the epicenter of contemporary dynastic conflicts. The commingling of the public and the private was the rule in the administration of contemporary governments generally and should have bothered no one. In this situation, however, familiarity did nothing to ease tensions.

The proprietary features of European dynastic monarchy made these rivalries all but inevitable and, once triggered, enduring. The title to patrimonial lands was understood as inalienable. Disputes passed from one generation to the next, either actively or in hibernation until someone chose to quicken them. Anticipating the extinction of their lines, heads of houses routinely drew up mutual succession agreements. However common, these arrangements were often very difficult to enforce, leaving the surviving house the holder of an unfulfilled contract. Local estates often challenged these agreements and turned to yet other dynasties to govern them. Distant, but nonetheless disappointed relatives of extinguished houses also reappeared to put themselves in the running. Territorial sovereigns were quite capable of signing several of these compacts with different parties, thereby increasing the likelihood of competing claimants. Dynastic intermarriage, though intended to foster good relations among ruling families, often led to problems which intensified rivalries. Patrimonial land, or the renunciation of it, was a routine part of dowries and other exchange relations in betrothal contracts. Disagreement over the meaning of these provisions and their implementation created, rather than eased, tensions between houses.

Whether the causes of these disagreements were recent or remote, they led to struggles which were conducted with single-minded tenacity by even the most lethargic of rulers. They were also pursued with utter disregard for larger interests of state, particularly those of a fiscal nature. Indeed, bankruptcy or near-bankruptcy was about the only condition that made contestants think twice about pursuing territorial rights. The armies of the competing houses of Habsburg and Valois grew substantially from the end of the fifteenth century to the Battle of Pavia in 1525, then dropped back a bit in size, and subsequently swelled again toward the middle of the sixteenth century. At that point, both houses had depleted their resources to a point where they had to pause for breath in their contest. Shaky finances had long limited Tudor England's pursuit of claims to Normandy and Guyenne in France.

Such epic persistence argues that more than simple property was at stake in the minds of the competitors, as indeed there was. For the emperor Charles V (ruled 1519–1556; also Charles I of Spain), King Francis I (ruled 1515–1547) of France, and many others, the loss of land was a personal insult, and the successful defense of land a point of individual honor. Charles's grandfather, the emperor Maximilian I (1493–1519), professed such values in two autobiographical works, *Theuerdank* (Noble mind; c. 1517), a thinly fictionalized account of his journey to claim the hand of Mary of Burgundy, and *Weisskunig* (The white knight; c. 1514), a more straightforward narrative of his battles against the Valois kings of France and refractory Netherlanders to preserve his wife's inheritance. Defending his patrimonial lands against Henry II of France in 1557 and 1558, Philip II of Spain believed that not only his lands, but also his honor and his reputation, were at stake.

Female Succession and Extinction of Houses. The extinction of ruling houses or their fallback to female succession always presented opportunities for conflicts over crowns. This situation, above all, may account for the frenetic pitch that dynastic rivalries reached in the Renaissance. An uncommonly large number of medieval ruling houses died out from the fourteenth to the beginning of the seventeenth centuries. The so-called Hundred Years' War (1338–1453) between France and England is a conspicuous early example. While commercial competition and disputes over feudal prerogatives had long been subjects of disagreement for the two realms, these turned into formal armed conflict only when the male ruling line of the French house of Capet died out in 1328. The question of succession rights to the French crown eventually became an issue which caught both countries up in episodic warfare for more than a century.

The Valois-Habsburg rivalry over Burgundy became violent following the death of Duke Charles the Bold in 1477. French claims to Burgundy, Flanders, Artois, Nevers, and Rethel went back to Capetian times, specifically to the marriage of Margaret of Flanders to Duke Philip, a son of King John II of France in 1369. In 1363 the nucleus of what was to be known as the duchy of Burgundy was made an appanage of the French crown and ruled by four successive Capetian dukes. Charles the Bold's demise left the rich patrimony in the hands of his daughter, Duchess Mary, and after her death in 1482 in those of her husband, the Habsburg Maximilian I, who was to become Holy Roman Emperor in 1493. Louis XI (ruled 1461–1483), the Valois king of France, decided to incorporate as much of the former patrimonial appanage as he could into his crown, and he actually succeeded in regaining ducal Burgundy and the Franche-Comté. His actions, however, deeply antagonized the Habsburgs, present and future, thus setting the stage for a great deal of future conflict.

East-central Europe lost all of its native royal houses in the fourteenth and fifteenth centuries. The medieval Polish ruling line, the Piasts, had died out in 1370 to be replaced for twelve years by the Angevin king of Hungary, Louis the Great. Following his death the Jagellonians, a Lithuanian princely family, succeeded to the crown on the promise that Lithuania and Poland would be united. Though the precise nature of this relationship would remain in dispute, the Polish Jagellonian kingship remained uncontested far longer than was the case in Bohemia and Hungary. Nevertheless, its extinction in 1572 left this realm, too, open to competing dynasties: the Habsburgs; the French Valois; the Transylvanian house of Bathory; and the Swedish Vasas.

Hungary, where the house of Árpád died out in 1290 and Bohemia, where the Přemyslids were extinct after 1306, were marked for acquisition by competing foreign dynasties for the next two hundred or more years. The houses of Luxembourg, Anjou, Habsburg, Wittelsbach, and the Polish Jagellonians all vied with one another for these thrones at one time or another. In justifying their candidacies, they called upon prior mutual succession agreements and hereditary rights through marriage. Both were stoutly resisted by estates or factions within them who insisted upon the privilege of electing their king. Should the ways of peace fail, war was often the result.

The ultimate victor in Bohemia and Hungary after 1526 was the Habsburg archduke Ferdinand I of Austria, the younger brother of Emperor Charles V. Without a royal crown but very eager to have one, Ferdinand was a man for whom membership in an important dynasty was the avenue to success, at least in Hungary. To a faction of the estates there, his chief attraction was his relationship to his older brother who, as king of Spain and emperor, might be called upon to finance the defense of the kingdom against the Turks. Fraternal relations were less important to him in Bohemia. There his chief competitors came from the Bavarian Wittelsbachs who had married into the ruling houses of the kingdom since the twelfth century. The Wittelsbach duke, Albrecht III (ruled 1438–1460) had been raised in Prague at the court of King Václav IV, who married twice into the Bavarian house. With the advent of the Protestant Reformation, the Wittelsbachs became early champions of Catholic orthodoxy. Ferdinand, by comparison, was more nuanced in matters of religion, a position that had greater appeal to Bohemia's Utraquists, an evangelical movement that won royal recognition during the fifteenth century. Ferdinand's triumphs were at the expense of yet another regional dynasty, the Polish Jagellonians. Indeed, the archduke's fear that the Polish king, Sigismund I, might ally himself with the Turks and end up as the ruler of kingdoms on Habsburg Austrian borders gave added urgency to his pursuit of the Bohemian and Hungarian crowns.

Armed Conflict. However much these dynastic shifts changed the internal political complexion of east-central Europe, they did not set off extended armed conflicts among the competing dynasties in the fifteenth and sixteenth centuries. The ultimate standard for this kind of struggle was set by the hegemonic competition between the Spanish Habsburgs and the French Valois in the west and south of Europe. Its chief arena was Italy, where succession problems also abounded, though of a somewhat different order than those in east-central Europe. The latter region was organized into kingdoms; the Italian peninsula knew such government—Naples, for example—but was home to many other kinds of polities as well. Flexible standards of legitimacy were common to several of them. Multiple claims to the city-states which dotted the peninsula reached back into the cloudiest recesses of medieval history. While local authorities often governed these places effectively, their staying power was unpredictable, which opened the way for

Plate 1. Clothing. Embroidered jacket worn by Margaret Laton. A jacket was worn with a skirt; the tabs at the bottom, called basques, extended below the waist. Front view. English; 1610–1620. VICTORIA AND ALBERT MUSEUM, LONDON/ART RESOURCE, NY

Plate 2. Correggio. *The Deposition* (Descent from the Cross). [See the entry on Correggio in this volume.] GALLERIA NAZIONALE, PARMA/SCALA/ART RESOURCE

Plate 3. Lucas Cranach the Elder. *Cupid Complaining to Venus.* Oil on wood; early 1530s; 81.3 x 54.6 cm (32 x 21.5 in.). [See the entry on Cranach in this volume.]
NATIONAL GALLERY, LONDON

Plate 4. Albrecht Dürer. *Self-Portrait.*
[See the entry on Dürer in this volume.]
ALTE PINAKOTEK, MUNICH/SCALA/ART RESOURCE

Plate 5. Decorative Arts. *Water Festival with Marine Monster,* one of the Valois Tapestries made in Brussels, c. 1573. In the left foreground are Margaret of Valois; Charles, duke of Lorraine; and Henry, king of Navarre (later Henry IV, king of France), husband of Margaret. Queen Catherine de Médicis, dressed in black, is seated on the barge in the center with her back to the viewer. 394 x 355 cm (155 x 140 in.). [See the entry on Decorative Arts in this volume.] GALLERIA DEGLI UFFIZI, FLORENCE/SCALA/ART RESOURCE, NY

Plate 6. Diplomacy. *Jean de Dinteville and Georges de Selve,* commonly known as *"The Ambassadors,"* by Hans Holbein the Younger. At the bottom foreground is a distorted skull that can be viewed correctly only from a vantage point to the left of and below the painting. Oil on oak; 1533; 207 x 210 cm (81.5 x 82.7 in.). [See the entry on Diplomacy in this volume, the entry on Holbein in volume 3, and the entry on Space and Perspective in volume 6.] NATIONAL GALLERY, LONDON/ART RESOURCE, NY

Plate 7. El Greco. *Saint Martin and the Beggar.* Oil on canvas; 1597–1599; 193.5 x 103 cm (76 x 40.5 in.). [See the entry on El Greco in this volume.] NATIONAL GALLERY OF ART, WASHINGTON, D.C./THE BRIDGEMAN ART LIBRARY

Plate 8. Jan van Eyck. *The Arnolfini Betrothal.* Oil on oak; 1434; 82 x 60 cm (32.25 x 23.5 in.). [See the article on Jan and Hubert van Eyck in this volume.] NATIONAL GALLERY, LONDON/SUPERSTOCK

Plate 9. Art in Florence. *The Annunciation* by Fra Filippo Lippi (c. 1406–1469). Late 1450s. Tempera on panel; 68.5 x 152 cm (27 x 60 in.). [See the entry on Florence, subentry on Art of the Fifteenth Century in this volume.] NATIONAL GALLERY, LONDON/THE BRIDGEMAN ART LIBRARY

Plate 10. Art in Florence. *Madonna and Child with Cherubim,* by Andrea della Robbia (1435–1525). Terra-cotta relief, glazed; c. 1485; 54.7 cm (21.5 in.) diameter. [See the entry Florence, subentry on Art of the Fifteenth Century in this volume.] NATIONAL GALLERY OF ART, WASHINGTON, D.C., ANDREW W. MELLON COLLECTION

Plate 11. Art in Florence. *Deposition* (Descent from the Cross), painted by Jacopo Pontormo (1494–1557) in the Cappella Capponi in the church of Santa Felicità in Florence. Oil on wood; c. 1525; 230 x 175 cm (90.5 x 69 in.). [See the entry Florence, subentry on Art of the Sixteenth Century in this volume.] ERICH LESSING/ART RESOURCE

Plate 12. Art in Florence. *Holy Family*, called the *Stroganoff Holy Family*, by Agnolo di Cosimo, called Bronzino (1503–1572). [See the entry Florence, subentry on Art of the Sixteenth Century in this volume.] PUSHKIN MUSEUM, MOSCOW/ART RESOURCE

Plate 13. Art in Florence. *Charity*, by Andrea d'Agnolo, known as Andrea del Sarto (1486–1530). Oil on canvas; 1518; 185 x 137 cm (73 x 54 in.). [See the entry Florence, subentry on Art of the Sixteenth Century in this volume.] MUSÉE DU LOUVRE, PARIS/ERICH LESSING/ART RESOURCE

other claimants to enter the competition. That Italy was comparatively rich only added to its attraction.

It was just such a situation which emerged there at the end of the fifteenth century. The focal points of the conflict were Naples and Milan. The former had been handed back and forth between rulers of Aragonese and Angevin origins from 1282, when Peter III of Aragon displaced Charles I of Anjou, a son of the Capetian king of France, Louis VIII. A long period of Aragonese rule followed between 1435 and 1494, during which Sicily was reunited with Naples. The extinction of the Sicilian Aragonese dynasty brought a claim to the title from the Valois ruler of France, Charles VIII, who had a number of reasons for his bid. One of his grandmothers was an Angevin. In addition, the last Angevin count of Provence, Charles III, had died in 1481 and bequeathed his titles, king of Naples among them, to the kings of France. In Aragon, King Ferdinand II (ruled 1479–1516 as the consort of Isabella of Castile) wished to preserve the Aragonese hold on Naples.

Both France and Aragon made some effort to settle their differences over Naples through negotiation, but no lasting agreement emerged. Charles VIII decided to go to Italy with an army in 1494, on the invitation of the ruler of Milan, Ludovico Sforza, who felt himself increasingly open to Florentine and Spanish aggression. Spain responded in kind. This situation became even more difficult to resolve when the French laid claim to Milan in 1498. A new king, Louis XII, the uncle of Charles VIII, was a son of Valentina Visconti, whose family had once governed the city. The French were willing to yield on Naples, but Louis seized Milan in 1499. This move was hotly contested by the Spanish; the Holy Roman Empire, which technically had suzerain rights over the city and its environs; and by other Italian governments.

The Spanish-French struggle in Italy became a Habsburg-Valois conflict as soon as Charles V became king of Spain in 1516 and Holy Roman Emperor in 1519. Charles was determined to continue the contest with the Valois for control of the Netherlands, where he had been raised. He was equally set on upholding Aragonese claims in Naples, along with Spanish interests generally throughout the Italian peninsula.

Milan eventually fell under Spanish control in 1535. In 1556 it became a Spanish appanage, though technically it remained a fief of the Holy Roman Empire. Though ducal Burgundy remained beyond Charles's grasp, he successfully retained the Habsburg hold over the rest of the Netherlands. The territory was increasingly linked with Spain, making the Habsburg territorial encirclement of France and its kings even more complete and the occasion of even deeper rivalry. During the sixteenth century the Catholic Valois kings of France would ally themselves with both the Ottoman Turks and German Protestant princes to curb the international reach of the House of Habsburg. Since the claims of the French ruling house also extended beyond the Pyrenees to Roussillon and Navarre, that border was also contested between the Habsburgs and the Valois, and later with the Bourbon rulers of France. In 1559 the Peace of Cateau-Cambrésis between Charles's son, Philip II of Spain, and Henry II of France brought some respite to this struggle, albeit to the distinct advantage of Spain. Philip's possession of the Franche-Comté was reaffirmed, as was his hold on the contested territories of Italy. Both Spain and France became preoccupied with internal affairs, in the French case with religious civil war. Nevertheless, these questions would all emerge again in the course of future conflicts, most notably in the Thirty Years' War (1618–1648).

BIBLIOGRAPHY

Allmand, Christopher. *The Hundred Years' War: England and France at War, c. 1300–c. 1450.* Cambridge, U.K., 1988. A topical overview.

Bonney, Richard. *The European Dynastic States, 1494–1660.* Oxford, 1991. A thorough survey.

Russell, Joycelyne. *Peacemaking in the Renaissance.* London, 1986. An unusually close study of the peace process in dynastic warfare.

Salgado-Rodriguez, Maria J. "The Habsburg-Valois Wars." In *The New Cambridge Modern History.* 2d ed. Vol. 2. Edited by G. R. Elton. Cambridge, U.K., 1990. Pages 377–400. A very clear account.

Vale, Malcolm. *The Angevin Legacy and the Hundred Years' War, 1250–1340.* Cambridge, Mass., 1990. Good background on competing dynastic claims.

PAULA SUTTER FICHTNER

EARLY MODERN PERIOD. "Early modern" or "early modern Europe" are terms often employed to describe the period of history following the Middle Ages and preceding the nineteenth century. The origins of early modern are obscure, and its exact chronological meaning varies. In addition, some scholars use the terms to assert a particular approach to English literature of the sixteenth and early seventeenth centuries.

Historians teaching in European universities have traditionally drawn a line between "medieval" and "modern." They typically see the date 1492 (Columbus's discovery of the New World), or 1494 (the French invasions of Italy, which began sixty-five years of war and political upheaval), or the more general date 1500 as the beginning of the modern era. The Protestant Reformation, which followed shortly afterward, seems to confirm an immense change. The beginning of great geographical, political, and religious changes persuaded European historians that the Middle Ages had given way to modern history. Scholars dealing exclusively with northern Europe especially preferred this division.

There are two problems with this approach. First, Italian history, especially that of the Italian Renaissance, does not fit comfortably into this time frame. Scholars of the Italian Renaissance generally agree that the Italian Renaissance began with the maturity of Petrarch (c. 1350) or the beginning of Florentine humanism (c. 1400), and that these dates marked the beginning of the modern world. Second, many historians believed that the traditional terms "medieval" and "modern" denoted too sharp a distinction be-

tween eras. In order to address these objections North American historians, especially authors of broad surveys of European history, began to use the term "early modern," which suggested the beginning of the modern era, but not the fully developed modern world of the nineteenth and twentieth centuries. This notion seems to have entered the English-language textbook tradition in the 1950s and 1960s, although it is difficult to pinpoint a precise book or date.

Possibly the most common meaning of early modern Europe today is Europe from the beginning of the Renaissance (1350 or 1400) to what is seen as another major historical turning point beginning with the French Revolution and concluding with the final defeat of Napoleon (1789–1815). Historians tend to see the Renaissance, Reformation, and Enlightenment as significant components of early modern European history.

A less common approach divides the period from about 1400 to 1815 into two. The Renaissance and Reformation era begins in 1350 or 1400 and ends with the outbreak (1618) or the conclusion (1648) of the Thirty Years' War. This era is followed by the early modern era, which runs until 1815.

While the term early modern is a product of the study of European history, it is also commonly used to define Japanese history from 1600 (the date of the last great medieval battle in Japanese history) to the establishment of the modern Japanese state in 1868. Early modern is seldom, if ever, employed in the historiography of any other parts of the world.

In the 1980s some scholars of English literature began to articulate a new ideological and methodological meaning for early modern. Instead of calling English literature written between 1500 and 1603 or 1660 Renaissance, they call it early modern. While both terms indicate the same chronological period, some literature scholars adopt the term early modern to make a statement of their scholarly approach, methods, and values. They reject the term Renaissance, which they define as an era in which a small group of elite males created great works of literature as expressions of their individuality. By contrast, early modern literature refers to a broader range of formal and informal writing of the period, especially of women and members of nonelite groups, whether or not the work can be judged "great." For these literary scholars early modern also means a rejection of traditional techniques of scholarship. Such scholars do not necessarily accept that the words of a work of literature present its meaning. Instead, they argue that meaning is found in the historical, cultural, and social context of the work. And they believe that it is the task of the scholar to employ the techniques of critical literary theory, and sometimes the cultural assumptions of the late twentieth century, in order to uncover meaning.

See also **Middle Ages**; **Renaissance**, *subentries on* **The Renaissance in Historical Thought** *and* **The Renaissance in Literary Interpretation**.

BIBLIOGRAPHY

Clough, Shepard B. et al. *A History of the Western World*. Vol. 2, *Early Modern Times*. New York, 1964. A typical early modern textbook covering European and North American history from the Italian Renaissance (c. 1400) to 1815.

Marcus, Leah S. "Renaissance/Early Modern Studies." In *Redrawing the Boundaries. The Transformation of English and American Literary Studies*. Edited by Stephen Greenblatt and Giles Gunn. New York, 1992. Pages 41–63. A clear statement of the differences between Renaissance and early modern in English literature as seen by a scholar committed to the early modern approach.

PAUL F. GRENDLER

EAST ASIA. *See* **Asia, East**.

EAST CENTRAL EUROPE, ART IN. Matthias Corvinus, king of Hungary (1458–1490), was a well-known friend of the arts. A devoted patron of Italian and humanistic culture and ideas, he maintained throughout his reign close contacts with Florence, Milan, and other cultural centers throughout western Europe. Upon his sudden death in 1490, Władysław II Jagiełło—king of Bohemia since 1471 and also a great patron of western European art—was elected to the throne of Hungary. His accession brought about the political and cultural union of Poland, Bohemia, and Hungary under the Jagiellonian dynasty, resulting in a kingdom that stretched from the Baltic to the Adriatic, and from Silesia to Transylvania. Both Władysław II (1490–1516) in Prague and his brother, Sigismund I (1506–1548) in Cracow, continued to disseminate western European Renaissance artistic styles and culture through their patronage, providing a significant cultural link between east central Europe and its western neighbors.

After the fall of the Jagiellonian dynasty in 1526, the house of Habsburg supplanted it as ruling dynasty of Bohemia and parts of Hungary. Through the Habsburgs, imperial artistic patronage and collections expanded, culminating with the activities of Emperor Rudolf II in Prague.

Cracow. The city of Cracow in the kingdom of Poland-Lithuania was the second locale in east central Europe to receive and foster Italian Renaissance artistic styles in a consistent manner and within a humanist cultural context. Italianate forms were transmitted to the Polish court of the Jagiellonian dynasty by Italian artists coming not directly from Italy itself, but rather via the courts of Matthias Corvinus in Hungary, and Władysław II Jagiełło in Bohemia.

The intellectual traditions of Cracow University (founded 1364) as well as the humanist predilections of the Jagiellonian King Sigismund I the Old (reigned 1506–1548), enabled a particular adaptation of Renaissance art to take shape in Cracow. Although the court was the major source of patronage for the new style, the Cracovian Renaissance was not characterized by a homogeneity in artistic styles or taste. Rather, artistic forms were mixed, generated by the intermingling of the new Italianate styles with the more traditional Gothic ones, as well as by the diversity of practices brought to the kingdom for the German-speaking land and the Low Countries.

Sigismund I had stayed at his brother Władysław's court in Bohemia from 1490 to 1493, where he could have come into contact with Italian art and culture. Even before taking the Polish throne in 1506, he may have called the Florentine stonemason, Francesco Fiorentino (Franciscus Florentinus; d. 1516) from the Buda court in 1602, thereby initiating a series of projects characterized by Italian, Tuscan forms. Whereas Italianate forms were desired for architectural and sculptural commissions, German, Polish and Netherlandish craftsmen were called upon for commissions in painting and the decorative arts. Even within architecture and sculpture Italians did not work

Sigismund Chapel, Cracow. COURTESY OF POLISH NATIONAL TOURIST OFFICE/PHOTOGRAPH BY EDWARD RYSINSKI

alone, but usually collaborated with artists from the German-speaking lands.

The niche tomb of Sigismund I's older brother, King Jan Olbracht (built 1502–1505; Cracow, Wawel Cathedral), was the first major work to exhibit the new Italian style. Francesco Fiorentino constructed the architectural surround for the tomb in the form of a triumphal arch, and decorated its surface with classical forms. The classical, triumphal arch shape serves as a reminder of the imperial aspirations of the Jagiellonian dynasty. The effigy of King Jan Olbracht within the niche, completed by a member (either Stanislas Stoss [b. 1527/28] or Jörg Huber) workshop of Veit Stoss (1438 or 1447–1533) conforms to a non-Italian, northern style. It has been interpreted not as an inharmonious addition to Fiorentino's classicizing arch, but rather as typical collaborative practice within Cracow between regional workshops.

The courtyard (1507–1536) at the royal Wawel castle is one of the earliest surviving arcaded castle courtyards outside of Italy. Here, Francesco Fiorentino, as well as Master Benedykt (fl. 1518–1529) and the Italian Bartolommeo Berrecci (c. 1480–1537), employed a Renaissance vocabulary of rounded arches and classical decorative motifs. The "Wawel-type" door and window stonemasonry, combining classical and Gothic decorative elements, first appeared at Wawel around 1510. Possibly of Hungarian origin, this type of masonry was transmitted by Cracow masons as far as Lithuania and is traditionally associated with Polish Renaissance art.

The Sigismund Chapel (1519–1531, Cracow Wawel Cathedral), designed and built for Sigismund I by Berrecci, represents the most rigorous use of Tuscan forms in sixteenth-century Poland, and was copied extensively throughout the kingdom until the seventeenth century. The structure is that of a central plan with an octagonal drum and round windows, capped by a dome and lantern. Decorated with a profusion of antique motifs, statuary, and complex mythical subject matter, the chapel has been interpreted on one level as a statement of the Jagiellonian rivalry with the house of Habsburg. The figure of Sigismund I is shown in a reclining position and appears to be asleep, a type which would be copied extensively and exclusively throughout the Polish kingdom. It is known that Sigismund I had been personally involved in overseeing its creation at every stage. The inscription, BARTHOLO FLORENTINO OPIFICE, stands as Berrecci's signature inside the cupola, a place usually reserved for a holy image or the patron's coat of arms, and thus suggests the importance of the architect as creator and his high status within the court. In 1575 the chapel was remodeled so that the effigy of Sigismund II August could be placed beneath that of his father, thus becoming what is often referred to as a "double-decker" tomb.

By the second half of the sixteenth century, Italian artists from the Veneto and Lombard lakes region determined the nature of the Italianate style in Poland. Representative projects were those by the Paduan Bernardo Morando, working from 1578 to 1600 for the Lord Chancellor Jan Zamoyski in Zamość, as well as Giovanni Battista Quadro's (d. 1590/91) Town Hall at Poznań (1550–1560). The forms of this so-called "second" Renaissance were chiefly architectural and sculptural, innovative for the combinations of Italian, German, and Netherlandish styles derived in part from engravings and pattern books. The work of the Florentine, Santi Gucci (1550–1600), who executed the tomb of King Stefan Bathory (reigned 1575–1586) as well as several residences and tombs for aristocratic patrons (for example, Baranów Castle, 1591–1606), serves as an example of the ornate, hybrid forms which have been loosely referred to as "Mannerist," although the style should be seen not merely as a derivative of its Italian counterparts, but as a creative solution to the problem of integrating several regional styles, including eastern ones, into the visual vocabulary.

Painting in Cracow was dominated by German and Polish schools and remained essentially Gothic in style throughout the first half of the sixteenth century. Tempera on panel was the traditional medium, and oil painting was not introduced until the 1530s. During the 1460s an interest in naturalism took the form of attention to detail, placement of figures in a landscape or architectural setting, and interest in physiognomy. Cracow had a strong tradition of miniature painting, represented by Stanisław Samostrzelnik (1480s–1541). A Cistercian monk from Mogiła, he painted the twelve miniatures for a *Liber genesis* of the Szydłowiecki family for Chancellor Krzysztof Szydłowiecki (1532) and illuminated the *Lives of the Gniezno Archbishops* (early 1530s; Warsaw, National Library) for the bishop of Cracow, Piotr Tomicki. Other painters commissioned in Cracow were the Nürnbergers, Hans Seuss von Kulmbach (1480–1522), who worked in the Church of St. Mary, and Hans Dürer (1490–1538), who worked on the altarpiece in the Sigismund chapel from 1535 to 1538. In the first decade of the sixteenth century a Cracow miniaturist workshop of uncertain attribution executed the *Codex of Balthasar Behem* (Cracow, Jagiellonian Library, Jagiellonian University), important for its detailed portrayals of the secular world of craftsmen and trades.

Prague. Under the patronage of Władisław Jagiełło, who was elected to the throne of Bohemia in 1471, and perhaps as his response to Matthias Corvinus's commissions in Silesia and Lusatia, Prague became a center for artistic production in which a fusion of Renaissance and Gothic forms prevailed during the first quarter of the sixteenth century.

In a move to reestablish the authority of the Luxembourg dynasty from which Władisław descended, the king called the German mason Benedikt Ried to Prague in 1489 to carry out important royal projects on the castle hill, called the Hradčany, including the Vladislav Hall (1493–1502), which exhibits the first, albeit impure, interpretation of Renaissance classicism in Bohemia. On the Ludvik Wing of the Hradčany Castle (so named after Władisław's son; 1500–c. 1510), Ried employed cross-mullion windows with Renaissance frames and cornices, perhaps a clear statement of the reception of the new Italianate aesthetic. It can be noted that the exterior contrasts markedly with the lyrical Gothic ribs in the vault. For that reason, the Vladislav Hall can be seen as a unique interpretation of western and local forms within the same monument, yielding the kind of solution that has been generally referred to as "vernacular."

In painting, the anonymous master of Litoměřice executed the fresco cycle dedicated to St. Wenzel (c. 1505) in the south transept of St. Vitus's Cathedral. It has been pointed out that while the figures in his compositions generally reflect his southern German training, his mastery of perspective demonstrates familiarity with Italian Renaissance pictorial conventions.

From the mid-sixteenth century, artistic patronage in Prague was driven largely by the Habsburg rulers. Ferdinand I (reigned in Bohemia and Hungary 1526–

Central European Art. *Mountain Landscape with Woodcutters* by Roelandt Savery. Oil on panel; 1610. KUNSTHISTORISCHES MUSEUM, GEMÄLDEGALERIE, VIENNA/ERICH LESSING/ART RESOURCE

1564) called artists from northern Italy to Prague. From 1535 to 1563 the Italian architect Paolo della Stella, followed by the German Bonifaz Wohlmut (d. 1579), constructed the Villa Belvedere on the Hradčany, the first of its type in east central Europe to be placed in an urban setting. The villa's structure is related to that of sixteenth-century Italian designs, characterized by a lower level in the style of Bramante and decorated with reliefs bearing classical subjects. Wohlmut's other projects in Prague exhibit an adherence to classical forms, such as the Serlianstyle organ lift at St. Vitus's Cathedral (1556–1561), and the Palladian ball court building in the Hradčany gardens (1567–1569).

Artistic culture in Prague attained new levels when the Emperor Rudolf II (b. Vienna, 1552; reigned in Hungary, 1572–1607 and in Bohemia, 1575–1611; Holy Roman Emperor, 1576–1612; d. Prague, 1612) moved his court to Prague in 1583. In the tradition of high Renaissance princely patronage and collecting, Rudolf II employed artists, humanists, alchemists, and scientists from throughout Europe. Already as early as 1604 the Netherlander Karel van Mander (1548–1606) had mentioned the Prague court as the most important place for an art lover to visit. His imperial *Kunstkammer,* described as a collection that mirrored the microcosm of the world over which Rudolf presided, has been declared as the most impressive of its time, and was used by his artists for study. Because of the breadth of Rudolf's patronage in the areas of painting, sculpture, goldsmithing, engraving, and stonecutting, and because individual artists often worked in contradictory ways, it has been suggested that Rudolfine art cannot be characterized by any single formal style.

From his father, Maximilian II (reigned in Bohemia, 1562–1575 and in Hungary 1563–1572; Holy Roman Emperor, 1564–1576) Rudolf had inherited several humanists and artists, notably the painter Giuseppe Arcimboldo (1527–1593) whose portrait of Rudolf II as Vertumnus (c. 1591) serves as an example of the complex, witty, and often epigrammatic iconography that characterized Rudolf's patronage, and that served to emphasize the learnedness of Rudolf himself, his courtiers, and his artists.

Among the artists whom Rudolf called to Prague in the 1580s were the painters Hans von Aachen (1552–1615), Bartholomaeus Spranger (1546–1611), Joseph Heintz (1564–1609), and Dirck de Quade van Ravesteyn, from whom the emperor commissioned allegorical works. Others such as Roelandt Savery (1576–1639), Pieter Stevens (c. 1567–c. 1625), and Joris Hoefnagel (1542–1601) produced still lifes, ani-

mal paintings, genre paintings, and landscape from study after nature. Rudolf had sent Savery to the Alps from 1606 to 1607 to record what he saw there, resulting in some of the first landscapes painted for nature by a Netherlandish artist (see for example Savery's *Mountain Landscape with Woodcutters,* 1610; Vienna, Kunsthistorisches Museum).

Sculptors called to court included the Netherlander Adriaan de Vries (c. 1560–1626), who was trained by Giambologna (1529–1608), whose allegorical bronze *Portrait Bust of Rudolf II* (1603; Vienna, Kunsthistorisches Museum) features Rudolf in ceremonial armor decorated with reliefs and carried by the Roman gods Jupiter and Mercury. The decorative arts were represented by the goldsmiths Paulus van Vianen (c. 1570–1613) and Wenzel Jamnitzer (1508–1585), among others, as well as the ivory carver Nikolaus Pfaff. Stone cutting flourished in the workshops of the Miseroni and Castrucci workshops (see for example the Castrucci *Landscape with a Bridge and Chapel,* 1596; Vienna, Kunsthistorisches Museum). Engravers such as Aegidus Sadeler II (c. 1568–1628), Hendrick Goltzius (1558–1617), and Martino Rota (c. 1520–1583) disseminated images of works from Rudolf's collection through the lands of the Empire and beyond.

See also **Cracow**; **Poland**; **Prague**; *and biographies of figures mentioned in this entry.*

BIBLIOGRAPHY

Białostocki, Jan. *The Art of the Renaissance in Eastern Europe.* The Wrightsman Lectures, vol. 8. Oxford, 1976.

Evans, R. J. W. *Rudolf II and His World: A Study in Intellectual History, 1576–1612.* Oxford, 1973.

Fučíková, Eliska, ed. *Rudolf II and Prague: The Imperial Court and the Residential City as the Cultural and Spiritual Heart of Central Europe.* Exhibition catalog, Prague, Czech Republic. London, 1997.

Karpowicz, Mariusz. *Artisti ticinesi in Polonia nel '500.* Bellinzona, Switzerland, 1987.

Karpowicz, Mariusz. *Artisti ticinesi in Polonia nel '600.* Lugano, Switzerland, 1983.

Kaufmann, Thomas DaCosta. *Court, Cloister, and City: The Art and Culture of Central Europe, 1450–1800.* Chicago, 1995.

Kaufmann, Thomas DaCosta. *The School of Prague: Painting at the Court of Rudolf II.* Translation and revision of his *L'École de Prague: La Peinture à la cour de Rodolphe II.* Paris, 1985.

Kozakiewicz, Helena, and Stefan Kozakiewicz. *Renaissance in Poland.* Warsaw, 1976.

Miłobędzki, Adam. *The Architecture of Poland; A Chapter of the European Heritage.* Translated by Teresa Baluk-Ulewiczowa. Cracow, 1994.

Mossakowski, Stanislaw. "Bartolomeo Berrecci à Cracovie: La chapelle Sigismond." *Revue de l'art* 101 (1993): 67–85.

Polen in Zeitalter der Jagiellonen, 1386–1572. Exhibition catalog, Schallaburg, Austria, 1986.

Prag um 1600: Kunst und Kultur am Hofe Rudolfs II. 2 vols. Exhibition catalog, Essen Villa Hügel and Vienna Kunsthistorisches Museum, 1988–1989. Freren, Germany, 1988–1989.

Scheicher, E. *Die Kunst- und Wunderkammern der Habsburger.* Vienna and Munich, 1979.

Seibt, Ferdinand, ed. *Renaissance in Böhmen.* Munich, 1985.

The Stylish Image: Printmakers to the Court of Rudolf II. Exhibition catalog by Mungo Campbell, National Gallery of Scotland. Edinburgh, 1991.

CAROLYN C. GUILE

EBERLIN, JOHANN VON GUENZBURG (c. 1470–1533), German Reformer and pamphleteer. Although considered only a minor Reformer, Eberlin was a prominent propagandist for the early Protestant movement. An apostate Franciscan, he is known especially for his attacks on the mendicant orders. Before becoming a Franciscan, probably around 1500, he served as a priest in the diocese of Augsburg and attended university in Basel and Freiburg, eventually attaining his master's degree. Thereafter he resided at Franciscan priories in Upper Alsace, Tü-

Johann Eberlin. Title page of *Ain klegliche klag* (Augsburg, 1521). ARCHIV FÜR KUNST UND GESCHICHTE, BERLIN/ AKG PHOTO

bingen, Basel, and Ulm. In these locations he was exposed to a reforming tradition that synthesized the ideals of the Franciscan observance with the reforming aspirations of prominent humanists within the order such as Paul Scriptoris in Tübingen and Konrad Pellican (1478–1556) in Basel.

During Lent 1521, in Ulm, Eberlin openly proclaimed his support for the cause of Martin Luther (1483–1546). Putting Ulm and the Franciscan order behind him, he traveled widely in Switzerland and southwestern Germany before arriving in Wittenberg in early 1522. During this time he penned his best-known work, a collection of fifteen pamphlets published anonymously under the title *Fünfzehn Bundesgenossen* (The fifteen confederates; Basel, 1521). These pamphlets contain a wide-ranging vision for social and ecclesiastical reform, including the statutes for an imaginary land of Wolfaria, which some interpreters hail as the first Protestant Utopia.

Eberlin remained in Wittenberg from 1522 until early 1524, aside from a brief tour of the southwest in the summer and autumn of 1523. In Wittenberg he immersed himself in the program of the Reformation while continuing his pamphlet writing. His ongoing interest in social reform is evident in a series of anonymous pamphlets including *Mich wundert, dass kein Geld im Land ist* (I wonder that there is no money in the land; 1524), which is modeled closely on Ulrich von Hutten's *Praedones* (The robbers; 1520). He also continued to focus on the details of practical ecclesiastical reform, dealing with matters such as clerical celibacy in *Wie gar gefährlich, so ein Priester kein Eheweib hat* (How very dangerous that a priest does not have a wife; 1522), and monasticism in *Wider den unvorsichtigen Ausgang vieler Klosterleute* (Against the imprudent, unreasonable departure of many cloistered; 1522) and *Wider den falschen Geistlichen, genannt die Barfüsser und Franziskaner* (Against the false religious known as the barefoot friars or Franciscans; 1523). New to his pamphlets, however, was an increasing concern with the central themes of Luther's theology, as evidenced in *Vom Missbrauch christlicher Frëiheit* (On the abuse of Christian liberty; 1522) and in published epistles to friends and former charges in Augsburg and Ulm.

In early 1524 Eberlin relocated to Erfurt, where he remained a full year despite his inability to secure a pastoral position. In 1526 he entered the service of Duke George II of Wertheim, eventually coming to direct the reformation of the church in the duke's territories. Unpublished writings from this period of Eberlin's life indicate not only his concern with the practical matters of ecclesiastical reform but also a continued commitment to a humanist pedagogical program. With the death of the duke in 1530, Eberlin was forced out of Wertheim, ending up as a pastor in the parish of Leutershausen. There he continued his reforming activities until his own death in 1533.

BIBLIOGRAPHY

Primary Work

Enders, Ludwig, ed. *Johann Eberlin von Günzburg*. Flugschriften aus der Reformationszeit, vols. 11, 15, 18. Halle, Germany, 1896–1902. Volume 11 is entitled *Ausgewählte Schriften* (Selected writings); volumes 15 and 18 are entitled *Sämtlichen Schriften* (Complete writings).

Secondary Works

Dipple, Geoffrey. *Antifraternalism and Anticlericalism in the German Reformation: Johann Eberlin von Günzburg and the Campaign against the Friars*. Aldershot, U.K., 1996. Analyzes Eberlin's writings from the perspective of early Reformation attacks on the clergy, and especially the mendicant orders.

Ozment, Steven. *The Reformation in the Cities: The Appeal of Protestantism to Sixteenth-Century Germany and Switzerland*. New Haven, Conn., and London, 1975. Provides partial translations of *The Fifteen Confederates*.

Peters, Christian. *Johann Eberlin von Günzburg ca. 1465–1533: Franziskanischer Reformer, Humanist und konservativer Reformator*. Gütersloh, Germany, 1994. The most recent authoritative biography in German.

GEOFFREY DIPPLE

ECONOMIC INTERPRETATIONS. *See* **Renaissance, Interpretations of the,** *subentry on* **Economic Interpretations.**

ECONOMIC THOUGHT. *See* **Banking and Money; Mercantilism; Usury.**

EDUCATION. Medieval Latin grammar education descended from classical education, although the dominance of monastic and cathedral educational centers in the early and central Middle Ages made medieval education unique. In addition, although older Roman grammar texts remained in use, the ubiquity of the primer and the Psalter for the teaching of reading and the sustained production and use of newer grammar books between the tenth and thirteenth centuries meant that Renaissance educators saw significant differences between Roman education and that of their medieval predecessors.

In the thirteenth and early fourteenth centuries there were significant increases in the availability of both primary and grammar education, and a consequent rise in the level of literacy among men particularly, and primarily above the level of the artisan and peasant classes. Even considering this, the greater attention paid to education by Renaissance thinkers, as well as a turn to rhetoric, the imitation of the classics (particularly Cicero), the production of newer textbooks (based on a more classical Latin or on Greek), and a new emphasis on method and the psychology of the child signify a major shift in the history of education.

The Beginnings in Italy. The Renaissance history of education begins with Petrarch's discovery, in 1350, of parts of the *Institutio oratoria* of the Roman orator and teacher Marcus Fabius Quintilianus, written originally about A.D. 94. The complete text, discovered in 1416 by Poggio Bracciolini, inspired a new humanistic philosophy of education. Quintilian presents an ideal—the training, from infancy to adulthood, of a perfect orator who is also a good man. The rhetorical education he describes was elite and, at the elementary level, inculcated within the home. Quintilian advised teaching methods that accommodated differing abilities and character and were sensitive to a child's psychology. He recommended a more humane, more moral, more practical, and broader education, with a deliberate sequencing of exercises, from the simple to the more complex, and constant reinforcement tailored to the individual. Children should intersperse studies with recreation. Quintilian eschewed rigidly applied rules and corporal punishment; the young, he thought, are naturally inclined to learn.

According to Quintilian, the grammar master dissects Latin and Greek poetry (in terms of both meaning and grammatical construction), teaching an analytical style of reading, composition, the liberal arts, and, finally, rhetoric. The bulk of the *Institutio* is devoted to the parts, nature, value, origin, and function of rhetoric, emphasis that was to be determinative for Renaissance education. One of the first printed books in Italy was a complete copy of Quintilian; one hundred editions of the *Institutio* were to be published over the next eighty years.

Also influential and similar in content was pseudo-Plutarch, *De pueris educandis* (On the education of children), translated from Greek into Latin by Guarino da Verona in 1411. The rediscovery of Cicero's *De oratore* and *Orator* in 1421 further reinforced the importance of rhetoric.

In 1404 Pier Paolo Vergerio (1370–1444) published *De ingenuis moribus* (On noble customs). Although often described as a treatise for the privileged (addressed as it is to Ubertino, the son of the lord of Carrara), it was copied and printed more than any other pedagogical treatise prior to Erasmus, and its influence traveled beyond the elite and beyond Italy. Vergerio argues for the importance of liberal studies, by which he means history, moral philosophy, and poetry, and the seven liberal arts (grammar, dialectic, rhetoric, music, arithmetic, geometry, and astronomy). He stresses training in eloquence and offers advice for teaching students wisely, keeping in mind differing tempers and mental abilities. He rejects harsh punishments and recommends a manageable curriculum. Instruction should be paced, allowing students to master one point before proceeding to the next. Vergerio recommends discussion and students teaching students. Finally, he requires that pupils be trained in body (the art of war) as well as in mind, inculcating virtue and wisdom through both. These ideas were to be repeated and developed throughout the Renaissance, although subsequent writers, more so than Vergerio, linked a classical education with Christian piety, civic values, and public service to the state or the prince.

Other Italian writers (Leonardo Bruni, Eneo Silvio Piccolomini, Leon Battista Alberti) emphasized the role of the study of letters in creating civic responsibility. Venetian humanists, such as Francesco Barbaro, insisted that a liberal education benefited the republic by enhancing the character and culture of its patriciate. Those teaching the humanities should emphasize effective enunciation and the importance of style—prime possessions for a person seeking a public or professional career. Italian humanist educators recommended writing exercises—paraphrasing poetry into prose, translating Greek into Latin and vice versa, and directly imitating model passages. Ciceronian declamations were to be read aloud, and large portions committed to memory. Latin was to be spoken among students both in and out of class. They stressed the importance of integrating breadth of learning with grace of style, a proficiency in literary form accompanied by a broad acquaintance with classical culture. In general, whether in the princely courts of northern Italy or among the merchants and professionals in Italian cities, the *studia humanitatis* became a sine qua non for secretarial, diplomatic, and political posts, and the mark of an educated person.

Humanist education moved quickly from Italian households into the grammar schools in the fifteenth century and very rapidly into the rest of Europe through the sixteenth century. One of the first (and most famous) to run a humanist school was Vittorino da Feltre (1378–1446), who established a boarding school, Casa Giocosa, at the court of Mantua in 1423 under the patronage of the Gonzaga dukes. Vittorino taught the Gonzaga children, children of noble families, and poor, promising children recommended by friends and family. He received them free of charge, beginning as young as four or five with reading and spelling. Instruction took place in Latin, through dictation and recitation, with stress on correct pronunciation. Students were expected to memorize impressive amounts of texts. Vittorino used Latin poets and historians (particularly Livy) to develop vocabulary and to study syntax and prosody. The goal of this training, which included Greek literature, was to enable students to compose both written and spoken Latin and Greek. Only with a select number of older pupils did Vittorino introduce the moral philosophies of Cicero, Aristotle, Plato, and the Stoics. Teachers were available to instruct students in mathematics, astronomy, and geometry. Vittorino made sure that students devoted time to games and to strenuous physical activity in an often spartan atmosphere. He stressed the development of mind, body, and character, and argued for the necessity of this training for those who sought to enter the professions or public service. Vittorino, whose commitment to teaching derived in part from a strong sense of Christian duty, also insisted that his pupils attend mass and go to confession often.

Another noted fifteenth-century school, the court school at Ferrara taught by Guarino Guarini (c. 1374–1460), the father of Battista Guarini, required memorization, repetition, catechism, composition, and imitation, but concentrated on content in both Latin and Greek texts in order to provide better understanding. Guarini worked through texts meticulously, defining terms, explaining context, and analyzing problems of interpretation. His students took detailed lecture notes and were encouraged to compile indexed books of reading notes. Subsequent humanist educators in Italy and elsewhere tended to repeat the ideas of Quintilian and Vergerio and to follow the practices of Vittorino and Guarini.

The humanist curriculum paid little attention to other subjects, with the exception of music, whose position as a liberal art was strengthened. Although there continued to be a focus on liturgical singing, instrument playing captured greater attention—especially instruments like the lute, viol, and clavichord that might be played in a domestic or court setting. Interest in classical Greek music led to production of different scales and melodies suited to different emotions and particularly applicable to madrigal singing. There was minimal attention to astronomy, mathematics, geometry, and natural science. Drawing was, at first, a subject for professional artists, but by the end of the fifteenth century, it gained in value, due in part to the elevation of artists in Renaissance society.

Humanist education existed side by side with martial training. For those boys who would not fight as soldiers, the physical side of their education consisted of ball games, dancing, archery, fencing, gymnastics, riding, and swimming. Most humanist educators insisted upon attendance at worship, regular confession, religious observance, and prayers.

Humanist educators understood that they were teaching potential advisers to princes and boys who, as men, would influence the public sphere. They recommended the moral lessons derived from classical texts and warned against using, for example, Ovid's racier texts or particular passages from Juvenal's *Satires*. They focused on inculcating a moral philosophy, often Stoical in complexion. Spirituality and religiosity are less in evidence, although this changed as humanist educational ideas moved north. Underlying this somewhat secularized education was the assumption that the classical virtues harmonized with Christian doctrine and piety. In practice, however, moral philosophy was often secondary to grammatical exercises and to style. The humanist method was adaptable to a variety of political and pedagogical contexts and could be presented as value-free, with pragmatic ends.

The example of Vittorino da Feltre and Guarino Guarini helped spread the *studia humanitatis* through Italian court culture. The *studia humanitatis* also spread beyond the courts. Prior to his stint at Ferrara, Guarini had been appointed by the commune of Verona to offer a classical Latin education to that city's children (1420–1430). His example, and that of others, spurred the growth of humanistic education in the 1430s, 1440s, and 1450s in towns throughout northern and central Italy. By the middle of the fifteenth century Venetian patricians, for example, were wholeheartedly committed to humanistic education, either in the public schools or in study with private teachers. By the 1470s southern Italian schools also began to hire humanistic masters. Paul Grendler estimates that by the end of the fifteenth century nearly all Latin schools in Italy were humanistic.

Latin School Texts. The turn to classical Latin texts created a demand for new Latin grammars. The most popular medieval grammar texts had been the late Roman grammars of Priscian, the *Dis-*

ticha Catonis (Sayings of Cato), and Donatus's *Ars minor* and variants, as well as a twelfth-century poetic grammar, the *Doctrinale puerorum*, of Alexander de Villa Dei. Grammar teachers in Italy at the beginning of the fifteenth century were using the same basic grammars and school authors that a thirteenth-century grammar teacher would have used. The *Ars minor* of Donatus continued to be in demand. The *Doctrinale* was printed in large numbers up to 1525, although rarely after that. Niccolò Perotti (1429–1480), taught by Vittorino da Feltre, wrote a very substantial manual of Latin grammar, *Rudimenta grammatices*, incorporating classical examples; it was first printed at Rome in 1473.

In Spain, Antonio de Nebrija (1441–1522) produced an elementary Latin grammar, *Introductiones latinae* (Latin introductions), in 1481. The second edition (c. 1487), dedicated to Queen Isabella, had parallel columns of Latin and Castilian, making it useful for Spanish readers. The *Introductiones* was reprinted often and exported all over Europe. In 1598 the Royal Council of Castile ordered that no other Latin grammar be used in Spain or Portugal. Nebrija also compiled the first Spanish-Latin dictionary in 1492.

In 1493 Aldus Manutius (1450?–1515), the great Italian printer and publisher of classical, and especially Greek, texts, published his *Institutiones grammaticae latinae* (Principles of Latin grammar), a comprehensive grammar with some basic Greek and Hebrew materials; it went through numerous editions. The preface attacks grammar masters who compose their own grammar exercises or force students to memorize medieval grammatical treatises. He recommends, instead, memorizing something of Cicero, Virgil, and other famous authors.

The most popular of all Renaissance grammar texts was the *Grammatica* (c. 1520) of Johannes Despauterius of 's-Hertogenbosch, which opened with an attack on the *Doctrinale*, although it followed the *Doctrinale* in its poetic, somewhat prolix presentation of Latin grammar. Despauterius gained popularity in France, Scotland, and the Low Countries, where his text became the basis for all Latin grammars until the twentieth century. It was incorporated into the Jesuits' grammar curriculum, although it was never popular in their Italian or German schools, and the Spanish insisted on using Nebrija. In 1572 the Portuguese Jesuit Manoel Alvares published *De institutione grammatica*, which became the official grammar text in Jesuit schools.

In Germany the elementary Latin grammar (*Enchiridion elementorum puerilium*; 1524) of Philipp

In the Schoolroom. From the signboard of a schoolmaster by Ambrosius Holbein (c. 1494–1519). 1516. Oeffentliche Kunstsammlung Basel/Art Resource, NY

Melanchthon (1497–1560) spread throughout Saxony, remaining in use until the eighteenth century. It consisted of short sentences, prayers, psalms, and fables that allowed students to learn grammar and vocabulary from reading and memorization, rather than beginning with rules and syntax.

In England about 1500 there was a flurry of new grammars published in connection with Magdalen College, Oxford, and with the grammar school at St. Paul's Cathedral, London. Some of these, despite acknowledged debts to Italian humanists, were not substantially different from medieval grammar texts. More clearly influenced by humanism was the *Rudimenta grammatices* of William Lily, headmaster at St. Paul's from 1512 to 1522. Lily's grammar was to become the basis, in 1540 and 1542, for two authorized royal Latin grammars, one in Latin, another in English. These were prescribed through the reigns of Protestant and Catholic rulers alike and well beyond the Renaissance.

A frequent practice in humanist grammar schools was the use of commonplace books, notebooks with topically arranged illustrative sentences in Latin and the vernacular. Beginners also used phrase books, extracts, and grammar exercises put together by their schoolmasters. All these practices could evolve only in an age when paper, pens, ink, and desks were more common in classrooms. By 1500 the quotations in commonplace books were being taken increasingly from classical texts, and double translation (from Latin to the vernacular and back again) was a schoolroom practice. The direct imitation of classical authors, in lieu of learning grammatical rules, was also recommended by Erasmus and Melanchthon. The northern humanists devoted some of their sharpest attacks to grammarians and their grammatical formularies, arguing, as does Roger Ascham, that "without doubt *grammatica* itself is sooner and surer learned by examples of good authors than by the naked rules of grammarians."

Desiderius Erasmus's *De copia verborum* (Foundations of the abundant style; 1512), an anthology of classical authors, was just the kind of text to encourage such reading, and through the sixteenth century it was printed in over a hundred editions, becoming the standard work in grammar schools throughout northern Europe. Also used in Renaissance schools were colloquies, fictional dialogues in classical style that provided models for speaking Latin outside the classroom. The most immediately popular of these was Erasmus's *Colloquia*, reprinted seven times within eighteen months of being published in 1518, then rewritten and enlarged, resulting in twelve editions between 1522 and 1533. Other popular colloquies were Juan Luis Vives's *Exercitatio linguae latinae* (Schoolboy dialogues; 1538) and the *Colloquiorum scholasticorum* (School colloquies; 1556) of Mathurin Cordier, the latter still in use in English schools in the nineteenth century.

In addition to grammars, commonplace books, anthologies, colloquies, and dictionaries, the humanist curriculum built on original Latin classical texts. Virgil and Ovid, medieval staples, remained in the curriculum, which now included Cicero's letters or Catiline speeches, Lucan, Sallust, Terence, and Livy, along with moral fables, Statius, some of Seneca, Horace, and Quintilian. From the very beginning readings in the classical tradition were balanced with reading of Psalms, the Old and New Testaments, and sometimes the church fathers. Later Latin writers (excluding the humanists themselves) were no longer acceptable.

Teaching Greek. Efforts to secure teachers of classical Greek in the West were largely unsuccessful until the Byzantine scholar Manuel Chrysoloras (c.

1350–1414) taught Greek at Florence (1396/97–1400) and at Pavia (1400–1403); some of his pupils were to become able teachers of Greek. Chrysoloras also produced *Erotemata sive quaestiones* (published 1476), a text of Greek accidence written in Greek. Subsequent Greek grammars were those of Theodore Gaza (c. 1445) and Constantine Lascaris (c. 1460). All these texts were adapted to a Latin-speaking environment, simplified, and provided with explanatory notes and Latin translations.

Students studying Greek could expect to begin with some easy Greek prose plus the Latin Gospels with a Greek version side by side. Aesop, Homer, and Hesiod followed, and then Isocrates, Plato, Herodotus, Xenophon, the dramatists, perhaps Plutarch and Demosthenes, or an anthology of parts of these texts. In general the range of Greek texts available in grammar schools throughout Europe was limited and did not include many Christian works, although the writings of John Chrysostom were oftentimes recommended.

The introduction of Greek into the school curriculum was first attempted by Guarino Guarini at Venice and by Vittorino da Feltre at Mantua. Vittorino taught Greek almost in lecture style—with explanations of mythology, geography, personages, uses by Latin writers, and some syntactical lessons. Latin translations were used side by side with the Greek. For Guarini, the goal of Greek learning was to aid Latin scholarship, although some students learned to translate from Greek to Latin. Students were not expected to write or speak Greek. Not until the last quarter of the fifteenth century, with the introduction of printed Greek texts, did Greek grammar become common in humanist schools in Italy; even so, it was normally taught to older students.

Greek remained a course of study for very few. In 1587 only 3 percent of the schoolboys in Venice were learning classical Greek. Except in Jesuit schools Greek probably remained on the margins of the humanist curriculum. The Greek component of the curriculum may have been most useful in deepening understanding of classical Latin literature and its underlying Greek culture.

The introduction of Greek into schools north of the Alps is difficult to trace. Reference to Greek in school statutes or in job descriptions of grammar masters does not guarantee that Greek was really being taught. The ideas of Erasmus, Melanchthon, and Vives—that boys be introduced to Greek early on—were not necessarily mirrored in practice. Greek was taught at Zwolle in 1516 and at St. Paul's in London under John Colet. Toward the end of the sixteenth century, Greek was available in most of the better English grammar schools, having been introduced at Eton by 1560. At Harrow, in 1591, Greek grammar started in the fourth form, followed by readings in Greek, particularly the Greek New Testament but also Demosthenes, Isocrates, Hesiod, and others. The first Greek grammar in English was written by Edward Grant at Westminster in the 1570s.

Expansion to France. Italian humanist educational ideals took French cities and their urban elites by storm. Led by the example of the centralizing but humanistically inspired King Francis I, large numbers of city leaders demanded, and funded, municipal classical grammar schools (called *collèges*) in the 1520s and 1530s. The curriculum was mediated through "the method and order of Paris." Humanist in complexion, it also included Christian, scholastic, and French elements, remaining somewhat wary of the Italian-Latin tradition. In Paris, by 1520, several university colleges had incorporated classical studies (both Latin and Greek) as the foundation of arts and theology. In addition, the Parisian masters had developed a progressive order of studies that moved from grammar to oratory and logic, ending with two years focused fundamentally on Aristotelian logic and natural philosophy. Students moved through the curriculum according to capacity. In the French grammar schools modeled on Paris, students were divided into classes by age and ability. Latin learning was graded, beginning with Cicero and Terence, moving on to Virgil, Ovid, Lorenzo Valla, Horace, and, finally, Sallust, Livy, and Juvenal. Frequent French translation into Latin was complemented with lessons in Greek grammar and some reading of Greek in Plato, Aristotle, and Xenophon. By the mid-sixteenth century nearly every town of sufficient size contained such a public school. Staffed by a principal and four to six teachers, each school normally taught several hundred students from a variety of social backgrounds. One of the most famous of these *collèges* was the Collège de Guyenne in Bordeaux, where Michel de Montaigne was educated. Mathurin Cordier (1479–1564), grammar master at Guyenne from 1534 to 1536, moved to Calvinist Geneva, where he brought the Guyenne model to the humanist curriculum of the Collège de la Rive.

The rationale for this burst of foundations and mobilization of resources (both pedagogical and material) was based on the educational and professional aspirations of town elites and the perceived value of a humanist education for buttressing the commonweal, honoring the king, and preserving the republic. As one French town put it, this education was "of greater profit to a community than are all the hospitals in the world." The movement barely touched village schools, however. Some French cathedral schools, most notably that of Carpentras under the guidance of Cardinal Jacopo Sadoleto (1477–1547), instituted a classical curriculum.

By the 1570s the *collèges* began to decline. Increasingly, there was a lack of funds and a dearth of qualified teachers. Town schools had become a battleground of religious orthodoxies, with large numbers of schoolteachers attracted to Protestantism while municipalities and the state tried to enforce Catholicism. By 1610 priests and religious orders were teaching an increasingly modified Renaissance curriculum, overlaid with religious training. In addition, after 1600 both church and crown expressed concern that society had too many educated laymen. Although the modified classical curriculum retained some force, it was gradually overshadowed by a French chauvinism that privileged the French language over Latin, French culture over Roman and Greek, and Christianity over paganism. Nor had the humanist curriculum won acceptance from the French aristocracy, which continued to prefer a military and practical training. For them humanist learning remained an ornament associated with Roman and Italian culture.

Spain and Portugal. Education in the humanities was a court phenomenon in fifteenth-century Spain and Portugal. The humanist court of Alfonso V (ruled 1416–1458) at Naples provided a conduit to Spain, as did Spanish contacts with Rome and Florence, and numbers of Spanish students attended Italian humanist schools, especially the Spanish College of San Clemente at the University of Bologna; Portuguese students were supported by the royal court to study at Paris. Humanism took root in Spain in the last quarter of the fifteenth century, with the patronage of Queen Isabella of Castile and the production of classical texts from Spanish printing presses. Beginning in the 1490s, Queen Isabella invited humanists such as Pietro Martire d'Anghiera (1447?–1526) and Lucio Marineo Siculo (d. 1533) to make the palace school into a Latin academy. The royal court hosted two schools of classical Latin, and aristocratic families began to hire humanist tutors, a practice they continued into the eighteenth century. The Portuguese court, by the beginning of the sixteenth century, had secured the tutorial services of Arias Barbosa, a Spanish scholar of Greek trained in Italy. Humanism in the Iberian peninsula, even during its heyday up to the 1530s, tended to be chauvinistic, with an emphasis on Spanish Roman writers such as Quintilian.

It is probable that humanist curricula began to be instituted in numerous independent or town Latin grammar schools of Spain and Portugal by the early sixteenth century, but there are no studies of this and no detailed analyses of texts and curricula. These Latin schools were competitive with church schools, and their rising numbers were such that, by 1600, they existed in hundreds of communities. Richard Kagan estimates that virtually every town of more than five hundred population had a humanist Latin school—a development that was not sustained in the seventeenth century. In the second half of the sixteenth century the Jesuits rapidly dominated the secondary schools of Spain and Portugal. By 1600 there were 118 Jesuit colleges in Spain's major towns and cities, educating perhaps ten to fifteen thousand boys a year.

Expansion to England and Scotland. The first humanistically oriented educational instruction in England was at Christ Church, Canterbury, where Prior William Sellyng taught Greek and Latin to the monks and to boys from Canterbury. Best known of the English humanist schools was that founded by John Colet at St. Paul's. Appointed dean in 1505, Colet (1466–1519) reformed the chapter and, in 1509, refounded the school to teach 153 students free. Colet appointed William Lily, a scholar who had traveled widely and had studied classical Latin and Greek in Italy, as schoolmaster. Lily taught Greek at St. Paul's and also produced several short guides to Latin grammar, *Brevissima institutio* (1548; the English part is entitled *A Shorte Introduction of Grammar*). Colet's instructions for his school required the use of Erasmian texts and emphasized Christian piety as much as good literature. The devotional aspect of Colet's foundation highlights his view of school as a sacred space, with attention to the prayers of schoolboys and the prominence of Christ as schoolchild. This more positive, almost sanctified, space for children partly explains the growing popularity of school foundations in England, as much as does the popularity of a humanist curriculum. It was Colet's successor as dean of St. Paul's, Richard Pace, who more clearly advocated an Italian humanist program.

A driving force behind the introduction of the *studia humanitatis* into English education was Desiderius Erasmus (c. 1466–1536), whose training in the classics as well as in the devotio moderna tradition led him to agree with Colet that education and piety are yoked. Erasmus visited England for the first time in 1499, becoming friends with Thomas More (1478–1535) and Colet. Erasmus's earliest pronouncements on humanist education were in the 1490s. In following his own adage that good authors form the mind well, he compiled a book of proverbs, *Adagia* (Adages; 1500), drawn from ancient authors. Erasmus visited England again in 1505, and returned in 1509 for his longest stay, during which time he wrote his *De ratione studii* (On the method of study; 1511), highly dependent on Quintilian but shaped to his generation, and his anthology *De copia*. *De ratione studii* argues for early acquaintance with Latin. Children should begin life speaking Latin, a task more easily accomplished in a wealthy household and less easily accomplished by students learning in a grammar school environment. Students should read extensively, for example in his *De copia*, and not simply memorize grammatical rules.

Erasmus's last essay on education, published in 1529, is *De pueris instituendis* (On the education of boys). It includes an attack on current pedagogical practices, especially in monastic schools. Erasmus recommends that parents either choose a public school or keep their child at home. Children should be molded from birth, and the proper education of children demands insightful and psychologically supportive pedagogues. Thomas More set up his household to function as a school along the lines advocated by Erasmus and reinforced by More's reading of Quintilian.

The most famous humanist school in England was the royal court, where the children of Henry VII and Henry VIII were educated along with children of noble families. Roger Ascham, schoolmaster to Elizabeth I, wrote his educational theories in the posthumously published *The Scholemaster* (1570). His theory and practice emphasized the reading of Greek and Latin texts, with double translations, supplemented with extensive readings from the Christian fathers. This second generation of humanist educators, which included Thomas Elyot (c. 1490–1546), saw education as a means toward reform of the commonwealth and community.

By the 1530s book inventories, school statutes, and the writings of grammar teachers show that in the better grammar schools in southern England, children were reading Cicero, Ovid, Horace, Quintilian, Aphthonius's *Progymnasmata* on rhetoric, and particularly Erasmus's *De copia*. The north of England was slower to embrace humanism in the grammar curriculum. The first clear indication comes from school statutes at York in 1547 and at East Retford in 1552. Most of these schools were large public institutions, in which the curriculum may have been humanist but the pedagogy remained strongly disciplinary.

In Scotland evidence for humanist education is fragmentary up to the 1560s, although the Latin grammar of Despauterius seems to have been popular. In about 1563 and again in 1576, George Buchanan proposed a humanistic curriculum for St. Andrews that he may have intended as a national model. Parts of this program may have been instituted at grammar schools in Perth, Aberdeen, Dundee, Dunbar, Stirling, Haddington, Edinburgh, and Glasgow, but the evidence is incomplete. Alexander Hume, the headmaster of Edinburgh grammar school, crafted a new school order in 1597 that followed some of Buchanan's curriculum. In Scotland there would appear to have been little consistency in the curriculum, with many grammar masters creating their own Latin texts within a humanist framework.

Expansion to Germany and the Low Countries. Early signs of humanism at the imperial court in Prague are somewhat fleeting. In 1442, however, Enea Silvio Piccolomini (later Pope Pius II) became acquainted with Ladislaus, the future king of Bohemia, at the court of the emperor Frederick III. In 1449 he composed a treatise, *De liberorum educatione* (On the education of children), for Ladislaus. Primarily derivative from earlier works, particularly Quintilian, it stressed the importance of Latin grammar, letter writing, and moral training for the young ruler, with some attention to the need to learn to speak in the vernaculars of one's subjects. Later, the Burgundian and Habsburg courts in Brussels, Bruges, and Vienna were open to a somewhat limited humanist presence.

Humanism reached Germany and the Low Countries more substantively through contacts at ecclesiastical councils, university student contacts, and via monasteries. A humanist education was available in the late fifteenth and the early sixteenth centuries at the abbeys of Sponheim and Adwerth, and probably also at Oudenburg Abbey and Korsendonk Priory. By the end of the fifteenth century, city schools in the Low Countries were a primary conduit for a humanist education. Latin studies at Bruges, Ghent, Deventer, Münster, Zwolle, Groningen, 's Hertogenbosch, Louvain, Oudenburg, the Hague, Amsterdam, Gouda, Alkmaar, and later Antwerp were descended from Italian humanism, sometimes filtered through the Parisian educational milieu or through the Collegium Trilingue in Louvain after 1517. Humanists in these city schools sometimes competed with, and sometimes collaborated with, the schools associated with the Brethren of the Common Life. In one case, when the Brethren's school at Liège was picked by the town council to be *the* Latin school, the interests of humanists blended with the textual and educational interests of the Brethren. In other cases the Brethren appear to have been marginalized by the new Latin schools, which could be quite large, with faculty broken down by forms (academic years) and academic specialty.

Juan Luis Vives, the Valencian scholar whose adopted home was Bruges, was, besides Erasmus, the most notable educational thinker in the Low Countries. His several plans of study culminated in his *De disciplinis libri xx* (Twenty books on education; 1531), in which he advocated public schools in every township, the equality of languages (accommodating the vernacular alongside Latin and Greek), the inductive nature of knowledge, associative learning, affection between schoolmasters and their boys, and the holy service of teaching children to better their God-given minds. While echoing many traditional humanist ideas, Vives was more original in his epistemology and his ideas on human psychology.

Throughout Germany and the Low Countries education took on an organized form, with specialized subjects and graded classes. In Zwickau, for example, a 1523 *Schulordnung* (school order) describes six classes. The lowest class learned Latin grammar and German, but the next already started the reading of humanist texts and beginning Greek. In classes four to one, students learned more Latin and Greek texts, including Cicero, Quintilian, Lucian, Aristophanes, and the New Testament in Greek. The second and first classes read the Old Testament (in Hebrew as well as in Latin and Greek translations), Homer, Euripides, Aristotle, Pliny, and Seneca. Neither the Lutheran Reformation nor the Catholic Counter-Reformation challenged this humanist curriculum, although each added more religious instruction. Philipp Melanchthon, in particular, promoted classical education in the service of biblical studies, most notably in his foundation speech, *In laudem novae scholae* (In praise of the new school), for the Nuremburg school in 1526, and in the small school he set up in his own home. In 1528 he offered a Latin curricular model that was implemented throughout Saxony and influential in all of Germany and in Denmark. Although level one was traditionally medieval, with added articles of faith

and biblical extracts, the children were to speak, and sing, in Latin. At level two the classical texts of Aesop's fables, Terence, Plautus, and Latin colloquies were introduced. Beyond this, students followed a Renaissance humanist curriculum in Latin and Greek, with the addition of some of Erasmus's works as well as scriptural texts, music, and, if possible, training in Hebrew. Increasingly, performance of Latin and Greek dramas entered the curriculum.

Similar humanistic curricula and purposes guided the educational plan for Hesse in 1526 (patterned on the Latin school curriculum at Marburg); the 1528 school ordinance written by Johannes Bugenhagen (and instituted at Brunswick, Hamburg, Lübeck, Bremen, Pomerania, Schleswig-Holstein, Brunswick-Wolfenbüttel, and cities in Denmark and Norway); and the Württemberg school system (ordered under Duke Christopher of Württemberg in 1559). It was at Strasbourg, in the gymnasium led by Johann Sturm (1507–1589), that students encountered the most thoroughly humanist curriculum. The Strasbourg Latin school was established in 1538, with Sturm as rector, in an effort to consolidate two earlier humanist schools. Sturm's students studied Latin grammar, rhetoric and dialectic based mainly on Cicero and Aristotle, Greek, mathematics, science, and biblical texts. Classical plays, orations, and defenses were presented on stage. Some Hebrew was introduced in the final year.

Sturm's school was divided into eight rigidly hierarchical classes with strict exams for promotion. Both the curriculum and the structure, as a model of classical pedagogy with a pietistic goal, influenced schools throughout the empire, in England (Sturm and Roger Ascham were correspondents), in the reform of Nîmes College (France), and throughout Europe. Many of the humanists who taught at Strasbourg produced grammar texts and scholarly editions for other classical schools in France, Germany, and Switzerland. Although the Strasbourg gymnasium was open, in theory, to sons of the poor, in practice it catered, at any one time, to about five hundred sons of the wealthier citizens.

The numerous printing presses in the Low Countries and Germany strengthened educational opportunities with the printing of grammars and of Greek and Latin texts. Sixteenth-century Germany saw an expansion in the number of schools, an explosion of printed schoolbooks, and increased efforts to regulate and standardize education. By the mid-sixteenth century a thoroughgoing humanist grammar education, buttressed by religious doctrine, was prescribed by the states and fully integrated into the needs of church and state in both Protestant and Catholic parts of Germany and the Low Countries.

The Jesuits. The Jesuits especially tended toward orderly regulation of the humanist curriculum. From the first, Jesuit colleges made the *studia humanitatis* a foundation of their curriculum, while their pedagogy—intensive explication of original texts and imitation of classical writers—was humanist albeit highly disciplined.

The Jesuits began to conduct schools for external students, beginning with a Jesuit-founded college at Gandía, Spain, in 1547 and another at Messina in Sicily in 1548. The instruction of others became a requirement of the order in the *Constitutions* (1559), and the Jesuits documented their successes and failures, and detailed their curricula, their textbooks, their discipline, and their methods of study. These culminated in the *Ordo studiorum* of 1551 and the *Ratio studiorum* of 1599; the latter was a methodical codification of Jesuit educational curriculum and administration.

Jesuit colleges were influenced by the method of instruction used at the University of Paris, by the humanist ideas described above (particularly Quintilian), and by their own pedagogical experiences. Jesuit education began with three graded and distinct levels of Latin grammar. Beginning Greek was originally taught at the fourth level, along with Latin humanities, although it was subsequently integrated into the lower levels of grammar in the *Ratio studiorum*. The humanities (reading in classical poetry and in Cicero) were then followed by rhetoric at the fifth level. In some schools these five levels were followed by philosophy and theology, with continued reading in Greek along with Latin and occasionally Hebrew. The schools were divided into distinct classes, graded to the capacity of each scholar, and highly dependent upon rigorous exercises—compositions, repetitions, corrections, disputations, and declamations. Students at a Jesuit college learned not only grammar, philosophy, and theology, but also mathematics, geography, history, and astronomy, all grounded in the original Latin texts. Jesuit colleges promoted public performances—theatrical representations, public debates and orations—that advertised their institutions. Along with the intellectual progress was a concern for the spiritual progress of the student; as noted by Ignatius in a letter to Ingolstadt in 1556, "Let them use every means to inculcate in their pupils, even in the youngest, the Catholic teaching, remembering that they are instructors in virtuous habits no less than in letters" (Quoted in Farrell, *The Jesuit Code of Liberal Education,* p. 139).

Jesuit education was free and attracted boys from all social classes, although the urban and scholastic orientation of the colleges tended to attract elites. Demand for Jesuit colleges put strains on the expanding order. In 1551 Ignatius of Loyola established the Collegio Romano, a high school in Rome for boys and young men, intending that it take a preeminent educational position within the order in the formation of future teachers. By the time Ignatius died (1556) Jesuits were conducting thirty-three colleges in seven European countries. By 1586 there were another 150 colleges, and, by 1600, a total of 236, ranging from Japan to Peru and Mexico. Jesuit colleges became models for Italian seminaries and the schools of other religious orders.

Education of Women. Christine de Pizan's prehumanist treatise *Cité des dames (The Book of the City of Ladies;* 1404–1405) argued that daughters, were they educated like sons, could learn as well as, and perhaps better than, men. In fact, however, educational treatises were nearly always written with the education of boys and the careers of men in mind. Nonetheless, the Renaissance saw a few treatises promoting classical education for women and arguing for their intellectual capacities, and it produced some prominent examples of classically educated women.

Positive attitudes toward the education of women in the Renaissance may have been influenced by Quintilian's examples of learned Roman women and his exhortation that both parents be as learned as possible. Humanists were also influenced by the number of powerful women in the northern Italian courts of the fifteenth century and the number of female rulers throughout sixteenth-century Europe.

The younger age at which humanists urged children to begin to learn, and their emphasis on an individualized home education, involved the nurse or mother. Enea Silvio Piccolomini, for example, refers to perfectly cultured mothers who serve as models for sons. And Jacopo Sadoleto, in his *De pueris recte instituendis* (On the right method of teaching boys; 1533), saw virtue and the discipline of learning grounded in the intellectual and moral qualities of both parents. Juan Luis Vives advocated the mother's role in perfecting the mother tongue, and a few humanists advocated speaking Latin at home.

Girls sometimes benefited from this home schooling. Erasmus argued that girls should be taught to study because it reduced idleness and led to virtue.

For Thomas More, a classical education gave his daughters greater access to a spiritual life, autonomy and equality in a companionate marriage, and the ability to learn wisdom. Most Renaissance writers who addressed the education of women saw the purpose as perfecting the women's roles in marriage, as mothers and early educators of their children, and as virtuous individuals. Some few, such as Vives, may have seen it also as preparatory to life in a convent—or at least a life of chastity. And a few writers suggest a link between classical education for women and civic life. Thomas Elyot, in his *Defense of Good Women* (1545), offers an example of a sophisticated, learned, and successful female ruler and defends the education of women as a way to improve themselves in all possible roles, including that of governing. Anne Marie van Schurmann's *On the Capacity of the Female Mind for Learning,* published in 1638, argued that the purpose of learning was an end in itself and suitable for both sexes.

Humanist pedagogy had the potential for giving women an intellectually distinctive role, but it envisioned no real revolution in their lives. Women continued to take on religious and household roles, with the added necessity of some learning.

One of the first treatises to address female education was Leonardo Bruni's letter to Battista da Montefeltro Malatesta, written about 1405. Bruni recommends a list of Latin classical and Christian authors from whose style she can perfect her Latin grammar and literary style and from whose moral principles she can learn. Although history, religion, moral philosophy, and poetry (that is, much of the new learning) are all brought to her attention, Bruni counsels her to study rhetoric only for the purpose of learning to write eloquently, for "to her [as woman] neither the intricacies of debate nor the oratorical artifices of action and delivery are of the least practical use, if indeed they are not positively unbecoming." And yet, Battista Malatesta practiced public discourses before visitors to her father's court, including an address to the emperor Sigismund in 1433. Additional treatises promoting the education of women include those of Maffeo Vegio, *De educatione liberorum* (1491), Juan Luis Vives, *De institutione feminae christianae* (1524), and Erasmus's colloquy ("The Abbot and the Learned Lady"; 1524).

The list of humanistically learned women in Renaissance Italy is long. Among Vittorino da Feltre's students must be counted the girls attached to the Gonzaga court. Cecilia Gonzaga (1425–1451) was introduced to the Greek Gospels at age seven by Vittorino and was writing Greek at age ten. Paola

Education of a Prince. Massimiliano Sforza attending to his lessons. Miniature, fifteenth century, from a manuscript in the Biblioteca Trivulziana, Milan (MS. 2167, fol. 13v). BIBLIOTECA TRIVULZIANA, MILAN/THE BRIDGEMAN ART LIBRARY

di Malatesta, mother of the Gonzaga children, was involved in the educational progress of her children, receiving written reports in Latin. Laura Cereta (1469–1499) of Brescia was educated by her father in classical Greek and Latin literature, and left behind a collection of letters. Isotta Nogarola of Verona (1418–1466) wrote Latin prose and poetry, corresponded with humanists, and participated in learned conferences and discourses. Cassandra Fedele (1465–1558), tutored by a humanist in Latin and Greek, delivered orations before members of the University of Padua, the people of Venice, the Venetian doge, and, at the age of ninety-one, before the queen of Poland, welcoming her to Venice. Battista Sforza (1446–1472), wife of the duke of Urbino, and Ippolita Maria Sforza (1445–1488) both made Latin addresses, including one to Pope Pius II; Ippolita was educated by humanist scholars and left two humanist works. Costanza Varano (1426–1447) was educated partly by her grandmother, Battista da Montefeltro; she made several public addresses and has left letters, orations, and poems. Olympia Morata (1526–1555), tutored by a German humanist at the court of Ferrara, mastered both Latin and Greek, and left behind a volume of poems, letters, and dialogues, some of which are in Greek. Dozens of other women in fifteenth- and sixteenth-century Italy might be named, although, increasingly, learned women were more likely to compose in the vernacular.

In Spain Queen Isabella, whose learning in Latin was acquired as an adult and was not very classical, supported her Latin tutor and companion, Beatriz Galindo, called La Latina. A more classically trained female humanist was Francisca de Nebrija, daughter of Antonio de Nebrija, who substituted for her father as a lecturer in humanities at Alcala in the early sixteenth century. Luisa Sigea, Latin tutor at the court of Portugal, wrote Latin poems and letters in more than one antique language. Another early sixteenth-century humanistically trained lady at the Spanish court was Ana Cervato; she memorized all of Cicero's orations, displaying an extensive knowledge of the classics. In Spain particularly, although also in Italy, a large number of these learned women, of whom there are many more in the sixteenth century, entered convents.

Learned humanist women, initially found in the urban and court culture of northern Italy or in Spanish court culture, soon appeared in northern Europe. In the early sixteenth century, for example, Margaret Blauer of Constance was a good Latinist, as were the daughters of Willibald Pirckheimer, an imperial counselor. The convents were homes of literary women and, although humanist learning arrived piecemeal in those convents, a number of nuns corresponded as humanists with other humanists. The subsequent dissolution of nunneries in those parts of Germany that converted to Protestantism was often met with successful proposals to continue these houses as schools for girls. The education offered in these schools, however, appears to have been largely catechetical, based on the study of Scripture and the German language, and not at all humanist.

In England there were voices raised in favor of educating women, and some success within selected households, but no larger institutional context. Women had not traditionally attended grammar schools in England. Thomas More's household provided a classical education to his three daughters and an adopted daughter, but his example was not widely followed. The daughters of King Henry VIII, Mary and Elizabeth, were taught by humanists. Vives's "plan of study" for Mary Tudor is a thoroughly classical curriculum, balanced with Christian Latin poets, the Latin Bible, the *Paraphrases* of Erasmus

and *Utopia* of Thomas More, with drills in both Latin and Greek. Elizabeth, tutored by Roger Ascham, was fluent in Latin, competent in Greek, and steeped in humanist culture. Her stepmother Catherine Parr studied Latin as an adult and supervised a translation of Erasmus's *Paraphrases*. Other women who seem to have benefited from the humanist tutors at the royal court include Jane and Katherine Grey and female members of the Seymour and Howard families. Since these families suffered disgrace, exile, or execution, they did not become models for later families. The Elizabethan aristocracy did not follow the royal lead, or the example set by Thomas More, in providing a household, humanist education for their daughters. In addition, the destruction of convents in England was done without planning alternative schools for girls. The education of women remained restricted to households and to the petty schools (elementary vernacular schools), with few opportunities for classical training.

The first female humanist of note in France was Margaret of Navarre (1492–1549), trained in Latin, Greek, and Hebrew, although her writings were in French and Italian. Another Margaret, the daughter of Francis I, was likewise humanistically trained and the patroness of humanists. The education that Mary Stuart received (and shared with her three future sisters-in-law and others) at the French royal court in the 1550s was not very different from that at the English court—mainly a reading of Latin drawn from classics and from Erasmus, with the purpose of instilling virtue. Her notebook of Latin exercises includes several humanistic arguments in favor of the education of women and a list of learned women, including Greek, Roman, and Italian Renaissance women. The subject of learned women formed the substance of an address she gave to the court at age fourteen. The humanist education available at court did not penetrate into the convent schools for girls in Scotland until well into the seventeenth century, however. Public schools in the cities were open to girls at the elementary level but not at the secondary (college) level. Therefore, most girls were not able to avail themselves of a humanist education, although they could learn to read and write.

There was one effort to establish a network of humanist schools for girls, patterned after the Jesuit model for boys. Mary Ward (1585–1645), an English recusant, learned in Latin and inspired by the English Jesuit college at Saint Omer, attempted to establish a European network of schools under the leadership of lay female teachers. Her Institute of the Blessed Virgin Mary was organized in 1609, and her followers were popularly called Jesuitesses. By 1631 the Institute had three hundred female lay teachers and ten houses supervising numerous schools, one of which, in Vienna, enrolled as many as five hundred pupils. The curriculum included Latin and Greek (as well as vernacular education), mathematics, and the performance of Latin plays. The order was suppressed in 1631. Ward was imprisoned, although she subsequently established another Institute; her followers have continued her work to the present.

Humanistically educated women became increasingly rare in the seventeenth century, as Bathsua Makin, a royal English governess, noted in her *Essay to Revive the Antient Education of Gentlewomen in Religion, Manners, Arts, and Tongues* (1673). She argued that women should receive a solid classical education, most especially in ancient languages. Makin herself taught these languages to women at court, but her efforts did not enlarge the public for the productions of learned female humanists.

Conclusion. Whether the humanist schools were German gymnasia, French public schools, Jesuit colleges, or others, throughout Europe the humanist curriculum created a culture of educated elites, mostly men, whose early training enabled them to communicate and grounded them in a cultural heritage that crossed regional, linguistic, and confessional lines. Regardless of whether the textbooks differed along confessional or national lines, the grammatical rules, methods of instruction, and classical texts remained very much the same. Thinking on educational matters flourished, nourished by the rediscovery of Quintilian, pseudo-Plutarch (a treatise known as *De pueris educandis*), and Cicero, and enhanced by treatises from many of the greatest writers of the Renaissance.

Humanist education was notable for its rapid expansion into the grammar schools of Europe from the early fifteenth century into the sixteenth century. This growth braked before the end of the sixteenth century as the supply of trained humanists exceeded the needs of society, and the attractions of business, other professional training, and modern languages successfully competed for attention. The humanist curriculum had remarkable staying power, however. The goals that fueled the continuing demand for a humanist education may have been, as Gerald Strauss has argued, both citizenship and subjectship—a method of teaching discipline and conditioning minds as much as an education in moral *exempla* and civic duty. Despite the call for an individualized and flexible pedagogy, the realities of such a demanding curriculum, particularly when implemented en masse, required discipline and order. The profound impact that this had on European culture has still not been adequately assessed.

See also **Classical Scholarship**; **Humanism**, *subentries on* **The British Isles**, **France**, **Germany and the Low Countries**, **Italy**, **Portugal**, *and* **Spain**; *and biographies of figures mentioned in this entry.*

BIBLIOGRAPHY

Primary Works

Ascham, Roger. *The Scholemaster by Roger Ascham.* Edited by Lawrence V. Ryan. Charlottesville, Va., 1967.

Erasmus, Desiderius. *The Collected Works of Erasmus.* Vol. 24: *De copia/De ratione studii.* Edited by Craig R. Thompson. Toronto, 1978.

King, Margaret L., and Albert Rabil, eds. *Her Immaculate Hand: Selected Works by and about the Women Humanists of Quattrocento Italy.* Binghamton, N.Y., 1983.

Vives, Juan Luis. *Vives: On Education: A Translation of the* De tradendis disciplinis *of Juan Luis Vives.* Edited by Foster Watson. Totowa, N.J., 1971.

Woodward, William Harrison. *Vittorino da Feltre and Other Humanist Educators.* Cambridge, U.K., 1897. Reprint, New York, 1963; Toronto, 1996.

Secondary Works

Charlton, Kenneth. *Education in Renaissance England.* London, 1965.

Chrisman, Miriam Usher. *Lay Culture, Learned Culture: Books and Social Change in Strasbourg, 1480–1599.* New Haven, Conn., 1982.

Farrell, Allan P. *The Jesuit Code of Liberal Education: Development and Scope of the Ratio Studiorum.* Milwaukee, 1938.

Garin, Eugenio. *Educazione umanistica in Italia.* Bari, Italy, 1966.

Garin, Eugenio, ed. *Il pensiero pedagogico dell'umanesimo.* Florence, 1958.

Giard, Luce, ed. *Les Jesuites à la Renaissance: Système educatif et production du savoir.* Paris, 1995.

Grendler, Paul F. *Books and Schools in the Italian Renaissance.* Aldershot, U.K. and Brookfield, Vt., 1995.

Grendler, Paul F. *Schooling in Renaissance Italy: Literacy and Learning, 1300–1600.* Baltimore, 1989.

Hartfelder, Karl. *Philipp Melanchthon als Praeceptor Germaniae.* Nieuwkoop, Netherlands, 1964.

Huppert, George. *Public Schools in Renaissance France.* Urbana, Ill., 1984.

Huppert, George. "Ruined Schools: The End of the Renaissance System of Education in France." In *Humanism in Crisis: The Decline of the French Renaissance.* Edited by Philippe Desan. Ann Arbor, Mich., 1991. Pages 55–67.

Kagan, Richard L. *Students and Society in Early Modern Spain.* Baltimore, 1974.

King, Margaret L. *Women of the Renaissance.* Chicago, 1991.

McQueen, John, ed. *Humanism in Renaissance Scotland.* Edinburgh, 1990.

Moog, Willy. *Geschichte der Padagogik.* Vol. 2: *Die Padagogik der Neuzeit von der Renaissance bis zum Ende des 17. Jahrhunderts.* 8th ed. Ratingen, Germany, 1967.

Moran, Jo Ann Hoeppner. *The Growth of English Schooling, 1340–1548.* Princeton, N.J., 1985.

Rabil, Albert, ed. *Renaissance Humanism: Foundations, Forms, and Legacy.* 3 vols. Philadelphia, 1988. See especially vol. 3, which has essays on humanism and education, humanism by country, and humanism by discipline.

Robey, David. "Humanism and Education in the Early Quattrocento: The *De ingenuis moribus* of P. P. Vergerio." *Bibliothèque d'humanisme et Renaissance* 42 (1980): 27–58.

Ross, James B. "Venetian Schools and Teachers, Fourteenth to Early Sixteenth Century: A Survey and a Study of Giovanni Battista Egnazio." *Renaissance Quarterly* 29 (1976): 521–566.

Schindling, Anton. *Humanistische Hochschule und freie Reichsstadt.* Wiesbaden, Germany, 1977.

Simon, Joan. *Education and Society in Tudor England.* Reprint, Cambridge, U.K., 1979.

Spitz, Lewis W., and Barbara Sher Tinsley. *Johann Sturm on Education: The Reformation and Humanist Learning.* St. Louis, 1994.

Strauss, Gerald. *Enacting the Reformation in Germany.* Aldershot, U.K. and Brookfield, Vt., 1993.

Warnicke, Retha M. *Women of the English Renaissance and Reformation.* Westport, Conn., 1983.

Woodward, William Harrison. *Studies in Education During the Age of the Renaissance, 1400–1600.* Cambridge, U.K., 1906. Reprint, New York, 1967.

JO ANN HOEPPNER MORAN CRUZ

EDWARD VI (1537–1553), king of England and Ireland (1547–1553). Edward VI was born at Hampton Court Palace to Henry VIII and Jane Seymour, Henry's third wife. He succeeded his father as king of England and Ireland and died prematurely at Greenwich of pulmonary tuberculosis. His reign, though brief, was auspicious, as it marked the official beginning of England's Protestant Reformation.

Education. The imprint of the northern Renaissance on Edward VI is to be seen most clearly in his remarkable schooling, the evidence for which, his notebooks for the period 1548–1552, constitutes the fullest extant record of a humanist education in Tudor England. Edward's chief tutor was Sir John Cheke, and his curriculum was the one Cheke had originally designed for undergraduates at Saint John's College, Cambridge. Edward began a rigorous, accelerated course of study in the classics and the Roman and Greek historians. For the Greek historians Edward possessed a chorographical index to Justin's Latin translation, given him by Peter Olivares, the Spanish humanist. Rhetorically, Edward's Latin essays, like the Greek orations he composed and delivered aloud, tested his ability to provide historical examples of moralistic precepts. The method was inspired by Aristotle's *Ethics;* Edward drew his examples from readings in contemporary European history. From William Buckley, a fellow of King's College, Cambridge, he acquired mathematics, as-

Edward VI. Anonymous portrait, 1542. BY COURTESY OF THE NATIONAL PORTRAIT GALLERY, LONDON

tronomy, cosmography, and the applied science of oceanic navigation: he owned and could use a quadrant, astrolabe, and dial ring. Geography buttressed this learning; he could name every creek, bay, and river in England. Christopher Tye, the composer, taught him music; Philip van Wilder, the lute; Jean Belmain, French; and Roger Ascham, the celebrated author of *The Scholemaster,* his neat italic penmanship. At fourteen, his schooling completed, Edward's learning surpassed that of most university graduates.

Edward's mentors were fervent Protestants, and the king's curriculum was devised to instill in him the tenets of "true religion." The arguments in his *Treatise against the Supremacy of the Pope,* penned at twelve, employed Aristotle's syllogisms, just as his essays in French on religious doctrine breathed, via Belmain, the spirit of Calvin. At his coronation Edward was hailed as England's Josiah, destined to purge the realm of popish "superstition." Evangelical preachers at court reinforced this message in weekly sermons, the most notable passages of which he studiously recorded. Aristotle's *Politics* he read in preparation for kingly duty, but neither his "Chronicle" of occurrences at court nor his so-called political papers and tracts are evidence that at fourteen he was really beginning to rule. The manuscripts, like his staged speeches in council, were based on notes supplied by royal secretaries: they show that he was following, not directing, the business of state. There are hints, however, of extracurricular exposure to the problems of princely power: consider the ninety-one written advices secretly given him by William Thomas, clerk of the privy council. Thomas, sojourner in Italy (1545–1549) and author of a *History of Italy* (1549) and the first Italian-English dictionary (1550), quoted Machiavelli to the effect that a prince must strive always to maintain a free hand. What the king thought of this counsel remains unknown.

Government. Edward VI played no part in making royal policy. The authority to govern during his minority lay technically with the sixteen executors of Henry VIII's will, the members of Edward's privy council. In fact, his elder uncle, Edward Seymour, duke of Somerset, assumed power in March 1547 as lord protector of the realm and governor of the king's person. A zealous Protestant, he abolished the Mass and all things deemed "idolatrous"—candles, shrines, processions, and images, as well as numerous aspects of a centuries-old popular religious culture (holy days, mystery plays, maypoles). Receipts from the sales of chantries helped fund his invasion of Scotland (September 1547), but garrisoning Scotland brought war with France, the costs of which nearly bankrupted England. When rebellious peasants challenged his authority in 1549, a cabal of councillors led by John Dudley, earl of Warwick, abolished the protectorate in a bloodless coup. Dudley (duke of Northumberland after October 1551) ruled from February 1550 as president of a council purged of rivals. He readmitted Somerset to the council, but when the former protector contemplated a countercoup, Dudley arrested him and rigged his trial (1551) and execution (1552).

A political pragmatist, Dudley governed effectively through a council packed with adherents. Abandoning Somerset's military stance, he made peace with France and reordered royal finance. Only in Ireland did he maintain an earlier policy of colonization and control, made all the more necessary, he reckoned, by the advancing Reformation. His political ambition dictated that he respect Edward VI's religious sincerity, giving Thomas Cranmer, archbishop of Canterbury, leeway to reform yet further the doctrines and liturgy of the Church of England. Cranmer's genius found expression in a Book of Common Prayer (rev. ed., 1552), linguistically one of the great pillars of English Renaissance culture. Hoping to preserve the godly Reformation, Edward VI sought to bar his Catholic sister, Mary, from succeeding him; at Northumberland's bidding, he tried to will his crown to the duke's daughter-in-law, Jane Grey, only days before dying. For giving Edward this treasonous advice, Northumberland was beheaded by Queen Mary I.

Art. Edward's reign witnessed important developments in the spread of Renaissance artistic styles. Italian and Netherlandish artists in England borrowed the new styles from France, thanks to the patronage of Protector Somerset and his steward, John Thynne. Thynne oversaw construction of Somerset House, the protector's London residence in the Strand (1550). The splendid, French-influenced classical facade of the house, preserved now only in John Thorpe's drawing, trumpeted the appearance of Renaissance architecture in England. In 1550 Northumberland sent John Shute to Italy to study classical architecture at first hand; Shute's descriptions, with engravings, were the first to be published in England (1563). At Edward VI's court, Guillim Scrots, a Fleming, served as king's painter, succeeding Hans Holbein the Younger (d. 1543) in that post. Edward VI employed an Italian sculptor and painter, Nicholas Bellin of Modena, to work on Henry VIII's elaborate Renaissance tomb, then under construction at Westminster. Bellin fabricated and painted Edward VI's funeral effigy, a remarkable (now-lost) piece of wax and wood in the tradition of Pietro Torrigiano's royal effigies.

See also **England**; **Tudor Dynasty**.

BIBLIOGRAPHY

Primary Work

Nichols, John Gough, ed. *Literary Remains of King Edward the Sixth.* 2 vols. London, 1857. Reprint, New York, 1964. Indispensable source of the king's papers and related contemporary documents. Nichols's lengthy introduction constitutes a scholarly, if dated, biography.

Secondary Works

Hoak, Dale. *The King's Council in the Reign of Edward VI.* Cambridge, U.K., 1976. Detailed analysis of the institutional setting of court politics, providing evidence of the genesis of Edward VI's state papers and Northumberland's control of the king's privy chamber and all information reaching the king.

Jordan, W. K. *Edward VI.* 2 vols. London, 1968–1970. Valuable for its citation of sources unavailable to Nichols, but Jordan's interpretations cannot always be trusted, as the author often misread or erroneously transcribed the manuscripts cited.

Needham, Paul Swope. "Sir John Cheke at Cambridge and Court." Ph.D. diss., Harvard University, 1971. Brilliant reconstruction (in chapter 4) of Edward VI's humanist education, based on the king's written schoolwork (now in the British Library and the Bodleian Library, Oxford).

DALE HOAK

EGUÍA PRESS. The press of Miguel de Eguía published classical and humanist works and editions of Erasmus and other theologians in Spain between 1523 and 1546. The total output was about 200 editions.

Miguel de Eguía was born in Estella (Navarre) about 1495, one of twenty-eight children of the wealthy and very devout merchant Nicolás de Eguía and Catalina Pérez de Jaso. Miguel was apprenticed in the press of Arnaldo Guillén de Brocar in Logroño and moved with him to Alcalá de Henares when Cardinal Cisneros invited Brocar to set up a press for his new university emphasizing biblical studies for a reformed clergy. Brocar's most important publication in Alcalá de Henares was the Complutensian Polyglot Bible, which was produced between 1514 and 1517 and on which Eguía undoubtedly worked. About 1518 Eguía married Brocar's daughter Maria, and he assumed the management of the press, acting in the role of printer for the university, when Brocar died in 1523. While printing in Alcalá, Eguía also operated presses in Valladolid and Toledo from 1524 to 1527 and produced a number of works in Logroño from 1527 to 1533.

About 130 works bear Eguía's name. His first signed publication in Alcalá de Henares was *Erudita in Dauiticos Psalmos expositio* (Learned exposition of the Psalms of David; 1523), and his further production reflected both the university's interest in liturgical and biblical studies and his personal commitment to the objectives of the new piety known as Illuminism, which was condemned as heretical in 1525. Among the important authors he published in this area were Desiderius Erasmus, Juan de Valdés, and Francisco de Vergara. Eguía was instrumental in popularizing the works of Erasmus in Spain. He published at least fifteen editions of Erasmus, including several religious works and his commentaries on the Gospels. To make the works of Erasmus accessible to those who could not read Latin, Eguía produced a number of translations in Castilian, beginning with the *Enchiridion, o Manual del Caballero Cristiano* (Enchiridion, or handbook of the Christian knight; 1526, no known copy; 2d ed., 1527), which enjoyed great success.

In Alcalá, Eguía also published two editions of Savonarola and three of St. Bonaventura; romances of chivalry; editions of classical authors such as Cur-

tius Rufus and Valerius Flaccus, Aristotle, Persius Flaccus, Seneca, Caius Julius Caesar, Valerius Maximus, Aesop, Plutarch, and Appian; a number of school texts by Elio Antonio de Nebrija, Lorenzo Valla, and Francisco de Vergara; several liturgical works; and a few historical works and royal laws.

Eguía's identification with adherents to the Illuminist heresy and his advocacy of Erasmus's works proved his undoing. Tried by the Inquisition as a crypto-Lutheran, he spent two years in prison (1531–1533), but was eventually acquitted of all charges of heresy. It is unlikely that he espoused anti-Catholic sentiments. After his release from prison Eguía returned to Estella, although the editions of the press in Alcalá continued to bear his name until the late 1530s, when Brocar's son Juan assumed control. Eguía printed several works there in 1546, perhaps in partnership with Adrian de Anvérez. Eguía's testament was drawn up on 23 October 1546 and gives evidence both of his firm attachment to the Catholic church and of his considerable wealth. The exact date of his death is unknown; there is evidence that he published an edition of "Horas romanas," now lost, in Estella in 1548.

See also **Alcalá de Henares, University of; Cisneros, Francisco Jiménez de; Erasmus, Desiderius.**

BIBLIOGRAPHY

Bataillon, Marcel. *Erasmo y España: Estudios sobre la historia espiritual del siglo dieziséis.* 2d ed. Mexico City, Mexico, 1966.

Goñi Gaztambide, J. "El impresor Miguel de Eguía, procesado por la Inquisición (c. 1495–1546)." *Hispania sacra* 1 (1948): 35–54.

González Navarro, Ramón. "El impresor navarro Miguel de Eguía, en Alcalá de Henares." *Principe de Viana* 42 (1981): 307–319.

WILLIAM A. PETTAS

EGYPT. *See* **Africa, North.**

EL GRECO (Doménikos Theotokópoulos; c. 1541–1614), late Renaissance painter from Crete. Doménikos, the son of a tax collector, was born in Candia (now Herakleion), the capital of Crete, then a Venetian possession. He was trained in the Byzantine style of painting and is first recorded as an independent master in 1563.

Italy. El Greco—as Doménikos came to be known—established himself in Venice in 1567. There, he slowly transformed his native idiom through his exposure to the light, color, vigorous brushwork, and principles of composition of Titian

El Greco. *Portrait of a Cardinal.* The identity of the sitter is uncertain. He may be Fernando Niño de Guevara (d. 1609), grand inquisitor at Toledo from 1599 to 1601. Or he may be one of two archbishops of Toledo, Gáspar de Quiroga (d. 1594) or Bernardo de Sandoval y Rojas (d. 1618). Oil on canvas; 170.8 × 108 cm (67.25 × 42.5 in.). THE METROPOLITAN MUSEUM OF ART, H. O. HAVEMEYER COLLECTION, BEQUEST OF MRS. H. O. HAVEMEYER, 1929

and Tintoretto. His (later) annotations to his copy of Vasari's *Lives of the Artists* (1568 ed.) disclose his love for both Venetian masters and his ambivalence toward Michelangelo, whom he considered the uncontested master of the human figure but wanting as a colorist and therefore as a painter. *The Purification of the Temple* (Washington D.C., National Gallery of Art) was probably painted during this Venetian sojourn, as it includes clumsily juxtaposed motifs borrowed from Michelangelo, Raphael, Titian, Veronese, and possibly Sebastiano Serlio, such as one would expect of an artist attempting to modify his style and imagery.

El Greco arrived in Rome by November 1570, where the miniaturist Giulio Clovio helped him obtain lodgings in the palace of Cardinal Alessandro Farnese. In Rome he had the opportunity to further his study of Renaissance painting and to frequent the humanist circle around the cardinal's librarian Fulvio Orsini, a great scholar of classical antiquity who acquired several of El Greco's works.

Spain. Due to a shortage of patronage, however, El Greco was compelled to move by July 1577 to Toledo in Castile, where he was awarded the commission for the *Disrobing of Christ* for the cathedral's sacristy (in situ). This picture, which couples sections of vivid naturalism with areas of unprecedented abstraction, merges different episodes from John's and Luke's account of Christ's Passion. Although the artist was criticized both for including the three Marys in his composition and for raising the heads of secondary actors above the head of Christ, he refused to make changes to his picture and filed a lawsuit to obtain rightful compensation for his work, eventually settling for much less than he had anticipated. In Spain, El Greco, who had embraced Italian Renaissance notions of artistic license and technical prowess, was working for an audience that deemed such ideas unacceptable.

The painter's annotations to his copies of Vasari's *Lives* and Vitruvius's *On Architecture* (1556 Italian ed.) offer testimony to his absorption of late sixteenth-century Italian mannerist theory. El Greco reportedly wrote treatises on painting and on architecture, now lost, which would have corroborated his interest in providing intellectual foundations for artistic practice, and thereby elevating the status of the artist.

El Greco was among the artists selected to provide altarpieces for the royal basilica of the Escorial, northwest of Madrid. His *Martyrdom of St. Maurice and the Theban Legion* (in situ), completed by the autumn of 1582, displeased King Philip II, who kept the painting, paid the artist less than he had requested, and ordered a new picture of the same subject from Romulo Cincinnato. A comparison of both works suggests that Philip was disturbed both by the inclusion of contemporary portraits in this episode from early Christianity, and by the displacement of the martyrdom scene to the distant middleground, on the left. Thus, as a result of his innovative methods of narration and composition, El Greco succeeded in alienating two of the most powerful patrons in Spain in less than five years.

El Greco returned to Toledo, where by 1585 he established a workshop capable of producing copies after his paintings, as well as frames and statues. In 1586 he obtained the important commission for *The Burial of the Count of Orgaz* for a chapel in Santo Tomé, Toledo (in situ; see the color plates in volume 1). This monumental picture depicts the moment when the heavens opened, and SS. Augustine and Stephen suddenly appeared in order to lower Gonzalo de Ruiz's corpse into his tomb. This fourteenth-century scene is witnessed by late sixteenth-century Toledan aristocrats and prelates, as Gonzalo's soul is lifted by an angel toward God in the "open Heaven of glory" hovering just above them. Gonzalo was reputed for his gifts to the church. This painting declares that good works are needed to obtain salvation and reveals the intercessory powers of saints. Both of these doctrines were vigorously disputed by Protestants.

Other Genres. El Greco was a powerful portrait painter, with remarkable gifts of psychological insight—witness *Gentleman with His Hand on His Breast* (1577–1579; Madrid, Prado) and the seated full-length *Cardinal Fernando Niño de Guevara* (c. 1600; New York, Metropolitan Museum). His mysterious, pantheistic *View of Toledo* (c. 1610; New York, Metropolitan Museum; see the color plates in volume 6)—vibrating with the energies of divine creation—opens a new chapter in the history of landscape painting, a genre he rarely explored.

El Greco, a learned, well-read, and extraordinarily inventive artist, re-created—in the Renaissance tradition of "ekphrasis"—a lost antique picture by Antiphilus of Alexandria, based on Pliny the Elder's description in his *Natural History: Boy Lighting a Candle* (c. 1570–1575; Naples, Capodimonte). Significantly, this work was painted at the time the artist frequented Orsini's circle in Rome.

The late, unfinished *Laocoön* (c. 1610–1614; Washington, D.C. National Gallery of Art) is El

Greco's only surviving mythological painting. Here, the artist departs radically from the canonical figural arrangement in the carved Hellenistic prototype (in the Vatican Museum) discovered a century earlier in Rome, and includes one male and one female nude—unwarranted by visual or textual sources—witnessing the death of Laocoön and his sons. Richard Mann's identification of the female nude as Venus (love causes the fall of Troy and Laocoön's demise), the male nude as Apollo (who exacts revenge upon Laocoön and his sons, according to two early accounts of the story), and the underlying meaning of this picture as a warning against the violation of the vow of chastity among the clergy (embodied by the Trojan priest Laocoön, who was unchaste), is compelling.

Style. El Greco developed one of the truly distinctive styles in painting, through his synthesis of Byzantine and sixteenth-century methods of paint handling, coloring, design, and composition. The abstracted corporeality of his figures—obtained through fluid brushwork and attenuated proportions—and the dynamic tensions of his pictorial spaces—attained by means of powerful diagonals, virtuoso foreshortenings, and brusque contrasts of tone and color—exalt their author's powers to transcend nature in order to express the divine.

El Greco's rhetorical style seems perfectly suited to convey the ideals of the Counter-Reformation. However, it was rapidly supplanted after his death due to a lack of talented followers and the introduction of the baroque style in Spain.

[El Greco's *St. Martin and the Beggar* appears in the color plates in this volume.]

BIBLIOGRAPHY

Brown, Jonathan. *The Golden Age of Painting in Spain.* New Haven, Conn., and London, 1991. Pages 69–88.

Brown, Jonathan, ed. *El Greco of Toledo.* Boston, 1982. Exhibition catalog, Toledo Museum of Art.

Brown, Jonathan, and Richard G. Mann. *The Collections of the National Gallery of Art, Systematic Catalogue: Spanish Paintings of the Fifteenth through Nineteenth Centuries.* Washington, D.C., 1990. See "El Greco," pp. 42–83. Includes thorough discussions of the *Purification of the Temple* and the *Laocoön.*

Hadjinicolaou, Nicos, ed. *El Greco of Crete: Proceedings of the International Symposium Held on the Occasion of the 450th Anniversary of the Artist's Birth, Iraklion, Crete, 1–5 September 1990.* Herakleion, Greece, 1995.

Marías, Fernando. "Greco, El." In *The Dictionary of Art.* Edited by Jane Turner. New York, 1996. Vol. 13, pp. 339–346.

MICHAËL J. AMY

ELIZABETH I (1533–1603), queen of England (1558–1603). The real Elizabeth is hard to discern through the poetic haze that surrounds her reputation. Scarcely a patron of Renaissance artists, she was the focus of much of their activity in England during her long reign. Educated as a humanist and a Protestant, Elizabeth was too careful with her money to spend it on art, architecture, or poets, but her court and her tastes inspired many of the creative efforts that mark her culturally brilliant reign.

Early Years. Daughter of Henry VIII and Anne Boleyn, Elizabeth's tastes were formed by her rigorous education. After her mother's execution in 1536, she was raised for the continental marriage market. Henry VIII's last wife, Katherine Parr, saw to it that Elizabeth had excellent tutors like Roger Ascham, and she became fluent in Greek, Latin, Italian, and French. In 1545 she translated Margaret of Navarre's *Mirror of the Sinful Soul* from the French and Erasmus's *Dialogue of Faith* from the Latin. Her skill as a linguist was such that she regularly surprised ambassadors with her linguistic accomplishments, and her knowledge of the classics was such that she could appreciate and use the elaborate mythological and historical references popular at the time.

Elizabeth's conception provoked Henry VII's split with Rome. Thus it is not surprising that her classical education was balanced with good Protestant training. She read the New Testament in Greek, the Greek and Latin fathers, and Protestant commentators like Philipp Melanchthon. In her youth she had a reputation for austere Protestant piety (and haughtiness).

By the time Elizabeth was twenty-one she had seen England move from the English Catholicism of Henry VIII through the stages of the Edwardian Reformation marked by the English Prayer Books of 1549 and 1552. Under her sister Mary, Elizabeth conformed to Roman Catholicism (as distinct from Henry VIII's nationalist Catholicism), but she was the center of Protestant hopes. Mary never trusted her sincerity, scrupling at Elizabeth's "heretical opinions, illegitimacy, and characteristics in which she resembled her mother." After Thomas Wyatt's rebellion, Mary was pressured by the Holy Roman Emperor's ambassador to execute Elizabeth, but fears that the next nearest heir, Mary, queen of Scots, would inherit the English throne and make England a province of Scotland prompted Mary's advisers to argue against Elizabeth's execution, saving her.

Early Reign. Elizabeth acceded to the throne on 17 November 1558, bringing to office a team of men who would make up the core of the government for much of her reign. William Cecil, created Lord Burghley in 1571, was the principal secretary of the Privy Council and the leader of the government until his death in 1598. Robert Dudley, created the earl of Leicester in 1564, became the queen's favorite in 1559. Elizabeth's infatuation with Dudley, a married man whose wife soon died under suspicious circumstances, gave him great influence. He remained one of Elizabeth's closest councillors until his death in late 1588.

The first task of Elizabeth's government in 1559 was the restoration of the Protestant religion. What form of Protestantism she wished to impose was less clear, though she clearly intended to restore the royal supremacy over the church. Her own faith is enigmatic. It is perhaps best described as a conservative, antipapal compound of Augustinianism, Lutheranism, and Catholicism, tempered with classical stoicism.

The Elizabethan settlement of religion enacted by Parliament in 1559 made her Supreme Governor of the Church and imposed on the nation the worship prescribed by the 1552 Book of Common Prayer, as glossed by a set of articles and injunctions that were issued to the ecclesiastical visitors who imposed it in June 1559. In some ways these new rules were more conservative than those of Edward VI, placing the communion table in the east end of the church "altar wise" and, through the "ornaments rubric," seeming to require Protestant ministers to dress like Catholic priests. It is not certain how much Elizabeth dictated the content of the articles and injunctions issued in her name.

In the first few years of her reign many expected Elizabeth to use her power to make further changes in religion. Catholic diplomats convinced themselves that she might marry a Catholic and convert. Protestants hoped for further reformation of her church, since it was a "leaden mediocrity," stranded on a theological sandbar somewhere between Rome and Geneva. Only after the Revolt of the Northern Earls in 1569, when English Catholics demonstrated their enmity to Elizabeth and Pope Pius V issued the bull *Regnans in excelsis* excommunicating her, did her regime become aggressively Protestant.

At about the same time, the Puritan movement began to take shape in response to Elizabeth's refusal to allow any further reformation of the church. She believed that she ruled under God and the law and that she had the duty to lead the church. She was unwilling even to allow Parliament to discuss further religious reform. Her bishops, though they desired more religious change, were forced to de-

Elizabeth victorious over the Armada. The Armada Portrait celebrates the defeat of the Spanish Armada, 1588. The queen's hand rests on the globe, suggesting her ambitions for England. Artist unknown. PRIVATE COLLECTION/THE BRIDGEMAN ART LIBRARY

fend the status quo against those who wanted a more reformed faith. Puritanism and presbyterianism were both results of the realization, dawning by 1571, that Elizabeth would keep the church as it was. The tension this created would increase throughout her reign. At the same time, Elizabeth was careful not to persecute Catholics only for their religion's sake. Francis Bacon, who knew her, said Elizabeth, not liking "to make windows into men's hearts and secret thoughts . . . tempered her law so as it restraineth only manifest disobedience . . . in impugning her Majesty's supreme power." However, she became increasingly intolerant of both Catholic and Puritan dissent as she grew older.

Mary, Queen of Scots, and the Armada. In 1568 Mary, queen of Scotland, fled into England, escaping the religious and political revolt stirred up there with English help. Elizabeth's second cousin, granddaughter of Henry VII's sister Margaret and James IV of Scotland, she was the clear heir to Elizabeth's throne—and a Catholic. Her presence was a political danger, underlining what Parliament had been telling Elizabeth since 1559: she had to marry. The question of Elizabeth's marriage became the spring that drove much of Elizabethan foreign policy for the first twenty years of her reign. After 1578 her single state seemed unalterable, turning her into the "Virgin Queen" celebrated by the poets of her court.

The Scottish queen would remain in England, a constant source of political trouble, until Elizabeth was finally convinced, by the discovery of the treasonous Babington Plot, to execute her in 1587. The man who proved Mary's treason was Francis Walsingham, a secretary to the Privy Council since 1573. Walsingham was, in effect, foreign secretary, managing a network of spies; he was a leading advocate of English intervention in the war between Philip II of Spain and the Dutch Protestants.

Working closely with Walsingham through the 1570s and 1580s was Sir Christopher Hatton. He had first come to the queen's attention in the 1560s, rising to be her favorite in the middle period of the reign. By 1587 she had made him lord chancellor, and, when he lay near death in 1591, she visited his home and fed him with her own hands.

Elizabeth kept her nation out of continental wars for the first two decades of her reign. However, Spain's attempts to suppress the Dutch revolt that began in the 1560s had to be met for strategic reasons. She preferred sending money, but eventually she sent men, leading England into war with Spain in 1585. One result was the Spanish Armada of 1588. The defeat of the Armada by weather and English gunnery was a glorious, defining moment in the English national consciousness. Elizabeth's appearance before her troops at Tilbury, wearing armor and declaring that, though she was a weak woman, she had the "heart and stomach of a king" who would stand with them in the fight, won her national affection. After that her accession day, 17 November, was a national holiday. But despite the defeat of the armada, the war continued through the next decade.

The 1590s were marked by war with Spain and revolt in Ireland. Irish revolts occurred frequently in Elizabeth's reign, but the last, thanks to Spanish help, went on for nine years, ending in the Irish peace of 1603—a settlement imposed at terrible cost in blood and money. It was reported that Elizabeth became "sick and ill" at the mere mention of rebellion in Ireland.

One of the most important players in the Irish wars was the earl of Essex, Elizabeth's last favorite. For ten years she showed the young man great favor while he sought military glory and failed to gain it. In September 1599 he rushed back from defeat in Ireland, burst into the queen's chamber, and saw her without her wig and makeup. After that she no longer protected him, and in 1601 he tried to seize the court and take control of the queen. He was executed.

By the time Elizabeth died on 24 March 1603, she was unpopular with her heavily taxed subjects and with her courtiers, who failed to receive advancement and fortune from their notoriously frugal queen. Though she resolutely refused to name her successor, her kingdom was inherited by Mary of Scotland's son, James VI of Scotland, known as James I in the English succession.

Classical Court Culture. Elizabeth imperiously presided over a brilliant Renaissance court. Styled officially "most worthy Empress from the Orkney Isles to the Mountains Pyrenee," she lived amid imperial pomp. The forms that pomp took tell us a great deal about how Elizabeth's presence shaped the English Renaissance.

Until the mid-1570s the dominant cultural models in the court were classical. Stoicism was the dominant philosophy among those of Elizabeth's generation: detachment and frugality, combined with a deep respect for the chances of fortune, served people well who had survived the 1540s and 1550s. Elizabeth herself, in a letter of comfort written in 1595, enunciated her stoical philosophy: "Observe this rule, that seeing griefs and troubles make haste enough, unsent for, to surprise us, there can be no folly greater than by fearing that which is not, or by over grieving for that which needs not, to overthrow the health of mind and body."

Given Elizabeth's stoical outlook, it is not surprising that the first tragedy written in English, *Gorboduc,* was modeled on Seneca and aimed at convincing the queen to marry Robert Dudley. Plays were popular entertainment at court, and when Elizabeth visited Oxford and Cambridge, the students offered her a banquet of theatrical productions on classical themes. Masques also depended on a knowledge of classical stories.

Painters employed by the court in this period were mostly foreigners. Hans Eworth, from Antwerp, had assumed Holbein's mantle as a portraitist in the later 1540s, continuing into the early 1570s. He made designs for masques, as well as for the play *Elizabeth I and the Three Goddesses* (1569), in which the queen is favorably compared to Pallas Athena, Juno, and Venus.

It might be safe to say that in this period Elizabeth's court was mastering the new idiom of female monarchy and learning to behave on continental models. The popularity of Thomas Hoby's translation of Baldassare Castiglione's *Il cortegiano (The Book of the Courtier),* first published in 1561, underscores this search for suavity.

Elizabeth I. The Blackfriars Portrait, a 1600 painting by Robert Peake, suggests the opulence of Elizabeth's court. COURTESY OF SHERBORNE CASTLE ESTATES

Elizabeth's early years were not a time of important cultural productivity. The foundations of her state were being laid, her church defined, and her treasury restocked. The mid-1570s saw a marked change in English culture, much of it stimulated by her court. Elizabeth was first celebrated as the Virgin Queen in 1578. No longer of childbearing age, Elizabeth assumed a new, quasi-mythical identity, celebrated for her barren virginity and garlanded with sobriquets like Gloriana, Diana, or Virginia.

The 1570s saw a burst of artistic activity. Foreign artists such as Federico Zuccaro were imported to portray Elizabeth and members of her court, and Protestant refugee artists made London their home. Painters like Lucas De Heere, Marcus Gheeraerts the Elder, and Isaac Oliver arrived as refugees. Oliver came as a child and apprenticed with the artist most closely associated with Elizabeth's court, the miniaturist Nicholas Hillyard.

Gothic Themes. Of course the classical idiom never left Elizabeth's court, but the later years of the reign saw her court increasingly attracted to Gothic themes. Chivalry was the watchword of Gloriana's court, and cultural production used its motifs. Edmund Spenser's *Faerie Queene* (1590–1596), an extended chivalric allegory, is one result of this mode

of expression. Chivalric romance was literally acted out at court tournaments, when champions would break lances in honor of the queen and their ladies.

The Faerie Queene may be linked to another of Elizabeth's pastimes, going on progress. She spent most of her summers traveling about southern England, visiting the homes of her courtiers, who both sought and feared her visits. Entertaining Elizabeth and her court could be devastatingly expensive, and huge homes were built in preparation for her arrival. Thus, although Elizabeth herself built no palaces, she inspired the building of many of the great Elizabethan houses, many designed by Robert Smythson as stages for royal pageants. When she visited Elvetham, the house of the earl of Hertford, in 1591, Elizabeth was entertained by an elaborate pageant enacted on an island crowned by a mock castle.

Sir Philip Sidney's *Arcadia* (1581, 1583–1584) is another example of Elizabethan court literature, with its complicated classical names and romantic themes, mixed with chivalric images. Tilting was added to the second version of the *Arcadia* to bring it up to fashion when it was first published in 1590. In the new version Elizabeth, as Helen, queen of Corinth, is fought for by the knights of Corinth and Iberia. Many characters in the composition can be clearly linked to Elizabethan politics, showing that courtiers often used classical language to disguise the political morals of their writing from all but their inner circles.

Elizabeth managed her court by keeping her courtiers in a perpetual attitude of chivalric adoration. In the accession tilt of 1581, four courtiers, "Four Foster Children of Desire," besieged the queen in the "Castle of Perfect Beauty," but she remained inviolate, a metaphor for the way she was treated by her court.

Elizabeth's reign was a great age for English music, and she directly patronized its greatest composers, Thomas Tallis and William Byrd. Though both men were Catholics, Elizabeth protected them. They wrote for the Chapel Royal, creating English settings for the English Prayer Book and Latin settings for Elizabeth's private services.

Elizabeth was imperious, stubborn, parsimonious, and very much a brilliant politician in her earlier years. As she grew older her political touch became less pleasing to her subjects as her other characteristics asserted themselves. Nonetheless, she inspired the Elizabethan Renaissance, providing its focus if not paying its bills. Her court consumed artistic production as it celebrated the product of its own imagination, Diana, Gloriana, Elizabeth Regina.

See also **Armada, Spanish; Chivalry,** *subentry on* **Arthurian Romance; Drama, English,** *subentry on* **Elizabethan Drama; Espionage; Music in England; Patronage,** *subentry on* **Literary Patronage in England; Poetry, English,** *subentry on* **Elizabethan Poetry; Puritanism;** *and biographies of figures mentioned in the entry.*

BIBLIOGRAPHY

Doran, Susan. *Monarchy and Matrimony: The Courtships of Elizabeth I*. London, 1996. A fine scholarly study of her matrimonial negotiations.

Erickson, Carolly. *The First Elizabeth*. New York, 1992. A critical, antiromantic biography, presenting Elizabeth as whimsical and petty.

Jenkins, Elizabeth. *Elizabeth the Great*. New York, 1958. A "personal" biography that pays little attention to high politics; it borders on being a novel.

Johnson, Paul. *Elizabeth I: A Study in Power and Intellect*. London, 1974. A good popular biography.

Jones, Norman L. *The Birth of the Elizabethan Age: England in the 1560s*. Oxford, 1993. Good for the politics of religion and succession in the first decade of the reign.

Levin, Carole. *"The Heart and Stomach of a King": Elizabeth I and the Politics of Sex and Power*. Philadelphia, 1994. A feminist study.

MacCaffrey, Wallace. *Elizabeth I*. London, 1993. The most historically reliable political biography.

Neale, J. E. *Queen Elizabeth I*. New York, 1934. Long the standard biography, though very nationalistic.

Strong, Roy. *The Cult of Elizabeth: Elizabethan Portraiture and Pageantry*. London, 1987.

Strong, Roy. *Gloriana: The Portraits of Queen Elizabeth I*. London, 1987.

Williams, Neville. *The Life and Times of Elizabeth I*. Garden City, N.Y., 1972. A good, well-illustrated popular biography lacking scholarly apparatus.

NORMAN L. JONES

ELYOT, THOMAS (c. 1490–1546), English writer, diplomat. Sir Thomas Elyot was one of the most prolific writers among the early English humanists and was especially important as a popularizer of Renaissance ideas and ancient history. His interests included political theory, education, the classical virtues, medicine, and contemporary political events. He also compiled the earliest English dictionary of classical Latin, published in 1538.

Elyot followed his father, a judge, into the legal profession. He probably studied at Oxford, although the records do not include his name, and at the Inns of Court. Having come to the attention of Henry VIII's great minister, Thomas Wolsey, Elyot was named clerk of the King's Council about 1523 and was knighted in 1530. He was a member of the circle of scholars who gathered at Sir Thomas More's home in Chelsea, where he met Thomas Linacre (who taught him about medicine) and Hans Holbein the Younger (who sketched his portrait).

When Wolsey fell from power after failing to secure Henry's divorce from Catherine of Aragon, Elyot also lost his office. His most famous work, *The Boke Named the Governour*, published in 1531, almost certainly represents an attempt to regain Henry's favor. It begins with chapters intended to flatter the king by praising monarchy as the finest form of government. Subsequent sections discuss the classical education appropriate for members of the governing class and the virtues that governors need to display, illustrated by examples drawn from ancient Greek and Roman history.

Perhaps because he was impressed by the *Governour*, Henry sent Elyot as an ambassador to Charles V in 1532. Elyot was not able to persuade Charles to cease opposing Henry's divorce of Catherine and returned in disgrace. In his later life he retired to a small country estate near Cambridge, where he wrote *The Castel of Helth*, an important popularization of the medical ideas of Galen, as well as political dialogues covertly criticizing Henry and praising Catherine of Aragon.

BIBLIOGRAPHY

Lehmberg, Stanford. *Sir Thomas Elyot, Tudor Humanist*. Austin, Tex., 1960. Describes Elyot's life and works.

Major, John M. *Sir Thomas Elyot and Renaissance Humanism*. Lincoln, Nebr., 1964. Considers Elyot's writings in the context of humanism.

STANFORD E. LEHMBERG

ELZEVIER PRESS. The founder of the seventeenth-century Dutch publishing house, Louis I Elzevier (Elzevir; 1546/47–1617), was born in Louvain. He came to Leiden as a Protestant refugee shortly after the foundation of the University of Leiden (1575), having previously worked in Antwerp with Christopher Plantin. Elzevier was active in Leiden as a bookseller and bookbinder, but his good relations with the university resulted in his appointment as beadle in 1586. Although his earliest publication dates from 1583, Elzevier did not become a regular publisher until 1592. His books, always printed by others, were almost without exception in Latin. In 1599, or possibly even earlier, he was the first in Europe to hold a book auction based on a printed catalog. The Elzeviers subsequently organized many such auctions in Leiden and The Hague.

Louis I was succeeded in 1617 by his sons Matthias (1564–1640) and Bonaventura (1583–1652), while his grandson Isaac (1596–1651), who had set up a printing house, was appointed university printer in 1620, using the oriental types of the great Leiden orientalist Thomas Erpenius. Matthias Elzevier sold his share in the firm to his oldest son, Abraham (1592–1652), who, together with Bonaventura, took over Isaac's printing establishment in 1625. This event marks the beginning of the great era of the Leiden Elzeviers.

During their partnership Abraham and Bonaventura published well over five hundred books as well as a large amount of academic ephemera, such as dissertations and orations. A substantial part of their publishing list consists of scholarly works by famous Leiden men, such as Gerardus Joannes Vossius, Hugo Grotius, and particularly Daniel Heinsius, who also acted as their adviser. Foreign scholars sent their books to Leiden, among them Galileo Galilei, whose *Discorsi e dimostrazioni matematichi* (Mathematical discourses and demonstrations) was published by the Elzeviers in 1638. They also produced fine editions of Roman classical authors, a series of descriptions of various countries and regions—the so-called Elzevier Republics—as well as many pirated editions of the works of contemporary French literary authors, all in small format. After the deaths of Abraham

Elzevier Press. The press was located in the courtyard at the right. From P. van der Aa, *Les délices de Leide, une des célèbres villes de l'Europe* (Leiden, 1712), p. 72.

and Bonaventura, Abraham's son Jean (1622–1661) continued the firm, first with Bonaventura's son Daniel (c. 1626–1680), then, after the latter's departure for Amsterdam, alone, concentrating mainly on the printing business. After Jean's premature death the Elzevier printing establishment in Leiden slowly declined until it was sold in 1713.

In 1638 Louis II Elzevier (1604–1670), grandson of Louis I, who at first had worked as a sales representative for Abraham and Bonaventura Elzevier, established himself as an independent publisher in Amsterdam. His publishing list was markedly different from that of the Leiden Elzeviers, with an emphasis on modern science and philosophy. Louis published work by Thomas Hobbes, Francis Bacon, Pierre Gassendi, John Milton, and above all René Descartes. In 1655 Louis began a partnership with his cousin Daniel (1626–1680), with whom he collaborated for nine years, after which the latter took over. Daniel had inherited the rights to many Leiden publications, which he reissued in Amsterdam together with a large variety of scholarly and literary works in Latin and French. Under a pseudonym he also published Jansenist tracts. Daniel was one of the greatest wholesale booksellers of his age, producing impressive assortment lists, such as his 1674 catalog, which contains some twenty thousand titles. With his death the Amsterdam branch came to an end.

Various members of the Elzevier family were active in The Hague and Utrecht. The branch in The Hague was founded by another son of Louis I Elzevier. It operated for more than seventy years in close cooperation with the Leiden and Amsterdam firms and organized many book auctions. The activity of the Elzeviers in Utrecht was of little importance. Josse Elzevier, Louis I's fourth son, started a modest bookshop there in 1600. He was succeeded by his son Pieter.

Although the Elzeviers were regularly accused by their authors of fickleness, their publications enjoyed a great reputation among scholars and collectors, both because of their editorial and their typographic qualities. The ever-increasing demand by bibliophiles for their books in the eighteenth and nineteenth centuries was particularly aimed at the so-called "petits Elzeviers" in small format. In consequence, numerous Elzevier bibliographies were published.

See also **Printing and Publishing**.

BIBLIOGRAPHY

Davies, D. W. *The World of the Elseviers, 1580–1712.* The Hague, Netherlands, 1960.

Willems, Alphonse. *Les Elzevier.* Brussels and Amsterdam, 1880.

P. G. HOFTIJZER

EMBLEM. A pan-European phenomenon, the Renaissance emblem in its canonical form was a three-part invention consisting typically of a titular inscription, a picture, and a short text, usually in verse, and ideally epigrammatic in form. The idea for the genre developed around the title the Milanese jurist Andrea Alciato (1492–1550) had chosen for his collection of illustrated epigrams from the Greek Anthology, a collection of ancient Greek poems first compiled in the tenth century. Heinrich Steyner published the collection in Augsburg in 1531 as *Emblematum liber.* The Latin juridical term *emblema* referred to various types of attached or inserted ornaments that did not fundamentally change the nature of the dish, drinking cup, or, metaphorically, the text to which they were attached. Steyner viewed Alciato's work as no more than a collection of illustrated poetry and failed to see the potential for understanding each combination of picture and text as a rhetorical unit in which all parts interacted with and commented upon each other. The picture presented the reader with a recognizable scene or symbolic collage, and the text then reoriented the reader's understanding of that scene with a new and unexpected message.

The Fortunes of Alciato's Emblems. In 1534 Christian Wechel published an edition in Paris that came closer to Alciato's intentions, and this edition set the generic standard for the following two centuries. Wechel's *Emblematum libellus* suggested quite forcefully the generic implications of combining certain kinds of epigrammatic texts with pictures by paying close attention to the visual unit formed by a double-page opening. In his edition, this unit usually contained a complete emblem, or at least the title, the picture, and most of the text. As this format was repeated, with title, picture, and epigram always in the same position within the page opening, it reinforced the impression that the picture and text were meant to be understood as an indissoluble unit. This unity was further underscored by the use of elaborate, decorative frames in later editions to enclose the picture with portions of the related text.

Most early editions of Alciato's emblems were published in France, first in Paris and then, after 1545, in Lyon; after 1560 the emblem began to attract wider interest, and editions of Alciato's work now began to issue regularly from Dutch and German presses, and later from Italian and Spanish presses, together with those still being published in Paris and Lyon. Wechel published the first French translation in 1536, and two other French versions were completed in the next fifty years. German, Italian, and Spanish translations, all published in France, followed by 1550. In all some 150 editions were published by the late eighteenth century, with the *editio optima,* a heavily commented one-thousand-page quarto volume, published by Tozzi in Padua in 1621. After this landmark edition, the first to contain all 212 emblems, only 18 more were published before the end of the eighteenth century, and 6 of those, all with crude woodcut illustrations, came from Spanish presses.

Very early, the work began to inspire imitators, first in France—with Guillaume de La Perrière's pioneering *Theatre des bons engins* (Theater of fine devices, 1540) and Gilles Corrozet's *Hecatomgraphie* (1540) together with slightly later works by Guillaume Guéroult, Barthélemy Aneau, and others—and then after 1555 in Italy and the Netherlands. By the end of the sixteenth century, emblem books were being composed and published throughout Europe and formed one of the vehicles of choice for disseminating humanist ideals. The first religious emblem books, composed by Arias Montanus (Catholic) and Georgette de Montenay (Protestant), were published in 1571. At the turn of the century, Jan David composed the first Jesuit emblem

In Auaros.

Septitius populos inter ditißimus omnes,
  Arua senex nullus quo magis ampla tenet.
Defraudans geniumáq; suum, mensasq; paratas,
  Nil præter betas, duráq; rapa uorat.
Cui simulem dicã hunc, inopem quem copia reddit,
  An ne asino? sic est, instar hic eius habet.
Nanq; asinus dorso preciosa obsonia gestat,
  Seq; rubo aut dura carice pauper alit.

D iiij

An Emblem of Alciato. "Against misers." From Andrea Alciato, *Emblematum libellus,* 1531.

book, the *Veridicus Christianus* (The true Christian; 1601). Having been accorded a place in the new Jesuit curriculum as prescribed in the definitive version of the *Ratio studiorum* (Plan of studies; 1599), emblems were also being composed in the schools. Throughout the first half of the seventeenth century, members of the highest classes in the Flemish Jesuit colleges each composed an emblem, and the production of the entire class was collected in commemorative albums painted by professional artists and calligraphers. In the seventeenth century Jesuits were heavily involved in the theoretical discussion of the emblematic forms, and in the use of these forms in the design of ceremonial decorations for courtly festivals, royal weddings, and the ceremonies surrounding the opening of the school year.

Given the expense involved in producing the extensive suites of engravings necessary to illustrate an emblem book, the finer examples were produced in polyglot editions for international audiences, especially in the emblem books of the Dutch artist, Otto van Veen, whose emblems of divine and secular love (*Amorum emblemata,* 1608; and *Amoris divini emblemata,* 1615), and his moralizing emblems based on quotations from Horace (*Q. Horatii flacci emblemata,* 1607) had great success throughout Europe. Another example is the 1619 German edition of Georgette de Montenay's *Emblemes, ou devises chrestiennes* (Christian emblems, or devices; 1571), with its texts in French, German, English, and Latin. In such books, the translations were often geared to the projected audience; hence, the German translation of de Montenay's work is aimed at the burgher class, while her French huitains (eight-line stanzas) were composed for a courtly audience. A similar intention to tailor La Perrière's emblems to a particular, but different, audience is evident in the English translation of *The Theater of Fine Devices* (c. 1593).

Emblems in Germany and England. The first German emblem books were published in the last quarter of the sixteenth century, and they quickly split into two traditions. The Latin emblem books of Nicolas Reusner (*Emblemata,* 1581) and Nicolaus Taurellus (*Emblemata,* 1595), together with the natural history emblems of Joachim Camerarius (1590, 1595, 1596, 1604) maintained the humanist tradition of Alciato and the Hungarian Johannes Sambucus, whose *Emblemata* were published along with a numismatic anthology in Antwerp by Christopher Plantin in 1564. In contrast, German books by Matthias Holzwart (1581) and others catered to the moralizing impulses of a rising burgher class and the rhetorical needs of Catholic and Protestant churches.

In England, emblems were known before 1550. For many years, there had been manuscript collections; English translations of continental emblem books; and Geffrey Whitney's anthology of English versions of emblems by Alciato, Sambucus, and Reusner, and devices by Claude Paradin (*A Choice of Emblems,* 1586). Despite this, England produced no illustrated emblem books of its own before the seventeenth century. The most famous of these were George Wither's *A Collection of Emblemes* (1635), which used Crispin de Passe's plates for Gabriel Rollenhagen's *Nucleus Emblematum* (1611–1613), and Francis Quarles's *Emblemes* (1635) and *Hieroglyphikes of the Life of Man* (1638), which adapted the Jesuit Herman Hugo's immensely popular *Pia desideria* (Pious desires; 1624) to the doctrinal requirements of the English church.

Device or Impresa. Even before Alciato invented the emblem, there existed another emblematic form, known in France as the *devise* and in Italy as the *impresa*. The first Italian *imprese* date from the middle of the fifteenth century, when they found a place on the *revers de medailles* of Antonio Pisanello (c. 1415–c. 1455). These combinations of a pictured sign and a short motto were used to identify individuals and permit their personal expression of an idealized view of the owner, or some military or amorous project of particular and personal importance. The fashion of anthologies of devices with biographical and technical commentary developed shortly after 1550 in France and in Italy, with the works of Paolo Giovio, *Dialogo dell'imprese militari et amorose* (Dialogue on military and amorous devices; 1555) and Claude Paradin's *Devises heroiques* (1551), and it was in these anthologies that most of the theorizing about the form took place, first in Italy, and then, after 1620, in France.

Applied Emblematics. While the European emblem produced very few literary masterpieces or anything close, the quality of engraving was sometimes very high, especially in France and the Low Countries, and these engravings often provided the motifs for interior decoration. Glassware, ceramic tiles, tapestries, and wall paintings regularly served as the vehicle for emblematic motifs that made some statement about the owner. Sometimes, as in the small room known as Lady Drury's oratory at Hawstead Hall (early seventeenth century), the emblematic motifs seem to form a meditational program for the owner or some member of the owner's family. The ceilings of several seventeenth-century Scottish residences were decorated with moralizing emblems, personal devices, and heraldic arms. By the eighteenth century, private residences were often elaborately decorated with suites of emblems, either painted or embedded in ceramic tiles as at Fliesenssal, near Hildesheim in Germany.

Emblems also provided building blocks for court masques in England and baroque theater in Germany. Even certain of Shakespeare's plays, including *The Winter's Tale,* where Father Time comes on stage to instruct the audience, and *Pericles,* with its *impresa* shields in the second act, contain numerous "naked emblems," that is, emblems in which the picture is described, but not shown. Elsewhere, the impact of emblematics is evident in the structure of poetry, sermons, and court propaganda, especially in the later years of the French religious wars.

By the end of the Renaissance, the emblem had evolved into a rhetorical vehicle that could be adapted to a wide variety of media and could carry a wide range of messages, from humanist precepts to religious doctrine, political propaganda, and satire.

See also **Alciato, Andrea**; **Graphic Arts.**

BIBLIOGRAPHY

Primary Work
Alciato, Andrea. *The Latin Emblems* and *Emblems in Translation*. Edited by Peter M. Daly, Virginia W. Callahan, and Simon Cuttler. 2 vols. Toronto, 1985.

Secondary Works
Bath, Michael. *Speaking Pictures: English Emblem Books and Renaissance Culture*. London and New York, 1994.
Daly, Peter M. *Literature in the Light of the Emblem*. Toronto, 1979.
Russell, Daniel. *The Emblem and Device in France*. Lexington, Ky., 1985.
Russell, Daniel. *Emblematic Structures in Renaissance French Culture*. Toronto, 1995.
Russell, Daniel. "Looking at the Emblem in a European Context." *Revue de littérature comparée* 64, no. 4 (1990): 625–644.

DANIEL RUSSELL

EMILIA, ART IN. Emilia-Romagna is one of the nineteen major regions (*paesi*) of Italy. Located in north-central Italy, it is bounded by Liguria and Piedmont to the west, by Lombardy and the Veneto to the north, by the Adriatic Sea to the east and Tuscany and the Marches to the south. Within this region, the western district is known as Emilia, and the eastern district is known as Romagna. However, the adjective "Emilian" frequently designates the entire region, which fostered important developments in Renaissance art, especially in the art of painting.

The Este and Ferrara. By the mid-fifteenth century the humanistic theoretical parameters that define Renaissance art were well established in Emilia, largely owing to the patronage and influence of the Este family, who as papal vicars were lords of Ferrara from the thirteenth century until 1452 and then (beginning with Borso d'Este) held the title of dukes of Ferrara, Modena, and Reggio until 1597, when the last legitimate Este duke died and Ferrara devolved to the possession of the Holy See. Under the marchese Leonello d'Este (ruled 1441–1450), the new artistic traditions of the humanistic Renaissance flourished. Indeed, Leonello was educated by the outstanding humanist Guarino Guarini, who founded an important tradition of humanistic learning at the Ferrarese court, and Leonello's own contacts with the Florentine humanist Leon Battista Alberti (author of seminal humanist commentaries on painting, sculpture, and architecture) and with such artists as Pisanello (Antonio Pisano), Jacopo Bellini, Andrea Mantegna, and Piero della Francesca, among others, provided him with a highly sophisticated understanding of contemporary art's theoretical and stylistic developments.

A patron of both literature and the visual arts, Leonello employed the Ferrarese painter Cosmè Tura to paint a series of images of the Muses for his personal study at the country palace of Belfiore, having conceived the idea for this series in collaboration with Guarino da Verona. Leonello's half-brother and successor Borso d'Este may not have been personally involved in the study of classical letters to quite the same extent, but nonetheless his patronage of both the visual and literary arts reveals a continued commitment to the new humanistic culture. His renovations to the fourteenth-century Palazzo Schifanoia at Ferrara, begun around 1465, included the famous Hall of the Months, the principal reception hall of the palace, which featured a fresco cycle designed by Tura and executed by Francesco del Cossa, Ercole de' Roberti, and others. The cycle included not only astrological and calendrical scenes but also scenes of courtly pageantry expressed in the Renaissance pictorial language of illusionistic space and classicizing form.

Duke Ercole I d'Este (ruled 1471–1505) similarly made major contributions to Emilian art, but his achievements in the area of city planning are especially noteworthy. In the early 1490s, the possibility of war between Ferrara and Venice led Ercole to undertake a vast building project designed to protect the vulnerable northern portions of the city by encompassing it within new defensive walls and improving access and communication with new, efficiently designed streets and a major new plaza, the Piazza Nuova. Ercole appears to have worked closely with his architects in the design of this new urban area, known as the "Herculean Addition," and the resulting design reveals a careful consideration of the humanistic theory of urban design set forth by Alberti in the fourth book of his treatise *De re aedificatoria* (1452).

Later fifteenth-century Ferrarese painting was characterized by a studied artificiality and enamel-like coloring, but by 1490 certain artists, especially Roberti, had begun to develop more naturalistic modes of drawing and coloring reminiscent of contemporary Venetian art. In the early decades of the sixteenth century Emilian traditions of painting took on a new identity consonant with the naturalism that eventually came to define north Italian art in general. Duke Alfonso I d'Este's selection of the Venetian

master Giovanni Bellini to complete one of the mythological paintings for his *camerino* (private study), and his subsequent choice of Bellini's brilliant young pupil Titian to complete the project, are perhaps symptomatic of this new taste, but it is in the work of Dosso Dossi (1479?–1542), painter to the ducal court, that we encounter the most completely developed indigenous example of this new Ferrarese naturalism, for example in his remarkable *Hercules and the Pygmies,* painted after 1534.

The Renaissance in Bologna. A similar pattern may be traced in another of the great artistic centers of Renaissance Emilia: Bologna. The Bolognese were certainly aware of the new developments in early fifteenth-century Florentine painting, and Florentine artists received important commissions in the city, as for example in the case of Paolo Uccello's altarpiece of the *Nativity* at San Martino (1437). Under the rule of Giovanni II Bentivoglio, godson of Leonello d'Este, such Ferrarese artists as Roberti and del Cossa also received numerous commissions in Bologna, which helped to establish a strong tradition of Renaissance style by the end of the fifteenth century. The arrival of Raphael's famous altarpiece of *St. Cecilia* in Bologna in 1515 encouraged the new tendency toward idealized naturalism already evident in the works of such Bolognese masters as Amico Aspertini and Francesco Francia. For example, their own fresco decorations for the Oratory of St. Cecilia at Bologna, begun around 1505, appear to be informed by the same quest for perfect grace and beauty that structured Raphael's early development.

Parma and Emilian Naturalism. The defining moment of Emilian naturalism ultimately occurred in Parma, in the work of the painter Antonio Allegri, called Correggio (1494–1534). Although Correggio does not appear to have traveled to Rome or Venice, he arrived at a form of tenderly lyrical naturalism based on theories of human proportions, anatomy, and color technique recalling developments in both of these centers, and perhaps also reflecting a knowledge of Leonardo's art theoretical precepts. Parma's annexation by the Papal States in the early sixteenth century brought about a general efflorescence of art patronage, of which Correggio was a major beneficiary, creating such works as the famous cycle of mythological frescoes for the private chambers of Giovanna da Piacenza, abbess of the Benedictine convent of San Paolo (1519); and the remarkable illusionistic fresco of the *Assumption of* *the Virgin* for the dome of Parma Cathedral (1522–1530).

The highly artificial quality or *maniera* that had been implicit in the divergent styles of Leonardo and Michelangelo and also became evident in the later works of Raphael had by this time been spread throughout the courts of central Italy, and had been carried even further northward by Raphael's pupils (especially Giulio Romano and Perino del Vaga) after the sack of Rome (1527). This new stylistic tendency, now called mannerism, involved the quasi-Platonic assumption that true beauty could not be known through the senses but only glimpsed through fantastic revelation, and was manifested in painting through expressive distortions of form and antinaturalistic color techniques. Like his Venetian contemporaries (for example, Titian), Correggio resisted this tendency, maintaining his naturalistic figural proportions and color. Correggio's younger contemporary in Parma, the painter Francesco Mazzola, called Il Parmigianino (1503–1540), employed a similarly naturalistic system of coloring, but unlike Correggio he experimented extensively with mannerist distortions of form. A typical example might be his *Madonna of the Long Neck* painted c. 1534–1540 for the Baiardi chapel in Santa Maria dei Servi, Bologna, but never completed; as has been demonstrated, the figural distortions in this work, including the Madonna's famously elongated neck, were actually inspired by Petrarchan poetic conceits aimed at the praise of feminine beauty.

The Carracci and the Reform of Painting.

By the second half of the sixteenth century, a great variety of mannerist styles had taken root in Emilia and Romagna, as throughout much of northern Italy. At Bologna, such mannerist artists as Prospero Fontana, Tommaso Laureti, and Ercole Procaccini were filling the churches with images of unearthly, artificial beauty, Fontana's extraordinary *St. Alexis Giving Alms* in the church of San Giacomo (1573) being a typical example. However, by the early1580s, three Bolognese painters belonging to the Carracci family, including Ludovico Carracci and his cousins Annibale and Agostino, began to articulate a distaste for these mannerist tendencies, which they regarded as vapid, overly polished, and utterly fantastic. They sought to reform the art of painting by returning to the example of nature in search of a more universally valid and meaningful style. The Carracci traced their stylistic roots to the most naturalistic northern Italian painters of the sixteenth century, including not only their Emilian predecessor Correggio, but also such

Venetian masters as Titian and Veronese, and the contemporary Umbrian master Federico Barocci. They established an art academy in which they taught the theoretical and practical bases of this new naturalistic style. Early Carracci works such as Annibale's *Madonna and Child with Six Saints* for the high altar of the church of Santi Ludovico e Alessio (c. 1588; now Pinacoteca Nazionale, Bologna) show these Correggesque and Venetian influences. However, since this style was founded on the assumption that a selective imitation of nature's most perfect forms would lead inevitably to the discovery of abstract, universal verities, the Carracci (especially Annibale in his Roman period, 1594–1609) developed in a progressively more idealizing direction, ultimately arriving at a style that is simultaneously abstract and naturalistic. The resulting style, now known as the baroque, came to dominate European art throughout the seventeenth century.

See also **Carracci Family; Correggio; Mannerism; Parmigianino.**

BIBLIOGRAPHY

Campbell, Stephen J. *Cosmè Tura of Ferrara: Style, Politics, and the Renaissance City, 1450–1495.* New Haven, Conn., and London, 1997.

Emiliani, Andrea, ed. *The Age of Correggio and the Carracci: Emilian Painting of the Sixteenth and Seventeenth Centuries.* Washington, D.C., 1986. Exhibition catalog.

Emiliani, Andrea, ed. *La pittura in Emilia e in Romagna: Il Seicento.* 2 vols. Milan, 1994.

Fortunati, Vera, ed. *La pittura in Emilia e in Romagna: Il Cinquecento.* 2 vols. Milan, 1995.

Rosenberg, Charles M. *The Este Monuments and Urban Development in Renaissance Ferrara.* New York, 1997.

Tuohy, Thomas. *Herculean Ferrara: Ercole d'Este, 1471–1505, and the Invention of a Ducal Capital.* Cambridge, U.K., 1996.

Volpe, Carlo. *La pittura nell'Emilia e nella Romagna: raccolta di scritti sul trecento e quattrocento.* Modena, Italy, 1993.

ANTHONY COLANTUONO

EMPIRE. *See* **Holy Roman Empire.**

ENCINA, JUAN DEL (c. 1468–1529/30), Spanish poet, playwright, musician. Born Juan de Fremoselle, Encina changed his surname by 1490. His father was a shoemaker. He took a law degree at the University of Salamanca and became a cathedral chorister in 1490. He next entered the service of Don Gutierre de Toledo, leaving it for that of Gutierre de Toledo's brother, the duke of Alba, in 1492. At the ducal court in Alba de Tormes, Encina was master of the revels, furnishing musical, poetic, and dramatic entertainment for the duke, the duchess, and their courtiers. Most of his extant works were created at Alba de Tormes between 1492 and 1500. From 1500 until his death, he pursued a clerical career under papal protection, although he was not ordained a priest until 1519.

Encina wrote hundreds of poems of all kinds, at least fourteen *églogas* (eclogues), or plays in verse, and is represented in the *Cancionero musical de palacio* (Palace music songbook) by sixty-one songs. His fourteen verse dramas are his most significant achievement. As these advance from playlets of a few hundred lines to the almost three thousand verses of the fourteenth eclogue, they also grow in artistry. In their internal evolution, a theater is born, although it does not really presage the high drama in Spain of the great years from 1580 to 1640. Encina's dramatic art is rather the voicing of a personal and artistic conflict between his dual vocations as an expositor inspired by Christianity and an advocate of neopagan courtly erotics. This double allegiance produces the dissonances that resound throughout the eighth, tenth, eleventh, twelfth, and fourteenth eclogues, and which the fourteenth most richly utters in an impossible but glorious attempt to harmonize them. It is ironic that Encina's dramaturgy, striving to evolve out of rusticity into the utmost refinement, should mainly endure in the form of a conventionalized rustic peasant patter called *sayagués* that the greatest later golden age playwrights, Tirso de Molina most of all, adopt when they cause country people to speak.

BIBLIOGRAPHY

Primary Works

Encina, Juan del. *Églogas completas de Juan del Enzina*. Edited by Humberto López-Morales. New York and Madrid, 1968. Its introduction is controversial and annotated solely as to variants, but this remains the handiest edition of Encina's plays.

Encina, Juan del. *Obras completas*. 3 vols. Edited by Ana M. Rambaldo. Madrid, 1978. The only edition of all Encina's extant writings, sparingly annotated.

Encina, Juan del. *Poesía lírica y cancionero musical*. Edited by R. O. Jones and Carolyn R. Lee. Madrid, 1975. Uncautious in the attribution of anonymous poems to Encina, this edition of all the lyrics and known musical settings of songs is nonetheless invaluable and unique, particularly in its analysis of the music.

Secondary Works

Andrews, J. Richard. *Juan del Encina: Prometheus in Search of Prestige*. Berkeley, Calif., 1959. Still the only comprehensive study.

Stern, Charlotte. "Juan del Encina's Carnival Eclogues and the Spanish Drama of the Renaissance." *Renaissance Drama* 8 (1965):181–195.

Sullivan, Henry W. *Juan del Encina*. Boston, 1976.

Ter Horst, Robert. "*Ut pictura poesis:* Self-Portrayal in the Plays of Juan del Encina." In *Brave New Words: Studies in Spanish Golden Age Literature*. Edited by Edward H. Friedman and Catherine Larson. New Orleans, La., 1966. Pages 1–18.

Wardropper, Bruce W. "Metamorphosis in the Theatre of Juan del Encina." *Studies in Philology* 59 (1962): 41–51. The single most influential analysis of the plays, contested by Sullivan.

ROBERT TER HORST

ENGINEERING. *See* **Technology.**

ENGLAND. The course of the Renaissance in England is nearly coterminous with the history of the Tudor dynasty. Renaissance ideas were only beginning to affect the country in 1485, when Henry VII won the throne in the Battle of Bosworth Field. They were firmly established in 1603, at the death of the last Tudor, his granddaughter Elizabeth I. They continued to flower during the reign of James I (1603–1625) but lost importance under his son Charles I as attention was diverted to governmental crises and the English Civil War.

The Early Tudor Period. Between 1455 and 1485 England had been torn by the dynastic strife known as the Wars of the Roses. The Yorkist kings Edward IV (1461–1483) and Richard III (1483–1485) supplanted the old line of Lancastrian monarchs, the last of whom, Henry VI, was murdered after losing the Battle of Barnet in 1471. Henry Tudor, whose ancestry was Welsh though he could claim a relationship with the Lancastrian line, left his exile in France and invaded England in 1485. On 22 August he was proclaimed king on the battlefield of Bosworth, where Richard was defeated and slain. Edward IV's two sons, the "princes in the Tower," had presumably been murdered on the order of Richard III, although their fate remains uncertain, and it is possible that Henry VII was responsible for their death. Two impostors, Lambert Simnel and Perkin Warbeck, later attempted to impersonate the princes, Edward V and Richard, duke of York, but both were easily apprehended. Simnel became a scullion in the royal kitchens; Warbeck was executed.

Henry VII married Elizabeth of York, the daughter of Edward IV and sister of the princes, thus ending the hostility between the two lines of succession. They had four children. Their older son, Arthur, was married to the Spanish princess Catherine of Aragon in 1501 but died in 1502. His younger brother, Henry, then became heir to the throne. A daughter, Margaret, was wed to King James IV of Scotland in the hope that the union would bring an end to the

England

hostility between the English and the Scots that had characterized the medieval period. It failed to do so, but a descendant of this marriage eventually succeeded to the English throne as King James I. A dynastic marriage was also arranged for the younger daughter, Mary, known as the "White Queen"; she was wed to the French king Louis XII.

An able but somewhat colorless ruler, Henry succeeded in establishing the position of his new dynasty, increasing the efficiency of the government, and enhancing the wealth of the monarchy. He was not himself much interested in intellectual affairs, although his mother, Lady Margaret Beaufort, did provide patronage for scholars and founded two colleges at Cambridge University as well as professorships at both Oxford and Cambridge.

The humanist ideas associated with the English Renaissance had begun to filter into England before

Henry VII's accession, and the earliest book printed in England antedated his coronation by a decade, but both humanism and printing became firmly established only during his reign. Latin and Greek had been taught occasionally at the universities by visiting scholars prior to 1485, and a few Englishmen had gone to Italy to study, but regular instruction in the classical languages did not begin until about 1500.

Henry VIII and the Reformation. For these reasons Henry VII used to be thought of as England's first Renaissance ruler, and the English Renaissance was often dated to 1485. More recent interpretations place the break between medieval and modern times—the point at which Renaissance ideas became dominant in England—in the decade of the 1530s and recognize Henry VIII, who reigned from 1509 to 1547, as the true Renaissance prince.

Handsome, dashing, well educated in classical Latin and theology, willing to spend money on learning and the arts, Henry seemed to personify many attributes of the Renaissance. The great humanist Sir Thomas More served as his lord chancellor in the 1530s; Hans Holbein was his court painter; Sir Thomas Elyot was for a time one of his secretaries. The Renaissance palace at Hampton Court, originally built by Thomas Wolsey, was taken over by Henry after the cardinal's fall and was the scene of many splendid entertainments. Great Renaissance pageantry adorned the meeting between Henry VIII and Francis I, the Renaissance king of France, at the Field of the Cloth of Gold in 1520. Saint Paul's School, founded early in Henry's reign by John Colet, the learned dean of Saint Paul's Cathedral, was the first grammar school to provide rigorous instruction in the classical languages. The Latin grammar written for Saint Paul's by William Lily (1527) was the first such exposition of classical Latin; Elyot's dictionary (1538) was the first volume to provide English equivalents for all the words in the classical Latin vocabulary. The grand tour, which often included protracted visits to Rome and Florence, became virtually obligatory as part of the education of young English aristocrats and gentlemen.

Henry's marital career was intermeshed with the Reformation of the English church. Immediately following his accession. Henry had married his brother's widow, Catherine of Aragon. For more than a decade the marriage was a happy one, but it was not blessed with a male heir to the throne. There was a daughter, Mary, but the kind did not believe that she would be accepted as his successor, so beginning in 1527 he sought to divorce Catherine in the hope that he might beget a son by a younger wife, Anne Boleyn. Papal consent was required, but Pope Clement VII was in no position to grant it, since Catherine's nephew Charles V had invaded Italy and his troops had sacked Rome that very year. Catherine, Charles, and Clement thus opposed the king's demand. Finally Henry, acting on advice from his chief minister, Thomas Cromwell, simply repudiated papal jurisdiction in England. Statutes passed by the Reformation Parliament in 1533 and 1534 named the king Supreme Head of the Church and cut the ties that had bound the English church to the papacy. The Church of England thus became an independent national body, espousing some of the Protestant teachings of Martin Luther. Henry, who had earlier written against Luther and been rewarded by the pope with the title "Defender of the Faith," came to see merit in a number of Lutheran doctrines and supported their adoption by his new religious establishment.

In May 1533 Henry's divorce was pronounced by Thomas Cranmer, the new archbishop of Canterbury. Henry and Anne had been secretly married in January and their daughter Elizabeth was born in September. In 1536 Henry discovered evidence that Anne had been unfaithful to him and had her beheaded. Catherine of Aragon died a natural death in the same year. Henry's third wife, Jane Seymour, bore him the son he so greatly desired in 1537 but shortly succumbed to complications following childbirth. He waited until 1540 to marry again. Thomas Cromwell, eager to forge an alliance between England and one of the Protestant states on the Continent, had arranged a marriage with Anne of Cleves, sister of the duke of Cleves, who ruled a small territory on the Rhine. But when Anne came to England, the king found her unattractive; Archbishop Cranmer pronounced their annulment soon after he officiated at their marriage. Cromwell lost favor with the king, partly because of this episode, and was executed in 1540. On the very day of Cromwell's death Henry married Catherine Howard who, like Anne Boleyn, was a niece of Thomas Howard, duke of Norfolk. Like Anne, Catherine was found guilty of adultery and was beheaded in 1542. Henry's last wife was Katherine Parr. Already a widow, though still relatively young, she was an intelligent woman who cared for the aging king and attempted to provide something like a mother's care for his children, especially Edward and Elizabeth, who had never had anything approaching a normal home. Both Katherine Parr and Anne of Cleves outlived the king.

One of the most important religious changes of Henry's reign was the dissolution of the monasteries. At the beginning of the Tudor period the religious houses owned as much as a quarter of all the land in the country. These estates had been given or bequeathed to the monks by pious men and women who wished to endow prayers for the repose of their souls. A survey of the religious houses undertaken by Thomas Cromwell revealed some corruption and immorality as well as a general lack of spirituality, but not all of this evidence should be accepted at face value, since the commissioners realized that they were expected to produce a justification for confiscation of monastic property. An act for the dissolution of the monasteries passed by Parliament in 1536 ordered the closing of the smaller monasteries and nunneries (those with annual incomes of two hundred pounds or less); their residents were permitted to transfer to the larger houses that remained

Henry VIII. Anonymous portrait of Henry handing over a charter to Thomas Vicary, 1541, commemorating the joining of the Barbers and Surgeons. BARBER'S HALL, LONDON/THE BRIDGEMAN ART LIBRARY

open or to renounce their vows. Most chose the latter course. The great abbeys were suppressed one by one in the next few years. A second statute, passed in 1540, legalized these closures and mandated the confiscation of all remaining monastic property. Former monastic possessions were managed by a new financial bureau, the Court of Augmentations, which paid small pensions to the former monks and nuns, larger ones to the former abbots and priors who had acquiesced in the dissolution of their houses. By the time of Henry VIII's death most of the monastic land had been sold to noblemen and members of the gentry, thus creating a vested interest in the continuation of the Reformation.

The loss of the monasteries was felt in various ways. Earlier they had been great centers of learning and the arts, but they no longer provided leadership in these areas. Humanistic scholarship had not affected them in any significant way. The great monastic libraries were dispersed. Some collections remained in cathedrals that had earlier been monastic in organization, like Canterbury and Durham, and others were acquired by the universities of Oxford and Cambridge or by private collectors. Perhaps the role of religious houses in providing suitable residences for single men and women, including women who lacked the necessary dowry to be married, had been their most valuable social service.

Much of the wealth confiscated from the religious houses was spent on warfare. Early in his reign, before the Reformation, Henry VIII had joined Pope Julius II in a Holy League intended to prevent the French from acquiring territory in Italy. The king personally commanded English troops at the famous Battle of the Spurs (1513), in which the French retreated chaotically, leaving several towns in northern France under English control. In 1520 his principal adviser, Cardinal Wolsey, attempted to secure the pacification of Europe by arranging the Treaty of London, but this scheme did not prove workable. Henry and his advisers were fearful of a Catholic attempt to invade England and restore the old religion. They spent vast amounts of money on fortifications and on renewed wars against France and Scotland (a traditional ally of the French). Following the Reformation, diplomatic alignments were almost always dictated by religious concerns.

The relationship between the Renaissance and the Reformation in England is complex. Renaissance ideas of skepticism and critical inquiry may have paved the way for a reconsideration of ecclesiastical government; a number of the leaders of the new church benefited from classical educations. But Sir Thomas More and Bishop John Fisher, two of the most learned men in the realm, became martyrs because they would not abjure the old faith. It is probably fair to say that the Reformation drew interest away from the Renaissance. Humanistic scholarship generally became less important after 1540, as England became engulfed in religious controversy.

During the years after 1536 two rival factions emerged at Henry's court. Reformers like Thomas Cromwell and Archbishop Cranmer advocated social and religious change, while conservatives led by Bishop Stephen Gardiner and Thomas Howard, duke of Norfolk, sought to block their proposals. Cromwell's fall, coupled with Cranmer's reluctance to oppose the conservative king, weakened the more liberal cause. Despite their relationship to Norfolk, neither Anne Boleyn nor Catherine Howard influenced the course of religion significantly. Jane Seymour and Katherine Parr held Protestant views and supported reform; on one occasion Catherine was charged with attempting to interfere in religious matters and influence the king, but she denied involvement and was pardoned. Shortly before the death of Henry VIII, both the duke of Norfolk and his son, the earl of Surrey, were found guilty of treason and sentenced to death. Surrey was executed in January 1547. Just before Norfolk's execution was to have been carried out, it was postponed because of the death of the king at the end of January 1547. Because no one wanted to mar a new reign with such an event, Norfolk was allowed to live, but he and Bishop Gardiner lost their political power to the reformers.

Edward and Mary. In his will Henry VIII provided for the possible succession of all three of his children—Edward, Mary, and Elizabeth—although both of the daughters had earlier been declared illegitimate when Henry divorced their mothers. Edward was the youngest but as a male had precedence. He was crowned when he was only nine years old but was not destined to attain maturity and died in 1553. Henry had named a large council of regents to rule England during his son's minority, but Edward's uncle, Edward Seymour, duke of Somerset, almost immediately assumed control of the government. As Protector, Somerset was the effective ruler for several years, but he found it difficult to deal with several rebellions that broke out in 1549 and lost power to John Dudley, duke of Northumberland,

who was the most important figure in the government for the remainder of Edward's reign.

Both Somerset and Northumberland approved of further reform in the church. Archbishop Cranmer was eager to introduce changes that had been resisted by the old king, and young Edward, having been tutored by Protestants, was enthusiastic about reform as well. Renaissance ideas had dominated his education. He was taught Latin and Greek by one of England's finest scholars, John Cheke, and was instructed in religion by Richard Cox, later bishop of Ely. Protestantism now reached its highest point in English history. Cranmer's first English-language Book of Common Prayer, introduced in 1549, was moderate in tone, but a revision promulgated in 1552 was radically reformed in character; it regarded the Communion as no more than a commemorative reenactment of the Last Supper and ordered the destruction of stone altars associated with the Catholic Mass. The Forty-Two Articles of Religion issued by Cranmer in 1553 also set out radical views on many theological issues.

In 1553 Edward died, probably from pneumonia and possibly tuberculosis. During his last days some of his advisers attempted to divert the succession to Lady Jane Grey, a distant relative of the king's and a reliable supporter of Protestant causes, for they knew that the accession of Mary Tudor would bring the restoration of the Catholic faith to which she had always adhered. But very few ordinary men and women approved of the scheme. As the older daughter of Henry VIII, Mary enjoyed general support, and she was crowned virtually without incident.

Mary undid the Reformation in two stages, restoring the Latin Mass in 1553 and the jurisdiction of the pope in 1554. Archbishop Cranmer was dismissed from office and placed under house arrest, while Reginald Pole, an English aristocrat who had spent the years since Henry VIII's break with the papacy living in Italy, was brought back to England to assume the archbishop's place. Pole acted as one of Mary's chief advisers, curiously enough dying on the same day as the queen herself.

Many people supported Mary's restoration of the Catholic faith, believing that the Edwardian reforms had gone too far in abolishing cherished ceremonies and beliefs. Those who clung to Protestant doctrines continued to worship in underground churches or fled to the Continent. Hundreds of English Protestants formed groups of Marian exiles in Frankfurt, Strasbourg, Geneva, and Zurich. Three hundred more remained in England to become martyrs for their faith. John Foxe's famous *Book of Martyrs* describes in excruciating detail the scenes in which they were burned at the stake, and many editions of his compilation, which attained great popularity, were illustrated with engravings depicting the death of such Protestant leaders as Archbishop Cranmer. He is known as one of the Oxford martyrs, since his execution took place there. Bishops Hugh Latimer and Nicholas Ridley were also burned at Oxford. Mary had taken Philip II of Spain, the son of Charles V, as her husband, but Philip had counseled leniency, so responsibility for the executions must rest with Mary herself. Since they had no children, despite Mary's delusions of pregnancy, the throne passed to her sister Elizabeth when she died in 1558.

Elizabeth I. The accession of Anne Boleyn's daughter ushered in what is often regarded as England's golden age. In her religious settlement of 1559 the queen restored the Church of England, which she tried to guide into a middle-of-the-road course somewhere between papal Rome and Calvinist Geneva. The queen took the title Supreme Governor of the Church, not Supreme Head, perhaps because of the view that no woman could be its head, but she intended to exercise the same control enjoyed by her father and brother. The Elizabethan Book of Common Prayer was based on Cranmer's second version but was modified to permit individual worshipers to hold diverse views about such matters as the theology of the Eucharist.

Excellently educated by the scholars Roger Ascham and John Cheke, Elizabeth knew Greek, was fluent in Latin (as she demonstrated in extempore orations when visiting the universities of Oxford and Cambridge), occasionally embarrassed foreign diplomats by understanding the private comments they expressed in their own languages, and was a proficient performer on the virginal, the keyboard instrument named to honor her status as the Virgin Queen. During her long reign Renaissance ideas dominated literature—the plays of Shakespeare offer only one example of the deep influence of ancient history and humanistic thought—and even such areas as state pageantry and medical practice demonstrated the pervading influence of classical antiquity. Both grammar school teaching and university curricula were reformed; Greek and classical Latin formed the basis of the education provided for members of the governing classes and for the clergy of the state church, and ancient history was avidly studied.

It was unfortunate for Elizabeth that much of her realm's energy had to be devoted to warfare, mainly the opposition to Catholic enterprises. Following Mary's death Philip II had suggested that he marry Elizabeth. When his suit was spurned he turned against her, and for the rest of the century England and other Protestant states were involved in conflict with Spain and the papacy. This conflict manifested itself in the Revolt of the Netherlands, where the Protestants in the Low Countries fought to throw off Spanish rule and Catholic persecution. Initially reluctant to become involved, Elizabeth finally accepted the argument that England, the chief Protestant power in Europe, had an obligation to aid beleaguered Protestants elsewhere. The famous Spanish Armada of 1588 represented Philip's attempt to put down the Dutch revolt and restore Catholicism in England, all in one campaign. Had he been successful Elizabeth would have been deposed and Philip would have assumed the throne once again, but the combination of English seamanship and a Protestant wind led to the destruction of much of the Spanish fleet and its forlorn return to Spain in defeat. Other Catholic threats to Elizabeth's security were the various plots associated with Mary, queen of Scots, who had been driven from Scotland by her Protestant subjects. For years Elizabeth granted her refuge in England, even though, as a granddaughter of James IV and Margaret Tudor, she was the leading Catholic contender for the English throne. But the discovery of Anthony Babington's conspiracy to assassinate Elizabeth in 1586 led to Mary's execution at Fotheringhay castle in 1587. The earl of Tyrone's rebellion in Ireland also marred Elizabeth's last years; it was only on her deathbed that she learned of his surrender.

Despite the various threats to Elizabeth's rule and the financial pressures induced by military activity, intellectual and artistic endeavors reached new heights during Elizabeth's years. Puritans might object to her refusal to allow further change in the church; Parliament might regret her failure to marry and object to her grants of monopolies to her friends; ordinary subjects might suffer under an unprecedented burden of taxation. But through it all the queen almost magically retained the love of her people.

The Early Seventeenth Century. Since Elizabeth left no direct heirs, the Tudor dynasty came to an end with her death in 1603. She was followed by James VI of Scotland, the son of Mary, queen of Scots, and Lord Darnley, grandson of Henry VII, from whom he inherited English royal blood going back to the marriage between Margaret Tudor and James IV.

A learned man himself, James wrote two treatises on political theory (*The Trew Law of Free Monarchies* and *Basilikon doron* [Royal gift]) and loved delivering lectures on history and politics. His court was a less happy place than Elizabeth's, for James suffered from financial difficulties, and his royal favorites were unpopular with political leaders.

As he rode from Edinburgh to London in 1603, James was met by a group of Puritans who gave him the Millenary Petition, a request for changes in the church supposedly signed by a thousand subjects. Among the reforms they demanded were simplified services, less elaborate church music, simpler vestments, more preaching, and an end to the use of wedding rings, which were believed to be popish because Catholics wore them. Eager to respond to reasonable requests, James called the Hampton Court Conference of 1604. Here Puritan leaders met with the king and some of the officers of the state church. The prospect of cooperation and compromise was dashed when the Puritans demanded the abolition of bishops, whom they regarded as popish innovations in the church, conservatives who blocked every attempt at reform. James, who felt that the episcopal hierarchy was a necessary complement to monarchy, then adjourned the conference. Its only lasting result was the so-called King James Bible, a new translation prepared by both Anglican and Puritan scholars and published in 1611. James himself had little to do with it, but the elegance of its prose style caused this "Authorized Version" to be used and loved for centuries.

James's personal motto was one of the Beatitudes, "Blessed are the peacemakers": he promptly pardoned Tyrone and made peace with Spain. A Spanish marriage was proposed for his son Charles, and when negotiations seemed endless Charles himself went to Spain to woo the Infanta. But she proved unwilling to marry anyone who was not a Catholic; Charles returned insulted and alienated and eventually married a French princess, Henrietta Maria, sister of Louis XIII. The marriage between James's daughter Elizabeth and Frederick, the elector Palatine, had unfortunate repercussions when Frederick's attempt to assume the Bohemian throne led to the outbreak of the bloody Thirty Years' War (1618–1648). Partly because he realized that England lacked the financial resources required for intervention, James attempted to remain outside the conflict, but many of his subjects believed that aid to the continental Protestants was a religious necessity, and England was dragged into unsuccessful naval campaigns against Spain and France.

A Royal Hunt. A courtier presents a slain deer to Queen Elizabeth. From George Turberville, *Noble Art of Venerie or Hunting.* BY PERMISSION OF THE FOLGER SHAKESPEARE LIBRARY

Throughout the early Stuart age classical learning continued to dominate education and literature. Court masques, some of them written by Ben Jonson, were based on classical mythology. They often involved elaborate scenery and costumes as well as music. Prominent courtiers and members of the royal family often played roles in them. An important revolution in architecture was manifest in the work of Inigo Jones. Originally employed as a designer of costumes and stage sets, Jones was later commissioned by James to erect a new Banqueting House in Whitehall and by his wife, Anne of Denmark, to build the Queen's House on the royal estate at Greenwich. These two buildings introduced the pure classicism of Vitruvius and Palladio into England. They inspired much later architecture and provided the basis from which Sir Christopher Wren developed his baroque style later in the century.

Renaissance ideas were thus still dominant at the time of James's death in 1625. The reign of his son Charles I was to see the country drawn into a civil war; the king's execution in 1649 was followed by a Puritan Interregnum in which such classical visions declined in importance.

Economic and Social History. The population of England grew rapidly during the sixteenth century after having remained stable throughout the later Middle Ages. Standing at about 2.75 million in 1540, it had reached about 4.1 million by the time of Elizabeth's death. Such an increase naturally put pressure on the realm's resources. Economic troubles were often blamed on the enclosure movement, in which open fields that had been planted with grain were replaced by fenced pastures for sheep. Landlords found enclosure profitable, for wool was England's chief export commodity, but the peasant farmers who had tilled the soil were often turned out of their homes and left unemployed. Many migrated to cities, but without special skills they found no jobs and sometimes resorted to robbery or begging. Their displacement was the occasion for Sir Thomas More's famous lament, in his *Utopia,* that "sheep do eat up men": there was ample food for the animals but not for the humans. The government attempted to deal with these social problems by issuing proclamations prohibiting enclosure (which were generally disregarded by the landlords) and by enacting a series of poor laws. The earliest, passed in 1536, unrealistically ordered beggars to be whipped until they found work; those who were old or infirm might receive relief, but only in the parish where they had been born. Revisions passed late in Elizabeth's reign were more compassionate and formed the basis for poor relief until the nineteenth century. Private philanthropy also provided a number of almshouses as refuges for the impoverished and infirm.

Economic distress was made worse by the debasement of the coinage, a scheme under which Henry VIII and Edward VI met their expenses by issuing coins that contained a larger percentage of base metals than was allowed in their fine silver and gold predecessors. Merchants soon realized that the coins were worth less, so they began demanding more of them in exchange for commodities. The obvious result was inflation. Prices, like the population, had generally been stable during the later Middle Ages. Inflation began to be felt toward the end of Henry VIII's reign. At the time of his death the price level was twice what it had been at his accession. In Elizabeth's great recoinage of 1560, all the debased coins were called in and replaced by newly minted ones of high quality, but prices continued to rise. They doubled again in the second half of the sixteenth century, reaching exceptional peaks in the 1590s, a decade of bad weather and poor harvests. Crime, disorder, and corruption grew during the "nasty nineties," in part because of this economic distress.

Exploration and Discovery. The growth of English sea power, which eventually gave rise to the British Empire, took place during the years when the influence of the Renaissance was at its height. Exploration and discovery began with John Cabot's voyage from Bristol to Nova Scotia in 1497. His son Sebastian sailed for both England and Spain. Still more famous are the exploits of the Elizabethan mariners John Hawkins and Sir Francis Drake. Hawkins opened up English trade with the Caribbean; Drake circumnavigated the globe between 1577 and 1580. More's *Utopia* (published in 1516) represents a humanist's attempt to imagine what a newly discovered state might be like, while the records of voyages compiled by Richard Hakluyt during Elizabeth's reign provide detailed documentation of the activities of the English sailors.

There were attempts at colonizing Virginia during Elizabeth's reign—the territory was named in her honor—but the settlement at Roanoke failed and finally disappeared. The first successful English colony in North America was Jamestown, planted in 1607. Anglican settlers were drawn to surrounding areas in Virginia, while a number of Puritans came to seek religious freedom in New England.

Conclusion. If one accepts Jakob Burckhardt's view that "the discovery of the world and of man" was an important aspect of the Renaissance, the relationship between Renaissance ideals and English expansion is close. Even more significant is the adoption of classical education emphasizing the study of Latin and Greek, the widespread desire to read the writings of classical antiquity, and the urge to emulate the great deeds of the ancient Greeks and Romans. Medical practice came to be based on the classical theory of the humors and complexions borrowed from Galen and introduced to England by Thomas Linacre, the founder and first president of the Royal College of Physicians. Classical ideals, including these medical theories, were popularized by the publications of Sir Thomas Elyot and Roger Ascham. The drama and poetry of Shakespeare, Sidney, Marlowe, and Milton depends heavily on ancient history and mythology and is full of classical allusion. Even architecture came to adopt the styles of antiquity. If the English state did not become a new Athens or Rome, it was not for want of trying.

In short, the England of Henry VIII, Elizabeth, and James I was also the England of the Renaissance.

See also **Armada, Spanish; Field of Cloth of Gold; Grand Tour; Puritanism; Stuart Dynasty; Tudor**

Dynasty; *and biographies of figures mentioned in this entry.*

BIBLIOGRAPHY

Coward, Barry. *The Stuart Age.* 2d ed. London, 1994. One of the best textbooks for the seventeenth century.

Dickens, A. G. *The English Reformation.* 2d ed. London, 1989. The classic account of the Reformation.

Elton, G. R. *England under the Tudors.* 3d ed. London, 1991. Written by the greatest Tudor scholar of the twentieth century, this remained the standard textbook for many years.

Guy, John. *Tudor England.* Oxford and New York, 1988. Now the best Tudor text.

Hale, J. R. *England and the Italian Renaissance.* London, 1954. An interesting account of Renaissance influences in England.

Neale, J. E. *Queen Elizabeth.* London, 1934. Despite its age, still the classic life of Elizabeth.

Scarisbrick, J. J. *Henry VIII.* Berkeley, Calif., 1968. The leading biography of Henry.

Willson, David Harris. *King James VI and I.* London, 1956. The standard life, harder on James than more recent works.

Youings, Joyce. *Sixteenth-Century England.* Harmondsworth, U.K., 1984. The most useful social history of the Tudor period.

STANFORD E. LEHMBERG

ENGLISH LITERATURE AND LANGUAGE.

By the end of the fifteenth century there was a written standard variety of English based on the administrative English of Chancery, which influenced the linguistic practices of London merchants and printers. However, there was no spoken standard dialect, giving William Caxton, England's first printer, occasion to marvel about the diversity of English speech. Despite the existence of a nascent literary standard, and despite a growing market for books in English due to the spread of printing and the emergence of a reading public largely educated in English, the principal language of traditional scholarship and of the new science at the end of the fifteenth century remained Latin.

Latin and English.

Latin's importance in England through the sixteenth century diminished while that of the English language increased. A number of factors contributed to these changes. The religious controversies of the Reformation foregrounded the importance and prestige of the vernacular. William Tyndale's English translation of the New Testament (1525) paved the way for the central role of the English Great Bible (1539) and the English Book of Common Prayer (1549) in the service of Henry VIII's new church of England, thus breaking the connection between church and Latin. The English language became a likely symbol of nationhood as well as of the national church, but the language needed to be perfected first.

Teachers, writers, and rhetoricians worried about the low prestige of English as compared with other European languages. They debated its merits as a medium of literary expression, its appropriateness for scholarship and for the faithful translation of classical works, the adequacy of its vocabulary for different purposes, and methods of improving and expanding it.

The Inkhorn Controversy.

The label "inkhorn" captures the tenor of the clash of attitudes regarding the capacity of English for eloquence and stylistic variety. Thomas Wilson, author of *The Arte of Rhetorique* (1553), recommended the cultivation of a plain oratory style by avoiding inkhorn terms (literary, pedantic, or bookish words) and speaking in an ordinary manner, and he attacked as obscure the use of learned coinages from Latin. George Pettie contended that borrowing from Latin was not only "the ready way to inrich our tongue, and make it copious," but unavoidable: "How we should speake any thing without blacking our mouthes with inke?" (Preface to *The Ciuile Conversation of M. Steeuen Guazzo,* 1581).

Over the course of the century, advocates of borrowing words from Greek and Latin attacked those who favored reliance on existing and historical native resources for building the eloquence of English. The former argued that loans from Latin, French, and Italian—neologisms—were necessary to augment the language. Middle English had absorbed a large influx of loanwords from French and Latin, so the practice itself was not new; what was new was the introduction of learned loanwords by translators or popularizers. The diplomat and scholar Sir Thomas Elyot was responsible for many Latin and Greek borrowings, such as "education," "encyclopedia," "metamorphosis," and "modesty," which are not attested before their appearance in his *Boke Named the Governour* (1531). Although the stated reason for borrowing from foreign word stocks was that they provided readily adaptable source terms, the persuasive argument was that the native word stock did not have sufficient resources to make the language eloquent. George Puttenham opined that native English substitutes for words, such as "enter into with violence" for the French "*broach*" or Latin "*penetrate,*" did not sound as good as the Latinate words (*The Arte of English Poesie,* 1589).

On the other side, purists advocated the use of existing English words to build the vocabulary, by compounding, affixation, or changing their meaning. They invoked ideas of linguistic purity and naturalness. The most prominent purist of the age, the Greek scholar Sir John Cheke, argued that English should be written "clean and pure, vnmixt and vnmangeled with borowing" (*Letter to Sir John Holby,* 1557). In his translation of Saint Matthew's Gospel he put his ideal into practice by substituting English words for classical terms, for example, "washing" for "baptism," "crossed" for "crucified," and "gainrising" for "resurrection." Both neologists and purists appealed to issues of style and eloquence. Other exponents of Englishness such as Edmund Spenser advocated the renovation of archaisms and dialect words to create a truly English diction. The debates continued into the seventeenth century before they were replaced by demands for the regulation of a now unruly language and for dictionaries of difficult words.

Structural Change. The greatest expansion of the English vocabulary occurred between 1580 and 1600. Despite the prominence given to linguistic borrowing, most of the innovation was created by affixation, compounding, and word-class shift. Spelling and orthography were scrutinized by reformers such as John Hart, who proposed radical changes in the spelling system, and traditionalists such as Richard Mulcaster, who opposed such meddling. The grammar of English, which underwent considerable change in the period, was not the object of such conscious attention. The standard third-person singular present tense inflection "-th" was joined by the northern, colloquial inflection "-es," which occurred occasionally in informal documents such as private letters and in poetry in the early part of the period, for the purposes of rhyme and rhythm. The use of the "dummy" auxiliary verb "do" was increasingly normal in negative and interrogative sentences: "How do'st thou feele thy selfe now?" versus "Why lookes your Grace so heavily to day?"; "He sends you not to murther me for this" versus "beleeve him not" (Shakespeare, *Richard III,* 1592–1593). The second-person plural pronoun "you" was a polite form for addressing an individual—by inferiors to superiors as well as a neutral form of address between social equals. By contrast, "thou" was ordinarily used for addressing a social inferior, but it could also be used in situations in which "you" would be normal, to express intimacy or affection on the one hand or anger or contempt on the other.

Shakespeare and his contemporaries encoded such emotional variety in their manipulation of the second-person plural in their dramatic writing. In *Twelfth Night* (1601–1602), Sir Toby Belch advises Sir Andrew Aguecheek to use the insulting *thou:* "If thou thou'st him some thrice, it shall not be amisse." By contrast, the old singular-plural contrast encoded in the opposition of *thou-you* was strictly observed in the Bible and in liturgy, possibly because the practice of Bible translation did not draw upon secular, colloquial, or literary linguistic practices.

The sixteenth century was also a period of stylistic experimentation. John Lyly's two-part didactic romance *Euphues* (1579–1580) deployed a style based on patterns of Latin rhetoric, with balanced or parallel clauses of moderate length. Spenser used English archaisms and dialect forms to juxtapose elaborate and vernacular language. The period saw the development of a multilayered vocabulary, with native English considered "low" by comparison with Latinate language. Finally, a standard or prestige variety of spoken English was recognized as "the vsuall speach of the Court, and that of London and the shires lying about London within lx. myles, and not much aboue" (Puttenham, p. 123).

See also **Biography and Autobiography; Drama, English; Fiction; Literacy; Pastoral; Poetry, English; Prose, Elizabethan; Satire.**

BIBLIOGRAPHY

Primary Works

Puttenham, George. *The Arte of English Poesie.* Edited by Gladys Doidge Willcock and Alice Walker. Cambridge, U.K., 1936. Originally published in 1589.

Wilson, Thomas. *The Arte of Rhetorique.* Edited by Thomas J. Derrick. New York, 1982. Originally published in 1553.

Secondary Works

Barber, Charles. *Early Modern English.* London, 1976. Classic, comprehensive history of literary and nonliterary varieties of the English language from 1500 to 1700.

Görlach, Manfred. *Introduction to Early Modern English.* Cambridge, U.K., 1991. Compendium of sources and descriptions of the English language from 1500 to 1700. Useful collection of excerpts from primary texts of the period.

Knowles, Gerry. *A Cultural History of the English Language.* London, 1997. An accessible social and cultural history of the English language, its structure and use.

SUSAN M. FITZMAURICE

ENGRAVING. *See* **Printmaking.**

EPERNON, JEAN-LOUIS DE NOGARET, DUC D' (1554–1642), "archi-mignon," or favorite, at the French court of Henry III, soldier and aristocrat at the courts of Henry IV and Louis XIII. Epernon was born at Caumont (Gers) into a modest Gascon noble family whose origins lay in the urban notability of Toulouse. With his elder brother Bernard, he studied at the Collège de Navarre in Paris as a student (1567–1570) before each sought his fortune as a Gascon cadet in the French civil wars. He looked for aristocratic protection, first in the household of Henry of Navarre (1574–1575) then from the king's brother François d'Alençon, duc d'Anjou (1576–1577). It was only following the Peace of Bergerac (1577) that he entered the king's household. Given important opportunities for service, Epernon was rewarded lavishly with governorships in the strategically vital fortresses and provinces of France—La Fère (1580), the Boulonnais (1583), Metz (1583), Provence (1585), and others. He was made captain-general of the French infantry (1580), first gentleman of the chamber (1582), and duke of Epernon (1582). Epernon's influence and wealth grew spectacularly and, with the death of the duke of Joyeuse in 1587, he accumulated his rival's spoils of power as well. Political cunning and stubbornness, coupled with military experience and accumulated wealth, ensured that he was not eclipsed after the death of Henry III. He remained a considerable force to be reckoned with at the court of the early Bourbon and retained regional influence in the southwest of France, partly through his marriage to the wealthy heiress Marguerite de Foix-Candale in 1587. Subsequently, he rebuilt the château of his birthplace at Cadillac into the lavish palace where he was eventually buried. Reliably Catholic in religion, his culture was martial and conventionally aristocratic.

See also **Joyeuse, Anne de.**

BIBLIOGRAPHY

Mouton, Léo. *Un demi-roi, le duc d'Epernon.* Paris, 1922.
Mouton, Léo. *Le duc et le roi. D'Epernon, Henri IV–Louis XIII.* Paris, 1924.

MARK GREENGRASS

EPIC. During the Renaissance, narrative poetry underwent significant transformations. Renewed esteem for classical epics as models for imitation initially promoted such changes. Subsequent theories of genre, inspired by mid-sixteenth-century discussions of Aristotle's *Poetics,* helped to codify this literary form, which is more precisely termed epic romance or romantic epic in a number of its most estimable versions, for example, *Orlando furioso* (Maddened Roland; 1532) and *The Faerie Queene* (1590; 1596). Full-fledged epic performances, such as Torquato Tasso's *Gerusalemme liberata* (Jerusalem delivered; 1580) and John Milton's *Paradise Lost* (1667; 1674), occur only late in the development of Renaissance culture; both stand on the verge of neo-classicism. These four works, however, best exemplify early modern narrative poems that warrant the label "Renaissance epic." They skillfully integrate classical and medieval traditions into vast, harmonious narratives that address major concerns in the cultures in which they participate.

Boiardo and Ariosto. In Italy, Matteo Maria Boiardo's (1441–1494) *Orlando innamorato* (Roland in love; 1483) represents the first stage of this process. It merges epic matter from French *chanson de geste*—the epic poems of eleventh- to thirteenth-century France—with the Arthurian lore of chivalric romance. Boiardo himself received a humanistic education at the famous school of Guarino Guarini in Ferrara. He wrote Latin love elegies and translated Greek classics. Such hallmarks of medieval romance as magic and wonder, erotic themes, and episodic structure characterize his narrative poem, but it also contains discernible affinities to Herodotus and Virgil that foreshadow the classicism of later Renaissance epic. In a spirit of playful detachment, Boiardo employs the romance convention of relying upon an authoritative source in retelling a tale. The discovery of Turpin's secret history of Orlando's love life serves as a premise that facilitates the interweaving of both martial and erotic themes in *Orlando innamorato.*

Ludovico Ariosto (1474–1533) composed *Orlando furioso* (1532, first complete publication) as a sequel to his Ferrarese compatriot's immense yet unfinished romance, *Orlando innamorato. Furioso* is saturated with classical echoes and imitations that broadcast its endorsement of the values of high Renaissance court culture in Italy. Moreover, it regularly satirizes the episodic structure of medieval romance by suddenly interrupting its story line and thus conspicuously confounding expectations of narrative continuity. However, Ariosto also demonstrates his regard for romance traditions by artfully merging them with classical imitations. For example, his reprise of Mercury's embassy to Aeneas in Carthage employs a magician in the heavenly messenger's role. Thus, Melissa's rescue of Ruggiero from Alcina's garden manages to echo classical epic by means of a figure from medieval romance. Ariosto's harmonization of diverse cultural legacies here entails no sharp conflict of values between rival traditions. Rather, it epitomizes a balanced assimilation of the two major legacies that he has inherited. Often he demonstrates a comparable parity in his imitation of classical precursors. Ovidian multiplicity of tales and erotic comedies of errors coexist with Virgilian gravitas when treating military and dynastic themes.

Analyses of Epic. Ariosto published the third and final edition of *Orlando furioso* in 1532 and died the following year. The extraordinary popularity of this poem inspired widespread emulation, but not until Torquato Tasso completed *Gerusalemme liberata* in the mid-1570s did European literature possess a narrative poem that truly rivaled Ariosto's accomplishment. Indeed, that rivalry became the topic of extensive theoretical debate over the nature of epic poetry in a spate of treatises that anatomized the constituent features and definitive examples of the genre. This sometimes contentious theorizing construed Ariosto and Tasso as exemplary alternatives, if not mighty opposites, in the practice of narrative poetry. However, such treatises derived ultimately from the "rediscovery" of Aristotle's *Poetics* and its increasingly wide circulation in the middle of the sixteenth century. Aristotle's brief manual, perhaps conveniently, contained rather limited consideration of narrative poetry and thus provided an opportunity to speculate with great freedom upon the genre that, thanks in good part to Ariosto, had captured the attention of Renaissance literati.

No narrative poet of consequence during the mid-sixteenth century escaped the influence of neo-Aristotelian reflections upon his art. Giangiorgio Trissino (1478–1550) wrote an epic in unrhymed hendecasyllables (thus setting a noteworthy precedent for Milton in *Paradise Lost*), *Italia liberata dai Goti* (Italy liberated from the Goths, 1547), whose subject was the expulsion of the Goths from Italy in the sixth century by Justinian and Belisarius. But he also paraphrased and expanded Aristotle's *Poetics* in the posthumously published fifth and sixth divisions of his own *Poetica* (1529; 1563). Giovanni Battista Pigna and Giombattista Giraldi (Cinzio) (1504–1573) wrote anti-Aristotelian treatises in defense of Ariostan romance—and, it should also be noted, of themselves, since they both also composed narrative romance. Bernardo Tasso (1493–1569), Torquato's father, revised his Ariostan romance, *L'Amadigi di Gaula* (1560), to make it better conform to neo-Aristotelian strictures.

Tasso. Torquato Tasso participated fully in this culture where theoretical reflection and poetic practice went hand in hand. Between the publication of his romance, *Rinaldo* (1562), and the completion of his epic, *Gerusalemme liberata,* in the mid-1570s, he wrote his *Discorsi dell'arte poetica* (Discourses on the art of poetry). Its central section offers a compelling synthesis of Ariostan variety and neo-Aristotelian unity of plot that persuasively rationalizes the narrative practices he brought to bear in *Gerusalemme liberata*. In England almost a century later John Milton credits neo-Aristotelian theorists of the mid-sixteenth century like Tasso with teaching "what the laws are of a true epic poem."

Tasso pointedly asserts the identity of epic and romance under the rubric of heroic poetry. This label sticks, as we can see, for example, in Sir Philip Sidney's (1554–1586) conferring upon it the distinction of being the supreme genre. "But if anything be already said in defence of sweet poetry," Sidney opines midway through *The Defence of Poesy* (1595), "all concurreth to the maintaining the heroical, which is not only a kind, but the best and most accomplished kind of poetry." Sidney's apologia concentrates upon the exceptional utility of heroic poetry as an instrument of moral education, and Tasso has recourse to the same claim in the allegory (first published 1582) he writes for *Gerusalemme liberata*. Likewise, Edmund Spenser will follow both Tasso's and Sidney's lead in the "Letter to Ralegh," which he appended to the first edition of *The Faerie Queene* (1590). However, the central aim of Tasso's neo-Aristotelian poetics is to integrate the legacies of both Ariostan romance and classical epic despite their formal and thematic differences. The challenge continues through the emergence of the novel, as the debates over literary theory between the Canon of Toledo and Don Quixote in Cervantes's great fiction decisively attest. Tasso did successfully integrate the two, though in an atmosphere of increasingly contentious critique, and thus set a daunting standard by which subsequent poets measured their efforts.

In *Gerusalemme liberata* Tasso "disciplines" romance by containing the extravagant adventures and fetching females typical of such poems within the unifying structure of a clearly determined plot. The geography of Tasso's epic itself exemplifies the boundaries of plot that continually reconfine wanderers within their borders. Even Rinaldo, who journeys beyond the pillars of Hercules to Armida's magic isle, is retrieved by a team of rescuers. He returns to the main theater of battle in Jerusalem, where the vast majority of the poem's action is either situated or recounted. Armida's beauty and magic, Clorinda's strange origins and remarkable career, and the pathos of Erminia's unrequited love (before and after her pastoral excursion) all ultimately play themselves out in this central locale. Moreover, these intriguing women further epitomize the vivid passions and exoticism of romance that Tasso retains within the providential framework of his epic.

Spenser. Although he was almost Tasso's exact contemporary, Edmund Spenser notably harked back to *Orlando furioso* as one of the two—the *Aeneid* is the second—dominant models for his epic romance. Indeed, John Harington (1561–1612) undertook his translation of Ariosto's poem as Spenser was composing *The Faerie Queene*. Harington's "Englishing" of the *Furioso* appeared within less than a year of the first edition of *The Faerie Queene*, and its elaborate apparatus reveals the remarkable process of reception by which Ariosto's poem was recast to accommodate changing criteria of literary value in the late 1500s.

From Virgil, Spenser derives the ideal of the poet as a national, if not an imperial, spokesman, and this initially defines his encomiastic attitude toward Elizabeth's reign. From Ariosto, however, he derives the interweaving of episodes and the erotic motives especially apparent in book 3; "many other adventures are intermeddled," Spenser remarks in the "Letter to Ralegh," "but rather as accidents than intendments." Still, Tasso's influence upon *The Faerie Queene* is also unmistakable, though it is confined to episodes such as the Bower of Bliss, whose destruction brings book 2 emphatically to a halt. The "Letter to Ralegh" has affinities both to Tasso's allegory of *Gerusalemme liberata* and to his concern with narrative structure: "a Poet thrusteth into the middest, even where it most concerneth him, and there recoursing to the thinges forpaste, and divining of things to come, maketh a pleasing Analysis of all." The second installment of *The Faerie Queene* (1596), on the other hand, bears virtually no traces of Tasso except for a reprise of the anticourt lament from the old shepherd during Erminia's pastoral retreat, a moment that indicates not only Spenser's astute deployment, on behalf of his own distress, of Tasso's reputation as a disgruntled courtier, but also his awareness of how Tasso's justification and exemplification of variety within a heroic poem had legitimated such practices. The sustained pastoralism of book 6 of *The Faerie Queene* epitomizes this daring inclusiveness. The notion of epic as a virtual encyclopedia of literary forms thus gains significant confirmation. John Milton implements this comprehensive agenda unforgettably in *Paradise Lost,* the grand finale of the genre's career in the Renaissance.

Milton. Because Milton's biblical epic fully imbibes the spirit of the Reformation, it also contains currents of thought contrary to such Renaissance notions as the dignity of man. Milton's theme of the Fall of man, although set in direct relation to human-kind's creation in the image of God, undercuts the optimism characteristic of early humanism's perspective upon our potential. More importantly, Milton's biblicism comes into conflict with his conscious imitation of classical epic, whose polytheism he refused to ignore or allegorize away. The proems that begin books 3, 7, and 9 were censured as "extrinsic" by Dr. Johnson, though, relenting, he queried, "Who would take away . . . superfluities so beautiful?" Tasso had voiced a similar criticism of Ariosto, who speaks at length in his own voice at the opening of each canto and thus falls short of the Homeric ideal of virtual anonymity that Aristotle praises. But the real crisis for Milton occurs in the proems to books 1 and 7 where he follows the classical convention of invoking the muse. Since such invocations amount to prayers, the divine addressee's identity poses a problem that Milton, as a Protestant poet, must clearly resolve. By the time he reaches the dramatic occasion of the Fall, he actually uses the proem of book 9, not as a prayer to the true divinity, but as an opportunity to expound the poetics of a new Christian heroism that transcends classical heroism and incorporates tragic experience.

Milton's reliance upon biblical authority legitimates his poetic enterprise in the same decisive way that dependence upon Holy Writ lent authority to leaders of the Reformation. Of course, scripture, in many places, is hardly perspicuous, so that the Protestant abandonment of interpretive tradition sometimes gives rise to both uncertainty and extreme subjectivity in a reader's response. Moments of this sort are discernible in *Paradise Lost,* but Milton also skillfully exploits the hazard of torturing the sacred text by making Satan the key exemplar of a self-serving exegete of God's word. Moreover, since retelling sacred stories in a classical manner is Milton's chief accomplishment as a Renaissance poet, it is noteworthy that he adopts a similar strategy in deploying narrative genres to recount biblical love. For example, he astutely exploits the tensions between epic and romance that regularly challenge narrative poets of the Renaissance by having Satan act as a romantic hero. Furthermore, he exposes the shortcomings of classical morality from a Christian perspective by assigning the attributes of pagan heroism to the fallen angels. Time and again Milton assimilates useable elements of inherited narrative forms without compromising his religious vision.

Sixteenth century Italian poets and theorists establish the clearest sense of the epic as a genre during the Renaissance, and the major English practitioners of this form, Edmund Spenser and John

Milton, composed their masterworks with conscious attention to these penninsular precursors. However, other significant accomplishments in narrative poetry deserve mention, especially because the political concerns of criticism since the 1970s have brought them into increasing prominence. Luís Vaz de Camões's (1524–1580) *Os Lusíadas* (1572) tells of Vasco da Gama's voyage around the Cape of Good Hope to India and thus makes modern history a subject for heroic poetry, which had customarily focused upon events more remote in time. Similarly, another Iberian poet, Alonso de Ercilla y Zúñiga (1533–1594), in *La Araucana* (1569–1578), chooses the Spanish conquistadors' efforts to subject the Indians of Chile as the central matter of his poem. In France, Agrippa d'Aubigné (1551–1630) in *Les Tragiques* (1616) concentrates upon religious strife between Catholics and Protestants. Such poems not only demonstrate the vitality and diversity of Renaissance work in the genre of epic; they also exemplify the more immediate engagement of imaginative writers with early-modern political developments.

See also **Aristotle and Cinquecento Poetics; Chivalry,** *subentry on* **Romance of Chivalry; Literary Theory, Renaissance; Pastoral; Poetics;** *and biographies of figures mentioned in this entry.*

BIBLIOGRAPHY

Grose, Christopher S. *Milton's Epic Process:* Paradise Lost *and Its Miltonic Background.* New Haven, Conn., 1973.

Guillory, John. *Poetic Authority: Spenser, Milton, and Literary History.* New York, 1983.

Javitch, Daniel. *Proclaiming a Classic: The Canonization of* Orlando Furioso. Princeton, N.J., 1991.

Lewalski, Barbara Kiefer. *"Paradise Lost" and the Rhetoric of Literary Forms.* Princeton, N.J., 1985.

Lewis, C. S. *Preface to* Paradise Lost. New York, 1961 (1942).

Looney, Dennis. *Compromising the Classics: Romance Epic Narrative in the Italian Renaissance.* Detroit, 1996.

Marinelli, Peter V. *Ariosto and Boiardo: The Origins of* Orlando Furioso. Columbia, Missouri, 1987.

Quint, David. *Epic and Empire: Politics and Generic Form from Virgil to Milton.* Princeton, N.J., 1993.

Rhu, Lawrence F. *The Genesis of Tasso's Narrative Theory: English Translations of the Early Poetics and a Comparative Study of Their Significance.* Detroit, 1993.

Ricks, Christopher. *Milton's Grand Style.* Oxford, 1963.

LAWRENCE F. RHU

EPICURUS AND EPICUREANISM. The Greek philosopher Epicurus (341–c. 271 B.C.) sought to answer the ethical question, What is the good life? He believed that a good life leads to a state of tranquility called *ataraxia,* attained by maximizing pleasure and minimizing pain. In order to dispel the chief causes of mental pain, fear of the gods and fear of punishment in life after death, he espoused a materialistic philosophy of nature in which all phenomena can be explained in terms of the chance collisions of atoms moving in infinite, void space. The atoms collide because their eternal downward motion is occasionally interrupted by random swerves, which also provided an explanation for human free will. Everything in the universe is composed of atoms. Epicurus considered the present world to be one in an unending series formed by such collisions. The qualities of physical objects depend on how the motions and configurations of their constituent atoms impinge on our sense organs. Epicurus relegated the gods to a beatified existence, in which they are unconcerned with human affairs, and he claimed that the human soul is material and mortal, leaving the body at the time of death, when its constituent atoms are dispersed through the universe.

Epicurean ideas were popularized in Latin in *De rerum natura* (On the nature of things), an epic poem by Lucretius (c. 99–55 B.C.), as well as in several writings by Cicero (106–43 B.C.), particularly his *Tusculanae disputations* (Tusculan disputations), *De finibus* (On the supreme good), *De natura deorum* (On the nature of the gods), *De divinatione* (On divination), and *De fato* (On fate). Seneca (c. 4 B.C.–A.D. 65) gave a sympathetic portrayal of Epicurean ethics because he considered the Epicurean combination of hedonism and asceticism compatible with the Stoic philosophy that he personally preferred. Because Epicurus was commonly misunderstood to advocate atheism and unrestrained sensuality, his philosophy had little following in the Christian Middle Ages.

Epicurean ideas, known largely through the writings of Cicero and Seneca, did not receive serious attention until the fifteenth century, when Italian humanists recovered the manuscript of Lucretius's poem. First edited by Poggio Bracciolini in 1417, *De rerum natura* finally became a permanent part of European intellectual resources when it was printed in 1473. Early interest in the recovered poem focused on Lucretius's literary style and, later, on Epicurean ethics. Further interest in Epicureanism was sparked by the recovery of *Lives of Eminent Philosophers* by Diogenes Laertius (third century A.D.), which was published by Ambrogio Traversari in 1431. This work, containing three letters and two collections of maxims by Epicurus himself, was a major source for knowledge of Epicureanism and other ancient philosophies. As a young man, Marsilio Ficino (1433–

1499) composed an appreciative commentary on *De rerum natura* but he later rejected Epicureanism. Epicureanism received serious consideration from Lorenzo Valla (1407–1457) in *De voluptate* (On pleasure), a discussion of Christian morality and Epicurean sensuality first published in 1431. Valla endorsed Epicurean hedonism as the closest of all the ancient philosophies to Christianity. Thomas More (1478–1535), like other Christian humanists, believed that the philosophies of the ancients had been superseded by Christianity, but he believed that the doctrines of antiquity could be transformed and incorporated into Christian ethics. Thus his Utopians follow the spirit of Christ's teachings even though they endorse the pleasure-seeking ethics of Epicurus.

The first serious consideration of Epicurean natural philosophy was undertaken by Pierre Gassendi (1592–1655), a French Catholic priest, who modified Epicurean physics and ethics in an attempt to render them compatible with Christian doctrine. Although Epicurean ideas were very influential in the seventeenth century, they continued to arouse suspicion about their implications for religion and morality.

BIBLIOGRAPHY

Primary Works

Diogenes Laertius. *Lives of Eminent Philosophers*. Translated by R. D. Hicks. 2 vols. Cambridge, Mass., 1980. Greek text with facing-page English translation.

Long, A. A., and D. N. Sedley. *The Hellenistic Philosophers*. 2 vols. Cambridge, U.K., 1987. Greek and Latin texts with English translation and commentary.

Lucretius Carus, Titus. *De rerum natura*. Translated by W. H. D. Rouse. Rev. ed. Cambridge, Mass., 1982. Latin text with facing-page English translation.

Secondary Works

Jones, Howard. *The Epicurean Tradition*. London and New York, 1989. Discusses the Epicurean tradition from classical times through the seventeenth century.

Osler, Margaret J., ed. *Atoms, Pneuma, and Tranquillity: Epicurean and Stoic Themes in European Thought*. Cambridge, U.K., 1991. Contains articles on Renaissance and early modern Epicureanism.

Osler, Margaret J. *Divine Will and the Mechanical Philosophy: Gassendi and Descartes on Contingency and Necessity in the Created World*. Cambridge, U.K., 1994. Full discussion of Gassendi's Epicurean project, especially in physics.

Sarasohn, Lisa T. *Gassendi's Ethics: Freedom in a Mechanistic Universe*. Ithaca, N.Y., 1996. Contains full discussion of Gassendi's Christianization of Epicurean ethics and political philosophy.

Schmitt, Charles B., et al., eds. *The Cambridge History of Renaissance Philosophy*. Cambridge, U.K., 1988. Indispensible reference work.

MARGARET J. OSLER

ERASMUS, DESIDERIUS (c. 1466–1536), humanist. Born in Rotterdam the illegitimate child of a priest, Erasmus received his education at the school of the Brethren of the Common Life at Deventer and at 's Hertogenbosch. After the death of his parents, he and his brother Pieter passed into the care of guardians, on whose advice the young men joined the Augustinian canons. In later years Erasmus complained that his guardians had exerted undue pressure. He did not renounce his vows but obtained a papal dispensation that allowed him to reside outside the monastery. In 1492 he was ordained to the priesthood, and a year later he entered the service of Hendrik van Bergen, bishop of Cambrai. In 1495 he was sent to Paris to study theology. He was lodged at the Collège de Montaigu, a hostel for poor students. It is not clear what lectures Erasmus attended during his stay in Paris, but he developed a strong distaste for the traditional scholastic method and increasingly turned to the study of classical literature. Scathing comments in letters to friends described the Paris professors as quibbling pseudotheologians and obscurantists. Finding the living conditions at the Collège de Montaigu unbearable, Erasmus struck out on his own and began to tutor the sons of wealthy families. He never obtained an academic degree at Paris, perhaps for financial reasons or because his illegitimate birth was an impediment.

The Humanist's Career. In 1499 he traveled to England in the company of one of his pupils, William Blount Lord Montjoy. During this and subsequent visits he made lifelong friends, among them Thomas More, whom he found highly congenial and whose scholarly interests he shared, and John Colet, who inspired him to pursue biblical studies. Through his friends, Erasmus was introduced to future patrons: William Warham, the archbishop of Canterbury, who conferred on him the benefice of Aldington in Kent; John Fisher, bishop of Rochester; and Cuthbert Tunstall, later to become bishop of London.

In 1506 he traveled to Italy, accompanying the sons of the royal physician Giovanni Battista Boerio. While in Turin, he obtained a doctorate in theology *per saltum,* that is, without fulfilling the usual residence requirements. The degree had little value in the eyes of theologians who had undergone the rigorous training at Paris, a fact that was repeatedly cast into his teeth. For a year he did editorial work for the printing house of Aldo Manuzio in Venice, where he enjoyed contact with fellow scholars and made use of Aldo's excellent collection of books and manuscripts. On hearing the news of Henry VIII's accession to the throne in 1509, Erasmus returned to England in the hope of patronage from a monarch his friends described as an enthusiastic champion of learning. His expectations were only modestly rewarded, however. He obtained a Lady Margaret lectureship at Cambridge and pursued his interest in biblical studies.

In 1514 he returned to the Continent, where the Burgundian chancellor, Jean Le Sauvage, procured for him a second benefice, a canonry at Courtrai. He converted both benefices into pensions, which enabled him to pursue his researches as an independent scholar. By this time he had made a name for himself through his publications, and in 1515 he was appointed councillor to Prince Charles (later Emperor Charles V). To be near the court at Brussels, he took up residence in Louvain and was co-opted into the faculty of theology at the university. It is not clear what, if any, functions this arrangement entailed. His relationship with the faculty was an uneasy one. His philological studies and their application to scriptural texts, seen as a controversial undertaking at the time, brought him in conflict with the theologians. During his years of residence at Louvain, Erasmus was frequently consulted on matters concerning the recently established Collegium Trilingue, an institution devoted to the teaching of the biblical languages. A similar institution (later to be known as the Collège Royal, or Collège de France) was planned in Paris under the patronage of the French king Francis I. Erasmus, who had been brought to the attention of the court by the humanist and antiquarian Guillaume Budé and the royal confessor Guillaume Petit, was invited to become its director. However, the political rivalry between the Habsburgs and the Valois made this an awkward proposition. Erasmus therefore declined the offer.

In the 1520s Erasmus was drawn into the Reformation debate. His position at Louvain became increasingly difficult because he was perceived as a supporter, if not the inspirational source, of the Lutherans. To escape the hostile climate, Erasmus moved to Basel, where the printer Johann Froben made a house available to him. He soon became the center of a scholarly circle including the Amerbach brothers, Johannes Oecolampadius, Ludwig Baer, Beatus Rhenanus, and Wolfgang Capito. Erasmus remained in Basel from the end of 1521 until 1529, when the city formally turned Protestant. At this point, he moved to Catholic Freiburg, where Archduke Ferdinand offered him lodgings. During the last decade of his life he became the focus of attacks from both Catholics and Protestants. Catholics questioned his orthodoxy; Protestants called him a hypocrite for his failure to support Luther. Erasmus died in Basel in 1536, on the way to his native Netherlands, where his presence had been requested by the regent Mary as a condition for continued payment of his councillor's pension.

Works. Erasmus was a scholar of unusual breadth of learning and a prolific writer. In 1523 he published a descriptive catalog of his works (revised 1530), to which he appended a plan for an edition of his collected works. He divided his writings into nine *ordines* or categories, covering respectively his pedagogical works and textbooks (1), his collection of proverbs (2), his correspondence (3), moral and devotional works (4, 5), his biblical studies (6, 7), his polemics (8), and his work on the church fathers (9). This arrangement was followed, with variations, in the posthumous *Opera omnia* published by the Froben Press in 1540 and has remained the basis of modern editions.

Pedagogical works and textbooks. Erasmus's pedagogical ideals are typical of the humanistic philosophy of education developed in fifteenth-century Italy. Most clearly formulated in his treatise *De pueris instituendis* (On the education of children; 1529), they are characterized by a strong belief in the human capacity for self-improvement. The individual, Erasmus said, was not born but made human by education. It was the solemn duty of parents to educate their children or to select a teacher who could provide the necessary moral and intellectual leadership. Erasmus abhorred physical punishment and recommended motivating learners by providing interesting material, a healthy challenge, and positive reinforcement. Curriculum and method are discussed in greater detail in three treatises: *De ratione studii* (The method of study; 1512), *Ratio verae theologiae* (The method of true theology; 1518), and *Antibarbari* (The antibarbarians; 1520), a defense of liberal studies against critics denying pagan authors a place in Christian education.

Erasmus's curricular proposals focus on language studies, the core subject of the *studia humanitatis*. He recommended beginning with classical Greek and Roman models to develop sound grammatical and stylistic principles. Although he subscribed to the traditional method of imitation, he broadened its meaning, describing it as a process of internalization and creative reshaping of the classical model. Discussing the subject in *Dialogus Ciceronianus* (The Ciceronian; 1528), he emphasized that the good writer must observe *aptum,* the classical ideal of accommodating one's speech to the time, subject, and audience. For Christian writers this meant adjusting classical idiom to reflect the spiritual community to which they belonged. Indeed, there is a Christian subtext to all of Erasmus's pronouncements on education. The overall purpose of studies was to provide a well-rounded education involving not only training of the intellect but also the development of a virtuous disposition. The ideal scholar embodied *docta pietas,* learned piety.

Erasmus began to compose texts for classroom use in Paris for the benefit of the young men he tutored. Later he revised and enlarged the material he had compiled and incorporated it in textbooks such as *De copia* (Foundations of the abundant style; 1512), a manual of composition; *De conscribendis epistolis* (On writing letters; 1522), a letter-writing manual; and *Colloquia* (The colloquies; first authorized edition, 1519), a popular collection of dialogues. Substantial additions to this last work changed its character, however, and transformed it from a schoolbook teaching basic Latin to a vehicle of social criticism and church reform. Erasmus also edited an epitome of Lorenzo Valla's *Elegances* (1529), a collection of proverbs, *Adagia* (The adages, the title of the enlarged edition based on the earlier *Collection of Adages;* 1500), *Parabolae sive similia* (Similes; 1514), and literary anecdotes, *Apophthegmata* (Apothegms; 1531). These collections were meant to give stylistic guidance to writers and provide them with commonplaces to embellish and enliven their compositions.

Correspondence. Over three thousand letters exchanged between Erasmus and his correspondents are extant today. The list of addressees reads like a "Who's Who" of the sixteenth century. Erasmus kept in contact with kings and popes, scholars and financiers, humanists and reformers. Many of the letters date from the second half of his life and were published by Erasmus himself. Between 1516 and 1519 selections of his correspondence appeared annually; thereafter new collections appeared in 1521, 1528, 1531, and 1532. They were eagerly studied by Erasmus's contemporaries not only for their content but also as models of style, as the marginal remarks of Renaissance readers indicate. Today Erasmus's correspondence constitutes a valuable source both for the biography of the humanist and for the intellectual, social, and religious history of Europe in his lifetime.

Translations and editions. When Erasmus was a young man, Greek texts and Greek teachers were rare. He himself was largely self-taught. His translation into Latin of Theodore Gaza's Greek grammar (1518) was a great service to students. His verse translations of two plays by Euripides (1506) were unprecedented. Until then this difficult task had been attempted only for individual scenes. His first translations of prose texts were in part undertaken for practice, Erasmus tells us. Among the authors whose works he translated were Isocrates's *Nicocles* (advice to a prince, which Erasmus coupled with his own *Institutio principis Christiani* [Education of a Christian prince]), selections from Plutarch's *Moralia,* and Lucian's satirical dialogues (a project he undertook jointly with Thomas More). In the context of his own career, he saw translations from classical authors as stepping stones to his magnum opus, the bilingual edition of the New Testament (for its controversial nature, see below under "Polemics").

Erasmus also produced a large number of critical editions of classical Latin authors (works by Cicero, Plautus, Pliny, Seneca, Suetonius, Terence, and others) and translations and editions of the church fathers. Among the latter the most important was his work on the edition of Jerome's *Opera omnia,* a collaborative project. Erasmus edited the volume of Jerome's letters and contributed a biography of Jerome, the first to take a historical rather than a hagiographical approach. Erasmus also contributed to an edition of Augustine's *Opera omnia* and edited or translated works of Ambrose, Basil, Cyprian, Chrysostom, Hilary, Irenaeus, and Origen. Erasmus's efforts to make the writings of the Fathers available to his contemporaries reflect the value he placed on them as witnesses to the scriptural text and as exegetes closer in time and spirit to the pristine church than the Scholastics whose method he disdained. In his prefaces to the various editions, Erasmus frequently stressed the fluidity of doctrine contained in their writings, using it as a plea for latitudinarianism and tolerance. In this sense his patristic editions may be regarded as part of a larger program to recall the church to its roots and promote a spirit of concord.

Political and social thought. Erasmus's thoughts about government are formulated in the *Education of a Christian Prince* (1516), dedicated to sixteen-year-old Prince Charles (the future Holy Roman Emperor, Charles V). He portrays the ideal ruler as the steward of God and the embodiment of divine goodness and justice. He is a father figure to his people, whose welfare must be his foremost concern. The tract belongs to the Mirror of Princes genre popular with Renaissance humanists but has a strong re-

Erasmus's *Adagia*. Title page of the 1523 edition.

ligious dimension characteristic of Erasmus's "Christian humanism." In this work, as in his *Querela pacis* (Complaint of peace; 1517) and in his exposition of the adage *Bellum dulce inexpertis* (War is sweet to the inexperienced; 1515), Erasmus promotes peace and the idea of a universal fellowship of human beings. Although Erasmus was not a pacifist in the strict sense of the word and accepted the concept of "just war," he disparages military solutions. In his exegesis of Psalm 28, subtitled *De bello Turcico* (On war against the Turks; 1530), he depicts the enemy as a scourge of God sent for the punishment of sins. He therefore calls for a reformation of morals, that is, for spiritual rather than military weapons. He furthermore proposes to settle conflicts through a mediation process. He tendered this advice also to the warring religious factions. In his exegesis of Psalm 83, subtitled *De sarcienda ecclesiae concordia* (On mending the concord of the church; 1533), he applied his political thought to the government of the church, suggesting a moratorium on the debate until a universal council could settle the differences.

Erasmus's concept of a Christian society is embodied in the later dialogues of the *Colloquies* and in the *Enchiridion militis Christiani* (Handbook of the Christian soldier; 1503), which he called a pattern of Christian life. His social thought is representative of the period. He envisages a tightly structured, patriarchal society built on Christian values. Erasmus addressed himself specifically to women in *Institutio Christiani matrimonii* (The Christian marriage; 1526), dedicated to Catherine of Aragon, and *De vidua Christiana* (Christian widowhood; 1529), dedicated to the emperor's sister Mary. Although his views on women are, on the whole, traditional, a more open-minded attitude is evident in his advocacy of education for women and in his emphasis on mutual respect and fellowship in marriage.

Devotional literature and theological works.

Erasmus has been called a "pre-reformer" or "reformer." Neither of these labels is entirely appropriate. The strict periodization and linear genealogy implied by the first term is rejected by most historians today. Nor can Erasmus be placed in the same category as Luther, Zwingli, or Calvin. He was a vocal critic of church abuses, but unlike the reformers, he did not advocate doctrinal changes or challenge the teaching authority of the church. The reform he envisaged was personal and spiritual. It meant embracing *philosophia Christi,* the philosophy of Christ exemplified in the gospels. Erasmus first outlined his religious thought in the *Handbook of the Christian Soldier*. It was Christocentric and Pauline in its emphasis on inner piety over external observance of rites. Linking the homiletic *Handbook* with the satirical *Moriae encomium* (Praise of folly; 1511, significant revisions in 1514), he noted that he was using different literary approaches but preaching the same message. The famous harangue delivered by Dame Folly lampoons human foibles in general but focuses on the self-importance and lack of spiritual values among theologians and clerics. It concludes with an exhortation to Christians to embrace what appears to be folly in the eyes of the world, that is, the simple-hearted devotion to Christ, which leads to the Kingdom of Heaven.

In 1504 Erasmus discovered a manuscript of Lorenzo Valla's notes on the New Testament. Following in the footsteps of the renowned Italian humanist, Erasmus began to collate biblical manuscripts and make notes on textual variants and errors in the translation or transcription. The result was a critical edition of the New Testament (1516), perhaps his most significant contribution to scholarship. The edition offered the Greek text (the first to become available in print) accompanied by a revised version of the Latin Vulgate. It was followed by annotations justifying the revisions and corrections. Of the prefatory essays explaining the nature of the undertaking and setting forth Erasmus's philosophy of Christ, *Paraclesis* and the *Method of True Theology* were published separately and found a wide readership. Erasmus continued his biblical studies with the *Paraphrases in Novum Testamentum (Paraphrases on the New Testament),* narrative interpretations of the biblical text, published in a series from 1522 on, and with expositions of individual psalms, published between 1515 and 1533.

Polemics. During the 1520s Erasmus came under increasing pressure to clarify his position in the confessional debate. He had given Luther limited support in the beginning, but voiced disapproval of his radical language. When he saw that the doctrinal changes advocated by Luther and other reformers would lead to a schism in the church, he distanced himself from the movement. He was reluctant, however, to enter the theological debate and would have preferred to remain on the sidelines. It was primarily to clear his name and defend himself against charges of crypto-Lutheranism that he took up his pen against the reformer in *De libero arbitrio diatribe* (Diatribe on free will; 1524). The thrust of this collation of biblical passages for and against the concept of free will was to demonstrate that, where scripture lacked clarity, the verdict must rest with the church. Luther replied sharply in *De servo arbitrio* (The bondage of the will), denying free will and insisting on the clarity of scripture. The extended polemic that followed drove a final wedge into the relationship of the two men, which had so far been one of mutual sufferance.

Many Catholic theologians regarded Erasmus's contribution to the debate as too little, too late. It did not remove all doubt about his orthodoxy. Erasmus had first raised the hackles of theologians with mordant criticism of their arrogance and obscurantism in *Praise of Folly. The Method of True Theology,* also sharply critical of the scholastic method, increased his unpopularity. It was, however, his edition of the New Testament and the accompanying annotations that involved him in a storm of doctrinal controversy. The book was greeted with enthusiasm by biblical humanists but seen as a challenge to the authority of the Bible by conservative theologians. In the sixteenth century it was widely believed that the Vulgate was the work of Jerome, commissioned by Pope Damasus and written under divine inspiration. Erasmus's introduction of stylistic changes to the text and his indication of errors and mistranslations led to charges of blasphemy. His annotations aroused suspicion as well. They were called heterodox and a source of inspiration to the reformers. Two other tracts, *De esu carnium* (On the eating of meat; 1522), which dealt with fasting and other church regulations, and *Exomologesis* (On confession; 1524), which examined the merit of secret aural confession, added to the suspicion that Erasmus was a Lutheran sympathizer.

From 1523 on, Erasmus's works were investigated by the theological faculty at Paris, whose judgment in theological matters was regarded as authoritative. Numerous passages in his works were censured. A formal condemnation was issued in 1531, calling forth a lengthy apologia on Erasmus's part. In the meantime his works had also been investigated by the Spanish Inquisition at the conference of Valladolid (1527). The Spanish court was, however, dominated by Erasmian supporters, and the investigation, stalled by the outbreak of the plague, was never resumed. Attacks by individuals, both Catholic and Protestant, dogged Erasmus until his death. His replies and justifications fill two of the ten folio volumes in the eighteenth-century edition of his *Opera omnia*.

Erasmus in Basel. Albrecht Dürer created this portrait of Erasmus in 1526, by which time he had moved to Basel. Intaglio print; 1526; 24.7 × 19 cm (10 × 7.5 in.). THE METROPOLITAN MUSEUM OF ART, FLETCHER FUND, 1919

Influence. Erasmus's principal merit as a scholar was his promotion of the philological method in biblical studies and his dissemination and popularization of pagan and Christian classics. He successfully combined Christian thought with the classical tradition to become the quintessential "Christian humanist." In his own time, even critics did not dispute that he was the reigning "prince of humanists." His admirers credited him with the single-handed revival of letters in Germany. For some years Erasmus enjoyed celebrity status. He was fawned over by correspondents and lionized by visitors who considered a journey to his home a cultural pilgrimage. Works like the *Handbook of the Christian Soldier, Praise of Folly,* and the *Colloquies* were translated into all major European languages.

Erasmus's reputation began to decline in the 1520s, however. His refusal to take sides in the Reformation debate was unpopular in an age of confessional zeal. The times were too turbulent for the voice of moderation to be heard. By the end of his life, he was attacked by reformers as a temporizer and by Catholics as a heretic. The Council of Trent, by means of the Index of Prohibited Books, banned some of his works outright and insisted that others be expurgated. This halted or sharply reduced the publication of his works in Italy, France, and Spain. Elsewhere his books, especially his manuals of instruction and his editions, remained in use. England in particular honored his memory. Katherine Parr, the widow of Henry VIII, sponsored a translation of the *Paraphrases*. Edward VI decreed that the translations should be made available in every parish church in England.

The Erasmian tradition also stayed alive in the Netherlands. At the end of the seventeenth century, Erasmus's reputation was revived by Arminians and Jansenists, who identified with his struggle against a prevailing orthodoxy. In the Enlightenment he was admired as the man who first presented a religion of reason. The twentieth century saw another resurgence of interest in Erasmus's writings, perhaps because ecumenism characterizes twentieth-century religious thought, perhaps also because two world wars made readers susceptible to Erasmus's pacifism. It is telling that an English translation of his *Complaint of Peace* by José Chapiro was presented to the United Nations in 1950.

The periodic rise and decline in Erasmus's reputation and the fate of his works reflect the prevailing intellectual climate of successive ages. The revival of interest in Erasmus's writings at the end of the seventeenth century resulted in the publication of *Opera omnia* by Jean LeClerc in 1703–1706. It remains the most complete edition of his works. Two editions in progress, which will provide a critical Latin text and the first comprehensive English translation of his works, attest to a continued interest in Erasmus. The increased accessibility of his works may remedy the fact that Erasmus has been in the twentieth century seen as a writer "plus célèbre que connu" (more celebrated than known), as Leon Halkin quipped in his introduction to *Les colloques d'Erasme*.

See also Bible, *on* Texts and Textual Criticism; Collège de France; Humanism.

BIBLIOGRAPHY

Primary Works

Erasmus, Desiderius. *Collected Works of Erasmus.* Toronto, 1974–. Modern English translation in progress.

Erasmus, Desiderius. *La correspondance d'Erasme.* Edited by Aloïs Gerlo and Paul Foriers. 12 vols. Brussels, Belgium, 1967–1984. The only complete edition of the correspondence in a modern language.

Erasmus, Desiderius. *Opera omnia Desiderii Erasmi Roterodami.* Amsterdam, 1969–. Critical Latin edition, in progress. Introductions to individual works in English, French, or German.

Erasmus, Desiderius. *Opus epistolarum Des. Erasmi Roterodami.* Edited by Percy S. Allen and H. W. Garrod. 12 vols. Oxford, 1906–1958. Standard Latin edition of correspondence.

Secondary Works

Augustijn, Cornelis. *Erasmus: His Life, Works, and Influence.* Translated by J. C. Grayson. Toronto, 1991. Focuses on Erasmus and the Reformation.

Bainton, Roland H. *Erasmus of Christendom.* New York, 1969. A classic narrative biography.

Boyle, Marjorie O'Rourke. *Erasmus on Language and Method in Theology.* Toronto, 1977.

Jardine, Lisa. *Erasmus, Man of Letters: The Construction of Charisma in Print.* Princeton, N.J., 1993. On Erasmus as publicist.

Mansfield, Bruce. *Interpretations of Erasmus, c. 1750–1920: Man on His Own.* Toronto, 1992.

Mansfield, Bruce. *Phoenix of His Age: Interpretations of Erasmus, c. 1550–1750.* Toronto, 1979.

McConica, James. *Erasmus.* Oxford, 1991. A concise intellectual biography.

Pabel, Hilmar, ed. *Erasmus' Vision of the Church.* Kirksville, Mo., 1995. Collection of essays.

Rummel, Erika. *Erasmus and His Catholic Critics.* 2 vols. Nieuwkoop, Netherlands, 1989.

Rummel, Erika. *Erasmus as a Translator of the Classics.* Toronto, 1985.

Tracy, James. *Erasmus of the Low Countries.* Berkeley, Calif., 1996. Biography, providing good political and cultural context.

Woodward, William Harrison. *Desiderius Erasmus: Concerning the Aim and Method of Education.* Cambridge, U.K., 1904. Reprint, New York, 1964. The only comprehensive study of Erasmus's philosophy of education.

ERIKA RUMMEL

ERAUSO, CATALINA DE (1592–c. 1650), Spanish soldier and adventurer. Catalina de Erauso was a Basque woman who lived most of her life dressed as a man and who became legendary when it was discovered in 1624 that this soldier with twenty years of New World service to the Spanish crown was female. Not quite a nun, the fifteen-year-old novice escaped from the convent in which her parents had placed her and began her adventurous man's life in the wide-open world of Spain's colonial American empire. A page to several masters in Spain, then a bold, brawling soldier in Peru and Chile, Erauso was sent back to Spain, in women's clothing, when her biological identity was revealed. With King Philip IV's life pension for her military service and Pope Urban VIII's dispensation to continue cross-dressing, she returned to Mexico in 1629, living out her days as a muleteer named Antonio de Erauso.

No original manuscript exists of *Historia de la monja alférez* (Story of the nun ensign), first published in 1829 and purported to be the autobiography she dictated or wrote in the 1620s. Archival documents attest to the existence and cross-dressed soldiering of Catalina de Erauso, but scholars disagree about the autobiography's author. Generally, the core of the story is believed to be hers, but elaborated on, and thus fictionalized, by later writers using literary models from the Spanish Renaissance like the picaresque novel, epic chronicles of discovery and conquest, fictionalized soldiers' tales, and conventions of dramas of intrigue, one of which is the 1626 play by Pérez de Montalbán, *La monja alférez*.

BIBLIOGRAPHY

Erauso, Catalina de. *Lieutenant Nun: Memoir of a Basque Transvestite in the New World.* Translated by Michele Stepto and Gabriel Stepto. Foreword by Marjorie Garber. Boston, 1996. Translation of the 1918 edition of *Historia de la Monja Alférez (Doña Catalina de Erauso) escrita por ella misma* (1624).

Erauso, Catalina de. *Vida i sucesos de la Monja Alférez. Autobiografía atribuida a Doña Catalina de Erauso.* Edited by Rima de Vallbona. Tempe, Ariz., 1992. Critical edition of the *Vida* and manuscript and published documents related to Erauso, including Fitzmaurice-Kelly's 1908 translation, *The Nun Ensign.*

CONSTANCE A. SULLIVAN

ERCILLA Y ZÚÑIGA, ALONSO (1533–1594), Spanish poet. Ercilla is the author of the most widely read epic poem of the Spanish Renaissance, *La Araucana,* published in Madrid in three parts (1569, 1578, and 1589). Born in Madrid to noble parents serving at the court of Spain's King Charles I (also Emperor Charles V), the young Ercilla grew up in the royal palace and became the future King Philip II's page at age fifteen. In this capacity, Don Alonso accompanied Philip to the Netherlands in 1548, and in 1554 followed him to England, where Philip celebrated his marriage to Mary Tudor. News of a revolt in Peru led by Francisco Hernández Girón in 1553 and 1554, and the death of Pedro de Valdivia, governor of Chile, at the hands of the indigenous Araucanians prompted Ercilla to ask permission to accompany the newly appointed viceroy, Andrés Hurtado de Mendoza, to Peru in 1555. After the pacification of the Girón rebellion, Ercilla followed Mendoza's son, Don García, to put down the Araucanian revolt in Chile.

The story of the war of Arauco, in present-day Chile, is narrated in the thirty-seven cantos of *La Araucana.* This epic partially breaks with the norms of its genre in that its pages combine history, poetry, and autobiography in a spectacularly vivid way. Provoked to duel with another soldier, the poet was jailed, then expelled from Chile by his commander, Don García, in 1558. We know that an impoverished and disillusioned Ercilla wrote to Philip II from Peru, asking for a "distribution of Indians." In 1561 Ercilla traveled to Panama to participate in the expedition against Lope de Aguirre, but arrived too late. After a long illness, the Spanish soldier-poet returned to Spain in 1563. There he married, wrote most of his *Araucana,* and engaged in small-scale business enterprises. He participated in the campaign against Portugal in 1580 and died in Madrid.

See also Epic; Spanish Literature and Language.

BIBLIOGRAPHY
Medina, José Toribio. *Vida de Ercilla.* 1916. Reprint, Mexico City, 1948.

ELIZABETH B. DAVIS

ESPIONAGE. Espionage (simply defined as the use of spies to obtain secret military or political information) has been practiced since the beginning of human history, but it took on new significance with the advent of permanent diplomacy in the Renaissance. Medieval espionage was mostly ad hoc, used in times of crisis to observe enemies, be they military, political, or personal. Ambassadors could always obtain some information, but the news they brought back was often superficial. Besides, as Bernard du Rosier wrote in 1436, the purpose of an ambassador was to serve the general welfare and promote peace, not to inquire into a state's secrets. Yet regardless of theory, everyone knew that ambassadors were often used as legalized spies, and escorts were usually assigned to keep an eye on them. In Venice members of the government were not allowed to speak privately to foreign ambassadors for fear of disclosing state secrets. Philippe de Commynes advised that ambassadors should be heard and then quickly sent home, and for each one received two should be sent out. Machiavelli's advice to Raffaello Girolami when he departed as ambassador to the emperor was less cynical: "A man who wants others to tell him what they know must tell them what he knows, because the best means for getting information is to give it" (*Chief Works, and Others,* trans. Gilbert, p. 117).

With the growth of resident embassies, ambassadors became more suspect, since their primary duty was to supply information to their governments. Although the Venetian scholar-diplomat Ermolao Barbaro reiterated in 1490 that an ambassador should not behave like a spy or pry into issues that did not officially concern him, his first duty, Barbaro affirmed, was to do and say whatever might best serve the preservation and aggrandizement of his own state. Given the intense rivalries among Italian city-states, the need for reliable information was critical, and the line between diplomacy and espionage became more ambiguous. Intelligence was gathered by whatever means possible, including bribing local officials and paying secret informers.

As the Reformation and religious wars heightened international tensions, espionage became even more vital. Bernardino de Mendoza built up a vanguard of spies while he was Spanish ambassador in Elizabethan London and expanded it after being moved to Paris. Spanish documents confirm that he had agents in key coastal towns on the Continent as well as in the English ports of Dover and Plymouth, with spies and pensioners inside the government itself. He communicated with the captive Mary, queen of Scots, through recusant Catholics, sometimes using the French ambassador as an intermediary. His most effective link to affairs in England was through several spies planted in the entourage of the pretender

Ciphers and Codes

Ciphers and codes were commonly used to provide secrecy in diplomatic correspondence. Ciphers were composed of mixed letter, number, or symbol substitutes for each plain text letter, and made unauthorized deciphering more difficult by multiplying the number of vowel substitutes, using various signs for nulls, doubles, and so on, and adding a list of code words or symbols for frequently used names and words.

With the growth of diplomacy and espionage, cryptography became essential. Although sophisticated systems of polyalphabetic substitutions (the key to modern cryptography) were developed by Leon Battista Alberti, Johannes Trithemius, Giambattista della Porta, and others, the normal secret writing used by diplomats and spies was a combination of letter substitution and a code list of name equivalents. Most Renaissance governments employed cipher secretaries; the noted lawyer and mathematician François Viète provided this service to the French king and his agents. Philip II's cipher secretary, Luis Valle de la Cerda, and Walsingham's skilled cryptanalyst, Thomas Phelippes, did the same for theirs. The following note of 15 March 1590 from Viète to Henry IV is revealing: "No doubt this [capture of a Spanish dispatch] will cause our enemies to change their ciphers. . . . They have already changed them many times, and one is amazed at their astuteness. But our cause is just and theirs is evil. Therefore, God will dispel their counsels and bless our own."

The basic structure of Bernardino de Mendoza's syllabic cipher of 1584–1586 was a substitutional alphabet of numbers, signs, and letters with suppressed frequencies of the most used letters:

A	B	C	D	E	F	G	H	I	L	M	N	O	P	Q	R	S	T	U	X	Y	Z
4	9	2	7	3	6	4	5	10	22	11	*E*	12	X	13	19	14	18	15	17	16	*Z*

Also represented is this cipher (generally by a two-digit number) were the commonly use digraphs:

BL	BR	DR	CH	CL	CR	FR	GU	PR	QU	TR
23	24	*Δ*	25	26	27	29	6+	33	20	34

In addition to these substitutions there was also a set of five signs representing the vowels once more and used as syllable endings when attached to their accompanying consonant symbols. This is the most characteristic feature of Mendoza's cipher. These syllable endings were:

A	E	I	O	U

The language itself provided the key to this interesting feature of the cipher. Most Spanish words are made up of combinations of two-letter syllables with a consonant as the first letter and a vowel as the last. This succession of consonant-vowel combinations is occasionally interrupted by the presence of an additional consonant, in which case the cryptographer merely inserts the accompanying sign for that letter and proceeds to the next syllable. Many Spanish words also end with one of the three busy consonants "n," "r," or "s," for which the cipher provided the following signs: ˏ, ʌ. Occasionally "l" or "m" stand at the end of a word, in which case they were represented by a dot (˙) above the preceding sign for an "l," and dot (.) below the preceding sign for an "m." Double letters, such as "ll," "rr," and "ss" were provided simply by placing a + over the letter to be doubled, and a null was created by inserting a small (°) above any legitimate symbol or letter, which thereby cancelled out its meaning.

Many proper nouns, titles, names of individuals, and a long list of frequently used words were ciphered by the separate use of arbitrary symbols, generally composed of short meaningless letter combinations or else two-digit numbers (sometimes underlined), which had no relation to the foregoing system. "Cardinal," for example, was ciphered 77, "kingdom" became xll, a "dispatch" was 33, and "so that" gal.

The following sentence from one of Mendoza's ciphered dispatches of 16 July 1585 will illustrate more clearly just how the cipher worked.

[ciphered text]
El dia siguiente siendo el Rey en Sanmor por haver buelto aqui
The next day at Sanmor, where the king had returned the previous night

[ciphered text]
aquella noche ha estar con la Reyna su muger tuvo consejo despues
to be with the queen his wife, he met after dinner for more than six

[ciphered text]
de comer mas de seys horas encerrado con su madre el cardinal de
hours behind closed doors in council with his mother, the cardinal of

[ciphered text]
Borbon, el duque de Lorena, el de Guissa, el de Joyossa, el de Pernon, y
Bourbon, the dukes of Lorraine, Guise, Joyeuse, and Epernon, and

[ciphered text]
Secretario Villaroe.
Secretary Villeroy.

to the Portuguese throne, Dom Antonio. One of these was a Portuguese named Antonio de Escobar, alias "Sanson"; another was the enigmatic Manuel de Andrada, alias "David," who was the most active of Mendoza's agents. Although Sanson and David had frequent contact, neither of them knew that the other was a spy for Spain. However, David was actually a double agent; he gave Mendoza the information he wanted and reported everything to Elizabeth's spymaster, Sir Francis Walsingham.

Certainly the most extensive and effective espionage network in the sixteenth century was that of Walsingham, who served as principal secretary and guardian of state secrets from 1573 to 1590. Elizabeth preferred spies to resident ambassadors, especially given the threats of Catholic infiltration, Spanish invasion, and imminent assassination. Spies were less expensive and usually provided more accurate information. With Walsingham supervising it, the Elizabethan secret service was more a personal operation than a bureaucratic system. Spies were recruited from many levels of society: disgruntled Catholics, men of any rank with a score to settle, criminal types who thrived on intrigue, and seekers of power or influence. Often they were obscure figures, but sometimes they were prominent individuals. The Italian philosopher Giordano Bruno, alias "Henry Fagot," was one such prominent figure, as were Nicolas Leclerc, seigneur de Courcelles, secretary of the French ambassador, and the talented but enigmatic author Christopher Marlowe. At its height in the 1580s, Walsingham's network included secret agents reporting from a dozen different locations in France (at least three in Paris), nine or ten in Germany, four in Italy, four in Spain, eight or more in the Low Countries, and others as far away as Constantinople. These numbers do not include the busy counterespionage agents in England such as Thomas Rogers, alias "Nicholas Berden," who were watching Catholics closely. It is safe to assume that little occurred anywhere in Europe of which Walsingham was not aware.

How was communication achieved and secrecy maintained with these ubiquitous agents? It was not, always. Spies were often discovered and caught, their messages intercepted and codes broken, and yet enough of them got through to make the effort worthwhile. Secret communications were often transported in diplomatic pouches through the regular post, which had been functioning in some countries since the middle of the previous century. When this occurred, the communications were always written in code or cipher, and sometimes partially disguised with invisible ink. Most often private couriers were employed to carry messages, while essential secrets were transmitted by more clandestine means. Sometimes these vital secrets were concealed inside the clothing of a consenting traveler; occasionally they were carried in a hidden compartment of a trunk or valise. Often, information was transmitted orally by a courier or by the agent himself. These techniques were widespread among all of the European states during the Renaissance.

See also **Diplomacy.**

BIBLIOGRAPHY

Alban, J. R., and C. T. Allmand. "Spies and Spying in the Fourteenth Century." In *War, Literature, and Politics in the Late Middle Ages*. Edited by C. T. Allmand. Liverpool, U.K., 1976. Pages 73–101. A good, documented look at fourteenth- and early fifteenth-century espionage.

Bossy, John. *Giordano Bruno and the Embassy Affair*. New Haven, Conn., 1991. A detailed and fascinating exposé of the identity of the spy Henry Fagot.

Haynes, Alan. *Invisible Power: The Elizabethan Secret Services, 1570–1603*. Stroud, N. H., 1992. The best of several surveys of Elizabethan espionage.

Kahn, David. *The Codebreakers: The Story of Secret Writing*. New York, 1967. Chapters 3 and 4 of this 1,164-page opus cover cryptography in the time of the Renaissance.

DE LAMAR JENSEN

ESTE, HOUSE OF. In 1393 Niccolò III d'Este succeeded his father, the marquis Alberto d'Este (ruled 1388–1393), inheriting Ferrara's papal vicariates and the imperial fiefs: Rovigo and the marquisates of Modena and Reggio. Ferrara and its territory had been held continuously by the Este since 1240, and as papal vicariates from 1329; the imperial fiefs had been held by them from the emperor sporadically over a century by 1393, and in unbroken succession half that time. Niccolò's charm and ebullience, with his long rule (he died in 1441), brought stability to the territory, perpetuating Este control over the region that incorporated the frontier between papal and imperial overlordship on the Italian peninsula. To the west and north about half the Este lands—which extended from the Adriatic to Liguria—were held from the emperor, the contiguous area southward was held from the pope. A potentially disastrous situation for an Este prince would arise should the emperor be at war on the peninsula against the pope, since the prince could not fight for both simultaneously; in response to this very threat Alfonso I (ruled 1505–1534) promoted the League of Cambrai (1508), with pope and emperor as allies.

Territorial Strategy. The Este, aware of strong local traditions and privileges, did not seek to

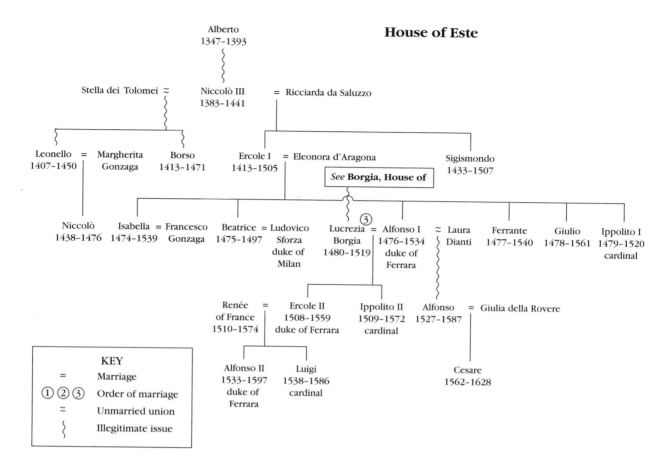

House of Este

KEY

=	Marriage
① ② ③	Order of marriage
≈	Unmarried union
⌇	Illegitimate issue

unify their state. Their predilection for the city of Ferrara meant that they resided and administered from there; lesser vicariates were controlled by Este appointees, and each imperial fief was under a resident Este-appointed governor. The pope's return to Rome from Avignon in 1378 and the end of the Great Schism with Martin V's election signaled the likely successful outcome, in the long run, of papal aims to restore the vicariates to direct papal rule. To avert this danger, the marquis Alberto in 1391 obtained investiture of the vicariates held by the Este from the pope; the pope's bull of legitimization for his bastard heir, Niccolò; and the cancellation of Este debts arising from long-standing nonpayment of the annual tax due to the pope (*censo*), any one of which was grounds for a vicar's dispossession.

According to character and opportunity Renaissance popes sought to recover the vicariates; in the case of the Este two military attempts, in the 1480s and 1510s, proved abortive, but finally in January 1598 the Este vicariates did devolve to the pope. Then Cesare d'Este (1597–1628), a cousin of the childless Alfonso II (ruled 1559–1597), chosen by the latter as his successor, was declared by the pope

to be ineligible because his father was illegitimate. Whereupon the Este moved to Modena, ruling their imperial fiefs from that city.

During the Renaissance the dynasty's apogee in terms of rank was achieved by Niccolò's son, Borso (ruled 1450–1471). In the course of the emperor Frederick III's 1452 visit to Ferrara, Borso became duke of Modena and Reggio and count of Rovigo, while in 1471 he was made duke of Ferrara by the pope; these titles were inherited by his successors. Este coats-of-arms reflected their status and were affixed prominently on their residences and on public buildings; likewise the Este devices (*imprese*), including the diamond and the unicorn, with their hidden meanings, asserted the family's unique distinction.

Given the expansionist ambitions of the major powers on the Italian peninsula in the fifteenth century and, from 1494, the peninsula's vulnerability to continental invasions, Este survival without considerable territorial loss until 1598 was remarkable. True, Niccolò III held Parma only from 1409 until 1420, and Rovigo was lost to Venice in 1484, but holdings increased when Niccolò III became lord of the Garfagnana in 1429, and when Alfonso I was enfiefed with Carpi in 1527. Este success stemmed in part from their ability to find a powerful ally in a crisis: Alfonso I had French military support against papal forces in 1510–1512. Involvement in wars was avoided when possible, but the princes were astute military commanders. Ercole I and Alfonso I for a time were *Gonfaloniere* (that is, standard-bearers) of the church, and Ercole II was appointed by Francis I as his lieutenant-general on the Italian peninsula in the Carafesca War against Philip II.

Marriage Alliances.

Matrimony was a tested means of forging state alliances, and Este princes' daughters were specifically educated for political marriage to a ruler, or potential one; for instance, the daughters of Ercole I, Isabella and Beatrice, married respectively the marquis of Mantua and the regent (shortly afterward duke) of Milan. Ercole had married Eleonora, daughter of the king of Naples, who held his kingdom from the pope, so that Ercole could anticipate his support should the pope move against Este vicariates. In 1502, faced with Cesare Borgia's military onslaught against vicars in the Romagna and the Marches in the name of Pope Alexander VI, his father, Alfonso I, reluctantly married the pope's daughter, Lucrezia. However, diplomatic marriages were not consistently satisfactory: in 1484 King Ferrante of Naples abandoned Ercole, who thereby lost Rovigo; the Borgia pope died in 1503, the year after his daughter's wedding.

Este males looked elsewhere than to marriage for sexual gratification, their power and wealth giving them ample scope. Reputedly, Niccolò III fathered some three hundred bastards. His eldest son and chosen successor, Leonello (ruled 1441–1450), was born of his most favored mistress, as was Borso, who was proclaimed ruler instead of Leonello's legitimate son, then merely twelve years old. On Borso's death government passed to Ercole I, who was Niccolò III's eldest legitimate son (aged ten at his father's death). Such inheritance strategy in the family's best interests—a minority tended to result in family feuds and citizens' revolts—became impossible as popes attained sufficient authority to impose succession according to canon law. Too many sons proved a danger to Este princes, notably because of rivalry. Shortly after Alfonso I's accession in 1505 a plot to assassinate him was led by a disgruntled younger brother and a natural half-brother.

The strong vein of piety evident in the Este princes did not deflect them from placing their surplus children in the church for a supposed vocation. From Ercole I's time the aim was to ensure that a scion of the dynasty became a cardinal who, leaving aside financial rewards, could benefit the ruler by informing him of the pope's intentions, while actively furthering family interests in Curia and conclave. Briefly in the second half of the sixteenth century there were two Este cardinals at the same time: Ippolito II and Luigi.

Este Patronage.

Particularly in the fifteenth century Este princes had sought the well-being of many influential citizens. Hence Ferrara, with its Este-sponsored university, was transformed by Ercole I into an exceptional planned Renaissance city.

Borso's library, well furnished with classical and humanistic manuscripts, was open to scholars, while another semipublic library was established in the 1460s at the Friary of San Domenico. The Este residences were richly embellished with artwork of all kinds, as were the city's numerous churches. It was largely Este commissions that encouraged a Ferrarese school of painters, notably Cosmè Tura, Francesco Cossa, and Ercole de' Roberti. Many of the works of art possessed by the Este, with their other movable property, were transferred to Modena late in 1597, leaving the associated buildings empty shells.

Este patronage was costly, and heavy taxation led to a disgruntled citizenry, but any anti-Este disturbances were harshly repressed. In the course of the Renaissance Este rule became increasingly despotic and egocentric. By Ercole II's time the court, previously associated with cultured poets like Matteo Maria Boiardo and Ludovico Ariosto, had become primarily sordid. Indeed after Borso the Este males, including the cardinals, appear essentially unattractive, often brutally cruel and vindictive, and consistently licentious.

See also **Borgia, Lucrezia; Ferrara.**

BIBLIOGRAPHY

Chiappini, Luciano. *Gli Estensi*. Milan, 1967.
Dean, Trevor. "Este." In *Die grossen Familien Italiens*. Edited by Volker Reinhardt. Stuttgart, Germany, 1992. Pages 245–258.
Dean, Trevor. *Land and Power in Late Medieval Ferrara: The Rule of the Este, 1350–1450*. Cambridge, U.K., 1988.
Gundersheimer, Werner L. *Ferrara: The Style of a Renaissance Despotism*. Princeton, N.J., 1973.
Tuohy, Thomas. *Herculean Ferrara: Ercole d'Este (1471–1505) and the Invention of a Ducal Capital*. Cambridge, U.K., 1996.

CECIL H. CLOUGH

ESTE, ISABELLA D'

(1474–1539), marchioness of Mantua, patron. An energetic and exceptionally cultivated figure of the northern courts, Isabella, the daughter of Duke Ercole I of Ferrara and Eleonora of Aragon, was raised in one of Italy's most refined centers of art and culture. She grew up surrounded by poets, painters, diplomats, and intellectuals. From Giovanni Battista Guarini and other humanist teachers she received a classical education uncommon for women of her time. On 11 February 1490 she married Francesco Gonzaga II, a soldier and marquess of Mantua (1466–1519). Her triumphal entry into his city (15 February) inaugurated the long career in which she earned fame as princess of Mantua and "first lady of the world."

She reared six children and wielded enormous influence over their careers. Her firstborn, Eleonora (1493–1550), married Francesco Maria della Rovere, duke of Urbino, and reigned with him over that neighboring court. Two other daughters, Ippolita (1502–1570) and Paola (1508–1569), entered convents. Her eldest son, Federico II (1500–1540), married Margherita Paleologo; he was named captain general of the church in 1521 and became duke of Mantua under the emperor Charles V in 1530. Her second son, Ercole (1505–1563), obtained the cardinal's hat, largely due to Isabella's persistent advocacy at the papal court. The third and youngest son, Ferrante (1507–1557), served in the imperial army and married Isabella di Capua.

Isabella was an avid reader, especially of vernacular literature; her collection of books included many romances, Greek and Latin codices, and a complete set of the Aldine editions. Her talents included dancing, singing, playing music, hunting, and riding. Her clothing designs were imitated throughout Europe, and a personal druggist concocted perfumes and cosmetics to her specifications. She loved to travel, usually without Francesco and sometimes incognito to avoid unwanted attention. Her passion for collecting made legendary the Gonzaga holdings of antiquities, tapestries, jewelry, clocks, majolica, musical instruments, medallions, and countless other valuables. With these and other objects she furnished her *camerini,* the exquisite private apartments in the Castello di San Giorgio and the Corte Vecchio where she entertained her closest friends. She was the object of portraits by Andrea Mantegna, Cosmè Tura, Leonardo da Vinci, Titian, and Giovanni Cristoforo Romano (among others) and of literary tributes by Ludovico Ariosto, Baldassare Castiglione, Pietro Bembo, and Gian Giorgio Trissino. Her art collection included additional works by the major artists of her generation, most prominently Mantegna, Lorenzo Costa, Francesco Francia, Ra-

Isabella d'Este. Portrait by Titian. Oil on canvas; 1534; 102 × 64 cm (40 × 25 in.). KUNSTHISTORISCHES MUSEUM, GEMÄLDEGALERIE, VIENNA/ERIC LESSING/ART RESOURCE

phael, Michelangelo, Dosso Dossi, Pietro Perugino, Leonardo da Vinci, Correggio, Giulio Romano, Antico, and Titian.

Often governing in Francesco's absence, Isabella earned a reputation for justice, diplomacy, tenacity, and wit in the exercise of her authority. During his Venetian imprisonment (August 1509–July 1510), she ruled independently, as she did again after his death from syphilis until Federico assumed his regency. Her energetic personal and political career is best reflected in her enormous correspondence, which archivists number around twelve thousand letters. These include intimate missives to family and close friends—many of which feature her shrewd political analysis—as well as ample records of her artistic patronage, management of Gonzaga affairs, and activities as a governor.

BIBLIOGRAPHY

Bellonci, Maria. *Private Renaissance*. New York, 1989. Epistolary novel based on Isabella d'Este's letters and on archival documents.

Brown, Clifford, and Anna Maria Lorenzoni. *Isabella d'Este and Lorenzo da Pavia: Documents for the History of Art and Culture in Renaissance Mantua*. Geneva, Switzerland, 1982.

Cartwright, Julia [Mrs. Henry Ady]. *Isabella d'Este, Marchioness of Mantua, 1474–1539: A Study of the Renaissance*. 2 vols. New York, 1903. Biography based on published sources.

Ferino Pagden, Sylvia, ed. *Isabella d'Este: Fürstin und Mäzenatin der Renaissance: "La prima donna del mondo"*. Vienna, 1994. Exhibit catalog with extensive bibliography.

Luzio, Alessandro, and Rodolfo Renier. *Mantova e Urbino: Isabella d'Este ed Elisabetta Gonzaga nelle relazioni famigliari e nelle vicende politiche*. Turin, Italy, 1893.

DEANNA SHEMEK

ESTIENNE FAMILY. The Estienne family of French printers and publishers was one of the most distinguished in Renaissance Europe, rivaling the Aldines of Venice in its contributions to humanistic scholarship, and was exceeded only by Plantin of Antwerp in the volume of its publications. The publishing house was founded by Henri I Estienne (c. 1470–1520) in Paris. He began in partnership with the German printer Wolfgang Hopyl in 1502, but within two years Estienne had gone into business for himself. By the time of his death, he had published at least 120 books, including works of theology, liturgy, and Aristotelian philosophy. Among his most famous authors were Jacques Lefèvre d'Étaples and Josse Clichtove.

Following Henri's death the publishing house passed to his widow and was managed with considerable success by her second husband, Simon de Colines. Henri I's second son, Robert I (1503–1559), at first worked for his stepfather but took over the business in 1526. He displayed impressive business, scholarly, and technical skills in building a firm that became one of the largest in Europe, publishing about five hundred titles during his tenure. Robert I is best known for his superb scholarly editions of the Bible, particularly in Greek and Latin, and also in Hebrew. His skills won him an appointment as royal printer in 1539. Royal grants also paid for the elegant Garamond types in Greek that distinguish many Estienne printings. Robert I's Bibles, however, also alarmed theologians at the Faculty of Theology at the University of Paris, who felt that some of his marginal comments were not orthodox. Such criticism provoked him to leave Paris for Geneva in 1550, smuggling most of his equipment with him. There he continued to publish Bibles and became a leading publisher of Protestant theology, notably of John Calvin's works.

Robert I was succeeded in Paris by his brother Charles (c. 1504–1564), a physician by training, who became royal printer between 1551 and 1561 and published about one hundred books. The best known is probably his collection of treatises on agriculture, the *Praedium rusticum* of 1554, better known in its translation, *L'agriculture et maison rustique de M. Charles Estienne* (1564), which was published after Charles's death by his son-in-law Jean Liébault. A third son of Henri I, François I, also published a few books in Paris (1537–1561), but almost all for his stepfather or brothers.

Robert I was succeeded in Geneva by his oldest son Henri II (1528–1598), who became one of the most distinguished scholar-publishers the world has ever known. By the terms of his father's will, he had to keep the precious equipment for publishing Greek texts in Geneva. He obtained subsidies from a variety of sources, including Ulrich Fugger, a Protestant member of the great German banking family, and King Henry III of France. His most important single publication is his five-volume *Thesaurus* of the Greek language (1572), a monumental reference work that, in updated versions, remains useful to scholars today. He never succeeded, however, in recovering all of its enormous cost. Henri also published a number of standard editions of Greek writ-

Robert Estienne. BIBLIOTHÈQUE NATIONALE, PARIS/ © COLLECTION VIOLLET

ers, including Herodotus, Thucydides, and Plato. He continued his father's involvement in Calvinist publishing, producing a number of standard works including Thédore de Bèze's version of the New Testament in several editions and George Buchanan's paraphrase of the Psalms. He also published polemical and satirical pieces of his own composition. Henri published about 170 titles in all. Robert I's third son, François II, was also a printer in Geneva from 1562 to 1582, but he was never very successful, usually working for others and producing only about seventeen books on his own.

The work of the Paris branch of the Estienne house was carried on by the second son of Robert I, Robert II (1530–1571), who succeeded his father and uncle as royal printer in 1561. His widow and her second husband, Mamert Pattisson, kept the house running until 1601; his widow alone continued operations until 1604; and his son, Robert III, ran the house from 1606 to 1631. Robert II published about 160 titles, his widow and Pattisson almost as many, and Robert III more than 90.

The Geneva branch of the house was taken over, shortly before the death of Henri II, by his son Paul (1566–1627), who published about thirty titles between 1593 and 1627. Finally, Paul's son Antoine (1592–1674), who returned to Catholicism and Paris, also became royal printer, and published about 130 titles between 1613 and 1664. For more than a century, the Estiennes played a commanding role in the European publishing business.

See also **Printing and Publishing.**

BIBLIOGRAPHY

Armstrong, Elizabeth. *Robert Estienne, Royal Printer: An Historical Study of the Elder Stephanus.* Cambridge, U.K., 1954. Expanded and rev. ed., Abingdon, U.K., 1986. An excellent study of the most prominent of the Estiennes.

Kingdon, Robert M. "The Business Activities of Printers Henri and François Estienne." In *Aspects de la propagande religieuse.* Edited by E. Droz. Geneva, Switzerland, 1957. Pages 258–275. A report of archival research on the business activities of these two family members in Geneva.

Renouard, Ant. Aug. *Annales de l'imprimerie des Estienne: Ou, histoire de la famille des Estienne et de ses éditions.* 2d ed., Paris, 1843. Reprint, New York, 1972. Still the most detailed and useful study of the entire family, including lists of their publications. These are necessarily incomplete, particularly for those in the family who as royal printers produced a significant number of government promulgations in addition to books for sale on their own account.

ROBERT M. KINGDON

ESTRÉES, GABRIELLE D'

ESTRÉES, GABRIELLE D' (c. 1573–1599), official mistress of French king Henry IV. Gabrielle was

Gabrielle d'Estrées. *Gabrielle d' Estrées in Her Bath* by an unknown French painter of the School of Fontainebleau. Oil; 115 × 103 cm (45 × 40.5 in.). MUSÉE CONDÉ, CHANTILLY/PHOTO BULLOZ

born at her family's manor in Coeuvres, Picardy. She was one of seven children of Antoine d'Estrées and Françoise Babou de la Bourdasière, both of whose families had risen to prominence in the 1500s through royal service. Of Gabrielle's many alleged lovers, only one, Roger de Saint-Lary, duke of Bellegarde, can be confirmed before she caught Henry IV's eye in November 1590.

Long estranged from his wife, Margaret of Valois, Henry IV had many mistresses over his lifetime, but the king and Gabrielle formed a relationship that deepened over the years. In 1594 she moved into the Louvre and received the unprecedented office of titular mistress of France; by 1596 she sat on the king's council, where she exercised considerable sway. She is credited with having decisively influenced Henry IV's conversion to Catholicism in 1593 and the historic accord reached with the Huguenots in the Edict of Nantes in 1598. Gabrielle also helped raise emergency funds that enabled the king to wrest Amiens from Spanish control in 1597, paving the way for peace the next year. She bore Henry IV three children, all of whom the king had legitimized by acts of the high court of Parlement. They were César, duke of Vendôme, Catherine-Henriette, and Alexandre, later grand prior of France. Against the better judgment of some of his advisers, Henry IV actively pursued the possibility of making Gabrielle his queen. However, her death in childbirth on 10 April 1599 dashed the king's hopes.

BIBLIOGRAPHY

Desclozeaux, Adrien. *Gabrielle d'Estrées, marquise de Monceaux, duchesse de Beaufort.* Paris, 1889. A dated but otherwise fine archivally based study.

Edwards, Samuel. *Lady of France: A Biography of Gabrielle d'Estrées, Mistress of Henry the Great.* London, 1964. A popular account that offers a sympathetic portrait of Gabrielle.

MICHAEL WOLFE

ETHNOGRAPHY OF THE NEW WORLD. The history of Renaissance ethnographies of the Americas centers on texts related to European travel and exploration. The Spanish voyages and conquests, in particular, provided one of the more dominant contexts in which a variety of ethnographic writings emerged. Among the principal Spanish authors of ethnographic texts were Gonzalo Fernández de Oviedo y Valdés (1478–1557), José de Acosta (1540–1600), Pedro de Cieza de León (1518–1554), Francisco López de Gómara (1511–1564), Bernal Díaz del Castillo (1492–1581), and Bartolomé de Las Casas (1474–1566). Other European writers wrote on ethnographic subjects as well.

People living during the Renaissance did not refer to the study of people and customs as ethnography or anthropology. Writings about those living in remote places appeared in a variety of contexts. Interest in issues of human culture and custom was relatively high, although there was not a community of sixteenth-century scholars who described themselves as ethnographers or anthropologists. Roughly twenty works were written in sixteenth-century Spain that may be considered "ethnographic." Books that described peoples living in remote places commonly went through numerous editions and reprints due to the high demand for such texts among the literate public. Acosta's *Historia natural y moral de Las Indias* (1590), for example, was translated into six languages and reprinted in twenty-two editions from 1590 to 1684, a simply enormous run of publication for the period. The genre of writing that outlined human customs and behavior was more generally called "moral history" or simply "history."

The question of whether one should observe people and places as a prerequisite to writing authoritatively harks back to an ancient debate between the Greek historians Herodotus and Thucydides. During the Renaissance, ethnographers resumed the debate about the proper ways to write a moral history. Early Renaissance writers wrote about others in a genre that may be called sedentary ethnography. Johann Boemus, a German Hebraist, published his *Omnium gentium mores* (The customs of all peoples; 1520) as a collection of human customs and behavior without having visited the peoples he described. Pietro Martire d'Anghiera (known also as Peter Martyr), an Italian scholar attached to the Spanish court of Ferdinand and Isabella, also employed a sedentary approach. Martire interviewed Europeans who had returned to Spain after having lived in the Americas, examined native artifacts, and inspected the captives that were brought back to Europe by ship. Observation "in the field" was generally not considered an essential part of ethnographic writing. Many Spanish authors emulated this journalistic style of ethnographic writing. López de Gómara, for example, took the travelogue of Hernán Cortes and used it as the basis for his description of the native populations of Mexico in his work *Historia general de Las Indias* (1552) without having traveled there himself.

As voyaging became a less dangerous enterprise, firsthand observation of a people became more common. Histories claiming to revise the earlier accounts of populations, places, and events emerged regularly from the printing presses at the end of the sixteenth century. Díaz del Castillo, a Spanish soldier who accompanied Cortes during his foray through Mexico, severely criticized López de Gómara in his book *Historia verdadera de la conquista de la Nueva España* (1575?) because Gómara had neither visited Mexico nor met the natives of central America. Díaz played heavily on the fact that he had been an eyewitness to the events and had personally observed the Aztec culture. Díaz's duty, as he saw it, was to rewrite the history of Cortes's "conquest" of Montezuma as well as the history of Aztec political, military, and economic organizations. Hence Díaz wrote the "truthful" history in response to the "fables" and "lies" that Gómara had spread in his book. José de Acosta criticized those who had not lived among the Indians and yet held as fact various unproved statements. The tendency to rewrite earlier sixteenth-century ethnographies also manifested itself in French ethnographies. Jean de Léry, a Calvinist missionary in Brazil, rewrote a version of André Thévet's *Les singularités de la France Antarctique* (1557), on the customs of the Tupinamba, one of the many tribes native to Brazil. One of his reasons for rewriting the ethnography was that, in Léry's opinion, Thévet's delore, which they mixed with their actual observations. A prominent theme throughout the early ethnographies was a focus on the marvelous and unusual aspects of foreign cultures. Cieza de Léon in his *La crónica del Perú* (1554) looked at the Incan culture through the framework of "strange things worthy to be known." Elsewhere José de Acosta, a Jesuit missionary and administrator, wanted to include all things "novel and strange" in his description of the Indian customs. The prose epic also was an important aspect of early ethnographies. American natives were frequently incorporated into a narrative structure that included literary elements of irony, dramatic tension, and climax. Chivalric romances, such as *Amadís de Gaula,* also had a strong influence on many of the early Spanish ethnographies. In addition, classical models provided a prototype by which to organize descriptions of the customs of other peoples. The writings of both the Roman Pliny and the Greek Herodotus provided earlier examples of ethnographic writing to which the Spanish authors frequently referred. The strange and the novel "matters of fact" were generally divided into social, economic, religious, military, and political categories. In sum, Spanish Renaissance ethnographies were an evocative blend of medieval, classical, and contemporaneous literary traditions.

See also **Americas; Travel and Travel Literature.**

BIBLIOGRAPHY

Primary Works

Acosta, José de. *The Natural and Moral History of the Indies.* Vols. 60 and 61. Issued by the Hakluyt Society. London, 1880. Translation of *La historia natural y moral de las Indias* (1608). Reprint, New York, 1970–1973.

Casas, Bartolomé de las. *La historia de las Indias* [History of the Indies]. Madrid, 1994

Cieza de León, Pedro. *The Discovery and Conquest of Peru: Chronicles of the New World Encounter.* Edited and translated by Alexandra Parma Cook and Noble David Cook. Translation of *La crónica de perú.* 1553. Durham, N.C., 1998.

Díaz del Castillo, Bernal. *The Conquest of New Spain.* Translation by J. M. Cohen of *Historia verdadera de la conquista de la Nueva España.* 1575?. Baltimore, Md., 1963.

Fernández de Oviedo y Valdés, Gonzalo. *Historia general y natural de las Indias* (The general and natural history of the Indies; 1535). Reprint, Asunción, Paraguay, 1944.

López de Gómara, Francisco. *Cortes: The Life of the Conqueror by His Secretary.* Edited and translated by Lesley B. Simpson. Berkeley, Calif., 1964. Translation of *Historia general de las Indias* (1552).

Secondary Works

Ford, Thayne R. "Stranger in a Foreign Land: José de Acosta's Scientific Realizations in Sixteenth-Century Peru." *Sixteenth century Journal* 29, no. 1 (spring 1998): 19–33.

Hodgen, Margaret T. *Early Anthropology in the Sixteenth and Seventeenth Centuries.* Philadelphia, 1964.

New World Indians. Tupi Indian "greeting of tears" from Jean de Léry's *Histoire d'un voyage fait en la terre du Bresil autrement dit Amerique,* 1578. RARE BOOK AND MANUSCRIPTS DIVISION, NEW YORK PUBLIC LIBRARY, ASTOR, LENOX AND TILDEN FOUNDATIONS

scription of the natives was full of the "most grotesque and bawdy tales." In *Histoire d'un voyage fait en la terre du Brasil* (1578) Léry attempted to set the record straight on a number of different issues related to the Tupinamba and the missionary work in Brazil. By the end of the sixteenth century a growing sentiment held that a writer had to travel to a location and observe the people in question to be considered authoritative.

Eyewitnessing, however, did not necessarily lead to the "accuracy" of an ethnographic account. Among those who had traveled to the Americas, many ethnographers had no qualms about extensively copying, or even plagiarizing, from medieval

Pagden, Anthony. *The Fall of the Natural Man: The American Indian and the Origins of Comparative Ethnology*. New York, 1982.

THAYNE R. FORD

EUCLID (fl. c. 295 B.C.), Alexandrian geometer. Euclid's work was reedited, revived, and reinvestigated throughout the Renaissance. The Euclidean corpus includes most prominently *Stoicheia* (*Elements*), as well as works on optics, music, and other mathematical subjects. This body of work served as a major resource for mathematicians, philosophers, and educators who were reformulating the role of mathematics in technology, natural philosophy, and logical reasoning. *Elements* in particular assumed enormous importance as it became available in various Latin and vernacular printed editions. The minor works of Euclid were influential for some important mathematicians. (Nicholas Copernicus, for example, refers to Euclid's *Optics* several times in marshaling evidence for his groundbreaking theory that the earth moves.) However, it was the Renaissance editions of *Elements* that most structured—and served as a stage for—new thinking on mathematics.

In the medieval tradition, most exposure to Euclid was fragmentary. Parts of Euclidean mathematics remained available throughout the Renaissance in editions of encyclopedic textbooks (editions of the works of Boethius, for example, or *De expetendis* [1501] by Giorgio Valla [1430–1500]) and in artists' handbooks. Throughout the age of printing, however, numerous scholars reexamined and taught anew the complete *Elements*. The complete thirteenth-century Arabic-Latin translation of the *Elements* by Joannes Campanus of Novara (d. 1296) was one of the first books published by the Venetian printing firm of Erhard Ratdolt (1482); it was also the first printed edition of *Elements*. The Campanus edition was challenged by the Greek-Latin translation (1505) of the humanist Bartolomeo Zamberti (b. c. 1473) and most sixteenth-century editions of *Elements* drew on these until the Greek-Latin translation of Federico Commandino (1509–1575) in 1572, which became the dominant version for the following centuries. Perhaps the greatest flowering of Renaissance learning as it took root in the Euclidean text, however, is exemplified by the 1574 *Elements* brought out by Christopher Clavius (1537–1612), the Jesuit mathematician. Clavius utilized the translations of Campanus, Zamberti, and Commandino; he added numerous problems for the new mathematical adept, composed whole treatises examining vari-

ous topics more fully than had Euclid, and added 671 of his own propositions to the 486 in the Greek text.

Renaissance editions included fifteen books in *Elements* instead of the now accepted thirteen. The teaching of the work often concentrated on the first six geometrical books, while the arithmetical books (7–10) were largely superseded by developments in algebra. The final books on solid geometry were worked over by the most advanced mathematicians of the age.

The first vernacular edition of *Elements* was published in Italian by Niccolò Tartaglia (1499–1557), a practical mathematics teacher, in 1543. (Commandino later translated his edition into Italian in order to compete with this notoriously popular version.) In the next generation, full translations also appeared in German (1558 and 1562), French (1564), and English (1570).

These vernacular editions were often aimed at artisans and practical men, but in fact the prefaces of Latin and vernacular editions alike emphasized the necessity of mathematical knowledge in both practical concerns and philosophical pursuits. It would be difficult to capture the excitement that the seemingly dull Euclidean text could engender, although some insight is afforded by a 1508 lecture printed in Luca Pacioli's edition of the *Elements* (1509). Pacioli (c. 1445–1517) spoke before a large audience whose members were among the most prominent citizens in Venice. The friar-mathematician emphasized the usefulness of Euclid in the practical concerns of navigation, architecture, and military engineering as well as the professions of medicine and law, and the philosophical pursuits of astronomy, natural philosophy, and theology. Indeed similar discussions can be found in the introductions written by Clavius (1574), Tartaglia (1556), John Dee (1570), and many others. The belief that Euclid imparted relevant knowledge both to philosophy and the mechanical arts was perhaps encouraged by the fact that the major commentaries cited by Renaissance scholars were those of the fifth-century Neoplatonic synthesizer Proclus and the more mechanically minded fourth-century geometer Pappus.

Pacioli included the text of his lecture (and a list of his attendees) directly before book 5 of the *Elements*. This book, which articulates a general theory of proportion, was among the most influential in the corpus. It served as a basis of commentary for many mathematicians, including Galileo Galilei. Proportional theory in its simplest form helped solve problems where the ratio $a:b$ is equivalent to $b:c$ and can be represented geometrically by similar triangles. One extreme term can be found given the other two; this rule was used in commercial calculation, simple scaling, and measuring problems, and for other practical concerns. But geometric and arithmetic proportionals could also be spun into advanced mathematics or could even be conceived as metaphorical—propaedeutic to notions such as a golden mean. The only other book that may have been as fruitful for Renaissance thinkers is book 10, which considers the ratios of rational and irrational numbers. In particular, Euclid here explained the method of exhaustion by which increasingly accurate approximations of the areas of curves can be made through a process of repeated inscription and superscription of polygons. This helped explain passages in Archimedes, and seemed to have led to investigation of infinitesimals, the groundwork from which calculus developed.

Philosophers too began to see Euclid as a necessary link in their understanding of both the Platonic and the Aristotelian traditions. Euclid himself had the status of an ancient philosopher, and one related to the major schools of Greek philosophy. Plato's legendary injunction "let no one untrained in geometry enter [my school]" was repeatedly recalled as a claim to the relevance of Euclid's work to the understanding of an essentially mathematically structured world. In fact, the author of *Elements* was often confused with Euclid of Megara, a disciple of Plato. This structure of the Euclidean text itself, meanwhile, paralleled aspects of the reigning Aristotelian logic in its use of deduction from axioms and postulates to more and more complicated theoretical proofs. Clavius argued for the importance of teaching Euclid as a logical tool in Jesuit schools, and the influential French educator Petrus Ramus (1515–1572) tried to capture Euclidean logic for more elementary students in his commentary *Scholae mathematicae* (1559).

The tight procedures of proof contained in Euclid's *Elements* offered certainty, and many Renaissance thinkers believed the work offered a more secure basis of knowledge than any precept, of logic, natural philosophy, or theology. Indeed, several successive professors of mathematics and astronomy at the University of Padua engaged in debate on the relative certainty of mathematics in the second half of the sixteenth century. Galileo continually appealed to geometry's sure progression from known precepts and axioms to the discovery of new theorems, as did Descartes after him. Euclid's work had not only spurred advanced mathematics and pene-

trated practical arts, philosophy, and education, but had become itself the avatar of knowledge.

See also **Aristotle and Aristotelianism; Logic; Mathematics;** *and biographies of figures mentioned in this article.*

BIBLIOGRAPHY

Primary Work

Euclid. *Elements.* Translated by Sir Henry Billingsley. 1570. With a "mathematicall praeface" by John Dee. Facsimile edition. London, 1967.

Secondary Works

Bulmer-Thomas, Ivor. "Euclid." *Dictionary of Scientific Biography.* New York, 1971. Volume 4, pages 414–437.

Homann, Frederick A. "Christopher Clavius and the Renaissance of Euclidean Geometry." *Archivum Historicum Societatis Jesu* 52 (1983): 233–246.

Mancosu, Paolo. "Aristotelian Logic and Euclidean Mathematics: Seventeenth-Century Developments of the *Questio de certitudine mathematicarum.*" *Studies in the History and Philosophy of Science* 23, no. 2 (1992): 241–265.

Murdoch, John E. "Euclid: Transmission of the Elements." *Dictionary of Scientific Biography.* New York, 1971. Volume 4, pages 437–459.

Rose, Paul Lawrence. *The Italian Renaissance of Mathematics: Studies in Humanists and Mathematicians from Petrarch to Galileo.* Geneva, 1976.

M. HENNINGER-VOSS

EUGENIUS IV (Gabriele Condulmer, Condulmaro; c. 1383–1447), pope (1431–1447). Born in Venice, the son of a merchant, Gabriele Condulmer became a cleric in 1397. The elevation of his uncle Angelo Correr as cardinal and subsequently as Pope Gregory XII (1406–1415) prompted Condulmer to seek his fortune at the papal court, where he was named bishop of Siena in 1407. Condulmer became a cardinal in 1408.

Facing the certainty of deposition by the Council of Constance (1414–1418), Gregory XII resigned his papal office in July 1415. At the same time, the status of his cardinals was recognized and they were enjoined to attend the Council of Constance, where Gabriele Condulmer, called "the Cardinal of Siena," participated in the special conclave that elected Cardinal Oddo Colonna as Pope Martin V, under whom the Latin church was reunited. The new pope named Condulmer legate for the March of Ancona in 1420–1421 and legate for Bologna in 1423–1424.

Condulmer never studied the arts, theology, or law at a university, nor did he show an interest in the new humanist learning, but he was committed to liturgical devotions and religious reading. From the beginning of his career he supported the reformed discipline and spiritual life instituted at the

Benedictine monastery of Santa Giustina in Padua, where his friend Ludovico Barbo had become abbot in 1409. Subsequently as pope, he confirmed and strengthened the papal constitution that governed the congregation of Santa Giustina. Cardinal Condulmer maintained similar relations of mutual respect and support with the Camaldolese Order and its general Ambrogio Traversari, who also served him—as did Ludovico Barbo—as envoy to the Council of Basel.

Cardinal Condulmer was elected pope at Rome on 3 March 1431, taking the name Eugenius IV. In the conclave, he had subscribed to an electoral capitulation, confirmed at his coronation, that required him to reform the church "in head and members," to hold the scheduled general council at Basel, to consult the cardinals on major matters relating to the government of the Papal States, and to create new cardinals only in accordance with the norms established at the Council of Constance. But when the Council of Basel, which had opened in July 1431, was only sparsely attended, Eugenius IV issued a bull in December 1431 that dissolved the synod. The council fathers at Basel rejected the dissolution as invalid. When the major princes, most of the prelates north of the Alps, and even the majority of his cardinals sided with the council, Eugenius IV was forced in December 1433 to revoke his bull of dissolution.

The council fathers now asserted the supreme authority of a general council in the church and established an organization by deputations and a mode of procedure that enabled them to act independently of papal direction and to publish decrees enacting reforms. In response to the persistent refusal of Eugenius IV to obey these decrees, the council initiated legal proceedings (31 July 1437) that threatened the pope with deposition. Eugenius IV countered with the bull *Doctoris gentium* (18 September 1437), in which he ordered the transfer of the synod to Ferrara for a council of reunion with the Greeks, thereby challenging the Council of Basel's invitation to the Greeks for a council of reunion (May 1437) at Basel or Avignon—but not in Italy.

In *Doctoris gentium* Eugenius IV reasserted the papacy's traditional claim to absolute monarchical authority in the church. The council fathers of Basel responded by deposing the pope from office on 25 June 1439. The outcome of the conflict was decided by the major kings and princes. It was a victory for Eugenius IV that representatives of the Greek church attended the papal countercouncil at Ferrara (1438) and Florence (1439), where the Latin church was

Pope Eugenius IV. Portrait medal.

represented primarily by prelates from northern and central Italy. In the decree *Laetentur coeli,* proclaiming on 6 July 1439 the union of the Latin and Greek churches at Florence, theological differences were deemphasized and the pope's position as supreme head of the universal church was acknowledged. In the East, the union was soon thereafter disavowed by the Greeks. *Laetentur coeli* was hailed by Eugenius IV and his supporters as an acknowledgment of his legitimacy and authority but did not convince the conciliarists.

In his struggle against the Council of Basel and its reform decrees, Eugenius IV achieved substantial but not complete success through concordats, which conceded to the major princes rights of nomination to benefices in return for an acknowledgment of papal powers of appointment and taxation. By the end of his pontificate, Eugenius IV had succeeded almost everywhere in Latin Christendom in reasserting absolute papal monarchy over the church, albeit at the price of concessions to secular princes and without having won over the clergy north of the Alps, many of whom remained supporters of conciliar authority.

As temporal ruler in Rome and the Papal States, Eugenius IV governed largely through others. His nephew Francesco Condulmer was named a cardinal (1431) and as chamberlain (1432–1440) was put at the head of the financial administration of the Roman church and the government of its temporal domains, followed in 1437 by his appointment as vice chancellor (1437–1453). In the first years of his pontificate, the Colonna family and their clients repeatedly challenged his rule and in May 1434 promoted a revolt. Disguised as a monk, Eugenius IV fled Rome, seeking refuge in Florence, and did not return until 1443. In the intervening years, the pope relied on warrior-prelates to subdue all opposition.

Of his nine years in exile from Rome Eugenius IV had spent six in Florence. However, the new humanist culture and trends in the arts appear to have been of little interest to a pope whom contemporaries praised primarily for his piety and concern for monastic reform. Meeting the challenge of the conciliar movement was the dominant feature of his pontificate.

See also **Basel, Council of; Conciliarism; Florence, Council of; Papacy.**

BIBLIOGRAPHY

Primary Works

Epistolae pontificiae ad Concilium Florentinum spectantes. Edited by George Hofmann. 3 vols. Rome, 1940–1946.

Platina (Bartolomeo Sacchi). "Liber de vita Christi ac omnium pontificum." In *Rerum italicarum scriptores = Raccolta degli storici italiani dal cinquecento al millecinquecento.* New ed. Edited by Giacinto Gaida. Città di Castello, Italy, 1913–1932. See Volume 3, part 1, pages 313–328, for the entry "Eugenius IIII."

Vespasiano da Bisticci. *The Vespasiano Memoirs: Lives of Illustrious Men of the Fifteenth Century.* Translated by William George and Emily Waters. 1963. Reprint, Toronto, 1997. See pages 17–30.

Secondary Works

Caravale, Mario, and Alberto Caracciolo. *Lo Stato pontificio da Martino V a Pio IX.* Torino, Italy, 1978.

Gill, Joseph. *Eugenius IV, Pope of Christian Union.* London, 1961. Decidedly apologetic.

Helmrath, Johannes. *Das Basler Konzil, 1431–1449: Forschungsstand und Probleme.* Köln, Germany, 1987.

Stieber, Joachim W. *Pope Eugenius IV, the Council of Basel, and the Secular and Ecclesiastical Authorities in the Empire: The Conflict over Supreme Authority and Power in the Church.* Leiden, Netherlands, 1978.

JOACHIM W. STIEBER

EUPHUISM. *See* **Lyly, John.**

EUROPE, IDEA OF. The period 1400 to 1700 saw an increasing confounding of the terms "Europe" and "Christendom" and the progressive displacement of Christendom by Europe. More narrowly in the period defined by Pope Pius II (1458–1464) and ending with Abraham Ortelius's first atlas (1570), the emotionally laden term *Christianitas* (Christendom), originally given both geographical definition and religious content by the Muslim menace, gradually yielded to the hitherto neutral, more secular term Europa, derived from classical mythology. Increasingly, nurtured by the humanists and aided by political and ecclesiastical events, Europe became endowed with geographical definition, political meaning, and cultural import.

From Christendom to Europe. Two myths, one classical the other Old Testament, served to locate Europe as the westernmost and smallest among the continents, the other two being Asia and Africa. The classical myth of the beautiful Europa, her rape and transport by Zeus westward from Phoenicia to Crete, associated Europe with Greece and its expansion throughout the Mediterranean. According to the Jewish contribution, one of the three sons of Noah, Japheth, had his progeny allocated by Josephus to Europe. These traditions of late antiquity represented Europe as the land of the Gentiles, the Greeks, and the Christians. Not only would Christians soon dwell there, but there Christendom would define itself geographically and emotionally under repeated Muslim onslaught and crusader counterassault. Yet in launching the First Crusade in 1095, Urban II used the word Europe. With the subsequent disintegration of Christendom in the later Middle Ages and the provincialization of the universal church, the growing ideological vacuum provided opportunity for the usurpation effected by the term Europe.

The decisive step that put Europe on a new trajectory of significance came with Pius II. Alert to the emerging formation of quasi-national groupings within an ailing Christendom increasingly confined to Europe and being deprived of its religious import, the pope appealed in a remarkable letter to the Ottoman sultan Muhammed II in 1461 that if he accepted baptism, Pius would offer him the adherence of all Europe, synonymous to the Christian world. Besides clearly identifying Christendom with Europe, Pius took the more decisive step of coining the adjective, creating *Europeos* (Europeans), and making the term equivalent to Christians. That a pope with a strong humanist background should so identify the Europeans gave more than casual authority and support to the emerging status of Europe as an idea. Less well recognized is the fact that Pius II introduced into the continuing policy of Renaissance popes the practice of moving at will from the role of spiritual pastor and leader of Christendom to the more expressly political role of territorial prince. Pius thus precipitated a process whereby the traditional, clearly defined religious enmity between the two religions might be displaced by the Turks inclusion in an emerging European state system.

Europe and the New Geography. Just as Christendom had earlier been religiously and locally defined by its conflict with Islam, so in the sixteenth century, as the Iberian peoples launched themselves into an age of expansion and discovery, the increasing global contacts would serve to promote the consolidation of Europe's geographical identity and cultural preeminence. At least in the writings of the geographers and cosmographers this process, only completed in the eighteenth and nineteenth centuries, would get its start. To Enea Silvio Piccolomini, before his becoming Pius II, the inhabitants of Asia were always considered inferior to the inhabitants of Europe. To Sebastian Münster in 1544, Europe, although smaller, surpassed the other continents in being more fertile, more cultivated, and more populous. The European ascendancy became visually imaged in the title pages to geography books picturing Europe as crowned, cuirassed, armed, and scientifically equipped, while the other continents appear in varying degrees of servility and undress. Ortelius's *Theatrum orbis terrarum* (Theater of the world) of 1570, the first formal atlas, conveys this invidious comparison, and in his *Thesaurus geographicus* of 1578 he equates *Christiani* and *Europaei*.

With the recovery of Strabo's *Geographia* for Latin scholarship in 1469, the new descriptive geography had its essential source for the attributes distinguishing Europe from the other continents. Strabo apparently drew upon Hippocrates, the first to articulate a climatic and environmental determinism for a people's character: In contrast to Asia, Europe's intense variety and very harshness produce opposing stimuli promotive of the warlike and the resourceful, of courage and prudence, its very variety working for its preeminent vitality, beauty, and enterprise. Although the smallest continent, Europe is totally autonomous, the most cultivated both agriculturally and politically, and the most densely populated, resourceful, and enterprising. Drawing upon the same common source, other writers conveyed this picture of Europe's distinctive superiority to the detriment of Asia, Africa, and America. Obversely, the myth of the noble savage served to further the consolidation of Europe's distinctiveness.

Machiavelli, Vives, and the Turk. Without any apparent indebtedness to Strabo and the new geographers, Machiavelli, that man best prepared to forget and forgo the term *Christianitas* and its connotations, applied the traditional notion of Europe's

Europe Personified. Engraving from Sebastian Münster's *Cosmographia,* 1527. ELSEVIER PUBLISHING PROJECTS, AMSTERDAM

internal variety and diversity to the political dimension. In scattered statements Machiavelli recognized the rich diversity of European countries. In contrast to Asiatic monarchical despotism, especially that of the Turk, exercised by a single ruler, he saw Europe as differently constituted both by the multiplicity of lands and by the diversity of their internal organization, including both monarchies and numerous republics. For the Spanish humanist J. L. Vives in 1526, this creative diversity had become dissensions; however, such dissensions now refer not to Christendom but to Europe—its peoples and its desired unity.

Conclusion. The Renaissance saw the decisive step taken among an intellectual leadership for the displacement of *Christianitas* by Europe and the definition of the ascendancy of this new emotional focus. After 1600, the development and identity of a thriving supranational community of scholars as a specifically European phenomenon, the *Respublica literaria* (Republic of letters), made possible by the common usage of the Latin language, served to reinforce the intellectual and cultural identity and sophistication of Europe. Yet it would take the better part of the seventeenth century for the idea of Europe in its multiple dimensions to be translated by tract and broadside from the learned study to the street.

BIBLIOGRAPHY

Burke, Peter. "Did Europe Exist before 1700?" *History of European Ideas* 1 (1985): 21–29. Sounds a useful cautionary note.

Céard, Jean. "L'image de l'Europe dans la littérature cosmographique de la Renaissance." In *La conscience européenne au XVe au XVIe siècle.* Actes du Colloque international organisé à l'École Normale Supérieure de Jeunes Filles (30 septembre–3 octobre 1980). Paris, 1982. Pages 49–63. Valuable for showing Strabo's influence upon Renaissance geographers in the exalting of Europe.

Chabod, Federico. *Storia dell'idea d'Europa.* Bari, Italy, 1971. A broad treatment, yet with some useful observations regarding Machiavelli's European awareness.

Hay, Denys. *Europe: The Emergence of an Idea.* Edinburgh, 1957. Fundamental, being the most effective study of the subject.

Margolin, Jean-Claude. "Conscience européenne et réaction à la menace turque d'après Le 'De dissidiis Europae et bello turcico' de Vives (1526)." In *Juan Luis Vives.* Edited by August Buck. Hamburg, Germany, 1981. Pages 107–140.

Pfeffermann, Hans. *Die Zusammenarbeit der Renaissancepäpste mit den Türken.* Winterthur, Switzerland, 1946. A most insightful study of the twofold papal policy toward the Turk, with its consequences for the beginnings of the European state system in the Renaissance.

Schulze, Winfried. "Europa in der frühen Neuzeit: Bergriffsgeschichtliche Befunde." In *Europäische Geschichte als historiographes Problem.* Edited by Heinz Duchhardt and Andreas Kunz. Mainz, Germany, 1997.

JOHN M. HEADLEY

EVANGELISM. *See* **Spirituali.**

EVERYDAY LIFE. *See* **Daily Life.**

EXPLORATION. Before the great seaborne reconnaissance of the fifteenth and sixteenth centuries, the geographical vision of Europeans hardly transcended the known world of the ancients. Firsthand experience and accurate information were for the most part confined to Europe itself, or the areas of Africa and Asia bordering the Mediterranean. What little was known of sub-Saharan Africa or the interior of western Asia had been gleaned through military and commercial contacts with the Muslim world. In the thirteenth century, a few European travelers—notably Giovanni di Piano Carpini, William of Rubruck, and Marco Polo—had penetrated the Mongol-dominated East, and their accounts stimulated hopes of increased trade and dreams of alliance with putative Asian Christians against the intervening power of Islam. The best-informed Europeans could not

agree on the circumference of the earth, much less make a reasoned evaluation of the Ptolemaic assertion (dating from the second century C.E.) that the Indian Ocean was landlocked, encircled by the joined mass of Africa and Asia, or of the widespread notion that the torrid equatorial zone of the earth was uninhabitable and impassable.

The period of the Renaissance brought an end to this epoch of geographic isolation and ignorance. From the early fifteenth century, Portuguese seamen began exploring southward in the Atlantic. By century's end, they had established a sea route around Africa to South Asia, while Christopher Columbus's voyages in the service of Castile had found lands westward across the Atlantic that were coming to be recognized as a hitherto-unknown continent. Over the next century and a half, this expansion of Europe's horizons led to the establishment of American colonial empires by the Spanish and Portuguese, and more tenuously by the Dutch, English, and French. Meanwhile, in the Old World, Europeans established a thriving commerce accompanied by partial territorial domination, in south Asia and the Far East, and instigated a large-scale transatlantic trade in African slaves. Although the Pacific retained many of its secrets, Europeans sailed and traded across its vast distances and began to discern the outlines of the Australian continent. Renaissance exploration and conquest greatly augmented knowledge of the earth and its peoples and conferred upon western Europe the wealth, geopolitical power, and cultural confidence that were the principal foundations of its dominance of the first modern centuries. Little wonder then that the Spaniard Francisco de Jérez could ask in 1547: "When, among the ancients or the moderns, have been seen such great undertakings of so few individuals to go conquering the unseen and the unknown in the face of so many people, in such diverse climates and reaches of the sea or across such distances?" (quoted in Maravall, *Antiguos y modernos,* p. 441).

Origins: A Technological Impetus? Why a movement of world historical significance arose when and where it did—over the course of the fifteenth century on the southwestern periphery of Europe—remains a question without tidy or entirely satisfying answers. Explanations for the dawning of the great age of exploration have focused, on the one hand, on techniques of shipbuilding, seamanship, and navigation, and on the other hand, on the motives that impelled a growing curiosity about the world beyond Europe. As we shall see, mentality rather than technology is the independent variable in this historical equation; examining motive rather than means yields the most satisfactory—if, inevitably, incomplete—understanding of the genesis of Renaissance exploration.

As the Renaissance dawned, three practical problems discouraged voyages beyond the familiar confines of the Mediterranean or the immediate coastal waters of the Atlantic. First, and most obvious, Europeans lacked accurate maps and charts of unfamiliar waters, and had little useful knowledge about oceanic currents or wind patterns. Second, European mariners had limited experience of sailing for long periods out of sight of land, and possessed only rudimentary understanding of the principles of navigation and primitive tools for its practice. Third, few ships of the time were well suited for long oceanic voyages or were particularly nimble in sailing under adverse wind conditions.

Solutions to these problems arose from the practice of seafaring exploration rather than the reverse. At first Portuguese explorers sailed small single-masted *barcas,* worthless against the wind but rowable in a pinch, and switched to caravels after 1440. While an improvement, early lateen-rigged caravels (usually from fifty to seventy tons, two-masted, and perhaps seventy-five feet long) had been developed for traditional coastwise navigation; far from being purposely built for the pioneers of oceanic reconnaissance, the caravels were utilized for lack of better options. Over time, Atlantic sailors adapted caravel design to allow square-rigging as well, creating the so-called *caravela redonda* (round caravel), which could accommodate hybrid combinations of canvas suited to the various wind conditions encountered on the high seas. As much longer voyages became the norm, the expanded hold required for necessary supplies and cargo drove the development of the much larger *naos,* or carracks (of nearly two hundred tons by 1500).

To an even greater extent than in the case of ships, the other limitations facing the mariners of the time—lack of cartographical information and of navigational skills—were to be effectively remedied only by the accumulated experience of voyages of exploration. In home waters, mariners could use coastal charts—called portolans in the Mediterranean and rutters in the north—to guide them into ports and away from reefs, tidal races, and other dangers. Charting unfamiliar shores was to be one of the great tasks and accomplishments of the explorers. Besides charts, sailors of the time had few navigational aids. Compasses remained primitive, and had

to be remagnetized periodically with a lodestone. Accurate knowledge about the variation of magnetic north from true north had to await the sixteenth-century innovations of men like the Portuguese royal cosmographer Pedro Nunes and the accumulation of observations from an array of locations. Assessment of latitude relied on observation of the North Star with quadrant or astrolabe, instruments difficult to manipulate with precision from a rolling deck. As the reconnaissance progressed, sailors would be forced to devise means of assessing their north-south position when Polaris disappeared below the horizon in equatorial or Southern Hemisphere waters. Measurement of east-west movement posed greater difficulties, which would not be solved until the development in the eighteenth century of accurate chronometers allowed calculation of longitude. In practice, then, Renaissance mariners relied on dead reckoning with the aid of simple devices like logs and traverse boards, as well as soundings to discern their approach to the coast.

Thus, unlike some more recent explosions of human curiosity, where new tools can be said to have inspired new uses, the Renaissance efflorescence of maritime exploration was not the product of dramatic technological innovation. Initially at least, the explorers of the age pushed out into the unknown Atlantic with the inadequate equipment of the past. To understand why they ventured forth it will be useful to examine the specific context of European endeavors at reconnaissance, the earliest of which were launched in the course of the fifteenth century from the Iberian kingdoms of Portugal and Castile.

Portuguese Pioneers, 1415–1500. Traditionally, historians date the great age of exploration from 1415 and the Portuguese capture of Muslim Ceuta opposite Gibraltar. This enterprise represented a revival of the Portuguese Reconquest, and seems to have inspired crusading devotion and a lasting curiosity about Africa in the prince Dom Henrique (Henry the Navigator; 1394–1460), who was twenty-one when he participated in the siege of Ceuta. His motivation seems to have been primarily military and religious, the desire to advance Christendom against Islam, perhaps by making contact with the legendary Prester John, thought to head a Christian kingdom to the southeast of Muslim North Africa. The prince's ambition to further the faith dovetailed with a powerful belief—reinforced by dabblings in astrology—in his own glorious destiny. In Ceuta, Dom Henrique may have learned some details of the trans-Saharan gold trade, and certainly he hoped to divert this commerce away from the Muslims. In 1420 Dom Henrique became head of the military Order of Christ, a position that could only sharpen his thirst for crusading glory. By then he had begun dispatching ships commanded by his retainers on missions into the Atlantic. In 1419 one of these voyages rediscovered Madeira, which along with the Canaries and Azores had likely been reached by Mediterranean sailors during the fourteenth century and largely forgotten since. The colonization of Madeira soon began to pay off, first with exports of timber and subsequently with sugar and wine prized across Europe. During the 1420s Dom Henrique also claimed the Canary Islands, but was opposed by Castile, which in 1479 won all rights in the Canaries. Dom Henrique's efforts met greater success in the Azores, far to the west, which from the 1430s were explored and colonized under his aegis.

Apart from the revenue it generated, this island hopping marked a diversion from the main thrust of Portuguese voyaging. [See the map in the entry Africa, Sub-Saharan.] Dom Henrique's ships reached the first major milestone in exploring the coast of Africa in 1434, when Gil Eanes rounded Cape Bojador (in 26° north latitude), the previous southern limit of European coasting. Expeditions led by Nuno Tristão passed Cape Blanco and found the mouth of the Senegal (16°8′ north latitude) in 1444 and of the Gambia (13°28′ north latitude) in 1446. Meanwhile, Dinis Dias (fl. 1440–1484) reached Cape Verde in 1444. Alvise Cà da Mosto (a Venetian in Dom Henrique's service) and Diogo Gomes explored the Cape Verde Islands and pushed farther south in 1455 and 1456, and Pedro da Sintra reached Sierra Leone (below 9° north) by 1460. By then trade in ivory, gold dust, and slaves had been established on the Senegambian coast. From 1419 to 1460 Portuguese mariners made at least thirty-five voyages in West African waters. Scholars debate the number directly sponsored by Dom Henrique, but few would deny his status as the prime mover of this unprecedented reconnaissance.

Dom Henrique died in 1460. Initially, King Afonso V (ruled 1438–1481) evinced little interest in further voyages, but eventually the king granted the trading concession south of Sierra Leone to the merchant Fernão Gomes in return for a fixed rent and an undertaking to continue exploration. Gomes proved extremely able, and between 1469 and 1475 he reaped handsome profits and sponsored exploration of another vast section of the African coast. By the end of Gomes's lease in 1475, his sailors had explored beyond the Bight of Benin toward Cameroon.

Fernando Po discovered the sizable island of Bioko in the Bight of Bonny (Bight of Biafra), while in 1474 Lopo Gonçalves and Rui de Sequeira found the southward turning of the coast and, crossing the equator, sailed past Cape López (0°47′ south latitude). Navigation had been complicated beyond Sierra Leone because the North Star dropped below the horizon but the Portuguese addressed the problem as early as 1484, when King John II (ruled 1481–1495) impaneled a commission of experts to codify a system for determining latitude by observing the meridian transit of the sun. Their efforts led to a useful guidebook—the *Regimento do estrolabio e do quadrante* (Manual for the astrolabe and quadrant)—that was used by Portuguese mariners from the late 1480s and published by 1509.

Gomes consolidated the commerce established in earlier decades and opened up for Portugal the more lucrative Guinea trades in malagueta pepper from the Grain Coast, gold from the Gold Coast, and true pepper from the Benin Kingdom. The slave trade grew rapidly as well; one expert estimates that the Portuguese took 150,000 blacks from West Africa before 1500. Afonso V, now intrigued by the potential of this commerce, entrusted the African enterprise to his son Dom John rather than renewing Gomes's concession in 1475. When the prince succeeded as John II in 1481, he established the Guinea trade as a direct crown monopoly, and the next year ordered the construction of a castle at São Jorge da Mina (Elmina) on the Gold Coast. This post quickly outstripped the *feitorias* (factories, trading posts) established on the Senegambian coast as the richest center of the African trade.

Beginning in 1475 the war between Portugal and Castile over the Castilian succession spilled over into Atlantic waters. While the Portuguese suffered a heavy defeat in Iberia itself, they won the naval war and the Treaty of Alcáçovas of 1479 barred the Castilians from sailing past Cape Bojador. The next decade saw several significant voyages patronized by John II. In 1483 Diogo Cão pushed southward past the mouth of the Congo River to Cape Santa María at about 13° south latitude. A second Cão voyage reached nearly to the Tropic of Capricorn in 1486.

A rumor circulated upon Cão's return from his first voyage that he had found a passage into the Arabian Sea. The story was groundless, but reveals lingering geographical confusion as well as contemporary perceptions of John II's ambitions. And in 1487 the king took three initiatives to resolve key questions posed by Portuguese exploration. First, he sent ambassadors inland from the Guinea coast to seek Prester John and a land route across Africa; little evidence of these missions survives but they seem to have reached Timbuktu as well as the courts of inland rulers like the Oni of Ife. Next he sent Afonso Paiva and Pero de Covilhã via the Mediterranean and Red Seas to Aden, Paiva to seek Prester John in "Middle India" (Ethiopia), while Covilhã would proceed to India to gain commercial and navigational knowledge of the Indian Ocean. Paiva died before fulfilling his orders, but Covilhã took ship to India and traveled the Malabar Coast from Goa to Calicut before turning back. In 1490 Covilhã was in Cairo, whence he sent a report to the king lauding Calicut as a crucial port for the spice trade and providing some information on sailing routes from East Africa to India. On his own initiative Covilhã traveled from Cairo to Mecca disguised as a pilgrim; by 1493 he was in Ethiopia, where he spent the last thirteen years of his life in the service of the emperor.

Most significantly, John II sent Bartolomeu Dias (c. 1450–1500) to sea in 1487 to seek the southern extremity of Africa and a route around it. Before Christmas he reached Hottentot Bay (26°8′ south latitude). Farther south, Dias's caravels moved out to sea seeking a favorable wind and sailed on a southwesterly course for about two weeks before finding the westerlies in the region of 40° south latitude. Running east, they passed the cape without seeing it, and turning to the north found the southeastern coast of Africa, sailing as far as the Great Fish River (33°28′ south latitude). On the return, Dias saw the cape, which he dubbed the Cape of Storms. Back in Lisbon by December 1488, Dias reported to the king, who preferred to call it the Cape of Good Hope.

These explorers demonstrated two important truths: Dias that Africa could be rounded by sea, and Covilhã that at least the northern reaches of the Indian Ocean comprised a zone of routine navigation. The passage to India, it now seemed clear, should not require the slow blind groping that had characterized Portuguese progress down the West African coast. Therefore it is surprising that nearly nine years passed before another Portuguese expedition under Vasco da Gama (c. 1460–1524) ventured forth to capitalize on this welcome news. The delay is most plausibly explained by internal political distraction including John II's death in 1495 and the succession of Manuel I (ruled 1495–1521). It is also worth considering that the new knowledge gained in the late 1480s provided no encouragement for the crusading dreams that had spurred Portuguese exploration. There was no sign of a potential eastern ally against the Muslims. An entrée into the spice trade held obvious attractions, but the Portuguese delay in exploiting this opportunity supports the idea that commercial advantage had been only a secondary motive of Portugal's overseas ventures.

The famous expedition of Vasco da Gama sailed from Lisbon in 1497, accompanied at first by Dias, who was bound for Elmina. Rather than coasting, da Gama sailed down the open ocean from the Cape Verde Islands. After a record thirteen weeks out of sight of land, skill or luck brought his ships to the southwestern African coast perhaps one hundred miles north of the Cape of Good Hope. From there they sailed south into the zone of the westerlies, doubled the cape and proceeded up the East African coast, reaching Mozambique (15° south latitude) in March 1498. Here they first met Muslim traders and were directed up the coast to the thriving port of Malindi (3°12′ south latitude), where they hired the Gujarati pilot Ahmed ibn Majid to guide the fleet to India. In May 1498 da Gama anchored at Calicut. Despite the hostility of the dominant Arab merchants and the unsuitability of his trade goods—designed for the less sophisticated commerce of Guinea—da Gama managed to secure a cargo of cinnamon and pepper. He returned to Lisbon by September 1499, after a difficult passage of the Indian Ocean and a skilled traversal of the Atlantic. Carried by the southeast trade winds to equatorial waters, da Gama made his way north to the Cape Verdes and finally to the Azores before catching the westerlies home. The round trip had included about ten months at sea. [See the map in the entry Asia, East.]

While da Gama had lost half his ships and two-thirds of his men to shipwreck, scurvy, and other hazards, he had succeeded in finding the basic sailing route that would open to Europeans the commerce of South Asia, and eventually of the Spice Islands and the Far East. Manuel I wasted no time in commissioning a second voyage by a much larger fleet under Pedro Álvares Cabral (1460s–1520), who sailed in 1500. Cabral attempted to follow da Gama's course south from the Cape Verdes but was blown farther west, raising the coast of Brazil near 17° south latitude in April. The fleet landed, and after unsatisfactory attempts to communicate with the natives and instruct them in Catholicism, Cabral decided to proceed to India, though not before ordering a ship back to Portugal to report the discovery. Sailing from Brazil in May, Cabral's fleet reached Calicut in September 1500, having unwittingly encountered the land that would become Portugal's foothold in the New World.

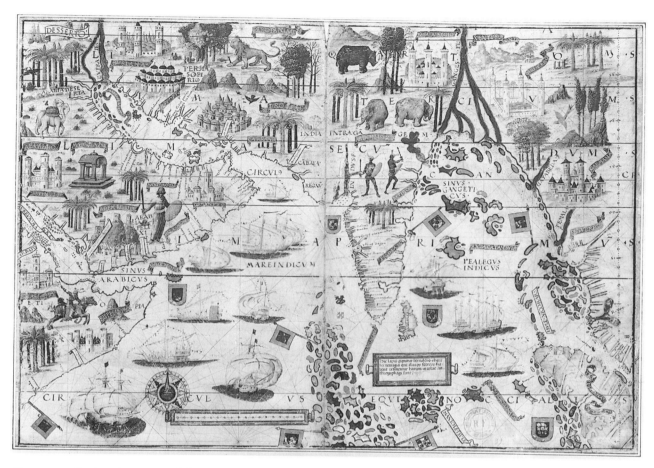

Portuguese Exploration. Map of the Indian Ocean dedicated to King Manuel I of Portugal; 1519. BIBLIOTHÈQUE NATIONALE DE FRANCE, PARIS, RES GE DD683 (2R)

Columbus and the Western Route. During the fifteenth century Castilian sailors from the Andalusian ports had explored the Canaries and attempted to penetrate the West African trade opened by Portugal. Movement into the Canary Islands gained new impetus after Castile's claims there were affirmed in 1479. With the War of Succession over, Ferdinand (ruled 1474–1516) and Isabella (ruled 1474–1504) turned to completing the peninsular reconquest and strengthening the royal state in Castile. In 1486 they first received the Genoese mariner Christopher Columbus (1451–1506), who turned to them after failing to interest John II of Portugal in his project to discover a western route to East Asia. Columbus was an experienced sailor, having participated in Portuguese voyages into the North Atlantic and as far south as Elmina. His idiosyncratic readings of various texts by the Florentine Paolo dal Pozzo Toscanelli (1397–1482), Ptolemy, Marco Polo, and Pierre d'Ailly led him to calculate the equatorial circumference of the earth at around 18,700 miles

(three-quarters of the true figure of 24,900 miles). This underestimate, compounded by the errors of Ptolemy and later writers who had vastly exaggerated the eastward extension of Asia, led Columbus to believe that a sea voyage of less than 3,000 miles separated the Canaries from Japan. He presented this vision to Ferdinand and Isabella, who impaneled a commission of experts to evaluate his plan. Reporting in 1486 and 1487, the experts rejected Columbus's calculations. Through patrons close to Isabella, Columbus managed to win reconsideration of his scheme from another royal commission in 1491. Again the experts were skeptical, but this time he secured crown backing, spelled out in capitulations of April 1492.

Columbus's squadron, consisting of a *nao* and two caravels, departed from Palos (near Huelva) in August and sailed to Gomera in the Canaries. After refitting and provisioning there, Columbus sailed into the unknown western ocean in September, making landfall in the Bahamas at San Salvador (24°

north latitude, longitude 74°40′ west) or Samana Cay (23°3′ north latitude, longitude 73°45′ west) on 12 October 1492. Columbus found no use there or in his subsequent cruising of the Caribbean for his Arabic interpreter or the letter he carried from the monarchs addressed to the Great Khan, but he remained convinced that his ships had reached the approaches of Asia. Leaving the crew of the foundered *nao* (the *Santa María*) to establish a settlement on the north coast of Hispaniola, Columbus turned back for Spain in January 1493. After a difficult voyage, he put in at Lisbon in March. Following a wary interview with John II, Columbus was allowed to sail home to Palos, whence he journeyed to meet Ferdinand and Isabella in Barcelona in April.

The monarchs moved quickly to authorize a second voyage and to register Castile's claim to the new discoveries. They secured a series of bulls from the Spanish pope Alexander VI (reigned 1492–1503) adjudicating to Castile all past and future discoveries in the region Columbus had explored and establishing a line of demarcation (about four hundred miles west of the Azores and Cape Verde Islands) between Castilian and Portuguese spheres of control. One of the bulls seemed to threaten the Portuguese monopoly on West African trade, prompting John II in 1494 to negotiate the Treaty of Tordesillas with Ferdinand and Isabella. This agreement shifted the line of demarcation about one thousand miles further west (to longitude 46°37′ west by modern reckoning), securing the Guinea trade, the eastern route to India, and as it happened Brazil for Portugal, while adjudicating the bulk of the yet-undiscovered Americas to Castile.

A second, larger fleet under Columbus as admiral sailed from Cádiz via the Canaries in the autumn of 1493, reaching Dominica (15°20′ north latitude, longitude 61°20′ west) in the Lesser Antilles in November. This second voyage saw the exploration of much of the West Indies. While Columbus continued to distinguish himself as a navigator, events of this voyage highlighted his incapacity to govern the Spanish settlers of the new colony (the first settlement having been wiped out by the natives in Columbus's absence). Leaving his brother Bartolomeo in charge, Columbus returned to Spain in June 1496 to counter negative reports of his administration.

Although his favor was waning, Columbus was able to win royal support for a third voyage. By 1496 the explorer had begun affecting the dress of a Franciscan and displayed a mounting obsession with mystical Christian prophecy and apocalypticism. His third expedition, launched in 1498, made landfall at Trinidad and reconnoitered a stretch of the north-

eastern coast of South America before veering northwest to Hispaniola. Observing the huge flow of fresh water off the mouth of the Orinoco, Columbus arrived at the conclusion that the biblical Eden was nearby. By contrast, Hispaniola was hardly a paradise when Columbus returned. The admiral dealt clumsily with the aftermath of a settlers' revolt and in 1500 endured the indignity of deportation to Spain in chains at the hands of a royal judge who had been sent out to investigate conditions on the island.

Despite his erratic behavior, Columbus was allowed to undertake a fourth voyage in 1502. He explored the coast of Central America from modern-day Honduras to Panama. Sailing north toward Hispaniola in ships heavily damaged by shipworm, the fleet was forced to take refuge in Jamaica, where Columbus and most of his men were marooned for nearly a year. The admiral returned to Spain in November 1504, preceded by an incoherent letter he had written to the sovereigns while awaiting rescue, in which he ranted at length about his election by God to bring about the reconquest of Jerusalem and thus signal the end of times. Columbus's career was effectively over, and he died in 1506, still believing that his voyages had brought him close to Asia.

Discoveries Interpreted and Expanded. While Columbus still lived, others began to discern the true nature of the lands to the west. As early as 1493, Pietro Martire d'Anghiera (1457–1526), an Italian scholar writing at the court of Spain, referred to Columbus's discovery as "the New World." John Cabot (c. 1450–c. 1498), a Venetian serving Henry VII of England (ruled 1485–1509), sailed from Bristol in May 1497, and crossing the North Atlantic reached Newfoundland in June and explored the island's seaward coastline. Although the expedition had been inspired by reports of Columbus's success, the English did not expect to find Asia within a month's voyage; when Cabot returned he was hailed for finding a new island. The next spring Cabot left Bristol on a second voyage. One ship soon returned to port, while Cabot and the four other vessels were lost without a trace. The region of Cabot's discovery was revisited around the turn of the century by three Portuguese expeditions under the command of Gaspar Corte-Real in 1500 and 1501 and his brother Miguel in 1502. The most extensive voyage was Gaspar's second, which reached Labrador, Newfoundland, and Nova Scotia. Both brothers were lost at sea in the course of their explorations, but their efforts facilitated the establishment of a Portuguese cod fishery on the Grand Banks, which left traces in tax records as early as 1506.

The north and east coasts of South America were being partially reconnoitered as well. In 1499 the Andalusian Vicente Yáñez Pinzón explored near the mouth of the Orinoco, while Alonso de Ojeda coasted northwest from the vicinity of Cayenne (5°5′ north latitude, longitude 52°8′ west) to Trinidad and the Gulf of Paria and then westward as far as La Guajira (12° north latitude, longitude 72° west), discovering Curaçao and the Gulf of Maracaibo along the way. In the latter area, the Spaniards saw native villages built on pilings and dubbed the region Venezuela, or "Little Venice." The vast extent of South America became more evident as a result of the Portuguese voyage of 1501 and 1502 led by Gonçalo Coelho to examine the western regions found by Cabral in 1500. The Florentine Amerigo Vespucci (1454–1512) accompanied Coelho, whose flotilla coasted along Brazil from about 5° to 25° south latitude, returning to Portugal via West Africa. In his accounts of this voyage and another he undertook with Coelho in 1503 and 1504, Vespucci greatly exaggerated his own role in the enterprise as well as the distance traversed to the south. In published form, though, Vespucci's vivid tracts, one of which insisted that the western lands constituted a *mundus novus* (New World), won him such great fame that the cartographer Martin Waldseemüller dubbed the new continent America (from Amerigo) on his world map of 1507.

The dissemination of Vespucci's narratives convinced informed opinion in Europe that America was indeed a new continent lying between Europe and Asia. In the first decades of the sixteenth century a variety of Castilian coasting expeditions along Central America and the Yucatán Peninsula dispelled the remaining hopes of an easy water passage through America. Vasco Núñez de Balboa traversed the isthmus in 1513 and became the first European to see the western reaches of the "Great South Sea," the Pacific Ocean. Pedrarias de Ávila, named in the same year royal governor of the isthmian province of Darien, promoted an energetic exploration of both coasts of the region.

Meanwhile, the Portuguese were consolidating a foothold in the Indian Ocean and moving into the archipelagoes of Southeast Asia. Vasco da Gama returned to the Malabar coast in 1502 at the head of a powerfully armed fleet; he coerced trading concessions by shelling Calicut and defeating an Arab armada in a pitched sea battle. In the following years fleets led by the first viceroy, Francisco de Almeida,

continued the violent penetration of African and Indian ports. Almeida's successor, Afonso de Albuquerque (1453–1515), put Portugal's power in the region on a firm footing by establishing strong fortified bases at Goa in 1510, Malacca on the Malay Peninsula in 1511, and Ormuz on the Persian Gulf in 1515. Dispatched by Albuquerque from Malacca, António de Abreu and Francisco Serrão explored the Moluccas between 1512 and 1514 and initiated the direct Portuguese penetration of the islands' spice trade.

The status of the Moluccas was the central issue motivating what Samuel Eliot Morison deemed "the greatest voyage in recorded history," the circumnavigation of the earth from 1519 to 1522 led by Ferdinand Magellan (c. 1480–1521) and Juan Sebastián del Cano (1476–1526). The Portuguese Magellan, who had participated in the capture of Malacca, formed the opinion that a relatively narrow sea separated the Moluccas from South America, and that therefore the rich spice islands might fall within the Castilian zone were the Tordesillas line to be extended over the pole and through the Eastern Hemisphere. Like Columbus, Magellan underestimated the distance between Europe and Asia, but he was quite sensible to propose that he could test his theory by sailing south around the American continent into the ocean beyond. Such an expedition could have no possible attraction for the Portuguese crown, so Magellan successfully put his proposal to Charles I of Spain (ruled 1516–1556).

Both Manuel I of Portugal and Pope Leo X (reigned 1513–1521) protested the plan, but nevertheless Magellan sailed from Seville in 1519 at the head of five ships. His fleet made its first American landfall near 49° south latitude in Patagonia, well to the west of the Tordesillas line. Proceeding south and then westerly through the strait, Magellan lost two ships but negotiated a harrowing passage into the Pacific (Magellan gave this name to the "South Sea" of Balboa) in thirty-eight days. Catching fair winds most of the way, the three ships sailed north and northwest, crossing the equator at about longitude 125° west, and then westward to Guam and on to the Philippines in March 1521. The Pacific crossing had taken 106 days, during which the crew suffered grave effects of hunger and scurvy while Magellan enjoyed ample opportunity to contemplate his underestimate of the ocean's breadth. In April 1521 the explorer was killed in an affray with Philippine natives, and the Castilian Juan Sebastián del Cano led the expedition, reduced now to two ships, south to the Moluccas. His flagship, *Victoria,* evaded capture by the Portuguese and returned via the Cape of Good Hope to Spain carrying a lucrative cargo of East Indies cloves. Del Cano reached Sanlúcar de Barrameda in September 1522, the first navigator to have rounded the globe. The distance separating South America from the East Indies should have provided confirmation of Portugal's claims, but the canny Spanish king would not relent so easily, and in the Treaty of Zaragoza of 1529 he managed to extract a large monetary payment from John III of Portugal (ruled 1521–1557) in return for renouncing his "rights" in the Moluccas. Although the Philippines also lay within the Portuguese sphere, Castilian possession of that archipelago, discovered by Magellan, was never disputed.

Subsequent Exploration to 1600. The most astounding phase of Renaissance exploration ended with the *Victoria*'s return to Andalusia in 1522. In a little over a century, Iberian navigators had determined the shape and extent of Africa and much of the Asian coastline and archipelagoes. They had found and begun to explore and colonize an unexpected continent and the vast ocean beyond, and had established European settlement in the tropics. The exact measure of the earth and true cartographical precision would have to await solution of the problem of determining longitude, but the lengthy voyages of the *Carreira da India,* and above all Magellan's circumnavigation, had so far established distances and routes and the relative positions of the continents as to forever dispel the geographic errors of authorities like Ptolemy and Toscanelli. Traditional credulity about the marvels of the unknown—dog-headed men, sea monsters, maelstroms blocking the outlets of mysterious seas—began to wane as well, as firsthand experience of foreign lands, seas, and people became common in Europe.

Some illusions were extraordinarily persistent, such as that of a Northwest Passage around America; this dream motivated increasingly desperate efforts by mariners serving France, England, and Holland, nations eager for a share of Asian trade through waters uncontrolled by their Iberian rivals. Sailing for the French king, Giovanni da Verrazano (1485?–1528) traced the Atlantic seaboard of North America from Cape Fear south to Florida and then north as far as Maine in 1524. He passed without entering the Chesapeake Bay and the mouth of the Hudson before returning to France, and concluded that the mainland in that latitude was of isthmian width. In two voyages between 1534 and 1536, Jacques Cartier (1491–1557) continued this French endeavor, ex-

ploring the north coast of Newfoundland, the Labrador Strait, and the Gulf of St. Lawrence and then navigating the river up to the rapids near the present site of Montreal. In a final voyage of 1541, Cartier attempted—without lasting success—to plant a colony on the lower St. Lawrence.

English attempts to find the elusive passage began with the voyage of Martin Frobisher (c. 1535–1594) of 1576; Frobisher found the bay that bears his name at around 62° north latitude on the southeast of Baffin Island, and mistook it for a strait. Two further voyages were marked by courage in the face of grim Arctic conditions, but little accomplishment. The three voyages of John Davis (c. 1550–1605) from 1585 through 1587 probed the strait between Greenland and Baffin Island, in fact the entry into a true Northwest Passage that became navigable only in the era of nuclear submarines. Voyaging in Netherlandish service, Henry Hudson (d. 1611) explored the eponymous river to the head of navigation in 1609. On two previous expeditions for the English Muscovy Company in 1607 and 1608, Hudson had searched the Arctic waters of the Old World for a Northeast Passage before being thwarted by the ice pack of the Barents Sea. Turning to the northwest on his final voyage, under English sponsorship, in 1610, Hudson cruised into the great bay that carries his name, believing that he had found the Pacific. Hudson died there, cast adrift by mutineers, but his explorations spurred subsequent expeditions to the bay and the eventual establishment of the English fur trade there.

Far to the south, other geographic illusions proved nearly as durable. The legend of the golden South American kingdom of El Dorado drew adventurers far into the interior of the continent. The first was Gonzalo Pizarro (c. 1502–1548), brother of the conqueror of Peru, who led a violent and star-crossed expedition over the Andes into the upper Amazon Basin in 1540 and 1541. Failing in the quest for El Dorado, this mission produced one tangible result when Francisco de Orellana and a small party navigated the Amazon to its mouth in 1541 and 1542. El Dorado would lure many other explorers, including the Englishman Walter Ralegh (1554–1618) on his final venture in 1617, when he sailed up the Orinoco in search of the reputed golden treasure of Guiana. A similar legend, of the wealthy cities of Cíbola, enticed Spanish seekers—most famously Francisco Vázquez de Coronado (c. 1510–1554) between 1540 and 1542—into the North American southwest.

Extensive penetration of the Spanish-American lands was of course a feature of the era of conquistadores in the first half of the sixteenth century, though it is largely misleading to characterize the great captains like Hernán Cortés and Francisco Pizarro as explorers. Their achievements were military and imperial above all, while less successful conquerors may be remembered primarily for charting unknown territory. For example, in 1523 Cristóbal de Olid explored Honduras and Pedro de Alvarado the Mayan heartland of Guatemala, while Diego de Almagro from 1535 to 1537 and Pedro de Valdivia in 1540 and 1541 led the first European penetrations of Chile in southwestern South America. Large areas of the interior, especially in Portuguese Brazil, remained utterly uncharted, but by the middle of the sixteenth century Europeans had gained some notion of all of the great river systems of South America. Meanwhile, except for the region of Tierra del Fuego and Cape Horn south of the Strait of Magellan, Spanish and Portuguese vessels had traced the entire coast of the continent.

The mammoth Pacific remained the great unknown. A disastrous Spanish mission meant to follow up Magellan's circumnavigation left Corunna in 1525 under the command of Francisco García de Loaysa, but encountered grave difficulties in the Strait of Magellan and the Pacific in 1526 and faltered entirely amid conflict with the Portuguese in the Moluccas, along the way costing the lives of Loaysa, Juan Sebastián del Cano, and a host of sailors. The English seaman Francis Drake (c. 1540–1596) succeeded in circumnavigating the earth from 1577 through 1579, along the way pioneering an alternate route through the southern straits and exploring along the west coast of North America, perhaps past San Francisco Bay as far as Bodega Bay (38°20′ north latitude). Perhaps more significant, however, was the achievement of Felipe de Salcedo and Andrés de Urdaneta (the latter a survivor of the Loaysa fiasco), who sailing in 1565 on behalf of Miguel López de Legazpi, the Spanish conqueror of the Philippines, established a workable east-west sailing route across the Pacific from the archipelago to Acapulco on the Mexican coast. This would be the track of the Manila galleons, which carried the trade of American silver for Chinese silks across the Pacific in the great age of the Spanish empire. With the establishment of this commerce, Europeans now traded and traveled on a regular basis across all of the oceans of the world.

Besides fomenting enhanced knowledge of the dimensions and contours of the globe and a vast increase in physical and commercial mobility, this age of exploration had darker consequences as well. For many other peoples "discovered" by Europeans, the encounter brought violent disruption and demographic catastrophe. It is sadly ironic that the good intentions that underlay Christianizing efforts—a sincere aspect of the Iberian expansion in particular—could prove just as destructive as the rapacity of armed adventurers or the greed of planters. But where earlier historians doubtless erred in celebrating the exploits and "civilizing mission" of explorers, colonizers, and missionaries, there is reason to be wary as well of scholarship that finds mutual incomprehension the chief characteristic of contacts between human cultures, and reduces the legacy of Renaissance exploration to one of unspeakable cruelty and ecological disaster. Certainly most of the actors in these initial encounters failed to transcend ethnocentrism and contempt for difference. It is, however, equally certain that no cross-cultural understanding could ever arise in the absence of contact between the diverse peoples of the world. For better or worse, European seaborne explorers and those who followed in their wakes effected the mutual introductions of most branches of the human family. Truly we can still hold with Jules Michelet that "to this era, more than to all its predecessors, belong two phenomena: the discovery of the world, and the discovery of mankind" (*Histoire de France au XVIe siècle: La Renaissance*, p. 8).

See also **Africa, North; Africa, Sub-Saharan; Americas; Asia, East; Travel and Travel Literature;** *and biographies of Afonso de Albuquerque, Francisco de Almeida, Christopher Columbus, Vasco da Gama, and Ferdinand Magellan.*

BIBLIOGRAPHY

Primary Works

Brito, Bernardo Gomes de, comp. *The Tragic History of the Sea, 1589–1622.* Edited by C. R. Boxer. London, 1959. Translation of *História trágico-marítima* (2 vols., 1735–1736). Vivid contemporary accounts of shipwrecks in the Portuguese Carreira da India.

Cohen, J. M., ed. and trans. *The Four Voyages of Christopher Columbus, Being his Own Log-Book, Letters, and Dispatches with Connecting Narrative Drawn from the Life of the Admiral by His Son Hernando Colón and Other Contemporary Historians.* Harmondsworth, U.K., 1969. Useful and readable extracts from the principal sources.

Hakluyt, Richard. *The Principal Navigations, Voyages, Traffiques, and Discoveries of the English Nation.* 1589, 1598–1600. 12 vols. Glasgow, 1903–1905. An extraordinary compilation that aimed, quite successfully, to spur English overseas efforts. Good one-volume selections include Hakluyt, *Voyages and Discoveries,* edited by Jack Beeching (Harmondsworth, U.K., 1972), and *The Portable Hakluyt's Voyages,* edited by Irwin R. Blacker (New York, 1965).

Ley, Charles D., ed. *Portuguese Voyages, 1498–1663.* London and New York, 1947. Contemporary accounts of the da Gama and Cabral voyages, and of Portuguese explorers in Africa and the Far East.

Pigafetta, Antonio. *The First Voyage Around the World (1519–1522): An Account of Magellan's Expedition.* Edited by T. J. Cachey Jr. New York, 1995. Translation of *Viaggio attorno al mondo* (1522). A participant's chronicle of the circumnavigation.

Purchas, Samuel. *Hakluytus Posthumus or Purchas His Pilgrimes: Contayning a History of the World in Sea Voyages and Lande Travells by Englishmen and Others.* 1625. 20 vols. Glasgow, 1905–1907. A sequel to Hakluyt, by a less talented compiler.

Ralegh, Walter. *The Discoverie of the Large and Bewtiful Empire of Guiana.* 1596. London, 1928.

Works Issued by the Hakluyt Society. 1st ser. (100 volumes) and 2d ser. (189 vols. through 1998). London, 1847–. An invaluable resource, presenting a wide array of contemporary accounts of exploration and travel.

Secondary Works

Boxer, C. R. *The Portuguese Seaborne Empire, 1415–1825.* London, 1969.

Chaunu, Pierre. *Conquête et exploitation des nouveaux mondes (XVIe siècle).* Paris, 1969.

Diffie, Bailey, and George Winius. *Foundations of the Portuguese Empire, 1415–1580.* Minneapolis, 1977.

Fernández-Armesto, Felipe. *Before Columbus: Exploration and Colonisation from the Mediterranean to the Atlantic, 1229–1492.* London, 1987.

Hale, J. R. *Renaissance Exploration.* New York, 1968.

Kelsey, Harry. *Sir Francis Drake: The Queen's Pirate.* New Haven, Conn., 1998.

McAlister, Lyle. *Spain and Portugal in the New World, 1492–1700.* Minneapolis, 1984.

Maravall, José Antonio. *Antiguos y modernos: Visión de la historia e idea de progreso hasta el Renacimiento.* 2d ed. Madrid, Spain, 1986.

Michelet, Jules. *Histoire de France au XVIe siècle: La Renaissance.* 1855. Paris, 1930.

Morison, Samuel Eliot. *The European Discovery of America: The Northern Voyages, A.D. 500–1600.* New York, 1971.

Morison, Samuel Eliot. *The European Discovery of America: The Southern Voyages, A.D. 1492–1616.* New York, 1974.

Parry, J. H. *The Age of Reconnaissance.* New York, 1963. Remains the best survey of the topic.

Parry, J. H. *The Discovery of South America.* New York, 1979.

Phillips, J. R. S. *The Medieval Expansion of Europe.* Oxford, 1988.

Phillips, William D., Jr., and Carla Rahn Phillips. *The Worlds of Christopher Columbus.* Cambridge, U.K., 1992.

Russell-Wood, A. J. R. *A World on the Move: The Portuguese in Africa, Asia, and America, 1415–1808.* New York, 1993.

Schurz, William Lytle. *The Manila Galleon.* New York, 1939.

Spate, O. H. K. *The Spanish Lake.* Minneapolis, 1979.

Subrahmanyam, Sanjay. *The Career and Legend of Vasco da Gama.* Cambridge, U.K., 1997.

Ure, John. *Prince Henry the Navigator.* London, 1977.

Verlinden, Charles. *The Beginnings of Modern Colonization.* Translated by Yvonne Freccero. Ithaca, N.Y., 1970.

Zerubavel, Eviatar. *Terra Cognita: The Mental Discovery of America.* New Brunswick, N.J., 1992.

JAMES M. BOYDEN

EXPULSIONS OF JEWS. *See* **Conversos; Antisemitism.**

EYCK, JAN VAN, AND HUBERT VAN. A Netherlandish family of artists, probably from Maaseick, near Maastricht, the brothers Hubert, Jan, and Lambert van Eyck were painters, as was their sister Margaret (the last two are sparsely documented). Jan's epitaph in St. Bavo's, Ghent, included armorials, suggesting that the family belonged to the gentry.

Hubert (Hubrecht; Lubrecht; c. 1370–1426). Documents regarding the career and works of Hubert van Eyck are largely conjectural. In 1409 a *Magister Hubertus, pictor* was paid for panels ordered by the members of the chapter of Our Lady's church in Tongeren. In 1413 a Master Hubert executed a panel bequeathed by Jan de Visch van der Capelle to his daughter, a Benedictine nun near

Jan van Eyck. *Virgin and Child with Chancellor Rolin.* Nicolas Rolin (1376–1462) was chancellor of Burgundy during the reign of Philip the Good (ruled 1419–1467). Wood; c. 1435; 66 × 62 cm (26 × 24.5 in.). MUSÉE DE LOUVRE, PARIS/SUPERSTOCK

Grevelingen. These masters may or may not be identical with Hubert van Eyck. Hubert is more securely attested in Ghent between 1422 and 1426. There he made two designs for a painting for the town magistrates, may have begun an altarpiece for the funeral chapel of Robbrecht Portier and his wife in the church of the Savior, and started the monumental *Adoration of the Lamb* or Ghent Altarpiece (dedicated 6 May 1432, St. Bavo, Ghent) for Jodocus (Joos) Vijd and Elisabeth Borluut. He died before its completion, however, and his brother Jan took over the project.

The dedicatory inscription on the frame of the Ghent Altarpiece states that it was begun by Hubert and finished by Jan, but the precise nature of Hubert's contribution has vexed scholars for centuries, and one even argued that Hubert created a sumptuous sculptural framework for the altarpiece, while Jan did the painting. The homogeneous execution of the altarpiece has made it difficult to distinguish Jan's contribution from that of another painter, although infrared photographs revealed two underdrawing styles below the paint surface, one consistent with Jan's other works, another distinct. Hubert may well have designed, prepared, underdrawn, and begun painting the altarpiece, while Jan completed the majority of the painting.

The altarpiece consists of two tiers, each with four hinged wings. When closed for weekday masses and during Lent, it presents an *Annunciation* in the upper register, foretold by the prophets and sibyls in the lunettes above, and on the bottom register kneeling donors praying before their patron saints rendered in grisaille (shades of gray) to resemble stone sculptures. When opened, the upper register reveals the enthroned Christ, the Virgin, and St. John the Baptist, flanked by music-making angels and life-size nude images of Adam and Eve. The bottom register depicts all the saints, apostles, martyrs, patriarchs, prophets, and confessors converging to adore the Lamb of God. The lost predella (a painted platform at the foot of the altarpiece), mentioned by a later chronicler, represented Hell. The whole was probably encased in an elaborate carved frame. The Ghent Altarpiece has been the most praised Flemish painting from the time of its creation, lauded by countless beholders for its beauty, realism, and technical mastery. It has influenced numerous other painters, and was enacted in tableaux-vivants staged by Ghent citizens in 1458 on occasion of the "Joyous Entry" of Philip the Good, duke of Burgundy, after he suppressed the rebellious city.

Jan (before 1395–1441). According to sixteenth-century Ghent sources, Jan van Eyck trained under Hubert, and may have begun as a book illuminator. He is first documented in August 1422 in The Hague, already a mature artist serving John III, count of Holland (John of Bavaria, ruled 1419–1425). In 1423 Jan became official court painter, with two assistants. No actual works from this period survive, although scholars speculate as to echoes of lost paintings in other pictures and drawings. The death of John III terminated Jan's employment. He is next recorded in Bruges, where on 19 May 1425 Philip the Good (ruled 1419–1467) engaged him as court painter and *varlet de chambre,* a post (also held by Jan at The Hague) denoting personal service to the ruler, but not predicated on the profession of an artist. This title designated its bearer as a member of the ruler's *familia,* extended to him valuable benefits including room, board, and medical services, and made him subject to the laws of the court rather than those of the city. Jan's reputation was clearly established by this time, for Philip already knew of "his aptness in the art of painting" and counted on his loyalty and honesty. Throughout their association the duke greatly valued Jan and remunerated him generously. Indeed, when in 1435 the ducal exchequer sought to reduce Jan's salary and pension in accordance with a general program of austerity, Philip dispatched a stern letter ordering prompt and full payment, for he "would never find a man equally to his liking nor so outstanding in his art and science." Reciprocally, the prestige of his employer enhanced Jan's renown domestically and internationally.

Jan's service under Philip entailed frequent travels, both between numerous ducal residences and abroad on diplomatic missions. He worked in Lille on the newly built ducal palace from 1425 until at least 1428; in Bruges from 1431 until his death; at Hesdin in 1432; and in Brussels in 1433. His only unequivocally documented foreign journey, from October 1428 to December 1429, took him to the Iberian Peninsula as part of an embassy negotiating marriage between Philip the Good and Isabella of Portugal. Jan was required to paint a portrait of Isabella for Philip's approval (a standard practice for dynastic marriages). While waiting for the ducal reply, the ambassadors made a pilgrimage to Santiago de Compostela and paid visits to several rulers on the Iberian Peninsula. As a *varlet de chambre,* Jan was not merely a craftsman, but also a courtier, and traveled as such. Ducal accounts record several

Hubert and Jan van Eyck. *Adoration of the Lamb.* The polyptych, also called the Ghent Altarpiece, is in the church of St. Bavo, Ghent, Belgium. SCALA/ART RESOURCE

"secret missions to distant lands" undertaken by Jan on Philip's behalf. As a courtier, moreover, Jan could travel on assignments unrelated to art: on 26 August 1426 he was paid for performing a certain pilgrimage in Philip's name. However, Jan's travels to Italy and the Holy Land, proposed by many scholars, are conjectural.

Works. Jan executed a variety of projects for the duke, as well as for private patrons in court circles. He decorated Philip's residences, and probably participated in staging lavish festivities on such occasions as the wedding of Philip and Isabella, and the tournament between Philip and the duke of Bedford held in Lille in June 1427. He also served as an agent in procuring works of art and services of other masters: in 1439 he hired Jean Creve of Bruges to paint gold

initials in a book for Philip, and in 1441 he bought the duke some paintings. In 1435, moreover, Jan gilded and painted six statues and tabernacles for the facade of the town hall of Bruges. His paintings ranged from portraits of his employers, to religious pictures, to scenes of women bathing, and merchants going over their accounts (the latter two lost, but recorded in Italian collections), as well as a *Mappamundi* (that is, a map of the world), which he probably produced in collaboration with a cartographer at Philip's court. Most of these works do not survive, but those that do often bear Jan's signature. He was almost unique among his contemporaries in signing his paintings, usually in Latin, and frequently including his motto, *Als Ich Can,* apparently punning on his name (and possibly playing on a common medieval scribal phrase, "As I was able, but not as I wished"), which seems simultaneously to signal humility and pride.

Jan's works for members of Philip's entourage are those best known today, for they alone are preserved. The *Virgin and Child with Chancellor Rolin* (c. 1435; Paris, Louvre) was commissioned by the ducal chancellor for his family chapel at Autun; the *Portrait of Baudouin de Lannoy* (early 1430s; Berlin, Gemäldegalerie) depicts the governor of Lille and one of the leaders of the embassy to Portugal; the *Arnolfini Betrothal* (1434; London, National Gallery; see the color plates in this volume) was painted for a member of the Italian colony in Bruges, traditionally identified as Giovanni Arnolfini, a Lucchese merchant who supplied most of Philip's silks and velvets—the identity of the sitters, however, was reconsidered in the late twentieth century. (Not only are the double-portrait format and the narrative subject uncommon, but the painting also bears a florid, legalistic signature declaring "Jan van Eyck was here" on the back wall of the room—above the convex mirror, which reflects the interior backwards and reveals two witnesses in the doorway). Anselm Adornes, a Genoese aristocrat in Bruges who was prominent in the civic and court affairs, purchased from Jan two pictures of *The Stigmatization of St. Francis* (Turin, Galleria Sabauda, and possibly Philadelphia, Museum of Art), which he willed to his daughters in 1470. Georg van der Paele (d. 1443), canon of St. Donatian's in Bruges, commemorated his founding of a chaplaincy by commissioning a large painting of *Virgin and Child with SS. Donatian and George,* which included his portrait (1436; Bruges, Groeningemuseum). Jan also painted a *Portrait of His Wife, Margaretha* (1439; Bruges, Groeningemuseum).

Jan's fame resounded well outside the Burgundian territories. Indeed, the earliest eulogies of his art come from Italy, where his work was admired and sought after: Italian humanists, including Bartolomeo Fazio and Cyriac of Ancona, as well as fifteenth-century inventories reveal that King Alfonso I of Naples, the Medici of Florence, the Este of Ferrara, Ottaviano della Carda at Urbino, and other Italian worthies eagerly collected Jan's paintings. In the sixteenth century Georgio Vasari ascribed to Jan the invention of oil painting. Actually, this technique had been employed since the Middle Ages, but Jan clearly took it to new levels of proficiency and refinement. By systematically layering multiple coats of tinted oil glazes, he created enamel-like surfaces that possessed both depth and translucency. The use of fine glazes also enabled him to blend brushstrokes to the point of imperceptibility, and to build up painted images gradually and in minute detail. In addition to oil painting Jan probably also used other media, including tempera and watercolors. He is, moreover, believed to have produced book illuminations: the miniatures by Hand G in the *Turin-Milan Hours* (c. 1416–1441; Turin, Museo Civico d'Arte Antica) have been associated with Jan's oeuvre on stylistic and technical grounds.

Jan's work is distinguished by a meticulous depiction of the physical world: one can discern in his pictures individual hairs and highlights on jewels in the foreground, and entire cityscapes, landscapes, and a wealth of human activity rendered on an almost microscopic scale in the background. He paid particular attention to sumptuous display, presenting with striking tangibility the shimmer of costly textiles and metalwork, and rich architectural interiors furnished with marble columns, carved relief, pictorial tiles, and oriental carpets. His emphasis on the material opulence likely reflected the values and desires of his courtly clientele. The extraordinary elaboration of pictorial detail, moreover, is evident not only in finished paintings, but also in preparatory drawings, the most famous being *St. Barbara* (1437; Antwerp, Koninklijk Museum voor Schoone Kunsten), an unfinished painting that Jan made into an independent, signed picture.

The complexity of the visual world within Jan's paintings, and the combination of everyday details with religious allegories have given birth to the notion of "disguised symbolism," postulated by Erwin Panofsky, according to which every narrative element within these pictures—light effects, flora, architectural elements, gestures of characters—bears theological significance, which can be decoded with the help of contemporary texts. Numerous scholars, influenced by Panofsky, have sought to uncover such "hidden" meanings in Jan's paintings. In the late twentieth century, however, Panofsky's theories came under criticism and reevaluation, and technical examinations as well as socio-historical inquiries into early Netherlandish painting became popular.

Jan's work influenced artists both in the Netherlands and abroad in Germany, Italy, and Spain. Karel van Mander, the first historian of Netherlandish art, extolled Jan as the founder of northern Renaissance artistic tradition. He occupies this position in scholarly literature to this day.

See also **Netherlands,** *subentry on* **Art in the Netherlands.**

BIBLIOGRAPHY

Archival Documents and Early Sources

Baxandall, Michael. "Bartholomaeus Facius on Painting." *Journal of the Warburg and Courtauld Institutes* 27 (1964): 90–107. Translation of *De viris illustribus* (MS., 1456, Lorenzo Mehus, ed. Florence, 1745).

Mander, Carel van. *The Lives of the Illustrious Netherlandish and German Painters*. 4 vols. Edited by Hessel Miedema Doornspijk, Netherlands, 1994. Translation of *Schilder-boeck* (1604).

Paviot, Jaques. "La vie de Jan van Eyck selon les documents écrits." *Revue des archéologues et historiens d'art de Louvain* 23 (1990): 83–93.

Weale, W. H. James. *Hubert and John van Eyck: Their Life and Work*. London, 1908.

Secondary Works

Dhanens, Elisabeth. *Hubert en Jan Van Eyck*. Antwerp, 1980.

Duverger, Jozef. "Jan van Eyck as Court Painter." *Connoisseur* 194 (1977): 172–79.

Hall, Edwin. *The Arnolfini Betrothal*. Berkeley, Calif., 1994.

Panofsky, Erwin. *Early Netherlandish Painting*. Cambridge, Mass., 1953.

Purtle, Carol J. *The Marian Paintings of Jan van Eyck*. Princeton, N.J., 1982.

Sterling, Charles. "Jan van Eyck avant 1432." *Revue de l'art* 33 (1976): 7–82.

Van Asperen de Boer, Johan Rudolph Justus. "A Scientific Reexamination of the Ghent Altarpiece." *Oud Holland* 93 (1979): 141–214.

MARINA BELOZERSKAYA

FABER STAPULENSIS. *See* **Lefèvre d'Étaples.**

FABRICIUS OF AQUAPENDENTE, GIROLAMO

(c. 1533–1619), Italian anatomist. Fabricius was born at Aquapendente, a small village north of Rome, from which he moved to Padua, where he studied with the great anatomist Gabriele Falloppio (c. 1523–1562). He succeeded Fallopio as teacher of anatomy at the University of Padua upon the latter's death. In 1565 he was nominated professor of anatomy and surgery in the medical school at Padua. He retired in 1613 and died six years later.

In 1594 Fabricius convinced the Venetian government to build a permanent anatomical theater that is still preserved. As a surgeon and physician he enjoyed a high professional reputation. He had a difficult character, however, and had bitter disagreements with relatives and students, who included Caspar Bartholin (1585–1629), Ole Worm (1588–1654), and especially William Harvey (1578–1657). Almost all of Fabricius's treatises were published in the latter part of his life, a first group around 1600, another group in his later years. Manuscripts and 167 anatomical tables, plus 300 color plates he produced in 1600, are preserved in the library of St. Mark in Venice.

Fabricius's surgical works are collected in his *Pentateuchos cheriurgicum* (Five surgical books; 1592, augmented 1619). It conformed to the Hippocratic and Galenic tradition and was the most complete surgical treatise of the time. It contains many plates illustrating his instruments, including two plates illustrating an orthopedic device that apparently was used to correct injuries and deformities.

Fabricius's importance for the history of medicine rests more on his anatomical and embryological works and for the influence he exerted on Harvey, who frequently cited him. His treatise *De venarum ostiolis* (On the "doors" of the veins; 1603) reports observations of the valves of the veins he made in 1574. Fabricius suggested that their function was to slow down the centrifugal flow of blood for even distribution and to strengthen the walls of the veins. He observed that if, after ligating the vein, one pressed upon it with a finger, one could observe the valve in action—a technique later used by Harvey in studying the blood's circulation.

The anatomical observations of Fabricius were centered around three aspects of each organ: its structure, its action, and its utility. He devoted several treatises to the anatomy of various sensory organs and their function, in some cases expressing, unwillingly, his disagreement with Aristotle and Galen. His primary research field, however, was the study of fetal anatomy, which was conducted mainly along Galenic lines. His embryological works include *De formatione ovi et pulli* (On the formation of the egg and the fowl; 1621) and *De formato foetu* (On the formed fetus; 1603). The latter includes comparative studies of reproductive organs in different animals. His study of the placenta is the most original part of the treatise, limiting the use of the term (introduced by Realdo Colombo; c. 1516–1559) to the discoidal type found in humans and some mammals, including rabbits, mice, rats, and guinea pigs.

In his last years Fabricius published several physiological treatises, including one on respiration and its instruments in 1615 and another on the movement of animals in 1618. These were probably influenced by his contacts with the new generation of scientists, and particularly Galileo Galilei (1564–1642), who had left Padua in 1610. Fabrizi seems to have been the first to apply physical laws to the study of the body's movements, anticipating the analogous researches of Galileo and of Giovanni Borelli (1608–1679). These works were an effort to transcend the limits of purely anatomical description, but they were not as successful as his other writings.

BIBLIOGRAPHY

Adelmann, Howard Bernhardt, ed. and trans. *The Embryological Treatises of Hieronymus Fabricius of Aquapendente.* 1942. 2d ed. 2 vols. Ithaca, N.Y., 1967.

Zanobiò, Bruno. "Fabrici, Girolamo." In *Dictionary of Scientific Biography.* Edited by Charles C. Gillispie. Vol. 4. New York, 1971. Pages 507–512.

BERNARDINO FANTINI

FACEZIE. The plural form of the Latin name "facetiae," frequently used by Cicero, identified brief, witty mottoes and pungent satirical sayings, which are best represented in Latin literature in the work of Valerius Maximus (early first century) and Macrobius (early fifth century).

Humanists, in general, were greatly inspired by these classical models. Poggio Bracciolini (1380–1459), for example, drew from various sources to gather up to 272 such sayings, writing them out in excellent Latin between 1438 and 1452. His purpose was to display how expressive Latin can be even when dealing with humble and everyday issues.

In the fifteenth century *facezie* began to be incorporated into special literary collections. Ludovico Carbone of Ferrara (1435–1485) wrote 108 of them, partly derived from Poggio Bracciolini, in the Italian vernacular. Toward the end of the fifteenth century two anonymous versions (one in prose, the other in octaves) of the *Buffonerie del Gonnella* (Jests of Gonnella) appeared, as well as the collection by Arlotto Mainardi (1396–1484), *Motti e facezie del piovano Arlotto* (Sayings and witticisms of the priest Arlotto).

In the sixteenth century Lodovico Domenichi (1515–1564), coached in Florentine elegance, transcribed 455 *facezie* (1548–1562), which he derived partly from Giovanni Pontano's *De sermone* (1509) and partly from Angelo Poliziano's *Dette piacevoli.* In Domenichi's version the *facezie* acquired a more literary character than those of the fifteenth-century humanists.

In *Il cortegiano* (*The Book of the Courtier;* 1528), Baldassare Castiglione expounds a theory about *facezie:* classifying them into "festivities" and "sayings." He thereby widens the scope of their function, which—unlike the function of *facetiae* in classical rhetoric—is not used just as a persuasive tool, but now encompasses the characterization of a new type of man, *vir facetus* (man of wit), who displays the agility of his wit in public assemblies and law courts and also in conversation with friends.

See also **Italian Literature and Language.**

BIBLIOGRAPHY

Bracciolini, Poggio. *Facezie.* Edited by Stefano Pittaluga. Milan, 1995.

Carbone, Lodovico. *Facezie.* Edited by Gino Ruozzi. Bologna, Italy, 1989.

Domenichi, Lodovico. *Facezie.* Rome, 1923.

Greco, Aulo, ed. *Facezie italiane del'400 e '500.* Rome, 1945.

Mainardi, Arlotto. *Motti e facezie del piovano Arlotto.* Collected by Gianfranco Folena. Milan, 1953.

MAUDA BREGOLI-RUSSO

FACTION. It is an apparent paradox of Renaissance history that faction was generally condemned even while it remained a permanent feature of political life. There are, however, valid reasons for this. On the one hand factions usually connoted for people then, as now, informal, sectional interest groups attempting to achieve particular political ends rather than those of the body politic as a whole. Hence their inadmissibility according to the political ideals of the age, which saw peace, harmony, and the achievement of the well-being of the whole community as the goals of government. From the thirteenth century these ideals were reinforced by Aristotelian political philosophy, which spread the concept of the common good as the touchstone of good government. Accordingly, those involved in political life were expected to set aside all concern for private or sectional interest in order to act for the general welfare. As faction was felt to represent the antithesis of this fundamental principle, it was necessarily condemned.

These attitudes were connected with the very real destructive effects that faction had on the body politic. Where factional conflict was especially prevalent, as in Italy, endemic party strife led to sporadic war, exile, destruction of life and property, and the disruption of normal human activities. Part of its disruptive force was seen in its subversion of justice and effective government, which often meant the collapse of republican governments and the loss of liberty to a tyrant.

Reasons for Factions. Given these obviously negative aspects of faction, contemporaries could often explain its existence only in terms of human sin. Greed, pride, and avarice were the motives most frequently cited as inspiring factional conflict, while charity and humility were the means to restore unity and concord. Yet there were very concrete reasons for the formation of factions—reasons that were generally ignored by the political thought of the time. In particular the conviction that it was possible to separate public from private interest neglected the fact that government policy and the way in which it was executed had very profound effects on private concerns. Access to power could be essential for the protection or promotion of personal interests, as well as for the satisfaction of notions of status and prestige. Hence the "rivalry for office" frequently denounced as the root of conflict, but which reflected a concern for personal success or even survival. Further, within governing groups differences could arise over policy, not least because differing interests caused people to take different points of view. In such cases each side might see its own position as the common good, and feel justified even in fighting for it. In this they could obtain support from a few authors, including the eminent jurist Bartolus da Sassoferrato (1314–1357), who accepted that a party might on occasion represent the common good, and thereby become a valid legal entity.

The situation was further complicated by the nature of loyalties in a world where government power was necessarily limited, and many needs of life continued to be satisfied through personal contacts, whether of friendship, neighborhood, or, especially, family, which remained the principal source of wealth, status, and power for the upper classes. Such personal connections, reinforced as they were by private interest, could be more important for one's existence than action by the state, while the latter might be profoundly influenced by the private attachments of those in government. Hence, the tendency of personal groupings to compete with the state as the focus of political loyalties, while the difficulty of obtaining an impartial application of the laws contributed to the resentments which fed factional strife.

Clearly, different political forms dealt more or less effectively with these problems. In traditional principalities with an established ruling family, political issues tended to be less divisive because some major ones, such as the distribution of power, had been mainly decided, while others were determined by a restricted group. Provided the ruler acted according to traditional expectations and satisfied powerful interests, harmony could generally be maintained, especially as a single figure existed at the vertex of the political structure and possessed the ultimate authority to decide potentially divisive disputes. Yet, even here, factional conflict did occur, if the central figure failed to fulfill his role adequately or adopted policies which offended important sections of the political nation. This was the case, for example, in fifteenth-century England and sixteenth-century France, while by the sixteenth century the development of government bureaucracy and the court exacerbated the phenomenon of court factions attempting to influence a prince. In republics, especially those in Italy, where political forms were still sometimes in flux, more areas remained open to dispute, more people tended to be involved in the political process, and there was greater difficulty in resolving the disputes that arose. Serious disagreements tended, therefore, to emerge relatively frequently, and to escalate into political and even physical conflict before the issues at stake could be settled, often by the complete defeat of one faction or another and/or by the emergence of a lord whose unique power allowed him to decide issues and quell disputes.

Elements Giving Rise to Faction. For faction to arise, division was necessary within the ruling group. Such division generally took the form of a conflict between powerful clans. Repeatedly contemporaries describe factions in terms of the great families who headed them and who often gave them their names, from the Lambertazzi and Geremei of thirteenth-century Bologna to the Medici and Albizzi of fifteenth-century Florence to the Strumieri and Zambarlani parties formed in the sixteenth century in the Friuli region of northeastern Italy, around the Della Torre and Savorgnan clans. Outside Italy factional conflict was similarly associated with leading noble and even royal families, whether the Armagnacs and Burgundians of early fifteenth-century France, the Yorkists and Lancastrians of fifteenth-century England, or the rival Guise, Bourbon, and Montmorency of sixteenth-century France. It is fairly evident why such figures should be at the center of political groupings in a world before the development of modern political parties. Frequently of noble origin and with military skills, they possessed the wealth, status, and political influence necessary to attract wide support and emerge as political leaders. Such men were not prepared to take a secondary political role and were generally prepared to fight, if necessary, to assert themselves.

In some of the above cases, it is fairly clear why these prominent figures should have become engaged in factional conflict. In the monarchies the problem was repeatedly created by lack of leadership at the center: royal insanity, minorities, and young and impressionable kings all raised the question of who would provide effective government. Those closest to the throne naturally attempted to do so, as their honor and duty, but also because it served their interests of power and income. However, the interests and policies of these leading figures could clash to a degree which escalated into a major struggle for power. In the Italian cases the sources of the political conflict are sometimes less clear. On occasion the problem seems to have arisen from an imbalance within the ruling group caused by one family's gaining exceptional prominence, forcing other leading clans to band together to preserve their own political influence. Such, for example, seems to have been the origin of the pro- and anti-Guinigi factions in late fourteenth-century Lucca and the pro- and anti-Medici parties in early fifteenth-century Florence.

On other occasions chroniclers trace the origin of faction simply to personal animosity between great families, such as the disdain of the aristocratic Donati for the nouveaux riches Cerchi, so frequently cited as the source of the Black-White conflict in late thirteenth-century Florence. Such assertions should not be dismissed, as they reflect contemporary concepts of honor and vendetta, and help account for the primary division around which a faction could emerge. In fact the feud between the Cerchi and Donati (fueled by economic rivalries) helped polarize powerful families and create an escalating spiral of violent confrontation. The Florentine chronicler Dino Compagni (c. 1285–1324) shows us how this personal rivalry could, in the fluctuating and complex world of late thirteenth-century Florentine politics, turn into political conflict. According to Compagni it caused the Cerchi to seek support among disaffected sections of the Florentine population, from prominent commoners to guildsmen dissatisfied with recent political developments to Ghibellines (the pro-imperial party) by now in large part excluded from political life. The connection with the Ghibellines extended the conflict by bringing the Cerchi external support in the Ghibelline cities of Pisa and Arezzo, and foreign policy became a more serious issue once the Donati denounced their rivals to the pope as enemies of the papal (Guelf) party.

In the end, then, the factions developed from the level of personal rivalry to that of important political principles which could divide the whole political class. On the Black side lay Florence's traditional Guelf loyalty to the papacy; on the White, its equally traditional commitment to liberty from external intervention (now threatened by the pope), combined, according to some historians, with a general goal of social reconciliation.

Compagni's account rightly reminds us of the importance of external connections and intervention in the creation of factions. Repeatedly, what were limited internal conflicts turned into major factional strife because foreign powers intervened or internal opposition found support abroad. It was the conflict between pope and emperor that transformed local divisions into the international parties of Guelf and Ghibelline, whose power depended on finding much wider backing than a locality could provide. Similarly the king of France's desire for greater influence in Flanders lay behind the emergence of the Lilies (Leliaerts) and Claws (Clauwaerts) parties in that county in the thirteenth and fourteenth centuries, and Edward III's manipulation of the supply of wool to the Flemish cloth industry created a dominant pro-English party in 1338, at the start of the Hundred Years' War.

The socioeconomic aspects of faction at which Compagni hints are not always so easy to identify, and their importance has tended to be questioned by historians rejecting simplistic applications of Marxist theory. Social and economic issues were certainly in evidence during the thirteenth and fourteenth centuries, when population growth and then its rapid contraction led to aspirations or grievances on the part of the disadvantaged classes and to conflicts between aristocratic and popular parties, both led by members of the (as usual) divided elite. If, subsequently, economic issues were of less obvious importance, they did not disappear. For example, taxation was one of the factors affecting the formation of anti-Medici groups in mid-fifteenth-century Florence, and an anticorruption program of tax reduction and reform was the main plank in the Burgundian propaganda against the Armagnacs in early fifteenth-century France. Again, in the sixteenth century, as Edward Muir has shown, the Savorgnan feud with other noble families in Friuli became connected with the local peasants' grievances against their lords, as well as with urban rivalries and foreign alliances.

The role of principle in faction remains controversial; it has tended to be minimized in recent historiography, which emphasizes the classic concept of faction as concerned merely with self-interest and lacking any "ideological" content. Undoubtedly, higher principles were often used to cloak self-interest, but equally, self-interest could lead to the assumption of particular political ideals. An excellent example of the latter is offered by the Medici-Albizzi confrontation in Florence during the 1420s and 1430s. When the Albizzi group contemplated narrowing the political class, the Medici evidently opposed the idea, thereby emerging as the representatives of broad government and of the existing constitution, as well as supporters of the political interests of a relatively broad section of the citizen body. More cynical was the manner in which disaffected nobles of France (whether the Burgundians in the early fifteenth century or the leaders of the War of the Public Weal in 1464–1465) repeatedly veiled their self-interested motives behind claims to be acting for good government and the general welfare.

Nevertheless, such claims were taken seriously and were important in winning wider support. They therefore confirm that ideals could be influential in creating a strong political grouping as well as in justifying what might be interpreted as treasonable behavior. The same is true of the highest principle of all—religion—in sixteenth-century France. While it is not always clear whether nobles joined the Huguenot cause through conviction or for political advantage, religion was the most compelling motive justifying rebellion, and served as the only factor uniting diverse groups into a common cause. Even in the case of court factions, so concerned with promoting private interests through personal influence, higher principles were not completely forgotten. At the court of King Henry VIII of England, religion remained an important element in factional controversy. And in the rivalry between Ruy Gómez de Silva and Fernando Alvarez de Toledo, duke of Alba, at the court of Philip II of Spain (r. 1556–1598), foreign policy does seem to have been at stake, even if this has recently been interpreted as a purely self-interested quarrel.

Thus factions, while often originating in personal conflicts among prominent families, could radiate outward to affect wider groups and acquire complex significance. It is perhaps this capacity to attract multiple meanings and conflicts that explains why factions tend to come in pairs and why they so often succeeded in spreading throughout and beyond a ruling group.

Structure and Organization of Factions.

Along with the question of what factions were about goes the related issue of how they were formed and held together. Given parties' informal and even illegal character, their tendency to form around major families, and the nature of loyalties mentioned above, their main cohesive force was necessarily personal bonds. Around the leading figures of each side gathered their relatives, including those by marriage, dependents and retainers, and those whose interests and loyalties deeply attached them to one or the other side. Recently, of such personal attachments, the role of client-patron relationships has been given particular emphasis. It is clear that prominent figures, whether the Cerchi, the Medici, or the Savorgnan, did attempt to win political support by showing themselves willing and able to do favors for less powerful people, while one of the strengths of nobles everywhere was the political and personal patronage they could wield. However, it is exaggerated to see patronage as more than one element in the formation of factions. We must remember that clients often sought favors from various patrons, thus preventing the formation of one particularly strong bond, and that receiving small personal favors was not necessarily sufficient to cause a person to commit himself to political activity by definition dubious.

Moreover, as patronage itself was entered into for the sake of interests, how much it influenced political behavior depended on a continuing calculation of where one's interests lay. People's concepts of their interests and their loyalties were affected by many factors other than patronage; by, for example, the question of how events and policies would affect themselves, or by loyalty to higher principles such as religion. All this helps to explain why patronage and personal bonds did not always succeed in committing people decisively to one side or another, for ultimately a number of factors might influence a person's sense of where his best interests and highest loyalties lay.

The need to persuade people to commit themselves to a faction helps explain the efforts made to distinguish parties visibly and to create an effective party structure. When noble families were involved, this might take the form of wearing the family's colors or livery, or using special symbols, from handshakes to flowers. On occasion a minimum of formal organization might be achieved by the creation of the "companies" mentioned by chroniclers or by the oaths and written pacts used by opposing currents in fifteenth-century Florence. The most organized of such formal structures were those of the Guelf and

Ghibelline parties, which gained a degree of legitimacy through their connection with pope and emperor, respectively, and a more permanent and committed membership as a result of the long-term, severe conflict in which they engaged. These parties developed institutions with officials and councils imitating and even rivaling those of the city-state, and their organizations on occasion survived long after the papal–imperial struggle had lost much of its significance. However, even such structures could not always guarantee real or long-term loyalty. In general, factional alignments remained amorphous groupings of limited staying power, whose adherents shifted according to the pattern of issues, interests, and power prevailing at the time.

Overcoming Faction. Although contemporaries were not always aware of the deeper sources of faction, they did try to find means of extirpating them. Some of the methods used were of very limited efficacy, such as the highly emotional pacifications arranged among warring families or the frequently given exhortations to charity, forgiveness, and peace. The repeated appeals to place public before private interest, including those of civic humanism, did not touch the real political issues at stake, and even oaths imposed to commit citizens to constitutional behavior were easily broken. At a deeper level institutional means were sought to prevent faction. Some writers, such as Marsilio of Padua and the religious reformer of Florence, Girolamo Savonarola, remained convinced that guaranteeing sovereignty to the people and maintaining strict controls over an elected executive would prevent any sectional interest from dominating. Others saw that more was necessary. Niccolò Machiavelli suggested public institutions to deal with personal resentments and suspicions of subversive activity, but when faced with the phenomenon of the Medici, he could suggest only that it was better to temporize than to act against overly powerful citizens. Some, in despair, concluded that the only way to achieve peace and stability was to entrust ultimate power to one individual: the solution of Dante in the early fourteenth century and of Jean Bodin in the late sixteenth century.

However, some republics did succeed in solving the problem—lucky ones, like Venice and Nürnberg, which did not have to deal with an unruly nobility and which succeeded in stifling the "rivalry for office" by effectively closing the political class. By providing relatively good government and general prosperity, they could avoid provoking popular grievances and at least claim to be satisfying the universal goal of the common good.

See also Bourbon Family and Dynasty; Guise-Lorraine Family; Medici, House of; Montmorency Family; Wars of Religion; *and biographies of figures mentioned in this entry.*

BIBLIOGRAPHY

Primary Works

Bartolus da Sassoferrato. "A Tract on the Guelfs and Ghibellines." Translated by Ephraim Emerton. In Emerton's *Humanism and Tyranny: Studies in the Italian Trecento.* Cambridge, U.K., 1925. Pages 253–284. Translation of *Tractatus de guelphis et gebellinis.*

Compagni, Dino. *Dino Compagni's Chronicle of Florence.* Translated by Daniel E. Bornstein. Philadelphia, 1986.

Secondary Works

Boyden, James M. *The Courtier and the King: Ruy Gómez de Silva, Philip II and the Court of Spain.* Berkeley and Los Angeles, 1995.

Heers, Jacques. *Parties and Political Life in the Medieval West.* Translated by David Nicholas. Amsterdam and New York, 1977.

Kent, Dale V. *The Rise of the Medici: Faction in Florence, 1426–1434.* Oxford, 1978.

Lansing, Carol. *The Florentine Magnates: Lineage and Faction in a Medieval Commune.* Princeton, N.J., 1991.

McFarlane, Kenneth Bruce. *England in the 15th Century: Collected Essays.* London, 1981.

Meek, Christine. *Lucca 1369–1400: Politics and Society in an Early Renaissance City-State.* Oxford, 1978.

Muir, Edward. *Mad Blood Stirring: Vendetta and Factions in Friuli during the Renaissance.* Baltimore, 1993.

Skinner, Quentin. *The Foundations of Modern Political Thought.* Vol. 1, *The Renaissance.* Cambridge, U.K., 1978.

Vaughan, Richard. *John the Fearless: The Growth of Burgundian Power.* London, 1966.

PAULA C. CLARKE

FAIRS. In the high Middle Ages (eleventh to thirteenth centuries) fairs became a significant feature of economic activity, and by the end of that period they existed in large numbers all over northwestern Europe. Information about eastern Europe and Italy is less readily available, but paradoxically, economic retardation in the former and precociousness in the latter were inhibiting factors in fair development. Most fairs were of only local importance, an expansion of a weekly market into an annual event lasting a few days, often coinciding with the feast of a locally revered saint. A much smaller number acquired a wider regional or national standing, sometimes attracting merchants from a foreign country but without acquiring a truly international role. The English fairs of St. Ives, Boston, and Winchester, which were visited by Flemish merchants buying wool and sell-

Fairs. Market scene at Antwerp. Anonymous painting. ROYAL MUSEUM OF FINE ARTS, BRUSSELS, BELGIUM

ing cloth, are classic examples of this type. The annual cycle of six fairs in Flanders, comprising two at Ypres and one each at Bruges, Torhout, Lille, and Messines, were larger but did not rise much more above a regional status than did their English counterparts. The only true international fairs were the cycle of Champagne (in northeastern France), with two each at Troyes and Provins, and one each at Lagny and Bar-sur-Aube. By the end of the twelfth century these were the most vibrant centers of trade in Europe, where Italians exchanged Levantine and Mediterranean products for northern cloth brought by merchants from the Low Countries, France, and England. These fairs may be singled out also as the only ones where, before the fifteenth century, money itself, whether in metallic form or in the guise of international bills of exchange, was a commodity. This helped to maintain the importance of the Champagne fairs until about the 1320s, even though as centers for trade in wares they had been declining for at least forty years.

A downturn in the economic climate in the fourteenth century caused a severe and widespread decline in fair activity. Recovery in the fifteenth and sixteenth centuries was patchy and accompanied by changes in the nature of many fairs, whatever their degree of importance. At first it appeared that Chalon-sur-Saône in Burgundy might survive as an international successor to the Champagne fairs, but even before 1400 Geneva, Switzerland, had secured the inheritance. For much of the fifteenth century its four fairs, spaced through the year, were thronged with merchants from the Rhineland, the Low Countries, Italy, Spain, and all of France, dealing in merchandise, bullion, and financial instruments. In 1420 the French dauphin, later Charles VII, established fairs in Lyon, in Burgundy. Initially, these benefited from merchants coming to Geneva, but later the two places became keen rivals. A turning point came in 1463 when Louis XI altered the dates of the Lyon fairs to coincide with those of Geneva. One early indication of the shift in importance was the transfer of a branch of the Medici bank from Geneva to Lyon in 1465, and by the early sixteenth century the former was deeply overshadowed by the latter. The quarterly fairs of Lyon dominated Europe for the greater part of that century. They supported a prosperous trade in merchandise, especially silks and spices, but are best known for their role in the international money market. Loans were arranged there, bills cleared, and interest rates established. By the 1580s financial business was shifting to Besançon, another town conveniently situated on the borders of France and the Empire. Besançon flourished until well into the seventeenth century, purely as a money fair acting in close cooperation with similar fairs in Piacenza and Genoa in Italy and Medina del Campo in Spain.

The major Flemish fairs did not survive into the later Middle Ages and those of the northern Low Countries never attained more than regional significance. The fifteenth century saw the establishment of a cycle of four important fairs at Antwerp and Bergen op Zoom in Brabant. Paradoxically, the growth of Antwerp as a major international center of trade and finance in the early sixteenth century caused these fairs to decline. Part of the rationale of all fairs was that they allowed a temporary suspension of local privileges and monopolies to encourage visitors, but since Antwerp was an open city in this respect it did not need the fairs. In the early 1560s the English Merchant Adventurers Company, whose cloth trade provided a major stimulus to the fairs in the fifteenth century, tried vainly to restrict its members' business to the traditional fair structure of both towns. This conservatism was a defense mechanism against the company's Hanseatic rivals, who operated a flourishing year-round trade in English cloth at Antwerp.

In England many of the smallest fairs simply died out. Others changed their character and even increased their catchment area by specializing in one or two products or types of livestock, often combining this with an annual labor hiring function. Some relics still survive under regional names, such as mop fairs or goose fairs, though very few retain any of their ancient characteristics. Among the few nationally significant fairs in this period, the most important were those at Bristol; at Beverley in Yorkshire, which acquired three fairs between 1534 and 1555; and above all at Stourbridge, near Cambridge. The last, unheard of in earlier times, flourished until the eighteenth century and was patronized by customers from all over England.

In northern Europe the great fair at Scania, in southern Sweden, survived until the mid-sixteenth century. Although generally regarded merely as a herring fair, it was also a general distribution point for much of the west Baltic region. Apart from Scania the Hanseatic towns had little use for fairs and their civic ordinances prevented visiting English and Dutch merchants from penetrating the interior to patronize fairs in northern Germany and Poland. The most important German fair was that of Frankfurt am Main. Some historians have questioned whether this was an international fair or simply one serving a very large regional market. Since textiles brought from Italy and southern Germany were sent from the fair to the Low Countries, with English and Dutch cloth distributed in the opposite direction, there seems no reason to doubt its international status. In the sixteenth century the fair became important for financial transfers between Germany and the Low Countries, but activity was not on the scale of Lyon and the other southern fairs. Leipzig may be mentioned as the second German fair town and for its book fair, which still survives.

BIBLIOGRAPHY

Brésard, Marc. *Les foires de Lyon aux XVe et XVIe siècles.* Paris, 1914.

Dietz, Alexander. *Frankfurter Handelsgeschichte.* Vol. 1. Frankfurt, Germany, 1910.

Recueils de la Société Jean Bodin, vol. 5. *La foire.* Brussels, Belgium, 1953.

Thompson, James Westfall. *The Frankfurt Book Fair: The Francofordiense Emporium of Henri Estienne.* Reprint. New York, 1968. Originally published in 1911.

Verlinden, O. "Markets and Fairs." In *Cambridge Economic History of Europe.* Edited by M. M. Postan, E. E. Rich, and Edward Miller. Vol. 3. Cambridge, U.K., 1963. Pages 119–153.

T. H. LLOYD

FAMILY AND KINSHIP. Kinship loomed large in the life of the Renaissance. It was referred to by a variety of terms, among them lineage, house, *casa,* race, blood, and family. None of these are precise equivalents of what present-day anthropologists call kinship, and "family" was particularly ambiguous, since it was also the commonest way of referring to the household.

Structures. As defined by the incest prohibitions of the Roman Catholic Church, kinship comprised everyone with a common ancestry going back four generations (that is, extending out to third cousins), as well as the spouses of these relatives and some connected by godparentage. Some secular laws gave inheritance rights to descendants of even more remote common ancestors. In reality, however, kinship was perceived more narrowly, limited to individuals whose names were known and who saw each other from time to time. The perception varied according to social position and wealth.

The standard way of reckoning descent was through males. Mothers were invisible in most genealogies. As a member of a lineage, an individual belonged to a group of agnates, people related by blood through male progenitors. However, maternal blood relatives were also important. Bilateral descent was very much in the consciousness of the period, in spite of the greater emphasis on patrilines, and relatives with no connection by blood were also important. The church included both affinity and consanguinity in its definition of kin, and in-law relationships were the prime objective of many marriages.

Kinship and Power.

Kinship was different for the powerful than for the majority of people. Ordinary people did not have the resources to know as many distant relatives, whereas the elite could claim knowledge of even remote ancestors. The largest, most extended families were those in the upper levels of society. This was the era of dynasties, not only royal dynasties, but noble, patrician, and mercantile ones as well. Names of dynasties were at least as important as the names of individuals. Scholars have shown how important dynastic considerations were in the Renaissance, even in Italy, calling into question Jakob Burckhardt's influential characterization of the age as the cradle of modern individualism. It can be argued that the chief players were not individuals but collectivities like the Colonna and Orsini families of Rome, the Medici and Strozzi families of Florence, the extended Contarini family of Venice, the Fuggers of Augsburg, the ruling Habsburgs of Austria and Spain, the ruling Tudors of England, and the ruling Valois of France.

First among the symbols of powerful families were these surnames. The use of surnames was fairly new in the early fifteenth century and was at first associated only with important families, who based them either on the names of illustrious ancestors or on the names of territories whose possession was the basis of their power. More visible symbols were coats of arms, which decorated houses, furniture, the clothing of servants, and a variety of other things, including public works erected by popes and marked with the arms of their families. Houses were family symbols, too, whose size and appearance proclaimed power and wealth.

Inheritance was the key to family power in modest families as well as great ones. Property was passed down through a succession of individuals who were expected to preserve and enhance what they received. It was in this period that primogeni-

ture slowly spread to more and more sectors of society, since it had the advantage of preventing the fragmentation of patrimonies.

Individuals and Families.

There was hardly an aspect of an individual's life that was not affected by kinship, especially for someone in an important family. Nobles and patricians were acutely aware of their ancestors and constructed genealogies that were sometimes partly fictional, in which, for example, the founder of a lineage was a legendary hero of antiquity. Preserving the memory of ancestors appropriated aspects of Christianity, with elaborate funerary ceremonies, monuments, and the endowment of family chapels, which have preserved the names of some great families.

Every member of a great family shared in the family's reputation. How much this was also true of lower-class individuals is difficult to know. Great families overshadowed other families, almost seeming to be the only families, as indeed they were in the eyes of the state. The loss of family honor was a collective burden. An individual convicted of a serious crime not only shamed his kin but also might cause them to lose for generations to come the legal privileges they enjoyed as members of a noble family. Short of anything so drastic, any injury to family honor was nevertheless serious. Women had a special responsibility for maintaining the honor of their husbands' families by being above reproach sexually. All kinsmen got involved in rivalries with other families; feuds and vendettas were a feature of Renaissance culture.

It was assumed that individual desires would be subordinated to the needs of kinship. Marriage choices were based on what benefited the family, as were career choices. Family members in positions of power had an obligation to help their kin. Wealthier kinsmen were expected to come to the rescue of impecunious relatives. Even in the lower classes the first source of help for paupers was kin, but the laws in England, for example, obligated only fairly close relatives, like grandparents and aunts or uncles, to support kin. Members of great families assumed they had a right to approach distant relatives for help.

Nepotism. The system of family obligations and family power can be summed up in the word "nepotism." Far from being thought of as corrupt, favoritism toward one's family was admired. The most famous examples are found in the Renaissance papacy. In the course of what was usually a short reign, a pope would act quickly to advance the careers and status of his relatives, most often the immediate family of a sister, dispensing titles, bestowing property, arranging prestigious marriages, and, most notably, naming nephews as cardinals. Popes did on a grand scale what anyone did if he—or she—could. Royal ladies-in-waiting, for example, took care of husbands, brothers, and children. Whenever possible, the goal was to put a relative in a position where the family would benefit from future favors and, most important, acquire something that was hereditary.

See also **Marriage**.

BIBLIOGRAPHY

Primary Work

Alberti, Leon Battista. *The Albertis of Florence: Leon Battista Alberti's Della Famiglia.* Translated by Guido A. Guarino. Lewisburg, Pa., 1971. Reveals how a man like Alberti perceived family and kinship.

Secondary Works

Diefendorf, Barbara B. *Paris City Councillors in the Sixteenth Century: The Politics of Patrimony.* Princeton, N.J., 1983.

Goody, Jack, Joan Thirsk, and E. P. Thompson, eds. *Family and Inheritance: Rural Society in Western Europe, 1200–1800.* Cambridge, U.K., 1976.

James, Mervyn. *Family, Lineage, and Civil Society: A Study of Society, Politics, and Mentality in the Durham Region, 1500–1640.* Oxford, 1974.

Kent, Francis William. *Household and Lineage in Renaissance Florence: The Family Life of the Capponi, Ginori, and Rucellai.* Princeton, N.J., 1977.

Klapisch-Zuber, Christiane. *Women, Family, and Ritual in Renaissance Italy.* Translated by Lydia Cochrane. Chicago, 1985.

Kuehn, Thomas. *Law, Family, and Women: Toward a Legal Anthropology of Renaissance Italy.* Chicago, 1991.

BEATRICE GOTTLIEB

FAMOUS MEN AND WOMEN. The tradition of famous men and women, or *uomini famosi* and *donne illustri,* achieved considerable importance in Renaissance times, constituting perhaps the most significant form of monumental secular art of that period. The primary purpose of the revival of this ancient tradition in art and literature was to establish the immortality of a group of classically inspired heroes and heroines that adorned princely palaces and civic buildings, constituting a humanist-inspired thematic content that could be political, philosophical, intellectual, or personal.

Petrarch's *De viris illustribus* (On famous men), the first since antiquity, and Boccaccio's *De casibus virorum illustrium* (On the lives of famous men) and his *De mulieribus claris* (On famous women) served as the initial inspiration for the revival of this classical tradition in Italian trecento (fourteenth-century) art.

Famous Hero. *Man with a Broadsword* by Bramante. PINACOTECA DI BRERA, MILAN/ALINARI/ART RESOURCE

During this century cycles of heroes are known to have existed in Naples, Padua, Siena, Florence, and Rome. The earliest of these, painted in the 1340s by Giotto (1276–1337) for King Robert of Naples (1278–

1343, reigned 1308–1343), probably involved the collaboration of Petrarch (1304–1374). Though women were present in Giotto's series (now destroyed), it appears they were "wives" of the male heroes, smaller in dimension and placed in a lower position.

During the fifteenth century, cycles of famous men flourished in Italy. From 1407 to 1414, Taddeo di Bartolo decorated the ante-chapel of the Palazzo Pubblico in Siena with nine famous figures from republican antiquity. The Trinci family of Foligno commissioned, in about 1413, a Sala dei Giganti that included twenty Roman kings, statesmen, and generals. The humanist approach of these early examples is clear not only in the selection of famous men from classical history but also in the literary form of their accompanying *tituli* (inscriptions beneath the figures) that followed classical models. Cycles of classical heroes appear to have reached an even greater popularity in the second quarter of the quattrocento (fifteenth century). The proliferation of such cycles was meant to provide the "example of example" to contemporary Italians in matters of civic rule by serving political and didactic purposes; accompanying *tituli* pressed home the message. A variety of inscriptions ranging from 1438 to 1475 assist us in dating the twenty-three hero frescoes (including two women) of the Sala del Consiglio in the Palazzo Communale of Lucignano. This grouping has been connected with Dante's notion of the greatness of Rome—including its Hebraic inheritance, its development of Christian law, the founding of the "new" Rome, and the destiny of Rome to rule the world. Northern Italian cycles of famous men (for example, in the Castel Roncolo near Bolzano) exhibited a tendency to be more chivalric. Though most fifteenth-century cycles are painted, some sculptured examples are known, such as a relief series, now dispersed, by Desiderio da Settignano (1430–1464). The second half of the fifteenth century saw the publication of Vespasiano da Bisticci's *Lives*—a collection of biographies of popes, prelates, princes, nobles, and humanists—and witnessed increasing humanist enthusiasm reflected in the proliferation of painted cycles of famous heroes. A series of Roman warriors was painted by Domenico Ghirlandaio (1449–1494) for the Palazzo della Signoria in Florence, and Donato Bramante (1444–1515) painted a series of warriors for the Casa Panigarola in Milan (two of which survive in the Brera Gallery) and another of sages for a house in Bergamo (now lost). It was also during this period that a series of famous women, which probably accompanied a now-lost series of famous men, was painted; one panel of this series survives in the Andrew W. Mellon Collection (Washington, D.C., National Gallery of Art), and has been associated with Neroccio dei Landi (1447–c. 1500), Luca Signorelli (1445–1523), and the Griselda Master (fl. 1490).

Though the sixteenth century saw a distinct decline in the number of such cycles, it also witnessed the most brilliantly innovative of all, Raphael's (1483–1520) Stanza della Segnatura in the Vatican, where, on four walls, famous philosophers, jurists, poets, and theologians are represented in historical settings and mingling in conversation with one another, rather than arranged in rows with accompanying *tituli*. Perhaps the greatest and best-known collection of heroes was brought together in this century by Paolo Giovio (1483–1552) in his collection of portraits known as the Templum Virtutis. It is also in this century that Giorgio Vasari (1511–1574) wrote his *Le vite de' piu eccellenti architteti, pittori, et scultori italiani* (trans. *Lives of the Artists*, 1550), which was accompanied by engraved portraits of each artist. This was the first biographical collection of lives of artists, thus realizing an idea first expressed by Cicero, who had lamented that artists had not been included in the first steps—taken during his lifetime—to record the deeds of famous men lest their memories be forgotten.

See also biographies of Boccaccio, Petrarch, and other figures mentioned in this entry.

BIBLIOGRAPHY

Cheles, Luciano. *The Studiolo of Urbino: An Iconographic Investigation.* University Park, Pa., 1986.

Joost-Gaugier, Christiane L. "Dante and the History of Art: The Case of a Tuscan Commune. Part 1: The First Triumvirate at Lucignano." "Part 2: The Sala del Consiglio at Lucignano." *Artibus et Historiae* 21 (1990): 15–30; 22 (1990): 23–46.

Joost-Gaugier, Christiane L. "Giotto's Hero Cycle in Naples: A Prototype of Donne Illustri and a Possible Literary Connection," *Zeitschrift für Kunstgeschichte* 43 (1980): 311–318.

Mode, Robert. "*The Monte Giordano Famous Men Cycle of Cardinal Giordano Orsini and the 'Uomini Famosi' Tradition.*" Ph. D. dissertation, University of Michigan, 1970.

Mommsen, Theodor E. "Petrarch and the Decoration of the Sala Virorum Illustrium in Padua." *Art Bulletin* 34 (1952): 95–116.

Rubinstein, Nicolai. "Political Ideas in Sienese Art: The Frescoes by Ambrogio Lorenzetti and Taddeo di Bartolo in the Palazzo Pubblico." *Journal of the Warburg and Courtauld Institutes* 21 (1958): 179–207.

CHRISTIANE L. JOOST-GAUGIER

FARNESE, HOUSE OF. The Farnese were a family of military men and landholders in southern Tuscany and the northern part of the Papal States, ele-

House of Farnese

Alessandro
1468–1549
Pope Paul III

Bosio II Sforza = Costanza   Pier Luigi = Gerolama   Paolo   Ranuccio
                             1503–1547   Orsini
                             duke of Parma
                             and Piacenza

Charles V
Holy Roman Emperor

Guido Ascanio
Sforza di Santafiora
1518–1564
cardinal

Vittoria = Guidobaldo II
          della Rovere

Alessandro
1520–1589
cardinal

Ottavio
1524–1586
duke of Parma
and Piacenza

= Margaret
of Austria

Ranuccio
1530–1565
cardinal

Orazio
1531–1553

Maria = Alessandro
of Braganza   1545–1592
              duke of Parma
              and Piacenza

Margharita = Ranuccio
Aldobrandini   1569–1622
              duke of Parma
              and Piacenza

Odoardo
1573–1626
cardinal

KEY

=   Marriage

⦚   Illegitimate issue

Odoardo
1612–1646

Ranuccio II
1630–1694

---

vated to princely status by Pope Paul III Farnese. In the Middle Ages and the Renaissance, the Farnese were politically important especially in the area between the Lake of Bolsena, Viterbo, and Orvieto. For the most part Guelf partisans, they furnished a number of distinguished mercenary captains to Florence, Venice, and the papacy in the fifteenth century. The fortunes of the family took a dramatic turn with the election in 1534 of Cardinal Alessandro Farnese to the papal throne as Paul III (reigned 1534–1549), and with the extraordinary extent of his nepotism.

Three of the pope's grandsons were added to the college of cardinals: Guido Ascanio Sforza di Santafiora (1518–1564), son of his daughter Costanza, and his namesake Alessandro (1520–1589) and Ranuccio (1530–1565), sons of his son Pier Luigi (1503–1547). Another grandson, Ottavio (1524–1586) became prefect of Rome. In 1537 Pier Luigi was made duke of the newly created duchy of Castro, as well as commander in chief of papal troops. More important and controversial was the alienation of church lands by Paul III in order to forge in 1545 the duchy of Parma

and Piacenza for his family. Despite opposition by Emperor Charles V (ruled 1519–1558), Pier Luigi became the first duke. His rule was short-lived. By his tactlessness and strong-arm tactics against the local elite, Pier Luigi provoked a conspiracy and was assassinated in 1547. His son Ottavio succeeded him as the second duke.

Political power and territorial acquisition were strategies for aggrandizing the family. Another was through marriage alliances. Pier Luigi married Girolama Orsini, a member of one of the oldest Roman noble families. His sister Costanza married into the aristocratic Sforza family. Paul III controlled the marriages of his grandchildren as well. His greatest coup was the union of his grandson Ottavio with Margaret, illegitimate daughter of Emperor Charles V. Although the couple was notoriously at odds, Ottavio and Margaret eventually did have children, thus assuring Farnese succession to Parma and Piacenza. Pier Luigi's daughter Vittoria was married to the duke of Urbino. Another son of Paul III, Orazio (1531–1553), married the illegitimate daughter of the

OCTAVIVS·FARNESIVS·CAMERINI·DVX
MARGARITAM·CAROLI·V·IMP·FILIAM
PAVLO·III·PONTIFICE·MAX·AVSPICE
SIBI·DESPONDET·ANNO·SAL·∞D·XXXIX

A Farnese Marriage. Pope Paul III presides at the betrothal of his grandson Ottavio
Farnese to Margaret of Austria, daughter of Emperor Charles V, 1539. Mural by Taddeo
Zuccaro in the Palazzo Farnese, Caprarola. ALINARI/ART RESOURCE

French king Henry II. Thus, Paul III achieved the transformation of the Farnese into a great Italian princely house.

Among his grandsons, Cardinal Alessandro stands out. Appointed vice-chancellor of the church in his mid-teens, he was showered with so many benefices by the pope that he became one of the richest cardinals. Although he developed into a shrewd and successful diplomat, posterity remembers him primarily as a great art collector and generous patron of writers and artists. He was responsible for the completion of the magnificent Farnese palace in Rome, and the building of many churches, most famously the Jesuit church of the Gesù in Rome, and the decoration of the Cancelleria, also in Rome. Other outstanding building projects were a villa on the Palatine Hill in Rome and the great Farnese villa in Caprarola.

Alessandro's brother Ottavio ruled Parma and Piacenza during a particularly difficult time. He openly defied his grandfather, Pope Paul III, after whose death he became politically dependent on King Philip II of Spain (ruled 1556–1598), the half-brother of his wife Margaret of Austria, Spanish regent of the Netherlands from 1559 to 1567. The main object of Ottavio's policy was the preservation of the duchy for his descendants. His only son, Alessandro (1545–1592), lived as a youth at the Spanish court and became entirely hispanicized. He garnered fame as one of the greatest military leaders of his age, fighting for Spain in the wars of Dutch independence. Alessandro was instrumental in preserving the southern Netherlands as part of the Spanish Empire. As duke of Parma, he was more authoritarian than his father, centralizing the state at the expense of the nobility.

Alessandro's son Ranuccio (1569–1622) may be the best-known of the Farnese dukes. During his long reign of thirty years he presided over the formation of an absolute state, promulgating laws, streamlining administrative offices, constructing massive monuments to the Farnese and building the outsized ducal palace in Parma. He continued his father's policy of suppressing heresy and supporting the Jesuits. Endowed by Ranuccio, their college for young nobles in Parma became a famous educational institution with students from all Italian states and from abroad. Ranuccio also founded the University of Parma in 1601; it still existed at the end of the twentieth century.

At Ranuccio's death his brother, Cardinal Odoardo Farnese (1573–1626), assumed the regency of the duchy for his nephew and namesake Odoardo (1612–1646). During his twenty-year reign, Duke Odoardo was able to play a more independent role in Italian politics than his predecessor. Spain, a vassal state of which Parma and Piacenza had been for almost a century, was in decline as a great power. Odoardo, and after him his son Ranuccio II (1630–1694), tried to consolidate their rule over all their territories, including Castro, which led to the War of Castro (1642–1644) with the papacy. The seizure of Castro by Pope Innocent X in 1649 diminished Farnese possessions.

The Farnese line in Parma and Piacenza came to an end with the last two dukes, Ranuccio II's sons, Francesco (1678–1727) and Antonio (1679–1731). Their sister Elisabetta (1692–1766) married King Philip V of Spain (ruled 1700–1746), and the duchy passed through inheritance to the Spanish Bourbon.

As a family, the Farnese followed a consistent political program: after they became rulers, their first objective was to preserve Parma and Piacenza in their power. They strongly supported the Catholic church in their territories, favoring especially the Jesuits. Their close alliance with Spain in the sixteenth century gave way to more complex diplomatic maneuvering between the Holy Roman Empire, France, and Italian states in the seventeenth. Patrons of artists and architects, the Farnese contributed splendid buildings above all to Rome and Parma. The most significant patrons of the family were Pope Paul III and his grandson, the second cardinal Alessandro Farnese.

See also **Parma; Paul III.**

BIBLIOGRAPHY

Drei, Giovanni. *I Farnese: Grandezze e decadenza di una dinastia italiana*. Rome, 1954. Solid and informative.

I Farnese: Arte e collezionismo. Milan, 1995. Exhibition catalog with rich and up-to-date bibliography.

Robertson, Clare. *Il Gran Cardinale: Alessandro Farnese, Patron of the Arts*. New Haven, Conn., and London, 1992. Study of Cardinal Alessandro and his patronage. Good bibliography.

ELISABETH G. GLEASON

FEDELE, CASSANDRA (Fidelis; 1465–1558), Venetian writer and humanist scholar. Cassandra Fedele was born in Venice. Although she had among her kinsmen a bishop, an attorney, and a physician, her father, Angelo Fedele, never acquired a profession. Nothing is known about her mother, Barbara Leoni, or her mother's family. Her father introduced Cassandra to Latin grammar and the Roman orators and poets. When she reached the age of twelve, he sent her to Gasparino Borro, a monk, who taught her Greek grammar, philosophy, the sciences, and Aristotelian dialectics.

From the beginning, Angelo Fedele represented Cassandra as a child prodigy. She delivered Latin orations standing before the assembled faculty at the University of Padua, the Venetian Senate, and before the doge himself. At twenty-two, Fedele saw her first book go to press, a work with four letters and an oration (*Oratio pro Bertucio Lamberto* [Oration in honor of Bertucio Lamberti]; Modena, 1487). Before she reached the end of her twenties, her vita began to appear in encyclopedias of famous men and women.

Fedele's chief professional achievement lay in the vast correspondence she maintained with both local and far-flung friends and patrons over several decades. Like male humanists before her, she exchanged perhaps thousands of letters with some of the most celebrated men and women of her day. Only a fraction of these letters survive. Although Fedele never held an academic appointment, she corresponded with the leading Aristotelian at the University of Padua, Niccolò Leonico Tomei, and she met regularly with a number of prominent Paduan humanists. She also maintained warm friendships through letters with the chancellor of Florence, Bartolomeo Scala, with his daughter Alessandra, who had played the part of Sophocles's Antigone and who wrote Greek verse, and with Alessandra's teacher, the poet Angelo Poliziano. Fedele exchanged letters with royalty throughout Europe, including every Italian queen, duchess, and marchise in Baldassare Castiglione's *Il cortegiano* (*The Book of the Courtier*; 1528).

Fedele came close to accepting an academic appointment with Queen Isabella and King Ferdinand of Spain. For eight years she corresponded with the queen and her representatives, but war put an end to her plans in 1495. She married in 1498, but in 1520 her husband died, leaving Fedele a widow, childless, and almost penniless. She shared cramped quarters with her sister's family until 1547, when Pope Paul III responded to her plea for assistance by securing an appointment for her as prioress at the orphanage of San Domenico di Castello. In 1556, Fedele made her last public appearance—she delivered an oration welcoming the queen of Poland to Venice. Of her writings, only two published books survive: one the pencil-slim volume of letters she published when she was a girl; the other, a 1636 Paduan edition of her works containing 123 letters and 3 orations, *Cassandrae Fidelis epistolae et orationes* (The letters and orations of Cassandra Fedele).

Cassandra Fedele was the most renowned woman scholar of her time. She accepted the gender ideology of her era and believed in the "natural" inferiority of the female sex. In her literary self-presentation, she foregrounded her small stature, her physical weakness, her maladies, the sluggishness of her mind, her inability to write stylishly, and her deference toward men. Thus Fedele, or—if not Fedele herself—the two deeply redacted editions of her letters that have survived, offered later generations of women writers a model very different from that of Laura Cereta and the early Venetian feminists who were driven by personal goals rather than social issues.

See also biography of Laura Cereta.

BIBLIOGRAPHY

Primary Work

Cereta, Laura. *Collected Letters of a Renaissance Feminist.* Edited and translated by Diana Robin. Chicago, 1997. Includes letters addressed to Cassandra Fedele.

Secondary Works

King, Margaret L., and Albert Rabil Jr., eds. *Her Immaculate Hand: Selected Works by and about the Women Humanists of Quattrocento Italy.* Binghamton, N.Y., 1983. Includes selected letters by Cassandra Fedele in translation.

Labalme, Patricia. "Venetian Women on Women: Three Early Modern Feminists." *Archivio Veneto* 5, no. 117 (1981): 81–108.

Robin, Diana. "Cassandra Fedele (1465–1558)." In *Italian Women Writers: A Bio-Bibliographical Sourcebook.* Edited by Rinaldina Russell. Westport, Conn., 1994. Pages 119–127.

Robin, Diana. "Cassandra Fedele's Epistolae (1488–1521): Biography as Effacement." In *The Rhetorics of Life-Writing in Early Modern Europe: Forms of Biography from Cassandra Fedele to Louis XIV.* Edited by Thomas F. Mayer and D. R. Woolf. Ann Arbor, Mich., 1995. Pages 187–203.

DIANA ROBIN

FEDERICO DA MONTEFELTRO (1422–1482), Italian military leader, patron of the arts. Signore (lord) of Urbino from 1444, first as its count, then from 1474 as its second duke, and highly esteemed as a mercenary general, Federico channeled his wealth into patronage of the arts, briefly elevating his state to an outstanding cultural center.

The illegitimate son of Count Guidantonio, he came to rule his father's papal vicariates at the behest of Urbino's citizens, after his half-brother's murder there. From 1474 he was Gonfaloniere of the church, knight of the Neapolitan Order of the Ermine, and knight of the Garter. Already in 1453 Flavio Biondo's "Italia illustrata" differentiated him as the contemporary role model for an aspiring young Italian prince. His reputation rested on four bases: a remarkably successful military career, political acumen, lavish patronage of the arts, and promotion of humanistic learning.

Federico was trained for military command from the age of sixteen, under Niccolò Piccinino and then under Francesco Sforza. His trustworthiness, tenacity, and careful campaigns brought him fame and fortune. From 1451 until his death, his annual military contracts, exceptionally for the whole year (rather than for the eight months of likely fighting in a year) and renewable, were with the king of Naples. From 1460 (except for twelve months from mid-1473), he was simultaneously general of the forces of the league concerned to maintain the Peace of Lodi. Financial rewards fluctuated, but from 1474 until his death he was contracted to receive from the king almost 120,000 Neapolitan ducats annually as a retainer for his generalship and for a small personal army of cavalry and infantry. This was apart from the league's stipend and gratuities from the pope. His own force preserved his state from expansionist neighbors, notably Sigismondo Pandolfo Malatesta. As a royal client, Federico could anticipate that no pope was likely to rescind effectively his vicariates; to ensure further security, he promoted a web of marriage alliances between ruling dynasties of the Romagna and the Marches. Federico's military career provided employment within his state and helped ensure low and stable taxation, despite his prodigious spending for "magnificence" from 1465. His building program was notable. Besides building defensive frontier fortresses (particularly in case he died while his son was a minor), he rebuilt Urbino's Montefeltro palace and the cathedral on a lavish scale and in accord with humanistic precepts. More modest refurbishments enhanced other towns of the state, particularly Gubbio, which was protected by a fortress on the hill above and beautified within its walls by a fine ducal palace. Federico employed, among others, Luciano Laurana and Francesco di Giorgio Martini as architects, and Piero della Francesca and Justus of Ghent as painters. The highly original interior decoration of the Urbino palace, especially its set of eleven Flemish tapestries of the

Trojan War, was a tastemaker. Vittorino da Feltre, who taught the ten-year-old Federico in Mantua, stimulated his classical learning and stressed to him the obligations of a Christian prince. One outcome was the Urbino palace library, partially formed by purchases from Fiorentino Vespasiano da Bisticci, which was open to scholars. They dedicated their works to Federico, hoping for patronage, and hence their contemporary writings in manuscript, and even (rarely) as printed books, enhanced the library's core of classical texts.

BIBLIOGRAPHY

Primary Works

Bisticci, Vespasiano da. "Commentario de la vita di Federico, Duca di Urbino." In *Le vite.* Edited by Aulo Greco. 2 vols. Florence, 1970–1976. Vol. 1, pp. 354–416. The best edition of Bisticci translated by W. G. Waters as *Memoirs: Lives of Illustrious Men of the Fifteenth Century* London, 1926. Pages 83–114. (Reissued under the title *Renaissance Princes, Popes, and Prelates,* New York, 1961.)

Paltroni, Pier Antonio. *Commentari della vita e gesti dell'illustrissimo Federigo, Duca d'Urbino.* Edited by Walter Tommasoli. Urbino, Italy, 1966.

Secondary Works

Clough, Cecil H. *The Duchy of Urbino in the Renaissance.* London, 1981.

Clough, Cecil H. "Federigo da Montefeltro: The Good Christian Prince." *Bulletin of the John Rylands University Library of Manchester* 67, part 1 (1984): 293–348.

Clough, Cecil H. "Federico da Montefeltro and the Kings of Naples: A Study in Fifteenth-Century Survival." *Renaissance Studies* 6 (1992): 113–172.

Tommasoli, Walter. *La vita di Federico da Montefeltro, 1422–1482.* Urbino, Italy, 1978.

CECIL H. CLOUGH

FEMINISM. For two millennia before the Renaissance women were silent before the authority of men. During the Renaissance a new female voice emerged. By the end of the Renaissance women had begun to see themselves in new ways. These were the first feminists, advocates not only of equality and education but of taking control of their lives.

Humanism and Feminism.

Renaissance humanism was midwife to the emergence of the feminist voice. Between 1399 and 1402 Christine de Pizan (1365–c. 1430) corresponded with several French writers over the moral value of Guillaume de Lorris's *Roman de la rose* (Romance of the rose; 1265), to which Jean de Meun had written a continuation and which popularized traditional male views of women. She argued that the novel, not woman, was morally deficient. During the same period she read a recent French translation of Boccaccio's *De claris mulieribus* (On famous women; c. 1360–1374), a book extolling the public accomplishments of 104 mostly classical women. Pizan wrote *Le livre de la cité des dames* (1405; trans. *The Book of the City of Ladies*) in which she cited many of Boccaccio's examples but interpreted them differently. She refused to identify women with their sexuality, as Boccaccio had done in several cases, and when the sources emphasized sexual deviance, as in the case of Semiramis, who committed incest with her son, Pizan attributed her behavior to the state of civilization at the time she lived. As for the differences between men and women, she conceded only that men were physically stronger and insisted that women and men were on equal footing in terms of character. Thus she believed in the possibility of extraordinary achievement for any woman of virtue. She recognized that the differences between men and women were culturally generated—women, she said, were not as learned as men because they were not sent to school and did not participate in the public arena, where one learns many things—but she did not advocate changing women's social status. Nonetheless, hers was a boundary-shifting book, and she was the first genuine feminist.

A few women humanists in Italy experienced but did not identify social oppression. Isotta Nogarola (1418–1466), Cassandra Fedele (1465?–1558), and Laura Cereta (1469–1499), among others, hoped their learning would bring acceptance by learned men, but all failed to gain it. In an exchange with a male humanist, Ludovico Foscarini, Nogarola absolved Eve of responsibility for the fall by accepting the misogynist perception of Eve as weak. Fedele urged women to study but warned that it brought no outward reward, only personal delight. Cereta alone expressed optimism that women could gain equality by applying themselves to learning, asserting that their failure to do so was their own fault and urging them to cultivate their minds more avidly than their dress or makeup.

Early in the sixteenth century feminists appeared in France, notably Louise Labé (c. 1524–1566), a poet who urged women to take up scholarly pursuits, and Madeleine (c. 1520–1587) and Catherine (1542–1587) des Roches who presided over a salon known as the school of learning or academy of honor and were encouraged by the humanists who attended it to pursue their studies and publish their work. They were thus unusual among learned women of the Renaissance in that they participated fully in an intellectual culture with men.

Feminist Consciousness. From the late fifteenth until the mid-sixteenth century the feminist voice became more audible and more assertive. The first women in England to defend women (Jane Anger, 1589; Ester Sowernam, Rachel Speght, and Constantia Munda, 1617) were writing *self*-defenses. While many of the early participants in the *querelle des femmes* (the woman question) were said to be engaged in play or self-conscious paradox and could have written on either side, it is impossible to imagine any of these later women writing a brief against themselves; all responded with outrage to the stereotyping of their sex.

Although these writers identified traditional spiritual virtues with women, they saw men as also capable of such qualities, reintroducing Pizan's notion that true virtue is the same for both sexes. Hence, it could be said that the virtuous person is androgynous. A number of women in London from the 1570s until the 1620s acted out their androgyny through cross-dressing and were often referred to as hermaphrodites. In January 1620 King James I ordered ministers to preach against cross-dressing in their sermons. In February a treatise titled *Hic mulier, or, The Man-Woman* was published, reaffirming the idea that women have a fixed nature. In one week another treatise appeared, *Haec-vir, or, The Womanish Man,* which proclaimed that "to conclude *Custome* is an Idiot." Differing as it does from one time or place to another, culture cannot reflect the laws of nature: the English mourn in black, the Romans mourned in white; "I see not but we may mourne in *Greene, Blue, Red.*" Here was something prophetically novel.

During these same years in France similar radical stirrings were in the air. Between the assassination of Henry IV in 1610 and the majority of Louis XIV after he survived the civil wars of the Fronde, which ended in 1653, the salon tradition was introduced, largely through the impetus of two female regents who governed France during their children's minorities. When the influence of Marie de Médicis (regent, 1610–1614) ended in 1630, Louise-Marguerite de Lorraine, princesse de Conti, left the court and established a salon-in-exile at her château at Eu. There she wrote her memoirs of the court of Henry IV and read them at her salon, then handed the manuscript over to writers in her circle, asking them to rewrite it for publication as a novel. This practice became a pattern crucial to the early history of the French novel. The novels created at Eu used a historical setting to develop plots composed equally of political and amorous adventures. They were written by men and women alike, but a woman's name was attached to each.

In the 1620s, 1630s, and 1640s the *femme forte* (strong woman), portrayed as a Christian Amazon fighting, hunting, shooting, and riding and dressed like a man while engaged in these pursuits, appeared in French novels emerging from the salons. During the Fronde women exercised great power in France on both sides; many fought as warriors. It was during these years that Madeleine de Scudéry published *Artamène, ou le grand Cyrus* (1649–1653), initially a political novel but, as the Fronde ended, changing direction and focusing on intellectual matters through dialogue. The years 1653–1660 were important in establishing a change from the *femme forte* to the *précieuse* (lay intellectual). The novels of Scudéry and others thereafter chronicled the salon life of intellectual conversation.

During the same half century three Italian women expressed strong feminist views. Lucrezia Marinella, the author of *La nobiltà et l'eccellenza delle donne, co' diffetti e mancamenti de gli huomini* (The nobility and excellence of women, with the defects and vices of men; 1600, augmented edition 1601), written in response to Giuseppe Passi's diatribe *I donneschi diffetti* (The defects of women; 1599), reveals great learning and skill in formal debate. She is the first female writer to confront male authorities directly (Passi and Aristotle in the 1600 edition, supplemented by Boccaccio, Sperone Speroni, Torquato Tasso, and Ercole Tasso in the 1601 edition). All of them, she says, generalize from one woman or some women to all women. Marinella expresses the hope that women will "wake themselves from the long sleep which oppresses them." In Moderata Fonte's *Il merito delle donne* (The worth of women; 1600) seven Venetian noblewomen document female inequality in Venice (for example, exclusion from education, withholding of dowries), thus making an explicit connection between misogynist assumptions and social practice. One speaker urges women to "wake up, and claim back our freedom, and the honor and dignity men have usurped from us for so long." The intent here is not entirely rhetorical. Arcangela Tarabotti's *La tirannia paterna* (Paternal tyranny), published posthumously as *La semplicità ingannata* (Innocence deceived; 1654), denounces the practice by which young girls—like Arcangela—were forced into convents by parents who wished to avoid having to provide them dowries.

In many of these texts women begin to see themselves as actors who must shape their own destiny. Before the end of the seventeenth century European feminists had developed a consciousness of themselves as a group. Although Mary Wollstonecraft's *Vindication of the Rights of Woman* (1792) was the first clear call to change the conditions under which women lived, her feminist forebears in the Renaissance prepared the way.

See also **Querelle des Femmes**; **Women**; *and biographies of women mentioned in this entry.*

BIBLIOGRAPHY

Beilin, Elaine V. *Redeeming Eve: Women Writers of the English Renaissance.* Princeton, N.J., 1987.

Benson, Pamela. *The Invention of the Renaissance Woman.* University Park, Pa., 1992.

DeJean, Joan. *Tender Geographies: Women and the Origins of the Novel in France.* New York, 1991.

Jordan, Constance. *Renaissance Feminism: Literary Texts and Political Models.* Ithaca, N.Y., 1990.

Kelso, Ruth. *Doctrine for the Lady of the Renaissance.* Urbana, Ill., 1956. Especially useful for her bibliography of 891 items.

King, Margaret L. *Women of the Renaissance.* Chicago, 1991.

Labalme, Patricia H., ed. *Beyond Their Sex: Learned Women of the European Past.* New York, 1980.

Lerner, Gerda. *The Creation of Feminist Consciousness.* New York, 1993.

Maclean, Ian. *The Renaissance Notion of Woman: A Study in the Fortunes of Scholasticism and Medical Science in European Intellectual Life.* Cambridge, U.K., 1980.

Maclean, Ian. *Woman Triumphant: Feminism in French Literature, 1610–1652.* Oxford, 1977.

Smith, Hilda L. *Reason's Disciples: Seventeenth-Century English Feminists.* Urbana, Ill., 1982.

Woodbridge, Linda. *Women and the English Renaissance: Literature and the Nature of Womankind, 1540 to 1620.* Urbana, Ill., 1984.

ALBERT RABIL

FERDINAND I (1503–1564), Holy Roman Emperor (1558–1564), king of Hungary and Bohemia (1526–1564). Born in Spain, Ferdinand was the second son of Infanta Juana, the eventual heiress to the throne of Castile, and her husband, Archduke Philip, the son of the emperor Maximilian I. After his older brother Charles became Holy Roman Emperor in 1519, Ferdinand received the Austrian patrimonial lands of his house, thus beginning the split between the German and Spanish branches of the Habsburg dynasty. He married the sister of Louis, king of Hungary and Bohemia, and after Louis's death in the Battle of Mohács (1526), he succeeded to the two crowns. As king of Hungary and Bohemia, Ferdinand was on the front line of defense against the expansion of the Ottoman Turks, who in 1529 threatened Vienna itself. Although he failed to recapture Hungary fully from his lifetime opponent, Sultan Süleyman the Magnificent, Ferdinand did stitch to-

Emperor Ferdinand I. Portrait by Martin Rota, 1575.

gether the defenses of central Europe enough to keep the Turks at bay.

An energetic and capable ruler, Ferdinand set up an administrative structure of financial, secretarial, and consultative offices widely imitated throughout Germany. A devout though flexible Catholic, Ferdinand believed that the church could be preserved only through moral and educational reform. It was in part his persistent prodding and knack for reconciling differences that brought the Council of Trent to a relatively successful conclusion in 1563. He was also a major force behind the 1555 Peace of Augsburg, which conferred a temporary measure of religious calm on Germany.

Having departed from Spain in 1518, Ferdinand spent some time at the court of his Aunt Margaret in Mechelen. There he was deeply touched by the moderate Christian Reform of Erasmus; he remained committed to it for the rest of his life. He tried, in vain, to bring the Dutch humanist to the University of Vienna. Nevertheless, Ferdinand's court in Vienna drew an array of sympathetic intellectuals, moderate Catholics such as Johannes Faber (1478–1541), who may have suggested the *cuius regio eius religio* formula of the Peace of Augsburg, and irenic Protestants, such as one of Ferdinand's physicians, Johannis Crato (1519–1585).

Ferdinand was a generous, eclectic, and knowledgeable patron of arts and learning. A lover of music, his reorganization of the imperial chapel choir in 1527 under Arnold von Bruck attracted Netherlandic musicians and composers who raised both performance and programming standards to exceptionally high levels. Major composers such as Jakobus Vaet and Philippe de Monte (1521–1603) served as directors during the reign of Ferdinand's son, the emperor Maximilian II (ruled 1564–1576). Ferdinand's extensive coin collection became the core of the numismatic holdings of the Austrian National Library. Several talented painters served him at various points in their careers. In 1562 he brought the extravagant mannerist Giuseppe Arcimboldo (c. 1530–1593) from Milan to Vienna. Ferdinand ennobled the painter Jakob Seisenegger (1505–1567) in 1558 after twenty-eight years of service, during which Seisenegger painted a series of strikingly expressive portraits of Ferdinand and several of his children. Ferdinand ordered reforms at the University of Vienna in 1533, 1537, and in 1554 that substantially furthered not only the study of the classical languages but also contemporary scholarship in the field. In 1523 he founded a chair for Greek at the university, and in 1535 one for Hebrew.

See also **Austria**; **Habsburg Dynasty**; **Holy Roman Empire**.

BIBLIOGRAPHY

Fichtner, Paula Sutter. *Ferdinand I of Austria: The Politics of Dynasticism in the Age of the Reformation.* Boulder, Colo., and New York, 1982. An overview of Ferdinand's career.

Hilger, Wolfgang. *Ikonographie Kaiser Ferdinands I.* Vienna, 1969.

Lhotsky, Alphons. *Festschrift des kunsthistorischen Museums zur Feier des fünfzigjährigen Bestands.* 2 vols in 3. Horn, Austria, 1941–1945. Still a definitive account of the collections, many of which trace their origins to the early modern period.

PAULA SUTTER FICHTNER

FERDINAND OF ARAGON (Ferdinand the Catholic; 1452–1516), king of Aragon (as Ferdinand II; 1479–1516), king of Castile (as Ferdinand V; 1474–1504), king of Sicily (as Ferdinand II; 1468–1516), and king of Naples (as Ferdinand III; 1504–1516). Ferdinand of Aragon and Isabella of Castile (1451–1504) are known to posterity as the *Reyes Católicos* (Catholic sovereigns), an honorific title granted them by the papacy.

Ferdinand was born in Sos, Aragon, the son of John II by his second wife, Juana Enríquez. King John, looking for allies to help in a civil war in his domains, arranged a marriage in 1469 for his son with Isabella of Castile on terms that were disadvantageous to his son.

Ferdinand and Isabella. A succession struggle broke out in Castile after King Henry IV's death in 1474 when Isabella, his half-sister, with assistance from Ferdinand, took the throne away from her adolescent niece, Juana. After Portugal invaded Castile in support of Juana's faction, Isabella improved the marriage contract for her husband, whose prestige was augmented when he inherited Aragon in 1479. Thereafter, Ferdinand and Isabella cooperated in a famously harmonious "union of crowns," although the queen's personal life seems to have been unfulfilled due to her husband's philandering. The king brilliantly used his legitimate children as diplomatic pawns: After his two oldest, Isabella and the heir apparent John, died early, that left Juana to be sent to Austria, María to go to Portugal, and Catalina (as Catherine of Aragon) to marry Arthur, prince of Wales, and then Henry VIII of England.

Ferdinand and Isabella resolved upon a strategy of keeping factions at bay with a succession of wars. When Andalusian aristocrats invaded Muslim Granada in 1481 the monarchs made the long struggle their own. After Granada fell in 1492 its Muslims were later converted and dispersed. In Aragon, however, Ferdinand allowed large concentrations of superficially converted Muslims. Ferdinand instituted the Inquisition in 1478 under royal, not papal, control to police orthodoxy and feed the royal treasury from expropriations. The Inquisition was the only institution shared by church and state. Pressure from the grand inquisitor convinced the crown in 1492 to expel or convert all remaining Jews.

Ferdinand and Isabella next directed their energies toward southern Italy. Pope Alexander VI was by birth an Aragonese subject of Ferdinand, and he favored the king with a so-called Holy League against France. After Naples was taken from the French in 1503 by Golzalo Fernandez de Córdoba (the Grand Captain), the kingdom remained under Spanish rule for the next two and a half centuries. Ferdinand emerged as a major player in Italian politics with wide-ranging influence. Another arena for Spanish arms in cooperation with Italian finance opened in the Western Hemisphere, when Christopher Columbus's second, third, and fourth voyages showed the full extent of his finds.

Ferdinand's Legacy. Isabella's death in 1504 ended the union of crowns. Under her will the Castilian succession went to their daughter Juana (Joan the Mad) and her husband, Philip "the Handsome" (Philip I of Spain, 1504–1506). After being excluded from succession in Castile, the king first thought to set a return by marrying Isabella's rival and niece, Juana *"La Excelente Señora,"* but instead took as bride in 1505 Germaine de Foix, niece of King Louis XII. After Philip I's death (1506) Ferdinand, as stipulated by a clause in Isabella's will, returned in 1507 and within a few years incorporated Navarre into Castile. Before dying at Madrigalejo, he prepared the advent of his grandson, Charles V (1500–1558), king of Spain (as Charles I, 1516–1556) and Holy Roman Emperor (as Charles V, 1519–1556).

That succession inadvertently formed a united Spain; one with control over part of Italy and an incipient empire in the Americas. Less auspiciously, Ferdinand bequeathed military conflicts for which his subjects were financially unprepared, his militant Catholicism left festering divisions, and the aristocracy of Castile retained economic control. He has been much admired by Spaniards because he was their last Spanish ruler before their land passed to foreign dynasties. Machiavelli is more ambivalent than they about Ferdinand, despite presenting him in *The Prince* as an admirable "new" ruler who from being a weak king rose through his own efforts to become first prince of Christendom. He found Ferdinand to be a sly fox who preached peace and mutual trust, yet was the enemy of both. Machiavelli thought Ferdinand's religiosity no more than a pretext to extract money from the church, to justify attacks on neighbors, and to indulge in "pious cruelty" by harassing and looting his subjects.

Ferdinand and the Renaissance. Because his Sicilian and Neapolitan associations gave him an admiration for Italian culture, Ferdinand promoted humanism in his Aragonese realms. He was patron to Lucius Marineus Siculus and Antonio Geraldi and encouraged the study of Latin to equip his diplomatic service, the first such corps created outside Italy. Elio Antonio de Nebrija, who returned from Italy to compile the first grammar book (1492) of a modern language (Castilian), was followed by Peter Martyr of Anghiera, who chronicled Spain's exploration, and Lucius Marineus Siculus, who was from 1484 to 1496 professor at Salamanca. Hebrew, Latin, and Greek were taught at the University of Alcalá (founded 1508) and incorporated in a Polyglot Bible (1514–1517). Following Italian examples, Juan del Encina (1468–1529) and Lucas Fernández (c. 1474–

Ferdinand of Aragon. Portrait by an unknown artist, originally from the collection of Henry VIII. THE ROYAL COLLECTION © HER MAJESTY QUEEN ELIZABETH II

1542) set eclogues and songs in pastoral surroundings.

In painting, Pedro Berruguete shows Italian influence, but the style favored by Ferdinand's court continued to be northern European. Painters in the Hispano-Flemish manner include John of Flanders and Michael Zittow and the sculptors Hans Wass and Gil de Siloé. Architecture blended florid native medievalism in a goldsmith-inspired Plateresque style on the façade of the Escuelas Mayores at the University of Salamanca (1525) and in Valladolid for the Church of San Pablo by Siloé and the Hospital of Santa Cruz (1487–1491) by Enrique de Egas.

An idealized full-length portrait of the king, kneeling at prayer with his family, is prominent in the anonymous *Virgin of the Catholic Sovereigns* (c. 1490), now held at the Prado Museum. An anonymous double portrait bust of the sovereigns at the convent of Santa María de Gracia (Ávila) is more realistic. The Royal Chapel in Granada's Cathedral has painted wooden reliefs (1520–1522) by Felipe Vigarny that present the king on horseback and, at the same location, his recumbent form is displayed on Domenico Fancelli's marble sepulchre (1512–1517).

See also **Isabella of Castile.**

BIBLIOGRAPHY

Congreso de Historia de la Corona de Aragon, Fifth. *Pensamiento politico, politica internacional y religiosa de Fernando el Católico.* Saragossa, Spain, 1956.

Fernández-Armesto, Felipe. *Ferdinand and Isabella.* New York, 1991. Brief topical coverage is thorough up until Isabella's death.

Hillgarth, J. N. *The Spanish Kingdoms.* Vol. 2, *1410–1516: Castilian Hegemony.* Oxford, 1978. Well written, with an excellent bibliography.

Mattingly, Garrett. *Renaissance Diplomacy.* Boston and London, 1955. Deals with Ferdinand's foreign policy through his diplomatic agents.

Merriman, R. B. *The Rise of the Spanish Empire.* Vol. 2, *The Catholic Kings.* New York, 1918. Old but balanced appraisal.

Suárez Fernández, L., and M. Fernández Álvarez. *La España de los Reyes Católicos (1474–1516).* 2 vols. Madrid, 1969. Most comprehensive coverage of the joint reign.

Vincens Vives, J. *Historia critica de la vida y reinado de Fernando II de Aragón.* Saragossa, Spain, 1962. First volume of uncompleted work ends with 1481.

MARVIN LUNENFELD

FERNÁNDEZ DE CÓRDOBA, GONZALO

(1453–1515), Spanish military commander. Known for reorganizing the army and extending Castilian military power to Granada and Italy, Fernández came to be known as *el gran capitán* (the great captain) because of his victories and was celebrated in contemporary Spanish literature.

Fernández went from his home in Córdoba to the Castilian court in 1466, and by the mid-1470s he was a major figure in Spanish military affairs. Fernández strengthened the army by enlarging the infantry, organizing troops into units of six thousand known as *tercios,* and equipping soldiers with pikes, swords, javelins, and muskets. He led the army in the final stages of the campaign against the Muslim kingdom of Granada, and he negotiated the kingdom's surrender in 1492. In 1495 he took an army to Italy to support the Aragonese kingdom of Naples against King Charles VIII of France, whose invading force he helped drive out of Italy. In 1500 he returned to Italy when Spanish and French kings agreed to conquer Naples and partition its territories. By 1502 the victors were quarreling over their spoils, and in 1503 Fernández evicted French forces from the kingdom of Naples.

In 1504 he became the first Spanish viceroy of Naples. He held the post until recalled to Spain in 1507, but he returned to Italy at the head of an army following the French victory at the Battle of Ravenna in 1512. He died in Granada in 1515. His reorganization of the Spanish army survived until the mid-seventeenth century, and it contributed to the effectiveness of Spanish forces in the Americas as well as in Europe.

BIBLIOGRAPHY

De Gaury, Gerald. *The Grand Captain: Gonzalo de Cordoba.* London and New York, 1955.

Purcell, Mary. *The Great Captain: Gonzalo Fernández de Córdoba.* New York, 1962.

JERRY H. BENTLEY

FERRARA. [This entry includes two subentries, one on the history of the city and territory of Ferrara in the Renaissance and the other on artists active in Ferrara.]

Ferrara in the Renaissance

The classical-style sixteenth-century female bust set over the right-hand doorway of the west facade of Ferrara's cathedral (*duomo*) is popularly known as "Madonna Ferrara," legendary founder of the city. Ferrara's name originated in a Roman settlement cultivating low-grade wheat (*farro*) on the right bank of the Po River. During the Renaissance the city increased considerably in size, deriving much wealth from the rich agricultural lands of the associated vicariates, under the essentially peaceful rule of the Este.

Population. The August 1601 census of Ferrara's twenty-four parishes totaled 32,869 individuals, including 1,478 religious (clerics, monks, friars), 454 nuns, and 1,530 Jews; additionally, the population of the outlying territory of the former duchy of Ferrara totaled much the same. In January 1598 the duchy (as it had become) of Ferrara passed from the Este to direct papal rule, whereupon a large painted canvas was sent by Ferrara to Loreto depicting the new governor, Cardinal Pietro Aldobrandini, the pope's nephew, kneeling in thanks to God before a silver votive effigy of the Madonna of Loreto, whose robe bore a representation of Ferrara.

The plebiscite of 1310 reveals Ferrara's population as almost two-thirds that of 1601, with 3,740 males, presumably heads of households (women, children, servants, and the religious were not included) in thirty-two districts (*contrade*). The returns detailed (perhaps not entirely reliably) categories,

Ferrara. Covered staircase in the Palazzo del Corte (now the Palazzo Communale), 1503. ALINARI/ART RESOURCE

professions, and occupations: for instance, 217 magnates, 218 foreigners, and 24 Jews. Clearly the dominance of the Guild of Judges and Notaries was already well established, with 10 judges and 283 notaries, testimony to the city's extensive legal and administrative controls over its inhabitants. There were 12 medical practitioners, 1 dentist, 10 teachers of grammar, 96 shoemakers, and 109 tailors, yet only 2 masons. In the 1490s the city's Jewish population notably increased, following the 1492 expulsion of Jews from Spain and Sicily, and the following decades witnessed a further influx from the kingdoms of Naples and Portugal.

The City and Its Government. Despite the Black Death and its aftermath, by the mid-fifteenth century there was settlement beyond the walls, causing Duke Borso d'Este to extend them to the south. In the early 1490s Duke Ercole I considerably extended the walls to the north, taking in the Certosa of Santa Maria degli Angeli and the Este palace of Belfiore (sacked by Venetian forces a decade earlier), thereby almost doubling the city's enclosed area (this latter extension is the Herculean Addition). Concomitantly the duke authorized redevelopment within the walls on classical lines by the Ferrarese architect Biagio Rossetti. Principal thoroughfares were broadened and crooked alleys considerably straightened. A wide road—the Corso Giovecca— replaced the ditch that prior to the extension was immediately outside the city walls; it proceeded over a mile in a straight line from the castle (*Castelvecchio* [San Michele]) to the north gate of the new city wall. One goal of the planning was to place at the city's heart its main buildings: the Este *Corte* and castle, the fourteenth-century Gothic city hall (Palazzo della Ragione), and the cathedral. Public squares brought light and air into the city. Hence Ferrara was the earliest sizable planned Renaissance city, predating Turin by some seventy years.

Theoretically Renaissance Ferrara and its territory were subject to papal authority, but from the early thirteenth century this had been delegated in perpetuity through the legitimate male line to the Este as papal vicars. Communal government, based on male citizenship and guild membership, maintained a hollow semblance of power, for it elected as a matter of form each succeeding Este vicar as lord (*signore*). Ferrara's citizens, mindful of their free commune's internecine struggles, preferred princely rule by a dynasty that fostered public well-being. Revolts were few, and most originated in rivalry between Este family members.

The *signore*'s authority was essentially absolute by the terms of his communal election and in virtue of papal authority as vicar; moreover, the lord controlled nomination to all important offices, which he filled with Este clients. The commune dealt with matters regulated by the city's statutes, such as weekly street cleaning. It was responsible for the homes for widows built in 1401 (in Via Mortara) and for the elegant Market Hall (*Loggia de' Mercanti*) of 1473. Even so, all the city council's decisions were subject to the *signore*'s approval. Foreign relations were the responsibility of the Este, save for contentious rights claimed by Venice relating to Adriatic trade and annual fairs; these claims, asserted by means of a resident Venetian consul (*vicedomino*) were much resented after Ferrara's defeat by Venice in the war that ended in 1484, when the Este duke's territory was reduced by the loss of Rovigo and Polesine lands.

The Este lords, though holding imperial fiefs, usually resided in Ferrara and the lands surrounding. Their quest for "magnificence" in the fifteenth century especially resulted in exceptional Renaissance architecture in Ferrara, though some buildings were lost in the 1570 earthquake and its aftershocks. The city's international reputation was established in 1438 when Pope Eugenius IV chose its cathedral as the compromise venue for a council which aimed at reconciling the Eastern and Western churches. The cathedral, dedicated to St. George, possessed as a relic an arm of the saint, patron of the city.

The Este. The castle was built in 1383 following an uprising against the dynasty; it incorporated a former city gate, the Torre de' Leoni, wherein were the dungeons and torture chambers, and on its outside wall over the moat were displayed state criminals in metal cages. The castle was heavily fortified as a refuge for the prince, but at the end of the fifteenth century Duke Ercole I assigned it to his heir, Alfonso I, as his residence. Already in 1472 it had been connected by a covered walkway to the Palazzo del Corte, where Duke Ercole lived, and which was the subject of incessant renovations over the next thirty years. The Este had several summer palaces, including Belriguardo (eight miles outside the city), Belfiore (brought into the city in the 1490s), and Schifanoia, which had been begun by Alberto d'Este in the 1390s, probably for guests. Sculpted effigies were erected at prominent locations within the city. Charitable institutions that contributed to the city's well-being received generous Este patronage, notably the Hospital of Santa Anna for the sick, founded in 1444 by Ferrara's bishop. Churches and associated religious buildings were founded or extensively renovated at Este expense, including

the nunnery of Corpus Domini of the Order of St. Clare, whose church within the convent contains the tombs of Lucrezia Borgia and her husband, Duke Alfonso.

Like the Medici of Florence, the Este avidly promoted public spectacles. Borso had a piazza before the Palazzo Schifanoia cleared for tournaments, and Ercole I favored theatrical performances in his palazzo's courtyard; in the sixteenth century very lavish divertissements were associated with Este weddings and the annual carnival, whose processions were along the Giovecca. The city's culture was largely that of the Este and their court. In 1391 Alberto, while on a pilgrimage to Rome, obtained a papal bull which, among other privileges, granted the city a university; Alberto's statue, showing him as a pilgrim clutching the papal bull, is in a niche outside the cathedral. Alberto had a new palace built for the university, which for a decade or so from the 1440s enjoyed an international reputation when Guarino da Verona instructed in the *studia humanitatis*. Borso later re-created the institution, giving an emphasis to law and medicine.

In the late fifteenth century the wealthy nobility had family palaces built in Renaissance style, a dominant feature being external decoration with classical motifs in terra-cotta, the Palazzo Magnanini (now Roverella) on the Giovecca is one example. Overspending by the princes from the 1470s brought increasing taxation; consequently, a neglect of public and private property characterized the sixteenth century. Drainage suffered, bringing malaria, which though unidentified as such brought a rise in the death rate in the late summer months. As the sixteenth century waned a general decline in the city's lifestyle was paralleled by court decadence, a sorry end to almost four centuries of Este rule.

See also **Este, House of.**

BIBLIOGRAPHY

Primary Works

Bonasera, Francesco. *Forma veteris urbis Ferrariae.* Florence, 1965.

Secondary Works

Beloch, Karl Julius. *Bevölkerungsgeschichte italiens.* 2d ed. Revised by Margherita Piazzolla-Beloch and W. Hageman. 3 vols. Leipzig and Berlin, 1965. See vol. 2, pp. 108–115.

Lanzoni, Ermanno, and Anna Chiara Venturini. *Ferrara: Una città nella storia.* Ferrara, Italy, 1984.

Noyes, Ella. *The Story of Ferrara.* London, 1904.

Rosenberg, Charles M. *The Este Monuments and Urban Development in Renaissance Ferrara.* Cambridge, U.K., 1997.

Zeri, Bruno. *Saper vedere l'urbanistica: Ferrara di Biagio Rossetti, la prima città moderna europea.* Turin, Italy, 1971.

CECIL H. CLOUGH

Art in Ferrara

The history of art in Renaissance Ferrara properly begins in the late fourteenth century when the ruling family, the Este, became actively engaged in artistic patronage.

Early Este Patronage. During the reigns of Nicolò II (1361–1388) and Alberto V (1388–1393) d'Este, four important centers of future artistic activity were constructed: the Castelvecchio and Palazzo Schifanoia in 1385, the Palazzo Paradiso in 1388, and the villa Belfiore in 1391 (subsequently destroyed). Although records document a number of painters living in Ferrara during this period, it is not possible to connect surviving notices with any specific works. Remnants of mural decorations dating from the late fourteenth and early fifteenth centuries have been found in the Schifanoia and Paradiso palaces. These fresco fragments reveal that the Este shared the pan-European preference for chivalric and courtly themes. Illuminations in late-fourteenth-century Ferrarese guild statutes show a variety of influences, including those of the Paduan, Bolognese, and Lombard schools.

Probably the most significant artistic developments in Ferrara during the reign of Nicolò III d'Este (1393–1441) were the foundation of a new Dominican monastery, Santa Maria degli Angeli, close to the villa Belfiore; the construction of Belriguardo, a hunting lodge and villa located about twelve miles (twenty kilometers) southeast of the city; and the commission of a spectacular, International-style, illuminated manuscript, the so-called Bible of Nicolò III (Vatican Barberini), executed in the early 1430s. Most notable among the artists working on this manuscript was the north Italian illuminator Luchino Belbello da Pavia.

Nicolò's son and successor, Leonello (1441–1450), significantly changed the tenor of the Ferrarese court through his strong interest in humanist culture, which was reinforced through his association with such distinguished scholars as Guarino da Verona. During his reign the marquis commissioned and purchased works by artists such as Pisanello, Jacopo Bellini, Andrea Mantegna, and Rogier van der Weyden. Perhaps most emblematic of Leonello's humanistic orientation were two projects begun during his reign and completed by his brother and successor, Borso (1450–1471): the elaborately ornamented

study at Belfiore, decorated with intarsie by Arduino da Baiso (fl. 1406–1454) and a cycle of the Muses, executed by Angelo Macagnino (fl. 1447–1456), Michele Pannonino (c. 1400–1464), and Cosmè Tura (c. 1430–1495) and based on a program probably drawn up by Guarino; and a bronze equestrian monument to his father, Nicolò III. The commission for the latter project was based on a competition in which Leon Battista Alberti may have played a decisive role. The work was executed by two sculptors associated with the circle of Donatello: Antonio di Cristoforo (1443–1459) and Nicolò Baroncelli (fl. 1434–1453).

Emergence of a Ferrarese School. Borso d'Este's reign witnessed the emergence of an identifiable Ferrarese school of painting. Of the many artists employed by the duke, the painters Cosmè Tura and Francesco del Cossa (c. 1435–1476/77), and manuscript artists Taddeo Crivelli (c. 1425–1479), Franco dei Russi (fl. c. 1453–1482), and Guglielmo Giraldi del Magro (1445–1490) are perhaps the best known.

Cosmè Tura. Tura, who is generally acknowledged as the founder of Ferrarese painting, was responsible for designs for tapestries and silverware and also created an elaborately painted and stuccoed chapel in Belriguardo. His best-known surviving works are a pair of organ shutters painted for the cathedral of Ferrara in 1469 (Ferrara, Museo del Duomo), and the panels associated with an altarpiece that he executed for the Roverella chapel in San Giorgio fuori le Mura, Ferrara, in the mid-1470s (London, National Gallery; Rome, Colonna Collection; Paris, Louvre; and elsewhere). His style, which demonstrates a knowledge of the work of the Paduan artist Francesco Squarcione and of Flemish traditions, is characterized by wiry, nervous figures clothed in angular, linear drapery. These figures are often set into elaborately ornamented architectural settings or in front of landscapes that evince the typical stratified rocky vistas of the Paduan school.

Francesco del Cossa. Francesco del Cossa is best known for the frescoes that he painted in the late 1460s in the Sala dei Mesi (Room of the months) in the Palazzo Schifanoia, Ferrara. The Schifanoia was expanded and decorated at the end of Borso's reign and, in its present form, affords a shadowy glimpse of what the much larger and more elaborately frescoed Este villas of Belfiore and Belriguardo must have looked like. The three-tiered frescoes in the Sala dei Mesi are the work of several different artists. With their combination of astro-mythological scenes in the upper two zones and densely interwoven vignettes of Ferrarese courtly life in the palace and countryside in the lowest zone, these images, which combined erudition and splendor, celebrate the Este court as a center of earthly virtue and enlightened rulership. The duke's commitment to personal magnificence was also manifested in the bronze statue of Borso by Nicolò Baroncelli, erected by the commune in front of the Palazzo della Ragione in Ferrara in 1454. Shortly after completing his work in the Schifanoia, Cossa, who was apparently dissatisfied with his position in Ferrara, left the city to work in Bologna. His style, which is visible not only in the Schifanoia frescoes but also in the panels of an altarpiece done for Griffoni chapel in San Petronio, Bologna, between 1472 and 1473 (London, National Gallery; Milan, Brera; Washington, D.C., National Gallery), exhibits both the bony, nervous figural style of Tura and the greater three-dimensional monumentality of Piero della Francesca. Cossa's works also echo Tura's style in their depiction of clinging, sharply folded, metallic clothing and illogical, densely ornamented architectural backdrops and fantastic stony, stratified landscapes.

Illumination. The contributions of Taddeo Crivelli and Franco dei Russi are best exemplified in the images found in one of the most lavishly illuminated books of the entire fifteenth century, the two-volume "Bible of Borso d'Este" (1456–1459; Modena, Biblioteca Estense). This bible, with its hundreds of lavishly embellished pages, is a veritable encyclopedia of Ferrarese manuscript illumination. The art of a third illuminator, Guglielmo Giraldi, may be seen in the pages of a bible that he executed for the monks of the newly erected Certosa di Ferrara (1467–1476; Ferrara, Museo Civico, Palazzo Schifanoia), and in an illuminated copy of Dante's *Divine Comedy* produced for the duke of Urbino in the early 1480s, a project on which he and Franco dei Russi collaborated (Vatican City, Biblioteca apostolica vaticana). Ferrarese manuscript illumination in this period is characterized by both sophistication and eclecticism, and shows a range of stylistic influences from the Burgundian, Tuscan, Lombard, and Paduan schools.

The Late Fifteenth and Sixteenth Centuries.

Borso's successor, Ercole I (1471–1505), is probably best known for his intense involvement in architectural projects, including substantial additions to the ducal palace, the enlargement of the apse of the cathedral of Ferrara, and the extension of the walls of the city to the north in order to create a massive new urban area known as the Addizione

Art in Ferrara. *Virgin and Child Enthoned* from the Roverella Altarpiece by Cosimo Tura (c. 1430–1495), c. 1474. NATIONAL GALLERY, LONDON/FOTO MARBURG/ART RESOURCE

Erculea. Biagio Rossetti (c. 1447–1516), the architect of the cathedral project, has also been given credit for planning the addition to Ferrara. Although he is still acknowledged as the designer of some of the most significant structures within the addition, including the Palazzo dei Diamante and Santa Maria della Consolazione, it now appears that Rossetti played a more supervisory role on the larger project.

Ercole de' Roberti. One of the most versatile artists employed by Ercole I was Ercole de' Roberti (c. 1456–1496). Roberti was probably trained in Cossa's shop. A salaried court painter by 1487, he was responsible for decorating the newly constructed apartments of the duchess Eleanora of Aragon (1473–1493) in the Castelvecchio in the early 1490s and for making significant contributions to the elaborate fresco program in Belriguardo. Roberti was a highly inventive artist whose emotional narrative style, visible in the predella panels from the Griffoni Altarpiece (1473; Vatican City, Pinacoteca Vaticana) and a pair of passion scenes from a Bolognese altarpiece (1480s; Dresden, Gemäldegalerie Alte Meister), seems to have been particularly suited to the intense devotional piety practiced by both the duke and duchess. In addition to serving as court painter, Roberti also designed the church of Santa Maria in Vado and an ill-fated colossal equestrian monument dedicated to the duke. Ercole I's increasing interest in narrative art is evident in the work of a number of local artists he employed, including the painters Gian Francesco Maineri (fl. 1489–1506) and Lodovico Mazzolino (c. 1480–after 1528), and the sculptor Guido Mazzoni (c. 1450–1518). Mazzoni's highly veristic, impassioned polychrome terracotta *Lamentation* (c. 1483–1485; Ferrara, Il Gesù) particularly reflects the growing taste for emotional religious imagery.

The Reign of Alfonso I. Ercole's son Alfonso I (1505–1534) continued the family tradition of creating sumptuous suburban and rural retreats by building the paradisal villa Belvedere on an island in the Po River. This *delizia* (delight), as the Este villas were known, which was destroyed in the seventeenth century, incorporated carefully planted flower beds and groves, ingenious fountains, and a palace embellished with terrazzo floors and lavish frescoes by such artists as Dosso Dossi.

Alfonso greatly expanded the ducal collection of antiquities and aggressively sought to employ not only local artists but also ones with international reputations, including the painters Giovanni Bellini, Raphael, and Titian, and the sculptor Antonio Lombardo, all of whom contributed to the decoration of the duke's private *camerini* (small rooms) in the corridor connecting the Este palace to the Castelvecchio.

The local artists who most clearly define the character of Ferrarese art during Alfonso I's reign are the brothers Dosso Dossi (Giovanni Lutero; c. 1490–1541/42) and Battista Dossi (Battista Lutero; c. 1490/95–1548) and Garofalo (Benvenuto Tisi; 1481–1559). Dosso's contributions to the decorations of the *camerini* included a *Bacchanal* (London, National Gallery) and a cycle of scenes from the Aeneid (Birmingham, Barber Institute of Art; Ottawa, National Gallery of Canada). Typical of Dosso's style are his numerous mythological and allegorical paintings, including his *Apollo* (Rome, Borghese Gallery) and the luminescent *Allegory of the Origins of Painting* (Vienna, Kunsthistorisches Museum), and the extensive cycle of allegorical frescoes that he painted with Battista in the Castello del Buonconsiglio in Trent (1531–1532).

In addition to his work on the Trent project, Battista was responsible for numerous decorations in the ducal palace, the Castello, and various Este villas in and around Ferrara. In his capacity as court artist, he designed a series of influential arboreal allegories that were woven into tapestries for the duke. The style of the Dossi demonstrates both the influence of Venetian art in the handling of light and landscape and a fondness for figural idealization and strong narrative gestures drawn from a wide variety of sources, including Giorgione, Raphael, Michelangelo, and antiquity.

Garofalo is best known for his numerous devotional paintings and altarpieces, including a magnificent polyptych that he executed with Dosso's assistance for the church of San Andrea in Ferrara (c. 1530–1532; Ferrara, Pinacoteca Nazionale), and for the cycle of allegorical paintings and portraits he did in the Sala del Tesoro (Room of the treasure) in the Palazzo Costabili (c. 1510; Ferrara, Palazzo di Ludovico il Moro). This artist's accessible and attractive style is closely related to that of the Dossi, exhibiting the influence of both Venetian painting and the art of Lorenzo Costa and Raphael.

The last Este. During the reigns of the last two Este rulers of Ferrara, Ercole II (1534–1459) and Alfonso II (1559–1597), the ongoing decorations of the ducal apartments and reception rooms in the Palazzo Ducale, Castelvecchio, and villas were carried out by the Dossi, Garofalo, Girolamo da Carpi (c. 1501–c. 1556), and others. In addition to his work as a painter, Girolamo was also responsible for the design of one of the last of the Este suburban retreats, the Montagna di San Giorgio, on the extreme eastern side of Ferrara. Il Bastianino (Sebastiano Filippi; 1532–1602) contributed to the character of Ferrarese art in the later portion of the century. Many of his paintings, including the *Last Judgment* in the apse of the cathedral of Ferrara (1577–1580) and the frescoes in the Salone dei Giochi (Room of games) in the Castelvecchio (c. 1575), show a curious combination of a soft, shimmering luminosity with a powerful Michelangelesque figural style.

See also **Este, House of**; *and biographies of figures mentioned in this entry.*

BIBLIOGRAPHY

Baruffaldi, Girolamo. *Vite de' pittori e scultori ferraresi.* Ferrara, 1844. Reprint, Bologna, Italy, 1972.

Bentini, Jadranka, and Luigi Spezzaferro. *L'impresa di Alfonso II: Saggi e documenti sulla produzione artistica a Ferrara nel secondo cinquecento.* Bologna, Italy, 1987.

Franceschini, Adriano. *Artisti a Ferrara in età umanistica e rinascimentale. Testimonianze archivistiche.* 3 vols. Ferrara, Italy, 1993–1997.

Hermann, Hermann Julius. *La miniatura estense.* Translated by Giovanna Valenzano. Modena, Italy, 1994. Translation of *Zur Geschichte der Miniaturmalerei am Hofe der Este in Ferrara* (1900).

Mottola Molfino, Alessandra, and Mauro Natale, eds. *Le muse e il principe: Arte di corte nel Rinascimento padano.* 2 vols. Modena, Italy, 1991.

Rosenberg, Charles M. *The Este Monuments and Urban Development in Renaissance Ferrara.* Cambridge, U.K., and New York, 1997.

CHARLES M. ROSENBERG

FERRARA-FLORENCE, COUNCIL OF. *See* **Florence, Council of.**

FERREIRA, ANTÓNIO (1528–1569), Portuguese poet and dramatist. Ferreira was born in Lisbon. His father was a member of the household of the duke of Coimbra, and António always remained faithful to this important family.

One-quarter of Ferreira's life was spent at the University of Coimbra (1543?–1555/56), where he studied canon law and became steeped in humanistic learning. This Portuguese university, originally located in Lisbon, had been refounded at Coimbra in 1537, and Ferreira, therefore, lived through a particularly dynamic period in its history. Though he was not enrolled in the famous Colégio das Artes

(College of Arts), which flourished as an independent institution from 1547 to 1555, he knew Diogo de Teive, who taught there, and he may have had some contact with George Buchanan. His two comedies and the famous tragedy, *Castro,* were written and performed during this period. Leaving the university for the royal service in Lisbon was a profound shock, and in many poems he complained of the difficulty of pursuing humanistic ideals in the corrupt atmosphere of the capital. His brief marriage to Maria Pimentel occurred at an unknown date, but probably between 1557 and 1560; his courtship and her early death are the subject of much of his writing in these years. Sometime in the 1560s he remarried. In 1567 he was appointed *desembargador* (judge), and in 1569 he died, prematurely, in the great plague of that year.

António Ferreira's poetry and plays are the most perfect expression of Renaissance classicism and humanism in Portugal. Alone among his contemporaries he avoided the traditional Iberian meters and composed exclusively in classical and Italian poetic forms, some of which he introduced to Portugal. He was also the only sixteenth-century poet of importance never to have written in Spanish. Despite his reliance on Petrarchan and classical models, some of his love poetry is of considerable originality. The purpose of much of his other writing is to create in Portugal an awareness of the moral and aesthetic ideals associated with humanism. His collected works, to which he gave the patriotic title of *Poemas Lusitanos* (1598), are dedicated to a group known as the *bons espritos* (good spirits), formed partly by the poet's friends but also by important public figures such as kings John III and Sebastian and Cardinal Prince Henry.

Ferreira's masterpiece is the verse tragedy *Castro* (c. 1553–1558) which is based on an incident from Portuguese history, the judicial murder of Inês de Castro in 1355. Ferreira, like his contemporaries in Italy and France, follows the model of Seneca but modifies the Roman view of fate to take account of the Christian concept of free will. In this way he is able to explore, with great psychological penetration, the options open to a ruler faced with a difficult problem of conscience. In the play Ferreira succeeded in combining love poetry with the moral and political concerns of Christian humanism.

Ferreira, together with Luis de Camões (in *The Lusiads,* Canto 3; 1572), is particularly associated with the dissemination of the myth of Inês de Castro. The tragedy has, therefore, tended to eclipse Ferreira's other writings, whose importance has only recently begun to be fully appreciated.

BIBLIOGRAPHY

Primary Works

Ferreira, António. *Poemas Lusitanos.* Edited by T. F. Earle. Lisbon, 1999. A modern edition of the first edition of 1598.

Ferreira, António. *The Tragedy of Inês de Castro.* Translated by John R. C. Martyn. Coimbra, Portugal, 1987.

Secondary Works

Dias, José Sebastião da Silva. *A política cultural da época de D. João III* (Cultural politics in the period of King John III). Coimbra, Portugal, 1969. The most complete study of the Portuguese university in the Renaissance.

Earle, T. F. *The Muse Reborn: The Poetry of António Ferreira.* Oxford, 1988.

T. F. EARLE

FESTIVALS.

Renaissance festivals may be usefully classified in several different ways: as religious, civic, or courtly; as annual or for unique occasions; as popular and folkloric or elite and learned; and, finally, according to whether they were celebratory of the religious and social order or subversive of it. No category of these classifications was entirely discrete, for there was much overlapping of tone and circumstance. Thus, in violation of the final distinction, an old tradition in some cities authorized the rabble to confiscate the valuable canopy under which a fervently cheered sovereign or pope had just ridden. At Ferrara in 1598, even Pope Clement VIII's horse was seized as legitimate booty. Nevertheless, this division between "establishment" feasts and subversive ones is the one most in tune with the concerns of contemporary scholarship, and the most useful for a general discussion.

Celebration of the Existing Order.

Both religious and civic pageantry, often overlapping, aimed at representing the established order in a favorable light, at creating an impression of harmony and security.

Religious feasts and processions. The comforting calendar of religious feasts and processions, with their repeated allusions to the drama of the Crucifixion and redemption, to the afterlife and to the church's role in salvation, suggested a purposeful, coherent view not just of human history but of the universe. When civic officials took part in religious processions, as for example on Palm Sunday in Venice and on various occasions in other cities, the arrangement implied a perfect integration of the spiritual and secular realms of life.

For Italian city-states, patronal feast days were the equivalent of today's Bastille Day (France) or Independence Day (United States). In Florence, vassal towns brought symbolic tribute on the Feast of Saint John the Baptist (June 24), and there were often parades with patriotic floats. In Siena, the Assumption of the Virgin (August 15) was the national holiday. Procession-minded Venice celebrated not only the Feast of Saint Mark (April 25), but also several other holidays recalling the saint's connection with the republic.

State occasions. Civic pageantry proper aimed at presenting a similarly harmonious and unified view of the state and of society. When, for example, the processions of triumphal entries and those for local ceremonies put the head of state and other government officials on display to the people in the company of foreign ambassadors, delegations of foreign merchants, and representatives of local guilds and confraternities, these public arrangements implied a harmony among the various classes of society and even among the nations of Christendom.

The routes taken by civic processions similarly suggested an integration of church and state and of ruler and ruled. Entering sovereigns stopped at the city gates to receive greetings from the town fathers and then proceeded to the cathedral, to be received there by the bishop and to make a show of personal devotions. Only thereafter were they free to go to the palace designated for their residence. In some cities, such as Naples with its five *seggi* (seats), they stopped at designated points of the entry route to receive the homage of local authorities. New popes, in their procession to take possession of Saint John Lateran, paused to accept the civil allegiance of the Jewish colony in Rome and to confirm its civil rights. New sovereigns in England and France noted messages from various groups in their first grand progress through London and Paris. Even allowing for the desire to flatter in official accounts, it seems clear that public enthusiasm on such state occasions was enormous. Awareness of injustices could be suspended temporarily in civic pride, and the staging of entries and state processions must have been a force for civic peace.

Royal and dynastic weddings. Civic unity was promoted also by celebrations for royal and noble weddings, which, if the bride came from elsewhere, often included joyous entries as well as a series of courtly entertainments. When, as often happened, the marriage signaled a political alliance, like that of the Florentine duke Cosimo I to the daughter of the

Feast of Saint John the Baptist. A Florentine guild honors John the Baptist, patron saint of Florence. Distemper on wood. MUSEO NAZIONALE DEL BARGELLO, FLORENCE/ERICH LESSING/ART RESOURCE

Spanish viceroy of Naples in 1539, the themes of the entry decorations were heavily political. Subsequent courtly entertainments might include banquets, indoor pageants, tournaments or other chivalric contests, fireworks, and, especially in Italy, the playing of comedies. Early on, for example in Ferrara for the 1502 wedding of Lucrezia Borgia and Alfonso d'Este, comedies of Plautus were played in Italian. Later in the century, as at Florence in 1539, original neoclassical comedies in the vernacular, called *commedie erudite* (learned comedies), were put on. Wedding festivities were, in fact, after carnival, the principal occasion for the staging of comedies. Mantua, Ferrara, and Florence were particularly important in the early development of the genre. In 1548, on the occasion of a visit of Catherine de Médicis, Florentine merchants in Lyon sponsored the first production of a neoclassical comedy in France.

Elaborate nuptial festivities became common also in northern Europe. The wedding of the Danish king Frederick II in 1572 had banquets, a tournament, and a grand passage of the bride through the streets of Copenhagen. The 1589–1590 celebrations for the wedding of the Scottish king James VI (later James I of England) to Anne of Denmark apparently included the playing of comedies both in Latin and in Danish, first at Oslo and then at the Danish court. Northern European courtly entertainments eventually became more elaborate than the Italian, moving toward the lavish style of the baroque. At Copenhagen, for the 1634 wedding of Prince-Elect Christian, guests saw a ballet, two musical comedies, and an extremely elaborate, symbol-laden display of fireworks. The art of court festivals became an international affair. Italians were often employed in the north, and the English architect Inigo Jones, who had Italian experience, almost certainly designed festival material for Hamburg in 1603. English actors performed in Germany and Denmark.

The humanistic civic celebration. Humanistically minded professors and students in various places amused themselves at times by reviving classical festivals or by celebrating events in Roman history. This practice was carried furthest in the Roman *Studium* (university), where in the late fifteenth century Julius Pomponius Laetus and some colleagues renewed observance of the Palilia, which had originally been an agricultural festival but was celebrated in classical times also as the anniversary of the building of Rome by Romulus. In early years of the revival there was scarcely more than a banquet and a Latin oration in praise of the city. In 1501 the celebration moved to the Campidoglio, the ancient Capitolium, with participation of officials from the Vatican and from the city government, which had its seat on the hill; then, in 1513, it was the occasion for the most remarkable humanistic and learned festival of the Renaissance.

Festival. Sketch of costumes and set for an intermezzo by the Florentine theatrical designer Bernardo Buontalenti (1531–1608). BIBLIOTECA NAZIONALE CENTRALE, FLORENCE, PAL.C.B. 3.53, VOL. II, FOL. 30v–31

The new pope, Leo X, a Medici from whom everyone expected great things, asked the city government to grant honorary Roman citizenship to his brother Giuliano and nephew Lorenzo, and the flattered officials resolved to do the thing with as much style as possible. Making the ceremony coincide with the Palilia, they commissioned the construction on their Capitoline Hill of an enormous neoclassical theater, with temporary statues and paintings that evoked moments of ancient history. Paintings and inscriptions concentrated on the supposedly cordial relations between early Romans and Etruscans, the latter being deemed the ancestors of the Medici and other Florentines. Proceedings included a mass (the sole Christian element), a Latin oration in praise of Rome and of the Medici, the presentation of a diploma of citizenship, an elaborate banquet of more than twenty courses, a complex pageant recited in Latin, and a playing of Plautus's *Poenulus* in Latin, with both male and female roles being filled by male students. Afterward, the Romans had fierce pride in what they had done. The quality of Latin enunciation, in this birthplace of the tongue, was especially remarked upon. Here at Rome in the High Renaissance, Latin made one of its last stands as the dominant language of literature as well as of erudition. Pope Leo X authorized annual celebration of the Palilia, but there was never again such humanistic splendor.

Festivals of Misrule or Subversion.

While civic festivals have been studied mainly by historians of art, literature, and ideas, those festivals that served as safety valves of popular resentment or as subversions of public order have attracted attention since the 1970s from anthropologists, semioticians, social historians, and sociologists. An undoubted ancestor of many Renaissance festivals of this kind can be seen in the Roman Saturnalia, celebrated around the time of the winter solstice. During one stage of the ancient feast, the social order was turned upside down. Masters and slaves wore each others' clothes, and the former served the latter at table. Whether the Saturnalia weakened or strengthened the fabric of Roman society is a matter of scholarly debate, and a similar uncertainty underlies interpretation of related festivals in the Renaissance.

The Feast of Fools. The Feast of Fools (Latin *Festum Stultorum,* French *Fête des Fous,* German *Narrenfest*) was long celebrated in religious communities over most of western Europe shortly after Christmas, near the time of the old Saturnalia. Hierarchy was reversed as a young cleric or monastic novice was elected bishop, and things normally held sacred were made fun of, notably in mock masses. Some places observed, more or less in association with the Feast of Fools, a *Festum Asinorum* (Feast of Asses), in which a donkey was brought into church and both priest and congregation brayed at particular points of the liturgy. High church officials understandably took steps to suppress such customs, and by the sixteenth century they were in decline. Secular festivals of misrule continued, however, to prosper.

Abbeys of misrule. In the fifteenth and sixteenth centuries, France and some other countries had organizations, especially of young men, that were sometimes called abbeys or kingdoms of misrule (French *abbayes de maugouvert*). These associations elected abbots or kings who led them in a variety of activities for regular festivals like Christmas and carnival, and also in conducting *charivaris* (shivarees) to humiliate henpecked husbands and their domineering wives, or the partners of May-December marriages. In sixteenth-century England, on a higher social plane, a court lord of misrule was sometimes appointed for Yuletide celebrations. George Ferrars, holding that appointment from King Edward VI, staged a mock triumphal entry into London on 3 January 1552.

If the abbeys of misrule were often agents of social conformity in punishing those who transgressed against social norms, sometimes, when they had mainly patrician members, they abandoned their burlesque nature altogether to participate in official pageantry. Thus the Lyonese Enfants de la Ville went out in fine costumes to greet kings or other great personages about to make triumphal entries into their city. At other times, as a considerably body of surviving songs and literary compositions attests, the abbeys were simply purveyors of good fun. They were clearly not always organs of subversion.

Carnival. By far the most important annual feast of "transgression," carnival was celebrated over most of central and western Europe, at least until the Reformation, when it was suppressed, along with Lent, in some but not all Protestant areas. Although its celebration had once begun on Twelfth Night, close to the time of the old Saturnalia, during the Renaissance it was confined in most places to the last few days before Lent, whose dates varied with that of Easter. It was a period of licensed, authorized transgression, of "the world turned upside down," that drew much of its force from the fact of being limited in duration. The form of celebrations varied enormously with local tradition. Masking was perhaps the most nearly universal element, although it was sporadically forbidden in reaction to various excesses. In really bad times, as at Rome in the years following the Sack of 1527, the celebration of carnival itself was suspended, but it was perhaps the most popular of all annual festivals, and people did not give it up easily.

Rome had one of the most elaborate series of carnival entertainments and may serve as a sort of example. Setting the annual program was the privilege and responsibility of the city government on the Campidoglio, which had, however, to get papal approval (and help with expenses). Nearly all events took place in the week between the last two Sundays

A Horse Race. *Palio in Florence* by Giovanni Toscani (d. 1430). Tempera and gold on canvas; 1418; 42.1 × 139.5 cm (16.5 × 55 in.). THE CLEVELAND MUSEUM OF ART, HOLDEN COLLECTION, 1916.801

before Lent. There were several footraces: one for young men, one for Jews, one for old men, and, occasionally, one for prostitutes. There were also horse races, bullfights, and games involving other animals, some of them very cruel to the modern sensibility. Several games took place on the second Sunday, at a hill outside the walls called Testaccio. Certain other days saw chivalric competitions for young patricians. The grandest chivalric contest during the period was a 1565 tournament held in the Vatican's Belvedere courtyard, handsomely recorded in engravings. On Shrove Thursday the main pageant of carnival was held in Piazza Navona, then called the Agone, with a parade that included the single senator and the three *conservatori* (officials) of the city government, and floats depicting allegorical, historical, or mythological subjects. Prominent literati planned the floats, and first-rate artists sometimes decorated them.

The Roman celebrations thus included both learned and popular elements, both aristocratic and plebeian. While there was much blowing off of steam and relieving of tensions, truly subversive elements were scarcely visible. The pageant often flattered the reigning pope, as when that of 1536 recreated the ancient triumph of Paulus Aemilius in allusion to Paul III. The masking was no doubt politically risky, and popes forbade disguising for the purpose of mocking the clergy or religious ceremonies. Carnival harassment of the Jews was also specially forbidden, a clear indication that such a thing was not unlikely.

Among other Italian carnivals, those in Florence and Venice were especially elaborate. In 1513, the Compagnia del Broncone and the Compagnia del Diamante, companies of young Florentines analogous to the French abbeys of misrule, staged competing parades through town. The first had chariots portraying golden ages of the past and the present (in allusion to the recent return to power of the Medici), and the second depicted the three ages of man. Comedies were often performed for carnival in Florence, as in other Italian cities, and there arose a special lyric genre of *canti carnascialeschi* (carnival songs), which was cultivated by, among other poets, Lorenzo de' Medici, the Magnificent, the city's ruler in the late fifteenth century.

Venice had a particularly long celebration of carnival, beginning on Twelfth Night. The official climax came on Shrove Thursday, when the doge and other officials presided over a bizarre commemoration of a twelfth-century victory over the patriarch of Aquileia entailing a mock judicial condemnation of a bull and three hundred pigs and real executions of them, after a cruel chase around the Piazzetta. In the Piazza San Marco, there were sometimes parades that mocked the official ones of the republic, without, however, much bitterness, since virtually no one in prosperous Venice wanted to change the system of government. As in Florence, many carnival activities were carried out by groups of wellborn young men, here called Compagnie delle Calze. These groups sometimes staged pageants in the piazza on specially erected platforms. They also held performances of comedies, usually in private houses. Many strangers came to town during the Venetian carnival, both for the spectacles and for the masking, which was particularly extended and free.

If the official activity of Italian carnivals was scarcely subversive, and often even supportive of government, in Germany its main manifestations seem to have been more daring. During the early years of the Reformation, carnival parades and floats in several cities mocked the pope and Roman Catholic clergy. At Nürnberg in 1539, on the other hand, the main float, a ship, satirized the principal Protestant preacher, who was an enemy of carnival pleasures. Nervous city authorities everywhere tried to prevent such embarrassments.

Nürnberg, home of the popular writer Hans Sachs (1494–1576), was a center for the production of German carnival plays, *Fastnachtsspiele*. Although much shorter than the neoclassical comedies of Italy, the German plays resembled them in concentrating their satire on timeless human failings, such as miserliness, vanity, and unseemly lust. Institutions were, for the most part, spared. Sachs's "The Inquisitor and All His Soup Cauldrons" is unusual in its bitter satire of the venality of a monk with the pointed name of Doctor Romanus.

France offers the exceptional example of a carnival celebration that turned to terrible violence. In the Dauphiné town of Romans, social and sectarian tensions had been high for some time when in 1580 revelers with reactionary views took advantage of the license and confusion of carnival to massacre a large number of reform-minded revelers.

Scholarly opinion is divided as to whether the irreverence and "world turned upside down" of carnival and other festivals of misrule served only as a safety valve for high spirits and social resentments or helped, in the long run, to develop a true revolutionary spirit and to reform society. The Russian literary historian Mikhail Bakhtin won support for the latter view, but there is much skepticism, and the multiple, disparate aspects of misrule celebrations make the question very complex.

See also **Carnival**; **Charivari**; **Drama**, *subentry on* **Erudite Comedy**; **Parades, Processions, and Pageants**; **Ritual, Civic**; **Violence**.

BIBLIOGRAPHY

Bakhtin, Mikhail. *Rabelais and His World*. Translated by Helene Iswolsky. Boston, 1968. Translation of *Tvorchestvo Fransua Rable* (1965). See chapter 3, "Popular-Festive Forms and Images in Rabelais," pp. 196–277. A controversial literary study with a Marxist interpretation of Renaissance carnival as well as of Rabelais.

Béhar, Pierre, and Helen Watanabe-O'Kelly, eds. *Spectaculum Europaeum. Manuel de l'histoire du spectacle en Europe de la fin du seizième au milieu du dix-huitième siècle. Theatre and Spectacle in Europe from the End of the Sixteenth to the Middle of the Eighteenth Century—a Handbook*. Forthcoming. Individual sections in English or in French. A valuable guide to courtly festivals in many European countries during the late Renaissance as well as in the baroque period.

Burke, Peter. *Popular Culture in Early Modern Europe*. New York and London, 1978. See chapter 7, "The World of Carnival," pp. 178–204. An excellent interpretive study.

Cruciani, Fabrizio. *Il teatro del Campidoglio e le feste romane del 1513, con la ricostruzione architettonica del teatro di Arnaldo Bruschi*. Milan, 1968. Excellent study of a humanistic festival, with edition of the main sources.

Davis, Natalie Zemon. *Society and Culture in Early Modern France*. Stanford, Calif., 1975. See chapter 4, "The Reasons of Misrule," pp. 97–123. A pioneering study of "abbeys of misrule" in sixteenth-century France.

Le Roy La Durie, Emmanuel. *Carnival in Romans*. Translated by Mary Feeney. New York, 1979. Translation of *Le Carnaval de Romans* (1979). Careful analysis by a social historian of a 1580 French carnival celebration that led to a massacre.

Scribner, Bob. "Reformation, Carnival, and the World Turned Upside Down." *Social History 3* (1978):303–329. Study of twenty-four German carnivals during the Reformation.

Sebeok, Thomas A., and Marcia E. Erickson, eds. *Carnival!* Berlin, New York, and Amsterdam, 1984. Includes short essays by semioticians Umberto Eco and V. V. Ivanov dealing respectively with the comic of carnival and with a theory of that festival as the inversion of bipolar opposites.

Strong, Roy. *Art and Power: Renaissance Festivals 1450–1650*. Berkeley Calif., 1984. The best general study of courtly festivals in the Renaissance.

Wade, Mara R. *Triumphus Nuptialis Danicus: German Court Culture and Denmark: The "Great Wedding" of 1634*. Wiesbaden, Germany, 1996. An introductory chapter, pp. 17–56, has much information about courtly festivals in Germany and Scandinavia during the late Renaissance.

BONNER MITCHELL

FICINO, MARSILIO (1433–1499), Florentine translator and philosopher. Marsilio Ficino's father was a court physician to Cosimo de' Medici and intended a medical career for his son, who eventually became well versed in Aristotle's logic, natural science, and metaphysics, as well as in the questions raised by his commentators, among them the Arab pharmacologists and astronomer-astrologers, astrology and Aristotelian philosophy being integral to a physician's training. Throughout his career Marsilio wrote on medical matters, and health and cure remained guiding metaphors for him as both teacher and philosopher. Jungians, interestingly, have approached him as an important precursor of depth psychology and holistic therapy, though many of his arguments and nostrums we would now characterize as New Age.

Translator and Philosopher. From the onset Marsilio was drawn to Platonic philosophy by way of the Latin tradition, and he studied the works of Apuleius, Calcidius, Macrobius, and Boethius as well as those of Augustine and Aquinas, and possibly of other Scholastics such as William of Conches, Albertus Magnus, and Henry of Ghent, all of whom he mentions (though apart from Aquinas his debt to these and other medieval thinkers awaits exploration). He soon realized he needed to learn Greek, however, and by the late 1450s he had acquired sufficient facility—perhaps under Francesco da Castiglione—to draft out Latin translations, for his own personal use, of such ancient poetic texts as the Orphic Hymns and Hesiod's *Theogony*. By the 1460s he had also paraphrased four technical treatises by Iamblichus, along with Hermias's *Phaedrus* commentary. Presumably he was also working on translations of Plato and Plotinus, since he was clearly familiar with them from the early 1460s, long before he produced his definitive translations of their complete works.

By 1462 his scholarly brilliance had been brought to the notice of Cosimo, who asked him to translate Plato's works from a newly acquired codex, giving him a house in Florence and in 1463 a small villa at Careggi along with a farm property to provide him with income. Hardly had Ficino embarked on this monumental task than Cosimo, having bought a codex of the *Corpus Hermeticum,* asked him to render it, too, into Latin. This he promptly did under the title of the opening treatise, *Pimander.* (In the sixteenth century it was published with the unattributed commentaries of a French disciple, Jacques Lefèvre d'Étaples, which later readers assumed were Ficino's.)

By August 1464 Ficino had finished ten Plato dialogues and Cosimo, rather memorably, ordered him to read *Parmenides* and *Philebus* to him on his deathbed. By 1468 he had completed first drafts of the canon. These he subsequently revised and published in the astrologically propitious year of 1484, along with introductions (*argumenta*) and the first version of a commentary on *Timaeus* and a subsequently enormously influential commentary on the *Symposium* (which he had meanwhile translated into Italian himself). A second edition of the Plato appeared in Venice in 1491 and was thereafter printed many times, becoming, though subject to revisions, the unrivaled Latin version. Ficino consulted earlier humanist translations where available, notably those of Leonardo Bruni, but he arrived at his own independent judgments and was soon acknowledged as Plato's preeminent Latin translator.

In 1469, having finished an Italian translation of Dante's *De monarchia,* he abandoned his long metaphysically oriented commentary on *Philebus* (the subject of a course of public lectures) and embarked on an eighteen-book summa in the medieval tradition but full of Platonizing arguments and references to the "ancient theologians"—Zoroaster, Hermes, Orpheus, Pythagoras, and others. A major work of metaphysics, it is entitled *Platonic Theology,* recalling the title of Proclus's masterpiece, and subtitled *On the Immortality of the Soul,* echoing one of Augustine's titles. Finished by 1474, it was not published until 1482. Meanwhile, Ficino was ordained a priest in 1473 and the following year wrote Italian and Latin versions of *De Christiana religione* (On the Christian religion), drawing on earlier anti-Jewish and anti-Muslim polemicists. Eventually, he was given several ecclesiastical livings and became a canon of Florence's cathedral (a striking bust still adorns the south nave wall). At one point he was promoted as a candidate for the bishopric of Cortona.

In 1477 he drafted an attack on judicial or predictive astrology and in 1479 a medical treatise, *Consiglio contro la pestilenza* (Advice against the plague). In the 1480s he translated all of Plotinus's *Enneads* into Latin and supplied the opening books with probing commentary, the latter with more perfunctory analyses. The result in 1492 was the magnificent *Plotini Enneades.* In 1496 he published his principal Plato commentaries (though some were still incomplete): on *Parmenides;* on the passage on the nuptial number in book 8 of the *Republic;* on the *Sophist;* and, in their final versions, on *Philebus, Phaedrus,* and *Timaeus.* In 1497 he published Latin translations of various Neoplatonic treatises by Porphyry, Iamblichus, Synesius, Proclus, Psellus, and others. In the meantime he also translated, and wrote an interspersed series of commentaries on, the works of Dionysius the Areopagite (fl. c. A.D. 500), for us a Christian follower of Proclus, but for Ficino and the vast majority of his contemporaries the Athenian convert of St. Paul mentioned in Acts 17:34. Dionysius's mystical Neoplatonizing writings were thus held to be the foundation stone, along with the Gospels and St. Paul's Epistles, of Christian philosophy. In his final years, Ficino angrily attacked the dead Savonarola, and died in 1499 while still engaged in a commentary on St. Paul's epistle to the Romans, which includes corrections of the Vulgate's Latin against the Greek text.

In addition to these monumental scholarly endeavors, Ficino sustained a correspondence with well over a hundred of the intellectual, ecclesiastical, and signorial elite of Florence, and with notable figures elsewhere in Italy and Europe, including John Colet in England. His twelve books of Latin letters (translated into Italian in the next century), along with other letters that have come to light, constitute a remarkably rich testimony to his influence as a teacher, friend, counselor, and priest. Finally, he composed a number of sermons, exhortations, prefaces, prayers, consolations, and philosophical opuscula, some of them in the vernacular, others in Latin.

Ficino's Platonism. Ficino's Platonism is a complex tissue of ideas and arguments made all the more difficult by his prolixity and repetitiveness, by his wide-ranging eclecticism, by his synthesizing goals as both medical theorist and philosopher, and by the variety and general difficulty of his sources. From the outset, he was convinced not only that the central tenets of Platonism were reconcilable with Christian belief but also that Platonic metaphysics was the "net" that would capture the reason and the enthusiasms of the *ingeniosi,* the intellectually gifted. In this he was emboldened by the example of Augustine, whose works he studied and who served in many ways as his model, though Ficino's program was more radical than Augustine's and closer to the irenic goals of Origen, Eusebius, and the Cappadocian fathers. He ignored, for instance, Augustine's vehement attack on *Asclepius,* because of its statue magic, preferring instead to adopt Lactantius's laudatory account of Hermes Trismegistus, its purported author, as a gentile prophet who had foreseen the coming of Christ and the triumph of the church. This spoke to his lifelong conviction that God had providently supplied pagan antiquity with a line of prophets and a philosophical theology, a *prisca theologia* (ancient theology), that paralleled the line of the Hebrew prophets and ultimately derived from the same source in Zoroaster and before him perhaps in Enoch. This ancient, essentially poetic theology, which culminated in Plato, had expounded the same truths given to the Hebrews by Moses, and both traditions contained prophecies of the coming Messiah and intimations of the mysteries of the Passion, the Redemption, and the Trinity.

Following the Neoplatonists, and notably Proclus, Ficino supposed that Plato, though taught ethics by Socrates, had learned his metaphysics from such Pythagorean teachers as Philolaus and the followers of Parmenides the Eleatic, and had espoused their monism and their mathematical perspectives on cosmology and the world's structure. Thus Plato's *Parmenides,* with its series of nine propositions concerning the existence and the nonexistence of the One, and his *Timaeus,* with its memorable myth of the demiurge's creation of the world inspired by the idea of order, its subsequent sallies into ratio, harmony, and musical theory, and its presentation of a triangle-based physics, were for Ficino, as for the Neoplatonists before him, the two climactic dialogues. Other dialogues were ancillary, though out-

Marsilio Ficino. Portrait medal attributed to Niccolò Fiorentino. Before 1500. ©THE BRITISH MUSEUM, LONDON

standing among them were the *Sophist, Philebus, Symposium, Phaedrus,* and *Republic,* to which Ficino devoted his longest commentaries.

This is not to deny that the tenth book of *Laws,* the Platonic second and sixth epistles, the myth of alternating world cycles in the *Statesman,* and passages in a number of other dialogues figure prominently and constantly in his analyses. But it does underscore his concern not so much with the ethical issues of the earlier Socratic dialogues as with the theogony and cosmogony (and their accompanying eschatology) of the later dialogues; that is, with the metaphysics of the descent of the intelligible realm of Mind from the transintelligible source of all being, the One beyond being, and then of Soul and of all individual souls led by the World-Soul from Mind, and, finally, of the sensible world from Soul. This is the visionary scheme that was arrived at by Plato's great third-century interpreter Plotinus, Neoplatonism's founder, whom Ficino considered "even more profound sometimes than Plato himself" and whose system he mastered from his early years and then read back into Plato and into the poetic dicta of the ancient sages.

Ficino's Christianity. But Ficino was not only a Plotinian. As a devout Christian he sought to arrive at an accommodation of Plotinian metaphysics with Christian theology, without ignoring the differences between them. In particular he sought to take the Plotinian epistemological-psychological account of the soul's descent into plurality and then of its reascent, first to a state of unity in itself, and thence to union with Soul, with Mind, and finally with the One, and to accommodate it to the Pauline account of our membership in the body of one Christ. Haunting him here was Paul's reference in 2 Cor. 12 of his being "caught up to the third heaven." Here Ficino emphasized the roles first of love and its idealizing and sublimating powers (as articulated by Diotima in the *Symposium* and by Socrates in *Phaedrus*), then of the will (*voluntas*), with its goal of unalloyed joy (*gaudium*), and finally of intellectual understanding by way of Platonic dialectic, the intuitive *intelligentia* of the angels, not the discursive reasoning of ordinary thinking. His weaving together of voluntarist and intellectualist positions into the fabric of a philosophy of intellectual love had a profound effect on Renaissance love theory, but so too did his theory of the divine madness, which he combined with a Christian-Platonic vision of prayer, contemplation, mystical ascent, and union of mind with Mind, of the intellectual soul with Christ as the Wisdom and Understanding of God. This goal of divine union formed the foundation stone of his arguments for the soul's immortality (proclaimed as a dogma at the Lateran Council of 1512–1517, in part perhaps because of his championship of its Platonic reasonability). Thus Ficino helped articulate a new conception of the ideal Christian not as saint or simple believer so much as ecstatic thinker, as enraptured philosopher, even if in doing so he espoused semi-Pelagian positions that deemphasized human sinfulness and resurrected the old Socratic assumption that error, not sin, is the source of human woe.

If Ficino's psychological adaptation of the Platonic tradition to Christian ends was successful and uncontested (for the most part by) other fifteenth-century theologians, his cosmological and magical speculations were less easily tolerated. His *De vita* (On life; 1489) in particular ran into Curial opposition, though he did manage to avoid formal censure. The opposition was understandable. Besides containing a bizarre and daunting amount of medical, astrological, and pharmacological lore, it explores ancient magic theory. Its third book in particular has daring speculations on the efficacy of amulets, talismans, and affective demonology; on the astrology of nativities; on the human spirit as the soul's pneumatic vehicle, envelope, or chariot; and on the World-Spirit as the World-Soul's chariot linking the World-Soul to the World-Body. This World-Spirit is subject to manipulation in ways similar to the magical and medical ways one can manipulate an individual human spirit (itself traditionally divided into natural, vital, and animal).

However, *De vita* (one of the first treatises to deal with the pathology of a particular occupation) contains a fascinating account of scholarly melancholy and, more generally, of the unity and harmony of the cosmos and of the correspondence and interrelationships of the various levels of being under the governance of the stars as benevolent instruments of a divine providence rather than of a malevolent fate. Ficino is one of the most eloquent proponents in the Renaissance of this vision both of an animate universe, of a living, unitary, essentially musical Nature, and of man as the angelic demon-magus on the middle rung of creation's ladder, uniting both the sensible and intelligible realms. Human beings constitute the microcosm at the heart of the great Man that is God's macrocosm, the harmonic universal creature full of grace and truth. Ficino's Platonism, in short, leads him to a Christian anthropocentric cosmology centered on the intellectual soul, and to a cosmocentric psychology centered on the universe's living harmony.

Ficino's Legacy. Many aspects of this complex interweaving of philosophy, theology, magic, music, medicine, astrology, numerology, and ratio theory still await investigation, though his achievements as a scholar, translator, and interpreter continue to receive scholarly plaudits. If Ficino has retained his position as the great Platonicus of his age, he has also emerged as one of its exemplary magi—a paradigm that was only eclipsed by the advent of Enlightenment ideals. But, while there is no doubting Ficino's European impact for over two centuries (he was the guiding spirit for the Cambridge Platonists as late as the mid-seventeenth century), doubt has always been voiced whether he was the head of a Platonic Academy, even in the sense of an informal group of signori, artists, scholars, poets, ecclesiastics, diplomats, and other distinguished men of affairs. For though he had an extensive network of friends, correspondents, and admirers, few if any embraced his Platonic metaphysics in toto, and the notion of his being the head of an academy is probably the invention of sixteenth-century Medicean propagandists bent on emphasizing the role of Lorenzo as a patron of learning and the arts. Even so, ample testimony speaks to his being acknowledged by contemporaries as one of the luminous thinkers of his time; and he was among the first to reap the rewards of having his works printed, thus acquiring a rapid exposure and celebrity across Europe. A defining figure in the history of Western philosophy and culture, he remains above all a signal witness to the preoccupations, ideals, and energies of Italy's greatest age.

BIBLIOGRAPHY

Works by Ficino

Commentary on Plato's "Symposium" on Love. Translated by Sears Jayne. Dallas, Tex., 1985. Translation of Ficino's *Symposium* commentary (1484).

The Letters of Marsilio Ficino. Translated by Members of the Language Department of the School of Economic Science, London. 5 vols. London, 1975–.

Marsilio Ficino and the Phaedran Charioteer. Edited and translated by Michael J. B. Allen. Berkeley, Calif., 1981. An edition of the *Phaedrus* commentary.

Opera omnia (Collected works). Basel, Switzerland, 1576. Reprint, Turin, Italy, 1962.

The "Philebus" Commentary. Edited and translated by Michael J. B. Allen. Berkeley, Calif., 1975.

Théologie platonicienne de l'immortalité des âmes. Edited by Raymond Marcel. 3 vols. Paris, 1964–1970. French translation of *Theologia Platonica* (1482).

Three Books on Life: A Critical Edition and Translation. Edited and translated by Carol V. Kaske and John R. Clark. Binghamton, N.Y., 1989. An edition of the *De vita libri tres* (1489) with a comprehensive introduction.

Secondary Works

Allen, Michael J. B. *Icastes: Marsilio Ficino's Interpretation of Plato's "Sophist".* Berkeley, Calif., 1989. Contains studies on aspects of Ficino's metaphysics, cosmology, philosophy of art, and demonology; also a text and translation of his *Sophist* commentary (1496).

Allen, Michael J. B. *Nuptial Arithmetic: Marsilio Ficino's Commentary on the Fatal Number in Book VIII of Plato's "Republic".* Berkeley, Calif., 1994. Contains studies on aspects of Ficino's numerology and his views on time, the golden age, prophecy, fate, and providence; also a text and translation of the commentary (1496).

Allen, Michael J. B. *The Platonism of Ficino: A Study of His "Phaedrus" Commentary, Its Sources and Genesis.* Berkeley, Calif., 1984. An introduction to Ficino's Neoplatonism.

Allen, Michael J. B. *Plato's Third Eye: Studies in Marsilio Ficino's Metaphysics and Its Sources.* Aldershot, U.K., 1995. A collection of fifteen essays.

Allen, Michael J. B. *Synoptic Art: Marsilio Ficino on the History of Platonic Interpretation.* Florence, 1998. Studies of Ficino's views on the ancient theology, Socrates, and the history of Platonism; on Plato's expulsion of the poets; and on Platonic dialectic.

Chastel, André. *Marsile Ficin et l'art.* Geneva, 1954. Reprint, 1975. Still the best introduction to Ficino's impact on the visual arts.

Field, Arthur. *The Origins of the Platonic Academy of Florence.* Princeton, N.J., 1988. An excellent introduction to Ficino's early years.

Hankins, James. *Plato in the Italian Renaissance.* 2 vols. Leiden, Netherlands, 1990. The authoritative synoptic account.

Kristeller, Paul Oskar. *Marsilio Ficino and His Work after Five Hundred Years.* Florence, 1987. A supplement to Kristeller's own *Supplementum,* with a complete bibliography (up to 1986) and various lists and indices.

Kristeller, Paul Oskar. *The Philosophy of Marsilio Ficino.* Translated by Virginia Conant. New York, 1943. Reprint, Gloucester, Mass., 1964. The authoritative account.

Kristeller, Paul Oskar. *Supplementum Ficinianum.* 2 vols. Florence, 1937. An invaluable supplement (though in Latin) to the study of Ficino, with many additional texts.

Tomlinson, Gary. *Music in Renaissance Magic: Toward a Historiography of Others.* Chicago, 1993. A suggestive work on Ficino's influence on music.

Walker, D. P. *Spiritual and Demonic Magic: from Ficino to Campanella.* London, 1958. Reprint, Notre Dame, Ind., 1975. The seminal study on Ficino's magic theory and its influence.

Wind, Edgar. *Pagan Mysteries in the Renaissance.* Rev. ed. New York, 1968. A rich book, exploring, among many other themes, Ficino's influence on Renaissance art and culture.

MICHAEL J. B. ALLEN

FICTION, ELIZABETHAN. More than one hundred works of extended prose fiction were published in England during the Elizabethan period (1558–1603), and evidence suggests they had a wide readership. They shared many characteristics of the novel, even if failing to meet strict definitions of the genre, and ranged in length from pamphlets of some 15,000 words to tomes of 200,000, although most were in the region of 30,000 words.

Elizabethan fiction has not enjoyed a favorable critical reputation. Dismissed as mere sources of Shakespeare's plays or clumsy beginnings of a genre that first blossomed only in the eighteenth century, the works have suffered from misunderstanding of the way they were read at the time and the role they played.

Oral Culture. The ground out of which Elizabethan fiction grew was oral culture. While contemporaneous art and literature contain some images of solitary reading, reading aloud in a group would seem to have been the most common mode of transmission. Thus John Lyly's *Euphues: The Anatomy of Wit* (1578) is often scorned as clumsy and boring, but it was stylistically the most influential work of the period. It achieved this position by virtue of its aural values—intricate patterns of complex alliteration, rhythmical phrasing, and repetition structure the prose.

Because the oral mode made the reception of fiction collective, it not only ensured a larger potential audience than private reading but also meant that responses could be enhanced by the group experience, in the way that a film seen in a crowded cinema is different from the video watched at home. In the fiction this added potential could take the simple form of gestures of recognition toward the audience. George Pettie, for example, flirts with his female audience in *A Petite Pallace of Pettie His Pleasure* (1576; a collection of stories in the "euphuistic" style later elaborated by Lyly), and George Gascoigne, in *The Adventures of Master F. J.* (1573; sometimes claimed to be the first English novel), tells readers that their discretion permits him to say what he does. A different form of collectivity was the author presenting a social perspective that readers could share, such as Sir Philip Sidney's mockery of peasants in *The Countess of Pembroke's Arcadia* (1590) and Robert Greene's celebration of a peasant getting the better of a knight in *Greenes Never Too Late* (1590).

The Development of Commercial Publishing. A decisive element in the growth and change of Elizabethan fiction was the development of commercial publishing. Many authors of the day could make some claim to gentility, even without family connection, by virtue of a university education. Whereas manuscript circulation was restricted to a select upper-class group, publications in print were available to anyone with the money. Furthermore, a printed book might be assumed to be the product of paid labor, which was incompatible with gentility. Thus many writers made excuses for going into print: a friend took the book to the printer against the author's will (Pettie), or it was not written for money (Gascoigne, in the 1575 revision of his work of 1573), or friends demanded it be printed (Barnaby Rich; *Farewell to Military Profession,* 1581). But by the end of the century this pretense was the subject of mockery; print had become the accepted medium.

The accommodation to print had effects that went well beyond the mechanics of publication. Although fiction continued for some time to reflect the personal quality of oral culture, by the end of the century it had adjusted to the indirectness of the market. John Lyly (1554?–1606), in *Euphues* and its sequel, *Euphues and His England* (1580), contrived a strong sense of authorial presence. Similarly, Sir Philip Sidney (1554–1586) had written the first version of the *Arcadia* (the *Old Arcadia,* c. 1580) for reading to his sister and her friends, and his revision of about 1584 retained some of that quality. The elaborated style of this pastoral romance of love and politics gave it a directness comparable to Lyly's, and it became an influential model.

In the work of Robert Greene (1558?–1592), the first professional writer in English (that is, earning his living by writing), the change from oral to print culture begins to be marked. The first of his more than thirty works, *Mamillia* (1580), and his *Gwydon-*

ius, the Card of Fancy (1584) imitated Lyly's style, but he turned to Sidney in 1588 in *Pandosto* (which Shakespeare adapted for *The Winter's Tale*) and even more so in *Menaphon* (1589), which was called "Greene's *Arcadia.*" In his last works, a series of "crime" stories referred to as his "Conny-catching pamphlets" (1591–1592), he was blatantly commercial but, in the fashion of tabloid journalism, incorporated his readers into his social-critical perspective. His stories often depend on strong social attitudes; he reverses Lyly's misogyny and in almost all his work the heroic characters are women, figures of integrity who stand for individual choice against traditional hierarchy.

Like Greene, Thomas Lodge (1558–1625), whose *Rosalynde* (1590) provides the plot of *As You Like It,* was commercially oriented, but, unlike Greene, he developed no ideological perspective, and his work had considerably less popular success.

The work of Thomas Nashe (1567–c. 1601) best illustrates the contradictory effects of this literary evolution. A writer of extraordinary verbal agility, Nashe constantly parodies literary conventions and tests the limits of language. *The Unfortunate Traveller* (1594; his only fiction sufficiently controlled to resemble a novel) combines conventions of oral narration with insistence on the written nature of the work. In this book he concludes the description of a battle, for example, with "What is there more as touching this tragedy that you would be resolved of? Say quickly, for now is my pen on foot again."

Thomas Deloney (1543?–1600) creates no personal presence in his works, but, writing about tradespeople, he offers an artisan perspective. In *Jack of Newbury* (c. 1597) he emphasizes the value of productivity over hierarchy, projecting ideology in a way that adequately compensates for the lack of authorial presence.

By the end of Elizabeth's reign, fiction had become thoroughly adapted to print. Oral conventions were no longer functional, but authors had found other ways of communicating effectively in the new medium.

See also biographies of figures mentioned in this entry.

BIBLIOGRAPHY

Primary Works

Klein, Holger, David Margolies, and Janet Todd, eds. *Early English Prose Fiction.* Selected by Salzburg Centre for Research on the Early English Novel. Cambridge, U.K., 1997. CD-Rom.

Salzman, Paul, ed. *An Anthology of Elizabethan Prose Fiction.* Oxford, 1987. Contains texts of George Gascoigne, *The Adventures of Master F. J.;* John Lyly, *Euphues: The Anatomy of Wit;* Robert Greene, *Pandosto: The Triumph of Time;* Thomas Nashe, *The Unfortunate Traveller;* and Thomas Deloney, *Jack of Newbury.*

Secondary Works

Margolies, David. *Novel and Society in Elizabethan England.* London, 1985.

Maslen, R. W. *Elizabethan Fictions: Espionage, Counterespionage and the Duplicity of Fiction in Early Elizabethan Prose Narratives.* Oxford, 1997.

Salzman, Paul. *English Prose Fiction 1558–1700: A Critical History.* Oxford, 1995.

DAVID MARGOLIES

FIELD OF CLOTH OF GOLD. Between 7 and 24 June 1520, Henry VIII of England and Francis I of France met amid feasting and chivalric feats that were thought extravagant even by the standards of the Renaissance. Contemporaries came up with the name "Field of Cloth of Gold" to describe the sight of so many luxuriously dressed nobles and servants. Despite the attention this event has received, it was only of momentary importance in Anglo-French relations and intra-European politics.

The universal peace concluded in London in 1518 promised a new era of harmony between France, England, Spain, and the Holy Roman Empire. Henry VIII and his chief minister, Thomas Cardinal Wolsey, enhanced their own stature by acting as arbitrators to preserve the peace between the Habsburgs, who ruled the Empire and Spain, and Francis I. Francis I hoped that a meeting of reconciliation in 1519 with

Henry VIII would produce an Anglo-French alliance sealed by a marriage between the dauphin and Princess Mary, Henry's daughter.

However, tensions increased in 1519 after Francis I's rival, King Charles of Spain, was elected to succeed his grandfather, Maximilian I, as Emperor Charles V, threatening a Habsburg encirclement of France. The meeting between Henry and Francis was postponed to 1520. The new emperor was most anxious that Henry meet with him instead of Francis, and Francis was most anxious to forestall any such interview. Henry and Wolsey saw an opportunity to magnify the Tudor king's stature and honor among European princes by holding meetings with both Charles and Francis, demonstrating that Henry held the balance of power between the two.

In March 1520 Wolsey, acting as commissioner for both Henry and Francis, produced a treaty stipulating that Henry and Francis would meet near Guînes in early June and engage in "feats of arms." In late May Henry met Charles V in Canterbury during three days of feasting and dancing. The two monarchs affirmed the 1518 treaties and the political status quo of Europe.

Henry and his entire court then set sail for France, while at the Val Doré thousands of laborers completed work on magnificent tents, pavilions, and stands for spectators. Outside Ardres the French nobility had erected their magnificent tents of velvet and cloth of gold. King Francis's grand tent, made of

Field of Cloth of Gold. Anonymous painting. THE ROYAL COLLECTION © HER MAJESTY QUEEN ELIZABETH II

cloth of gold, was supported by two masts from a ship tied together and surmounted by a life-size statue of St. Michael. Henry outdid Francis by building a temporary palace outside Guînes with a brick foundation, an edifice of timber and canvas fashioned to look like brick, and large windows.

On 7 June the kings and their retinues of equal number proceeded to the Val Doré and halted at the opposite ends of the valley, as if arrayed for battle. Then, at the sound of a trumpet, Henry and Francis, leaving their attendants behind, galloped toward each other, as if to engage in combat. Halting at a spot marked by a spear, the two kings embraced. After withdrawing to a nearby tent, they emerged an hour later and ordered their nobles to embrace each other.

The "feats of arms," consisting of jousting at the tilt, open-field tournaments, and combat on foot, commenced on 9 June. Valorous acts of chivalry between the English and the French were meant to strengthen the embrace of reconciliation. Henry and Francis joined together as challengers against teams of noblemen. The only contest between Henry and Francis appears to have been an impromptu wrestling match, in which Francis bested Henry.

On Sunday 10 June, Francis dined with Queen Catherine of Aragon at Guînes, while Henry dined with Queen Claude at Ardres. In a frivolous episode a week later, Francis surprised Henry in his bedchamber early in the morning and declared himself the English king's prisoner. A few days later, Henry surprised Francis at Ardres as the French king was getting out of bed. On 23 June, in the tournament field, Wolsey, accompanied by a papal legate, three cardinals, and twenty-one bishops, sang a solemn high mass, after which Wolsey conferred the papal benediction on the two kings and proclaimed a plenary indulgence for all those present. The next day, at the conclusion of the tournaments, the kings bade each other farewell and vowed to build in the Val Doré a chapel dedicated to Our Lady of Friendship and a palace where they could meet each year.

In 1521, after Francis provoked Charles V and the pope to war, Henry and Wolsey abandoned their roles as arbitrators and repudiated reconciliation with France by allying England with the emperor. In the aftermath the Field of Cloth of Gold appeared as mere diplomatic frivolity.

See also **Diplomacy.**

BIBLIOGRAPHY

Anglo, Sydney. *Spectacle, Pageantry and Early Tudor Policy.* Oxford, 1969.

Russell, Joycelyne G. *Field of Cloth of Gold.* New York, 1969.
Scarisbrick, J. J. *Henry VIII.* Berkeley, Calif., 1968.

JOHN M. CURRIN

FILARETE (Antonio Averlino; c. 1400–1469), Italian sculptor and architect. Antonio di Piero Averlino, known as Il Filarete, was born in Florence and probably trained as a goldsmith like his contemporaries Lorenzo Ghiberti and Filippo Brunelleschi. Although he remained a champion of *fiorentinità* throughout his life, his activity unfolded primarily outside of Florence, in Milan, Bergamo, and Rome, where he is believed to have died in 1469. Like his two more famous countrymen, he divided his attention between sculpture and architecture. Unlike them, he also entered the literary arena and wrote what amounts to the first illustrated architectural treatise of the Renaissance, on which his fame chiefly rests.

Sculptural and Architectural Work. Filarete's early work was focused on sculpture (medals, plaquettes, and so forth), for which he achieved enough recognition to earn an invitation to Rome to design and execute the new bronze doors for St. Peter's. The work, interrupted by travels and other activities, spanned the decade from 1433 to circa 1445 and constitutes Filarete's answer to Ghiberti's Baptistery doors in Florence. Yet no two approaches could be more distinct, for Filarete's historiated panels display a conflict between tradition and innovation characteristic of his whole oeuvre. On the one hand, scale, panel layout and format, decorative scroll motifs, and representations of figures and buildings *all'antica* (in the ancient style) speak of his commitment to the revival of antiquity; on the other, the treatment of the narrative, the absence of a coherent perspectival schema, and the crowded compositions recall late medieval practices. Filarete's few architectural works—in Milan, the Ospedale Maggiore, interventions to the Castello Sforzesco and the cathedral, a chapel for Francesco Sforza, and perhaps the Banco Mediceo; in Bergamo, interventions to the cathedral—testify to a similar imbrication of old and new. As far as we can assess he adopted the Lombard architectural idiom of medievalizing forms and richly carved and decorated polychrome surfaces despite passionate professions of adherence to the Florentine "modern manner."

Architectural Treatise. Nowhere is the clash between these two approaches more evident than in Filarete's architectural treatise (*Trattato di architettura;* c. 1461–1464). Written for Duke Francesco Sforza, during Filarete's sojourn in Milan, the

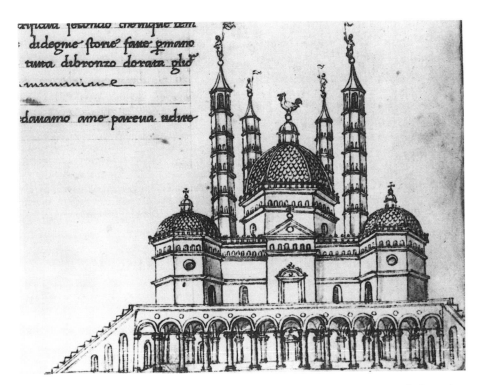

Filarete's City of Sforzinda. Design for a public building for the ideal city of Sforzinda. Drawing; c. 1455–1460.

treatise remained in manuscript form. Nevertheless, it was widely enough disseminated and reached a number of Italian and European (even Ottoman) courts through copies dedicated to Piero de'Medici; Alfonso, duke of Calabria; Matthias Corvinus, king of Hungary; and others. Still, unlike Leon Battista Alberti's *De re aedificatoria* (On the art of building), which was written at about the same time and was subsequently published, translated, and commented on in several editions and languages, Filarete's text did not command sustained interest after the fifteenth century. This pattern of reception (also reflected in the dearth of modern scholarship) is perhaps the most eloquent testimony of the transitional nature of the treatise and the residual medievalism that inflects its structure, format, individual topics, language, and illustrations.

Indeed, the treatise reads like a cross between Vitruvius's *De architectura,* the obligatory reference text for all Renaissance writers on architecture, and the late-medieval literary genre of romances and *novelle*. Thus, while Filarete seeks to advise the reader on city layout, building design, and deployment of ornament, he also develops a complex narrative complete with plot, characters, dialogue, and literary embellishments on the political and artistic educa-tion of a young prince by his architect. To a certain extent this idiosyncratic format is a function of the reader Filarete envisages: the work is not addressed to architects and workmen and it is neither a work on theory nor a manual on how to build, though both types of recommendations abound. Instead, it is aimed at the princely patron who must be swayed away from late-fourteenth-century forms so as to assure the victory of the new style. In this sense the treatise is about patronage as well as political responsibilities, about constructing civic and personal identity through architectural magnificence, and about the nearly physical pleasure of building. In choosing a narrative genre Filarete also responded to the context for which the treatise was intended: read out loud to guests at banquets, much like the romances it resembles, it was meant to divert as much as to teach. However appropriate, these oral qualities were ultimately an anachronism in a predominantly text-based culture and contributed to the work's gradual eclipse.

Relationship with Antiquity. The multitude of themes Filarete broaches and his proselytizing tone, the very peculiarities of his text, document the excitement of discovery and interpretation that a newly negotiated relationship with antiquity entailed. Probably chief among the themes Filarete thrusts into the foreground is that of the city. Although in designing Sforzinda, his prototype of the ideal city, he responds to the building explosion of the late fourteenth century, he draws heavily on classical sources, on Plato's *Atlantis,* and on the encomiastic literature on cities (especially rich in Byzantium) probably provided him by the the humanist Francesco Filelfo, his presumed collaborator in this venture. The mythic and symbolic functions that Filarete associates with the founding and embellishment of cities were very appealing both to the patrons and architects of succeeding generations. Indeed, despite its unresolved geometry, the centrally planned, star-shaped Sforzinda affected conceptions of the city well into the sixteenth century, from the urban renewal schemes of Alfonso II in Naples to the design of fortified cities like Palmanova (1593) in northeastern Italy.

Filarete's sense of his historical moment characterized by the revival "in our city of Florence of the antique way of building" lends the whole work a note of energy and urgency. His attempt to export the Florentine manner was one way to help the process on its way. Another was to explain Vitruvius's words with images and to illustrate the ancient ruins in his text. This strategy set another powerful precedent. Visually conceived and written in the Tuscan vernacular, his presentation of the columnar orders and their proportions, of the human analogy, of the spectrum of meanings carried by ornament, and of the precedents set by the ancients offered an alternative model to that of Alberti. His equation of the purification of the classical architectural forms with that of the classical literary corpus was equally powerful: thus presented, the simultaneous recovery of Cicero and of Roman architecture seemed inevitable. It also signaled that the recuperation project depended equally on words and images, exegesis and reconstruction, and that the paths of humanists and architects necessarily intersected. The extraordinary proliferation of collaborative undertakings in the next century proved him right.

See also **Architecture,** *subentry on* **Architectural Treatises***; and biographies of figures mentioned in this entry.*

BIBLIOGRAPHY

Primary Work

Filarete, Treatise on Architecture. 2 vols. Facsimile edition and translation with an introduction by John Spencer. New Haven, Conn., 1965.

Secondary Works

Cannata, Pietro. "Le placchette del Filarete." In *Italian Plaquettes.* Vol. 22 of *Studies in the History of Art.* Washington, D.C., 1989. Pages 35–53.

Necipoglu, Gulru. "Plans and Models in Fifteenth- and Sixteenth-Century Ottoman Practice." *Journal of the Society of Architectural Historians* 45 (1986): 224–243.

Onians, John. "Alberti and Filarete: A Study in Their Sources." *Journal of the Warburg and Courtauld Institutes* 34 (1971): 96–114.

Scafi, Alessandro. "Filarete e l'Ungheria: L'utopia universitaria di Mattia Corvino." *Storia dell'arte* 81 (1994): 137–168.

Seymour, Charles, Jr. "Some Reflections on Filarete's Use of Antique Visual Sources." *Arte Lombarda* 38, no. 9 (1973).

Tigler, Peter. *Die Architekturtheorie des Filarete.* Berlin, 1963.

ALINA A. PAYNE

FILELFO, FRANCESCO (1398–1481), Italian humanist and Hellenist. For forty years Francesco Filelfo virtually ruled Milan as its cultural dictator. By the early 1430s he was acclaimed as the leading Hellenist in Italy. In Florence, then the European capital of humanism and the Greek revival, his rivals gossiped that his scholarship was of little consequence and that he was vain and quarrelsome. The slander of his Florentine critics stuck, and still survives in Renaissance historiography today, despite his long prominence in Milan, his enduring friendships with eminent princes, churchmen, and scholars, and the fame of his learned letters, which by 1521 had been published in forty-one editions.

Filelfo was born on 25 July 1398 in Tolentino. He studied law and rhetoric with Gasparino Barzizza at the University of Padua. At seventeen he taught rhetoric and moral philosophy at Vicenza. In 1420 he journeyed to Constantinople where he remained for seven years, studying Greek with John Chrysoloras and eventually marrying the latter's daughter. In 1423–1424 Filelfo traveled as the personal envoy of the Byzantine emperor Manuel Paleologus to Poland, Hungary, and Adrianople, a province of the Turks.

In September 1427, accompanied by his wife Theodora and their infant son, Filelfo returned to Venice with a substantial library of Greek books. An outbreak of plague ended his hopes of founding a humanist school in Venice. In 1428 he departed for Bologna, where he taught rhetoric and moral philosophy at the university until civil war broke out there that summer.

In 1429 he assumed the professorship of Greek at the University of Florence. Crowds thronged to hear him lecture on ancient Greek authors then little known in the West. His patrons included the most influential men in the city, including Cosimo de'

Medici, Palla Strozzi, and Leonardo Bruni. In 1431, when civil war broke out in Florence, he fell out of favor with Cosimo and lost his university post. Later that year, when the Medici were temporarily banished, he was reinstated. Nearly murdered by an assassin in May 1433, he fled from Florence when the Medici took power in 1434.

From 1435 to 1438 he taught at Siena, where he survived a second assassination attempt. He taught briefly at Bologna, and in 1439 he became court poet to the duke of Milan, and professor of rhetoric at Pavia. His wife died in 1441; a year later he married the Milanese noblewoman Orsina Osnaga. With the exception of the period when a republican regime replaced the monarchy in Milan in 1447–1450, and the year he taught at Rome, 1475–1476, Filelfo enjoyed the uninterrupted patronage of the dukes of Milan until 1481. During the Milan years, he embarked on two grand tours of Italy. In 1453 he read from his works at the princely courts of Mantua, Ferrara, Urbino, Rome, and Naples, where King Alfonso crowned him poet-laureate. In 1456 he made a second such tour, adding Bologna, Cesena, and Perugia to his itinerary.

After the death of his second wife in 1453, he married Laura Maggiolini, who died in 1476. That same year assassins took the life of his patron, Duke Galeazzo Maria Sforza of Milan. In the summer of 1481, Filelfo left Milan to occupy the Chair of Greek at the University of Florence. He died on 31 July, before the academic year began.

Despite the urban turbulence around him, outbreaks of plague, the two attempts on his life, and his losing battle to support his family, his productivity never slowed. His major works include his Horatian *Satyrae* (1434); two Plutarchan dialogues, *Commentationes de exilio* (On exile; 1440) and *Convivia Mediolanensia* (Milanese symposia; 1443); a Virgilian epic poem, *Sforziad* (c. 1450); the Horatian polymetric *Carmina varia* or *Odae* (Odes; 1449; published 1497); the satirical epigrams *De iocis et seriis* (Light and serious verses; 1465), written in the style of Martial; his Ciceronian treatise *De morali disciplina* (On moral philosophy; 1473; published 1552); and his magnum opus containing forty-four poems in Greek, *De psychogogia* (1459). Filelfo also chronicled his life in a forty-eight-volume letter-book, his *Epistolae* (1477; published 1502), a work that, while it paints the events and personalities of his age in graphic detail, has yet to be translated into English. His translations from the Greek include Lysias's *Murder of Eratosthenes,* Xenophon's *Agesilaus* and the *Constitution of Sparta,* Aristotle's

Francesco Filelfo. Copper engraving. THE GRANGER COLLECTION

Rhetoric (1434), and Plutarch's *Lives of Lycurgus and Numa.*

As the first major scholar of Greek in Italy, Filelfo occupies a place beside the foremost humanists of his day: Francesco Barbaro, Leonardo Bruni, Poggio Bracciolini, and Lorenzo Valla. Not a philosopher or a theologian but a poet, satirist, and moralist, he modeled himself on Horace, Virgil, and Juvenal. His one philosophical work, although thoroughly Neoplatonic, is decidely not Christian.

See also **Humanism,** *subentry on* **Italy.**

BIBLIOGRAPHY

Primary Works

Filelfo, Francesco. *Commentationes florentinae de exilio.* In Eugenio Garin, ed., *Prosatori latini del quattrocento.* Milan, 1952. Pages 494–567.

Filelfo, Francesco. *Odae, Satyrae.* In *Poeti latini del quattrocento.* Edited by Francesco Arnaldi, Lucia Gualdo Rosa, and Liliana Monti Sabia. Milan, 1964.

Secondary Works

Kraye, Jill. "Francesco Filelfo, Virtues and Vices; A Re-examination of His Sources." *Bibliothèque d'Humanisme et Renaissance* 43 (1981): 129–140.

Robin, Diana. *Filelfo in Milan: Writings, 1451–1477.* Princeton, N.J., 1991.

Robin, Diana. "A Reassessment of the Character of Francesco Filelfo." *Renaissance Quarterly* 36 (1983): 202–224.

Robin, Diana. "Unknown Greek Poems of Francesco Filelfo." *Renaissance Quarterly* 37 (1984): 173–206.

DIANA ROBIN

FINANCE AND TAXATION. The greatest challenge faced by Renaissance governments was financing their diverse activities. The effort involved extracting funds from citizens, who often were reluctant to part with money and who, as was common in premodern society, did not reflexively accept the rights of the state in this sphere. Consequently, the history of Renaissance public finance is one of expedience and experimentation, of tension between ruler and ruled. The ever increasing costs of the era, stemming primarily from the increased frequency and scope of wars, caused financial crises, from which evolved significant fiscal innovations.

Taxation. The basic means of raising revenue was through taxes of various kinds: taxes on goods and services, on exports and imports, on salaries, and on property and land. The most sophisticated tax systems were those developed by northern and central Italian towns. Their intense commercial development and broad range of fiscal activities dating back to the Middle Ages gave the towns greater experience in handling the vagaries of finance. By the fifteenth century cities such as Florence, Milan, and Venice possessed articulated fiscal apparatuses that brought in money from diverse sources.

Florence, for example, employed taxes on an impressive array of services and activities within the city, known locally as *gabelle.* The *gabelle* have sometimes been portrayed as indirect taxes, but they were both direct and indirect exactions. They included taxes on wages and salaries, on wine, meat, oil, and various other foodstuffs, on the flow of goods through the city gates, on criminal proceedings, and on the salaries of soldiers. There were even taxes on brothels and the earnings of prostitutes and on gambling profits. Florence's neighbor Siena had some forty-eight *gabelle* on the books in the fourteenth century, a number that prompted one observer to comment that "all was taxed except the air and water." In Florence, Siena, and throughout Italy, the sale of salt was a government monopoly (*dogana*). Citizens bought their salt directly from the state, which artificially controlled supply and manipulated the price. During emergencies such as war, states required "forced" purchases by citizens, whereby locals were ordered to buy a certain amount of salt for an elevated price.

For much of the fourteenth century the Florentines avoided direct taxation. In 1427 officials instituted the *catasto,* an assessment of the wealth upon which a form of graduated income tax was based. All inhabitants of Florence and the Florentine state were assessed. The formula was a sophisticated one, which included deduction for dependents (200 florins per "mouth") and exemption for movables and business profits. Land was taxed according to a percentage of its value.

France. By the late fifteenth century in France the tax on land, the *taille,* became a major source of revenue. The *taille* grew out of the *fouage,* a tax used as an expedient to raise money during the Hundred Years' War (1337–1453). Although the *fouage* was canceled in the aftermath of the conflict, it received a new lease on life, together with a new name, and became a major source of income. Louis XI derived some two-thirds of his income from the *taille.* French kings supplemented their income with other taxes, notably *aides* (excise taxes on commodities such as wine) and the *gabelle,* which in France was a tax on salt, more akin to the Italian *dogana.* The *gabelle* brought in modest amounts of money, constituting about 4 percent of revenue in the later fifteenth century. This was significantly less than what an Italian state usually derived from its salt *dogana.* The *aides* provided up to 30 percent of income at about the same time.

More so than in Italy, there remained in France a deep-rooted feeling among the citizenry that taxes were temporary expedients necessary in times of crisis but onerous and unnecessary in times of peace. Kings continually had to justify taxation. In the late fourteenth century, influenced by popular pressure, the king temporarily canceled taxes. Such expedients seriously compromised revenue, and on several occasions, notably in the fourteenth and early fifteenth centuries, hard-pressed French monarchs resorted to the dubious expedient of debasing the coinage. The debasements of 1427 reduced the silver content of Parisian *gros* to a mere 20 percent. Kings saw their revenues increase greatly, but their kingdoms saw a concomitant rise in social tensions. Debasement was less common in Italy and virtually nonexistent in England. The reliability of French royal revenue increased greatly under the so-called bourgeois king, Louis XI (1461–1483), whose economic policies, both in government finance and in fostering manufacture throughout the kingdom, did much to bolster revenue.

Finance and Taxation. Paying taxes, from a Sienese book cover. Tempera on wood; 1343; 41 × 24.8 cm (16 × 9.75 in.). THE METROPOLITAN MUSEUM OF ART, ROGERS FUND, 1910 (10.203.3)

England and elsewhere. The English tax system was somewhat more stable than the French model. From the Middle Ages, English kings had succeeded in putting together a centralized apparatus. They relied particularly on taxes on imports and exports (notably on wool), on movables, and on clerical incomes. A tradition of direct taxation dated back to the beginning of the millennium with the so-called Danegeld and was well entrenched by the fifteenth century. In the seventeenth century a tax on hearths was a major source of revenue, although never so important as in France. In the fractured German states, taxes on tolls and customs were of the greatest importance. Holland meanwhile relied on a combination of taxes on real property, customs duties, and a variety of commodities.

In all instances, taxation required the consent of the people. In northern Italian republics this usually came from city councils; in England and France from Parliament and the Estates General, respectively. Monarchs attempted to evade these bodies, sometimes with notable success. Tensions between representative bodies and sovereigns over taxation and money were legion and form much of the backdrop of the internal political history of Renaissance states.

Collection of taxes. States were always faced with the problem of how to collect taxes, and even potent regimes had difficulty reaching into the pockets of its citizenry. Many Italian cities dealt with the issue by resorting to tax farming, wherein the state sold the right to collect a tax to an individual contractor in return for a flat fee. The fee was less than what the tax farmer stood to earn, but it was advantageous to the state because it assured the speedy and reliable turnover of funds. This was particularly helpful in time of war, when quick turnover of money was of paramount importance. Tax farming was practiced elsewhere, notably in England, where direct collection did not become widespread until the late seventeenth century. It was also common in France, where charges of peculation and unfair profits often followed officials. The inequalities in the French system were exacerbated by exemptions and special privileges that lightened taxation on some (nobles) and increased it on others (bourgeoisie and peasantry).

State Borrowing. Even in the best of circumstances, states were rarely able to meet all their expenses. To make up the shortfall, governments resorted to borrowing money. In Italy borrowing took the form of forced loans and voluntary loans imposed on citizens. The forced loan was an exaction that required the lender to pay the state a certain sum based on assessment of his wealth. A typical rate was one florin per one-thousand-lire assessment. In return the lender was offered interest, usually from 5 to 15 percent of the principal. The local government assigned repayment to lucrative *gabelle*, such as on wine or salt. The voluntary loan differed from the forced loan in that it was not mandatory. Usually assessed on selected wealthy individuals or clergy, it offered a higher return than the forced loan. In times of war, cities relied heavily on both forced and voluntary loans. During its fight with Milan in 1403, Florence raised nearly 400,000 florins, more than the typical yearly budget of a middle-size Italian state.

Recourse to loans was common throughout Europe. The archdukes of Tyrol relied greatly on loans from the Fugger bank, in return for which they gave lucrative concessions on copper and silver mines. King Francis I of France borrowed 300,000 francs (at $8\frac{1}{3}$ percent interest) from Parisian businessmen in 1543. Fifty-five years later the French debt increased to 300 million francs. Meanwhile the Spanish monarchy during the reign of Charles V borrowed heavily both at home and from Genoese bankers. The debt to the Genoese stood at one point at 14 million *ducados*.

In England and France there was long history of seeking money from the clergy. This was also true in Italy, where requests for money from the clergy grew steadily with the increase in incidence of war from the mid-fourteenth to mid-fifteenth centuries. At the same time, Italy also witnessed a sharp increase in Jewish lending. Throughout north and central Italy (Florence, Siena, Volterra, Perugia, Assisi, Bologna, Mantua, Modena), Jews, in many cases only recently established in their cities, paid forced loans to help cover military and other expenses. The advantage in seeking loans from Jews was that they could be bullied into paying, threatened with imprisonment or removal from the city. The regular citizenry often evaded loans, particularly in time of war and great crisis, when they feared that they would likely receive neither interest nor principal in return. However, the increased involvement of Jews in local affairs brought resentments and recriminations. In the fifteenth century, led by Bernardino of Siena and others, there was movement to limit Jewish participation in local Italian affairs.

Funded Public Debt. Difficulty repaying loans was a chronic problem faced by states. Large sums borrowed during wars often outstripped the resources—usually indirect taxes—pledged to repay them. Several states responded by establishing funded debts, aimed at converting short-term obligations into more long-term ones. The Venetians were the leaders, establishing the so-called *monte*

vecchio (old mountain) in 1262. The Florentines followed with their *monte* (mountain) in 1345. The Florentine *monte* called for the consolidation of all outstanding loans and repayment at a single fixed rate of 5 percent. The innovation radiated out elsewhere. Several of Florence's Tuscan neighbors, including Siena, Lucca, and Pisa, soon consolidated their debts, as did the Genoese in 1405. The Dutch funded their debt in the sixteenth century, while the English did so in the seventeenth century.

The measures enjoyed some notable successes. The Florentine *monte* was described at the beginning of the fifteenth century as "the heart of this body that we call the city." Astute Florentine officials enhanced its appeal by allowing credits to be transferable. This opened up a secondary market in which the wealthy could speculate, thus making the *monte* an attractive investment for the monied classes. Soon after its implementation, the Florentines began offering a *monte d'un due*, offering interest of twice the standard 5 percent, and a *monte d'un tre*, offering triple the standard rate. Although the city eventually rescinded these privileges, the opportunities to make more than the par value on the *monte* shares continued. In the fifteenth century virtually all well-to-do Florentine families had some share of their wealth invested in the public debt. This was not true in neighboring cities such as Pisa, Lucca, and Siena, which did not permit transfer or speculation.

Positive results were also achieved in Holland and England. The Dutch public debt, or *renten* (from the French *rentes*), functioned in many ways like the earlier Italian models. Like the Florentines, the Dutch allowed a "free market" in *renten* shares (life and hereditary annuities), which enhanced confidence and attracted investors. The English debt was organized similarly, with the exception that it was managed not by the state but by the Bank of England. In this regard it resembled the Genoese public debt, which was managed by the Bank of St. George. Like its Dutch predecessor, the English public debt was particularly effective at handling the enormous fiscal pressures of war. The scholars who studied the innovation in both countries have spoken in glowing terms of "financial revolutions" produced thereby.

The establishment of funded public debts represents a creative response to the growing fiscal demands of the era. These fiscal demands were propelled into the stratosphere by the enormous cost of warfare, brought on by the technical innovations of the "military revolution," which permitted conflict on an unprecedented scale. It has been argued that the frenetic search for funds and increased volume of spending brought more rigorous and systematic fiscal practices which in turn gave rise for the first time to the concept of a national budget. Likewise, the increased reliance on lending has been credited with producing closer links between the ruling and monied classes, converting, as it were, private interest into public interest through shared economic destiny. The development brought with it the precondition for the modern state.

See also **Banking and Money**; **Usury**.

BIBLIOGRAPHY

Braddick, Michael J. *The Nerves of State: Taxation and the Financing of the English State, 1588–1714.* Manchester, U.K., 1996.

Brewer, John. *The Sinews of Power: War, Money and the English State, 1688–1783.* London and Boston, 1989.

Caferro, William. *Mercenary Companies and the Decline of Siena.* Baltimore, 1998.

Dickson, P. G. M. *The Financial Revolution in England.* London and New York, 1967.

Ehrenberg, Richard. *Capital and Finance in the Age of the Renaissance.* London, 1928.

Lane, Frederic C. *Venice and History: The Collected Papers of Frederic C. Lane.* See "The Funded Debt of the Venetian Republic 1262–1482," pp. 87–98. Baltimore, 1966.

Molho, Anthony. *Florentine Public Finances in the Early Renaissance, 1400–1433.* Cambridge, Mass., 1971.

Tilly, Charles. *Coercion, Capital, and European States, A.D. 990–1992.* Oxford, 1990.

Tracy, James D. *A Financial Revolution in the Habsburg Netherlands: Renten and the Renteniers in the County of Holland, 1515–1565.* Berkeley, Calif., 1985.

Wolfe, Martin. *The Fiscal System of Renaissance France.* New Haven, Conn., 1972.

WILLIAM CAFERRO

FIORENTINO, NICCOLÒ

(Niccolò di Forzore Spinelli; 1430–1514), Florentine medalist. Considered the finest portraitist among fifteenth-century medalists, Niccolò Fiorentino combined bold likenesses with uninspired reverse compositions to dominate—and define—the Florentine school of medals in the late fifteenth and early sixteenth centuries. Niccolò cast five medals bearing his signature: Sylvestro Daziari, Bishop of Chioggia; Antonio Geraldini, poet laureate and ambassador; Alfonso I d'Este, Marquess of Ferrara; Lorenzo the Magnificent de' Medici of Florence; and Antonio Della Lecia, a Florentine merchant. Based on these verifiable medals, an extremely large, and unlikely, body of work—more than 150 medals—has been attributed to Niccolò or his circle.

Niccolò was born in Florence, coming from a family of artists, particularly goldsmiths. His grandfather, Niccolò di Luca Spinelli (d. 1422?), was one of the original competitors for the Baptistery doors of Flor-

Niccolò Fiorentino. **Portrait Medal of Lorenzo the Magnificent.** MUSEO NAZIONALE DEL BARGELLO, FLORENCE/SCALA/ ART RESOURCE

ence in 1401, while his great-uncle was Spinello Aretino (1350/52–1410), the prolific and popular late fourteenth-century painter working in a derivative style of Giotto. Niccolò's father Forzore (1397–1477) and his uncle Cola (c. 1377/84–1458) ran a respectable goldsmith *bottega* (workshop) in Florence, where Niccolò probably apprenticed in the mid-1440s. He is recorded in 1468 as engraving seals for Charles the Bold in Burgundy, but returned to Florence by 1471, where he married Alexandra di Leonardo di Lorenzo Paoli. In 1484 Niccolò repaired the great silver seal for the Arte dei Giudici e Notai (the judicial and notary guild) in Florence. He filed his first tax return in 1480 and filed again in 1498. He probably visited Rome in the mid-1480s when he cast a medal of Sylvestro Daziari (1485), and he was paid in 1492 for a silver medal for Alfonso I d'Este of Ferrara. Leonardo da Vinci's notebooks (c. 1504–1505) record Niccolò's advice on the specifics of how a stream might be diverted in Flanders.

Sir George Hill divided Niccolò's medals into seven basic categories: (1) signed medals; (2) those relating to Rome; (3) medals of Frenchmen (presumably cast c. 1494–1495 during the French invasion of Italy); (4) medals generally related to Florentine personalities; (5) medals of Savonarola; (6) medals somewhat distantly related to Niccolò but still in the "Florentine" style; and (7) medals depicting famous

Florentine literary figures (Petrarch, Dante, Boccaccio) and other medals for popular consumption.

However artificial these divisions may be, they highlight the issues surrounding a clear definition of Niccolò's style. His portraits are infused with an uncompromising naturalism and boldness, heightened by his insistence that an effigy reach the borders of the medal. Though all of his signed medals depict men, Niccolò was equally adept at portraying women, as his attributed portraits of Nonina Strozzi Barbigia, Costanza Rucellai, and Giovanna Albizzi Tornabuoni attest. Sometimes Niccolò's reverses approach elegance, such as the Three Graces used for the medal of Giovanna Tornabuoni (also used for a medal of Pico della Mirandola). More often, however, his reverse compositions represent a frustrating indifference to quality and exhibit monotonous repetition of antique sources, usually with little attempt to personalize the symbol to a specific patron. These issues seem not to have bothered his contemporaries, however, as he and his workshop provided medals to most of the leading families of Florence and many distinguished patrons in Rome.

Niccolò's reverses largely draw on ancient sources; Spinelli's reuse of the same imagery for various patrons may indicate that the artist's workshop dealt in ready-made objects; in such a case, the patron's portrait would be joined to a pre-made reverse. In effect, this practice may have made portrait medals, which represented humanist ideals in durable materials, available to a growing middle class.

See also **Coins, Medals, and Plaquettes.**

BIBLIOGRAPHY

Flaten, Arne R. "Niccolò Spinelli and the Image of Humanism: Portrait Medals and the Late Quattrocento Florentine Art Market." Doctoral dissertation in progress, Indiana University.

Heiss, Aloïss. *Les médailleurs de la Renaissance.* 9 vols. Paris, 1880–1892. Vol. 5, 1885.

Hill, George Francis. *A Corpus of Italian Medals of the Renaissance before Cellini.* 2 vols. London, 1930. Reprinted Florence, 1984.

ARNE R. FLATEN

FIREARMS.   While the invention of firearms took place during the Middle Ages, arms makers of the Renaissance made many improvements and brought firearms to a high degree of perfection. By the sixteenth century, armies and individuals made great use of firearms in warfare and hunting.

The Later Middle Ages.   Hand-held firearms were invented in western Europe during the second quarter of the fourteenth century. They were a development, in reduced proportions, of early forms of cannon, prototypical examples of the latter being documented by around 1325. Firearms arose from the introduction of gunpowder into Europe from China, perhaps via Moorish Spain, some time in the thirteenth century. The extent of the military applications of gunpowder in Asia at that time remains a matter of debate. In Europe, however, the military potential of gunpowder was widely realized by approximately 1350, from which time the evolution of artillery and firearms progressed steadily.

An early hand cannon (the term "handgun" first appears toward the end of the fourteenth century) consisted of little more that a barrel and a stock. The first barrels were cast in brass or bronze in the shape of a small vase with a circular opening at the narrow end (the muzzle) joined by a tubular recess to a cavity in the wider end (the breech). Shortly thereafter barrels generally took the form of faceted cylinders, without a widening at the breech. A small hole, called the touchhole, was drilled into the breech, perpendicular with, and joining to, the inside of the barrel recess.

The barrel was lashed to a wooden shaft by metal bands or was cast with a socket in the breech end, into which the shaft could be inserted. By the early fifteenth century barrels were also being made of iron, sometimes forged with a rod extending from the breech end, which served as a stock. By the late 1400s iron was the predominant material for gun barrels. Hand cannon were frequently made with a short hook extending from the underside of the stock or barrel, by which the gun could be steadied on the edge of a wall or other fixed object to facilitate aim and guard against recoil.

To load the weapon, a measured quantity of gunpowder (the charge) was poured down the barrel and tamped firmly in place with a rod (later known as a ramrod). A projectile could then be inserted into the barrel. The earliest projectiles shown in European sources are short arrows, probably made of metal or reinforced wood. These were soon replaced by circular stone, and later lead bullets wrapped in a small piece of cloth (the patch) to ensure a tight fit and to seal in the charge. A small amount of gunpowder (later known as priming powder) was poured into a shallow counter-sunk recess at the opening of the touchhole. To fire the weapon, it was aimed with one hand while a smoldering brand or slow-burning taper (known as a match) was applied with the other hand to the powder in the touchhole, which in turn caused the charge in the breech to explode, thereby propelling the bullet from the muz-

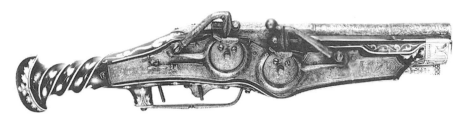

Firearm. Double-barreled wheellock pistol made for Emperor Charles V by Peter Pech. Etched barrel; stock and butt inlaid with engraved ivory; c. 1540; 49 cm (19.375 in.) long. THE METROPOLITAN MUSEUM OF ART, GIFT OF WILLIAM H. RIGGS, 1913 (14.25.1425)

zle. This is the basic principle underlying all muzzle-loading firearms.

Improvements during the Renaissance.

The hand cannon of the fourteenth and early fifteenth century were relatively crude weapons with only limited military capabilities. By the end of the fifteenth century, however, firearms had improved enough in practicality and effectiveness to begin having a significant and ever-increasing impact on the way in which warfare was conducted in Europe and, through European colonization, around the world. Several basic improvements made firearms more portable, more reliable, and easier to use. Barrels were made longer and more slender, so that they looked more like modern gun barrels than miniature cannon. A small, shallow cup called the priming pan was added to the side of the breech at the touchhole. Fitted with a pivoted cover, it securely held the priming powder in place. Whereas earlier hand cannon had been fired with the stock held under the arm or over the shoulder like a bazooka, the more contoured gun stocks that developed from about 1475 onward were designed for firing from the cheek or the shoulder, allowing for better aim.

The most significant development by far was the invention of various types of gun locks, the firing mechanisms that permitted a gun to be held with two hands and fired by means of a trigger device. The first, and one of the most enduring, of these was the matchlock. The term, as with the name of other lock mechanisms, refers both to the lock itself and to a firearm so equipped.

The matchlock. The development of the matchlock made firearms highly portable and relatively reliable. It was also a comparatively simple, efficient, yet sturdy mechanism; therefore, it could be produced in large numbers and was easy to use, easy to repair, and strong enough to withstand hard use. These factors combined in the late fifteenth century to make the matchlock musket the first type of firearm with which it was both practical and effective to equip large numbers of troops. At its simplest, the basic mechanism consists of a pivoted, serpentine arm (the cock) fitted with jaws in which the end of a slow burning cord (the match) was held. This was mounted on a plate on the outside of the stock. The trigger engaged an internal lever that pivoted the jaws of the cock into the priming pan, igniting the charge and firing the gun. Because of its simplicity and durability, the matchlock musket remained the standard infantry weapon in Europe up to the mid-seventeenth century, long after more sophisticated lock mechanisms had been developed. The matchlock also made firearms usable as hunting weapons and, therefore, of interest to the nobility. As a consequence, from the early 1500s, more finely made and decorated firearms were created for nonmilitary pastimes, such as hunting and target shooting, and as luxury items.

The wheellock. The next major innovation in firearms technology was the wheellock, which was invented in the late fifteenth century, probably in northern Italy. The wheellock was the first fully self-contained firearm. Rather than a slow-burning match, the jaws of the cock held a piece of iron pyrites against a serrated wheel mounted on the side of the stock at the touchhole. A quick rotation of the wheel, powered by an internal spring, struck sparks from the pyrites in the priming pan and ignited the charge in the barrel. The wheellock had several advantages over the matchlock. The absence of a smoking match made the wheellock less susceptible to damp weather and eliminated the smoky clouds that heralded the movement of matchlocks. The wheellock also made a pistol-size weapon practical because it could be kept primed and at the ready and worn on a belt or carried in saddle holsters. In response to the advent of wheellock pistols, the first laws against the carrying of concealed firearms were enacted in the early sixteenth century.

The disadvantages of the wheellock were that it was more expensive and complicated to make than the matchlock, more complex to use and maintain, and costlier to repair if broken. For these reasons it never became a common infantry weapon during the Renaissance. Wheellock pistols and carbines (short rifles), however, quickly became important cavalry weapons, supplanting the heavy lance as the primary weapon of the armored cavalry by the 1600s. With the creation of the wheellock, firearms were widely adopted by the nobility, both for military and for sporting purposes.

The flintlock. Developed in the first decade of the seventeenth century by the French gunmaker Marin Le Bourgeois, the flintlock became the most reliable and effective type of firing mechanism for the next two centuries. It was a refinement of an earlier form of lock, known as the snaphaunce, which was used throughout Europe from the late sixteenth to the mid-seventeenth century. The flintlock mechanism takes its name from the piece of flint held in the jaws of the cock. In operation the cock is drawn back to an intermediary position, or half cock (a safety position, ready for loading), and a firing position of full cock. The powder in the priming pan is kept in place by a pivoted L-shaped cover (the steel, or frizzen). When a flintlock is fired the cock snaps forward in a downward arc, causing the flint to scrape rapidly down the frizzen, simultaneously uncovering the priming pan and sending a shower of sparks into the priming powder, which ignites the charge in the barrel. By the mid-seventeenth century, flintlock pistols were rapidly replacing wheellocks as the predominant cavalry weapon. Matchlock infantry muskets were also superseded by flintlock muskets at about the same time. Flintlocks could be made simply and sturdily enough to withstand the rigors of field service. They could also be refined to meet the needs of hunters and marksmen.

Rifling. Another great innovation in firearms technology of the Renaissance was rifling, a process in use in Germany possibly as early as around 1500 but rarely found before the mid-sixteenth century. Most military firearms of the period were smooth bore, meaning that the interior of the gun barrel (the bore) had smooth sides. A rifled barrel has a series of loosely spiraling grooves (usually from three to five) cut into the interior of the barrel along the entire length of the bore. The effect is to cause the projectile (usually a round musket ball) to spiral as it is shot from the muzzle, propelling it with greater velocity, range, and accuracy. Rifled barrels were more expensive to produce and required frequent cleaning. Most military firearms, therefore, remained smooth bore, while weapons for hunting and other sporting purposes were frequently rifled.

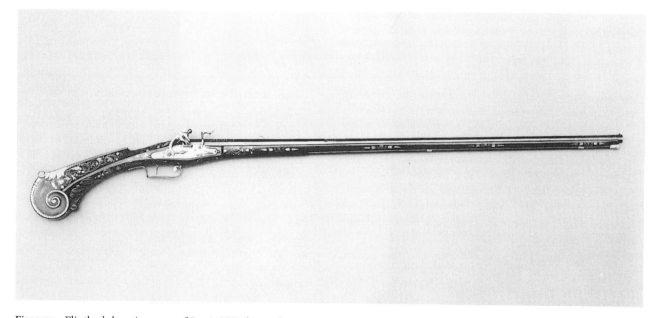

Firearm. Flintlock hunting gun of Louis XIII, king of France, attributed to Pierre Le Bourgeoys of Lisieux (d. 1627). Steel, brass, silver, gold, wood, mother-of-pearl; c. 1615; 140 cm (55 in.) long. THE METROPOLITAN MUSEUM OF ART, ROGERS AND HARRIS BRISBANE DICK FUND, 1972

Luxury arms. Along with the rapid profusion of military firearms, by 1525 ornately decorated firearms also began to be made. Gun stocks were delicately inlaid with bone, horn, ivory, mother-of-pearl, sheets of brass or silver, and gold or silver wire. Stocks were also carved in relief or veneered with exotic woods, ivory, or even tortoiseshell. The leading gun stockers employed all the marquetry techniques found in the finest furniture and architectural woodwork. The steel parts of the gunlocks and other fittings were chiseled and chased in high and low relief, etched, engraved, silvered, or gilt. From the mid-sixteenth century onward, ornate firearms were considered an essential part of a nobleman's armory. They were commissioned as hunting weapons, presentation pieces, diplomatic gifts, and works of decorative art.

Centers of Production.

By the middle of the sixteenth century virtually every significant geographic region in Europe included one or more cities renowned for the manufacture of firearms. Among the best known were Brescia, Italy; Munich; Augsburg; Nürnberg; Brunswick; Dresden; Vienna; Prague; Suhl, in Thuringia; Paris; St.-Étienne; Liège; Maastricht; Utrecht; and London.

See also **Artillery**; **Warfare**.

BIBLIOGRAPHY

Blackmore, Howard L. *Guns and Rifles of the World.* New York, 1965.

Blair, Claude. *Pistols of the World.* New York, 1968.

Blair, Claude, ed. *Pollard's History of Firearms.* London, 1983.

Hayward, John F. *The Art of the Gunmaker.* 2 vols. New York, 1962–1963.

Norman, A. V. B., and Don Pottinger. *A History of War and Weapons, 449–1660: English Warfare from the Anglo-Saxons to Cromwell.* New York, 1966.

Schedelmann, Hans. *Die grossen Büchsenmacher: Leben, Werke, Marken vom 15. bis 19. Jahrhundert.* Braunschweig, Germany, 1972.

DONALD J. LAROCCA

FIRENZUOLA, AGNOLO (1493–1543), Florentine vernacular writer. Michelangiolo (Agnolo) Girolamo Firenzuola was the son of Bastiano Firenzuola, a Florentine notary. After early education in Florence, Agnolo was sent to Siena and Perugia to study law and at the age of twenty-five completed his studies, motivated more by his father's desire to prepare him for the notarial profession than by personal conviction. In order to secure a promising career for his son, Bastiano urged Agnolo to enter a monastery. As it did for other humanists at this time, the ecclesiastical career brought Firenzuola to Rome, where in 1518 he was appointed Roman attorney (*procuratore*) for the Vallombrosian order. At the papal courts of Leo X and Clement VII, Firenzuola came into contact with the social and intellectual elite of his time.

In Rome he began the first phase of his literary activity (1518–1526), associating with influential figures and illustrious men of letters, including his old friend Pietro Aretino (1492–1556). The turning point of his career in Rome was in 1523, when he met a woman known (in his work) under the pseudonym of Costanza Amaretta (Bitter Constancy), whom he describes as the source of his literary inspiration. Through her influence, as he recalls in his free adaptation of Apuleius's *L'asino d'oro* (The golden ass; published 1550), he was able to abandon the "asinine" world of law to pursue his scholarly vocation. Firenzuola's first literary success came in 1524 with a treatise on Italian orthography titled *Discacciamento delle nuove lettere inutilmente aggiunte nella lingua toscana* (The expulsion of the new letters unnecessarily added to the Tuscan language), in which he defends the purity of the Italian language against Gian Giorgio Trissino's attempt to introduce Greek letters into the Italian alphabet. The treatise caught the attention and admiration of his contemporaries, including Pietro Bembo, who encouraged him to continue his literary endeavors. In the same year Firenzuola composed *Ragionamenti d'amore* (Discourses on love), which was not only a sign of his commitment to the vernacular but also a useful illustration of the evolution of the Italian novella, which in the sixteenth century was becoming more classical, closely linked to the dialogue form. *Ragionamenti,* a collection of short stories modeled on Giovanni Boccaccio's *Decameron* (1353), effectively shows how the two genres harmoniously come together.

Despite his dedication to a literary vocation, Firenzuola became disillusioned by the short-lived popularity of his works. Deeply saddened by the death of Amaretta (1525) and suffering from syphilis, in 1526 he withdrew from public life. In 1538 Firenzuola began writing again after moving to Prato as newly appointed abbot of the Vallombrosian monastery of San Salvatore a Vaiano. In Prato he enjoyed the patronage and support of the city's most influential families before falling victim to social enmity and financial misfortune. His last works include *Dialogo delle bellezze delle donne* (Dialogue on the beauty of women), which he completed in 1541; *La prima veste dei discorsi degli animali* (The first version of the animals' discourses), a collection of tales of Indian origin; two comedies; and a translation of Horace's *Ars poetica*. Firenzuola's treatise on feminine beauty, including its external aspects, has long been considered a fundamental text of the Italian Renaissance for its exemplary illustration of the close relationship between Platonic philosophy and the figurative arts.

BIBLIOGRAPHY

Primary Works

Firenzuola, Agnolo. *The Bawdy Tales of Firenzuola*. Translated by Jules Griffon. Covina, Calif., 1967.

Firenzuola, Agnolo. *On the Beauty of Women*. Translated and edited by Konrad Eisenbichler and Jacqueline Murray. Philadelphia, 1992.

Firenzuola, Agnolo. *Opere*. Edited by Adriano Seroni. Florence, 1958.

Firenzuola, Agnolo. *Opere di Agnolo Firenzuola*. Edited by Delmo Maestri. Turin, Italy, 1977.

Secondary Works

Cropper, Elizabeth. "On Beautiful Women, Parmigianino, *Petrarchismo*, and the Vernacular Style." *Art Bulletin* 58, no. 3 (1976): 374–394.

Murray, Jacqueline. "Agnolo Firenzuola on Female Sexuality and Women's Equality." *Sixteenth Century Journal* 22 (summer 1991): 199–213.

Riviello, Tonia Caterina. *Agnolo Firenzuola: The Androgynous Vision*. Rome, 1986.

Rogers, Mary. "The Decorum of Women's Beauty: Trissino, Firenzuola, Luigini, and the Representation of Women in Sixteenth-Century Painting." *Renaissance Studies* 2, no. 1 (1988): 47–88.

GIUSEPPE FALVO

FISCHART, JOHANN (1546 or 1547–1590), German Protestant author. Fischart was the greatest German prose writer of the second half of the sixteenth century. He is regarded as a difficult but intriguing author whose prose is filled with random tonal associations and who delighted in coining arcane words. In many ways his work anticipated German Dadaism.

Fischart grew up in Strasbourg and attended the gymnasium (high school) that had developed into one of the leading humanist schools in Germany under the direction of the educator Johann Sturm. In 1562 Fischart was placed under the supervision of the family friend and noted humanist author Caspar Scheidt. After his schooling, Fischart traveled to the Netherlands, France, England, Italy, and Switzerland. In 1574 he received a law degree from the University of Basel. At that time his lifelong collaboration with his brother-in-law, the printer Bernhard Jobin, began. After working as a lawyer at the imperial high court in Speyer, Fischart was appointed Amtmann (prefect) in Forbach in Lorraine. He died, probably victim of a plague, in 1590.

Fischart published over seventy works in prose and verse, representing various literary genres, often using pen names or pseudonyms. Prompted by the reassertion of Catholic power in Strasbourg, which had become Protestant earlier in the century, the militantly Protestant Fischart published a number of anti-Catholic pamphlets of which *Die wunderlichst unerhörtest Legend und Beschreibung des abgeführten, quartirten, gevierten und viereckechten Vierhörnigen Hütleins* (The strangest and most shocking legend and description of the four-cornered hat; 1580) is the best known. Based on a Huguenot satire, this satirical mini-epic describes the alleged unholy alliance between Lucifer and the papacy; in this work, the Jesuits in particular are singled out for his scorn.

Different in tone and intention is Fischart's poem *Das glückhafft Schiff von Zürich* (The fortunate ship of Zürich; 1576), in which he describes the arduous boat trip between Zurich and Strasbourg undertaken by a delegation of Zurich citizens on a single day in June 1576. The poem celebrates the value of hard work, perseverance, and the importance of good neighborly relations. The year 1577 saw the publication of two satirical works, *Flöh Hatz/Weiber Tratz* (Hunting of fleas/Defiance of women), in which Fischart, from the perspective of a flea, offers humorous observations on the female anatomy, hygiene, and dress, as well as *Das Podagrammisch Trostbüchlein* (Consolation of the gout), an ironic encomium of gout.

The work on which Fischart's reputation rests, however, is his combined adaptation and translation of the first book of François Rabelais's *Gargantua*. Published in three ever-expanding editions (1575, 1582, 1595), the *Affentheurlich naupengeheurliche Geschichtklitterung* (Adventurous, whimsically vast story scribble) is a work in which Fischart indulges his passion for punning, wordplay, free association, and other verbal acrobatics. The translation, which constitutes approximately a quarter of the text, provides the pretext for a flood of digressions, amplifications, and additions.

Fischart's lack of concern for intelligibility might have contributed to his disappearance into near oblivion in the seventeenth century. However, since the eighteenth century and the romantic period, readers have shown a renewed interest in his works.

See also **Satire**.

BIBLIOGRAPHY

Primary Works

Fischart, Johann. *Flöb Hatz, Weiber Tratz*. Edited by Alois Haas. Stuttgart, Germany, 1967.

Fischart, Johann. *Das glückhafft Schiff von Zürich*. Edited by Alois Haas. Stuttgart, Germany, 1967.

Fischart, Johann. *Sämtliche Werke*. Edited by Hans-Gert Roloff, Ulrich Seelbach, and W. Eckehart Spengler. Vol. 1 published. Bern, Switzerland, 1993–.

Secondary Works

Kühlmann, Wilhelm. "Johann Fischart." In *Deutsche Dichter der frühen Neuzeit (1450–1600)*. Edited by Stephan Füssel. Berlin, 1993. Pages 589–612. Excellent article in German with good bibliography of secondary literature.

Wailes, Stephen L. "Johann Fischart." In *Dictionary of Literary Biography*. Vol. 179, *German Writers of the Renaissance and Reformation 1280–1580*. Edited by James Hardin and Max Reinhart. Detroit, Mich.; Washington, D.C.; and London; 1997. Pages 55–62. Concise, most recent article with bibliography of most important works of primary and secondary literature.

Weinberg, Florence M. *Gargantua in a Convex Mirror: Fischart's View of Rabelais*. New York; Bern, Switzerland; and Frankfurt, Germany; 1986. Only full-length, very critical study in English of Fischart's main work.

ECKHARD BERNSTEIN

John Fisher. Anonymous portrait. NATIONAL PORTRAIT GALLERY, LONDON

FISHER, JOHN (1469–1535), English churchman. Born in Beverley, Yorkshire, where his father was a mercer, John Fisher spent his youth in Rochester, the cathedral city halfway between London and Canterbury. After attending the cathedral school there, Fisher studied at Cambridge, where he was influenced by the new teachings of the humanists. He was largely responsible for Lady Margaret Beaufort's foundation of two new colleges, Christ's and St. John's, and he himself gave St. John's four fellowships as well as lectureships in Greek and Hebrew. He served briefly as master of Queens' College, bringing Erasmus to teach there, and was chancellor of the university as well as the first Lady Margaret Professor of Divinity.

Fisher's career in the church began with his appointment as bishop of Rochester in 1504. His conservative views soon became apparent. Like Henry VIII, he opposed Martin Luther's view of the sacraments and his doctrine of salvation by faith alone. He also wrote refuting the reformed teachings of John Oecolampadius on the Eucharist. His theology embraced the Augustinian doctrine of justification by grace alone and a patristic understanding of the Mass. His support of the papacy was tempered by respect for the decisions of general councils. In 1512 he was nominated to attend the Lateran Council, but in the end he did not go to Rome.

When the king began to seek a divorce from his first wife, Catherine of Aragon, Fisher became Catherine's chief adviser and advocate. He was unwise enough to listen to the tale of Elizabeth Barton, the holy maid of Kent, who prophesied the king's death should he proceed with the divorce. The act attainting Elizabeth, passed in 1534, also condemned Fisher and his friend Sir Thomas More. They were committed to the Tower and interrogated at length; both refused to swear the succession oath required of them.

Fisher's execution may have been prompted by news that Pope Paul III had created him a cardinal in May 1535. Henry was unwilling to allow the cardinal's hat to be received in England, and he ordered Fisher to be put to death on 22 June. A frail septuagenarian, he could not have lived much longer.

Immediately acknowledged to be a Catholic martyr, Fisher became a model for the Counter-Reformation episcopate, and his views were influential in doctrinal discussions at the Council of Trent. Like More, he was beatified in 1886 and canonized as a saint in 1935. His portrait, sketched by Hans Holbein the Younger, is part of the royal collection at Windsor Castle.

BIBLIOGRAPHY

Bradshaw, Brendan, and Eamon Duffy, eds. *Humanism, Reform, and the Reformation: The Career of Bishop John Fisher.* Cambridge, U.K., 1989. A collection of essays on Fisher's career and beliefs.

Rex, Richard. *The Theology of John Fisher.* Cambridge, U.K., 1991. A fine study, placing Fisher's theology in the context of humanism and the Reformation.

Reynolds, E. E. *Saint John Fisher.* Rev. ed. Wheathampstead, U.K., 1972. The standard biography, but Catholic hagiography.

Surtz, Edward. *The Works and Days of John Fisher, 1469–1535.* Cambridge, Mass., 1967. An earlier examination of Fisher's theology, written by a leading Jesuit scholar.

STANFORD E. LEHMBERG

FLANDERS. *See* **Netherlands.**

FLAVIUS MITHRIDATES (Shmuel ben Nissim ben Shabbatai Abu al-Faraj; c. 1450–1483), Italian scholar. Flavius Mithridates is the best known of the names he adopted after converting to Christianity in or about 1470. (Others include Guglielmo Raimondo Moncada, Siculus, and Romanus.) Born in Grigento in Sicily sometime around 1450, he embodied Sicilian Jewish culture from at least two major points: He was fluent in a variety of languages, including Hebrew, Aramaic, Arabic, Latin, and perhaps some Ethiopic, which he used in order to translate, and he taught the brand of Kabbalah that was dominant in the island: Abraham Abulafia's "ecstatic" (or "prophetic") Kabbalah.

On Good Friday 1481 Mithridates delivered a sermon on the passion in the presence of Pope Sixtus IV, in which he spoke about Jewish arcana without referring to Kabbalistic concepts or texts. Resorting to classical, Christian, and Jewish texts, he attempted to demonstrate that Christ's passion was already adumbrated in ancient Jewish sources, including one that he designated as Vetus (Old) Talmud.

Mithridates was an itinerant scholar. He visited Aragon in 1474–1475, where he attempted to convert Jews. He taught theology at the University of Rome and, between 1482 and 1484, in Louvain, Basel, Tübingen, and Cologne. Mithridates taught Giovanni Pico della Mirandola in Florence and also influenced scholars such as Johann Reuchlin, Rudolf Agricola, and Konrad Summerhart. He served as a cleric in Messina before 1474 and received the priorate of Cefalù but had to leave the country for an unknown reason. He returned to Viterbo and was arrested in 1489.

Mithridates translated part of the Koran into Latin, as well as the book of Job and some Jewish philosophical writings. More than any other person, he contributed to the initial encounter between Christian intellectuals of the Renaissance, especially Pico della Mirandola, and the Jewish Kabbalah. Mithridates translated a long series of Kabbalistic treatises from Hebrew into Latin, and sold them to the young count of Mirandola, whom he also taught Oriental languages.

These translations represent mainly the Italian Kabbalistic traditions, especially the writings of Abraham Abulafia and Menahem Recanati, but also some Ashkenazi esoteric and Spanish Kabbalah writings. The translations, though performed by someone who had a fine understanding of the many complex topics expounded in them, are nevertheless biased. Short additions and semantic choices reveal the translator's intention to portray Kabbalah as close to some Christian tenets, and as more magical than the original sources. Most of the translations are extant in three manuscripts found in the Vatican Library, and their content has been meticulously analyzed in Wirszubski's monograph on Pico.

It was from these extensive translations, which were, as Wirszubski conclusively demonstrated, sometimes colored by Mithridates's Christian and magical biases, that Pico learned most of what he knew about Kabbalah. Mithridates's role in introducing a new speculative corpus in Renaissance thought can be compared only to that of Marsilio Ficino (1433–1499). As a translator Mithridates mediated between a sort of literature that was practically unknown to the Christian intellectuals in the West, but he also offered his own understanding of the material.

BIBLIOGRAPHY

Primary Work

Mithridates, Flavius. *Sermo de pasione domini* (Sermon on the passion). Edited by Chaim Wirszubski. Jerusalem, Israel, 1963.

Secondary Works

Idel, Moshe. "The Ecstatic Kabbalah of Abraham Abulafia in Sicily and Its Transmission during the Renaissance." *Italia judaica* 5 (1995): 330–340.

Secret, François. "Qui était l'orientaliste Mithridate?" *Revue des études juives* 116 (1957): 96–102.

Simonsohn, Shlomo. "Some Well-Known Jewish Converts during the Renaissance." *Revue des études juives* 148 (1989): 17–52.

Wirszubski, Chaim. *Pico della Mirandola's Encounter with Jewish Mysticism.* Cambridge, Mass., 1989.

MOSHE IDEL

FLETCHER, JOHN. *See* **Drama, English,** *subentry on* **Jacobean Drama.**

FLORENCE. [This entry includes three subentries, one on the history of the city and territory of Florence in the Renaissance and the other two on artists active in Florence in the fifteenth century and in the sixteenth century.]

Florence in the Renaissance

This city on the Arno River became the hub of Renaissance Italian culture. A center of banking, commerce, and textiles, Florence (Firenze) was, along with Venice, Milan, Rome, and Naples, one of the five powers and two great independent republics (the other being Venice) of Italy. As of 1434 the Medici, a wealthy and powerful banking and merchant family, dominated Florentine politics. By the century's end the Medici had been expelled (1494) and Florence had fallen under the influence of the friar Girolamo Savonarola; after his death in 1498, the city was ruled by a coalition of patricians. In 1512 the Medici returned as *signori* (lords), but were exiled again in 1527. Florence suffered increasing turmoil during its last years as a republic before the Medici returned in 1530. They became dukes of Florence and, in 1569, grand dukes of Tuscany.

Origins. Excavation in the mid-1980s of the city's main square, the Piazza della Signoria, revealed evidence of prehistoric settlements. Destroyed in the civil wars between the factions of Marius and Sulla, the town was refounded as a walled city during the time of Julius Caesar. The Roman legacy of Florentia, as it was called, can be seen in today's street plan, the center still laid out in the typical Roman grid with its main thoroughfares, the *decumanus maximus* and *cardo maximus,* and their parallel streets crossing at right angles. Florentia's economic development—it served as a seat of provincial government, port (the Arno then being navigable even upstream from Florence), and commercial center during the Roman empire—presaged its importance during the Renaissance.

Florence suffered sieges, attacks, or occupations by the Goths, Byzantines, and Lombards, but survived to become an important bishopric and a county nominally subject to the Holy Roman Emperor. In 1081 Henry IV attempted to depose and dispossess Florence's ruler, Countess Matilda of Tuscany, over her support of his opponent, Pope Gregory VII. Florence alone among Matilda's Tuscan possessions remained faithful to her. Florence's identity as a Guelf (pro-papal) city was thus established, though such sympathies would not keep it from going to war against the papacy in 1375. Prior to her death in 1115, Matilda granted it substantial privileges. Beginning in 1125 with the conquest of its nearby rival, Fiesole, Florence embarked on a policy of Tuscan expansion that would culminate, in the mid-sixteenth century, with its acquisition of Siena. By 1138 it was a commune with its own consuls, men from powerful families who made foreign policy, governed the city, and carried out justice.

The Florentine Constitution. By the first part of the thirteenth century, Florence had twenty-one guilds, divided into seven major (judges and notaries; international cloth merchants, or *calimala;* wool manufacturers; bankers; silk manufacturers; physicians and apothecaries; and furriers) and fourteen minor guilds (mostly shopkeepers and artisans like winesellers and blacksmiths). Though both major and minor guildsmen were eligible for political office, the major guilds enjoyed greater access. Guild members numbered no more than six thousand by the late fourteenth century; thousands of lower-class workers, including those employed in the cloth industry, had no trade guild and were thus excluded from political participation. *Accoppiatori* (scrutinizers) examined the qualifications of those theoretically eligible for office, eliminating, for instance, men who owed taxes, and then placed the names of those approved into leather bags (*borse*). Offices were filled not by voting but by random drawing of names from the *borse*. Only about 10 to 15 percent typically passed the scrutiny. It stands to reason that any faction able to control the *accoppiatori* could control Florentine politics.

Florence's Signoria (city council) comprised nine priors: eight standard-bearers (*gonfalonieri*) and the standard-bearer of justice (*gonfaloniere di giustizia*). They sat for a two-month term. The Signoria was advised by two colleges, the Twelve Good Men (Dodici Buonomini), who served three-month terms, and a group of sixteen also called standard-bearers (Sedici Gonfalonieri), who sat for four months. Two extraordinary commissions (*balìe*) also existed: the Ten of War (Dieci di Balìa) and the Eight of Public Safety (Otto di Guardia e di Balìa), the latter created in 1380 by the merger of the secret political police force and a six-month extraordinary committee. The *balìe* gained power during the fifteenth century, by which time the Otto had begun to function as a court as well as an investigative bureau. Over a dozen other magistracies carried out administrative functions in the city and its domain. A group of permanent civil servants, including the chancellor (appointed for life and, beginning in the late fourteenth

Sources of Knowledge about Renaissance Florence

More is known about, and has been written on, Florence than any other premodern city. One reason for this attention is its prominence in creating and molding Renaissance culture. The center of art and humanism for much of the fourteenth and fifteenth centuries, Florence claimed Dante Alighieri, Francesco Petrarca (Petrarch), and Giovanni Boccaccio as native sons; its chancellors included prominent humanists like Coluccio Salutati, Leonardo Bruni, and Poggio Bracciolini; the most important artists of the Renaissance (many, like Donatello, Domenico Ghirlandaio, and Sandro Botticelli, natives of the city) found commissions there. Tuscan, the local dialect, became the basis for modern Italian with the vernacular work of Dante.

Beyond Florence's considerable importance per se is the survival of unusually rich—in some cases, incomparable—documentation for its history. Many of these sources are located in the State Archive of Florence (Archivio di Stato di Firenze). Others are held in Florence's great libraries, including the Biblioteca Laurenziana (Laurentian Library) and the Biblioteca Nazionale di Firenze (National Library of Florence). Though the republican and ducal regimes kept and consulted records, it was not until the 1840s and 1850s, during the reign of Grand Duke Leopold II (Habsburg) of Tuscany, that the archives were centralized.

Taken together, these sources have no parallel in richness, variety, and continuity. Only for Florence, for instance, do records of legislative deliberations reach back to the thirteenth century. The *Libri fabarum* (books of the beans, a reference to the casting of yes or no votes by black and white beans, respectively) list not only bills that passed but also those that failed; nowhere else in Europe do such records exist for the late Middle Ages and Renaissance. For many issues the city council called in respected citizens who spoke for or against; summaries of their remarks offer a unique window into the intricacies of domestic and foreign policies, factions, and political strategies.

In 1427, preparing to levy a new tax, the city took a special census, the *catasto*. Each head of household in all parts of Tuscany controlled by Florence had to compile a declaration of assets and liabilities. The family's principal residence was exempt from taxation; deductions were allowed for debts and dependents. These records, which took three years to redact, remain almost intact and constitute a font of information about the society of Florence: demography, social classes, sources and ownership of wealth, financial strategies,

and the like. A second exhaustive census ordered by Grand Duke Cosimo I de' Medici in 1552 serves as a kind of bookend for Florentine social geography during the Renaissance.

Heads of households, especially those of the merchant classes, often kept *ricordanze* or *ricordi,* a combination of household ledger, memoir, diary, and chronicle. Over one hundred such diaries are extant for Renaissance Florence; in contrast scholars have found but a single such merchant's diary for Renaissance Genoa. *Ricordi* reveal business dealings, marriages, and other important areas. Other private records include those from the archives of leading families like the Strozzi and Medici.

In addition the Florentines developed institutions, some of them unique, whose records remain vital for historians. The Monte delle Doti, or public dowry fund, was created in 1425. An investment in this state-backed, fixed-term fund was guaranteed to pay a projected sum as part of the dowry once the marriage was consummated. Historians have also probed the extant records of Florence's funded public debt (Monte Comune, founded in 1345) and public charitable pawnshop (Monte di Pietà, which opened in 1496).

Florentine history is further enriched by the vast extant documentation for corporations and city bureaucracies. The former include monasteries, convents, and charitable associations—there were 163 known confraternities in Renaissance Florence—as well as trade guilds (*arti*) and the Guelf faction (Parte Guelfa). The archives of the Otto di Guardia e di Balìa, established in 1378 as a secret political police force and revived by 1380, reveal much about crime, prostitution, and other hidden activities. For the sixteenth century the records of the health board (Ufficiali di Sanità) and of extraordinary commissions like one dealing with the aftermath of Arno floods show the city's attempts to cope with nature and the environment.

A highly legalistic society like that of Florence depended on notaries, whose main function was the drawing up of contracts or other legal documents: wills, marriage agreements, real estate transactions, and the like. Government agencies also employed notaries to keep minutes of meetings and transcribe documents. Each notary kept a copy of the contracts he wrote; tens of thousands of these volumes survive. These records represent only a sample of the kinds of documentation available for scholars of Renaissance Florence.

century, a respected humanist), gave the system continuity despite the rapid rotation of offices.

Legislation was introduced by the Signoria, which also had power over foreign relations. A temporary chairman, or *proposto,* presented a bill for discussion. If the Signoria wished, it could debate by itself in a *pratica ristretta,* or it could invite interested and informed parties (a *pratica non ristretta*) for their counsel. The records of these discussions, called *consulte e pratiche,* were recorded by the chancellor and his scribes; some of the great lights of the Renaissance, like Leonardo Bruni and Coluccio Salutati, took the notes. If the bill passed by a two-thirds' majority, it was forwarded to the legislative bodies, originally two in number: the Council of the People (Consiglio del Popolo) and the Council of the Commune (Consiglio del Comune), with about three hundred members each. These bodies could reject the bill, but otherwise had little power. In the second half of the fifteenth century, however, the Medici created the Council of One Hundred and the Council of Seventy, which gained power at the expense of the old bodies. An approved bill was registered as a law, or *provvisione.* A public assembly of all the citizens, the Parlamento, was called rarely, generally in times of emergency.

With the expulsion of the Medici in 1494, the new regime eliminated organs of government, including the Seventy and One Hundred, considered instruments of tyranny. In their place it established a Great Council of some three thousand members. But beginning in 1530, with the return of the Medici, the inner oligarchy redrew the constitution. Preferring a Medici *signore* to what they considered the evils of popular government, these patricians invited Alessandro de' Medici (d. 1537) to become *capo* (head) and, shortly thereafter, "duke of the republic of Florence." Reforms removed the old Signoria for a new executive body, the Magistrato Supremo, which was to share power with the duke; the Great Council was replaced by the Council of Two Hundred and the Senate of Forty-Eight, appointment to both of which was for life.

Florence established a sophisticated if complicated court system. The *podestà* was, as of 1207, the highest juridical officer and a noble foreigner with Guelf loyalties; the Florentines hoped thus to ensure impartiality. Some cases fell under the jurisdiction of guild courts. Others were handled by the tribunal of the archbishop, which occasionally wrestled with secular courts for jurisdiction over issues like the validity of marriage. Until 1537 three different courts adjudicated most criminal offenses: the Otto di Guar-

dia e di Balìa, the Executors of the Ordinances of Justice, and the courts of the *podestà;* thereafter, the second two were consolidated in the Otto, though, as late as 1560 and despite ducal attempts at centralization, twenty-seven other bodies exercised criminal-justice functions.

The Conservatori di Leggi (conservators of laws), established in 1429, oversaw execution of the law and the behavior of public officials. From the late thirteenth century on, civic auditors reviewed the accounts of those entrusted with public funds. Auditing, and meting out fines and other punishments to public officials, became increasingly important by the mid-sixteenth century, when mishandling of public moneys became tantamount to robbing the duke. By that time auditors could examine suspects under torture, and were motivated to undertake their responsibilities zealously by the prospect of being granted a share of any recovered sums. During the duchy offices like the Magistrato Supremo and Pratica Segreta exercised some judicial functions. So busy did the latter become, with its jurisdiction over issues in Florence's subject towns, that one of his advisers wrote to Duke Cosimo de' Medici that the Pratica would have to add Saturday meetings.

Politics. The strife between landed nobility and the increasingly important merchant classes hastened the formation of trade guilds by the late twelfth century. The corporations served to protect and standardize trades and to counter the power of the magnates, whose vendettas and street violence helped give contemporaries the impression that Florence was a place of turmoil in contrast to Venice, "the most serene republic." Such violence would make Dante wonder, as he journeyed through the *Inferno,* why Florentines hated each other so much.

By the middle of the thirteenth century, the commune had forced restrictive legislation on the magnates. The political dominance of the guilds was confirmed in 1293–1295, during the priorate of Giano della Bella, by the Ordinances of Justice. These laws forbade those not enrolled in a trade guild from holding most offices, effectively excluding the magnates from politics; identified troublemaking magnates by name and forced them to post a bond against their good behavior; and increased penalties for violence. These ordinances tried to distinguish the *magnati* or *grandi* from the *populares* or *popolani:* magnates from people. The "people," however, tended to fall into two groups: *popolo grasso* (literally, "the fat," meaning "rich") and *popolo minuto,* the middle and lower classes. Nor did the bit-

Republics of Florence and Siena

25 Miles
25 Kilometers

Marco, was in fact a dangerous political conspiracy of wool carders and beaters. Several attempts to organize wool workers' brotherhoods ended in executions of the leaders. Repeated proclamations and ordinances tried to outlaw gatherings of workers. Unrest culminated in 1378 with the revolt of the Ciompi, poor cloth workers demanding their own guilds and finding themselves in a strange alliance with some of the ruling class, including the wealthy rentier Salvestro de' Medici. The Ciompi and the broader government they forced on the patricians were suppressed only in 1382.

The experience of 1378–1382 ushered in a conservative, restricted oligarchy that realized that the interests of trade guilds were not necessarily identical to its interests. Legislation over the next several decades tightened the rules for holding office while ensuring at least nominal participation by all guilds. The main foreign-policy issue was preventing the expansion of other Italian powers; thus from 1375 to 1378 the Guelf city fought the papacy in the "War of the Eight Saints" when Gregory XI attempted to reconstitute the papal states in the Romagna.

This was hardly the last Italian crisis Florence would face. Two wars, one against Duke Giangaleazzo Visconti of Milan, another against the Angevin prince Ladislaus, ended only with their deaths in 1402 and 1414, respectively. War with Milan was reprised in the 1420s. A costly attempt to conquer Lucca in 1429 dragged on until 1433, ending in Florence's ignominious withdrawal. These foreign-policy crises, coupled with a fiscal emergency in the 1420s that revealed bitter disagreements within the oligarchy over tax reform, opened the way for the rise of two factions, one led by the Albizzi, the other by the Medici. Although historians have sometimes called the Albizzi the more patrician and the Medici the more popular of the two groups, kin and patronage ties were probably more important in factional loyalty.

Though suffering exile in 1433, the Medici under Cosimo the Elder (d. 1464) emerged triumphant by 1434. Head of the family's huge bank, Cosimo dispensed favors shrewdly and enjoyed unrivaled connections beyond Florence. By controlling the scrutiny of the *accoppiatori,* making use of existing institutions and advocating new ones, relying on the power of the *balìe,* and distributing patronage—including lavish public spending—he and his family ruled from behind the scenes until 1494. They preserved the facade of republicanism and, dwelling in their private residence, carefully presented themselves not as *signori* but as citizens; in the sixteenth

terness of factional politics disappear. Dante consigned Filippo Argenti to the fifth circle of hell, rejoicing in his rival's eternal torment; later, the poet encountered the Ghibelline leader Farinata degli Uberti, who called Dante and his kin bitter enemies. By 1300 the Guelfs, having defeated the Ghibellines, split into two hostile factions, the Whites (among them, Dante) and the Blacks. The victory of the Blacks resulted in the exile of Dante and other Whites in 1302.

The problems of communal politics, exacerbated by military defeats (notably, Montecatini in 1315 and Altopascio in 1325), led Florentines on three different occasions to invite in a *signore* to restore order. The last of these, Walter of Brienne, supported by magnates and the *popolo minuto,* established himself as ruler for life, but was driven out in 1343 after less than a year. Following this failed experiment, the guilds established a broad-based regime that should not, however, be confused with democracy. The following decades sharpened Florentine factionalism. The Albizzi family claimed to represent Florence's traditional Guelf interests even though the Guelfs, having long since defeated the Ghibellines, had lost their original identity. This faction also tended to favor old money and to be distrustful of the "new men" who gravitated to the Ricci faction.

The unguilded cloth workers of Florence had begun agitating for a share of political power. In 1317 the wool guild charged that a workers' benevolent and pious group, a confraternity meeting at San

century the Medici dukes would move first to the Palazzo della Signoria, later to the immense Pitti Palace. The Medici appeased some enemies by making marriage alliances with them, and they retained the loyalty of many patricians who feared broader, more popular government by allowing them access to offices they expected as their birthright. The Medici kept close control over foreign policy, attempting to maintain a balance among the five Italian powers but also reversing Florentine tradition by establishing close ties with Milan. This balance was achieved by the Peace of Lodi of 1454–1455, a nonaggression treaty signed by Milan, Venice, Florence, the papacy, and Naples, each of which had established more or less permanent ambassadors at the other courts. Cosimo was succeeded by his son Piero (d. 1469) and then by Lorenzo "the Magnificent" (d. 1492). Lorenzo's marriage into the Orsini, a powerful Roman senatorial family, symbolized the Medici's evolving outlook, one that allowed them to take advantage of ties beyond Florence. In 1478 Lorenzo and his brother, Giuliano, were targets of assassins, part of a revolt masterminded by the rival Pazzi family. Giuliano was stabbed to death; Lorenzo, though wounded, survived. The aftermath was a far worse bloodbath as Medici adherents had their revenge through murder or exile. The affair resulted in war against Naples and the papacy that ended with the personal diplomacy of Lorenzo himself and, ultimately, political power more firmly in his grasp.

Medici domination of republican Florence did not long outlive Lorenzo. The Dominican friar Girolamo Savonarola (d. 1498) settled in Florence in 1489, became prior of San Marco in 1491, and began preaching an apocalyptic, reformist, and prophetic message to crowds of Florentines. A contemporary, Luca Landucci, considered Savonarola to have been sent by God, and noted that there were many Florentines who would have walked through fire for him. The friar urged Florentines to reform their lives and their government, and warned them to expect purge and punishment before salvation. He established pious youth organizations, and called on Florentines to destroy "vanities" like "pagan" art (Botticelli, falling under Savonarola's influence, burned some of his own works). The arrival in Italy of Charles VIII, king of France, in 1494 seemed the fulfillment of Savonarola's preaching. Piero di Lorenzo de' Medici capitulated to Charles and was soon exiled, along with many members of his family. The departure of the Medici opened the field to Savonarola and his followers, the *Piagnoni* (Snivelers). Within just a few years, however, Savonarola's pro-French policy, an-

tithetical to the anti-France position of Pope Alexander VI, his condemnation of worldly vanity (which struck the pope a little too close to home), and his defiance of both a ban on preaching and a papal excommunication, led to his fall, and in 1498 he was executed by hanging in the Piazza della Signoria. The shocking vicissitudes of the period beginning in 1494 would lead historians Niccolò Machiavelli and Francesco Guicciardini to look back on the Laurentian period as one of prosperity and peace.

Having had an unpleasant taste of popular government under Savonarola, Florence's patricians moved to avoid a repeat of it. One of them, Piero Soderini, became *gonfaloniere* for life in 1502. Ten years later Soderini's pro-French policy and his attempt to steer a course between broad-based government and patrician oligarchy lay in shambles; he fled Florence as the Medici, led by Cardinal Giovanni de' Medici (the future Pope Leo X and the son of Lorenzo) and supported by the emperor, returned. This time they established themselves as lords, ruling until 1527, when they left peacefully following the sack of Rome and the humiliation of the Medici pope, Clement VII, by troops of Emperor Charles V. The years 1527–1530 represented Florence's final fling with republicanism. The new regime suppressed the *balìe*, reestablished the Great Council, and took the interesting though dubious step of naming Jesus Christ king of the city. Clement VII, however, reconciled with Charles V, and in 1529 pro-Medici forces besieged Florence. Despite seizing the assets of the trade guilds and taking thousands of florins, never repaid, from the Monte di Pietà (the public charitable pawnshop), the regime capitulated in 1530.

Textbooks often dismiss Florentine history after 1530 as a sad tale of decline. Florence, however, a duchy as of 1532, became the capital of an important medium-sized state and, as of 1537, was ruled by one of the most talented of the Medici, Cosimo I (d. 1574). Part of Cosimo's success lay in his near-workaholic habits, which, until he abdicated in favor of his son Francesco in 1564, gave him unprecedented control over Florentine matters. Part of that control stemmed from his ability to exploit institutions that could serve his purposes. He ruled through the use of powerful small magistracies whose membership he controlled, and he promoted the careers of talented outsiders, "new men" who owed their positions to him. Nonetheless, Florence's old patriciate survived almost intact; 90 percent of the men appointed to the Senate during the sixteenth century came from families who had served in the Signoria the century before. Cosimo realized an old Florentine dream, the conquest and permanent attachment to Tuscany of Siena in 1557, and in 1569 won the title of grand duke of Tuscany. Culture throve under his regime as Florence once again became a center of intellectual and artistic life.

Money, Finance, and Economy. Florence's monetary system was bimetallic, with coins of gold, used mainly in international transactions, as well as of silver or copper, which dominated small and local business. The city gave its name to the famous gold florin (*fiorino d'oro*), first struck in 1252 and containing about 3.5 grams of twenty-four-carat gold. By the sixteenth century the florin was replaced by the gold *scudo,* of inferior fineness. The *lira* was not minted but was a money of account. It was divided into *soldi* and *denari* (twenty *soldi* to the *lira* and twelve *denari* to the *soldo,* similar to the old English system of pounds, shillings, and pence). When first minted, the florin was the equivalent of twenty *soldi,* or one *lira.* By 1410 the florin was worth eighty *soldi,* or four *lire;* five *lire* by the 1450s; six *lire* by the 1480s; seven *lire* by 1502. The result of the florin's appreciation was a loss in average wages, as expressed in gold, of about 50 percent from about 1350 to 1500, a development that surely favored employers. But since local transactions were often made in silver and copper, the worker's purchasing ability was not drastically lessened.

Although moneys of account were used elsewhere, the Florentine custom of maintaining written ledgers meant that *lire* were the common currency of bookkeeping. So accepted was the *lira* that in 1430 one Florentine merchant proffered the precocious suggestion, not acted upon, that it be printed as paper money. The Florentines did, however, devise or exploit other useful banking practices. Financial institutions routinely transferred sums as debits or credits to their customers' current accounts, or accepted drafts drawn against them. By the mid-sixteenth century, for instance, the Medici paid some creditors or accepted payments from debtors through their accounts, some at least temporarily running a deficit, in the Monte di Pietà. While the typical Florentine worker would not have had a bank account, he or she could present a written draft, perhaps for wages owed, to a bank for cash. Tax declarations show that even artisans, probably motivated by the deductibility of some of these sums, kept written records of their debtors and creditors.

Ironically, in a city whose wealth rested in part on international banking, average Florentines who needed credit had few options. In 1430 the Signoria reached an agreement with Florence's Jews that made pawnbroking their virtually exclusive domain in return for the Jews' paying a tax on their lending. In response to a clear economic need and grounded in a fifteenth-century revival of anti-Semitism, the councils passed a law in 1495 creating the Monte di Pietà and calling for the expulsion of the Jews. Those needing small loans—often not the poor but the middle class—could receive them at 5 percent, less than what Jewish lenders charged, at the Monte di Pietà. By the 1530s the Monte di Pietà paid 5 percent interest on deposits, and thus took on some of the functions of a bank.

Like other European states Florence experienced a growing need for revenue by the mid-thirteenth century. By the late 1330s indirect taxation accounted for about 75 percent of the government's income and was sufficient in times of peace. Emergencies such as war required additional revenue from interest-bearing forced loans (*prestanze*), the amounts owed by each household being determined by citizen committees that were hardly immune to fraud or pressure. Those forced to make loans became the state's creditors in the Monte Comune, or funded public debt, created in 1345. By the late fourteenth century the government felt pressure to service this growing debt and to respond to accusations of fraud and injustice. Citizens who had not paid their taxes were, moreover, barred from public office and sometimes threatened with imprisonment in the Stinche, Florence's debtors' prison, so complaints about the *prestanze* had serious political implications. War with Milan further stressed the fisc in the 1420s. City councils heard pleas for tax reform that would impose the burden objectively on all assets but with clearly identified deductions allowed. Thus was born the *catasto* (1427), modeled after a Venetian tax of the same name, to be levied on both Florence and its Tuscan territory.

Altogether some 60,000 households submitted tax documents covering about 265,000 inhabitants. Foreigners, mercenaries, and clergy in the city were not subject to the *catasto;* they may have comprised an additional 22,000 or more inhabitants (some temporary). Of the total of 265,000, about 40,000, roughly one in seven, lived in Florence itself, and held a disproportionate share of taxable wealth: about two-thirds. A smaller cohort of about a hundred Florentines controlled one-fifth of Tuscany's taxable wealth. Since a family's dwelling was exempt from taxation regardless of its worth, the *catasto* may

Florence. View of Florence from the nearby hills, 1490. MUSEO DI FIRENZE COM'ERA, FLORENCE/ALINARI/ART RESOURCE

have encouraged the rich to spend lavishly on their homes.

Some subject towns claimed that historic liberties rendered them immune to the tax. Others, like Volterra, undertook revolts that were put down with armed might. Many areas succeeded in evading the tax, and subsequent cadastral surveys (undertaken every three years) did not even attempt to include the rest of Florentine Tuscany. The *catasto* had greater success, however, in placing the tax burden on households rather than on neighborhoods, and seems to have eliminated some of the fraud of forced loans. In other ways the *catasto* proved the universality of cheating on taxes. Since dowries were deductible from taxable assets, many fathers overstated the size of their dotal commitments. A prominent scholar of the *catasto* has argued that its demand for precision about not only wealth but also personal facts, such as the ages of household members, helped change Florentine views about the importance of knowing one's age. Ultimately the *catasto* failed, and following the Pazzi conspiracy of 1478, was replaced by the *decima scalata* (a graduated direct tax) that was permanently adopted in 1495, after the expulsion of the Medici.

Florence's economic power derived principally from two industries: banking and textiles. By the late thirteenth century, with the triumph of the Guelf faction, Florentine banks won important business from the papacy and from the kingdom of Naples. Among the perquisites of the former concession was the collecting of papal taxes throughout Europe. The Na-

ples connection yielded a Florentine monopoly on that kingdom's grain trade. Great banking families, including the Bardi, Peruzzi, and Acciaiuoli, found themselves amassing unprecedented capital through branches that spanned the continent. The English crown's default at the outset of the Hundred Years' War ruined several of Florence's banks by 1346, but their fall only seemed to clear the way for new entrepreneurs like the Medici, who achieved political power through their wealth and then used that power to forward their business interests.

Of even greater importance was the wool industry. Florence's high-quality wool cloth found a market just as the Flemish cloth industry was stagnating in the first half of the fourteenth century. Good raw wool, imported from England, Spain, and elsewhere, was spun by thousands of country women and then woven into cloth on looms. Until the mid-fourteenth century women dominated the weaving trade, but were then replaced by German immigrant males. By the late sixteenth century, following the removal of power from and the restructuring of the guilds in 1532, women once again flocked to the trade, and constituted nearly two-thirds of wool weavers by 1604. According to the fourteenth-century chronicler Giovanni Villani, as many as thirty thousand men and women worked in cloth production before 1348. Turning raw wool into fine finished cloth was a labor-intensive, sometimes backbreaking process that included shearing, washing, sorting, combing, carding, spinning, weaving, dyeing, stretching, and cutting. The men who owned the wool firms, of which there were some two hundred during the Renaissance, belonged to the wool (*lana*) guild. The skilled or semiskilled workers who owned equipment necessary to production could enjoy middle-class prosperity. But the bulk of those whose labor went into wool production had no trade guild and were prevented from organizing. With the Ciompi revolt of 1378, they succeeding briefly in establishing their own guild.

Smaller but still important was Florence's silk industry, which through the Renaissance produced high-quality, luxury goods. The captains of this industry belonged to their own trade guild. Women played important roles in cultivating mulberry trees, harvesting the leaves on which the silkworms fed, caring for the silk cocoons, and spinning the raw silk into thread. As with the wool industry, women tended to carry out production tasks associated with plain cloth, not with fine, highly decorative textiles.

Population, Geography, Social Life.
Compared with coastal cities like Genoa, Pisa, and Venice, Florence through the twelfth century remained small and provincial; city walls constructed in 1172 enclosed an area about two-thirds that of Pisa. But beginning in the late twelfth century, Florence, though not endowed with a particularly strategic location or with fertile plains, grew rapidly into a large, prosperous town. By 1284 the city walls could not contain the expanding population, and had to be enlarged. New walls, completed in 1333 in anticipation of continued growth, enclosed about five square kilometers.

Contemporaries in the late 1330s and modern historians alike put the population at around 120,000, making Florence one of Europe's five largest cities. The Black Death, which in 1348 killed as many as half the inhabitants, reappeared every ten years or so, preventing the population from reaching its pre-plague level until the nineteenth century. In 1427 Florence held about forty thousand permanent inhabitants, not including clergy and foreigners. The 1552 census counted about sixty thousand residents, including clergy. The population was unusually literate; Giovanni Villani claimed that as many as ten thousand boys attended schools, and historians suggest that between a quarter and a third of Florentine males could read and write.

Until 1343 Florence was divided into six districts (*sestieri*), each associated with a city gate. Thereafter, it was reorganized into four quarters (*quartieri*): Santo Spirito, on the left bank of the Arno, and Santa Croce, San Giovanni, and Santa Maria Novella on the right bank. Each quarter was divided into four *gonfaloni* (a reference to the military standard, for each was the territorial entity from which the militia was supposed to be drawn). Florentines identified not only with their quarter and *gonfalone*, but also with their local parishes, of which the city boasted nearly sixty during the Renaissance.

The surrounding countryside (*contado*), much of which was owned by Florentine families, provided much of the city's victuals. Annonary laws regulating the sale (place, price, amount) of important comestibles assured that the capital city would remain the market of enforced choice for farmers. The land was worked predominantly by sharecropping (*mezzadria*). In 1427, 25 percent of all peasant households were sharecroppers, who paid half of what they produced to their landlords and who made up some of the very poorest Tuscans. Sharecroppers often found, however, that their landlords acted as their patrons, lending them money and arranging marriages and dowries.

Florence had an important Jewish community by the early thirteenth century. Jews were generally kept out of trade guilds, though there were a few exceptions: several Jews enrolled in the physicians' guild in the fifteenth century, for instance. Some Jews enjoyed the title *civis*, citizen, though not until the eighteenth century did they gain eligibility for civic offices. By the fifteenth century they were relegated to a very few professions, notably pawnbroking. As a rule of thumb, Florence's Jews fared better under the Medici than under popular republican regimes. An attempt in 1495 to expel them failed when a fiscal crisis made the city fathers think twice about the loss of an important source of revenue.

Corporations formed the social basis of Renaissance Florence and, in some ways, the family could be seen as the most basic corporation. Marriage, therefore, was serious business. Male guardians devised strategies to obtain dowries that would permit respectable marriages for their dependent girls, for the right marriage could bring wealth and honor to a family, reconcile political opponents, and create amity. Indeed, the very word for forming a marriage alliance—*parentado*—can be loosely translated as "making relatives."

Middle- and upper-class city girls married by their late teens, whereas men tended to stay single until established financially, often in their late twenties. The patrician Buonaccorso Pitti, an adventurer, entrepreneur, and professional gambler, did not marry until he was about thirty-eight. He reported in his diary that through a marriage broker he approached

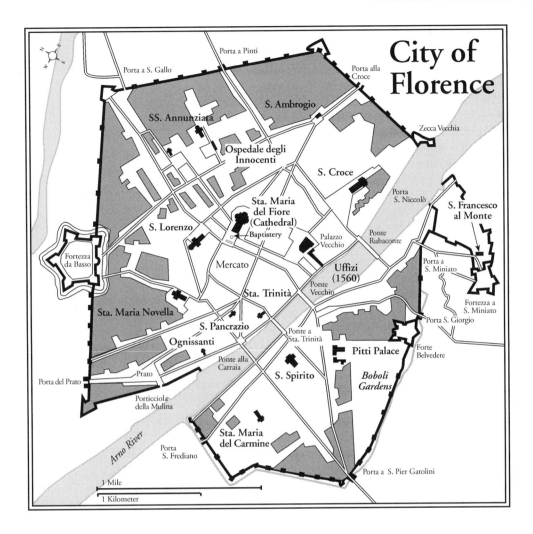

City of Florence

Porta a Pinti
Porta a S. Gallo
Porta alla Croce
S. Ambrogio
SS. Annunziata
Zecca Vecchia
Ospedale degli Innocenti
S. Croce
Porta S. Niccolò
Sta. Maria del Fiore (Cathedral)
S. Francesco al Monte
S. Lorenzo
Baptistery
Palazzo Vecchio
Ponte Rubaconte
Fortezza da Basso
Mercato
Uffizi (1560)
Porta a S. Miniato
Sta. Trinità
Ponte Vecchio
Sta. Maria Novella
Fortezza a S. Miniato
S. Pancrazio
Porta S. Giorgio
Ognissanti
Ponte a Sta. Trinità
Pitti Palace
Forte Belvedere
Ponte alla Carraia
Porta del Prato
Prato
S. Spirito
Boboli Gardens
Porticciola della Mulina
Sta. Maria del Carmine
Arno River
Porta S. Frediano
Porta a S. Pier Gatolini

1 Mile
1 Kilometer

the del Palagio family for a bride. In making this *parentado* Pitti hoped his new in-laws would help him to patch up his relationship with a third family. Marriage was too important to leave to the whims of love, and was brokered, as Pitti's case shows, by serious-minded men. Given the mortality of women during their childbearing years, men could expect to marry more than once. Not unusual was Gregorio Dati, one of seventeen children, who married four times in the name, as he put it, of God and good fortune.

Marriages were typically arranged by written contracts drawn up by notaries. The details of the dowry and any restrictions on it were listed. Most such contracts required that dowries be placed in real estate, government funds, or other safe investments. On the death of either spouse, the dowry normally reverted to the woman's family. For merchants like Gregorio Dati, dowries brought vital infusions of capital. In his diary Dati expressed the hope that his impending marriage with its forthcoming dowry might provide

a thousand florins he needed for a partnership in the silk business. Later, planning another partnership, he counted on getting about six hundred florins from his soon-to-be wife, and expressed the desire of every marriageable Florentine man: "I hope that I may find a woman with a dowry as large as God might be pleased to grant."

Art and Culture. Florence's enduring fame rests on its place in Renaissance culture. Yet no one has ever provided a satisfactory answer to the question of why Florence produced and nurtured such a concentration of men and women of genius. Some scholars argue that the fifteenth century brought economic stagnation, and that the wealthy saw art and buildings as sound investments during hard times. Others argue that a robust economy supported spending on culture; thus, the Renaissance had a real economic cause. Regardless, there is no doubt that some of Florence's wealthiest men and women created convivial places for discussion and learning, and that individuals, corporations, and the city itself commissioned much art. The humanists Coluccio Salutati, Niccolò Niccoli, Poggio Braccio-lini, Marsilio Ficino, Angelo Poliziano, and Giovanni Pico della Mirandola all worked in Florence. In the early sixteenth century the diplomat and historian Bernardo Rucellai and his progeny hosted gatherings of Florentine patricians in the Orti Oricellari, the gardens of the palace built by Leon Battista Alberti for Bernardo's father, Giovanni. Strolling amid flora that Bernardo had selected from references in clas-sical literature, Machiavelli explained to the literati gathered there the principles of his *Discourses;* in-deed, scholars trace the political realism of Machia-velli and Francesco Guicciardini to modes of thought developed by participants in the Rucellai garden conversations.

Two generations earlier Cosimo de' Medici gath-ered prominent humanists interested in Plato and gave them employment and places to meet, and he and his descendants were active in their discussions. One modern scholar argues that humanist acclama-tion of Cosimo the Elder was not mere adulation of a valued patron by Medici clients, but a way for re-publicans to check the ambition of the Medici by tying them to classical models of restraint. The Med-ici even showed some toleration for dissent. The hu-manist Alamanno Rinuccini wrote a scathing attack on the Medici in the wake of the Pazzi rebellion. Not long thereafter Rinuccini found himself employed by the Medici. In the next century Duke Cosimo I de' Medici enticed an opponent, the poet Benedetto Varchi, to return from exile.

Though the old idea that the Medici ran an art school in which the young Michelangelo perfected his craft has long been disproved, the Medici and other patrons did seek out the best artists and hu-manists of the day. The competition for commissions itself spurred creativity. Writing in the sixteenth cen-tury, the artist Giorgio Vasari argued that the great-ness of Florentine art resulted from the "spirit of criti-cism" in Florence—a kind of capitalistic cultural atmosphere, almost—that led to the freeing of the mind and a disdain for mediocrity. One example of competition was the search in 1401 for a sculptor to design new doors for Florence's Baptistery, a building of both civic and religious importance. Prominent artists including Donatello, Filippo Bru-nelleschi, and Lorenzo Ghiberti submitted panels de-picting the sacrifice of Isaac, with the last's earning him the commission. The entries submitted by Bru-nelleschi and Ghiberti are among the first examples of a radical departure from Gothic style.

Art held important symbolic value. Florence en-visioned itself as a free republic battling against tyr-anny and had long identified with David; different versions of this biblical boy-warrior show the devel-opment of Renaissance taste. In 1408 Donatello carved a marble David that was to decorate a buttress on the outside of the Duomo and had been com-missioned by the Opera di Santa Maria del Fiore, the board of overseers of the church. It shows a young classical warrior, fully clothed, almost Stoic in his quiet contemplation of victory. A bronze done by Donatello some twenty-five later for Cosimo de' Medici shows a completely different treatment. This David, his face modeled on the Roman boy Antin-oüs, is sensual, androgynous, and nude, the first free-standing nude since antiquity and a figure de-signed for private display. Michelangelo's David, created in 1504 for the city itself for a public space, is modeled on Hellenic sculpture and may also rep-resent the ideal hero (art historians have noted that Michelangelo's version of this Jewish youth is not circumcised).

Florence's grain market, Or San Michele (which also became the center of an important cult and con-fraternity), contains exterior niches for which the trade guilds commissioned sculptures representing their crafts. Among these was Donatello's masterful St. Mark (1411–1413), carved for the linen guild. Fi-lippo Brunelleschi designed the gallery of the Os-pedale degli Innocenti, the foundling hospital, on a commission from the wool guild, evidence that char-ities and confraternities were as caught up as other patrons in the desire to display the latest in art. Pri-vate palaces made a statement about the desire for great architecture and for quiet living space in the midst of the city. Among the notable *palazzi* are those of the Medici (Michelozzo Michelozzi), Gondi (Giuliano da Sangallo), Strozzi and Antinori (Giuli-ano da Maiano), and Rucellai (Leon Battista Alberti).

See also **Lodi, Peace of; Medici, Cosimo de'; Medici, Cosimo I; Medici, Lorenzo de'; Medici, House of; Pazzi Conspiracy; Savonarola, Girolamo;** *and biographies of artists, humanists, and historians mentioned in this entry.*

BIBLIOGRAPHY

Primary Works

Brucker, Gene A., ed. *The Society of Renaissance Florence: A Documentary Study.* New York, 1971. A superb collection of documents on the social history of Florence, edited by the foremost American historian of the field.

Brucker, Gene A., comp. and ed. *Two Memoirs of Renaissance Florence: The Diaries of Buonaccorso Pitti and Gregorio Dati.* Translated by Julia Martines. New York, 1967; repr.

Prospect Heights, Ill., 1991. The diaries of Pitti, a powerful Florentine patrician and entrepreneur, and Dati, a middle-class silk merchant, covering the late fourteenth through early fifteenth centuries.

Landucci, Luca. *A Florentine Diary from 1450 to 1516, Continued by an Anonymous Writer till 1542.* Translated by Alice de Rosen Jervis. London and New York, 1927. An eyewitness account of events in Florence by a Savonarola sympathizer. Translation of *Diario fiorentino dal 1450 al 1516.*

Machiavelli, Niccolò. *Florentine Histories.* Translated by Laura F. Banfield and Harvey C. Mansfield Jr. Princeton, N.J., 1988. Florence's history as compiled, on commission from the Medici, by an astute political observer. Translation of *Istorie fiorentine.*

Two Renaissance Book Hunters: The Letters of Poggius Bracciolini to Nicolaus De Niccolis. Translated by Phyllis Walter Goodhart Gordan. New York, 1974. Nearly one hundred letters by the famous Florentine chancellor and humanist, a key figure among intellectuals seeking to recover lost works by ancient Roman writers.

Secondary Works

Becker, Marvin. *Florence in Transition.* 2 vols. Baltimore, 1967–1968. The evolution from communal to territorial state and the increasingly complex institutions created in the course of this change.

Brackett, John K. *Criminal Justice and Crime in Late Renaissance Florence, 1537–1609.* Cambridge, U.K., 1992. Analyzes the Florentine criminal justice system in the late Renaissance.

Brucker, Gene A. *Renaissance Florence.* Rev. ed. Berkeley, Calif., 1983. An excellent thematic overview of Florence's history and culture for a general readership.

Cochrane, Eric. *Florence in the Forgotten Centuries, 1527–1800.* Chicago, 1983. Colorful and well written; an impressionistic work for a general readership with several chapters on the late Renaissance.

Goldthwaite, Richard A. *The Building of Renaissance Florence: An Economic and Social History.* Baltimore, 1980. Argues that investment in building in the fifteenth century brought about maturing of the Florentine economy; a wealth of detail about money, wages, trades, and the like.

Henderson, John. *Piety and Charity in Late Medieval and Renaissance Florence.* Oxford, 1994. The charitable and devotional work of Florence's many confraternities.

Herlihy, David, and Christiane Klapisch-Zuber, eds. and trans. *Tuscans and Their Families: A Study of the Florentine Catasto of 1427.* New Haven, Conn., 1985. A groundbreaking work, based on quantitative analysis of the famous 1427 tax census. Translation and edition of *Les Toscans et leurs familles: Une étude du "catasto florentin de 1427."* Paris, 1978.

Klapisch-Zuber, Christiane. *Women, Family and Ritual in Renaissance Italy.* Translated by Lydia Cochrane. Chicago, 1985. Essays on a wide variety of topics, including families, wet nursing, dowries, and childhood in Renaissance Tuscany.

Kuehn, Thomas. *Law, Family, and Women: Toward a Legal Anthropology of Renaissance Italy.* Chicago, 1991. The impact of law and the legal system on the lives of Florentine women.

Litchfield, R. Burr. *Emergence of a Bureaucracy: The Florentine Patricians, 1530–1790.* Princeton, N.J., 1986. Catalogs the resilience of the Florentine elite over the *longue durée.*

Menning, Carol Bresnahan. *Charity and State in Late Renaissance Italy: The Monte di Pietà of Florence.* Ithaca, N.Y., 1993. A scholarly work exploring the history of Florence's charitable pawn shop.

Molho, Anthony. *Marriage Alliance in Late Medieval Florence.* Cambridge, Mass., 1994. Based on the Monte delle Doti; reconstructs marriage and investment strategies as well as patterns of wealth and socialization.

Phillips, Mark. *The Memoir of Marco Parenti: A Life in Medici Florence.* Princeton, N.J., 1987. The life of a Florentine silk merchant and Medici opponent reconstructed from his memoirs, account books, and letters.

Trexler, Richard C. *Public Life in Renaissance Florence.* Ithaca, N.Y., 1980. Social interaction and public ritual in the Renaissance city.

CAROL BRESNAHAN MENNING

Art of the Fifteenth Century

Florence witnessed a remarkable flowering of arts in the course of the fifteenth century. The term "art" (*arte*) had a different meaning in that period, however: *arte* denoted diverse activities resulting in some product, as well as the name of a guild that supervised a given enterprise. Producers of "art" were usually designated by the more specific name associated with the craft they practiced, for example, painter. Objects produced by craftsmen were viewed largely in terms of their function, rather than their aesthetic qualities.

Although Florence was one of numerous centers of artistic production in the fifteenth century, its preeminence was significantly enhanced by self-promotion: it is to Florentine theorists and historians of art, such as Leon Battista Alberti (1404–1472), who wrote influential treatises on painting (*De pictura;* 1435), sculpture (*De statua;* c. 1433), and architecture (*De re aedificatoria libri X;* c. 1450), and Giorgio Vasari (1511–1574), who composed the *Lives of the Painters, Sculptors, and Architects* (1550, 1568) and heavily emphasized Florentine accomplishments, that we owe much of the information about the period, along with the Florentine bias that still dominates the study of Renaissance art.

Crucial to the development of arts was the civic pride of Florence, as well as the wealth and ambition of its merchants and bankers. The Medici, Pitti, Rucellai, Strozzi, and other prominent families competed to sponsor public projects and erect grand residences for the glory of God, the country, and themselves.

Architecture. The physical appearance of fifteenth-century Florence was significantly enhanced by the architectural and urban designs of Filippo Brunelleschi (1377–1446), which drew on classical

385

forms and methods of construction. Brunelleschi's Dome of the Florence Cathedral (1420–1436; see the color plates in volume 1) came to dominate the city and proclaim its power and glory far beyond its walls. His Ospedale degli Innocenti (begun c. 1419; see the illustration in the entry on Art, subentry on Renaissance Art, in volume 1) reintroduced a system of measurements and proportions based on Pythagoras's writings, giving rise to a new style of architecture of symmetry and harmony, further enhanced by classical elements. For the church of San Lorenzo (c. 1425–1470s) Brunelleschi designed an elegant and structurally clear interior based on early Christian three-aisled basilicas and an ancient system of ratios (work probably completed under Michelozzo di Bartolomeo; see the illustration in the biography of Brunelleschi in volume 1). He gave full fruition to his classically inspired ideas in the Old Sacristy of San Lorenzo (1419–1428), the family chapel commissioned by Giovanni di Averardo de' Medici and the Pazzi Chapel in Santa Croce (c. 1433–1461). A highly versatile and talented artist—trained as a goldsmith, practicing as a sculptor, engineer, and architect—Brunelleschi was greatly admired in his own day and for centuries following.

The Medici, who unofficially ruled the city from 1434 to 1494, financed numerous private and public projects. They erected a monumental palazzo (Palazzo Medici-Riccardi, 1445–1460), designed by Michelozzo di Bartolomeo, which influenced palazzo architecture for the next century. They sponsored the construction of a new church and monastery of San Marco, where Cosimo Il Vecchio established the first public library in Europe. They also financed the transformation of the church of San Lorenzo, as well as building several villas in the countryside (a common practice of prosperous Florentines), the one at Poggio a Caiano, refurbished by Giuliano da Sangallo for Lorenzo the Magnificent (mid-1480s), being the most famous.

The Rucellai family immortalized their name through Palazzo Rucellai (begun c. 1453; see the illustration in the biography of Alberti in volume 1) designed by Leon Battista Alberti; a family chapel (1464–1467) in San Pancrazio; and a new splendid facade on the church of Santa Maria Novella (c. 1456–1470), also planned by Alberti, with their sponsorship of the project proclaimed in large Latin letters. Architectural undertakings were deemed the most prestigious form of self-expression, and Giovanni Ruccelai recorded in his diary that he viewed his palazzo as his major achievement. Great *palazzi* along with renovated churches transformed Florence, visibly proclaiming its prosperity and cultural ambitions, and influenced architectural developments well beyond its frontiers. Churches and *palazzi,* moreover, provided further opportunities for visual display, as their exteriors and interiors were embellished with other forms of art.

Sculpture. The adornment of the city was sponsored not only by wealthy families, but also by public institutions and civic authorities. The most celebrated sculptural projects, for example, were financed by the guilds, for both their own honor and the fame of Florence. Thus, the guilds paid for the enrichment of the exterior of the public granary, the Orsanmichele, which also housed a miraculous image of the Madonna. Leading Florentine guilds had been assigned to decorate the building with statues of their patron saints set in sculpted niches in the fourteenth century, but most of the work did not proceed until the early fifteenth century. The figures, carved in marble or cast in bronze, were placed in elaborately decorated niches, some of them more costly than the statues within. Lorenzo Ghiberti (c. 1378–1455) produced the bronze *St. John the Baptist* (1405–1417) for the Arte di Calimala (refiners of imported woolen cloth, who were the oldest guild, also responsible for commissioning Ghiberti's Baptistery doors. More than eight feet tall, *St. John* was the largest bronze statue to be cast in Italy for centuries. Ghiberti also cast *St. Matthew* (1419–1422) for the Arte del Cambio (bankers), and *St. Stephen* for the Arte della Lana (wool guild). Nanni di Banco (1380/1385–1421), meanwhile, carved the *Four Crowned Martyrs* (1410s) for the Arte di Pietra e Legname (workers in stone and wood). Donatello (1386?–1466) executed three figures: a marble *St. Mark* (1411–1415) for the Arte dei Linaiuoli e Rigattieri (linen weavers and peddlers), a marble *St. George* (c. 1415–17, Florence, Museo Nazionale) for the Arte dei Corazzai e Spadai (armorers and sword makers), and a bronze *St. Louis of Toulouse* (c. 1422–1425, Florence, Museo di Santa Croce) for the Parte Guelpha, later moved to Santa Croce and replaced by Andrea del Verrocchio's bronze *Christ and Doubting Thomas* (1465–1483) created for the Mercanzia (merchants guild).

These sculptors also contributed to other civic undertakings. Donatello and Nanni di Banco adorned the cathedral and Campanile. Ghiberti executed two sets of monumental gilded bronze doors for the Baptistery. The set illustrating the New Testament (1403–1424) is famous for the competition preceding its commission (1401), in which Ghiberti's proposal

Domenico Ghirlandaio. *Funeral of St. Francis of Assisi.* Fresco in the Sassetti Chapel, church of S. Trinità, Florence.
ALINARI/ART RESOURCE

won over Brunelleschi's (competition was the standard way of assigning public works). Ghiberti's second pair of doors (1425–1452), devoted to the Old Testament and often called the *Gates of Paradise,* presented biblical narratives, enacted by classical style figures, in spaces of remarkable depth, complexity, and coherence. [See the color plates in volume 3.] The economic prosperity of Florence and her civic pride nourished such great public projects.

The Florentines also used sculpture to honor or commemorate illustrious or prominent citizens. Leonardo Bruni, the chancellor of Florence and a great humanist scholar, was thus immortalized at the expense of the Republic: Bernardo Rossellino carved an elaborate wall tomb (1444–1451, Santa Croce; see the illustration in the biography of Bruni in volume 1) depicting Bruni, hands folded on one of his books, in eternal sleep on a bier draped with heavy brocade upheld by eagles. As a pendant to Bruni's memorial, Desiderio da Settignano was commis-

sioned to carve the tomb of Carlo Marsuppini (after 1453, Santa Croce), another humanist chancellor.

Portrait busts became a fashionable mode of commemoration in the second half of the century. They were consciously derived from ancient types. Antonio Rossellino's bust of the humanist Matteo Palmieri (1468; see the illustration in the biography of Palmieri in volume 4) and Benedetto da Maiano's bust of Pietro Mellini (1474; both Florence, Bargello) presented the sitters' faces in minute and unflattering detail, deliberately recalling Roman Republican portraiture in which signs of age and wear connoted the life of virtuous service to the state. Alongside such mature portraits, patrons also commissioned likenesses of beautiful women, such as Andrea del Verrocchio's *Bust of a Young Lady* (1480s; Florence, Bargello), and children. Desiderio da Settignano's exquisite *Head of a Child* (c. 1460; Washington, D.C., National Gallery of Art) is modeled so subtly as to convey the effect of soft baby skin. Much of

Florentine sculpture thus reflected interest in naturalistic forms and classical sources.

Painting. In addition to sculpture, interiors of ecclesiastical and secular buildings were embellished with paintings, both frescoes and panels. Fra Angelico (1400–1455), a Dominican friar and the leading painter in Florence in the 1430s, helped by his assistants, painted frescoes in the forty-four friars' cells, corridors, and chapter house of the convent of San Marco (1438–1445), patronized by Cosimo de' Medici. He also painted the altarpiece devoted to the *Virgin and Saints* (c. 1440) for the high altar of the convent's church. Masaccio became famous as a consequence of his work on the frescoes narrating the life of St. Peter in the Brancacci Chapel in Santa Maria del Carmine (c. 1425–1428), on which he collaborated with Masolino. (The cycle was completed in the early 1480s by Filippino Lippi.) Masolino painted in an elegant and flowing style; Masaccio produced monumental figures situated in convincing pictorial spaces. His ability to create a rational and inhabitable space is particularly evident in the fresco of the *Trinity* in Santa Maria Novella (c. 1427; see the color plates in volume 4), painted over the tomb of a member of the Lenzi family. The patron and his wife are shown kneeling in front of the Trinity set in a painted chapel rendered with so convincing a use of illusion as to prompt scholars to calculate its exact dimensions were it to be translated into an actual interior. Later in the century Francesco Sassetti, manager of the Medici bank from 1463, ordered a fresco cycle from Domenico Ghirlandaio for his chapel in Santa Trinità. The scenes devoted to the *Life of St. Francis* (1483–1486) included portraits of the patron and his employers. The chapel's altarpiece depicting the *Nativity and Adoration of the Shepherds* (1485), also by Ghirlandaio, exhibited the influence of not only ancient architecture and sculpture, but also the Portinari Altarpiece (late 1470s; Florence, Uffizi; see the color plates in volume 4) by Hugo van der Goes that had been recently imported to Florence from Flanders. Thus, an interest in classical revival coexisted with a fascination with the works of contemporary foreign craftsmen.

Family chapels, such as Sassetti's, served as a locus where the living could pray for their ancestors' and their own salvation and so honor God and their family. They manifested their owners' piety and devotion, as well as their lineage and social standing. Frescoes devoted to the owner's patron saint set the tone for the chapel, but more important, as indispensable for the performance of the mass, were the liturgical accouterments—a crucifix, chalice, vestments, manuscripts, candlesticks, and the like—often made of precious materials and thus more costly than the paintings on the walls or over the altar. Tombs holding the bodies of family members, often carved in stone, completed these ensembles.

Interiors of palazzi contained fresco decorations of both religious and secular nature (80 to 90 percent of Renaissance paintings were religious). Benozzo Gozzoli (1420–1497), trained by Fra Angelico, painted frescoes in the chapel of Palazzo Medici with a continuous panorama depicting the Journey of the Magi (c. 1459), set in the Tuscan countryside dotted with Medici villas. The Medici belonged to a confraternity called the Company of the Magi, and the choice of frescoes reflected this affiliation: members of the family were portrayed in the narrative in the guise of the Magi. Benozzo also included himself, wearing a hat bearing his signature. The color scheme, abundant detail, and disposition of figures in the landscape recalled and imitated costly and prestigious Flemish tapestries, for which many domestic fresco cycles served as a relatively inexpensive substitute. Over the altar of the chapel stood the painting of the *Adoration of the Child* (late 1450s; Berlin, Gemäldegalerie), the final destination of the Magi, painted by Fra Filippo Lippi.

Another remarkable domestic fresco ensemble was produced by Andrea del Castagno (1421–1457), whose other major frescoes—the *Last Supper* and the *Passion* (1447)—adorned the refectory of the convent of Sant' Apollonia in Florence. In the loggia of the Villa Carducci at Legnaia, outside Florence, Castagno painted a series of *Famous Men and Women* (1448; Florence, Uffizi), a subject popular throughout Italy among learned patrons seeking to model themselves on great scholars and statesmen. Castagno's figures included three Florentine military leaders (Pippo Spano, Farinata degli Uberti, Niccolo Acciaioli), three illustrious women (the Cumaean Sibyl, Queen Esther, Queen Tomyris), and three Florentine literary giants (Dante, Petrarch, Boccaccio). The larger-than-life-size standing worthies were placed in a continuous illusionistic portico lined with simulated revetments of marble, granite, and porphyry.

In addition to frescoes, panel paintings adorned Florentine domestic and ecclesiastical interiors. Palla Strozzi, one of the richest men in Florence, commissioned Gentile da Fabriano to paint an exquisitely detailed *Adoration of the Magi* panel (1423; Florence, Uffizi) for his family chapel in Santa Trinità. The fine quality of the work and quantities of gold in the panel and its elaborate frame reflected the wealth of the patron.

Sandro Botticelli (1445–1510), whose stylized pictorial manner is distinguished by elegant lines of swaying draperies and exaggerated body language, painted numerous religious and secular panels. For Benedetto di Ser Francesco Guardi del Cane he produced the *Annunciation* (1489–1490; Florence, Uffizi) intended for Sta. Maria Maddalena dei Pazzi. For the Medici he executed several mythological scenes, including *Camilla and the Centaur* (after 1482), likely ordered by Lorenzo de Pierfrancesco de' Medici for his Florentine palazzo at the time of his 1482 wedding; the *Primavera* (c. 1482?; see the color plates in volume 1), set in the garden of Venus, probably originally a *spalliera* or a decorative wall paneling for the private apartments of the same owner; and the *Birth of Venus* (c. 1484–1486; all Florence, Uffizi; see the color plates in volume 4) seen at Lorenzo di Pierfrancesco's villa at Castello in the sixteenth century.

Antonio del Pollaiuolo, who collaborated with his brother Piero, also produced mythological scenes for the Medici. Lorenzo de' Medici, who collected such images and encouraged much of the classical style art in Florence, acquired Pollaiuolo's paintings of the Labors of Hercules. The originals were painted on canvas and do not survive, but their copies on small panels by Pollaiuolo himself are preserved: they show *Hercules and the Hydra* and *Hercules and Antaeus* (c. 1460; Florence, Uffizi), the latter also rendered in a small bronze group (c. 1470s; Florence, Bargello), and reveal Pollaiuolo's fascination with human anatomy portrayed in violent action. Pollaiuolo's *Apollo and Daphne* (n. d.; London, National Gallery), based on Ovid's *Metamorphoses,* may have been painted for Lorenzo. Pollaiuolo also made engravings such as the *Battle of the Nudes* (c. 1465; New York, Metropolitan Museum of Art; see the illustration in the entry on the Human Body in Renaissance Art), designed embroidery patterns for the life of St. John the Baptist vestments for the Florentine Baptistery, and bronze tombs for Pope Sixtus IV and Innocent VIII (1484–1493; Rome, St. Peter's).

Florentine homes were further decorated with *cassoni*—wooden chests, highly fashionable in the fifteenth century, for storing cloth made for brides. Often painted with narratives taken from Greek and Roman history and mythology as well as from the Bible, they taught lessons of female virtue—fidelity, chastity, for example. Apollonio di Giovanni and Marco del Buon Giamberti's *Story of Esther* (c. 1450–

Filippino Lippi. *Portrait of a Youth.* Oil on panel; c. 1485; 51 × 35.5 cm (20 × 14 in). NATIONAL GALLERY OF ART, WASHINGTON, D.C., ANDREW W. MELLON COLLECTION.

1455; New York, Metropolitan Museum of Art) exemplifies their decorative and lively style.

Individual portraits, commemorating marriages or ancestors, as well as images of the Virgin and Child rendered in painting, glazed terra-cotta, or wood, were also common in Florentine residences and reflected the twin concerns of family pride and religious devotion.

Other Arts. Florentine "intarsia"—pictorial panels composed of colored wood inlays—were much admired in their day. Fascination with linear perspective, a technique for conveying three-dimensional receding space in two-dimensional media, stimulated illusionistic depictions of objects and spaces in flat wood mosaics, as in paintings. Such intarsia decorating the north vestry of the Florence Cathedral executed by Antonio Manetti and Agnolo di Lazzaro (1436–1445) and augmented by Giuliano da Maiano (1460–1465) were eagerly emulated across Italy. The intarsia "in perspective" in Piero de' Medici's *studietto* in the Palazzo Medici (c. 1456–1459; lost) were greatly praised. Florentine intarsia masters were consequently sought by patrons outside the city, as were other craftsmen.

Another innovative technique, developed in Florence by Luca della Robbia (1399/1400–1482), was the art of glazing terra-cotta sculptures and reliefs. Luca ran an active workshop, passing on his formula and his business to his nephew and successor Andrea della Robbia (1435–1525). Their glazed terracottas, exemplified by the *Madonna and Child* on Orsanmichele, decorated buildings around the city and served as outdoor shrines and as private devotional images.

Manuscript illumination was another important branch of Florentine artistic production patronized by the Medici and their peers, as well as by those outside the city. The Florentine book dealer Vespasiano di Bisticci supplied numerous worthies of Italy; he was instrumental, for example, in assembling a distinguished library for the duke of Urbino, Federigo da Montefeltro.

This discussion focused on individual media, yet it is important to bear in mind that Florentine artists frequently practiced several crafts. Andrea del Verrocchio, who trained Leonardo da Vinci, ran a workshop that produced sculpture in stone, bronze, silver, and terracotta, as well as paintings on panel; the multiple skills of Brunelleschi and the Pollaiuolos have been noted above. A Renaissance Florentine artist's economic success was predicated on flexibility and diversification.

See also biographies of artists and patrons mentioned in this entry.

BIBLIOGRAPHY

Primary Works

Alberti, Leon Battista. *On Painting*. Edited by Martin Kemp. Translated by Cecil Grayson. London, 1991.

Alberti, Leon Battista. *On the Art of Building in Ten Books*. Edited and translated by Joseph Rykwert, Neil Leach, and Robert Tavernor. Cambridge, Mass., 1988.

Vasari, Giorgio. *Lives of the Painters, Sculptors and Architects*. Translated by Gaston du C. de Vere, New York, 1996 from *Vite de' più eccelenti pittori scultori, ed architettori*. Edited by G. Milanesi. 9 vols. Florence, 1877–1885.

Secondary Works

Andres, Glenn, John M. Hunisak, and Richard Turner. *The Art of Florence*. 2 vols. New York, 1987.

Borsook, Eve. *The Companion Guide to Florence*. London, 1973.

Brucker, Gene. *Renaissance Florence*. New York and London, 1969.

Burke, Peter. *The Italian Renaissance: Culture and Society in Italy*. Princeton, N.J., 1987.

Goldthwaite, Richard A. *The Building of Renaissance Florence*. Baltimore, 1980.

Goldthwaite, Richard A. *Wealth and Demand for Art in Italy, 1300–1600*. London and Baltimore, 1993.

Gombrich, Ernst H. "The Early Medici as Patrons of Art." *Italian Renaissance Studies*. Edited by Ernst Fraser Jacob. London, 1960.

Jenkins, A. D. Fraser. "Cosimo de' Medici's Patronage of Architecture and the Theory of Magnificence." *Journal of the Warburg and Courtauld Institutes* 33 (1970): 162–170.

Painting and Illumination in Early Renaissance Florence, 1300–1450. New York, 1995. Exhibition catalog.

Saalman, Howard. *Filippo Brunelleschi: The Cupola of Santa Maria del Fiore*. London, 1980.

Thomas, Anabel. *The Painter's Practice in Renaissance Tuscany*. Cambridge, 1995.

Thornton, Peter. *The Italian Renaissance Interior, 1400–1600*. New York, 1991.

Trexler, Richard. *Public Life in Renaissance Florence*. Ithaca, N.Y., 1991.

Turner, Richard A. *Renaissance Florence. The Invention of a New Art*. New York, 1997.

Wackernagel, Martin. *The World of the Florentine Renaissance Artist: Projects and Patrons, Workshop and Art Market*. Princeton, N.J., 1981.

MARINA BELOZERSKAYA

Art of the Sixteenth Century

Florentine painting evolved in the sixteenth century from high Renaissance style through mannerism and other forms. The city and especially its Medici rulers continued to be a fountain of patronage for some of Italy's best-known artists.

Leonardo and Michelangelo, 1501–1508.

During the opening years of the sixteenth century, when Piero Soderini was administrative leader of the Florentine Republic, both Leonardo da Vinci and Michelangelo Buonarroti were active in the city. Their work from this time was to have far-reaching consequences for Florentine art, and, together, they brought about what is now commonly referred to as the high Renaissance classical style. Both masters were involved in the design of large-scale fresco scenes that celebrated the military victories of the Republic of Florence for the Council Chamber in the Palazzo della Signoria. Leonardo's *Battle of Anghiari* (c. 1503–1506; destroyed) was executed using an experimental technique that had disastrous results, and the painter returned to Milan in 1508 having completed only a small section of the work. Michelangelo's scene of the *Battle of Cascina* (work on cartoon, c. 1504–1506; fresco never realized) was also abandoned when he left Florence to enter the service of Pope Julius II in 1506.

Although neither project was ever finished, the preparatory cartoons (lost) did expose artists in Italy

FLORENCE: ART OF THE SIXTEENTH CENTURY

and elsewhere to many of the stylistic and compositional innovations of the proposed mural decorations. Benvenuto Cellini called the cartoons *la scuola del mondo* (the school for the world) because through them artists could draw on Leonardo's study of the animated movements of man and horse engaged in furious battle (see the copy after Leonardo's central group by Rubens; c. 1615; Paris, Louvre), and on Michelangelo's interest in the heavily muscular, expressive male nude (see Bastiano da Sangallo's copy after Michelangelo in Holkham Hall, Norfolk). In these years Michelangelo also worked on the monumental statue of *David* (1501–1505; Florence, Accademia; see the color plates in volume 3), which was set up in Piazza della Signoria as a symbol of Florentine liberty, and on a painting of the *Holy Family* (*Doni Tondo;* c. 1503; Florence, Uffizi; see the color plates in volume 4), which presents a subtle interaction of grandiose figures defined through sharply outlined forms.

Raphael, resident in Florence from 1505 to 1508, immersed himself in the art of the city, paying particular attention to the latest work of Leonardo and Michelangelo. Assimilating the innovations of these masters—in terms of how the figures were grouped and force of feeling—Raphael achieved a clarity of style that encapsulates the qualities of early sixteenth-century classicism.

Progression of Style, 1509–1516. The years 1509 to 1516 were dominated by Fra Bartolomeo and Andrea del Sarto. By 1509 Leonardo, Michelangelo, and Raphael had left Florence, and, in the following decade, Fra Bartolomeo (Baccio della Porta; 1475–1517) and Andrea del Sarto (1486–1530) became the city's leading artists. The former painter, who had entered the Dominican Order in 1500 after a period of intense reflection on the preaching of Girolamo Savonarola, studied the work of Leonardo and, as his mature style displays, painted in a restrained and monumental manner that is entirely in keeping with the spirit of high Renaissance classicism. His altarpiece of *God the Father between Saints Mary Magdalen and Catherine of Siena* (1509; Lucca, Museo Nazionale di Villa Guinigi) is characterized by majestic forms, subtle effects of lighting and color, and a carefully balanced composition. This painting also shows Fra Bartolomeo's debt to Venetian traditions (the friar had visited Venice in 1508), especially to the art of Giorgione and his circle, in the rendering of the distant landscape bathed in light and enriched with atmospheric effects. In

many ways, the poised and graceful style of Fra Bartolomeo developed in parallel with Raphael's work.

Influences from Leonardo, Raphael, and Michelangelo, as well as from Fra Bartolomeo, can be discerned in the work of Andrea del Sarto, who had trained in the shop of Piero di Cosimo from 1498 to 1508. In 1509–1510 del Sarto executed five episodes from the *Life of Saint Filippo Benizi* for the atrium of SS. Annunziata, Florence. The scenes display well-drawn figures with carefully articulated gestures who move within rhythmically designed, luminous landscapes. The soft brushwork betrays an understanding of Leonardo's *sfumato* (modeling by subtle gradations of light and dark), which enhances the effects of color in these compositions. A greater monumentality is to be found in a later fresco for SS. Annunziata, the *Birth of the Virgin* (1513–1514), which, in the light of early sixteenth-century developments, presents an up-to-date revision of Domenico Ghirlandaio's earlier fresco on this theme. Though massive, the smiling women by del Sarto move gracefully within the splendid domestic interior, which also contains balletic angels. However, the rhythmic movements of these figures, the ambiguity of their facial expressions, and the subtlety of the color scheme all go beyond the measured dignity of high Renaissance classicism. Instead, these features anticipate aspects of mannerism. Del Sarto's collaborators and assistants (Franciabigio, Pontormo, Rosso Fiorentino) also worked on Marian themes in SS. Annunziata from about 1513 to 1516 and as a group they represent the most progressive current in Florentine painting of the mid-1510s. [See del Sarto's *Charity* in the color plates in this volume.]

Pontormo and Rosso Fiorentino, 1516–1529. The work of Jacopo Carucci da Pontormo (1494–1557) evolved from the ambiguous classicism of his SS. Annunziata fresco of the *Visitation* (1514–1516), which displays an unusual figural composition and strident color combinations, towards the highly idiosyncratic *Joseph in Egypt* (c. 1518; London, National Gallery), which can justifiably be defined as mannerist. Commissioned as part of a series of paintings for the Florentine Palazzo Borgherini, the *Joseph*'s composition is diffuse, with anxious figures who roam about a bizarre architectural setting that opens up to reveal a Germanic landscape. That the artist does not depict space in a conventional way in the work undermines the narrative flow. This results in a general feeling of disquiet.

Less disconcerting is Pontormo's lunette fresco of *Vertumnus and Pomona* (1520–1521) in the Medici villa at Poggio a Caiano, which Pope Leo X had decided to decorate (the Medici family returned from exile in 1512). In the lunette, where a group of relaxing gods is positioned against a sunlit wall, Pontormo blends a vibrant naturalism with a love of pattern, line, and color. The artist subsequently replaced the lyricism of these designs with the tormented spiritual force of the frescoed scenes of the *Passion* (1523–1526; Florence, Certosa di Galluzzo) inspired by Albrecht Dürer prints. But the most poignant of these paintings is in the altarpiece of the *Lamentation* (1525–1528; Florence, Capponi Chapel, S. Felicita; see the color plates in this volume). With the decoration of this chapel, the first stage of Florentine mannerism reached full maturity. Pontormo's altarpiece, therefore, displays a mass of attenuated forms, idiosyncratic in detail, that rise and hover in no apparent pattern in the picture. The artist uses line for ornamental effect, while the bright and sometimes jarring color combinations contribute to the picture's strange though poetic intensity.

Rosso Fiorentino (Giovanni Battista di Jacopo Rosso; 1494–c. 1540), like Pontormo, emerged from del Sarto's workshop and alongside the latter painters was involved in the decoration of SS. Annunziata. Rosso's contribution to the cycle, the *Assumption of the Virgin* (1513–1514), displays all the hallmarks of the emerging mannerist style in Florence: dramatic contrasts of color, eccentric forms, and well-characterized figures. These aspects of his art matured, so that by the time he painted the *Deposition* (1521; Volterra, Pinacoteca Comunale), the colors he used had become more unnatural, forms more distorted, and the composition more fragmented. The uncontrolled force and bitter struggle of the *Moses Defending the Daughters of Jethro* (c. 1523; Florence, Uffizi; see the illustration in the entry on Mannerism) is inspired by the expressive power of Michelangelo's art. In this picture Rosso manipulated lighting effects on the naked bodies, which results in a highly unnatural abstraction of anatomical form.

While Pontormo and Rosso developed their own highly individual style within the mannerist current of the 1520s, del Sarto maintained the measured dignity of the classical style. His fresco of the *Last Supper* (1526–1527; Florence, S. Salvi) exhibits a clearly organized figural and spatial composition in which a sensitive use of color emphasizes naturalism.

Painting and Sculpture at the Medici Court, 1530–1563. By the end of 1530 del Sarto was dead, and Rosso had abandoned Italy for France; Pontormo, meanwhile, remained active as a painter until the 1550s, working on a variety of Medici projects with his former pupil, Agnolo Bronzino (1503–1572).

Bronzino became court artist to Cosimo I de' Medici (1519–1574), who, through spectacular patronage of the arts, created a court whose magnificence rivaled the proudest and most splendid courts of Europe. Building on the illustrious tradition of Medici art patronage, Cosimo I attracted many artists and architects to his court so that he could enhance the glory and power of his name and of the Medici dynasty. In 1539, as part of the celebrations for Cosimo's marriage to Eleonora of Toledo (1522–1562), Bronzino set to work on the decoration of a chapel for the duchess in the Palazzo della Signoria (by 1540 Cosimo had made this palace his main residence). This artistic ensemble, comprising fresco decorations and an altarpiece, is the epitome of the grace of the high *maniera* style, the culminating phase of mannerism. In the ceiling decoration of *Allegorical Figures and Saints* Bronzino displays an interest in sculptural forms, which are based on a close study of antique statuary and the art of Michelangelo and Bandinelli. The accomplished drawing of the *Saints* is sharp and precise, and, throughout the ceiling, there is an obvious use of bright color and clear light. The *Stories from the Old Testament* that decorate the walls of the chapel are filled with muscular figures whose anatomies are defined with the painter's characteristic clarity of line. These designs are ultimately indebted to the art of Michelangelo, but Bronzino, with great invention, constantly adapted Michelangelesque prototypes to suit his own requirements.

As court artist, Bronzino executed state portraits of Cosimo I and his family [see the illustration in the biography of Cosimo I de' Medici in volume 4]; these propagandist images helped to consolidate the power and prestige of the Medici family. In the portrait of *Eleonora of Toledo and her Son* (1545; Florence, Uffizi), the painter's technical prowess comes through in the lavish display of the brocaded gown and jewels. The incomparable elegance of the image derives from the painter's emphasis on the aloofness of the duchess and the marmoreal, highly polished forms of the composition.

By 1555 Bronzino had lost his position as Cosimo's favored artist, and in this year Giorgio Vasari became artistic superintendent of a grand project to transform the Palazzo Vecchio (formerly called the Palazzo della Signoria). The complex decorative program that he devised glorifies the Medici dynasty and Cosimo's rule, and the style of these works represents the epitome of the Florentine *maniera*. Earlier

Andrea del Sarto. *Birth of the Virgin.* Fresco in the church of SS. Annuziata, Florence.

in 1543–1545 Francesco Salviati (1510–1563), who had trained with del Sarto, decorated the Sala dell'Udienza in the Palazzo Vecchio with frescoes from the *Life of Camillus;* these scenes were also intended as an allegory of Cosimo's reign.

Under Cosimo the art of sculpture flourished too. Baccio Bandinelli (1493–1560), who was particularly favored by the duke, emerged as the most important sculptor in Florence in 1534, the year when Michelangelo left Florence for Rome and of the unveiling of Bandinelli's *Hercules and Cacus* (Florence, Piazza della Signoria), commissioned by Clement VII. However, Michelangelo, active in the city in the 1520s and

1530s, continued to exert an important influence over Florentine sculpture until his death in 1564. Bandinelli's *Hercules,* a pendant to Michelangelo's *David,* is conceived as a static group of figures in which there is little place for the dramatic tension of Michelangelo's art. Bandinelli was also involved in designing a bronze portrait bust of Cosimo (commissioned 1545; Florence, Palazzo Pitti) in competition with Cellini. Cosimo evidently favored Bandinelli's conventional public image of a ruler over Cellini's more revealing, psychologically suggestive study. Cellini, however, was more successful with the *Perseus* group (1545–1553), another commission

393

from Cosimo, who also employed the services of the sculptors Niccolò Tribolo (1500–1550) and Pierino da Vinci (1530–1553) for the decoration of the gardens of the Medici villa at Castello.

In the late 1550s Bartolomeo Ammanati (1511–1592), with support from Michelangelo and Vasari, emerged as an important sculptor at Cosimo's court. Competing with Bandinelli and Cellini for Medici patronage, Ammanati secured for himself the commission of the Neptune fountain (c. 1559–1575; Florence, Piazza della Signoria), which is filled with allusions to Cosimo and his son Francesco. The ponderous marble Neptune contrasts with the smaller bronze figures around the basin that were cast later by assistants; in their attenuated forms and graceful demeanor, these later statues display all the hallmarks of the high *maniera* from the reign of Francesco I. For the Palazzo Vecchio, Ammanati designed the *Juno Fountain* (fragments; c. 1563; Florence, Bargello) whose complex iconographic program refers to Cosimo and Eleonora.

Art and Patronage under Francesco I, 1564–1587.

In 1564 Cosimo I passed much of the responsibility for government to his son Francesco (1541–1587), who ordered the redecoration of certain areas of the Palazzo Vecchio for his marriage in 1565 to Joanna of Austria. Within the palace Francesco had Vasari build him a private apartment, which included the famous *studiolo* (1570–1575). Vasari directed a large group of painters and sculptors on the decoration of this small space, whose iconography, devised by Vincenzo Borghini, focuses on man's control of nature through art and science (Francesco I was passionate about alchemy). Among the best known contributions to the *studiolo* is Alessandro Allori's (1535–1607) *Pearl Fishers,* which exhibits a concern for tender color combinations and fantastic landscapes. In this composition the painter also displays a debt to Bronzino, his former master, in the polished surfaces of the anatomies and in the confident drawing of the forms.

Bronze statuettes were commissioned for the *studiolo* from a number of sculptors, including Giambologna (Jean Boulogne; 1529–1608), who executed the *Apollo* (1570s; in situ). Though intended for a niche, the work is based on the *figura serpentinata* (serpentine line). The *Apollo* is a perfect expression of the art of its time, as displayed in the elegance, poise, and impeccable finish of its late *maniera* style. However, Giambologna's work for the Medici family culminated in the more vigorous and monumental *Rape of the Sabines* (1581–1583;

Florence, Loggia dei Lanzi), a statue in which the complexity of the multiple viewpoint reaches its full potential. The group, composed of three interlocking figures engaged in energetic movement, is characterized by a vitality and freedom of invention that were to interest the sculptors of the seventeenth century.

Francesco's interest in alchemy and the natural sciences is also manifested in the fountain-grottoes that Bernardo Buontalenti (1531–1608) designed for him. The interaction between art and nature is a feature of the facade of the Grotto (Florence, Boboli Gardens), which Buontalenti designed (upper section only) from 1583, which incorporates a fantastic display of natural rock formations. These organic, elemental qualities are also to be found inside, where roughly hewn rocks and dripping stalactites create an atmospheric space in which Michelangelo's *Slaves* were once housed. These links between art and nature that Francesco evidently delighted in reemerge in the work of Giambologna, whose Apennine fountain (c. 1580) was set into the gardens of the Medici villa designed by Buontalenti at Pratolino.

By 1587, when Ferdinando I de' Medici (1548–1609) came to power, certain Florentine painters were reforming the excesses of the late *maniera*. Foremost among them was Santi di Tito (1536–1603), who made a return to naturalism and who looked to the best examples of both Roman and Florentine classicism of the high Renaissance. In sculpture, Giambologna was still active and, in the service of Ferdinando, worked on a group of equestrian statues that enhanced the status and power of the Medici.

See also biographies of individual artists mentioned in this entry.

BIBLIOGRAPHY

Avery, Charles. *Florentine Renaissance Sculpture.* London, 1970.

Barocchi, Paola, ed. *Palazzo Vecchio: Committenza e collezionismo medicei: Firenze e la Toscana dei Medici nell'Europa del cinquecento.* Florence, 1980.

Berti, Luciano. *Pontormo e il suo tempo.* Florence, 1993.

Briganti, Giuliano, ed. *La pittura in Italia: Il cinquecento.* Milan, 1987.

Cox-Rearick, Janet. *Dynasty and Destiny in Medici Art: Pontormo, Leo X, and the Two Cosimos.* Princeton, N.J., 1984.

Franklin, David. *Rosso in Italy.* New Haven, Conn., and London, 1994.

Freedberg, Sydney J. *Painting in Italy, 1500–1600.* Harmondsworth, U.K., 1971.

Gibbons, Mary Weitzel. *Giambologna: Narrator of the Catholic Reformation.* Berkeley, Calif., 1995.

Gregori, Mina, ed. *Mural Painting in Italy: The Sixteenth Century.* Bergamo, Italy, 1997.

Kinney, Peter. *The Early Sculpture of Bartolomeo Ammanati.* New York, 1976.

McCorquodale, Charles. *Bronzino.* London, 1981.

Padovani, Serena. *Fra' Bartolomeo e la scuola di San Marco.* Venice, 1996.

Pope-Hennessy, John. *Italian High Renaissance and Baroque Sculpture.* London, 1963.

Shearman, John. *Andrea del Sarto.* Oxford, 1965.

Shearman, John, and C. Coffey. *Maestri toscani del cinquecento.* Florence, 1978.

FLAVIO BOGGI

FLORENCE, COUNCIL OF. The Council of Florence (1438–1445) was the culmination of a concerted effort that began in the thirteenth century to reunite the Eastern and Western churches. Divisive influences included languages, cultures, and past politics, especially resentment over the Sack of Constantinople (1204). Topics of theological dissension included the procession of the Holy Spirit from the Son (and the use of the word *Filioque* in the Creed), the Eastern use of leavened bread in the Eucharist, papal claims to supreme power, and the doctrine of Purgatory. Despite negotiations, culminating in an abortive union at the Second Council of Lyons (1274), these issues were unresolved by the beginning of the fifteenth century.

The advance of the Turks, threatening Constantinople, left the Eastern emperors eager for Western aid. Once the Great Schism had ended, Pope Martin V (1417–1431) undertook negotiations for ecclesiastical union. His successor, Eugenius IV (1431–1447) continued this effort. The Council of Basel (1431–1449) took a hand in these negotiations, but its majority faction was unwilling to move to a site in Italy acceptable to the Greeks. A substantial minority, led by Cardinal Giuliano Cesarini, was willing to accept transfer of the council. Soon its representatives were working together with Eugenius to bring the Greeks to Italy. In November 1437 the emperor John VIII Palaeologus and his entourage sailed for Venice. Eugenius already had decreed the transfer of the Council of Basel to Italy. Eventually he settled on Ferrara as the site. Cesarini and others of like mind left Basel for the council of union.

The first session of the Council of Ferrara was held by Cardinal Nicholas Albergati on 8 January 1438. Eugenius IV arrived in February, but questions of precedence and protocol had to be resolved before the Greeks arrived in March. Although the emperor played a leading role, the principal spokesmen were Mark Eugenicus of Ephesus and Bessarion of Nicaea, who would come to opposite conclusions about the possibility of union. Public theological discussion did not begin until June, when the doctrine of Purgatory was made the initial topic of debate. By October attention had shifted to the legitimacy of the Western addition of the word *Filioque* to the Creed.

The council was proceeding slowly, and other problems, including penury and disease, complicated matters. Cosimo de' Medici offered the hospitality of Florence and financial support. The council agreed to move, and Eugenius IV set out in January 1439. The Greeks arrived in February and agreed to make the procession of the Holy Spirit the chief topic of discussion, convinced that other problems would fall into place if this issue were resolved. Much of the public debate, beginning in March, turned on the authenticity and interpretation of key passages from the church fathers. Although Eugenius remained unconvinced, grounds for agreement were discerned by Bessarion and other proponents of union. The emperor and the patriarch of Constantinople, Joseph II, whose health was failing, also supported union. By June 1439 negotiations for the formulation of a statement on the procession of the Holy Spirit for inclusion in the decree of union were under way. The final version of this statement was incorporated into the decree *Laetentur coeli* (6 July 1439). It declared that the Latin *Filioque* and the Greek statement that the Spirit proceeds from the Father through the Son mean the same thing. The text, formulated as a constitution of Eugenius with the consent of the emperor and the Eastern delegates, also included statements on the Eucharist, purgatory, and papal primacy.

Meanwhile, the Council of Basel was taking measures to suspend Eugenius, even to depose him. In June 1439 the assembly declared that conciliar supremacy was a truth of the faith. On 25 June a decree deposing the pope was ratified. Thereafter Duke Amadeus VIII of Savoy was elected to reign as Pope Felix V. Buoyed by the Florentine union, Eugenius replied with the bull *Moyses* (4 September 1439), in which he reasserted papal sovereignty and denounced conciliar pretensions. Eugenius provided theological arguments in support of this bull by sponsoring a debate between Cardinal Cesarini, championing conciliar supremacy, and the Dominican theologian Juan de Torquemada, advocating papal sovereignty. Thereafter envoys of Basel and its pope, Felix V, vied with Eugenian diplomats, among them Nicholas of Cusa, for the allegiance of prelates and princes. By the time of Eugenius's death in 1447, only the Holy Roman Empire had not submitted to Rome, and it was negotiating terms. The next pope,

Nicholas V (1447–1455), would remove the last obstacles to Rome's triumph.

The Council of Florence, however, did not cease working for ecclesiastical union. The Armenians accepted union on 22 November 1439, which was recorded in a bull notable for its statement on seven sacraments. Representatives of the Egyptian Copts also came to Florence, and a decree announcing their union with the Latins was issued on 4 February 1442. During the next year, Eugenius prepared to return to Rome. He had been driven from the Eternal City a decade before, but his political fortunes had improved dramatically. After a few months of residence in Siena, the pope entered Rome on 28 September 1443. The council was transferred to the Lateran, the site of the cathedral of Rome. There it heard encouraging reports on the progress of a crusade against the Turks being led by Cardinal Cesarini. This good news, however, was followed in 1444 by word that the cardinal had perished in the defeat of the crusading host at Varna. Later that year the Syrians of Mesopotamia accepted union. The Chaldeans and Maronites of Cyprus did likewise in August 1445. Negotiations also were held with the king of Bosnia, who renounced Manichaeism. The council seems thereafter to have passed quietly out of existence, without a formal dissolution. Eugenius recorded many of its achievements on the doors that he had Filarete prepare for the Vatican basilica.

The Council of Florence was a great success for Eugenius, helping him withstand secular and ecclesiastical enemies. Moreover, the council proved to be a great meeting place for scholars such as George Gemistus Pletho and a major market for manuscript books, especially Greek texts. Thus it was a significant event in Renaissance cultural history. Moreover, the Medici benefited from the prestige of having hosted the council of union. Much of this success, however, proved illusory. Union with Rome was not well received in the East, and the papacy proved unable to help repel the Turkish threat. Pope Nicholas V complicated the fortunes of Constantinople on the eve of the climactic siege by Mehmed II (1453) by trying to use military aid as a lever to win full implementation of the Florentine decree of union. After the Turks triumphed and the last Palaeologus emperor fell, the Greek church eventually reverted to its traditional doctrines and practices. The Florentine union was rejected by many as nothing more than an effort by the popes to oppress the Eastern churches.

See also **Christianity,** *subentry on* **Orthodox Christianity; Conciliarism.**

BIBLIOGRAPHY

Concilium florentinum documenta et scriptores. 11 vols. Rome, 1940–1976.

Gill, Joseph. *The Council of Florence.* Cambridge, U.K., 1959.

THOMAS M. IZBICKI

FOLENGO, TEOFILO (Girolamo Folengo; 1491–1544), Italian macaronic poet. Teofilo Folengo was born near Mantua to a noble but impoverished family. He became a Benedictine monk in 1509 and lived in various monasteries until 1525, when he was expelled from the order. He was readmitted in 1534.

Folengo is best known for his works in macaronic, a hybrid literary language that combined Latin morphology and grammar with lexical and sometimes syntactical elements of Italian and various dialects. A late-fourteenth-century product of Paduan university culture, macaronic was typically adopted for works that parodied classical language and genres, often by focusing on the "low" themes of food and material or corporeal needs. Folengo, however, was the first to use macaronic for a work of epic theme and length.

In 1517 and 1521 Folengo, using the pseudonym Merlin Cocai, published the first and second editions of his macaronic works, the *Maccheronee.* The second edition contained four works: *Zanitonella,* a series of elegies and eclogues celebrating the love of the peasant Tonino for Zanina, in which the courtly love lyric is parodied; the *Moschaea* (The war of the flies), modeled on the pseudo-Homeric *Batrachomyomachia;* his masterpiece, *Baldus,* expanded from the seventeen books of 1517 to twenty-five; and a collection of verse letters and epigrams. Folengo also wrote several works in Italian, among which are *Orlandino* (Little Orlando; 1526), a comic account of the epic hero Roland's childhood, written under the pseudonym Limerno Pitocco; and *L'Umanità del Figliuol di Dio* (The humanity of the Son of God; 1533). In *Caos del Triperuno* (The chaos of the threefold man; 1526), an allegory that treats comic and religious themes, three of Folengo's alter egos speak macaronic, Latin, and Italian.

With his *Baldus,* Folengo makes direct reference to the Carolingian chivalric epic and to comic reworkings of this tradition, such as Luigi Pulci's *Morgante.* The other principal target of Folengo's parody, on both linguistic and thematic levels, is the classic epic, especially that of his fellow Mantuan poet, Virgil. Baldus, the eponymous hero of the poem, is born to the daughter of the king of France at the home of a peasant outside Mantua. The first part (books 1–11) tells of Baldus's rustic childhood and youth; in the second part (books 12–25) Baldus leaves home and undertakes an initiatory journey to various mysterious places, the last of which is the Inferno.

Folengo's treatment of canonical literary forms and languages in a carnivalesque manner places him firmly within the anticlassicist tradition of the sixteenth century. The explosive plurilingualism that characterizes his major works, the heterogeneity of materials and techniques that he adopts, and his meticulously "anthropological" attention to peasant society and its vernacular, make him one of the most original exponents of the Italian Renaissance. His eclectic experiments with the intersections between elite and popular traditions were the index of a serious questioning of the hegemonic status of courtly culture; Folengo's works exerted a significant influence on authors such as François Rabelais and Giambattista Basile, and on the future development of the mock-epic genre.

BIBLIOGRAPHY

Primary Works

Folengo, Teofilo. *Opere*. Edited by Carlo Cordié. Milan and Naples, Italy, 1977. Edition of Folengo's macaronic (with Italian translation) and Italian works, some in abridged versions, with an appendix of the works of earlier macaronic poets.
Folengo, Teofilo. *Il Baldo*. Translated by Giuseppe Tonna. 2 vols. Milan, 1958. Bilingual macaronic-Italian edition.

Secondary Works

Bonora, Ettore, and Mario Chiesa, eds. *Cultura letteraria e tradizione popolare in Teofilo Folengo*. Milan, 1979. Proceedings of a 1977 conference on Folengo by leading Italian scholars.
Russell, Anthony Presti. "Epic Agon and the Strategy of Reform in Folengo and Rabelais." *Comparative Literature Studies* 34 (1997): 119–148. Study of the two authors' parodic rewriting of the epic tradition.
Segre, Cesare. "*Baldus*, la fantasia e l'espressionismo." *Strumenti critici* 7 (1992): 315–326. Study of significance of Folengo's linguistic and thematic experimentalism in the context of Renaissance classicism.

NANCY L. CANEPA

FOLK ART. *See* **Popular Culture.**

FONTE, MODERATA (Modesta Pozzo; 1555–1592), Italian writer. Born into a family of Venetian citizens—her father was a lawyer employed at the ducal palace—Fonte became an orphan at one year of age and was raised by relatives. After acquiring her elementary education in a convent, she learned to read and write Latin at home—according to the biographical sketch written by Nicolò Doglioni in 1593 and published in her main work—by having her younger brother repeat the lessons heard at the school from which she collected him. Married to Filippo de' Zorzi, a lawyer in the service of the republic, Fonte had four children and died in childbirth at the age of thirty-seven.

Her first publication was *Le feste* (Celebrations; 1582), an allegorical entertainment performed for the doge Nicolò da Ponte on Saint Stephen's day in 1581. It represents a dispute between an Epicurean and a Stoic on whether virtue or pleasure is more desirable for mankind. The Eritrean sibyl is called in to reconcile the two opposing views, and the performance ends with the praise of Venice as the fitting home of poetry and the arts. In 1582, much in the religious spirit of the Counter-Reformation, Fonte published *La passione di Christo* (The passion of Jesus Christ), followed, ten years later, by *La resurretione di Giesù Christo nostro Signore* (The resurrection of Jesus Christ): both poems are written in octave stanzas and follow the Gospels closely. More significant is her *Tredici canti del Floridoro* (The thirteen cantos of Floridoro; 1581), an unfinished chivalric romance, which recounts the adventures of many knights and anticipates some of the themes found in Fonte's mature work. Floridoro, a foolhardy and ineffectual young man, foreshadows the faults and failures of which Fonte later accuses the male sex. In the confrontation between the twin sisters Risamante and Biondaura, who compete for the possession of the kingdom left by their father, Fonte anticipates two female characterizations that animate the dialogue authored in the last years of her life: one of a woman brought up conventionally and well endowed in feminine charms, and the other of a virginal woman-warrior who surpasses men in wisdom and bravery. The fourth canto opens with a eulogy of women, who possess natural intelligence and courage and would be capable of any undertaking, whether intellectual or military, but whose potential capacities are hidden and hampered by an education that is intentionally lower than that available to men.

Moderata Fonte is best known for her dialogue, *Il merito delle donne* (The worth of women), written around 1592 and published posthumously in 1600. Like most Renaissance dialogues, this work purports to relate a conversation that has occurred among friends on a predetermined subject, but it varies in the fact that the discussion takes place exclusively among women who, in defiance of traditional injunctions to silence, authoritatively expound their views and come to a series of reasoned and appropriate conclusions. The chosen topics are also new and daring, for they range from women's position in the family and society, and men's behavior toward them, to a variety of disciplines and contemporary interests, including natural sciences, medicine, philosophy, and politics. Among the seven Venetian ladies of varied age and family status who participate in the discussions, the outstanding character is Corinna, an unmarried woman who defiantly proclaims her choice of a life of celibacy, independence, and intellectual pursuit. She leads the conversation in the first part of the dialogue and opens it in the second to a wide range of subjects, thus implicitly claiming for women the theoretical and practical knowledge that can liberate them from their position of inferiority. The revisionary value of the dialogue becomes evident in the conclusion, where women's social and emotional bondage is declared to be an abuse perpetrated by men against nature and the natural relations between the sexes.

Fonte is mentioned in a few sixteenth- and seventeenth-century publications about Venice or about women. She was known by Lucrezia Marinella and Arcangela Tarabotti, who also wrote in defense of women, and features prominently in Luisa Bergalli's anthology of Italian women's poetry published in Venice in 1726. No claim, however, can be made of Fonte's possible influence on the work and lives of these women writers. The rediscovery of her work began in the 1970s, when women scholars began to give Moderata Fonte a prominent place in the line of feminist thought that stretches from Christine de Pizan—also Venetian born—and reaches into the theoretical debates of our own time.

See also **Querelle des Femmes**; **Women**, *subentry on* **Women and Literature**.

BIBLIOGRAPHY

Primary Work

Fonte, Moderata. *The Worth of Women: Wherein Is Clearly Revealed Their Nobility and Their Superiority to Men*. Edited and translated by Virginia Cox. Chicago, 1997.

Secondary Works

Chemello, Adriana. "Gioco e dissimulazione in Moderata Fonte." In Moderata Fonte, *Il merito delle donne*. Edited by Adriana Chemello. Venice, 1988. Pages ix–lxiii.

Cox, Virginia. "Moderata Fonte and *The Worth of Women*." In Moderata Fonte. *The Worth of Women: Wherein Is Clearly Revealed Their Superiority to Men*. Edited and translated by Virginia Cox. Chicago, 1997. Pages 1–23.

Labalme, Patricia H. "Venetian Women on Women: Three Early Modern Feminists." *Archivio veneto,* 5th ser., 117 (1981): 81–109.

Malpezzi Price, Paola. "Moderata Fonte." In *Italian Women Writers: A Bio-Bibliographical Sourcebook*. Edited by Rinaldina Russell. Westport, Conn., 1994. Pages 128–137.

RINALDINA RUSSELL

FOOD AND DRINK. Although the basic outlines of the Renaissance diet would be familiar to anyone living today, the way Europeans thought about food and drink was quite different. Patterns of fasting and feasting were set by the Christian calendar; a system of humoral physiology inherited from the Greeks informed their ideas about what was healthy to eat, and the courtly fashion of banqueting was consciously distinguished from the food of the masses.

The Staples of the European Diet. Bread was the single most important element in the European diet for all social classes. It was not only central to the Christian religion in the form of the Eucharist, but was the principle agricultural commodity and constituted the basic staple of all meals. Wealthier Europeans preferred fine white bread made of carefully bolted wheat flour. Less refined brown bread containing more bran and sometimes including barley or rye—or in times of need beans or chestnuts—furnished the tables of the lower classes. Typically, before the use of individual plates for each diner, bread was also used as a trencher, on which other foods were placed. Cooked grains were also prominent in the diet, and were easier and cheaper to prepare, not requiring a bread oven. In the south various forms of porridge (*pulmentum, polenta*) were made of cooked barley or millet. In the north spelt or oatmeal was used more commonly. In extreme poverty vetches and lupines could supplant cultivated grains. Rice was a relatively recent introduction and was grown primarily in Lombardy by the fifteenth century.

The most common drink in southern Europe was wine, and entire regions were devoted to the production and trade in wine. Monasteries whose monks made wine for use in the Catholic mass maintained many of the oldest vineyards. Although the majority of wines were locally manufactured and consumed, there was a large export trade from regions such as Bordeaux. Expensive sweet wines were also imported from Crete and Madeira, and stronger spirits, such as aqua vitae for medicinal purposes, brandy, and whisky, were distilled. In northern Europe beer or ale was the most common beverage, and many households brewed their own. In some regions, such as Normandy and the southwest of England, cider pressed from apples was the usual drink. In eastern Europe mead was still made from fermented honey. Water was rarely consumed by itself, probably for fear of contamination, although it was typically mixed with wine. Whether the water was meant to dilute the wine or the wine to improve the water was a matter for debate in the Renaissance.

The preferred fat is another major distinction between southern and northern European diets in the Renaissance. Olive oil dominated in the south and butter in the north. As an animal product, however, butter was theoretically banned during Lent, and there was a concerted effort to enforce the use of oil in the north. Animal fats such as pork or goose might also figure prominently in the diet in certain regions.

Animal products. The most commonly raised domestic animals included cows, sheep, and goats. Their milk was used to make a wide variety of fresh and aged cheeses, the most renowned of which, Placentia, came from Piacenza (near Parma). As meat, these animals were typically consumed young as veal, lamb, and kid, or in mature form. Pigs were also important throughout Europe and were preserved in numerous ways as sausages and hams. Food from the annual slaughter could thus be consumed throughout the year. Domestic fowl included chickens, ducks, geese, and pigeons. Hunting wild game was also still common throughout Europe, although the privilege to shoot venison or boar might be reserved for the nobility. Small wild birds such as turtledoves and ortolans were also commonly eaten, as well as rabbits, hares, and even hedgehogs.

Depending on the location, fish were also extremely important in the European diet. In the Mediterranean, along the Atlantic coasts, and in the Baltic marine fish were either consumed locally or preserved for export. From the north herring and stockfish (cod) were among the preserved fish, in the south anchovies, sardines, and botargo (salted belly of tuna) were prepared. These products were all important during Lent, when they could be transported inland. The major river systems provided salmon and trout, and fishponds could provide a steady supply of fish to an inland community. Whale meat and porpoise were also among the more expensive and elegant foods available.

Vegetable products. Fruits and vegetables were an integral part of the European diet, although physicians typically warned against excessive consumption of these. Generally the poorer a family, the greater the proportion of their diet consisted of vegetables. The sixteenth century was a period of demographic growth; inflation and a drop in real wages increasingly constrained the average worker to spend a greater proportion of household income on cheaper foods, such as grains and vegetables. This meant less meat was consumed, and may have been part of a general deterioration in the diet of average Europeans. Some vegetables were specifically associated with the lower classes: beans, cabbage, garlic, and onions in particular. Conversely, peaches and melons became very popular in European courts.

As flavoring agents, Renaissance cooks depended on native herbs such as parsley, basil, oregano, marjoram, thyme, sage, tarragon, fennel, dill, bay, coriander, sorrel, saffron, and mustard. There was also a vibrant trade in spices from Asia and Africa, in which the Venetians were most successful. Late medieval and Renaissance cuisine is characterized by the liberal use of spices. Because of their exorbitant cost, as a result of being carried via overland routes and handled by various middlemen before they reached Europe, spices became a powerful marker of social status. The more heavily one could season a dish, the more wealthy and impressive one would seem. The idea that spices were used to mask the odor of rancid meat makes little sense; clearly anyone who could afford spices could also afford fresh meat. Apart from the spices still used in Europe in the twentieth century—pepper, cinnamon, cloves, nutmeg, ginger, and cardamom—there were a number of others commonly imported. "Grains of Paradise," or melegueta pepper, was brought from the west coast of Africa until the Portuguese feared it would cut into their pepper profits and banned its import in the sixteenth century. Galangal, a southeast Asian relative of ginger, was also well known, as were cubebs and long pepper, now virtually unknown in Europe. The importance of spices cannot be overstated, and it should be remembered that Columbus was primarily looking for spices, not a New World. Sugar, used liberally as a spice in this period, later formed the backbone of several New World slave economies, in the Caribbean and Brazil especially. The attempt to find a sea route directly to Asia for spices also inspired the Portuguese to travel around the southern tip of Africa and eventually to found colonies in India, Indonesia, and China.

The Columbian exchange. Although many New World food products did not gain wide acceptance until long after the Renaissance, these crops made their first appearance in Europe after being introduced by Columbus and later explorers. Tomatoes, potatoes, corn (maize), peppers (capsicum), certain species of squash and beans, turkeys, allspice, as well as chocolate are all of American origin. In many cases they simply filled a position in the cuisine formerly held by another plant. Corn, for example, was made into polenta, and potatoes into

Eating and Drinking. Woodcut of a princely banquet by Michael Wohlgemuth from *Der Schrein Od'Schatzbehalter* by Stephan Prater (Nürnberg, Anton Koberger, 1491). THE METROPOLITAN MUSEUM OF ART, ROGERS FUND, 1919 (19.49.4)

dumplings or gnocchi. In much of Europe, though, these foods were consciously avoided. Tomatoes—possibly because of their poisonous relatives in the Solanaceae family, but also because of Renaissance ideas of nutrition and fear of watery vegetables—did not catch on in northern Europe for centuries. However, some medical theorists did consciously promote the use of tobacco, another American product.

Ideas about Food. Attitudes toward food in Renaissance culture were informed by several different traditions and range across a spectrum from the extremely austere and ascetic to the grossly indulgent. For the average European, the patterns of fast and feast were set by the seasons and the requirements of the Christian calendar.

The Christian calendar. Holidays were liberally strewn throughout the Christian year, and indi-

vidual localities might also celebrate their own patron saints with festivals and lavish feasts. But no celebration typifies better the spirit of excess than carnival, or *carne–val* from the word "meat." Ostensibly, the festival was designed as a way to consume all remaining meat prior to Lent, in which meat was proscribed, but it became an opportunity to "turn the world upside down" and indulge the appetite for all things carnal—food, sex, and violence. The festival culminated in Mardi Gras (Fat Tuesday) and often included a staged battle between the fat personification of Carnival bearing sausages and an old thin woman armed with a herring representing Lent. It has been suggested that this temporary subversion of the normal rules of behavior acted as a "safety valve" that actually reinforced regular social roles throughout the rest of the year. It certainly did accentuate the common perception that the monotonous paucity of most European's daily fare could be legitimately relieved by such bouts of gluttony.

It is also revealing that popular fairy tales and stories of Cockaigne or *Sclaraffenland,* the magical land of plenty, envision happiness as an eternal feast in which food presents itself to be eaten without any labor and rivers of wine flow endlessly. Giovanni Boccaccio's story of the land of Bengodi (*Decameron*, 1353; eighth day, third story) with its mountain of Parmesan cheese from which the inhabitants hurl macaroni is one version, and the painter Pieter Brueghel's vision of Cockaigne is another. Something of this carnivalesque spirit is also captured in François Rabelais's *Gargantua and Pantagruel* (1532–1534), in which incredible amounts of rustic food, like sausages and tripe, and buckets of wine are consumed by insatiable giants.

In stark contrast to these scenes were the official fasts. Lent, extending forty days from Ash Wednesday to Easter, was the most important although not the only time meat, milk, butter, and eggs were forbidden. A dispensation from strict adherence could be purchased, and apparently rules were bent. At one point both beaver's tail and puffin were defined as fish products and therefore suitable for Lent. Otherwise most Europeans did survive on fish and vegetables, but for some consumers this might not involve any hardship at all. Rare and exotic fish or opulent displays of fruit enabled the wealthy to overlook the original purpose of Lent as a period of public atonement for sins. After the Protestant Reformation, Lenten rules were dispensed with in Protestant lands, but rulers would sometimes initiate "political" Lents, as did Queen Elizabeth of England, to prevent the supply of meat from dwindling and its price from soaring.

Beyond the mild austerities of Lent, a strong ascetic impulse remained in Christian practice, particularly among certain monastic orders. The Carthusians, for example, abstained from flesh permanently as a way of heightening spirituality. There were also cases of holy women undergoing rigorous fasting and sometimes even starving themselves to death.

Nutritional theory.

The second major system that influenced European foodways in the Renaissance was nutritional theory. Using humoral physiology as inherited from Greek and Arab physicians, Renaissance theorists could categorize every food according to its dominant properties and predict how they might affect the individual consumer. According to this theory, human health consists of a balance of four bodily fluids: blood, phlegm, choler, and bile. One particular humor tends to dominate in each individual and determines that person's complexion (that is, temperament or constitution)—sanguine, phlegmatic, choleric, melancholic.

Equally, all plants and animals have their own complexion. Although there was wide disagreement among dietary authors about how specific foods should be categorized, flavor was the dominant factor. Spicy, aromatic, and salty foods were all classified as hot and dry and were thought to increase hot and dry (choleric) humors in the body. This might be advantageous for those distempered or inclined toward an excess of phlegmatic humors, and thus food acts as a counterbalance for regulating the complexion. Conversely, sour or styptic foods and condiments were considered cold and dry and could be used not only to treat the bilious patient, but also to temper or correct excessively "hot" dishes. It is possible that many popular food combinations were originally designed with this dietary logic in mind. For example, cold and moist pork could be corrected with hot and dry mustard. Sweet dishes (hot and moist) might be balanced with sour (cold and dry) condiments.

Beyond their dominant humors, individual foods were also assigned specific properties: power to open or close the body's passages, aid digestion, induce sweat, promote sleep, and so forth. Thus, the order of a meal was considered important. Certain foods should precede other foods, and foods prone to putrefaction, like melons and cucumbers, should never be allowed to rest at the top of the stomach where they might go bad before being digested. The list of rules and the resulting arguments waged in professional circles was endless. The number of dietary guides published in the Renaissance was also prodigious. All this attests to the importance of this topic to Renaissance thinkers and the role of food as an essential part of the maintenance of health.

Food Texts: Cookbooks, Banquets, and Carving Manuals. From the evidence provided by the first cookbooks, cuisine in the early Renaissance was not very different from that of preceding centuries. The only major novelty was the appearance of distinctly regional styles as opposed to the more international character of medieval cuisine. The first printed cookbook, *De honesta voluptate* (1475) by Bartolommeo Sacchi, called Platina, contains recipes borrowed from an earlier compilation of one Maestro Martino of Como, chef to the patriarch of Aquilea. His recipes still bear many medieval features such as heavy use of spices and sugar, as well as unique ingredients such as almond milk, rosewater, defrutum (reduced grape must), and verjus (juice of unripe grapes). Platina's work, which also contains much nutritional and historical information, was the best-selling book about food in the entire period. It was translated from Latin into Italian, German, and Dutch; was expanded in a French version; and ran through dozens of editions through the sixteenth century. The following recipe gives a good impression of the flavors and techniques of early Renaissance cooking:

Crusta ex cicuribus (Pigeon Pie)

If you want to make a pie of pigeon or some other bird: first boil them and when almost cooked, lift them out of the pot. Then cut them into pieces and fry them in a pan with a lot of fat. Then put them into a dish or crock that has been well greased, with the crust on the bottom. This recipe won't be harmed if you add plums and cherries or some other sour fruit. Then [in a separate pot] take verjus and eight eggs (more if you have guests or less if fewer) and some broth, stir it up with a spoon. To this parsley, marjoram, and mint minced with a knife, which can be cut up and mixed in. Then put it near the fire but far from the flames. Cook slowly; it is necessary that it not boil. Meanwhile stir it all with a spoon until it sticks to the spoon. Lastly, put this broth into the piecrust, near the fire, and when it becomes compact and cooked, serve it to your guests. (Author's translation)

Distinct regional cookbooks were also written in other parts of Europe. Among these is the *Libro di cucina* of Roberto da Nola, written in Naples but revised and published in Spain in 1525. In Germany the *Kuchenmeystery* appeared in 1485; the English

Boke of Cokery in 1500; and in Flanders, the *Boexken van Cokereyn* in 1510. All these reflect, to a certain extent, ingredients and flavor combinations unique to these regions.

Another typically Renaissance work is the *Banchetti* (1549) of Christoforo di Messisbugo, a Bavarian at the Este court of Ferrara. His descriptions of banquets held there reveal a preference for a profusion of sights, sounds, textures, and flavors intended to dazzle guests. With no apparent logical order from course to course, and literally hundreds of dishes in succession, these banquets seem aesthetically comparable to the mannerist paintings of the same period as well as to the poems Ludovico Ariosto produced at this court.

The most massive and comprehensive cookbook of the Renaissance was the *Opera* (1570) of Bartolomeo Scappi, chef to Pope Pius V. Scappi had access to all the latest kinds of kitchen equipment, which are lavishly illustrated in his tome; among them are the fork, recently introduced as standard tableware. His recipes, hundreds in all, mark a definitive break with the Middle Ages and are distinctly Italian. The recipes for pasta and stews in particular approach their recognizable modern form. A diminished emphasis on spices and sugar may be due to their reduction in cost in the sixteenth century, and possibly a loss of their function as markers of social status.

Apart from cookbooks designed for actual use, several other food-related genres became popular in the Renaissance. One of these was the archaeologically minded history of eating habits among the ancient Greeks and Romans. Typical in an era obsessed with classical antiquity, these works attempt to reconstruct what foods were eaten, in what order, and in what social setting. Pedro Chacon's *Triclinio* (1590), Johan Stuckius's *Antiquitatum convivialium* (1597), and Erycius Puteanus's *Reliquiae convivii prisci* (1598) are three examples of this genre.

Guides for kitchen management and carving also became best-sellers at Renaissance courts. Vincenzo Cervio's *Il trinciante* (1581) offers elaborate instructions for the neophyte carver on how to present everything from tiny fowl to exotic fruits. The *Ufficio dello scalco* by Domenico Romoli and a similar manual titled *Dello scalco* by Giovan Battista Rossetti, also on the duties demanded of the office of *scalco* (carver, or steward), reflect the increasing importance and professionalization of banquet managers, as well as the dominant role of etiquette, fashion, and proper service among Renaissance elites.

To conclude, there was a glaring gap between the food consumed by the upper classes as described in these works and the food consumed by the less fortunate, whose experiences are obviously less well documented. The social differences in diet appear to have only worsened in the course of the sixteenth century and well into the seventeenth, and subsistence crises continued to threaten the existence of marginalized peoples throughout Europe. This pronounced separation of elite and popular culture continued well into the modern era.

BIBLIOGRAPHY

Bell, Rudolph M. *Holy Anorexia*. Chicago and London, 1985.

Camporesi, Piero. *Bread of Dreams*. Translated by David Gentilcore. Cambridge, U.K., 1989. Translation of *Il pane selvaggio*.

David, Elizabeth. *Harvest of the Cold Months*. New York, 1995.

Faccioli, Emilio, ed. *L'arte della cucina in Italia*. Turin, Italy, 1987.

Firpo, Luigi, ed. *Gastronomia del Rinascimento*. Turin, Italy, 1974.

Flandrin, Jean-Louis. "Distinction Through Taste." In *A History of Private Life*. Edited by Philippe Ariès and George Duby. Cambridge, Mass., 1987. Vol. 3, pp. 265–307.

Flandrin, Jean-Louis. "Internationalisme, nationalisme et régionalisme dans la cuisine." In *Manger et boire au Moyen Age*. 2 vols. Edited by Denis Menjot. Nice, France, 1984.

Forster, Robert, and Orest Ranum, eds. *Food and Drink in History*. Baltimore, 1979.

Goody, Jack. *Cooking, Cuisine, and Class*. Cambridge, U.K., 1982.

Grieco, Allen. *Classes sociales, nourriture, et imaginaire alimentaire en Italie*. Lilles, France, 1987.

Hémardinquer, Jean-Jacques, ed. *Pour une histoire de l'alimentation*. Paris, 1970.

Henisch, B. A. *Fast and Feast*. University Park, Pa., 1976.

Jeanneret, Michel. *A Feast of Words: Banquets and Table Talk in the Renaissance*. Translated by Jeremy Whiteley and Emma Hughes. Cambridge, U.K., 1981.

Margolin, Jean-Claude, and Robert Sauzet. *Pratiques et discours alimentaires à la Renaissance*. Paris, 1982.

Mennell, Stephen. *All Manners of Food: Eating and Taste in England and France from the Middle Ages to the Present*. Oxford, 1985.

Mintz, Sidney W. *Sweetness and Power: The Place of Sugar in Modern History*. Harmondsworth, U.K., 1985.

Montanari, Massimo. *The Culture of Food*. Translated by Carl Ipsen. Oxford, 1994. Translation of *Fame e l'abbondanza*.

Montanari, Massimo. *Nuovo convivio*. Rome, 1991.

Moulin, Léo. *Les liturgies de la table: Une histoire culturelle du manger et du boire*. Anvers, Belgium, 1988.

Revel, Jean-François. *Culture and Cuisine*. New York, 1982.

Riley, Gillian. *Renaissance Recipes*. San Francisco, 1993.

Schivelbusch, Wolfgang. *Tastes of Paradise*. New York, 1992.

Scully, Terence. *The Art of Cookery in the Middle Ages*. Woodbridge, U.K., 1995.

Tannahill, Reay. *Food in History*. New York, 1988.

Toussaint-Samat, Maguelonne. *History of Food*. Translated by Anthea Bell. Oxford, 1992.

Vehling, Joseph Dommers. *Platina and the Rebirth of Man*. Chicago, 1941.

Visser, Margaret. *The Rituals of Dinner.* New York, 1991.

Westbury, David Alan Bethell. *Handlist of Italian Cookery Books.* Florence, 1963.

Wheaton, Barbara Ketcham. *Savoring the Past.* Philadelphia, 1983.

KENNETH B. ALBALA

FORGERIES. Where the arts flourish, so too does the art of forgery, the deliberate attempt to present one's own work as the work of someone else, whether it be a famous contemporary or a creator from a bygone era. Because it entails intentional deception, forgery has been deplored even in cultures where adherence to tradition may count for as much as originality. Two aspects of Renaissance aesthetic sensibility offered lucrative temptations for those with large ambitions and small scruples: the veneration of antiquity and favorable conditions for the contemporary arts.

Forgery flourished across the arts. As writers aimed at an ever-expanding public through print, the publishing process itself offered a sheltering anonymity to those with ulterior motives. The bootleg press throve on authors who took a more famous author's name, and publishers who did likewise, producing, for example, imitation editions by Aldo Manuzio on cheap paper with cheap type. Copyright law was in its infancy; the best most authors and publishers could hope for was a privilege, a government-generated statement of their rights to publication. In the graphic arts, supplying a print with Albrecht Dürer's characteristic initials could sell it fast, even when any attentive eye could spot the imposture at once. All told, forgery could pay, and handsomely; the Renaissance was a forger's renaissance across every medium. As the forgers prospered, they in turn sparked a progressive sharpening of the criteria for establishing authenticity of texts and artifacts—that other venerable Renaissance tradition, the *beffa* or practical joke, sat hard with its victims.

Of all the varieties of forgery, the forgery of antiquities took pride of place. Because the humanist movement explicitly styled itself as a revival of ancient aesthetic standards for language and art, young writers and artists alike were trained first to *imitate* their ancient predecessors and then to *emulate* them by creating new work in the ancient spirit. Versatility was an integral part of this classical training, because creative endeavors shared in one basic analytical vocabulary. This vocabulary derived from a course of rhetorical training first established in classical Greece and subsequently adapted by the Romans to equip young men for public life; hence terms originally tailored to

Forgery. *The Naming of John the Baptist,* stone plaque carved in 1642 by Georg Schweigger, after Albrecht Dürer's 1510 woodcut *Death of the Virgin.* The "AD" monogram and 1510 date are on a detachable panel (at the lower left, above the dog), the back of which bears the signature proving the forgery. © THE BRITISH MUSEUM

speechmaking were eventually applied as well to poetry, music, and the visual arts, consistently emphasizing such qualities as harmony, beauty, authority, and persuasiveness as the ideals for composition. The universality of this classical aesthetic system facilitated the proverbial versatility of Renaissance creative life—and a similar versatility among Renaissance forgers, who often worked in a variety of media.

Yet the line between imitation and forgery could be finely drawn: the very young Michelangelo, who apparently copied every image in sight, also began to fake engravings by the German engraver and painter Martin Schongauer (1445/50–1491) in pen and ink, deliberately yellowing his paper to make it look more authentic. According to another story, whose shifting details suggest it has been embroidered, he sculpted a sleeping Cupid, "antiqued" it, and buried it, setting up a colossal *beffa* and knowingly committing forgery. When he revealed himself as the forger, however, he lifted the *beffa* into another plane: by successfully passing off his work as ancient, Michelangelo claimed, in effect, that his ability to *imitate* the ancients had reached the stage of *emulation;* his ability to compose in the ancient style proved his supreme competence as a contemporary artist.

The same set of distinctions between imitation, emulation, and forgery can be seen operating in the most famous unmasking of a forgery to occur in the Renaissance. In the mid-fifteenth century, Lorenzo Valla, a historian and councillor of the king of Naples, Alfonso V of Aragon, took a careful look at the venerable text known as the Donation of Constantine, which detailed that emperor's transfer of temporal power—and a lavish set of objects—into the hands of Pope Sylvester I, providing a firm documentary foundation for papal involvement in politics ever afterward. Valla's keen sense of literary style, honed by familiarity with a broad range of Latin writers, alerted him to the fact that the Donation could not possibly have been written in the fourth century. Aware of the devastating effect his discovery would have on the temporal claims of the papacy (his patron, King Alfonso, was strongly antipapal), Valla exposed the fraud in a treatise of 1440, *De falso credita et ementita Constantini donatione.* But Valla, as a good humanist, did more than reveal this important document as a medieval forgery (of the eighth century): he also supplied his own corrected version of the text as it *should* have read, in a reasonable fifteenth-century imitation of fourth-century Latin. Because of his proud claim to authorship, his "improved" Donation of Constantine is not a forgery, but, like Michelangelo's reclaimed *Sleeping Cupid,* a tour de force.

It is surprising, given Valla's exploit, that the most successful forger of the Renaissance should so easily have eluded the critical senses of his finely trained contemporaries. But Giovanni Nanni (1543/44–1607), a Dominican preacher from the old Etruscan city of Viterbo, was an exquisite critic himself. After years of activity in Genoa, he suffered a nearly fatal abscess of the brain and retired to his native haunts in the 1480s. Turning his attention to Viterbo's Etruscan past, he began a lively second career as an antiquarian. From a pair of manuscripts acquired in his Genoese days and a variety of stone inscriptions, in Greek, Latin, Etruscan, and Egyptian hieroglyphs, all extracted from the antiquity-laden ground around Viterbo, he made astounding discoveries about ancient Etruscan history. These he began to circulate under the Etruscan surname of Annius, and it is as

Johannes Annius of Viterbo that he is remembered today. Elaborating on a medieval Roman legend, he reported that Noah, safely delivered from the Flood, traveled to Italy by raft, took a new name, Janus, and established a kingdom in what would later become Viterbo. Given the descent of Etruscan culture from the Hebrew patriarch, it was no surprise when Annius revealed that the Etruscan language, with its retrograde script, was actually an evolved form of Aramaic, and that there were countless parallels between Etruscan tradition and biblical revelation. Most significantly for his own subsequent career, he "proved" that Noah/Janus was the precursor to the papacy. His collected papers, the *Commentaria Fratris Joannis Annii Viterbiensis super opera diversorum auctorum de antiquitatibus loquentium* (Commentaries of Friar Johannes Annius of Viterbo on the works of divers authors speaking about antiquities), were published in 1498 by the papal printer Eucharius Silber, and frequently reprinted in the sixteenth and seventeenth centuries.

A truly inspired forger, Annius was also an inspired critic. He established exacting criteria for determining the authenticity of ancient texts, insisting that sources must corroborate one another independently—and then showed how his spurious creations met these standards. Meanwhile, he applied himself to the reading of genuine Etruscan inscriptions and achieved the first real progress toward their interpretation. The combination of Annius's rigorous philological and archaeological method with the attractiveness of his conclusions blinded many contemporaries to the glaring discrepancies in his work; in 1499, he was appointed by Pope Alexander VI to the position of Master of the Sacred Palace, or chief theological adviser to the pope. He was later appointed chief censor in Rome.

Pope Alexander's successors, Julius II (1503–1513), Leo X (1513–1521), and Clement VII (1523–1534), all continued to believe in the story of Noah/Janus and his connection with the popes; this is why, for example, Noah figures so prominently on Michelangelo's Sistine Chapel ceiling. Martin Luther's use of Annius to prove some of his own contentions about the papacy began to raise suspicions about the friar from Viterbo, but his texts and some of his conclusions still enjoyed a surprising vogue well into the seventeenth century.

See also **Classical Antiquity, Discovery of; Classical Scholarship.**

BIBLIOGRAPHY

Grafton, Anthony E. *Forgers and Critics: Creativity and Duplicity in Western Scholarship.* Princeton, N.J., 1990.

Jones, Mark ed. *Fake? The Art of Deception.* London, 1990.

Stephens, Walter E. "Berosus Chaldaeus: Counterfeit and Fictive Editors of the Early Sixteenth Century." Ph.D. dissertation, Cornell University, Ithaca, N.Y., 1979.

Stephens, Walter E. *Giants in Those Days: Folklore, Ancient History, and Nationalism.* Lincoln, Nebr., and London, 1989.

INGRID D. ROWLAND

FORTIFICATIONS.

The new bastioned fortifications of the Renaissance represented both a technical architectural development and a political phenomenon of considerable importance. The development of fortifications capable of resisting gunpowder artillery and accommodating the new weapons in a defensive role had obvious military significance. Recently the so-called military revolution debate has pushed bastioned military architecture center stage in arguments about changing patterns of early modern warfare. By slowing the pace of war, it is argued, the new fortifications allowed minor powers to defy great ones, increased the size of armies needed to carry out lengthy sieges, prevented the triumph of the Habsburgs in the Netherlands, and laid the foundations for the militarized, centralized states of seventeenth-century Europe. Less controversially, belts of new urban fortifications changed the face of the cities of post-Renaissance Europe. Questions are also raised about the role of urban citadels in consolidating the power of late-Renaissance regimes. The technical development that perhaps prompted some of these wider changes can best be explained by examining the principles of the medieval fortifications that were supplanted by Renaissance bastions and ramparts.

From Medieval to Renaissance Fortifications.

Medieval fortifications throughout Europe presented high walls and towers, capped with crenellations, from which defenders dropped or shot missiles down onto besiegers. Traditional options for attack included undermining the foundations (a very lengthy process), battering a breach in the walls under fire from above, or an assault on the upper fighting galleries from timber siege towers that were highly vulnerable to catapult artillery and incendiary devices, and which required major bridgeworks over the moat before they could be moved close to the walls. Defenders could often hold out until the arrival of relief, or the onset of winter forced a siege to be raised.

The advent of effective and increasingly mobile gunpowder-powered artillery in the mid-fifteenth century briefly, but dramatically, changed the balance of advantage in favor of the attackers. Slender walls and towers were dangerously exposed to cannon fire, and were ill-adapted to accommodate defensive guns. The challenge was met with a variety of responses; initially and most commonly by the thickening and lowering of preexisting walls and towers. The construction of low, wide, gun galleries in front of the main walls represented an early design initiative, which provided both a solid obstacle and a gun platform from which near-horizontal defensive fire could be aimed at attackers. A well-preserved mid-fifteenth-century example of this kind of external gun gallery may still be seen running around the base of the Castelnuovo in Naples. Purpose-built, thick-walled, gun towers were a common northern and central European solution. These towers housed numerous levels of gun emplacements from which a heavy weight of defensive fire could be delivered, albeit from generally small guns and at the cost of noisy, smoke-filled firing chambers. Such gun towers were built in Italy also as late as the 1520s in Lucca and the 1530s in Assisi.

However, it was the Italians who pioneered the development of wide, low, largely solid gun platforms, known as *bastioni* or *baluardi,* built to the same level as the walls connecting them. This allowed relatively heavy guns to be mounted in open positions and moved easily around the defensive perimeter. Originally circular or horseshoe-shaped in plan, by the end of the fifteenth-century bastions with a pointed, polygonal, or triangular footprint were being designed by architects such as Giuliano da Sangallo, Antonio da Sangallo the Elder, Baccio Pontelli, and Francesco di Giorgio Martini. The pointed shapes allowed every part of the perimeter to be swept by defensive fire, without the "blind spots" that could never be entirely avoided with round towers. Set in deep ditches, the bastions and the thick, earth-filled ramparts connecting them presented a low profile to enemy siege guns, and were capable of mounting a formidable defense from the heavy guns mounted on the forward "faces" and the smaller pieces which swept the faces of adjacent bastions from the "flanks." The pointed bastion was the key element in the Renaissance system of fortification that by the mid-sixteenth century was known throughout Europe as the *trace Italienne* (Italian trace).

Italy was not of course the only country to respond architecturally to the challenge of gunpowder artillery. Further research may well support French claims to a share in the early development of the bastion to sit beside their undoubted leadership in the development of modern gunpowder artillery,

Fortified City. Planned fortress city of Palmanova in northeastern Italy, showing bastions and moat. From Brann and Hohenberg, *Civitas orbis terrarum* (Cologne, 1597). BY PERMISSION OF THE BRITISH LIBRARY

and their tactical use of artillery in a series of successful sieges against English fortifications in France in the closing stages of the Hundred Years' War (1337–1453). Italy, however, was the principal theater for the series of conflicts between the royal houses of France and Spain between 1494 and 1559, which meant that the peninsula became a testing ground for the perfection of bastioned fortification. Before Charles VIII of France invaded Naples in 1494, Italy had already witnessed Francesco di Giorgio's fortress designs for the duchy of Urbino and the Aragonese kingdom of Naples. Many of the principles of the new fortifications were set out in his treatise on architecture, and in the revealing sketches of his schemes and projects that illustrate the various manuscript editions.

Pointed fortifications probably first appeared in detached outworks, such as the barbicans defending the gates in many of Francesco di Giorgio's illustrations, or the pillboxes (*capannati* to the Italians, *caponnières* to the French) that were often added to the bases of round medieval towers to provide ditch-level fire bases. Baccio Pontelli's fortress of Ostia (1483–1486) is a well-restored example of such an early transitional fortification. It includes one partly flanked polygonal bastion tower, a triangular barbican, low-level gunports in the towers, and a level platform connecting all of the upper works. At Ostia, however, new works are combined with circular towers, and the generally high profile of the works are reminiscent of medieval rather than Renaissance forms. Pointed bastions with lower profiles and the

characteristic scarped (wedge-shaped, angled thickening) bases appear in Giuliano da Sangallo's new fortress of Poggio Imperiale (from 1487), guarding the Florentine frontier with Siena. Fully developed bastioned systems appeared only in the early 1500s, and it was not until the second quarter of the century that they can truly be said to represent a new orthodoxy. By the end of the sixteenth century, however, a second phase of development had taken place, with very considerable increases in the size of the bastions and ramparts, and the width of the ditches into which they were sunk. It was this final phase of development that was to change the face of Europe's cities, as the high towers came down and subsequent urban expansion was severely restrained by thick belts of ramparts and bastions.

Complete Renaissance Systems. The *trace Italienne* was first used on a complete circuit of city walls at the papal naval base of Civitavecchia between 1516 and 1520. In 1544 Antwerp, in Flanders, became the first major city in northern Europe to boast a complete new bastioned circuit, and many other Low Countries towns were equipped with bastions before the end of the sixteenth century as both Spain and the United Provinces invested heavily in fortifications during the Eighty Years' War (1568–1648). Between 1548 and 1555, Milan became the biggest Italian city to be comprehensively refortified with bastions, and a number of Mediterranean cities in the front line against the Turks (Palermo, Messina, and Lecce in Italy; the new city of Valetta on Malta; and the Venetian colonies in Crete and Cyprus) led the way in the south. Elsewhere progress was often much slower, and the best early examples of complete Renaissance systems are generally to be found in relatively small new foundations: Acaya in Puglia (1521–1535); Portoferraio on the island of Elba (from 1548); Sabbioneta in Lombardy (1560s); Livorno in Tuscany (1575–1590); and the French frontier towns of Villefranche-sur-Meuse and Vitry-le-Françoise, and the imperial fortress town of Mariembourg, near Liège (all built in the middle years of the sixteenth century by Italian architects in foreign service).

The most spectacular surviving bastioned fortification is the Venetian stronghold of Palmanova, which was constructed between 1593 and 1600 on the eastern frontier of the republic, near Udine. The town inside the ramparts was laid out on radial lines, with a series of satellite *piazze* (squares) surrounding a hexagonal central *piazza d'armi* (place of arms), served by three main radial roads from the gates. Palmanova was defended by nine bastions, set around a regular polygon, making it the largest regular fortress completed in mainland Europe during the sixteenth century (although the Venetian fortifications of Nicosia, Cyprus, boasted eleven bastions). Georg Braun and Frans Hogenberg's bird's-eye view of Palmanova (1598) did much to propagate the ideal of a completely integrated fortress and city plan, but the urban development was never properly completed. Only the street layout and the monuments around the central square matched the regular geometry of the plan.

Elsewhere, entirely new fortifications for large established cities proved enormously costly and often gave rise to difficulties over the properties that were to be excluded or threatened with destruction by the modern works, which occupied a much wider swath of land than had medieval walls. Milan's refortification, although completed, caused great stresses. The refortification of Rome had been abandoned in the 1540s because of the immense costs of an eighteen-kilometer circuit and the difficulty of identifying a shorter defensive line that did not exclude important monuments. The surviving bastions and ramparts of the city of Lucca, one of the best preserved of all late-Renaissance urban fortifications, took from 1544 to 1650 to complete [see the illustration in the entry on Lucca in volume 3].

The time taken to complete Lucca's great civic enterprise goes far toward explaining why in so many cities a self-contained urban citadel seemed (at least to the princes and foreign rulers involved in the project) a more practical solution that could be completed quickly at reasonable cost. In many parts of late-medieval Europe, moreover, fortresses already dominated the important towns. This was particularly true of the centralized states where royal fortresses—the Tower of London, the Bastille in Paris, Moscow's Kremlin, and even the post-1453 Castle of the Seven Towers in Constantinople—provided strong points for urban defense and powerful symbols of monarchical rule. The relatively petty rulers of Renaissance Italy played the same game. Fortresses dominated late-medieval Milan, Verona, Ferrara, Mantua, and Naples, while the republics of Florence and Venice secured their subject cities by the same means. Thus, the practicalities of modern defense and a well-established tradition of urban fortresses were combined in numerous projects for new urban citadels.

The Florentine construction of the new citadel in defeated Pisa in 1509 set a pattern for the century. Florence itself was secured for the Medici-imperial cause after the defeat of the last republic in 1530 by the construction of the five-bastioned Fortezza da Basso (from 1534), which straddled the northern walls, strengthening and dominating that section of the city. Its designer, Antonio da Sangallo the Younger (1484–1546), also built a fortress for Pope Paul III in defeated Perugia (from 1540), and began the transformation of the Vatican precinct in Rome into a formidable fortified enclave. Sangallo also laid down the plan (completed by others after his death) for the fortress-palace of Caprarola northwest of Rome, an impressive pentagonal structure with miniature bastions around the base and a circular central courtyard that, in formal terms, represented very clearly the marriage of the new military architecture with that of the residential palace. More often than not, however, the new urban citadel was primarily military in function and was seen by theorists such as Alberti or Francesco di Giorgio, as well as by citizens, as a potent symbol of repressive and authoritarian rule. In Italy alone the sixteenth century was to see further new fortresses in Florence (the Belvedere), Pistoia, Arezzo, Cortona, Siena, Livorno, Naples (Sant'Elmo), Siracusa, Palermo, Brescia, Parma, Piacenza, Casole, and Turin. Francesco Paciotto's design for a regular pentagonal fortress at Turin (1564–1566) proved to be a seminal design. Paciotto was commissioned in 1567 by the Spanish rulers of the Netherlands to build the citadel of Antwerp on near-identical lines. The Antwerp citadel was the first of a series of six such fortresses that were planned by the Spanish authorities to secure their hold over the chief cities of the Low Countries. Had all the program been completed as planned, it would have been the most extensive coordinated campaign of repressive fortress construction in Europe, and possibly a unique instance of a large-scale construction program in different cities, all exclusively modeled on a single Turin-Antwerp prototype.

If citadels often became instruments of central power, and the new bastioned defensive circuits the means by which cities could again be defended in a new age of gunpowder artillery, the fortifications of the fifteenth and sixteenth centuries exercised a profound influence on Europe's landscape and townscape, as well as on the political and military history of the Continent.

See also **Artillery**; **Warfare**.

BIBLIOGRAPHY

De la Croix, Horst. "The Literature of Fortification in Renaissance Italy." *Technology and Culture* 6 (1963): 30–50.

De la Croix, Horst. "Military Architecture and the Radial City

Plan in Sixteenth-Century Italy." *Art Bulletin* 42 (1960): 263–290.

Duffy, Christopher. *Siege Warfare.* 2 vols. Volume 1, *The Fortress in the Early Modern World, 1494–1660.* London, 1979.

Hale, J. R. *Renaissance Fortification: Art or Engineering?* London, 1977.

Hale, J. R. *Renaissance War Studies.* London, 1983. Contains many articles on fortification, including the author's seminal paper "The Early Development of the Bastion: An Italian Chronology, c. 1450–1534."

Parker, Geoffrey. *The Military Revolution: Military Innovation and the Rise of the West, 1550–1800.* Cambridge, U.K., and New York, 1988.

Pepper, Simon, and Nicholas Adams. *Firearms and Fortifications: Military Architecture and Siege Warfare in Sixteenth-Century Siena.* Chicago, 1986.

SIMON PEPPER

FORTUNE. The notion that the external circumstances and vicissitudes of human life were governed by chance was widespread during the Renaissance. It was not only an ingredient of common belief, but found expression in popular artistic and literary imagination. *Fortuna* was depicted as a goddess precariously balancing on a sphere symbolizing her constant changeableness, or as turning a large wheel carrying four persons who rose and fell as their circumstances in life shifted. A popular superstition rather than a religious belief in Renaissance times, *Fortuna* in ancient Rome was indeed worshiped as a goddess; this belief was gradually eliminated from Christian notions in the course of the Middle Ages, but never entirely lost its popularity. With the development of late-medieval and Renaissance urban life with trade, interregional commerce, banking, and nascent capitalism, individuals and families did rise and fall with their economic success or failure, and change of fortune became an important ingredient of popular consciousness. At the same time, the frequency of wars and the shifts in dynastic and aristocratic powers, along with popular suffering served to underline the continuous presence of changing fortunes.

Petrarch and Salutati. The first of the literary and philosophical considerations of fortune that was written in response to these circumstances was also the most popular, and exercised its influence through manuscripts and then printed editions up to the mid-eighteenth century. This was none other than Petrarch's *De remediis utriusque fortunae* (Remedies for both kinds of fortune). Written around 1354, it addresses the state of mind of mankind: "Forever beset by fretful cares, which are not merely trivial and useless, but harmful and noisome, we are wracked by the present, and tormented by the past and future, so that we seem to fear nothing worse than not to be sufficiently wretched at all times." *Remedies* is divided into two books: in the one *Ratio* (Reason) counsels *Gaudium* (Joy) on the false expectations offered by good fortune, while in the other *Dolor* (Sorrow) is urged to face the difficulties of life with courage.

Petrarch (1304–1374) in a letter of his old age to Tommaso del Garbo (1366) explains why he wrote about "something I either know or believe is about nothing." He further says that "in writing nothing about fortune but remedies about what is called 'fortune,' I included what seemed either to soothe or to inspire the human spirit." For the most part, his counsels were based on the Stoic view of Seneca that moral attitudes were sufficient to cope with fortune; but there was also at times a Christian element that saw fortune as in part the work of divine providence. Petrarch also included in this work the first Renaissance treatise on the dignity of man. His views later influenced Giovanni Boccaccio's work, *De casibus virorum illustrium* (On the accidents of illustrious men; 1355–1374). More important, Petrarch's *Remedies* became over the next four centuries a popular handbook on how to conduct one's everyday life and on how to find one's proper place in the world.

Coluccio Salutati (1331–1406), perhaps the most important figure in transmitting Petrarchan humanism, completed a treatise, *De fato et fortuna* (On fate and fortune) in 1396. This was a major theological, philosophical, and humanistic work. "Fortune" was to be regarded in the context of divine providence, astrological determinance, and "chance." Salutati thought fortune was real; he defined it as a rare, unanticipated consequence of an unintended cause. But it was more than that; it was the occasion for the dramatic poetical and visual image of the goddess from antiquity to his own time, which Salutati recounts as an element of both folk culture and high arts. The legends of fortune are mythology, admirable for their aptness or charm, but not to be taken seriously. True fortune is an expression of divine providence acting through human and natural events. It could, in its occasional violation of ordinary historical and natural events, be viewed theologically as an action of God's *potentia absoluta* (absolute power) transcending what ordinarily occurs. The work also includes Salutati's Latin translation of a passage on fortune from Dante's *Divina Commedia*. But *fortuna* should not be confused with ordinary accidental or chance happenings, called *casus* by philosophers. This distinction is important because Renaissance discussions were for the most part concerned with moral attitudes, political behavior, and historical events expressed sometimes in poetry and art, sometimes in essays, histories, and works of political thought.

Poggio Bracciolini. One such work was Poggio Bracciolini's *De Varietate fortunae* (On the vicissitudes of fortune). Written after 1442 and first circulated in 1448, it was dedicated to Pope Nicholas V. This work is of historical interest apart from its central theme of the many kinds of calamitous events happening to political and religious leaders that may be attributed to fortune. In it is one of the first surveys of the then surviving ruins of ancient buildings in the city of Rome, presented as witnesses to the power of fortune in destroying the ancient Roman capital. Its discussion of the theory of fortune is limited to an interchange between "Poggio" and "Antonio" (Loschi), the one promoting Aristotle because he gives a definition of "fortune" as the unforeseen outcome of an unintended cause, and the other promoting Cicero for his more practical counsels of temperance and fortitude in resisting the gifts and blows of fortune. Its central content is a detailed survey of the rise and fall of military and political leaders both in antiquity and in Poggio's own times. Interestingly, he also includes the Mongol, Mameluke, and Turkish conquests of his own epoch. After a graphic description of the power struggles and sad outcomes involving the clerical hierarchy of his own times, well known to him from his years as apostolic secretary, Poggio ends his work with a remarkable account of the vicissitudes of life in India.

In 1453 Poggio returned to Florence as chancellor in the regime of Cosimo de' Medici. His thoughts on the subject of fortune, which he had essentially described but had not theorized about in the above work, were put forth in his disquisition *De miseria humanae conditionis* (The misery of the human condition) of 1455. It is the very gifts of fortune, so avidly sought after, that bring mankind its troubles. "The most ample dignities, principalities, kingdoms and empires we know are nothing else than the enticements of fortune. . . . And certainly all anxieties, all the troubles of life, all diseases of the soul are contracted from the gifts of fortune." Poggio had a realistic, even cynical view of the life of the men he had known personally and of those he knew by reputation and by his readings. His view was not exceptional, but in this epoch of widespread striving after wealth and power, was almost taken for granted.

Earthly life itself seemed to many Renaissance writers to be characterized by the ebb and flow of fortune. Not untypical was the short fantasy written in the early 1430s by Leon Battista Alberti entitled *Fatum et fortunae* (On fate and fortune). Alberti depicted life as a turbulent river surrounding a craggy island. Newborn souls slipped into the waters and sought to make their way. Those who fared worst were those who sought to ride the river's surface on floats and were dashed madly around. The safer ones were those who entrusted themselves to fortune and to their own efforts to swim.

Niccolò Machiavelli. Possibly the best known exponent of fortune was the political writer and historian Niccolò Machiavelli (1469–1527). His famous chapter twenty-five of *Il principe* (The prince) certainly conceives of fortune in the same way as Poggio had, taking for granted its pursuit by all men seeking or exercising wealth or power, but also believing they could in some way, though highly limited, achieve control over it. But fortune, which is thought of as time combined with historical and natural circumstances, or vicissitudes, keeps changing, and it can only be controlled if men themselves can change with it. Machiavelli also thinks that highly motivated and powerful men can impose their will on circumstances. In his words—so objectionable to so many—"Fortune is a woman, and it is necessary, if you wish to master her, to conquer her by force. . . . She lets herself be overcome by the bold rather than those who proceed coldly."

For Machiavelli, as in the case of Poggio and some other Renaissance writers, "Fortune" is sometimes thought of as surrogate to fate or to divine providence, but this is spoken cautiously because of the danger of its being thought sacrilegious. Machiavelli is very explicit in a passage in his *Discorsi sopra la prima deca di Tito Livio* (Discourses on Titus Livy; completed by 1519):

And thus Titus Livy, who has given an account of all the above troubles, concludes by saying, "Fortune thus blinds the minds of men when she does not wish them to resist her power." . . . It certainly is the course of Fortune, when she wishes to effect some great result, to select for her instrument a man of such spirit and ability that he will recognize the opportunity which is afforded him. And thus, in the same way, when she wishes to effect the ruin and destruction of states, she places men at the head who contribute to and hasten such ruin. . . . I repeat, then, as an incontrovertible truth, proved by all history, that men may second fortune, but cannot oppose her; they may develop her designs, but cannot defeat them. But men should never despair on that account: for not knowing the aims of Fortune, which she pursues by dark and devious ways, men should always be hopeful, and never yield to despair, whatever troubles or ill fortune may befall them.

Sentiments such as this, with which Petrarch, but perhaps not Poggio, would have agreed, epitomize the combination of realism and a sense of human possibility that prevailed in the Renaissance and continued in some way in succeeding ages.

See also **Dignity of Man; Political Thought;** *and biographies of figures mentioned in this entry.*

BIBLIOGRAPHY

Primary Works

Alberti, Leon Battista. *Dinner Pieces. A Translation of the Intercenales.* Translated by David Marsh. Binghamton, N.Y., 1987. See *Fate and Fortune [Fatum et Fortunae],* pp. 23–27.

Bracciolini, Giovanni Poggio. *De varietate fortunae.* Edited by Outi Merisalo. Helsinki, Finland, 1993.

Machiavelli, Niccolò. *The Prince and the Discourses.* Translated by Christian E. Detmold. New York, 1940.

Machiavelli, Niccolò. *Il Principe e Discorsi sopra la prima deca di Tito Livio.* Edited by Sergio Bertelli. Milan, 1960.

Petrarca, Francesco. *Petrarch's Remedies for Fortune Fair and Foul: A Modern English Translation of De remediis utriusque Fortunae with a Commentary.* Translated by Conrad Rawski. 5 vols. Bloomington and Indianapolis, Ind., 1991.

Salutati, Coluccio. *De fato et fortuna.* Edited by Concetta Bianca. Florence, 1985.

Secondary Works

Cioffari, Vincenzo. "The Function of Fortune in Dante, Boccaccio, and Machiavelli." *Italica* 24 (1947):1–13.

Doren, Alfons. "Fortuna im Mittelalter und in der Renaissance." *Vorträge der Bibliothek Warburg* 2 (1922–1923): 71–115.

Fowler, W. Warde. "Fortune (Roman)." *Hastings Encyclopedia of Religion and Ethics.* New York, 1914. Vol. 1, pp. 98–104.

Heitmann, Klaus. *Fortuna und Virtus: Eine Studie zu Petrarcas Lebensweisheit.* Cologne, Germany, 1958.

Patch, Howard R. *The Goddess Fortuna in Medieval Literature.* New York, 1974.

Pitkin, Hanna Fenichel. *Fortune Is a Woman: Gender and Politics in the Thought of Niccolò Machiavelli.* Berkeley, Calif., 1984. See chapter 6, "Fortune," pp. 138–169.

Tarlton, Charles. *Fortune's Circle.* Chicago, 1970.

Trinkaus, Charles. *Adversity's Noblemen: The Italian Humanists on Happiness.* New York, 1965. Reprint with additional material.

CHARLES TRINKAUS

FOUNDLINGS. *See* **Orphans and Foundlings.**

FOUQUET, JEAN. *See* **France,** *subentry on* **Art in France.**

FOXE, JOHN (1517–1587), Protestant church historian and martyrologist. Foxe was born in Boston, Lincolnshire, and educated at Oxford, where he remained as a fellow of Magdalen College until resigning in 1545 under pressure for his Protestant views.

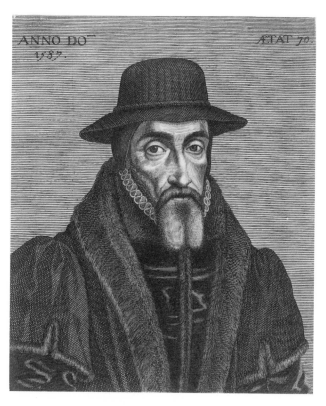

John Foxe. Portrait from the title page of *The Book of Martyrs.* © THE BRITISH MUSEUM, LONDON

He found employment as tutor to the children of William Lucy at Charlecote, where he married Agnes Randall of Coventry in 1547, and subsequently joined the London household of the reform-minded duchess of Richmond as tutor to the three oldest children of her late brother Henry Howard, earl of Surrey. There he met John Bale, whose commentary on Revelation (*The Image of Both Churches*; 1545) shaped Foxe's sense of church history, and he formed a lasting bond with the oldest child, Thomas, subsequently duke of Norfolk.

After being ordained deacon by Nicholas Ridley in 1550 and beginning to preach in London, Foxe fled to the Continent in the spring of 1554 to escape Mary's interrogators. In Basel, where he settled, Foxe barely sustained his family by working for the Protestant printer Johann Oporinus while he pursued his major project, an expanded version of the account of Lollard martyrs that he had published in Strasbourg in 1554 as *Commentarii rerum in ecclesia gestarum* (A commentary on the history of the church), using reports of persecution under Mary that had been sent from England to Edmund Grindal to bring his story to the present. After the expanded version appeared in August 1559, Foxe returned to Elizabeth's England, where he was ordained a priest in Saint Paul's Cathedral by his friend Grindal, now bishop of London.

Foxe could have risen to a prominent position in the church, but his reluctance to make the necessary compromises, initially over clerical vestments, persisted throughout his career. He devoted most of his energies to continuing his work on martyrology, which made him famous when the first English edition appeared in 1563 as the *Actes and Monuments of These Latter and Perilous Days,* an immense folio volume three times the length of the 1559 version, published by John Day with more than fifty woodcuts. Foxe continued to gather new information for the 1570 version of his *Book of Martyrs,* as it was popularly known, which appeared in two folio volumes that doubled the length of the 1563 edition. In the 1570 version Foxe answered his detractors while taking his story back to include early Christian martyrs, drawing heavily upon the fourth-century *Ecclesiastical History* of Eusebius. He continued to tinker with the *Actes and Monuments,* making deletions as well as additions, in editions of 1576 and 1583; a posthumous Elizabethan edition appeared in 1596.

Foxe's works include an apocalyptic drama from his Basel years, *Christus triumphans* (1556); the well-known *Sermon of Christ Crucified* (1570) preached at Paul's Cross (an outdoor pulpit in London); and an unfinished commentary on Revelation that he was working on at his death. He was known chiefly, however, for his enormously influential *Actes and Monuments.* This served English Protestants as a polemical history of the survival of the true church, on the Continent as well as in England (Foxe borrowed from Jean Crespin's *Livre des martyres* [1554] among other sources), and of the triumph of the English church under Elizabeth. Foxe suppressed doctrinal differences among his martyrs to present a picture of a unified Protestant church, yet his portraits of heroic suffering under persecution provided powerful models of resistance for those who would oppose the established church in England. He adapted conventions and values he had learned from classical biography, using contemporary materials that included accounts of examinations for heresy and descriptions of the conduct of martyrs at the stake, to fashion a new kind of Protestant hero that was to influence such leading nonconformist writers of the next century as John Milton, John Bunyan, and the Quaker leader George Fox.

BIBLIOGRAPHY

Primary Work
Foxe, John. *The Acts and Monuments of John Foxe.* Edited by Josiah Pratt. 8 vols. London, 1877.

Secondary Works
Haller, William. *Foxe's Book of Martyrs and the Elect Nation.* London, 1963.
Loades, David, ed. *John Foxe and the English Reformation.* London, 1997.
Mozley, James F. *John Foxe and His Book.* London, 1940. Reprint, New York, 1970.

JOHN R. KNOTT

FRACASTORO, GIROLAMO (c. 1478–1553), Italian anatomist. Born in Verona of a noble family, Fracastoro studied in Padua with the Aristotelian philosopher Pietro Pomponazzi (1462–1525), the anatomist Alessandro Benedetti (1450–1512), and the physicians Marcantonio della Torre (1481–1511) and Pietro Prapolini. Man of the Renaissance, he studied mathematics, medicine, botany, geology, astronomy, and philosophy. He acquired an extensive knowledge of Latin and Latin literature, establishing a close relationship with Pietro Bembo (1470–1547), the greatest Latinist of the time. He married in 1500 but his wife died before 1541. They had a daughter and three sons, two of whom died young in 1516.

In 1501 Fracastoro was appointed a lecturer in logic at the University of Padua. After a career as a professor at Padua and a physician, he retired before 1534 to his father's villa in Caffi, fifteen miles from Verona, dedicating himself to private practice and to study. Held in esteem in ecclesiastical circles, he was named official physician *(medicus conductus)* of the Council of Trent.

Doctor and poet, in his time Fracastoro enjoyed a solid reputation as an astronomer, mathematician, and geographer. He contributed to the new geography and cartography that were required after the voyages of exploration. Also interested in cosmography, in 1538 he wrote an astronomical treatise in which, slightly before Nicolaus Copernicus (1473–1543), he proposed a new interpretation of Ptolemaic theory. In this work he attempted to explain diffraction in terms of different densities of air. He also studied mechanics, in particular vibratory motion, and experimented with magnets and the compass.

Fracastoro participated in philosophical debates and wrote three dialogues. The first was devoted to aesthetics and discussed beauty and the aim of poetry; the second discussed his theory of knowledge and the functions of the intellect; and the third was concerned with the nature of the immortal soul, treating the soul's control over "vital spirits" and sensations.

Fracastoro's scientific reputation rests on two major works, both devoted to epidemic diseases: the poem in Latin hexameter, *Syphilis sive morbus gallicus* (Syphilis or the French disease; 1530, with a final version in 1547), which he dedicated to Bembo, and the treatise *De contagione et contagiosis morbis et eorum curatione* (On contagion and contagious diseases and their care; 1546), which assured him lasting fame in the history of epidemiology. His theory of contagion was based upon airborne "particles" or "seeds" that have an "antipathy" for the animal organism and provoke an alteration of its humors, thus producing the disease. In a related work, *De causis criticorum dierum* (On the causes of critical days; 1538), Fracastoro rules out astral influences and number mysticism as their causes, insisting that the cause must be found in the nature of the disease itself, the crisis being the result of the body's reaction to modification of its humors.

Fracastoro's *De contagione* was published together with his *De sympathia et antipathia rerum* (On the sympathy and antipathy of things; 1546), both directed against explanations of natural phenomena in terms of "occult qualities." Sympathy and antipathy, for him, explains magnetism, why a sponge absorbs water, and why some bodies are more receptive than others to particular diseases. He compared the action of certain diseases to that of poisons or of mythical animals whose glance was believed to be fatal because of the antipathy of their *species spirituales* to the spirits of the human body. He described various infectious diseases, including typhus and tuberculosis, and tried to explain how contagion takes place and why some diseases are contagious and others not. He emphasized receptivity as a possible explanation of the fact that, even in the most terrible epidemic, some escape.

Fracastoro's theory has often been considered as the first statement of the modern theory that infectious diseases are transmitted by a living agent. There is little evidence to support this claim. His theory, however, was the most advanced contribution within the Galenic culture of his time to debates that had been going on since the Black Death of the fourteenth century. He saw contagion as "an infection that passes from one thing to another," comparing it to the emanations of an onion. Fracastoro further discerned a relationship between contagion and putrefaction. He thought that putrefying bodies emit invisible corpuscles that are communicable, which explains why one rotten apple infects the whole barrel. For him, contagion is "a similar corruption of the substance of a particular combination which passes from one thing to another and is originally caused by the infection of imperceptible parts."

Fracastoro's originality lies in the mechanisms he associated with the diffusion of diseases. He distinguished three ontologically different types of contagion: by direct contact with a sick person (*cumtagium,* or touching with, in the strict sense); by indirect contact through *fomites* ("tinders"); and at a distance through the air, originating with a sick person. He appears to have been the first to use the word *fomites* as a technical term for substances deposited on or in clothing and wood and to describe the transferred infectious agent as "seedlets of contagion" *(seminaria contagionis)*. They are sticky gelatinous substances that remain adherent to objects, as in the traditional idea of "sticky venomous atoms." Fracastoro suggests that *seminaria* are able to propagate and engender themselves, "just as spirits do." They have specific affinities for plants, animals, and organs or fluids in the body. The term *seminara* is now usually interpreted as "germs," but nowhere does Fracastoro specify that they are living organisms.

BIBLIOGRAPHY

Primary Works

Fracastoro, Girolamo. *Fracastoro's Syphilis.* Translated by Geoffrey Eatough. Liverpool, U.K., 1984.

Fracastoro, Girolamo. *Syphilis sive morbus gallicus.* 1530. Translated by N. Tate. Edited by Heneage Wynne-Finch. London, 1935.

Fracastoro, Girolamo. *De sympathia et antipathia rerum liber unus. De contagione et contagiosis morbis et curatione libri III.* 1546. Translation of *De contagione* by W. C. Wright. New York and London, 1930.

Secondary Works

Baumgartner, Leona, and John F. Fulton. *A Bibliography of the Poem Syphilis, sive Morbus gallicus by Girolamo Fracastoro, of Verona.* New Haven, Conn., 1935.

Garrison, Fielding H. "Fracastorius, Athanasius Kircker, and the Germ Theory of Disease." *Science,* no. 31 (1910): 500–502.

Howard-Jones, Norman. "Fracastoro and Henle: A Reappraisal of Their Contribution to the Concept of Communicable Disease." *Medical History* 21 (January 1977): 61–68.

Nutton, Vivian. "The Reception of Fracastoro's Theory of Contagion: The seed That Fell among Thorns?" *Osiris* 2d ser., 6 (1990): 196–234.

Nutton, Vivian. "The Seeds of Disease: An Explanation of Contagion and Infection from the Greeks to the Renaissance." *Medical History* 27 (January 1983): 1–34.

Temkin, Oswei. *The Double Face of Janus.* Baltimore, Md., 1977. See chapter 31, "An Historical Analysis of the Concept of Infection," pp. 456–471.

Bernardino Fantini

FRANCE. [This entry includes two subentries, one on the history of the kingdom of France in the Renaissance and the other on artists active in France.]

The Kingdom of France

In the age of the Renaissance, here somewhat arbitrarily defined as extending from 1461 to 1617, France was preoccupied with foreign and civil wars. The period was one of radical change. Apart from the advent of humanist culture, which in turn fed into religious heterodoxy, striking economic and social shifts occurred, accompanied by numerous governmental reforms.

Politics, Diplomacy, and War. Until 1589 the kingdom was ruled by the Valois dynasty. Louis XI (1461–1483) was succeeded by his son Charles VIII (1483–1498), and he by his cousin of the branch of Orléans, Louis XII (1498–1515). There followed Francis I (1515–1547) of the line of Angoulême, his son Henry II (1547–1559), and then the latter's three sons, Francis II (1559–1560), Charles IX (1560–1574), and Henry III (1574–1589). The next two kings, Henry IV (1589–1610) and Louis XIII (1610–1643), belonged to the family of Bourbon. Several female regents also ruled: Anne de Beaujeu (during the minority of her younger brother, Charles VIII), Louise of Savoy (during the absence in Italy and Spain of her son, Francis I), Catherine de Médicis (widow of Henry II and regent in the early parts of the reigns of Charles IX and Henry III), and Henry IV's widow, Marie de Médicis (in the first years of the reign of her son, Louis XIII). The so-called Salic law prevented accession by a queen in her own right and the transmission of a claim to the throne through a female line. Nevertheless, women regents and other highborn noblewomen played a notable part in French politics.

Louis XI. Louis XI's regime was marked by the consolidation of French territory. His economic policies, together with his endeavors to weaken the power of the magnates and make use of persons of lesser rank, did much to break down feudal structures. In 1465 Duke Francis of Brittany and Charles the Bold, son of the duke of Burgundy, joined the king's brother, Charles de Berry, to oppose Louis XI in the League of the Public Weal. Unable to defeat the League militarily, the king eventually imposed his authority by dividing his opponents. His diplomacy managed to neutralize the English king, Edward IV, the ally of Louis's principal enemy, Charles the Bold, who became duke of Burgundy in 1467. The king came to a temporary understanding with the German emperor, Frederick III. The death in battle of Charles the Bold in 1477 allowed Louis to occupy Burgundy, Artois, and Franche-Comté, but the marriage of the emperor's son, Maximilian, to

Charles's heiress, Mary of Burgundy, obliged France to withdraw from the two latter territories. The extinction of the Angevin line by the death of Duke René and his heirs enabled the absorption of the semi-independent appanages of Anjou and Maine into the royal domain, as well as Provence, which had previously owed fealty to the emperor. The appanage of Guyenne also reverted to the crown with the death of the king's brother.

Against these successes, the subsequent marriage of Mary of Burgundy's son, Philip the Fair, to Joan, the daughter of the dual sovereigns of Spain, Ferdinand of Aragon and Isabella of Castile, foreshadowed Habsburg hegemony in Europe. The product of this union, the future emperor Charles V, was to rule what remained of the Burgundian inheritance together with Spain and much of Italy and Germany, thus encircling France. Louis XI's diplomacy also had the unforeseen consequence of drawing French arms into Italy. He did little to support the claim of the Angevin line to the kingdom of Naples before the death of René of Anjou, but his own son and successor, Charles VIII, was to lead an invasion of the peninsula. Louis's alliance with Francesco Sforza, the usurper of Milan, slighted the claims of the Orléanist branch of the French royal dynasty, which was descended on the maternal side from the Visconti, the former rulers of the duchy. Louis of Orléans, the future Louis XII, was to assert his right to Milan.

Charles VIII. After the death of Louis XI a strong reaction against his policies was evident at a meeting at Tours in 1484 of the national representative body, the Estates General, where a struggle took place between the supporters of Anne de Beaujeu and those of Louis of Orléans to see who should be regent in the boyhood of the new king, Charles VIII. After losing this contest, Louis of Orléans set up a coalition with Duke Francis of Brittany and waged war unsuccessfully against the government of Anne de Beaujeu in the years 1485–1488. Charles began to rule personally from 1491 and, after the death of the duke of Brittany, married the duke's heiress, Anne. However, Brittany did not observe the Salic law, and Anne of Brittany retained control of the duchy. In 1494 Charles VIII traversed Italy at the head of a French army to make good his claim to the kingdom of Naples. A league of Italian states formed in his rear, and he had to fight his way out at the Battle of Fornovo (1495). The garrison he left behind in Naples surrendered in the following year. This first invasion is customarily associated with the importation

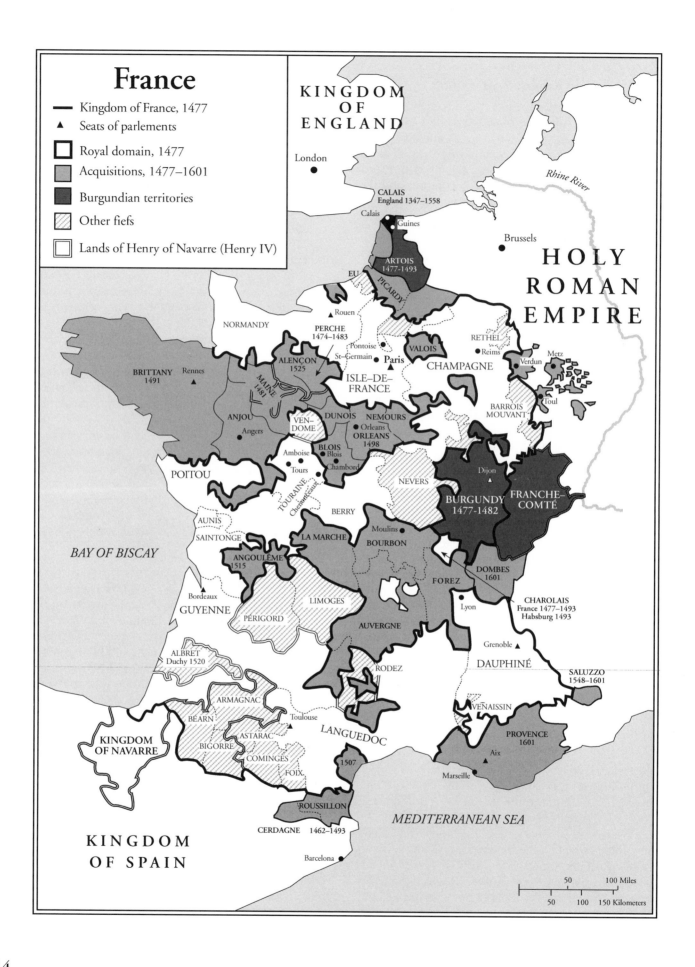

France

- —— Kingdom of France, 1477
- ▲ Seats of parlements
- ☐ Royal domain, 1477
- Acquisitions, 1477–1601
- Burgundian territories
- Other fiefs
- Lands of Henry of Navarre (Henry IV)

KINGDOM
OF
ENGLAND

London

Rhine River

CALAIS
England 1347–1558
Calais
Guines

Brussels

HOLY
ROMAN
EMPIRE

EU

PICARDY

ARTOIS
1477–1493

NORMANDY

Rouen

PERCHE
1474–1483

Pontoise
St–Germain
Paris

VALOIS

RETHEL

Reims

Metz

Verdun

Toul

BRITTANY
1491

Rennes

ALENÇON
1525

ISLE–DE–
FRANCE

CHAMPAGNE

BARROIS
MOUVANT

MAINE
1481

ANJOU

Angers

VEN–
DOME

DUNOIS

NEMOURS

Orleans

BLOIS
Amboise   Blois

ORLEANS
1498

POITOU

Tours
Chambord

TOURAINE
Chenonceaux

NEVERS

BURGUNDY
1477–1482

Dijon

FRANCHE–
COMTÉ

BERRY

AUNIS
SAINTONGE

LA MARCHE

Moulins

BOURBON

Forez
DOMBES
1601

BAY OF BISCAY

ANGOULÊME
1515

Bordeaux

GUYENNE

LIMOGES

PÉRIGORD

AUVERGNE

FOREZ

Lyon

CHAROLAIS
France 1477–1493
Habsburg 1493

Grenoble

DAUPHINÉ

SALUZZO
1548–1601

ALBRET
Duchy 1520

RODEZ

VENAISSIN

ARMAGNAC

BÉARN

Toulouse

ASTARAC

LANGUEDOC

PROVENCE
1601

Aix

KINGDOM
OF NAVARRE

BIGORRE

COMINGES

FOIX

1507

Marseille

ROUSSILLON

KINGDOM
OF SPAIN

CERDAGNE   1462–1493

MEDITERRANEAN SEA

Barcelona

	50		100 Miles
50	100	150 Kilometers	

414

of Renaissance art and manners into France, although Italian cultural influence was evident earlier.

Louis XII. When Charles VIII died without heirs in 1498, it was the former rebel duke of Orléans who became king as Louis XII. Having put aside his wife Jeanne, the saintly daughter of Louis XI, the new king married the former queen, Anne of Brittany. Louis XII evicted Ludovico Sforza from Milan and partitioned Naples with Ferdinand of Aragon. Subsequent disagreement between France and Spain resulted in armed conflict, the defeat of the French at Cerignola (1503), and their withdrawal. In 1508 Louis XII was associated with many of the rulers of Europe in the League of Cambrai, designed to curb the expansion of the Venetian republic. His victory at Agnadello extended French dominion in north Italy, but this provoked the warrior pope, Julius II, to form the Holy League against France.

The king attempted to depose the pope by calling a council of the church at Pisa, and when this failed, he resorted to military means. The victory gained at Ravenna in 1512 was offset by the death of the brilliant young French general, Gaston de Foix, the ruler of extensive lands bordering the Pyrenees. Ferdinand of Aragon, who had married Gaston's sister, Germaine de Foix, after the death of Isabella of Castile, occupied Spanish Navarre in the name of his wife. In Italy the defeat of the French army at Novara in 1513 obliged Louis XII to withdraw his forces across the Alps. Anne of Brittany died in 1514. Shortly before his death in 1515, Louis married Mary Tudor, the sister of Henry VIII of England. The martial character of his reign rallied the French nobility in his support. His benevolence and generosity earned him the title "the father of his people." Apart from Pierre de Rohan, marshal de Gié, who quarreled with Louise of Savoy and was tried for treason in the years 1504–1506, his principal minister was Cardinal Georges d'Amboise. The king pleased Louise by arranging the marriage of his daughter Claude to her son, the heir presumptive to the crown, Francis of Angoulême.

Francis I. The French Renaissance reached its apogee under the next king, Francis I, whose reign was marked by rivalry with Henry VIII and, more particularly, with Charles V, king of Spain in 1516 and emperor in 1519. Francis's rule was authoritarian in tone, although noble faction increased at his court in his last years. Soon after his accession he launched a fresh invasion of Italy and won a signal victory against the Swiss defenders of Milan at Marignano. He then made an agreement with Pope Leo X, known as the Concordat of Bologna (1516), whereby the pope could collect the first year's revenues from newly appointed French bishops, and the king gained the right to nominate the higher clergy to benefices. Although his sister, Margaret of Angoulême, sympathized with some of the early leaders of French Protestantism, the king took a firm stand against the Reformation. This did not prevent him from making alliances with Protestant princes in Germany against Charles V. The chancellor, Cardinal Antoine Duprat, was the principal minister until his death in 1535. Anne de Montmorency, constable of France, played an important military and advisory role in the years 1528–1541. The king's mother and sister also wielded considerable influence, as did some of his mistresses in his later years.

In 1520 Francis I and Henry VIII met amid much panoply at the Field of the Cloth of Gold, near Guines. However, the English king chose to ally himself with Charles V in the war that began in the following year. During this conflict Montmorency's predecessor as constable, Charles de Bourbon, deserted to the emperor, who gave him military command. In 1525 Francis was defeated and captured at the Battle of Pavia, and remained a prisoner in Spain until the Treaty of Madrid in 1526. Queen Claude having died, Francis married the emperor's sister, Eleanor, under the terms of the treaty, which also required two of the king's sons to be held in Spain until the payment of a ransom. The king soon negotiated a coalition against the emperor known as the League of Cognac, and war resumed until the Treaty of Cambrai in 1529. Further indecisive wars were fought in 1536–1538 (ended by the truce of Nice) and 1542–1544 (concluded with the Treaty of Crépy). In this period Francis I not only made use of the German Protestant princes, but also entered into an alliance with the Turkish sultan, Süleyman the Magnificent, to harry the emperor in eastern Europe and the Mediterranean.

Henry II. Henry II continued his father's rivalry with the Habsburgs. His invasion of Lorraine in 1552 resulted in the capture of Metz, Toul, and Verdun, towns promised him by his German Protestant ally, Maurice of Saxony. French troops were also in Scotland to aid the young Mary, queen of Scots, against the English. Mary was the niece of Francis, duke of Guise, a leading nobleman and general. Henry gave Guise command of an army in Italy in 1556 but had to recall him when his rival Montmorency, now restored to favor, was defeated when he tried to relieve Saint-Quentin on the northeast frontier in the following year. This disaster was mitigated by the capture of Calais from the English by Guise in 1558. The son and successor of Charles V in Spain and the Netherlands, Philip II, had married the Catholic English queen Mary, so that the Habsburg threat to France seemed stronger than ever. Gaspard de Coligny, a nephew of the constable, defended Saint-Quentin after his uncle's defeat and capture, but he eventually surrendered and was taken to Brussels, where he became a Calvinist.

Henry II's government was riven between the families of Montmorency and Guise and another powerful favorite, the marshal de Saint-André. The king's mistress, Diane de Poitiers, whom he created duchess of Valentinois, played an important part in muting this rivalry in the last years of the reign. However, Guisard influence increased when Henry II's eldest son, Francis, was married to Mary, queen of Scots. The king died from a jousting accident in July 1559 during the celebrations in Paris to mark the marriage of his daughter, Elisabeth de Valois, with Philip II of Spain under the terms of the Peace of Cateau-Cambrésis. This treaty was dictated by the financial bankruptcy of the combatants. It provided for the French retention of Calais, Metz, Toul, and Verdun, and the renunciation of French claims in Italy, Franche-Comté, and the southern Netherlands. The series of wars in Italy was replaced by internal conflicts in which a nobility accustomed to foreign campaigns turned its attention to the factious and religious troubles at home.

Francis II. At fifteen Francis II was too old for a formal regency, and his wife's uncles, Francis of Guise and Charles, cardinal of Lorraine, assumed the reins of government. They pursued a policy of repressing heresy at a time when Calvinism was at its flood tide, especially among the nobility. A client of the Guise, Michel de l'Hôpital, was appointed chancellor but, as it turned out, did not support religious persecution, and in fact had more in common with Henry II's widow Catherine de Médicis, who had been excluded from influence first by Diane de Poitiers and then by the Guise, and was now waiting in the wings. Religious riots and demonstrations among the lower orders were answered by trials and executions.

The new converts to Calvinism found powerful protectors. Apart from Coligny, two other nephews of Constable Montmorency, François Dandelot, colonel general of the infantry, and Cardinal Odet de Châtillon, bishop of Beauvais, supported their cause. Within the Bourbon branch of the royal family, Antoine, king of Navarre through his marriage to Jeanne d'Albret, heiress to the Foix and Albret lands in the south, and his brother, Louis of Condé, were also sympathetic to the Reformed faith. Antoine proved fickle in his religious allegiance, but his wife remained staunchly Protestant.

Condé led the forces opposing the Guise. In the spring of 1560 an armed plot to remove the young king from their tutelage failed at the château of Amboise. Condé was arrested for complicity and condemned to death. Toward the end of the year an Estates General was convened in which opposition to the regime was voiced. At this juncture the death of Francis II allowed L'Hôpital and the queen mother to take charge of the government. Condé was pardoned, and Antoine, whose hopes of becoming regent in the minority of Charles IX were frustrated by the appointment of Catherine de Médicis, had to content himself with the post of lieutenant general of the kingdom.

Charles IX. The regent's attempt to provide freedom of worship for the Huguenots, as those of the Reformed faith came to be called, was resisted by a triumvirate of Montmorency, Guise, and Saint-André. The massacre of a Protestant congregation at Wassy in the spring of 1562 persuaded the queen mother to appeal to Condé, but it was the triumvirs who took possession of the young king and his mother. Three inconclusive civil wars followed in the 1560s in which the triumvirs, together with Antoine de Bourbon and Louis of Condé, met their deaths. Jeanne d'Albret died on 9 June 1572, after negotiating the marriage of her son, Henry of Navarre, with Margaret of Valois, the daughter of Catherine de Médicis.

This union was intended to reconcile the warring factions, but the monarchy suddenly changed course and authorized the massacre of the Protestant nobles gathered in Paris for the wedding. The killing began on Saint Bartholomew's Day (24 August 1572), spread to Protestants in general, and continued for several weeks in the provinces. Coligny was the most notable victim. Navarre and his cousin, Henry of Condé, were spared at the price of converting to Catholicism. The massacre was a turning point in the wars. The Huguenots, who had used constitutional arguments to justify their resistance, added radical doctrines on the nature of political obligation and the deposition of tyrants to their ideological arsenal. Dissident Catholic noblemen, led by Henri de Damville, son of Constable Montmorency, allied with the Huguenot republic that formed in the south and were known as politiques. Charles IX died in May 1574 and was succeeded by his brother, Henry III.

Francis I. Antoine Macault reads to Francis and his court from his translation of Diodorus of Sicily. Anonymous; 1532. MUSÉE CONDÉ, CHANTILLY, FRANCE/GIRAUDON/ART RESOURCE

Henry III. The new king returned from Poland, where he had been elected sovereign, and soon found himself involved in a war against a Huguenot-politique coalition led by his younger brother, Francis of Alençon (duke of Anjou from 1576). A peace in 1576 granted such favorable terms to the Protestants that a Catholic League, dominated by the Guise, persuaded a meeting of the Estates General to force

417

the king to revoke it. A peace was patched up in 1577, but another indecisive war occurred in 1580.

Henry III now found himself isolated between the two powerful factions of Guise and Bourbon. He advanced the fortunes of two favorites, Jean-Louis de Nogaret, duke of Epernon, and Anne, duke of Joyeuse, in an effort to create his own party, and encouraged his brother, Alençon-Anjou, to intervene against Spain in the Netherlands. The royal court became notorious for its duels and intrigues, and also, by way of reaction, for its bouts of ostentatious piety led personally by the king. At the same time Henry III displayed a third side to his nature with the intellectual pursuits of the so-called Palace Academy and the instigation of governmental reforms.

In 1584 the death of Alençon-Anjou made the reconverted Protestant, Henry of Navarre, heir presumptive to the throne and provoked a revival of the Catholic League, allied with Philip II of Spain and Pope Sixtus V. Henry III pretended to cooperate with the League, but Navarre and Henry of Guise, the son of Francis of Guise, each won victories, while Joyeuse was killed and Epernon discredited. The king was humiliated and driven from his capital by a revolutionary branch of the League known as "The Sixteen." He secured his revenge by having Henry of Guise and his brother, the cardinal of Guise, murdered during a further meeting of the Estates General. The League responded by vilifying and deposing Henry III in favor of Navarre's Catholic uncle, the cardinal of Bourbon. In April 1589 the king united his forces with those of Henry of Navarre. In August the two were advancing on Paris when the last Valois was assassinated by a Leaguer fanatic.

Henry IV. Even before his accession as Henry IV, Navarre was under pressure to return to the Catholic faith he had abandoned on escaping from court in 1576. Many of Henry III's Catholic supporters deserted the new king, while the Huguenots distrusted his intentions, especially when he promised to maintain the Gallican, or French Catholic, church. His military talents enabled him to defeat the new leader of the League, Charles of Mayenne, brother of the martyred Henry of Guise, and to hold off Spanish armies that invaded France from the Netherlands. Mayenne established a rival national government in the name of Charles X, the cardinal of Bourbon, but the latter's death in 1590 as a prisoner of Henry IV obliged him to convene an Estates General to elect a Catholic successor. The Leaguer estates finally met for this purpose in 1593, and the king chose this moment to return to Catholicism. Elements of the

League continued to resist, even after Pope Clement VIII had granted Henry absolution in 1595. Most Leaguer towns and magnates surrendered or were bought over in 1594 and 1595, but the war with Spain continued and the last Guisard lord, the duke of Mercœur, held out in Brittany. In March 1598 Mercœur accepted terms. A month later the king issued the Edict of Nantes, giving substantial privileges to the Huguenots, who had refused to participate in the war with Spain and even threatened to turn their arms against their former leader. In May negotiations were concluded at Vervins for a peace with Spain's Philip II.

For four decades France had been the arena for a European struggle between the forces of Reformation and Counter-Reformation. Spanish, Italian, English, German, and Dutch forces had all played a part in the conflict. The combination of religious passions and factious dissidence on the part of the nobility had severely disrupted government and society. A major factor in the achievement of peace had been a series of popular revolts in the later stages of the wars. In the face of social anarchy the higher orders had shelved their differences and looked to the crown to restore order. The minister who did most to foster the recovery of agriculture in the postwar period was Maximilien de Béthune, duke of Sully. His colleagues, Pomponne de Bellièvre and Brûlart de Sillery, who followed Bellièvre as chancellor of France, helped to restore stability in government.

The so-called peaceful years of Henry IV were not, however, without their conflicts. A war with Savoy, during which the king's companion in arms Charles de Gontaut, baron of Biron, plotted against his sovereign, occurred in 1600–1601. There was a tax revolt in Poitiers and Limoges in 1602, and a conspiracy involving Charles of Auvergne, the illegitimate son of Charles IX, and other nobles was uncovered in 1604. Henry IV encountered armed opposition from the Huguenot magnate, Henry of Turenne, duke of Bouillon, and had to invade his independent principality of Sedan in 1606. The problem of succession was solved by the annulment of the king's marriage with Margaret of Valois and his union with Marie de Médicis, who gave birth to the future Louis XIII in 1601. Henry IV's mistresses also had important political roles. Gabrielle d'Estrées helped to negotiate the settlement with Mercœur, while her successor, Henriette d'Entragues, was involved in some of the plots against her royal lover in the last decade of the reign.

The most significant developments in foreign affairs concerned growing tensions in Germany. In

1609 a succession crisis occurred in the territories of Cleves-Jülich, bordering the southeast Netherlands and commanding the Rhine. Henry IV was about to lead an army to aid the Protestant princes opposing Habsburg interests when he was assassinated by a fanatic inspired by the tyrannicidal teachings of the former Catholic League on 14 May 1610.

The regency of Marie de Médicis. For seven years after the death of Henry IV, his widow, Marie de Médicis, ruled France. The high court of the Parlement of Paris confirmed her as regent, although, as with the regency of her distant cousin, Catherine de Médicis, in the minority of Charles IX, her claim could have been challenged by a Bourbon prince of the blood, in this case Henry II of Condé, son of Henry I of Condé, who had died in 1588. Condé and other magnates repeatedly challenged the new government. The regent relied upon her late husband's ministers, Nicolas de Villeroy, who conducted foreign policy, Pierre Jeannin, who replaced Sully in the management of the finances, and the chancellor, Brûlart de Sillery. Concino Concini, an Italian adventurer and husband of the queen mother's confidante, Leonora Galigai, rose to prominence and took the title of marshal d'Ancre. Marie de Médicis restricted the army that Henry IV had been about to lead into Germany to a local action, and began to negotiate a marriage between the boy king, Louis XIII, and the daughter of Philip III of Spain, Anne of Austria.

In January 1614 Condé led a revolt of discontented magnates against the regent's policies but accepted, under the Treaty of Sainte-Ménehould (May 1614), the promise of pensions and the convening of the Estates General as the price of peace. The estates met in Paris from October 1614 to March 1615. They accomplished little because of the divisions between the clergy, the nobility, and the third estate, which was represented mainly by officeholders. Throughout much of 1615 Condé and Bouillon tried to involve the Huguenots in their protests against the Spanish match. However, the marriage took place in November, after which Condé and his associates once more raised the banner of revolt. A pacification was achieved at Loudun in May 1616, granting Condé further pensions and a place on the royal council.

Meanwhile the veteran councilors were replaced by newcomers, including Armand Duplessis, the future Cardinal Richelieu. Rivalry between Condé and Concini led to the arrest of the former. Noble resentment against Concini continued to build until, on 24 April 1617, he was killed by the royal guards in a coup planned by Charles d'Albert, later duke of Luynes, who had won the favor of Louis XIII. The king exiled his mother to Blois and installed a new regime. The regency had been another period of instability, but one far less intense than the civil wars of 1562–1598. Like those wars, it was accompanied by an outpouring of printed political propaganda. The French Renaissance left not only a legacy in humanist literature but also a body of political theory that influenced European thinking for centuries to come.

Economy and Population. The population of France began to increase in the late fifteenth century and accelerated until about 1570, when it probably attained 19 million persons. Thereafter it began to decline in the later religious wars, and slowly recovered lost ground in the early seventeenth century.

More than eight out of every ten French men and women were peasants involved in agriculture. The proportion of townspeople rose from about 10 percent of the total population at the beginning of the Renaissance to perhaps 15 percent a century and a half later. Among those enjoying privileged status, the clergy composed about 2 percent of the population, and the nobility somewhat less.

A variety of languages were spoken. Latin was the language of the church, the universities, and the law. The Edict of Villers-Cotterêts (1539), which was mainly concerned with procedural law reforms, represented the first official attempt to make French the standard tongue. Basque was spoken at the western end of the Pyrenees and Breton in the northwest, while four different Romance languages were employed in the south. Every province, and even every subprovince, had its own local dialect or patois. Rabelais satirized this linguistic chaos when he had his fictional giant, Pantagruel, meet a scholar from Limoges whose affected Latinisms clashed with his Limousin patois.

Agriculture. Agricultural production revived after the Hundred Years' War, when abandoned land was brought back into cultivation. The unit of economic exploitation was the seigneury, which involved rights over land and rights over people. The seigneury was divided into the reserve, which the seigneur's agents farmed directly, and that part in which the peasantry had individual tenures and communal rights. During the fifteenth century many seigneurs alienated much of their reserve to village corporations or *communautés*. In the next century these *communautés* became encumbered with debts and often sold off common lands. Grain prices doubled during the century before the Wars of Religion and redoubled in the second half of the sixteenth century, fluctuating wildly in times of crisis. Inflation was caused primarily by the importation of foreign silver, and to a lesser extent by population growth. It has been argued that the price rise, together with the wars in Italy and a more extravagant lifestyle, had an adverse economic effect upon the rural nobility, who were replaced in the seigneuries by newcomers. It is certainly true that there was an infusion of urban capital into country estates in this period and that peasant dues fixed by local law diminished in purchasing power. Many seigneuries did in fact change hands, but there is also evidence to show that some seigneurial families of ancient lineage managed their estates well and even augmented their holdings.

Rural society. Serfdom, which bound the peasant to his lord so closely that his tenures as well as his person were at the seigneur's disposal, had become rare by the sixteenth century. Most peasants were enfranchised, although they were obliged to pay annual dues (*cens*) and were subject to such impositions as fees for the sale of land rights (*lods et ventes*), labor on the seigneurial reserve (*corvée*), and compulsory use of the seigneur's mills, ovens, and winepresses (*banalités*). Moreover, civil and criminal justice was administered by seigneurial officers, although with right of appeal to royal courts. In many parts of France dues were paid in kind (*champart*) rather than in cash, a circumstance that benefited the seigneur during the price rise. Peasants were also obliged to pay church tithes (*dîme*) and the royal poll tax (*taille*).

In the first half of the sixteenth century, changes in the laws of usury allowed the extension of rural loans (*rentes*) to both seigneurs and peasants. This was the means by which capital from the towns could be invested in land. It often resulted in foreclosure and the transfer of property. New owners were likely to employ a system of sharecropping (*métayage*), by which seed, stock, and implements were provided by the investor, who took a proportion of the crop (usually half) in return. This could lead to the expropriation of peasant tenures and the reduction of peasants to landless laborers or vagrant poor.

In the south, where a system of equal inheritance was mandated under Roman law, population growth fragmented tenures and estates into small uneconomic parcels. Elsewhere in France, land aggregation was often the rule under changing economic conditions.

Through all these changes the village remained the center of rural communal life. The parish priest (*curé*), the notary, the officers of the seigneury, and better-off peasants (*laboureurs*) were its principal inhabitants. It also housed the rural artisanate of blacksmiths, cobblers, and wheelwrights, together with small shopkeepers and, in some areas, weavers and dyers. Some villages were divided between two or more seigneuries, while large seigneuries might incorporate several villages.

Cities and merchants. Population grew even more quickly in the towns than it did in the countryside, partly because of an influx of expropriated peasants and other migrants, and partly because of the extension of government agencies into comparatively small centers. In the middle of the sixteenth century, Paris had grown to some 250,000 persons. The next largest towns were Rouen (75,000), Lyon (58,000), Orléans (47,000), and Bordeaux (33,000). Marseille, Nantes, and Rennes were soon to exceed 40,000. A score of intermediate towns ranged between 10,000 and 30,000, and 40 or more held 5,000 to 10,000 citizens and their families. Well over 100 smaller places qualified as towns through their defensive walls or their charters of self-government. Many of these were in fact no more than large villages. In his endeavor to counterbalance the nobility by familial inheritance, Louis XI fostered municipal growth through special privileges and the establishment of trading fairs. He revised municipal charters to benefit town notables at the expense of popular franchises, and he and his successors developed a special kind of seminoble rank (*noblesse de cloche*).

Louis XI also supported large merchant enterprises in the Mediterranean and the northern seas. Under Francis I, Breton and Norman sailors voyaged to the Americas in search of trade. Dieppe rivalled Rouen as a center for northern commerce, and Marseille had a prosperous trade with the Levant. The Biscayan ports of Bordeaux, Bayonne, and La Rochelle traded primarily with Spain, even in times of war. Textile manufacturers produced goods for export in Rouen and the towns along the Somme and the Oise. Rough fustian was made in Poitou and luxury fabrics in Tours and Lyon. Lyon became the hub of international credit, attracting north Italian and south German bankers.

Much of the capital necessary for commerce and manufacturing was diverted into other channels, such as investment in land and government office. Borrowing by the crown to finance war engrossed credit that might otherwise have been available for private enterprise. A banking syndicate was set up at Lyon in 1555 to consolidate and amortize royal debts, and when it failed four years later a second syndicate undertook the task. Lyon was also a center for the printing industry. The wages of artisans did not keep pace with the inflation, and major strikes of printing workers occurred in 1529 and 1539. Associations of artisans were illegal. Master craftsmen and manufacturers were organized into guilds that were licensed by the crown (*métiers jurés*) or by civic authorities (*métiers libres*). The commercial expansion of the towns was halted by the civil wars in the later sixteenth century but began to recover in the peaceful years of Henry IV.

Government and Society.

The king of France was the focus of national loyalty and the directive force in government. His authority was legitimated by divine sanction, as signified by anointing at his coronation, by private dynastic right, and by his public role as the head of the mystical body of the kingdom. Conceptions of his primary function began to change in the sixteenth century from giving justice to making law. His power was not unlimited. Claude de Seyssel, the humanist diplomat and archbishop under Louis XII, described it in *La monarchie de France* (Monarchy of France; 1519) as bridled by religion, justice, and constitutional forms. Two generations later Jean Bodin, the most influential political thinker of the time, wrote in his *Six livres de la république* (Six books of the commonweal; 1576) that the essence of royal sovereignty was making law without consent. There were, however, some things that Bodin believed the king could not do, such as overriding the fundamental laws of succession, or taxing without consent, except in cases of emergency. During the Renaissance the king no longer governed through his household, although household officers still played an important part at court. Nor did he rely upon his vassals for armed force, although the feudal procedure of summoning the nobility for military service (called the ban) was invoked at times in the sixteenth century. Some instruments of national government, such as the representative body of the Estates General and the high court of the Parlement of Paris, had come into existence in the early fourteenth century.

The royal council.

The center of royal government was the council, which made decisions in four areas of administration: the church, justice, finance,

and the military (see diagram). It consisted of an inner group (*conseil étroit*) for major policy decisions, usually containing the two highest officials of the realm, the constable, who was responsible for military matters, and the chancellor, who was the head of the judiciary, as well as four to ten other trusted advisers, who were usually princes of the blood, cardinals, or magnates. Larger committees (*conseil privé, conseil des affaires*) dealt with routine administration and judicial appeals. Legislation was enacted in the form of edicts or ordinances, sealed by the chancellor, and sent to an appropriate court, usually the Parlement, for registration before it became effective law. A college of notaries and secretaries, whose members gained automatic nobility, provided necessary administrative staff to the council and the household, although many of them were purely honorary and performed no effective function.

More significant in the running of the royal council were the secretaries of the commandments of the king, also called secretaries of the finances, who recorded decisions and prepared correspondence for the king's signature. Under Charles VIII, Louis XII, and Francis I, one such secretary, Florimond Robertet, became so indispensable that the office of secretary of state was created in his image. In 1547 four offices of secretary of state were established, each responsible for a particular quadrant of France and for diplomatic correspondence with countries beyond the borders of the provinces he administered. These high officials married into each other's families and constituted a network that barred entrance to newcomers for several generations.

Also important to the working of the council were the masters of requests, who had at first handled petitions sent to the household, and subsequently were given high judicial rank and sent on temporary commissions of inquiry in the provinces. They came to organize much of the routine business of the council and were the ancestors of the intendants sent permanently into the provinces in the seventeenth century. The first intendants of justice went to the provinces to enforce the peace treaties during the religious wars.

The church.

The role of the monarchy in the administration of the French Catholic, or Gallican, church was traced by supporters of the church's independence from Rome to Clovis, the first Christian Merovingian king (481–511). By the Pragmatic Sanction of Bourges (1438) the Gallican church could elect its bishops through cathedral chapters and thus had a certain independence from king as well as

French Administration in the Later Sixteenth Century

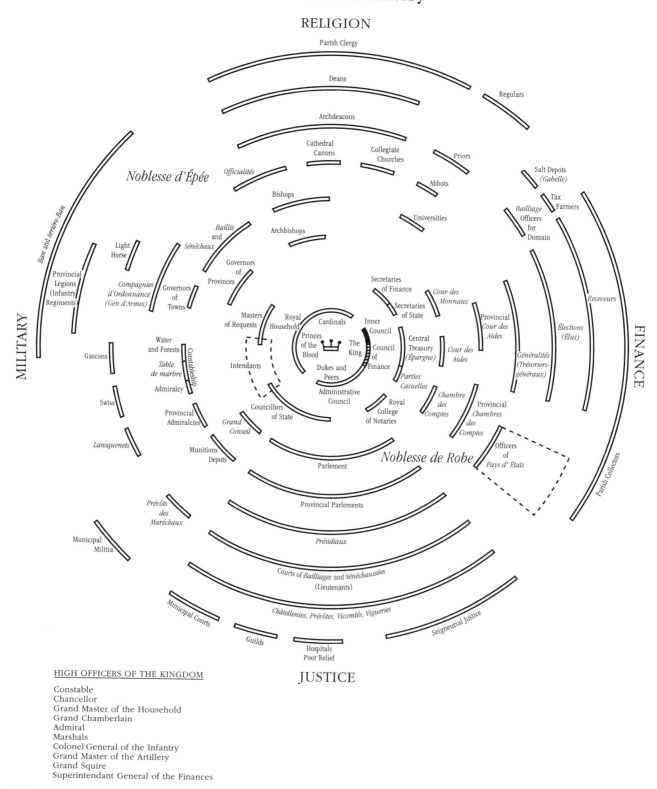

RELIGION

Parish Clergy

Deans

Regulars

Archdeacons

Cathedral Canons

Collegiate Churches

Priors

Salt Depots (*Gabelle*)

Officialités

Noblesse d'Épée

Bishops

Abbots

Tax Farmers

Bailliage Officers for Domain

Archbishops

Universities

Ban and Arrière-Ban

Baillis and Sénéchaux

Governors of Provinces

Light Horse

Secretaries of Finance

Cour des Monnaies

Provincial *Cour des Aides*

Receveurs

Provincial Legions (Infantry Regiments)

Secretaries of State

Élections (*Élus*)

Compagnies d'Ordonnance (Gen d'Armes)

Governors of Towns

Masters of Requests

Royal Household

Cardinals

Inner Council

Central Treasury (*Épargne*)

Cour des Aides

Généralités (*Trésoriers-généraux*)

Gascons

Water and Forests

Table de marbre

Princes of the Blood

The King

Council of Finance

Parties Casuelles

MILITARY

Constableship

Intendants

Admiralcy

Dukes and Peers

Administrative Council

Royal College of Notaries

Chambre des Comptes

Provincial *Chambres des Comptes*

FINANCE

Swiss

Provincial Admiralcies

Grand Conseil

Councillors of State

Lansquenets

Munitions Depots

Parlement

Noblesse de Robe

Officers of *Pays d' États*

Provincial Parlements

Prévôts des Maréchaux

Présidiaux

Parish Collectors

Municipal Militia

Courts of *Bailliages* and *Sénéchaussées* (Lieutenants)

Municipal Courts

Châtellenies, Prévôtes, Vicomtés, Viguieries

Seigneurial Justice

Guilds

Hospitals Poor Relief

JUSTICE

HIGH OFFICERS OF THE KINGDOM

Constable
Chancellor
Grand Master of the Household
Grand Chamberlain
Admiral
Marshals
Colonel General of the Infantry
Grand Master of the Artillery
Grand Squire
Superintendant General of the Finances

Reforms and overlapping jurisdictions make this diagram a very approximate guide.

Source: *Society in Crisis* by J. H. M. Salmon. Copyright © by J. H. M. Salmon. Reprinted with permission of St. Martin's Press, Incorporated.

number of *élections* increased from 70 to 143. The *épargne* continued to function but received only a portion of taxes actually paid. The central bureau of finance was run by controllers and intendants of finance and directed after 1562 by a superintendant of finance, who became one of the great officers of state.

The army. The core of the French standing army was the heavily armored lancers, known as *gens d'armes* or *compagnies d'ordonnance,* created toward the end of the Hundred Years' War. Each cavalryman was supported by five auxiliaries, so that a company of 100 lances consisted of 600 men. This was the elite body in which the rural nobility sought to pursue their vocation of arms. The 9,000 men in the *gendarmerie* expanded to 12,000 under Louis XI. Most of the companies were placed under the command of provincial governors and tended to serve their commanders, rather than the king, during the religious wars. In the fifteenth century an infantry force known as *francs-archers* had been drawn from, and supported by, rural villages. These proved unsatisfactory and were replaced by provincial legions of harquebusiers and pikemen. If these contingents became outdated by the growing sophistication of small arms and battle tactics, the French field artillery proved itself the best in Europe. During the Italian wars French armies contained a high proportion of Swiss and German mercenaries. In the early religious wars, when the royal army has been estimated at some 72,000 men, fully one-third were hired foreign troops.

The supreme military commander under the king was the constable of France, supported by two marshals, who were increased to four by Francis I. Other important military dignitaries were the colonels general of the cavalry and the infantry, and the grand master of the artillery. The admiral of France was effectively a military officer, since there were few royal fighting ships, and the monarchy adopted the practice of impressing armed merchant vessels in time of need.

The nobility. In the sixteenth century, relations between the nobility were governed by clientage rather than the feudal ties of vassalage, although these still existed. The hierarchy descended from princes of the blood, peers of France (much increased in number by Henry III from the original twelve), dukes and marquesses, through counts, viscounts, barons, and chevaliers, to the lowly dignity of *écuyer* (squire). The upper ranks of the society of orders were more fluid in the sixteenth century than

in preceding or subsequent times. In the Middle Ages many of the traditional nobility had held posts in the administrative bureaucracy, but with the advent of formal venality of office the men of the sword tended to serve only as military officers or as lancers in the *gendarmerie,* as high clerics or diplomats, or in posts reserved for the nobility of race, such as governors or lieutenants general of provinces, governors of garrison towns, and *baillis* (now deprived of judicial authority).

Access to nobility could be gained by paying the *franc-fief* and living nobly (without indulging in commerce or manual labor) for three generations, by the purchase of special licenses, or by knighthood in battle. Whether of new or old lineage, country squires and their superiors were attracted by the splendors of the Renaissance royal court and flocked there in search of patrons and pensions. At first the concept of nobility was based upon inherent virtue, but as the century wore on and the old nobility began to feel challenged, antiquity of lineage was emphasized.

Nobility through office in the top rank of the robe bureaucracy (a chancellor or first president) was personal and transmissible, but for intermediate posts, such as an ordinary judgeship in a sovereign court, it did not become hereditary until an office had been held by a family for three generations. Had it not been for the continuing creation of new offices, hereditary officeholding would have blocked the path of ascension to newcomers. Families of financiers climbed through the fiscal administration, and bourgeois notables bought judicial offices for sons they had had trained in law.

While the men of the robe respected the ethos of the warrior nobility, they developed their own collective mentality and ensured that their eldest sons were married to other robe families. Younger sons often sought assimilation with the sword through military service. Since noble marriage was a matter of property as well as dynasty, it was not unknown for impecunious sword nobles to seek wealthy dowries below their social level.

On several occasions in the later sixteenth century, reforming ordinances were passed with the object of eventually dismantling the system of venality. No administration proved able to carry through such a reform and buy out the officeholders. Tenure in office restricted the authority of the crown and has been described as a new feudality. The final institutionalization of venality occurred in 1604 with an edict known as the *paulette,* but even then the system was nearly undone by resolutions passed at the Estates General of 1614–1615.

In the seventeenth century the crown began to reduce the independence of municipal governments and found means to circumvent judicial impediments to executive control by creating a new layer of officials known as intendants, who were sent permanently into the provinces with revocable commissions. Nevertheless, these new commissioners were drawn from the ranks of the robe and more often than not cooperated with provincial governors and local courts. In this sense the absolutist regime that came into existence at this time can be depicted as an alliance of the crown and the elite orders to exploit the unprivileged.

Renaissance France is more clearly distinguished from the preceding and subsequent ages in terms of art, literature, and ideas than it is by way of socioeconomic and institutional contrasts. France had been, and remained, a primarily rural and hierarchical society, although the sixteenth century saw an increase in urban population and subtle shifts in the nature of the seigneury. Until the advent of Louis XIV to personal power the high nobility continued to challenge royal government, but not in the feudal terms prevailing before Louis XI. Similarly, popular uprisings occurred in the seventeenth century, but these were directed against the fiscal agents of the crown rather than the seigneurs who had been the target of medieval jacqueries. Royal authority increased in the first half of the Renaissance period, and was exercised more systematically after the anarchy of the Wars of Religion. The trend entailed larger royal armies, greater centralization, and a growing sense of national unity. It was buttressed by theories of absolutism propounded in the later religious wars to counter doctrines of legitimate resistance and popular participation in government. Like the Estates General, the counterpart of these ideas, now expressed in the Enlightenment language of popular sovereignty and natural right, was to reemerge in the French Revolution.

See also **Bourbon Family and Dynasty; Concordats; Field of Cloth of Gold; Pavia, Battle of; Resistance, Theory of; Tyrannicide; Valois Dynasty; Wars of Italy; Wars of Religion;** *and biographies of figures mentioned in this entry.*

BIBLIOGRAPHY

Baumgartner, Frederic J. *Change and Continuity in the French Episcopate: The Bishops and the Wars of Religion, 1547–1610.* Durham, N.C., 1986. An excellent survey of the church.

Baumgartner, Frederic J. *France in the Sixteenth Century.* New York, 1995. Contains chapters on the monarchy, the church, the nobility, and the people. Also discusses the judiciary and Renaissance culture.

Benedict, Philip, ed. *Cities and Social Change in Early Modern France.* 2d ed. London and New York, 1992. Contains studies of five sixteenth-century cities with an overview.

Collins, James B. *The State in Early Modern France.* Cambridge, Mass., 1995. Describes the government of France in the seventeenth and eighteenth centuries, but has a good introduction on the earlier period.

Diefendorf, Barbara D. *Beneath the Cross: Catholics and Huguenots in Sixteenth-Century Paris.* New York, 1991. Covers the government and social structure of Paris, stressing religious aspects.

Greengrass, Mark. *France in the Age of Henri IV: The Struggle for Stability.* London, 1995.

Harding, Robert R. *Anatomy of a Power Elite: The Provincial Governors of Early Modern France.* New Haven, Conn., 1978.

Hayden, J. Michael. *France and the Estates General of 1614.* London, 1974. A thorough account of the regency of Marie de Médicis and the Estates General.

Holt, Mack P. *The French Wars of Religion, 1562–1629.* Cambridge, U.K., 1995. A very readable account, extending beyond the period. Has a prologue on Gallicanism and reform.

Major, J. Russell. *Representative Government in Early Modern France.* New Haven, Conn., 1980. Particularly good on provincial estates.

Neuschel, Kristen B. *Word of Honor: Interpreting Noble Culture in Sixteenth-Century France.* Ithaca, N.Y., 1989. Investigates the nature of noble clientage.

Roelker, Nancy Lyman. *One King, One Faith: The Parlement of Paris and the Religious Reformations of the Sixteenth Century.* Berkeley, Calif., 1996. On the mentality of the Parisian magistracy.

Salmon, J. H. M. *Society in Crisis: France in the Sixteenth Century.* 2d ed. London, 1979. Part 1 analyzes the structure of French government and society; part 2 provides a narrative.

Schalk, Ellery. *From Valor to Pedigree: Ideas of Nobility in France in the Sixteenth and Seventeenth Centuries.* Princeton, N.J., 1986.

Sutherland, N. M. *The French Secretaries of State in the Age of Catherine de Médici.* London, 1962. A classic institutional study.

Wolfe, Martin. *The Fiscal System of Renaissance France.* New Haven, Conn., 1972.

J. H. M. SALMON

Art in France

The Renaissance in France is often thought to begin with the reign of Francis I (1515–1547). Yet strong medieval traditions in the arts subsisted, giving way slowly to the influence of Italian artists and artisans who brought fashionable new styles to France. The fusion of local and imported elements allowed France to develop its own particular brand of classicism, with an emphasis on the decorative arts and, in architecture, on the château. In the later part of the century, the Wars of Religion (1562–1598) dev-

Art in France. *Pietà of Villeneuve-lès-Avignon* by Enguerrand Quarton (1410–1466). Oil on wood; c. 1455; 1.63 × 2.19 m (5.3 × 7.2 ft.). MUSÉE DE LOUVRE, PARIS/ERICH LESSING/ART RESOURCE

astated art and patronage. A self-absorbed court, tormented imagery, and narrative art characterize the end of the Valois dynasty. With the beginning of the Bourbon and the reign of Henry IV (1589–1610), a slow process of rebuilding began.

The "Late Gothic" in France. In late-medieval France the focus of art production was largely religious, with Gothic cathedrals at its center. Stonework adorning church architecture, interior sculptural groups, stained glass, and manuscript illumination, particularly in lavish books of hours, together form the backdrop of visual culture for both clergy and laity in France at the dawn of the Renaissance.

In the early fifteenth century, the French-speaking duchy of Burgundy, later incorporated into the French crown, had been an important site for patronage of northern artists such as Rogier van der Weyden, Hubert and Jan van Eyck, and Claus Sluter, as well as a central promoter of late-medieval ideals of chivalry. In fifteenth-century France the courtly arts flourished alongside (often mirroring) religious art production in such dreamily beautiful books as the *Livre du Cuer d'Amours Espris* of King René of Anjou. Tapestries, among them the contemplative *Lady and the Unicorn* cycle (c. 1500), lined aristo-cratic halls with courtly figures and emblems placed on a rich "millefeuille" (thousand-flower) backdrop.

Jean Fouquet (c. 1420–1481) stands out among painters in the later fifteenth century. He produced sensitive portraits, altarpieces and gorgeous books of hours (such as the Hours of Étienne Chevalier), and the almost surreal *Virgin and Child* of the Diptych of Melun (1450–1460), for which Charles VII's mistress, Agnès Sorel, may have served as a model. Flemish traditions made their influence felt in southern as in northern France; the *Pietà* of Villeneuve-lès-Avignon (c. 1455, possibly by Enguerrand Quarton), with its stark lines, somber colors, and chiseled figures, is one of the most striking paintings of the second half of the fifteenth century. With the church of Hagia Sophia silhouetted against the abstracted gold background, Christ's broken body memorializes the fall of Constantinople in 1453.

Transitions and Continuities. Dialogue between France and Italy continued throughout the fifteenth and sixteenth centuries. As the influence of Italy began to be felt especially strongly in the second quarter of the sixteenth century, during the reign of Francis I, the Gothic nonetheless maintained a strong presence. Gothic typefaces flourished in books alongside humanist roman and italic typefaces. Popular woodcuts, often hand colored, depicted religious themes (but also satire, courtly scenes, and prodigies), and adopted new forms only slowly, as did church architecture, which continued to employ the elaborate style known as "flamboyant Gothic." In sculptural groups depicting the dying Christ in Pietàs and entombment groups in churches throughout France, Renaissance forms were melded with the traditional arrangement of figures, developing a syntax in which the figures interact more dramatically with one another (as, for instance, in Ligier Richer's *Entombment* at the church of St.-Étienne in St.-Mihiel). New styles brought from Italy could thus update local compositional modes without revolutionizing them.

Likewise, early manifestations of Italian influence in architecture often involved the application of classical decorative motifs to essentially Gothic structures. St.-Eustache in Paris (1532–1589 and 1624–1654) possesses a basically Gothic floor plan, but with classical capitals and rounded rather than pointed arches. Many churches built over the course of the century manifest the different styles through which architecture passed in the period.

It was the château that became the principal site of architectural innovation in the French Renaissance; under Louis XII the châteaux of Blois, Amboise, and Gaillon were remodeled. Under Francis I more châteaux, both royal and noble, were built— Chambord (1519–1540), Azay-le-Rideau, Écouen, and Madrid (now destroyed)—and Blois was further renovated. Chambord's plan is that of a medieval castle, but its famous roof, with a luxuriant profusion of dormers, towers, turrets, and lanterns, exemplifies the fusion of French Gothic structure and Italian Renaissance ornament of the early French Renaissance.

The Problem of "Fontainebleau."

Francis's most famous project was the expansion and renovation of the château of Fontainebleau, outside of Paris. Starting around 1528, the project attempted to "import" the Italian Renaissance into France.

By the early sixteenth century, the territories that would become modern France had been assembled under one crown. With imperial pretentions, and following in the footsteps of his predecessors, Francis sought to conquer Italy, but initial success was followed by his defeat and capture at the Battle of Pavia in northern Italy in 1525. After a period of captivity in Spain, he returned to Paris, where he decided on a strategy of cultural conquest: to bring the best of Italy to France.

Francis had earlier persuaded Leonardo da Vinci to retire to France; he had agents in Italy collecting books, medals, antiquities, modern painting and sculpture, and casts of numerous pieces of antique sculpture. After the sack of Rome by imperial armies in 1527, with artists dispersed and disposed to travel to France, Fontainebleau became the founding moment for the assimilation of Italian style into the visual culture of France (though many of the workers were also French and Flemish).

Italian art and artists. The Italian mannerists Francis hired brought a style whose elegance, ornamentality, and even eccentricity, fused well with the flamboyant Gothic. Francis's collection of art (much of which was disastrously housed in the baths at Fontainebleau) included such famous mannerist works as Agnolo Bronzino's *Venus, Cupid, Folly, and Time* and Benvenuto Cellini's famous golden saltcellar, made for Francis himself [see the illustration in the "Decorative Arts" entry in vol. 2]. Among the Italians brought by Francis to Fontainebleau were Niccolò dell'Abate, Andrea del Sarto, Benvenuto Cellini, Sebastiano Serlio, and Giorgio Ghisi. But the most influential were Rosso Fiorentino (1494–1540) and Francesco Primaticcio (1504–1570). Rosso and Primaticcio were jointly responsible for the fresco decoration of the apartments of Fontainebleau, with Primaticcio continuing Rosso's work after the latter's death in 1540.

The Galerie François I at Fontainebleau, completed in the 1530s by numerous artists working under Rosso's direction, is widely considered one of the finest works of mannerist art outside Italy, and it may well be the most complicated and abstruse iconographic ensemble of the period anywhere in Europe. The gallery coordinates two- and three-dimensional modes and different media: large narrative frescoes, small fresco medallions and friezes, stucco of varying scales in high and low relief, and woodwork. [See the illustration to the entry on Patronage, subentry on Patronage of the Arts.] The narrative frescoes depict obscure mythological narratives and allegorical representations of Francis I himself, involving both violent action and solemn ritual. For the gallery, Rosso invented the stucco "strapwork"—curving, leather-like ornamentation, which had a strong influence (via prints) on northern European art. The use of stucco by both Rosso and Primaticcio also influenced Italian interior design.

Fontainebleau's abundant style of ornamentation, fruit, flowers, and putti (small figures of children), expresses the richness and magnificence of Francis's political and cultural aspirations. This abundance may be most easily visible in Primaticcio's stucco decoration for the chamber of the duchess of Étampes, Francis's mistress: there, arrangements of delicate, elongated female forms rhyme visually with fruit and children, framing scenes less allegorical than hedonistic. An abundance of serpentine figures absorbed in the pursuit of pleasure characterizes Primaticcio's work in the château's Galerie d'Ulysse, the ballroom, and the baths, most of which have been destroyed.

The "School of Fontainebleau." What has come to be known as the French Renaissance in the visual arts is inextricably linked to the slippery designation "School of Fontainebleau." This term was first devised in the early nineteenth century by Adam von Bartsch in his classic study of Renaissance and early modern prints, *Le peintre-graveur* (1803–1821); Bartsch used the term to indicate the printmakers who worked in the orbit of the painters and other artisans brought by Francis I to Fontainebleau. Prints "after" Fontainebleau include an initial group of etchings such as the relatively inelegant works of Antonio Fantuzzi and the master known as IΦV, and the more sophisticated, graceful productions of the Master L. D. (or Léon Davent) and Jean Mignon. Etching produces a shallowly incised plate and could not be produced in large quantities. Engravers, however (including Domenico del Barbiere, Pierre Milan and René Boyvin), were able to produce works that take full advantage of the medium's potential for deep chiaroscuro (light and dark), and also for mass production. Through these engravers, the imagery of Fontainebleau reached a wide audience. Boyvin engraved many works by Léonard Thiry (both active midcentury), a Flemish painter and draftsman who had worked at Fontainebleau; Thiry's designs add a sinuous grotesquerie to Rosso's mythological themes.

The Arts of Aristocratic Living.

The explosion of printing in the late fifteenth and early sixteenth centuries facilitated the publicizing of "styles" of all kinds, including architectural and ornamental styles. With images of their monarch's visual style available to them, those with the means to pay for imitations might commission buildings and objects that suited their notion of modern luxury.

By the late sixteenth century many observers criticized excesses in building and particularly in ornamentation, echoing critiques of fashionable dress. In the middle of the century, Jacques Androuet du Cerceau (c. 1520–c. 1585) published a wide variety of ornament prints, designs for decorative arts, and images of architecture, most famously *Les plus excellens bastiments de France* (The most excellent buildings of France, 1579). Androuet du Cerceau was criticized by his rival Philibert de L'Orme for being a fanciful draftsman with no knowledge of building. But such collections were a significant force for popularizing not only individual luxury objects but the very idea of luxury.

Through widely disseminated prints, Fontainebleau ornamental motifs and Italian grotesques had wide reverberations in the so-called decorative arts, including furniture, ceramics, metalwork, and textiles. There was a great deal of crossover between trades, particularly between engravers and metalworkers. Étienne Delaune (c. 1519–1583) is a particularly interesting example: censured for practicing goldsmithery effectively without a license, he became a successful designer of metalwork—medallions, luxury objects, armor—as well as producing narrative prints, both mythological and religious.

Classicizing ornamental forms fused with local traditions characterize the work of Léonard Limosin in enamel and in the ceramics known as St.-Porchaire, which uses strapwork, antique grotesques, and "moresque" (Moorish) interlace motifs in blue and brown on a cream-colored background. Bernard Palissy (1510–1589), perhaps the most famous decorative artist of sixteenth-century France, was also a naturalist, protogeologist, and unrepentant Protestant (although he worked willingly for the Catholic monarchy). Palissy's brightly hued ceramics are dotted with figures of plants, amphibians, and other creatures cast from life; they inspired numerous nineteenth-century replicas.

National Style and the Assimilation of the Antique.

In his *Défense et illustration de la langue française* (1549), Joachim du Bellay urges French writers not simply to introduce classical vocabulary into French, but to "devour" classical authors in order to "transform themselves into them." Though the classicism of the French Renaissance in the visual arts may appear to our eye to be a purely Italian import, in reality this classicism had a specifically French agenda. Under the guidance of Francis I and of Henry II, France was to become the "new Rome," its relationship to antiquity no longer mediated by Italy.

The assimilation of the antique. The artists of Fontainebleau brought a stylized interpretation of antiquity to France, but they were not its only conduit. Before their arrival, Jean Duvet (c. 1485–1561), an engraver and goldsmith to Francis I and later

Henry II, had already appropriated elements of classicism from Marcantonio Raimondi and Andrea Mantegna. Duvet's solid, stately, densely shaded forms settle sculpturally into their compositions and are ornamented with lyrical lines that add movement, though not the mannered elegance more typical of artists of the Fontainebleau school. Like Duvet, many French writers and artists traveled to Rome or copied Italian prints, seeking to emulate classical style.

Gradually, French architecture began to incorporate more Italian structural elements, integrating the surface application of classical ornament with the use of the classical orders, arcaded loggias, and squared windows and doorways. In his sojourn at Fontainebleau during the 1540s, Sebastiano Serlio developed a new style of column broken at intervals by rusticated (roughened) stone rings, a style that was widely adopted in France. Other characteristically French elements included experiments with staircases and with ornamental brickwork.

The work done on the Louvre under Henry II represents the pinnacle of sixteenth-century French classicism. Designed by Pierre Lescot (c. 1515–1578), the remodeling of the Cour Carrée (square court) and its new western wings made idiosyncratic use of the classical orders and retained the slate-covered roofing of French buildings, using a pitched roof that—along with the large windows, double-columned pavilions, and abundant surface decoration—would be characteristic of later châteaux.

The sculptor Jean Goujon (1510–1568) produced the bas-relief sculpture whose heavy but not ungraceful figures, sheathed in elaborately modeled drapery folds, adorn the upper tiers of the facades, as well as the monumental caryatids of the Salle des Caryatides. Goujon, whose stonework is reminiscent of Duvet's engraving, is best known for the nymphs of the Fontaine des Innocents in Paris.

Along with Lescot, France's most important architect of the period was Philibert de l'Orme (Delorme; c. 1515–1570), whose most famous surviving work is the chateau of Anet, built for Diane de Poitiers, mistress of Henry II, after her fall from favor at Henry's death in 1559. De l'Orme is best known for his writings, *Nouvelles inventions pour bien bastir à petits frais* (New inventions for building well at little cost, 1561) and *Architecture* (1567), in which he sought to develop a French style of architecture, drawing on both the theory of the classical orders and practical knowledge of building techniques.

National artists, national genres. While architecture "à l'antique" (in the ancient style) served

French goals for sixteenth-century French artists and writers, art historians in the nineteenth and early twentieth centuries sought to disavow Italian influence by seeking a properly "national" art in painting, despite the relative unimportance of painting in sixteenth-century France. They focused on the Clouet family and on the figure of Jean Cousin, making them icons of "French" art of the Renaissance.

As previous court portraitists had done, the Clouet family—Jean (c. 1485–1540) and François (c. 1520–1572)—produced ceremonial portraits of kings and noblemen, as well as numerous albums of portrait drawings. Perhaps most closely associated with the mythology of the French Renaissance are the half-length nude portraits of women produced by the Clouet family and other artists, depicting delicately adorned figures in curtained interiors who sit at dressing tables or in their bath. Objects of great curiosity on the part of modern viewers, they have been interpreted as queens and princesses, as courtesans and brides-to-be, as admiring and as bitingly satirical images. In nationalist histories of art they were (and still are) used as metaphors for the purity of a national art devoid of Italian influence, their elegance conceived as the very image of French refinement.

Along with the Clouet family, "Jean Cousin" (in reality a father, c. 1490–1560, and son, c. 1522–1594, of the same name) was portrayed as the savior of French painting from pernicious Italian influence, a notion bolstered by the elder Cousin's intellectual status as author of the *Livre de perspective* (1560), a treatise on perspective. Yet few paintings can be attributed to either father or son; both were more active in prints and designs for decorative arts, including stained glass and the elaborate gold confection given to Henry II by the city of Paris on the occasion of his ceremonial entry. Cousin *père* worked on decorative designs for the entry, and the painting for which he is best known, the languorous nude inscribed *Eva prima Pandora,* was probably painted at the same time, since its inscription echoes a motto from the entry, "Lutetia Nova Pandora." Paris was to be the "new" Pandora, receiving only the beneficial, and not the negative, gifts of the gods to the mythical first woman.

The End of the Renaissance in France.

The last forty years of the sixteenth century, and the early years of the seventeenth, were a time of crisis and fragmentation in the arts as well as in life.

Art in France. *Saint Martin and the Beggar* by Jean Fouquet (c. 1420–1477 or 1481). Miniature from a book of hours made for Étienne Chevalier, secretary to King Charles VII, painted c. 1455. MUSÉE DE LOUVRE, PARIS/GIRAUDON

Conflict and festivity: Narrative arts in the time of the last Valois kings. France witnessed its first episodes of Protestant image-breaking in the 1520s, but the main negative effects of the Reformation on art production in France were the Wars of Religion, which devastated the French population and economy in the second half of the sixteenth century. France became a battleground for the international struggle between Catholic and Protestant powers. Under the regency of Catherine de Médicis (1560–1589), Italian artists returned to fashion, but their influence was the object of intense nationalist critique.

From the 1560s on, war consumed much of the money and energy that might have been used to produce art. The court became increasingly self-absorbed, and devoted its creative energies to ceremony and performance. Throughout the century, the ceremonial entries of royalty had involved poets (including Pierre de Ronsard) and artists (such as Jean Cousin, already mentioned in this capacity) in collaborative work to plan celebrations that included elaborate processions, wooden architecture painted with triumphal and allegorical motifs, and feasting (at tables adorned with elaborate sculpted sugar centerpieces). Such ceremonies had long been commemorated with illustrated books, but more and more frequently, entries, marriages, and religious processions were documented in paintings and tapestries (such as the Valois tapestries, which depict festivities during the reign of Henry III, 1574–1589). Dance, music, costume, and mythological themes were increasingly incorporated into productions such as Balthasar de Beaujoyeulx's *Balet comique de la Reine* (Comic ballet of the Queen, 1581), the first of a long series of theatrical court ballets.

At the same time, polemical paintings and prints deployed tiny figures engaged in violent action, wars, colonial conflict, and, frequently, Catholic or Protestant atrocities. Prints were used for propaganda by various parties, with particularly vicious satire aimed at Catherine de Médicis and her last reigning son, Henry III.

Restoration and renovation. After the assassination of Henry III in 1589 and a period of bitter civil war, Henry IV acceded to the throne in Paris in 1594, ushering in the Bourbon dynasty. The complicated drama of late Valois forms finds an echo in the mythological paintings of the "second" school of Fontainebleau, artists (many of them Flemish) working under Henry IV's patronage. Ambroise Dubois, Martin Fréminet, and Toussaint Dubrueil (1561–1602) deployed complicated, cascading figures, extreme perspective, and obscure narratives. Among Dubrueil's vertiginous paintings is a series, based on Pierre de Ronsard's patriotic epic, *La Franciade* (1572), that adorned the château of St.-Germain en Laye. The drama of the portraits of Frans Porbus (1569–1622), for instance, his portrait of Henry's second queen, Marie de Médicis, is in their presentation of the royal personage framed by ornate costume and decor.

Working outside the court's orbit, the late Renaissance school of Lorraine claims two idiosyncratic masters, Jacques Bellange (c. 1574–1616) and Jacques Callot (1592–1635). Bellange perfected a technique of emotionally charged, muted chiaroscuro using engraving along with a pointillist etching technique: soft, diffuse shadows with planes of white and darker lines, dramatic placement of fig-

ures in radical perspective. In his engravings, Jacques Callot employed popular imagery, particularly the piquant characters of the *commedia dell'arte,* exaggerating their billowing costume and pinched bodies; his style is recognizable but muted in the documentary series *Grandes misères de la guerre* (Great miseries of war).

A relatively indifferent patron of the arts, Henry IV left his most decisive mark on the urban landscape of Paris, which the former Huguenot famously declared was "worth a mass." He began modernizing the city, commissioning the Pont Neuf (the "new bridge") and the sober and beautifully coherent Place Royale, now the Place des Vosges, to encourage the nobility to establish residences in Paris. At the same time, Parisian "hôtels particuliers" (elaborate private residences) flourished, along with country estates and the development of the French formal garden. French royal patronage of Flemish (Rubens) and Italian (Orazio Gentileschi) masters both echoed Francis's Renaissance and set the stage for the new art celebrating the reign of the absolutist Louis XIV.

See also **Francis I; Henry IV.**

BIBLIOGRAPHY

Amico, Leonard. *Bernard Palissy: In Search of Earthly Paradise.* New York, 1996.

The French Renaissance in Prints from the Bibliothèque Nationale de France. Los Angeles, 1994. Exhibition catalog.

Blunt, Anthony. *Art and Architecture in France 1500–1700.* New York, 1973.

Brugerolles, Emmanuelle, and David Guillet. *The Renaissance in France: Drawings from the École des Beaux-Arts, Paris.* Translated by Judith Schub. Cambridge, Mass., 1995.

Bryant, Lawrence M. *The King and the City in the Parisian Royal Entry Ceremony.* Geneva, 1986.

Chastel, André. *French Art: The Renaissance, 1430–1620.* Paris, 1995.

Dimier, Louis. *French Painting in the Sixteenth Century.* New York, 1904.

Béguin, Sylvie et al. *La Galerie François Ier au château de Fontainebleau.* 2 vols. Paris, 1972.

Panofsky, Dora and Erwin. "The Iconography of the Galerie François I at Fontainebleau." *Gazette des Beaux-Arts* 1076 (September 1958): 113–190.

Strong, Roy. *Art and Power: Renaissance Festivals 1450–1650.* Suffolk, U.K., 1984.

Thomson, David. *Renaissance Architecture: Critics, Patrons, Luxury.* Manchester, U.K., 1993.

Yates, Frances. *Astraea: The Imperial Theme in the Sixteenth Century.* London, 1975.

Zerner, Henri. *L'art de la Renaissance en France: L'invention du classicisme.* Paris, 1996.

Zerner, Henri. *The School of Fontainebleau: Etchings and Engravings.* New York, 1969.

REBECCA E. ZORACH

FRANCESCO DI GIORGIO MARTINI

FRANCESCO DI GIORGIO MARTINI (Francesco Maurizio di Giorgio di Martini; 1439–1501), Sienese painter, sculptor, architect, theorist, engineer. One of the outstanding personalities of the Italian Renaissance, Francesco di Giorgio Martini administered a versatile workshop that produced private devotional panels and painted *cassoni* (marriage chests), manuscript illuminations and altarpieces, illustrated architectural treatises, and sculptures in wood as well as bronze. He designed both secular and ecclesiastical buildings but was valued above all by contemporary rulers as an expert in military fortifications. Since the sixteenth century his reputation has rested primarily on two editions of his *Trattati di architettura civile e militare* (Treatise on civil and military architecture). Richly illustrated compendiums on the theory and practice of architecture, engineering, and the military arts, they were highly influential and widely copied. Leonardo da Vinci knew them, and Baldassarre Peruzzi and Sebastiano Serlio, among others, studied them in the sixteenth century. Even though he does not discuss painting and sculpture specifically in the treatises, Francesco reveals the importance he placed on the expression of *invenzione* (invention) through *disegno* (drawing). This emphasis on the idea and *disegno* rather than autograph execution characterizes his work as a whole.

Siena, 1439–1476. Although Francesco's life is copiously documented, nothing certain is known about his training, and verifiable information about his art and architecture remains scant. He probably received his initial instruction in painting and sculpture, and perhaps in military architecture, from Vecchietta, who trained most of the leading Sienese artists of the second half of the fifteenth century. His engineering background derived from Mariano Taccola, several of whose engine designs he copied into a small notebook variously dated from the mid-1460s to the mid-1470s (Vatican Library, Ms. Urb. Lat. 1757). Many of Taccola's drawings concern hydraulic engineering, a field in which Francesco worked throughout his career, beginning in 1469, when he served as co-superintendent of works at the *bottini,* Siena's underground network of aqueducts.

All of the early documents identify Francesco as a painter, yet his activity in this field is not recorded until the early 1470s, when he would have been a mature artist. What he was doing during the 1460s is unclear. Perhaps he assisted Vecchietta, who served as a fortifications expert throughout the Sienese territory from 1467 to 1470; more likely, he worked as a military architect in southern Italy.

The most compelling work of art associated with Francesco's early years is a more than life-size figure of St. John the Baptist carved in wood for Siena's confraternity of San Giovanni Battista della Morte (Siena, Museo dell'Opera del Duomo). Inspired by the harrowing bronze effigy of St. John cast for the Sienese Cathedral in 1457 by the Florentine Donatello, Francesco's *Baptist* announces the vital energy and drama that also animate his finest bronze reliefs, the *Deposition of Christ* (1474–1477; Venice, Santa Maria del Carmine) and the *Flagellation* (1480–1485; Perugia, Galleria Nazionale dell'Umbria). Whether the *Baptist* can be associated with a small payment record of 1464, as the scholarship maintains, is arguable, for there is no record of such a figure in the confraternity's inventories prior to 1470. Moreover, there is nothing in Francesco's oeuvre prior to the 1470s that evinces such expressive depth, and as a type the *Baptist* resembles several male figures in his *Coronation of the Virgin* (1472–1474; Siena, Pinacoteca Nazionale).

This *Coronation* altarpiece, painted for the chapel of Saints Catherine and Sebastian at Monteoliveto Maggiore, near Siena, was followed by a *Nativity* altarpiece (1475–1476; Siena, Pinacoteca Nazionale) commissioned by the Sienese Olivetan community at Porta Tufi. As Francesco's only securely dated extant paintings, these monumental images occupy a special place in his pictorial oeuvre; yet both were produced with varying degrees of workshop participation. The same is true of virtually all of the paintings assigned to him, including his devotional images, addressed to a more traditional audience, and his *cassoni,* whose literary subjects, inspired by antiquity, were designed for a more discerning clientele. Despite a range of quality, however, the ideas and designs of all of these works are attributable to Francesco, who enriched the local visual tradition by looking to antiquity and to Florentine as well as north Italian art.

Urbino, 1476/7–1489. Francesco's career in architecture, which he later extolled as "the highest of the arts," matured in the first half of the 1470s. Sometime after 1474 he dedicated a codex containing drawings of war engines, fortifications, and mechanical devices (London, British Museum, Harley Ms. 3281, Cod. 197 *b* 21) to Federico da Montefeltro, the duke of Urbino and captain general of the papal armies, offering to serve him as a modern Vitruvius might serve a modern Caesar. This petition for employment evidently bore fruit, for by 1477 Francesco was in Gubbio commissioning local artists to execute his designs in a room at the ducal residence and working on the fortifications at Costacciaro. Documents indicate that he was already empowered to act on behalf of the duke in artistic matters. One of Francesco's principal tasks in Urbino was to complete the ducal palace, left unfinished by his predecessor Luciano Laurana in 1472. The works attributed to Francesco during this period (c. 1476–1482) include the wing that extends from the palace toward the cathedral; the Giardino Pensile, or garden terrace; and a helicoidal ramp that leads from the residence to the large ducal stables, called the *Data,* which he also designed. His ecclesiastical architecture in Urbino, dating from the early 1480s, include three of the city's most notable monuments: the cathedral, the monastery of San Bernardino, and the convent of Santa Chiara.

Francesco worked on several fortifications throughout Federico's duchy during the late 1470s and 1480s. His fortresses at Cagli, Sassofeltrio, Tavoleto, and Serra S. Abbondio are discussed in his treatises, as are Mondavio and Mondolfo, designed for Federico's son-in-law Giovanni della Rovere. Francesco's fortress designs, which aimed to eliminate vulnerable spaces along perimeters, addressed the problems posed by an increasing use of artillery. He developed polygonal plans as well as round and angled bastions that allowed for protection of the enceinte while being resistant to cannon fire.

The evolution of the treatises, known in an early and a late edition, remains the most polemical issue associated with Francesco's career. Although cogent evidence has been adduced for dating the early treatise, which survives in two principal versions (Turin, Biblioteca Reale, Ms. Salluzziano 148; and Florence, Biblioteca Medicea-Laurenziana, Ms. Ashburnham 361), to the years immediately preceding Francesco's departure for Urbino (c. 1475–1476); most scholars prefer to see it as postdating rather than antedating his experiences in Urbino. The proponents of this theory typically favor a date between 1482 and 1486, but late-twentieth-century studies advance that date still further to 1487–1489. A similar difference of opinion exists about the second treatise, also known in two principal versions (Siena, Biblioteca Comunale degli Intronati, Ms. S.IV.4; and Florence, Biblioteca Nazionale, Ms. Magliabechiano II.I.141). Again, the dates vary widely, from as early as 1487–1489 to after 1496. These chronological issues are complicated further by the fact that none of the principal manuscripts is holograph and by the conten-

Francesco di Giorgio Martini. Portrait plaque of Battista Sforza attributed to Francesco. PALAZZO DUCALE, URBINO/ THE BRIDGEMAN ART LIBRARY

tion that many of the drawings accompanying these texts are workshop products.

The most notable difference between Francesco di Giorgio's treatises and the earlier theoretical writings of Leon Battista Alberti and Filarete (Antonio Averlino) lies in the systematic use of illustrations, which serve not only to complement the text but as an additional source of information. While Francesco's first treatise is essentially a profuse catalog of information that ranges from military to civil architecture and engineering, the second treatise is structured as a humanist discourse in the Aristotelian tradition. Bracketed in the preamble and conclusion by a discussion of the role of *disegno,* "be it in the process of invention or the explanation of ideas," is Francesco's claim that an explicit affinity exists between drawing, "which in our times is considered base and inferior to many other mechanical arts," and arithmetic and geometry, thus projecting his endeavors into the realm of the liberal arts. What intervenes between the first and second versions of the treatises are humanist ambitions, undoubtedly supported by the duke, and a translation of Vitruvius (dated c. 1482–1487; bound with Magliabechiano II.I.141).

Francesco's reputation as an architectural consultant resulted in commissions throughout Italy after the duke's death. In 1484 the painter Luca Signorelli secured Francesco's designs for the church of Santa Maria del Calcinaio at Cortona, which best exemplifies his preference for architecture characterized by clear plans and solid white walls relieved by a framework of gray sandstone elements.

Siena, Milan, and Naples, 1489–1501.

During the 1490s Francesco's services were repeatedly sought at the most prestigious Italian courts. In 1490 he was in Milan at the request of Duke Giangaleazzo Maria Sforza to advise on the cathedral's lantern tower, and from there he traveled to Pavia with Leonardo da Vinci, again as a consultant. During the same year he designed fortresses for Virginio Orsini in Abruzzo, and beginning in 1491 he made several trips to Naples to inspect fortresses throughout the south Italian kingdom (1492) and to plan the fortifications of the Castelnuovo (1497).

Sienese authorities began to solicit Francesco's repatriation in 1485 to attend to the needs of his city and its territory. When he returned permanently, in 1489, the government was once again in the hands of powerful families that had endured long periods of exile, and it was with this faction that Francesco allied himself. At this time he effectively became Siena's chief architect and engineer and formed a business partnership with Pandolfo Petrucci, the rising political star. Francesco also resumed his activities as a painter and sculptor in Siena. Assisted by his lifelong collaborator Giacomo Cozzarelli, he cast two bronze angels (1489–1492) for the high altar of Siena Cathedral, and together with Luca Signorelli and Pietro di Francesco Orioli almost certainly he participated in the monochrome fresco decorations of the Bichi Chapel (c. 1490–1494). Elected twice to Siena's principal governing body, Francesco di Giorgio apparently prospered throughout his career, purchasing three houses in Siena as well as a farm in Urbino. He died at his farm near Siena.

See also **Architecture,** *subentry on* **Architecture in the Renaissance.**

BIBLIOGRAPHY

Primary Work

Franceso di Giorgio Martini. *Trattati di architettura, ingegneria e arte militare.* Edited by Corrado Maltese and transcribed by Livia Maltese Degrassi. 2 vols. Milan, 1967. Treatises on architecture, engineering, and military arts.

Secondary Works

Bellosi, Luciano, ed. *Francesco di Giorgio e il Rinascimento a Siena, 1450–1500.* Milan, 1993. Exhibition catalog.

Betts, Richard J. "On the Chronology of Francesco di Giorgio's Treatises: New Evidence from an Unpublished Manuscript." *Journal of the Society of Architectural Historians* 36, no. 1 (1977): 3–14.

Christiansen, Keith, Laurence B. Kanter, and Carl Brandon Strehlke, eds. *Painting in Renaissance Siena, 1420–1500.* New York, 1988. Exhibition catalog.

Dechert, Michael S. A. "The Military Architecture of Francesco di Giorgio in Southern Italy." *Journal of the Society of Architectural Historians* 49 (June 1990): 161–180.

Fiore, Francesco Paolo, and Manfredo Tafuri, eds. *Francesco di Giorgio architetto.* Milan, 1993. Exhibition catalog.

Galluzzi, Paolo, ed. *Prima di Leonardo: Cultura delle macchine a Siena nel Rinascimento.* Milan, 1991.

Scaglia, Gustina. *Francesco di Giorgio: Checklist and History of Manuscripts and Drawings in Autographs and Copies from ca. 1470 to 1687 and Renewed Copies (1764–1839).* London, 1992.

Toledano, Ralph. *Francesco di Giorgio Martini: Pittore e scultore.* Milan, 1987.

Weller, Allen Stuart. *Francesco di Giorgio, 1439–1501.* Chicago, 1943.

ARTHUR F. IORIO

FRANCIS I (1494–1547), king of France (1515–1547). Francis was the son of Charles, count of Angoulême, and Louise of Savoy. He succeeded his cousin Louis XII on the French throne on 1 January 1515. He was twice married, first to Louis's daughter, Claude de France (1514), and second to Eleanor of Portugal (1530), sister of the emperor Charles V. A notorious philanderer, Francis had numerous mistresses, the most famous being Anne de Pisseleu, duchess of Étampes, who became very influential politically after 1532.

Francis and his sister, Margaret, were brought up by their mother at Cognac until they were invited to court by Louis XII, who placed them in the care of Pierre de Rohan, seigneur de Gié, at the château of Amboise. Louise of Savoy, however, remained in charge of her children's education, which contemporaries saw as unusually enlightened. But Francis became primarily a man of action, who excelled in various outdoor sports, and spent much of his time hunting. He and his court led a nomadic existence vividly evoked by Benvenuto Cellini in his *Autobiography*. Whenever the king visited a town for the first time he was given an *entrée joyeuse* (joyful entry), which, in its most elaborate form, included street theatricals and the erection of temporary monuments adorned with adulatory inscriptions and appropriate symbols. The king's personal emblem was the salamander, and his device—"Nutrisco et

Francis I of France. Portrait, c. 1525–1530, by Jean Clouet (c. 1485–c. 1540). Musée du Louvre, Paris/The Bridgeman Art Library/SuperStock

extinguo"—may be translated as "I feed upon the good [fire] and put out the evil one."

Foreign and Domestic Policy. Popularly known as *le roi chevalier* (the knight-king), Francis spent much of his reign fighting. In 1515 he invaded the duchy of Milan, which he claimed as his by right of descent from Valentina Visconti. He wrested the duchy from Maximilian Sforza after defeating the duke's Swiss army at Marignano (13 September 1515). In 1519 Francis put himself forward as candidate for Holy Roman Emperor, but the German electors chose Charles of Habsburg who already ruled the Netherlands, Spain, and Franche-Comté. As emperor, Charles became the most powerful ruler in Christendom and Francis's lifelong enemy. In 1521 war broke out between them, which led to Francis's loss of Milan and culminated in his defeat and capture at Pavia (24 February 1525). He remained a prisoner in Spain until 1526, when he was released after promising in the Treaty of Madrid to surrender Burgundy to the emperor. When he broke his word, France entered a new round of hostilities, which lasted until the end of Francis's reign, save for brief respites after the Treaty of Cambrai (1529) and the truce of Nice (1538).

In 1538 Francis, acting under the influence of his chief minister, Anne de Montmorency, constable of France, tried to recover Milan by peaceful means. Charles accepted an invitation to visit the French court but failed to satisfy the king's Milanese aspirations. Montmorency's influence accordingly waned and there was a return to war, which ended with the Treaty of Crépy (1544). In fighting the emperor, Francis sought allies in various quarters. He met Henry VIII at the Field of the Cloth of Gold (1520) and again at Boulogne (1532), but Henry eventually sided with Charles and captured Boulogne (1544). Francis also courted the papacy, meeting Clement VII at Marseilles (1533) and Paul III at Nice (1538). He also intrigued with the German Protestant princes and the Ottoman Turks. Christian opinion was shocked when a combined Franco-Turkish fleet attacked Nice and Francis allowed the Barbary corsair, Barbarossa, to use the port of Toulon as a base (1543).

Francis I was strongly authoritarian. This was demonstrated as early as 1516 by the imposition on his subjects of the Concordat of Bologna, an agreement reached with Pope Leo X that satisfied a long-standing papal demand for the abolition of the Pragmatic Sanction of Bourges (1438). The agreement, which legalized royal nominations to major ecclesiastical benefices in France, was bitterly resisted by the Parlement of Paris, the highest court of law under the king, and also by the University of Paris, but both were overruled. Policy decisions were taken by the king assisted by his council, but royal legislation was effective only insofar as it could be enforced by a relatively small civil service. The crown generally respected local privileges and customs handed down from the Middle Ages.

Two major royal weaknesses were the tax system, which was riddled with exemptions and anomalies, and the largely decentralized and corrupt fiscal administration. Revenue accruing from direct and indirect taxes fell far short of the king's ever-growing military needs. Francis was obliged to borrow from foreign bankers, mostly Italians, and to resort to a variety of expedients, notably the sale of royal offices and the alienation of parts of the royal domain. He launched a system of public credit secured by the revenues of the city of Paris and created a central treasury (*Trésor de l'épargne*). He also prosecuted several financiers, notably Jacques de Beaune-Semblançay, whose execution is a major stain on the king's generally humane record.

At the local level, Francis was dependent on the support of the high nobility, more particularly those who served as provincial governors. The only noble defector was Charles III, duc de Bourbon, who turned traitor in 1523 and became one of the emperor's principal army leaders. A major domestic problem Francis had to face was the growth of the Protestant heresy. At first he vacillated, condemning heresy while protecting individual scholars like Jacques Lefèvre d'Étaples, who held evangelical views. But the king rallied to the cause of orthodoxy after the affair of the Placards in October 1534, which threatened public order. He endorsed repressive measures taken by the Parlement in conformity with the Faculty of Theology of the University of Paris, and in 1545 sanctioned a massacre of Waldensians.

Artistic and Literary Patronage. Francis I was an outstanding builder. His earliest palaces, or châteaux, were built in the Loire Valley at Amboise, Blois, and Chambord. One of his most original creations was the Façade of the Loggias at Blois, which was inspired by Donato Bramante's loggias at the Vatican. Chambord, built between 1519 and 1540, is mainly remarkable for the plan of its keep: a Greek cross with a double spiral staircase in the middle. Two people have been suggested as its designers: Domenico da Cortona, a pupil of Giuliano da Sangallo, and Leonardo da Vinci, but the latter's influence can only have been posthumous since he died in 1519. It was following his conquest of Milan that Francis invited Leonardo, who was sixty-five years old at the time, to settle in France. He was given the manor of Cloux outside Amboise, where he spent the last three years of his life. He seems not to have painted anything for the king, but some of his notes and drawings date from his time in France, and by 1545 several of his major works, including the *Mona Lisa,* had passed into the king's collection. Another major Italian artist whom the king briefly employed was Andrea del Sarto.

In 1528 Francis began rebuilding the Louvre. He erected a château, popularly called Madrid, in the Bois de Boulogne, remodeled Saint-Germain-en-Laye, built Villers-Cotterêts, and began transforming Fontainebleau. The most unusual feature of Madrid was the brightly colored terra-cotta decoration inside and out designed by Girolamo Della Robbia, a member of the famous Florentine family. At Fontainebleau, a team of Italian artists, led by Giovanni Battista di Jacopo, il Rosso Fiorentino, and Francesco Primaticcio, created a distinctive style of interior decoration combining fresco painting with stucco.

Francis had been interested in art since childhood. When Federigo Gonzaga, the future duke of Mantua, visited his court in 1516, art was among the topics they discussed. Some of the most important works in Francis's collection were gifts from popes and Italian princes. In 1518 Leo X sent him four paintings by Raphael, including a St. Michael, a Holy Family, and a portrait of Joanna of Aragon. In 1533 Clement VII gave him a casket with carved panels of crystal by Valerio Belli. By 1525 the king's collection comprised a significant number of paintings by artists of the high Renaissance. Among his artistic agents were Battista della Palla, who sent him Michelangelo's *Hercules,* an early work now lost, and Pietro Aretino, who, in addition to introducing Rosso to the king, sent him paintings by Titian, including the famous portrait in profile now in the Louvre.

Although mainly interested in Italian art, Francis turned to Flanders for portraiture. Many chalk drawings of the king and members of his court by Jean Clouet or his son François have survived. Sculpture entered Francis's collection later than painting. Primaticcio returned from Rome in 1541 with plaster casts of ancient statues, mostly from the papal collection at the Belvedere, which were turned into bronzes by Giacomo Barozzi da Vignola at a foundry set up at Fontainebleau. Other works in Francis's collection included tapestries, most of them imported from Brussels and Antwerp, and precious objects made by Benvenuto Cellini, the Florentine goldsmith and sculptor who visited France in 1537 and 1540–1545. On Cellini's second visit he was given a studio at the Petit Nesle in Paris. Francis and his courtiers allegedly visited Cellini in this studio as he worked on his *Jupiter.* Other works made by Cellini for Francis included a bronze relief of the *Nymph of Fontainebleau* and the famous saltcellar, now in Vienna.

Francis I has been called *"père des lettres"* (father of letters). Even in his youth, according to Baldassare Castiglione, he was more respectful of men of letters than was the average French nobleman. His tutor, François Dumoulin, was a humanist and a prolific author. As king, Francis had several scholars in his entourage, notably Guillaume Budé, who wrote for him *L'institution du prince.* Francis liked books. A chest containing his favorite reading—mostly ancient histories and medieval romances—followed him on his travels. He also enlarged the library at Blois, which he had inherited, and employed agents in Italy and elsewhere to acquire precious classical manuscripts, many of them in Greek, for his library at Fontainebleau. The two royal libraries were integrated in 1544, eventually forming the nucleus of the present Bibliothèque Nationale in Paris, just as the king's paintings came to be the nucleus of the Louvre collection. In 1540 Francis ordered many of his books to be superbly bound in tooled leather, a task continued more lavishly by his successor. Printing was another of the king's interests. Three special fonts of Greek characters (*grecs du roi*) were cut by Claude Garamond at Francis's expense.

The occult sciences—astrology, alchemy, and the Kabbalah—which were believed to hold the key to the secret forces animating the universe, also interested the king. In 1517 he promised to found a college for the study of classical languages not as yet taught at the University of Paris, but no serious steps were taken until 1530, when Francis created four royal professorships (*lecteurs royaux*)—two in Greek and two in Hebrew—to which others were added later. The Collège de France traces its origin to this royal foundation.

In the sixteenth century Francis I was commonly called "*le grand roi François*" (the great king Francis). Later centuries have been less complimentary, presenting him rather as a playboy. Modern historians have redressed the balance by pointing to his reign's constitutional significance and its impressive cultural legacy.

See also **Field of Cloth of Gold; France; Valois Dynasty.**

BIBLIOGRAPHY

Primary Works

Bourrilly, V.-L., ed. *Journal d'un bourgeois de Paris sous le règne de François Ier (1515–1536)*. Paris, 1910.

Catalogue des actes de François Ier. 10 vols. Paris, 1887–1908.

Ordonnances des rois de France: Règne de François Ier. 9 vols. Paris, 1902–1989.

Secondary Works

Cox-Rearick, Janet. *The Collection of Francis I: Royal Treasures.* New York, 1996.

Hamon, Philippe. *L'argent du roi: Les finances sous François Ier.* Paris, 1994.

Jacquart, Jean. *François Ier.* Rev. ed. Paris, 1994.

Knecht, R. J. *Renaissance Warrior and Patron: The Reign of Francis I.* New York, 1994.

Lecoq, Anne-Marie. *François Ier imaginaire: Symbolique et politique à l'aube de la Renaissance française.* Paris, 1997.

R. J. KNECHT

FRANCIS II (1544–1560), king of France (1559–1560). Francis was the first son of Henry II and Catherine de Médicis. His birth ten years after his parents' marriage was regarded as miraculous, but he did not inherit their robust constitutions and was sickly throughout his short life. In 1558 he married Mary, queen of Scots, the daughter of James V and Mary of Guise. Francis became king in July 1559, when Henry was fatally injured while jousting. Henry left the new king a realm facing major problems. Most serious were the religious divisions, as the Calvinists had increased their numbers substantially despite Henry's efforts at repression. Francis was fifteen and did not need a regent, but his youth dictated that someone else take control of the government. The Guise, uncles of his queen, filled that role, although his mother had greater influence than usually acknowledged. Other major figures of Henry's court were excluded, including the Bourbons, who as princes of royal blood felt that they merited authority. Their exclusion in favor of the Catholic Guise solidified their commitment to Protestantism, especially for Louis of Condé, who became involved in a Huguenot plot to rescue Francis from the Guise. The plot was revealed to the government before the conspirators could reach the court at Amboise. Several hundred were killed around Amboise or later executed. Condé was condemned to death but avoided the supreme penalty. The Tumult (or Conspiracy) of Amboise was the only significant event of the reign, as Francis died in December 1560 and was succeeded by his nine-year-old brother, Charles IX. No significant cultural developments occurred during Francis's reign. François Clouet painted the best-known portrait of him.

BIBLIOGRAPHY

Cloulas, Ivan. *Catherine de Médicis.* Paris, 1979. Covers his life well since there is no biography of Francis II.

Sutherland, N. M. *Catherine de Medici and the Ancien Régime.* London, 1966.

FREDERIC J. BAUMGARTNER

FRANCIS XAVIER (1506–1552), early member of the Jesuits, missionary to India, Indonesia, and Japan. Born in the castle of Xavier in the kingdom of Navarre, Francis Xavier was the youngest of three sons and two daughters of Dr. Juan de Jassu, president of the Royal Council of Navarre, and Maria de Azpilcueta. In 1525 he matriculated at the University of Paris, receiving his baccalaureate in early 1529 and his licentiate in 1530. While at the university he was a stipendiary at the College of Sainte-Barbe, headed by the Portuguese humanist Diogo de Gouveia. He then taught at the College of Dormais-Beauvais.

While in Paris, Xavier met Ignatius of Loyola, also a student at the university, and in 1534 took vows with five others, thereby forming the Society of Jesus under the leadership of Ignatius. The group decided to accompany Ignatius to Jerusalem or else enter the service of the pope. They traveled to Venice in late 1536, but hostilities between Venice and the Turks made the pilgrimage impossible. Throughout his stay in Italy, Xavier preached, instructed children in Christian doctrine, and ministered to the sick. While in Rome, he served as the first secretary of the Society of Jesus, which Pope Paul III formally recognized as a religious order on 27 September 1540.

At the request of King João III of Portugal for missionaries to serve in Asia, Ignatius of Loyola named Francis Xavier, who in 1540 traveled to Portugal in the company of D. Pedro Mascarenhas, Portugal's ambassador to Rome. Upon his arrival in Lisbon at the end of June of that year, Xavier attended to the spiritual needs of those at Court, ministered to those being held prisoners by the newly-founded Portuguese Inquisition, and prepared for his voyage to India. Armed with a papal brief naming him apostolic nuncio, Xavier sailed from Lisbon in April 1541 and arrived in Goa in May of the following year. Upon his arrival in India, he busied himself with the spiritual needs of both the Portuguese and the newly converted Indians. He then went to the Pearl Fishery Coast, located in southeast India across from Sri Lanka, where he ministered to the newly converted poor pearl fishers, the Paravas, for a year. In November 1543 Xavier returned to Goa, where he made solemn vows in the Jesuit order. He then sailed to the southwestern coast of India in January 1544 and baptized more than ten thousand Macuans in Travancore, after which he returned to southeast India to work again with the Paravas.

In 1545, after spending a brief time in Cochin and four months in São Tomé de Meliapor, Xavier sailed to Malacca in present-day Malaysia. He remained there until early January 1546, when he set sail for Ambon, where he proselytized from January to June 1546. From June to April of the following year he did the same in the Spice Islands of Moro and Ternate. By July 1547 Xavier had returned to Malacca, where he heard news about Japan and met a Japanese refugee from Kagoshima, who, along with two countrymen, accompanied him to India for instruction in the Christian faith.

After a year of missionary work in India, in April 1549 Xavier sailed for Japan via Malacca in the company of two Jesuits and the three Japanese mentioned above. The first Catholic missionary to Japan, he arrived in Kagoshima on the island of Kyushu on 15 August 1549 and remained in Japan until November 1551. After preparing a Japanese catechism using

RETRATO: DE: MICER: FRANCISCO: XAVIER, DA: ORDEM: DA: COMPⁿ: DE: IESV. Anno. 1542.

Francis Xavier. Anonymous portrait, 1542.

the Latin alphabet, Xavier traveled to Hirado and Yamaguchi. He then visited the emperor in Kyoto, after which he stayed at Funai (today Oita). En route back to India, Xavier received news that Ignatius of Loyola in 1549 had named him provincial of the Jesuit missions from the Cape of Good Hope to China and Japan. While in India, he set about reorganizing and re-forming the Jesuits under his authority. Hoping to bring Christianity to China, he set sail from Goa on 17 April 1552 with instructions from the viceroy to accompany Diogo Pereira's embassy to the emperor. Pereira was a close friend and one of the wealthiest Portuguese in sixteenth-century Asia. In Malacca the governor of the outpost refused to allow Pereira's embassy to continue on, and Xavier attempted to enter China clandestinely via the island of Sancian near Macao. Arriving there at the end of August, Xavier took ill and died that December. Buried on the island, his incorrupt body was exhumed the following year and taken to Goa in 1554, where it remains—an object of veneration. Xavier was beatified by Pope Paul V in 1619 and canonized three years later by Pope Gregory XV.

An indefatigable traveler who spent much of the last twelve years of his life in transit, Xavier emphasized that it was essential for missionaries to learn the languages and customs of the people they hoped to convert. He was also a strong advocate for a native clergy. In 1927 Pope Pius XI named Xavier patron of all missions.

See also **Asia, East; Missions, Christian.**

BIBLIOGRAPHY

Georg Schurhammer, S. J.'s monumental *Francis Xavier: His Life, His Times,* translated by M. Joseph Costelloe, S. J., 4 vols. (Rome, 1973–1982), supersedes all of the earlier biographies. Xavier's correspondence has been edited by Georg Schurhammer and Josef Wicki, S. J., *Epistolae S. Francisci Xaverii aliaque eius scripta,* 2 vols. (Rome, 1944–1945). John W. O'Malley, *The First Jesuits* (Cambridge, Mass., 1993), places the activities of Xavier and his companions in historical perspective.

FRANCIS A. DUTRA

FRANCK, SEBASTIAN (1499–1542), German theologian, historian, printer, publicist. Franck's early years in Donauwörth are undocumented. Although he attended universities at Ingolstadt (1515–1517), where the humanist educators Jacob Locher, Johannes Aventinus, and Urbanus Rhegius taught, and at Heidelberg (1518–?), his formal education proved less important than experience and wide reading. After Heidelberg he served as a Catholic priest and later as Lutheran pastor until 1528. He then left the pastorate and moved to Nürnberg with his wife, Ottilie Beham (Behaim), sister of Barthel (1502–1540) and Sebald (1500–1550), two Nürnberg painters who studied under Albrecht Dürer. In Nürnberg Franck learned the printer's art, translated, and wrote. The preface to his 1530 *Chronica und Beschreybung der Türkey* (Chronicle and description of Turkey) proclaims in embryo his new spiritualism.

The year 1531 found him in Strasbourg with other dissidents, including Johann Bünderlin (1499–after 1544), Michael Servetus (1511–1553), and Caspar von Schwenckfeld (1489–1561). His *Chronica, Zeytbuch und Geschychtbibel* (Chronicle, chronology, and Bible of history; 1531) angered Erasmus (c. 1466–1536), whom Franck deeply respected, and Martin Bucer (1491–1551), and led to jail and expulsion in December 1531. A citizen of Ulm in 1534, Franck held unorthodox views that soon provoked enmity, forcing him to publish his work elsewhere, despite employment at Hans Varnier's press. Expelled in late 1539, he moved with his seriously ill wife and large family to Basel. There he worked at Nicholas Brylinger's press, remarried after Ottilie's death, and continued until his death in October 1542 to publish and write.

Sources as diverse as the Bible, Plato, Nicholas of Cusa, Plotinus, Erasmus, and Seneca inform Franck's "rational spiritualism," which holds that every human contains a portion of the divine Word, and the free will to accept or reject it. Acceptance assures moral activity and salvation; it cannot be mediated. Franck's spiritualist belief that the Logos/Christ redemptive principle is omnipresent involves the rejection of all externals in religion (churches, sacraments, orthodoxy) and of Christ's historic centrality. Because the loving God is present throughout his creation (but greater than it—panentheism), knowledge of nature and history, if interpreted by one's inner Word, leads to knowledge of God. Christ's crucifixion answered a human, not a divine, need: though important, it is insufficient for salvation.

Franck's spiritualism and skepticism led him to question all depictions of religion, especially those by Catholic historians. His *Geschichtsbibel* (the modernized spelling), the earliest Reformation-inspired revision of traditional Augustinian historiography, best shows his originality. Its "Heretic Chronicle" literally turns earlier interpretation upside down, while church and state affairs occupy separate chronicles. The *Weltbuch* (1534) marks a notable, if weak, effort to integrate Africa, Asia, and the New World into world history—a direct application of universal spiritualism to history.

Franck's influence is not easily traced beyond Dirck Coornhert (1522–1590) and Gottfried Arnold (1666–1714), although a group of *Franckisten* appeared briefly in the Netherlands. More important are the silent witnesses: twenty-five editions of his pamphlet, *Trunckenhayt* (Drunkenness), including three Dutch and two Czech; sixteen German editions of his *Geschichtsbibel* by 1585 and seven Dutch editions by 1595; and thirteen editions of the *Sprichwörter* (Proverbs). A heavy borrower, Franck impressed a powerful originality upon everything he translated or wrote. Though he had "little Greek and less Hebrew," his command of German made him, after Luther, a key influence on that language.

BIBLIOGRAPHY

Primary Work

Franck, Sebastian. *Two Hundred and Eighty Paradoxes or Wondrous Sayings.* Translated by E. J. Furcha. Lewiston, N.Y., 1986.

Secondary Works

Dejung, Christoph. *Wahrheit und Häresie: Untersuchungen zur Geschichtsphilosophie bei Sebastian Franck.* Zurich, Switzerland, 1980.

Hayden-Roy, Patrick. *The Inner Word and the Outer World. A Biography of Sebastian Franck*. New York, 1994.

Kaczerowsky, Klaus. *Sebastian Franck: Bibliographie*. Wiesbaden, Germany, 1976.

Kintner, Philip. *Studies in the Historical Writings of Sebastian Franck (1499–1542)*. Dissertation: Yale University, 1957; Ann Arbor Microfilms, 1983.

Teufel, Eberhard. *Landräumig*. Neustadt an der Aisch, Germany, 1954.

PHILIP L. KINTNER

FRANCO, VERONICA (1546–1591), Venetian courtesan poet. Veronica Franco was born in Venice, the daughter of a procuress, Paola Fracassa, and Francesco Franco, a merchant. Her family had a coat of arms because they were native-born citizens who belonged by hereditary right to a professional caste that made up the government bureaucracy and Venetian confraternities. Married off to Paolo Panizza in the early 1560s in what was probably an arranged marriage, she separated from him soon after. She bore six children from different men but only three survived beyond infancy.

Franco became a *cortigiana onesta* (honest courtesan) in the mid- to late 1560s; she provided men with intellectual and cultural pleasures as well as physical ones. Her intellectual life began with sharing her brothers' education by private tutors in the family home, and she frequented literary gatherings in Venice during the 1570s and 1580s. She captured the interest of Domenico Venier (1517–1582), a Venetian poet and the head of the most renowned vernacular literary academy in Venice, who became her reader and protector. A frequent visitor to his private literary salon, Franco composed sonnets and *capitoli* in terza rima for exchange with male poets. By her mid-twenties, Franco was requesting sonnets for publication from male poets for anthologies that she assembled to commemorate men of the Venetian elite. In 1575 she published a volume of her own poetry, *Terze rime*.

In her poems, Franco is forthright about her profession; she is often erotic, even sexually explicit. Her frankness challenges the literary poses adopted by male poets who repeat the idealizing clichés of Petrarchan poetry that praise a reserved, unattainable woman, rarely speaking in her own voice. The verse form used by Franco (the *capitolo* in terza rima) was often used for poetic debate. She used the form to challenge her male opponents, foregrounding her verbal skills and sexual independence.

Franco also published in 1580 a volume of fifty letters, *Lettere familiari a diversi* (Familiar letters to diverse persons). The first is written to Henry III of Valois and the twenty-first is to Jacopo Tintoretto, the Venetian painter. The letters show her in a variety of daily activities—playing music, sitting for a portrait, organizing a dinner party, engaged in literary activities. They are inspired by ancient authors, particularly Cicero's and Seneca's familiar epistles, which were translated into Italian by members of the Venier academy. The epistolary genre allowed Franco to position herself as judge and stoic adviser, writing as a courtesan-secretary to advise patricians who have been led astray by passion unmoderated by reason.

In 1580 Franco was brought to trial by the Venetian Inquisition to counter the accusation of Ridolfo Vannitelli, her sons' tutor, that she practiced magical incantations in her home. Her own defense, the help of Domenico Venier, and probably the predisposition of the inquisitor freed her from the charges. When she died in Venice at forty-five, she was impoverished. The trial had damaged her reputation and she experienced grave financial losses owing to the plague of 1575–1577.

BIBLIOGRAPHY

Primary Works

Franco, Veronica. *Lettere dall'unica edizione del 1580 con proemio e nota iconografica*. Edited by Benedetto Croce. Naples, Italy, 1949. Edition of *Lettere familiari a diversi*.

Franco, Veronica. *Poems and Selected Letters*. Edited and translated by Ann R. Jones and Margaret F. Rosenthal. Chicago, 1998. Bilingual edition and translation into English of Veronica Franco's *Terze rime* and a selection of letters from her *Lettere familiari a diversi*.

Franco, Veronica. *Rime*. Edited by Stefano Bianchi. Milan, 1995. Critical edition of Franco's poems.

Franco, Veronica, and Gaspara Stampa. *Rime*. Edited by Abd-el-kader Salza. Bari, Italy, 1913. Edition of *Terze rime*.

Secondary Works

Bassanese, Fiora A. "Private Lives and Public Lies: Texts by Courtesans of the Italian Renaissance." *Texas Studies in Language and Literature* 30, no. 3 (1988): 295–319.

Diberti-Leigh, Marcella. *Veronica Franco: Donna, poetessa e cortigiana del Rinascimento*. Ivrea, Italy, 1988.

Jones, Ann Rosalind. *The Currency of Eros: Women's Love Lyric in Europe, 1540–1620*. Bloomington and Indianapolis, Ind., 1990.

Phillippy, Patricia. "'Altera Dido': The Model of Ovid's *Heroides* in the Poems of Gaspara Stampa and Veronica Franco." *Italica* 69 (1992): 1–18.

Rosenthal, Margaret F. *The Honest Courtesan: Veronica Franco, Citizen and Writer in Sixteenth-Century Venice*. Chicago, 1992.

MARGARET F. ROSENTHAL

FRENCH INVASIONS OF ITALY. *See* **Wars of Italy.**

FRENCH LITERATURE AND LANGUAGE. The Renaissance was a period of intense renewal and radical transformation in French literature, a period during which centuries-old traditions of lyric poetry, theater, and narrative were gradually abandoned in favor of classicizing traditions that endured to the twentieth century. The period produced much of the finest poetry in the French language and two of the greatest works of world literature written in French—François Rabelais's satirical mock epic cycle *Gargantua* and *Pantagruel* and Michel de Montaigne's *Essays*.

Precisely when the Renaissance occurred in France is a subject of some disagreement among modern scholars. The term is often used as a convenient synonym for the sixteenth century, to designate the period beginning roughly with the Italian Wars (1494) and ending with the Wars of Religion and the Edict of Nantes (1598) or the death of Henry IV (1610). Legitimate claims can be made for an early Renaissance in the late fifteenth century, when the influence of the Italian writers Petrarch and Boccaccio first becomes discernible in French literature. But in the eyes of contemporary Frenchmen the new era of arts and letters we now call the Renaissance began later, during the reign of Francis I (1515–1547), whose deliberate policy of promoting both classical scholarship and avant-garde writing in the vernacular earned him the enduring title of "père des arts et des lettres" (father of arts and letters). The various influences that shaped this new movement—religious and political influences as well as literary and artistic ones—made for a highly complex cultural phenomenon quite distinct from those of other European countries, fraught with ideological and aesthetic tensions that were fully resolved with the emergence of Cartesianism and French neoclassicism in the reign of Louis XIII (1610–1643). These developments marked the fulfillment of Renaissance literary impulses and the beginning of an entirely new period of French literature.

Influences and Distinctive Features.

Because the Renaissance arrived so late in France, nearly two centuries after it began in Italy, it was inspired and shaped by influences quite different from those that gave rise to the Italian Renaissance, and these account for many of its distinctive features.

Christian humanism, Reformation, Wars of Religion.

Most significant, perhaps, is the fact that the French Renaissance began not primarily as a classical revival but as a religious movement. Its impetus came not from Italy but from northern Europe,

where the aims and methods of humanism had been successfully applied to the texts of the Greek New Testament, the Greek and Latin church fathers, and even the Hebrew Bible. France being the center of scholastic theology and an old political opponent of the papacy, the French avant-garde was naturally more interested in returning to the founding texts of the Christian religion than to the pure sources of pagan eloquence and poetry.

The single most important figure for the first generation of French Renaissance writers was Erasmus, whose heroic efforts to edit and retranslate the Greek New Testament, to understand Christianity in essentially historical and moral terms, and to reform the church on the model of the earliest Christian communities were seen to mark a decisive turn that would eventually lead to a rebirth of the paleo-Christian church. Clément Marot (1496?–1544) translated three of Erasmus's antimonastic colloquies, composed allegorical poems about the thousand-year exile and imminent return of "la belle Christine" (the primitive Christian church), and heeded the injunctions of the *Paraclesis* by translating forty-nine psalms into French verse that could be sung by shopkeepers and plowmen as they worked. Erasmus's literary techniques were as influential as his biblical scholarship and theology. The corrosive irony of satirical works like the *Praise of Folly* and the *Colloquies* had a decisive influence on François Rabelais (1483?–1553), whose works are filled with biting Erasmian satire against scholastic theology, monasticism, the papacy, and warmongering Christian princes.

Another important figure for the first generation of French Renaissance authors was Martin Luther (1483–1546), whose doctrine of justification by faith alone had a profound and lasting influence on Margaret of Navarre (1492–1549) and thus on the circle of young writers she patronized, including the young John Calvin (1509–1564). From her earliest poems (for example, *Le miroir de l'âme pécheresse;* Mirror of the sinful soul, 1531) through her secular plays and *chansons spirituelles* (spiritual songs) to the vast works of her final years (for example, *Les prisons*), Margaret combined Lutheran theology and late-medieval mysticism in representations of humble or wretched souls utterly incapable of just action who are nevertheless saved without merit by the inscrutable mystery of God's grace.

Later in the sixteenth century, when the Reformation shattered all hopes of realizing a reformed Catholic church and France became engulfed in a bloody civil war (1562–1598), religion continued to give a distinctive cast to French literature. In 1562 the Catholic poet Pierre de Ronsard (1524–1585) wrote powerful anti-Protestant polemics (*Discours des misères de ce temps;* Discourse on the calamities of this time), while the Protestant writer Henri Estienne (1528–1598) ridiculed the superstitious beliefs and practices of the Catholic church in an eclectic satire titled *Apologie pour Hérodote* (Apology for Herodotus; 1566). Among the many works inspired by the Wars of Religion is a great masterpiece unimaginable in any other context: *Les tragiques,* a violent epic centering on the St. Bartholomew's Day Massacre (1572), written in the late 1570s by the fanatically Protestant soldier-humanist-poet Agrippa d'Aubigné (1552–1630).

Classical literature and philosophy. Another distinctive feature of the French Renaissance arises from the fact that when French writers first began turning to classical literature for inspiration, many more works of classical antiquity had been recovered from oblivion than had been available to Italian writers of the fourteenth and fifteenth centuries. Moreover, those works were far better understood, thanks to nearly two centuries of Italian and northern philology. And because of the new technology of printing with moveable type, they were infinitely more accessible.

Of particular importance in this regard was a vast corpus of Greek literature that had been largely inaccessible before 1453, when the fall of Constantinople to the Turks drove Greek scholars to the West with their learning and their libraries. By the time the Renaissance began in France, it was possible to learn Greek and read printed works both in Greek and in Latin translation. Indeed, the very first Renaissance scholar in France, Guillaume Budé (1467–1540), was universally recognized as the greatest Hellenist in the world.

This advanced state of classical studies had a determining influence on writers in the vernacular. Rabelais knew enough Greek to lecture and publish commentaries on the texts of Hippocrates and Galen and to compose original prose and poetry in Greek. The classical authors who influenced his own fiction the most were Lucian, Plutarch, and Plato—Greek authors who had been unpublished and unreadable before the end of the fifteenth century and the beginning of the sixteenth. By the next generation, the young poets Ronsard, Joachim du Bellay (c. 1522–1560), and Jean-Antoine Baïf (1532–1589) studied not only Virgil and Horace but also Homer and Pindar in the normal course of their studies in Paris. An intense enthusiasm for these and other Greek and Latin poets is what led them directly to their own calling as poets in the vernacular.

Michel de Montaigne (1533–1592) was raised speaking classical Latin as his first language. As a schoolboy he played the leading role in neo-Latin humanist tragedies and read Ovid for pleasure, when his tutor was not watching. He knew vast quantities of classical poetry and prose by heart. But the classical authors Montaigne held in highest esteem were Plutarch and Seneca, whose unpretentious, ruminative style inspired him to develop a form of writing very different from the affected Ciceronianism of earlier Italian prose writers like Pietro Bembo. A few years later Agrippa d'Aubigné learned classical Latin, Greek, and Hebrew by the age of six and soon thereafter mastered the extant literatures in all three languages.

While Latin eloquence was never a major preoccupation in the French Renaissance, and Cicero was never the central figure he had been in Italy, classical philosophy played a decisive role from the beginning. Plato, especially in Marsilio Ficino's Latin translations but occasionally also in the original Greek, was widely read and admired. A few French writers seem to have been serious Platonists but most merely borrowed the language of Platonism for poetic effect (for example, Maurice Scève and Ronsard) or for satirical purposes (for example, Rabelais). Socratic irony and skepticism were at least as influential as Platonic idealism for Renaissance writers from Rabelais to Montaigne.

Other important Greek philosophies were known chiefly through Latin literature: academic skepticism through Cicero's philosophical writings, Epicureanism through Lucretius, and Stoicism through Seneca. Nevertheless, the radical brand of skepticism known as Pyrrhonism became influential following the publication of works by the third-century skeptic Sextus Empiricus in 1562, as did a new stoicism following Guillaume du Vair's French translation of Epictetus at the turn of the seventeenth century. While Renaissance writers vigorously rejected Aristotelianism in its scholastic guise they were strongly influenced by Aristotle's moral works: the *Politica,* the *Economica,* and especially the *Ethica* (especially the *Nicomachean Ethics*). The *Poetics,* which was published for the first time only at the turn of the sixteenth century, became influential only late in the century.

Italian literature. Because the Renaissance had already entered its final stages in Italy by the time it began in France, French writers of the sixteenth century often looked to Italian literature for new ways of writing in the vernacular. Poets, especially, engaged in an intense rivalry with their Italian predecessors and counterparts. Serious interest in Italian culture is often said to have begun in 1494, when the Italian Wars waged by Charles VIII (1483–1498), Louis XII (1498–1515), and Francis I brought these French monarchs face to face with an artistic culture more exquisite than any they had previously known. Distinct traces of Italian influence are indeed discernible in French art and literature in the late fifteenth century, especially in allegorical scenes inspired by Petrarch's *Trionfi,* and as early as 1511 the poet Jean Lemaire de Belges (c. 1475–c. 1525) devoted an entire work, *La concorde des deux langages* (Harmony of the two languages), to the idea of a marriage of French and Italian literary traditions.

But a far more important phase of Italian influence began in the 1530s in the cosmopolitan French city of Lyon, where a large population of cultivated Italians resided and great numbers of Italian books were published. It was here that Petrarch's *Canzoniere* (Book of songs) first became the touchstone for a new kind of French poetry and the single most important model to be imitated and bested. Maurice Scève (c. 1500–1560) became so obsessed with Petrarch that he set out to locate the burial site of Petrarch's Laura. His putative discovery of Laura's tomb in Avignon in 1533 was a much-publicized event that marked the beginning of a Petrarchan age. Clément Marot soon translated six sonnets and a *canzone* from the *Canzoniere* and wrote what may well be the first original sonnet in French. In 1544 Scève himself published the first French "*canzoniere*" in direct imitation of Petrarch: *Délie, object de la plus haute vertu* (Délie, object of the highest virtue). Five years later, Joachim du Bellay went one step further by promoting the Petrarchan sonnet as a quasi-classical form as worthy of imitation as the Horatian ode, and by publishing his own French *canzoniere,* the first consisting entirely of sonnets (*L'olive;* 1549 and 1550).

From this point forward the Italian sonnet replaced all native lyric forms as the standard medium for love poetry. French poets were virtually required to practice pointed imitation of single sonnets of the *Canzoniere,* to mimic certain mannerisms of Petrarch's Italian imitators, and to produce composed collections of sonnets devoted to a single lady, all in imitation of Petrarch. This new tradition, which continued well into the seventeenth century, was accompanied by an ironic counterpoint known as anti-

Petrarchism, best illustrated by du Bellay himself in his "Contre les Pétrarquistes" (1553) and by Pierre de Ronsard in an ironic elegy "A son livre" (To his book; 1556).

After Petrarch, the most influential Italian works were Boccaccio's *Decameron,* Castiglione's *Il cortegiano* (trans. *The Book of the Courtier*), and Ludovico Ariosto's *Orlando furioso.* This last work inspired no comparable romance in French but was widely read and provided a well-known repertory of characters, situations, and soliloquies that became a fixed point of reference in literature of all genres. At the end of the sixteenth century and well into the seventeenth, Italian pastoral works by Torquato Tasso and Battista Guarini exercised a powerful influence over the French imagination.

Although Italian influences remained strong throughout most of the sixteenth century, a reaction against Italianism arose in the last third of the century, fueled in part by anti-Roman religious sentiment during the Wars of Religion. Henri Estienne gave clear expression to this reaction in his *Deux dialogues du nouveau français italianisé* (Dialogues on the new Italianized French; 1578) and *De la précellence du langage français* (The surpassing excellence of the French tongue; 1579), which condemn the contamination of French by Italian and proclaim the natural superiority of French. In the seventeenth century Francesco Berni and Giambattista Marino were much admired and imitated, but otherwise Italian literature was almost totally eclipsed by new works from Spain, including Cervantes's *Don Quixote* and *novelas ejemplares* (exemplary stories), which were immediately translated and became universal points of reference.

Phases of the French Renaissance. The century and a quarter between the coronation of Francis I and the death of Louis XIII was a period of continuous transformation and renewal that produced works of the greatest imaginable diversity. For all its complexity and diversity, however, the literary Renaissance can be seen to evolve through four more-or-less distinct phases corresponding roughly to four successive generations of writers.

First phase. The generation that wrote during the reign of Francis I—a generation that includes Rabelais, Margaret of Navarre, and Marot—typically used the forms and conventions of medieval literature to express an antimedieval ideology. Marot's earliest poems, which he collected in the *Adolescence Clémentine* (1532), are allegorical narratives in the tradition of the *Roman de la rose* and short lyrics in the medieval "fixed forms" (ballades and rondeaux), which nevertheless proclaim the beginning of a new era of reformed spirituality. Margaret of Navarre wrote several secular plays indistinguishable in form and style from medieval farces, but which express a powerful blend of evangelical mysticism and Lutheran theology that is entirely new. Rabelais adopted the forms and conventions of medieval chivalric epic in his *Pantagruel* (1532) and *Gargantua* (1534) to debunk medieval learning and piety and to illustrate through his hero's comic exploits the benefits of the new learning and piety of Erasmian humanism.

In the later 1530s and the 1540s these authors gradually freed themselves from the constraints of medieval forms and modes. Margaret of Navarre was the most conservative, composing spiritual farces and vast allegorical poems to the very end of her life, yet even she turned to Boccaccio as a model for her unfinished *Heptameron*. Marot was somewhat more adventurous, abandoning allegory and the "formes fixes" in favor a short form he called the *épigramme* (in fact a single-strophe ballade in a new guise), verse epistles about his scrapes with religious orthodoxy, and Psalm translations that could be sung as French chansons. The most innovative writer of this generation was Rabelais, whose *Tiers livre de Pantagruel* (Third book of Pantagruel; 1546) and *Quart livre de Pantagruel* (Fourth book of Pantagruel; 1552) moved so far beyond the norms of medieval chivalric epic as to constitute an entirely original form of heroic narrative more consistent with the new humanistic ideology he had been promoting from the beginning. During these same years Scève composed his revolutionary Petrarchan *canzoniere*, *La Délie*, using a ten-line ballade strophe—a native French form more than four centuries old.

Second phase. Beginning in 1549 the poets collectively known as the Pléiade attempted to make a clean break with medieval tradition by systematically rejecting all forms and conventions of their own vernacular literature and forging an entirely new literature modeled directly on Greek and Roman models. Their explicit purpose in doing so was to sweep away a millennium of postclassical barbarism, to raise French from a vulgar to a classical language, and to endow France with the kind of cultural prestige that Homer and Virgil, Pindar and Horace, Demosthenes and Cicero had bestowed upon ancient Greece and Rome.

This ambitious program was spelled out by du Bellay in his *Défense et illustration de la langue fran-* çaise (Defense and illustration of the French language; 1549), a vigorous, tendentious manifesto that claims to mark the most significant turning point in the history of French literature. Du Bellay put his own program into practice by publishing, together with the *Défense,* a collection of thirteen odes modeled closely on the odes of Horace. The following year du Bellay's friend and collaborator Ronsard published a much larger collection of odes in four books, the first of which begins with an even more brazen innovation: thirteen "Pindaric odes" faithfully re-create the tripartite lyric structure (strophe, antistrophe, epode), the soaring élans, and the characteristic metaphors and lexical tics of Pindar's Olympian and Nemaean odes.

These collections resembled nothing ever before written in French and set the tone for an entire generation of poets and playwrights. In 1552 another member of the Pléiade, Étienne Jodelle (1532–1573), composed and staged what he intended as the first classical tragedy in French, *Cléopâtre captive,* which the Pléiade celebrated by sacrificing a live goat in imitation of the pagan Dionysian mysteries associated with tragedy, and the first classical comedy in French, *Eugène.* Although the former is in fact quite unlike Greek or Roman tragedy in its static, elegiac lyricism, it is conspicuously classical in its subject, form (five acts punctuated by choruses), and style, and thus marks a clean break with medieval mystery plays, moralities, and farces, as Horatian and Pindaric odes do with medieval ballades, rondeaux, and allegories.

Near the end of this classicizing phase of the French Renaissance, Jean Antoine Baïf founded the Académie de Poésie et de Musique (1570) devoted to the re-creation of Greek lyric (music and poetry) in French. One of its principal innovations was the so-called *vers mesurés,* based like Greek and Latin verse on patterns of long and short syllables (quantity), rather than on the number of syllables in a line, like traditional French verse. This experiment in classical metrics was a logical extension of the original project of the Pléiade but it eventually failed. French literature could accommodate lyric forms and conventions imported from classical literature, but the language proved incompatible with a system of metrics so alien to its essential nature.

Third phase. As classicizing literature lost its novelty, the new forms and styles borrowed from antiquity began to appear more constraining than liberating. And as the horrors of civil war became more frequent and intense, the dream of a new golden age of classical literature began to appear pathetically irrelevant. Around the time of the St. Bartholomew's Day Massacre (24 August 1572), a new generation of writers began expressing violent passions and intense inwardness with an air of spontaneity and subjective authenticity that appeared to defy the constraints of literary form and classical decorum, inaugurating the period sometimes referred to as the baroque. This period is far more diverse than earlier periods and is characterized by bold experimentation with well-assimilated classical genres and conventions, resulting in unclassifiable works that have no apparent antecedents in classical or medieval literatures.

The oldest and most influential member of this generation is Montaigne, who knew ancient history and vast quantities of classical Latin verse by heart and admired the classicizing poetry of du Bellay and Ronsard but chose to write in a manner that is decidedly anticlassical in form, style, and purpose. His famous *Essais* (1580, 1588, 1595) are, as their title suggests, not a work of literature at all but rather "exercises," "attempts," "trials," or "experiments," in which the author puts his own natural faculties to the test by trying out his own judgment on various topics. The object of these tests is anything that comes to mind—a passage of Virgil's *Aeneid* or a symptom of Cicero's vanity, thumbs or gallstones, philosophy or sex. But their real subject is always the author himself, who makes himself known through his own subjective judgments. The result is an entirely original expression of an individual consciousness at work and a new vision of the world that is fluid, subjective, relativistic, and skeptical.

The greatest writer of the period after Montaigne is d'Aubigné, who was also a great student of classical literature and a fervent admirer of Ronsard. In an early collection of love poetry, *Le printemps* (Spring; written c. 1571–1573), d'Aubigné retained the lyric forms introduced by the Pléiade—sonnets, odes, and "stances"—but exploded the conventional metaphors of erotic poetry with violent and gruesome images of carnage, destruction, and martyrdom. In *Les tragiques* (begun in 1577–1578, published in 1616 and again before 1630) he went much further, combining heterogeneous elements of epic, satire, martyrology, and universal history in a vast, apocalyptic vision of the defeat of the Protestants in the Wars of Religion and their ultimate triumph at the Last Judgment.

Other characteristic works of this generation include vast encyclopedic miscellanies like *La semaine, ou création du monde* (The week, or the creation of the world; 1578) by Guillaume de Salluste Du Bartas (1544–1590), a sprawling seven-book verse amplification of Genesis 1:1–2:3 that achieves astonishing effects through a highly mannered style and aspires to contain everything known about nature; *Les bigarrures* (1583) by Étienne Tabourot (1549–1590), a handbook of verbal tricks—rebuses, puns, double entendres, anagrams, spoonerisms—illustrated by copious examples from classical literature and facetious anecdotes from contemporary life; and *Le moyen de parvenir* (How to succeed; 1610) by François Béroalde de Verville (1556–c. 1629), a parody of the philosophical banquet in dialogue form with no beginning, no end, and no apparent direction, but a clearly satirical purpose expressed through ribald banter and obscene jokes spoken by thousands of historically identifiable guests.

Fourth phase: Libertinism and transition to neoclassicism. Writers of the first decades of the seventeenth century, though often excluded by modern scholars from the Renaissance, continued the literary experiments of the preceding generation in a different way, revitalizing familiar genres and forging new ones to represent with greater immediacy the passions of the soul and express with a greater realism the kind of individual subjectivity invented by Montaigne. They also marked the transition to a new period in French literature characterized by decorum, order, and restraint based on Cartesian rationalism and neoclassical aesthetic doctrines.

Theater became the most popular form of literature in this period. The first professional playwright, Alexandre Hardy (c. 1572–c. 1632), represented murder, rape, and adultery on stage in action-packed, pathos-laden "baroque" tragedies that conspicuously flout classical decorum and the Aristotelian unities. Mixed genres like tragicomedy and the pastoral play, and highly irregular tragedies based on romances and nouvelles, were the norm rather than the exception. The period drew to a close when Jean Mairet (1604–1686) staged the first entirely regular tragedy (*Sophonisbe*, 1634) and the young Corneille (1606–1684) used the device of the play within a play to reflect on the power and the nobility of the theater (*L'illusion comique*, 1636).

In poetry, "libertine" poets like Théophile de Viau (1590–1626) and Marc-Antoine de Saint-Amant (1594–1661) gave new life to an exhausted tradition by singing with astonishing vigor and immediacy the pleasures of the tavern and the brothel, the wretchedness of poverty and fear, and the communion of the poetic genius with nature and his muse, all in lyric forms first invented by the Pléiade (sonnets, odes, elegies) but with occasional gestures back to Marot as well. With the death of this generation, lyric poetry virtually ceased in France, not to return until the early nineteenth century.

As for narrative prose, first-person autobiographical narratives abounded, culminating in the *Discours de la méthode* (1637), in which René Descartes (1596–1650) adopted the subjective first-person and the radical skepticism of Montaigne's *Essais* in order to find a way out of the epistemological impasse that Montaigne had made famous in his "Apologie de Raimond Sebond." Drawing inspiration from Montaigne, French nouvelles, libertine poetry, and the Spanish picaresque novel, Charles Sorel (1599–1674) created the first authentic novel in French, *L'histoire comique de Francion* (1623, 1626, 1633).

With the virtual disappearance of lyric poetry and the advent of regular neoclassical tragedy, Cartesian rationalism, and an entirely new prose genre with no antecedent in antiquity or the Middle Ages, the French Renaissance can safely be said to have ended.

Genres, Authors, Works. Many important works of the French Renaissance are difficult to classify by genre, partly because generic categories were not as discrete as they became after the Renaissance, partly because authors so often created new forms and meanings by deliberately combining elements from various genres and traditions. Nevertheless, a clear evolution within certain general categories is evident throughout the period.

Long narrative. *Les illustrations de Gaule et singularités de Troie* (1510–1513) by Jean Lemaire de Belges is often considered the earliest major work of the Renaissance. This massive three-volume prose narrative traces French origins back to the Trojans and to Noah. Though essentially medieval in its fantastical ahistoricism, its encyclopedic form, and its archaic style, it was nevertheless enormously influential on later writers, including Rabelais and Ronsard, and can be considered a masterpiece of late Gothic, pre-Renaissance prose fiction.

Renaissance prose fiction can truly be said to begin with Rabelais, whose four books of Pantagruel are the greatest, most original works of the French Renaissance. Taking their inspiration from the tradition of late medieval chivalric epics, the first two books combine robust popular humor and astounding erudition to recount the birth, education, and epic exploits of giant heroes who are saved from ignorance and barbarity by a humanist education in moral philosophy, law, medicine, and the Bible, and who in turn save the world from Scholasticism, monasticism, and political tyranny. The sequels to *Pantagruel* abandon most vestiges of medieval popular culture to explore the limits of human knowledge and understanding through an inconclusive quest undertaken by the hero's perplexed companion, Panurge (*Le tiers livre*), and to explore the abuses of ideology and power through an equally inconclusive allegorical sea voyage in quest of a nonexistent "Holy Bottle" (*Le quart livre*). (The posthumous *Cinquième livre de Pantagruel*, 1562, that completes this voyage is almost certainly apocryphal, though composed largely of early drafts written and rejected by Rabelais himself.)

A contemporaneous work that has only recently begun to attract serious critical attention, *Les angoisses douloureuses qui procèdent d'amours* (The painful anguish that results from love; 1538) by Hélisenne de Crenne (c. 1500–c. 1555), grows out of an entirely different narrative tradition, medieval romance. Heavily indebted to Boccaccio's *Fiammetta*, this charming work relates an unhappy adulterous love affair between a married lady, Hélisenne, and her lowborn suitor, Guenelic, in three first-person narratives that examine with astonishing analytical precision the psychology of love.

Although Renaissance writers from the second generation onward considered epic to be the noblest of all classical genres, the Renaissance did not produce a single classicizing epic. Ronsard tried and failed, publishing a mere four books of his national epic, *La franciade,* after twenty years of labor (1572). The fragment is a laborious, servile imitation of Homer and Virgil in the service of the late medieval Trojan legend made famous by Jean Lemaire. With *Les tragiques* d'Aubigné succeeded where Ronsard had failed, taking Lucan's historical epic as his model and focusing with real conviction on current events rather than on a patently absurd, legendary prehistory. But in doing so he stretched epic beyond the breaking point, fusing many different genres into a highly original work and a unique vision that allowed no further imitation.

Arising out of a long pastoral tradition, Honoré d'Urfé's (1567–1625) sprawling, unfinished pastoral romance, *L'Astrée* (1607, 1610, 1619, 1627), portrayed a highly idealized society of aristocratic shepherds living in the golden-age forests of fifth-century Gaul. Centering on a fateful misunderstanding between a faithful lover, Céladon, and his faithful lady,

Astrée, but meandering through a labyrinth of secondary plots, it extends the kind of analytical precision developed earlier by Hélisenne de Crenne to a whole range of amorous sentiments and situations and to exquisite distinctions in the psychology of love. Frequently cited but rarely read today, it was one of the most popular and influential works of the seventeenth century and prepared the way for the *préciosité* and sentimental novels of the next generation.

As *L'Astrée* was being completed, Sorel published the first seven books of his *Francion* (1623), which arises out of very different narrative traditions to inaugurate the realistic novel in France. Veering in and out of pornography, it traces the adventures of a young nobleman in his pursuit of a former prostitute, Laurette, and of a beautiful Italian lady, Naïs, satirizing fools of all classes and professions—courtiers, magistrates, pedants, poets—while extolling the authentic wherever it may be found. Completed in 1627 and revised in 1633, it remained, with the ethereal *Astrée,* one of the best sellers of the century.

Short narrative. Short, realistic, funny, often obscene tales in the tradition of the medieval *fabliaux* were written well into the sixteenth century. In the mid-fifteenth century a collection of one hundred such tales, narrated by different speakers in imitation of Boccaccio, appeared in Burgundy under the title *Cent nouvelles nouvelles* (1462, published 1486), inaugurating a new tradition in France that continued throughout the Renaissance. Several similar collections were composed in the early sixteenth century but survive only in manuscript. The most prominent of these, the *Nouvelles récréations et joyeux devis* by Bonaventure des Périers (c. 1510–c. 1544), was published posthumously in 1558.

By far the greatest work of this kind is Margaret of Navarre's unfinished *Cent nouvelles,* published posthumously under the misleading but enduring title *Heptameron* (1559). The collection is the first to include serious and even tragic stories about love between the sexes, and to introduce long discussions among its ten narrators about the significance of each story. Later collections developed both of these innovations. "Histoires tragiques" became a distinct genre with Pierre Boaistuau's (1517–1566) translations (1559) and with François de Belleforest's (1530–1583) adaptations (1560–1580) of Matteo Bandello's *Novelle.* And discussions among fictional storytellers burgeoned into full-blown frame narratives that gradually overwhelmed the stories in collections like Noël du Fail's (c. 1520–1591) *Propos*

rustiques (Rustic chats; 1547) and *Contes et discours d'Eutrapel* (Stories and speeches of Eutrapel; 1585), Jacques Yver's (1520–c. 1571) *Printemps* (Spring; 1572), Bénigne Poissenot's (c. 1558–c. 1586) *Été* (Summer; 1583), and Guillaume Bouchet's (c. 1514–1594) *Serées* (Evening conversations; 1584, 1597, 1598). Whether concerned with peasants, bourgeois, or nobles, these collections share a common concern for realism that distinguishes them from most forms of longer narrative.

Lyric poetry. In the late Middle Ages poetry was considered a species of rhetoric and served an essentially epideictic function: glorifying the Virgin Mary and praising princes, celebrating alliances and births, mourning disasters and deaths, and so on. To this function the so-called *grands rhétoriqueurs* of the late fifteenth and early sixteenth centuries—the last of whom include Guillaume Cretin (c. 1465–1525) and Jean Lemaire de Belges—brought a technical virtuosity that indulged in elaborate special effects of rhyme and meter. Mellin de Saint-Gelais (c. 1491–1558) and Clément Marot began their careers in this tradition, but soon began to write in new ways in the court of Francis I—especially Marot, whose mature work includes verse epistles, elegies, eclogues, epigrams, sonnets, and psalms.

The city of Lyon produced several major poets in the 1530s and 1540s, often referred to collectively as the École de Lyon. The first and greatest of these is Scève, whose *Délie* fused elements of Platonic idealism, Alexandrian preciousness, the Petrarchan literary project, and a uniquely abstract, cerebral form of expression, in the first coherent collection of love poems devoted to a single lady. Pernette du Guillet (c. 1518–1545), often identified as the real Délie, returned the compliment in abstract Platonizing love poems (epigrams, chansons, elegies) addressed to Scève and collected in a posthumous volume titled *Rimes* (1545). The greatest woman poet of the Renaissance was another Lyonnaise, Louise Labé (c. 1520–1566), whose *Œuvres* (1555) include three long elegies and twenty-four sonnets. These highly original poems express an erotic urgency often more reminiscent of Catullus and Ronsard than of Petrarch and Scève, and make Guillet's fussy, frigid epigrams pale by comparison.

The poetic revolution of the Pléiade began in 1549 with the simultaneous publication of two dense, demanding books by du Bellay designed to illustrate the theory of the *Défense et illustration:* a collection of sonnets explicitly intended to rival Petrarch's *Canzoniere,* titled *L'olive,* and the book of thirteen odes explicitly intended to rival Horace's *Carmina*, titled *Vers lyriques*. While the individual poems of these collections may remain too close to their models to succeed as creative imitations, the collections themselves are meticulously composed in such a way as to rival the architecture of their models. Ronsard's parallel efforts in the *Odes* (1550) and *Amours* (1552) are relatively uncomposed but contain freer, more creative adaptations in their individual poems. The *Amours*, especially, combine lyric and epic conventions by assimilating the poet's lady, Cassandre, to Homer's Cassandra of Troy. While du Bellay systematically promoted an ideal of poetry based on art (imitation), Ronsard promoted an opposing ideal based on nature (inspiration). Ronsard's famous "Ode à Michel de L'Hospital" (1552) is a kind of answer to du Bellay's *Défense et illustration* in this respect.

Du Bellay's greatest works are his later sonnet collections written in Rome: *Les regrets* (1558), which traces a poetic itinerary in 191 sonnets, from elegiac nostalgia through satiric animus to pure encomium, and *Les antiquités de Rome* (1558), a melancholy meditation on time and empire. Ronsard went on to publish successive books of odes and love sonnets—most notably the *Continuation des amours* (1555 and 1556) addressed to a village girl, Marie, and the *Sonnets pour Hélène* (1578), addressed to a lady at court, Hélène de Surgères. In 1560 he published his complete works (*Œuvres*) in four books, which he reorganized and expanded (eventually to ten books) in frequent reeditions to the end of his life.

Other members of the Pléiade, including Pontus de Tyard (1521–1605), Baïf, Olivier de Magny (1529–1561), Jacques Peletier du Mans (1517–1582), and Rémy Belleau (c. 1528–1577), followed in the footsteps of du Bellay and Ronsard. In later years two younger poets continued the tradition of Ronsard's *Amours* in diametrically opposed directions: the suave court poet Philippe Desportes (1546–1606) eclipsed Ronsard with collections of sweeter, gentler ("doux-coulant"), more accessible sonnets like *Les amours de Diane* and *Les amours d'Hippolyte* (1573), while the Protestant firebrand Agrippa d'Aubigné wrote violent, blood-drenched sonnets addressed to the niece of Ronsard's Cassandre in his unpublished *Hécatombe à Diane* (written 1571–1573). As the religious wars became more gruesome, a new generation of poets, both Catholic and Protestant, turned increasingly from love lyric and pagan mythology to devotional lyric and meditations on death: François de Malherbe (1555–1628) in his "Lar-mes de Saint Pierre" (1587); Jean de Sponde (1557–1595) in his "Stances et sonnets de la mort" (published posthumously in 1598); Jean-Baptiste Chassignet (c. 1570–c. 1635) in his *Mépris de la vie et consolation contre la mort* (Contempt of life and consolation against death; 1594); Jean de La Ceppède (c. 1548–1623) in a sonnet cycle inspired by Loyola's *Spiritual Exercises,* the *Théorèmes sur le sacré mystère de notre rédemption* (Speculations on the holy mystery of our redemption; 1613–1621).

In the early seventeenth century Malherbe disavowed the stylistic and sentimental excesses of his earlier manner to write measured, decorous odes on official events and affairs of state, like the stately "Prière pour le roi, allant en Limousin" (A prayer for the king on his way to Limousin; 1605), and to define a new classical aesthetic in his critical annotations on Desportes's style. Before classicism could triumph, however, a generation of libertine freethinkers and free spirits—Théophile de Viau, Saint-Amant, and Tristan L'Hermite (c. 1601–1655)—produced some of the most unclassical and original poetry of the Renaissance, ranging from descriptions of vast landscapes to evocations of macabre visions and disgusting inns, from Epicurean love elegies and erotic nature poems to ebullient cabaret poems in praise of food.

Theater. Mystery plays, farces, and *sotties* continued to be staged and even printed in great numbers throughout the first half of the sixteenth century and beyond, and exerted an enormous influence during the first phase of the Renaissance: Rabelais probably played in farces while a medical student and his work reveals an intimate familiarity with popular comic theater; Marot may have been a member of the "Enfants sans soucy" (Carefree youths), one of several *confréries* (guilds) devoted to writing and performing farces; Margaret of Navarre wrote several farces of her own. Farce survived as a vital tradition to the beginning of the seventeenth century, as the examples of Tabarin (1584–1626) and early Molière (1622–1673) attest.

The second phase of the Renaissance broke with this tradition by producing deliberately classicizing plays in French. The first attempt at tragedy was a biblical tragedy by the reformer Théodore de Bèze (1519–1605), *Abraham se sacrifiant* (1550). This was followed shortly by Jodelle's first attempts at classical tragedy (*Cléopâtre captive,* 1552, and *Didon se sacrifiant,* 1555), and comedy (*Eugène,* 1552). Neoclassical plays by Jodelle's humanist successors became increasingly dramatic as they approached

Plautine models of comedy and Senecan, eventually even Sophoclean and Euripidean, models of tragedy. Jacques Grévin (1538–1570) wrote the first historical tragedy, *César* (1561), and two successful comedies, *La trésorière* and *Les ébahis* (1561); Baïf produced a good adaptation of Plautus's *Miles gloriosus* in *Le brave* (1567) and Pierre Larivey (c. 1540–1619) adapted Italian comedy to the French stage with works like *Les esprits* (1579). Robert Garnier (1545–1590) brought humanist tragedy to its highest point with six works on both Roman historical and Greek epic-tragic themes, ranging from a *Porcie* (1568) and a *Cornélie* (1574) to a *Troade* (1579) and an *Antigone* (1580).

A tradition of biblical tragedy flourished meanwhile with *Saül le furieux* (1572) and *La famine, ou les Gabeonites* (1573) by Jean de la Taille (c. 1533–1608), and with Garnier's *Les juives* (1583). Tragicomedy became a separate genre with Garnier's *Bradamante* (1582). Theoretical writings showing the influence of Aristotle's *Poetics* began to appear with an important *Art de la tragédie* (1572) by Jean de la Taille and an *Art poétique* (begun 1574, published 1605) by Jean Vauquelin de la Fresnaye (1535–1606).

The theatrical explosion of the early seventeenth century produced works as different in form and inspiration as the humanist tragedies of Antoine de Montchrestien (c. 1575–1621)—for example, *Sophonisbe* (1596) and *Hector* (1604); Hardy's violent, irregular, "baroque" tragedies and tragicomedies based on modern novellas and classical romances as often as on ancient history or legend—for example, *La force du sang* (after 1614, published 1625) and the eight-play cycle *Théagène et Cariclée* (published 1623); a pastoral drama, *Les Bergeries* (1619), by Honorat de Racan (1589–1670); Théophile de Viau's tragedy *Pyrame et Thisbée* (1623); a pastoral tragedy and tragicomedy by Mairet, *La Sylvie* (1628) and *La Sylvanire* (1631); and Corneille's comedies and irregular tragedies—as in *La place royale* (1633) and *Le Cid* (1637).

Dialogue. As the canonical form of philosophy for both ancients and modern humanists, dialogue was a much practiced form in the Renaissance for a variety of diverse purposes. At one extreme, the *Cymbalum mundi* (The cymbal of the world; 1537), usually attributed to Bonaventure des Périers and clearly inspired by Lucian and Erasmus, represents a thieving Mercury, scoundrel innkeepers, squabbling theologians, and talking dogs in a corrosive satire so ambiguous and so antimetaphysical as to appear atheistic to many readers. At another extreme, a pallid dialogue by Pontus de Tyard, titled *Le solitaire premier* (The first solitary; 1552) and clearly inspired by Leone Ebreo's *Dialoghi d'amore,* is little more than a catechism in Platonic theories of poetry, played out by the learned narrator and his docile lady pupil, Pasithée. Other notable examples include *Le débat de Folie et d'Amour* (Debate between Folly and Love; 1555), a witty parable by Louise Labé, and the posthumous *Dialogues* (1565) by Jacques Tahureau (1527–1555), which present conversations about the foolishness of the world between Démocritic and Cosmophile. Many of the unclassifiable works of the third phase (for example, Béroalde de Verville's *Moyen de parvenir*) are in fact monstrous hybrids of dialogue and nouvelle traditions.

See also **Drama, French; Pléiade; Poetics,** *subentry on* **French Poetics; Rhétoriqueurs;** *and biographies of figures mentioned in this entry.*

BIBLIOGRAPHY

Primary Works

Aubigné, Agrippa d'. *Œuvres.* Edited by Henri Weber. Paris, 1969.

Conteurs français du seizième siècle. Edited by Pierre Jourda. Paris, 1965.

Du Bellay, Joachim. *Œuvres poétiques.* Edited by Henri Chamard, completed by Yvonne Bellenger. 8 vols. Paris, 1908–1985 and 1982–1985.

Labé, Louise. *Œuvres complètes.* Edited by François Rigolot. Paris, 1986.

Lemaire de Belges, Jean. *Œuvres complètes.* Edited by Jean Stecher. 4 vols. 1882–1891. Reprint, Geneva, 1972.

Margaret of Navarre. *Heptaméron.* Edited by Michel François. Paris, 1967.

Margaret of Navarre. *The Heptameron.* Translated by Paul A. Chilton. Harmondsworth, U.K., 1984.

Marot, Clément. *Œuvres poétiques complètes.* Edited by Gérard Défaux. 2 vols. Paris, 1990–1993.

Montaigne, Michel de. *Complete Essays.* Translated by Donald M. Frame. Stanford, Calif., 1958.

Montaigne, Michel de. *Essais.* Edited by Pierre Villey and V. L. Saulnier. 2 vols. Paris, 1965.

Poètes du seizième siècle. Edited by Albert-Marie Schmidt. Paris, 1953.

Rabelais, François. *The Complete Works of François Rabelais.* Translated by Donald M. Frame, with a foreword by Raymond C. La Charité. Berkeley, Los Angeles, and Oxford, 1991.

Rabelais, François. *Œuvres complètes.* Edited by Mireille Huchon. Paris, 1994.

Ronsard, Pierre de. *Œuvres complètes.* Edited by Jean Céard, Daniel Ménager, and Michel Simonin. 2 vols. Paris, 1993–1994.

Saint-Amant, Marc-Antoine Girard de. *Œuvres.* Edited by Jacques Bailbé and Jean Lagny. 5 vols. Paris, 1967–1979.

Scève, Maurice. *The "Délie" of Maurice Scève.* Edited by I. D. McFarlane. Cambridge, U.K., 1966.

Sorel, Charles. *Histoire comique de Francion*. Edited by Fausta Garavini. Paris, 1996.

Le théâtre du dix-septième siècle. Edited by Jacques Scherer. 2 vols. Paris, 1975.

Traités de poétique et de rhétorique de la Renaissanace. Edited by Francis Goyet. Paris, 1990.

Urfé, Honoré. *L'Astrée* (excerpts). Edited by Jean Lafond. Paris, 1984.

Viau, Théophile de. *Œuvres poétiques*. Edited by Jeanne Streicher. 2 vols. Geneva, 1958–1967.

Secondary Works

Balmas, Enéa. *La Renaissance II: 1548–1570*. Paris, 1974.

Castor, Grahame. *Pléiade Poetics: A Study in Sixteenth-Century Thought and Terminology*. Cambridge, U.K., 1964.

Clements, Robert J. *Critical Theory and Practice of the Pleaide*. 1942. Reprint, New York, 1970.

Cruickshank, John, ed. *French Literature and Its Background*. Vol. 1: *The Sixteenth Century*. London, 1968.

Friedrich, Hugo. *Montaigne*. Edited by Philippe Desan. Berkeley, Calif., 1991. Translated from the original German (1967) by Dawn Eng.

Giraud, Yves, and Marc-René Jung. *La Renaissance I: 1480–1548*. Paris, 1972.

Holyoake, S. John. *An Introduction to French Sixteenth-Century Poetic Theory: Texts and Commentary*. Manchester, U.K., and New York, 1972.

Kaiser, Walter. *Praisers of Folly: Erasmus, Rabelais, Shakespeare*. Cambridge, Mass., 1963.

McFarlane, I. D. *Renaissance France, 1470–1589*. London and New York, 1974.

Morel, Jacques. *La Renaissance III: 1570–1624*. Paris, 1973.

Screech, Michael A. *Rabelais*. Ithaca, N.Y., 1979.

Simone, Franco. *The French Renaissance: Medieval Tradition in Shaping the Renaissance in France*. London, 1969. Translation by H. Gaston Hall of *Il rinascimento francese* (1961).

EDWIN M. DUVAL

FROBEN PRESS. For almost a century—from 1491 to 1587—the Froben press in Basel was among the leading printing and publishing establishments of Europe. Its founder was Johannes Froben (or Frobenius) (1460–1527), who was born in the German city of Hammelburg. After having worked with the renowned publishing firm of Anton Koberger in Nürnberg, he moved to Basel where he published his first book in 1491, an octavo edition of the *Biblia Latina*. It was printed in a minute gothic typeface of Froben's own design, which already at this early stage demonstrated his great concern with the physical appearance of books. In 1494 Froben formed a partnership with Johannes Petri; seven years later the two men joined forces with Johannes Amerbach, the greatest Basel printer of his day and a scholar in his own right. Their production was almost exclusively oriented toward large format publications on canon law and scholastic theological works, including numerous editions of the Vulgate and the works of the church fathers. It was Amerbach, one of the pioneers

of Renaissance textual criticism, who taught Froben always to look for the best manuscripts and devote meticulous editorial care to his editions.

The firm of Petri, Froben, and Amerbach would last for nearly two decades (1494–1513). Petri died in 1511, followed by Amerbach in 1513, after which Froben took over the latter's house and printing office in the Totengässlein. In 1510 he had married Gertrud Lachner, daughter of the prominent local bookseller Wolfgang Lachner, with whom he started a new partnership after Amerbach's death. During the five years of their collaboration Lachner, who was a commercial genius, was in charge of the firm's management and international sales, while Froben saw to the printing and design of their books. In these years the Froben press had an increasing variety of solid but elegant typefaces and sizes at its disposal, among which were some fine roman, italic, and Greek fonts modeled after Italian cuts. Furthermore, Froben hired the services of great artists such as Urs Graf and the brothers Ambrosius Holbein and Hans Holbein (1497–1543) for the design of monumental woodcut frontispieces, title borders, and typographic ornaments, including his famous printer's mark: a caduceus with a snake and dove (based on Matthew 10:16, "Behold, I send you out as sheep in the midst of wolves; so be wise as serpents and innocent as doves"). Few of Froben's books, however, have individual text illustrations.

During the 1510s and 1520s, Froben's activities took a decisive turn. The premises of his printing establishment became the meeting place of a circle of young humanist scholars. They included Beatus Rhenanus; Bruno; Basilius and Bonifacius Amerbach, sons of Johannes Amerbach; Sigismundus Gelenius; Henricus Glareanus; Johannes Oecolampadius; and Conradus Pellicanus. They brought Froben interesting manuscripts, gave editorial advice, provided translations, and acted as proofreaders.

Yet the greatest asset of Johannes Froben's press was Desiderius Erasmus of Rotterdam (c. 1466–1536). While in England, he had been working on a new edition of his *Adages*, to be published by the renowned Parisian printer Jodocus Badius. However, through the maneuvers of Erasmus's book agent, the printer's copy was diverted to Froben, who had already produced a pirated edition of the *Adages* in 1513. In spite of these dealings Erasmus, who first visited Basel in 1514, struck up a friendship with the printer. He collaborated with Froben on the great edition of the works of Saint Jerome and maintained a close association with the Froben press until his death in 1536.

Erasmus played a major part in the realization of many of Froben's most ambitious publications. These included the numerous multivolume folio editions of the Latin and Greek church fathers, such as Jerome (1516), Chrysostom (1517), Cyprian (1520), Ambrose (1527), and Augustine (completed after Froben's death, 1528–1529), and Erasmus's own Latin and Greek edition of the New Testament (1516). But even more important, not least from a commercial point of view, were Erasmus's own writings. Of all the publications of Erasmus, nearly half were printed for the first time by Froben and many were reprinted more than once by him. Among these works we find the *Adages,* of which a new, authorized edition came out in 1515, *The Praise of Folly* (1515), the *Handbook of the Christian Soldier* (1516), and the first edition of the *Colloquies* (1518; edited without Erasmus's consent by Beatus Rhenanus). The immense popularity of these works can be gauged not only from their successive editions but also, in the case of *The Praise of Folly,* from surviving information about its sale figures. The book, which was published together with a satire by Seneca, came out in an edition of 1,800 copies in March 1515, just in time for the Frankfurt book fair. By 17 April, the majority had already been sold, and on 30 April, Froben had to begin printing a new edition.

This close association with Europe's leading humanist was beneficial not only to Froben. At a time when authors at best received a number of copies of their work as a reward for their efforts, Erasmus was exceptionally well paid by his printer, pocketing an annual allowance of 200 guilders as well as a percentage of the revenues brought in by his work. On the other hand, the pressure exerted on him by Froben to publish was great; Erasmus later regretted having at times given in to Froben's supplications when he was not yet fully satisfied with his work. The publication of Erasmus's Greek and Latin edition of the New Testament in 1516, for instance, was hastened because Froben feared the competition of its Spanish counterpart, the polyglot Bible edited at Alcalà. Although the six volumes of this Complutensian Polyglot were printed between 1514 and 1517, it was, to Froben's great relief, not officially published until 1522. These pressures occasionally gave rise to tensions. Erasmus complained about the "forced labor" demanded from him, or that he was not paid properly, or that Froben had shortened his texts. When Froben published Rhenanus's unauthorized and sloppy edition of the *Colloquies* in 1518, Erasmus retaliated by allowing an old friend, the Louvain printer Thierry Martens, a corrected edition in 1519.

The congenial, Christian humanist atmosphere in Froben's workshop, which for a long time remained relatively undisturbed by the increasing turmoil of the Reformation, was much appreciated by many of the members of the European intellectual elite. After the death of Aldo Manuzio in 1515, Froben was generally heralded as the great Venetian printer's only true successor. In a letter written to Erasmus in 1516, the Dutch humanist Maarten van Dorp praised Froben as the "prince of publishers." In the same year, Henricus Glareanus described him as the "common friend of all scholars." As Froben was no scholar himself, he was commended particularly for his technical skills and splendid typography: "exquisite, elegant, and beautiful beyond all others" are the words used by the French scholar Nicolas Bérault in a letter to Erasmus in March 1519 to describe Froben's type. And Erasmus himself, in a letter of December 1526 to the physician Thebald Fettich, wrote: "There is, in my opinion, no one more worthy of your favor than Froben, and no workshop can serve the interests of the great authors better than his."

All in all, Froben's total production over a period of thirty-six years amounts to more than five hundred books, the majority of which consists of weighty theological works in Latin and Greek, edited according to the new and exacting standards of northern European Renaissance scholarship, and many works of Erasmus. During the last phase of his life he would turn to well-printed publications of popular classical and modern authors in small formats, by which he set a typographical standard for many contemporary printers. Around 1520, at the height of his career, he published some fifty titles per year. Curiously, none of his books are in German.

Johann Froben died in 1527, much lamented by his family and friends. He was succeeded by his illegitimate son Hieronymus (1501–1563), who contrary to his father had received an academic education. Hieronymus published a few books in his own name in 1520, but during the life of his father was mainly concerned with the firm's administration. In or about 1528 he began a partnership with his stepmother's new husband, Johannes Herwagen, and from 1529 onward he cooperated also with his brother-in-law, Nicolaus Episcopius. In 1531 he moved the firm's premises to the "Zum Luft" house in the Bäumleingasse, where Erasmus, who remained a close friend of the family, would spend the last year of his life and eventually, on 12 July 1536, breathe his last.

Between 1527 and 1563, the firm produced an impressive publishing list of over four hundred titles,

From the Froben Press. A page from Plutarch's *Moralia,* printed by Froben in 1542.
BIBLIOTHÈQUE NATIONALE, PARIS, RES. J. 103

in which Erasmus continued to have an important place. Many new editions of his books were produced and in 1540 his collected works, edited by his friends, were published by Froben and Episcopius. But they also moved into new directions, not previously explored by Johannes Froben. They published important works in science and medicine, among which were excellent new editions of the writings of the classical Greek physicians Hippocrates (1558) and Galen (1562).

After Hieronymus's death in 1563 the firm would pass to his sons Ambrosius (1537–1602) and Aurelius Erasmus, who together published another forty books, the most important of which is an edition of the Hebrew Talmud (1578–1581). Following an unsuccessful attempt to set up a new press in Freiburg im Breisgau, Ambrosius handed the Basel officina, now much declined, over to his son Hieronymus II in 1585, who sold it two years later. It was the ignominious end of one of Europe's greatest printing and publishing houses.

See also **Printing and Publishing; Typography,** *and biography of Desiderius Erasmus.*

BIBLIOGRAPHY

Allen, P. S. *Erasmus: Lectures and Wayfaring Sketches.* Oxford, 1934.

Gewerbemuseum. *Johann Froben und der Basler Buchdruck des 16. Jahrhunderts.* Exhibition catalog. Basel, Switzerland, 1960.

Heckethorn, C. W. *The Printers of Basle in the XV and XVI Centuries: Their Biographies, Printed Books, and Devices.* London, 1897. Includes at pp. 91–111, 114, and 130 the only printed bibliography of the Froben press, which, however, is in urgent need of an update.

Wackernagel, Rudolf, ed. *Rechnungsbuch der Froben und Episcopius, Buchdrucker und Buchhändler zu Basel, 1557–1564.* 1881. Reprint, Vaduz, Lichtenstein, 1985.

P. G. HOFTIJZER

FROTTOLA. *See* **Music,** *subentry on* **Secular Vocal Music.**

FUGGER FAMILY. The Fuggers were German merchants and bankers, famous for their economic power and political influence. Hans Fugger, a weaver who settled in Augsburg in 1367, prospered in the textile trade. At the death of his son Jakob in 1469, the Fuggers were among Augsburg's wealthiest families. The family business achieved greatness under Jakob's youngest son, Jakob II (1459–1525), nicknamed "the Rich." The secret of his success was lending large sums to rulers (especially Maximilian I of Habsburg) and accepting as security the control of their sources of revenue, especially mining properties. Beginning in Tirol in 1485, Jakob II established monopolistic control of silver and copper mines in Tirol, Hungary, and Slovakia.

Jakob also became deeply involved in papal financial administration. In 1514, for example, he granted large loans to secure papal approval of the irregular election of Albrecht of Brandenburg as archbishop of Mainz, and then the bank administered the infamous indulgence of 1517 for Saint Peter's basilica, criticized by Martin Luther, which secretly gave Albrecht half of the contributions so that he could repay the Fuggers. The outstanding example of Fugger power was their role in the election of the Habsburg Charles V as emperor in 1519. Jakob mobilized the money needed to bribe the German

Jakob Fugger II. Portrait of Jakob Fugger II (1459–1525) in his counting house by M. Schwarz. 1518. HERZOG-ANTON ULRICH MUSEUM, BRAUNSCHWEIG, GERMANY/AKG BERLIN

electoral princes to favor the Habsburg candidate, a total of 850,000 florins, of which Jakob provided 543,000. As security for the loan, Charles granted valuable privileges in Spain, including control of rich mercury and silver mines. Although Jakob often thought the emperor ungrateful, he repeatedly provided new loans for Habsburg wars against France, the Barbary states, and the Turks. When he died in 1525, the capital assets of his company were more than two million gulden. While Jakob's backing of the Habsburgs' rise to power may have been risky, it was also profitable, producing a tenfold increase in assets since 1511.

Jakob Fugger had no children. After his death his nephew Anton (1493–1560) managed the company. Anton struggled to preserve Fugger power, defending his Hungarian and Spanish mining rights against nativist attacks on foreign capitalists. He backed financially Archduke Ferdinand's claim to the Hungarian throne and also his election as the next emperor. Although Anton favored a peaceful religious settlement in Germany and was dismayed by the emperor's decision to attack the Protestants, during the Schmalkaldic War (1546–1547) he provided the money that made possible the imperial victory. After the war, Anton attempted to reduce his financial involvement in Spain, but having already lent so much, he found it difficult to pull back. The bankruptcy of Charles's son Philip II in 1557 was a terrible blow. Although the Fuggers' nominal capital resources were still enormous, most of them were locked up in unredeemable loans to Philip. Under Anton's management, capital assets continued to grow (to a total of 5.6 million florins), but the bank became dangerously overcommitted to Spain (3 million of these assets represented loans to Spain and another 782,000 to the Spanish-ruled Netherlands). The firm was hard-pressed to pay off its own creditors and short of cash to pursue new opportunities for investment.

The generation that succeeded Anton was far less talented. The firm remained solvent under Anton's son Marcus (manager, 1560–1591), but it could no longer undertake major loans. It endured additional Spanish bankruptcies in 1575 and 1607 and by 1641 could claim solvency only on the unrealistic assumption that all of Spain's debts would be repaid. After 1650 the company was dissolved.

The Fugger firm is often (but incorrectly) credited with publication of newsletters based on reports from company agents working abroad and thus is often credited with an important role in the early history of journalism. In reality, the so-called Fugger newsletters are a miscellaneous collection of reports on events and conditions abroad during the period 1568–1604, not published until the twentieth century. Some of these probably come from reports by company agents, but many were extracted from early German newspapers and from a handwritten newsletter circulated by an early Augsburg news service. The collection was compiled for his own use by Count Philip Eduard Fugger (1546–1618), who hired copyists who produced the lengthy manuscript in which these documents were transmitted to modern times. But there is no evidence that the Fugger firm or any member of the family ever circulated (even in manuscript form) a newsletter reporting on contemporary events. In 1923, Victor Klarwill published a volume, *Die Fugger-Zeitungen,* based on the seventeenth-century manuscript preserved in the Austrian State Archives; it was published in English as *The Fugger News-Letters* in 1924. In 1926, a "second series" of *The Fugger News-Letters* was published in English translation; apparently this material, which dealt mainly with English affairs during the reign of Queen Elizabeth I, was never published in German.

The Fuggers were patrons of art and learning. Jakob II commissioned portraits by Thoman and Hans Burgkmair, Hans Holbein the Elder, and Albrecht Dürer. In 1522 he commissioned a painting by Giulio Romano for the German church in Rome. He built the earliest German example of a Renaissance family burial chapel in Augsburg's Carmelite church. His unique creation was the Fuggerei, a community of over fifty residences intended to provide working-class housing. Anton was one of the first Germans to collect ancient coins, bronzes, and marble. He transformed the family residence into a Renaissance-style palace. Hans Jakob (1516–1575) formed a great collection of books, which he sold in 1571 to the duke of Bavaria. It became the foundation for the great Bavarian State Library. Hans (1531–1598) constructed the Schloss Kircheim (1578–1582), the most expensive of the Fugger building projects and an impressive example of late Renaissance architecture, and a library with decor inspired by Nero's Domus Aurea (Golden house) at Rome. He also collected ancient sculpture and coins and became an expert on the detection of forged antiquities. The family also supported musicians, including the organists Paul Hofhaimer, Othmar Luscinius, and Gregor Alichinger, the lutenist Melchior Neusidler, and the composer Orlando di Lasso. More than forty collections of printed music were dedicated to members of the family.

See also **Banking and Money; Germany, Art in.**

BIBLIOGRAPHY

Burkhardt, Johannes, ed. *Vorträge und Dokumentation zum 500 jährigen Jubiläum.* Weissenhorn, Germany, 1994.

Ehrenberg, Richard. *Capital and Finance in the Age of the Renaissance.* Translated by H. M. Lucas. 1928. Reprint, New York, 1985. Abridged translation of *Das Zeitalter der Fugger* (1896).

Pölnitz, Götz, Freiherr von. *Die Fugger.* 1960. Reprint, Tübingen, Germany, 1981. General work based on his many earlier publications (all in German), especially the biographies *Jakob Fugger,* 2 vols. (Tübingen, Germany, 1949–1951) and *Anton Fugger,* 3 vols. (Tübingen, Germany, 1958–1986).

Smith, Geoffrey Chipps. "Fugger." In vol. 11 of *The Dictionary of Art*. London, 1996. Pages 817–820.

Strieder, Jacob. *Jacob Fugger the Rich*. Translated by Mildred L. Hartsough. 1931. Reprint, Westport, Conn., 1984. Translation of *Jacob Fugger der Reiche* (1926).

CHARLES G. NAUERT

FUNERALS. *See* **Death.**

FURIÓ CERIOL, FADRIQUE (1527–1592), Valencian humanist and political theorist. Born of the Valencian nobility, Furió Ceriol began his study of rhetoric, ancient languages, and history at the University of Valencia. Like many Spanish intellectuals of the mid-sixteenth century, he continued his education abroad, at the universities of Paris and of Louvain.

In 1556 Furió Ceriol published a Latin dialogue entitled *Bononia,* in which he presented several humanist arguments in favor of the translation of scripture into the vernacular. His ideas sparked a controversy in Spain, where the Inquisition had placed such translations on its *Index* of banned books in 1551. Charles V came to Furió Ceriol's aid, assigning him to the retinue of Prince Philip, later King Philip II of Spain, in whose employ he remained for the rest of his life. Furió Ceriol made his greatest contribution, both as an adviser and as a political theorist, with the publication of his *El consejo i consejeros del principe* (Of councils and counselors) in 1559. In this work, ostensibly a prescriptive treatise on the ideal counselor, the Valencian advocated the preservation of regional laws, languages, and institutions, as well as the inclusion of advisers of different nationalities in the king's inner circle. This federalist vision of empire informed the foreign policy of the faction led by the king's favorite, Ruy Gómez, prince of Eboli, who sought a diplomatic solution to the upheaval in the Spanish Netherlands in the 1570s. Although Philip II ultimately turned to the more martial views espoused by the duke of Alba's faction, he continued to favor the humanist at court, naming him royal historian. Furió Ceriol died in Valladolid in 1592.

BIBLIOGRAPHY

Primary Works

Furió Ceriol, Fadrique. *El concejo y consejeros del príncipe (1559)*. Madrid, 1993.

Furió Ceriol, Fadrique. *Of councils and Counselors (1570) by Thomas Blundeville; an English Reworking of El consejo i consejeros del principe (1559) by Frederico Furio Ceriól*. Gainesville, Fla., 1963.

Secondary Work

Sevilla Andrés, Diego, ed. *El concejo y consejeros del principe, y otras obras*. By Fadrique Furió Ceriol. Valencia, 1952.

BENJAMIN A. EHLERS